Introduction to
SOCIOLOGY

Seagull
Edition

12e

Select Sociology Titles From W. W. Norton

Introduction to
SOCIOLOGY

Seagull 12e

Anthony Giddens
LONDON SCHOOL OF ECONOMICS

Mitchell Duneier
PRINCETON UNIVERSITY

Richard P. Appelbaum
UNIVERSITY OF CALIFORNIA,
SANTA BARBARA

Deborah Carr
BOSTON UNIVERSITY

W. W. NORTON & COMPANY
Independent Publishers Since 1923

W. W. NORTON & COMPANY has been independent since its founding in 1923, when William Warder Norton and Mary D. Herter Norton first published lectures delivered at the People's Institute, the adult education division of New York City's Cooper Union. The firm soon expanded its program beyond the Institute, publishing books by celebrated academics from America and abroad. By midcentury, the two major pillars of Norton's publishing program—trade books and college texts—were firmly established. In the 1950s, the Norton family transferred control of the company to its employees, and today—with a staff of four hundred and a comparable number of trade, college, and professional titles published each year—W. W. Norton & Company stands as the largest and oldest publishing house owned wholly by its employees.

Editor: Michael Moss
Editorial Assistant: Angie Merila
Project Editor: Caitlin Moran
Managing Editor, College: Marian Johnson
Managing Editor, College Digital Media: Kim Yi
Production Manager: Stephen Sajdak
Media Editor: Eileen Connell
Associate Media Editor: Ariel Eaton
Media Project Editor: Danielle Belfiore
Media Editorial Assistant: Alexandra Park
Ebook Production Manager: Sophia Purut
Marketing Manager, Sociology: Julia Hall
Interior Design: Marisa Nakasone
Design Director: Rubina Yeh
Photo Editor: Catherine Abelman
Permissions Consultant: Elizabeth Trammell
Director of College Permissions: Megan Schindel
Composition: Graphic World
Manufacturing: Transcon

Library of Congress Cataloging-in-Publication Data

Names: Giddens, Anthony, author.
   Title: Introduction to sociology / Anthony Giddens, London School of Economics, Mitchell Duneier, Princeton University, Richard P. Appelbaum, University of California, Santa Barbara, Deborah Carr, Boston University.

Description: Seagull 12e [edition] | New York : W.W. Norton & Company, [2021] | Includes bibliographical references and index.
Identifiers: LCCN 2020047531 | **ISBN 9780393428216** (paperback) | ISBN 9780393537963 (epub)

Subjects: LCSH: Sociology.

Classification: LCC HM585 .G53 2021 | DDC 301--dc23
LC record available at https://lccn.loc.gov/2020047531

1 2 3 4 5 6 7 8 9 0

Brief Contents

Contents

Part II: The Individual and Society 55

Part III: Structures of Power 237

11

12

16

17

Part V: Social Change in the Modern World 703

20

Preface

We wrote this book with the belief that sociology plays a key role in modern intellectual culture and occupies a central place within the social sciences. We have aimed to write a book that combines classic theories of sociology with empirically grounded studies and examples from real life that reveal the basic issues of interest to sociologists today. The book does not bring in overly sophisticated notions; nevertheless, ideas and findings drawn from the cutting edge of the discipline are incorporated throughout. We hope it is a fair and nonpartisan treatment; we endeavored to cover the major perspectives in sociology and the major findings of contemporary American research in an evenhanded, although not indiscriminate, way.

MAJOR THEMES

The book is constructed around eight basic themes, each of which helps give the work a distinctive character. One of the central themes is the **micro and macro link**. At many points in the book, we show that interaction in micro-level contexts affects larger, or macro-level, social processes, and that these macro-level processes influence our day-to-day lives. We emphasize that one can better understand a social situation by analyzing it at both the micro and macro levels.

A second theme is that of the **world in change**. Sociology was born out of the transformations that wrenched the industrializing social order of the West away from the ways of life that characterized earlier societies. The world created by these changes is the primary object of sociological analysis. The pace of social change has continued to accelerate, and it is possible that we stand on the threshold of transitions as significant as those that occurred in the late eighteenth and nineteenth centuries. Sociology has prime responsibility for charting the transformations of the past and grasping the major lines of development taking place today.

Another fundamental theme is the **globalization of social life**. For far too long, sociology has been dominated by the view that societies can be studied as independent and distinct entities. But even in the past, societies never really existed in isolation. In current times, we can see a clear acceleration in processes of global integration. This is obvious, for example, in the expansion of international trade across the world, or the rapid spread of the deadly coronavirus disease around the globe. The emphasis on globalization also connects closely with the interdependence of the industrialized and developing worlds today.

The book also focuses on the importance of **comparative study**. Sociology cannot be taught solely by understanding the institutions of any one particular society. Although we have focused our discussion primarily on the United States, we have balanced it with a rich variety of materials drawn from other cultures. These include research carried out in other Western countries and in Russia and eastern European societies, which are currently undergoing substantial changes. The book also includes much more material on developing countries than has been usual in introductory texts. In addition, we strongly emphasize the relationship between sociology and anthropology, whose concerns often overlap. Given the close connections that now mesh societies across the world and the virtual disappearance of many types of traditional social systems, sociology and anthropology have increasingly become indistinguishable.

A fifth theme is the necessity of taking a **historical approach** to sociology. This involves more than just filling in the historical context within which events occur. One of the most important developments in sociology over the past few years has been an increasing emphasis on historical analysis. This should be understood not solely as applying a sociological outlook to the past but as a way of contributing to our understanding of institutions in the present. Recent work in historical sociology is discussed throughout the text and provides a framework for the interpretations offered in the chapters.

Throughout the text, particular attention is given to a sixth theme—issues of **social class, gender, and race**. The study of social differentiation is ordinarily regarded as a series of specific fields within sociology as a whole—and this volume contains chapters that specifically explore thinking and research on each subject (Chapters 8, 10, and 11, respectively). However, questions about gender, race, and class relations are so fundamental to sociological analysis that they cannot simply be considered subdivisions of the field. Thus many chapters contain sections concerned with the ways that multiple sources of social stratification shape the human experience.

A seventh theme is that a solid grasp of **sociological research methods** is crucial for understanding the world around us. A strong understanding of how social science research is conducted is crucial for interpreting and making sense of the many social "facts" that the media trumpet.

The final major theme is the relationship between the **social and the personal**. Sociological thinking is a vital help to self-understanding, which in turn can be focused back on an improved understanding of the social world. Studying sociology should be a liberating experience: The field enlarges our sympathies and imagination, opens up new perspectives on the sources of our own behavior, and creates an awareness of cultural settings different from our own. Insofar as sociological ideas challenge dogma, teach appreciation of cultural variety, and allow us insight into the working of social institutions, the practice of sociology enhances the possibilities of human freedom.

ORGANIZATION

Every chapter in the Twelfth Seagull Edition follows the same structure, making it easier for students to study. Each chapter opens with an attention-grabbing question that challenges students' misconceptions about the topic.

Each chapter is broken down into four sections:

1. Basic concepts
2. Important theories
3. Current research
4. Unanswered questions

At the end of each section, students have the opportunity to test themselves with integrated "Concept Check" quizzes. The Twelfth Seagull Edition also features "Big Picture" concept maps that integrate the learning objectives, key terms, "Concept Checks," and "Thinking Sociologically" activities into a handy one-stop review tool at the end of each chapter.

The chapters follow a sequence designed to help students achieve a progressive mastery of the different fields of sociology, but we have taken care to ensure that the book can be used flexibly and will be easy to adapt to the needs of individual courses. Chapters can be deleted or studied in a different order without much loss. Each has been written as a fairly autonomous unit, with cross-referencing to other chapters at relevant points.

In this edition, racial and ethnic categorizations are considered proper nouns and thus are capitalized. As Temple University journalism professor Lori Tharps notes, "Black with a capital B refers to people of the African diaspora. Lowercase black is simply a color" (Tharps, 2014). In the same way, "White" as a racial category acknowledges the functions of this label in society. Racial designations are not neutral markers of skin tone, but socially constructed categories whose meanings and boundaries shift over time and place. Treating these categories as proper nouns recognizes them as such (Appiah, 2020).

WHAT'S NEW IN THE TWELFTH SEAGULL EDITION

Chapter 1 (What Is Sociology?): A new chapter opener discusses how the education system was forced to make rapid changes in response to the 2020 coronavirus pandemic, and how the tools of sociology can help make sense of the pandemic's social toll. The impact of the pandemic on education is used as a unifying example throughout Part 1, helping to explain social construction in the college experience, the disruption to social order that can result from quickly moving classes online, and how the pandemic has affected social change. Additionally, the "Development of Sociological Thinking" section has been streamlined for space and clarity.

Chapter 2 (Asking and Answering Sociological Questions): Table 2.2, "Opinion of the United States: Comparison of Selected Nations," has been updated with the most recently available data. In the section on research methods, subsections on recent examples have been clarified to indicate what research method is being illustrated.

Chapter 3 (Culture and Society): A new table, "Applying Sociology to Culture," highlights contemporary applications for important concepts presented in the chapter. Data updates throughout the chapter include: an updated chapter opener with more recent data on social media usage; updated data in the section on values and norms on smoking among American adults as an example of changing norms; more recent data in the industrial societies section on the percentage of the world that lives and works in urban areas; and updated data on poverty and food insecurity in the section on the Global South.

Chapter 4 (Socialization and the Life Course): The "Agents of Socialization" section includes desocialization as a new key term. The discussion of schools as agents of socialization considers changing patterns in the ratio of boys to girls in high school STEM classes. The discussion of the mass media as an agent of socialization has been expanded to address the benefits and detriments of time spent using technologies such as smartphones, social media, and video games. The discussion of work as an agent of socialization features new research on the growing trend of working from home. The "Socialization Through the Life Course" section features new data on child labor practices around the world, an updated definition for young adulthood, new research on divorce rates in midlife, and a new discussion of the growing number of older adults as a proportion of the population and changing trends in social roles for older adults. The "Theories of Socialization" section connects the looking glass self theory to the core themes of symbolic interactionism. This section also expands the discussion of Carol Gilligan's theory of moral development to include feminist critiques of the theory. A new table, "Applying Sociology to Socialization and the Life Course," highlights contemporary applications for important theories presented in the chapter.

Chapter 5 (Social Interaction and Everyday Life in the Age of the Internet): A new table, "Applying Sociology to Social Interaction," highlights contemporary applications for important concepts presented in the chapter. In Part 4, the question on to what extent electronic communication can substitute for face-to-face communication has been updated with new data on Facebook usage.

Chapter 6 (Networks, Groups, and Organizations): The chapter title has been changed to "Networks, Groups, and Organizations" to account for the reordering of the chapter. A new chapter opener discusses COVID-19's ability to rapidly spread via one virus carrier by following one real-life example in NYC. The chapter opener COVID-19 discussion informs the updated "Networks" section at the beginning of "Basic Concepts." A new table, "Applying Sociology to Networks, Groups, and Organizations," applies sociological theories on groups to contemporary examples.

Chapter 7 (Conformity, Deviance, and Crime): A new "Applying Sociology to Deviance" table offers contemporary examples for theories discussed in the chapter. Figure 7.4, "Support for the Death Penalty in the United States," has been updated with the most recent available data. Figure 7.5, "Crime Rates in the United States, 1995–2018," has been updated with the most recent available data.

Chapter 8 (Stratification, Class, and Inequality): The new chapter opener discusses Alexandria Ocasio-Cortez's rise to national prominence and the increasing popularity of socialism in U.S. politics. The chapter opener has been updated with 2019 data regarding the national totals for student loan, credit card, and automobile loan debts. Figure 8.1, "Mean Household Income by Income Group, 1967–2018," has been updated with the most recent data available. In the "Basic Concepts" section, Jeff Bezos's net worth has been updated for 2020 and the average amount of household debt in the United States has been updated with the most recent data available. Figure 8.2, "Median Earnings of Young Adults, 2018," has been updated with the most recent data available. The section on Erik Olin Wright has been expanded to add more background on Wright's work and how he was influenced by Marx. A new "Applying Sociology" table highlights contemporary examples for theories discussed in the chapter. The "Research on Social Stratification" section now discusses research from Rachel Sherman's 2017 book, *Uneasy Street: The Anxieties of Affluence*. Data on the unemployment rate has been updated with the most recent available data, with COVID-19's impact on the economy in mind. The income ranges for all socioeconomic levels have been updated with 2019 data, while the section on the "underclass" has been removed. Figure 8.3, "Americans Living in Poverty, 2018," has been updated with the most recent data available. Figure 8.4, "Families with Children under 18 in Poverty, 2018," has been updated with the most recent data available. The use of "elderly" has been removed from the chapter and replaced with terminology such as "older adults," "65+ population," "retirement age," etc. Figure 8.6, "Distribution of Income in the United States, 1967–2018," and Figure 8.7, "Percentage of the U.S. Population on Welfare, 1970–2015," have been updated with the most recent available data.

Chapter 9 (Global Inequality): The chapter opener now discusses the three wealthiest men in the world. The percentage of the world's wealth that billionaires have has been updated with the most recent available data. Research regarding how billionaires have been affected by the COVID-19 pandemic has been incorporated into the opener. A new figure 9.1, "The Distribution of the World's Wealth, 2019," now shows where wealth is concentrated around the word. In "Basic Concepts," the concept of GNI has now replaced GDP. Global Map 9.1, "Rich and Poor Countries: The World by Income, 2020," has been updated with the most recent available data. The "Low-Income Countries" section has been expanded to discuss the economies in low-income countries. This section also now includes a lengthier discussion of family size and how this correlates to a country's income level. A new section, "Is Global Economic Well-Being Improving?" has been added, which discusses how economic well-being has improved globally between 1999 and 2019. A new section, "Going Beyond Purely Economic Measures of Well-Being," has been added, which addresses the issues inherent in relying on World Bank income categories in determining global well-being. A discussion regarding the difference between relative and absolute poverty has been added to this section. A 2019 list of conclusions the United Nations has made via the Capabilities Approach regarding social well-being has also been added to this section. An explanation of neoliberalism and Keynesianism has replaced the section on market-oriented theories. A discussion concerning the rise of East Asian economies as related to dependency theory has been added to the "Dependency Theories" section. The section on world-systems theory now builds on the concept of global commodity chains as they relate to world-systems theory. The example of Apple relying on global commodity chains has been updated to include how an iPhone 11 Pro Max is made. A new section, "The Theory of Global Capitalism," which discusses global capitalism as defined by William Robinson, has been added. A new "Applying Sociology to Global Inequality" table highlights contemporary applications for theories presented in the chapter. The projected world population increase for 2100 has been updated with the most recent available data. The "Health" section now includes COVID-19 infection and mortality rates, as well as a discussion concerning its global spread and how it has affected the global economy. Global Map 9.2, "Hunger Is a Global Problem," has been updated with the most recent available data. Figure 9.2 (previously Figure 9.1), "Extreme Poverty by Region, 1990 and 2018," has been updated with the most recent available data. Research regarding the rise of far-right nationalist politics throughout Europe has been added to the "What Does Rapid Globalization Mean for the Future of Global Inequality?" section. Figure 9.3 (previously 9.2), "Share of the Total Income Going to the Top 1%, 1900–2015," has been updated with the most recent available data.

Chapter 10 (Gender Inequality): The percent of women holding Fortune 500 CEO slots has been updated with the most recent available data. In the "Sociological Theories of Gender Inequalities" section, a new table, "Applying Sociology to Gender," highlights contemporary applications for theories discussed in the chapter. A 2017 study regarding women and the college majors they're studying has been added to Part 3. Figure 10.1, "Women's Participation in the Labor Force in the United States, 1948–2018," Figure 10.2, "Occupational Segregation," and Figure 10.3, "The Gender Pay Gap," have been updated with the most recent available data. The section "Global Gendered Inequalities in Economic Well-Being" has been fully updated with the most recent available data. A 2016 study by Pew Research Center regarding how sharing chores impacts marriage has been added. The "Gender Inequality in Politics" section has been updated with the most recent data available. Research on women-dominated professions and what women earn (compared to men) in these same fields has been updated with the most recent data available.

Chapter 11 (Race, Ethnicity, and Racism): The section on institutional racism has been fully updated and now discusses George Floyd's death, the subsequent protests, and how this has impacted the way racial inequality is discussed in the United States. A new table, "Applying Sociology to Race," highlights contemporary applications for theories discussed in the chapter. The "Hispanics and Latinos in the United States" section has been updated with the most recent available data. The percentage of the U.S. population that is foreign born has been updated with the most recent available data. Graduation rate and dropout rates according to racial group have been updated in the "Educational Attainment section." Figures 11.2A and 11.2B, "Percentage of Population with a High School Diploma, 2019" and "Percentage of Population with Bachelor's Degree, 2019," have been updated with the most recent available data. The "Employment and Income" section has been completely updated with the most recent data available. Figure 11.3, "Real Median Income by Race and Hispanic Origin, 1967–2018," has been updated. The "Health" section now discusses how COVID-19 has unequally impacted different racial groups. The number of Black and Hispanic members of Congress has been updated.

Chapter 12 (Aging): The chapter opening discussion now discusses how COVID-19 has impacted the older adult population. The number of older adults making up the U.S. population has been updated with the most recent available data. Life expectancy for men and women has also been updated. Figure 12.1, "Average Life Expectancy at Birth in the United States, 1900–2018," has been updated with the most recent available data. The projected older adult population in 2060 has been updated with 2019 data. The "Biological Aging" section now includes data regarding how many older adults have been infected with and died from COVID-19. A new table, "Applying Sociology to Aging," highlights contemporary applications of theories discussed in the chapter. The number of older adults receiving Social Security and how much of their income it represents has been updated with the most recent available data. Figure 12.4, "Older Population in Poverty by Race, 2017," has been updated. The "Social Isolation" section expands on how COVID-19 has further isolated the older adult population. A discussion regarding how ageism intensified during the COVID-19 pandemic was added to the "Prejudice" section. The "Health Problems" section has been updated with the most recent data available. Table 12.2 (previously Table 12.1) has been updated. The "Unanswered Questions" sections have been updated with the most recent available data. All instances of "elderly" have been replaced by terminology such as "older adults," "retirement age," "65+ population," etc.

Chapter 13 (Government, Political Power, and Social Movements): The Freedom House data regarding the number of countries classified as "free" has been updated. The members of the Trump cabinet in the "Power Elite" section have been updated to be more recent. A new table, "Applying Sociology to Government, Political Power, and Social Movements," highlights contemporary applications for theories discussed in the chapter. The "Role of the Military" section has updated the amount of money that the United States has spent on the War on Terror as of 2020. Figure 13.1, "World's 15 Largest Military Budgets, 2019," has been updated with the most recent available data. The percent of the population that identifies as Democrat, Republican, and Independent has been updated as of December 2019. The number of women represented in the federal government has been updated with the most recent available data in "The Political Participation of Women" section. The number of people using the Internet globally has been updated with the most recent available data in the "Political Participation in the United States" section. This data has also been broken down by age, race, and gender. The number of people lacking adequate food and the number of people in danger of extreme food shortage has been updated with the most recent available data. Survey responses from Americans regarding how many trust the government and how many would prefer a larger government have been updated in the "Is Democracy in Trouble?" section.

Chapter 14 (Work and Economic Life): The chapter opener now expands on Pou Chen's subsidiary, Yue Yuen, and its refusal to comply with a Cambodian Arbitration Council ruling in 2017. The opener now uses the Yue Yuen example to elaborate on how global supply chains have transformed the world economy. GNI has replaced the use of GDP in this chapter. Walt Disney's purchase of 21st Century Fox in 2019 has been added to the "Types of Capitalism" section. The discussion of managerial capitalism now includes more information on company ownership as well as an updated discussion of how large corporations have moved much of their production overseas. The section on post-Fordism has been expanded so that it now includes a discussion of how global supply chains and developments in artificial intelligence have affected workers. Data on Walmart's worldwide revenues and employees has been added. In "Mass Customization," the number of apps available to Android and Apple users has been added. The key term definition for "flexible production" has been revised. The "Informal Economy" section has been expanded in order to include a discussion of the vulnerable status of many domestic and migrant workers across the globe. The "Corporations and Corporate Power" section has added research on some of the largest and most recent mergers and acquisitions. Table 14.2, "Corporate Globalization: The World's 50 Largest Economies (in Billions of Dollars), 2018," has been updated with the most recent available data. The "Transnational Corporations" section now mentions and includes an image of the MSC Gülsün, the largest container ship in the world. Figure 14.1, "Work Stoppages Involving 1,000 Workers or More, 1947–2019," has been updated with the most recent available data. Figure 14.2 (previously Figure 14.3), "Unemployment Rate in the United States, 1947–2020," has been updated with the most recent available data. A new section, "Unequal Pay," has been added in "Current Research on Work and Economic Life," which discusses CEO-worker wage gaps. A new figure, Figure 14.3, "Americans' Paychecks, 1984–2018," has been added. The "Unemployment" section has been expanded and now highlights how unemployment rates have impacted different racial and ethnic groups in distinct ways. This section also includes research on the unemployment rate in the United States during the COVID-19 crisis and discusses how COVID-19 has impacted the job market and global economy. Updated data on the difference in earnings between unionized and non-unionized workers has been added, as well as data on unionized workers according to industry. Research on the minimum wage in "Low-Wage Work" has been updated to the most recent available data. Figure 14.4 (previously Figure 14.3), "The Rise of the Service Sector, 1900–2018," has been updated with the most recent available data. The discussion on automation has been significantly expanded to include updated research on off-shoring and white-collar jobs, and it now includes a more in-depth discussion of companies such as Amazon and Uber. A new table, "Applying Sociology to Work and Economic Life," highlights contemporary applications of theories discussed in the chapter. A more up-to-date, expanded version of the Knowledge Economy Index (KEI) has been included in the chapter, along with an accompanying discussion, list, and critique of how the KEI doesn't always correctly measure economic success.

Chapter 15 (Families and Intimate Relationships): The "Symbolic Interactionist Approaches" section now includes research by Christopher Carrington on how same-sex couples "do gender." The "Feminist Approaches" section has been expanded to include how economic factors can affect the gendered allocation of household roles. A new table, Table 15.1, "Applying Sociology to Families," highlights contemporary applications of theories discussed in the chapter. The "Contemporary Perspectives in the Sociology of Families" section now includes 2017 survey data concerning beliefs about gender roles. A new section, "Dating and Courtship," has been added, which highlights how courtship has changed drastically from the eighteenth century to the twenty-first century. This section includes coverage of how twenty-first-century dating apps have transformed courtship, changing attitudes toward same-sex dating, and how dating partners from different racial, ethnic, and religious backgrounds has become more common. Figure

15.1, "Median Age at First Marriage, 1890–2019," has been updated with the most recent available data. The "Race, Ethnicity, and American Families" section has updated data on Native American, Hispanic and Latino, Black, and Asian families using the most recent available research. Figure 15.3, "Living Arrangements for White and Black Children, 2019," has been updated. A new section on multiracial families has been added. The "Hispanic and Latinx-Origin Families" section has been expanded to include research on the effects of parental deportation and separation on children's well-being. The section on Black families now highlights the differences between U.S.-born and immigrant Blacks. It also includes a discussion of the increasing rates of interracial marriage. This section has been expanded to include a summary of E. Franklin Frazier's book *The Negro Family in the United States* and how his research has been received by contemporary scholars. The "Nonmarital Childbearing" section has been revised to include more research on how cohabitating unions vs. marital unions affect children. The "Class-Based Cultural Practices" section has been significantly revised to include a discussion on child-rearing habits and class. The discussion of divorce has been streamlined and now highlights more general discussions of how family instability affects the well-being of children. Figure 15.5, "Divorce Rates in the United States, 1920–2018," has been updated. The "Repartnering and Stepparenting" section (previously "Remarriage and Stepparenting") has been renamed and expanded. Figure 15.6, "Rise of Single-Parent Families, 1970–2019," has been updated. The "Same-Sex Couples" section has been updated to include recent developments, such as same-sex marriage being legalized in Taiwan in May 2019. "Unanswered Questions" has now been renamed "Contemporary Questions." Data on adoption rates between same-sex and different-sex couples have been added.

Chapter 16 (Education): The chapter opener quiz and discussion have been replaced with the previous edition's Chapter 1 opener and discussion. This opener discusses the history of the college admission process at Ivy League universities. A new table, "Applying Sociology to Education," highlights contemporary applications for concepts discussed in the chapter. The "Children Left Behind" section has updated with the most recently available data regarding funding for schools in poor vs. wealthy neighborhoods. The "School Discipline" section includes updated data on the percent of Black students enrolled in school vs. the percent of Black students referred to law enforcement. The "Race and The 'Acting White' Thesis" section now includes data on reading and math assessment scores between White, Black, and Hispanic students. In the "Gender and Achievement" section, the discussion of differences between testing scores among boys and girls has been updated with the most recent available research. "Global Perspectives: Education and Literacy in the Developing World" has updated global illiteracy rates. Global Map 16.1, "Adult Literacy Rates Worldwide (15 years and older)" has been updated with the most recent available data. "Education and the Technology Gap" now discusses access to electronic devices during the COVID-19 pandemic. "Is Homeschooling a Substitute for Traditional Schooling?" now discusses how the COVID-19 pandemic impacted students and their parents differently as they transitioned to remote learning. The percent of foreign students studying STEM at American universities has been updated in "Who Benefits from 'International Education'?" The number of American students studying abroad has been updated with the most recent available data.

Chapter 17 (Religion in Modern Society): The "Secularization: The Sociological Debate" section now includes 2018 survey data concerning how important religion is to individuals around the world. This section now discusses the rise and popularity of Christianity in sub-Saharan Africa. The number of Christians globally has been updated with the most recent available data. The projected growth rate of the global Muslim population has been updated with 2020 data. The Muslim population in Indonesia has been updated with the most recent available data. In "Religion in the United States" data concerning the rise of the religiously unaffiliated in the

United States has been updated. The "Catholicism" section has updated data concerning how often Catholics attend church. "Other Religious Groups" has updated data on the percent of American Jews that practice Reform Judaism. This section also includes updated data regarding the percentage of U.S. adults who identify as Jewish. Political affiliation among White evangelical Protestants in the United States has been updated with the most recent available data. A new table (Table 17.1), "Applying Sociology to Religion in Modern Society," highlights contemporary applications of theories discussed in the chapter. "Is Religious Violence on the Rise?" adds that cyberattacks are now globally considered one of the top threats to national security.

Chapter 18 (The Sociology of the Body: Health, Illness, and Sexuality): In the chapter opener, the percentages of obese American adults by gender and race have been updated. Map 18.1, "Percentage of the U.S. Adults Classified as Obese (BMI > 30), 2018," has been updated with the most recent available data. In Part 1, the percentages of the U.S. population that identify as bisexual, lesbian, or gay have been updated. A new table, "Applying Sociology to the Body," highlights contemporary applications for theories discussed in the chapter. In Part 3, the most "fatal" jobs list has been updated according to the most recent available data. A new discussion of life expectancy as it correlates to education has been added. Early life mortality data according to race and ethnicity have been updated. The median wealth of Black, White, and Hispanic households has been updated. A lengthier discussion regarding health differences among White and Black people has been added. Data regarding the gender gap in life expectancy have been updated. The number of people lacking access to safe water has been updated. Data regarding the number of people newly infected with or killed by AIDS/HIV has been updated. Global Map 18.2, "The Number of HIV-Positive People around the World," has been updated with the most recent available data. Data regarding the percentage of high schoolers who have had sexual intercourse by age 18 has been updated from 2011–2015. Recent research regarding the number of LGBT students who have been bullied in school has been added. Data regarding the percent of the population in support of same-sex marriage in the United States has been added for 2019. The list of countries which have legalized same-sex marriage has been updated. In Part 4, the distribution of income in the United States has been updated. The number of Americans suffering from eating disorders has been updated.

Chapter 19 (Population, Urbanization, and the Environment): This chapter has been thoroughly revised with a new emphasis on the environment and climate change. The chapter opener discussion has been updated with a comparison between the world's population 2,000 years ago and the current population of the United States, according to 2018 U.S. Census data. The opener has also been revised with more recent research on the rapidly increasing global population and what this means for sustainability. Part 1 has updated data on which countries have the highest crude birth rates. By reviewer request, the discussion on fertility vs. fecundity has been removed and a more indepth discussion on crude death rates has been added in its place. This section also explains how and why crude death rates can be misleading, using updated data from the World Bank. The "Dynamics of Population Growth" section now includes more up-to-date data on how much the world population is increasing each year. Part 2 now includes a lengthier discussion on how the transition to large-scale urban living in the twentieth century has had enormous consequences for the environment. The "Urbanism as a Way of Life" section has been streamlined for length and clarity. The section on Jane Jacobs now highlights the continuing impact of her book *The Death and Life of Great American Cities*. The section on Saskia Sassen includes a lengthier discussion on the interlinking relationships within global cities between prosperous business districts and nearby impoverished areas. A new section that discusses the percentage of the world population living in cities has been added to "A Brief

History of Urbanization." Research regarding the spread of COVID-19 in urban areas has been added. A new section, "Urbanization in the United States," has been added. "The Decline of Rural America?" now includes U.S. Census data that compares the rural population percentages from the 1950s to 2017. This section includes more information on health issues endemic to the rural United States, as well as recent survey data on whether Americans would prefer to live in rural, urban, or suburban locations, according to age. The section on "Suburbanization" has absorbed the "History of Suburbs" subsection and includes a history of suburbanization and race. A new section, "Explosive Urbanization in the Global South," which discusses rural-urban population shifts throughout the global south, has been added. Another new section, "The New Ecological Paradigm in Sociology," highlights changes in thinking about human-environmental relations within the field of sociology from the 1970s through the present. The section on "Global Environmental Threats" now includes a discussion on per-person consumption throughout the world. A new section, "Global Warming and Climate Change: Welcome to the Anthropocene," includes recent data on worldwide energy use, with a new figure illustrating global energy consumption from 1990 up until 2040. This section also highlights the findings of the Intergovernmental Panel on Climate Change (IPCC) 2014 report on how to mitigate the effects of global warming, as well as the negative impact that global warming has had on Indigenous peoples. This section includes data and analysis on the consequences that global warming, population growth, and urbanization will have on urban areas throughout the world. A new section, "Loss of Biodiversity," highlights a May 2019 report concerning the effects of global climate change on species extinction. A new section, "Food Security," details recent IPCC research on global food production. A new section, "Environmental Injustice," includes a discussion on sociologist Robert Bullard and his research on environmental justice. Sections on "Addressing Climate Change—What Is Being Done?" and "The Politics of Climate Change: National Action to Stop Global Warming" have been added, which include the current U.S. approach to climate change. This section highlights the Trump Administration's climate skepticism and the U.S. withdrawal from the Paris Agreement. The section on sustainable development now includes a lengthier discussion on possible ways to achieve sustainable development as well as recent data on the accelerated increase of major greenhouse gases. A new section, "Environmental Social Movements," highlights social movements and demonstrations to protest government inaction on climate change—this section especially focuses on Greta Thunberg's demonstrations against the Swedish government. A new table (Table 19.1), "Applying Sociology to Population, Urbanization, and the Environment," highlights contemporary applications for theories discussed in the chapter. Part 4 now includes a Marxist critique of Malthus's argument that overpopulation will result in starvation. A new section, "Sustainable Development or Adaptation to the Inevitable?" considers how consumers have been urged to purchase ecofriendly products in order to combat climate change, as well as critiques of this method.

Chapter 20 (Globalization in a Changing World): In the chapter opener, the number of films produced in India and Nigeria in 2019 have been added. In Part 3, the number of satellites floating around the earth have been updated. The number of people globally using the Internet has been updated with the most recent available data. The combined revenues of the world's 500 largest transnational corporations in 2018 has been added. A discussion concerning the Australian bush fires, their link to climate change, and the damage they created has been added. Data concerning the distribution of the world's wealth has been updated. The cost of subsidies made to farmers in the United States and in Europe has been updated with more recent data. Data concerning the number of patent applications made in high-income countries has been updated. In Part 4, a new table, "Applying Sociology to Globalization in a Changing World," highlights contemporary applications for theories discussed in the chapter.

ACKNOWLEDGMENTS

During the writing of all twelve editions of this book, many individuals offered comments and advice on particular chapters and, in some cases, large parts of the text. They helped us see issues in a different light, clarified some difficult points, and allowed us to take advantage of their specialized knowledge in their respective fields. We are deeply indebted to them. Special thanks go to Aleksandra Malinowska, who worked assiduously to help us update data in all chapters and contributed significantly to the editing process.

We would also like to thank the many readers of the text who have written with comments, criticisms, and suggestions for improvements. We have adopted many of their recommendations in this new edition.

Ryan Acton, University of Massachusetts Amherst
Ryan Alaniz, California Polytechnic State University
Lindsay Anderson, University of Tennessee at Martin
Cristina Bradatan, Texas Tech University
Joseph Boyle, Brookdale Community College
Andrew Butz, Portland Community College
Emily Campbell, College of the Holy Cross
Rob Crosnoe, University of Texas at Austin
Luciano N. Cruz, Moreno Valley College
Janette Dill, University of Akron
Nancy Downey, University of Nevada, Reno
David Embrick, Loyola University Chicago
Kathryn J. Fox, University of Vermont
Kelly Fulton, University of Texas at Austin
Farrah Cambrice, Prairie View A&M University
Robert Gallagher, Broward College
Chad Goldberg, University of Wisconsin–Madison
Matthew Green, College of DuPage
Kerry Greer, University of British Columbia
Heather Guevara, Portland Community College
Drew Halfmann, University of California, Davis
Gregory Hamill, Oakton Community College
Ted Henken, Baruch College (CUNY)
Cedric Herring, University of Illinois at Chicago
Olivia Hetzler, County College of Morris
Nicole Hindert, Northern Virginia Community College
Christine Ittai, University of Central Florida
Hanna Jokinen-Gordon, Florida State University
Tony S. Jugé, Pasadena City College
Xavia Karner, University of Houston
Kevin Keating, Broward College
Alissa King, Kirkwood Community College
Megan Klein, Oakton Community College
Christopher Knoester, Ohio State University
Jenny Lê, Bellevue College
Alexander Lu, Francis Marion University
Timothy Madigan, Mansfield University of Pennsylvania
Aaron Major, University at Albany (SUNY)

Robert Mackin, Texas A&M University
John Malek-Ahmadi, College of Western Idaho
Catherine Marrone, Stony Brook University (SUNY)
Noriko Matsumoto, University of Vermont
Mike McCarthy, Marquette University
Stephanie Medley-Rath, Lake Land College
Mohsen M. Mobasher, University of Houston–Downtown
Glenda Morling, Kellogg Community College
Julie Netto, Western Connecticut State University
Roger Neustadter, Northwest Missouri State University
Erik Nielsen, Pennsylvania State University
Lauren Norman, Delta State University
Mary Pattillo, Northwestern University
Margaret Preble, Thomas Nelson Community College
Lina Rincon, Framingham State University
Chunhui Ren, Delta State University
Teresa Roach, Florida State University
Christina Ryder, Missouri State University
Randall Salm, College of Southern Maryland
Kim Smith, Portland Community College
Pamela J. Smock, University of Michigan
David Tabachnick, Muskingum University
Ahoo Tabatabai, Columbia College of Missouri
Vaso Thomas, Bronx Community College, CUNY
Lori A. Tuttle, SUNY Jefferson Community College
Oliver Wang, California State University, Long Beach
Amanda White, St. Louis Community College
Claire Whitlinger, Furman University
Daniel Wilson, Montgomery College
Rowan Wolf, Portland Community College
Jane Zavisca, University of Arizona

We have many others to thank as well. We are extremely grateful to project editor Caitlin Moran, production manager Stephen Sajdak, and editorial assistant Angie Merila for managing the myriad details involved in producing this book. Media editor Eileen Connell and associate media editor Ariel Eaton deserve special thanks for creating all the rich materials, including the InQuizitive course, test bank, DVDs, and other instructor-support materials that accompany the book. Cat Abelman and Elyse Rieder painstakingly researched the best photos to grace these pages. Art director Rubina Yeh, designer Marisa Nakasone, and Kiss Me I'm Polish showed exceptional flair and originality in designing and illustrating the book.

We are also grateful to our editors at Norton, Steve Dunn, Melea Seward, Karl Bakeman, Sasha Levitt, and Michael Moss, who have made many direct contributions to the various chapters, and have ensured that we made reference to the very latest research. We would also like to register our thanks to a number of current and former graduate students—many of whom are now tenured professors at prestigious universities—whose contributions over the years have proved invaluable: Wendy Carter, Joe Conti, Francesca Degiuli, Audrey Devine-Eller, Neha Gondal, Neil Gross, Black Hawk Hancock, Dmitry Khodyakov, Paul LePore, Alair MacLean, Ann Meier, Susan Munkres, Josh Rossol, Sharmila Rudrappa, Christopher Wildeman, David Yamane, and Kathrin Zippel.

RESOURCES FOR STUDENTS AND INSTRUCTORS

For Students

InQuizitive

InQuizitive—Norton's adaptive learning platform—delivers a personalized sequence of questions to each student and provides answer-specific feedback in an engaging, game-like environment. With each activity organized around the chapters' signature four-part structure, the revised InQuizitive course for the Twelfth Seagull Edition of *Introduction to Sociology* includes interactive questions on the new "Applying Sociology" tables as well as new questions that ask students to recall and apply theoretical concepts introduced in Chapter 1. Each InQuizitive activity has been streamlined so that there are no more than 50 questions per chapter.

"Writing for Sociology" online tutorials

These tutorials strengthen essential skills such as evaluating sources, developing research questions, choosing a research method, and crafting an effective introductory paragraph. Each tutorial includes concept check questions as well as short answer prompts that can serve as a springboard for papers. Students receive full credit for completing each tutorial, and instructors can review their answers within the Norton gradebook, adjusting grades if they choose. The tutorials offer students low-stakes opportunities to strengthen their writing skills before they start working on a writing assignment.

(New) Everyday Sociology Blog Online Quizzes

Everyday Sociology Blog quizzes on current events show students how understanding sociological theory and methods can enhance their understanding of the world around them. These chapter-based 2–3 question quizzes give instructors a low-stakes but structured way to bring current events into the classroom.

Ebooks

Norton Ebooks give students and instructors an enhanced reading experience at a fraction of the cost of a print textbook. The ebook for *Introduction to Sociology* can be viewed on—and synced among—all computers and mobile devices and allows students to take notes, bookmark, search, highlight, and even read offline.

For Instructors

Resources for Your LMS

A free customizable coursepack for *Introduction to Sociology*, Twelfth Seagull Edition, enables instructors to incorporate student activities and assessment materials into Blackboard or other learning management systems. The coursepack includes integration links to the following resources, organized by chapter:

- Writing for Sociology Tutorials
- Everyday Sociology Blog quizzes
- Key-term flashcards and matching quizzes
- Census activities (select chapters)

Sociology in Practice Videos

The popular Sociology in Practice video series features over ten hours of clips drawn from documentaries by independent filmmakers. Organized by topics such as gender, inequality, and race, the videos are ideal for initiating classroom discussion and encouraging students to apply sociological concepts to popular and real-world issues.

Interactive Instructor's Guide
The easy-to-navigate Interactive Instructor's Guide makes lecture development easy with an array of teaching resources that can be searched and browsed according to a number of criteria. Resources include chapter outlines, discussion questions, suggested readings, class activities, video clips and exercises, and practical advice for how to teach effective online classes.

Lecture PowerPoints
This fully customizable classroom presentation tool features Lecture PowerPoint slides with bulleted classroom lecture notes in the notes field that will be particularly helpful to first-time teachers. The Lecture PowerPoint images include alt text, and the slides are designed to be used with screen readers.

Art PowerPoints and JPEGs
All of the art from the book, sized for classroom display, is available in PowerPoint and JPEG formats. Alt text is included, and the slides are designed to be used with screen readers.

Test Bank
Norton uses evidence-based models to deliver high-quality, pedagogically effective quizzes and testing materials. The framework to develop our test banks, quizzes, and support materials is the result of a collaboration with leading academic researchers and advisers. Questions are classified by section and difficulty, making it easy to construct tests and quizzes that are meaningful and diagnostic. With over 2,000 questions, the thoroughly revised and updated test bank for *Introduction to Sociology*, Twelfth Seagull Edition, includes 15 percent brand-new questions. The *Introduction to Sociology* test bank also includes 5–7 questions per chapter drawn from each chapter's InQuizitive activity; delivering the same questions to students in both formative and summative assessment will increase the likelihood they'll retain the material after the course has ended.

Norton Testmaker brings Norton's high-quality testing materials online. Create assessments for your course from anywhere with an internet connection, without downloading files or installing specialized software. Search and filter test bank questions by chapter, type, difficulty, learning objectives, and other criteria. You can also edit questions or create your own. Then, easily export your tests to Microsoft Word or Common Cartridge files for import into your LMS.

The Study of Sociology

We live in a world today that is increasingly complex. What makes this possible? Why are the conditions of our lives so different from those of earlier times? How will our lives change in the future? To what extent are things that seem natural actually socially constructed? Does the individual matter? These types of questions led to the study of sociology. As you read this text, you will encounter examples from different people's lives that will help answer these important questions.

In Chapter 1, we explore the scope of sociology and learn what insights the field can bring, such as the development of a global perspective and an understanding of social change. Sociology is not a body of theories everyone agrees on. As in any complex field, the questions we raise allow for different answers. In this chapter, we compare and contrast differing theoretical traditions.

Chapter 2 explores the tools of the trade and considers how sociologists do research. A number of basic methods of investigation are available to explore the social world. We must be sure that the information underlying sociological reasoning is as reliable and accurate as possible. The chapter examines the problems encountered when gathering such information and indicates how best to deal with them.

1

What Is Sociology?

What percentage of college students were enrolled exclusively in online courses in 2017?

A   5%

B   16%

C   28%

D   40%

TURN THE PAGE FOR THE CORRECT ANSWER.

O nline college courses have become ever more popular in the past decade. Remote learning is more flexible, and thus more convenient for many students, especially those who hold jobs while pursuing degrees, and less costly for universities. Many exclusive, private institutions, however, have resisted the trend, claiming that in-person learning is far more effective. In 2020, a worldwide state of emergency forced virtually every U.S. college and university to switch to remote learning overnight, leading to a situation that may impact higher education for many years to come.

In late winter of 2020, the global pandemic known as COVID-19 hit the U.S. education system with the force of a major earthquake. As the number of people infected by this new strain of a potentially deadly virus increased day by day, public officials began urging people to cancel public events and limit inessential social intercourse in the hope that "social distancing" would check and eventually stop the contagion. Soon more draconian measures became necessary. Thus, on Friday, March 13, 2020, President Donald Trump declared a state of national emergency. One by one, governors and mayors of deeply affected areas passed ordinances closing down brick-and-mortar businesses, restaurants, entertainment venues, and public institutions.

Although it was known that those under 20 years of age without preexisting medical conditions were at minimal risk of dying from COVID-19, they could easily contract the virus in the classroom and pass it on to their elders and others at risk. Within a few days of the president's declaration, therefore, colleges and universities began shutting their dorms on short notice and sending students home for the rest of the semester. School districts across the United States followed suit, announcing that they too would be closing down for an indefinite period. Each institution—public or private—was left to its own devices to figure out how to conduct a massive switch to remote learning within a week or two.

The pandemic placed a great burden not only on educators but also on working parents who were suddenly called upon to find some-

THE ANSWER IS B.

LEARNING OBJECTIVES

1 Basic Concepts

Learn what sociology covers as a field and how everyday topics are shaped by social and historical forces. Recognize that sociology involves not only acquiring knowledge but also developing a sociological imagination.

2 The Development of Sociological Thinking

Learn how sociology originated and understand the significance of the intellectual contributions of early sociologists.

3 Modern Theoretical Approaches

Be able to identify some of the leading theorists and the concepts they contributed to sociology. Learn the different theoretical approaches modern sociologists bring to the field.

4 How Can Sociology Help Us?

Understand how adopting a sociological perspective allows us to develop a richer understanding of ourselves and the world.

one to supervise their children at home, just as they themselves were dealing with the threat of impending unemployment and the need to protect older relatives more vulnerable to the disease. Many could not afford day care, while those who could were often nervous about leaving children in places where they could contract the virus. As the crisis escalated, day cares too began closing, leaving parents with no alternative but to keep their children at home, or with anybody they could find. The rapid rise in fatalities soon led governors across the country to issue "shelter in place" ordinances that shut down all inessential businesses and services and forced people indoors indefinitely. Although some could continue working remotely from home, millions more found themselves out of work, at least into the indefinite future, and wondering about their future once the virus ran its course. Indeed, many found themselves more stressed about logistics than about the actual disease.

The rapid change to distance learning for all classes highlighted inequalities among students that traditional campus life often obscured.

This massive upheaval amplified changes and societal trends in the works since the early twenty-first century. Online classes, for example, though peripheral to and even resisted by many private elite institutions, were already common at state universities and commuter schools due to their cost-effectiveness and convenience for less affluent or unconventional students who need to work while attending school. During the pandemic, however, everyone—regardless of their knowledge of online teaching tools—was forced to enter a virtual classroom operated by programs such as Zoom and Webex and adjust their pedagogical methods accordingly. In an unexpected reversal of fortune, faculty at less prestigious institutions now had a considerable advantage over their more privileged colleagues, who were rushed through the essentials by hastily organized online workshops that they often had difficulty following.

The problems facing K-12 education were of a different sort. Although some school districts around the country already used programs such as Google Classroom to assist in teaching, many, especially in poorer regions, still relied on traditional in-person pedagogical methods that were not easily adaptable to screens. Moreover, many parents, especially those of low economic status, who suddenly found themselves pushed into the role of teacher, had no idea how to navigate these online tools, let alone teach others how to use them.

On top of dealing with these trying circumstances, parents had to be on constant alert to ensure that their children were attending online classes rather than checking social media, playing games, watching videos, or chatting with friends. Now that even education was reduced to an electronic device, it was virtually impossible to limit screen time or combat children's obsession with computer games and social media. Cooped up in their homes week after week, parents were likewise glued to the screens as they sought fresh news about the pandemic or tried to sift through the barrage of advice on how to deal with this new reality.

The pandemic exacerbated not only social trends, but also social inequalities and vulnerabilities. Some college students were able to come home to economically stable and secure environments, where they could complete the semester in relative comfort; however much the national emergency disrupted their immediate educational plans, it was unlikely to stop them from reaching their long-term professional goals. Those less affluent, however, sometimes from the very same classes, often returned to cramped households in lower income areas more vulnerable to contagion and thus less conducive to serious study. Bombarded by reports of an imminent economic crisis, these students were also more likely to be stressed by the possibility of financial restraints jeopardizing their educational and professional future.

As students participated in Zoom sessions from their homes, the economic disparities between them could be easily visible from their screens. At college they were used to playing on the same sports teams, eating in the same cafeterias, and living in the same dorms with roommate assignments generated by lottery. Whereas everyday college life disguised many of the disparities, now socioeconomic differences were visible for all to see. One student might be staring into a Zoom session with a background from her parents' vacation home on the coast of Maine, while another might be on lying on a small bed, the only space to work in a tiny room that had no room for a desk. It was no wonder that many students at either end of the economic spectrum chose to keep their camera off (Casey, 2020).

Although we are by no means ignorant of these stark differences in our everyday lives, we all go through life with a certain limited perspective and certain moments give rise to a heightened consciousness. When the average person suddenly "takes note," they are using what C. Wright Mills called the **sociological imagination**, a phrase he coined in 1959 in a now-classic book (Mills, 2000; orig. 1959). Mills tried to understand how the average person in the United States understood his or her everyday life. According to Mills, each of us lives in a very small orbit, and our worldview is limited by the social situations we encounter on a daily basis. These include the family and the small groups we are a part of, the school we attend, and even the dorm in which we live. All these things give rise to a certain limited perspective and point of view.

The average person, according to Mills, doesn't really understand their personal problems or social situation as part of any kind of larger framework or series of goings-on. Mills argued that we all need to overcome our limited perspective. What is necessary is a certain quality of mind that makes it possible to understand the larger meaning of our experiences. This quality of mind is the sociological imagination.

sociological imagination The application of imaginative thought to the asking and answering of sociological questions. Someone using the sociological imagination "thinks himself away" from the familiar routines of daily life.

social structure The underlying regularities or patterns in how people behave in their relationships with one another.

When some students on a Zoom class start taking note of the social backgrounds of their peers, they are connecting their individual experience to a conception of the larger **social structure**. If the on-campus college experience itself functioned to obscure the differences between students, the remote learning experience gives rise to a sudden recognition of the difference in home environments.

1 BASIC CONCEPTS

The scope of sociological study is extremely wide, but in general, sociologists ask themselves certain questions that help to focus the sociological imagination and provide them with the concepts that motivate research. These questions that orient the discipline include, How are the things that we take to be natural actually socially constructed? How is social order possible? Does the individual matter? How are the times in which we are living different from the times that came before?

Social Construction

There is a basic flaw in human reasoning that goes something like this: The things that we see before us are inevitable. They are natural and cannot be changed. What sociology teaches us is that, in many ways, we are freer than we think—that the things we think are natural are actually created by human beings. We might consider the question we started this chapter with as an example: The on-campus college experience, with students congregating in large lecture halls and living in dorms, is a **social construction** located in a specific historic moment. Who would have ever thought that in a matter of weeks the entire system could be transformed? Yet, now we are more aware than ever that many aspects of a college education can actually be undertaken remotely. There is nothing natural about a campus education.

Another example comes from everyday experiences with sex and gender. A baby is usually born with either a penis or a vagina. By way of that characteristic, the baby begins a process of being assigned to the category of "boy" or "girl." This distinction is extremely important because the baby's sex is almost always the first thing you want to know before you interact with him or her. If you can't figure it out, you may ask the parents.

Is this true of any other characteristic? You usually don't need to know the race of a baby before interacting with him or her. You don't need to know the economic class of a baby. Most babies today, regardless of their economic standing, are dressed in mass-produced clothes from stores such as Baby Gap or Target. In general, most parents do not try to signal the class of their baby with his or her garments. The same principle applies to race and ethnicity. Some parents will dress their baby to affiliate with a certain race or ethnic group, but—except on holidays—this practice is less commonplace. Not as many people feel they need to know the race of a baby to interact with the infant.

Sex is different. If you are a parent, you do not want someone coming up to your baby boy and asking, "Is it a boy or a girl?" So what do you do to avoid this scenario? You dress your baby in blue if he is a boy or in pink if she is a girl. Some parents do not do this at the beginning—until they start getting asked that question. Then they start dressing their baby in a certain way so that people will stop asking. Of course, even if you do dress your baby in the traditional blue or pink, there may still be people who come up and ask, "Is it a boy or a girl?" But it is not something that will happen often, because most people are pretty good at reading social cues—such as a blue or pink cap.

Now, the fact that many people need to know the sex of a baby suggests that we interact differently depending on whether we think the baby is a boy or a girl. If a baby is a boy, a

> **social construction** An idea or practice that a group of people agree exists. It is maintained over time by people taking its existence for granted.

People interact differently with babies based on the baby's gender. How do sociologists analyze these interactions?

person might walk up and say something in a traditional masculine style, such as "Hey, bud! How you doin'?" If it's a girl, the person might say something that is more appropriate for a little girl or more in keeping with the norms of traditional femininity. Eventually, we get to the point where these interactions start to mold the kind of person the baby becomes. Children come to see themselves as being either a boy or a girl. They start to move their bodies like a little boy or a little girl. They know that this is how others see them, and they know that when they go out onto the street, they occupy the role of boy or girl. This happens through a process of interaction.

Even though it is not simply a natural occurrence that a person starts to behave as a boy or a girl, many of us are raised to believe that the differences between men and women are purely biological. Sociologists disagree. Does this mean that sociologists want to dismiss the role of biology? No. The goal of sociology is not to try to teach you that the biological realm is a residual category with a minor role in explaining human behavior. One purpose of sociology is to disentangle what is biological from what is socially constructed. It is in part to try to determine how social phenomena relate to biological phenomena. Most sociologists admit that there is a place for the biological. However, many studies show that the things that the average human being thinks are biological, and thus natural, are actually socially constructed. We will explore several of these issues in later chapters.

The more you start to think about disentangling what is natural from what is socially constructed, the more rigorously you will begin to think like a sociologist.

Social Order

Before students were sent home in the spring of 2020 to learn remotely, the social order of a campus classroom was part of our routine experience: A professor looks out onto a lecture hall and sees a roomful of silent students taking notes and exhibiting self-control and discipline. There must be somebody in the room who wishes that he or she were doing yoga instead, or who would like to turn around and say something to a friend in the back. But the fact of the matter is that almost everyone appears to be doing the same thing: sitting quietly, listening, taking notes (or at least pretending to). How can we explain this orderly behavior? How can we explain the existence of social order in a lecture hall or in a society? We certainly need social order to get through the day, but how can we understand it?

Sociologists have offered up many different explanations to try to answer such questions. One explanation is that it is rational for individuals to act this way. Students know it is in their self-interest to sit quietly and pay attention. Perhaps a student hopes to apply to graduate school and wants to get a letter of recommendation from the professor. This goal motivates the student to respond to the classroom environment: The professor's willingness to write a letter is an incentive for good behavior. The recommendation acts as an incentive, stimulating the response of the student who wants it. The student tries to make a good impression, all the while keeping in mind that if he or she turns around and talks to the friend in the back week after week instead of listening, the professor might write an unflattering letter or refuse to write one at all. This explanation based on self-interest and incentives is what economists would use to explain most things. While some sociologists adopt such theories, most find such explanations to be based on an all-too-narrow conception of human nature. They therefore appeal to a different set of theories.

socialization The social processes through which children develop an awareness of social norms and values and achieve a distinct sense of self. Although socialization processes are particularly significant in infancy and childhood, they continue to some degree throughout life. No individuals are immune from the reactions of others around them, which influence and modify their behavior at all phases of the life course.

Thus, another explanation for social order is the existence of norms. It is a norm of social life that when students come into a classroom, they sit and take notes and pay attention. We learn and internalize norms as young people through a process called **socialization**. Once we have internalized a norm, we tend to follow through with the expectations of the norm in most of our interactions. Norms are important to sociologists because they explain some of the ways in which we are inside society and, simultaneously, society is inside us.

Yet another explanation for social order focuses on beliefs and values. Perhaps students place a value on the classroom, on the university, or on higher education. If this is the case, then the social order upheld in classrooms is more than a norm. The lecture hall is a symbol of a greater whole, a sacred place that is part of a larger moral universe. Students sit quietly because they believe professors in this ceremonial order deserve respect, maybe even deference.

It is important to keep in mind that we do not need to choose among these theories. Multiple factors can operate together. All these explanations address the question of social order from a sociological perspective. As such, the existence of social order is not taken for granted. For the average person, the question of social order arises in response to disruptions or breaks in that order. When students began doing remote learning during the COVID-19 pandemic, it was no longer necessary to look directly at the lecturer and pretend to be paying attention. Many students would turn their cameras off for long periods of time and the professor could not know if someone was doing yoga while listening, or whether they were listening at all.

The average person who sees an event such as the attacks on the World Trade Center and the Pentagon on September 11, 2001, or the Sandy Hook school shooting on December 14, 2012, may ask, "How could this event have happened?" The sociologist reverses that question and instead asks, "How is it that disruptions in the social order do not happen more frequently?"

How do sociologists explain the typical orderly behavior in a lecture hall?

Agency and Structure

A long-standing debate in the social sciences revolves around questions of free will and determinism. For example, a deterministic framework would predict that where an individual ends up in life is significantly, if not entirely, influenced by the position into which he or she is born. The sociological imagination can be quite deterministic in that it pushes us to see that, in many ways, the lives of individuals are quite determined by their social roles, gender, race, and class. Yet we would not want you to take away the lesson that individuals are trapped or controlled like puppets.

Take the example of college admissions. It is true that Ivy League graduates have a significantly higher average income than graduates of state-level schools. This difference in income would suggest that the place at which one attends college is a crucial determinant of one's success in later life. However, conventional studies looked only at students who had the same SAT scores and grades; they did not factor in other, personal characteristics that may have had an effect on later success in life.

In 2002, Alan Krueger and Stacy Dale published a study comparing the average yearly incomes of students who had attended an Ivy League college with those who had been admitted to an Ivy League school but chose to attend a state-level college instead. Despite an apparent disparity in opportunities for students who attended Ivy League versus non–Ivy League universities, Krueger and Dale discovered that the average salaries of the two groups of students were essentially the same. However, this study was extended and updated in 2011 and found that there were some notable exceptions to these outcomes. The 2011 study found that for Black and Hispanic students from households with less-educated parents, earning degrees from Ivy League universities did matter (on capitalization of racial and ethnic groups, see preface). While the popular conception that attending elite institutions guarantees future success may not be true for all students, it does appear that racial and socioeconomic disparities do matter for some groups of students (2002; 2011; Gladwell, 2005).

Sociologists tend to think in probabilities. They look at the probabilities that people will end up in certain living situations on the basis of characteristics, de-emphasizing to some extent the power of the individual. However, the sociological imagination does leave room for the person to have an impact, even as we acknowledge that he or she is constrained.

Think about a girl from a working-class family whose parents have active sociological imaginations and a very deterministic understanding of their child's life chances. The parents did not go to college. Instead, they entered the workforce after high school, and they expect that their daughter will do the same. When the teenager tells her parents that she would like to go to college and be a lawyer, the parents

Tocqueville described nineteenth-century Americans as a nation of joiners. Is that still true?

might think of the probability of an individual from their class position achieving such a goal—how unlikely it is. They might tell their child to consider the odds against her and encourage her to pursue a different goal so that she will not be disappointed. What if she took this advice with a grain of salt and applied to college anyway? She would be no different from many of your classmates—and possibly even you. Many of you can think of people who started out just like this, with similar constraints, but who ended up in college due to their refusal to accept the odds as their fate.

Social Change

Another question sociologists ask is how people live in light of the social transformations of their time. For today's generation of college students and their parents, these questions will revolve around whether the world will ever be the same after the COVID-19 pandemic, but questions about social change go back to the beginnings of the field of sociology.

In 1831, Alexis de Tocqueville, a French aristocrat and one of the first great social theorists, visited the United States from France. He wanted to understand how the conditions of democracy and equality were possible. Ever since the publication of his resulting study, *Democracy in America* (1969; orig. 1835), the United States has been viewed through the lens of sociology as a nation of joiners in which, more so than in Europe, people are involved in many groups and activities. Yet sociologists constantly revisit questions about whether the way we live today is different from how we lived in earlier times, and one of the enduring questions is whether Americans are less involved today in public-spirited activities than in the past.

Another great theorist, Max Weber (1947; orig. 1922), looked at the way the world had been changing due to the influence of massive large-scale organizations, and how the emergence of an organizational society and large bureaucratic organizations had changed and transformed social life. Karl Marx, in *Capital* (1977; orig. 1867), examined how industrialization had changed the structure of an entire society, transforming the relationships of individuals to their work and to one another from feudalism to capitalism. Émile Durkheim, in *The Division of Labor in Society* (1964; orig. 1893), discussed how the historical changes wrought by industrialization and urbanization had led to the increasing specificity of the roles individuals filled, and how this specialization functioned to benefit society as a whole. These sound like abstract topics, but they were central to understanding how the world was changing at particular times.

In recent decades, sociologists have focused more and more on the rise of the Internet and how it has transformed everyday life. During the COVID-19 pandemic, many of these changes were not only on full display, but were transformed into a new social reality.

CONCEPT CHECKS

1 What is the sociological imagination, according to C. Wright Mills?

2 How does sociology help us disentangle what is biological from what is socially constructed?

3 How does the concept of social structure help sociologists better understand social phenomena?

2 THE DEVELOPMENT OF SOCIOLOGICAL THINKING

When students start studying sociology, many are puzzled by the diversity of approaches they encounter. Indeed, sociologists often disagree about how to study human behavior and how best to interpret research results. Why is this? Why can't sociologists agree more consistently, as natural scientists seem to do? The answer is bound up with the very nature of the field. Sociology is about our lives and our behavior, and studying ourselves is the most complex endeavor we can undertake. To understand this complexity, sociologists are guided by the four questions we've discussed: How are the things we take to be natural actually socially constructed? How is social order possible? Does the individual matter? How are the times in which we live different from those that came before?

Theories and Theoretical Approaches

Auguste Comte

Auguste Comte (1798–1857)

The French philosopher Auguste Comte (1798–1857) invented the word *sociology* to describe the discipline he wished to establish. Comte believed that the scientific method could be applied to the study of human behavior and society, and that this new field could produce knowledge of society based on scientific evidence. Comte believed that sociology, as the scientific study of social life, should model itself after physics; he initially called the subject *social physics*, a term that many of his contemporaries used. Comte also felt that sociology should contribute to the welfare of humanity by using science to predict and control human behavior. His ideas about social planning were predicated on an understanding that society and the social order are not natural or preordained by a divine power, but rather are constructed by individuals. Later in his career, Comte drew up ambitious plans for the reconstruction of French society in particular, and for human societies in general, based on scientific knowledge. The question of whether sociologists should seek to serve humanity with their work is one that sociologists still ask.

Émile Durkheim

Although Émile Durkheim (1858–1917) drew on aspects of Comte's work, he thought that many of his predecessor's ideas were too speculative and vague and that Comte had not successfully carried out his program—to establish sociology on a scientific basis. To have a scientific basis, according to Durkheim, sociologists must develop methodological principles to guide their research. Sociology must study **social facts**—aspects of social life that shape our actions as individuals, such as the state of the economy or the influence of religion. Durkheim's famous first principle of sociology was "Study social

social facts According to Émile Durkheim, the aspects of social life that shape our actions as individuals. Durkheim believed that social facts could be studied scientifically.

facts as things!" By this principle, he meant that social life can be analyzed as rigorously as objects or events in nature.

Like a biologist studying the human body, Durkheim saw society as a set of independent parts, each of which could be studied separately. These ideas drew on the writings of Herbert Spencer, who also likened society to a biological organism. Each of a body's specialized parts—such as the brain, heart, lungs, and liver—contributes to sustaining the life of the organism. These specialized parts work in harmony with one another; if they do not, the life of the organism is threatened. So it is, according to Durkheim, with society. For a society to endure over time, its specialized institutions—such as the political system, the economy, the family, and the educational system—must function as an integrated whole. Durkheim referred to this social cohesion as **organic solidarity**. He argued that the continuation of a society depends on

Émile Durkheim (1858–1917)

cooperation, which presumes a general consensus among its members regarding basic values and customs.

Another theme pursued by Durkheim, and by many others since, is that societies exert **social constraint** over their members' actions. Durkheim argued that society is far more than the sum of individual acts; when we analyze social structures, we study characteristics that have a "firmness" or "solidity" comparable to those of structures in the physical world. Think of a person standing in a room with several

doors. The structure of the room constrains the range of the person's possible activities. The position of the walls and doors, for example, defines routes of exit and entry. Social structure, according to Durkheim, constrains our activities in a parallel way, limiting what we can do as individuals. It is "external" to us, just as the walls of the room are.

Durkheim's analysis of social change was based on the development of the **division of labor**; he saw it as gradually replacing religion as the basis of social cohesion and providing organic solidarity to modern societies. He argued that as the division of labor expands, people become more dependent on one another because each person needs goods and services that those in other occupations supply.

Another of Durkheim's famous studies (1966; orig. 1897) analyzed suicide. Although suicide seems to be a personal act, the outcome of extreme personal unhappiness, Durkheim showed that social factors such as **anomie**—a feeling of aimlessness or despair provoked by

organic solidarity According to Durkheim, the social cohesion that results from the various parts of a society functioning as an integrated whole.

social constraint The conditioning influence on our behavior of the groups and societies of which we are members. Social constraint was regarded by Durkheim as one of the distinctive properties of social facts.

division of labor The specialization of work tasks by means of which different occupations are combined within a production system. All societies have at least some rudimentary form of division of labor, especially between the tasks allocated to men and those performed by women. With the development of industrialism, the division of labor became vastly more complex than in any prior type of production system.

anomie The concept first brought into wide usage in sociology by Durkheim to refer to a situation in which social norms lose their hold over individual behavior.

modern social life—influence suicidal behavior. Suicide rates show regular patterns from year to year, he argued, and these patterns must be explained sociologically. According to Durkheim, processes of change in the modern world are so rapid and intense that they give rise to major social difficulties, which he linked to anomie. Traditional moral controls and standards, formerly supplied by religion, largely break down under modern social development, and this breakdown leaves many individuals feeling that their lives lack meaning. Durkheim later focused on the role of religion in social life. In his study of religious beliefs, practices, and rituals, *The Elementary Forms of Religious Life* (1965; orig. 1912), he explored the importance of religion in maintaining moral order in society.

Karl Marx

Karl Marx (1818–1883)

Karl Marx (1818–1883)—a German economic, political, and social theorist—also sought to explain social changes arising from the Industrial Revolution; however, his ideas contrast sharply with those of Comte and Durkheim. When he was a young man, his political activities brought him into conflict with the German authorities; after a brief stay in France, he settled in exile in Britain. Much of his writing focuses on economic issues, but because he was concerned with connecting economic problems to social institutions, his work is rich in sociological insights.

Marx's viewpoint was founded on what he called the **materialist conception of history**. According to this view, it is not the ideas or values human beings hold that are the main sources of social change, as Durkheim claimed. Rather, social change is prompted primarily by economic influences. The conflicts between classes—rich versus poor—provide the motivation for historical development. In Marx's words, "All human history thus far is the history of class struggles."

Though he wrote about various phases of history, Marx concentrated on change in modern times. For him, the most important changes were bound up with the development of **capitalism**. Those who own capital—factories, machines, and large sums of money—form a ruling class. The mass of the population makes up a class of wage workers, a working class, who do not own the means of their livelihood but must find employment provided by the owners of capital. Capitalism is thus a class system in which conflict is inevitable because it is in the interests of the ruling class to exploit the working class and in the interests of the workers to seek to overcome that exploitation.

According to Marx, in the future, capitalism will be supplanted by a society with no divisions between rich and poor. He didn't mean that all inequalities would disappear. Rather, societies will no longer be split into a small class that monopolizes economic and political power and a large mass of people who benefit little from the wealth their work creates. The economic system that will develop in response to capitalist conflict will be characterized by communal ownership and will lead to a more equal society than we know at present.

Marx's work had a far-reaching effect on the twentieth-century world. Until the fall

materialist conception of history The view developed by Marx according to which material, or economic, factors have a prime role in determining historical change.

capitalism An economic system based on the private ownership of wealth, which is invested and reinvested in order to produce profit.

of Soviet communism at the end of the twentieth century, more than a third of the earth's population lived in societies whose governments derived inspiration from Marx's ideas. In addition, many sociologists have been influenced by Marx's ideas about class divisions.

Max Weber

Max Weber (1864–1920)

Like Marx, the German-born Max Weber (pronounced "Vay-ber," 1864–1920) cannot be labeled simply a sociologist, because his interests spanned many areas. His writings covered the fields of economics, law, philosophy, and comparative history as well as sociology, and much of his work also dealt with the development of modern capitalism. He was influenced by Marx but was also critical of some of Marx's major views. For instance, he rejected the materialist conception of history and saw class conflict as less significant than did Marx. In Weber's view, economic factors are important, but ideas and values have just as much effect on social change.

Some of Weber's most influential writings analyzed the distinctiveness of Western society compared with other major civilizations. He studied the religions of China, India, and the Near East, thereby making major contributions to the sociology of religion. Comparing the leading religious systems in China and India with those of the West, Weber concluded that certain aspects of Christian beliefs had strongly influenced the rise of capitalism. He argued that the capitalist outlook of Western societies had not emerged, as Marx supposed, only from economic changes. In Weber's view, cultural ideas and values shape society and affect individual actions.

One of the most persistent concerns of Weber's work was the study of **bureaucracy**. A bureaucracy is a large organization that is divided into jobs based on specific functions and staffed by officials ranked according to a hierarchy. Industrial firms, government organizations, hospitals, and schools are examples of bureaucracies. Weber saw the advance of bureaucracy as an inevitable feature of our era. Bureaucracy enables large organizations to run efficiently, but at the same time, it poses problems for effective democratic participation in modern societies. Bureaucracy involves the rule of experts who make decisions without consulting those whose lives are affected by these decisions.

Some of Weber's writings also address the character of sociology itself. He was more cautious than either Durkheim or Marx in proclaiming sociology to be a science. According to Weber, it is misleading to imagine that we can study people by using the same procedures by which we use physics or biology to investigate the physical world. Humans are thinking, reasoning beings; we attach meaning and significance to most of what we do, and any discipline that deals with human behavior must acknowledge this fact.

Neglected Founders

Although Comte, Durkheim, Marx, and Weber are foundational figures in sociology, other thinkers from the same period made important contributions. Very few women

bureaucracy A type of organization marked by a clear hierarchy of authority and the existence of written rules of procedure and staffed by full-time, salaried officials.

Table 1.1

INTERPRETING MODERN DEVELOPMENT

DURKHEIM	1.	The main dynamic of modern development is the **division of labor** as a basis for social cohesion and **organic solidarity**.
	2.	Durkheim believed that sociology must study **social facts** as things, just as science would analyze the natural world. His study of suicide led him to stress the influence of social factors, qualities of a society external to the individual, on a person's actions. Durkheim argued that society exerts **social constraint** over our actions.
MARX	1.	The main dynamic of modern development is the expansion of **capitalism**. Rather than being cohesive, society is divided by class differences.
	2.	Marx believed that we must study the divisions within a society that are derived from the economic inequalities of capitalism.
WEBER	1.	The main dynamic of modern development is the **rationalization** of social and economic life.
	2.	Weber focused on why Western societies developed so differently from other societies. He also emphasized the importance of cultural ideas and values on social change.

or members of racial minorities had the opportunity to become professional sociologists during the "classical" period of the late nineteenth and early twentieth centuries. Even the foundational figures in sociology frequently ignored women and racial minorities, at the same time that they were creating the first theories to systematically address inequality, stratification, subjective meaning, and exploitation. As a result, the few women and members of racial minorities who conducted sociological research of lasting importance often remain neglected by the field. These individuals and the theories they developed deserve the attention of sociologists today.

Harriet Martineau

Harriet Martineau (1802–1876)

Harriet Martineau (1802–1876), born and educated in England, has been called the "first woman sociologist." As with Marx and Weber, her interests extended beyond sociology. She was the author of more than 50 books, as well as numerous essays, and was an active proponent of women's rights and the abolition of slavery. Martineau is now credited with introducing sociology to England through her translation of Comte's founding treatise of the field, *Positive Philosophy* (Rossi, 1973). Additionally, she conducted a systematic study of American society during her extensive travels throughout the United States in the 1830s, which is the subject of her book *Society in America* (1962; orig. 1837).

Martineau is significant to sociologists today for several reasons but in particular for her methodological insight. First, she argued that when one studies a society, one must focus on all its aspects, including key political, religious, and social institutions. Second, she insisted that an analysis of a society must include all its members, a point that drew attention to the conspicuous absence of women's lives from the sociology of that time. Third, she was the first to turn a sociological eye on previously ignored issues and institutions, including marriage, children, domestic and religious life, and race relations. Finally, like Comte, she argued that sociologists should do more than just observe; they should also act in ways that benefit society.

W. E. B. Du Bois

W. E. B. Du Bois (1868–1963)

W. E. B. Du Bois (1868–1963) was the first African American to earn a doctorate from Harvard University. Among his many contributions to sociology, perhaps most important is the concept of "double consciousness," a way of talking about identity through the lens of the experiences of African Americans (Morris, 2015). He argued that American society lets African Americans see themselves only through the eyes of others: "It is a particular sensation, this double consciousness, this sense of always measuring one's soul by the tape of a world that looks on in amused contempt and pity. One ever feels his two-ness—an American, a Negro, two souls, two thoughts, two unreconciled strivings, two warring ideals in one dark body, whose dogged strength alone keeps it from being torn asunder" (1903). Du Bois made a persuasive claim that one's sense of self and one's identity are greatly influenced by historical experiences and social circumstances—in the case of African Americans, the effect of slavery, and, after emancipation, segregation and prejudice.

Throughout his career, Du Bois focused on race relations in the United States; as he said in an oft-repeated quote, "The problem of the twentieth century is the problem of the color line" (Du Bois, 1903). His influence on sociology today is evidenced by continued interest in the questions he raised, particularly his concern that sociology must explain "the contact of diverse races of men" (Du Bois, 1903). Du Bois was also the first social researcher to trace the problems faced by African Americans to their social and economic underpinnings, a connection that most sociologists now widely accept. Finally, he connected social analysis to social reform. He was one of the founding members of the National Association for the Advancement of Colored People (NAACP) and a longtime advocate for the collective struggle of African Americans.

Later in his life, Du Bois became disenchanted by the lack of progress in American race relations. He moved to the African nation of Ghana in 1961 when he was invited by the nation's president, Kwame Nkrumah, to direct the *Encyclopedia Africana,* a government publication in which Du Bois had long had an interest. He died in Ghana in 1963. Although Du Bois receded from American life in his later years, his impact on American social thought and activism has been particularly profound, with many ideas of the Black Lives Matter movement informed by his writings (Morris, 2015).

Understanding the Modern World:
The Sociological Debate

From Marx's time to the present, many sociological debates have centered on Marx's ideas about the influence of economics on the development of modern societies. According to Marx, the stimulus for social change in the modern era resides in the pressure toward constant economic transformation produced by the spread of capitalist production.

Capitalism is a vastly more dynamic economic system than any other that preceded it. Capitalists compete to sell their goods to consumers; to survive in a competitive market, firms have to produce their wares as cheaply and efficiently as possible. This competition leads to constant technological innovation because increasing the effectiveness of the technology used in a particular production process is one way in which companies can secure an edge over their rivals. There are also strong incentives to seek new markets in which to sell goods, acquire inexpensive raw materials, and make use of cheap labor power. Capitalism, therefore, according to Marx, is a restlessly expanding system pushing outward across the world. This is how Marx explained the global spread of Western industry.

Subsequent Marxist authors have refined Marx's portrayal. However, numerous critics have set out to rebut Marx's view, offering alternative analyses of the influences shaping the modern world. Virtually everyone accepts that capitalism has played a major part, but other sociologists have argued that Marx exaggerated the effect of purely economic factors in producing change and that capitalism is less central to modern social development than he claimed. Most of these writers have also been skeptical of Marx's belief that a socialist system would eventually replace capitalism.

One of Marx's earliest and most acute critics was Max Weber, whose alternative position remains important today. According to Weber, noneconomic factors have played the key role in modern social development. Weber's celebrated work *The Protestant Ethic and the Spirit of Capitalism* (1977; orig. 1904) proposes that religious values—especially those associated with Puritanism—were of fundamental importance in creating a capitalistic outlook. This outlook did not emerge, as Marx had supposed, only from economic changes.

Weber's understanding of the nature of modern societies, and the reasons for the spread of Western ways of life across the world, also contrasts substantially with that of Marx. According to Weber, capitalism—a distinct way of organizing economic enterprise—is one among other major factors shaping social development in the modern period. Underlying these capitalist mechanisms, and in some ways more fundamental than those mechanisms, is the effect of science and bureaucracy. Science has shaped modern technology and will presumably do so in any future society, whether socialist or capitalist.

CONCEPT CHECKS

1 According to Émile Durkheim, what makes sociology a social *science*? Why?

2 According to Karl Marx, what are the differences between the two classes that make up a capitalist society?

3 In what key ways did Weber's interpretation of modern development differ from that of Marx?

Bureaucracy is the only way of organizing large numbers of people effectively and therefore inevitably expands with economic and political growth. The developments of science, modern technology, and bureaucracy are examples of a general social process that Weber referred to collectively as **rationalization**. Rationalization means the organization of social, economic, and cultural life according to principles of efficiency, on the basis of technical knowledge.

Which interpretation of modern societies, that deriving from Marx or that coming from Weber, is correct? Scholars are divided on the issue. Moreover, within each camp are variations, so not every theorist agrees with all the points of one interpretation. The contrasts between these two standpoints inform many areas of sociology.

3 MODERN THEORETICAL APPROACHES

Although the origins of sociology were mainly European, over the last century, the subject has become firmly established worldwide, and some of the most important developments have taken place in the United States.

Symbolic Interactionism

The work of George Herbert Mead (1863–1931), a philosopher teaching at the University of Chicago, influenced the development of sociological thought, in particular through a perspective called **symbolic interactionism**. Mead placed particular importance on the study of language in analyzing the social world. According to him, language allows us to become self-conscious beings aware of our own individuality. The key element in this process is the **symbol**, something that stands for something else. For example, the word *tree* is a symbol by which we represent the object tree. Once we have mastered such a concept, Mead argued, we can think of a tree even if none is visible. Symbolic thought frees us from being limited in our experience to what we can actually see, hear, or feel.

Unlike animals, according to Mead, human beings live in a richly symbolic universe. This idea applies even to our very sense of self. Each of us is a self-conscious being because we learn to look at ourselves as if from the outside—as others see us. When a child begins to use "I" to refer to that object whom others call "you" (himself or herself), the child is exhibiting the beginnings of self-consciousness.

All interactions among individuals, symbolic interactionists say, involve an exchange of symbols. When we interact with others, we constantly look for clues to discern what type of behavior is appropriate in the context and interpret what others are up to. Symbolic interactionism directs our attention to

rationalization A concept used by Weber to refer to the process by which modes of precise calculation and organization, involving abstract rules and procedures, increasingly come to dominate the social world.

symbolic interactionism A theoretical approach in sociology developed by George Herbert Mead that emphasizes the role of symbols and language as core elements of all human interaction.

symbol One item used to stand for or represent another, as in the case of a flag symbolizing a nation.

George Herbert Mead
(1863–1931)

the detail of interpersonal interaction and how that detail is used to make sense of what others say and do. For instance, suppose two people are on a first date. Each spends a good part of the evening sizing the other up and assessing how the relationship is likely to develop, if at all. Neither wishes to be seen doing this too openly, although each recognizes that it is going on. Both individuals are careful about their own behavior, being eager to present themselves in a favorable light; but, knowing this, both are looking for aspects of the other's behavior that reveal his or her true nature. A complex and subtle process of symbolic interpretation shapes their interaction.

Functionalism

Symbolic interactionism has been criticized for concentrating too much on things that are small in scope. Symbolic interactionists have struggled to deal with larger-scale structures and processes—the very things that a rival tradition of thought, **functionalism**, emphasizes. Functionalist thinking in sociology was originally pioneered by Comte, who saw it as closely bound up with his overall view of the field.

To study the function of a social activity is to analyze its contribution to the continuation of the society as a whole. The best way to understand this idea is by analogy to the human body, a comparison that Comte, Durkheim, and other functionalist authors made. To study an organ such as the heart, we need to show how it relates to other parts of the body. When we learn how the heart pumps blood, we understand its vital role in the continuation of the organism's life. Similarly, analyzing the function of some aspect of society, such as religion, means examining its role in the continued existence and health of a society. Functionalism emphasizes the importance of moral consensus in maintaining order and stability in society. Moral consensus exists when most people share the same values. Functionalists regard order and balance as the normal state of society—this social equilibrium is grounded in a moral consensus among the members of society. According to Durkheim, for instance, religion reaffirms people's adherence to core social values, thereby helping to maintain social cohesion.

Functionalism became prominent in sociology through the writings of Talcott Parsons (1902–1979) and Robert K. Merton (1910–2003), each of whom saw functionalist analysis as providing the key to the development of sociological theory and research. Merton's version of functionalism has been particularly influential.

In his work, Merton distinguished between manifest and latent functions. **Manifest functions** are those known to, and intended by, the participants in a social activity. **Latent functions** are consequences of that activity of which participants are unaware. Merton used the example of a rain dance performed by the Hopi tribe of Arizona and New Mexico. The Hopi believe that the ceremony

functionalism A theoretical perspective based on the notion that social events can best be explained in terms of the functions they perform—that is, the contributions they make to the continuity of a society.

manifest functions The functions of a type of social activity that are known to and intended by the individuals involved in the activity.

latent functions Functional consequences that are not intended or recognized by the members of a social system in which they occur.

will bring the rain they need for their crops (manifest function). This is why they organize and participate in the dance. But using Durkheim's theory of religion, Merton argued that the rain dance also promotes the cohesion of Hopi society (latent function). A major part of sociological explanation, according to Merton, consists in uncovering the latent functions of social activities and institutions.

Robert K. Merton (1910–2003)

Merton also distinguished between functions and dysfunctions. To look for the dysfunctional aspects of social behavior means to focus on features of social life that challenge the existing order. For example, it is incorrect to suppose that religion is always functional—that it contributes only to social cohesion. When two groups support different religions or different versions of the same religion, the result can be major social conflicts, causing widespread social disruption. Thus, wars have often been fought between religious communities—as in the struggles between Protestants and Catholics in European history.

For much of the twentieth century, functionalist thought was considered the leading theoretical tradition in sociology, particularly in the United States. In recent years, its popularity has declined as its limitations have become apparent. While this was not true of Merton, many functionalist thinkers—Talcott Parsons is an example—unduly stressed factors leading to social cohesion at the expense of those producing division and conflict. In addition, many critics claim that functional analysis attributes to societies certain qualities they do not have. Functionalists often wrote as though societies had "needs" and "purposes," even though these concepts make sense only when applied to individual human beings.

Conflict Theories

Functionalism and symbolic interactionism are not the only modern theoretical traditions of importance in sociology. A third influential approach is **conflict theory**. In general, conflict theories underscore the role of coercion and power in producing social order. Social order is believed to be maintained by domination, with power in the hands of those who possess the greatest political, economic, and social resources; historically, those with power would include White men with ample economic and political resources. Two particular approaches typically classified under the broad heading of conflict theories are Marxism and feminist theories.

Marxism

Marxists, of course, all trace their views back to the writings of Karl Marx, but today, some schools of Marxist thought take very different theoretical positions.

In all its variations, **Marxism** differs from non-Marxist traditions of sociology in that its adherents view sociology as a combina-

> **conflict theory** A sociological perspective that emphasizes the role of political and economic power and oppression as contributing to the existing social order.
>
> **Marxism** A body of thought deriving its main elements from the ideas of Karl Marx.

tion of sociological analysis and political reform. Marxism is supposed to generate a program of radical political change. Moreover, Marxists lay more emphasis on conflict, class divisions, power, and ideology than do many non-Marxist sociologists, especially those influenced by functionalism. The concept of **power** is of great importance to Marxist sociologists and to sociology in general. Power refers to the ability of individuals or groups to make their own interests count, even when others resist. Power sometimes involves the direct use of force but is almost always accompanied by the development of ideas (**ideologies**), which are used to justify the actions of the powerful. Power, ideology, and conflict are always closely connected. Many conflicts are about power because of the rewards it can bring. Those who hold the most power may depend on the influence of ideology to retain their dominance, but they are usually also able to use force if necessary.

Feminism and Feminist Theory

Feminist theory is one of the most prominent areas of contemporary sociology. This development is notable because gender issues are scarcely touched upon in the work of the major figures who established the discipline. The success of feminism's entry into sociology required a fundamental shift in the discipline's approach.

Many feminist theorists' experiences in the women's movement of the 1960s and 1970s influenced their work as sociologists. Like Marxism, **feminism** links sociological theory and political reform. Many feminist sociologists have been advocates for political and social action to eliminate the inequalities between women and men in both the public and the private spheres.

Feminist sociologists argue that women's lives and experiences are central to the study of society. Historically, sociology, like most academic disciplines, has presumed a male point of view. Concerned with women's subordination in society, feminist sociologists highlight gender relations and gender inequality as important determinants of social life in terms of both social interaction and social institutions such as the family, the workplace, and the educational system. Feminist theory emphasizes that gendered patterns and gendered inequalities are not natural but socially constructed. (We will cover this point in more detail in Chapter 10.)

Today, feminist sociology focuses on the intersection of gender, race, and class. A feminist approach to the study of inequality

power The ability of individuals or the members of a group to achieve aims or further the interests they hold. Power is a pervasive element in all human relationships. Many conflicts in society are struggles over power, because how much power an individual or group is able to achieve governs how far they are able to put their wishes into practice.

ideologies Shared ideas or beliefs that serve to justify the interests of dominant groups. Ideologies are found in all societies in which there are systematic and ingrained inequalities among groups. The concept of ideology connects closely with that of power, since ideological systems serve to legitimize the power that groups hold.

feminist theory A sociological perspective that emphasizes the centrality of gender in analyzing the social world and particularly the uniqueness of the experience of women. There are many strands of feminist theory, but they all share the desire to explain gender inequality in society and to work to overcome it.

feminism Advocacy of the rights of women to be equal with men in all spheres of life. Feminism dates from the late eighteenth century in Europe, and feminist movements exist in most countries today.

has influenced new fields of study, such as men's studies, sexuality studies, and LGBTQ studies. Taken together, these theoretical perspectives underscore power imbalances and draw attention to the ways that social change must entail shifts in the balance of power—consistent with the overarching themes of conflict theories.

Rational Choice Theory

Max Weber thought that all behavior could be divided into four categories: (1) behavior oriented toward higher values, such as politics; (2) behavior oriented toward habit, such as walking to school on a familiar path; (3) behavior oriented toward affect (emotions), such as falling in love; and (4) behavior oriented toward self-interest, such as making money. Behavior in the last category is often called "instrumental," or "rational," action. In recent years, many sociologists have adopted an approach that focuses on this type of behavior. This approach has led numerous scholars to ask under what conditions human behavior can be said to constitute rational responses to opportunities and constraints.

The **rational choice approach** posits that if you could have only a single variable to explain society, self-interest would be the best one. A person who believes in this approach might even use it to explain things that seem irrational. One popular rational choice theory sees decisions to marry as maximizing self-interest in a marriage market; this understanding might explain why marriage has declined the most in poor African American communities with low rates of employment. The explanation—that it is not in the self-interest of women to marry men who cannot support them (Wilson, 1987)—goes against competing explanations suggesting that poor African Americans don't marry because they don't share mainstream values. The rational choice argument sees the decline as having little to do with values and much to do with self-interest under existing conditions. According to this theory, if employment rates for Black men were to change, so would the number of "eligible" men and the desire of women to marry them.

Rational choice theorists find few irrational mysteries in life. One of the few some note is love, which they define as the irrational act of substituting another person's self-interest for one's own (Becker, 1991). But such a definition makes it difficult to distinguish among basic altruism, friendship, and romantic love. Indeed, although a rational choice approach often can be useful, it cannot explain some aspects of life. Consider an angry driver who tries to teach a tailgater a lesson by tailgating the tailgater. Self-interest does not explain this action, because the "teacher" is unlikely personally to reap the benefits of a lesson well learned (Katz, 1999).

Postmodern Theory

Advocates of **postmodernism** claim that the classic social thinkers' idea that history has a shape—it "goes somewhere" and leads to progress—has collapsed. No longer do any "grand narratives," or metanarratives—overall conceptions of history or society—make any sense (Lyotard, 1985). In fact, there is no such thing as history. The postmodern world is not destined, as Marx hoped, to be a social-

> **rational choice approach** More broadly, the theory that an individual's behavior is purposive. Within the field of criminology, rational choice analysis argues that deviant behavior is a rational response to a specific social situation.
>
> **postmodernism** The belief that society is no longer governed by history or progress. Postmodern society is highly pluralistic and diverse, with no "grand narrative" guiding its development.

ist one. Instead, it is dominated by the new media, which "take us out" of our past. Postmodern society is highly pluralistic and diverse. As countless films, videos, TV programs, and websites circulate images around the world, the many ideas and values we encounter have little connection with our local or personal histories. Everything seems constantly in flux: "[F]lexibility, diversity, differentiation, and mobility, communication, decentralization and internationalization are in the ascendant. In the process our own identities, our sense of self, our own subjectivities are being transformed" (Hall, Held, and McGrew, 1988).

One important theorist of postmodernity, Jean Baudrillard (1929–2007), believed that electronic media created a chaotic, empty world. Despite being influenced by Marxism in his early years, Baudrillard argued that the spread of electronic communication and the mass media reversed the Marxist theorem that economic forces shape society. Instead, he asserted, social life is influenced above all by signs and images. In a media-dominated age, Baudrillard said, meaning is created by the flow of images, as in TV programs. Much of our world is now a make-believe universe in which we respond to media images rather than to real persons or places. Is "reality" television a portrayal of social "reality," or does it feature televised people who are perceived to be "real"? Do hunters in Louisiana really look and act like the Robertson family on *Duck Dynasty*, and do the tough guys in *Amish Mafia* resemble the peaceful Amish who live and work in Lancaster County, Pennsylvania? Baudrillard would say no and would describe such images as "the dissolution of life into TV."

Theoretical Thinking in Sociology

So far, we have been discussing theoretical approaches—broad orientations to the subject matter of sociology. Theoretical approaches are distinct from theories. Theories are more narrowly focused and represent attempts to explain particular social conditions or types of events. Theories are usually formed during the research process and in turn suggest other problems for subsequent research. An example would be Durkheim's theory of suicide, referred to earlier in this chapter.

Sociologists do not share a unified position on whether theories should be specific, wide-ranging, or somewhere in between. Merton (1957), for example, argued that sociologists should concentrate on what he called theories of the middle range. Rather than attempting to create grand theoretical schemes (in the manner of Marx, for instance), sociologists should develop more modest theories. Middle-range theories are specific enough to be tested by empirical research, yet sufficiently general to cover a range of phenomena.

Consider the theory of relative deprivation, which holds that how people evaluate their circumstances depends on the persons to whom they compare themselves. Thus, feelings of deprivation do not conform directly to the level of material poverty one experiences. A family living in a small home in a poor area, where everyone is in similar circumstances, is likely to feel less deprived than a family living in a similar house in a neighborhood where other homes are much larger and other people more affluent.

Assessing theories in sociology, especially theoretical approaches, is a challenging and formidable task. The fact that there is no single theoretical approach that dominates the whole of sociology might be viewed as a limitation. But this is not the case: The jostling of rival theoretical approaches and theories actually highlights the vital-

Microsociology focuses on small-scale face-to-face interactions (left), while macrosociology analyzes large-scale forces (right). How might a microsociologist and a macrosociologist analyze this food court differently?

ity of the sociological enterprise. In studying human beings (ourselves), theoretical variety rescues us from dogma. Human behavior is complex, and no single theoretical perspective could adequately cover all its aspects. Diversity in theoretical thinking provides a rich source of ideas for research and stimulates the imaginative capacities so essential to progress in sociological work.

microsociology The study of human behavior in the context of face-to-face interaction.

macrosociology The study of large-scale groups, organizations, or social systems.

Levels of Analysis: Microsociology and Macrosociology

An important distinction among the theoretical perspectives we've discussed in this chapter involves the level of analysis at which each is directed. The study of everyday behavior in situations of small-scale face-to-face interaction is called **microsociology. Macrosociology,** by contrast, is the analysis of large-scale social systems, such as the political system or the economy. It also includes analysis of long-term processes of change, such as the development of industrialization. Although micro analysis and macro analysis may seem distinct from each other, in fact, the two are closely connected (Giddens, 1984; Knorr-Cetina and Cicourel, 1981).

Macro analysis is essential for understanding the institutional background of daily life. The ways in which people live their everyday lives are shaped by the broader institutional framework. Consider a comparison of the daily cycle of activities in a medieval culture and in an industrialized urban environment. In modern soci-

CONCEPT CHECKS

1 What are the differences between symbolic interactionism and functionalist approaches to the analysis of society?

2 How do rational choice theorists explain human behavior?

3 What role does theory play in sociological research?

4 How are macro and micro analyses of society connected?

eties, we are constantly in contact with strangers—however indirect and impersonal. No matter how many indirect or electronic relationships we enter into, even the most complex societies require the presence of other people. While we may opt to just text or e-mail an acquaintance, we can also choose to fly thousands of miles to spend the weekend with a friend.

Micro studies, in turn, are necessary for illuminating broad institutional patterns. Face-to-face interaction is the basis of all forms of social organization, no matter how large scale. In studying a business corporation, we could analyze the face-to-face interactions of directors in the boardroom, staff working in their offices, or workers on the factory floor. We would not gain a clear picture of the whole corporation in this way, because some of its business involves e-mail, phone calls, and printed materials. Yet we could certainly contribute significantly to understanding how the organization works.

Later chapters will give further examples of how interaction in micro contexts affects larger social processes and how macro systems in turn influence the more confined settings of social life.

4 HOW CAN SOCIOLOGY HELP US?

As we discussed at the beginning of the chapter, sociological thinking is relevant to your day-to-day life—from understanding the profound impact of the COVID-19 pandemic to the actual value of going to a fancy college. C. Wright Mills emphasized these practical applications of sociology when developing his idea of the sociological imagination. When we observe the world through the prism of the sociological imagination, we are affected in several important ways.

First, sociology allows us to see the social world from many perspectives. If we properly understand how others live, we better understand their problems. Practical policies that lack an informed awareness of the ways of life of the people they affect have little chance of success. Thus, a White social worker operating in a predominately Black community won't gain the confidence of its members if he or she isn't sensitive to the differences in social experiences of Whites and Blacks in the United States.

Second, we are better able to assess the results of public-policy initiatives. For example, a program of practical reform may fail to achieve its goals or may produce unintended negative consequences. Consider the large public-housing blocks built in city centers in many countries following World War II. The goal was to provide high standards of accommodation for low-income groups from slum areas and to offer shopping amenities and other civic services close at hand. However, research later showed that many people who moved to the large apartment blocks felt isolated and unhappy. High-

In her book *$2.00 a Day: Living on Almost Nothing in America,* sociologist Kathryn Edin explains how one unintended consequence of welfare reform was a dramatic increase in households with children living on $2 or less a day.

rise apartment blocks and shopping malls in poorer areas often became dilapidated and provided breeding grounds for muggings and other violent crimes.

Third, and perhaps most important, sociology can provide us with self-enlightenment—increased self-understanding. The more we know about our own behavior and how our society works, the better chance we have to influence our futures. Sociology doesn't just help policy makers make informed decisions. Those in power may not always consider the interests of the less powerful or underprivileged when making policies. Self-enlightened groups can benefit from sociological research by using the information gleaned to respond to government policies or form policy initiatives of their own. Self-help groups such as Alcoholics Anonymous (AA) and social movements such as the environmental movement are examples of social groups that have directly sought practical reforms, with some success.

Finally, developing a sociological eye toward social problems and developing rigorous research skills opens many career doors—as industrial consultants, urban planners, social workers, and personnel managers, among other jobs. An understanding of society also serves those working in law, journalism, business, and medicine.

Those who study sociology frequently develop a social conscience. Should sociologists themselves agitate for programs of reform or social change? Some argue that sociology can preserve its intellectual independence only if sociologists remain neutral in moral and political controversies. Yet are scholars who remain aloof more impartial in their assessment of sociological issues than others? No sociologically sophisticated person can be unaware of the inequalities, the lack of social justice, or the deprivations suffered by millions of people worldwide. It would be strange if sociologists did not take sides on practical issues, and it would be illogical to ban them from drawing on their expertise in doing so.

We have seen that sociology is a discipline in which we often set aside our personal views to explore the influences that shape our lives and those of others. Sociology emerged as an intellectual endeavor along with the development of modern societies, and the study of such societies remains its principal concern. But sociologists are also preoccupied with the nature of social interaction and human societies in general.

Sociology has major practical implications for people's lives. Learning to become a sociologist shouldn't be a dull academic endeavor but rather an exciting pursuit! The best way to make sure the pursuit is exciting is to approach the subject in an imaginative way and to relate sociological ideas and findings to your own life.

CONCEPT CHECKS

1 Describe three ways that sociology can help us in our lives.

2 What skills and perspectives do sociologists bring to their work?

THE BIG PICTURE

Chapter 1
What Is Sociology?

1 **Basic Concepts**

p. 7

2 **The Development of Sociological Thinking**

p. 12

LEARNING OBJECTIVES

Learn what sociology covers as a field and how everyday topics are shaped by social and historical forces. Recognize that sociology involves not only acquiring knowledge but also developing a sociological imagination.

Learn how sociology originated and understand the significance of the intellectual contributions of early sociologists.

TERMS TO KNOW

sociological imagination • social structure • social construction • socialization

social facts • organic solidarity • social constraint • division of labor • anomie • materialist conception of history • capitalism • bureaucracy • rationalization

CONCEPT CHECKS

1. What is the sociological imagination, according to C. Wright Mills?
2. How does sociology help us disentangle what is biological from what is socially constructed?
3. How does the concept of social structure help sociologists better understand social phenomena?

1. According to Émile Durkheim, what makes sociology a social science? Why?
2. According to Karl Marx, what are the differences between the two classes that make up a capitalist society?
3. In what key ways did Weber's interpretation of modern development differ from that of Marx?

Exercises: Thinking Sociologically

1. Healthy older Americans often encounter exclusionary treatment when younger people assume they are feebleminded and thus overlook them for jobs they are fully capable of doing. How would functionalism and symbolic interactionism explain the dynamics of prejudice against the elderly?

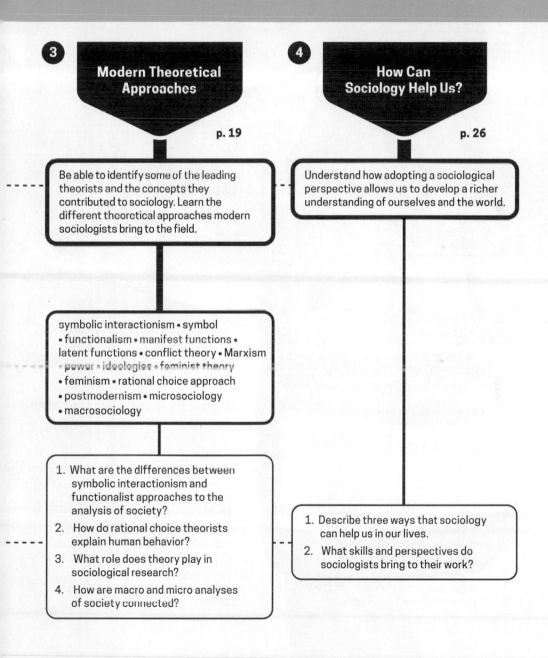

3 **Modern Theoretical Approaches**

p. 19

Be able to identify some of the leading theorists and the concepts they contributed to sociology. Learn the different theoretical approaches modern sociologists bring to the field.

symbolic interactionism • symbol • functionalism • manifest functions • latent functions • conflict theory • Marxism • power • ideologies • feminist theory • feminism • rational choice approach • postmodernism • microsociology • macrosociology

1. What are the differences between symbolic interactionism and functionalist approaches to the analysis of society?

2. How do rational choice theorists explain human behavior?

3. What role does theory play in sociological research?

4. How are macro and micro analyses of society connected?

4 **How Can Sociology Help Us?**

p. 26

Understand how adopting a sociological perspective allows us to develop a richer understanding of ourselves and the world.

1. Describe three ways that sociology can help us in our lives.

2. What skills and perspectives do sociologists bring to their work?

2

Asking and Answering Sociological Questions

Sociology today

A relies increasingly on statistical studies that use big datasets.

B has no place for empathy.

C relies too much on qualitative methods to be a science.

TURN THE PAGE FOR THE CORRECT ANSWER.

When was the last time you posted on a friend's Facebook page, liked a photo, or changed your relationship status? Many of us use social networking to keep up with friends and family and share details about our lives with a wider audience. Indeed, Facebook not only allows us to keep up with those we care about, but it also serves as a detailed record of our social relationships.

In recent years, scholars have taken data from our Facebook pages to ask questions about whom we interact with, whom we befriend, and whom we love. One study claimed that Facebook could predict whether our romantic relationships would last. To make this argument, they drew on a large dataset of more than 1 million individuals in romantic relationships, as well as their Facebook friends—a total of nearly 380 million Facebook users. They found that if two people were romantic partners, and their friendship groups overlapped a great deal, meaning they had the same group of friends, they had a higher likelihood of staying together (Backstrom and Kleinberg, 2013).

If your answer to the question on the previous page was that sociology today relies more and more on studies that, like this one, use big data, then you are correct. Increasingly, studies are relying on statistical or **quantitative methods** and computer programs that make it possible to analyze the vast amounts of data the Internet generates. These methods allow sociologists to process more data than ever before.

Even as we reap all the scientific potential that can be seen in the age of big data, we must also contend with its potential arrogance. Some researchers feel more confident than ever before in the claims that can be made from big datasets. Researchers who have never been to a slum, nor have any personal relationship to a single poor person, feel they can speak with authority about inequality and poverty from a study based on interesting statistical correlations. In the age of big data, empathy and

LEARNING OBJECTIVES

1 Basic Concepts

Learn the steps of the research process. Name the different types of questions sociologists address in their research—factual, theoretical, comparative, and developmental.

2 Asking and Answering Sociological Questions: Historical Context

Contrast Park's and Ogburn's visions of sociology as a science. Understand their influence on contemporary sociological research.

3 Asking and Answering Sociological Questions Today: Research Methods

Familiarize yourself with the methods available to sociological researchers, and recognize the advantages and disadvantages of each.

4 Unanswered Questions

Understand how research methods generate controversies and ethical dilemmas for sociologists.

THE ANSWER IS A.

involvement with communities and people under study are less frequently the basis of social scientific insights. But if you answered *b*—sociology has no place for empathy—that would not be correct either.

Sociology has a rich tradition that also includes **qualitative methods**, which rely on observations, interviews, and archival data. Here, personal involvement and empathy count for a great deal, though most of the insights in qualitative studies also derive from other kinds of sociological thinking. While quantitative analyses may make use of numerical data (such as that collected in surveys or Facebook friend lists), qualitative analyses may use data derived from interactions, interviews, conversations, or observations of a social scene. For example, a qualitative study of the same question asked in the Facebook study of romantic relationships might use fewer cases to focus on richer details of how individuals dissolve their relationships. In *Uncoupling*, Diane Vaughan (1986) explored this question by using interviews with people who broke up to better understand how relationships end.

Does the reliance on qualitative methods make sociology less of a science? It does not. Do quantitative methods make sociology more scientific? They do not. When many people think of a "science," they typically imagine fields like physics or chemistry. Yet, as we shall see, what makes chemistry and physics a science is not the sample size or even the subject matter, but rather a set of values that can be deployed in any research. In this chapter, we begin by discussing those values to clarify the meaning of *science* in social science.

> **quantitative methods** Approaches to sociological research that draw on objective and statistical data and often focus on documenting trends, comparing subgroups, or exploring correlations.
>
> **qualitative methods** Approaches to sociological research that often rely on personal and/or collective interviews, accounts, or observations of a person or situation.

1 BASIC CONCEPTS

Regardless of whether it is quantitative or qualitative, sociological research that is striving to be scientific tries to meet basic scientific standards (King, Keohane, and Verba, 1994).

First, the goal of sociological research is *inference*. By this we mean that when we make observations particular to a specific setting or group, the goal is to be able to generalize beyond that specific entity to others of its kind. In other words, while sociologists cannot collect data about the whole world, they are able to use more limited data to make broader claims about phenomena they cannot directly observe (King et al., 1994). Take as an example *Uncoupling*. If Diane Vaughan limited her claim to the 103 interviews she recorded, this material on its own would not constitute a sociological analysis. Moving beyond these interviews to make more general claims about how we—as humans—form and break romantic relationships is part of what makes her analysis scientific.

Second, sociologists must ensure that other researchers can retrace the paths to their findings. Ideally, others in the scientific community can reproduce their results.

The procedures researchers use for collecting and analyzing data should be public; the reliability of research data can only be verified if the ways in which that data were collected and processed are made explicit to the scientific community, allowing other researchers both to learn from the methods used and to address the limitations of these methods. What's more, careful documentation of the way one arrives at conclusions about the social world allows research findings to be comparable even when conducted by researchers at different times.

Third, the conclusions of all scientific research, including sociology, are uncertain. This might be surprising. Isn't the purpose of studying the social world to be able to make forceful arguments about it? The values of science sometimes demand that we do the opposite. The scientific validity of inferences can be assessed only if researchers are clear about all the sources of their uncertainty. In sociology, like any science, the highest status is conferred on those who are honest about how certain their conclusions really are. Sociologists need to specify all the possible sources of uncertainty in their study.

All three of the previous standards of empirical research are found in both the natural sciences and the social sciences. They are also shared by quantitative and qualitative social science. It is important to highlight a fourth element that is emphasized more in the social sciences—particularly in qualitative research. This is called *reflexivity*. For social scientists, it is particularly important to acknowledge that the investigator is a crucial part of the world she studies and cannot necessarily divorce herself from it. This includes power dynamics among subjects and the ways in which personal values or personal identity influence both the nature of the questions asked and the interpretation of data. Social scientists must thus be ready to reflect on how the way they are part of the social scenes they study may affect the kinds of conclusions they draw. For example, a middle-class researcher studying a poor population should be clear about how his or her class position influenced a sociological argument or the relations with subjects.

These four principles help identify work that is living up to the highest ideals of social science. Some good scientific work might not necessarily be strong in all the areas at once, but the goal of social science should be to achieve as many of them as possible. While these principles are useful for understanding how sociology can strive to be a science, they don't provide a practical guide for how one might begin defining and going on to answer a research question. To do this, we now consider the research process.

The Research Process

In order to understand the way sociology asks and answers questions, it is helpful to think of the research it does as a process. We can better understand the main concepts of research design by breaking down the process into seven stages of research, beginning with the definition of a research question and ending with the dissemination of the study findings.

1. Define the Research Problem

All research starts with a research problem. This problem may be an area of factual ignorance about, say, certain institutions, social processes, or cultures. A researcher might seek to answer questions such as: What proportion of the population holds strong religious beliefs? Are people today disaffected with "big government"? How far does the economic position of women lag behind that of men? Do LGBTQ and straight teens differ in their levels of self-esteem?

The best sociological research begins with problems that are also puzzles. A puzzle arises not simply from a lack of information but also from a gap in our understanding. Much of the skill in producing worthwhile sociological research consists in correctly identifying puzzles.

Rather than just answering the question "What is going on here?" skilled researchers try to illuminate why events happen as they do. Thus, we might ask, Why are patterns of religious belief changing? What accounts for the recent decline in the proportion of the population voting in presidential elections? Why are women poorly represented in science and technology jobs? What are the characteristics of high schools with high levels of bullying?

In looking at this painting by Brueghel, we can observe the number of people, what each is doing, and the style of the buildings. But without the title, *Netherlandish Proverbs*, these facts tell us nothing about the picture's meaning. In the same way, sociologists need theory as a context for their observations.

No piece of research stands alone. One project may lead to another because it raises issues the researcher had not previously considered. A sociologist may discover puzzles by reading the work of other researchers in books and professional journals or by being aware of social trends. For example, an increasing number of public health programs have sought to treat the mentally ill while they continue to live in the community rather than confining them in asylums. Sociologists might be prompted to ask, What has caused this shift in attitude toward the mentally ill? What are the likely consequences for the patients themselves and for the rest of the community?

2. Review the Literature

Once a research problem is identified, the sociologist must review related research: Have previous researchers spotted the same puzzle? How have they tried to solve it? What aspects of the problem has their research left unanalyzed? Have they looked only at small segments of the population, such as one age group, gender, or region? Drawing on others' ideas helps the sociologist clarify the relevant issues and the appropriate research methods.

3. Make the Problem Precise

A third stage involves clearly formulating the research problem. If relevant literature already exists, the researcher may have a good idea of how to approach the problem. At this stage, hunches sometimes become **hypotheses**—educated guesses about what is going on. For the research to be effective, the researcher must formulate a hypothesis in such a way that the factual material gathered will provide evidence either supporting or disproving it.

hypotheses Ideas or educated guesses about a given state of affairs, put forward as bases for empirical testing.

4. Work Out a Design

The researcher then decides how to collect the research materials, choosing from a range of methods based on the study objectives as well as the aspects of behavior under study. For some purposes, a survey (usually involving questionnaires) might be suitable. In other circumstances, interviews or an observational study might be appropriate.

5. Carry Out the Research

Researchers then proceed to carry out the plan developed in step 4. However, during the actual research, unforeseen practical difficulties may arise that force the researcher to rethink his or her initial strategy. For example, it might prove impossible to contact certain questionnaire recipients or interview subjects. A business firm or government agency might not let the researcher carry out the work as planned. Yet omitting such persons or institutions from the study could bias the results, creating an inaccurate or incomplete picture of social reality. For instance, a researcher studying how business corporations have complied with affirmative action programs might find that companies that have not complied do not wish to be studied.

6. Interpret the Results

Once the information has been gathered, the researcher's work is not over—it is just beginning! The researcher must analyze the data, track trends, and test hypotheses. Most important, researchers must interpret their results in such a way that they tell a clear story and directly address the research puzzle outlined in step 1. Although it may be possible to reach clear answers to the initial questions, many investigations are ultimately not fully conclusive.

7. Report the Findings

The research report, usually published as a journal article or book, provides an account of the research question, methods, findings, and the implications of the findings for social theory, public policy, or practice. This stage is only final in terms of the individual project. Most reports identify unanswered questions and suggest new questions for further research. All individual research investigations are part of the continuing process of research within the sociological community.

Reality Intrudes!

The preceding sequence of steps is a simplified version of what happens in actual research projects. These stages rarely succeed each other so neatly; the difference is like that between the recipes outlined in a cookbook and the actual process of preparing a meal: Deviations can sometimes be necessary and beneficial. Experienced cooks often don't work from recipes at all, yet they might cook better meals than those

CONCEPT CHECKS

1 Compare and contrast qualitative and quantitative research methods.

2 What are the seven steps of the research process?

3 What is a hypothesis?

who do. Following fixed schemes can be unduly restricting; much outstanding sociological research would not fit rigidly into this sequence, though it would include most of the steps outlined here.

2 ASKING AND ANSWERING SOCIOLOGICAL QUESTIONS: HISTORICAL CONTEXT

When sociology began as a discipline, it was a highly theoretical field. It consisted of much armchair speculation, and many of the notions it developed about how the world worked were not well grounded in evidence. But in the 1920s, there developed in American sociology, largely at the University of Chicago, a more intense commitment to the idea that such theoretical speculations were not enough—that sociology as a discipline needed to ground its concepts and theories in facts and data.

This goal for sociology was represented in two figures, both of whom were professors at the University of Chicago: Robert Park (1864–1944) and William Ogburn (1886–1959). Park's beliefs about how to make social research more scientific came from his background, both as a student of philosophy in Europe and as a reporter for the *Minneapolis Star*. He was interested in developing theories but wanted them to relate directly to the actual lives of people and to be based on the careful accumulation of evidence about people's lives. He told his students that to do real research they needed to get the seat of their pants dirty, to wear out their shoe leather to discover the truth.

Park thought that the most important thing for a sociologist to do was to go around all the neighborhoods of the city and find out what was going on by meeting the people who were the subjects of the sociologists' theories. Following Park's lead, the University of Chicago's sociology department used the city as a laboratory. Its sociologists took on roles in the community to see how the community's members lived, conducting interviews and firsthand observations. Their research reports tended to be highly systematic, well written, and oriented toward improving conditions in the city and around the United States.

William Ogburn, however, Park's colleague in the department of sociology at the University of Chicago, didn't believe that the future of sociology lay in shoe leather, well-written books, findings that could not be quantified, or efforts to influence public policy. These, he thought, were the domain of ethics, religion, journalism, and propaganda. In his presidential address to the American Sociological Society, he argued that sociology needed to become a science (Ogburn, 1930). The goal, he argued, was not "to make the world a better

(left) William Ogburn (1886–1959) and (right) Robert Park (1864–1944)

place in which to live" or to set forth "impressions of life" or to "[guide] the ship of state" but only to "[discover] new knowledge." Ogburn wanted sociology to be a field that looked a lot more like the natural sciences in both its presentation and its orientation. Whereas Park had clear ideas about what the subject matter of sociology should be (immigration and the life of the city), Ogburn believed sociologists could study anything that could be measured with numbers.

These two figures, Park and Ogburn, coexisted at the University of Chicago for many years, each committed to his own vision of sociology as a science. For Park and his students, the personal, emotional, and scientific side of sociology complemented the aspiration to develop explanations about the social world. We can see this legacy in the work of young sociologists today. But the legacy of William Ogburn is no less significant. The value of statistics and scientific methodologies for understanding the world has never been greater, in part because of the massive amount of data and information being collected on the Internet. More than ever before, business and government need people who can analyze this material and who are disposed to think about the world in a scientific way.

3 ASKING AND ANSWERING SOCIOLOGICAL QUESTIONS TODAY: RESEARCH METHODS

Let's look at the various **research methods** sociologists currently employ (Table 2.1). Whereas many fields have one main method, modern sociology embraces a variety of methodologies. People trained in sociology end up developing a wide range of research skills, which makes them quite versatile after graduation. Here are the basic methods used today, with examples drawn from recent research.

research methods The diverse methods of investigation used to gather empirical (factual) material. Different research methods exist in sociology, but the most commonly used are fieldwork (or participant observation) and survey methods. For many purposes, it is useful to combine two or more methods within a single research project.

ethnography The firsthand study of people using observation, in-depth interviewing, or both; also called *fieldwork*.

participant observation A method of research widely used in sociology and anthropology in which the researcher takes part in the activities of the group or community being studied.

Ethnography

One widely used qualitative method is **ethnography**, or firsthand studies of people using observations, interviews, or both. Here, the investigator socializes, works, or lives with members of a group, organization, or community. In the case of **participant observation**, the researcher participates directly in the activities he or she is studying. Other ethnographers, by contrast, may

Table 2.1

THREE OF THE MAIN METHODS USED IN SOCIOLOGICAL RESEARCH

RESEARCH METHOD	STRENGTHS	LIMITATIONS
Ethnography	Usually generates richer and more in-depth information than other methods. Can provide a broader understanding of social processes.	Can be used to study only relatively small groups or communities Findings might apply only to groups or communities studied; not easy to generalize on the basis of a single fieldwork study.
Surveys	Make possible the efficient collection of data on large numbers of individuals. Allow for precise comparisons to be made among the answers of respondents.	Material gathered may be superficial; if questionnaire is highly standardized, important differences among respondents' viewpoints may be glossed over. Responses may be what people profess to believe rather than what they actually believe.
Experiments	Influence of specific variables can be controlled by the investigator. Are usually easier for subsequent researchers to repeat.	Many aspects of social life cannot be brought into the laboratory. Responses of those studied may be affected by the experimental situation.

observe at a distance and not participate directly in the activities under observation. An ethnographer cannot simply be present in the group she studies but must explain and justify her presence to its members. The researcher must gain and sustain the cooperation of the community to achieve worthwhile results.

For a long while, research based on participant observation excluded accounts of the hazards or problems involved, but more recently, fieldworkers have been more open. Frequently, fieldworkers experience feelings of loneliness and frustration, the latter occurring especially when group members refuse to talk frankly with them. Some types of fieldwork may be physically dangerous; for instance, a researcher studying a delinquent gang might be seen as a police informer or might become unwittingly embroiled in conflicts with rival gangs.

In traditional works of ethnography, accounts provided little information about the observer because ethnographers were expected to present objective reports. More recently, ethnographers have increasingly spoken about their connection to the people under study. For example, a researcher might discuss how her race, class, or gender affected the work, or how the power differences between observer and observed distorted the dialogue between them.

Sociologist Alice Goffman spent six years doing participant observation research for her study of the impact of intensive policing on young Black men.

Advantages and Limitations of Fieldwork

Successful ethnography provides rich information on the behavior of people in groups, organizations, and communities, as well as information on how these people understand their own behavior. Once we look inside a given group, we can better understand not only that group but also broader social processes.

But fieldwork has its limitations. Only fairly small groups or communities can be studied. Much also depends on the researcher's skill in gaining the confidence of the individuals involved. Also, a researcher could identify so closely with the group that he loses the perspective of an objective outside observer. Or a researcher might draw conclusions that are more about his own effect on the situation than he or his readers realize. Interpreting ethnographies usually involves problems of generalizability because we cannot be sure that what we find in one context will apply in others, or even that two different researchers will draw the same conclusions when studying the same group.

A Recent Example of an Ethnography

When Alice Goffman was a graduate student, she spent six years in an intensely policed poor Black neighborhood. She was interested in the social situation of large numbers of Black men who were on the run from the criminal justice system. She became part of the everyday life of a group of boys who were known as the 6th Street Boys, writing about them in her book *On the Run* (Goffman, 2014). Goffman's research cast new light on the struggles of men who were dipping and dodging the police and worrying that any encounter would result in their imprisonment. By spending time with them every day for many years, Goffman was able to see that for these men, activities, relations, and localities that others relied on to maintain a decent and respectable identity were transformed into a system that authorities used to locate, arrest, and confine them. The police and the courts became dangerous to interact with, as did showing up to work or going to places such as hospitals. Instead of a safe place to sleep, eat, and find acceptance and support, their childhood homes were transformed into a "last known address," one of the first places police looked for them. Close relatives, friends, and neighbors became potential informants.

Surveys

Quantitative methodologists have a range of analytical tools and data resources at their disposal, but surveys are the most commonly used. When conducting a **survey**, researchers ask subjects to provide answers to structured questionnaires, which are administered in person, over the phone, mailed or emailed to a select group of people. This group is known as a **population**. While ethnographies are best suited for in-depth studies of small slices

> **survey** A method of sociological research in which questionnaires are administered to the population being studied.

of social life, survey research produces information that is less detailed but can be generalized to the population as a whole.

Standardized and Open-Ended Questions

Two types of questions are used in surveys. With *standardized*, or *fixed-choice*, questions, only a fixed range of responses is possible—for example, Yes, No, Don't know or Very likely, Likely, Unlikely, Very unlikely. Such questions have the advantage that responses are easy to count and compare because only a small number of categories are involved. However, because they do not allow for subtleties of opinion or verbal expression, they may yield restrictive, if not misleading, information.

Open-ended questions, by contrast, typically provide more detailed information because respondents may express their views in their own words, and the researcher can ask follow-up questions to probe more deeply into what the respondent thinks. However, the lack of standardization means that responses may be difficult to compare statistically.

In surveys, all the items must be readily understandable to interviewers and interviewees alike. Questions are usually asked in a set order. In large national surveys undertaken by government agencies and research organizations, interviews occur more or less simultaneously across the country. Those who conduct the interviews and those who analyze the results could not work effectively if they constantly had to check with one another about ambiguities in the questions or answers.

Questionnaires should also accommodate the characteristics of respondents. Will they see the point of a particular question? Might it offend them? Do they have enough information to answer usefully? Will they answer at all? A questionnaire's terminology might be unfamiliar; for instance, "What is your marital status?" might better be asked as, "Are you single, married, separated, or divorced?" Most surveys are preceded by pilot studies, which reveal problems with the survey not anticipated by the investigator. A **pilot study** is a trial run in which just a few people participate. Any difficulties can then be ironed out before the main survey takes place.

Sampling

Often sociologists are interested in the characteristics of large numbers of individuals—for example, political attitudes of the American population as a whole. In such situations, researchers concentrate on a **sample**, or a small proportion of the overall group. Usually, the results from a properly chosen sample can be generalized to the total population. Studies of only 2,000–3,000 voters, for instance, can accurately indicate the attitudes and voting intentions of the entire population. But to achieve such accuracy, we need a **representative sample**; the group of individuals studied must be typical, or representative, of the population as a whole. Because **sampling** is highly complex, statisticians have developed rules for working out the correct size and nature of samples.

population The people who are the focus of social research.

pilot study A trial run in survey research.

sample A small proportion of a larger population.

representative sample A sample from a larger population that is statistically typical of that population.

sampling Studying a proportion of individuals or cases from a larger population as representative of that population as a whole.

random sampling Sampling method in which a sample is chosen so that every member of the population has the same probability of being included.

A particularly important procedure that ensures that a sample is representative is **random sampling**, in which every member of the sample population has the same probability of being included. The most sophisticated way of obtaining a random sample is to assign each member of the population a number and then use a computer to generate a random list from which the sample is derived—for instance, by picking every tenth number. Random sampling is often done by researchers doing large population-based surveys, aimed to capture the behaviors or attitudes of the overall U.S. population. For qualitative researchers interested in a particular population, such as street vendors or gangsters, it simply would not make sense to try to draw a random sample.

Advantages and Disadvantages of Surveys

Surveys are widely used in sociological research for several reasons. Questionnaire responses can be more easily quantified and analyzed than material generated by most other research methods; large numbers of people can be studied; and, given sufficient funds, researchers can employ a specialized agency to collect the responses. The scientific method is the model for this kind of research since surveys give researchers a statistical measure of what they are studying.

However, many sociologists are critical of the survey method. They argue that findings whose accuracy may be dubious—given the relatively shallow nature of most survey responses—can nonetheless appear to be precise. Also, levels of nonresponse are sometimes high, especially now that so many people use cell phones and no longer have landlines at home. Furthermore, some published studies are based on results derived from little more than half a sample, though normally there is an effort to recontact nonrespondents or to substitute them with other people. Although little is known about those who do not respond to surveys or who refuse to be interviewed, we do know that people often experience survey research as intrusive and time-consuming. One development that may hold great promise for learning about public opinion is the rise of new statistical techniques for surveying the online conversation that is taking place quite naturally on the Internet.

In addition to the decennial census, the U.S. Census Bureau conducts the American Community Survey, contacting more than 3.5 million households to collect data on education, housing, and employment.

A Recent Example of a Survey

One of the most famous contemporary surveys is the General Social Survey, which has been administered to Americans since 1972. It is sometimes called the "pulse of America," as it has tracked the social life of Americans for decades. Since 1985, however, it has also been administered outside the United States to obtain comparative data. One of its most significant and controversial findings of recent years came from an analysis of the number of real-life "friends" Americans were reporting. The results suggested that Americans had fewer confidants than in the past, and that a growing number couldn't name a single person with whom they shared "important matters." The implication was that Americans were growing lonelier (McPherson, Smith-Lovin, and Brashears, 2006).

How did the researchers evaluate whether friendships were declining over time? What accounts for this decline? The study was based on face-to-face interviews with a nationally representative sample of nearly 1,500 American adults. All had participated in the long-running General Social Survey and were asked questions about their social networks. Specifically, they were asked to identify people with whom they had discussed "matters [that are] important to [them]" in the past six months. On average, they named 2.08 people in 2004, compared to 2.94 people in 1985. The proportion of respondents who reported that there was no one with whom they discussed important matters jumped from 10 percent in 1985 to 25 percent in 2004.

measures of central tendency The ways of calculating averages.

correlation coefficients The measure of the degree of correlation between variables.

mean A statistical measure of central tendency, or average, based on dividing a total by the number of individual cases.

mode The number that appears most often in a given set of data. This can sometimes be a helpful way of portraying central tendency.

median The number that falls halfway in a range of numbers; a way of calculating central tendency that is sometimes more useful than calculating a mean.

standard deviation A way of calculating the spread of a group of numbers.

degree of dispersal The range or distribution of a set of figures.

experiment A research method by which variables can be analyzed in a controlled and systematic way, either in an artificial situation constructed by the researcher or in a naturally occurring setting.

Some social scientists are not convinced that these findings support the claim that Americans are isolated or lonely. Rather, some argue that "weak" social ties, such as those with acquaintances, may be perfectly acceptable and rewarding for some people; these people may actually prefer to have many casual acquaintances rather than a handful of deep friendships. University of Toronto sociologist Barry Wellman (1994), for example, believes that the study offers important findings about "intimate ties," but he questions whether these findings should be taken as evidence that Americans are lonely and isolated. Rather, he notes that people's overall ties are actually increasing compared to previous decades, due in part to the Internet.

Experiments

Experiments are often used in the natural sciences and psychology, as they are considered the best method for ascertaining *causality*, or the influence of a particular factor on a study's outcome. In an experimental situation, the researcher directly controls the circumstances being studied. In a typical experiment, people are randomly assigned to two groups. The first, called an *experimental group*, receives some special attention based on the researcher's theory; the second, the *control group*, does not receive this attention. The subjects usually do not know to which group they have

STATISTICAL TERMS

Research in sociology often makes use of statistical techniques in the analysis of findings. Some are highly sophisticated and complex, but those most often used are easy to understand. The most common are **measures of central tendency** (ways of calculating averages) and **correlation coefficients** (measures of the degree to which one variable relates consistently to another).

There are three methods of calculating averages, each of which has certain advantages and shortcomings. Take as an example the amount of personal wealth (including all assets, such as houses, cars, bank accounts, and investments) owned by 13 individuals. Suppose the 13 own the following amounts:

1.	$0	8.	$80,000
2.	$5,000	9.	$100,000
3	$10,000	10.	$150,000
4.	$20,000	11.	$200,000
5	$40,000	12.	$400,000
6	$40,000	13.	$10,000,000
7.	$40,000		

The **mean** corresponds to the average, arrived at by adding together the personal wealth of all the people and dividing the result by the number of people in the sample (13). The total is $11,085,000; dividing this amount by 13, we calculate the mean to be $852,692.31. The mean is often a useful calculation because it is based on the whole range of data provided. However, the mean can be misleading when one or a small number of cases is very different from the majority. In this example, the mean is not in fact an appropriate measure of central tendency, because the presence of one very large figure, $10,000,000, skews the picture. One might get the impression, when using the mean to summarize these data, that most of the people own far more than they actually do.

In such instances, one of two other measures may be used. The **mode** is the figure that occurs most frequently in a given set of data. In our example, it is $40,000. The problem with the mode is that it doesn't take into account the overall distribution of the data—that is, the range of figures covered. The most frequently occurring case in a set of figures is not necessarily representative of the distribution as a whole and thus may not be a useful average. In this example, $40,000 is too close to the lower end of the figures.

The third measure is the **median**, which is the middle of any set of figures; here, this would be the seventh figure, again, $40,000. Our sample includes an odd number of figures, 13. If there were an even number—for instance, 12—the median would be calculated by taking the mean of the two middle cases, figures 6 and 7. As with the mode, the median gives no indication of the actual range of the data being measured.

Sometimes a researcher will use more than one measure of central tendency to avoid giving a deceptive picture of the average. More often, a researcher will calculate the **standard deviation** for the data in question. This is a way of calculating the **degree of dispersal**, or the range, of a set of figures—which in this case goes from $0 to $10,000,000.

Correlation coefficients offer a useful way of expressing how closely connected two (or more) variables are. When two variables correlate completely, we can speak of a perfect positive correlation, expressed as 1.0. When no relation is found between two variables—they have no consistent connection at all—the coefficient is 0.0. A perfect negative correlation, expressed as −1.0, exists when two variables are in a completely inverse relation to one another. Perfect correlations are never found in the social sciences. Correlations of the order of 0.6 or more, whether positive or negative, are usually regarded as indicating a strong degree of connection between whatever variables are being analyzed. Positive correlations on this level might be found between, say, social class background and voting behavior.

been assigned and seldom know the purpose of the experiment, though this is not always the case.

A classic example is the 1971 experiment carried out by Philip Zimbardo (1992), who set up a make-believe jail, randomly assigning some student volunteers to the role of guard and other volunteers to the role of prisoner. His aim was to see how role-playing would affect changes in attitude and behavior. The results shocked the investigators. Students who played guards quickly assumed an authoritarian manner; they displayed real hostility toward the prisoners, verbally abusing and bullying them. The prisoners, by contrast, showed a mixture of apathy and rebelliousness—a response often noted among inmates in actual prisons. These effects were so marked and the level of tension so high that the experiment had to be called off at an early stage. The results, however, were important: Zimbardo concluded that behavior in prisons is more

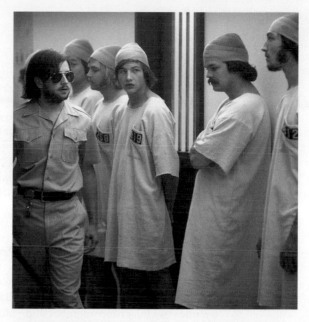

From his jail experiment, Zimbardo concluded that behavior in prisons is influenced more by the nature of the prison itself than by the individual characteristics of those involved.

influenced by the nature of the prison situation than by the individual characteristics of those involved.

Advantages and Disadvantages of Experiments

The advantage of experimental studies is that researchers can test a hypothesis under highly controlled conditions established by the researcher. The ability to control experimental conditions, however, is also the principal weakness of experimental studies, which in many ways are artificial. To the extent that the laboratory fails to duplicate a natural setting, it is difficult to generalize the results of laboratory experiments to the larger society. We can bring only small groups of individuals into a laboratory setting, and, in such experiments, people know they are being studied and may behave unnaturally. As a result, sociologists sometimes use field experiments, in which a real-life situation is simulated as accurately as possible.

A Recent Example of an Experiment

In 1994, a group of sociologists launched an experiment to find out if it makes a difference to move people from high-poverty ghetto neighborhoods to low-poverty neighborhoods. People who responded to an advertisement offering vouchers for new apartments were randomly assigned to two groups—those who were given the opportunity to move (experimental group) and those who weren't (control group).

Why did the experimenters compare the fates of two groups who both applied for vouchers, one of which got them and one of which didn't? Why not compare people who got the vouchers against those who did not apply in the first place? In fact, the study kept data on all three groups. The ones who applied but did not receive vouchers had more in common with the ones who got to move, because they also wanted to escape from their current circumstances. The best comparison is between two groups that wanted to move. They are alike in all characteristics except for whether they actually stayed in place or experienced a new living condition.

Following the groups since the mid-1990s, researchers made some important discoveries. For example, people who moved did not do much better in the labor market than those who stayed behind. But the movers tended to be much happier, and they experienced decreased levels of obesity when compared with those who did not get to move.

Comparative Historical Research

Comparative research is of central importance in sociology because it enables researchers to document whether social behavior varies across time and place and by one's social group membership. Most comparative work is quantitative in that researchers aim to document whether behaviors and attitudes change over time and place; thus, a consistent metric is required to make comparisons. Consider the American rate of divorce—the number of divorces per thousand married people. Divorce rates rose rapidly in the United States after World War II, reaching a peak in 1979. Since then, the divorce rate has dropped by nearly a quarter, with only 15.7 marriages per 1,000 ending in divorce in 2018 (Allred, 2019)—a statistic expressing profound changes in the area of sexual relations and family life. Do these changes reflect specific features of American society? We can find out by comparing divorce rates in the United States with those in other countries. The comparison reveals that although the U.S. rate is higher than the rate in most other Western societies, the overall trends are similar.

Theda Skocpol's comparative research showed how major historical revolutions grew into much more radical movements than contemporaries could have predicted.

The most influential way of doing comparative research is through historical research. One classic study that investigated a much longer period and applied comparative research in a historical context was Theda Skocpol's *States and Social Revolutions* (1979), one of the best-known studies of social change. To produce a theory of the origins and nature of revolution grounded in detailed empirical study, Skocpol looked at processes of revolution in three historical contexts: the 1789 revolution in France, the 1917 revolution in Russia (which brought the Communists to power and established the Soviet Union, which was eventually dissolved in 1989), and the revolution of 1949 in China (which created Communist China).

By analyzing a variety of documentary sources, Skocpol was able to develop a powerful explanation of revolutionary change, one that emphasized underlying social structural conditions. She showed that social revolutions are largely the result of unintended consequences. Before the Russian Revolution, for instance, various political groups were trying to overthrow the regime, but none of these groups—including the Bolsheviks (Communists), who eventually came to power—anticipated the revolution that occurred. A series of clashes and confrontations gave rise to a process of social transformation that was much more radical than anyone had foreseen. At the time that Skocpol wrote, existing theories basically related the emergence of revolutions to the strength of social movements, and these to class relations. Skocpol showed, first, that state structures are as important as class relations and more important than the strength of the revolutionary movements; and second, that these state structures are heavily influenced by international events (for instance, revolutions come in the wake of a breakdown in state authority often due to lost international wars).

A Recent Example of Comparative Research

Such studies as those pioneered by Theda Skocpol rely on qualitative methods of historical research, which depend on careful comparisons of a small number of cases. One of the costs of such approaches has been that sociologists have derived their understandings from some very famous revolutions or wars, while ignoring most of the world altogether.

In recent years, Andreas Wimmer has taken up an alternative approach to historical sociology. He uses formal modeling and statistical techniques to analyze hundreds of cases at the same time, rather than a few famous ones. Unlike scholars who go to the library and pull existing data off the shelf, Wimmer has found it necessary to create his own datasets to answer age-old questions. In his approach, what happened in Haiti or in Latin America counts no less than what went on in Holland or in Europe more generally—though these latter places have tended to be studied much more frequently and thus count more heavily in existing theories. Wimmer's work therefore goes against the grain of most historical sociology that tends to focus mainly on Europe at the expense of Africa and the Americas. (It is not just Latin America that has figured infrequently in historical sociology; even North America is eclipsed by the usual focus on Europe.)

In his monumental book *Waves of War* (2012), Wimmer used this approach to study war as a sociological phenomenon, drawing on large original datasets. He found that if we look at all wars that occurred throughout history, a major shift has occurred. Prior to the nineteenth century, most wars were driven by conquest, or the desire of states to achieve or throw off a cer-

CONCEPT CHECKS

1 What are the main advantages and limitations of ethnography as a research method?

2 Contrast the two types of questions commonly used in surveys.

3 What is a random sample?

4 Discuss the main strengths of experiments.

READING A TABLE

When reading sociological literature, you will often come across tables. They sometimes look complex but are easy to decipher if you follow the few basic steps outlined here; with practice, these will become automatic. (See Table 2.2 as an example.) Do not succumb to the temptation to skip over tables; they contain information in concentrated form that can be read more quickly than would be possible if the same material were expressed in words. By becoming skilled in the interpretation of tables, you will also be able to check how justified the conclusions a writer draws actually are.

1. Read the title in full. Tables frequently have long titles that represent the researcher's attempt to state accurately the nature of the information conveyed. The title of Table 2.2 gives, first, the subject of the data; second, the fact that the table provides material for comparison; and third, the fact that data are given only for a limited number of countries.
2. Look for explanatory comments, or notes, about the data. A source note at the foot of Table 2.2 indicates that the data were obtained from the Pew Research Center, a large international survey organization. It also notes that data were not available for all nations for all years. Footnotes may say how the material was collected or why it is displayed in a particular way. If the researcher did not gather the data but instead used findings originally reported elsewhere, a source will be included. The source sometimes gives you some insight into how reliable the information is likely to be and tells you where to find the original data. In Table 2.2, the source note makes clear that the data have been taken from one international organization.
3. Read the headings along both the top and the left-hand side of the table. (Sometimes tables are arranged with "headings" at the foot rather than the top.) These tell you what type of information is contained in each row and column. In reading the table, keep in mind each set of headings as you scan the figures. In our example, the headings on the left name the countries involved, while those at the top refer to the proportion of the population who hold a "favorable" opinion of the United States and the years for which data are available.
4. Identify the units used; the figures in the body of the table may represent cases, percentages, averages, or other measures. Sometimes it may be helpful to convert the figures to a form more useful to you: If percentages are not provided, for example, it may be worth calculating them.
5. Consider the conclusions that might be reached from the information in the table. Most tables are discussed by the author, and what he or she has to say should, of course, be considered. But you should also ask what further issues or questions the data might suggest. How might you explain some of these declines? Or the sudden and precipitous drops?

tain balance of power in their region. More recently, wars have been driven by ethnic and nationalist concerns. According to Wimmer, whereas Karl Marx once proclaimed that the twentieth century would be the age of revolutionary class struggle, it turned into the age of ethno-nationalist conflict. Using a global dataset of his own creation, Wimmer found that the existence of nationalist organizations in a territory more than doubles the probability of war at any time. It is unlikely that a researcher using a qualitative approach with small numbers of cases would have come up with such a finding, because such an approach would have focused on positive cases (i.e., on a handful of nationalist wars), rather than systematically comparing a large number of pre-nationalist contexts with nationalist ones.

Table 2.2

OPINION OF THE UNITED STATES: COMPARISON OF SELECTED NATIONS

Several interesting trends can be seen from the data in this table. First, the extent to which people hold favorable attitudes toward the United States varies considerably across nations. Second, although there are strong national and regional patterns of support for the United States, we also see considerable historical variation within nations. For example, in Egypt, one-third held favorable views in 2006, yet this proportion has steadily gone downward and bottomed out at 10 percent in 2014. Yet some nations show a steep and sudden drop rather than a steady decline. While two-thirds of Mexicans held a favorable view through much of the 2000s, this share had plummeted to 36 percent by 2019.

PERCENTAGE OF PERSONS WHO HOLD A "FAVORABLE" (VS. "UNFAVORABLE") OPINION OF THE UNITED STATES

COUNTRY	2005	2006	2007	2008	2009	2010	2011	2012	2013	2014	2015	2017	2018	2019
China	42	47	34	41	47	58	44	43	40	50	44	-	-	-
Egypt	-	30	21	22	27	17	20	19	16	10	-	-	-	-
France	43	39	39	42	75	73	75	69	64	75	73	46	38	48
Germany	42	37	30	31	64	63	62	52	53	51	50	35	30	39
Indonesia	38	30	29	37	63	59	54	-	61	59	62	48	42	42
Japan	-	63	61	50	59	66	85	72	69	66	68	57	67	68
Jordan	21	15	20	19	25	21	10	12	14	12	14	15	-	-
Mexico	-	-	56	47	69	56	52	56	66	63	66	30	32	36
Pakistan	23	27	15	19	16	17	12	12	11	14	22	-	-	-
Poland	62	-	61	68	67	74	70	69	67	73	74	73	70	79
Russia	52	43	41	46	44	57	56	52	51	23	15	41	26	29
S. Korea	-	-	58	70	78	79	-	-	78	82	84	75	80	77
Spain	41	23	34	33	58	61	64	58	62	60	65	31	42	-
Turkey	23	12	9	12	14	17	10	15	21	19	29	18	-	20
U.K.	55	56	51	53	69	65	61	60	58	66	65	50	50	57
U.S.	83	76	80	84	88	85	79	80	81	82	83	85	79	81

SOURCE: Wike et al., 2020.

4 UNANSWERED QUESTIONS

Although the research methods of sociology have become quite advanced over the past 50 years, many open or unanswered questions still cause much disagreement among sociologists.

Can Sociology Identify Causes and Effects?

One of the main problems faced in research methodology is the analysis of cause and effect. One difficult causal relationship to understand is an association in which one social context produces a certain effect. For example, if you live in a poor neighborhood, some sociologists think you are more likely to be unemployed or obese. But is the neighborhood the cause, or is it the other way around? Isn't it also possible that the kinds of people who would be unemployed or obese tend to gravitate toward living in certain kinds of neighborhoods? Although one of the main tasks of sociology is to identify causes and effects, there is a crisis of confidence among many scholars that such a goal is not as easily attained as once thought.

How Can Social Research Avoid Exploitation?

All research involving human beings can pose ethical dilemmas. A key question for sociologists is whether research poses risks to subjects that are greater than the risks those subjects face in their everyday lives. For example, ethnographers and field researchers conducting research in areas with high crime rates potentially risk getting their subjects arrested with their writings or getting themselves arrested simply for observing and participating in the lives of the people whom they are trying to understand. Although a great deal of sensitivity to such issues exists in contemporary social science, one largely unanswered question relates to exploitation: Are social scientists benefitting at their subjects' expense? Most studies don't address such questions, and some social scientists are never forced to think seriously about them. The question of exploitation arises more in qualitative field studies than in quantitative research, but it must be considered whenever people's careers come to depend on the advancement of sociological knowledge. For example, if a scholar earns money on a book based on cooperation with research subjects, should that money be shared with the subjects?

Can We Really Study Human Social Life in a Scientific Way?

To answer this question, we must first understand what *science* means. Science is the use of systematic methods of **empirical investigation**, the analysis of data, theoretical thinking, and the logical assessment of arguments to develop a body of knowledge about specific subject matter. According to this definition, sociology is a scientific endeavor.

empirical investigation Factual inquiries carried out in any area of sociological study.

However, sociology is not equivalent to a natural science. Unlike natural phenomena and animals, humans are self-aware beings who confer sense and purpose to what they do. We can't describe social life accurately unless we grasp the concepts that people apply in their own behavior. For instance, to describe a death as a suicide means knowing what the person intended when he died. Suicide can occur only when an individual has self-destruction actively in mind. If he accidentally steps in front of a car and is killed, he cannot be said to have committed suicide.

The fact that we cannot study human beings in the same way as we can study objects in nature is an advantage to sociological researchers, who profit from being able to pose questions directly to those they study: other human beings. In other respects, sociology encounters difficulties not present in the natural sciences. People who are aware that their activities are being scrutinized may not behave normally; they may consciously or unconsciously portray themselves in a way that differs from their usual attitudes. They may even try to "assist" the researcher by giving the responses they believe she wants.

CONCEPT CHECKS

1 How are the ethical dilemmas that social scientists face different from those that other researchers encounter in the physical or the biological sciences?

2 Why should sociologists be concerned about the exploitation of the people they study?

THE BIG PICTURE

Chapter 2
Asking and Answering
Sociological Questions

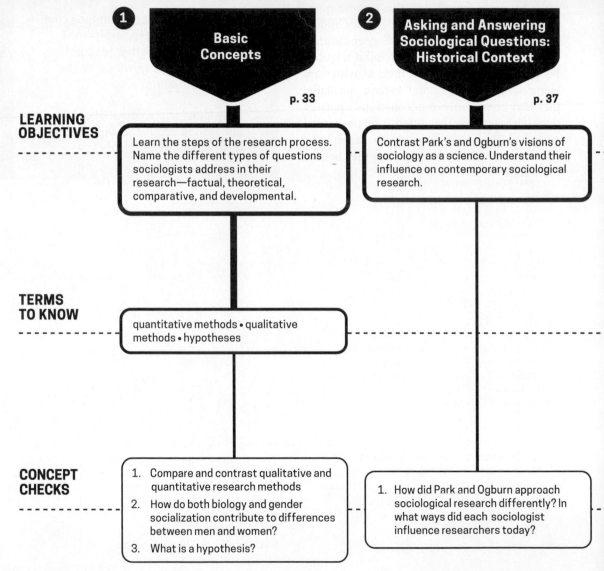

1 **Basic Concepts** p. 33

2 **Asking and Answering Sociological Questions: Historical Context** p. 37

LEARNING OBJECTIVES

Learn the steps of the research process. Name the different types of questions sociologists address in their research—factual, theoretical, comparative, and developmental.

Contrast Park's and Ogburn's visions of sociology as a science. Understand their influence on contemporary sociological research.

TERMS TO KNOW

quantitative methods • qualitative methods • hypotheses

CONCEPT CHECKS

1. Compare and contrast qualitative and quantitative research methods
2. How do both biology and gender socialization contribute to differences between men and women?
3. What is a hypothesis?

1. How did Park and Ogburn approach sociological research differently? In what ways did each sociologist influence researchers today?

Exercises: Thinking Sociologically

1. Suppose the dropout rate in your local high school increased dramatically. Faced with such a serious problem, the school board offers you a $500,000 grant to study the sudden increase. Following the recommended procedures outlined in the text, explain how you would conduct your research. What hypotheses might you test? How would you prove or disprove them?

2. Explain the advantages and disadvantages of documentary research. What will it yield that will be better than experimentation, surveys, and ethnographic fieldwork? What are its limitations compared with those approaches?

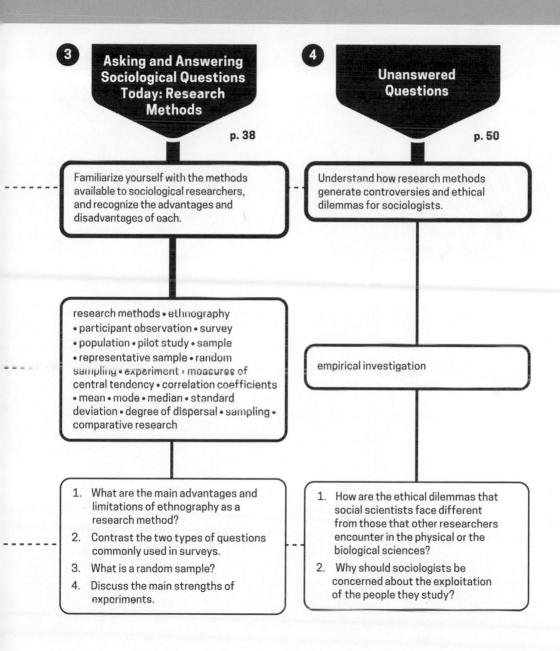

3 Asking and Answering Sociological Questions Today: Research Methods

p. 38

Familiarize yourself with the methods available to sociological researchers, and recognize the advantages and disadvantages of each.

research methods • ethnography • participant observation • survey • population • pilot study • sample • representative sample • random sampling • experiment • measures of central tendency • correlation coefficients • mean • mode • median • standard deviation • degree of dispersal • sampling • comparative research

1. What are the main advantages and limitations of ethnography as a research method?
2. Contrast the two types of questions commonly used in surveys.
3. What is a random sample?
4. Discuss the main strengths of experiments.

4 Unanswered Questions

p. 50

Understand how research methods generate controversies and ethical dilemmas for sociologists.

empirical investigation

1. How are the ethical dilemmas that social scientists face different from those that other researchers encounter in the physical or the biological sciences?
2. Why should sociologists be concerned about the exploitation of the people they study?

PART

II

The Individual and Society

We start our exploration of sociology by looking at the connections between individual development and culture and by analyzing types of societies from the past and present. Although our personalities and outlooks are influenced by our culture and society, we actively re-create and reshape the cultural and social contexts in which our activities occur. Chapter 3 examines the unity and diversity of human culture. We consider how human beings differ from and resemble nonhuman animals, and we analyze variations among human cultures. Chapter 4 discusses socialization, concentrating on how the human infant develops into a social being.

Because socialization continues throughout the life course, we also analyze the relationships among young, middle-aged, and older people. Chapter 5 explores how people interact in everyday life and identifies the mechanisms people use to interpret what others say and do. The study of social interaction reveals a great deal about the larger social environment. Chapter 6 focuses on social groups, networks, and organizations, and how individuals interact in various settings. Chapter 7 looks at deviance and crime. We can learn about the way a population behaves by studying people whose behavior deviates from accepted patterns.

Culture and Society

What is the effect of social media, such as Facebook, on young adults' sense of themselves?

A   always positive

B   more often positive than negative

C   more often negative than positive

D   always negative

TURN THE PAGE FOR THE CORRECT ANSWER.

By September 2019, Facebook had grown to more than 2.45 billion monthly active users worldwide, including 1.62 billion daily users (Facebook, 2019). This extensive use of social media is often believed to have a positive effect, especially on young people, who frequently spend hours posting status updates and photos on Facebook, Instagram, Twitter, and similar social networking sites. Nearly nine out of every ten young Americans (ages 18 to 29) report engaging in social networking, enabling them to connect with a large number of "friends," which ideally provides them with a stronger sense of social connection (Perrin and Anderson, 2019).

In fact, surveys of Americans of all ages have found that Facebook users report having a slightly greater number of close relationships than do average Americans, and in turn, they receive slightly more emotional support and companionship (Pew Research Center, 2011c; Pew Research Center, 2014d). Yet research on the emotional effects of social media on young people paints a much less rosy picture. Multiple studies of young adults have found that people who used social media more frequently felt slightly worse over time, whereas those who reported increased direct interaction with their friends tended to feel better over time (Kross et al., 2013; Shakya and Christakis, 2017).

One possible explanation has to do with self-esteem—how people feel about themselves. There is some evidence that as social media interaction increases, self-esteem decreases, especially among women (Leif et al., 2012). Frequent social media users often closely monitor their friends' posts, making unfavorable comparisons with their own lives. They are also more likely to be attentive to unfavorable responses to their own posts. One study found that young people with low self-esteem tend to complain about their lives on their social media pages, which in turn provokes negative responses, contributing to a downward emotional spiral (Forest and Wood, 2012).

Pop singer Taylor Swift may not be a sociologist, but her insights square with the recent research:

We are dealing with a huge self-esteem crisis. These girls are able to scroll pictures of the high-light reels of other people's lives, and they're

THE ANSWER IS C.

LEARNING OBJECTIVES

1 Basic Concepts

Know what culture consists of and recognize how it differs from society.

2 The Sociological Study of Culture

Learn about the "cultural turn" and sociological perspectives on culture. Understand the processes that changed societies over time.

3 Research Today: Understanding the Modern World

Recognize the legacies of colonialism and the effects of globalization on your own life and the lives of people around the world.

4 Unanswered Questions

Understand the debate over the influence of biological and cultural factors on behavior. Learn how the Internet and global culture influence local cultures.

stuck with the behind-the-scenes of their own lives. They wake up and they look at their reflection in the mirror, and they compare it to some filtered, beautiful photo of some girl who's really popular and seems like she has it all together. (NPR, 2014)

The correct answer, unfortunately, is *c*: The effect of social media on young adults' sense of themselves is more often negative than positive.

Nor are such effects of social media limited to the United States. China, now the world's second-largest economy (and rapidly closing on the world's largest—the United States), claims more than 829 million Internet users (Internet World Stats, 2019), and its own versions of Google (*Baidu*), Facebook (*Renren*), and Twitter (*Sina Weibo*). Although Facebook is currently banned in China, China's own social media sites are widely used, with nearly two-thirds of Chinese over 18 plugged in (Pew Research Center, 2016e).

China's social media sites have been described by Chinese sociologist Liu Neng as "a place of escape" from the pressures of school, parental expectations, and even (as long as politics are not discussed) government censorship. The widespread use of social media encourages self-expression, a trait far more common among Chinese youth than among their parents' generation (Rabkin, 2011). Young people in China increasingly rely on social media to form relationships, advertise their accomplishments, and flaunt their sense of worth. One study of university students in China found that students with higher self-esteem were more likely to post comments on social media sites; students with lower self-esteem presumably feared receiving unfavorable feedback (Wang et al., 2012). Chinese culture places an extremely high value on academic achievement and success in general. While no studies have yet focused on the relationship between the extent of social media use and self-esteem among young Chinese, it seems reasonable to conclude that in China, as in the United States, it is common for young people to compare their own posts with those of their friends; many will find such comparisons hurtful.

The lives of everyone on the planet are becoming increasingly interdependent. Few places on earth can escape radio, television, air travel (and its throngs of tourists), cell phones, or the Internet. A few generations ago, some peoples' ways of life might have been untouched by the rest of the world. Today, these same people use tools made in the United States, Europe, or Japan; wear clothing manufactured in China, the Dominican Republic, or Bangladesh; and share personal information and photos on social media sites. While Facebook and Twitter are banned in China, a growing number of tech-savvy young Chinese are able to break through what has been termed the "Great Chinese Firewall." But Renren, Sina Weibo, and other Chinese social media sites openly copy Facebook and Twitter. As their content converges with that of their non-Chinese counterparts, it would seem that a global culture is emerging across the planet.

Some of the forces that contribute to such a global culture are discussed throughout this book:

- Television, which brings U.S. culture into homes throughout the world daily and which adapts other cultural products for the U.S. audience

- The emergence of a unified global economy, with businesses whose factories, management structures, and markets span continents and countries
- "Global citizens," such as managers of large corporations (or university professors), who may spend so much time crisscrossing the globe that they identify with a global, cosmopolitan culture rather than with their own nation's culture
- A host of international organizations—including UN agencies, regional-trade and mutual-defense associations, multinational banks and other global financial institutions, and international labor and health organizations—that are creating a global political, legal, and military framework
- Electronic communications (cell phones, email, the Internet), which make instantaneous communication with almost any part of the planet an integral part of daily life in the business world
- The exploding use of smartphones and other devices, and the associated rise of social media such as Facebook and Twitter

Yet the emergence of a global culture is far from self-evident. In fact, there is considerable evidence to the contrary. The Internet, while exposing billions of people around the world to ideas that often challenge some of their most cherished cultural beliefs and values, also has resulted in a strengthening of those beliefs and values in many places. Although the force of globalization can often seem to be irresistible, sweeping away everything in its path, globalization has also resulted in outright resistance to the homogenization of local cultures along European and North American lines.

In this chapter, we explore the nature of culture and society in their many forms, and how they are being reshaped by the many changes occurring in the world today.

1 BASIC CONCEPTS

The sociological study of culture and society began with Émile Durkheim in the nineteenth century. The work of early sociologists strongly reflected the values of highly educated Europeans who often assumed that "primitive" cultures were inferior and lagged behind modern European "civilization." However, two destructive world wars, fought largely among European countries that claimed to be the most "civilized" cultures on earth, helped discredit that belief. Sociologists now recognize that there are many different cultures and societies, each with distinctive characteristics. The task of social science is to understand this diversity, which is best done by avoiding value judgments.

Culture consists of the values the members of a group hold, the norms they follow, the material goods they create, and the languages and symbols they use to construct their understanding of the world, including both speech and writing. Some elements of culture, especially people's beliefs and expectations about one another and about the world they inhabit, are components of all social relations. Culture therefore refers to the ways of life of individual members or groups within a society—their manner of dress, their marriage customs and family life, their patterns of work, their religious ceremonies, and

culture The values, norms, and material goods characteristic of a given group. Like the concept of society, the notion of culture is widely used in sociology and the other social sciences (particularly anthropology). Culture is one of the most distinctive properties of human social association.

their leisure pursuits. The concept also covers the goods they create—bows and arrows, plows, factories and machines, computers, books, and dwellings. We should think of culture as a "design for living" or a "tool kit" of practices, knowledge, and symbols acquired through learning, rather than by instinct, that enable people to live in society (Kluckhohn, 1949; Swidler, 1986).

A **society** is a system of interrelationships that connects individuals. The word *society*—like the word *social*—derives from a Latin term for the ties that bind people together, ties that make sustained human interaction possible. Such bonds can be informal—such as friendship or family—or formal, such as religious organizations, businesses, or entire nations. One characteristic of societies, at least as sociologists see them, is that they are relatively enduring over time. For this to occur, societies require some degree of common culture—a set of shared values to guide behavior. No society could exist without culture, and conversely, no culture could exist without a society.

society A group of people who live in a particular territory, are subject to a common system of political authority, and are aware of having a distinct identity from other groups. Some societies, such as hunting and gathering societies, are small, numbering no more than a few dozen people. Others are large, numbering millions. Modern Chinese society, for instance, has a population of more than a billion people.

cultural universals Values or modes of behavior shared by all human cultures.

marriage A socially approved sexual relationship between two individuals. Marriage historically has involved two persons of opposite sexes, but in the past decade marriage between same-sex partners has been legalized in a growing number of states and nations throughout the world. Marriage normally forms the basis of a family of procreation—that is, it is expected that the married couple will produce and bring up children.

Cultural Universals

When common features of human behavior are found in virtually all societies, they are called **cultural universals**. Among the cultural characteristics shared by all societies, two in particular stand out. All cultures incorporate ways of communicating and expressing meaning, and all cultures depend on material objects in daily life. There is no known culture without a grammatically complex language, or which lacks physical objects that share common cultural meanings. Additionally, all cultures possess some recognizable form of family system in which there are values and norms associated with the care of children. The institution of **marriage** is a cultural universal, as are religious rituals and property rights—although what constitutes marriage, how many spouses one is entitled to, and what is considered acceptable behavior both within and outside the marriage can vary considerably from culture to culture. All cultures also practice some form of incest prohibition—the banning of sexual relations between close relatives. Other cultural universals include art, dance, bodily adornment, games, gift-giving, joking, and rules of hygiene.

Marriage is an example of a cultural universal, a value shared by all human cultures.

nonmaterial culture Cultural ideas that are not themselves physical objects.

material culture The physical objects that a society creates that influence the ways in which people live.

values Ideas held by individuals or groups about what is desirable, proper, good, and bad. What individuals value is strongly influenced by the specific culture in which they happen to live.

Variations clearly exist within each category. Consider the prohibition against incest. Most often, incest is regarded as sexual relations between members of the immediate family, but among some peoples, it includes cousins and, in some instances, all people bearing the same family name. There have also been societies in which a small proportion of the population engages in incestuous practices. This practice was the case within the ruling class of ancient Egypt, when brothers and sisters were permitted to have sex with each other.

Sociologists and anthropologists distinguish between two forms of culture: **nonmaterial culture**, the cultural ideas that are not themselves physical objects, and **material culture**, the physical objects that a society creates. We discuss each form of culture in turn.

Nonmaterial Culture

Nonmaterial culture comprises the nonphysical components of culture, including values and norms, symbols, language, and speech and writing.

Values and Norms

Values are abstract ideals. For example, being faithful to one marriage partner is a prominent value in most Western societies, but in some other cultures, a person may have several wives or husbands. Some cultures value individualism, whereas others emphasize shared needs. Is it possible to describe an "American" culture? Although the United States is culturally diverse, we can identify several characteristics of a uniquely American culture. First, it reflects a particular range of values shared by many, if not all, Americans, such as the belief in the merits of individual achievement or in equality of opportunity. Second, these values are connected to specific norms: For example, it is usually expected that people will work hard to achieve occupational success (Bellah et al., 1985; Parsons, 1964). Third, it involves the use of material artifacts created mostly through modern industrial technology, such as cars, mass-produced food, clothing, and so forth.

People in China hold a much stronger belief in the importance of collective effort. Modesty is a strongly held virtue, as reflected in the adage (attributed to Confucius): "When walking in the company of three, there must be one I can learn from." Although an American who boasts about his or her self-made success might seem vulgar to the Chinese, some Chinese seem to be changing their values in this regard: *China's Got Talent* premiered in 2010 on a Shanghai TV station.

Even within American society, values may conflict. Some groups or individuals might value traditional religious beliefs, whereas others might favor progress and science. Some people might prefer lavish material comfort, whereas others might favor simplicity. In a modern age characterized by the global movement of people, ideas, goods, and information, cultural values will inevitably conflict. Sociological

research suggests that such conflicts foster a sense of frustration and isolation
(Bellah et al., 1985).

Norms are principles or rules of social
life that everyone is expected to observe.
Norms of behavior in marriage include the
way husbands and wives are supposed to
behave toward their in-laws: In some soci-

eties, they are expected to develop a close relationship; in others, they keep a clear
distance. Like the values they reflect, norms vary across cultures. In the United States,
for example, while a woman might wear a hat if it is in fashion, most do not regularly
cover their hair and neck with a headscarf. Some more traditional Muslim cultures
have a norm calling for women to wear headscarves as a religiously required sign of
modesty. While a few highly conservative Muslim cultures might enforce this rule on
some women who prefer to dress otherwise, cultural norms regarding dress are often
widely accepted; as a result, women in traditional Muslim cultures often prefer to wear
headscarves and other forms of more traditional clothing.

Cultural conflict occurs when norms perceived as culturally incompatible col-
lide. The use of veils by Muslim women in predominantly Christian countries, for
example, has led to cultural conflict in France (which in 2011 began to enforce a
ban on veils in public places) and some other European countries with large immigrant populations from the Middle East or North Africa. In the United States, Europe,
and even predominantly Muslim Turkey, religious Muslim women who insist on wearing headscarves often clash with prevailing beliefs that emphasize the separation of
church and state, or the belief that a headscarf symbolizes women's subservience to
male-generated beliefs and thus threatens women's rights (Elver, 2012).

The tension between subgroup values and national values came to a head in 2011 when
the French government banned Muslim women from wearing full-face veils in public.

Norms, like the values they reflect, also change over time. For example, beginning in 1964, with a U.S. Surgeon General's report that linked smoking with serious health problems, the U.S. government waged a highly effective campaign to discourage people from smoking. A strong social norm favoring smoking—once associated with independence, sex appeal, and glamour—has now given way to an equally strong social norm depicting smoking as unhealthful, unattractive, and selfish. In 2017, only 14 percent of American adults smoked (Centers for Disease Control and Prevention, 2018a), one-third of the percentage in 1964, when the Surgeon General's report was issued.

Symbols

The **symbols** expressed in speech and writing are the chief ways in which cultural meanings are formed and expressed. But they are not the only ways. Both material objects and aspects of behavior can generate meanings. A **signifier** is any vehicle of meaning—any set of elements used to communicate. The sounds made in speech are signifiers, as are the marks made on paper or other materials in writing. Other signifiers include dress, pictures or visual signs, modes of eating, forms of building or architecture, and many other material features of culture (Hawkes, 1977). Styles of dress, for example, normally signify differences between the sexes. Until relatively recently, women in American culture wore skirts and men pants. In some other cultures, this practice is reversed: Women wear pants and men skirts (Leach, 1976).

Semiotics—the analysis of nonverbal cultural meanings—opens up a fascinating field for sociology because it allows us to contrast the ways in which different cultures are structured. For example, the buildings in cities are not simply places where people live and work; they often have a symbolic character. In traditional cities, the main temple or church usually sat on high ground in or near the city center to symbolize the all-powerful influence of religion. In modern societies, by contrast, the skyscrapers of big business often occupy that symbolic position. Of course, material culture is not simply symbolic but also includes actual, practical objects vital for catering to physical needs—for example, the tools or technology used to acquire food, make weaponry, construct dwellings, and so forth. We have to study both the practical and the symbolic aspects of material culture to understand it completely.

Language

Language demonstrates both the unity and the diversity of human culture because there are no cultures without language, yet there are thousands of languages spoken in the world. Although languages with similar origins have words in common with one another—for example, German and English—most major language groups have no words in common at all.

Language is involved in virtually all our activities. In the form of ordinary speech, it is the means by which we organize most of what we do. (We will discuss the importance of talk and conversation in social life in Chapter 5.) However, language is involved not just in mundane activities but also in ceremony, religion, poetry, and many other spheres. One of its most distinctive features is that it allows us to extend the scope of our thought and experience. Using language, we can convey information about events remote in time or space and can discuss things we have never seen. We can develop abstract concepts, tell stories, and make jokes.

Languages—indeed, all symbols—are representations of reality. Symbols may signify things we imagine, such as mathematical formulas or fictitious creatures, or they may represent (that is, "re-present," or make present again in our minds) things initially experienced through our senses. Human behavior is oriented toward the symbols we use to represent "reality," rather than toward the reality itself—and these symbols are determined within a particular culture. When you see a four-footed furry animal, for example, you must determine which cultural symbol to attach to it. Do you decide to call it a dog, a wolf, or something else? If you determine it is a dog, what cultural meaning does that convey? In American culture, dogs are typically regarded as household pets and lavished with affection. In Guatemalan Indian culture, however, dogs are more often seen as guards or scavengers and are treated with an indifference that might seem cruel to Americans. Among the Akha of northern Thailand, dogs are seen as food, and they are treated accordingly. The diversity of cultural meanings attached to the word *dog* thus requires an act of interpretation.

In the 1930s, the anthropological linguist Edward Sapir and his student Benjamin Lee Whorf advanced the **linguistic relativity hypothesis**, which argues that language influences our perceptions of the world because we are more likely to be aware of things if we have words for them (Lucy, 1997; Wolff and Holmes, 2011). For example, expert skiers and snowboarders use terms such as *black ice, corn, powder,* and *packed powder* to describe different snow and ice conditions to more readily perceive potentially life-threatening situations that would escape the notice of a novice. In a sense, then, experienced winter athletes have a different perception of the world—or, at least, a different perception of the alpine slopes—than do novices.

Language also helps give permanence to a culture and identity to a people. Language outlives any particular speaker or writer, affording a sense of history and cultural continuity. It may seem that the English language is becoming increasingly global, as a primary language of both business and the Internet. Yet local attachments to language persist, often out of cultural pride. For example, the French-speaking residents of the Canadian province of Québec are so passionate about their linguistic heritage that they often refuse to speak English, the dominant language of Canada, and they periodically seek political independence from the rest of Canada. Minority languages are sometimes even outlawed by the majority government: Turkey restricts the use of the Kurdish language; similarly, the "English-only" movement in the United States seeks to restrict the language of education and government to English, even though numerous other languages are spoken throughout the country.

Speech and Writing

All societies use speech as a vehicle of language. However, there are other ways of expressing language—most notably, writing. The invention of writing marked a major

linguistic relativity hypothesis A hypothesis, based on the theories of Sapir and Whorf, that perceptions are relative to language.

transition in human history. Writing first began as the drawing up of lists: Marks made on wood, clay, or stone served to keep records about significant events, objects, or people. For example, a mark, or sometimes a picture, might represent each tract of land possessed by a particular family or set of families (Gelb, 1952). Writing began as a means of storing information and as such was closely linked to the administrative needs of the early civilizations. A society that possesses writing can locate itself in time and space. Documents can be accumulated that record the past, and information can be gathered about present-day events and activities.

Written documents, or texts, have qualities distinct from the spoken word. The effect of speech is limited to the contexts in which words are uttered. Ideas and experiences can be passed down through generations in cultures without writing, but only by word of mouth. Texts, on the other hand, can endure for thousands of years, and through them, all varieties of writers from past ages can address us directly. This is why documentary research is so important to historians.

Material Culture

Material culture consists of the physical objects that a society creates that influence the ways in which people live. These include consumer goods, from clothes to cars to houses; the tools and technologies used to make those goods, from sewing machines to computerized factories; and the towns and cities that serve as places for people to live and work. A central aspect of a society's material culture is technology.

Today, material culture is rapidly becoming globalized, largely through modern information technology such as the computer and the Internet. Although the United States has been in the forefront of this technological revolution, most other industrial countries are catching up. In fact, it no longer makes sense to speak of an exclusively "U.S. technology" any more than it makes sense to speak of a U.S. car. The iPhone, for example, contains hundreds of components that are sourced from some 200 manufacturers across the planet, embodying technology developed in Japan, South Korea, Taiwan, Europe, and the United States (Minasians, 2016). Another example of the globalization of material culture is the way that classrooms and department stores the world over increasingly resemble one another, and the fact that McDonald's restaurants are now found on nearly every continent.

CONCEPT CHECKS

1 Describe the main elements of culture.

2 What role does culture play in society?

3 Identify three examples of cultural universals.

4 What is the linguistic relativity hypothesis?

2 THE SOCIOLOGICAL STUDY OF CULTURE

It is easy to assume that we are so thoroughly shaped by culture that we never escape its influence. In fact, that is how most sociologists thought about culture until the 1990s (Inglis, 2005). Most sociologists took for granted the importance of culture without seriously considering how it worked in daily life.

Culture and Change: A "Cultural Turn" in Sociology?

The phrase **cultural turn** describes sociology's recent emphasis on understanding the role of culture in daily life. One result has been to challenge the assumption that culture rigidly determines our values and behaviors. Instead, the sociologist Ann Swidler (1986) has characterized culture as a "tool kit" from which people select different understandings and behaviors. Thus, some people can choose to dye their hair, wear nose rings, and tattoo their bodies but still accept their parents' traditional ideas about sexual restraint. Because people participate in many different (and often conflicting) cultures, the tool kit can be quite large and its contents varied (Bourdieu, 1990; Sewell, 1992; Tilly, 1992).

Our cultural tool kits include a variety of "scripts" that we can draw on—and even improvise on—to shape our beliefs, values, and actions. The more appropriate the script is to a particular set of circumstances, the more likely we are to follow it—and recall events that conform to it long after they have occurred (D'Andrade, 1995; DiMaggio, 1997). For example, imagine that you are a woman walking alone in an unfamiliar city late at night and suddenly encounter a male stranger who begins to cross the street toward you, stating as he approaches, "Excuse me, may I ask you a question?" Your choice of cultural script will shape your response. A popular cultural script—honed by film and television entertainment, reality TV, and politicians—is to fear such encounters, especially if you are female (Glassner, 1999). As a result, instead of hearing him out, you quickly turn and head for the safety of a nearby all-night restaurant. Later, when retelling the story, you might recall the stranger as taller and more menacing than he was—traits consistent with American cultural scripts about such encounters.

Now imagine that you are the man in this encounter, perhaps an out of town businessman trying to find your hotel in an unfamiliar neighborhood. You see a woman walking on the other side of the street, and as you cross to ask for directions, she turns and disappears into a restaurant. Your experience would be very different from that of the woman: You are concerned about the late hour, worried about being lost, and stunned by her response. Perhaps when you return home you will describe this event as evidence that people in this city are cold and indifferent to strangers.

In studying this case in light of the cultural turn, sociologists would attempt to understand the different cultural scripts involved and why each person might have chosen those scripts. How did physical appearance influence their different experiences? What words were spoken, and what meanings did those words convey? What did the two people's "body language" communicate? Sociologists would also consider alternative scripts that might have altered the experience of each participant. For example, the woman might have chosen the script of "Good Samaritan," viewing the approaching stranger as potentially in need of assistance and thereby offering to help. Or the man might have recognized that a lone woman would feel threatened and instead have chosen a less confrontational script—perhaps remaining on his side of the street and beginning with a soft-spoken, "Excuse me, can you please tell me the way to my hotel? I seem to be lost."

The cultural turn in sociology reveals that there is no single "reality" to social encounters and that multiple cultural scripts can play out in any situation. The challenge

cultural turn Sociology's recent emphasis on the importance of understanding the role of culture in daily life.

of sociology is to understand people's differing realities, the scripts that they follow, and the reasons they choose one set of scripts over another (Bonnell and Hunt, 1999; Chaney, 1994; Glassner, 1999; Hays, 2000; Long, 1997; Seidman, 1997; Sewell, 1999; Smith and West, 2000; Swidler, 2001).

Sociologist Wendy Griswold has identified four elements of any culture that constitute a complex cultural system, which she terms the "cultural diamond," with the four elements representing the four points of a diamond. These four elements include both material and nonmaterial cultural objects; the creators or producers of cultural objects; the receivers of cultural objects, who don't just passively accept these objects but rather actively make meaning out of them; and the larger social world, comprising the economic, political, social, and cultural patterns in any particular society. Each of the four elements of the cultural diamond interact with the other three, resulting in six possible linkages that shape a society's culture. Cultural sociology, as Griswold sees it, is especially concerned with one of the six linkages: that between cultural objects (both material and nonmaterial) and the social world (Griswold, 2013).

Early Human Culture: Greater Adaptation to Physical Environment

Human culture and human biology are intertwined. Understanding how culture is related to the physical evolution of the human species can, in turn, help us understand the central role of culture in shaping our lives. To understand the forms of society that existed before modern industrialism, we call on the historical dimension of the sociological imagination.

Given both the archaeological evidence and the similarities in blood chemistry and genetics between chimpanzees and humans, scientists believe that humans evolved from apelike creatures on the African continent some 4 million years ago. The first evidence of humanlike culture dates back 2 million years. Early humans fashioned stone tools, hunted animals and gathered nuts and berries, harnessed the use of fire, and established a highly cooperative way of life. Because early humans planned their hunts, they must have had some ability for abstract thought.

Culture enabled early humans to compensate for their physical limitations, such as lack of claws and sharp teeth and slower running speed relative to that of other animals (Deacon, 1998). It freed humans from dependence on the instinctual responses to the environment that are characteristic of other species. The larger, more complex human brain permitted greater adaptive learning in dealing with major environmental changes such as the Ice Age. For example, humans figured out how to build fires and sew clothing for warmth. Through greater flexibility, humans could survive unpredictable challenges in their surroundings and shape the world with their ideas and their tools. In an instant of geological time, we became the dominant species on the planet.

Yet early humans were closely tied to their physical environment because they lacked the technological ability to modify their surroundings in significant ways (Bennett, 1976; Harris, 1975, 1978, 1980). Their ability to secure food and make clothing and shelter depended on physical resources close at hand. Cultures varied widely according to geographic and climatic conditions, from deserts to rain forests, the frozen Arctic to temperate areas. Human inventiveness spawned a rich tapestry of cultures around the world. As you will see later in this chapter, however, modern

Compare the material culture of (top left) the Inuit building an igloo in Canada, (bottom left) a Bedouin woman beside her tent in the Sahara desert, and (right) an Embera man hollowing out a canoe.

technology and other forces of globalization pose both challenges and opportunities for future global cultural diversity.

The Earliest Societies: Hunters and Gatherers

For all but a tiny part of our existence on this planet, human beings have lived in small **hunting and gathering societies**, often numbering no more than 30 or 40 people (see Table 3.1). Hunters and gatherers gain their livelihood from hunting, fishing, and gathering wild edible plants. Such cultures still exist in some parts of the world, such as in India, a few arid parts of Africa, Australia, the Arctic, and the jungles of Brazil and New Guinea. Most such cultures, however, have been destroyed or absorbed by the spread of Western culture. Currently, only about 5 million people in the world support themselves through hunting and gathering—less than 0.1 percent of the world's population (Hitchcock and Beisele, 2000).

Compared with larger societies—particularly modern societies such as the United States—there was little inequality in most hunting and gathering groups; everyone lived in what would today be regarded as extreme poverty. Because necessary material goods

hunting and gathering societies Societies whose mode of subsistence is gained from hunting animals, fishing, and gathering edible plants.

Table 3.1

TYPES OF HUMAN SOCIETY

TYPE	PERIOD OF EXISTENCE	CHARACTERISTICS
Hunting and gathering societies	50,000 B.C.E. to the present Now on the verge of complete disappearance.	Consist of small numbers of people gaining their livelihood from hunting, fishing, and the gathering of edible plants. Few inequalities. Differences of rank limited by age and gender.
Agrarian societies	12,000 B.C.E. to the present Most are now part of larger political entities and losing their distinct identity.	Based on small rural communities, without towns or cities. Livelihood gained through agriculture, often supplemented by hunting and gathering. Stronger inequalities than among hunters and gatherers. Ruled by chiefs.
Pastoral societies	12,000 B.C.E. to the present Today mostly part of larger states; their traditional ways of life are being undermined.	Range from a few hundred people to many thousands. Depend on the tending of domesticated animals for their subsistence. Marked by distinct inequalities. Ruled by chiefs or warrior kings.
Traditional societies or civilizations	6000 B.C.E. to the nineteenth century All traditional states have disappeared.	Very large in size, some numbering millions of people (though small compared with industrialized societies). Some cities exist, in which trade and manufacturing are concentrated. Based largely on agriculture. Major inequalities exist among different classes. Distinct apparatus of government headed by a king or emperor.

were limited to weapons for hunting, tools for digging and building, traps, and cooking utensils, there was little difference among members of the society in the number or kinds of material possessions; there were no divisions between rich and poor. Differences in position or rank were based on age and gender; men were almost always the hunters, while women gathered wild crops, cooked food, and brought up the children.

The oldest and most experienced men usually had an important say in major decisions affecting the group, but differences in power were much less distinct than in larger types of society. Hunting and gathering societies were usually participatory rather than competitive: All adult male members assembled in the face of important decisions or crises.

Hunters and gatherers moved about a good deal within fixed territories, around which they migrated from year to year. Because they lacked animal or mechanical means of transport, they could take very few goods or possessions with them. Many hunting and gathering communities did not have a stable membership; people often moved between camps, or groups split up and joined others within the same territory.

Hunters and gatherers had little interest in developing material wealth; their main concerns were with religious values and ritual activities. Members participated regularly in elaborate ceremonies and spent time preparing the dress, masks, paintings, or other sacred objects used in such rituals.

Hunters and gatherers are not merely primitive peoples whose ways of life no longer hold interest for us. Studying their cultures demonstrates that some of our institutions are far from natural features of human life. We shouldn't idealize the circumstances in which hunters and gatherers lived, but the lack of inequalities in wealth and power and the emphasis on cooperation are reminders that the world of modern industrial civilization cannot necessarily be equated with progress.

Pastoral and Agrarian Societies

About 15,000 years ago, some hunting and gathering groups started raising domesticated animals and cultivating fixed plots of land as their means of livelihood. **Pastoral societies** relied mainly on domesticated livestock, whereas **agrarian societies** grew crops (practiced agriculture). Some societies had mixed pastoral and agrarian economies.

Depending on the environment, pastoralists reared cattle, sheep, goats, camels, or horses. Some pastoral societies exist in the modern world, especially in areas of Africa, the Middle East, and Central Asia. They are usually found in regions of dense grasslands or in deserts or mountain regions. Such regions are not amenable to agriculture but may support livestock.

At some point, hunting and gathering groups began to sow their own crops rather than simply collect those growing in the wild. This practice developed as horticulture, in which the group cultivated small gardens by the use of simple hoes or digging instruments. Like pastoralism, horticulture provided a more reliable food supply than hunting and gathering and therefore could support larger communities. Because they were not on the move, people who practiced horticulture could develop larger stocks of material possessions than people in either hunting and gathering or pastoral communities.

From about 6000 B.C.E. onward, we find evidence of societies larger than, and different from, any that existed before. These societies, which were based on settled agriculture and the development of cities, led to pronounced inequalities in wealth and power, and were ruled by kings or emperors. Because writing was present and science and art flourished, these societies are often called civilizations.

The earliest civilizations developed in the Middle East, mostly in fertile river areas. The Chinese Empire originated in about 1800 B.C.E., at which time powerful states also existed in what are now India and Pakistan. By the fifteenth century C.E., large civilizations also existed in Mexico and Latin America, including the Aztecs of the Mexican peninsula and the Incas of Peru.

pastoral societies Societies whose subsistence derives from the rearing of domesticated animals.

agrarian societies Societies whose means of subsistence are based on agricultural production (crop growing).

Most traditional (premodern) civilizations were also empires: They conquered and incorporated other peoples (Kautsky, 1982). This was true, for instance, of traditional Rome and China. At its height in the first century C.E., the Roman Empire stretched from Britain in northwest Europe to beyond the Middle East. The Chinese Empire covered most of the massive region of East Asia now occupied by modern China.

Industrial Societies

What happened to destroy the forms of society that dominated the whole of history up to two centuries ago? The answer, in a word, is **industrialization**—the emergence of machine production based on the use of inanimate power resources (such as steam or electricity). The industrialized, or modern, societies differ from any previous type of social order in several key respects, and their development has had consequences stretching far beyond their European origins.

Industrialization originated in eighteenth-century Britain as a result of the Industrial Revolution, a complex set of technological changes between 1750 and 1850 that affected people's means of gaining a livelihood. These changes included the invention of new machines (such as the spinning jenny for creating yarn, patented in 1770), the harnessing of power resources (especially water and steam) for production, and the use of science to improve production methods. Because discoveries and inventions in one field lead to more in others, the pace of technological innovation in **industrialized societies** is extremely rapid compared with that of traditional social systems.

In even the most advanced of traditional civilizations, most people worked on the land. By contrast, in industrialized societies today, the majority of the employed population works in factories, offices, or shops. And slightly more than half of all people (55 percent) live and work in urban areas (United Nations, 2018). The largest cities are vastly larger than the urban settlements of traditional civilizations. In cities, social life becomes impersonal and anonymous, and many encounters are with strangers. Large-scale organizations, such as business corporations or government agencies, influence the lives of virtually everyone.

The political systems of modern societies are more developed than forms of government in traditional states; in the latter, monarchs and emperors had little influence on the customs of most of their subjects, who lived in self-contained villages. With industrialization, transportation and communication became much more rapid, promoting a more integrated "national" community.

The industrialized societies were the first **nation-states**—political communities with clearly delimited borders and shared culture, rather than vague frontier areas that separated traditional states. Nation-state governments have extensive powers over many aspects of citizens' lives, framing laws that apply to all those living within their borders. The United States is a nation-state, as are virtually all other societies in the world today.

The application of industrial technology not only has served peaceful processes of economic development but also has altered

industrialization The process of the machine production of goods.

industrialized societies Strongly developed nation-states in which the majority of the population works in factories or offices rather than in agriculture, and most people live in urban areas.

ways of waging war, creating weaponry and modes of military organization much more advanced than those of nonindustrial cultures. Together, superior economic strength, political cohesion, and military superiority account for the worldwide spread of Western culture over the past two centuries.

nation-states Particular types of states, characteristic of the modern world, in which governments have sovereign power within defined territorial areas, and populations are citizens who know themselves to be part of single nations.

Sociology first emerged as a discipline as industrial societies developed in Europe and North America, and it was strongly influenced by the changes taking place at that time. As we saw in Chapter 1, the major nineteenth-century sociological theorists (Durkheim, Marx, and Weber) all sought to explain these sweeping changes. While they differed in their understanding and their predictions about the future, all shared a belief that industrial society was here to stay, and, as a result, the future would in many ways resemble the past.

For Durkheim, this vision of the future meant the increasing importance of what he termed "organic solidarity"—a growing division of labor, with all members of society engaged in highly specialized roles (or *functions*, in Durkheim's terminology), with functional interdependence resulting in ties that bind the members of society together. Marx, on the other hand, argued that industrial society's division into social classes hampered its technological potential because the capitalist class reaped all the benefits of advanced technologies at the expense of the working class. In his view, a working-class revolution was required to create a classless society, a new form of industrial society in which everyone prospered. Weber focused on the rise of what he termed *rational-legal society*, best seen in modern bureaucracies. This he viewed as a highly efficient form of social organization that was, unfortunately, simultaneously destructive of human freedom and potential—or, as he referred to it in his memorable phrase, an "iron cage." While Weber anticipated that from time to time charismatic leaders might emerge to challenge this trend, ultimately their power would become routinized, and the long march of the bureaucrat would continue.

While Durkheim, Marx, and Weber's theoretical understanding of the emerging industrial society still has relevance, contemporary theorists have shed new light on the ways in which culture and society are changing in the modern world. We're experiencing a transition to a new type of society that is no longer based primarily on manufacturing or low-paying service work, but rather relies increasingly on information technology, artificial intelligence, and robotics to replace human labor in a growing range of jobs—from unskilled labor slinging hamburgers to the highly skilled work of engineers, accountants, and other professionals. We are entering, in other words, a "postindustrial" society, a topic we will discuss in detail in Chapter 14. In the next section of this chapter, we consider recent research on some of the current issues that confront global societies.

CONCEPT CHECKS

1 Compare the three main types of premodern societies.

2 What transformations led to the development of civilizations?

3 What does the concept of industrialization mean?

4 How has industrialization weakened traditional social systems?

3 RESEARCH TODAY: UNDERSTANDING THE MODERN WORLD

From the seventeenth to the early twentieth century, Western countries established colonies in numerous areas previously occupied by traditional societies. Although all these colonies have by now attained independence, the process of **colonialism** helped shape the social map of the globe as we know it today. In some regions, such as North America, Australia, and New Zealand, which were only thinly populated by hunting and gathering or pastoral communities, Europeans became the majority population. In North America, the native population was greatly reduced by the spread of European diseases, as well as through conquest (Diamond, 1999). This form of colonialism is sometimes referred to as *settler colonialism* because it took the form of large-scale European settlement (Veracini, 2010). In other areas, including much of Asia, Africa, and South America, the local populations remained in the majority and were governed by the colonial powers, largely for the benefit of the home country.

Societies created through settler colonialism, including the United States, have become industrialized. Those with large native populations ruled by colonial administrators experienced a much lower level of industrial development, largely because much of the wealth produced in these societies was realized by the colonial powers. These included South Asia, as well as much of Africa and Latin America. Colonialism had come to an end by the mid-twentieth century, and today, many of these societies are experiencing rapid economic growth. Some, such as India and Brazil, are currently major drivers of global economic growth (Nederveen Pieterse, 2011).

There is no agreed-upon way of classifying countries in terms of their degree of industrialization. While it was once common to distinguish between "developed" and "developing" countries, it is not surprising that members of the latter category objected to being characterized as "developing," on the grounds that it privileged the "developed" countries of the world as being somehow more advanced. They saw this both as an invidious cultural judgment and as ignoring the role of colonialism in shaping their adverse economic situations. Among sociologists, a commonly used distinction is between the "global north" and the "global south," since most (but not all) of what was once referred to as the industrialized world is found in the Northern Hemisphere, while most (but not all) of what was called the developing world lies in the Southern Hemisphere.

These different ways of characterizing the world today highlight the importance of language and reflect an increased sensitivity, at least among scholars of globalization, to the ways in which words can shape our perceptions, unconsciously elevating some societies to a more "advanced" status, while unconsciously denigrating others. We shall use the terms *global north* and *global south*, imperfect as they are, because they are least likely to imply a judgment about which is culturally preferable.

It is important to recognize that power relations are culturally embedded. The French sociologist Pierre Bourdieu (1986) introduced the concept of **cultural capital**, the accumulated cultural knowledge within a society that confers power and sta-

colonialism The process whereby Western nations established their rule in parts of the world away from their home territories.

cultural capital The accumulated cultural knowledge within a society that confers power and status.

tus (Barker, 2004). In Bourdieu's formulation, there are three kinds of cultural capital, each of which is strongly influenced by one's socioeconomic position in society: the first is what a person embodies in his or her very person (for example, one's way of dressing and speaking, and one's mannerisms); the next is reflected in the material objects one possesses (such as one's home, car, or computer); and the last is socially determined by larger institutions (such as the academic credentials required for a particular job). In the United States, for example, a person could be said to possess a great deal of cultural capital if he or she were articulate and persuasive in English language skills; had access to high-end computers and the software required to run complex business programs; and possessed the advanced degrees necessary for a highly paid job with an investment firm.

Although there are always exceptions, those who possess the cultural capital valued in any society enjoy clear advantages over those who do not. Since cultural capital reflects socioeconomic status, it can reinforce existing patterns of economic and political inequality.

The Global South

As previously mentioned, the majority of countries in the global south—South Asia, Africa, and South America—are in areas that underwent colonial rule. A few colonized areas gained independence early, such as Haiti, which became the first autonomous Black republic in 1804. The Spanish colonies in South America acquired their freedom in 1810, while Brazil broke away from Portuguese rule in 1822.

Some countries that were never ruled from Europe were nonetheless strongly influenced by colonial relationships. China, for example, was compelled from the seventeenth century on to enter into trading agreements with European powers, which assumed government control over certain areas, including major seaports. Hong Kong was the last of these. Most nations in the global south have become independent states only since World War II, often following bloody anticolonial struggles. Examples include India, which shortly after achieving self-rule split into India and Pakistan, a range of other Asian countries (such as Malaysia, Myanmar, and Singapore); and countries in Africa (such as Algeria, the Democratic Republic of Congo, Kenya, Nigeria, and Tanzania).

Although they may include peoples living in traditional fashion, these countries differ from earlier forms of traditional society. Their political systems, following Western models, make them nation-states. Although most of the population still lives in rural areas, a rapid process of city development is occurring. Although agriculture remains the main economic activity, many crops are produced for sale in world markets. These countries are not merely societies that have somehow "lagged behind" the more industrialized areas; they emerged from contact with Western industrialism, which has undermined the more traditional systems.

The World Bank estimates that 736 million people, or nearly 10 percent of the world's population, are living in extreme poverty, which is defined as subsisting on $1.90 or less per day (World Bank, 2018a). Furthermore, the United Nations Food and Agriculture Association also estimates that as of 2018, an estimated 820 million people worldwide experienced hunger, and upwards of 2 billion people experienced food insecurity (UN Food and Agriculture Association, 2019b). Almost all of these people live in the global south and half live in sub-Saharan Africa. A third of the world's poor and hungry live in South Asia, in countries such as India, Pakistan, Indonesia, and Bangladesh (World Bank, 2018a). China, however, has made great strides; some 850 million people were lifted out of poverty between 1990 and 2019 (World Bank, 2019k). A substantial number of the poor—some 25.9 million people—live on the doorstep of the United States, in the Caribbean and Central and South America (World Bank, 2018a). Despite progress toward achieving the Sustainable Development Goals, which call for ending poverty by 2030, major challenges still remain, particularly in South Asia and sub-Saharan Africa, where most of the world's poor live. The global economic crisis in 2008 had an acutely destructive impact on people living in poverty, particularly women (UN Economic and Social Commission for Asia and the Pacific, 2010). Most of the gains in reducing global poverty and hunger have resulted from economic growth in China and East Asia.

Global poverty shouldn't be seen as remote from the concerns of Americans. Whereas in previous generations, the bulk of immigrants to the United States came from European countries, recent years have seen waves of Hispanic immigrants, nearly all from Latin America. Some U.S. cities, such as Los Angeles and Miami, have become international gateways to Latin America and are bursting with new immigrants who maintain trading connections with their home countries.

In most societies, poverty is worst in rural areas. Malnutrition, lack of education, low life expectancy, and substandard housing are most severe in the countryside, especially where arable land is scarce, agricultural productivity low, and drought or floods common. Women are usually more disadvantaged than men. For instance, they often work longer hours and, when paid at all, earn lower wages. (See Chapter 10 for a lengthier discussion of gender inequality.)

The poor in the global south live in conditions almost unimaginable to North Americans. Many have no permanent dwellings apart from shelters made of cartons or loose pieces of wood. Most have no running water, sewage systems, or electricity. Nonetheless, millions of poor people also live in the United States, and there are connections between poverty in America and global poverty. This is true of the descendants of the Black slaves brought over by force centuries ago, and it is true of more recent, and willing, immigrants who have arrived from Latin America, Asia, and elsewhere. Although immigrants and their children make up only 13 percent of the U.S. population, they account for a quarter of all those living in poverty in the United States (Center for Immigration Studies, 2016).

Some formerly impoverished countries have successfully embarked on a process of industrialization. Referred to as the **emerging economies**, they include Argentina, Brazil, Chile, China, India, Mexico, Singapore, South Korea, and Taiwan. The rates of economic growth of the most successful countries, such as those in East Asia, are several times those of the Western industrial economies.

The East Asian emerging economies are investing abroad as well as promoting growth at home. China is investing in mines and factories in Africa, elsewhere in East Asia, and in Latin America. South Korea's production of steel has increased by nearly 50 percent in the last decade, and its shipbuilding and electronics industries are among the world's leaders (World Steel Association, 2013). Singapore is becoming the major financial and commercial center of Southeast Asia. Taiwan is an important presence in the manufacturing and electronics industries. All these changes have directly affected the United

emerging economies Developing countries, such as India and Singapore, that over the past two or three decades have begun to develop a strong industrial base.

States. In fact, the "rise of the rest" (Zakaria, 2009) is arguably the most important aspect of global economic change in the world today.

It is worth noting that a country's economic growth does not necessarily mean that its citizens are happier or feel more secure. A growing body of research suggests the opposite: As countries industrialize, their general sense of well-being does not increase and may even decline. Even in China, despite unprecedented rates of economic growth that have elevated hundreds of millions of Chinese into middle-class status, the most recent research suggests that people's happiness—at least as measured on

Women wait in line for food in Calcutta, India. Why does poverty disproportionately affect women around the world?

a "life satisfaction" index—is actually lower than it was two decades ago, before China's "growth miracle" took off (Easterlin, 2001, 2003, 2010; Easterlin and Sawangfa, 2010; Easterlin et al., 2010, 2012; Inglehart, 1997).

Contemporary Industrial Societies: Cultural Conformity or Diversity?

The study of cultural differences highlights the influence of cultural learning on behavior, which can vary widely from culture to culture. For example, in the United States, we eat oysters but not kittens or puppies, both of which are regarded as delicacies in other parts of the world. Westerners regard kissing as a normal part of sexual behavior, but in other cultures, the practice is either unknown or regarded as disgusting.

Cultural Conformity

All cultures serve as an important source of conformity. For example, when you say that you subscribe to a particular value, you are probably voicing the beliefs of your family members, friends, teachers, or others who are significant in your life. When you choose a word to describe some personal experience, that word acquires its meaning in a language you learned from others.

American high school and college students often see themselves as especially non-conformist. Like the body piercers and tattooists of today, the hippies of the 1960s and the punks of the 1980s all sported distinctive clothing styles, haircuts, and other forms of bodily adornment. Yet how individualistic were they? Were their styles actually "uniforms," just as navy blue suits or basic black are "uniforms" among conservative businesspeople?

There is, in fact, an aspect of conformity to their behavior—conformity to their own group. When you buy a seemingly unique article of clothing to express your individuality, that garment was likely created by the design department of a global manufacturer that studied the current tastes of consumers and then ordered the mass production of your "unique" garment. When you listen to music, it is most likely the same kind that your friends listen to.

cultural appropriation When members of one cultural group borrow elements of another group's culture.

One of the challenges for all cultures is to instill in people a willingness to conform. Encouraging conformity is accomplished in two ways (Parsons, 1964; orig. 1951). First, members learn the norms of their culture starting from childhood, with parents playing a key role. When learning is successful, the ingrained norms become unquestioned ways of thinking and acting; they appear "normal." (Note the similarity between the words *norm* and *normal*; they share a common root.) Second, social control comes into play when a person fails to conform adequately to a culture's norms. Social control often involves informal punishment, such as rebuking friends for minor breaches of etiquette, gossiping behind their backs, or ostracizing them from the group. Formal forms of discipline might range from parking tickets to imprisonment (Foucault, 1975). Émile Durkheim argued that punishment not only helps guarantee conformity among those who would violate a culture's norms and values but also vividly reminds others what the norms and values are.

Cultures differ, however, in how much they value conformity. Research shows that Chinese culture lies at one extreme in terms of valuing conformity (Hofstede, 1997; Minkov and Hofstede, 2012), while at the other extreme lies American culture, ranking among the world's highest in cherishing individualism. Americans pride themselves on their independence of spirit, represented by the lone bald eagle, the U.S. national symbol. Globalization—from Starbucks and McDonald's to the widespread use of the Internet and smartphones—is exposing many young Chinese to more individualistic Western values.

Cultural Appropriation

Cultural appropriation occurs when members of one cultural group borrow elements of another's culture, such as when a person who is not an American Indian dons a feathered headdress on Halloween or when a non-Japanese person wears a

On the left, members of a 1970s commune relax outdoors. On the right, punks hang out on a street corner in the 1980s. Though their distinctive styles set them apart from mainstream society, these people are not as nonconformist as they may think they are. Both subcultures pictured here conform to the norms of their respective social groups.

kimono. Rock music became popular when White musicians—from Elvis Presley to the Rolling Stones—drew on African American blues and gospel, appropriating key musical elements that were then introduced to largely White audiences in Europe and the United States. While the history of music, art, and even language shows that cultural appropriation is widespread, sociologists have raised the question: When is it offensive to take on elements of a culture to which you don't belong? Sometimes even the most well-intentioned and seemingly benign decisions to borrow the cultural style of another group can be understood quite differently by those who come from that culture.

Controversy abounded at Yale when an instructor publicly questioned the validity of an email from administrators with proposed guidelines for Halloween costumes.

Sociologist George Lipsitz (1997) has argued that when a majority or dominant culture appropriates elements of a minority culture, particularly one that has historically suffered oppression at the hands of the majority, it is especially important that those doing the appropriation be extremely sensitive to the historical meaning and contemporary significance of the cultural forms being appropriated. In October 2015, the campus of Yale University broke out in controversy over a series of emails written by administrators about Halloween. The uproar began when the college's Intercultural Affairs Committee sent an email advising students to avoid costumes that "threaten our sense of community or disrespect, alienate or ridicule segments of our population based on race, nationality, religious belief or gender expression." A few days later, a Yale instructor and wife of the deputy director of one of the college's dorms wrote a pointed response that questioned whether it was appropriate for college administrators to police the costumes of young adults. In an email to the dorm residents, she asked, "Is there no room anymore for a child or young person to be a little bit obnoxious, a little bit inappropriate or provocative, or yes, offensive?" This email set in motion a series of protests, with many students calling for her resignation. Many felt that she was dismissing the power of harmful stereotypes to further degrade marginalized groups. Ultimately, in early 2016, the instructor and her husband stepped down from their posts in residential life.

Although no hard-and-fast rules can resolve such conflicts, Lipsitz argues that we should always be aware of what is at stake: Sometimes cultural appropriation can reduce an entire way of life to demeaning stereotypes that exacerbate historically unequal power relations. For this reason, many schools have banned the use of Native American mascots.

Cultural Diversity

Small societies tend to be culturally uniform, but industrialized societies involving numerous **subcultures** are themselves culturally

subcultures Values and norms distinct from those of the majority, held by a group within a wider society.

diverse, or multicultural. As processes such as slavery, colonialism, war, migration, and contemporary globalization have led to populations settling in new areas, societies have emerged that are cultural composites: Their population comprises groups from diverse cultural and linguistic backgrounds. In modern cities, for example, many subcultural communities live side by side.

Subcultures not only imply different cultural backgrounds or different languages within a larger society, but they include segments of the population that have different cultural patterns. Subcultures might include Goths, computer hackers, hippies, Rastafarians, and fans of hip-hop. Some people identify with a particular subculture, whereas others move among several.

Culture helps perpetuate the values and norms of a society, yet it also offers opportunities for creativity and change. Subcultures and **countercultures**—groups that reject prevailing values and norms—can promote views that represent alternatives to the dominant culture. Social movements or groups with common lifestyles are powerful forces of change within societies, allowing people to express and act on their opinions, hopes, and beliefs. For example, throughout most of the twentieth century, gays and lesbians formed a distinct counterculture in opposition to dominant cultural norms. In a few cities, such as San Francisco, New York, and Chicago, gays and lesbians lived in distinct enclaves and even developed political power bases. Over time, their political claims and lifestyle became more and more acceptable to mainstream Americans, so much so that gay marriage was legalized nationwide in 2015. Today, gays and lesbians are no longer a counterculture. As the wider society has increasingly embraced their demand to be included in the institution of marriage, gays and lesbians have embraced one of the most significant institutions of mainstream society.

U.S. schoolchildren are frequently taught that the United States is a vast melting pot that assimilates subcultures. **Assimilation** is the process by which different cultures are absorbed into a mainstream culture. Although virtually all peoples living in the United States take on some common cultural characteristics, many groups strive to retain a unique identity. In fact, identification based on race or country of origin persists in the United States, particularly among African Americans and immigrants from Asia and Latin America (Parekh, 2010). Research has found that migrants to the United States have gradually adopted the label of "American"; however, scholars still point to a segmented assimilation where certain groups have better opportunities by which to enter U.S. society (Sezgin, 2012).

A more appropriate metaphor for American society than the assimilationist melting pot might be the culturally diverse salad bowl in which all the ingredients, though mixed together, retain their original flavor and integrity, thereby contributing to the richness of the salad as a whole. This viewpoint, termed **multiculturalism**, calls for respecting cultural diversity and promoting the equality of different cultures (Anzaldúa, 1990).

As we have seen, in many modern industrial nations, young people have their own subcultures. Youth subcultures typically revolve around musical preferences and distinctive styles of dress, language (especially slang), and behavior. Like

countercultures Cultural groups within a wider society that largely reject the values and norms of the majority.

assimilation The acceptance of a minority group by a majority population in which the new group takes on the values and norms of the dominant culture.

multiculturalism A condition in which ethnic groups exist separately and share equally in economic and political life.

The origins of hip-hop culture can be traced back to DJ Kool Herc (left), who brought the Jamaican disc jockey tradition of "toasting" to New York in the mid-1970s. M.I.A. (right) represents one aspect of widening appeal of hip-hop across cultural lines, arguably for better and for worse.

all subcultures, however, they still accept most of the norms and values of the dominant culture.

Consider the patchwork that is hip-hop. Although it emerged as a subculture in the Bronx, New York, in the mid-1970s, hip-hop owes much of its identity to Jamaica. The first important hip-hop DJ, Kool Herc, was a Jamaican immigrant, and rapping derives from the Jamaican DJ tradition of "toasting," chanting stories into microphones over records. The story of hip-hop is a lesson in the fluidity of contemporary cultural identity. The music is built around beats from other records, but in "sampling" from recordings, hip-hop artists often do something more significant: They sample identities, taking on the characteristics of subcultures that can be considerably foreign to them.

Hip-hop's reach has widened over time. Rappers and rap groups from Queens and Long Island—such as Run-DMC, LL Cool J, and Public Enemy—recorded some of the first great hip-hop albums. By the end of the 1980s, the music had a national presence in the United States, as L.A. artists such as N.W.A and Ice T developed gangsta rap, which soon had outposts in Oakland, New Orleans, Houston, and elsewhere. White rappers such as Kid Rock and Eminem, following in the footsteps of the Beastie Boys, pioneered a rap-rock synthesis, and a Filipino American crew known as the Invisibl Skratch Piklz revolutionized turntable techniques. Hip-hop soon became a global form. Mathangi "Maya" Arulpragasam, better known by her stage name "M.I.A.," is of Sri Lankan Tamil descent and used the cultural milieu of West London to help shape her specific style.

The sampled beats of hip-hop can contain nearly anything. The secret is transformation: A portion of an earlier song, recast to fit a new context, can take on an entirely different meaning while still retaining enough of its former essence to create a complicated and richly meaningful finished product. In many ways, hip-hop is a music of echoes—rappers revisiting the funk music and "blaxploitation" films of the 1970s (Black action movies often criticized for glorifying violence and presenting Blacks in negative stereotypes); suburban fans romanticizing inner-city street styles. Hip-hop is the soundtrack to an emerging global culture that treats the looks, sounds, and byways of particular subcultures, or particular moments in time, as raw material for the creation of new styles.

What does hip-hop tell us about cultural diversity? On the one hand, its history of incorporating an ever-wider circle of influences and participants demonstrates that what is "normal" in one community can quickly be adopted in another community far away, through dissemination via vinyl records, digital samples, and other media. On the other hand, the controversies that hip-hop has generated suggest that such cultural crossings also bring uncertainty, misperception, and fear. Finally, hip-hop's evolution suggests that even in a global culture, subcultural distinctions retain an important aura of authenticity. Even today, hip-hop describes aspects of social realities that most Americans would prefer not to contemplate.

Subcultures also develop around types of work associated with unique cultural features. Long-distance truckers, coal miners, Wall Street stockbrokers, computer programmers, professional athletes, corporate lawyers, and artists, for example, form

Table 3.2

APPLYING SOCIOLOGY TO CULTURE

CONCEPT	APPROACH TO CULTURE	CONTEMPORARY APPLICATION
Cultural Appropriation	When members of one cultural group borrow elements of another group's culture.	A non-Native American wearing a feathered headdress on Halloween.
Subcultures	Segments within a population that develop distinct cultural patterns.	Young people whose cultural patterns and identities develop from and around skateboarding, video games, or certain types of music.
Countercultures	Groups that reject mainstream norms and values and thus question the status quo	The anti-vaccine movement.
Assimilation	The process by which the cultures of minority populations are absorbed into mainstream culture.	The increasing use of white wedding dresses by immigrants from countries where this is not a cultural norm.
Multiculturalism	The movement advocating respect for cultural diversity and promoting the equality of all cultures	Changes in college curricula that place greater emphasis on the culture and contributions of non-Western societies.

subcultures that value (respectively) physical strength, bravery, shrewdness, knowledge, speed, material wealth, and creativity. However, they seldom stray far from the dominant culture. Even professional thieves share most of the values of U.S. society: They marry and raise children; like most Americans, they want to accumulate wealth, power, and prestige; they eat with knives and forks, drive on the right side of the road, and try to avoid trouble as much as possible (Chambliss, 1988).

ethnocentrism The tendency to look at other cultures through the eyes of one's own culture, and thereby misrepresent them.

cultural relativism The practice of judging a society by its own standards.

Cultural Identity and Ethnocentrism

Every culture displays unique patterns of behavior. If you have traveled abroad, you know that aspects of daily life taken for granted in your own culture may not be part of everyday life elsewhere. Even in countries that share the same language, you might find customs to be quite different. The expression *culture shock* is an apt one. Often people feel disoriented when immersed in a new culture because they have lost familiar cultural reference points and have not yet learned how to navigate in the new culture.

Almost any familiar activity will seem strange if described out of context. Western cleanliness rituals are no more or less bizarre than the customs of some Pacific groups who knock out their front teeth to beautify themselves or of certain South American tribal groups who place discs inside their lips to make them protrude, believing that this enhances their attractiveness. We cannot understand these practices and beliefs separately from the wider cultures of which they are a part. A culture must be studied in terms of its own meanings and values—a key presupposition of sociology. Sociologists seek to avoid **ethnocentrism**, which is the judging of other cultures in terms of the standards of one's own. We must remove our own cultural blinders to see the ways of life of different peoples in an unbiased light. The practice of judging a society by its own standards is called **cultural relativism**.

Applying cultural relativism can be fraught with uncertainty and challenge. Not only is it hard to see things from a completely different point of view, but sometimes, troubling questions arise. Does cultural relativism mean that all customs and behaviors are equally legitimate? Are there any universal standards to which all humans should adhere? Consider the ritual of female genital cutting, or what opponents have called "genital mutilation." This is a painful cultural ritual, practiced in certain African, Asian, and Middle Eastern societies, in which the clitoris and sometimes all or part of the vaginal labia are removed with a knife or a sharpened stone and the two sides of the vulva are partly sewn together as a means of controlling sexual activity and increasing the

CONCEPT CHECKS

1 Give examples of subcultures that are typical of American society.

2 Why is cultural appropriation considered problematic by some?

3 What is the difference between cultural ethnocentrism and cultural relativism?

sexual pleasure of the man. The World Health Organization (2017) estimates that more than 200 million girls and women today have undergone female genital cutting.

In cultures where female genital cutting has been practiced for generations, it is regarded as normal. A study of 2,000 men and women in two Nigerian communities found that 9 out of 10 women interviewed had undergone clitoridectomies, a form of genital cutting, in childhood; the large majority favored the procedure for their own daughters, primarily for cultural reasons. However, a significant minority believed that the practice should be stopped (Ebomoyi, 1987). Female genital cutting is regarded with abhorrence by most people from other cultures and by a growing number of women in the cultures where it is practiced (el Dareer, 1982; Johnson-Odim, 1991; Lightfoot-Klein, 1989). These differences in views can result in a clash of cultural values, especially when people from cultures where female genital cutting is common migrate to countries where the practice is illegal.

In France, for instance, a country with a large North African immigrant population, many African mothers arrange for traditional clitoridectomies to be performed on their daughters. Some have been tried and convicted under French law for mutilating their children, but these African mothers have argued that they were engaging in the same cultural practice that their own mothers had performed on them, that their grandmothers had performed on their mothers, and so on. They have complained that the French are ethnocentric, judging traditional African rituals by French customs. Feminists from Africa and the Middle East, while themselves strongly opposed to female genital cutting, have criticized Europeans and Americans who sensationalize the practice by calling it "backward" or "primitive" without seeking any understanding of the underlying cultural and economic circumstances (Wade, 2011; Knop, Michaels, and Riles, 2012). In this instance, globalization has led to a clash of cultural norms and values that has forced members of both cultures to confront some of their most deeply held beliefs. The role of the sociologist is to avoid knee-jerk responses and to examine complex questions carefully and from as many angles as possible.

4 UNANSWERED QUESTIONS

We face many unanswered questions in the sociological study of culture and society. One of the oldest debates concerns whether we are more likely to be shaped by biological factors or social ones. More recently, many debates have focused on the role of the Internet, and on globalization more generally, in shaping the modern world. We now turn to some of these unanswered questions.

Does Nature or Nurture More Powerfully Influence Human Behavior?

Because humans evolved as part of the world of nature, one would assume that human thinking and behavior are the result of biology and evolution. In fact, one of the oldest (and still unresolved) controversies in the social sciences is the "nature/nurture" debate: Are we shaped by our biology, or are we products of learning through life's experiences—that is, of nurture? Whereas biologists and some psychologists emphasize biological factors, sociologists stress the role of learning and culture. They also argue that because human beings can make conscious choices, neither biology nor culture wholly determines human behavior.

> **sociobiology** An approach that attempts to explain the behavior of both animals and human beings in terms of biological principles.

The nature/nurture debate has raged for more than a century. For example, in the 1930s and 1940s, many social scientists focused on biological factors, with some seeking (unsuccessfully) to prove that a person's physique determined his or her personality. In the 1960s and 1970s, scholars in different fields emphasized culture. Some social psychologists argued that even severe mental illness was the result of society labeling some behavior as unusual rather than the consequence of biochemical processes (Scheff, 1966). Today, partly because of new understandings in genetics and brain neurophysiology, the pendulum is again swinging toward the side of biology.

The resurgence of biological explanations for human behavior began in 1975, when the evolutionary biologist Edward O. Wilson published *Sociobiology: The New Synthesis*. The term **sociobiology** refers to the application of biological principles to explain the social activities of animals, including human beings. Wilson argued that genes influence not only physical traits but also behavior. For instance, some species of animals perform elaborate courtship rituals leading to sexual union and reproduction. Human courtship and sexual behavior, according to sociobiologists, involve similar rituals. Also, in most species, males are larger and more aggressive than females. Some suggest that genetic factors explain why, in all known human societies, men tend to hold positions of greater authority than women.

One way in which sociobiologists illuminate the relations between the sexes is through the idea of "reproductive strategy," a pattern of behavior developed through evolutionary selection that favors the chances of survival of offspring. The female body has a larger investment in its reproductive cells than the male—a fertilized human egg takes nine months to develop. Thus, women will not squander that investment and are

Sociologists argue that our preferences for particular body types are not biologically ingrained but rather shaped by cultural norms of beauty communicated through magazine ads, commercials, and movies.

instincts Fixed patterns of behavior that have genetic origins and that appear in all normal animals within a given species.

not driven to have sexual relations with many partners; their overriding aim is the care and protection of children. Men, on the other hand, desire to have sex with many partners, which is a sound strategy in terms of preserving the species. This view, it has been suggested, explains differences in sexual behavior and attitudes between men and women.

Sociobiologists do not argue that genes determine 100 percent of our behavior. For example, depending on the circumstances, men can choose to act in nonaggressive ways. Yet, even though this argument seems to add culture as another explanatory factor in describing human behavior, social scientists have condemned sociobiology for claiming that a propensity for particular behaviors, such as violence, is somehow "genetically programmed" (Seville Statement on Violence, 1990).

Different biological factors interact with, and respond to, environmental inputs. It has been difficult to find compelling, substantive data on the interaction between biology and experience. But more evidence is coming out of studies of brain development. Beginning in the womb, genes interact with hormones to shape the child's development (Stiles, 2011).

Most sociologists today acknowledge a role for nature in determining attitudes and behavior, but with strong qualifications. For example, no one questions that newborn babies have basic human reflexes, such as "rooting" for the mother's nipple and responding to the human face (Cosmides and Tooby, 1997; Johnson and Morton, 1991). But it is a leap to conclude that because babies have human reflexes, adult behavior is governed by **instincts**—biologically fixed patterns of action found in all cultures.

Sociologists now ask how nature and nurture interact to produce human behavior. They acknowledge that all known human cultures have some common characteristics—for example, language, forms of emotional expression, rules for raising children or engaging in sexual behavior, and standards of beauty (Brown, 1991). But they also recognize that there is enormous variety in *how* these common characteristics play out: It is not some biological disposition that makes American men feel attracted to a *particular* type of woman. Rather, it's their exposure to magazine ads, TV commercials, and movies that transmit culturally specific standards of female beauty.

Because humans think and act in many different ways, sociologists do not believe that "biology is destiny." If biology were all-important, we would expect all cultures to be similar, if not identical. Yet this is hardly the case. For example, pork is forbidden to religious Jews and Muslims, but it is a dietary staple in China. All cultures have standards of beauty and ornamentation, but what constitutes beauty in one culture may constitute the opposite in another (Elias, 1987; Elias and Dunning, 1987; Foucault, 1988). However, some feminist scholars have argued that with global access to Western images of beauty on the Internet, cultural definitions of beauty throughout the world are growing narrower and increasingly emphasize the slender physique that is so cherished in many Western cultures (Sepúlveda and Calado, 2012).

In 2008, a special issue of the *American Journal of Sociology* was dedicated to the nature/nurture debate, specifically the relationship between genetics and social influences on human behavior (Bearman, 2008). The studies generally concluded that while genetics are important, how genes might affect behavior depends largely on the social context. For example, a study of obesity among adolescents found that social and behavioral factors, such as a family's lifestyle (for example, how much time a family spends watching TV or how often a family skips meals), have a significant effect on the likelihood that children will end up overweight, even when both parents are heavy (Martin, 2008). Similarly, an international study of gender differences in mathematical ability found that such differences varied widely across countries, with differences in high mathematical performance between men and women reflecting the country's level of gender inequality rather than purely biological factors (Penner, 2008). Even alcoholism is strongly affected by social context: While a specific gene has been identified as increasing one's propensity for alcohol dependence, a strong family support system can greatly reduce that risk (Pescosolido et al., 2008).

Sociologists' main concern, therefore, is with how behavior is learned through interactions with family, friends, schools, television, and every other facet of the social environment. Early child rearing is especially relevant to this kind of learning. Human babies have a large brain, requiring birth relatively early in their fetal development, while their heads can still pass through the birth canal. As a result, human babies must spend a number of years in the care of adults, during which time the child learns his or her society's culture. All cultures therefore provide for childhood socialization, but the processes vary greatly from culture to culture. An American child learns the multiplication table from a classroom teacher, whereas a child in the forests of Borneo learns to hunt with older members of the tribe.

Perhaps recent scientific advances in brain neurophysiology and genetics will tip the balance more toward emphasizing the role of nature in shaping human behavior. But for the present, most sociologists would conclude that both nature and nurture interact in complex and as yet imperfectly understood ways to shape who we are and how we behave.

Does the Internet Promote a Global Culture?

Many believe that the rapid worldwide growth of the Internet is hastening the spread of a global culture resembling the cultures of Europe and North America. Belief in such values as equality between men and women, the right to speak freely, democratic participation in government, and the pursuit of pleasure through consumption are diffused throughout the world over the Internet. Moreover, Internet technology itself seems to foster such values: Global communication, seemingly unlimited (and uncensored) information, and instant gratification all characterize the new technology.

Yet it may be premature to conclude that the Internet will sweep aside traditional cultures. Cyberspace is becoming increasingly global, and evidence shows that the Internet is, in many ways, compatible with traditional cultural values, perhaps even a means of strengthening them. This is especially likely to be true in countries that seek to control the Internet, censoring or blocking unwanted content and punishing those whose postings violate traditional values. One example is Saudi Arabia, a monarchy that officially enforces a highly conservative form of traditional Islam. The Saudi government not only routinely filters or blocks Internet content but also uses it to disseminate official propaganda. Content deemed "harmful," "anti-Islamic," or "offensive" is blocked, including any criticism of the royal family, and messaging apps such as Telegram and WhatsApp are restricted. In order to sell its iPhone in the kingdom, Apple had to remove the device's built-in FaceTime app. Social media is heavily monitored, and cyber dissidents—for example, those who defend women's or minority rights

According to Freedom House, two-thirds of Internet users live in countries where criticism of the government is subject to censorship. In addition to censoring Facebook and Twitter, governments are increasingly targeting messaging apps like WhatsApp and Telegram.

or criticize traditional religious beliefs—are likely to receive steep fines and severe punishment. In 2016, a Saudi individual was sentenced to 10 years in prison and 2,000 lashes for "spreading atheism" on Twitter (Freedom House, 2016).

Yet at the same time, even under such repressive conditions, the Internet provides a space for self-expression and discussion, albeit within limits. Saudis are some of the most active social media users in the world and are the largest adopters of Twitter in the Arab world. Women, for example, who comprise more than half of all Internet users in Saudi Arabia, are able to engage in Internet discussions that would be forbidden in public, such as those about women's health issues.

The Internet has sometimes been described as an echo chamber, in which people seek out like-minded others whose postings reinforce their own beliefs (Manjoo, 2008; Sunstein, 2012). For example, one study of a Jewish ultraorthodox religious group found that the Internet helped to strengthen the community, providing a forum for communication and the sharing of ideas (Barzilai-Nahon and Barzilai, 2005). In this sense, the Internet may be splitting society into what can be thought of as digitally linked tribes with their own unique cultural beliefs and values—sometimes even in conflict with the dominant culture. Examples from youth subcultures in recent years would include hippies, punks, skinheads, Rastas, Goths, gamers, rappers, and dancehall enthusiasts. Such subcultures sometimes emerge when ethnic minority youth seek to create a unique cultural identity within the dominant culture, often through music, dress, hairstyle, and bodily adornment such as tattoos and piercing. They are often hybrids of existing cultures: For example, dancehall, like reggae, which originated as part of a youth culture in Jamaica's poor neighborhoods, today has spread to the United States, Europe, and anywhere there has been a large Caribbean migration (Niahh, 2010).

Finally, of course, the Internet can be used to build a community around ideas that directly threaten the dominant culture. Al-Qaeda, ISIS, and other radical Islamist jihadists rely on the Internet to spread their ideas, attract new recruits, and organize acts of violence. Suicide bombers routinely make videos celebrating their imminent deaths, videos that are posted on jihadist websites (and occasionally even YouTube) to reach a wider audience of current and potential believers. Extremist groups from all faiths (Christian, Jewish, Muslim) have found the Internet to be a useful tool (Juergensmeyer, 2008).

Does Globalization Weaken or Strengthen Local Cultures?

The world has become a single social system as a result of growing ties of interdependence, both social and economic, that affect everyone. But it would be a mistake to think of increasing globalization simply as the growth of world unity. Rather, it is primarily the reordering of time and distance in social life as our lives are increasingly influenced by events far removed from our everyday activities.

Globalizing processes have brought many benefits to Americans, such as a much greater variety of goods and foodstuffs. At the same time, those processes have helped create some of the most serious problems American society faces, such as global climate change, the threat of terrorism, and the loss of jobs to low-wage workers in other countries.

The growing global culture has provoked numerous reactions at the local level. Many local cultures remain strong or are experiencing rejuvenation, partly out of the concern that a global culture, dominated by North American and European cultural values, will corrupt the local culture. For example, extremist Islamist movements in Afghanistan, in the tribal areas of Pakistan, in Yemen, and elsewhere in the Middle East seek to impose traditional tribal values, often prohibiting the consumption of alcohol, requiring men to grow full beards, and forbidding women from working outside their homes or being seen in public with men who are not their spouses or relatives. In some cases, violations of these rules are punished, sometimes by death. These movements can be understood partly as a rejection of the spread of Western culture—what Osama bin Laden referred to as "Westoxification" (Juergensmeyer, 2001).

The resurgence of local cultures is evident in the rise of **nationalism**, a sense of identification with one's people expressed through a common set of strongly held beliefs. Nationalism can be highly political, involving attempts to assert the power of a nation based on a shared ethnic or racial identity over people of a different ethnicity or race. The strife in the former Yugoslavia, and in parts of Africa and the former Soviet Union, bear tragic witness to the power of nationalism. The world of the twenty-first century may well witness responses to globalization that celebrate ethnocentric nationalist beliefs, promoting intolerance and hatred rather than acceptance of diversity.

New nationalisms, cultural identities, and religious practices are constantly being forged throughout the world. When you socialize with students from the same cultural background or celebrate traditional holidays with friends and family, you are sustaining your culture. The very technology that helps foster globalization also supports local cultures: The Internet enables you to communicate with others who share your cultural identity, even when they are dispersed around the world. A casual search of the web reveals thousands of pages devoted to different cultures and subcultures.

Although sociologists do not fully understand these processes, they often conclude that despite the powerful forces of globalization, local cultures remain strong. But it is too soon to tell whether and how globalization will result in the homogenization of the world's cultures, the flourishing of many individual cultures, or both.

How Easily Do Cultures Change?

In 1922, one of sociology's early founders, William F. Ogburn, introduced the notion of **cultural lag**—the idea that cultural changes take time to catch up with changes in technology, resulting in challenges for societies undergoing rapid transformation (Ogburn, 1964). In the modern world, changes in material culture precede changes in nonmaterial culture, often resulting in a host of social problems. For example, recent advances in synthetic biology, such as gene editing, have made it relatively easy (and inexpensive) to alter specific genes, opening up the possibility of creating new life forms with unique (and presumably desirable) properties.

One experiment, currently under serious consideration, involves altering the genes in thousands of white-footed mice on Nantucket Island, rendering them resistant to Lyme disease. Once altered, the mice would spread the gene to the offspring of the roughly one million mice on the island, eventually eradicating a disease that afflicts many of the island's residents. Gene editing could also be used to create a strain of malaria-resistant mosquitoes, thereby eliminating an illness that kills hundreds of thousands of children every year. It might even be used, in the perhaps not-so-distant future, to design human offspring—children who excel as students, athletes, or musicians (Specter, 2017; Ledford, 2016)!

Gene-editing techniques may hold great promise, but "rewriting the code of life" (as it has been described) raises a host of ethical questions. Apart from the possibility of disastrous unintended consequences, such as the creation of new Frankenstein-like species that bring unknown dangers, gene editing is seen by some as playing God, a violation of widely shared values (McFadden, 2016). Such concerns have led the U.S. National Academy of Sciences and National Academy of Medicine to develop guidelines for modifying human genes (Reardon, 2015). Scientific knowledge has, in this case, greatly outstripped long-standing values, which may well slow the adoption of this new technology.

Chinese students exit Maotangchang School at 11 P.M. after a 16-hour day of studying for gaokao, the country's college entrance exam.

China, which has undergone a transformation in recent years that is in many ways historically unprecedented, provides another illustration of cultural lag. Thirty years ago, China was completely closed to foreign businesses. Government bureaucrats, who controlled every economic institution, ran its economy. From large factories to small businesses to collective farms—all were owned and run by the state. The Chinese government also sought to control most aspects of Chinese culture: Media were state run, education was tightly managed to promote values that the ruling Communist Party deemed appropriate, and any signs of disagreement were closely monitored and often punished. Wall posters would denounce behavior that deviated from acceptable norms, while many universities and public places had loudspeaker systems that would frequently broadcast inspirational messages or criticize bad behavior.

Today, China appears to be a vastly different place, especially in the more developed coastal and large metropolitan areas. While some key industries remain state owned, most of the economy is now in private hands. European, American, Japanese, and other foreign firms are flocking to China in large numbers, bringing with them the cultural values of their home countries. China's rapidly growing economy has lifted hundreds of millions of people into middle-class status, turning them into consumers not only of products but also of information. China now claims more than 1.5 billion cell phone users (Chinese Ministry of Industry and Information Technology, 2018), opening up many Chinese to foreign sources of information and culture. Although the Chinese government still censors search engines, websites, blogs, and Twitter feeds it deems critical of central government policies, a great deal of dissent is now tolerated. Importantly, many Chinese are now exposed to cultural norms and values that 30 years ago were considered unthinkable.

Have these changes significantly altered Chinese culture so that it is becoming more Western? While superficially this may seem to be the case, in some ways, traditional Chinese culture has remained remarkably durable. Take one example: instilling in China's leading scientists and engineers a strong cultural value for the kinds of innovative thinking that can lead to technological breakthroughs. In the United States, such thinking is highly culturally valued. One result in the business world has been the creation of such innovative brands as Apple, Facebook, and Twitter. Such brands often achieve worldwide cachet—so much so that after the iPhones 6 and 6 Plus were introduced in October 2014, Apple was forced to divert stock from India to better meet the demand in China, which is one of its fastest-growing markets (Mukherjee, 2014; Chen, 2014).

To date, China's economic growth has been based largely on manufacturing and assembling products for foreign firms, rather than innovating new brands that capture global markets. Chinese scientists and engineers are known for their strong work ethic—for putting in long hours at diligent labor in their effort to innovate. Yet, thus far, the results have been mainly improving on foreign designs, rather than developing truly unique Chinese breakthroughs. During the past decade, the Chinese government has sought to change this situation. It has invested vast sums of money in higher education and science parks in the hope of spurring technological breakthroughs that will result in Chinese brand-name products that consumers the world over will want to buy. Yet, so far, these efforts have not succeeded. Why haven't they?

There are many reasons, but one has to do with a long-standing cultural tradition emphasizing the importance of memorization and rote learning, which produces stunning results on standardized tests but discourages the kind of "outside-the-box," more analytical thinking that can contribute to truly innovative breakthroughs (Wilsdon and Keeley, 2007). The Chinese cultural value that emphasizes test-taking as the key measure of one's ability dates back to the sixth and seventh centuries, when entrance into prestigious government jobs was first based on passing a difficult examination (Miyazaki, 1981). Every year, millions of Chinese students now take the dreaded two- to three-day exam known as the *gaokao*, which determines not only whether they will go to college, but also what college they will go to, and, ultimately, their life prospects. Hopeful parents often hire expensive private tutors, and students spend months (if not years) in preparation (Sudworth, 2012).

As a result, Chinese students do extraordinarily well when tested. In 2012, on a standardized test administered to over half a million fifteen-year-olds in sixty-five countries, Chinese students scored higher than students from any other country on science, reading, and math. U.S. students, by way of comparison, ranked twentieth in science, seventeenth in reading, and twenty-seventh in math (OECD, 2014b). Yet despite their superior performance, Chinese students do not often come up with creative, breakthrough ideas after they graduate, whether in the laboratory or in business (Parker and Appelbaum, 2012).

In an effort to change this situation, the Chinese government recently instituted an educational reform plan calling for more flexible college admissions policies modeled, in part, on the U.S. approach; letters of recommendation and extracurricular activities are now supposed to be considered (Wang, 2010; *Chronicle of Higher Education*, 2010). There is little evidence, however, that such official edicts have had any effect on students' relentless preparation for the *gaokao* or on college admissions committees' decisions.

Cultural beliefs and practices that have been in existence for nearly 1,500 years do not change easily.

CONCEPT CHECKS

1 Explain the nature/nurture debate. How is recent sociological research on the relationship between genetics and social influences on human behavior contributing to this debate?

2 How is the Internet affecting local cultures?

3 What is "cultural lag"? Think of a time when U.S. society has grappled with the implications of a new technology.

THE BIG PICTURE

Chapter 3
Culture and Society

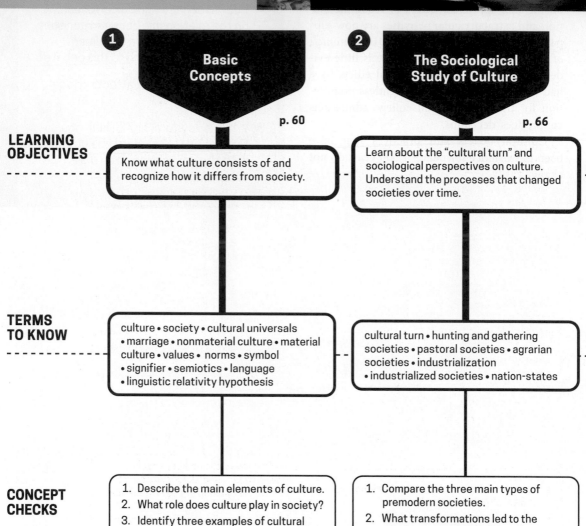

1 Basic Concepts
p. 60

2 The Sociological Study of Culture
p. 66

LEARNING OBJECTIVES

Know what culture consists of and recognize how it differs from society.

Learn about the "cultural turn" and sociological perspectives on culture. Understand the processes that changed societies over time.

TERMS TO KNOW

culture • society • cultural universals • marriage • nonmaterial culture • material culture • values • norms • symbol • signifier • semiotics • language • linguistic relativity hypothesis

cultural turn • hunting and gathering societies • pastoral societies • agrarian societies • industrialization • industrialized societies • nation-states

CONCEPT CHECKS

1. Describe the main elements of culture.
2. What role does culture play in society?
3. Identify three examples of cultural universals.
4. What is the linguistic relativity hypothesis?

1. Compare the three main types of premodern societies.
2. What transformations led to the development of civilizations?
3. What does the concept of industrialization mean?
4. How has industrialization weakened traditional social systems?

Exercises: Thinking Sociologically

1. Mention at least two cultural traits that you would claim are universals; mention two others you would claim are culturally specific traits. Use case study materials from different societies to show the differences between universal and specific cultural traits. Are the cultural universals you have discussed derivatives of human instincts? Explain your answer.

2. What does it mean to be ethnocentric? How is ethnocentrism dangerous in conducting social research? How is ethnocentrism problematic among nonresearchers in their everyday lives?

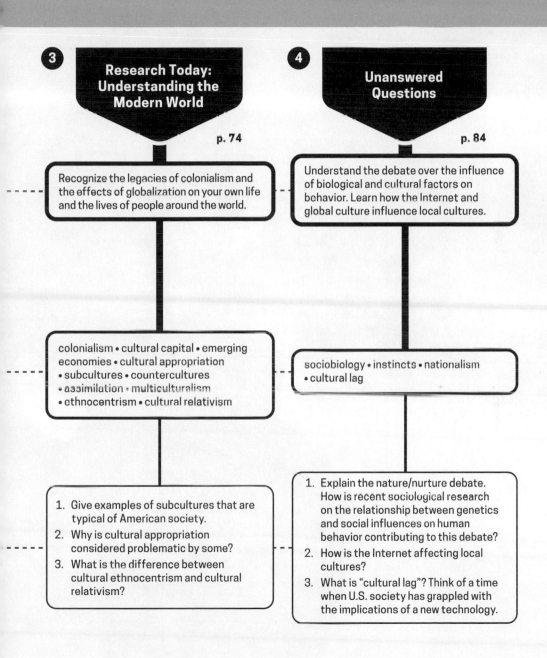

3

Research Today: Understanding the Modern World

p. 74

Recognize the legacies of colonialism and the effects of globalization on your own life and the lives of people around the world.

colonialism • cultural capital • emerging economies • cultural appropriation • subcultures • countercultures • assimilation • multiculturalism • ethnocentrism • cultural relativism

1. Give examples of subcultures that are typical of American society.
2. Why is cultural appropriation considered problematic by some?
3. What is the difference between cultural ethnocentrism and cultural relativism?

4

Unanswered Questions

p. 84

Understand the debate over the influence of biological and cultural factors on behavior. Learn how the Internet and global culture influence local cultures.

sociobiology • instincts • nationalism • cultural lag

1. Explain the nature/nurture debate. How is recent sociological research on the relationship between genetics and social influences on human behavior contributing to this debate?
2. How is the Internet affecting local cultures?
3. What is "cultural lag"? Think of a time when U.S. society has grappled with the implications of a new technology.

4

Socialization and the Life Course

Which of the following is considered the "most important" value that parents in the United States should instill in their children today?

A Creativity

B Being responsible

C Religious faith

D Obedience

TURN THE PAGE FOR THE CORRECT ANSWER.

When you think about the kind of parent you might someday be, what values do you hope to instill in your children? Would you like them to be successful? Creative? Well-mannered? Kind? Obedient? Religious? In 2014, the Pew Research Center asked more than 3,000 parents in the United States to indicate which of 12 qualities they believed were "most important" to instill in their children. "Being responsible" ranked first, followed closely by "hard work" and "helping others" (Parker, 2014). "Creativity" was in the middle of the pack, while "religious faith" rated second to last.

LEARNING OBJECTIVES

1 Basic Concepts

Understand how the four main agents of socialization contribute to social reproduction. Learn the stages of the life course, and see the similarities and differences among cultures.

2 Theories of Socialization

Compare and contrast the theories of child development according to Mead, Cooley, Piaget, Freud, and Chodorow.

3 Research on Socialization Today: Race Socialization

Learn how recent research reveals the ways that parents teach children about the meaning of racial identity.

4 Unanswered Questions

Consider the influence of social factors, especially mass media and social media, on gender learning. Analyze a new approach to combating bullying.

These data show that American parents hold nearly universal beliefs that children should be kind, responsible, productive members of society; more than 90 percent of those polled ranked responsibility and hard work as "important," and 86 percent each rated "helping others" and "being well-mannered" as very important. Think about the ways that your parents, schoolteachers, siblings, friends, and even your boss at your most recent job instilled such values in you. Whether lecturing you on "being responsible," serving as a positive role model, or praising you for a job well done, these efforts are examples of **socialization**, or the lifelong process of learning the norms, values, behavior, and social skills appropriate to your social position, such as your age, gender, or social class.

Try to recall the lessons you learned on your first day of kindergarten. These are likely very different from the messages you received at your college orientation session when you first arrived on campus. A core aspect of socialization is that the lessons one learns must be appropriate to one's level of maturity. For example, the Pew study found that parents of teenagers are more likely than parents of younger children to emphasize independence and good manners, while parents of young children are slightly more likely to rate a child's creativity as highly important.

The lessons that parents deem essential for their children also vary over historical time. In the classic *Middletown* studies, a sociological examination of everyday life in the quintessentially "middle American" city of Muncie, Indiana,

THE ANSWER IS B.

in the early 1920s, researchers asked parents what traits they valued in their children. The most commonly named trait was "obedience" (Lynd and Lynd, 1929). When residents of Muncie were interviewed again, more than 50 years later, however, the value of "obedience" was barely uttered, giving way to "autonomy" and "independence" (Alwin, 1988).

These changes reflect larger shifts in the roles and opportunities facing young people; in earlier historical periods when most children would grow up to work in factories or farms, obedience would be a valued and useful trait on the job. By the late twentieth century, however, when children would grow up to become white collar professionals, their career prospects would depend on their capacity for independent thinking and creativity. In this way, socialization reflects not only the social position that a child has, but the positions that a child will someday occupy.

The examples just cited illustrate the important sociological concept of socialization, or the ways we learn to become human. Socialization is the process whereby an infant gradually becomes a self-aware, knowledgeable person, skilled in the ways of his or her culture and historical time period. It also describes the processes whereby preschool-age children learn to be students, students learn to be workers, and childless persons learn to become parents. Most social roles we hold in life seem "natural" but actually involve intense socialization, or learning how to successfully navigate one's roles and relationships throughout the **life course**.

Socialization is a key mechanism contributing to **social reproduction**—the process whereby societies have structural continuity over time. During socialization, especially in the early years, children learn the ways of their elders, thereby perpetuating their values, norms, and social practices across the generations. All societies have characteristics that endure over time, even though their members change as individuals are born and die. North American society, for example, has many distinctive social and cultural characteristics that have persisted for generations—such as the fact that English is the main language spoken.

Socialization connects different generations to one another (Turnbull, 1983). The birth of a child alters the lives of those who are responsible for the child's upbringing—who themselves undergo new learning experiences. Older people, while of course remaining parents, forge a new set of relationships with another generation when they become grandparents. Although cultural learning is much more intense in infancy and early childhood than later in life, learning and adjustment continue through the life course.

In the sections to follow, we continue the theme of nature interacting with nurture introduced in the previous chapter. We first explore the main agents of socialization—families, schools, peers, and the media—considering how socialization contributes to social reproduction. We then analyze human development from infancy to early

socialization The social processes through which children develop an awareness of social norms and values and achieve a distinct sense of self. Although socialization processes are particularly significant in infancy and childhood, they continue to some degree throughout life.

life course The various transitions and stages people experience during their lives.

social reproduction The process of perpetuating values, norms, and social practices through socialization, which leads to structural continuity over time.

childhood, identifying the main stages of change. Different writers have offered a number of theoretical interpretations of how and why children develop as they do, and we describe and compare these, including theories that explain how people develop gender identities. We introduce recent research on the process of race socialization, exploring the ways that parents teach children about the meaning of racial identity. To conclude the chapter, we consider questions surrounding the influence of social factors on gender learning, as well as the issue of bullying and what we can do about it.

1   BASIC CONCEPTS

Agents of Socialization

Sociologists often speak of socialization as occurring in two broad phases, involving numerous **agents of socialization**—that is, groups or social contexts in which significant processes of socialization occur. Primary socialization, which occurs in infancy and childhood, is the most intense period of cultural learning. It is the time when children learn language and basic behavioral patterns that form the foundation for later learning. The family is the main agent of socialization during this phase. Secondary socialization occurs later in childhood and in maturity. In this phase, other agents of socialization, such as schools, peer groups, organizations, the media, the workplace, religious organizations (as we discuss in Chapter 17), and even the government become socializing forces.

Social interactions in these contexts help people learn (and unlearn) the values, norms, and beliefs of their culture. Importantly, socialization is a lifelong process and does not end in childhood. Additionally, socialization can be a process of learning, relearning, and unlearning. For instance, **resocialization** refers to the process whereby people learn new rules and norms when entering a new social world. For instance, mild resocialization might occur if we move to a different nation and must learn a new language, customs, eating habits, and basic rules of etiquette, such as bowing rather than shaking hands with a new colleague. A more extreme form of resocialization may occur if we enter an institution such as the military or prison, where individuals often need to learn an entirely new set of rules, schedules, and modes of interacting with others. For instance, taken-for-granted freedoms, such as being able to snack whenever we want, are curtailed in highly structured settings like the military, where meals are scheduled and ritualized. Likewise, **desocialization** entails unlearning rules and shedding the privileges associated with a particular role, such as an athlete who has retired from competitive sports.

Socialization can happen in the present, where we learn as we go, or it may occur far in advance of our adopting a social role or participating in a particular social world. **Anticipatory socialization** refers to the process whereby

agents of socialization Groups or social contexts within which processes of socialization take place.

resocialization The process whereby people learn new rules and norms upon entering a new social world.

desocialization The process whereby people unlearn rules and norms upon exiting a particular social world.

anticipatory socialization The process whereby we learn about a social role in advance of enacting the role.

we learn about what a particular role might entail before we enter it. For instance, parenting classes for pregnant women and their partners provide guidance that won't be used for several months. Summer camps for high school students prepare young people to someday live away from home or at college, independent from one's parents. As we shall soon see, many individuals and institutions—from parents to schools—play a critical role in the socialization process.

Families

Because family systems vary widely, the infant's range of family contacts is not standard across cultures. The mother tends to be the most important individual in the child's early life, but the nature of relationships between mothers and their children is influenced by the form and regularity of their contact. This, in turn, is conditioned by the character of family institutions and their relation to other groups in society.

In modern societies, most early socialization occurs within a small-scale family context. Most American children grow up within a domestic unit containing one or two parents and perhaps one or two other children. In many other cultures, by contrast, aunts, uncles, and grandparents are part of a single household and serve as caretakers even for very young infants. Even within U.S. society family contexts vary widely. Some children grow up in single-parent households; some have two mother figures and/or two father figures (divorced parents, stepparents, or same-sex parents). Many women with families work for pay outside the home and return to their paid work soon after the birth of their children. In spite of these variations, families normally remain the major agent of socialization from infancy to adolescence and beyond, in a sequence of development connecting the generations.

The centrality of family as an agent of socialization has changed throughout history. In most premodern societies, the family into which a person was born determined the individual's lifelong social position. In modern societies, social position is not inherited at birth, yet the region and social class of the family have a distinct effect on patterns of socialization. Children pick up ways of behavior characteristic of their parents or others in their neighborhood or community. Varying patterns of child-rearing and discipline, together with contrasting values and expectations, are found in different sectors of large societies. For instance, sociologist Annette Lareau (2011) observed parents and children in their own homes and found that working-class parents and middle-class parents approach child-rearing in different ways. Working-class parents promote what Lareau refers to as the *accomplishment of natural growth;* their children enjoy long periods of unstructured free time, often spent with friends and extended family members. In contrast, upper-middle-class parents practice what

Annette Lareau found that upper-middle-class parents engage in "concerted cultivation," actively monitoring their child's development.

Lareau calls *concerted cultivation*, actively fostering their kids' talents by enrolling them in a range of structured educational and extracurricular activities and closely monitoring their development. This latter approach provides children with the opportunities and skills necessary not only to succeed in school and, later, in the workforce, but also to maintain their social-class position.

Of course, few of us unquestionably adopt our parents' outlook. This is especially true in the modern world, where change is pervasive. Moreover, the very existence of a range of socializing agents in modern societies leads to divergences among the outlooks of children, adolescents, and parents.

Schools

Schools are another important socializing agent. Although schooling is a formal process, whereby students pursue a defined curriculum of subjects, schools are agents of socialization in more subtle respects. For instance, children must be punctual to class, stay quiet during lessons, and observe rules of discipline. They must accept the authority of the teaching staff. In some school systems, students say the Pledge of Allegiance to the American flag each morning and celebrate "Constitution Day" (Westheimer, 2007). This is also a way through which the government, another agent of socialization, instills in children cultural values such as patriotism. Teachers' reactions affect the expectations children have of themselves, which in turn become linked to their job experience when they leave school. Peer groups are often formed at school, and the system of age-based classes reinforces their influence.

Another key mechanism through which schools socialize children is the hidden curriculum; the **hidden curriculum** refers to the subtle ways that boys, girls, and those who do not identify as a single gender, middle class versus working class, and Black versus White are exposed to different messages and curricular materials from their teachers. In Chapter 16, we delve much more fully into the ways that schools socialize children, often unwittingly perpetuating race, class, and gender inequalities. For instance, think about the kind of classes you and your fellow students took in high school. You might have found that students from economically disadvantaged backgrounds were "tracked" into classes like automotive repair, whereas wealthier classmates were channeled into college-prep classes (Oakes and Guiton, 1995). Likewise, boys historically were encouraged to take advanced science, technology, engineering and math (STEM) classes, whereas girls were not (Basow, 2004). These patterns have changed in the past decade, and girls are now enrolled in high-level high school math and science courses like calculus, algebra, and chemistry at the same rate as their male classmates, with the exception of computer science and engineering (National Science Foundation, 2018). In this way, schools have perpetuated the status quo, including social inequalities.

hidden curriculum Traits of behavior or attitudes that are learned at school but not included in the formal curriculum—for example, gender differences.

peer group A friendship group composed of individuals of similar age and social status.

Peer Relationships

The **peer group** consists of individuals of a similar age. In some cultures, particularly small, traditional societies, peer groups are formalized as **age-grades** (normally confined to males), with ceremonies or rites that mark the transition from one age-grade to another. Those within a particular age-grade generally maintain close connections throughout their lives. Peers may experience rites of passages together, such as kindergarten graduation, religious rites like *bar* or *bat mitzvahs* and confirmation, or drivers' ed or SAT prep. These events are developmental markers and are also experiences that build feelings of unity among peers.

Children construct gender meanings through the games they play with their peers.

Although the family's importance in socialization is obvious, it is less apparent, especially in Western societies, how significant peer groups are. Yet even without formal age-grades, children over the age of four or five usually spend a great deal of time in the company of friends who are the same age. Given the high proportion of working parents whose children play together in day-care centers, peer relations are even more important today than before (Corsaro, 1997; Harris, 1998).

In her classic book *Gender Play* (1993), sociologist Barrie Thorne explores how children learn what it means to be male or female. (You will learn three classic theories of gender socialization later in this chapter.) Rather than seeing children as passively learning the meaning of gender from their parents and teachers, Thorne examines how children actively create and re-create the meaning of gender in their interactions with one another. The social activities that schoolchildren do together can be as important as other agents for their socialization.

Thorne spent two years observing fourth- and fifth-graders at two schools in Michigan and California, sitting in the classroom with them and observing their activities outside the classroom. She watched games—such as "chase and kiss," "cooties," and "goin' with," as well as children teasing one another—to learn how children construct and experience gender meanings in the classroom and on the playground.

Thorne found that peer groups greatly influence gender socialization, particularly as children talk about their changing bodies. The social context determined whether a child's bodily change was experienced with embarrassment or pride. As Thorne (1993) observed, "If the most popular girls started menstruating or wearing bras (even if they didn't 'need to'), then other girls wanted those changes too. But if the popular girls didn't wear bras and hadn't. . . gotten their periods, then these developments were seen as less desirable."

Peer relations have a significant effect beyond childhood and adolescence. Informal groups of people of similar ages, at work and in other situations, are usually of enduring importance in shaping individuals' attitudes and behavior. Thorne's research is a

age-grade The system found in small traditional cultures by which people belonging to a similar age group are categorized together and hold similar rights and obligations.

powerful reminder that children are social actors who help create their social world and influence their own socialization. Still, the effect of societal and cultural influences is also tremendous: Children's activities and values are also determined by influences such as the media.

Mass Media

Newspapers, periodicals, and journals flourished in the West from the early 1800s onward but had a limited readership. It was not until the early 1900s that such printed material became part of the daily experience of millions of people, influencing their attitudes and opinions. The spread of **mass media** soon included electronic communication—radio, television, audio recordings, videos, and online communication, including social networking sites such as Facebook, Twitter, and Instagram. Today, it is a rare American who goes a day (or even an hour) without reading an article, watching a video, or listening to a podcast online. In fact, more than 90 percent of teens go online at least once a day, while nearly a quarter (24 percent) use the Internet "almost constantly" (Lenhart, 2015). Fully 70 percent of all Americans and 86 percent of young adults (ages 18–29) use social media, with Facebook being the most widely used platform (Pew Research Center, 2017b). Young adults are also tethered to their smartphones. Nearly all (94 percent) adults between ages 18 and 24 own a smartphone, and they check their phones an average of 86 times a day. By contrast, the overall U.S. population ages 18 to 75 checks just 47 times a day (Deloitte, 2018).

Americans also spend a large portion of their leisure time consuming more traditional forms of media. According to the American Time Use Survey, Americans watched an average of nearly three hours of television per day in 2015, representing more than half of their total leisure time (U.S. Bureau of Labor Statistics, 2016a). However, in recent years smartphone use has surpassed television viewing, especially for young people. According to data from market research firm Nielsen, young adults ages 18 to 34 spend just under two hours per day watching live and time-shifted TV, yet 3.5 hours per day on the web or apps on their smartphone or tablets (Lee, 2019).

Media, in all its forms, has a powerful impact on our lives, and it is particularly influential in shaping the beliefs, behaviors, social interactions, and relationships of children, teens, and young adults. For instance, children and adolescents often model the gender roles and practices that they see on their favorite television shows. Fashion magazines, music videos, and more recently, social media's fashion influencers are also cited as powerful influences on girls' body image, or their beliefs about "ideal" body weight and physique (Fardouly and Vartanian, 2018; Grabe, Ward, and Hyde, 2008). Yet media can also teach children about topics with which their parents may be less familiar or comfortable, and can provide information and even a sense of solace for children who may be lacking support in their communities. For example, television shows like *I Am Jazz*, a reality show about the daily life of transgender teenager Jazz Jennings, has been praised for teaching messages of acceptance and providing a role model for children who may be conflicted about their own gender identity (*Time*, 2014). Trans youth also may use social media like Instagram to bolster and support fellow trans youth as they choose how to present themselves (Rutten, 2018).

mass media Forms of communication, such as newspapers, magazines, radio, and television, designed to reach mass audiences.

The study of the impact of media on youth is a critically important topic, with extensive research focused on the effect of television, film, popular music, and other media on propensities toward aggression and violence. Classic studies by George Gerbner (1986) and his collaborators analyzed samples of prime-time and weekend daytime TV for all major American networks each year for more than two decades dating back to 1967. They charted the number and frequency of violent acts and episodes for a range of programs, defining violence as physical force directed against the self or others by which physical harm or death occurs. Their database included

Americans of all ages spend the majority of their leisure time consuming media, which can function as a powerful agent of socialization, especially for young kids and adolescents.

observations on 2,816 television programs; they also coded 34,882 characters according to many thematic, demographic, and activity categories (Media Education Foundation, 1997). On average, 80 percent of programs contained violence, with a rate of 7.5 violent episodes per hour. Children's programs showed even higher levels of violence, although killing was less common. Cartoons depict the highest number of violent acts and episodes of any type of television program (Gerbner et al., 1986). The level and number of media sources portraying extreme violence has only increased since that time, with video games, Internet displays, and cell phone displays showing graphic violence in games like *Grand Theft Auto, Fortnite,* and *Mortal Kombat* (Huesmann, 2007).

The reason these trends are troubling is that decades of research document that witnessing violence, whether in person, via a recorded image like a live-actor television show or movie, or even in cartoons, increases the chances that a child will behave aggressively. In a now-classic experiment by psychologist Albert Bandura, children watched an adult play with tinker toys and a Bobo doll (a five-foot-tall inflated plastic doll). In one condition, the adult began by assembling the tinker toys for about a minute and then turned his attention to the doll. He approached the doll, punched it, sat on it, hit it with a mallet, tossed it in the air, and kicked it around the room while shouting things such as "Hit him in the nose." He did this for nine minutes while the child watched. Bandura had different versions of the experiment. In some cases, the child observed an actual actor; in another, the child witnessed a videotaped actor; and in a third, the child watched a cartoon version of the aggression. In the control-group condition, the actor worked with the tinker toys for the full 10-minute observation period. Relative to the control group, all three experimental groups of children subsequently engaged in more aggressive play, although a gradient emerged, where the effects of the actual actor were most powerful, followed by the videotaped actor and then the cartoon. Yet, in all three cases, the child imitated and acted out the aggressive play he or she had witnessed.

Given the powerful ways that violent media may socialize children into aggressive behaviors, researchers have become interested in studying how video games (especially violent video games) affect children. Nearly three-quarters of teenagers play video games on their phone, computer, or a console such as PlayStation, Xbox, or Wii, including 84 percent of teenage boys and 59 percent of teenage girls (Lenhart, 2015). Given what we've learned about socialization, is this a potentially harmful trend?

Researchers are finding that violent video games may affect youth in similar ways as violent television images. For instance, rapid-action games with very violent imagery may desensitize players to violence (Englehardt et al., 2011). Yet emerging research also shows that some video games can have positive effects on children and their families. Roughly 55 percent of parents believe that playing video games helps families spend more time together (Entertainment Software Association, 2014). Research carried out by an association of manufacturers of video games may be biased, so researchers have also carried out independent studies. Emerging research shows that some video games like Wii Fit can strengthen intergenerational relations, especially if grandchildren and grandparents play these games together (Costa and Veloso, 2016). And recent work by neuroscientists and psychologists finds that some types of fast-paced video games dubbed "brain games" boost children's brain stimulation, cognitive development, spatial abilities, problem-solving skills, and even self-esteem (Granic, Lobel, and Engels, 2014).

Mass media is an important influence on socialization in all forms of society. Few societies in current times, even among more traditional cultures, remain untouched by the media (Huesmann, 2007). Electronic communication is accessible even to those who cannot read or write, and in the most impoverished parts of the world, it is common to find people owning radios, television sets, and smartphones. In this way, people throughout the globe are exposed not only to cultural messages from their own societies, but increasingly to cultural and media images from across the world—a topic we will explore more fully in Chapter 20.

As new technologies evolve, researchers will be particularly interested in documenting how they help and hurt. In the past decade or two, for instance, social scientists have documented the benefits and problems linked to excessive smartphone use. Many benefits have been documented, including helping people to stay in touch with friends and family far away, providing an easily accessible source of information and job opportunities, and even tracking one's own health and fitness (Silver et al., 2019). However, other evidence suggests that smartphones prevent people from separating their personal and work lives, perpetuate a culture of round-the-clock work and responsiveness to work-related demands, and diminishing writing, emotional expression, and communication skills as smartphone users increasingly interact via terse text and instant messaging (Wagner, 2015).

Work

Work, in all cultures, is an important agent of socialization, although only in industrial societies do large numbers of people go to places of work separate from the home. In communities where people farmed nearby land or had workshops in their dwellings, work was not as distinct from other activities. In industrialized countries, joining the workforce ordinarily marks a much greater transition in an individual's life than beginning work in traditional societies. Over the past two decades, however, rising numbers of workers carry out their jobs at home, fueled in part by email and the Internet, although the overall numbers are still modest. About 5 percent of U.S. workers, numbering more than 8 million, worked exclusively at home in 2015—a steep increase over the 3 percent rate in 2000. As many as one in four do at least some paid work at home, with the option of working at home more common among professional and managerial workers (Bureau of Labor Statistics, 2016d).

The work environment often poses unfamiliar demands, perhaps calling for major adjustments in the person's outlook or behavior. For example, when young people enter the workforce, they learn skills such as independence, self-efficacy, personal responsibility, responsibility for

Flight attendants, and other service workers, must learn to manage their emotions on the job. Arlie Hochschild referred to this as "emotion work."

others, and how to develop effective relationships with nonfamily members (Greenberger and Steinberg, 1981). In addition to mastering the specific tasks of their job and internalizing cultural norms that guide appropriate professional behavior, many workers also need to learn how to "feel" on the job. Sociologists have explored in-depth how individuals learn to manage their emotions in the workplace, focusing on ways that workers learn to hide negative emotions so they can foster good relationships with customers or manage the emotional distress they feel when they encounter sad or gruesome experiences on the job. Sociologist Arlie Hochschild (1983) has documented the ways that workers, especially women workers, learn to feel and then display socially acceptable emotions at work. For instance, flight attendants learn to keep a calm and cool demeanor, even when dealing with a surly passenger or flying through extreme turbulence. Health-care workers, police officers, firefighters, and soldiers also must learn how to manage feelings such as fear, sadness, and disgust to do their job (e.g., Underman and Hirshfield, 2016). Schoolteachers and principals must remain calm and supportive, even when the children they work with act out (Maxwell and Riley, 2016). In these ways, individuals are socialized into the varied and complex skills they require to succeed in the workplace.

Social Roles

Through socialization, individuals learn about **social roles**—socially defined expectations for a person in a given social position. The social role of doctor, for example, encompasses a set of behaviors that all doctors should assume, regardless of their personal opinions or outlooks. Because all doctors share this role, we can speak in general terms about the professional behavior of doctors, regardless of the specific individuals who occupy that position.

Some sociologists, particularly those associated with the functionalist school, regard social roles as unchanging parts of a society's

social roles Socially defined expectations of an individual in a given status or social position.

People often exhibit multiple social identities simultaneously, sometimes seemingly conflicting ones.

culture; they are social facts. According to this view, individuals learn the expectations for social positions in their particular culture and perform these roles largely as they have been defined. Social roles do not involve negotiation or creativity. Rather, they prescribe, contain, and direct an individual's behavior. Through socialization, individuals internalize social roles and learn how to carry them out.

This view, however, is mistaken. It suggests that individuals simply take on roles rather than creating or negotiating them. In fact, socialization is a process in which humans can exercise agency; we are not simply passive subjects waiting to be instructed or programmed. Individuals come to understand and assume social roles through an ongoing process of social interaction.

Identity

The cultural settings in which we grow up influence our behavior, but that does not mean that humans lack individuality or free will. The fact that from birth to death we are involved in interaction with others certainly conditions our personalities, values, and behavior. Yet socialization is also at the origin of our individuality and freedom. In the course of socialization, each of us develops a sense of identity and the capacity for independent thought and action.

The concept of identity in sociology is multifaceted. Broadly speaking, **identity** relates to people's understandings about who they are and what is meaningful to them. These understandings are formed in relation to certain attributes that take priority over other sources of meaning. Some of the main sources of identity are gender, sexual orientation, nationality, ethnicity, and social class. Sociologists often speak of two types of identity: social identity and self-identity (or personal identity). These types are analytically distinct but closely related to each other.

Social identity refers to the characteristics that other people attribute to an individual—markers that indicate who, in a basic sense, that individual is. At the same time, these characteristics place that individual in relation to others who share the same attributes. Examples of social identities are student, parent, lawyer, Muslim, homeless, Asian, dyslexic, and married. All individuals have more than one social identity, reflecting the many dimensions of their lives. A person

identity The distinctive characteristics of a person's (or a group's) character that relate to who he is and what is meaningful to him. Some of the main sources of identity include gender, sexual orientation, nationality or ethnicity, and social class.

social identity The characteristics that are attributed to an individual by others.

could simultaneously be a parent, an engineer, a Catholic, and a city council member. This plurality of social identities can be a source of conflict.

Most individuals organize meaning and experience in their lives around a primary identity that is continuous across time and place. Sometimes people organize their lives around the identity that is most *salient* or personally meaningful and important. For instance, if being a devout follower of one's faith is very salient to an individual, they may eat particular foods, wear certain types of clothing, choose to socialize largely with fellow members of the community, and hold beliefs consistent with their religious teachings (Stryker and Serpe, 1994).

> **master status** A single identity or status that overpowers all the other identities one holds.
>
> **self-identity** The ongoing process of self-development and definition of our personal identity through which we formulate a unique sense of ourselves and our relationship to the world around us.

Sociologist Everett Hughes noted that some identities can overpower all the other traits an individual possesses; these identities are referred to as **master statuses**. Race, sex, age, and visible body features are among the most common master statuses. For instance, people who are morbidly obese may find that many of their interactions and behaviors are tied to their large bodies, in part because the social structure is organized in such a way as to remind them constantly of their weight; these reminders include such things as narrow airplane or movie theater seats, lack of clothing options, and disapproving looks and comments by others. A person who happens to weigh 300 pounds might also be a parent, a schoolteacher, a best friend, and a computer whiz, yet others who interact with the individual may only see the weight and may treat them accordingly.

Social identities involve a collective dimension. They mark ways that individuals are the same as others. Shared identities—predicated on common goals, values, or experiences—aside from forming an important base for social movements, serve as a powerful source of personal meaning or self-worth.

If social identities mark ways in which individuals are the same as others, **self-identity** (or personal identity) sets us apart as distinct individuals. Self-identity refers to the process of self-development through which we formulate a unique sense of ourselves and our relationship to the world. The notion of self-identity draws heavily on the work of symbolic interactionists. Our constant negotiation with the outside world shapes our sense of self, linking our own personal and public worlds. Though the cultural and social environment is a factor in shaping self-identity, individual agency and choice are key.

Tracing the changes in self-identity from traditional to modern societies, we can see a shift away from the fixed, inherited factors that previously guided identity formation, such as membership in social groups bound by social class or ethnicity. People's identities are now more multifaceted and less stable, owing to urban growth, industrialization, and the breakdown of earlier social formations. Individuals have become more socially and geographically mobile. Freed from the homogeneous communities of the past, people now find that other sources of personal meaning, such as gender identity, sexual orientation, or political beliefs play a greater role in their sense of identity.

Today we have unprecedented opportunities to create our own identities. We are our own best resources in defining who we are, where we have come from, and where we are going. Now that the traditional signposts of identity have become less essential, the social world confronts us with a dizzying array of choices about who to be, how to live, and what to do, without offering much guidance about which selections to make. The decisions we make in our everyday lives—about what to wear, how to behave, and how to spend our time—help make us who we are. Through our capacity as self-conscious, self-aware human beings, we constantly create and re-create our identities.

Socialization through the Life Course

The transitions through which individuals pass during their lives may seem biologically fixed—from childhood to adulthood and eventually to death. But the stages of the human life course are social as well as biological. They are influenced by cultural differences and material circumstances in various types of societies. For example, in most contemporary wealthy western nations, death is usually thought of in relation to old age because most people enjoy a life span of 79 years or more. In traditional societies of the past, however, more people died at younger ages than survived to old age.

Childhood

In modern societies, childhood is considered a distinct stage of life between infancy and adolescence. Yet the concept of childhood has developed only over the past two or three centuries. In earlier societies, young people moved directly from a lengthy infancy into working roles within the community. The French historian Philippe Ariès (1965) has argued that childhood did not exist in medieval times. In the paintings of medieval Europe, children are portrayed as little adults, with mature faces and the same style of dress as their elders. Children took part in the same work and play activities as adults, rather than in the childhood games we now take for granted.

Duccio da Buoninsegna's *Madonna and Child*, painted in the thirteenth century, depicts the infant Jesus with a mature face. Until recently, children in Western society were viewed as little adults.

Right up to the twentieth century, in the United States and most other Western countries, children were put to work at what now seems a very early age. There are countries in the world today, in fact, where young children do full-time work, sometimes in physically demanding circumstances (for example, in coal mines). According to the International Labor Organization, more than 152 million child laborers—one in every 10 children globally—are working today (U.S. Department of Labor, 2018). The ideas that children have rights and that child labor is morally repugnant are recent developments that have not yet been achieved worldwide.

Because of the long period of childhood that we recognize today, societies now are, in some respects, more child-centered than traditional ones were. But a child-centered society, it must be emphasized, is not one in which all children experience love and care from parents or other adults. The physical and sexual abuse of children and trafficking of child labor are realities, albeit statistically rare ones, of family life in present-day society. Yet the recognition of children as a social problem has come to light only relatively recently. Rates of child abuse are difficult to calculate, due to disagreement regarding definitions of child abuse and children's fear or inability to report abuse (U.S. Department of Health and Human Services, 2016). Most experts agree that roughly 3 million reports of child abuse are made to law enforcement authorities each year; roughly 75 percent of these cases involve neglect, followed by physical abuse (17 percent), and sexual abuse (8 percent).

It is possible that as a result of changes in modern societies, childhood as a distinct stage is again diminishing. Some observers have suggested that children now grow up so fast that this is in fact the case. They point out that even small children may watch the same television programs and use the same apps as adults, thereby becoming much more familiar early on with the adult world than did preceding generations. Yet others counter that children today are coddled by their "helicopter" parents, shielded from hardships and challenges that prior generations experienced (Lemoyne and Buchanan, 2011). Critics note that practices like giving children trophies for participating in a sport, rather than excelling in a sport, spare children from some of the difficult lessons that adults must learn about competition, competence, and self-sufficiency.

The Teenager

The idea of the teenager also didn't exist until the early twentieth century, when compulsory education and child-labor laws were enacted. Prior to that time, teenagers were not required to attend school, so adolescence was a time for working in fields and factories and for marrying and bearing children. Today, by contrast, adolescence is considered a time to learn, grow, and make choices about the kind of adult one wants to someday become.

The biological changes involved in puberty (the point at which a person becomes capable of adult sexual activity and reproduction) are universal. Yet in many cultures, these do not produce the turmoil and uncertainty often found among young people in modern societies. In cultures that foster age-grades, for example, which hold ceremonies that signal a person's transition to adulthood, the process of psychosexual development seems easier to negotiate. Adolescents in such societies have less to "unlearn" because the pace of change is slower. There is a time in Western societies when children are required to put away their toys and break with childish pursuits. In traditional cultures, in which children already work alongside adults, this process of unlearning is much less jarring.

In Western societies, teenagers are betwixt and between: They often try to act like adults, but they are treated by law as children. They may wish to go to work, but they are required to stay in school. Teenagers in the West live in between childhood and adulthood, growing up in a society subject to continuous change.

Young Adulthood

Young adulthood, also referred to as "emerging adulthood," is typically defined as roughly ages 20 to 30 (Arnett, 2000). This period is considered a transition between the carefree years of childhood and adolescence, and the responsibilities of marriage,

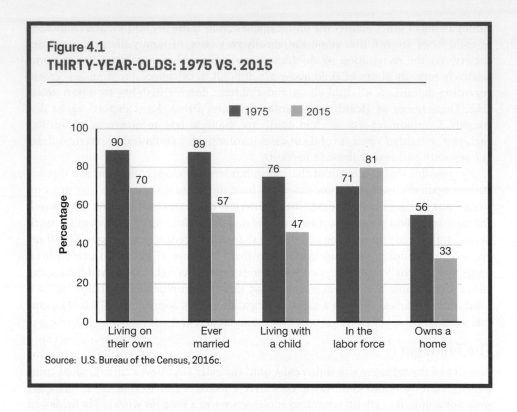

Figure 4.1
THIRTY-YEAR-OLDS: 1975 VS. 2015

1975   2015

	Living on their own	Ever married	Living with a child	In the labor force	Owns a home
1975	90	89	76	71	56
2015	70	57	47	81	33

Source: U.S. Bureau of the Census, 2016c.

parenthood, and home ownership that often accompany mid-adulthood. Part of the reason for the emergence of this distinctive life course stage is that scholars have observed a "delayed transition to adulthood" among young people in the late twentieth and early twenty-first centuries. Particularly among affluent groups, people in their early twenties take the time to travel, go to college or graduate school, try out a few different jobs, and explore sexual, political, and religious affiliations. The importance of this postponement of the responsibilities of full adulthood is likely to grow, given the extended period of education and career exploration many people now undergo.

Although it is difficult to pinpoint exactly when one makes the "transition to adulthood," sociologist Frank Furstenberg has identified five benchmarks that are considered critical to the adulthood transition: leaving the home of one's parents, finishing school, getting married, having a child, and being financially independent. In 1960, fully 65 percent of men and 77 percent of women had achieved all five milestones by age 30. In 2010, by contrast, only 25 percent of men and 39 percent of women had done all five by their thirtieth birthdays (Furstenberg, 2010; Kennedy and Furstenberg, 2013). These statistics clearly show that the transition to adulthood is being delayed today and that some benchmarks historically considered as signifiers of adulthood, such as becoming a parent, may be less central to one's identity as an adult in the twenty-first century (Figure 4.1).

Although social critics (and anxious parents) wring their hands and lament that young people today "refuse to grow up," Furstenberg offers a much more positive interpretation of these data. Young adults today have the opportunity to pursue education and "try out" many professions and romantic partners before settling on one career or one spouse. This period of exploration allows young people to figure out a life that works best for them in the long term. Young people today also have the option *not* to make particular transitions, without fear of stigma. For instance, young people are more likely than ever before to cohabit rather than marry, to stay single, and to remain child-free (Furstenberg, 2010). Young people themselves also adhere to a much broader view of what "adulthood" is, defining it in terms of abstract traits like self-reliance and happiness, rather than the attainment of particular milestones like homeownership (Henig, 2010).

Midlife

Most young adults in the wealthy industrialized world can expect to live well into old age. In premodern times, few could anticipate such a future with much confidence. Death through sickness or injury was much more frequent among all age groups than it is today, and women faced a high rate of mortality in childbirth. Given these advances in life expectancy, a "new" life course stage has been recognized in the twentieth century: midlife, or middle age (Cohen, 2012).

Midlife, the stage between young adulthood and old age, is generally believed to fall between the ages of 45 and 65. However, midlife is distinct from other life course stages in that there is not an "official" or legal age of entry. For example, American youth become legal adults at age 18, whereas age 65 is generally believed to signify the transition to old age and the receipt of retirement benefits. One's entry to midlife, by contrast, tends to be signified by the social roles one adopts (or relinquishes). While some scholars believe that menopause, or the loss of reproductive potential, signals women's transition to midlife, others believe that for both men and women, midlife is marked by transitions such as the "empty nest" stage (when children leave the family home).

Midlife is also a psychological turning point where men and women may assess their past choices and accomplishments and make new choices that prepare them for the second half of life. Keeping a forward-looking outlook in middle age has taken on a particular importance in modern societies. Most people do not expect to be doing the same thing their whole lives, as was the case for the majority in traditional cultures. For example, midlife persons today are more likely than ever to divorce, a phenomenon that has been called "gray divorce." One of the reasons why people in their 50s and 60s are ending their marriages is that they recognize that they have many years of life ahead and are choosing to leave behind unsatisfying marriages and instead opting for singlehood or new romantic partnerships (Brown and Lin, 2012).

Later Life

Old age has been reinvented in recent decades, as older adults comprise an increasingly large share of the population both in the United States and worldwide. In 1900, just 4 percent of the U.S. population was age 65 or older. By 2018, that proportion exceeded 15 percent. The older population is projected to double by 2060, at which point nearly one in four Americans will be an older adult (U.S. Administration on Aging, 2016). The same trend is found in all industrially advanced countries. Alongside these population shifts, the social roles of older adults have shifted as well.

In traditional societies, older people were accorded great respect. Among cultures that included age-grades, the elders usually had a major—often the final—say in matters

1 What is social reproduction? What are some specific ways that the four main agents of socialization contribute to social reproduction?

2 Compare and contrast social roles and social identities.

3 What are the five stages of the life course, and what are some of the defining features of each stage?

4 Describe how the life course stage of childhood has changed since medieval times.

5 How is midlife different from the life course stages of childhood and old age?

of importance to the community. Within families, the authority of both men and women increased with age. In industrialized societies, by contrast, older people tend to lack authority within both the family and the social community.

Transition to the age-grade of elder in a traditional culture often marked the pinnacle of an individual's status. In modern societies, retirement brings the opposite. No longer living with their children and often having retired from paid work, older people may find it difficult to make the final period of their life rewarding. People used to think that those who successfully coped with old age relied on their inner resources, becoming less interested in the material rewards of social life. Although this assumption may be true, it seems likely that in a society in which many are physically healthy in old age, an outward-looking view will become more prevalent. With advances in medical technologies, older adults are living and staying healthier longer than ever before. These extensions in life span have been accompanied by expanded opportunities for lifelong learning, with many older adults learning new skills and pursuing new leisure activities. Those in retirement might find renewal in the "third age," in which a new phase of education begins. (See also the discussion of lifelong learning in Chapter 12.)

2   THEORIES OF SOCIALIZATION

One of the most distinctive features of human beings, compared with other animals, is that they are self-aware. How should we understand the emergence of a sense of self—the awareness that the individual has a distinct identity separate from others? During the first months of life, the infant possesses little or no understanding of differences between human beings and material objects and has no awareness of self. Children do not grasp concepts such as "I," "me," and "you" until the age of two or later. Only gradually do they understand that others have distinct identities, consciousnesses, and needs separate from their own.

The processes through which the self emerges and develops is much debated among contrasting theoretical perspectives. To some extent, this debate stems from the fact that the most prominent theories about child development emphasize different aspects of socialization. The American philosopher and sociologist George Herbert Mead mainly considered how children learn to use the concepts of "I" and "me."

Charles Horton Cooley demonstrated the importance of other individuals for shaping a child's sense of self. Jean Piaget, the Swiss student of child behavior, studied many aspects of child development, but his best-known writings concern **cognition**—the ways in which children learn to think about themselves and their environment. Sigmund Freud and Nancy Chodorow focused on how children learn about gender differences and develop a gender identity.

G. H. Mead and the Development of Self

Because Mead's ideas underlie a general tradition of theoretical thinking, symbolic interactionism, they have had a broad impact in sociology. Symbolic interactionism emphasizes that interaction between human beings occurs through symbols and the interpretation of meanings (see Chapter 1). But Mead's work also describes the main phases of child development, concentrating on the emergence of a sense of self.

According to Mead, infants and young children develop as social beings by imitating the actions of those around them. Play is one way in which this development occurs. A small child will make mud pies, having seen an adult cooking, or will dig with a spoon, having observed someone gardening. Children's play evolves from simple imitation to more complicated games in which a child of four or five years old will act out an adult role. Mead called this "taking the role of the other"—learning what it is like to be in the shoes of another person. At this stage, children acquire a developed sense of self. Children achieve an understanding of themselves as separate agents—as a "me"—by seeing themselves through the eyes of others. We achieve self-awareness, according to Mead, when we learn to distinguish the "me" from the "I." The "I" is the unsocialized infant, a bundle of spontaneous wants and desires. The "me" is the **social self**. Individuals develop **self-consciousness**, Mead argued, by coming to see themselves as others see them.

A further stage of child development occurs when the child is eight or nine years old, the age at which children take part in organized games rather than unsystematic play. During this period, children begin to understand the values and morality that govern social life. To learn organized games, children must understand the rules of play and notions of fairness and equal participation. Children at this stage learn to grasp what Mead termed the **generalized other**—the general values and moral rules of the culture in which they are developing.

Charles Horton Cooley and the Looking-Glass Self

Charles Horton Cooley was an early-twentieth-century sociologist who studied self-concept, or the ways we view and

cognition Human thought processes involving perception, reasoning, and remembering.

social self The basis of self-consciousness in human individuals, according to the theory of G. H. Mead. The social self is the identity conferred upon an individual by the reactions of others. A person achieves self-consciousness by becoming aware of this social identity.

self-consciousness Awareness of one's distinct social identity as a person separate from others. Human beings are not born with self-consciousness but acquire an awareness of self as a result of early socialization. The learning of language is of vital importance to the processes by which the child learns to become a self-conscious being.

generalized other A concept in the theory of G. H. Mead, according to which the individual comes to understand the general values of a given group or society during the socialization process.

According to Cooley, our self-concept is based on our interpretations of how others, such as our teachers and classmates, perceive us.

think about ourselves. How do we come to view ourselves as humorous or cranky? Intelligent? Kind-hearted? Cooley argued that the notions we develop about ourselves reflect our interpretations of how others see us. His theory of the **looking-glass self** proposes that the reactions we elicit in social situations create a mirror in which we see ourselves. For example, if others regularly laugh at our jokes, we may perceive that they view us as funny, and in turn, view ourselves as such. Likewise, if our classmates and teachers praise us for our intelligent remarks in class, we may in turn start to view ourselves as smart.

Over time, mixed empirical evidence has led to reformulations of Cooley's classic theory. One refinement suggests that individuals take action to bring others around to their own views of themselves, rather than passively accepting what others think of them. For example, a student who sees herself as very intelligent may regularly answer questions in class, in an effort to ensure that her classmates also view her as very intelligent (Yeung and Martin, 2003). In this way, youth are not merely passive recipients but rather active agents in shaping others' perceptions. Despite critiques and refinements of looking glass self theory, this perspective exemplifies core themes of symbolic interactionism, and sets the groundwork for other theories that underscore the importance of perceptions and negotiations in shaping human behaviors and identities (for example, see labeling theory of deviance in Chapter 7).

Jean Piaget and the Stages of Cognitive Development

Piaget emphasized the child's active capability to make sense of the world. Children do not passively soak up information, but instead, select and interpret what they see, hear, and feel. Piaget described distinct stages of cognitive development during which children learn to think about themselves and their environment. Each stage involves the acquisition of new skills and depends on the successful completion of the preceding ones.

Piaget called the first stage, from birth up to about age two, the **sensorimotor stage**. At this stage, infants learn mainly by touching objects, manipulating them, and physically exploring their environment. Until age four months or so, infants cannot differentiate themselves from their environment. For example, a child will not realize that his or her own movements cause the sides of the crib to rattle. Objects are not differentiated from persons, and the infant is unaware that anything exists outside his or her range of vision. The infant gradually learns to

looking-glass self According to Cooley's theory, the reactions we elicit in social situations create a mirror in which we see ourselves.

sensorimotor stage According to Jean Piaget, a stage of human cognitive development in which a child's awareness of his or her environment is dominated by perception and touch.

distinguish people from objects, realizing that both have an existence independent of his or her immediate perception of them. The main accomplishment of this stage is children's understanding that their environment has distinct and stable properties.

The next phase, the **preoperational stage**, is the one to which Piaget devoted the bulk of his research. During this stage, which lasts from age two to age seven, children master language and use words to represent objects and images in a symbolic fashion. A four-year-old might use a sweeping hand, for example, to represent the concept airplane. Piaget termed the stage "preoperational" because children are not yet able to use their developing mental capabilities systematically. Children in this stage are **egocentric** in the sense that they interpret the world exclusively in terms of their own position. The child does not understand, for instance, that others see objects from a different perspective. Holding a book upright, the child may ask about a picture in it, not realizing that the person sitting opposite can see only the back of the book.

Children at the preoperational stage are not able to hold connected conversations with another person. With egocentric speech, what each child says is more or less unrelated to what the other speaker has said. Children talk together but not to one another in the same sense as adults. During this stage, children have no general understanding of categories of thought that adults take for granted: concepts such as causality, speed, weight, or number. Even if the child sees water poured from a tall, thin container into a shorter, wider one, he or she will not understand that the volume of water remains the same—and the child will conclude that there is less water because the water level is lower.

A third period, the **concrete operational stage**, lasts from age 7 to age 11. During this phase, children master abstract, logical notions such as causality. A child at this stage of development will recognize the false reasoning involved in the idea that the wide container holds less water than the narrow one, even though the water levels are different. The child becomes capable of carrying out the mathematical operations of multiplying, dividing, and subtracting. Children by this stage are much less egocentric. In the preoperational stage, if a girl is asked, "How many sisters do you have?" she may correctly answer, "One." But if asked, "How many sisters does your sister have?" she will probably answer, "None," because she cannot see herself from the point of view of her sister. The concrete operational child can easily answer such a question.

The years from 11 to 15 cover the **formal operational stage**. During adolescence, the developing child becomes able to grasp highly abstract and hypothetical ideas. When faced with a problem, children at this stage are able to review all the possible ways of solving it and go through them theoretically to reach a solution. The young person at the formal operational stage can understand why some questions are trick ones. To the question, "What creatures are both poodles

preoperational stage A stage of cognitive development, in Piaget's theory, in which the child has advanced sufficiently to master basic modes of logical thought.

egocentric According to Piaget, the characteristic quality of a child during the early years of his or her life. Egocentric thinking involves understanding objects and events in the environment solely in terms of one's own position.

concrete operational stage A stage of cognitive development, as formulated by Piaget, in which the child's thinking is based primarily on physical perception of the world. In this phase, the child is not yet capable of dealing with abstract concepts or hypothetical situations.

formal operational stage According to Piaget's theory, a stage of cognitive development at which the growing child becomes capable of handling abstract concepts and hypothetical situations.

and dogs?" the individual might not be able to give the correct reply but will understand why the answer "poodles" is right and will appreciate the humor in it.

According to Piaget, the first three stages of development are universal; but not all
adults reach the formal operational stage. The development of formal operational thought
depends in part on processes of schooling. Adults of limited educational attainment tend
to continue to think in more concrete terms and retain large traces of egocentrism.

Sigmund Freud's Theory of Gender Identity

Perhaps the most influential, and controversial, theory of the emergence of gender
identity is that of Sigmund Freud. According to Freud, the learning of gender differences in infants and young children centers on the possession or absence of the penis.
"I have a penis" is equivalent to "I am a boy," while "I am a girl" is equivalent to "I lack a
penis." Freud is careful to say that it is not just the anatomical distinctions that matter;
the possession and absence of the penis are symbolic of masculinity and femininity, of
power and lack of power, respectively.

Major objections have been raised against Freud's views, particularly by feminists
but also by many other authors (Coward, 1984; Mitchell, 1975). First, Freud seems to
identify gender identity too closely with genital awareness; other more subtle factors
are surely involved. Second, the theory seems to depend on the notion that the penis
is superior to the vagina, which is thought of as just a lack of the male organ. Yet why
shouldn't the female genitals be considered superior to those of the male?

Nancy Chodorow's Theory of Gender Identity

Although many writers have used Freud's approach in studying gender development,
they have modified it in major respects. An important example is the sociologist Nancy
Chodorow (1978, 1988), who argues that learning to feel male or female derives from
the infant's attachment to the parents from an early age. Children become emotionally
involved with the mother because she is the most dominant influence in their early lives.
At some point, this attachment has to be broken for the child to achieve a separate sense
of self—to become less closely dependent.

Chodorow argues that the breaking process
occurs in a different way for boys and girls.
Girls remain closer to the mother—able, for
example, to go on hugging and kissing her
and imitating what she does. Because there is
no sharp break from the mother, the girl, and
later the adult woman, develops a sense of self
that is more continuous with other people.
Her identity is more likely to be merged with
or depend on another's: first her mother's, later
a man's. In Chodorow's view, this process of
development fosters sensitivity and emotional
compassion in women.

Boys gain a sense of self via a more radical rejection of their original closeness to the

Nancy Chodorow argues that boys are socialized to
be less attached to, or dependent on, their parents
at an earlier age than girls.

mother, forging their understanding of masculinity from what is not feminine. They learn not to be "sissies" or "mama's boys." As a result, boys are relatively unskilled in relating closely to others; they develop more analytical ways of looking at the world. They take a more active view of their lives, emphasizing achievement, but they have repressed their ability to understand their own feelings and those of others.

Chodorow's work has met with various criticisms. Janet Sayers (1986), for example, has suggested that Chodorow does not explain the struggle of women, particularly in current times, to become autonomous, independent beings. Women (and men), Sayers points out, are more contradictory in their psychological makeup than Chodorow's theory suggests. Femininity may conceal feelings of aggressiveness or assertiveness, which are revealed only obliquely or in certain contexts (Brennan, 1988). Chodorow has also been criticized for her narrow conception of the family based on a White, middle-class model. What happens, for example, in one-parent households or, as in many Chicano communities, in families where children are cared for by more than one adult (Segura and Pierce, 1993)?

These criticisms don't undermine Chodorow's work, however. Her ideas remain important because they teach us a good deal about the nature of femininity and help us understand the origins of "male inexpressiveness"—the difficulty men have in revealing their feelings to others (Balswick, 1983).

Table 4.1

APPLYING SOCIOLOGY TO SOCIALIZATION AND THE LIFE COURSE

THEORY	APPROACH TO UNDERSTANDING SOCIALIZATION	CONTEMPORARY APPLICATION
G. H. Mead theory of self	Children learn to adopt the perspectives of others, and thus become self-aware.	A child may feel proud when a parent praises them. By adopting the parent's perspective, they become aware of their own good behavior.
Cooley's looking glass self	Our self-concept is based on our perceptions of how others see us.	A college student feels accepted and popular when they receive lots of "likes" on their Instagram photo.
Piaget's cognitive development model	As children mature, they gradually acquire skills and capacities in reasoning, with the final stage encompassing abstract reasoning.	Young teens may gravitate to poetry and symbolic song lyrics because they have the capacity to understand abstractions.
Psychoanalytic perspectives	Freud and Chodorow believe that gender identity develops out of one's attachment to and separation from parents.	Cisgender girls may mimic the clothing and personal style of their mothers, whereas cisgender boys mimic their fathers.
Gilligan's moral development theory	Men and women use different moral criteria in their decision-making, due to early socialization processes.	Men and women on a jury may react very differently to a defendant, as they may apply different values when assessing the motive and behavior.

CONCEPT CHECKS

1 According to Mead, how does a child develop a social self? How is this view similar to, and different from, Cooley's perspective?

2 What are the four stages of cognitive development, according to Piaget?

3 How do Chodorow's and Gilligan's theories help us understand the influence of socialization on gender?

4 Name one feminist critique of Chodorow.

Carol Gilligan's Theory of Moral Development

Carol Gilligan (1982) further developed Chodorow's analysis, concentrating on the images adult women and men have of themselves and their attainments. Women, she agrees with Chodorow, define themselves in terms of personal relationships and judge their achievements in terms of their ability to care for others. Women's place in the lives of men historically has been that of caretaker and helpmate. But the qualities developed in these tasks are devalued by men, who see their own emphasis on individual achievement as the only form of success. Women's concern with relationships appears to men as a weakness rather than as the strength that in fact it is.

Gilligan carried out intensive interviews with about 200 American women and men of varying ages and social backgrounds. She asked a range of questions concerning their moral outlook and conceptions of self. When asked, "What does it mean to say something is morally right or wrong?" the men mentioned abstract ideals of duty, justice, and individual freedom, whereas the women raised the theme of helping others. The women were more tentative in their moral judgments than the men, seeing possible contradictions between following a strict moral code and avoiding harming others. Gilligan suggests that this outlook reflects the traditional situation of women, anchored in caring relationships, rather than the outward-looking attitudes of men. Women's views of themselves are based on successfully fulfilling the needs of others, rather than on pride in individual achievement (Gilligan, 1982). Gilligan's work has been widely critiqued by feminist scholars, however, on the grounds that it essentializes gender differences and reifies the (mis)perception that women are innate caregivers (Senchuk, 1990). If indeed women abide by an ethic of care, it is likely a function of societal expectations rather than inherent differences in men's and women's morality. Gender roles are socially constructed and evolve over time, so theories that emphasize innate differences between men and women or boys and girls may not be sufficient to characterize our ever-changing world.

3 RESEARCH ON SOCIALIZATION TODAY: RACE SOCIALIZATION

Socialization research flourished in the 1970s, 1980s, and 1990s, as researchers explored the ways that social changes, like shifting gender roles, women's widespread entry into the paid labor force, and increased reliance on paid child care, affected childhood socialization. Yet socialization research can help us understand other contemporary social issues, such as the ways that Black families cope with violence and prejudice, and how parents socialize children to respect individual differences in our increasingly diverse society.

Race Socialization

In recent years, the daily news has all too often reported incidents involving police officers killing unarmed Black men. On the heels of these tragedies, many African American parents struggle not only to explain these events to their children but also to raise their children (especially their sons) to navigate and thrive in this increasingly uncertain world (Canedy, 2016). Many parents realize that it is not accurate to tell children that we live in a color-blind world and should instead teach the next generation to respect people from all backgrounds and walks of life.

How did you learn about your racial or ethnic background? Did your parents ever teach you what it means to be a White, Black, Asian, or Latino American? Or whether, as a member of a particular ethnic or racial group, there are certain ways you should act? Sociologists have recently explored the process of **race socialization**, which refers to the specific verbal and nonverbal messages that older generations transmit to younger generations regarding the meaning and significance of race, racial stratification, intergroup relations, and personal identity (Lesane-Brown, 2006).

The research team of sociologist Tony Brown and psychologist Chase Lesane-Brown has conducted rich and important work on race socialization, investigating the messages that parents teach, how these messages have changed over time, and the effects of this socialization on children's lives. Their work rests on the assumption that ethnic minority parents (especially Black parents) must socialize their children to be productive members of society, just as White parents do, yet they also face an additional challenge: raising children with the skills to survive and prosper in a society that often devalues Blackness. As part of race socialization, Black parents also may prepare their children to understand their heritage, cultures, and what it means to belong to a racial group that historically has occupied a low and stigmatized status in the United States (Brown and Lesane-Brown, 2006).

Their research shows that while parents of all racial and ethnic groups discuss their heritage with their children, parents of color—especially Black parents—do so more often than White parents. For example, in one study, the researchers asked parents, "How often does someone in your family talk with your child about (his/her) ethnic/racial heritage?" (Brown et al., 2006). They found that Black, Hispanic, Asian, Native Hawaiian/Pacific Islander, American Indian, and multiracial families were significantly more likely than White families to discuss their ethnic/racial heritage with their young children. In fact, the odds of discussing children's ethnic/racial heritage in non-White families were 1.9 to 4.7 times the odds for White families.

What exactly do Black parents teach their children about race, race stratification, and race relations? Lesane-Brown, Brown, and colleagues (2005) developed a detailed index capturing the specific messages and lessons that parents pass down to their children,

> **race socialization** The specific verbal and nonverbal messages that older generations transmit to younger generations regarding the meaning and significance of race.

noting of course that families may vary in what they say and how they say it. Among the messages encompassed in race socialization are color blindness (e.g., "race doesn't matter"), individual pride (e.g., "I can achieve anything"), group pride (e.g., "I'm proud to be Black"), distrust of other racial or ethnic groups (e.g., "don't trust White people"), and deference to other racial or ethnic groups (e.g., "Whites are better than Blacks"). The lessons that Black adolescents and college students found to be the most useful, however, were those that emphasized pride and color blindness, such as "race doesn't matter" and "with hard work, you can achieve anything regardless of race" (Lesane-Brown et al., 2005).

Race is socially constructed, as we shall see in Chapter 11, so the experiences of racial minorities and understandings of race change across time and space. Given tremendous changes in the opportunities facing Black Americans throughout the twentieth century and dramatic declines in levels of racism, have the messages that Black parents transmit to their children changed over time? In a 2006 study, Brown and Lesane-Brown examined data from a sample of Black Americans ages 17 to 101 in 1980. The subjects were asked about the racial lessons they had learned from their parents. Specifically, they were given the question: "When you were a child, were there things your parents or the people that raised you taught you to help you know what it is to be Black?" If respondents answered yes, they were asked the open-ended question, "What are the most important things they did or told you?" The researchers also classified people based on the time period in which they turned age 16 to explore the ways that historical context might have shaped their early socialization experiences. Subjects were classified based on whether they came of age pre–*Brown v. Board of Education* (before 1957), during the era of civil rights protests (1957–1968), or after the peak of the civil rights protests (1969–1980).

Brown and Lesane-Brown (2006) identified five main themes from their open-ended questions. The messages of racial socialization were individual pride, racial-group pride, deference to and fear of Whites, color blindness, and the belief that Whites are prejudiced. However, the frequency with which these themes were mentioned varied across generations. Black parents were more likely to transmit messages about deference to and fear of Whites during periods of blatant racial segregation and legalized brutality (pre–*Brown v. Board of Education* birth cohort). Although the researchers expected that parents would transmit more "color-blind" messages to their children in the later post–civil rights era, they did not find support for their hypothesis. Rather, messages of racial equality were more frequently transmitted to children during the early pre–*Brown v. Board of Education* era; the researchers concluded that Black parents may feel particularly compelled to assert that all groups are equal during the historical period when that assertion was contested most passionately by Whites.

What are the consequences of race socialization? Brown and Lesane-Brown (2006) found that the messages one receives during childhood have far-reaching implications for one's political attitudes and behaviors, including whether one supports voting for Black candidates and whether one believes that Blacks and Whites have the same chance to get ahead with respect to work and education. In other research, these scholars found that ethnic/race socialization is linked with better academic performance in elementary school. Interestingly, they found a curvilinear association, meaning that the positive

In our increasingly global society, it's more important than ever for teachers—and other agents of socialization—to promote positive racial identities.

effects of race socialization were most evident among children who had received moderately frequent messages; the positive effects were less evident among those who had parent-child conversations about their racial background either very frequently or very infrequently (Brown, Tanner-Smith, and Lesane-Brown, 2009).

Understanding race socialization will become increasingly important for future cohorts of young people. In our rapidly globalizing society, children and young people will need to develop the skills and capacities to negotiate multicultural contexts in their everyday lives (Priest et al., 2014). Children of all ethnic and racial backgrounds will require the skills and attitudes to think positively about racial, ethnic, and cultural diversity. Parents, teachers, and other agents of socialization must also promote positive racial attitudes, counter negative attitudes, and enable effective responses to racism when it occurs. Although race socialization historically has focused on raising Black children to fit in and get ahead in a racist world, scholars today recognize that White children, too, should be socialized to recognize and fight racism when they see it unfold (Priest et al., 2014).

CONCEPT CHECKS

1 What are the key lessons learned through the process of racial socialization?

2 Why is race socialization important in contemporary society?

4 UNANSWERED QUESTIONS

Although studies of socialization have become quite advanced over the past century, many open or unanswered questions are still the subject of much disagreement among sociologists. Some of the most significant have to do with **gender role socialization**—the learning of **gender roles** through social factors such as the family and the media. In recent years, however, researchers have become increasingly interested in how older children learn antisocial behaviors such as bullying; it is only by knowing how bullying is learned that we can figure out ways to stop it.

Are Gender Differences Caused by Social Influences?

Many studies have examined the degree to which gender differences are the result of social influences. Studies of mother-infant interaction show differences in the treatment of boys and girls, even when parents believe their reactions to both are the same. Adults asked to assess the personality of a baby give different answers according to whether they believe the child is a girl or a boy. In one experiment, five young mothers were observed interacting with a six-month-old called Beth. They smiled at her often and offered her dolls to play with. She was seen as "sweet" and as having a "soft cry." The reaction of a second group of mothers to a child the same age, named Adam, was noticeably different. They offered him a train or other "male" toys to play with. Beth and Adam were actually the same child, dressed in different clothes (Will, Self, and Datan, 1976).

Gender Learning

Gender learning by infants is almost certainly unconscious. Before a child can label itself as either a boy or a girl, the child receives preverbal cues. For instance, male and female adults usually handle infants differently. Women's cosmetics contain scents different from those the baby might associate with males. Systematic differences in dress, hairstyle, and so on provide visual cues for the infant in the learning process. By age two, children have a partial understanding of what gender is. They know whether they are boys or girls, and they can usually categorize others accurately. Not until age five or six, however, does a child know that a person's sex does not change, that everyone has gender, and that sex differences between girls and boys are anatomically based.

Parents play a pivotal role in gender learning, often unintentionally. A child's earliest exposure to what it means to be male or female comes from his or her parents. From the time their children are newborns, parents interact with their daughters and sons differently. They may dress their sons in blue and daughters in pink, or speak to girls in softer and gentler tones than they do with boys. One classic study found that parents have different expectations for their sons and daughters as early as one day after they are born, where infant girls are described as "soft" and "pretty" and boys as "energetic" and "strong" (Rubin, Provenzano, and Luria, 1974). It's not surprising, then, that

gender role socialization The learning of gender roles through social factors such as schooling, the media, and family.

gender roles Social roles assigned to each sex and labeled as masculine or feminine.

as children become toddlers, parents (especially fathers) engage in more rough-and-tumble play with boys and hold more give-and-take conversations with girls (Lytton and Romney, 1991).

Even parents who are sensitive to gender-equity issues and who challenge the notion of the male/female dichotomy may send subtle messages related to gender—messages that the developing child internalizes. Sex-role stereotypes and subtle messages about appropriate gender-typed behavior are so powerful that even when children are exposed to diverse attitudes and experiences, they may revert to stereotyped choices—especially in sociocultural and historical contexts that adhere to gender-typed social roles and expectations (Haslett, Geis, and Carter, 1992). Children may even deny the reality of what they are seeing when it doesn't conform to their gender expectations. For instance, a child whose mother is a doctor may state that only men are doctors, and women are nurses (Sheldon, 1990).

Children's toys and activities also tend to follow stereotypical patterns. Studies of children's bedrooms in the contemporary United States consistently find that girls' rooms have more pink decoration and more dolls, whereas boys' rooms tend to have more blue tones, sports equipment, and vehicles (Pomerleau et al., 1990). A simple visit to a department store or a big-box store illustrates the dominance of gender stereotypes, as retailers typically categorize their products by gender. Even toys that seem gender neutral are not so in practice. Vanda Lucia Zammuner (1986) studied the toy preferences of children between 7 and 10 years of age in Italy and Holland; they included stereotypically masculine or feminine toys as well as toys presumed not to be gender-typed. The children and their parents were asked which toys were suitable for boys and which for girls. There was close agreement between the adults and the children. On average, the Italian children chose gender-differentiated toys more often than the Dutch children—a finding that conformed to expectations because Italian culture holds a more traditional view of gender divisions than does Dutch society. As in other studies, girls from both societies chose gender-neutral or boys' toys far more often than boys chose girls' toys.

But these stark gender divides are historically bound. Cultural analyses have found that the "blue is for boys, pink is for girls" divide is a twentieth-century social construction. In the nineteenth century and early decades of the twentieth century, boys and girls wore similar colors, mostly white (Paoletti, 2012). However, in the post-war era in the United States, the pink-blue gender divide emerged, and persisted on and off throughout the late twentieth century. Yet the trend appears to be coming full circle, with retailers and shoppers alike abandoning this convention. For example, in 2015, Target, the nation's largest retailer, stopped dividing its toy departments into "boy" and "girl" sections and also discontinued the pink- and blue-colored walls previously used to draw attention to gender-typed toys. Recognizing that nearly every product for children is gender-typed, Target management also stopped dividing up other departments, such as bedding, by gender. Boys and girls might be equally likely to want a Star Wars or a Dora the Explorer comforter (Luckerson, 2015). The move was triggered, in part, by shoppers' concerns regarding the needless gender labeling of toys. Most famously, shopper Abi Bechtel noted a sign in Target's toy section differentiating "building sets" and "girls' building sets." The notion that gender-neutral toys are healthy for all children is rapidly spreading, with more and more manufacturers abandoning gender-typed colors and designs of their toys.

In her "Pink & Blue" project, photographer Jeong Mee Yoon records girls' obsession with the color pink. What are the implications of the gender-typed packaging and color coding we see in children's toys and clothing?

Like children's toys, children's books and television shows teach important, though subtle, lessons about gender. In the 1970s, Lenore Weitzman and her colleagues analyzed gender roles in some of the most widely used preschool children's books and found several clear differences in gender roles (Weitzman et al., 1972). Males played a much larger part in the stories and pictures than did females: they outnumbered females by a ratio of 11 to 1. When animals with gender identities were included, the ratio was 95 to 1. The activities of males and females also differed. The males engaged in adventurous pursuits and outdoor activities demanding independence and strength. When girls did appear, they were portrayed as passive and were confined mostly to indoor activities. Girls cooked and cleaned for the males or awaited their return. Much the same was true of the adult characters. Women who were not wives and mothers were imaginary creatures such as witches and fairy godmothers. In all the books analyzed, not a single woman held an occupation outside the home. By contrast, the men were depicted as fighters, policemen, judges, kings, and so forth.

More recent research suggests a slight change but notes that the bulk of children's literature remains the same (McCabe et al., 2011). Children's books feature many more men and boys as lead characters than women and girls. Even when characters are animals, they tend to be male (McCabe et al., 2011). The specific messages conveyed in children's books are often quite traditional as well. Fairy tales, for example, still embody traditional attitudes toward gender and expectations for boys' and girls' ambitions. In versions of fairy tales from several centuries ago, the idea that "someday my prince will come" usually implied that a girl from a poor family might dream of wealth and fortune. Today that notion is tied to the ideals of romantic love. Some observers have noted that the popular Disney movie *Frozen* is a small step toward chipping away at such stereotypes. The lead character, Anna, discovers that her "handsome prince" is actually a cruel liar. Anna goes on to find her happy ending when she reconnects with her estranged older sister, Elsa, although Anna does eventually find true love with her ruggedly handsome suitor, Kristoff the iceman (Guilford, 2014).

Although there are exceptions, analyses of children's television programs and video games match the findings about children's books. In the most popular cartoons and games, most leading figures are male, and males dominate the active pursuits (Leaper and Bigler, 2018). Similar images appear in the commercials advertising children's foods and toys. For instance, researchers recently examined the ways that boys and girls are portrayed in children's programming on three networks: the Disney Channel, Cartoon Network, and Nickelodeon (Hentges and Case, 2013). Boy characters outnumbered girls 3 to 2, and there was some evidence that characters were depicted behaving in stereotypical ways, where boys were more likely to be aggressive "rescuers" and girls were more likely to show affection.

How Do Children Learn to Bully? Can They Unlearn?

Parents, grandparents, teachers, religious leaders, and children's television shows from *Sesame Street* to *Thomas and Friends* to *Spongebob Squarepants* teach the importance of being kind to everyone. So how is it possible that by the time students reach middle school or high school, many treat each other cruelly? Bullying is an everyday part of adolescents' life. More mild forms of bullying include teasing or rudely excluding a classmate from a seat at the cafeteria lunch table. In its more extreme forms, physical threats and cyberbullying—or taunting and humiliating peers online—have led to dire outcomes, with dozens of bullied teens committing suicide in recent decades, including 12-year old Florida middle-school student Rebecca Ann Sedwick who jumped from a concrete silo tower to her death. In 2018, fully 58 percent of teens said they were the target of cyberbullying, which encompassed name-calling, spreading false rumors, sexting, and physical threats (Anderson, 2018). Rates of bullying are even higher for LGBT students (Schneider et al., 2012). A 2015 study found that nearly 60 percent of LGBT students reported feeling physically unsafe at school (Kosciw et al., 2016).

What accounts for the widespread cruelty that teens subject one another to, despite having been taught in elementary school to treat one another with kindness? Peers

A recent study found that middle schools that enlisted influential students in anti-bullying campaigns experienced a 30 percent decrease in reports of student conflict.

learn to bully in much the same way that they learn other positive and negative behaviors, through imitation and reinforcement. *Imitation* refers to the mimicking of the behaviors of others, especially those who hold social power, such as popular students or clique leaders. *Reinforcement* refers to the process whereby we learn to perform behaviors that are rewarded and avoid behaviors that are punished. Multiple studies show that the most popular students tend to be the perpetrators of abuse, whereas students who are less popular or emotionally insecure tend to be victims (Cook et al., 2010). Students may want to imitate the popular students they look up to and may join in on the bullying out of fear that refusing to do so may render them susceptible to abuse and isolation (Forsberg, Thornberg, and Samuelson, 2014).

Part of the reason bullying tends to spike in early adolescence is that it's the time when children most strongly identify with their peers (Gavin and Furman, 1989). Between the ages of 10 and 14, children show deficiencies in their ability to resist peer influence (Steinberg and Monahan, 2007). Both this increased identification with their peers and an inability to resist peer influence (perhaps out of fear of being victimized oneself) make adolescence a time when peers are particularly influential on children (Rubin, Bukowski, and Parker, 2006).

Yet just as popular students often are the ones whose bad behavior is modeled by others, their good behavior also can be modeled. For this reason, researchers now suggest that bullying-prevention programs in schools must not merely involve teachers and principals, but also enlist popular students as allies. One recent study of 56 New Jersey middle schools found that when the most influential students—known as "social referents" or "social influencers"—played a leadership role in anti-bullying campaigns, more students in the school reported anti-bullying attitudes, levels of bullying dropped, and more students did things to raise awareness of bullying, like purchasing yellow bracelets to publicly display their opposition to cruel behavior in their schools (Paluck, Shepherd, and Aronow, 2016). As one of the researchers explained, "We think the best way to change social norms is to have these student influencers speak in their own voices. Encouraging their own messages to bubble up from the bottom using a grassroots approach can be very powerful." This research provides compelling evidence that peers can play an important role in the socialization process by modeling pro-social as well as antisocial behavior.

Sociological research on socialization reveals the complex ways that individuals continue to learn the norms, values, behaviors, and social practices of the particular (and often overlapping) subgroups to which they belong over the life course. As we learned in this chapter's opening, the lessons and values passed down from generation to generation can shift dramatically over time, reflecting historical shifts in the social and economic opportunities that young people face and the roles that they will someday occupy. Gender and race socialization are two subtypes of socialization that change dramatically over time, as gender and race are socially constructed and their meanings and experiences change across time and place. As we will see in Chapters 10 (Gender Inequality) and 11 (Race, Ethnicity, and Racism), systems of gender and racial inequality have changed dramatically over the past century and will continue to do so into the future. These changes will continue to reshape the ways that gender and racial socialization processes unfold for future cohorts of young people.

CONCEPT CHECKS

1 How does the media contribute to gender role socialization?

2 How do parents and other adults reinforce gender roles?

3 Why are adolescents more likely than young children to bully their peers?

4 How might school systems effectively combat bullying?

THE BIG PICTURE

Chapter 4
Socialization and
the Life Course

1 Basic Concepts — p. 100

2 Theories of Socialization — p. 114

LEARNING OBJECTIVES

Understand how the four main agents of socialization contribute to social reproduction. Learn the stages of the life course, and see the similarities and differences among cultures.

Compare and contrast the theories of child development according to Mead, Cooley, Piaget, Freud, and Chodorow.

TERMS TO KNOW

socialization • life course • social reproduction • agents of socialization • resocialization • desocialization • anticipatory socialization • hidden curriculum • peer group • age-grade • mass media • social roles • identity • social identity • master status • self-identity

cognition • social self • self-consciousness • generalized other • looking-glass self • sensorimotor stage • preoperational stage • egocentric • concrete operational stage • formal operational stage

CONCEPT CHECKS

1. What is social reproduction? What are some specific ways that the four main agents of socialization contribute to social reproduction?
2. Compare and contrast social roles and social identities.
3. What are the five stages of the life course, and what are some of the defining features of each stage?
4. Describe how the life course stage of childhood has changed since medieval times.
5. How is midlife different from the life course stages of childhood and old age?

1. According to Mead, how does a child develop a social self? How is this view similar to, and different from, Cooley's perspective?
2. What are the four stages of cognitive development, according to Piaget?
3. How do Chodorow's and Gilligan's theories help us understand the influence of socialization on gender?
4. Name one feminist critique of Chodorow.

Exercises: Thinking Sociologically

1. Concisely review how an individual becomes a social person according to the three leading theorists discussed in this chapter: G. H. Mead, Jean Piaget, and Sigmund Freud. Which theory seems most appropriate and correct to you? Explain why.

2. Consuming alcoholic beverages is one of many things we do as a result of socialization. Suggest how the family, peers, schools, and mass media help establish the desire to consume alcoholic drinks. Of these influences, which force is the most persuasive? Explain.

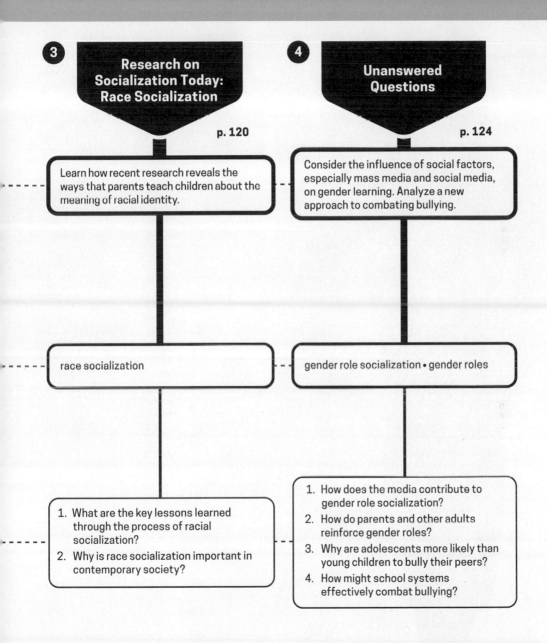

3

Research on Socialization Today: Race Socialization

p. 120

Learn how recent research reveals the ways that parents teach children about the meaning of racial identity.

race socialization

1. What are the key lessons learned through the process of racial socialization?
2. Why is race socialization important in contemporary society?

4

Unanswered Questions

p. 124

Consider the influence of social factors, especially mass media and social media, on gender learning. Analyze a new approach to combating bullying.

gender role socialization • gender roles

1. How does the media contribute to gender role socialization?
2. How do parents and other adults reinforce gender roles?
3. Why are adolescents more likely than young children to bully their peers?
4. How might school systems effectively combat bullying?

5

Social Interaction and Everyday Life in the Age of the Internet

Imagine you are in need of assistance in a crowded subway car. A person nearby who is listening to her iPod will probably:

- **A**   willingly provide you help.

- **B**   begrudgingly provide you help.

- **C**   react angrily to your request for help.

- **D**   ignore your request for help altogether.

TURN THE PAGE FOR THE CORRECT ANSWER.

Does the use of an iPod affect public social conduct? This is the question asked by Christine Miranda, a junior at Princeton University who wanted to know how receptive iPod users were to strangers. Comparing the behavior of individuals using iPods with those not using them, she embarked on a study in New York's subway system and began to document interactions between iPod users and nonusers on the 6 train on the east side of Manhattan.

You might expect that iPod users on the subway would be unwilling or unhappy to speak with you (answers *b*, *c*, or *d*). Given that someone listening to music via headphones is preoccupied with another task, you would probably be wary about approaching them. People not wearing the trademark white earbuds likely appear more open to conversation, (literally) more able to hear what you have to say.

LEARNING OBJECTIVES

1 Basic Concepts

Understand the core concepts of the "impression management" perspective. Recognize how we use impression management techniques in everyday life.

2 Theories of Social Interaction

Understand why the study of social interaction is of major importance in sociology. Learn the four zones of personal space. Learn what ethnomethodology is.

3 Contemporary Research on Social Interaction

Understand how social interaction and broader features of society are closely related.

4 Unanswered Questions

Consider how face-to-face interactions remain important in the age of the Internet.

Miranda's study put this commonsense hypothesis to the test. Boarding a subway car, she noted whether people possessed iPods; their positioning in relation to her; and their race, sex, and approximate age. In addition to observing users' and nonusers' responses to interactions, she noted cues such as body language and facial gestures, and recorded exchanges between users and nonusers, as well as interactions involving auditory interruptions, invasions of physical space, and sexual offenses.

Sometimes Miranda simply observed naturally occurring interactions; for example, she observed the responses of users and nonusers to a panhandler petitioning for donations. At other times, she acted as the "confederate," or intruder, interrupting an iPod user to ask about the train's last stop. She asked similar questions of nonusers as well, seeking to determine whether iPod users were less eager or less willing to respond.

Miranda found that iPod users seemed just as open to providing useful information as nonusers. Thus, answer *a* is actually correct. Among the iPod users, no one she asked seemed to mind removing their headphones long enough to provide an answer; indeed, the users she asked seemed more courteous than the nonusers. Having offered the information requested, however, iPod users promptly went back to listening to their music. (Similarly, nonusers who were reading when she asked

THE ANSWER IS A.

them went back to their newspapers or books, and those engaged in conversation went back to talking.)

Corroborating the popular hypothesis just detailed, most subway riders, Miranda discovered, perceived iPod users as less approachable. So, while most users seemed happy to offer information that was requested of them, they were less likely than nonusers to be asked in the first place. Indeed, Miranda noted: "The personal stereo presents an opportunity to block off the outside environment and to reduce the likelihood of being approached, but when social conduct does occur, the user's behavior is not much different from the nonuser's."

She concluded that while the personal stereo presents the illusion of separation, making a user appear less approachable, this "wall can be easily broken when we simply disrupt a person's personal space with words or actions." It may initially take a bit more effort to get the attention of an iPod user, whose senses may be somewhat dulled compared with those of a more alert nonuser. However, when a true attempt is made to get an iPod user to interact (for example, by asking a pointed question), the iPod user seems as open to interruption as the nonuser. After the interaction, however, it is generally understood that iPod users will go about their own business without acknowledging those around them.

1 BASIC CONCEPTS

When we published the first edition of this book, the study of face-to-face communication was a well-settled territory. There is reason to think, however, that social interaction over the past decade or so has undergone a major transformation because of the Internet. In this chapter, we will review the traditional findings of the field, but we will also ask how we must modify those findings in light of the rise of email, Twitter, iPhone apps, and social networking sites like Facebook. We will first learn about the ways we use impression management techniques in our daily interactions. We then move on to analyze the nonverbal cues (facial expressions and bodily gestures) all of us use when interacting with one another. Finally, we focus on the ways in which our lives are structured by daily routines, paying particular attention to how we coordinate our actions across space and time.

Impression Management: The World as a Stage

Sociologist Erving Goffman and other writers on social interaction often use notions from theater in their analyses. The concept of the social role, for example, originated in a theatrical setting. Broadly speaking, **roles**

roles The expected behaviors of people occupying particular social positions. The idea of social role originally comes from the theater, referring to the parts that actors play in a stage production. In every society, individuals play a number of social roles.

status The social honor or prestige that a particular group is accorded by other members of a society. Status groups normally display distinct styles of life—patterns of behavior that the members of a group follow. Status privilege may be positive or negative.

social position The social identity an individual has in a given group or society. Social positions may be general in nature (those associated with gender roles) or more specific (occupational positions).

impression management Preparing for the presentation of one's social role.

are socially defined expectations that a person in a given **status** (or **social position**) follows. To be a teacher is to hold a specific position; the teacher's role consists of acting in specified ways toward pupils. Goffman (1973) sees social life as played out by actors on a stage (or on many stages) because how we act depends on the roles we play at a given time.

People are sensitive to how others see them and use many forms of **impression management** to compel others to react to them in the ways they wish them to. Although we may sometimes do this in a calculated way, usually we do this without conscious attention. When going on a job interview, a person will typically dress more formally and try to put their best foot forward; however, when going out with friends, they might dress down, use slang, and act in ways that may not impress a prospective employer.

A central insight of social interaction based on Goffman's work is that every human being possesses a self that is fragile and vulnerable to embarrassment, or even humiliation, at every turn. People are intensely attuned to what others think of them and how others view them. That's part of the reason why we're so careful about what we post on Facebook and why we cringe if we're tagged by friends in unflattering or embarrassing photos. Seeking approval and respect, individuals want to "save face" at every turn. In social interactions, human beings tend to collaborate with others to make sure that the interaction ends without embarrassment for anyone. As a stage, social life has many players, and they must collaborate to make each scene work.

Think of examples from your own life when people did not collaborate with you. If you go to a club and someone with whom you don't want to talk approaches you, you will likely try to end the interaction in a way that spares the other person embarrassment. If you were simply to tell the person, "Get lost!" rather than help him or her save face, that would be highly unusual. This is because there is a norm of collaboration by which human beings try to move through life without embarrassing or humiliating others. When this collaboration does not occur, the interaction stands out.

The pose that we adopt depends a great deal on our social role, but no particular role dictates any specific presentation of self. A person's demeanor can be different depending on the social context. For instance, as a student, you have a certain status and are expected to act a certain way when you are around your professors. Some pupils will enact the self-presentation of the dutiful student, while others will assume an uncaring or apathetic pose.

How are technologies such as webcams, email, and smartphones transforming the ways we interact with one another?

Some sociological studies suggest that in poor inner-city schools whose student bodies comprise largely minorities, students afraid of being accused of "acting white" will adopt a personal style that is more "street" than studious. However, this appearance may not give an accurate sense of how capable a student really is. A student who takes on the demeanor of the street may be studying just as hard as classmates who take on the demeanor of the mild-mannered scholar.

Adopting Roles

For an example of collaboration in impression management that also borrows from the theater, let's look at one particular study in some detail. James Henslin and Mae Biggs (1971, 1997) studied a specific, highly delicate type of encounter: a woman's visit to a gynecologist. At the time of the study, male doctors carried out most pelvic examinations, hence the experience was (and sometimes still is) fraught with potential ambiguities and embarrassment for both parties. Men and women in the West are socialized to think of the genitals as the most private part of the body, and seeing, and particularly touching, the genitals of another person is ordinarily associated with intimate sexual encounters. Some women feel so worried by the prospect of a pelvic examination that they refuse to visit the doctor, male or female, even when they suspect there is a strong medical reason to do so.

Henslin and Biggs analyzed material collected by Biggs, a trained nurse, from a large number of gynecological examinations. They interpreted what they found as occurring in several typical stages. Adopting a dramaturgical metaphor, they suggested that each phase could be treated as a distinct scene, in which the parts the actors play alter as the episode unfolds. In the prologue, the woman enters the waiting room preparing to assume the role of patient and temporarily discarding her outside identity. Called into the consulting room, she adopts the "patient" role, and the first scene opens. The doctor assumes a businesslike, professional manner and treats the patient as a proper and competent person, maintaining eye contact and listening politely to what she has to say. If the doctor decides an examination is called for, he tells her so and leaves the room. Scene One is over.

As the doctor leaves, a female nurse comes in. She is an important stagehand in the main scene shortly to begin. She soothes any worries the patient might have, acting as both a confidante—knowing some of the "things women have to put up with"—and a collaborator in what is to follow. Crucial to the next scene, the nurse helps alter the patient from a person to a "nonperson" for the vital scene—which features a body, part of which is to be scrutinized, rather than a complete human being. In Henslin and Biggs's study, the nurse supervises the patient's undressing, taking the patient's clothes and folding them. Most women want their underwear to be out of sight when the doctor returns, so the nurse makes sure that this is so. She guides the patient to the examining table and covers most of the patient's body with a sheet before the physician returns.

The central scene now opens, with the nurse as well as the doctor taking part. The presence of the nurse helps ensure that the interaction between the doctor and the patient is free of sexual overtones and provides a legal witness should the physician be charged with unprofessional conduct. The examination proceeds as though the patient's personality were absent; the sheet across her separates the genital area from the rest of her body, and her position does not allow her to watch the examination itself. Save for any specific medical queries, the doctor ignores her, sitting on a low stool out of her line of vision. The patient collaborates in becoming a temporary non-person, not initiating conversation and keeping any movements to a minimum.

In the interval between this scene and the final one, the nurse again plays the role of stagehand, helping the patient become a full person once more. After the doctor has left the room, the two may again engage in conversation, the patient expressing relief that the examination is over. Having dressed and groomed herself, the patient is ready to face the concluding scene. The doctor reenters and, in discussing the results of the examination, again treats the patient as a complete person. Resuming his polite, professional manner, he conveys that his reactions to her are in no way altered by the intimate contact with her body. The epilogue is played out when the patient leaves the physician's office, resuming her identity in the outside world. The patient and the doctor have thus collaborated in such a way as to manage the interaction and the impression each participant forms of the other.

Audience Segregation

Although people cooperate to help one another "save face," they also endeavor individually to preserve their own dignity, autonomy, and respect. One of the ways in which people do this is by arranging for "audience segregation" in their lives. In each of their roles, they act somewhat differently, and they try to keep what they do in each role distinct from what they do in their other roles. This means that they can have multiple selves. Frequently, these selves are consistent with one another, but sometimes, they are not. People find it very stressful when boundaries break down or when they cannot reconcile their role in one area of their life with their role in another.

For example, we may have two friends who do not like each other. Rather than choose between them, we will spend time with both friends but never mention to either friend that we are close with the other. Or some people live very different lives at home and at work. For example, due to discrimination against gays and lesbians, someone who appears "straight" at work may live happily with a same-sex partner at home. Like all people who engage in audience segregation, they show a different face to different people.

Audience segregation implicitly encourages impression management. Some people maintain two different Facebook pages, one linked to family members or coworkers and another linked to friends and peers. Why might someone do this? Our Facebook pages are a strategy to "impression manage," or to carefully and selectively portray an image of ourselves to the outside world. On your "professional" page, you might try to convey an image of a respectable student and employee by carefully curating the information and images you post. By contrast, on your personal page, you might post photos that present a more fun and carefree version of yourself.

Goffman saw social life as a precarious balancing act, but he also studied those instances in which audience segregation could not be maintained. He conducted an ethnographic study of St. Elizabeth's, a mental hospital in Washington, D.C., described in his book *Asylums*. St. Elizabeth's was a place where the barriers among different spheres of life (sleep, play, and work) did not exist. In such an environment, which Goffman called a "total institution," human beings need to adapt to the fact that their private spheres are limited. Other examples of "total institutions," in which all aspects of life are conducted in the same place, include prisons, monasteries, and army boot camps.

Civil Inattention

When passersby—either strangers or intimates—quickly glance at each other and then look away again, they demonstrate what Goffman (1967, 1971) calls **civil inattention**. Civil inattention is not the same as merely ignoring another person. Each individual indicates recognition of the other person's presence but avoids any gesture that might be taken as too intrusive. Can you think of examples of civil inattention in your own life? Perhaps when you are walking down the hall of a dormitory, trying to decide where to sit in the dining hall, or simply walking across campus? Civil inattention to others is something we engage in more or less unconsciously, but it is of fundamental importance to the existence of social life, which must proceed efficiently, and sometimes among total strangers, without fear. When civil inattention occurs among passing strangers, an individual implies to another person that she has no reason to suspect his intentions, be hostile to him, or in any other way specifically avoid him.

The best way to see the importance of this process is by thinking of examples when it doesn't apply. When a person stares fixedly at another, allowing her face to openly express a particular emotion, it is frequently with a lover, family member, or close friend. Strangers or chance acquaintances, whether encountered on the street, at work, or at a party, virtually never hold the gaze of another in this way. To do so may be taken as an indication of hostile intent. It is only where two groups are strongly antagonistic to one another that strangers might indulge in such a practice. Even friends in close conversation need to be careful about how they look at one another. Each individual demonstrates attention and involvement in the conversation by regularly looking at the eyes of the other but not staring into them. To look too intently might be taken as a sign of mistrust about, or at least failure to understand, what the other is saying. Yet if each party does not engage the eyes of the other at all, each is likely to be thought evasive, shifty, or otherwise odd.

Nonverbal Communication

Social interaction requires numerous forms of **nonverbal communication**—the exchange of information and meaning through facial expressions, gestures, and body movements. Nonverbal communication, sometimes called "body language," often alters or expands on what is said with words. In some cases, our body language may convey a message that is at odds with our words.

Face, Gestures, and Emotion

One major aspect of communication is the facial expression of emotion. Paul Ekman and his colleagues have developed what they call the Facial Action Coding System (FACS) for describing movements of the facial muscles

civil inattention The process whereby individuals in the same physical setting glance at each other and quickly look away to indicate awareness of each other but not intrusiveness.

nonverbal communication Communication between individuals based on facial expression or bodily gesture rather than on language.

that give rise to particular expressions (Ekman and Friesen, 1978). By this means, they have tried to inject some precision into an area notoriously open to inconsistent or contradictory interpretations—for there is little agreement about how emotions are to be identified and classified. Charles Darwin, one of the originators of evolutionary theory, claimed that basic modes of emotional expression are the same in all human beings. Although some have disputed the claim, Ekman's research among people from widely different cultural backgrounds seems to confirm Darwin's view. Ekman and W. V. Friesen carried out a study of an isolated community in New Guinea whose members had previously had virtually no contact with outsiders. When they were shown pictures of facial expressions conveying six emotions (happiness, sadness, anger, disgust, fear, and surprise), the New Guineans were able to identify these emotions.

According to Ekman, the results of his own and similar studies of different peoples support the view that the facial expression of emotion and its interpretation are innate in human beings. He acknowledges that his evidence does not conclusively demonstrate this view, and it may be that widely shared cultural-learning experiences are involved; however, his conclusions are supported by other types of research. Irenäus Eibl-Eibesfeldt (1972) studied six children born deaf and blind to see to what extent their facial expressions were the same as those of sighted and hearing individuals in particular emotional situations. He found that the children smiled when engaged in obviously pleasurable activities, raised their eyebrows in surprise when sniffing at an object with an unaccustomed smell, and frowned when repeatedly offered a disliked object. Because the children could not have seen other people behaving in these ways, it seems that these responses must be innately determined.

Paul Ekman's photographs of facial expressions from a tribesman in an isolated community in New Guinea helped test the idea that basic modes of emotional expression are the same among all people. Here the instructions were to show how your face would look if (clockwise from top left) your friend had come and you were happy; your child had died; you saw a dead pig that had been lying there a long time; you were angry and about to fight.

Using the FACS, Ekman and Friesen identified a number of the discrete facial-muscle actions in newborn infants that are also found in adult expressions of emotion. Infants seem, for example, to produce facial expressions similar to the adult expression of disgust (pursing the lips and frowning) in response to sour tastes. But although the facial expression of emotion seems to be partly innate, individual and cultural factors influence what exact form facial movements take and the contexts in which they are deemed appropriate. How people smile—for example, the precise movement of the lips and other facial muscles—and for how long both vary among cultures.

No gestures or bodily postures have been shown to characterize all, or even most, cultures. In some societies, for instance, people nod when they mean no, the opposite of Anglo-American practice. Gestures that Americans tend to use a great deal, such as pointing, seem not to exist among certain peoples (Bull, 1983). Similarly, a straightened forefinger placed in the center of the cheek and rotated is used in parts of Italy as a gesture of praise but appears to be unknown elsewhere.

Like facial expressions, gestures and bodily posture are continually used to fill out utterances and convey meanings when nothing is actually said. All three can be used to joke, show irony, or express skepticism. The nonverbal impressions that we convey often inadvertently indicate that what we say is not quite what we actually mean. Blushing is perhaps the most obvious example, but innumerable other subtle indicators can be picked up by other people. Genuine facial expressions tend to evaporate after four or five seconds. A smile that lasts longer could indicate deceit. An expression of surprise that lasts too long may indicate deliberate sarcasm—to show that the individual is not, in fact, surprised after all.

On the Internet, it is very difficult to capture dimensions of emotion that are present only with facial expression. At first, the need that Internet users felt to approximate facial gestures resulted in at least two common faces:

:) or :-)

As time passed, a need for greater subtlety resulted in other widely understood variations, such as this winking smiley face:

;-)

Email may once have been devoid of facial expression, but today, the average email user expects to insert different emotions into a message. Strongly felt sentiments might be typed in all capitals, a gesture that is considered "shouting." The strong need that human beings feel to communicate with their faces has also led to other innovations, like Skype and FaceTime. But, in general, people who communicate over the Internet or even the phone lack the benefit of seeing the faces of their conversational partners as they speak.

Why and how does this lack of face-to-face contact matter for human relationships and interactions? On the phone, whether it's a cell phone or landline, an individual will frequently talk for a longer stretch of time than he or she would in face-to-face conversation. Unable to see the face of a conversational partner, the speaker can't as readily adjust what he or she is saying in response to clues from the listener that he or she "gets it." Yet, the phone maintains at least some immediacy of feedback that email and text messages, to a lesser extent, lack. This is why in email disputes, people who

Gestures and bodily poses vary by culture.

are unable to make mutual adjustments in response to verbal or facial cues will end up saying much more—communicated in the form of long messages—than they would need to say in spoken conversation.

Which is best? Would you prefer to make your point via email or text message, over the phone or Skype, or in person? Using sociological insights such as these might make you prefer electronic communication at some times and face-to-face communication at others. For example, if you are dealing with a powerful person and want to get your thoughts across, you may want to avoid a situation where the person can signal with facial gestures that your idea is silly and thus intimidate you, inhibiting you from making all your points. The power to signal with facial gestures is one of the things people do to control the flow of a conversation. On the other hand, face-to-face communication gives you an opportunity to try out an idea on someone more powerful than you without going too far down the road if the person is actually unreceptive.

Response Cries

Certain kinds of utterances are not talk but consist of muttered exclamations, or what Goffman (1981) has called **response cries**. Consider Lucy, who exclaims, "Oops!" after knocking over a glass of water. "Oops!" seems to be merely an uninteresting reflex response to a mishap, rather like blinking your eye when a person moves a hand sharply toward your face. It is not a reflex, however, as shown by the fact that people do not usually make the exclamation when alone. "Oops!" is normally directed toward others present. The exclamation demonstrates to witnesses that the lapse is only minor and momentary, not something that should cast doubt on Lucy's command of her actions.

Phrases like "Oops!" or "My bad!" are used only in situations of minor failure, rather than in major accidents or calamities—which also demonstrates that the exclamation is part of our controlled management of the details of social life. Moreover, these phrases may be used by someone observing Lucy rather than by Lucy herself, or they may be used to sound a warning to another. *Oops* is normally a short sound, but the *oo* may be prolonged in some situations. Thus, someone might extend the sound to cover a critical moment in performing a task. For instance, a parent may utter an extended "Oops!" or "Oops-a-daisy!" when playfully tossing a child in the air. The sound covers the brief phase when the child may feel a loss of control, reassuring him and probably at the same time developing his understanding of response cries.

This may all sound very contrived and exaggerated. Why bother to analyze such an inconsequential utterance in such detail? Surely we don't pay as much attention to what we say as this example suggests? Of course we don't—on a conscious level. The crucial point, however, is that we take for granted the immensely complicated, continuous control of our appearance and actions. In situations of interaction, we are never expected simply to be present. Others expect, as we expect of them, that we will display what Goffman calls "controlled alertness." A fundamental part of being human is continually demonstrating to others our competence in the routines of daily life.

Focused and Unfocused Interaction

In many social situations, we engage in what Goffman calls **unfocused interaction** with others. Unfocused interaction takes place whenever individuals exhibit awareness of one another's presence. This is usually the case anywhere large numbers of people are assembled, as on a busy street, in a theater crowd, or at a party. When people are in the presence of others, even if they do not directly talk to them, they continually communicate nonverbally through their posture and facial and physical gestures.

Focused interaction occurs when individuals directly attend to what others say or do. Goffman calls an instance of focused interaction an **encounter**. Much of our day-to-day life consists of encounters with other people—family, friends, colleagues—frequently occurring against the background of unfocused interaction with others. Small talk, seminar discussions, games, and routine face-to-face contact (with ticket clerks, waiters, shop assistants, and so forth) are all examples of encounters.

Encounters always need "openings," which indicate that civil inattention is being discarded. When strangers meet and begin to talk at a party, the moment of ceasing civil inattention is always risky because misunderstandings can easily occur about the nature of the encounter being established (Goffman, 1971). Hence, making eye contact may first be ambiguous and tentative. A person can then act as though he or she had made no direct move if the overture is not accepted. In focused interaction, each person communicates as much by facial expression and gesture as by the words actually exchanged.

Goffman distinguishes between the expressions an individual "gives" and those he "gives off." The first are the words and facial expres-

response cries Seemingly involuntary exclamations individuals make when, for example, they are taken by surprise, drop something inadvertently, or want to express pleasure.

unfocused interaction Interaction occurring among people present in a particular setting but not engaged in direct face-to-face communication.

focused interaction Interaction between individuals engaged in a common activity or in direct conversation with one another.

encounter A meeting between two or more people in a situation of face-to-face interaction. Our daily lives can be seen as a series of different encounters spread out across the course of the day. In modern societies, many of these encounters are with strangers rather than with people we know.

sions people use to make certain impressions on others. The second are the cues that others may spot to check a person's sincerity or truthfulness. For instance, a restaurant owner listens with a polite smile to the statements of customers about how much they are enjoying their meal. At the same time, he is noting how pleased they seemed to be while eating the food, whether a lot is left over, and the tone of voice they use to express their satisfaction.

Think about how Goffman's concepts of focused and unfocused interaction, developed mainly to explain face-to-face social encounters, apply to the current age. Can you think of a way in which unfocused interaction occurs on Facebook or Twitter? In some of these online communities, anyone can have an awareness of who else is online without being in direct contact with them. On Twitter, people are constantly broadcasting status updates about what they are doing at that moment. These status updates make it possible for people in unfocused interaction to have even more control over how they are perceived than people who are merely in one another's presence. Instead of unconsciously revealing their facial expressions or posture as they would in face-to-face encounters, people can consciously craft the message or tweet they wish to broadcast.

Interaction in Time and Space

Understanding how activities are distributed in time and space is fundamental to analyzing encounters and understanding social life in general. All interaction is situated—it occurs in a particular place and has a specific duration in time. Our actions over the course of a day tend to be "zoned" in time as well as in space. Thus, for example, most people spend a zone—say, from 9:00 A.M. to 5:00 P.M.—of their daily time working. Their weekly time is also zoned: They are likely to work on weekdays and spend weekends at home, altering the pattern of their activities on the weekend days. As they move through the temporal zones of the day, they often are also moving across space; to get to work, they may take a bus from one area of a city to another or perhaps commute from the suburbs. When we analyze the contexts of social interaction, therefore, it is often useful to look at people's movements across **time-space**.

The concept of **regionalization** will help us understand how social life is zoned in time-space. Take the example of a private home. A modern house is regionalized into rooms, hallways, and floors (if there is more than one story). These spaces are not just physically separate areas but are zoned in time as well. The living room and kitchen are used mostly in the daylight hours; the bedrooms, at night. The interaction that occurs in these regions is bound by both spatial and temporal divisions. Some areas of the house form **back regions**, with "performances" taking place in **front regions**. At times, the

time-space When and where events occur.

regionalization The division of social life into different regional settings or zones.

back region Areas apart from front-region performance, as specified by Erving Goffman, in which individuals are able to relax and behave informally.

front region Settings of social activity in which people seek to put on a definite "performance" for others.

clock time Time as measured by the clock, in terms of hours, minutes, and seconds, as opposed to measuring it by the rising and setting of the sun.

whole house can become a back region. Once again, this idea is beautifully captured by Goffman (1973):

> [On] a Sunday morning, a whole household can use the wall around its domestic establishment to conceal a relaxing slovenliness in dress and civil endeavor, extending to all rooms the informality that is usually restricted to kitchen and bedrooms. So, too, in American middle-class neighborhoods, on afternoons the line between children's playground and home may be defined as backstage by mothers, who pass along it wearing jeans, loafers, and a minimum of make-up.

Clock Time

In modern societies, the zoning of our activities is strongly influenced by **clock time**. Without clocks and the precise timing of activities, and thereby their coordination across space, industrialized societies could not exist (Mumford, 1973). Today, the measuring of time by clocks is standardized across the globe, making possible the complex international transport systems and communications we now depend on. World standard time was first introduced in 1884 at a conference of nations held in Washington, D.C. The globe was then partitioned into 24 time zones, one hour apart, and an exact beginning of the universal day was fixed.

Fourteenth-century monasteries were the first organizations to try to schedule the activities of their inmates precisely across the day and week. Today, there is virtually no group or organization that does not do so. The greater the number of people and resources involved, the more precise the scheduling must be. Eviatar Zerubavel (1979, 1982) demonstrated this concept in his study of the temporal structure of a large modern hospital. A hospital must operate on a 24-hour basis, and coordinating the staff and resources is a highly complex matter. For instance, the nurses work for one time period in ward A, another time period in ward B, and so on, and are called on to alternate between day- and night-shift work. Nurses, doctors, and other staff, plus the resources they need, must be integrated in both time and space.

Social Life and the Ordering of Space and Time

The Internet is another example of how closely forms of social life are bound up with our control of space and time. The Internet makes it possible for us to interact with people we never see or meet, in any corner of the world. Such technological change rearranges space—we can interact with anyone without moving from our chair. It also alters our experience of time, because electronic communication is almost immediate. Until about 50 years ago, most communication across space required a duration of time. If you sent a letter to someone

CONCEPT CHECKS

1 What is impression management?

2 Why do we segregate our audiences in daily life?

3 Describe several ways in which individuals communicate their emotions to one another.

4 Compare and contrast focused and unfocused interaction.

5 How does time structure human life?

abroad, there was a time gap while the letter was carried by ship, train, truck, or plane to the person to whom it was written.

People still write letters by hand today, of course, but instantaneous communication has become basic to our social world. Our lives would be almost unimaginable without it. We are so used to being able to switch on the TV and watch the news, make a phone call, or email a friend in another state or country that it is hard for us to imagine what life would be like otherwise.

2   THEORIES OF SOCIAL INTERACTION

Erving Goffman

Many of the concepts we have already reviewed were developed by Erving Goffman, the sociologist who did the most to create a new field of study focused on **social interaction**. Goffman believed that sociologists needed to concern themselves with seemingly trivial aspects of social behavior. His work on social interaction is just one example of the broader sociological subfield called microsociology. Sociologist Harold Garfinkel conceived this term to describe a field of study that focused on individual interaction and communication within small groups. This subfield stood in stark contrast with earlier sociological work, which historically had examined large social groups and societal-level behaviors.

The study of social interaction reveals important things about human social life. Passing someone on the street or exchanging a few words with a friend seem like minor and uninteresting activities, things we do countless times a day without giving them any thought. Goffman argued that the study of such apparently insignificant forms of social interaction is of major importance in sociology and, far from being uninteresting, is one of the most absorbing of all areas of sociological investigation. There are three reasons for this view.

First, our day-to-day routines, with their almost constant interactions with others, give structure and form to what we do; we can learn a great deal about ourselves as social beings, and about social life itself, from studying them. Our lives are organized around the repetition of similar patterns of behavior from day to day, week to week, month to month, and year to year. Think of what you did yesterday, for example, and the day before that. If they were both weekdays, in all probability, you got up at about the same time each day (an important routine in itself). You may have gone off to class fairly early in the morning, making a journey from home to school or college that you make virtually every weekday. You perhaps met some friends for lunch, returning to classes or private study in the afternoon. Later, you retraced your steps back home or to your dorm, possibly going out later in the evening with other friends.

Of course, the routines we follow from day to day are not identical, and our patterns of activity on weekends usually contrast with those on weekdays. If we make a major change in our life, such as leaving college to take a job, alterations in our daily routines are usually necessary, but then we establish a new and fairly regular set of habits again.

Second, the study of everyday life reveals to us how humans can act creatively to shape reality. Although social behavior is guided to some extent by forces such as roles, norms,

social interaction The process by which we act and react to those around us.

and shared expectations, individuals also have **agency**, or the ability to act, think, and make choices independently (Emirbayer and Mische, 1998). The ways that people perceive reality may vary widely based on their backgrounds, interests, and motivations. Because individuals are capable of creative action, they continuously shape reality through their decisions and actions. In other words, reality is not fixed or static—it is created through human interactions.

Third, studying social interaction in everyday life sheds light on larger social systems and institutions. All large-scale social systems, in fact, depend on the patterns of social interaction we engage in daily. This idea is easy to demonstrate. Consider the case of two strangers passing on the street. Such an event may seem to have little direct relevance to large-scale, more permanent forms of social organization. But when we take into account many such interactions, they are no longer irrelevant. In modern societies, most people live in towns and cities and constantly interact with others whom they do not know personally. Civil inattention, a concept discussed earlier, is one of the mechanisms that gives public life—with its bustling crowds and fleeting, impersonal contacts—its distinctive character.

Cultural norms frequently dictate the acceptable boundaries of personal space. In the Middle East, people frequently stand closer to each other than is common in the West.

Edward T. Hall—Personal Space

There are cultural differences in the definition of **personal space**. In Western culture, people usually maintain a distance of at least three feet when engaged in focused interaction with others; when standing side by side, they may stand closer together. In the Middle East, people often stand closer to each other than is thought acceptable in the West. Westerners visiting that part of the world are likely to find themselves disconcerted by this unexpected physical proximity.

Edward T. Hall (1969, 1973), who worked extensively on nonverbal communication, distinguishes four zones of personal space. Intimate distance, of up to one and a half feet, is reserved for very few social contacts. Only those involved in relationships in which regular bodily touching is permitted, such as lovers or parents and children, operate within this zone of private space. Personal distance, from one and a half to four feet, is the normal spacing for encounters with friends and close acquaintances. Some intimacy of contact is permitted, but this tends to be strictly limited. Social distance, from 4 to 12 feet, is the zone usually maintained in formal settings such as interviews. The fourth zone is that of public distance, beyond 12 feet, preserved by those who are performing to an audience.

agency The ability to think, act, and make choices independently.

personal space The physical space individuals maintain between themselves and others.

Table 5.1

APPLYING SOCIOLOGY TO SOCIAL INTERACTION

CONCEPT	APPROACH TO SOCIAL INTERACTION	CONTEMPORARY APPLICATION
Impression Management	When people's sensitivity to the way they are perceived by others causes them to manipulate situations so that others respond to them according to how they wish to be perceived.	Students and those working from home manipulating background images on Zoom to conceal things about their surroundings that they don't wish others to see.
Audience Segregation	When people act differently in particular situations.	People maintaining two separate Instagram accounts—one for family, the other for coworkers or friends.
Civil Inattention	When passersby glance at each other, then look downward in order to avoid eye contact that may be interpreted as overly intrusive.	Young men on the street staring straight into each other's eyes and interpreting this gesture as a threat and goad to physical violence.
Nonverbal Communication	Communication via gesture or facial expression rather than through words.	Using emojis to express emotions in text messages when the sender's face is not visible to the receiving party.
Response Cries	An expression uttered by someone who has made a mistake to indicate that it should not cast doubts on their power of judgment, aptitude, or competence.	A person exclaiming "my bad" or "oops" after discovering that he or she has been wrong about something.
Focused and Unfocused Interaction	When people pay explicit attention to what others say or do vs. when they simply exhibit awareness of others' presence	Friends getting together to talk to each other vs. friends attending to their own electronic devices while in each other's company.
Personal Space	A distance of one to four feet between people is deemed normal during human encounters	People having trouble interacting with others when a six-foot social distancing rule is put into effect during the COVID-19 pandemic.

In ordinary interaction, the most fraught zones are those of intimate and personal distance. If these zones are invaded, people try to recapture their space. We may stare at the intruder as if to say, "Move away!" or elbow him or her aside. When people are forced into proximity closer than they deem desirable, they might create a kind of physical boundary: A reader at a crowded library desk might physically demarcate a private space by stacking books around its edges (Hall, 1969, 1973).

Harold Garfinkel: Ethnomethodology

Although we routinely use nonverbal cues in our own behavior and in making sense of the behavior of others, much of our interaction is done through talk—casual verbal exchange—carried on in informal conversations with others. We can make sense of what is said in conversation only if we know the social context, which does not appear in the words themselves. Take the following conversation (Heritage, 1985):

A: *I have a fourteen-year-old son.*
B: *Well, that's all right.*
A: *I also have a dog.*
B: *Oh, I'm sorry.*

What do you think is happening here? What is the relationship between the speakers? What if you were told that this is a conversation between a prospective tenant and a landlord? The conversation then becomes sensible: Some landlords accept children but don't permit their tenants to keep pets. Yet if we don't know the social context, the responses of individual *B* seem to bear no relation to the statements of *A*. Part of the sense is in the words, and part is in the way in which the meaning emerges from the social context.

The most inconsequential forms of daily talk presume complicated, shared knowledge brought into play by those speaking. In fact, our small talk is so complex that it has so far proved impossible to program even the most sophisticated computers to converse with human beings. The words used in ordinary talk do not always have precise meanings, and we "fix" what we want to say through the unstated assumptions that back it up. If Maria asks Tom, "What did you do yesterday?" the words in the question themselves suggest no obvious answer. A day is a long time, and it would be logical for Tom to answer, "Well, at 7:16, I woke up. At 7:18, I got out of bed, went to the bathroom, and started to brush my teeth. At 7:19, I turned on the shower. . . ." We understand the type of response the question calls for by knowing Maria, what sort of activities she and Tom consider relevant, and what Tom usually does on a particular day of the week, among other things.

Ethnomethodology is the study of the "ethnomethods"—folk or lay methods— that people use to make sense of what others do and particularly of what they say. We all apply these methods, normally without giving any conscious attention to them. This field was created by Harold Garfinkel, who, along with Goffman, was one of the most important figures in the study of micro interaction.

Garfinkel argued that to understand the way people use context to make sense of the world, sociologists need to study the "background expectancies" with which we organize ordinary conversations. He highlighted these in some experiments he undertook with student volunteers (1963). The students were asked to engage a friend or relative in conversation and to insist that casual remarks or general comments be actively pursued to make their meaning precise. If someone said, "Have a nice day," the student was to respond, "Nice in what sense, exactly?" "Which part of the day do you mean?" and so forth. One of the exchanges that resulted ran as follows (*S* is the friend; *E*, the student volunteer) (Garfinkel, 1963):

S: *How are you?*
E: *How am I in regard to what? My health, my finances, my school work, my peace of mind, my . . . ?*
S: *(red in the face and suddenly out of control): Look! I was just trying to be polite. Frankly, I don't give a damn how you are.*

Why do people get so upset when apparently minor conventions of talk are not followed? The answer is that the stability and

> **ethnomethodology** The study of how people make sense of what others say and do in the course of day-to-day social interaction. Ethnomethodology is concerned with the "ethnomethods" by which people sustain meaningful interchanges with one another.

1 What is microsociology?

2 What are three reasons it is important to study daily social interaction?

3 What are the four zones of personal space?

4 How did Garfinkel's students create tense situations?

meaningfulness of our daily social lives depend on the sharing of unstated cultural assumptions about what is said and why. If we weren't able to take these for granted, meaningful communication would be impossible. Any question or contribution to a conversation would have to be followed by a massive "search procedure" of the sort Garfinkel's subjects were told to initiate, and interaction would simply break down. What seem at first sight to be unimportant conventions of talk, therefore, turn out to be fundamental to the very fabric of social life, which is why their breach is so serious.

Note that in everyday life, people on occasion deliberately feign ignorance of unstated knowledge. This may be done to rebuff others, poke fun at them, cause embarrassment, or call attention to a double meaning in what was said. Consider, for example, this classic exchange between parent and teenager:

P: *Where are you going?*
T: *Out.*
P: *What are you going to do?*
T: *Nothing.*

The responses of the teenager are effectively the opposite of those of the volunteers in Garfinkel's experiments. The teenager declines to provide appropriate answers at all—essentially saying, "Mind your own business!"

The first question might elicit a different response from another person in another context:

A: *Where are you going?*
B: *I'm going quietly round the bend.*

B deliberately misreads A's question to convey worry or frustration in an ironic manner. Comedy and joking thrive on such deliberate misunderstandings of the unstated assumptions involved in talk. There is nothing threatening about this behavior, so long as the parties concerned recognize that the intent is to provoke laughter.

3 CONTEMPORARY RESEARCH ON SOCIAL INTERACTION

Interactional Vandalism

Conversations are one of the main ways in which our daily lives are maintained in a stable and coherent manner. We feel most comfortable when the tacit conventions of small talk are adhered to; when they are breached, we can feel threatened, confused, and insecure. In most everyday talk, conversants are carefully attuned to the cues they get from others—such as changes in intonation, slight pauses, or gestures—to facilitate smooth conversation. By being mutually aware, conversants "cooperate" in opening and closing interactions and in taking turns to speak. Interactions in which one party is conversationally "uncooperative," however, can give rise to tensions.

> **conversation analysis** The empirical study of conversations, employing techniques drawn from ethnomethodology. Conversation analysis examines details of naturally occurring conversations to reveal the organizational principles of talk and its role in the production and reproduction of social order.

Garfinkel's students created tense situations by intentionally undermining conversational rules as part of a sociological experiment. But what about situations in the real world in which people make trouble through their conversational practices? One study investigated verbal interchanges between pedestrians and street people in New York City to understand why passersby so often see such interactions as problematic. The researchers used a technique called conversation analysis to compare a selection of street interchanges with samples of everyday talk. **Conversation analysis** is a methodology that examines all facets of a conversation for meaning—from the smallest filler words (such as *um* and *ah*) to the precise timing of interchanges (including pauses, interruptions, and overlap).

The study looked at interactions between black men—many of whom were homeless or addicted to drugs or alcohol—and women who passed by them on the street. The men often tried to initiate conversations with passing women by calling out to them, paying them compliments, or asking them questions. But something "went wrong" in these conversations, because the women rarely responded as they would have in a normal interaction. Even though the men's comments were rarely hostile in tone, the women tended to quicken their step and stare fixedly ahead. The following shows attempts by Mudrick, a black man in his late fifties, to engage women in conversation (Duneier and Molotch, 1999):

Mudrick begins this interaction when a white woman who looks about twenty-five approaches at a steady pace:
1. *Mudrick: I love you, baby.*
She crosses her arms and quickens her walk, ignoring the comment.
2. *Mudrick: Marry me.*
Next, it is two white women, also probably in their mid-twenties:
3. *Mudrick: Hi, girls, you all look very nice today. You have some money? Buy some books.*
They ignore him. Next, it is a young black woman.
4. *Mudrick: Hey, pretty. Hey, pretty.*
She keeps walking without acknowledging him.
5. *Mudrick: 'Scuse me. 'Scuse me. I know you hear me.*
Then he addresses a white woman in her thirties.
6. *Mudrick: I'm watching you. You look nice, you know.*
She ignores him.

Negotiating smooth "openings" and "closings" to conversations is a fundamental requirement for urban civility. These crucial aspects of conversation were highly problematic between the men and women in this study. Where the women resisted the men's attempts at opening conversations, the men ignored the women's resistance and persisted. Similarly, if the men succeeded in opening a conversation, they often refused to respond to cues from the women to close the conversation once it had got-ten underway (Duneier and Molotch, 1999):

1. *Mudrick: Hey, pretty.*
2. *Woman: Hi, how you doin'?*
3. *Mudrick: You alright?*
4. *Mudrick: You look very nice, you know. I like how you have your hair pinned.*
5. *Mudrick: You married?*
6. *Woman: Yeah.*
7. *Mudrick: Huh?*
8. *Woman: Yeah.*
9. *Mudrick: Where the rings at?*
10. *Woman: I have it home.*
11. *Mudrick: Y' have it home?*
12. *Woman: Yeah.*
13. *Mudrick: Can I get your name?*
14. *Mudrick: My name is Mudrick. What's yours?*

She does not answer and walks on.

In this instance, Mudrick made 9 out of the 14 utterances in the interaction to initiate the conversation and to elicit further responses from the woman. From the transcript alone, it is quite evident that the woman is not interested in talking, but when conversation analysis is applied to the tape recording, her reluctance becomes even clearer. Even when she does respond, the woman delays all her responses, while Mudrick replies immediately, his comments sometimes overlapping hers. Timing in conversations is a very precise indicator; delaying a response by even a fraction of a second is adequate in most everyday interactions to signal the desire to change the course of a conversation. By betraying these tacit rules of sociability, Mudrick was practicing conversation in a way that was technically rude. The woman, in return, was also technically rude in ignoring Mudrick's repeated attempts to engage her in talk. It is the technically rude nature of these street interchanges that make them problematic for passersby to handle. When standard cues for opening and closing conversations are not adhered to, individuals feel a sense of profound and inexplicable insecurity.

The term **interactional vandalism** describes cases like these in which a subordi-nate person breaks the tacit rules of everyday interaction that are of value to the more powerful person. The men on the street often do conform to everyday forms of speech in their interactions with one another, local shopkeepers, the police, relatives, and acquain-tances. But when they choose to, they subvert the tacit conventions for everyday talk in a way that leaves passersby disoriented. Even more than physical assaults or vulgar verbal abuse, interactional vandalism leaves victims unable to articulate what has happened.

This study of interactional vandalism provides another example of the two-way links between micro-level interactions and forces that operate on the macro level. To the men on the street, the women who ignore their attempts at conversation appear distant, cold, and bereft of sympathy—legitimate "targets" for such interactions. The women, mean-while, may often take the men's behavior as proof that they are indeed dangerous and

interactional vandalism The deliberate subversion of the tacit rules of conversation.

best avoided. Interactional vandalism is closely tied up with overarching class, gender, and racial structures. The fear and anxiety generated in such mundane interactions help reinforce the outside statuses and forces that, in turn, influence the interactions themselves. Interactional vandalism is part of a self-reinforcing system of mutual suspicion and incivility.

Interactional Vandalism Online

The Internet creates spaces in which less powerful people can make their superiors accountable in ways they never were before. Think of all the blogs in which workers talk anonymously about their bosses or situations in which workers forward rude messages from their boss to other employees. Because of the Internet, powerful people are less able to segregate their audiences—treating some people poorly behind the scenes and treating others very nicely in public.

The concept of "trolling" might be seen as an interactional mode that shares certain, though not all, aspects of interactional vandalism. A troll is a person who is anonymously disruptive

By approaching a woman on the street and trying to initiate a conversation, Mudrick engaged in interactional vandalism.

of the taken-for-granted purposes of an online space such as a message board. As such, he or she might post deliberately provocative items. Such provocations might have the effect of undermining the civility that is a foundation for the kind of communication the site's founders envisioned. Or the controversies raised by trolls can sometimes increase traffic to the site.

To what extent is trolling an example of interactional vandalism of the kind found in face-to-face communication on the sidewalk? Like the poor black men who act sincere as they pretend not to understand that a two-second pause is a signal to close a conversation, a troll will pretend not to understand certain assumptions of the conversational world for the specific purpose of being disruptive. Like the poor men on the street, the troll will write as if they are a sincere member of the group who perhaps does not understand certain things, while at a deeper level, they know precisely what they are doing.

Some readers of a comment posted by a troll might be lured further into the interaction, while others will attempt to restore normal order by dismissing the troll's actions. In interactional vandalism on the sidewalk, a less powerful person is subverting normal interaction to undermine the taken-for-granted control of someone in a superordinate position. In trolling, the parties are often anonymous, so it's not always possible to know what the actual power dynamics are. Are the anonymous people, in fact, less powerful members, or could they be very well-known members of the community who are using the board to further their own agenda?

Interaction on the "Digital Street"

Recently, sociologists have looked at how the proliferation of smartphones and the rise of social media are changing how boys and girls interact in public spaces. For teenagers in low-income urban areas, the street has long served as a hub of social life and dating. Street interactions between boys and girls may incorporate aspects of both courtship and the incivility that characterizes street talk between adult men and women who are strangers. Today, these encounters are reshaped online, or what urban sociologist Jeffrey Lane refers to as the "digital street." Lane (2018) studied a cohort of teenagers in Harlem and found that boys and girls had changed the experience of public space by using social media to buffer interaction. Whereas boys were more visible and acted more dominant toward girls on the sidewalk, girls gained visibility and control online.

While for some of the boys in Lane's study, social media provided *another,* alternative way to call out to girls, other boys engaged girls digitally *instead* of on the sidewalk. Messaging girls in private, rather than approaching them face to face on the sidewalk, shielded boys from public rejection in front of their friends when advances went unmet. But private messages were not necessarily the best strategy. Christian, one of the teenagers in Lane's study, explained that "a girl hates" when a boy writes "a million messages, like, 'What's up, I'm trying to talk to you.'" Instead, Lane found that a girl would rather a boy like one of her photos and then leave the girl to make the next move. The use of social media enabled ways to communicate at different distances and paces that steered teens either away from or toward meetings in person.

Lane argued that girls and, to a lesser extent, boys were safer with social media. But traditionally gendered norms of interaction and roles also carried forward. For instance, boys and girls alike articulated the pressure on young women to objectify their bodies online. "Girls get naked for likes," said one 18-year-old girl in Lane's research. False identity was another issue. Unlike in physical space, appearance and person may decouple online in the case of "fake pages" or "catfishes"—profiles that depict someone other than its user. The possibility of a fake page created trust issues among boys and girls, and these issues were compounded by the fact that law enforcement used profiles designed to mimic girls in the neighborhood to monitor and gather intelligence on boys of interest.

The role of social media raises new questions of how people come to find and know each other today. Do people have more understanding or even control over the people around them and their potential meetings? Or are people newly vulnerable online?

The Macro-Micro Link: Anderson's *Streetwise*

In his book *Streetwise: Race, Class, and Change in an Urban Community* (1990), Elijah Anderson describes social interaction on the streets of two adjacent urban neighborhoods, noting that studying everyday life sheds light on how the individual building blocks of infinite micro-level interactions create social order. He is particularly interested in understanding interactions when at least one party was viewed as threatening. Anderson shows that the manner in which many blacks and whites interact on the streets of a northern city in the United States has a great deal to do with the structure of racial stereotypes, which itself is linked to the economic structure of society. In this way, he reveals the link between micro interactions and the larger macro structures of society.

Anderson begins by recalling Erving Goffman's description of how social roles and statuses come into existence in particular contexts or locations:

> When an individual enters the presence of others, they commonly seek to acquire information about him or bring into play information already possessed. . . . Information about the individual helps to define the situation, enabling others to know in advance what he will expect of them and they may expect of him. (Anderson, 1990)

Following Goffman's lead, Anderson (1990) asked what types of behavioral cues and signs make up the vocabulary of public interaction. He concluded that skin color, gender, age, companions, clothing, jewelry, and the objects people carry help identify them, allowing assumptions to be formed and communication to occur. Movements (quick or slow, false or sincere, comprehensible or incomprehensible) further refine this public communication. Factors such as time of day or an activity that "explains" a person's presence can also affect how and how quickly the image of "stranger" is neutralized. If a stranger cannot pass inspection and be assessed as "safe," the image of predator may arise, and fellow pedestrians may try to maintain a distance consistent with that image.

According to Anderson, the people most likely to pass inspection are those who do not fall into commonly accepted stereotypes of dangerous persons: "Children readily pass inspection, while women and white men do so more slowly, black women, black men, and black male teenagers most slowly of all." In showing that interactional tensions derive from outside statuses such as race, class, and gender, Anderson makes clear that we cannot develop a full understanding of the situation by looking at the micro interactions themselves. This is how he makes the link between micro interactions and macro processes.

Anderson argues that people are streetwise when they develop skills such as "the art of avoidance" to deal with their felt vulnerability toward violence and crime. According to Anderson, whites who are not streetwise do not recognize the difference between different kinds of black men (e.g., middle-class youths versus gang members). They may also not know how to alter the number of paces to walk behind a suspicious person or how to bypass bad blocks at various times of day. In these ways, social science research can help you understand how a very ordinary behavior—navigating one's way through the city streets—reveals important lessons about the nature of contemporary social interaction.

Immediate assumptions based on race, gender, class, and style of dress, among other signs and behavioral cues, affect the way strangers interact. Elijah Anderson's study of social interaction between strangers on urban streets showed a strong connection between such micro-level interactions and the creation of social order.

The Cosmopolitan Canopy

Although public space can often be a site of tension and anxiety, the sociologist Elijah Anderson argues in *The Cosmopolitan Canopy* (2011) that social interaction in urban spaces is not all doom and gloom. There are many places where people of different backgrounds actually get along. For Anderson, the racially and ethnically diverse spaces he has studied offer "a respite from the lingering tensions of urban life as well as an opportunity for diverse peoples to come together." They are what he calls "pluralistic spaces where people engage with one another in a spirit of civility, or even comity and goodwill."

On the basis of in-depth observations of public areas in his long-time home of Philadelphia, Anderson reports on various important sites in the city. These include the Reading Terminal Market, Rittenhouse Square, and the Galleria Mall. The first two are venues dominated by middle- and upper-middle-class norms and values, while the Galleria caters to the tastes of the black working classes and the poor. All three sites, however, are spaces in which various kinds of people meet, agree to lay down their swords, carry on their life routines, and, in many cases, enjoy themselves.

Anderson begins with an ode to Philadelphia's indoor farmer's market—the downtown Reading Terminal Market. A regular at the market for decades, he paints a loving portrait of the many types of people who congregate there, including the population of Amish vendors. The patrons range from corporate executives to construction workers to senior citizens in poor health. They are all "on their best behavior" as they eat and shop for food and other items.

What is it about this space that causes people to "show a certain civility and even an openness to strangers"? To begin, the city is divided into two kinds of human beings: the open-minded people, whom he calls "cosmos" (shorthand for cosmopolitan), and the close-minded, whom he calls "ethnos" (shorthand for ethnocentric). As Anderson sees it, Reading Terminal Market is filled with open-minded people. Through a kind

of people watching, each contributes to the creation of the cosmopolitan canopy. It is literally the sight of so many kinds of people in one another's physical presence, as well as participation in what one sees, that reinforces the idea of a "neutral space." Whites and minorities who have few opportunities for such interaction elsewhere can relax and move about with security. Blacks, however, understand that their status there is always provisional, meaning that at any moment, they are subject to dramatic situations in which whites fail to treat them with the respect they deserve.

The dynamic that Anderson highlights over and over is the self-fulfilling nature of the interaction: The interaction and the sight of it makes it so. Most who come are probably repeat players, and they have long visualized different kinds of people getting along in the space. For newcomers, on the other hand, such visualiza-

Community pools are an example of what Elijah Anderson refers to as a cosmopolitan canopy, an area where diverse groups of people can come together and engage in a "spirit of civility."

tion of tolerance is "infectious." In the Ritten-house Square Park and the streets surrounding it, other social cues serve to bring about similar results. There is, for example, a fountain and a statue of a goat that attract mothers, nannies, and children. The sight of "public mothering" is a cue that indicates this is a civil place. A sense of safety and protection underlies good behavior and, in turn, leads to a virtuous circle of other acts of good will. Dog walkers are also crucial, with interaction naturally occurring between them and others (including children) as they form a critical mass in the park throughout the day. In a similarly positive encounter, when an elderly white woman has trouble standing up, a man sitting on a nearby bench rises and offers his hand to help. As Anderson notes: "Those of us who observed this act realized that we ourselves might expect such help or be called upon to render it."

CONCEPT CHECKS

1 What is interactional vandalism?

2 What does Anderson mean by the term "streetwise"?

3 How would you explain the street harassment that women often experience?

4 Can you identify any examples of cosmopolitan canopies in your neighborhood?

The Galleria is a different story. Anderson describes it as the "ghetto downtown," a community of close-minded poor blacks ("ethnos") in one mall. What makes it a canopy, albeit not a cosmopolitan one, is that various elements of the black community—the "street" and the "decent"—can coexist here. People feel free to be themselves, "loud and boisterous and frank in their comments, released from the inhibitions they might feel among Whites." The code of the street threatens to undermine the public order at any moment, but everyone is on their best behavior, with security guards reinforcing decorum. Nevertheless, Anderson stresses that through a negative feedback loop, this place has a self-reinforcing negative reputation among cosmopolitan whites and blacks. It arises from cues the nonwhite population on the streets around the mall give off and culminates in occasional deeply disturbing incidents such as the "flash mob"—high school students organized through Facebook and Twitter who suddenly appear on the downtown streets "wreaking havoc on businesses and terrifying pedestrians." Anderson continues: "As quickly as this storm appears out of the blue, it is over, but the effects are lasting, powerfully redefining the public spaces of the canopy zone" (98).

4 UNANSWERED QUESTIONS

How Do We Manage Impressions in the Internet Age?

The concept of "audience segregation" helps us understand some of the dilemmas of electronic communication. Many people are very sensitive about having things sent to their business email address if they don't want their coworkers or supervisors to know about them. Thus, they maintain different addresses for home (back region) and office (front region), a practice that is increasingly important because many companies have policies against sending personal email from a company's computer.

Or consider the social situation of a copied message. You write a message to a friend asking her whether she prefers to go to the early show or the late show. You also tell your friend that you have a new boyfriend whom you hope she'll like. She replies and copies the other people who are thinking of going to the movie, many of whom you never intended to tell about the new romance. Suddenly, the audience segregation you had imagined has broken down.

In recent years, undergraduate students have posted pictures of themselves drinking at parties, or even naked, only to discover that future employers conducted web searches before making hiring decisions. Some students have even found themselves expelled from their colleges for posting inappropriate Facebook photos or comments. For example, in April 2017, Harvard University rescinded admissions offers to at least 10 students who circulated offensive memes within a private Facebook group for prospective Harvard students. Another example of blurring audiences is the case of sexting; a high school student may send a revealing photo of herself to her boyfriend, only to have him forward it to the entire school—whether out of cruelty or by mistake. Personal catastrophes such as these, and ones far worse, occur frequently in the age of email and smartphones.

What Happens When Dating Moves Online?

How did you meet your last romantic partner? Perhaps you met at a party or sat next to each other in your introduction to sociology course. Can you remember what it was that drew you to him or her? Was there something subtle or unexpected that signaled to you there might be an attraction, like a tone of voice, a wink, or light touch to the shoulder? Or did you already have a clear-cut notion of the kind of person you wanted to date—maybe someone tall, or who shared your religious background, or who had professional goals similar to your own—and you carefully surveyed those whom you saw as an "appropriate" partner, before making your move?

While popular music suggests that two strangers will lock eyes across a crowded room and true love will follow, in our current digital age, meetings often happen in a far less romantic and more strategic way. According to a recent survey of more than 2,000 Americans 18 years of age or older, 15 percent of adults have used a mobile dating app or website (Smith, 2016). Dozens of smartphone apps like Tinder, Hinge, Bumble, Adventurely, and Happn allow people to search through endless photos of eligible partners and screen them, or "swipe right," based on personal preferences like education, occupation, age, height, body weight, gender, sexual orientation, and race. Usage is particularly high among young adults: More than a quarter (27 percent) of 18- to 24-year-olds have used a mobile dating app or website. Two-thirds of those who meet potential partners online have gone out on a date.

Although apps may take the romance and intrigue out of dating, they do fulfill a practical function. Young people can shop for a date in exactly the same way they would shop for a new car; they can specify precisely what they want and search for potential partners who possess those traits. From a sociological perspective, many apps provide strong evidence that norms of "homogamy," or dating and marrying a partner similar to oneself, are still pervasive in U.S. society. New studies also show that apps provide evidence of "hypergamy," or the preference for women, typically, to partner with a man with richer socioeconomic resources than her own.

For instance, sociologist Kevin Lewis (2013) analyzed data from more than 126,000 dating site users and found that users tended to show the greatest interest in those of their same ethnic background. He analyzed only the first message sent and first reply of each user. He found the strongest tendency to initiate contact within one's own race among East and South Asians and Indians and weakest among whites. He found that while users would respond to a message from someone from a different ethnic or racial group, this open-mindedness was relatively short-lived; most would promptly return to their old patterns of communicating only with members of their own group.

A social network analysis study of online dating in site users found that norms of homogamy are still pervasive in the United States.

Lewis's analyses also uncovered evidence that users hold dating preferences consistent with "highly gendered status hierarchies." For instance, women tend to seek out men with more education and more income than they themselves have. Although men also sought educated partners, they tended to show greatest interest in women with a college education—"no more and no less." Racial hierarchies also emerged. White men, Lewis found, enjoyed a privileged position, receiving the most initial messages, while black women received the fewest.

Additionally, more than a quarter of online daters report having been contacted in a way that made them feel harassed or uncomfortable. Not surprisingly, perhaps, a significant gender difference exists here: 42 percent of women complained about this type of contact, compared with 17 percent of men (Pew Research Center, 2013b). It turns out that online dating interactions tend to be gendered as well. One study of nearly 15,000 men and women found that men are far more likely to initiate online exchanges than are women, an unfortunate asymmetry because

> women who initiate conversations have greater odds of success with equally desirable partners than women who wait to be messaged, but women are much less likely to seize the initiator advantage. In other words, by relying on men to initiate a relationship, women often forego the promise of online dating and are left wondering where all the good men have gone. (Kreager et al., 2014)

The authors conclude that rather than placing men and women on an equal footing when it comes to establishing intimate partnerships, online dating actually reproduces gender inequality. Whether in a crowded bar or sheltered by the initial privacy of their mobile phones, women are less likely to make the first move, and this reluctance works to their disadvantage. The study's message to women is clear: Don't be shy. As the study notes, "Women should not be discouraged from sending messages if they want to contact attractive partners" (Kreager et al., 2014).

It remains unclear whether online dating is preferable to meeting the old-fashioned way. On the plus side, it provides access to a large number of potential partners in an initially anonymous setting, which may be of special benefit for those too shy or introverted to initiate direct face-to-face contact. The use of online questionnaires, which permit would-be partners to determine whether they are compatible before they ever meet, ideally provides a relatively safe way to winnow out poor choices. Yet the very anonymity of online dating invites deception, ranging from the unintentional (are most people accurate judges of their best personality traits?) to outright deception (lying about one's age, physical characteristics, or even marital status). One study concludes:

> Deliberate deception is unlikely, however, to account for the entire difference between online and offline impression formation. Even when deception is not an issue, face-to-face interaction still conveys information that cannot be gleaned readily from CMC [Computer Mediated Communication]. In particular, CMC is unlikely to convey experiential attributes as effectively as face-to-face interactions. (Finkel et al., 2012)

Online dating may be efficient, easy, and increasingly common, but it has yet to prove that it's preferable to locking eyes across a crowded room.

To What Extent Can Electronic Communication Substitute for Face-to-Face Communication?

In modern societies, we are constantly interacting with others whom we may never see or meet. Almost all our everyday transactions, such as buying groceries or making a bank deposit, bring us into contact—but indirect contact—with people who may live thousands of miles away. The banking system, for example, is international. Any money you deposit is a small part of the financial investments the bank makes worldwide.

Some people are concerned that the rapid advances in communication technology, such as email, the Internet, e-commerce, and social media, will only increase this tendency toward indirect interactions. More than two-thirds (69 percent) of all U.S. adults are on Facebook, with fully 74 percent visiting the site at least once a day (Perrin and Anderson, 2019). Among Facebook users, 7 percent say they are connected to people they have never met in person (Hampton, Gulet, and Purcell, 2011). Now that email, social networking sites, and electronic discussion groups have become facts of life for many people in industrialized countries, it is important to ask, what is the nature of these interactions and what new complexities are emerging from them?

Our society is becoming "devoiced," some claim, as the capabilities of technology grow ever greater. According to this view, as the pace of life accelerates, people are increasingly isolating themselves; we now interact more with our televisions and computers than with our neighbors or members of the community. Some researchers conclude that the substitution of email for face-to-face communication has led to a weakening of social ties and a disruption of techniques used in per-

Individuals, including world leaders, often prefer face-to-face interaction because it provides critical information not available via electronic communication.

sonal dialogue for avoiding conflict. Further, online communication seems to allow more room for misinterpretation, confusion, and abuse than more traditional forms of communication (Friedman and Currall, 2003).

compulsion of proximity People's need to interact with others in their presence

Many Internet enthusiasts, however, disagree. They argue that social relations continue to thrive and might even be facilitated by frequent online communication (Hampton et al., 2011; Wellman, 2008). Far from being impersonal, they argue, online communication has many inherent advantages that cannot be claimed by more traditional forms of interaction such as the telephone and face-to-face meetings. The human voice, for example, may be far superior in terms of expressing emotion and subtleties of meaning, but it can also convey information about the speaker's age, gender, ethnicity, or social position—information that could be used to the speaker's disadvantage. Electronic communication, it is noted, masks all these identifying markers and ensures that attention focuses strictly on the content of the message. This can be a great advantage for women or other traditionally disadvantaged groups whose opinions are sometimes devalued in other settings (Locke and Pascoe, 2000). Electronic interaction is often presented as liberating and empowering because people can create their own online identities and can speak more freely than they would elsewhere.

Recent research shows that social networking may even enhance social integration and friendships (Hampton et al., 2011). A national survey conducted by the Pew Internet and American Life Project reports that persons who use social networking sites are more trusting, have more close relationships, receive more emotional and practical social support, and are more politically engaged than those who do not use such sites. For many people, online relationships are quite meaningful. Further, people can communicate with those who don't share their geographic region; perhaps you have reconnected via Facebook with childhood friends who live hundreds of miles away.

Who is right in this debate? How far can electronic communication substitute for face-to-face interaction? Sociologists Deirdre Boden and Harvey Molotch (1994) argue that there is no substitute for face-to-face interaction. They argue further that humans have a true need for personal interaction, which they call the **"compulsion of proximity."** People put themselves out to attend meetings, Boden and Molotch suggest, because situations of copresence (for reasons documented by Goffman in his studies of interaction) provide much richer information about how other people think and feel, and about their sincerity, than any form of electronic communication. Only by actually being in the presence of people who make decisions affecting us in important ways do we feel able to learn what is going on and feel confident that we can impress them with our own views and our sincerity. "Co-presence," Boden and Molotch (1994) say, "affects access to the body part that 'never lies': the eyes, the 'windows on the soul.' Eye contact itself signals a degree of intimacy and trust; co-present interactants continuously monitor the subtle movements of this most subtle body part."

CONCEPT CHECK

1 Is face-to-face interaction, or copresence, an important aspect of human action? Why or why not?

THE BIG PICTURE

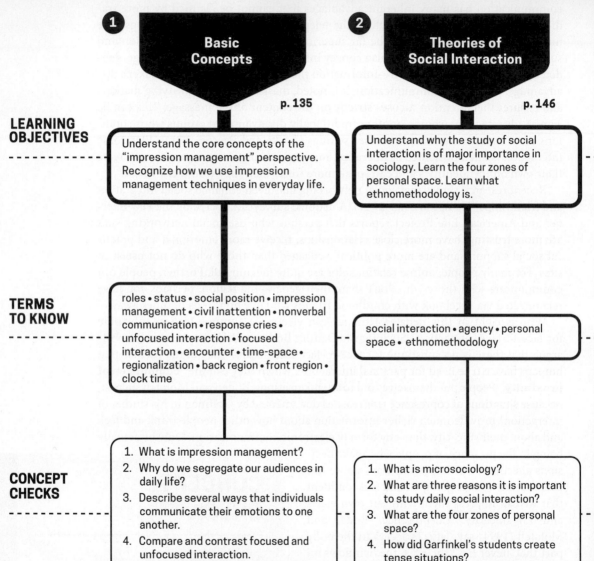

1 **Basic Concepts**

p. 135

2 **Theories of Social Interaction**

p. 146

LEARNING OBJECTIVES

Understand the core concepts of the "impression management" perspective. Recognize how we use impression management techniques in everyday life.

Understand why the study of social interaction is of major importance in sociology. Learn the four zones of personal space. Learn what ethnomethodology is.

TERMS TO KNOW

roles • status • social position • impression management • civil inattention • nonverbal communication • response cries • unfocused interaction • focused interaction • encounter • time-space • regionalization • back region • front region • clock time

social interaction • agency • personal space • ethnomethodology

CONCEPT CHECKS

1. What is impression management?
2. Why do we segregate our audiences in daily life?
3. Describe several ways that individuals communicate their emotions to one another.
4. Compare and contrast focused and unfocused interaction.
5. How does time structure human life?

1. What is microsociology?
2. What are three reasons it is important to study daily social interaction?
3. What are the four zones of personal space?
4. How did Garfinkel's students create tense situations?

Exercises: Thinking Sociologically

1. Identify the important elements to the dramaturgical perspective. This chapter shows how such a perspective might be applied in viewing the ministrations of a nurse to his or her patient. Apply the theory to account for a plumber's visit to a client's home. Are there any similarities? Explain.

2. Smoking cigarettes is a pervasive habit found in many parts of the world and a habit that could be explained by both microsociological and macrosociological forces. Give an example of each that would be relevant to explain the proliferation of smoking. How might your suggested micro- and macro-level analyses be linked?

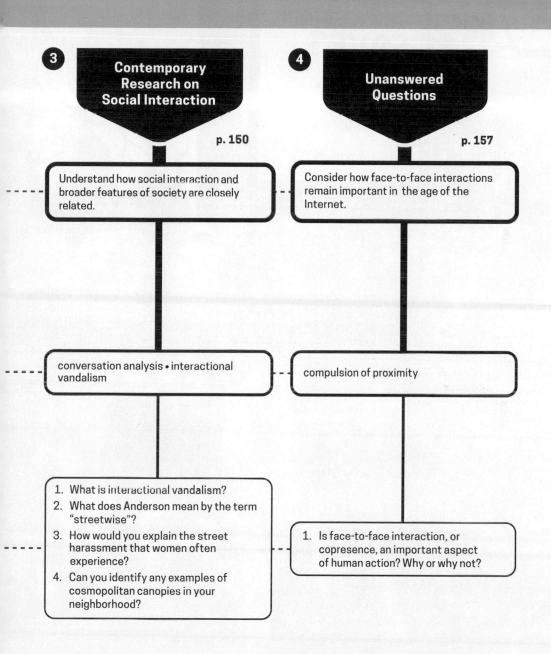

3 Contemporary Research on Social Interaction

p. 150

Understand how social interaction and broader features of society are closely related.

conversation analysis • interactional vandalism

1. What is interactional vandalism?
2. What does Anderson mean by the term "streetwise"?
3. How would you explain the street harassment that women often experience?
4. Can you identify any examples of cosmopolitan canopies in your neighborhood?

4 Unanswered Questions

p. 157

Consider how face-to-face interactions remain important in the age of the Internet.

compulsion of proximity

1. Is face-to-face interaction, or copresence, an important aspect of human action? Why or why not?

6

Networks, Groups, and Organizations

How many people can ultimately contract COVID-19 if a single carrier of the virus is allowed to go about his life unchecked?

- **A** 200
- **B** 5000
- **C** 25,000
- **D** 59,000

TURN THE PAGE FOR THE CORRECT ANSWER.

magine all the people to whom one average individual is directly and indirectly bound. The spread of COVID-19 can actually help us visualize the gigantic networks to which we are all consciously and unconsciously bound. Difficult as it may be to believe, the correct answer here is, in fact, d) 59,000 (Snow, 2020)! To understand just how quickly the virus can travel, let us take a look at "patient zero," the first person in the metropolitan New York area to be diagnosed with COVID-19.

On March 2, 2020, New Rochelle resident Lawrence Garbuz, an attorney and founding partner of a Manhattan law firm, tested positive for the new coronavirus. Most likely he caught the virus locally as he had not travelled to any of the countries already hit by the pandemic. Knowing the speed with which the illness could spread, health investigators immediately began retracing the attorney's steps and alerting those with whom he had spent time in the days leading up to his diagnosis. By March 10, the single case had grown to a cluster of 90, and by March 12, New York State Governor Andrew Cuomo had imposed a mile-radius coronavirus containment zone around the city of New Rochelle.

networks Sets of informal and formal social ties that link people to each other.

The situation in New Rochelle can best be understood through the lens of sociology, most notably through the concept of the social **network**, that is, all the direct and indirect connections that link one particular individual or group with other people or groups. Following the footsteps of the investigators in this case, we can trace the network of this individual by examining the trajectory of the contagion.

In the week prior to his diagnosis with COVID-19, Garbuz, a member of a tight-knit Modern Orthodox Jewish community who commutes daily on the Metro-North railway to his office in Manhattan, had had personal contact with between 800 and 1,000 people at two events that he had attended on the same day: a joint bar and bat mitzvah at the Young Israel of New Rochelle synagogue, and the funeral service of Marek Appell, a 91-year-old Holocaust survivor. Not long afterwards, Garbuz fell ill and was taken by a neighbor to a local hospital, where he was initially diagnosed with pneumonia. Only four days later was he tested for the new coronavirus. In the time between

LEARNING OBJECTIVES

1 Basic Concepts

Learn the variety and characteristics of networks and groups, as well as the effect they have on individual behavior. Know how to define an organization and understand how organizations developed over the last two centuries.

2 Theories of Networks, Groups, and Organizations

Learn Max Weber's theory of organizations and view of bureaucracy. Understand the importance of the physical setting of organizations and Michel Foucault's theory of surveillance. Understand the importance of social networks and the advantages they give some people.

THE ANSWER IS D.

his hospital admission and the test, Garbuz came into contact with dozens of physicians, nurses, medical technicians, orderlies, and other patients. Once health officials learned of the diagnosis, they reached out to administrators at SAR High School and Yeshiva University, where Garbuz's 14-year-old daughter and 20-year-old son were students. Classes at both institutions were immediately cancelled and teachers and students who had come in contact with the Garbuz's children were ordered to self-quarantine. Within two weeks, 46 students, faculty, and parents at the high school had tested positive, as had Garbuz's wife and children, the neighbor who had driven him to the hospital, and dozens of other individuals who had spent time with him during that period. In addition, many of the people who had socialized with Garbuz at the bar/bat mitzvah or funeral service had gone on to attend other bar mitzvahs or social functions before realizing that COVID-19 had surreptitiously entered their midst. By mid-April, the total number of infected in Westchester County had exceeded 24,000, making it the tenth-hardest-hit county in the United States.

3 Contemporary Research on Networks and Groups

Learn what the term "McDonaldization" means. Understand how social networks can influence you in unexpected ways. Discover how the Internet has transformed relationships between groups and social networks.

4 Unanswered Questions

Learn what Robert Michels meant by the iron law of oligarchy. Consider how information and communication technology is transforming organizations.

As we can see from this scenario, Garbuz's network encompassed people he knew both directly (his friends and family) and indirectly (his friends' friends and families). Also included in his network were the organizations in which he participated directly (his temple and law firm) and indirectly (his children's high school and university, the local medical facility). As he was an active member of a large religious community that spilled over into neighboring towns, the virus was able to quickly penetrate the county, spreading anxiety across the region.

Practically overnight, life in the local Jewish community was totally transformed: the activities that had always helped bound it together—synagogue services, Shabbat dinners, bar and bat mitzvahs, weddings, and funerals—were now proscribed by social-distancing ordinances issued by the government, while school and daily prayers shifted to video-conferencing platforms. In the words of one local rabbi, "Between the first Tuesday and the second Tuesday, it all changed."

The shock experienced by members of the community as they struggled to adjust to this new disconnected reality was captured by a comment posted on Facebook by Garbuz's wife, Alina Lewis. Updating her friends on her husband's condition, she exclaimed: "He is trying to comprehend a world where no one goes out, no social gatherings, no religious services, no Purim!!"

In this chapter we will consider the importance of social networks to every aspect of our existence, from matters of life and death to getting a job. We will also study different kinds of groups, the ways in which their size affects our behavior, and the nature of leadership. In addition, we will explore how group norms promote conformity, often to disastrous ends. We will then proceed to examine the role played by organizations in American society, look at major theories of modern organizations as well as at the ways in which organizations are changing in the modern world due to the impact of technology and the prominence of the Internet in our group life. We will end by discussing the debate over the decline in social capital and social engagement in the United States today.

1   BASIC CONCEPTS

Networks

Networks are crucial aspects of human life. On the one hand, they can lead to the death of large numbers of people, as occurred in the COVID-19 pandemic. But they also can serve us in many positive ways. You are likely to rely on your networks for a broad range of contacts, from getting into a sorority or fraternity to scoring a summer internship. But understanding how these networks work highlights important differences between biological and social outbreaks (Kucharski, 2020). When a virus spreads through a population, the closer the contact between people, the greater the chance for infection. But in social life, the opposite can also be true. Sociologist Mark Granovetter (1973) demonstrated that there can be enormous strength in "weak ties," particularly among higher socioeconomic groups. Upper-level professional and managerial employees are likely to hear about new jobs through connections such as distant relatives or remote acquaintances. Such weak ties can be of great benefit because relatives or acquaintances tend to have very different sets of connections from one's closer friends, whose social contacts are likely to be similar to one's own. Among lower socioeconomic groups, Granovetter argued, weak ties are not necessarily bridges to other networks and so do not really widen one's opportunities (see also Knoke 1990; Marsden and Lin 1982; Wellman, Carrington, and Hall 1988).

Most people rely on their personal networks to gain advantages, but not everyone has equal access to powerful networks. In general, whites and men have more advantageous social networks than do ethnic minorities and women. Some sociologists argue, for example, that women's business, professional, and political networks are fewer and weaker than men's, so that women's power in these spheres is reduced (Brass 1985). Yet as more and more women move up into higher-level occupational and political positions, the resulting networks can foster further advancement. One study found that women are more likely to be hired or promoted into job levels that already have a high proportion of women (Cohen, Broschak, and Haveman 1998).

The Internet as Social Network

Our opportunities to belong to and access social networks have skyrocketed in recent years due to the Internet. Until the early 1990s, when the World Wide Web was developed, there were few Internet users outside of university and scientific communities. By the end of 2017, however, an estimated 287 million Americans were using the Internet (Internet World Stats 2017), and while 52 percent of American adults used the Internet in 2000, 89 percent were online in 2018 (Pew Research Center 2019b). With such rapid communication and global reach, it is now possible to radically extend one's personal networks. Fully 57 percent of American teens have made new friends online (Lenhart 2015). It also enables people who might otherwise lack contact with others to become part of global networks. For example, people too ill to leave their homes can join online social networks or consult message boards, people in small rural communities can now take online college courses (Lewin 2012), and long-lost high school friends can reconnect via Facebook.

Launched in 2004, Facebook has more than 2.45 billion monthly active users and is one of the most popular tools for building online social networks.

The Internet fosters the creation of new relationships, often without the emotional and social baggage or constraints that go along with face-to-face encounters. In the absence of the usual physical and social cues, such as skin color or residential address, people can get together electronically on the basis of shared interests, such as gaming, rather than similar social characteristics. Factors such as social position, wealth, race, ethnicity, gender, and physical disability are less likely to cloud the social interaction (Coate 1994; Jones 1995; Kollock and Smith 1996). In fact, technologies like Twitter allow people from all walks of life to catch glimpses into the lives of celebrities (as well as noncelebs).

One limitation of Internet-based social networks is that not everyone has equal access to the Internet. Lower-income persons and ethnic minorities are less likely than wealthier persons and whites to have Internet access. But while a digital divide remains, the gaps have narrowed considerably in recent years. For example, in 2000, 81 percent of American adults in households earning $75,000 or more a year used the Internet, compared to just 34 percent of those who made less than $30,000. By 2019, however, this nearly 50 percent gap had narrowed to 16 percent, with 82 percent of those who make less than $30,000 per year now using the Internet (Pew Research Center, 2019b). There remains a larger gap in usage by level of education: While 97 percent of adults with a college degree are Internet users, that proportion drops to 65 percent for those with less than a high school education. A similar gap in Internet use exists between young adults (ages eighteen to twenty-nine) and older adults (ages sixty-five and older): While 100 percent of young adults are using the Internet, the same can be said of only 73 percent of older adults. This pattern is not limited to the United States; rates of Internet use are creeping up across the globe, enabling individuals to connect with anyone in the world who shares their interests.

Groups

Much of importance in life occurs through some type of social group. You and your roommate make up a social group, as do the members of your introductory sociology class. A **social group** is a collection of people who have a common identity and who regularly interact with one another on the basis of shared expectations concerning behavior. People who belong to the same social group identify with one another, expect one another to conform to certain ways of thinking and acting, and recognize the boundaries that separate them from other groups or people. In our need to congregate and belong, we have created a rich and varied group life that gives us our norms, practices, and values—our whole way of life.

We sometimes feel alone, yet we are seldom far from one kind of group or another. Every day, nearly all of us move through various social situations. We hang out with friends, study with classmates, play team sports, and go online to meet people who share our interests.

But just being in one another's company does not make a collection of individuals a social group. People milling around in crowds, waiting for a bus, or strolling on a beach make up what is called a **social aggregate**—a collection of people who happen to be together in a particular place but do not significantly interact or identify with one another. People waiting together at a bus station, for example, may be aware of one another, but they are unlikely to think of themselves as a "we"—the group waiting for the next bus to Poughkeepsie or Des Moines. By the same token, people may make up a **social category**—people sharing a common characteristic such as gender or occupation—without necessarily interacting or identifying with one another. The sense of belonging to a common social group is missing.

Group life differs greatly in how intensely members experience it. Beginning with the family—the first group to which most of us belong—many of the groups that shape our personalities and lives are those in which we experience strong emotional ties. This is common not only for families but also for groups of friends, including gangs and other peer groups, all of which are known as primary groups. **Primary groups** are small groups characterized by face-to-face interaction, intimacy, and a strong sense of commitment. Members of primary groups often experience unity, a merging of the self with the group into one personal "we." The sociologist Charles Horton Cooley (1864–1929) termed such groups "primary" because he believed that they were the basic form of association, exerting a long-lasting influence on the development of our social selves (Cooley, 1964; orig. 1902).

In contrast, **secondary groups** are large and impersonal and seldom involve intense emotional ties, enduring relationships, powerful commitments to the group itself, or a feeling of unity. Examples of secondary groups include businesses, schools, work groups, athletic clubs, and governmental bodies. We rarely feel we can be ourselves in

social group A collection of people who regularly interact with one another on the basis of shared expectations concerning behavior and who share a sense of common identity.

social aggregate A simple collection of people who happen to be together in a particular place but do not significantly interact or identify with one another.

social category People who share a common characteristic (such as gender or occupation) but do not necessarily interact or identify with one another.

primary groups Groups that are characterized by intense emotional ties, face-to-face interaction, intimacy, and a strong, enduring sense of commitment.

secondary groups Groups characterized by large size and by impersonal, fleeting relationships.

What makes the people in the image on the left a social aggregate and the people on the right a social group?

a secondary group; rather, we are often playing a role, such as employee or student. Cooley argued that while people belong to primary groups mainly because membership is fulfilling, people join secondary groups to achieve a specific goal: to earn a living, get a college degree, or compete on a sports team. Secondary groups may become primary groups. For example, when students taking a course together socialize after class, they create bonds of friendship that constitute a primary group.

For most of human history, nearly all interactions took place within primary groups. This pattern began to change with the emergence of larger agrarian societies, which included such secondary groups as those based on governmental roles or occupations. Today, most of our waking hours are spent within secondary groups, although primary groups remain a basic part of our lives.

Some early sociologists, such as Cooley, worried about a loss of intimacy as more and more interactions revolved around large, impersonal organizations. However, what Cooley saw as the growing impersonality and anonymity of modern life may also offer increasing tolerance of individual differences. Primary groups often enforce strict conformity to group standards (Durkheim, 1964; orig. 1893; Simmel, 1955). Secondary groups are more likely to be concerned with accomplishing a task than with enforcing conformity.

Conformity

Not so long ago, the only part of the body that American teenage girls were likely to pierce was the ears—one hole per ear, enough to hold a single pair of earrings. For the vast majority of boys, piercing was not an option. Today, earrings are common for men. From teenage boys to male professional athletes to college students, a growing number of males now sport multiple earrings. Pressure to conform to the latest styles is especially strong among teenagers and young adults, among whom the need for group acceptance is often acute.

While sporting earrings or the latest style of jeans may seem relatively harmless, conformity to group pressure can lead to destructive behavior, such as drug abuse or even murder. For this reason, sociologists and social psychologists have long sought to understand why most people tend to go along with others and under what circumstances they do not.

Going Along with the Group: Asch's Research

Some of the earliest studies of conformity to group pressures were conducted by psychologist Solomon Asch (1952). In a classic experiment, Asch asked subjects to decide which of three lines of different length most closely matched the length of a fourth line (Figure 6.1). The differences were obvious; subjects had no difficulty making the correct match. Asch then arranged a version of the experiment in which the subjects were asked to make the matches in a group setting, with each person calling out the answer in turn. In this version, all but one of the subjects were actually Asch's confederates. Each confederate picked as matches two lines that were clearly unequal in length. The unwitting subject, one of the last to answer, felt enormous group pressure to make the same match. Amazingly, one-third of the subjects gave the same answer as the others in the group at least half the time, even though that answer was clearly wrong. They sometimes stammered and fidgeted when doing so, but they nonetheless yielded to the unspoken pressure to conform to the group's decision. Asch's experiments showed that many people are willing to discount their own perceptions rather than buck group consensus.

Figure 6.1
THE ASCH TASK

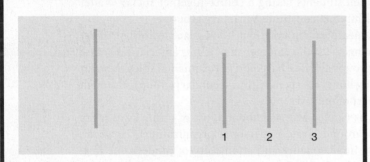

In the Asch task, participants were shown a standard line (left) and then three comparison lines. Their task was simply to say which of the three lines matched the standard line. When confederates gave false answers first, one-third of participants conformed by giving the wrong answer at least half the time.

Obedience to Authority: Milgram's Research

Another classic study of conformity was conducted by Stanley Milgram (1963). Milgram's work was intended to shed some light on what happened in Nazi Germany during World War II. How could ordinary German citizens have gone along with, and even participated in, the mass extermination of millions of Jews, Romanies (Gypsies), homosexuals, intellectuals, and others whom the Nazis judged to be inferior or undesirable?

Obedience is a kind of conformity, and Milgram sought to find its limits. He wanted to see how far a person would go when ordered by a scientist to give another person increasingly powerful electric shocks. So he set up an experiment that he told the subjects was about memorizing pairs of words. In reality, it was about obedience to authority. Milgram's study would not be permitted today, because the deception of subjects and its potential for doing psychological harm would violate current university ethics standards.

The subjects who volunteered for the study were supposedly randomly divided into "teachers" and "learners." In fact, the learners were Milgram's confederates. The teacher was told to read pairs of words from a list that the learner was to memorize. Whenever the learner made a mistake, the teacher was to give him an electric shock by flipping a switch on a fake but official-looking machine. The control board indicated shock levels ranging from "15 volts—slight shock" to "450 volts—danger, severe shock." For each mistake, the voltage was to be increased, until it reached the highest level. In reality, the learner, who was usually concealed from the teacher by a screen, never received any shocks.

As the experiment progressed, the learner began to scream out in pain for the teacher to stop delivering the shocks. (The screams, which grew louder as the voltage rose, had actually been prerecorded.) Milgram's assistant, who was administering the experiment, exercised his authority as a scientist and, if the teacher tried to quit, ordered the teacher to continue administering shocks. The assistant would say things such as "the experiment requires that you continue," even when the learner was tearfully protesting—even when he shrieked about his "bad heart."

The teacher was confronted with a major moral decision: Should he obey the scientist and go along with the experiment, even if it meant injuring another human being? Much to Milgram's surprise, over half the subjects administered the shocks until the maximum voltage was reached and the learner's screams had subsided into an eerie silence as he presumably died of a heart attack. How could ordinary people so easily obey orders that would turn them into possible accomplices to murder?

The answer, Milgram found, was surprisingly simple. Although it is obvious that soldiers in training will obey orders given by someone in a position of power or authority, ordinary citizens will often do the same—even if those orders have horrible consequences. From this experience, we can learn something about Nazi atrocities during World War II, which were Milgram's original concern. Many of the ordinary Germans who participated in the mass executions in concentration camps did so on the grounds that they were just following orders. Milgram's research has sobering implications for anyone who thinks that only "others" will bend to authority, but "not me" (Zimbardo, Ebbesen, and Maslach, 1977).

Organizations

People frequently band together to pursue activities that they cannot do by themselves. A principal means of accomplishing such cooperative actions—whether it's

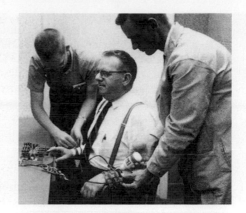

The Milgram experiment required participants to "shock" the confederate learner (seated). The research participant (top) helped apply the electrodes that would be used to shock the learner. An obedient participant (middle) shocks the learner in the "touch" condition. More than half obeyed the experimenter in this condition. After the experiment, all the participants were introduced to the confederate learner (bottom) so they could see he was not actually harmed.

organization A large group of individuals with a definite set of authority relations. Many types of organizations exist in industrialized societies, influencing most aspects of our lives. While not all organizations are bureaucratic, there are close links between the development of organizations and bureaucratic tendencies.

formal organization A group that is rationally designed to achieve its objectives, often by means of explicit rules, regulations, and procedures.

raising money for ALS research, winning a football game, or becoming a profitable corporation—is the **organization**, a group with an identifiable membership that engages in concerted collective actions to achieve a common purpose (Aldrich and Marsden, 1988). An organization can be a small primary group, but it is more likely a larger secondary one. Universities, religious bodies, and business corporations are all examples of organizations. Such organizations are a central feature of all societies, and their study is a core concern of sociology.

Organizations tend to be highly formal in modern industrial and postindustrial societies. A **formal organization** is designed to achieve its objectives, often by means of explicit rules, regulations, and procedures. The modern bureaucratic organization, discussed later in this chapter, is a prime example of a formal organization. As Max Weber (1979; orig. 1921) recognized almost a century ago, there has been a long-term trend in Europe and North America toward formal organizations, in part because formality is often a requirement for legal standing. For a college or university to be accredited, for example, it must satisfy explicit written standards governing everything from grading policy to faculty performance to fire codes. Today, formal organizations are the dominant form of organization throughout the world.

Social systems in the traditional world developed as a result of custom and habit. Modern organizations are designed with definite aims and housed in buildings or physical settings constructed to help realize those aims. Organizations play a more important part in our everyday lives than ever before. Besides delivering us into this world (hospital), they also mark our progress through it (school) and see us out of it when we die (hospital, funeral home). Even before we are born, our mothers, and often our fathers, are involved in birthing classes, pregnancy checkups, and so forth, all carried out within hospitals and other medical organizations. Today, every child born is registered by government organizations, which collect information on all of us from birth to death. Most people today die in a hospital—not at home, as was once the case—and each death must be formally registered with the government.

It is easy to see why organizations are so important today. In the premodern world, families, relatives, and neighbors provided for most needs—food, the instruction of children, work,

CONCEPT CHECKS

1 According to Granovetter, what are the benefits of weak ties? Why?

2 What is the difference between social aggregates and social groups? Give examples that illustrate this difference.

3 Describe the main characteristics of primary and secondary groups.

4 What role do organizations play in contemporary society?

and leisure-time activities. In modern times, many of our requirements are filled by people we never meet and who might live and work thousands of miles away. Substantial coordination of activities and resources—which organizations provide—is needed in such circumstances.

But the tremendous influence organizations have on our lives cannot be seen as wholly beneficial. Organizations often take things out of our own hands and put them under the control of officials or experts over whom we have little influence. For instance, we are required to do certain things the government tells us to do—pay taxes, obey laws, fight wars—or face punishment. As sources of social power, organizations can subject people to dictates they may be powerless to resist.

2 THEORIES OF NETWORKS, GROUPS, AND ORGANIZATIONS

In-Groups and Out-Groups

The "sense of belonging" that characterizes social groups is sometimes strengthened by scorning other groups (Sartre, 1965; orig. 1948). This is especially true of racist groups, which promote their identity as superior by hating "inferior" groups. Jews, Catholics, African Americans and other people of color, immigrants, and gay people historically—and Muslims more recently—have been the targets of such prejudice in the United States. This sense of group identity created through scorn is dramatically illustrated by the website rantings of a racist skinhead group called Combat 18 (1998): "We are the last of our warrior race, and it is our duty to fight for our people. The Jew will do everything to discredit us, but we hold that burning flame in our hearts that drove our ancestors to conquer whole continents."

Such proud, disdainful language illustrates the sociological distinction between in-groups and out-groups. **In-groups** are groups toward which one feels loyalty and respect—the groups that "we" belong to. **Out-groups** are groups toward which one feels antagonism and contempt—"those people." At one time or another, many of us have used in-group/out-group imagery to trumpet what we believe to be our group's strengths vis-à-vis another group's presumed weaknesses. For example, fraternity or sorority members may bolster their feelings of superiority—in academics, sports, or campus image—by ridiculing the members of a different house. Similarly, a church may hold up its "truths" as the only ones, while native-born Americans may accuse immigrants—always outsiders upon arriving in a new country—as ruining the country for "real Americans."

Reference Groups

We often judge ourselves by how we think we appear to others, which Cooley termed the "looking-glass self." Groups as well as individuals provide the standards by which we

in-groups Groups toward which one feels particular loyalty and respect—the groups to which "we" belong.

out-groups Groups toward which one feels antagonism and contempt—"those people."

Advertising creates a set of imaginary reference groups meant to influence consumers' buying habits by presenting unlikely, often impossible, ideals to which consumers aspire.

make self-evaluations. Robert K. Merton (1968; orig. 1938) elaborated on Cooley's work by introducing the concept of the **reference group**—a group that provides a standard for judging one's attitudes or behaviors (see also Hyman and Singer, 1968). Family, peers, classmates, and coworkers are crucial reference groups. However, you don't have to belong to a group for it to be a reference group. Regardless of his or her station in life, a person may identify with the wealth and power of Fortune 500 corporate executives, admire the contributions of Nobel Prize–winning scientists, or be captivated by the glitter of Hollywood stars. Although few of us interact socially with such reference groups, we may take pride in identifying with them, glorify their accomplishments, and even imitate the behavior of their members. This is why it is critical for children—minority children in particular, whose groups are often represented with negative stereotypes in the media—to be exposed to reference groups that model positive standards of behavior.

Reference groups may be primary (such as the family) or secondary (such as a group of soldiers). They may even be fictional. One of the chief functions of advertising is to create a set of imaginary reference groups that will influence consumers' buying habits. For example, when cosmetic ads feature thin models with flawless complexions, the message is simple: "If you want to look as though you are part of an ingroup of highly attractive, eternally youthful women, buy this product." In reality, the models seldom have the unblemished features depicted; instead, the ideal features are constructed through artful lighting, photographic techniques, and computer enhancement. Similarly, the happy-go-lucky, physically perfect young men and women seen sailing or playing volleyball or hang gliding in beer commercials have little to do with the reality of most of our lives—or, indeed, with the lives of the actors in those commercials. The message, however, is otherwise: "Drink this beer, and you will be a member of the carefree in-group in this ad."

reference group A group that provides a standard for judging one's attitudes or behaviors.

dyad A group consisting of two persons.

The Effects of Size

Another significant way in which groups differ has to do with their size. Sociological interest in group size can be traced to Georg Simmel (1858–1918), a German sociologist who studied and theorized about the impact of small groups on people's behavior. Since Simmel's time, small-group researchers have examined the effects of size on both the quality of interaction in the group and the effectiveness of the group in accomplishing certain tasks (Bales, 1953, 1970; Homans, 1950; Mills, 1967).

Dyads

The simplest group, which Simmel (1955) called a **dyad**, consists of two people. Simmel reasoned that dyads, which involve both intimacy and conflict, are likely to be simultaneously intense and unstable. To survive, they require the full attention and cooperation of both parties. If one person withdraws from the dyad, it vanishes. Dyads are typically the source of our most elementary social bonds, often constituting the group in which we are likely to share our deepest secrets. But dyads can be fragile. That is why, Simmel believed, numerous cultural and legal supports for marriage—an example of a dyad—are found in societies in which marriage is regarded as an important source of social stability.

Triads

Adding a third person changes the group relationship. Simmel used the term **triad** to describe a group of three people. Triads tend to be more stable than dyads because the presence of a third person relieves some of the pressure on the other two members to always get along and energize the relationship. In a triad, one person can temporarily withdraw attention from the relationship without necessarily threatening it. In addition, if two of the members have a disagreement, the third can play the role of mediator, as when you try to patch up a falling-out between two of your friends.

On the other hand, alliances (sometimes termed *coalitions*) may form between two members of a triad, enabling them to gang up on the third and thereby destabilize the group. Alliances are most likely to form when no one member is clearly dominant and when all

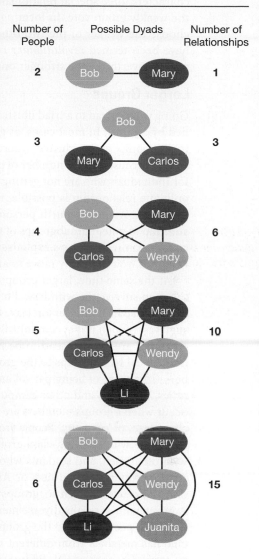

Figure 6.2
DYADS

Number of People	Possible Dyads	Number of Relationships
2	Bob — Mary	1
3	Bob, Mary, Carlos	3
4	Bob, Mary, Carlos, Wendy	6
5	Bob, Mary, Carlos, Wendy, Li	10
6	Bob, Mary, Carlos, Wendy, Li, Juanita	15

The larger the number of people, the greater the possible number of relationships. Note that this figure illustrates only dyads; if triads and more complex coalitions were to be included, the numbers would be still greater (4 people yield 10 possibilities). Even a 10-person group can produce 45 possible dyads!

triad A group consisting of three persons.

three members are competing for the same thing—for example, when three friends are given a pair of tickets to a concert and have to decide which two will go. The TV series *Survivor* provides many examples of alliance formation, as the program's characters forge special relationships with one another to avoid being eliminated in the weekly group vote. In forming an alliance, a member of a triad is most likely to choose the weaker of the two other members as a partner, if there is one. In what have been termed *revolutionary coalitions*, the two weaker members form an alliance to overthrow the stronger one (Caplow, 1956, 1959, 1969).

Larger Groups

Going from a dyad to a triad illustrates an important sociological principle first identified by Simmel: In most cases, as groups grow in size, their intensity decreases while their stability and exclusivity increase. Larger groups have less intense interactions, simply because a larger number of potential smaller group relationships exist as outlets for individuals who are not getting along with other members of the group. In a dyad, only one relationship is possible; in a triad, three different two-person relationships can occur. Adding a fourth person leads to six possible two-person relationships, in addition to potential subgroups of three. In a 10-person group, the number of possible two-person relationships explodes to 45 (Figure 6.2)! When one relationship doesn't work out, you can easily move to another, as you probably often do at large parties.

At the same time, larger groups tend to be more stable than smaller ones because they can survive the withdrawal of some members. A marriage or romantic relationship falls apart if one person leaves, whereas an athletic team or drama club routinely survives, though it may temporarily suffer from the loss of its graduating seniors.

Larger groups also tend to be more exclusive because it is easier for members to limit social relationships to the group itself and to avoid relationships with nonmembers. This sense of being part of an in-group, or clique, is sometimes found in fraternities, sororities, and other campus organizations. Cliquishness is especially likely to occur when a group's members are similar in such social characteristics as age, gender, class, race, or ethnicity. People from rich families, for example, may be reluctant to fraternize with working-class groups, men may prefer to go to the basketball court with other men, and students who belong to a particular ethnic group (for example, African Americans, Latinos, or Asian Americans) may seek out one another in the dorm or cafeteria. Even so, groups do not always restrict relationships with outsiders. A group with a socially diverse membership is likely to foster a high degree of interaction with people outside the group (Blau, 1977). For example, if your social group or club has members from different social classes or ethnic groups, you are more likely to appreciate such social differences from firsthand experience and seek them out in other aspects of your life.

Beyond a certain size (perhaps a dozen people), groups tend to develop a formal structure. Formal leadership roles may arise, such as president or secretary, and official rules may be developed to govern what the group does.

Theories of Organizations

Max Weber developed the first systematic interpretation of the rise of modern organizations. Organizations, he argued, are ways of coordinating the activities of human beings or the goods they produce in a stable way across space and time. Weber emphasized that the development of organizations depends on the control of information, and he stressed the central importance of writing in this process. An organization needs written rules to function and files in which to store its "memory." Weber saw organizations as strongly hierarchical, with power tending to concentrate at the top. Was Weber right? It matters a great deal, for Weber detected a clash as well as a connection between modern organizations and democracy that he believed had far-reaching consequences for social life.

Bureaucracy

All large-scale organizations, according to Weber, tend to be bureaucratic in nature. The word *bureaucracy* was coined in 1745 by Jean-Claude Marie Vincent de Gournay, who combined the word *bureau*, meaning both an office and a writing table, with the suffix *cracy*, a term derived from the Greek verb meaning "to rule." **Bureaucracy** is thus the rule of officials. The term was first applied only to government officials, but it gradually came to refer to large organizations in general.

From the beginning, the concept was used disparagingly. De Gournay spoke of the developing power of officials as "an illness called bureaumania." The nineteenth-century French novelist Honoré de Balzac saw bureaucracy as "the giant power wielded by pygmies." This view persists today. Bureaucracy is frequently associated with red tape, inefficiency, and wastefulness. Others, however, have seen bureaucracy as a model of carefulness, precision, and effective administration. Bureaucracy, they argue, is the most efficient form of human organization, because, in it, all tasks are regulated by strict procedures.

Weber's account of bureaucracy steers between these two extremes. A limited number of bureaucratic organizations, he pointed out, existed in traditional civilizations. For example, a bureaucratic officialdom in imperial China was responsible for the overall affairs of government. But only in modern times have bureaucracies developed fully.

According to Weber, the expansion of bureaucracy is inevitable in modern societies; bureaucratic authority is the only way of coping with the administrative requirements of large-scale social systems. However, as we will see, Weber also believed bureaucracy exhibits a number of major failings that have important implications for modern social life.

To study the origins and nature of bureaucratic organizations, Weber constructed an **ideal type** of bureaucracy. (*Ideal* here refers not to what is most desirable but to a pure form of bureaucratic organization, one that accentuates certain features of real cases so as to pinpoint essential characteristics.) Weber (1979; orig. 1921) listed several characteristics of the ideal type of bureaucracy:

1. **There is a clear-cut hierarchy of authority.** Tasks in the organization are distributed

bureaucracy A type of organization marked by a clear hierarchy of authority and the existence of written rules of procedure and staffed by full-time, salaried officials.

ideal type A "pure type," constructed by emphasizing certain traits of a social item that do not necessarily exist in reality. An example is Max Weber's ideal type of bureaucratic organization.

as "official duties." A bureaucracy looks like a pyramid, with the positions of highest authority at the top. A chain of command stretches from top to bottom, thus making possible the coordination of decisions. Each higher office controls and supervises the one below it in the hierarchy.

2. **Written rules govern the conduct of officials at all levels of the organization.** This does not mean that bureaucratic duties are just a matter of routine. The higher the office, the more the rules tend to encompass a wide variety of cases and to demand flexibility in their interpretation.

3. **Officials work full time and are salaried.** Each job in the hierarchy has a definite and fixed salary attached to it. Individuals are expected to make a career within the organization. Promotion is possible on the basis of capability, seniority, or a combination of the two.

4. **There is a separation between the tasks of an official within the organization and his or her life outside.** The home life of the official is distinct from his or her activities in the workplace and is also physically separated from it.

5. **No members of the organization own the materials with which they operate.** The development of bureaucracy, according to Weber, separates workers from the control of their means of production. In traditional communities, farmers and craft workers usually had control over their processes of production and owned the tools they used. In bureaucracies, officials do not own the offices they work in, the desks they sit at, or the office machinery they use.

Weber believed that the more an organization approaches the ideal type of bureaucracy, the more effective it will be in reaching its goals. He likened bureaucracies to sophisticated machines operating according to rational principles (see Chapter 1). Yet he also recognized that bureaucracy could be inefficient and that many bureaucratic jobs are dull, offering little opportunity for creativity. Although Weber feared that the bureaucratization of society could have negative consequences, he concluded that bureaucratic routine and the authority of officialdom were the prices we pay for the technical effectiveness of bureaucratic organizations. Since Weber's time, the bureaucratization of society has become more widespread. Critics of this development who share Weber's initial concerns have questioned whether the efficiency of rational organizations comes at a cost greater than Weber imagined. The most prominent of these critiques is known as the "McDonaldization" of society, which we will discuss later in this chapter.

While bureaucracy is often associated with long lines and excessive paperwork, it can also be an efficient way to organize modern societies. Here, a young woman attends a Dream Relief workshop, where undocumented immigrants can apply for work permits and deportation deferrals.

Formal and Informal Relations within Bureaucracies

Weber's analysis of bureaucracy gave prime place to **formal relations** within organizations, relations as stated in the organization rules. Weber had little to say about the informal connections and small-group relations that exist in all organizations. But in bureaucracies, informal ways of doing things often allow for a flexibility that couldn't otherwise be achieved.

In a classic study, Peter Blau (1963) looked at **informal relations** in a government agency that investigated possible income-tax violations. Agents who came across difficult cases were supposed to discuss them with their immediate supervisor; the rules of procedure stated that they should not consult colleagues at their same level. Most agents were wary about approaching their supervisors, however, because they felt it might suggest a lack of competence on their part and reduce their chances for promotion. Hence, they usually consulted one another, violating the official rules. This breaking of the rules not only helped provide concrete advice but also reduced the anxieties involved in working alone. A cohesive set of loyalties representative of a primary group thus developed among those working at the same level. The problems these workers faced, Blau concludes, were probably addressed more effectively as a result. The group was able to develop informal procedures that allowed for more initiative and responsibility than the formal rules of the organization permitted.

Informal networks tend to develop at all levels of organizations. At the top, personal ties and connections may be more important than the formal situations in which decisions are supposed to be made. For example, meetings of boards of directors and shareholders supposedly determine the policies of business corporations. In practice, a few members of the board often run the corporation, making their decisions informally and expecting the rest of the board to approve them. Informal networks of this sort can also stretch across different corporations. Business leaders from different firms frequently consult one another informally and may belong to the same clubs and social circles.

John Meyer and Brian Rowan (1977) argue that formal rules and procedures are usually quite distant from the practices an organization's members actually adopt. Formal rules, in their view, are often "myths" that people profess to follow but that have little substance in reality. The rules serve to legitimize—to justify—ways in which tasks are carried out, even while these ways may diverge greatly from how the rules say things are supposed to be done. Formal procedures, Meyer and Rowan point out, often have a ceremonial or ritual character. People make a show of conforming to them but get on with their real work using other, more informal procedures. For example, rules governing ward procedure in a hospital help justify how nurses act toward patients. Thus, a nurse will faithfully fill in the chart at the end of a patient's bed but will actually check progress by means of other, informal criteria—how the patient looks and whether the patient seems alert and lively. Rigorously

> **formal relations** Relations that exist in groups and organizations, as laid down by the norms, or rules, of the official system of authority.
>
> **informal relations** Relations that exist in groups and organizations developed on the basis of personal connections; ways of doing things that depart from formally recognized modes of procedure.

© Wiley Ink, inc./Distributed by Universal Uclick via Cartoonstock

Bureaucracies are often perceived as inefficient and fraught with red tape.

keeping up the charts impresses the patients and keeps the doctors happy, but it is not always essential to the nurse's assessments.

Deciding how much informal procedures help or hinder the effectiveness of organizations is not a simple matter. Systems that resemble Weber's ideal type tend to give rise to a multitude of unofficial ways of doing things. This workaround happens partly because the flexibility that is lacking ends up being achieved by unofficial tinkering with formal rules. For those in dull jobs, informal procedures often create a more satisfying work environment. Informal connections among officials in higher positions may be effective in ways that aid the organization as a whole.

Table 6.1

APPLYING SOCIOLOGY TO NETWORKS, GROUPS, AND ORGANIZATIONS

THEORY	APPROACH TO UNDERSTANDING GROUPS	CONTEMPORARY APPLICATION
Weber's theory of organizations and bureaucracy	A bureaucracy is a type of organization with a clear hierarchy of authority, written rules of procedure, and full-time, salaried officials.	Students at a large university may be frustrated by red tape and bureaucracy, as they consult many different offices before arriving at an answer to a question about their tuition bill.
Foucault's theory of surveillance	In hierarchical organizations, persons with lower levels of authority and status are especially susceptible to surveillance, including direct oversight by superiors, and the monitoring of one's personal records like employment history.	Salesclerks at discount chain stores are monitored by hidden cameras, by having managers check to make sure their cash drawers equal their sales each night, and other forms of oversight.
Simmel's theory of group size	Human interactions are shaped by group sizes. Larger groups have less intense interactions, because a larger number of potential smaller group relationships exist as outlets for individuals who are not getting along with other members of the group.	A college student is nervous about living with just one roommate (dyad), in case they don't get along, and two roommates (triad), in case the other two "gang up" on her. A larger setting, like a group house or sorority, provides a greater number of less intense social ties.
Merton's reference group theory	Reference groups provide a standard for judging one's attitudes or behaviors. Humans use as reference groups people they know as well as people they don't (e.g., media figures).	A star high school athlete feels very confident in their abilities, as they rank first in their school. However, when they compare their feats to Olympians their age, or when they compete in varsity sports in college, their own skills may feel less stellar in comparison.

The Control of Time and Space

Michel Foucault (1971, 1975) showed that the architecture of an organization is directly involved with its social makeup and system of authority. By studying the physical characteristics of organizations, we can shed new light on the problems Weber analyzed. The offices Weber discussed abstractly are also architectural settings—rooms, separated by corridors. The buildings of large firms are sometimes actually constructed as a hierarchy, in which the more elevated one's position, the nearer to the top of the building one's office is; not for nothing does "the top floor" refer to those who hold ultimate power in an organization.

In many other ways, the geography of an organization affects its functioning, especially when systems rely heavily on informal relationships. Physical proximity makes forming primary groups easier, whereas physical distance can polarize groups, resulting in a "them" and "us" attitude between departments.

The arrangement of rooms, hallways, and open spaces in an organization's buildings provides basic clues to how the organization's system of authority operates. In some organizations, people work collectively in open settings. Because of the dull, repetitive nature of certain kinds of industrial work, such as assembly-line production, regular supervision is needed to ensure that workers sustain the pace of labor. The same is often true of routine work carried out by telephone operators who respond to calls for information and who sit together where their activities are visible to their supervisors. Foucault laid great emphasis on how visibility, or lack of it, in the architectural settings of modern organizations influences and expresses patterns of authority. The level of visibility determines how easily subordinates can be subject to **surveillance**—the supervision of activities in organizations. In modern organizations, everyone, even those in relatively high positions of authority, is subject to surveillance; but the lowlier a person is, the more his or her behavior tends to be scrutinized.

> **surveillance** The supervising of the activities of some individuals or groups by others in order to ensure compliant behavior.

Surveillance takes two forms. One is the direct supervision of the work of subordinates by superiors. Consider the example of a school classroom. Pupils sit at tables or desks, usually arranged in rows, all in view of the teacher. They are supposed to look alert or be absorbed in their work. Of course, the extent to which this actually happens depends on the abilities of the teacher to command attention and the inclinations of the children to do what is expected of them.

In addition to direct supervision of subordinates' work, surveillance also takes the form of files, records, and work histories.

1 When groups become large, why does their intensity decrease but their stability increase?

2 What does the term *bureaucracy* mean?

3 Describe five characteristics of an ideal type of bureaucracy.

timetables The means by which organizations regularize activities across time and space.

The second type of surveillance is subtler but equally important. It consists of keeping files, records, and case histories about people's work lives. Weber realized the importance of written records (nowadays usually computerized) in modern organizations but did not fully explore how they could be used to regulate behavior. Employee records usually provide complete work histories, including personal details and often character evaluations. Such records are used to monitor employees' behavior and assess recommendations for promotion. In many businesses, individuals at each level in the organization prepare annual reports on the performances of those in the level just below them. In schools, transcripts are used to monitor students' performance as they move through the organization. Records are kept on file for academic staff, too.

Organizations cannot operate effectively if employees' work is haphazard. In business firms, as Weber pointed out, people are expected to work regular hours. Activities must be consistently coordinated in time and space, something promoted by both the physical settings of organizations and the precise scheduling of detailed **timetables**, which regularize activities across time and space. In Foucault's words, timetables "efficiently distribute bodies" around the organization. They are a condition of organizational discipline because they organize, or schedule, the activities of large numbers of people. If a university did not observe a lecture timetable, for example, it would soon collapse into complete chaos.

3 CONTEMPORARY RESEARCH ON GROUPS

The "McDonaldization" of Society?

George Ritzer (1993) developed a vivid metaphor to express his view of the transformations in industrialized societies. He argues that we are witnessing the "McDonaldization" of society—"the process by which the principles of the fast-food restaurant are coming to dominate more and more sectors of American society as well as the rest of the world." Ritzer uses the four guiding principles of McDonald's restaurants—efficiency, calculability, uniformity, and control through automation—to show that our society is becoming ever more rationalized.

If you have visited a McDonald's in two different countries, you will have noticed that few differences exist between them. The interior decoration may vary slightly, and the language used will most likely differ, but the layout, the menu, the procedure for ordering, the uniforms, the tables, the packaging, and the "service with a smile" are virtually identical. The McDonald's experience is designed to be the same whether you are in Bogota or Beijing. No matter where they are, McDonald's customers can expect quick service with a minimum of fuss and a standardized product that is reassuringly consistent. The McDonald's system is constructed to maximize efficiency and minimize human responsibility and involvement in the process. Except for certain key tasks, such as taking orders and pushing the Start and Stop buttons on cooking equipment, the restaurants' functions are highly automated and largely run themselves.

Ritzer argues that society as a whole is moving toward this highly standardized and regulated model. Many aspects of our daily lives, for example, now involve automated systems and computers instead of human beings. Email and texts are replacing letters and phone calls; e-commerce is threatening to overtake trips to the store; ATMs outnumber bank tellers; and prepackaged meals provide a quicker option than cooking. And if you have recently tried to call a large organization such as an airline, you know that it is almost impossible to speak to a human being. Automated touch-tone information services are designed to answer your requests; only in certain cases will you be connected to a live employee. Ritzer, like Weber before him, is fearful of the harmful effects of rationalization on the human spirit and creativity. He argues that McDonaldization is making social life more homogeneous, more rigid, and less personal.

Personal Taste

Are our music choices a matter of personal taste or an example of conforming behavior? We tend to think of the music we listen to as an intensely personal choice made independently of the people around us and one that reflects our individual personalities and preferences. How much, however, do our group memberships and social networks shape our most personal of decisions, such as our aesthetic tastes?

Social scientists Matthew Salganik, Peter Dodds, and Duncan Watts (2006) conducted research to test the effects of the influence of social networks on musical choices. To do so, they created an artificial cultural market on a website named Music Lab. More than 14,000 participants registered with the site and were asked to listen to music by bands with which they were unfamiliar and then rate how much they liked the songs. If they liked the music, they could download songs. The researchers first divided their sample into two groups. Those in the control group were unable to use the website to see what other participants were listening to. Members of the experimental, or "treatment," group,

Ritzer argues that more and more sectors of American society are adopting the principles of the fast-food industry. The Swedish furniture chain IKEA has applied McDonald's guiding principles to the furniture shopping experience with its low prices, predictable and controlled environment, and huge global presence.

or the "social influence" group, were able to see what other participants on the site were listening to as well as downloading. The social influence group was further placed into eight "worlds," and participants could see only the rankings and number of down-loads of people in their world.

The researchers found that in the social influence groups, the most popular songs were more popular than those in the control group—that is, when participants knew what songs were favored by others, they were more likely to favor those songs them-selves. The most popular song in each world was also different, providing further evi-dence of the importance of group influence. This suggests that the determinants of popularity in music were based on the listener's social "world." That is, the "intrinsic" quality of the music mattered less than the number of people in each world who were listening to the song, giving it high ratings, and downloading it.

The authors of the study described the effect of social networks as a "cumulative advantage" where "if one object happens to be slightly more popular than another at just the right point, it will tend to become more popular still. As a result, even tiny, ran-dom fluctuations can blow up, generating potentially enormous long-run differences among even indistinguishable competitors—a phenomenon that is similar in some ways to the famous 'butterfly effect' in chaos theory" (Watts, 2007). The butterfly effect proposes that small variations may produce large variations in the long-term behavior of a system or organism. Salganik, Dodds, and Watts's study revealed the impact of our social networks, which are now increasingly virtual networks, on our music decisions.

Studying how consumers make decisions is a part of a much deeper sociological tra-dition that is concerned with conformity, propaganda, and the question of how leaders have persuaded whole populations to take part in horrific deeds. The Holocaust, which claimed the lives of more than 6 million Jews and millions of others, left many social scientists searching to understand how, why, and under what conditions ordinary peo-ple would conform to authority. Many students who have seen or read about Stanley Milgram's laboratory experiments or the "make-believe jail" experiment (discussed in Chapter 2) tend to think that they would not conform to the demands of an authority figure as the study participants did. Yet the Music Lab study reveals how social envi-ronments affect our behavior and how we all, at times, conform to the movements of larger social groups, even when it comes to something as personal as the music we like.

Obesity

One major public health problem that sociologists have studied in recent years is obe-sity. In the United States today, the number of obese people has been growing steadily. More than one-third (39.8 percent) of American adults are obese, and 18.5 percent of children and teenagers ages 2 to 19 are obese (Hales et al., 2017). Although obesity may have a significant biological component, significant social factors should not be ignored. Most obviously, sociologists have discovered that particular communities, sometimes known as "food deserts," are short of healthy food options. Poor inner-city neighborhoods tend to have fewer grocery stores and health food outlets, and more fast-food restaurants than do wealthier neighborhoods (Walker, Keane, and Burke, 2010). More controversial has been the finding by sociologist Nicholas Christakis of Harvard Medical School and social scientist James Fowler of the University of Califor-nia, Davis, that having fat friends can make you fat.

Their study, titled "The Spread of Obesity in a Large Social Network over 32 Years," published in *The New England Journal of Medicine* (2007), showed that obesity was "contagious." Christakis and Fowler found that if one person became obese, then persons closely connected to him or her had a greater chance of becoming obese. If a person once considered a "friend" became obese, then one's own chances of becoming obese increased by 57 percent. However, a mere neighbor's weight change had no effect on one's body weight.

The media were eager to report the findings of the Christakis and Fowler study. It was the first-ever study to examine the ways that one's social networks affected one's body weight. The researchers had access to a unique data source that allowed them to ask questions such as, How do one's friends affect one's weight? Does it matter if one's friends live nearby or far away? Christakis and Fowler analyzed data from a sample of 12,067 adults who were followed over a period of 32 years, from 1971 to 2003. These adults were participants in the renowned Framingham Heart Study. The data source revealed with whom the study participants were friends and who was a spouse or sibling or neighbor. It also obtained information on each person's address and body weight at each interview point.

Because of their unique data and rigorous methodology, the researchers could rule out competing explanations for their findings. For example, because they had data from many time points throughout the 32-year study, they could ascertain the order in which events unfolded. It was not the case that obese people would simply seek out similar-weight people as friends. Rather, Christakis noted, there was a "direct, causal relationship." Christakis and Fowler also found that it didn't matter whether one's friend lived near or far; they found that a friend who lived 500 miles away had just as powerful an impact on one's own weight as a friend who lived across the street.

The study also found that the "contagion" of body weight was not due to the fact that friends might share lifestyles, hobbies, and dietary choices—such as eating large meals together or discouraging one another from exercising. If it's not the "birds of a feather flock together" explanation or "gluttony loves company" explanation, what accounts for the spread of body weight? The authors believe that their study is a testimony to the power of social norms. People develop their ideas about what is an acceptable body type by looking at the people around them. Christakis stated: "People come to think that it is okay to be bigger since those around them are bigger, and this sensibility spreads."

However, the researchers were adamant that Americans should not come away thinking that it is wise or healthy to abandon their obese friends. Rather, Christakis noted, it is good for one's health to have friends, period: "It is unlikely that severing ties with people on the basis of any of their particular traits—as some have supposed that our results might suggest—would necessarily be beneficial." Instead, they concluded that overweight or obese people could befriend a healthy-weighted person and

CONCEPT CHECKS

1 What does Ritzer mean by the concept "McDonaldization" of society?

2 What evidence do Watts et al. have for their claims about social influence on personal taste?

3 How do Christakis and Fowler explain the spread of obesity through social networks? Why are some researchers critical of their findings?

then allow themselves to be influenced by the positive model set by the healthy-weight friend.

Other researchers have criticized their methods. Lyons (2011) and other statisticians have argued in scathing critiques that the researchers did not properly use their statistics and that most of the association was due to error. However, even the most skeptical critics of Christakis and Fowler's work do acknowledge that human health and health behaviors are powerfully shaped by one's peers and significant others, although they would not go so far as to say that it is "contagion," instead suggesting that people associate with others like themselves, or they may model and influence each other's behaviors.

4   UNANSWERED QUESTIONS

Is Democracy Meaningless in the Face of Increasingly Powerful Bureaucratic Organizations?

Even in democracies such as the United States, government organizations hold enormous amounts of information about us, from records of our birth dates, schools attended, and jobs held, to data on income used for tax collecting and information for issuing driver's licenses and allocating Social Security numbers. Because we don't have access to the files of most government agencies, such surveillance activities can infringe on the principle of democracy.

The diminishing of democracy with the advance of modern forms of organization worried Weber a great deal (see also Chapter 13). What especially disturbed him was the prospect of rule by faceless bureaucrats. After all, Weber reasoned, bureaucracies are necessarily specialized and hierarchical. Those near the bottom of the organization inevitably carry out mundane tasks and have no power over what they do; power resides with those at the top. Weber's student Robert Michels (1967; orig. 1911) invented a phrase: "Who says organization says oligarchy." It has come to refer to this loss of power, in large-scale organizations and, more generally, in a society dominated by organizations. Michels called this concept the **iron law of oligarchy**. **Oligarchy** means "rule by the few." According to Michels, the flow of power toward the top is an inevitable part of an increasingly bureaucratized world—hence the "iron law."

Was Michels right? It surely is true that large-scale organizations involve the centralizing of power. Yet there is reason to believe that the iron law of oligarchy is not quite as hard and fast as Michels claimed. The connections between oligarchy and bureaucratic centralization are more ambiguous than he supposed.

First, unequal power is not just a function of size. Marked differences of power exist even in modest-sized groups. In a small business, for instance, in which the

iron law of oligarchy A term coined by Weber's student Robert Michels meaning that large organizations tend toward centralization of power, making democracy difficult.

oligarchy Rule by a small minority within an organization or society.

activities of employees are directly visible to the directors, much tighter control might be exerted than in larger organizations. As organizations expand in size, power relationships often become looser. Those at the middle and lower levels may have little influence over policies forged at the top. However, because of the specialization and expertise involved in bureaucracy, people at the top may lose control over many of the administrative decisions made by those lower down.

In many modern organizations, power is often delegated downward from superiors to subordinates. The heads of huge corporations are so busy coordinating different departments, coping with crises, and analyzing budget and forecast figures that they have little time for original thinking. Consequently, they delegate consideration of policy issues to others, whose task is to develop proposals. Many corporate leaders admit that, for the most part, they simply accept the conclusions given to them.

How Are Late-Modern Organizations Reinventing Themselves?

For quite a long while in Western societies, Weber's model, closely mirrored by Foucault's, held fast. In government, hospital administration, universities, and business organizations, bureaucracy was dominant. Even though, as Peter Blau showed, informal social groups always develop in bureaucratic settings, and are in fact effective, it seemed as though the future might be what Weber had anticipated: constantly increasing bureaucratization.

Bureaucracies still exist in the West, but Weber's idea that a clear hierarchy of authority, with power and knowledge concentrated at the top, is the only way to run a large organization is starting to look archaic. Numerous organizations are overhauling themselves to become less, rather than more, hierarchical.

In the 1960s, Burns and Stalker concluded that traditional bureaucratic structures could stifle innovation and creativity in cutting-edge industries. In today's electronic economy, few would dispute these findings. Departing from rigid vertical command structures, many organizations are turning to "horizontal," collaborative models to become more responsive to fluctuating markets. In this section, we examine some of the forces behind these shifts, including globalization and information technology, and consider some of the ways in which late-modern organizations are reinventing themselves.

Anyone who draws money from a bank or buys an airline ticket depends on a computer-based communication system. Because data can be processed instantaneously in any part of the world linked to such a system, there is no need for physical proximity among those involved. As a result, **information and communication technology** has allowed many companies to reengineer their organizational structures (Attaran, 2004; Bresnahan et al., 2002; Castells, 2000, 2001; Kanter, 1991; Kobrin, 1997; Zuboff, 1988). Such changes, while good for efficiency, can have negative as well as positive consequences for the individuals within the organization.

For example, one company found the sales of some of its products falling and needed to reduce costs. The traditional route would have been to lay off staff. Instead, the firm set up as independent consultants those

information and communication technology
Forms of technology based on information processing and requiring microelectronic circuitry.

who would have been laid off. The company then bought back a substantial proportion of the former employees' working time for a number of years but also left them free to work for other clients. The idea was that the new arrangement would provide the corporation with access to the skills of its former employees but at a cheaper rate because it no longer provided office space or company benefits (pension, health insurance, and so on). The former employees, in turn, had the opportunity to build up their own businesses. Initially, at least, the arrangement has worked well for both parties. In such a scheme, though, the burden is on the former employees, because they have to compensate for the loss of benefits with new business.

This is just one example of how large organizations have become more decentralized and flexible (Burris, 1998). Another example is the rise of telecommuting. A good deal of office work can now be carried out by remote workers using the Internet and other mobile technologies, such as smartphones and tablets, to work at home or somewhere other than their employer's primary office. In 2016, 43 percent of workers spent some time working remotely, while 20 percent of employees worked remotely all of the time. People are also spending more time working remotely: Currently, nearly one-third of remote workers are working outside the office 80 percent or more of the time, up from about a quarter of workers in 2012 (Gallup, 2017).

We see the highest proportions of remote workers in industries such as transportation and computer/information systems as well as arts, design, entertainment, and media. Remote workers are typically older (50+) and college educated, and they work in salaried professional or managerial positions.

To reduce costs and increase productivity, large firms may set up information networks connecting employees who work from home with the main office. In 2009, the computer company Cisco released a study of its own employees, which found that

For many, the word *corporation* conjures up images of a boring gray office. Yet, firms like Google are creating their own corporate cultures, offering perks like yoga classes and free food.

telecommuting significantly increased productivity, work-life flexibility, and job satisfaction. The company reportedly accrued annual savings of $277 million in productivity by allowing employees to telecommute and telework. In addition to productivity gains, Cisco estimates that its telework and telecommuting policies have resulted in a reduction of the company's carbon footprint, saving approximately 47,320 metric tons of greenhouse gas emissions due to avoided travel (Cisco, 2009). It is estimated that if all the workers whose jobs are compatible with working at home could do so, the savings would total over $700 billion each year and reduce the need for Persian Gulf oil imports by 37 percent (Global Workplace Analytics, 2014).

One reason that telecommuting increases productivity is that it eliminates commuting time, thereby permitting greater concentration of energy on work. Hartig, Johansson, and Kylin (2003) found that telecommuters actually spend more time on paid work when working at home than their counterparts do when working in the office. Employers view these longer hours as a primary benefit of telecommuting (International Telework Association and Council, 2004). However, these new work arrangements are not perfect. First, the employees lose the human side of work; computer monitors are no substitute for face-to-face interaction with colleagues and friends at work. Second, telecommuters experience isolation, distraction, and conflicting demands of work and home responsibilities (Ammons and Markham, 2004). In addition, female telecommuters face more stress from increased housework and childcare responsibilities (Ammons and Markham, 2004; Olson, 1989; Olson and Primps, 1984). In recent years, however, some large corporations have opted to buck this trend in remote work by terminating or scaling back their work-from-home policies, including Best Buy, Yahoo, and Bank of America, citing an effort to boost collaboration and communication (Gallup, 2017).

On the other hand, management cannot easily monitor employees working off-site (Dimitrova, 2003; Kling, 1996). While this lack of supervision may create problems for employers, it allows employees greater flexibility in managing their nonwork roles, thus contributing to increased worker satisfaction (Davis and Polonko, 2001). Telecommuting also creates new possibilities for older and disabled workers to remain independent, productive, and socially connected (Bricourt, 2004). Finally, telecommuting is contributing to new trends in housing and residential development as space for home offices becomes more of a priority. With people able to work at a distance from city centers, residential development no longer needs to be tied to commuting practices.

While computerization has resulted in increased flexibility and a reduction in hierarchy, it has created a two-tier occupational structure composed of technical "experts" and less-skilled production or clerical workers. In these restructured organizations, jobs have been redefined more in terms of technical skill than rank or position. For expert professionals, traditional bureaucratic constraints are relaxed to allow for creativity and flexibility (Burris, 1993). Although professionals benefit from this expanded autonomy, computerization makes production and service workers more visible and vulnerable to supervision (Wellman et al., 1996; Zuboff, 1988). For instance, organizations can now monitor work patterns to the point where they can count the number of seconds per phone call or keystrokes per minute, which in turn can lead to higher levels of stress for employees.

Granted, workplace computerization does have some positive effects. It has made some of the mundane tasks of clerical jobs more interesting. It can also promote social networking (Wellman et al., 1996). Office computers can be used for recreation; private exchanges with coworkers, friends, or family; and work-related interaction. And, as in the case of telecommuting, computerization can contribute to greater flexibility for workers to manage both their personal and professional lives.

Can the Traditional Organization Survive?

Traditionally, identifying the boundaries of organizations has been fairly straightforward. Until recently, organizations were generally located in defined physical spaces, such as an office building, a suite of rooms, or, in the case of a hospital or university, a campus. In addition, the mission or tasks of an organization were usually clearcut. A central feature of bureaucracies, for example, was adherence to a defined set of responsibilities and procedures for carrying them out. Weber's bureaucracy was a self-contained unit that intersected with outside entities at limited and designated points.

We have already seen how the physical boundaries of organizations are being broken down by the capacity of information technology to transcend countries and time zones. The same process is affecting the work that organizations do and the way in which it is coordinated. Many organizations no longer operate as independent units. A growing number are finding that they run more effectively when they are part of a web of complex relationships with other organizations and companies. No longer is there a clear dividing line between the organization and outside groups. Globalization, information technology, and trends in occupational patterns mean that organizational boundaries are more open and fluid than they once were.

In *The Rise of the Network Society* (1996), Manuel Castells argues that the "network enterprise" is the organizational form best suited to a global, informational economy. By this he means that it is increasingly impossible for organizations (large corporations or small businesses) to survive if they are not part of a network. What enables networking to occur is the growth of information technology, whereby organizations around the world are able to enter into contact and coordinate joint activities through an electronic medium. Castells cites several examples of organizational networking that originated in diverse cultural and institutional contexts but nevertheless all represent what he calls "different dimensions of a fundamental process"—the disintegration of the traditional, rational bureaucracy.

Organizations can function as networks via the powerful alliances formed between top companies. Increasingly, the large corporation is less and less a big business and more an "enterprise web"—a central organization that links together smaller firms. IBM, for example, used to be a highly self-sufficient corporation, wary of partnerships with others. Yet in the 1980s and early 1990s, IBM joined with dozens of U.S.-based companies and more than 80 foreign-based firms to share strategic planning and cope with production problems.

Decentralization is another process that contributes to organizations functioning as networks. When change becomes more profound and more rapid, highly centralized Weberian-style bureaucracies are too cumbersome and too entrenched in their ways to cope. Stanley Davis (1988) argues that as business firms and other organizations come to be networks, they go through a process of decentralization by which power and responsibility are devolved downward throughout the organization, rather than remaining concentrated at the top.

Networked organizations offer at least two advantages over more bureaucratic ones: They can foster the flow of information, and they can enhance creativity. As we've seen, bureaucratic hierarchy can impede the flow of information: One must go through the proper channels, fill out the right forms, and avoid displeasing people in higher positions. These processes not only hinder the sharing of information but also stifle creative problem solving. In networked organizations, when a problem arises, instead of writing a memo to your boss and waiting for a reply, you can simply pick up the phone or dash off an email to the person responsible for working out a solution. As a result, members of networked organizations learn more easily from one another than do bureaucrats. It is therefore easier to solve routine dilemmas and to develop innovative solutions to all types of problems (Hamel, 1991; Powell and Brantley, 1992; Powell, Koput, and Smith-Doerr, 1996).

CONCEPT CHECKS

1 What is the iron law of oligarchy?

2 How are technology and globalization transforming traditional organizations?

3 What is the difference between networked and bureaucratic organizations?

1 Basic Concepts

p. 168

2 Theories of Networks, Groups and Organizations

p. 175

LEARNING OBJECTIVES

Learn the variety and characteristics of networks and groups, as well as the effect they have on individual behavior. Know how to define an organization and understand how organizations developed over the last two centuries.

Learn Max Weber's theory of organizations and view of bureaucracy. Understand the importance of the physical setting of organizations and Michel Foucault's theory of surveillance. Understand the importance of social networks and the advantages they give some people.

TERMS TO KNOW

networks • social group • social aggregate • social category • primary groups • secondary groups • organization • formal organization

in-groups • out-groups • reference group • dyad • triad • bureaucracy • ideal type • formal relations • informal relations • surveillance • timetables

CONCEPT CHECKS

1. According to Granovetter, what are the benefits of weak ties? Why?
2. What is the difference between social aggregates and social groups? Give examples that illustrate this difference.
3. Describe the main characteristics of primary and secondary groups.
4. What role do organizations play in contemporary society?

1. When groups become large, why does their intensity decrease but their stability increase?
2. What does the term bureaucracy mean?
3. Describe five characteristics of an ideal type of bureaucracy.

Exercises: Thinking Sociologically

1. According to George Simmel, what are the primary differences between dyads and triads? Explain, according to his theory, how the addition of a child would alter the relationship between a husband and wife. Does the theory fit this situation?

2. The advent of the Internet, cloud computing, and the computerization of the workplace may change our organizations and relationships with coworkers. Explain how you see modern organizations changing with the adoption of newer information technologies.

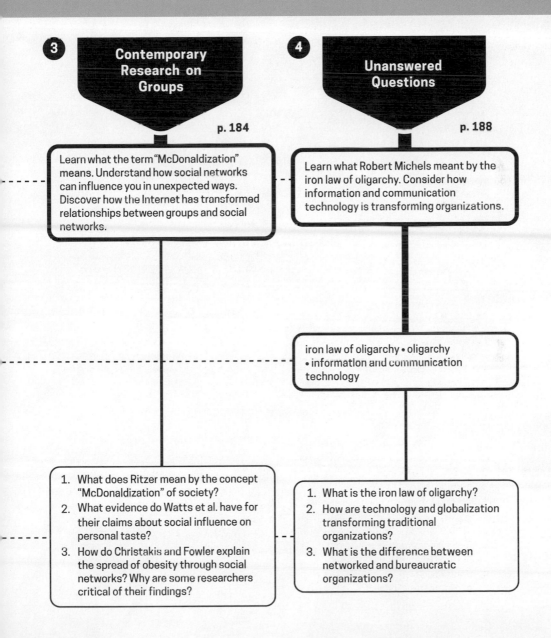

3 **Contemporary Research on Groups**

p. 184

Learn what the term "McDonaldization" means. Understand how social networks can influence you in unexpected ways. Discover how the Internet has transformed relationships between groups and social networks.

1. What does Ritzer mean by the concept "McDonaldization" of society?
2. What evidence do Watts et al. have for their claims about social influence on personal taste?
3. How do Christakis and Fowler explain the spread of obesity through social networks? Why are some researchers critical of their findings?

4 **Unanswered Questions**

p. 188

Learn what Robert Michels meant by the iron law of oligarchy. Consider how information and communication technology is transforming organizations.

iron law of oligarchy • oligarchy • information and communication technology

1. What is the iron law of oligarchy?
2. How are technology and globalization transforming traditional organizations?
3. What is the difference between networked and bureaucratic organizations?

Conformity, Deviance, and Crime

Members of the Mafia commit crimes in order to:

- **A** terrorize other citizens.
- **B** become respectable members of society.
- **C** extort money.
- **D** destroy communities and the government.

TURN THE PAGE FOR THE CORRECT ANSWER.

f you have ever watched a film like *The Godfather* or *Goodfellas*, you probably think of mobsters as quite exotic. Like drug dealers or vagrants, members of the Mafia appear to us as social deviants, individuals who don't conform to normal standards. Yet, while some members of the Mafia are violent criminals who could never achieve a typical existence, most mobsters ultimately end up exiting the world of crime and living respectably over the course of their lives.

This essential fact was discovered by Francis Ianni in a classic study that made many people question their basic assumptions about the mob. Ianni had grown up in a Mafia family, and he wrote his dissertation about the relatives whom he had known since childhood. Central to Ianni's work is the claim that Mafia members commit crimes to engage in a "quiet and determined push toward respectability" (Gladwell, 2014). Like other American immigrants, the Mafia members he studied sought to realize the American dream but found themselves barred from many of the resources and institutions available to other citizens. Crime became the primary vehicle through which Mafia families moved into the mainstream of American society. But once they had the money to start their own legitimate businesses, they did move on.

While members of the Lupollo clan may have started as "rule breakers" working as bootleggers in the Prohibition era, Ianni notes that of the 42 members of the Lupollo clan, only 4 were engaged in criminal activities four decades later in 1972, with the majority of profits from illegal activities reinvested into legal enterprises. Over time, the family increasingly separated their illegal businesses from their legal businesses. By the end of the twentieth century, families like the Lupollo clan had become fully integrated members of mainstream society, moving from rule breakers to conformists.

LEARNING OBJECTIVES

1 Basic Concepts

Learn how we define deviance and how it is related to social power and social class. Recognize the ways in which we encourage conformity.

2 Society and Crime: Sociological Theories

Know the leading sociological theories of crime and how each is useful in understanding deviance.

3 Research on Crime and Deviance Today

Recognize the usefulness and limitations of crime statistics. Understand that some individuals or groups are more likely than others to commit, or be the victims of, crime. Familiarize yourself with some of the varieties of crime.

4 Unanswered Questions

Explore the different explanations for the decline in crime. Think about the best solutions to reduce crime. Consider the ways in which individuals and governments can address crime.

THE ANSWER IS B.

Further, even when engaged in illegal activities, Mafia members maintained a clearly organized leadership structure and followed strict codes of family loyalty, mutual aid, and secrecy. In this way, the Mafia also acted as rule creators.

We have learned in previous chapters that social life is governed by norms that define some kinds of behavior as appropriate in particular contexts and others as inappropriate. **Norms** are principles or rules that people are expected to observe; they represent the "dos and don'ts" of society. Ianni found that while members of the Mafia may break some of the rules that many of us follow in mainstream society, they also follow their own set of norms to regulate behavior. Ianni describes the business of the Lupollo clan as governed by a strict set of rules about family loyalty and mutual aid. As such, members of the Mafia may have different definitions of who is "deviant" and who is "conformist."

Actually, we are all rule breakers as well as conformists. We are all also rule creators. For example, most American drivers may break the law on the freeways, but in fact, they've developed informal rules superimposed on the legal rules. When the legal speed limit is 65 mph, most drivers don't go above 75 mph or so, and they drive more slowly through urban areas. As a result, when we study deviant behavior, we must consider which rules people are observing and which ones they are breaking. Nobody breaks all rules, just as no one conforms to all rules. The behaviors that are defined as deviant may even change over time.

The study of deviant behavior reveals that none of us is as normal as we think. It also shows that people whose behavior appears incomprehensible or alien can be seen as rational beings when we understand why they act as they do. Indeed, if we can understand members of the Mafia as citizens working in pursuit of respectability, we might also consider how contemporary gang members, drug dealers, or homeless people might also be following a stable set of norms that may differ from our own—and that they may even aspire to live by a set of norms similar to our own.

> **norms** Rules of conduct that specify appropriate behavior in a given range of social situations. A norm either prescribes a given type of behavior or forbids it. All human groups follow definite norms, which are always backed by sanctions of one kind or another, varying from informal disapproval to physical punishment.

1 BASIC CONCEPTS

The study of deviance, like other fields of sociology, directs our attention to social power, which encompasses gender, race, and social class. When we look at deviance from, or conformity to, social rules or norms, we always have to consider the question: Whose rules? As we shall see, social norms are strongly influenced by divisions of power and class.

What Is Deviance?

Deviance may be defined as nonconformity to a set of norms that a significant number of people in a community or society accept. No society can be divided simply between those who deviate from norms and those who conform to them because most people sometimes transgress generally accepted rules of behavior. Although a large share of all deviant behavior (such as committing assault or murder) is also criminal and violates the law, many deviant behaviors—ranging from making bizarre fashion choices to joining a religious cult—are not criminal. By the same token, many behaviors that are technically "crimes," such as underage drinking or exceeding the speed limit, are not considered deviant because they are quite normative (see Figure 7.1). Sociologists tend to focus much of their research on behaviors that are both criminal and deviant because such behaviors have importance for the safety and well-being of our nation.

Although most of us associate the word *deviant* with behaviors that we view as dangerous or unsavory, assessments of deviance are truly in the eye of the beholder, as our next example will illustrate. Kevin Mitnick has been described as the "world's most celebrated computer hacker." To computer hackers everywhere, Mitnick is a pathbreaking genius whose five-year imprisonment in a U.S. penitentiary was unjust and unwarranted—proof of how misunderstood computer hacking has become with the spread of information technology. To U.S. authorities and high-tech corporations, Mitnick is one of the world's most dangerous men. A recent study found that hackers—the leading cause of data breaches—were responsible for 48 percent of data breaches in 2018 (Verizon, 2018). Mitnick was captured by the FBI in 1995 and later convicted of downloading source code and stealing software allegedly worth millions of dollars from companies such as Motorola and Sun Microsystems. As a condition of his release from prison in January 2000, Mitnick was barred from using any communications technology other than a landline telephone. He successfully fought this legal decision and gained access to the Internet. He now is a consultant and best-selling author who teaches others about computer security (Mitnick and Simon, 2011).

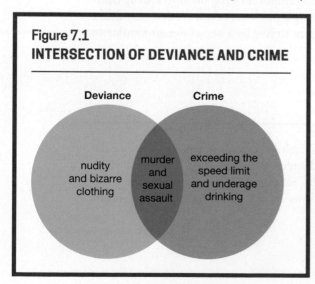

Figure 7.1
INTERSECTION OF DEVIANCE AND CRIME

Deviance

Crime

nudity and bizarre clothing

murder and sexual assault

exceeding the speed limit and underage drinking

Over the past decade or so, hackers have gradually evolved from a little-noticed population of computer enthusiasts to a much-reviled group of deviants who are believed to threaten the very stability of the information age. Yet, according to Mitnick and others in the hacker community, such depictions could not be further from the truth. Hackers are quick to point out that most of their activities are not criminal. Rather, they are primarily interested in exploring the edges of computer technology, trying to uncover loopholes and discover the extent to which it is possible to penetrate other computer systems. Once they discover flaws, the "hacker ethic" demands that they share information publicly. Many hackers have even served as consultants for large corporations and government agencies, helping them defend their systems against outside intrusion.

Deviance does not refer only to individual behavior; it concerns the activities of groups as well. Heaven's Gate was a religious group whose beliefs and practices were different from those of the majority of Americans. The cult was established in the early 1970s when Marshall Herff Applewhite made his way around the West and Midwest of the United States preaching his beliefs, ultimately advertising on the Internet in the early 1990s his belief that civilization was doomed and the only way people could be saved was to kill themselves so their souls could be rescued by a UFO. On March 26, 1997, 39 members of the cult followed his advice in a mass suicide at a wealthy estate in Rancho Santa Fe, California.

The Heaven's Gate cult represents an example of a **deviant subculture**. Its members were able to survive fairly easily within the wider society, supporting themselves by running a website business and using the Internet to recruit new members. They had plenty of money and lived together in an expensive home in a wealthy California suburb.

deviance Modes of action that do not conform to the norms or values held by most members of a group or society. What is regarded as deviant is as variable as the norms and values that distinguish different cultures and subcultures from one another. Forms of behavior that are highly esteemed by one group may be regarded negatively by others.

deviant subculture A subculture whose members hold values that differ substantially from those of the majority.

sanction A mode of reward or punishment that reinforces socially expected forms of behavior.

Norms and Sanctions

We most often follow social norms because, as a result of socialization, we are used to doing so. Individuals become committed to social norms through interactions with people who obey the law. Through these interactions, we learn self-control. The more numerous these interactions, the fewer opportunities we have to deviate from conventional norms. Over time, the longer we interact in conventional ways, the more we stand to lose by not conforming (Gottfredson and Hirschi, 1990).

All social norms carry **sanctions** that promote conformity and protect against nonconformity. A sanction is any reaction from others that is meant to ensure that a person or group complies with a given norm. Sanctions may be positive (the offering of rewards for conformity) or negative (punishment for behavior that does not conform). They can also be formal or informal. Formal sanctions are applied by a specific group or agency to ensure that a particular set of norms is followed. Informal sanctions are less organized and more spontaneous reactions to nonconformity, such as when a student's friends teasingly accuse him

CONCEPT CHECKS

1 How do sociologists define deviance?

2 Is all crime deviant? Is all deviance criminal? Why?

3 Contrast positive and negative sanctions.

of working too hard or being a nerd if he spends an evening studying rather than going to a party.

Courts and prisons represent the main types of formal sanctions in modern societies. The police are charged with bringing offenders to trial and possibly to imprisonment. **Laws** are norms defined by governments as principles their citizens must follow; sanctions are used against people who do not conform to those principles. Where there are laws, there are also crimes because **crime** constitutes any type of behavior that breaks a law.

It is important to recognize, however, that the law is only a guide to a society's norms.

2 SOCIETY AND CRIME: SOCIOLOGICAL THEORIES

Any satisfactory account of the nature of crime must be sociological because what crime is depends on the social institutions of a society. Contemporary sociological thinking about crime emphasizes that definitions of conformity and deviance vary based on one's social context. Modern societies contain many subcultures, and behavior that conforms to the norms of one subculture may be regarded as deviant outside it; for instance, a member of a gang may feel strong pressure to prove himself by stealing a car. Moreover, wide divergences of wealth and power in society greatly influence criminal opportunities for different groups. Theft and burglary, not surprisingly, are carried out mainly by people from the poorer segments of the population; embezzlement and tax evasion are by definition limited to persons in positions of some affluence.

Functionalist Theories

Functionalist theories argue that crime occurs when the aspirations of individuals and groups do not coincide with available opportunities. The disparity between desires and fulfillment will lead to deviant behavior.

Crime and Anomie: Durkheim and Merton

Émile Durkheim and Robert Merton argued that deviant behavior is the result of the structure of modern societies. Durkheim's notion of **anomie** suggests that in modern societies, traditional norms and standards become undermined without being replaced by new ones. Anomie exists when there are no clear standards to guide behavior in a given area of social life. Under such circumstances, Durkheim believed, people feel disoriented and anxious; anomie therefore heightens dispositions to suicide.

Durkheim saw crime and deviance as inevitable and necessary elements in modern societies. According to Durkheim, people in the modern age are less constrained

laws Rules of behavior established by a political authority and backed by state power.

crime The result of any action that contravenes the laws established by a political authority.

anomie A concept first brought into wide usage in sociology by Durkheim to refer to a situation in which social norms lose their hold over individual behavior.

than they were in traditional societies. Because there is more room for individual choice in the modern world, inevitably there will be some nonconformity. Durkheim recognized that modern society would never be in complete consensus about the norms and values that govern it.

Deviance is also necessary for society, according to Durkheim. First, deviance has an adaptive function: By introducing new ideas and social challenges, deviance brings about change. Second, deviance promotes boundary maintenance between "good" and "bad" behavior. A criminal event can provoke a collective response that heightens group solidarity and clarifies social norms. For example, residents of a neighborhood facing a problem with drug dealers might join together in the aftermath of a drug-related shooting and commit themselves to maintaining the area as a drug-free zone.

Durkheim's ideas on crime and deviance helped shift attention from explanations that focused on the problems of individuals to explanations focused on social forces. His notion of anomie was applied by the American sociologist Robert K. Merton (1957), who located the source of crime within the very structure of American society.

Merton modified the concept of anomie to refer to the strain put on individuals' behavior when accepted norms conflict with social reality. In American society—and, to some degree, in other industrial societies—values emphasize material success through self-discipline and hard work. Accordingly, it is believed that people who work hard can succeed regardless of their starting point in life. This idea is not in fact valid because most disadvantaged people have limited or no conventional opportunities for advancement, such as high-quality education. Yet those who do not "succeed" are condemned for their apparent inability to make material progress. In this situation, there is pressure to get ahead by any means, legitimate or illegitimate. According to Merton, then, deviance is a by-product of economic inequalities.

Merton split people into five possible types based on how they responded to the tensions between socially endorsed values and the limited means of achieving them (see Figure 7.2): *Conformists* accept generally held values and the conventional means of realizing them, regardless of whether they meet with success. Most of the population falls into this category. *Innovators* accept socially approved values but use illegitimate or illegal means to follow them. We might consider members of the Mafia to be innovators. While most Mafia members want to lead respectable lives by entering into mainstream

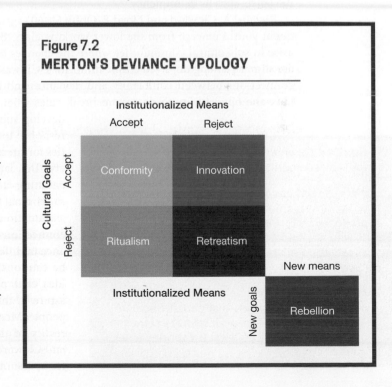

Figure 7.2
MERTON'S DEVIANCE TYPOLOGY

society, they need to acquire wealth through illegal activities to do so (Gladwell, 2014). *Ritualists* conform to socially accepted standards, though they have lost sight of their underlying values. They compulsively follow rules for their own sake. A ritualist might dedicate herself to a boring job, even though it has no career prospects and provides few rewards. *Retreatists* have abandoned the competitive outlook, rejecting both the dominant values and the approved means of achieving them. An example would be members of a self-supporting commune. Finally, *rebels* reject both the existing values and the means of achieving them but work to substitute new ones and reconstruct the social system. The members of radical political and religious groups, such as the Heaven's Gate cult, fall into this category.

Merton's writings addressed one of the main puzzles in the study of criminology: At a time when society as a whole was becoming more affluent, why did crime rates continue to rise? By emphasizing the contrast between rising aspirations and persistent inequalities, Merton identified a sense of **relative deprivation**, or the recognition that one has less than their peers, as an important element in deviant behavior.

Subcultural Explanations

Later researchers examined subcultural groups that adopt norms that encourage or reward criminal behavior. Like Merton, Albert Cohen saw the contradictions within American society as the main cause of crime. But while Merton emphasized individual deviant responses, Cohen saw the responses occurring collectively through subcultures. In *Delinquent Boys* (1955), Cohen argues that frustrated boys in the lower working class often join delinquent subcultures, such as gangs. These subcultures reject middle-class values and replace them with norms that celebrate nonconformity and deviance, such as delinquency.

Richard A. Cloward and Lloyd E. Ohlin (1960) agreed with Cohen that most delinquent youths emerge from the lower working class. But they argued that such gangs arise in subcultural communities where the chances of achieving success legitimately are slim, as among deprived ethnic minorities. Cloward and Ohlin's work emphasized connections between conformity and deviance: Individuals follow rules when they have the opportunity to do so and break rules when they do not. As a result, they develop subcultures with deviant values in response to a lack of legitimate opportunities for success as defined by the wider society. This lack of opportunity is the differentiating factor between those who engage in criminal behavior and those who do not.

Functionalist theories rightly emphasize connections between conformity and deviance in different social contexts. We should be cautious, however, about accepting the idea that people in poorer communities aspire to the same things as more affluent people. Most adjust their aspirations to the reality of their situation. Merton, Cohen, and Cloward and Ohlin can all be criticized for presuming that middle-class values

relative deprivation Deprivation a person feels by comparing himself with a group.

differential association An interpretation of the development of criminal behavior proposed by Edwin H. Sutherland, according to whom criminal behavior is learned through association with others who regularly engage in crime.

labeling theory An approach to the study of deviance that suggests that people become "deviant" because certain labels are attached to their behavior by political authorities and others.

Members of an El Salvadoran gang display their tattoos. The gangs, called *maras*, began in Los Angeles in the 1980s to protect themselves from established street gangs after their working-class families fled civil war in Central America. How might Cohen, Cloward, and Ohlin explain the emergence of the maras?

are accepted throughout society. It would also be wrong to suppose that only the less privileged experience a mismatch of aspirations and opportunities. Pressures toward criminal activity exist among other groups, too, as indicated by the white-collar crimes of embezzlement, fraud, and tax evasion, which we will study later.

Interactionist Theories

Sociologists studying crime and deviance in the interactionist tradition focus on deviance as a socially constructed phenomenon. Rejecting the idea that some types of conduct are inherently "deviant," they ask how behaviors get defined as deviant and why only certain groups get labeled as deviant.

Learned Deviance: Differential Association

In 1949, Edwin H. Sutherland advanced a notion that influenced much of the later interactionist work: He linked crime to what he called **differential association**. Differential association theory argues that we learn deviant behavior in precisely the same way we learn about conventional behavior: from our contacts with primary groups such as peers, family members, and coworkers. The term *differential* refers to the ratio of deviant to conventional social contacts. We become deviant when exposed to a higher level of deviant persons and influences, compared with conventional influences. In a society that contains a variety of subcultures, some individuals have greater exposure to social environments that encourage illegal activities.

Labeling Theory

One of the most important interactionist approaches to understanding criminality is **labeling theory**. It was originally associated with Howard S. Becker's (1963) stud-

According to interactionists, it's not the act of smoking marijuana that makes one a deviant, but the way others react to marijuana smoking.

ies of marijuana smokers. In the early 1960s, marijuana use was a marginal activity of subcultures rather than the lifestyle choice—an activity accepted by many in the mainstream of society—it is today (Hathaway, 1997). Becker found that becoming a marijuana smoker depended on one's acceptance by, and close association with, experienced users, as well as on one's attitudes toward nonusers. Because labeling theorists such as Becker interpret deviance as a process of interaction between deviants and nondeviants, it is not the act of marijuana smoking that makes one a deviant but the way others react to it. Thus, to understand the nature of deviance itself, labeling theorists seek to discover why some people become labeled "deviant."

People who represent law and order or who impose definitions of morality on others do most of the labeling. Thus, the rules by which deviance is defined express the power structure of society; such rules are framed by the wealthy for the poor, by men for women, by older people for younger people, and by ethnic majorities for minority groups. For example, many children wander into other people's gardens, steal fruit, or skip school. In an affluent neighborhood, parents, teachers, and police might regard such activities as relatively innocent. However, when they are committed by children in poor areas, they might be considered acts of juvenile delinquency.

Once a child is labeled a delinquent, he or she is stigmatized as a deviant and is likely to be considered untrustworthy by teachers and prospective employers. The child then relapses into further criminal behavior, widening the gulf between himself and orthodox social conventions. Edwin Lemert (1972) called the initial act of transgression **primary deviation**. **Secondary deviation** occurs when the individual accepts the label and sees himself as deviant. Research has shown that how we think of ourselves and how we believe others perceive us influence our propensity for committing crime. One study of a random national sample of young men showed that such negative self-appraisals are strongly tied to levels of criminality; in other words, the perception that one is deviant may in fact motivate deviant behavior (Matsueda, 1992).

Consider Luke, who smashes a shop window while out on the town with friends. The act may be called the accidental result of overly boisterous behavior. Luke might escape with a reprimand and a small fine—a likely result if he is from a respectable background and is seen as being of good character. The window smashing stays at the level of primary deviance. If, however, the police and courts hand out a suspended sentence and make Luke report to a social worker, the incident could become the first step on the road to secondary deviance. Forced to report to a law enforcement official, Luke may begin to see himself as a delinquent and act in ways that fit with this self-perception. The process of "learning to be deviant" tends to be reinforced by the very organizations set up to correct deviant behavior: prisons and social agencies.

According to conflict theorists, laws are not applied evenly across the population, with law enforcement targeting less powerful members of society such as drug users. Here, a member of a narcotics task force plans a drug bust.

Labeling theory assumes that no act is intrinsically criminal but may become so through the formulation of laws and their interpretation by police, courts, and correctional institutions. Although some critics of labeling theory argue that certain acts—such as murder, rape, and robbery—are prohibited across all cultures, this view is surely incorrect. Even within our own culture, killing is not always regarded as murder. In times of war, killing the enemy is approved, and, until recently, the laws in most U.S. states did not recognize sexual intercourse forced on a woman by her husband as rape.

We can more convincingly criticize labeling theory on other grounds. First, labeling theorists neglect the underlying processes that lead to the acts that are subsequently defined as deviant. Indeed, labeling certain activities as deviant is not arbitrary; differences in socialization, attitudes, and opportunities influence how far people engage in behavior likely to be labeled deviant. For instance, children from deprived backgrounds are on average more likely to steal than are richer children. It is not the labeling that leads them to steal so much as their background.

Second, it is not clear whether labeling actually has the effect of increasing deviant conduct. Delinquent behavior tends to increase after a conviction, but is this the result of the labeling itself? Other factors, such as increased interaction with other delinquents or learning about new criminal opportunities, may be involved.

Conflict Theory

Conflict theory draws on elements of Marxist thought to argue that deviance is deliberate and often political. Conflict theorists deny that deviance is "determined" by factors such as biology, personality, anomie, social

primary deviation According to Edwin Lemert, the actions that cause others to label one as a deviant.

secondary deviation According to Edwin Lemert, following the act of primary deviation, secondary deviation occurs when an individual accepts the label of deviant and acts accordingly.

conflict theory The argument that deviance is deliberately chosen and often political in nature.

disorganization, and labels. Rather, they argue, individuals choose to engage in deviant behavior in response to the inequalities of the capitalist system. Thus, members of countercultural groups regarded as deviant—such as supporters of the Black Power movement or gay liberation movement—are engaging in political acts that challenge the social order. More recently, the Occupy Wall Street and Black Lives Matter protesters were similarly engaging in political acts that challenge the social order.

Conflict theorists analyze crime and deviance in terms of the social structure and the preservation of power among the ruling class. For example, they argue that laws serve the powerful to maintain their privileged positions. These theorists reject the idea that laws are applied evenly across the population. Instead, as inequalities increase between the ruling class and the working class, law becomes the key instrument for the powerful to maintain order. This dynamic is evident in the criminal justice system, which has become increasingly oppressive toward working-class offenders or in tax legislation that disproportionately favors the wealthy. This power imbalance is not restricted to the creation of laws, however. The powerful also break laws, scholars argue, but are rarely caught. On the whole, these crimes are much more significant than the everyday crime and delinquency that attract the most attention. But, fearful of the implications of pursuing white-collar criminals, law enforcement instead targets less powerful members of society such as prostitutes, drug users, and petty thieves (Chambliss, 1988; Pearce, 1976).

Studies by Chambliss, Pearce, and others have played an important role in widening the debate about crime and deviance to include questions of social justice, power, and politics. They emphasize that crime occurs in the context of inequalities and competing interests among social groups.

Control Theory

Control theory posits that crime results from an imbalance between impulses toward criminal activity and the social or physical controls that deter it. Control theory assumes that people act rationally and that, given the opportunity, everyone would engage in deviant acts. One of the best-known control theorists, Travis Hirschi, argues that humans are fundamentally selfish beings who make calculated decisions about whether to engage in criminal activity by weighing the benefits and risks. In *Causes of Delinquency* (1969), Hirschi identifies four types of bonds that link people to society and law-abiding behavior, thus maintaining social control and conformity: attachment, commitment, involvement, and belief.

Attachment refers to emotional and social ties to persons who accept conventional norms, such as a peer group of students who value good grades and hard work. Commitment refers to the rewards obtained by participating in conventional activities and pursuits. For example, a high school dropout has little to lose by being arrested, whereas a dedicated student may lose his or her chance of going to college. Involvement refers to one's participation in conventional activities, such as paid employment, school, or community activities. The time spent in conventional activities means time not spent

control theory The theory that views crime as the outcome of an imbalance between impulses toward criminal activity and controls that deter it. Control theorists hold that criminals are rational beings who will act to maximize their own reward unless they are rendered unable to do so through either social or physical controls.

in deviant activities. Finally, beliefs involve holding morals and values that are consistent with conventional tenets of society. For example, people who believe that honesty and hard work are the keys to success may be less likely to resort to theft to get ahead in the world.

When sufficiently strong, these four elements help to maintain social control and conformity by rendering people unfree to break rules. If these bonds are weak, delinquency and deviance may result. Hirschi's approach suggests that delinquents have low levels of self-control that result from inadequate socialization at home or at school (Gottfredson and Hirschi, 1990).

Some control theorists see the growth of crime as an outcome of the increasing number of opportunities and targets for crime in modern society. As the population grows more affluent and consumerism becomes more central, more people own goods such as televisions, video equipment, computers, cars, and designer clothing—favorite targets for thieves. Residential homes are increasingly empty during the daytime as more women work outside the home. Motivated offenders can select from a broad range of suitable targets.

Many official approaches to crime prevention in recent years have focused on limiting the opportunities for crime via target hardening—making it more difficult for criminals to commit crimes by minimizing their opportunities to do so and intervening in potential crime situations. Control theorists argue that rather than changing the criminal, the best policy is to take practical measures to control the criminal's ability to commit crime by promoting the use of crime-deterring technologies and practices like community policing, private security services, house alarms, and even gated communities.

Target-hardening techniques and zero-tolerance policing have been successful at curtailing crime in some contexts; however, these measures do not address the underlying causes of crime and instead are aimed at protecting and defending certain

How are gated communities an example of target hardening? What are the social consequences of sequestering certain communities behind guards and gates?

elements of society from its reach. The growing popularity of private security services, alarm systems, and gated communities suggests that segments of the population feel compelled to defend themselves against others. This tendency is occurring not only in the United States but also in countries such as South Africa, Brazil, and those of the former Soviet Union, where a fortress mentality has emerged among the privileged.

These policies have another unintended consequence: As popular crime targets are "hardened," patterns of crime may simply shift from one domain to another. Target-hardening and zero-tolerance approaches may simply displace criminal offenses from better-protected areas to more vulnerable ones. Neighborhoods that are poor or lacking in social cohesion may well experience a growth in crime and delinquency as target hardening in affluent regions increases.

The Theory of Broken Windows

Target hardening and zero-tolerance policing are based on a theory known as *broken windows* (Wilson and Kelling, 1982), which arose from a study by the social psychologist Philip Zimbardo (1969). Zimbardo abandoned cars without license plates and with their hoods up in two social settings: the wealthy community of Palo Alto, California, and a poor neighborhood in the Bronx, New York. In both places, the cars were vandalized once passersby, regardless of class or race, sensed that the vehicles had been abandoned. Extrapolating from this study, Wilson and Kelling argued that any sign of social disorder in a community, even the appearance of a broken window, encourages more serious crime. One unrepaired broken window is a sign that no one cares, so breaking more windows—that is, committing more serious crimes—is a rational response by criminals to this situation of social disorder. Thus, minor acts of deviance lead to a spiral of crime and social decay.

In the late 1980s and 1990s, the broken windows theory underpinned policing strategies that aggressively focused on minor crimes such as traffic violations and drinking or using drugs in public. Studies have shown that proactive policing directed at maintaining public order can reduce the occurrence of more serious crimes, such as robbery (Sampson and Cohen, 1988). However, it remains unclear whether the broken windows theory is generalizable to all sorts of crime. Walking in a neighborhood where garbage and rubble are strewn across the sidewalk, we might be more likely to litter, but we might not necessarily be tempted to commit more serious crimes like murder. Lacking a systematic definition of disorder, the police can see almost anything as a sign of disorder and anyone as a threat. In fact, as crime rates fell throughout the 1990s, the number of com-

CONCEPT CHECKS

1 How do Merton's and Durkheim's definitions of anomie differ?

2 What is the core idea behind differential association theory?

3 What are two criticisms of labeling theory?

4 What are the root causes of crime, according to conflict theorists?

5 How does the theory of broken windows exemplify the core ideas of control theory?

plaints of police abuse and harassment went up, particularly by young, urban black men who fit the "profile" of a potential criminal.

Theoretical Conclusions

The contributions of the sociological theories of crime and deviance are twofold. First, these theories correctly emphasize that criminal and "respectable" behavior are not two discrete categories; rather, they are points along a continuum. The contexts in which particular types of activity are seen as criminal and punishable by law vary widely. Second, all agree that context is important; whether someone engages in a criminal act or comes to be regarded as a criminal is influenced by social learning and social surroundings.

In spite of its deficiencies, labeling theory is perhaps the most widely used approach to understanding crime and deviant behavior. It explains how some activities become defined in law as punishable, the power relations that form such definitions, and the circumstances in which particular individuals fall afoul of the law.

The way in which crime is understood directly affects the policies developed to combat it. For example, if crime is seen as the product of deprivation or social disorganiza-

Table 7.1

APPLYING SOCIOLOGY TO CRIME

THEORY	APPROACH TO UNDERSTANDING DEVIANCE	CONTEMPORARY APPLICATION
Functionalist Theory	Deviance serves the function of creating solidarity among the larger society.	In 2019, when a group of affluent parents that included Lori Loughlin was caught attempting to gain admission for their children to prestigious universities through a scheme of bribery and deception, parents and children across the country together shared outrage over this act of deviance.
Interactionist Theory	No act is objectively deviant— to understand the nature of deviance, we must understand the process through which some people get labeled deviant.	Diagnostic labels for certain psychiatric disorders—e.g. ADHD and depression—may add to the stigma associated with certain behaviors
Conflict Theory	The poor disproportionately violate norms and laws in response to their unequal position in society.	Immigrants without papers feel compelled to work "off the books."
Control Theory	Crime results from lack of social and physical controls that deter it.	Street sensors and cameras and other surveillance systems have contributed to lower crime rates in many cities
Broken Windows Theory	Minor acts of deviance must be controlled in order to avoid a spiral of crime and social decay.	Proactive policing focused on graffiti or drinking in public is believed by some to have the effect of lowering violent crime

tion, policies might be aimed at reducing poverty and strengthening social services. If criminality is seen as freely chosen, attempts to counter it will take a different form.

3   RESEARCH ON CRIME AND DEVIANCE TODAY

Research on criminal behavior helps us better understand how deviance arises and why we think of some things as deviant but not others.

Race and the Criminal Justice System

Much contemporary research on crime and deviance has focused on the relationship between race and the American criminal justice system. Today, many sociologists are interested in the ways we try to control, police, and punish deviant behavior—and how our legal system disproportionately punishes individuals of color—in particular, African American men.

Think back to our earlier discussion of the Italian American Mafia. In a later study titled *Black Mafia* (1974), Francis Ianni found that as Italian Mafia members moved out of crime and into the American mainstream, organized crime persisted—with new ethnic groups arriving to take control of former Mafia enterprises. Ianni considers whether this process of "ethnic succession" will occur in the case of black and Puerto Rican Americans, allowing them to take on the mafiosi mantle in the 1960s and 1970s.

Like members of the Italian American Mafia, new members of the black Mafia sought to lead respectable lives and escape urban poverty through illegal means. Ianni's analysis asks whether, over time, the black Mafia "can also follow the pattern of Italians and use these same monies as a basis for movement into legitimate areas" (Gladwell, 2014: 319). Ultimately, Ianni found that the black Mafia faced unique constraints in expanding its criminal organization beyond the ghetto and amassing sufficient wealth to reinvest in the legitimate economy. First, the black Mafia became overly dependent on the drug trade and was unable to diversify its criminal activities in the same way as the Italian Mafia had done. The drug trade upon which they depended would later receive extraordinary scrutiny and punitive action from the federal government and law enforcement officials. Second, they were never able to develop the kinds of relations with white politicians that once contributed to the stability of white organized crime.

Today, rates of mass incarceration linked to the drug trade have reached historic peaks. Police increasingly rely on new surveillance techniques to control crime and the drug trade in urban ghettos, which causes young black men to lead lives as fugitives "on the run" (Goffman, 2014; see Chapter 2). While organized crime may have provided a pathway "up and out" for Italian Americans, it seems to have had the opposite effect for black Americans (Ianni, 1974). Both historically and today, we see how race interacts with our criminal justice system to allow some deviants to enter mainstream society while cutting off those same pathways for others.

Mass Incarceration

Today, the United States locks up more people (nearly all men) per capita than any other country and has by far the most punitive justice system in the world. Although the United States makes up only 4.3 percent of the world's overall population, it accounts for more than 20 percent of the world's prisoners (Walmsley, 2018). The so-called "prison boom" began in the 1970s, with the number of inmates nearly quintupling—from roughly 100 inmates per 100,000 residents for most of the twentieth century to 486 inmates per 100,000 residents by 2004 (Pager, 2007). More than 2.1 million

A prison in Chino, California, is forced to house inmates in the gymnasium due to overcrowding.

people are currently incarcerated in American prisons and jails, with another nearly 4.7 million falling under the jurisdiction of the penal system (Walmsley, 2018; Kaeble and Glaze, 2016; McDonough, 2005; Slevin, 2005).

The American prison system employs more than 700,000 people and costs more than $81 billion annually to maintain (Wagner & Rabuy, 2017; Kyckelhahn, 2015; Slevin, 2005). The price of imprisoning an individual is enormous; it costs an average of $31,977 to keep a prisoner in the federal prison system for one year (Qureshi, 2016). The system has also become partially privatized, with private companies building and administering prisons to accommodate the growing inmate population. Critics claim that a "prison-industrial complex" has emerged. Large numbers of people—including bureaucrats, politicians, and prison employees—have vested interests in the existence and further expansion of the prison system.

Mass incarceration has had a particularly deleterious effect on black communities; indeed, African Americans make up around 33 percent of the current prison population, though they represent only 12 percent of the U.S. population (Gramlich, 2019b). In *The New Jim Crow*, legal scholar Michelle Alexander (2012) argues that mass incarceration creates a kind of caste system in the United States. According to Alexander, understanding mass incarceration means understanding not only the criminal justice system, but also the entire structure of policies and practices that stigmatize and marginalize those who are considered criminals (Alexander, 2012).

These policies and practices affect individuals even after they have been released from prison. In *Marked*, Devah Pager (2007) focuses on the difficulties former inmates face when attempting to find jobs upon release. Given that the ex-inmate population is approximately six times that of the inmate population, Pager argues that it is of critical importance to understand the types of policies governing prisoner re-entry into society (Pager, 2007). By conducting an experiment that involved having both black and white applicants apply to entry-level positions in Milwaukee, Pager found

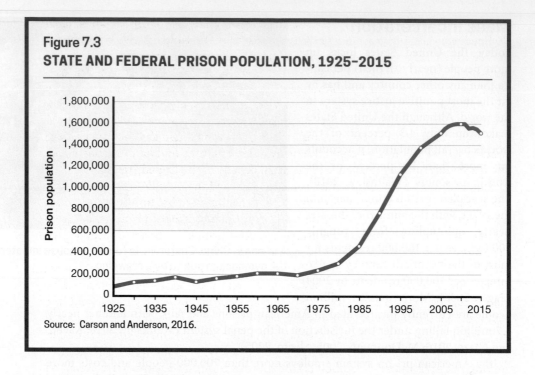

Figure 7.3

STATE AND FEDERAL PRISON POPULATION, 1925–2015

Source: Carson and Anderson, 2016.

that whites were much preferred over blacks, and non-offenders were much preferred over ex-offenders. Employers were half as likely to consider whites with a felony conviction as equally qualified non-offenders. For blacks, the effects were even greater. Black ex-offenders were only one-third as likely to receive a callback compared to non-offenders. But most surprising was the comparison of these two effects: Blacks with no criminal history fared no better than did whites with a felony conviction! Essentially, these results suggest that being a black male in America today is about the same as being a convicted criminal, at least in the eyes of Milwaukee employers. For those who believe that race no longer represents a major barrier to opportunity, these results represent a powerful challenge.

The Death Penalty

Like its mass incarceration rates, the United States' use of capital punishment (the death penalty) makes the country an unusual case compared to other liberal democratic nations. Support for capital punishment is high in the United States, though it has been steadily declining since peaking in the mid-1990s. In 2018, approximately 54 percent of adults surveyed said they favored the death penalty for people convicted of murder; 39 percent opposed it (Oliphant, 2019). This represents a significant shift from 1994, when 80 percent of those surveyed supported the death penalty and only 16 percent were opposed to it. Nevertheless, American support of capital punishment is unusual in an international political climate that has increasingly condemned the use of the death penalty.

In *Peculiar Institution: America's Death Penalty in an Age of Abolition*, David Garland (2010) discusses the political institutions and historical processes that explain the continuing use of the death penalty in the United States. While use of capital punishment declined from the 1940s to mid-1970s (by which time the United States had almost a decade without any executions), use of capital punishment has since increased. Today, between 20 and 40 executions are authorized annually; in 2018, 25 prisoners were executed (Death Penalty Information Center, 2018). From the 1770s to 1970s, the United States followed the example of many other Western nations, permitting capital punishment but steadily reducing its usage. Yet, today, it remains one of the last Western countries legally to permit the practice, and it relies upon capital punishment frequently to penalize violent criminals—a practice many other countries find hard to understand. What accounts for the persistence of the death penalty in the United States?

Some scholars have argued that something exceptional about American culture has allowed the death penalty to remain in place, despite abolition in other countries. However, Garland argues against this view. Rather, American "deviance" from an international trend toward abolishing the death penalty is better understood by looking at the specific historical circumstances, institutions, and social processes that produced this current state of affairs. In particular, Garland argues that three features of the American political system at the federal and state level—"the state's relative autonomy from the national state, the local control of the power to punish, [and] the political dominance of small groups"—explain the historical development of capital punishment in America. Though the Supreme Court had a number of opportunities to overturn the death penalty, concern for the separation of powers and "deference to shifting public sentiment" (Garland, 2010) has discouraged the court from ruling on behalf of the people.

While Garland's nuanced argument relates also to the emergence of liberalism and currents of humanitarian and democratic thought in Western nations, he suggests that the masses are generally in support of the death penalty, while elites will move to

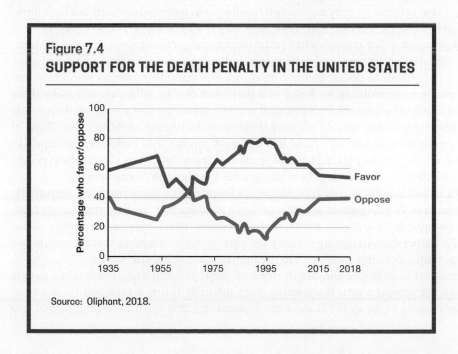

Figure 7.4
SUPPORT FOR THE DEATH PENALTY IN THE UNITED STATES

Source: Oliphant, 2018.

overturn it. In Western nations that have abolished the death penalty, governing elites like judges and legislators made the decision to abolish the death penalty—with or without the support of their citizens. By contrast, the U.S. Supreme Court has repeatedly left the question of capital punishment to the state courts. This unique feature of the American political system, rather than some essential feature of American culture, best accounts for the continued legality of the death penalty in the United States.

As a result of the way the U.S. legal system treats the most deviant of its criminals, the United States is regarded as a deviant nation on the international stage. However, Garland shows that this apparent deviance is actually a function of specific historical and political processes. By taking a historical and sociological approach to law, we see how the study of deviance can be applied even beyond individuals.

Security and Terrorism

In the aftermath of September 11, 2001, the United States began building an encompassing security apparatus to protect the country against the specter of global terrorism. Today, many activities we would have once considered mundane—flying home for the holidays, using public transportation, or calling our loved ones—have become sites of increased security and surveillance. In airports, subways, and federal government buildings nationwide, technologies such as metal detectors and X-ray machines have become commonplace. Do these new security measures protect us against potential threats?

In *Against Security*, Harvey Molotch asks if the securitization of numerous public spaces across the United States has indeed created a safer society—or if it has instead made us more fearful and less safe (Molotch, 2012). Molotch studies new security techniques used in restrooms, airports, and even the former site of New York City's Twin Towers to show how the United States has worked to create the appearance of order through the visible deployment of security personnel and surveillance technology. These extreme security measures treat all of us as potential deviants but have questionable value for weeding out those who may truly endanger public safety. Indeed, Molotch argues that measures like racial or physical profiling, designed to help security officers identify potentially dangerous individuals, can actually make it easier for those individuals to thwart security measures. For example, terrorists who know that wearing specific clothing, or being of a particular race or ethnicity, will make them more likely to be selected for additional security screening can simply send members of their organization who do not have these characteristics to avoid scrutiny. Thus, "if the profile is made into an official list, bad guys can use it to build their scheme"; in other words, profiling on the basis of specific characteristics can actually help people become deviants by showing them which rules they need to circumvent.

In response to these concerns, Molotch advocates for a more reasoned, empathetic approach to thinking about security. Molotch explains that "real security comes from the assemblage of artifacts, habits, and procedures, which mostly are already there" (217). Rather than designing security systems on the assumption that all individuals are potential deviants, he appeals to the human instinct toward "decency"—our natural instinct to help one another in times of need. Molotch argues that when people encounter someone who is drowning, they naturally throw a rope and do not need to be coerced to do so (193). As a result, measures that accord with the formal and informal norms of decency upon which a society already relies will be most effective in preventing deviant behavior.

Molotch's work suggests that our efforts to weed out deviants may not only be ineffective but may also make it more difficult to live together in a society. Our efforts to superimpose a foreign set of norms and regulations to create the appearance of security may dismantle the very mechanisms we already use to maintain social order. For example, consider a city neighborhood in which residents live in cramped, tenement-style housing amid shops and a bustling street life.

Have new security techniques created a safer society or do they just treat everyone like potential deviants, making us more fearful and less safe?

Individuals of different income levels live together and intermingle with residents on the streets, including street vendors, panhandlers, and the homeless. Crowds gather on the sidewalks, a cacophony of languages emanates from the apartments, and vendors call out to potential customers passing by.

To outsiders, this street scene might appear disorganized. They might wonder why police haven't cleared the sidewalk of panhandlers and the homeless or forced vendors to hawk their goods elsewhere. Like the creation of security systems, one could imagine creating highly controlled public spaces and making them available only to certain kinds of residents in an attempt to eliminate this apparent disorder. However, to neighborhood residents who are familiar with one another, the busy street may be one of the safest places in the city. Here, children playing outdoors can rely on the supervision of a whole cast of neighborhood regulars, like shop owners, who help maintain order. Jane Jacobs explored this idea in depth in *The Death and Life of Great American Cities,* where she found that "the public peace . . . of cities is not kept primarily by the police. . . . It is kept primarily by an intricate, almost unconscious, network of voluntary controls and standards among the people themselves, and enforced by the people themselves" (Jacobs, 1961). Like Jacobs, Molotch believes that social order is best maintained by practices that individuals themselves negotiate rather than practices imposed by a higher authority.

Reporting on Crime and Crime Statistics

Does American society really have more crime than other societies? Most TV and newspaper reporting is based on official crime statistics the police collect and the government publishes. Most of these reports are based on two sources: Uniform Crime Reports and victimization studies. Each has its own limitations and offers only a partial portrait of crime in American life.

Uniform Crime Reports (UCR) contain official data on crime that is reported to law enforcement agencies across the country that then provide the data to the FBI. UCR

Figure 7.5
CRIME RATES IN THE UNITED STATES, 1995–2018

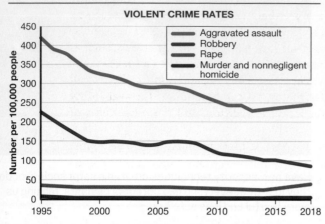

VIOLENT CRIME RATES

Legend:
- Aggravated assault
- Robbery
- Rape
- Murder and nonnegligent homicide

Y-axis: Number per 100,000 people
X-axis: 1995, 2000, 2005, 2010, 2015, 2018

Note: The murder and nonnegligent homicides that occured as a result of the events of September 11, 2001, are not included.

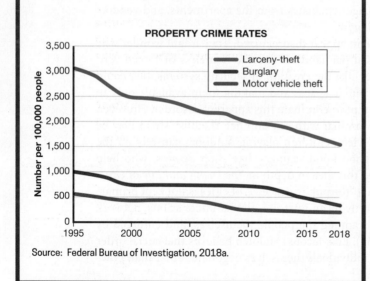

PROPERTY CRIME RATES

Legend:
- Larceny-theft
- Burglary
- Motor vehicle theft

Y-axis: Number per 100,000 people
X-axis: 1995, 2000, 2005, 2010, 2015, 2018

Source: Federal Bureau of Investigation, 2018a.

focus on "index crimes," which include serious crimes such as murder and nonnegligent manslaughter, robbery, forcible rape, aggravated assault, burglary, larceny/theft, motor vehicle theft, and arson (Figure 7.5). Critics of UCR note that the reports do not accurately reflect crime rates because they include only those crimes reported to law enforcement agencies; they don't, for example, include crimes reported to other agencies, such as the IRS. Some argue that by excluding crimes traditionally committed by middle-class persons, such as fraud and embezzlement, UCR reify the belief that crime is an activity of ethnic minorities and the poor.

Because UCR focus narrowly on crimes reported to the police, criminologists also rely on self-reports, or reports provided by the crime victims themselves. This second source of data is essential because some criminologists think that about half of all serious crimes, such as robbery with violence, go unreported. The proportion of less serious crimes that go unreported, especially small thefts, is even higher. Since 1973, the U.S. Bureau of the Census has been interviewing households across the country in its National Crime Victimization Survey (NCVS), which confirms that the overall rate of crime is higher than the index of reported crime. For instance, in 2018, less than 50 percent of violent crime was reported (43 percent), including just 33 percent of rape or sexual assaults, 62 percent of robberies, and 42 percent of simple assaults. Auto theft—a form of property crime—is the crime most frequently reported to the police (69 percent) (Gramlich, 2019a; Truman and Morgan, 2016).

Public concern in the United States focuses on crimes of violence—murder, assault, and rape—even though only about 13 percent of all crimes are violent (Federal Bureau of Investigation [FBI], 2016a). According to the FBI's 2018 Crime in the

United States Report, 1.2 million violent crimes occurred in the United States in 2018 (Federal Bureau of Investigation [FBI], 2018a). In the United States, the most common victims of murder and other violent crimes (with the exception of rape) are young, poor African American men in larger cities. The rate of murder among black male teenagers is more than five times the rate for their white counterparts, although this disparity has declined in recent years. In general, whether indexed by police statistics or the National Crime Victimization Survey, violent crimes, such as burglary and car theft, are more common in cities than in suburbs and more common in suburbs than in smaller towns. The most likely explanation for the overall high level of violent crime in the United States is a combination of the availability of firearms, the general influence of the frontier tradition, and the subcultures of violence in the large cities.

A notable feature of most crimes of violence is their mundane character. Most assaults and homicides bear little resemblance to the murderous, random acts of gunmen or the carefully planned homicides highlighted in the media. Murders generally happen in the context of family and other interpersonal relationships; the victim usually knows the murderer.

Victims and Perpetrators of Crime

Are some individuals or groups more likely to commit crimes or to become the victims of crime? Criminologists say yes—research and crime statistics show that crime and victimization are not randomly distributed among the population (Figure 7.6). Men are more likely than women, for example, to commit crimes; the young are more often involved in crime than are older people.

The likelihood of someone becoming a victim of crime is linked to the area where he or she lives. Inner-city residents run a much greater risk of becoming victims than do residents of affluent suburban areas. The fact that ethnic minorities are concentrated in inner-city regions appears to be a significant factor in their higher rates of victimization.

Gender and Crime

Like other areas of sociology, criminological studies have traditionally ignored half the population: Women are largely invisible in both theoretical considerations and empirical studies. Since the 1970s, important feminist works have noted the way in which criminal transgressions by women occur in different contexts than those by men and how assumptions about appropriate male and female roles influence women's experiences with the criminal justice system. Feminists

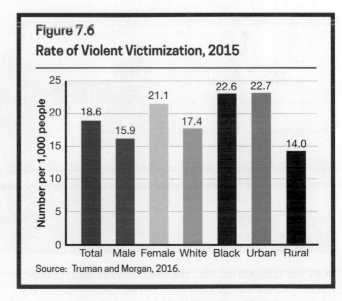

Figure 7.6
Rate of Violent Victimization, 2015

Total: 18.6
Male: 15.9
Female: 21.1
White: 17.4
Black: 22.6
Urban: 22.7
Rural: 14.0

(Number per 1,000 people)

Source: Truman and Morgan, 2016.

have also highlighted the prevalence of violence against women, both at home and in public.

Male and Female Crime Rates The statistics on gender and crime are startling. For example, of all crimes reported in 2018, nearly three-quarters of arrestees (73 percent) were men (OJJDP, 2019). There is also an enormous imbalance in the ratio of men to women in prison, not only in the United States but in all the industrialized countries. In 2017, women made up 7 percent of the state and federal prison populations in the United States (Bronson and Carson, 2019). There are also contrasts between the types of crimes men and women commit. Women's offenses rarely involve violence and are almost all small scale. Petty thefts such as shoplifting and public order offenses such as prostitution and public drunkenness are typical female crimes.

Perhaps the real gender difference in crime rates is smaller than the official statistics show. In the 1950s, Otto Pollak suggested that certain crimes perpetrated by women go unreported because women's domestic role enables them to commit crimes at home and in the private sphere. Pollak (1950) also argued that female offenders are treated more leniently because male police officers adopt a "chivalrous" attitude toward them. The suggestion that the criminal justice system treats women more leniently has prompted much debate. The "chivalry thesis" has been applied in two ways. First, police and other officials may indeed regard female offenders as less dangerous than men and excuse activities for which they would arrest males. Second, in sentencing for criminal offenses, women get sent to prison much less often than men.

A number of empirical studies have tested the chivalry thesis, but the results remain inconclusive. One difficulty is assessing the relative influence of gender compared with other factors such as age, class, and race. For example, older women offenders tend to be treated less aggressively than their male counterparts. Other studies have shown that black women receive worse treatment than white women at the hands of the police.

At 81 per 100,000 in 2017, the imprisonment rate for adult women is significantly lower than the imprisonment rate for adult men: 1,082 per 100,000.

Another perspective, which feminists have adopted, examines how social understandings about femininity affect women's experiences in the criminal justice system. One argument is that women receive harsher treatment when they have allegedly deviated from the norms of female sexuality. For example, young girls who are perceived to be sexually promiscuous are more often taken into custody than boys who are promiscuous. Such young women are seen as doubly deviant—not only breaking the law but also flouting appropriate female behavior. In such cases, they are judged less on the nature of the offense and more on their deviant lifestyle. Thus, the criminal justice system operates under a double standard, considering male aggression and violence as natural but female offenses as reflecting psychological imbalances (Heidensohn, 1985).

To make female crime more visible, feminists have conducted detailed investigations on female criminals—from girl gangs to female terrorists to women in prison. Such studies have shown that violence is not exclusively a characteristic of male criminality. Women are much less likely than men to participate in violent crime but are not always inhibited from doing so. Why, then, are female rates of criminality so much lower than those of men?

Some evidence shows that female lawbreakers often avoid coming before the courts because they persuade the police or other authorities to see their actions in a particular light. They invoke the "gender contract"—the implicit contract between men and women whereby to be a woman is to be erratic and impulsive on the one hand and in need of protection on the other (Worrall, 1990).

Yet differential treatment cannot account for the vast difference between male and female rates of crime. The reasons are probably the same as those that explain gender differences in other spheres: Male crimes remain "male" because of differences in socialization and because men's activities are still more nondomestic than those of most women. Further, control theory may also offer insights. Because women are usually the primary caregiver to their children and other relatives, they may have attachments and commitments that deter them from committing deviant acts. Imprisonment would have very high and undesirable costs both to women and to their kin.

Ever since the late nineteenth century, criminologists have predicted that gender equality would reduce or eliminate the differences in criminality between men and women, but as yet, crime remains a gendered phenomenon.

Crimes against Women In certain categories of crime—domestic violence, sexual harassment, sexual assault, and rape—men are overwhelmingly the aggressors and women the victims. Although each of these acts has been practiced by women against men, they remain almost exclusively crimes against women. It is estimated that one-quarter of women are victims of violence at some point, but all women face the threat of such crimes either directly or indirectly.

For many years, the criminal justice system ignored these offenses; victims had to persevere tirelessly to gain legal recourse. Even today, the prosecution of crimes against women is hardly straightforward. Yet feminist criminology has raised awareness of crimes against women and integrated such offenses into mainstream debates on crime. In this section, we examine the crime of rape, leaving discussions of domestic violence and sexual harassment to other chapters (see Chapters 10 and 15).

The extent of rape is very difficult to assess accurately. Only a small proportion of rapes comes to the attention of the police and is recorded in the statistics. In 2018, 433,648 cases of rape or sexual assault were reported in the United States (RAINN, 2019). However, from surveys of victims, we know that only about a third of instances of rape and sexual assault are reported to the police. At the same time, data from a nationally representative survey indicates that 1 in 6 women and 1 in 33 men in the United States have been victims of a rape or attempted rape (Tjaden and Thoennes, 2010).

The Gulabi Gang, also known as the Pink Vigilantes, fights against police corruption, domestic violence, and sexual abuse by physically attacking policemen who refuse to register rape cases and husbands who hit their wives.

A woman might not report sexual violence for many reasons. The majority of rape victims either wish to put the incident out of their minds or are unwilling to participate in the humiliating process of medical examination, police interrogation, and courtroom cross-examination. The legal process takes a long time and can be intimidating. Courtroom procedure is public, and the victim must face the accused. Proof of penetration, the identity of the rapist, and the fact that the act occurred without the woman's consent all have to be forthcoming. A woman may feel that she is the one on trial, particularly if her own sexual history is examined publicly, as is often the case.

Recently, women's groups have sought change in both legal and public thinking about rape, stressing that rape should not be seen as a sexual offense but as a violent crime. It is not just a physical attack but an assault on an individual's integrity and dignity. Rape is clearly related to the association of masculinity with power, dominance, and toughness. It is not primarily the result of overwhelming sexual desire but of the ties between sexuality and feelings of power and superiority. The sexual act itself is less significant than the debasement of the woman (Estrich, 1987). This campaign has managed to change legislation, and today, rape is generally recognized in law as a type of criminal violence.

In a sense, all women are victims of rape. Women who have never been raped may be afraid to go out alone at night, even on crowded streets, and may be almost equally fearful of being alone in a house or apartment. Susan Brownmiller (1975) has argued that rape is part of a system of male intimidation that keeps all women in fear. Those who are not raped are affected by the anxieties thus provoked and by the need to be more cautious in everyday aspects of life than men have to be.

Crimes against Gays and Lesbians

Feminists claim that understandings of violence are highly gendered and are influenced by perceptions about risk and responsibility. Because women are considered less able to defend themselves, common sense holds that they should modify *their* behavior to reduce the risk of victimhood. For example, not only should women avoid walking in unsafe neighborhoods alone and at night, but they also should avoid dressing provocatively or behaving in a manner that could be misinterpreted. Women who fail to do so can be accused of "asking for trouble." In a court setting, their behavior can be a mitigating factor in considering the perpetrator's act of violence (Dobash and Dobash, 1992; Richardson and May, 1999). It has been suggested that a similar logic applies in violent acts against gay men and lesbians.

Victimization studies reveal that gays and lesbians experience a high incidence of violent crime and harassment. In 2018, there were 1,196 anti-LGBT incidents affecting 1,445 victims (FBI, 2018b). Because sexual minorities remain stigmatized and marginalized in many societies, they are more often treated as deserving of crime rather than as innocent victims. Same-sex relationships are still seen as belonging to the private realm, whereas heterosexuality is the norm in public spaces. Lesbians and gay men who display their sexual identities in public are often blamed for making themselves vulnerable to crime, in a sense even provoking it. This notion ultimately denies both the essential personhood and rights of the victim. Such crimes have led many social groups to call for hate-crime legislation to protect the human rights of groups who remain stigmatized.

Crimes of the Powerful

Although there are connections between crime and poverty, it would be a mistake to suppose that crime is concentrated among the poor. Crimes by people in positions of power and wealth can have farther-reaching consequences than the often petty crimes of the poor. The term **white-collar crime**, introduced by Edwin Sutherland (1949), refers to crime affluent people commit. This category of criminal activity includes tax fraud, antitrust violations, illegal sales practices, securities and land fraud, embezzlement, the manufacture or sale of dangerous products, and illegal environmental pollution, as well as straightforward theft.

The most famous recent case of white-collar crime with obvious victims was the Bernie Madoff scandal. A trusted investment adviser, Madoff turned his wealth-management business into the largest Ponzi scheme in history, defrauding his clients—many of them senior citizens and charitable organizations—and robbing them of more than $18 billion.

The distribution of white-collar crimes is even harder to measure than that of other types of crime; most do not appear in the official statistics at all. Efforts to detect white-collar crime are limited, and rarely do those who are caught go to jail. Although the

white-collar crime Criminal activities carried out by those in white-collar, or professional, jobs.

One of the most high-profile white-collar criminals in recent memory is Bernie Madoff, a financier who choreographed the largest Ponzi scheme in U.S. history.

authorities regard white-collar crime more tolerantly than crimes of the less privileged, the amount of money involved in white-collar crime in the United States is 40 times greater than the amount involved in crimes against property, such as robberies, burglaries, larceny, forgeries, and car thefts (President's Commission on Organized Crime, 1986). Some forms of white-collar crime, moreover, affect more people than lower-class criminality does. An embezzler might rob thousands—or today, via computer fraud, millions—of people.

Corporate Crime **Corporate crime** describes the offenses large corporations commit. The increasing power and influence of large corporations and their global reach mean that they touch our lives in many ways—from producing the cars we drive and the food we eat to affecting the natural environment and the financial markets.

Corporate crime is pervasive and widespread. Both quantitative and qualitative studies of corporate crime have concluded that a large number of corporations do not adhere to legal regulations (Slapper and Tombs, 1999). Studies have revealed six types of violations: *administrative* (paperwork or noncompliance), *environmental* (pollution, permit violations), *financial* (tax violations, illegal payments), *labor* (working conditions, hiring practices), *manufacturing* (product safety, labeling), and *unfair trade practices* (anticompetition, false advertising).

Sometimes there are obvious victims; for instance, environmental disasters such as the 2010 Upper Big Branch coal mine explosion in West Virginia and the health dangers posed to women by silicone breast implants. One of the most devastating examples in recent years was the April 2013 fire and collapse of an eight-story commercial building, Rana Plaza, in Bangladesh. The death toll topped 1,100 with an additional 2,500 injured people rescued from the building. Rana Plaza housed several garment manufacturers. Although building inspectors had found cracks in the building days earlier and recommended that the building be evacuated and shut down, many of the garment workers were forced to return to work the following day.

As the Rana Plaza tragedy demonstrates, the hazards of corporate crime are all too real. But very often, victims of corporate crime do not see themselves as such. This is because in "traditional" crimes, the proximity between victim and offender is much closer; it is difficult not to realize that you have been mugged! In the case of corporate crime, greater distances in time and space mean that victims may not realize they have been victimized or may not know how to seek redress for the crime.

corporate crime Offenses committed by large corporations in society. Examples of corporate crime include pollution, false advertising, and violations of health and safety regulations.

Pollution, product mislabeling, and violations of health and safety regulations affect much larger numbers of people than petty criminality affects. However, the effects of corporate crime are often experi-

The collapse of Rana Plaza in Bangladesh, which killed at least 1,100 and injured another 2,500, is a tragic example of corporate crime.

enced unevenly within society. Those who are disadvantaged by other socioeconomic inequalities suffer disproportionately. For example, safety and health risks in the workplace tend to occur in low-paying occupations. Many of the risks from health care products and pharmaceuticals have affected women more than men, as in the case of contraceptives and fertility treatments with harmful side effects (Slapper and Tombs, 1999).

Cybercrime

It seems certain that the information and telecommunications revolution will change the face of crime. Internet-based fraud is one of the fastest-growing categories of crime. The annual cost of **cybercrime** worldwide is estimated to be $600 billion (Lewis, 2018). The 2019 Global State of SMB Cybersecurity report conducted by the Ponemon Institute and conducted on behalf of Keeper Security found that more than 76 percent of American companies experienced a cyberattack over the previous year, yet only 28 percent of security vio-

> **cybercrime** Criminal activities by means of electronic networks or involving the use of information technologies. Electronic money laundering, personal identity theft, electronic vandalism, and monitoring electronic correspondence are all emergent forms of cybercrime.

1 How does Devah Pager's study of former inmates support Michelle Alexander's argument that mass incarceration has created a new caste system in the United States?

2 According to David Garland, what accounts for the continued use of capital punishment in the United States?

3 Contrast the following two explanations for the gender gap in crime: behavioral differences and biases in reporting.

4 What are some consequences of white-collar crime?

lations were reported to the police, likely out of fears that negative publicity would damage the company's stock price or that competitors would steal valuable information (Computer Security Institute, 2011).

The global reach of telecommunications crime poses challenges for law enforcement in terms of detecting and prosecuting crimes. Police from the countries involved must determine the jurisdiction in which the act occurred and agree on extraditing the offenders and providing evidence for prosecution. Although police cooperation across national borders may improve with the growth of cybercrime, at present, cybercriminals have a great deal of room to maneuver.

At a time when financial, commercial, and production systems in countries worldwide are being integrated electronically, rising levels of Internet fraud and unauthorized electronic intrusions are potent warnings of the vulnerability of computer security systems. From the FBI to the Japanese government's anti-hacker police force, governments are scrambling to contend with new and elusive forms of cross-national computer activity.

4 UNANSWERED QUESTIONS

Why Have Crime Rates Gone Down?

Beginning in the 1990s, crime rates began to decline nationwide. In 2011, the Federal Bureau of Investigation announced that crime rates reached a 40-year low—even in the aftermath of the recession of 2008, bucking the conventional wisdom that poor economic conditions lead to elevated crime rates. Incredibly, rates of murder, rape, aggravated assault, and robbery, dropped considerably—though some cities (such as New York) experienced some increases in numbers of violent crime. That said, these increases pale in comparison to comparable figures in the 1990s (Oppel, 2011).

Criminologists nationwide have offered a number of different explanations for this decline. Some have suggested that better economic conditions and lower unemployment lead to decreased crime rates, though lower crime rates following the 2008 recession present a challenge to this theory. Others argue that citizens have become more adept at protecting themselves against crime through the use of sophisticated home security systems, while policing has become more targeted and disciplined, with police now using "hot-spot policing" to station officers around areas in which they know crime rates are relatively high. Still more scholars have suggested that the drop in crime may be related to decreasing cocaine and other illegal drug usage or even lower levels of lead in Americans' blood (which has been linked to higher levels of aggression in children) (Wilson, 2011).

As we have seen earlier in this chapter, one popular hypothesis is that mass incarceration is related to a lower crime rate. Given that the U.S. crime rate decreased over roughly the same period (beginning in the mid-1970s), this correlation might suggest that imprisonment is an effective deterrent for crime. Indeed, Americans today favor tougher prison sentences for all but relatively minor crimes. However, even if the prison system were expanded, it wouldn't significantly reduce the level of serious crime. Less than half of violent crimes result in arrest, and nearly half of arrests do not result in conviction (FBI, 2014c; FBI, 2014d). Further, America's prisons are so overcrowded that the average convict released from prison served less than half of their sentence (Kaeble, 2018).

About one-third of African American men are in the U.S. correctional system (NAACP, 2014; Gramlich, 2019b). In some major urban areas, counting those currently in prison, more than half of working-age African American men have criminal records (Alexander, 2011). Given that prisons often make offenders more hardened criminals, it is increasingly unclear whether imprisonment leads to a lower crime rate. The harsher and more oppressive prison conditions are, the more likely it is that inmates will be brutalized by the experience. Yet if prisons were attractive and pleasant places to live, would they have a deterrent effect?

Although prisons do keep some dangerous men (and a tiny minority of dangerous women) off the streets, evidence suggests a need for other means to deter crime. Robert Gangi, director of the Correctional Association of New York, said that "building more prisons to address crime is like building more graveyards to address a fatal disease" (quoted in Smolowe, 1994).

All in all, a sociological interpretation of crime makes clear that there are no quick fixes. The causes of crime, especially crimes of violence, are bound up with structural conditions of American society, including widespread poverty, the condition of the inner cities, and the deteriorating life circumstances of many young men.

Can We Reduce Crime through New Policing Techniques?

Some sociologists and criminologists have suggested that visible policing techniques, such as patrolling the streets, are reassuring for the public. Such activities support the perception that the police actively control crime, investigate offenses, and support the criminal justice system. But sociologists also see a need to reassess the role of policing in the late modern age. Policing, they argue, is now less about controlling crime and more about detecting and managing risks. Mostly it involves communicating knowledge about risk to other institutions in society that demand such information (Ericson and Haggerty, 1997).

According to this view, police are primarily "knowledge workers," spending time processing information, drafting reports, or communicating data. Consider the "simple" case of an automobile accident in Ontario, Canada. A police officer is called to the scene of an automobile accident involving two vehicles, with minor injuries and one drunk driver. The investigation takes one hour; the drunk driver is criminally charged with the impaired operation of a motor vehicle, causing bodily harm, and operating a motor vehicle under the influence of excess alcohol. The driver's license is automatically suspended for 12 hours.

Following this routine investigation, the officer spends 3 hours writing up 16 reports. Here, the role of police as brokers of information becomes clear:

- The provincial motor registry requires information about the location of the accident and the vehicles and people involved. This registry is used for risk profiling in accident-prevention initiatives, traffic management, and resource allocation.
- The automobile industry needs to know about the vehicles involved to improve safety standards, report to regulatory agencies, and provide safety information to consumer groups.
- The insurance companies involved need information to determine responsibility and make awards in the case. They also require police information to develop statistical profiles of risk to set premiums and compensation levels for clients.
- The public health system requires details on the injuries. This knowledge is used for statistical profiles and to plan emergency-service provision.
- The criminal courts require police information as material for the prosecution and as proof that the police properly investigated the scene and collected evidence.
- The police administration itself requires reports on the incident for both internal records and national computer databases.

This example reveals how police work is increasingly about "mapping" and predicting risk within the population.

The informational demands of other institutions, such as the insurance industry, now require that police gather and report information in a way that is compatible with the needs of outside agencies. Computerized systems and forms define the way in which police report information. Rather than writing narrative accounts, police input the facts of a case into standardized forms by checking off boxes and choosing among available options. The information is used to categorize people and events as part of creating risk profiles. But such close-ended reporting formats influence what police observe and investigate, how they understand and interpret an incident, and the approach they take in resolving a problem. This emphasis on information collection and processing can alienate and frustrate many police officers, who see a distinction between "real" police work (e.g., investigating crimes) and the bureaucratic "donkey work" of reports and paper trails.

In recent years, several high-profile court cases have attracted mainstream media attention around stop-and-frisk policies in major American cities. These policies work to put a visible police presence in communities with high crime rates by temporarily detaining and questioning individuals at an officer's discretion. In a decision declaring New York's stop-and-frisk policy to be unconstitutional, federal judge Shira A. Scheindlin declared that the frequent stops made by N.Y. police were in violation of the Fourth Amendment, which protects citizens from unreasonable searches and seizures. Judge Scheindlin's decision asks us to consider the effects of such policies in communities where individuals of color—overwhelmingly young men of color—are targeted by police officials on a near daily basis.

In *Punished: Policing the Lives of Black and Latino Boys* (2011), sociologist Victor Rios describes the lived experience of young black and Hispanic American men in Oakland, California. While Rios discusses much broader themes related to the policing of young men of color, temporary detainment policies such as stop and frisk contribute significantly to the "mass and ubiquitous criminalization of marginalized young people" (Rios, 2011). Rios documents the strain that policies like stop and

Sociologist Victor Rios documented how the pervasive presence of police created a culture of mistrust and resistance to authority for young black and Hispanic men in Oakland, California.

frisk place on heavily policed communities, and how young men respond to the pervasive presence of police and other authority figures in their schools and neighborhoods. For the men in Rios's study, negative interactions with police officers are a regular occurrence. These policies affect not only their daily lives but also the way in which they perceive themselves and their long-term life trajectories. Punitive policing created a culture of mistrust and resistance to authority, and even those who seldom broke the rules were perceived negatively by others in their community. In this setting, teachers and potential employers often interpreted innocuous behavior as acts of deviance or criminal activity and denied the young men access to the resources that could have helped them grow in positive ways.

Today, governments eager to appear decisive on crime favor work to increase the number and resources of the police. But it is not clear that a greater police presence translates into lower crime rates. In the United States, official statistics on violent crime rates and number of police cast doubt on such a link (Figure 7.7). This finding raises puzzling questions: If increased policing does not prevent violent crime, why does the public demand a visible police presence? What role does policing play in our society, and what role should it play?

Will New Surveillance Technologies Eliminate Deviance?

If you went about life knowing that a camera would record all your activities, would this knowledge encourage you to be a better rule follower? How about at work? Would it encourage you to do your job better, or to act in a more ethical manner? City officials in Oakland, California, and New York City seem to think so. In 2011, the Oakland police department mandated that its officers work with cameras attached to their

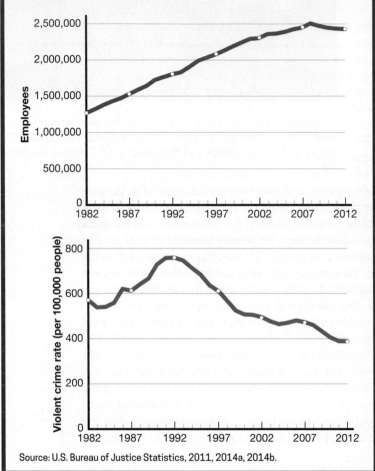

Figure 7.7

JUSTICE EMPLOYMENT AND CRIME RATES, 1982–2012

Although the number of police steadily increased between 1982 and 2012, the crime rate dropped, increased, and dropped again during this period. Therefore, no causal link can be made between the number of police and the crime rate.

Source: U.S. Bureau of Justice Statistics, 2011, 2014a, 2014b.

bodies to document arrests and traffic stops (Goode, 2011). Similarly, the tragic death of Eric Garner in 2014 at the hands of New York City police officers led New York's public to call for the use of body cameras for the NYPD (James, 2014; Glenza, 2011). In both cases, officials hope that body cameras will hold police accountable for their actions, address citizen concerns about abuse of power, and encourage more consistent adherence to codes of police behavior.

To sociologists, these cases raise a broader question about the relationship between deviance and privacy. In the absence of privacy—the assurance that you can go about your life without having a record of all your actions—is it possible to be anything *but* a rule follower? Further, if everyone is a rule follower, does this lead to a safer or more equitable society?

Based on our earlier discussions of crime prevention, you might be tempted to conclude that societies are always better off when people follow the rules. However, in some cases, not complying with the rules may facilitate social interactions, reduce power inequalities, or enable positive social change. Consider as an example social movements like the Arab Spring, where defiance of the law enabled individuals to demand democracy and respect for human rights. If constant government surveillance made it impossible for these individuals to break rules and engage in politically subversive acts, democratic movements in Egypt, Tunisia, Libya, and elsewhere may have never occurred.

You might also think back to the example used in the introduction of this chapter in which Mafia members broke the law to enter into mainstream society. If the police had access to a detailed record of all criminal activities linked to the Lupollo clan, the family may never have succeeded in becoming respectable. For the Lupollos, strict adherence to the rules might have offered fewer opportunities for upward mobility.

Finally, in everyday life, think about the role of white lies, or lies by omission, when speaking with someone you have only just met. On first dates, or meetings with potential employers—where stakes of the interaction are high—we may smooth social interactions by obscuring or selectively revealing the truth. In many ways, falsehoods and deviance from normative behavior are important in social life, helping us navigate new, complex social situations (Levy, 2014).

This discussion is particularly relevant in the context of recent revelations of surveillance and wiretapping conducted by the National Security Agency and other state bodies. Even data collection by private firms like Facebook and Google have raised new concerns about a citizen's right to privacy in the contemporary age. If the government and large corporations have the ability to track your movements, what you say online, and even what you say to close friends and family, is it still possible to be a rule breaker and deviate from norms in ways that may be conducive to social life?

On the one hand, new technologies can lead to what some legal scholars have referred to as "gap closure"—or the more thorough enforcement of laws regulating our conduct. Instead of hiring a police officer to watch an intersection all day and ticket people who run red lights, it may be more efficient to install a camera that can impartially capture all the rule breakers. The absence of human bias in law enforcement could lead to a more exact correspondence between laws and intended behaviors. However, as we have noted, the imperfect realization of certain norms may actually serve important social functions. What's more, "closing" the gap between certain rules and social expectations may lead to the rise of new gaps, perhaps in the ways that we interface with technologies or circumvent them to go about our lives (Levy, 2014).

Can We Prevent Crime by Building Stronger Communities?

Preventing crime and reducing fear of crime are both closely related to rebuilding strong communities. As we saw in our earlier discussion of the broken windows theory, one of the most significant discoveries in criminology in recent years is that the decay of day-to-day civility relates directly to criminality. For a long time, attention was focused almost exclusively on serious crime: robbery, assault, and other violent crime. More minor crimes and forms of public disorder, however, tend to have a cumulative effect. When asked to describe their problems, residents of troubled neighborhoods mention abandoned cars, graffiti, prostitution, youth gangs, and similar phenomena.

People act on their anxieties about these issues; they leave the areas in question if they can, buy heavy locks for their doors and bars for their windows, and abandon public places like parks. Fearful citizens stay off the streets, avoid certain neighborhoods, and curtail their normal activities and associations. As they withdraw physically, they also withdraw from roles of mutual support for fellow citizens, thereby relinquishing the social controls that formerly helped maintain civility within the community.

Community Policing

One popular idea to combat this development is to have police work closely with citizens to improve local community standards and civil behavior, using education, persuasion, and counseling instead of incarceration. **Community policing** implies not only involving citizens but also changing the outlook of police forces. A renewed emphasis on crime prevention rather than law enforcement can support a reintegration of policing with the community and reduce the siege mentality that develops when police have little regular contact with ordinary citizens.

To be effective, partnerships among government agencies, the criminal justice system, local associations, and community organizations have to include all economic and ethnic groups (Kelling and Coles, 1997). Government and business can act together to repair urban decay. One model is the creation of urban enterprise zones, which provide tax breaks for corporations that participate in strategic planning and invest in designated areas. To be successful, such schemes demand a long-term commitment to social objectives.

Emphasizing these strategies does not mean denying the links among unemployment, poverty, and crime. Rather, when coordinated with community-based approaches to crime prevention, these approaches can contribute directly and indirectly to furthering social justice. Where social order has decayed along with public services, other opportunities, such as new jobs, decline also. Improving the quality of life in a neighborhood by providing job opportunities and public services can lead to a revival of such areas.

Shaming as Punishment

The current emphasis on imprisonment as a means of deterring crime can cripple the social ties within certain communities. In recent years, **shaming**—a form of punishment that maintains the offender's ties to the community—has grown in popularity as an alternative to incarceration. Some criminologists see the fear of being shamed within one's community as an important deterrent to crime. As a result, the public's formal disapproval could deter crime as effectively as incarceration, without the high costs of building and maintaining prisons.

Criminologist John Braithwaite (1996) has suggested that shaming practices can take two forms: "reintegrative shaming" and "stigmatizing shaming." Stigmatizing shaming is related to labeling theory, discussed earlier, by which a criminal is labeled as a threat to society and is treated as an outcast. The labeling process and society's efforts to marginalize the individual reinforce that person's criminal conduct, perhaps leading

community policing A renewed emphasis on crime prevention rather than law enforcement to reintegrate policing within the community.

shaming A way of punishing criminal and deviant behavior based on rituals of public disapproval rather than incarceration. The goal of shaming is to maintain the ties of the offender to the community.

to future criminal behavior and higher crime rates.

The very different practice of reintegrative shaming works as follows: People central to the criminal's immediate community—such as family members, employers and coworkers, and friends—are brought into court to state their condemnation of the offender's behavior. At the same time, these people must accept responsibility for reintegrating the offender back into the community. The goal is to rebuild the individual's social bonds to the community as a means of deterring future criminal conduct.

Former Tampa police chief Jane Castor greets community members during the National Night Out, an initiative that fosters citizen involvement in crime prevention.

Japan, with one of the lowest crime rates in the world, has successfully implemented this approach. The process is based on a voluntary network of more than 500,000 local crime-prevention associations dedicated to facilitating reintegration into the community and on a criminal justice system that attempts to be lenient for this purpose. As a result, in Japan, only 5 percent of convicted individuals serve time in prison, compared with 30 percent in the United States. Reintegrative shaming is already a familiar practice in American social institutions such as the family. When a child misbehaves, the parent may express disapproval and try to make the child feel ashamed of her conduct but, at the same time, reassure her that she is a loved member of the family.

Could reintegrative shaming succeed in the U.S. criminal justice system? In spite of the beliefs that these tactics are "soft" on crime, that Americans are too individualistic to participate in community-based policing, and that high-crime areas are less community oriented, community networks have successfully worked with the police in preventing crime. These social bonds could also be fostered to increase the power of shame and to reintegrate offenders into local networks of community involvement.

CONCEPT CHECKS

1 Name three explanations for declining crime rates in the United States.

2 According to Victor Rios, why are policies like stop and frisk problematic?

3 What are police officers' primary tasks each day?

4 What are two specific ways by which community members can combat local crime?

THE BIG PICTURE

Chapter 7
Conformity, Deviance,
and Crime

1   Basic Concepts

p. 199

2   Society and Crime: Sociological Theories

p. 202

LEARNING OBJECTIVES

Learn how we define deviance and how it is related to social power and social class. Recognize the ways in which we encourage conformity.

Know the leading sociological theories of crime and how each is useful in understanding deviance.

TERMS TO KNOW

norms • deviance • deviant subculture • sanction • laws • crime

anomie • relative deprivation • differential association • labeling theory • primary deviation • secondary deviation • conflict theory • control theory

CONCEPT CHECKS

1. How do sociologists define deviance?
2. Is all crime deviant? Is all deviance criminal? Why?
3. Contrast positive and negative sanctions.

1. How do Merton's and Durkheim's definitions of anomie differ?
2. What is the core idea behind differential association theory?
3. What are two criticisms of labeling theory?
4. What are the root causes of crime, according to conflict theorists?
5. How does the theory of broken windows exemplify the core ideas of control theory?

Exercises: Thinking Sociologically

1. Summarize several leading theories explaining crime and deviance presented in this chapter: differential association, anomie, labeling, conflict, and control theories. Which theory appeals to you the most? Explain why.

2. Explain how differences in power and social influence can play a significant role in defining and sanctioning deviant behavior.

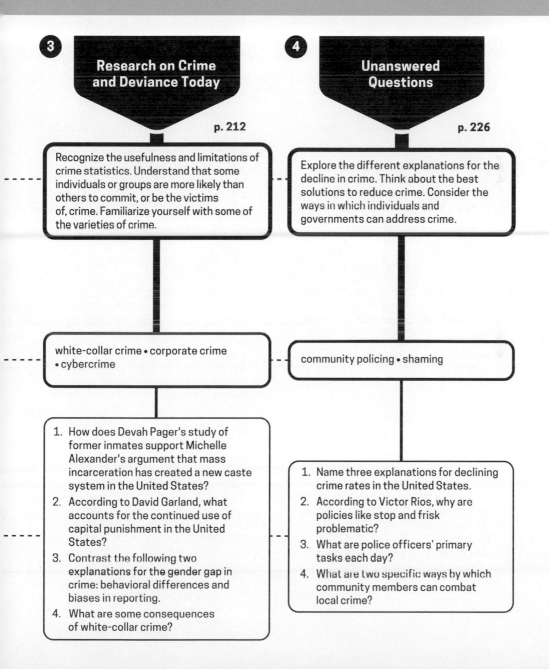

3

Research on Crime and Deviance Today

p. 212

Recognize the usefulness and limitations of crime statistics. Understand that some individuals or groups are more likely than others to commit, or be the victims of, crime. Familiarize yourself with some of the varieties of crime.

white-collar crime • corporate crime • cybercrime

1. How does Devah Pager's study of former inmates support Michelle Alexander's argument that mass incarceration has created a new caste system in the United States?
2. According to David Garland, what accounts for the continued use of capital punishment in the United States?
3. Contrast the following two explanations for the gender gap in crime: behavioral differences and biases in reporting.
4. What are some consequences of white-collar crime?

4

Unanswered Questions

p. 226

Explore the different explanations for the decline in crime. Think about the best solutions to reduce crime. Consider the ways in which individuals and governments can address crime.

community policing • shaming

1. Name three explanations for declining crime rates in the United States.
2. According to Victor Rios, why are policies like stop and frisk problematic?
3. What are police officers' primary tasks each day?
4. What are two specific ways by which community members can combat local crime?

Structures of Power

Power is an ever-present phenomenon in social life. In all human groups, some individuals have more authority or influence than others, and groups themselves have varying degrees of power. Power and inequality are closely linked. The powerful are able to accumulate valued resources, such as property and wealth; possession of such resources in turn generates more power.

In this part, we explore some of the main systems of power and inequality. Chapter 8 discusses stratification and class structure—the ways in which inequalities are distributed within societies. Chapter 9, on global inequality, examines the ways in which inequalities are distributed across societies. Chapter 10 analyzes the differ-ences and inequalities between men and women and how these inequalities are related to others based on class and race. Chapter 11, on ethnicity and race, examines the tensions between people who are physically or culturally different from one another. Chapter 12 discusses the experience of growing old and analyzes related social problems.

Chapter 13 examines the state, political power, and social movements. Governments are specialists in power; they are the source of the directives that influence many of our daily activities. However, they are also the focus of resistance and rebellion, political action that can lead to political and social change.

8

Stratification, Class, and Inequality

U.S. national politics and presidential elections have in recent years been heavily influenced by which of the founding fathers of sociology:

A Émile Durkheim

B Karl Marx

C Max Weber

TURN THE PAGE FOR THE CORRECT ANSWER.

LEARNING OBJECTIVES

1 Basic Concepts

Learn about social stratification and the importance of social background in an individual's chances for material success.

2 Theories Of Stratification In Modern Societies

Know the most influential theories of stratification, including those of Karl Marx, Max Weber, and Erik Olin Wright.

3 Research On Social Stratification Today

Know the class differences in U.S. society, what influences them, and how they are defined and determined. Recognize the ways in which the gap between rich and poor has grown larger. Learn the processes by which people become marginalized in a society and the forms this marginalization takes.

4 Unanswered Questions

Learn about competing explanations for why poverty exists and the means for combating it. Understand your own chances for social mobility. Learn how changes in the U.S. economy since the 1970s have led to growing inequalities.

In 2016, an unknown 29-year-old bartender named Alexandria Ocasio-Cortez (AOC) rose to national prominence when she defeated a powerful long-time incumbent congressman from her own party in the Democratic primary and went on to win the general election in New York's 14th congressional district. What was extraordinary about this feat was not simply that the candidate was a bartender, or still in her twenties, but that she was a self-identified socialist.

A socialist believes that government control of the economy—rather than a free-market capitalist system—will result in greater equality and democracy and be better for the working classes. Such ideas are currently more popular among young Americans now than during much of the twentieth century, when the country was generally averse to government interference in the economy. The correct answer to the opening question is *b*: These ideas are associated with one of the founders of sociology, Karl Marx.

By the end of 2016, the ideas of Karl Marx had reached the height of popularity in modern politics through the presidential campaign of Senator Bernie Sanders, and this laid the groundwork for the emergence of candidates like AOC in 2018. What was it about Sanders and AOC that was so indebted to Karl Marx? It was that they both viewed the capitalist system, driven by the constant search for profits, as the major problem facing American society. These profits had created massive wealth for a very small percentage of the population, while others such as the new generation of college graduates were struggling as never before. To cite one example, by the end of 2019, outstanding student loans had reached $1.5 trillion, in comparison with credit card debt ($1.08 trillion) and automobile loans ($1.19 trillion) (Board of Gover-

THE ANSWER IS B.

nors of the Federal Reserve System, 2020a). Graduates of the class of 2018 had an average of around $29,200 in student loan debt (Institute for College Access & Success, 2019). If you have a student loan, you are in good company: Two-thirds (65 percent) of graduating seniors have had to borrow to pay for the rising cost of higher education (Institute for College Access and Success, 2019). Politicians like Sanders and AOC highlight the economic and personal impacts of student debt and have made student loan forgiveness key aspects of their policy platforms.

Not all sociologists who are interested in inequality are concerned with capitalism, but the rise of socialist candidates in the United States has given new relevance to those scholars. We will discuss their work in this chapter, as well as others who are mainly interested in how differences in income and wealth affect one's life chances, from getting an affordable college education to enjoying a middle class lifestyle. Along the way, we will examine what sociologists have to say about social stratification—why social classes emerge, the reasons for social inequality, the degree to which a college education "pays off" in the sense of assuring a lifetime of earnings that will more than compensate for the cost of the education itself.

The differences explained here are directly related to the existence of inequalities within American society that result from class disparities. In this chapter, we will introduce a key concept of sociology: **social stratification**. By this we mean inequalities among individuals and groups that are determined not so much by individual personality or small-scale social situations but, more broadly, by attributes such as gender, age, race, ethnicity, or religious affiliation. The study of the interacting effects of these different sources of inequality, and the resulting experiences of oppression, is termed **intersectionality**.

In this chapter, we will focus on stratification with regard to societal inequalities based on social class—aspects of wealth, income, education, and lifestyle—although we will touch on gender, racial, and ethnic differences as well. In later chapters, we will consider more directly how gender (Chapter 10), race and ethnicity (Chapter 11), and age (Chapter 12) contribute to stratification.

Individuals and groups enjoy unequal access to rewards depending on their position within the larger stratification scheme. Stratification can thus be defined as **structured inequalities** between and among groups of people belonging to different classes, races, and genders. Sociologists see these inequalities as built into the economic and political system, rather than as resulting from individual differences or chance occurrences, such as being the most handsome or beautiful person in a class. We can picture stratification as the geological layering of rock in the earth's surface. Societies consist of strata in a hierarchy, with the more favored at the top and the less privileged nearer the bottom.

social stratification The existence of structured inequalities between groups in society in terms of their access to material or symbolic rewards. While all societies involve some forms of stratification, only with the development of state-based systems did wide differences in wealth and power arise. The most distinctive form of stratification in modern societies is class divisions.

intersectionality A sociological perspective that holds that our multiple group memberships affect our lives in ways that are distinct from single group memberships. For example, the experience of a Black woman may be distinct from that of a White woman or a Black man.

structured inequalities Social inequalities that result from patterns in the social structure.

1 BASIC CONCEPTS

Systems of Stratification

Historically, a few basic systems of stratification have existed in human societies: slavery, caste, and class. **Slavery** is an extreme form of inequality in which some individuals are literally owned by others as property. As a formal institution, slavery is illegal in every country and has almost completely disappeared.

Caste is associated with the cultures of the Indian subcontinent and the Hindu belief in rebirth. In caste systems, one's social status is given for life. This means that all individuals must remain at the social level of their birth throughout their life. It is believed that individuals who fail to abide by the rituals and duties of their caste will be reborn in an inferior position in their next life. Caste systems structure the type of contact that can occur between members of different ranks.

Class systems differ in many respects from slavery and castes. We can define a **class** as a large-scale grouping of people who share common economic resources that strongly influence the type of lifestyle they are able to lead. The concept of life chances, introduced by Max Weber, is the best way to understand what class means. Your **life chances** are the opportunities you have for achieving economic prosperity. The idea of life chances is important because it emphasizes that although class is a

Women from the Dalit caste (formally known as *untouchables*) earn a living as sewage scavengers in the slums of Ranchi, retrieving human waste from residential dry latrines and emptying the buckets into nearby gutters and streams.

powerful influence on what happens in our lives, it is not completely determining. Class divisions affect which neighborhoods we live in, what lifestyles we follow, and even which romantic partners we choose (Mare, 1991; Massey, 1996). But they don't fix people for life in specific social positions, as the older systems of stratification did. Class systems differ from slavery and castes in four main ways: Class systems are fluid, and movement is possible; positions are partly achieved; classes are economically based; and class systems are large-scale and impersonal. The chief bases of class are income, ownership of wealth, education, occupation, and lifestyle.

Let's begin our exploration of classes in modern societies by looking at basic divisions of income, wealth, educational attainment, and occupational status within the population as a whole.

Income

Income, which refers to wages and salaries earned from paid occupations plus money received from investments, serves as an important determinant of one's social position. One of the most significant changes over the past century has been the rising real income of the majority of the working population. ("Real income" is income excluding increases due to inflation, and provides a fixed standard of comparison from year to year.) Blue-collar workers, who typically perform physical labor such as manufacturing or construction work, now earn three to four times as much in real income in Western societies as their counterparts earned in the early 1900s, although they have seen their real income drop in the first two decades of the twenty-first century. Gains for managerial and professional workers, often known as "white-collar workers," have been higher still. In terms of earnings per person (per capita) and the range of goods and services their earnings can purchase, many Americans today are more affluent than any peoples have previously been in human history. One of the most important reasons for this is "increasing productivity"—output per worker—through technological development in industry. Another reason is almost everything we consume is now made in countries where wages are extremely low, keeping costs (and therefore prices) down. While this situation has been good for American consumers, it has not been so good for American workers, as we shall see later in this chapter, as well as in Chapters 9 and 14.

Even though real income has risen in the past century, these earnings have not been distributed evenly across groups. In other words, not everyone has shared equally in the growing productivity of the U.S. economy. Between 1993 and 2015, the average income of the bottom 99 percent of American households only grew by about 14 percent. In contrast, the income of the top 1 percent of households jumped nearly 95 percent (Saez, 2016). In 2018, the mean household income of the top 5 percent was around $416,520, according to the U.S. Census Bureau, compared to under $13,775 for the bottom 20 percent of American households (Semega et al., 2019) (Figure 8.1).

Since the 1970s, income inequality has been increasing dramatically; it is currently greater than at any time since 1928, the year before the Great Depression. In 1928, the richest 1 percent of families received nearly a quarter of all U.S. pretax income, while the bottom 90 percent (that is, everyone except the richest 10 percent) received about half. The Depression, which wiped out much of the wealth in the country and left millions unemployed, led to government policies aimed in part at protecting working- and middle-class Americans. President Franklin

slavery A form of social stratification in which some people are owned by others as their property.

caste A social system in which one's social status is held for life.

class systems A system of social hierarchy that allows individuals to move among classes. The four chief bases of class are ownership of wealth, occupation, income, and education.

class Although it is one of the most frequently used concepts in sociology, there is no clear agreement about how the notion should be defined. Most sociologists use the term to refer to socioeconomic variations among groups of individuals that create variations in their material prosperity and power.

life chances A term introduced by Max Weber to signify a person's opportunities for achieving economic prosperity.

income Money received from paid wages and salaries or earned from investments.

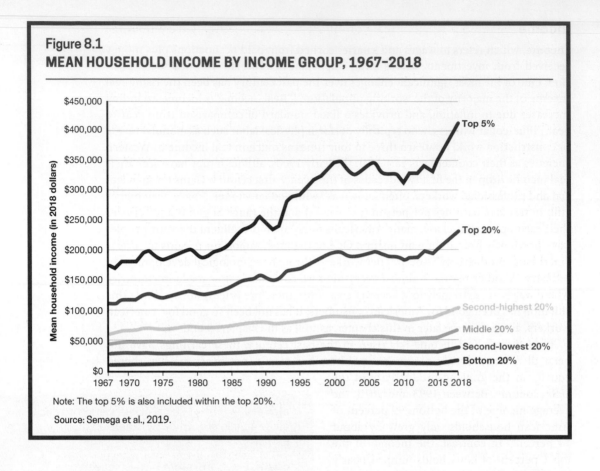

Figure 8.1

MEAN HOUSEHOLD INCOME BY INCOME GROUP, 1967–2018

Note: The top 5% is also included within the top 20%.

Source: Semega et al., 2019.

Delano Roosevelt's "New Deal," which created Social Security, welfare, housing, and many public works, resulted in the redistribution of income from the wealthiest Americans to working-class Americans. By 1944, the richest 1 percent of Americans were down to about a tenth of all U.S. pretax income, while the bottom 90 percent were up to two-thirds, an income distribution that remained until the end of the 1970s.

Today, the richest 1 percent are back up to over a quarter, while the lowest 90 percent are below half—for the first time since the U.S. government has kept records of income distribution. And inequality appears to be worsening. Between 1993 and 2018, the average income of American families rose by 30 percent; however, this growth was not shared evenly. The average income of the top 1 percent of all American families grew by 100.5 percent, while the average income of the bottom 99 percent rose by 18.3 percent. This means that the top 1 percent captured almost 50 percent of all gains in income over the period (Saez, 2018).

Wealth

Wealth is usually measured in terms of net worth: all the assets one owns (for example, cash, savings and checking accounts, investments in stocks and bonds, and real estate properties) minus one's debts (for example, home mortgages, credit card balances, loans that need to be repaid). Jeff Bezos, the richest person in the world in 2020, had an estimated net worth in that year of $110.5 billion, derived largely from the value of Amazon stock that he owns.

It is extremely difficult to get a truly accurate measure of wealth in the United States because the wealthiest Americans have ways of effectively hiding their wealth through trusts and foundations, as well as offshore tax havens and other tax shelters (Saez and Zucman, 2016). Nonetheless, some highly detailed (and mathematically sophisticated) efforts have recently been made to get a better picture of trends in wealth concentration (Piketty and Goldhammer, 2014; Piketty and Zucman, 2014; Saez and Zucman, 2016; Alvaredo, Atkinson, Piketty, and Saez, 2013). This research finds that trends in wealth inequality parallel those with income inequality: The rich are getting much, much wealthier relative to everyone else, mainly due to soaring top incomes. In the 1920s, before the Great Depression, the bottom 90 percent of Americans accounted for one-fifth of total wealth in the United States. In the mid-1980s, their share had risen to more than a third; but today, it has dropped to under a quarter. The vast majority of Americans are saddled with unpaid credit cards, and, as we learned in the chapter opener, many owe money for student loans, automobiles, and home mortgages.

The type of wealth one has also differs between the very rich and everybody else. Although most people make money from work, the wealthy often derive the bulk of their money from their investments, some of which may be inherited. Some scholars argue that wealth, not income, is the real indicator of social class because it is less sensitive to fluctuations due to shifting work hours, health, and other factors that might affect one's income in a given year. Much of the wealth of the wealthy lies in financial assets such as stocks, bonds, mutual funds, and other forms of investment, whereas for most Americans, their home is the principal form of wealth. For households whose net worth is in excess of $500,000, financial assets account for 75 percent of all wealth, only 13.5 percent comes from their homes. For all other households, homes account for more than half of their wealth, with only a third coming from financial assets (Board of Governors of the Federal Reserve System, 2020a; Shorrocks et al., 2019a).

Today, the average net worth of all American families is only $97,300, while the average net worth of the top 10 percent has grown to $1.6 million, the top 1 percent to $4 million and that of the top 0.1 percent, $111 million (Board of Governors of the Federal Reserve System, 2020a; Gold, 2017). Stated somewhat differently, the wealthiest 0.1 percent of Americans (160,700 families) have about as much wealth as the bottom 90 percent (144 million families) (Saez and Zucman, 2016). There are significant differences in net worth by race. The median net worth of White households was $171,000 in 2013, compared to $17,600 for Blacks (Dettling et al., 2017).

What are some of the reasons for the racial disparity in financial assets? The old adage "It takes money to make money" is a fact of life for those who start with little or no wealth. Because Whites, on average, have enjoyed higher incomes and levels of wealth than Blacks have, many Whites can accrue even more wealth, which they pass on to their children (Conley, 1999). But family advantages are not the only factors. Melvin Oliver and Thomas Shapiro (2006) argue that it is easier for Whites to obtain assets, even when they have fewer resources than Blacks do, because discrimination affects the racial gap in home ownership. Blacks are rejected for mortgages 60 percent more often than Whites are, even when they have the same qualifications and

wealth Money and material possessions held by an individual or group.

The recent subprime mortgage crisis left many Americans bankrupt. Blacks, Hispanics, and those living in the inner city were most likely to lose their homes.

creditworthiness. A recent study found that in 2016, Blacks were denied loans 21 percent of the time as compared to Whites who were denied 8.1 percent of the time (Yale, 2018). When Blacks do receive mortgages, they are more likely to take "subprime" mortgage loans that charge much higher interest rates. In 2006, 30 percent of Blacks took out subprime home loans, compared with 24 percent of Hispanics and 18 percent of Whites. Blacks and Hispanics were therefore especially hard hit by the recession of 2008; many were forced to default on their mortgage payments and, in many cases, lost their homes. Research shows that only a few lenders offer subprime loans, but those lenders focus on minority communities, whereas the prime lenders are unable or unwilling to lend in those communities (Avery, Canner, and Cook, 2005). According to a *New York Times* analysis of mortgage lending in New York City, Black households making more than $68,000 a year were nearly five times as likely to hold high-interest subprime mortgages as Whites of similar or lower income levels (Powell, 2009). Furthermore, the National Bureau of Economic Research conducted a study which was later published that showed that Black homebuyers were 103 percent and Hispanic homebuyers were 78 percent more likely to have high cost home mortgages as compared to Whites (Bayer, Ferreira, and Ross, 2018). These issues are particularly important because home ownership constitutes American families' primary means of accumulating wealth.

Financial assets are important because they provide a major source of funding if one wants to start a business or pay for a college education. For lower-income Americans (which includes many minorities), accumulating stocks or bonds in the hope of cashing them in to pay for their children's college education is not even a fantasy. In fact, it is more likely that people in this group owe far more than they own. In recent years, as credit has become more readily available, many Americans have gone increasingly into debt, using credit cards and refinancing their home mortgages to pay for their lifestyles rather than relying on their earnings. Total household debt exceeded $14.15 trillion in 2019, including $9.6 trillion for home mortgages, and, as noted at the beginning of this chapter, $1.08 trillion in credit card and $1.2 trillion in automobile loans

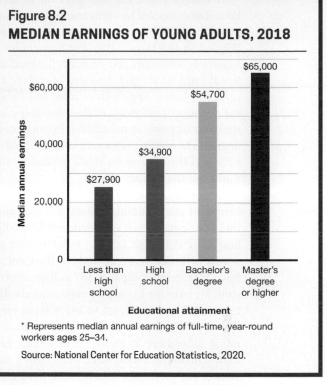

Figure 8.2
MEDIAN EARNINGS OF YOUNG ADULTS, 2018

* Represents median annual earnings of full-time, year-round workers ages 25–34.

Source: National Center for Education Statistics, 2020.

(Board of Governors of the Federal Reserve System, 2020a; Federal Reserve Bank of New York, 2020). That means that the average household with debt owes more than $130,000 (Federal Reserve Bank of New York, 2020).

Wealth is even more unequal globally. There are reportedly 2,153 billionaires in the world, with a combined net worth of more than $8.7 trillion (Kroll and Dolan, 2019a). According to some estimates, the wealthiest 1 percent now account for almost half of all global wealth (Shorrocks et al., 2019). We'll come back to this topic in Chapter 9.

Education

One thing that pays off in terms of income and wealth is a college education. In fact, education is one of the strongest predictors of occupation, income, and wealth later in life. In 2018, the median income of millenials (25 to 34 years old) with bachelor's degrees and full-time jobs was $54,700, compared to $34,900 for those who only graduated from high school, a gap of 57 percent (National Center for Education Statistics [NCES], 2019d). Moreover, the return on a college education has increased considerably over time: In 1966, for example, the income gap between those with a college degree and those with a high school diploma was only 24 percent (Pew Research Center, 2014c). A recent study by the Economic Policy Institute reports that in 2017, the hourly earnings of college graduates was nearly double that of people without a degree; 30 years ago, it was only two-thirds higher (Gould, 2018). In fact, over the long run, if one estimates the lifetime earnings of college graduates and subtracts the costs of going to college, the benefits outweigh the costs by a half million dollars on average (Autor, 2014).

A college education also pays off in terms of wealth. The median net worth of households headed by someone with a bachelor's degree was $163,700 in 2016, compared to $38,900 for households headed by someone with only a high school diploma (Eggleston and Hays, 2019). For households headed by high school dropouts, the difference is even more pronounced; the median net worth is $4,900. While a few exceptional individuals may drop out of college and go on to become billionaires (Microsoft's Bill Gates, Apple's Steve Jobs, and Facebook's Mark Zuckerberg come to mind), the chances of following in their footsteps is about as likely as becoming a billionaire rock star or professional athlete. Importantly, if you start college, it pays to finish your degree: The median net worth of households headed by someone who dropped out of college is the same as for those headed by someone with a high school diploma (U.S. Bureau of the Census, 2017f).

Of course, it matters which college you go to, what you major in, how much student loan debt you accumulate along the way, and—perhaps above all—the effort you put into your educational experience. While college graduates earn an average of $1 million more than high school graduates over the course of their careers, earnings vary widely by major. A recent study by the Center on Education and Workforce at Georgetown University compared 137 college majors and found that petroleum engineering students have the highest average annual salary, $176,000, while vocational rehabilitation majors earn the least, at $42,300 per year (Payscale, 2019).

Racial differences in levels of education also persist, which partly explains why racial differences in income and wealth persist as well. In 2016–2017, the highest high school graduation rates were among Asian Americans (91 percent), followed by Whites (87 percent), Hispanics (80 percent), Blacks (78 percent), and Native Americans (72 percent) (NCES, 2019b).

Importantly, as we will see later in this chapter, how much education one receives is often influenced by the social class of one's parents.

Occupation

In the United States and other industrialized societies, occupation is an important indicator of social standing. According to studies in which people rate jobs in terms of how "prestigious" they are, those requiring the most education are often—but not always—ranked most highly (Table 8.1). The top-ranked occupations appear to share one of two characteristics: They require a fair amount of either education or public service. These rankings have been fairly consistent for nearly four decades (Griswold, 2014). There are some interesting differences by age, however. Millennials seem more inclined than older Americans to value fame: Professional athletes, actors, and entertainers move up in the rankings (Harris, 2014).

Lifestyle

In analyzing class location, sociologists have traditionally relied on measures that are primarily economic, such as income or wealth. Some recent authors, however, seek to include cultural factors such as lifestyle and consumption patterns. According to this perspective, symbols and markers related to consumption are playing an ever-greater role in daily life. Individual identities are structured more around lifestyle choices—how to dress, what to eat, how to care for one's body, and where to relax—and less around traditional class indicators such as employment.

Table 8.1
RELATIVE SOCIAL PRESTIGE OF SELECT U.S. OCCUPATIONS

OCCUPATION	PRESTIGE SCORE	OCCUPATION	PRESTIGE SCORE
Physician	7.6	Farm manager	5.0
Architect	6.7	Real estate agent	4.9
Dentist	6.7	Carpenter	4.6
Airline pilot	6.6	Auto body repairperson	4.3
Registered nurse	6.5	Bank teller	4.2
Lawyer	6.4	Local delivery truck driver	4.2
Veterinarian	6.4	Salesperson in a store	3.9
Computer programmer	6.0	Hair stylist	3.8
Secondary-school teacher	6.1	Day-care aide	3.6
Sociologist	6.1	Waiter/waitress	3.6
Police officer	5.9	Bartender	3.6
Member of the clergy	5.8	File clerk	3.5
Actor	5.7	Cashier in a supermarket	3.4
Firefighter	5.7	Taxi driver	3.2
Musician in a symphony orchestra	5.6	Janitor	3.0
Electrician	5.2	Door-to-door salesperson	2.9

Note: Respondents were asked to rank the occupations' prestige on a scale of 1 to 9, with 1 as the least prestigious and 9 as the most prestigious.

SOURCE: Smith and Son, 2014.

The French sociologist Pierre Bourdieu saw social-class groups as identifiable according to their levels of "cultural and economic capital" (Bourdieu, 1984). Increasingly, individuals distinguish themselves not according to economic or occupational factors but on the basis of cultural tastes and leisure pursuits. Consider the growth in occupations related to convincing consumers that true happiness requires looking a certain way, buying a specific product, or being loyal to a particular brand. Advertisers, marketers, fashion designers, style consultants, interior designers, personal trainers, and webpage designers, to name but a few, are all involved in influencing cultural tastes and promoting lifestyle choices.

It would be difficult to dispute that stratification within classes, as well as among classes, now depends not only on occupational differences but also on differences in

CONCEPT CHECKS

1 How is the concept of class different from that of caste?

2 What are the principal determinants of social stratification?

3 What is the difference between wealth and income, and why does it matter for social stratification?

4 What are two examples of noneconomic indicators of one's social class?

consumption and lifestyle. The rapid expansion of the service economy and the entertainment and leisure industry, for example, reflects an increasing emphasis on consumption within industrialized countries. Modern societies have become consumer societies, and, in some respects, a consumer society is a "mass society" where class differences are overridden; thus, people from different class backgrounds may all watch similar television programs or shop for clothing in the same stores. Yet class differences can also become intensified through variations in lifestyle and "taste" (Bourdieu, 1984).

Despite the importance of cultural capital in signifying class, we must not ignore the critical role of economic factors in the reproduction of social inequalities. For the most part, individuals experiencing extreme social and material deprivations are not doing so as part of a lifestyle choice. Rather, their circumstances are constrained by factors related to the economic and occupational structure (Rank, Yoon, and Hirschl, 2003). Some Americans may not "choose" to buy clothes at Walmart and eat at McDonald's; they may simply be unable to afford to shop at higher-end stores and dine at gourmet restaurants.

2 THEORIES OF STRATIFICATION IN MODERN SOCIETIES

In this section, we look at some broad theories regarding stratification. Karl Marx and Max Weber developed the most influential approaches. Most contemporary theories of stratification are heavily indebted to their ideas.

Marx: Capitalism and the Analysis of Class

For many people, the word *capitalism* refers to a free-market economy, a system in which economic exchanges are essentially deregulated and occur through supply and demand. In a capitalist system, wealth is privately owned and is invested and reinvested to produce profit. But for Marx and his followers, it is impossible to define capitalism without reference to the classes that emerge through capitalism.

These are the groups of people who have a common relationship to the **means of production**—the means by which they gain a livelihood. In modern societies, the two main classes are the bourgeoisie and proletariat. The **bourgeoisie**, or capitalists, own the means of production. Members of the **proletariat**, or proletarians, by contrast, earn their living by selling their labor to the capitalists. The relationship between classes, according to Marx, is exploitative. During the working day, workers produce more than employers actually need to repay the cost of hiring them. This **surplus value** is the source of profit, which capitalists put to their own use.

Marx (1977; orig. 1867) believed that the maturing of industrial capitalism would create an increasing gap between the wealth of the minority and the poverty of the mass of the population, and he has been proven correct. Yet, he was not correct about everything. In his view, the wages of the working class could never rise far above subsistence level, while wealth would pile up in the hands of those owning capital. In addition, he claimed laborers would daily face work that was physically tasking and mentally tedious, as in many factories. At the lowest levels of society, particularly among those frequently or permanently unemployed, there would develop an "accumulation of misery, agony of labor, slavery, ignorance, brutality, moral degradation." Because of this accumulation, Marx concluded, the working class would eventually rise up and overthrow the capitalist system that was oppressing them. This revolution would then usher in a classless society in which technology replaced much of human labor, with everyone working together for the common good. He termed this system **communism**, common ownership of the means of production.

means of production The means whereby the production of material goods is carried on in a society, including not just technology but also the social relations between producers.

bourgeoisie People who own companies, land, or stocks (shares) and use these to generate economic returns.

proletariat People who sell their labor for wages, according to Marx.

surplus value In Marxist theory, the value of a worker's labor power left over when an employer has repaid the cost of hiring the worker.

communism A social system based on everyone owning the means of production and sharing in the wealth it produces.

Marx was right about the persistence of poverty in industrialized countries and in anticipating continued inequalities of wealth and income. He was wrong in supposing that the income of most of the population would remain extremely low. Most people in Western countries today are much better off materially than were comparable groups in Marx's day. Marx was also wrong in believing that a classless society—a communist utopia in which everyone shared equally in the fruits of their common labor—would inevitably result—unless that classless society is still to come, 150 years after the publication of his work.

Weber: Class and Status

There are three main differences between Weber's theory and that of Marx. First, according to Weber, class divisions derive not only from control or lack of control of the means of production, but also from economic differences that have nothing to do with property. Such resources include people's skills and credentials. Those in managerial or professional occupations earn more and enjoy more favorable conditions at work, for example, than do people in blue-collar jobs. Their qualifications, such as degrees, diplomas, and skills they have acquired, make them more "marketable" than others without such qualifications. At a lower level, among blue-collar workers, skilled craft workers secure higher wages than do the semiskilled or unskilled.

status The social honor or prestige a particular group is accorded by other members of a society. Status groups normally display distinct styles of life—patterns of behavior that the members of a group follow. Status privilege may be positive or negative.

pariah groups Groups who suffer from negative status discrimination—they are looked down on by most other members of society.

Second, Weber distinguished another aspect of stratification, which he called "status." **Status** refers to differences among groups in the social honor, or prestige, that others accord them. Status distinctions can vary independently of class divisions. Social honor may be either positive or negative. For instance, doctors and lawyers have high prestige in American society. **Pariah groups**, on the other hand, are negatively privileged status groups subject to discrimination that prevents them from taking advantage of opportunities open to others. The Jews were a pariah group in medieval Europe, banned from participating in certain occupations and from holding official positions.

Possession of wealth normally confers high status, but there are exceptions, such as Hollywood starlets who earn high salaries but lack the education or refinement typically associated with "status." In Britain, individuals from aristocratic families enjoy social esteem even after their fortunes have been lost, but individuals with "new money" are often scorned by the well-established wealthy. Whereas class is an objective measure, status depends on people's subjective evaluations of social differences. Classes derive from the economic factors associated with property and earnings; status is governed by the varying lifestyles that groups follow.

Third, Weber recognized that social classes also differ with respect to their power, or ability to enact change, command resources, or make decisions. Power is distinct from status and class, but these three dimensions often overlap. For example, on most college campuses, the president or provost has much greater power to change campus policies than does a cafeteria worker.

Weber's writings on stratification show that other dimensions besides class strongly influence people's lives. Most sociologists hold that Weber's scheme offers a more flexible and sophisticated basis for analyzing stratification than that provided by Marx.

Davis and Moore: The Functions of Stratification

Kingsley Davis and Wilbert E. Moore (1945) provided a functionalist explanation for stratification, arguing that it has beneficial consequences for society. They claimed that certain occupations in society, such as brain surgeons, are functionally more important than others, and that these positions require special skills. However, only a few individuals have the talents or experience appropriate to these positions. To attract the most qualified people, rewards need to be offered, such as money, power, and prestige. Davis and Moore determined that because the benefits of different positions in any society must be unequal, all societies must be stratified. They concluded that social stratification and social inequality are functional because they ensure that the most qualified people, attracted by the rewards society bestows, will fill the roles that are most important to a smoothly functioning society.

Davis and Moore's theory suggests that a person's social position is based solely on innate talents and efforts. It is not surprising that other sociologists have criticized their theory. For example, Melvin Tumin (1953) argued that the functional importance of a particular role is difficult to measure and that the social rewards bestowed on those in "important" roles do not reflect these people's actual importance. For instance, who is more important, a lawyer or a schoolteacher? If, on average, a lawyer earns four or five times the amount that a schoolteacher earns, does that earning potential accurately reflect his or her relative importance to society?

Tumin also argued that Davis and Moore overlooked the ways in which stratification limits the discovery of talent in a society. As we have seen, the United States is not entirely a meritocratic society. Those at the top have special access to economic and cultural resources, such as the highest-quality education that helps transmit their privileged status from one generation to the next. For those—even those with superior talents—who lack access to these resources, social inequality is a barrier to reaching their full potential.

Erik Olin Wright: Contradictory Class Locations

The career of the American sociologist Erik Olin Wright illustrates some of the most important changes in the U.S. class structure and system of inequality over the past half century. Influenced by the classical theories of Karl Marx, Wright was central to the creation of a group of scholars known as "no bullshit Marxists" who were interested in using empirical—largely quantitative—evidence to assess Marx's ideas in light of the times in which research was taking place.

In the 1980s, Wright was the first to recognize that the massive expansion of the middle class in American society posed a problem for Marx's theories because Marx viewed the class structure through the simple lens of owners and workers. Wright did not believe that middle-class people—and particularly the upper middle classes—could be understood using that classification. He argued, for example, that upper-middle class people such as managers controlled the working class while being simultaneously controlled by capitalist owners. In other words, these managers were essentially exploiting others while also being exploited.

This was a position that owed much to Marx but also incorporated ideas from Weber. According to Wright, there are three dimensions of control over economic resources in modern capitalist production, and these allow us to identify the major classes:

1. Control over investments or money capital
2. Control over the physical means of production (land or factories and offices)
3. Control over labor power

Members of the capitalist class have control over all of these dimensions of the production system. Members of the working class have control over none of them. Between these two main classes, however, are the groups whose position is more ambiguous: managers and white-collar workers. These people are in what Wright calls **contradictory class locations**, because they can influence some aspects of production but lack control over others. White-collar and professional employees, for example, must contract their labor power to employers to

> **contradictory class locations** Positions in the class structure, particularly routine White-collar and lower managerial jobs, that share characteristics with the class positions both above and below them.

make a living, in the same way manual workers do. Yet they have a greater degree of control over the work setting than do most people in blue-collar jobs. Wright terms the class position of such workers "contradictory" because they are neither capitalists nor manual workers, yet they share certain common features with each.

A large segment of the population—85 to 90 percent, according to Wright (1997)—falls into the category of those who must sell their labor because they do not control the means of production. Yet within this population is a great deal of diversity, ranging from the traditional manual working class to white-collar workers. To differentiate class locations within this large population, Wright considers two factors: the relationship to authority and the possession of skills or expertise. First, many middle-class workers, such as managers and supervisors, enjoy relationships to authority that are more privileged than those of the working class. Such individuals assist capitalists in controlling the working class by monitoring the work of other employees, for example, or by conducting personnel reviews and evaluations, and are rewarded by earning higher wages and receiving regular promotions. Yet these individuals remain under the control of the capitalist owners. In other words, they are both exploiters and the exploited.

The second factor that differentiates class locations within the middle classes is the possession of skills and expertise. According to Wright, middle-class employees possessing skills that are in demand in the labor market have a specific form of power in the capitalist system: They can earn a higher wage. The lucrative positions available to information technology (IT) specialists in the knowledge economy illustrate this point. Moreover, Wright argues, because employees with knowledge and skills are more difficult to monitor and control, employers secure their loyalty and cooperation by rewarding them accordingly.

Wright's ideas were central to carrying on the Marxist tradition through much of the past half century. Yet, toward the end of his life, he came to believe that a focus on the middle classes no longer was as important for Marxists. In an interview for this textbook, Wright said, "If I were to write a fifty-page text on how to think about class in the twenty-first century, I would begin by saying the problem of class is not the problem of the poor, the working class or the middle class. It's the problem of the ruling class—of a capitalist class that's so immensely wealthy that they are capable of destroying the world as a side effect of their private pursuit of gain."

Thus, in Wright's final studies, instead of focusing on the middle classes, he studied the democratization of the economy and the ruling class. His last book, published a few months after he passed away, was called *How to Be an Anticapitalist in the Twenty-First Century*.

CONCEPT CHECKS

1 According to Karl Marx, what are the two main classes, and how do they relate to one another?

2 What are the two main differences between Max Weber's and Karl Marx's theories of social stratification?

3 According to Kingsley Davis and Wilbert E. Moore, how does social stratification contribute to the functioning of society? What is wrong with this argument, according to Melvin Tumin?

4 What does Erik Olin Wright mean by "contradictory class location"? Give an example of a type of worker who falls in this category.

Table 8.2

APPLYING SOCIOLOGY TO STRATIFICATION

CONCEPTS	APPROACH TO INEQUALITY	CURRENT APPLICATION
Marxist Theories	The exploitation of working classes in capitalist societies is the key to understanding social and economic inequality in the contemporary world.	The presidential campaigns of Bernie Sanders, which gained wide traction in 2016 and 2020, were inspired in part by Marxist ideas
Weberian Theories	Status and power are as important as class in our understanding of social and economic inequality.	Journalists, writers, and scholars in an unequal society like the United States can hold status and exert power despite owning little capital.
Functionalist Theories	Inequality can be beneficial to society in so far as it inspires people to develop the skills and expertise necessary to excel at difficult jobs.	Entry level jobs in computer science are among the best paid, resulting in wide disparities between graduates in that field and most others. Computer science courses are among the most difficult at most universities, lending credence to a functional theory.
Contradictory Class Locations (theory developed by Erik Olin Wright in the 1980s, when the middle class was at the height of its political power)	Professional workers in modern capitalist society occupy contradictory positions: they exert control over the working classes, but remain subordinate to the upper classes.	This theory is of less relevance today than when it was developed in the 1980s. As Erik Olin Wright has observed, both the working class and the shrinking, downwardly mobile middle class of the twenty-first century is losing power due to a "capitalist class... so immensely wealthy that they are capable of destroying the world as a side effect of their private pursuit of gain."

3 RESEARCH ON SOCIAL STRATIFICATION TODAY

A Contemporary Portrait of the U.S. Class Structure

As we have already learned, a person's social-class position has a significant impact on their lifestyle. Most sociologists identify social classes in terms of wealth, income, and occupation, noting how social class influences consumption, education, health, and access to political power. The purpose of the following discussion is to describe broad class differences in the United States. Bear in mind that there are no sharply defined boundaries between the classes, and no real agreement among sociologists about where the boundaries should fall.

upper class A social class broadly composed of the more affluent members of society, especially those who have inherited wealth, own businesses, or hold large numbers of stocks (shares).

The Upper Class

The **upper class** consists of the very wealthiest Americans—those households earning more than $207,400, approximately 20 percent of all American households (Horowitz et al., 2020a). Most Americans in the upper class are wealthy but not superrich. They are likely to own a large suburban home and perhaps a vacation home as well, drive expensive automobiles, vacation abroad, and educate their children in private schools and colleges. At the lower levels of this group, a large part of income may come from salaried earnings. This group includes many professionals, from some doctors and lawyers to university administrators and possibly even a few highly compensated professors.

At the very top of the upper class are the superrich—people who have accumulated vast fortunes that permit them to enjoy a lifestyle unimaginable to most Americans. If one uses a cutoff of the richest 0.1 percent in terms of income, these are people whose income tops $7.3 million, roughly 140,000 Americans (Picchi, 2019). Their wealth stems in large part from their substantial investments, from stocks and bonds to real estate, and from the interest income derived from those investments. They include people who have acquired their wealth in a variety of ways: celebrities, professional athletes, the heads of major corporations, people who have made large amounts of money through investments or real estate, and those fortunate enough to have inherited great wealth from their parents.

A recent book by sociologist Rachel Sherman showed that the superrich and those below them in the top 1 percent are conscious of their unique and privileged social class position; some give generously to such worthy causes as the arts, hospitals, and charities (Sherman, 2017). Their homes are often lavish and sometimes filled with collections of fine art. Yet, whereas previous generations of wealthy people in America were proud of their class identity as indicated by such things as being listed in the social register, today's wealthy tend to downplay their money, experiencing the "anxieties of affluence" (Sherman, 2017).

Frequently they have attended the same exclusive private secondary schools (to which they also send their children). They sit on the same corporate boards of directors and belong to the same private clubs. Sherman found that they contribute large sums of money to their favorite politicians and are likely to be on a first-name basis with members of Congress and perhaps even with the president. Yet, their reasons for donating to charities and even political campaigns might be about more than having a significant influence on American politics (Domhoff, 2013). Many of the wealthiest are sensitive to the

Snapchat CEO Evan Spiegel poses for a photo in Los Angeles.

moral judgments that are made about their lifestyles. They thus expend a great deal of energy trying to confirm their moral worth in others' eyes. At times, this entails downplaying their wealth and minimizing their privilege, as well as making grand gestures to "give back" to society (Sherman, 2017).

The turn of the twenty-first century saw extraordinary opportunities for the accumulation of such wealth. Globalization is one reason. Entrepreneurs who are able to invest globally often prosper, by selling products to foreign consumers and making profits cheaply by using low-wage labor in developing countries. The information revolution is another reason for the accumulation of wealth. Young entrepreneurs with start-up, high-tech companies, such as Facebook founder Mark Zuckerberg and Yahoo! cofounder Jerry Yang, made legendary fortunes. In 2019, Zuckerberg was the sixth wealthiest person in the world, with an estimated net worth of $62.3 billion (Kroll and Dolan, 2019a).

As a consequence of globalization and the information revolution, the number of superrich Americans has exploded in recent years. At the end of World War II, only 13,000 people were worth $1 million or more in the United States. Today, the 400 richest Americans are worth $2.96 trillion; the cutoff to join this exclusive "club" is a net worth of $1.7 billion (Kroll and Dolan, 2019a). Unlike "old money" families such as the Rockefellers or the Vanderbilts, who accumulated their wealth in earlier generations and thus are viewed as a sort of American aristocracy, much of this "new wealth" is held primarily by entrepreneurs—including such recent arrivals as WhatsApp cofounder Jan Koum ($9.7 billion) and cofounder and CEO of SnapChat, Evan Spiegel ($2.0 billion).

While Americans have long glamorized and aspired to be part of this extraordinarily wealthy elite, perceptions of the superrich have changed in recent years. The recession that began with the financial collapse of 2007–2008, combined with growing income inequality, triggered movements such as Occupy Wall Street, during which protesters sought to bring attention to what they saw as greed, corruption, and undeserved political power among the very wealthy. A recent Pew Research Center poll found that nearly two-thirds believe that the rich-poor gap has increased over the past 10 years, and 6 out of 10 believe that the economic system is unfair, favoring the wealthy rather than everyone else. Slightly more than half (54 percent) would tax the rich and corporations to provide programs for the poor, although strong differences by political party exist on this issue. Such a redistribution of wealth is favored by 75 percent of Democrats and 51 percent of independents, but only 29 percent of Republicans (Pew Research Center, 2014b).

The Middle Class

Middle class is a catchall term for a diverse group of occupations, lifestyles, and people who earn stable and sometimes substantial incomes at primarily white-collar and highly skilled blue-collar jobs. It is generally considered to include households with income between $42,000 and $126,000 (dependent on the size of the household), which includes roughly 50 percent of all households (Snider, 2019; LaMagna, 2018). While the middle class was once largely White, today it is increasingly diverse—both racially and culturally—and includes African Americans, Asian Americans, and

middle class A social class composed broadly of those working in white-collar and lower managerial occupations.

Latinos. The middle class grew throughout much of the first three-quarters of the twentieth century but has been shrinking for most of the past four decades.

For many years, when Americans were asked to identify their social class, the majority claimed to be middle class (Boushey and Hersh, 2012). The reason lay partly in the pervasive cultural belief that the United States is relatively free of class distinctions; few people want to be identified as being too rich or too poor. Most Americans seem to think that others are not very different from their immediate family, friends, or coworkers. Since people seldom interact with those outside their social class, they tend to see themselves as being like "most other people," whom they then regard as being "middle class" (Kelley and Evans, 1995).

The perception that "we are all middle class" has changed in recent years, however. In public opinion polls taken in 2015, 47 percent of Americans identified as middle class, down from 53 percent in 2008 (Pew Research Center, 2015b). The 2008 recession was partly to blame, as well as the uneven economic recovery that followed. The stock market may have risen to record levels by 2014, but this increase did not benefit the majority of Americans. Eighty-five percent of self-described middle-class respondents to a 2012 survey said it had become more difficult for them to maintain their wealth in the ten years between 2001 and 2010, and reported declines in both income and net worth (Pew Research Center, 2012b).

The American middle class can be further subdivided into two groups: the upper middle class and the lower middle class.

The Upper Middle Class The upper middle class consists of highly educated professionals (for example, doctors, lawyers, engineers, and professors), mid-level corporate managers, people who own or manage small businesses and retail shops, and some large farm owners. Household incomes range quite widely, from about $126,000 to perhaps $188,000 (Snider, 2019). The lower half of the income category would include college professors, for example, while the higher end would include corporate managers and small business owners. The upper middle class includes approximately 19 percent of all American households (Kochhar, 2018). Its members are likely to be college educated (as are their children), with advanced degrees. They own comfortable homes, drive expensive late-model cars, have some savings and investments, and are often active in local politics and civic organizations. However, they tend not to enjoy the same high-end luxuries, social connections, or extravagances as do members of the upper class. Historically, their jobs have been secure and provided retirement, pension, and health benefits, yet many upper-middle-class persons—especially those working in finance and media—have been susceptible to layoffs and have seen their pension and home-value wealth shrink (U.S. Department of Commerce, 2010).

The Lower Middle Class The lower middle class consists of trained office workers (for example, secretaries and bookkeepers), elementary and high school teachers, nurses, salespeople, police officers, firefighters, and others who provide skilled services. This group, which includes about 40 percent of American households, is the most varied of the social-class strata and may include college-educated persons with relatively modest earnings, such as public elementary school teachers, and quite highly paid persons with high school diplomas only, such as skilled craftspeople (e.g., plumbers) and civil servants with many years of seniority. Household incomes in this group range from about $31,000 to $42,000 (Snider, 2019). The number of Americans who identify as "lower class" or "lower middle class" has increased in recent years. In 2008, roughly a quarter of all adults put themselves in this category; in 2012, fully a third so identified. The numbers have increased even more among millennials (from 25 percent to 39 percent) as young people become increasingly worried about their career prospects (Morin and Motel, 2012). As of 2016, 11 percent of individuals self-identify as lower class, and another 36 percent self-identify as lower middle class (Pew Research Center, 2016c).

Members of the lower middle class may own a modest house, although many live in rental units. Their automobiles may be late models, but not the more expensive ones. Almost all have a high school education, and some have college degrees. They want their children to attend college, although this goal usually requires work-study programs and student loans. They are rarely politically active beyond exercising their right to vote. Like upper-middle-class persons, lower-middle-class workers have seen their job security and financial security decline as a result of the 2008 recession, and these threats have disproportionately struck African Americans and persons who work in the public sector (Pitts, 2011).

While firefighters, police officers, and schoolteachers have historically enjoyed job security, this is no longer the case. Between 2009 and 2011, state and local governments throughout the United States laid off 429,000 workers (Pitts, 2011). For example, in June 2012, the New Orleans school system announced the layoffs of 200 teachers (Vanacore, 2012), while the impoverished city of Camden, New Jersey, witnessed the layoffs of nearly 250 firefighters, police officers, and city employees in 2011; public workers in dozens of other American cities have seen their pensions threatened (Kaplan and Eligon, 2012). Most recently, however, the impact of COVID-19 has raised the unemployment rate to 14.7 percent as of April 2020, while unemployment claims passed 40 million by the end of May 2020 (*New York Times,* 2020; Bureau of Labor Statistics, 2020c).

The Working Class

The **working class** includes primarily blue-collar workers such as mechanics and pink-collar laborers such as clerical aides. Household incomes range from about $20,000 to $40,000 (Elwell, 2014a), and at least two household members must work to make ends meet. Family income is just enough to pay the rent or the mortgage, put food on the table, and perhaps save for a summer vacation. The working class includes factory workers, mechanics, office workers, salesclerks, restaurant and hotel workers, and others who earn a modest weekly paycheck at a job that involves little control over the size of their income or working conditions. According to a Gallup poll from 2017, about 30 percent of Americans self-identify as working class (Bird and Newport, 2017). As you will see later in this chapter, many manufacturing jobs in the United States are threatened by economic globalization, and so members of the working class today are likely to feel insecure about their own and their family's future.

The working class is racially and ethnically diverse. While older members of the working class may own a home bought several years ago, younger members are likely to rent. The home or apartment is likely to be in a lower-income suburb or a city neighborhood. The household car, a lower-priced

working class A social class broadly composed of people working in blue-collar, or manual, occupations.

lower class A social class comprising those who work part-time or not at all and whose household income is typically lower than $31,000 a year.

model, is unlikely to be new. Most members of the working class are not likely to be politically active even in their own community, although they may vote in some elections.

Children of working-class families often bypass college and instead seek full-time work immediately after graduating from high school. However, high school graduates' employment and earnings prospects are bleak. While in 2019, the unemployment rate for people 25 and older with only a high school diploma was 3.7 percent, median weekly earnings were only $712; for high school dropouts, the situation was even worse, with 5.3 percent unemployed and median weekly earnings of $520 (U.S. Bureau of Labor Statistics, 2019n; Torpey, 2018). Rutgers University researchers studied high school graduates from the classes of 2009 to 2011 who did not go on to college; as of 2011, only 16 percent were working full time, 37 percent were unemployed and looking for work, 17 percent were unemployed and had given up on finding work, and 13 percent were hoping to up their current work hours from part time to full time (Van Horn et al., 2012). Of those who had found jobs, the median hourly wage was $7.50, just $0.25 above the federal minimum wage. These bleak employment prospects bode poorly for their futures; two-thirds of the high school graduates viewed important life transitions such as starting a family or owning a home as many years off in the future.

The Lower Class

The **lower class**, which overlaps with the working class to account for about 29 percent of American households, includes some full-time, low-wage workers and those who work part-time or not at all; their annual household income is typically lower than $31,000 (Kochhar, 2018; Snider, 2019). Most lower-class individuals live in cities, although some live in rural areas and earn a little money as farmers or part-time workers. Some manage to find employment in semiskilled or unskilled manufacturing or service jobs, ranging from making clothing in sweatshops to cleaning houses. Their jobs, when they can find them, are dead-end jobs, since years of work are unlikely to lead to promotion or substantially higher income. Their work is probably part-time and highly unstable, without benefits such as medical insurance, disability, or Social Security. Even if they are fortunate enough to find a full-time job, there are no guarantees that it will be around next month or even next week.

Many people in the lower class live in poverty. Very few own their own homes. Most of the lower class rent, and some are homeless. If they own a car at all, it is likely to be a used car. A higher percentage of the lower class is non-White than is true of other social classes (Lin and Harris, 2010). Members of the lower class do not participate in politics, and they seldom vote.

Social Mobility: Moving Up and Down the Ladder

The United States has long been hailed as the land of opportunity. "Rags-to-riches" stories abound, offering inspiring accounts of people such as Liz Murray, the homeless daughter of drug-addicted parents who ultimately graduated from Harvard University

(Murray, 2010). Movies and novels recount the triumphs of the secretary or mailroom worker who became a corporate vice president. Is it possible for a young person from a poor or working-class background to transcend class roots and become an upper-class professional? If yes, what factors contribute to their ascent up the social ladder?

Answers to these questions can be found in the study of **social mobility**, which refers to the upward or downward movement of individuals and groups among different class positions through changes in occupation, wealth, or income. Mobility can occur in one of two forms. **Intergenerational mobility** refers to social movement across generations; we can analyze where children are on the scale compared with their parents or grandparents. **Intragenerational mobility**, by contrast, refers to how far an individual moves up or down the socioeconomic scale during their working life. Another important distinction is between structural mobility and exchange mobility. Most mobility, whether intragenerational or intergenerational, is **structural mobility**—upward mobility made possible by an expansion of better-paid occupations at the expense of poorly paid ones. Most mobility in the United States since World War II has depended on continually increasing prosperity. In a hypothetical society with complete equality of opportunity—in which each person has the same chance of success as everyone else—there would be a great deal of downward as well as upward mobility. This is **exchange mobility**—an exchange of positions such that more talented people in each generation move up the economic hierarchy, while the less talented move down. In practice, however, no society approaches full equality of opportunity.

In a classic study of intergenerational mobility in the United States, sociologists Peter Blau and Otis Dudley Duncan (1967) found that long-range intergenerational mobility— that is, from working class to upper middle class—was rare. Why? Blau and Duncan concluded that the key factor behind occupational status was educational attainment. A child's education, however, is influenced by family social status; this, in turn, affects the child's social position later in life. Sociologists William Sewell and Robert Hauser (1980) later confirmed Blau and Duncan's conclusions. They added to the argument by claiming that the connection between family background and educational attainment occurs because parents, teachers, and friends influence the child's educational and career aspirations, and that these aspirations then become an important influence on the schooling and careers obtained throughout the child's life.

As we learned earlier in this chapter, French sociologist Pierre Bourdieu (1984, 1988) also examined the importance of family background to social status, but his emphasis was on the cultural advantages that parents can provide to their children. Bourdieu argued that among the factors responsible for social status, the most

social mobility Movement of individuals or groups between different social positions.

intergenerational mobility Movement up or down a social stratification hierarchy from one generation to another.

intragenerational mobility Movement up or down a social stratification hierarchy within the course of a personal career.

structural mobility Mobility resulting from changes in the number and kinds of jobs available in a society.

exchange mobility The exchange of positions on the socioeconomic scale such that talented people move up the economic hierarchy while the less talented move down.

cultural capital Noneconomic or cultural resources that parents pass down to their children, such as language or knowledge. These resources contribute to the process of social reproduction, according to Bourdieu.

important is the transmission of "**cultural capital**," or the cultural advantages that being from a "good home" confers. Wealthier families are able to afford to send their children to better schools, an economic advantage that benefits the children's social status as adults. Parents from the upper and middle classes are mostly highly educated themselves and tend to be more involved in their children's education—reading to them, helping with homework, purchasing books and learning materials, and encouraging their progress. Bourdieu noted that working-class parents are concerned about their children's education, but they lack the economic or cultural capital to make a difference.

Although Bourdieu focused on social status in France, the socioeconomic order in the United States is similar. Those who already hold positions of wealth and power can ensure that their children have the best available education, and this education will often lead them into the best jobs. Studies consistently show that a large majority of people who have "made money" did so by inheriting it or being given at least a modest amount initially—which they then used to make more. In U.S. society, it's better to start at the top than at the bottom.

One recent study of more than 40 million children and their parents found that social mobility in the United States has not changed much over the past 50 years. In fact, contrary to popular myth, social mobility has long been low, not high (Chetty et al., 2014). Among children born into the bottom fifth of the U.S. income distribution, only 7.5 percent wound up in the top fifth; two out of five remain poor as adults. By way of comparison, fully one-third of those born into the top fifth remained in the top

Higher education provides a path to upward mobility in the United States, but getting into college is often contingent upon one's social background.

fifth. While being born at the top is no guarantee one will remain there, the odds are far greater than for someone born at the bottom.

The study also found that there are significant differences in upward mobility by geographic area. For example, children from the bottom fifth of families who grow up in the Silicon Valley area near San Jose, California—the home of Stanford University, Apple, Google, Facebook, and countless other high-tech firms—have a 13 percent chance of reaching the top fifth; the odds of this happening for a child who grows up in Charlotte, North Carolina, is just 4 percent. Mobility is higher in areas that have less residential segregation and income inequality, better primary schools, higher family stability, and, importantly, greater "social capital" in the form of community involvement and personal networks (Chetty et al., 2014; Surowiecki, 2014).

Race and education play a major part in determining upward mobility. Sixty-three percent of Black children born into the bottom fourth of the U.S. income distribution remained in the bottom fourth, while only 4 percent made it into the top fourth. Among White children, 32 percent of those born into the bottom fourth remained there, while 14 percent made it into the top fourth. In other words, while upward mobility is not high for anyone, it is far lower for Blacks than it is for Whites. Differences in education account for at least part of the racial differences. Because schools remain highly segregated by race in many parts of the country, poor Black children often do not have the same educational opportunities as Whites do (Hertz, 2006).

One's parents' income has a strong effect on whether one goes to college. In 2016, 78 percent of young adults from the top 20 percent of American households were enrolled in postsecondary education, compared to just 28 percent of those in the bottom 20 percent (NCES, 2019b). One key reason is that children born into lower-income families are more likely to drop out of high school or, if they complete high school, do so without the preparation and grades that would qualify them for college (NCES, 2016b; Cameron and Heckman, 2001).

One of the most important avenues to upward intergenerational mobility is therefore higher education. One study found that at all income levels, a college education paid off. Children who earned a college degree were significantly more likely to earn more than their parents than were children who did not graduate from college. Moreover, the differences were largest for middle-class children, suggesting that the returns on education were greater for this group than for the very poor or the very wealthy (Haskins, 2009). Fully 60 percent of children from families in the top fifth of income earners graduated from college, whereas in the bottom fifth of earners, just 15 percent attained college degrees (Cahalan et al., 2016). Although a college degree may open the door to well-paying managerial and professional occupations, the returns on education, such as the economic payoff received in the workplace for each additional year of schooling or academic degree, is not equal for all Americans. As we will learn in subsequent chapters, each additional academic degree brings much richer financial and occupational rewards for men versus women and Whites versus Blacks and Latinos.

Further, the very process of applying to, being accepted to, and graduating from college, especially prestigious colleges, is shaped by one's social background. To obtain a "behind-the-scenes" look at who is accepted to prestigious colleges, sociologist Mitchell Stevens (2009) conducted an ethnographic study in which he spent a year and a half working in the admissions office of an elite New England college. The college was proud of its high academic standards, social conscience, and commitment to diversity. In practice, however, the admissions process often reproduced preexisting inequalities, Stevens found. Although admissions officers did strive for diversity in each entering class, they typically targeted Black and Latino students from economically advantaged backgrounds, rather than those from disadvantaged communities in the inner city or rural areas. Working-class Whites and ethnic minorities, even those with quite stellar records, often were left out in the cold. An NCES (2019b) study found that 37 percent of higher income students (top 20 percent) are enrolled at highly selective universities as compared to the 7 percent enrollment of students from the lowest 20 percent income.

Downward Mobility

Downward mobility is less common than upward mobility, yet the 2008 recession resulted in an uptick in the percentage of Americans who moved down the social ladder—either down from their parents' status (intergenerational mobility) or down from their own earlier economic status (intragenerational mobility). For example, one study found that a middle-class upbringing does not guarantee the same status over the course of a lifetime (Acs, 2011). One-third of Americans raised in the middle class—defined as those who grew up in households between the thirtieth and seventieth percentiles of the income distribution—fall out of the middle class as adults.

Downward intergenerational mobility also has increased in recent years. During the late 1980s and early 1990s, corporate America was flooded with instances in which

Men line up for a New York job fair. The 2008 recession was termed a "mancession" because the economic downturn impacted predominantly male professions like construction and manufacturing.

middle-aged men lost their jobs because of company mergers, takeovers, or bankruptcies. These executives either had difficulty finding new jobs or could only find jobs that paid less than their previous ones (Newman, 1999). Among the industries most strongly affected by the recent economic downturn were finance, construction, and real estate, which primarily employ men.

The most common type of downward intergenerational mobility is short-range downward mobility. Here, a worker moves from one job to another that is similar in pay and prestige (for example, from a routine office job to semiskilled blue-collar work). Although such moves may seem fairly minor, they are often accompanied by quite serious psychological costs and may create family strains. Men and women who stake their identity on having a well-paying and rewarding job may find themselves despondent working in a job that provides neither rich earnings nor the prestige and satisfaction that accompanied their prior job (Warner, 2010).

For women, both inter- and intragenerational downward mobility may have an additional source: divorce. One study found that women who divorced were between 31 and 36 percentage points more likely than their married counterparts to fall down the economic ladder (Acs, 2011). Studies also show that the fortunes of adult women change dramatically upon divorce. Newman (1999) tracked the experiences of upper-middle-class suburban mothers who found themselves struggling to maintain their former lifestyles after divorce. As we will learn more about in Chapter 15, women's standard of living drops by as much as 33 percent after divorce.

Ironically, the recent recession may have actually contributed to higher rates of female labor force participation. As in the Great Depression, so today women are generally paid less and maintain jobs that do not feel the effects of the economic downturn in the same way that predominantly "male" professions (e.g., construction or manufacturing) do. As a result, some scholars referred to the economic downturn as a "mancession," in which men suffered greater job losses than women did (Newman and Pedulla, 2010).

Poverty in the United States

In much of this chapter, we have been concerned with inequality between social classes, yet the fact that there is a gap between those at the top or middle, and those at the bottom does not necessarily mean that people at the bottom are very poor. One could imagine a society in which people at the top of the wealth distribution pay taxes that are high enough to ensure that those at the bottom have adequate resources. Or one could imagine a society in which people at the bottom feel less life satisfaction because they don't have as much as those above them, while at the same time having adequate resources for education and many of the most important health outcomes.

Therefore, in defining poverty, a distinction is usually made between absolute and relative poverty. **Absolute poverty** means that a person or family simply can't get enough to eat, or perhaps

absolute poverty Not meeting the minimal requirements necessary to sustain a healthy existence.

relative poverty Poverty defined according to the living standards of the majority in any given society.

poverty line An official government measure to define those living in poverty in the United States.

does not have access to adequate health care and education. People living in absolute poverty usually do not have access to healthy food or, in situations of famine, may even starve to death. Absolute poverty is common in the poorer developing countries. In many industrial countries, by contrast, **relative poverty** is essentially a measure of inequality. It means being poor as compared with the standards of living of the majority.

In the United States, there are many people who do not have the basic resources needed to maintain a decent standard of housing and healthy living conditions. In 2018, 38 million people, or roughly 12 percent of the population, lived below the poverty line. The rate of child poverty is even worse; one in six children lives in a household with income levels beneath the poverty line (Semega et al., 2019a). A recent UNICEF study reported that among the 35 wealthiest nations in the world, the United States has the seventh-highest child poverty rate, falling behind countries such as Spain, Mexico, and Romania (World Economic Forum, 2017). The largest concentrations of poverty in the United States are found in the South, inner cities, and rural areas. Among the poor, 18.5 million Americans (or 6 percent of the country) live in extreme poverty: Their incomes are only half of the official poverty level, meaning that they live at near-starvation levels (Stein, 2018). Therefore, the average poverty rate for the country masks major variations from state to state. Relatively well-off states such as New Hampshire, Vermont, Minnesota, and Massachusetts have about half as much poverty as do Louisiana, Mississippi, and New Mexico.

We are the richest democracy and yet we have one of the highest childhood poverty rates in the world. At the bottom of the class system in the United States are therefore the millions of people who live in poverty. Many do not maintain a proper diet and often live in neighborhoods marked by high crime rates, exposure to dangerous environmental conditions, and run-down, dilapidated homes. Poor persons are more likely than their richer counterparts to suffer from every possible health condition, ranging from heart disease to diabetes, and consequently, their average life expectancy is lower than that of the majority of the population. Thus, they experience absolute poverty. But unlike many countries in the developing world where poor people do not see much affluence around them, in the United States the poor are aware of the prosperity around them. Therefore, they must live with both absolute and relative poverty.

Measuring Poverty

What does it mean to be poor in the world's richest nation? The U.S. government currently calculates a **poverty line** based on cost estimates for families of different sizes. This calculation results in a strict, no-frills budget, which for a family of four in 2020 works out to an annual cash income of just over $26,200, or about $2,000 a month to cover all expenses (U.S. Department of Health and Human Services, 2020).

How realistic is this standard of poverty? Some critics, including the presidential administration of Donald Trump, believe it overestimates the amount of poverty. They point out that the current standard fails to consider noncash forms of income available

What does Newman's research reveal about the working poor? In 2017, more than 6.9 million Americans were among the working poor. Women are more likely than men to be among the working poor.

to the poor, such as food stamps, Medicare, Medicaid, and public housing subsidies, as well as "under-the-table" pay obtained from work at odd jobs that is concealed from the government (Joint Center for Housing Studies of Harvard University, 2014). Others counter that the government's formula greatly underestimates the amount of poverty because it overemphasizes the proportion of a family budget spent on food and severely underestimates the share spent on housing. According to some estimates, three-fourths of all U.S. families whose income is $15,000 a year (about what would be earned under the federal minimum wage) are spending more than half of their income on housing (Joint Center for Housing Studies of Harvard University, 2020). Still others observe that this formula dramatically underestimates the proportion of older adults (age 65+) who live in poverty (upwards of 7.2 million), because they spend a relatively small proportion of their income on food yet are faced with high health care costs (Carr, 2010; Cubanski et al., 2018).

The Working Poor

Many Americans fall into the **working poor**—that is, people who work at least 27 weeks a year but whose earnings are not high enough to lift them above the poverty line. In 2015, 5.6 percent of the labor force was not earning enough to stay out of poverty (BLS, 2017b). The federal minimum wage, the legal floor for wages in the United States, was first set in 1938 at $0.25 an hour.

working poor People who work but whose earnings are not enough to lift them above the poverty line.

The national federal minimum wage is now $7.25 per hour, although in February 2014, then-U.S. President Barack Obama issued an executive order to raise the minimum wage for federal contract workers to $10.10 an hour. Individual states can set higher minimum wages than that of the federal standard; in 2017 alone, 19 states raised their minimum wage, with the highest hourly minimum wages being in the District of Columbia ($14.00), Massachusetts ($12.00), and Washington state ($12.00). Although the federal minimum wage has increased over the years, it has failed to keep up with inflation; today's minimum wage is only two-thirds of the 1968 minimum wage, once the effects of inflation are considered (Elwell, 2014b).

In 2017, there were 6.9 million individuals among the working poor. The working poor are disproportionately non-White and immigrant; Hispanics and Blacks are twice as likely as Whites and Asian Americans to fall into this category. Education can make a significant difference in this regard: 13.7 percent of high school dropouts find themselves among the working poor compared to 6.2 percent of workers with a high school diploma, 3.2 percent with an associate's degree, and only 1.5 with a bachelor's degree or higher (BLS, 2019a).

Most poor people, contrary to popular belief, do not receive welfare payments; they earn too much to qualify for welfare. Only 5 percent of all low-income families with a full-time, full-year worker receive welfare benefits, and over half rely on public health insurance rather than employer-sponsored insurance. Research on low-wage, fast-food workers further reveals that many working poor lack adequate education, do not have health insurance to cover medical costs, and are trying to support families on poverty-level wages (Newman, 2000).

Poverty, Race, and Ethnicity

Poverty rates in the United States are much higher among most minority groups than among non-Hispanic Whites, even though more than 41 percent of the poor are White (Semega et al., 2019c). As Figure 8.3 shows, Blacks and Latinos experience more than double the poverty rate of Whites. Median household income among Hispanics was 75 percent of Whites' in 2018; among Blacks, it was only 61 percent (U.S. Census Bureau, 2019c). This discrepancy is because they often work at the lowest-paying jobs and because of racial discrimination. Asian Americans have the highest income of any group, but their poverty rate is also slightly more than that of Whites, reflecting the influx of relatively poor Asian immigrant groups.

The number of Blacks living in poverty has declined considerably in recent years. In 1959, 55 percent of Blacks were living in poverty; by 2018, that figure had dropped to 20.8 percent. A similar pattern holds for Hispanics: Poverty grew steadily between 1972 and 1994, peaking at

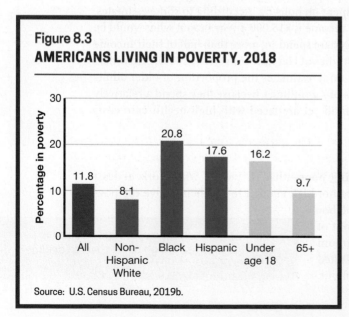

Figure 8.3
AMERICANS LIVING IN POVERTY, 2018

Source: U.S. Census Bureau, 2019b.

31 percent of the Hispanic population. By 2018, however, the poverty rate for Hispanics had fallen to 17.6 percent, including a decline of 2 percent from 2014 to 2015 alone. This decline is possibly because the unemployment rate has also dropped significantly for Hispanics in recent years, although it remains higher than that of Whites (U.S. Census Bureau, Semega et al., 2019c; Proctor, Semega, and Kollar, 2016; Krogstad, 2014).

The Feminization of Poverty

Much of the growth in poverty is associated with the **feminization of poverty**, an increase in the proportion of the poor who are women. Growing rates of divorce, separation, and single-parent families have placed women at a particular disadvantage, since it is extremely difficult for unskilled or semiskilled, low-income, poorly educated women to raise children by themselves while also holding down a job that could raise them out of poverty. As a result, in 2018, 39.1 percent of all single-parent families with children under 18 headed by women were poor, compared to less than 7.6 percent of married couples with children (Figure 8.4) (Semega et al., 2019a).

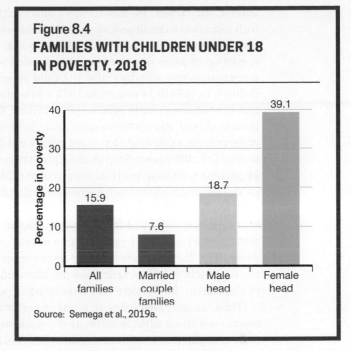

Figure 8.4

FAMILIES WITH CHILDREN UNDER 18 IN POVERTY, 2018

Source: Semega et al., 2019a.

The feminization of poverty is particularly acute among families headed by Hispanic women. Although the rate has declined by about one-third since its peak in the mid-1980s (it was 64 percent in 1985), 38 percent of all female-headed Hispanic families with children still lived in poverty in 2018. A similar proportion (38 percent) of female-headed African American families with children live in poverty; these percentages are considerably higher than those of either White (28 percent) or Asian (29 percent) female headed families (Fins, 2019).

A single woman attempting to raise children alone is caught in a vicious circle (Edin and Kefalas, 2005). If she has a job, she must find someone to take care of her children since she cannot afford to hire a babysitter or pay for day care. From her standpoint, she will take in more money if she accepts welfare payments from the government and tries to find illegal part-time jobs that pay cash not reported to the government rather than a regular full-time job paying minimum wage. Even though welfare will not get her out of poverty, if she finds a regular job, she will lose her welfare altogether, and she and her family may be even worse off economically.

Children in Poverty

Given the high rates of poverty among families headed by single women, it follows that children are the principal victims of poverty

feminization of poverty An increase in the proportion of the poor who are female.

in the United States. The United States ranks sixth among the world's wealthiest nations with respect to its child poverty rate. Nonetheless, that rate has varied considerably over the last 40 years, declining when the economy expands or the government increases spending on antipoverty programs and rising when the economy slows and government antipoverty spending falls. The child poverty rate declined from 27 percent of all children in 1959 to 14 percent in 1973, a period associated with both economic growth and the War on Poverty (1963–1969). During the late 1970s and 1980s, as economic growth slowed and cutbacks were made in government antipoverty programs, child poverty grew, exceeding 20 percent during much of the period. The economic expansion of the 1990s saw a drop in child poverty rates, and by 2002, the rate had fallen to 16 percent, a 20-year low (U.S. Bureau of the Census, 2003).

However, these patterns have reversed in recent years, due in part to the 2008 recession. Studies have found that child poverty surged during the past decade, erasing many of the gains in child well-being made in the last 20 years. Between 2006 and 2010, the child poverty rate rose by more than a quarter, reaching 22 percent—the highest level since 1993. The economic recovery since the recession may have improved the lives of the superrich, but the benefits have not filtered down to the poor. In 2018, 16.2 percent of children in the United States were living in poverty (Semega et al., 2019a).

The economic well-being of racial minority children and children of single mothers is even more dire. In 2018, 10.9 percent of non-Hispanic White children were poor, compared to 29 percent of Black children, 25.1 percent of Hispanic children, and 41 percent of children who lived in a single-mother household (Child Trends, 2019).

The 65+ Population in Poverty

Although relatively few persons age 65 and older live in poverty (9.7 percent), this aggregate statistic conceals vast gender, race, and marital status differences in the economic well-being of older adults. In 2018, older adult poverty rates ranged from just 3 percent among White married men to about 20 percent for Black women who live alone, and more than 20 percent for Hispanic women living alone (Semega et al., 2019b). As we noted earlier, these figures may actually underestimate how widespread older adult poverty is because poverty rates fail to consider the high (and rising) costs of medical care, which disproportionately strike older adults (Carr, 2010).

Because older people have, for the most part, retired from paid work, their income is based primarily on Social Security and private retirement programs. Social Security and Medicare have been especially important in lifting many older adults out of poverty. Yet people who depend solely on these two programs for income and health care coverage are likely to live modestly at best. In 2016, some 41 million retired workers were receiving Social Security benefits; their average monthly payment was just over $1,300 a month. Although Social Security was the main source of income for individuals ages 65 and older in 2016, it accounted for only 34 percent of their total income; most of the remainder came from investments, private pension funds, and sometimes earnings (Social Security Administration, 2016a).

Low-income households in particular are likely to rely heavily on Social Security: The lowest income group of adults 65 and older—the 20 percent with income under $13,500 annually—obtain an average of 81 percent of its income from Social Security benefits, compared to 15 percent for the highest income group. Yet even the combination of Social Security and private pensions results in modest retirement incomes for most people: In 2018, the median income for those 65 and older was $23,696 (Semega et al., 2019b).

A Special Case of Poverty: Homelessness

No discussion of poverty is complete without reference to the people who are traditionally seen as at the very bottom of the social hierarchy, **homeless** persons. The growing problem of homelessness is one of the most distressing signs of changes in the American stratification system. Homeless people are a common sight in nearly every U.S. city and town and are increasingly found in rural areas as well. Two generations ago, homeless populations were mainly elderly, alcoholic men who were found on the skid rows of the largest metropolitan areas. Today, they are primarily young single men, often of working age.

Because it is extremely difficult to count people who do not have a stable residence (Appelbaum, 1990), estimates of the number of homeless people vary widely. The most recent official government estimate is that on any given night in 2018 more than 553,000 people were homeless in the United States (Henry et al., 2018). About a quarter (24 percent) are chronically homeless. This last number has reportedly declined by

More than half a million people are homeless on any given night in the United States, 60 percent of whom are men.

as much as a third since 2007, due to an increase in permanent supportive housing for the previously homeless. The fastest-growing group of homeless people, however, consists of families with children, who make up more than a third (33 percent) of those currently homeless. An estimated 40 percent of the homeless are Black, 22 percent are Hispanic, and 1.2 percent are Native American (Henry et al., 2018).

Sadly, veterans, or the men and women who have served their country in the armed forces, have particularly high rates of homelessness, due in part to work-limiting physical and mental health problems triggered by combat. Nearly 38,000 veterans were homeless on any given night in January 2018, accounting for 9 percent of homeless adults. Many homeless veterans suffer from at least one chronic—and costly to treat—health condition (Haggerty, 2012). Veteran homelessness, like other forms of poverty, varies by race. Approximately 33 percent of all homeless veterans are African American, despite accounting for only 13 percent of the U.S. population. The good news is that veteran homelessness has reportedly declined by more than 48 percent since 2009 (Henry et al., 2018).

There are many reasons why people become homeless. About two-thirds reported having a problem with alcohol at some point during their lives, another two-thirds reported having a problem with drugs at some point, and nearly 60 percent have experienced a mental health problem. Additionally, insufficient income and lack of affordable housing are a lead cause (NLCHP, 2004, 2015). One reason for the widespread incidence of such problems among homeless people is that many public mental hospitals have closed their doors. The number of beds in state mental hospitals has declined by as many as half a million since the early 1960s, leaving many mentally ill people with no institutional alternative to a life on the streets or in homeless shelters. Such problems are compounded by the fact that many homeless people lack family, relatives, or other social networks to provide support.

The rising cost of housing is another factor, particularly in light of the increased poverty noted elsewhere in this chapter. Declining incomes at the bottom, along with rising rents, create an affordability gap between the cost of housing and what poor people can pay in rent. The share of renters paying more than 30 percent of income for rent has more than doubled since the 1960s, from 23 percent to 48 percent (Joint Center for Housing Studies of Harvard University, 2020). The burden of paying rent is extremely difficult for low-income families

CONCEPT CHECKS

1 What are the major social class groups in the United States today? Describe at least two ways (other than income) that these groups differ from one another.

2 Contrast intragenerational and intergenerational mobility.

3 According to classic studies of mobility in the United States, how does family background affect one's social class in adulthood?

4 Describe the demographic characteristics of the poor in the United States.

5 Why are women and children at a high risk of becoming impoverished?

whose heads of household work for minimum wage or slightly higher. Paying so much in rent leaves them barely a paycheck away from a missed rental payment and eventual eviction (National Low Income Housing Coalition, 2000).

4 UNANSWERED QUESTIONS

The rise in national popularity of socialist candidates such as AOC and Bernie Sanders has occurred at the same time that sociologists have been documenting important trends in inequality. Here we look at four of the fascinating and policy-relevant questions that have emerged from this continually evolving research. In the following section, we provide preliminary answers: Is inequality declining or increasing in the United States? Why are poverty rates rising in the United States? What can be done to combat poverty? How will these economic patterns affect your life?

> **Kuznets curve** A formula showing that inequality increases during the early stages of capitalist development, then declines, and eventually stabilizes at a relatively low level; advanced by the economist Simon Kuznets.

Is Inequality Declining or Increasing in the United States?

In 1955, the Nobel Prize–winning economist Simon Kuznets proposed a hypothesis that came to be widely accepted: the **Kuznets curve**, a formula showing that inequality increases during the early stages of capitalist development, then declines, and eventually stabilizes at a relatively low level (Figure 8.5). Studies of European countries, the United States, and Canada all suggested that inequality peaked in these places before World War II, declined through the 1950s, and remained roughly the same through the 1970s (Berger, 1986; Nielsen, 1994). In the post–World War II era, inequality declined in part due to economic expansion in industrial societies, which created opportunities for people at the bottom to move up,

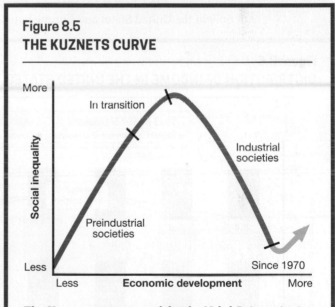

Figure 8.5
THE KUZNETS CURVE

The Kuznets curve, named for the Nobel Prize–winning economist who first advanced the idea in 1955, argues that inequality increases during early industrialization, then decreases during later industrialization, eventually stabilizing at low levels. Some evidence suggests that inequality may increase once again during the transition to postindustrial society.

Source: Nielsen, 1994.

and in part to government health insurance, welfare, and other programs aimed at reducing inequality.

Was Kuznets's prediction correct? Have we seen stabilization in levels of inequality? There is evidence that some capitalist economies have entered a fourth phase, one in which inequality is again increasing. In the United States, for example, during the past 30 years, the rich have gotten much richer, middle-class incomes have stagnated, and the poor have grown in number and are poorer than they have been since the 1960s. The gap between rich and poor is the largest since 1947, when the Census Bureau started measuring it, and the largest in the industrial world. Among industrialized countries, the United States has one of the most unequal distributions of household income (Denmark had the most equal; Organisation for Economic Co-operation and Development, 2014a). In 2015, the top 5 percent of households in the United States received 23.1 percent of total income, the highest 20 percent obtained 52 percent, while the bottom 20 percent received only slightly more than 3 percent (Figure 8.6) (U.S. Bureau of the Census, 2019c).

Most people are aware that the gap between rich Americans and all others has increased significantly since the 2008 recession. But the gap had been widening long before the recession. The reasons for this increase are many and debated, but globalization (whose role we consider in the next chapter) and the declining role of governments (discussed in Chapter 13) are likely two factors that have led to rising inequality not only in the United States and Europe but also in much of the world.

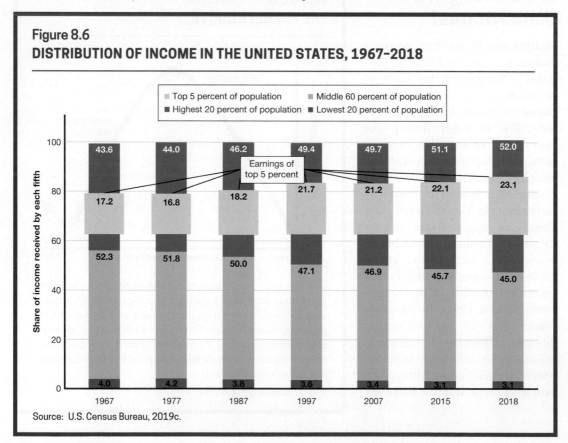

Figure 8.6
DISTRIBUTION OF INCOME IN THE UNITED STATES, 1967–2018

Source: U.S. Census Bureau, 2019c.

The Occupy Wall Street movement drew attention to rising income inequality in the United States.

Another indication of growing inequality (again, long before the recession) was the growing earnings gap between top corporate officials and average working Americans. In 2013, the CEOs of companies listed on the Standard & Poor's (S&P) stock index earned, on average, $11.7 million, 331 times the average worker compensation of $35,200. Thirty years ago, the S&P CEOs earned only 46 times as much as the average worker (Wong, 2014).

The ideas behind the Kuznets curve may have held true for much of the nineteenth and twentieth centuries, but whether it will hold true for the twenty-first century remains an open question.

Thomas Piketty: "Capital in the Twenty-First Century"

The most influential book on social stratification to appear in many years was written not by an American sociologist but by a French economist. Published in 2013, Thomas Piketty's book *Capital in the Twenty-First Century* (the title is intended to suggest an updating of Karl Marx's book by the same title, written nearly 150 years ago) examines changes in the sources and concentration of wealth in capitalist economies since the Industrial Revolution some two and a half centuries ago.

Although his book is long (700 pages), dense, and full of dozens of complicated tables and graphs, Piketty's conclusions can be stated simply: Unless an economy is growing rapidly—for example, because of technological breakthroughs or rapid population growth—increases in wealth will exceed economic growth. This situation, he shows, will inevitably result in a concentration of wealth—especially inherited wealth—and therefore growing inequality. Ever-increasing wealth inequality is therefore not an accident but rather an inevitable feature of almost all capitalist economic systems.

Piketty shows that this has been the case in most developed economies, with one major exception: the mid-twentieth century. During the period that included two world wars and the Great Depression, government policies (such as Roosevelt's New Deal), followed by periods of rapid economic growth, briefly reduced wealth inequality. But he argues that this reduction was an exception, and, in fact, we have once again entered a period of growing inequality. In the United States, for example, he shows that 60 percent of the increase in income in the past 30 years has gone to the richest 1 percent—a situation he calls "patrimonial capitalism" ("patrimonial" refers to a system in which power is concentrated in the hands of a few). This situation is of concern, he argues, because it is both politically untenable and economically unstable. To avoid a future crisis, he calls for a global tax on wealth.

Piketty's argument has been well received by sociologists since it provides an explanation for growing inequality that is supported by data and has the broad historical sweep of Marx and Weber.

Why Are Poverty Rates Rising in the United States? The Sociological Debate

Some theories see poor individuals as responsible for their own poverty, and other theories view poverty as produced and reproduced by structural forces in society. These approaches are sometimes described as "blame the victim" and "blame the system" theories, respectively. We shall briefly examine each.

There is a long history of attitudes holding the poor responsible for their own disadvantaged positions. For example, the poorhouses of the nineteenth century were grounded in a belief that the poor were unable—due to lack of skills, moral or physical weakness, absence of motivation, or below-average ability—to succeed in society. Social standing was seen to reflect a person's talent and effort; those who deserved to succeed did so, while others less capable were doomed to fail.

Such outlooks reemerged in the 1970s and 1980s as the political emphasis on entrepreneurship and ambition rewarded those who "succeeded" and held those who did not succeed responsible for their unfortunate circumstances. Often, explanations for poverty targeted the lifestyles and attitudes of poor people. Oscar Lewis (1968) proposed one of the most influential theories, which argues that poverty results from a larger social and cultural atmosphere into which poor children are socialized. The **culture of poverty** is transmitted across generations

culture of poverty The thesis, popularized by Oscar Lewis, that poverty is not a result of individual inadequacies but is instead the outcome of a larger social and cultural atmosphere into which successive generations of children are socialized. The culture of poverty refers to the values, beliefs, lifestyles, habits, and traditions that are common among people living under conditions of material deprivation.

A man reads from the scriptures in a nineteenth-century homeless shelter. According to the commonly held belief of the time, the poor were responsible for their circumstances due to lack of skills, motivation, or, as this engraving suggests, moral fiber.

because young people see little point in aspiring to something more. Instead, they resign themselves to a life of impoverishment.

The culture of poverty thesis was taken further by Charles Murray (1984), who controversially placed individuals who are poor through "no fault of their own"—such as widows or widowers, orphans, or the disabled—into a different category from those who are part of the **dependency culture**. This term refers to poor people who rely on welfare rather than entering the labor market. Murray argued that the growth of the welfare state undermines personal ambition and the capacity for self-help; welfare erodes people's incentive to work.

An opposite approach to explaining poverty emphasizes larger social processes that are difficult for individuals to overcome. In this view, structural forces within society—differences in opportunity that are associated with race, class, gender, ethnicity, occupational position, educational attainment, and so forth—shape the way in which resources are distributed (Wilson, 1996,

dependency culture A term popularized by Charles Murray to describe individuals who rely on state welfare provision rather than entering the labor market. The dependency culture is seen as the outcome of the "paternalistic" welfare state that undermines individual ambition and people's capacity for self-help.

2011). Advocates of this approach argue that the perceived lack of achievement among the poor is a consequence of their constrained situations, not a cause of it. Reducing poverty thus requires policy measures aimed at distributing income and resources more equally throughout society; such policy measures include child-care subsidies, a minimum hourly wage, and guaranteed income levels for families.

Surveys show that Americans are split on whether the poor are responsible for their plight. A Pew Research Center poll in 2018 found that 52 percent believe that poverty is the result of circumstances beyond people's control, while 31 percent believe it is because people do not do enough to lift themselves out of poverty. This represents a significant shift in opinion from 20 years earlier, when less than a third of respondents believed poverty to be caused by conditions beyond one's control, and more than half believed that the poor were responsible for their circumstances (Dunn, 2018). This shift in opinion may well reflect the lingering aftermath of the 2008 recession, which affected many working- and middle-class Americans, revealing to them that circumstances beyond one's control can adversely affect one's livelihood.

Both theories play a role in public debates about poverty. Critics of the "culture of poverty" thesis accuse its advocates of blaming the poor for circumstances beyond their control. They see the poor as victims, not as freeloaders. Most sociologists emphasize the systemic or structural causes of poverty. While individual initiative obviously plays a part, major advantages are conferred by being born higher up on the income and wealth ladder—and major disadvantages from being born at the bottom. Moreover, these advantages (or disadvantages) are amplified by what is happening in the U.S. economy. During a period of growth, new opportunities are created; a rising tide, as the expression goes, lifts all boats. During a time of economic decline, such as a recession, or stagnation, the poor suffer the most.

What Can Be Done to Combat Poverty?

In past economic downturns—beginning with the New Deal policies enacted by the FDR administration during the Great Depression of the 1930s—government transfers helped to blunt the effects. Unemployment insurance, welfare benefits, antipoverty programs, and government stimulus spending helped to create jobs, benefiting those at the bottom and thereby reducing inequality. These reforms also helped to reduce inequality in the long run by transferring wealth (in the form of higher taxes) from richer Americans to poorer Americans. Can contemporary government policies effectively reduce poverty?

Critics of government spending on poverty alleviation argue that it promotes "welfare dependency," meaning that poor people become materially and psychologically dependent on the very programs that are supposed to enable them to become independent. Others deny that such dependency is widespread. "Being on welfare" is a source of shame, they say, and most people on welfare usually try to escape from it.

Recently, we have seen a shift in public opinion with regard to the role of government in helping the poor. The Pew Research Center regularly asks a national sample of Americans whether they believe that "poor people today have it easy because they can get government benefits without doing anything in return," as opposed to "poor

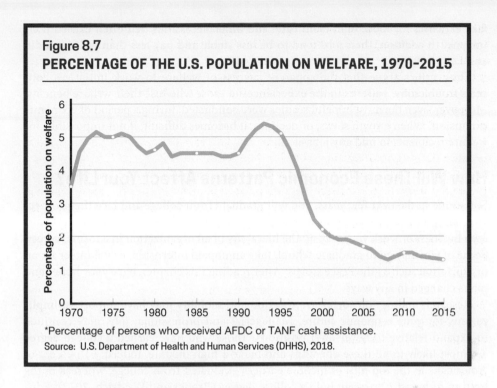

Figure 8.7
PERCENTAGE OF THE U.S. POPULATION ON WELFARE, 1970–2015

*Percentage of persons who received AFDC or TANF cash assistance.
Source: U.S. Department of Health and Human Services (DHHS), 2018.

people have hard lives because government benefits don't go far enough to help them live decently." The 2014 poll found that 47 percent chose the former option, while 43 percent chose the latter. Twenty years ago, the split was 53 percent to 39 percent. There has been a clear shift in opinion toward the belief that the government is failing to do enough to help the poor (Horowitz et al., 2020b).

President Bill Clinton enacted sweeping welfare reform designed to get people off the welfare rolls. In a sense, this law provided a test case of the "welfare dependency" thesis. The Temporary Assistance for Needy Families (TANF) program, which took effect in 1997, replaced earlier welfare programs by requiring that welfare recipients begin work after receiving benefits for only two years; families would be cut off entirely after a cumulative five years of assistance. Before this reform, the federal government imposed no time limits or work requirements on welfare recipients, many of whom are single mothers.

On the one hand, the welfare-to-work approach was a resounding success: It reduced welfare claims from 5.1 million families to 2.7 million families in the first three years. Employment rates did increase somewhat among welfare recipients, and the 61 percent of those who left welfare were able to find work. On the other hand, nearly one out of every five welfare recipients was unable to find work (or, indeed, any source of independent income), while another fifth was forced to rely on romantic partners, family members, or private charities for support. About half of those who did get a job wound up earning less than they had received on welfare; less than a quarter had health insurance through their employer (Loprest, 1999). For low-income mothers, the costs of leaving welfare for work can outweigh the advantages since they face expenses for food, rent, child care, and other necessities that often exceed their income. In addition, their jobs tend to be less stable and pay less than welfare (Edin and Lein, 1997).

Thus, critics argue that the apparent success of welfare-to-work initiatives conceals troublesome patterns in the experiences of those who lose their welfare benefits. Moreover, even the most hopeful studies were conducted during a period of economic expansion. When growth slows, or declines, it becomes difficult, if not impossible, for welfare recipients to find any jobs at all.

How Will These Economic Patterns Affect Your Life?

Sometime in the next few years, you will graduate from college and face the prospect of starting a career. Do you have any idea what you will do? Perhaps you will start your own business or work your way up the hierarchy of an organization in a formal career. Some of you may go to graduate school, take an unpaid internship, or volunteer for an organization such as the Peace Corps. After reading this chapter, have your hopes and plans changed in any way?

Research findings on social stratification and mobility may have important implications for your economic future. Managerial and professional jobs may continue to expand relative to lower-level positions. Those who have earned a college degree are most likely to fill these openings and make a high income. Indeed, 61 percent of Americans in the top fifth of income earners graduated from college, whereas in the bottom fifth, just 12 percent hold a college degree (Brooks and Weidrich, 2012). Educational attainment seems to be the key variable for upward mobility in the United States (Urahn et al., 2012).

Because you are a college student, chances are that one or both of your parents are college educated and that you grew up enjoying a middle-class lifestyle. If this was the case, what are the chances that you will wind up better off than your parents? A new study of intergenerational income mobility by Stanford researchers found that young people entering the workforce today are considerably less likely to outearn their parents than young people born two generations before them. While 90 percent of young people born in the 1940s went on to earn more than their parents, the same is true of just 50 percent of young people born in the 1980s. In other words, as one of the study's authors explained, "It's basically a coin flip as to whether you'll do better than your parents" (Wong, 2016; Chetty et al., 2016).

In addition, as a result of global economic competition, not nearly enough well-paid positions are open for all who wish to enter them. Even if a higher proportion of jobs is created at managerial and professional levels, the overall number of jobs available in the future may not keep pace with the number of people with college degrees seeking work. Reasons for this gap include the growing number of women entering the workforce and the increasing use of information technology in production processes. Because computerized machinery can now handle tasks—even highly complicated ones—that only humans could do before, many jobs may be eliminated.

Moreover, China, India, Brazil, and other countries are now part of a global workforce in which U.S. workers must compete for jobs. While this has been the case for some time with regard to manufacturing jobs—from automobiles to apparel to electronics—it is increasingly true for higher-skilled, higher-wage jobs as well. As we shall see in Chapter 14, many so-called "emerging economies" are now educating a growing number of scientists, engineers, and professionals who will be competing for jobs with U.S. college graduates. Although we are increasingly moving toward an interdependent, global economy, how these shifts will affect your jobs and careers—and stratification in the United States—is difficult to foresee.

CONCEPT CHECKS

1 Contrast the "culture of poverty" argument and structural explanations for poverty.

2 How has globalization affected the life chances of young adults in the United States today?

THE BIG PICTURE

Chapter 8
Stratification, Class, and Inequality

1 | **Basic Concepts** | p. 242

2 | **Theories of Stratification in Modern Societies** | p. 250

LEARNING OBJECTIVES

Learn about social stratification and the importance of social background in an individual's chances for material success.

Know the most influential theories of stratification, including those of Karl Marx, Max Weber, and Erik Olin Wright.

TERMS TO KNOW

social stratification • intersectionality • structured inequalities • slavery • caste • class systems • class • life chances • income • wealth

means of production • bourgeoisie • proletariat • surplus value • communism • status • pariah groups • contradictory class locations

CONCEPT CHECKS

1. How is the concept of class different from that of caste?
2. What are the principal determinants of social stratification?
3. What is the difference between wealth and income, and why does it matter for social stratification?
4. What are two examples of noneconoic indicators of one's social class?

1. According to Karl Marx, what are the two main classes, and how do they relate to one another?
2. What are the two main differences between Max Weber's and Karl Marx's theories of social stratification?
3. According to Kingsley Davis and Wilbert E. Moore, how does social stratification contribute to the functioning of society? What is wrong with this argument, according to Melvin Tumin?
4. What does Erik Olin Wright mean by "contradictory class location"? Give an example of a type of worker who falls in this category.

Exercises: Thinking Sociologically

1. If you were doing your own study of status differences in your community, how would you measure people's social class? Explain why you would take the particular measurement approach you've chosen. What would be its value(s) and shortcoming(s) compared with those of alternative measurement procedures?

2. Using occupation and occupational change as your mobility criteria, view the social mobility within your own family and explain why you think people in your family have moved up, moved down, or remained at the same status level. Apply these terms: upward and downward mobility, intragenerational and intergenerational mobility.

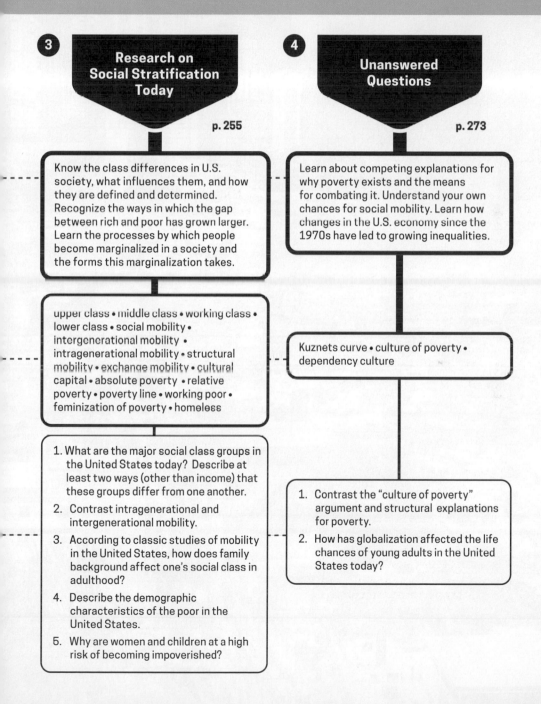

3

Research on Social Stratification Today

p. 255

Know the class differences in U.S. society, what influences them, and how they are defined and determined. Recognize the ways in which the gap between rich and poor has grown larger. Learn the processes by which people become marginalized in a society and the forms this marginalization takes.

upper class • middle class • working class • lower class • social mobility • intergenerational mobility • intragenerational mobility • structural mobility • exchange mobility • cultural capital • absolute poverty • relative poverty • poverty line • working poor • feminization of poverty • homeless

1. What are the major social class groups in the United States today? Describe at least two ways (other than income) that these groups differ from one another.

2. Contrast intragenerational and intergenerational mobility.

3. According to classic studies of mobility in the United States, how does family background affect one's social class in adulthood?

4. Describe the demographic characteristics of the poor in the United States.

5. Why are women and children at a high risk of becoming impoverished?

4

Unanswered Questions

p. 273

Learn about competing explanations for why poverty exists and the means for combating it. Understand your own chances for social mobility. Learn how changes in the U.S. economy since the 1970s have led to growing inequalities.

Kuznets curve • culture of poverty • dependency culture

1. Contrast the "culture of poverty" argument and structural explanations for poverty.

2. How has globalization affected the life chances of young adults in the United States today?

9

Global Inequality

Which three men topped the list of the world's richest people in early 2020?

A   Jeff Bezos, founder and CEO of Amazon; Mark Zuckerberg, founder and CEO of Facebook; and Warren Buffett, founder and CEO of Berkshire-Hathaway

B   Bill Gates, cofounder of Microsoft; Jeff Bezos, founder and CEO of Amazon; Mark Zuckerberg, founder and CEO of Facebook

C   Jeff Bezos, founder and CEO of Amazon; Bill Gates, cofounder of Microsoft; and Bernard Arnault, Chairman of LVMH Moet Hennessey Louis Vuitton

TURN THE PAGE FOR THE CORRECT ANSWER.

LEARNING OBJECTIVES

1 Basic Concepts

Understand the differences in wealth and power among countries.

2 Theories of Global Inequality

Learn several sociological theories for why some societies are wealthier than others, and understand the strengths and weaknesses of each.

3 Research on Global Inequality Today

Recognize the impact on people throughout the world of different economic standards of living, including one's health, diet, and educational opportunities.

4 Unanswered Questions

Understand the causes of inequality—both between countries and within countries—in the world today. Learn who makes up the global poor and whether the proportion of the population living in poverty is increasing or decreasing. Consider how globalization might shape global inequality in the future.

If you went out on a limb and guessed Jeff Bezos, Bill Gates, and Bernard Arnault—someone you most likely have never heard of—you were right! Even though most Americans have never heard of the French billionaire Bernard Arnault, in March 2020, he ranked third, with a net worth (the value of everything he owned minus everything he owed) of $76 billion. Bezos got top billing, with a net worth of $113 billion; Gates was not far behind with a net worth of $98 billion (Dolan, 2020). While the sources of Bezos's wealth (Amazon) and Gates's wealth (Microsoft) are known by just about everyone, "LVMH Moet Hennessey Louis Vuitton"—a giant corporation that is the world's largest maker of luxury goods—is hardly a household phrase. Among the products that propelled Arnault to third place: Louis Vuitton goods (you can pick up a pair of men's V.N.R. Sneakers for a mere $1,190; women's Denim Monogram Check Dresses go for only $2,250); TAG Heuer watches (prices range from $1,000 to $74,750); and Dom Perignon champagne (a bargain at $150 a bottle; a rare vintage once fetched the staggering sum of $84,700!).

The fortunes of these three men illustrate some important themes that will be developed throughout this chapter. Bezos's wealth stems from the retail revolution he launched—online shopping combined with home delivery. Amazon has made consumption virtually effortless, and now employs three-quarters of a million workers. It has also put many stores (along with the jobs they provided) out of business.

Amazon's success was made possible, in part, by Microsoft; Gates's computer/Windows software company played a major role in paving the way for today's virtual world, in which we can now engage in impulse buying on our smartphones or computers. Arnault, however, is a relative newcomer to the top tier of the world's richest people. While there have always been wealthy consumers (that $84,700 bottle of Dom Perignon champagne was sold at a New York City wine auction in 1959), there are now far more superrich in the world today than ever before in human history. Their wealth has made the sale of luxury goods, from private jets and yachts to $75,000 watches, a highly profitable busi-

THE ANSWER IS C.

ness for Arnault and others. The computer and retail revolutions, launched by Gates, Bezos, and other entrepreneurs, are a part of the story. **Globalization**—the increased economic, political, and social interconnectedness of the world—is another.

Over the past several decades, globalization has produced a skyrocketing number of billionaires. When Forbes first started keeping a list in 1987, it could identify only 140 billionaires throughout the world (Kilachand, 2012). By 2020, the most recent year for which Forbes has data, there were 2,095 billionaires, with a combined net worth of $8.0 trillion (Dolan, 2020). It should be noted that by March 2020 the world economy had already begun to slow as a result of the global COVID-19 pandemic. Billionaires weren't immune to the pandemic's financial effects: one year earlier, in March 2019, the world's billionaires were worth $8.7 trillion. Of these billionaires, 614 (29 percent) were from the United States, while China came in second with 389 billionaires (19 percent) (Dolan, 2020). While the United States still has the world's largest economy (China is rapidly closing in), the "rise of the rest" has brought great wealth to a growing number of people in other countries (Zakaria, 2009).

As globalization has created a growing number of billionaires, it has also resulted in growing inequality. The world's 2,095 billionaires could easily fit into a large lecture hall or movie theater. Despite accounting for an insignificant fraction of the world's 7.7 billion people, they own 2.0 percent of the world's wealth (the world's wealth is estimated at $361 trillion) (Shorrocks et al., 2019b). If we extend our lens beyond billionaires, to look at the richest 1 percent of the world's population, it turns out that the top 1 percent possesses almost as much of the world's wealth (45 percent) as the remaining 99 percent (Shorrocks et al., 2019b). The United States, by itself, accounts for 29 percent of the world's wealth (Figure 9.1) (Shorrocks et al., 2019b); yet within the United States, vast inequality also exists. According to Federal Reserve data, the richest 1 percent of U.S. households accounted for 32 percent of all the wealth in the country in 2019 (*US News*, 2019).

Globalization has produced opportunities for unthinkable wealth but also widespread poverty and suffering. Consider Mossammat Rebecca Khatun, a young woman who sewed clothing in the Rana Plaza industrial building in Bangladesh, often laboring 13 hours a day, six days a week, for weekly earnings unlikely to exceed $11. Rebecca, and thousands like her, made clothing for major European and U.S. brands and retailers. When Rana Plaza collapsed on April 24, 2013, 1,137 people died and thousands were injured. Rebecca was one of the lucky ones: She survived, buried alive for two days before rescuers reached her. But she lost her right foot and her entire left leg, and she still suffers from constant pain. Rebecca's mother, who worked in the same building, was not so fortunate: Her body was never found (Parveen, 2014). Billions of workers such as Rebecca are being drawn into the global labor force, many working in oppressive and unsafe conditions that would be unacceptable, if not unimaginable, under U.S. labor laws. And these are the fortunate ones. Those outside the global economy are frequently even worse off.

globalization The development of social and economic relationships stretching worldwide. In current times, we are all influenced by organizations and social networks located thousands of miles away. A key part of the study of globalization is the emergence of a world system—for some purposes, we need to regard the world as forming a single social order.

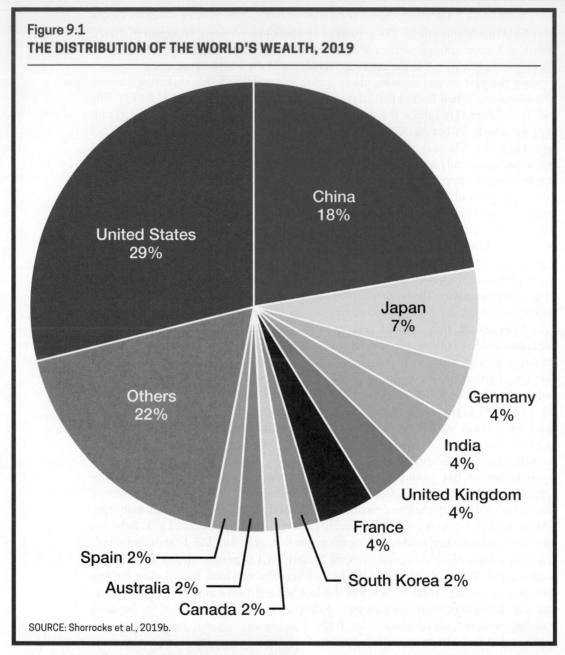

Figure 9.1
THE DISTRIBUTION OF THE WORLD'S WEALTH, 2019

China
18%

United States
29%

Japan
7%

Germany
4%

Others
22%

India
4%

United Kingdom
4%

France
4%

Spain 2%

Australia 2%

South Korea 2%

Canada 2%

SOURCE: Shorrocks et al., 2019b.

In the previous chapter, we noted vast differences in individuals' income, wealth, work, and quality of life. Just as we can speak of rich or poor individuals within a country, we can also talk about rich or poor countries within the world system. A country's position in the global economy affects how its people live, work, and die. In this chapter, we examine the differences in wealth and power among countries in the late twentieth and early twenty-first centuries. We examine differences in economic standards of living and then turn to a discussion of different theories on the causes of global inequality and what can be done about it. We conclude by considering some unanswered questions concerning economic inequality in an age of globalization. As we will see throughout this chapter, globalization has produced great wealth—as well as great inequality—both between and within countries.

1 BASIC CONCEPTS

Global inequality refers to the systematic differences in wealth and power among countries. These differences exist alongside differences within countries: Even the wealthiest countries have growing numbers of poor people. Yet it is important to remember that while some less wealthy nations, such as China, India, or Mexico are producing many of the world's superrich, there is still a huge difference between being poor in a wealthy nation such as the United States, and starving to death in a poor nation. Sociology's challenge is not merely to identify such differences but to explain why they occur—and how they might be overcome.

The most commonly used way to classify countries in terms of global inequality is to compare the wealth produced by each country for its average citizen. The gross national income, or **GNI**, is a measure of the total income earned as a result of a country's yearly output of goods and services, including any income earned abroad. We use GNI here, rather than the more commonly used gross domestic product (GDP), since the latter includes only income produced within the country. When divided by the number of people in a country, this provides one commonly used estimate of average (per person) income. The World Bank (Prydz and Wadhwa, 2019), an international lending organization that provides loans for development projects in poorer countries, uses this measure to classify countries as either high income (based on an annual 2019 average per person income greater than of $12,375), upper-middle income ($3,996–$12,375), lower-middle income ($1,026–$3,995), or low income ($1,025 or less). This system of classification is often used to show the vast differences in living standards that exist among countries. The World Bank in 2019 identified 80 countries (out of 218) as high income, 60 as upper-middle income, 47 as lower-middle income, and 31 as low income (World Bank, 2019g).

High-Income Countries

High-income countries are generally those that industrialized first, a process that began in England some 250 years ago and then spread to the rest of Europe, the United States, and Canada. In the 1960s, Japan joined their ranks, while Singapore, Hong Kong, and Taiwan did so only within the last several decades (Global Map 9.1). Most high-income countries are found in Europe, North America (United States, Canada), and the East Asian/Pacific region (Australia, New Zealand, Japan, South Korea, Singapore, Taiwan). There are also a few high-income countries in South America (Chile, Uruguay, Panama) and the Middle East (Israel; and such oil-rich countries as Saudi Arabia, Kuwait, and the United Arab Emirates), as well as a scattering of islands in the Caribbean (for example, The Bahamas, Puerto Rico). The average annual income for people living in

global inequality The systematic differences in wealth and power among countries.

GNI Gross National Income, a commonly used measure based on total income earned as a result of a country's yearly output of goods and services, including income earned abroad.

RICH AND POOR COUNTRIES: THE WORLD BY INCOME, 2020

Like individuals in a country, the countries of the world as a whole can be seen as economically stratified. In general, those countries that experienced industrialization the earliest are the richest, while those that remain agricultural are the poorest. An enormous, and growing, gulf separates the two groups.

High income: $12,376 or more

Upper middle income: $3,996–$12,375

Lower middle income: $1,026–$3,995

Low income: $1,025 or less

SOURCE: Prydz and Wadhwa, 2019; World Bank, 2020b.

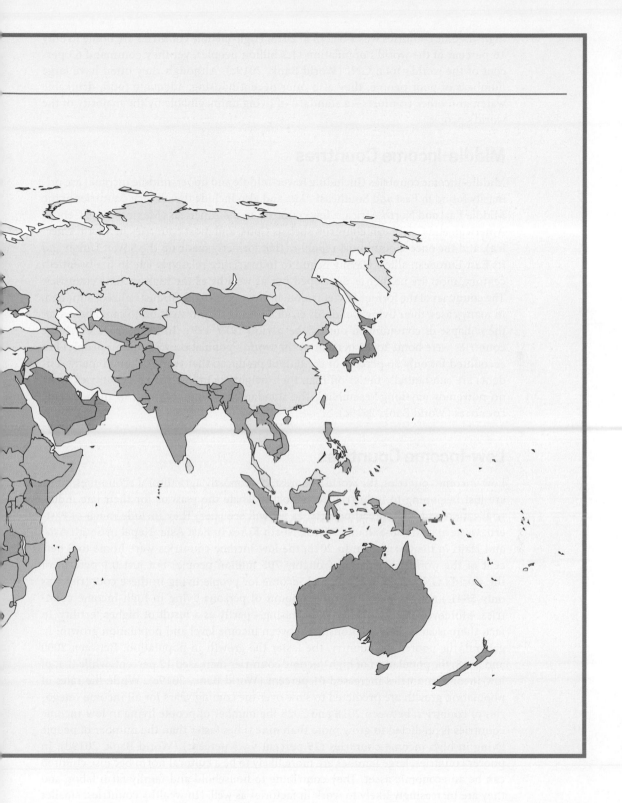

high-income countries was $44,275 in 2018. High-income countries are home to only 16 percent of the world's population (1.2 billion people), yet they command 63 percent of the world's total GNI (World Bank, 2019c). Although they often have large numbers of poor people, they also offer decent housing, adequate food, drinkable water, and other comforts—a standard of living unimaginable by the majority of the world's people.

Middle-Income Countries

Middle-income countries (including lower-middle and upper-middle income) are primarily found in East and Southeast Asia, and also include the oil-rich countries of the Middle East and North Africa, a few countries in the Americas (Mexico, some Central American and Caribbean countries such as Cuba, and most countries in South America), and the once-Communist republics that formerly made up the Soviet Union and its East European allies. Having begun to industrialize relatively late in the twentieth century, most are neither as developed nor as wealthy as the high-income countries. The countries of the former Soviet Union, however, are highly industrialized, although, in many cases, their living standards eroded during their transition to capitalism after the collapse of communism during the period 1979–1991. In 2018, middle-income countries were home to 75 percent of the world's population (5.7 billion people) but accounted for only 36 percent of the output produced that year. Although many residents are substantially better off than their neighbors in low-income countries, most do not enjoy anything resembling the standard of living common in high-income countries (World Bank, 2019c).

Low-Income Countries

Low-income countries, the world's poorest, have mostly agricultural economies; some are just beginning to industrialize. Scholars debate the reasons for their late industrialization and widespread poverty, as we will see later. They include much of eastern, western, and sub-Saharan Africa; North Korea in East Asia; Nepal in South Asia; and Haiti in the Caribbean. In 2018, the low-income countries were home to 9 percent of the world's population (roughly 705 million people) but just 0.1 percent of the world's GNI; the average annual income for people living in these countries was only $841 in 2018, one-fiftieth the amount of persons living in high-income countries. Moreover, this inequality is increasing—partly as a result of higher fertility. In fact, there is an inverse relationship between income level and population growth: In general, the poorer the country, the faster the growth in population. Between 2000 and 2018, the population of high-income countries increased 12 percent, while that of low-income countries increased 61 percent (World Bank, 2019e). While the rates of population growth are predicted to slow over the coming years for all income categories of countries, between 2018 and 2028 the number of people living in low-income countries is predicted to grow more than nine times faster than the number of people living in high-income countries (29 percent vs. 3 percent) (World Bank, 2019d). In poorer countries, large families are more likely to be a cultural norm because children can be an economic asset. They contribute to household and family farm labor, and they are increasingly likely to work in factories as well. (In wealthy countries, smaller families are the norm: in most families children do not typically contribute to household income, but instead depend on their parents' earnings for their lifestyles.) In many low-income countries, people struggle with poverty, malnutrition, and starvation. Most people live in rural areas, although in recent years, hundreds of millions of people have been moving to densely populated cities, where they live either in dilapidated housing or on the streets (see Chapter 19).

Is Global Economic Well-Being Improving?

Based on the World Bank's income categories, for the world as a whole, at least in terms of average incomes, there has been considerable progress over the last two decades. In only twenty years (1999–2019), the number of high-income countries has grown by 27; upper-middle-income countries by 20. As countries have moved up into the two upper-income categories, the number of lower-middle-income countries dropped by 10; low-income countries by 34 (Prydz and Wadhwa, 2019). And looking at the number of countries in each income category tells only part of the story, since when we look at the number of people in each category, the changes are even more striking. Twenty years ago, 60 percent of the world's population lived in low-income countries; today, the figure is only 9 percent. The number of people living in lower-middle-income countries grew from 15 percent to 35 percent; the number living in upper-middle-income countries grew from 10 percent to 35 percent. Significantly, however, the number of people living in high-income countries has been fairly constant at 15–16 percent over the 20-year period: the richest tier of nations remains a fairly exclusive club (Prydz and Wadhwa, 2019).

Much of this upward movement of people is the result of the economic success of two highly populous countries, China and India, which together account for more than a third of the world's population. After taking inflation into account, China's average income in 1998 was $800; by 2018, it had grown to $9,460, an historically unprecedented twelve-fold increase in only 20 years. China moved from the bottom of the lower-middle-income category to the top of the upper-middle-income category, and is poised to quickly join the ranks of high-income countries. Since China's 1.4 billion people account for nearly one out of every five persons on the planet, its economic success by itself has elevated a significant portion of the world population out of economic poverty. (We will focus on the reasons for China's success later in this chapter.) India's accomplishments are not quite as striking: Its average income grew from $410 in 1998 to $2,020 in 2018, a five-fold increase, enough to raise India from the low-income category to the lower-middle-income category—still a significant improvement for many of India's 1.4 billion people (Prydz and Wadhwa, 2019).

Going Beyond Purely Economic Measures of Global Well-Being

There are, however, a number of problems in using the World Bank income categories as measures of success. One problem is that using average income masks income inequality *within* each country. The average incomes for each economy, on which these data are based, are skewed upward when a relatively small portion of the population has extremely high incomes. China, for example, has raised several hundred million people out of poverty into middle-class status and, as we have seen, has many billionaires—yet China still has hundreds of millions of impoverished peasants. In contrast, the United States is in the upper ranks of high-income countries, with an average income in 2018 of $63,080 (World Bank, 2019d); yet the United States has more than a half million homeless people on any given day (Henry et al., 2018), and some 38 million people living in poverty (Fontenot et al., 2018).

This raises a second problem: Comparing countries on the basis of economic output alone may be misleading because GNI includes only goods and services produced for cash sale that are known to the government. Many people in low-income countries produce only for their own families or for barter, which involves noncash transactions. The value of their crops and animals is not reflected in the official statistics. The economy also includes paid work that is done "off the books"—the gardener or housekeeper who is paid by cash or check with no official records kept; the street vendor; illegal activities of all sorts. While this so-called informal sector is found in all countries, it is especially prevalent in poorer countries, where it may make an important contribution to the overall economy. According to a UN International Labour Organization estimate, as many as 60 percent of all workers in the world engage in some type of informal work, most of them in poorer countries (ILO, 2018).

A third problem with classifying countries on the basis of income alone is that it can be misleading, since it obscures the difference between absolute and relative poverty. **Absolute poverty** occurs when persons cannot acquire basic life needs, including food, clothing, and shelter; starvation is often a way of life for those in this category. **Relative poverty** occurs when persons are poor relative to others in their society; they may struggle to make ends meet while their neighbors can more easily put food on the table or pay the rent. Most poverty in the United States is relative poverty; most of the poor are not starving or homeless, and even homeless people are often able to find shelters and food kitchens. By way of contrast, almost everyone in the African country of Burundi, where an average income in 2018 of $280 makes it the poorest country in the world, lives in absolute poverty. In Burundi, half of the population is chronically hungry and agricultural production is too poor to meet the country's needs (World Food Programme, 2019).

Finally, economic output is not a country's whole story, since it fails to adequately capture important non-economic aspects of people's lives. The United Nations Human Development Program has developed a Multidimensional Poverty Index (MDPI) that combines 10 poverty-related indicators into a single weighted index, intended to provide a measure of *human development* rather than economic development alone. The indicators are grouped into three major categories that provide a broad picture of one's quality of life: *health* (nutrition, child mortality), *education* (years of schooling, school attendance), and *standard of living* (materials used as cooking fuel, household sanitation, access to potable drinking water, household electricity,

absolute poverty When persons cannot acquire basic life needs, including food, clothing, and shelter.

relative poverty When persons are poor relative to others in their society.

Capabilities Approach An approach to development that uses social indicators to emphasize the degree to which people are capable of achieving a life they value, given the opportunities they face.

adequately constructed housing, possession of such basic assets as a bicycle or refrigerator) (UNDP, 2019b). Based on this measure, the UN estimates that 1.3 billion people around the world live in poverty, twice the number as measured by income alone. The much higher numbers reflect aspects of poverty that are missed by purely economic indicators: the fact that more than a quarter of a billion children do not attend primary or secondary school, or 5.4 million children die before they reach the age of five (UNDP, 2019b).

This effort to measure aspects of human development, beyond purely economic growth, reflects a proposal first made by the Nobel Prize–winning Indian economist/philosopher Amartya Sen. Forty years ago, Sen argued that instead of focusing on purely economic indicators, what is important is the quality of life people are capable of achieving—the freedom to make fundamental life choices. Sen argued that indicators of such freedom were preferable to measures of income or wealth, since they reflected the capability people have to achieve the quality of life they prefer (Sen, 1979). Governments should be assessed not in terms of such measures as the average income of their country, but rather in terms of what their citizens are capable of achieving, given the public and private opportunities that are provided. For this reason, Sen's approach is termed the **Capabilities Approach**, since it emphasizes the degree to which people are capable of achieving a life they value, given the opportunities they face.

Sen's ideas (and efforts) shaped the United Nations' *Human Development Report*, an annual publication (first launched in 1990) that ranks countries on numerous social as well as economic indicators. The most recent *Report*, for example, distinguishes access to what it terms *basic capabilities* (early childhood survival, primary education, entry-level technologies, the ability to withstand minor life setbacks) from *more advanced capabilities* (high-quality health care and education, present-day technologies, the ability to withstand major life setbacks). This approach emphasizes the importance of the kinds of measures that sociologists, rather than economists, are likely to be concerned with. It has led the UN to some startling conclusions that are not evident from economic data alone (UNDP, 2019b):

- Although there has been success in raising incomes worldwide, such things as lack of basic schooling, infant mortality, and starvation remain global problems.
- While differences in *basic capabilities* have declined, a "new generation" of differences in *enhanced capabilities* is emerging; lack of access to high-quality education or technology will prove a barrier to those who are left behind in the years to come.
- Inequalities accumulate through life, often reflecting deep power imbalances: Where people lack power, they lack the ability to shape the institutions—from education to health care to jobs—that will affect the life prospects of their children.

CONCEPT CHECKS

1. Explain how the World Bank measures global inequality and discuss some of the problems associated with measuring inequality.

2. Compare and contrast high-income, middle-income, and low-income countries.

3. What is the Capabilities Approach to measuring well-being, and how does it provide a more sociological understanding of development than purely economic measures?

2   THEORIES OF GLOBAL INEQUALITY

What causes global inequality? How can it be overcome? In this section, we examine four different theories that have been advanced over the years to explain global inequality: neoliberal theories, dependency theories, world-systems theories, and global capitalism theories. Each approach has strengths and weaknesses. One shortcoming of all four is that they tend to underemphasize the role of women in economic development. By putting the theories together, however, we should be able to answer a question facing the 84 percent of the world's population living outside high-income countries: How can they move up in the world economy?

Neoliberal Theories

Neoliberalism refers to the belief that the best economic consequences will result if individuals are entirely free from governmental constraint to make their own economic decisions. Government bureaucracy should not dictate which goods to produce, what prices to charge, how much to pay workers, or whether businesses should be prevented from polluting the environment. Such decisions should be left to the businesses themselves, who will respond to what the market demands: You, the consumer, freely choose from among competing brands, perhaps taking into account the working and environmental conditions under which the product is made. Neoliberal economic theories assume that, in the long run, everyone will be better off if such economic freedom is maximized.

The word "liberal" in "neoliberalism" refers to freedom—in this case, the freedom for producers and consumers alike to make their own economic decisions. It became a part of economic thinking with the publication of Adam Smith's *The Wealth of Nations* in 1776, which argued that unrestricted industrial capitalism (which was then emerging) was the best avenue to economic growth. Liberal theories dominated economic belief until the 1930s, when the worldwide Great Depression caused the United States and other industrialized economies to question the belief that governments should play little or no role in the economy. A new economic theory called *Keynesianism*, which reflected the ideas presented in John Maynard Keynes's 1936 book *The General Theory of Employment, Interest and Money*, called for a greatly expanded role of government in order to repair the economic damage done by the Great Depression. These ideas held sway for a half century. By the 1960s, the United States was providing Social Security pensions for retirees, health insurance for the elderly (Medicare) and the poor (Medicaid), insurance for those who lose their jobs, and welfare programs for the very poor, as well as a host of regulations aimed at protecting consumers, workers, and the environment. By the mid-twentieth century, it was generally accepted in the United States and other industrialized nations that supposedly "free markets" did not necessarily produce the best outcomes for everyone: Left unregulated, markets could favor the rich and powerful, lead to recurring economic crises, and produce a widening gap between rich and poor.

neoliberalism The economic belief that free-market forces, achieved by minimizing government restrictions on business, will provide the greatest economic benefit to the widest range of people.

During the second half of the twentieth century, however, the old liberal economic ideas enjoyed a resurgence (hence the prefix "neo," or "new," in "neoliberalism"). Their success was due in large part to a small group of highly influential University of Chicago economists, whose ideas resonated with businesses and conservative politicians (Overtveldt, 2009; Valdes, 2008). These ideas helped to shape U.S. policies regarding low-income countries, especially in neighboring Latin America, where widespread poverty had made communism appealing to many peasants and workers. One strategy to counter such appeal, in the view of U.S. policymakers, was to help foster neoliberal capitalism in low-income countries, which would hopefully result in economic growth and thereby dampen the appeal of communism. The key was for these countries to open their borders to U.S. financed foreign-aid programs that provided money, expert advisers, and technology to low-income countries, paving the way for U.S. corporations to make investments there (Berger, 1986; Ranis, 1996; Ranis and Mahmood, 1992; Rostow, 1961; Warren, 1980).

One influential proponent of such theories was W. W. Rostow, an economic adviser to former U.S. president John F. Kennedy, whose ideas helped shape U.S. foreign policy toward Latin America during the 1960s. Rostow's explanation, termed **modernization theory**, argued that low-income societies could become "modern" (which meant resembling the United States and other high-income countries) only if they adopted modern economic institutions, technologies, and cultural values that emphasize savings and productive investment. According to Rostow (1961), the social institutions and traditional cultural values of low-income countries impeded their economic growth. One problem, it was argued, was that low-income countries' economies were overregulated by ineffective and often corrupt governments. Another concern was that their populations had cultural values favoring living for today rather than investing in the future, under the belief that poverty somehow reflected God's will. For low-income countries to "modernize," they needed to reduce the power and influence of corrupt government officials, jettison their traditional values and institutions, and invest in the future. The United States could facilitate this by providing low-cost loans for electrification, road and airport construction; providing technical assistance in the form of teachers, economic advisers, lawyers, and other consultants; and—importantly—get these countries to encourage U.S. firms to invest in factories and large-scale agricultural production. Opening low-income country economies to U.S. corporate investment was seen as key to economic growth. Rostow used an aeronautical metaphor that policy makers could easily understand to make his case. He argued that "traditional societies" could "take off" into sustained economic growth if they followed his prescriptions, finally achieving the "modern" stage he termed "high mass consumption." This transition would occur when countries invested at least 10 percent of their GNI into productive economic activities—under strict U.S. tutelage, of course.

Dependency Theories

During the 1960s, a number of sociologists and economists from the low-income countries of Latin America and Africa rejected Rostow's argument that their countries'

modernization theory A version of neoliberal development theory that argues that low-income societies develop economically only if they give up their traditional ways and adopt modern economic institutions, technologies, and cultural values that emphasize savings and productive investment.

economic poverty was due to their own cultural or institutional faults (Appelbaum, 2017). Instead, building on the theories of Karl Marx, they argued that contrary to Rostow and other neoliberal economists, capitalism was the problem, not the solution. In their view, global capitalist economic relations had made poor countries dependent on rich countries, locking them in a downward spiral of exploitation and poverty (hence the term **dependency theory**). To better understand how such exploitative relations worked, dependency theory introduced new concepts that emphasized the relational nature of powerful rich countries and relatively powerless poor countries (recall that modernization theory placed the blame for poverty on the poor countries themselves). According to dependency theory, the most advanced industrial countries are best understood as being **core** in the world economy, in that they extract the lion's share of profits from weaker countries; the low-income, largely agricultural countries are best understood as comprising a global economic **periphery**, in that they have a marginal role in the world economy and are thus dependent on the core countries for their trading relationships. The advanced industrial core countries (for example, the United States, Japan, and the countries of Western Europe) extract wealth, in the form of cheap labor and natural resources, from the poorer (and weaker) peripheral countries. In the view of dependency theory, this becomes a vicious downward cycle, in which the core countries in the world economy become richer, while the peripheral countries become increasingly impoverished.

Such exploitative core-periphery relations became a major force with **colonialism**, which dates back centuries but achieved its high point in the nineteenth and early twentieth centuries. Powerful nations colonized other countries to procure raw materials (such as petroleum, copper, and iron) for their factories and to control markets for the manufactured products. Although colonialism typically involved European countries establishing colonies in North and South America, Africa, and Asia, some Asian countries (such as Japan) had colonies as well.

Two British generals are served tea in Bangalore, India, which was part of the British Empire until 1947.

Even though colonialism largely ended after World War II, the exploitation did not: Corporations based in high-income countries continued to reap enormous profits from their branches in low-income countries. According to dependency theories, these global companies, often with the support of the powerful banks and governments of rich countries, established factories in poor countries, using cheap labor and raw materials to maximize production costs without governmental interference. In turn, the low prices for labor and raw materials prevented poor countries from accumulating the profit necessary to industrialize themselves. Local businesses that might have competed with foreign corporations were prevented from doing so. In this view, poor countries were forced to borrow from rich countries, thereby increasing their economic dependency.

Low-income countries are thus seen not as underdeveloped but as *misdeveloped* (Amin, 1974; Emmanuel, 1972; Frank, 1966, 1969a, 1969b, 1979; Prebisch, 1967, 1971). Except for a few local politicians and businesspeople serving the interests of the foreign corporations, people fall into poverty. Peasants must choose between starvation and working at near-starvation wages on foreign-controlled plantations and in foreign-controlled mines and factories. Dependency theorists rejected such exploitation, and some called for revolutionary changes that would push foreign corporations out of these countries altogether (Frank, 1966, 1969a, 1969b).

Whereas neoliberal theorists usually ignored political and military power, dependency theorists regarded the exercise of power as central to enforcing unequal economic relationships. Whenever local leaders questioned such unequal arrangements, their voices were suppressed. Unionization was usually outlawed, and labor organizers were jailed or killed. When people elected a government opposing these policies, it was likely to be overthrown by the country's military, often backed by armed forces of the industrialized countries. Dependency theorists cited many examples, such as the role of the CIA in overthrowing the Marxist governments of Guatemala in 1954 and the socialist government in Chile in 1973, and in undermining support for the leftist government in Nicaragua in the 1980s. In the view of dependency theory, global economic inequality was ultimately backed up by force: Economic elites in poor countries, backed by their counterparts in wealthy ones, used police and military power to keep the local population under control.

The Brazilian sociologist Fernando Henrique Cardoso, who served as Brazil's president from 1995 to 2002, argued that ending dependency did not always require revolutionary changes, as dependency theorists tended to argue. Rather, he claimed, some degree of **dependent development** was possible—that under certain circumstances, dependent countries can still develop economically, although only in ways shaped by their reliance on wealthier countries (Cardoso and Faletto, 1979). In particular, the governments of these countries could help steer a course between dependency and development (Evans, 1979). The rise of the East Asian economies was a case in point: Although Hong Kong, Taiwan, Singapore, and South Korea were the targets of investments from core countries such as the United States, thanks to strong governments and generally favorable world economic conditions, they eventually emerged from peripheral status and achieved significant economic development during the 1980s

dependency theories Marxist theories of economic development that argue that the poverty of low-income countries stems directly from their exploitation by wealthy countries and by the corporations that are based in wealthy countries.

core According to dependency theory, describes the most advanced industrial countries, which take the lion's share of profits in the world economic system.

periphery According to dependency theory, describes countries that have a marginal role in the world economy and are thus dependent on the core countries for their trading relationships.

colonialism The process whereby Western nations established their rule in parts of the world away from their home territories.

dependent development The theory that poor countries can still develop economically, but only in ways shaped by their reliance on the wealthier countries.

and 1990s (Amsden, Kochanowicz, and Taylor, 1994; Appelbaum and Henderson, 1992; Cumings, 1997; Evans, 1995; World Bank, 1997).

World-Systems Theory

World-systems theory builds on the concept of **global commodity chains**, worldwide networks of labor and production processes that extend from raw materials to the final consumer (Appelbaum and Christerson, 1997; Bair, 2009; Gereffi, 1995, 1996; Gereffi, Fernandez-Stark, and Psilos, 2011; Hopkins and Wallerstein, 1996). The globalization of production through commodity chains began to increase in the 1970s and accelerated throughout the twentieth and early twenty-first century (Chapter 14). The commodity chain approach emphasizes the increasingly globalized nature of production, as corporations based in high-income countries now outsource most of their manufacturing to independently owned contract factories in lower-income countries in search of the lowest costs and fewest environmental restrictions. As production goes global, lower-income countries compete with one another to get the factories. The most profitable part of the global commodity chain, typically headquartered in high-income countries, is made up of the brands that design the goods we all consume and the giant retailers that sell them. The least profitable part is found in low-income countries, and includes many of the low-wage factories that actually produce the goods.

Apple, a giant global corporation whose wide variety of consumer electronic products source their components from 200 principal suppliers (Apple, 2019), provides an excellent example of how commodity chains work. Consider the iPhone 11 Pro Max, whose 2020 sales price ranged from $1,000 to $1,450, depending on storage capacity. The iPhone actually costs only $491 to manufacture, once the cost of all its components are added up. The most profitable part of the its global commodity chain—design, creating brand identification, and marketing—is occupied by Apple, which is headquartered in Cupertino, located in California's famed Silicon Valley. Further down the commodity chain, where actual manufacturing occurs, the iPhone's most expensive component, the camera/image (costing $74 to make), was manufactured by the Korean corporation Samsung. The next most expensive item, the display/touchscreen (costing $67), was also mainly made by Samsung, although another Korean company, LG Display, also provided some screens. The numerous suppliers of its other components span the globe, requiring extremely tight coordination in order for Apple to meet its delivery goals. Although most people think of the iPhone as being made in China, what mainly occurs there is its final assembly (costing $21). This represents just 4 percent of its total cost, and only 1–2 percent of its retail price. Moreover, the factories that assemble iPhones in China—along with smartphones, tablets, computers, and other electronic gadgets for virtually all major consumer electronics corporations—are not even Chinese factories: they are owned by Foxconn, a global Taiwanese corporation that employs more than a million workers in China alone (Yang, Wegner, and Cowsky, 2019).

While the emergence of globalized commodity chains as a dominant form of manufacturing production has resulted in job loss in the United States, it has had the opposite effect in many of the countries where the jobs relocated. In East Asia in particular, commodity chains provided a pathway to economic development. China, for example, began its economic growth as the "world's factory," manufacturing everything from clothing and athletic shoes to the iPhone 11 Pro Max. Factory work in China is often dangerous and poorly paid; labor unions are controlled by the government, and workers have little choice but to suffer harsh conditions (Appelbaum and Lichtenstein, 2016). In one case that went viral in 2010, the pressure-cooker atmosphere demanded of the workers, reinforced by the Chinese government, resulted in despondent workers leaping from the upper floors of a giant Foxconn factory in south China; fourteen workers lost their lives (Ngai, Chan, and Selden, 2014). Yet at the same time, for many workers such manufacturing jobs have provided the first rung on the economic ladder, preferable to the impoverished rural lives they had left behind. And over several decades, Chinese factory workers became consumers, helping to drive China's emerging economy. The Chinese government invested heavily in science and technology, and, as we have seen, the Chinese economy took off, raising hundreds of millions out of poverty (Appelbaum et al, 2018).

Immanuel Wallerstein, the founder of world-systems theory, drew on ideas from both dependency theory and global commodity chains (Hopkins and Wallerstein, 1996). In Wallerstein's view, global commodity chains are best understood as containing core and peripheral activities that result in unequal and exploitative relations between countries. In our example, Apple's highly profitable design and marketing activities are core, while final assembly in Foxconn factories is peripheral. Moreover, what constitutes a core or peripheral commodity chain activity can change over time: Manufacturing was a highly profitable core activity in the mid-twentieth century, enabling U.S. workers in unionized factories to achieve middle-class status. But when manufacturing moved to poor countries, it often became a peripheral activity, generating low wages and little profit. Wallerstein added a third category to dependency theory's core and periphery: the **semiperiphery.** Semiperipheral countries are those that supply labor and raw materials to core industrial countries in the world economy, while at the same time profiting by extracting labor and raw materials from peripheral countries. Examples include Mexico in North America; Argentina, Brazil, and possibly Chile in South America; and some emerging economies of East Asia. The semiperiphery constitutes a kind of world middle class, and therefore offers the promise of economic growth to poorer countries in the periphery.

Wallerstein's **world-systems theory** sees the world capitalist economic system not merely as a collection of independent countries engaged in diplomatic and economic relations with one another, but rather as a single economic unit (Wallerstein, 1974a, 1974b, 1979, 1990, 1996, 2004). The ability of countries to move up, from periphery to semiperiphery or from semiperiphery to core, is severely limited, but it does sometimes happen. Many East Asian countries, for example, have moved from the periphery to the semiperiphery—and some regions of those countries, such as those containing their leading cities, increasingly resemble the core. China, as previously noted, in world-systems terms seems soon to join the core.

global commodity chains Worldwide networks of labor and production processes that extend from raw materials to the final consumer.

semiperiphery Semi-industrialized, middle-income countries that extract profits in the form of cheap labor and raw materials from peripheral countries, while at the same time providing labor and raw materials to the core industrial countries.

world-systems theory Pioneered by Immanuel Wallerstein, this theory emphasizes the interconnections among countries based on the expansion of a capitalist world economy. This economy is made up of core, semiperiphery, and periphery countries.

The reasons for such successes are debated, but world-systems theory would attribute them, at least in part, to their strong states. Unlike neoliberal theories, world-systems theory argues that strong governments do not necessarily interfere with economic development, but rather can be key in promoting it. Considerable research now suggests that in some regions, such as East Asia, successful economic development has been state-led. Strong governments contributed in various ways to economic growth in the emerging economies of East Asia during the 1980s and 1990s (Amsden, Kochanowicz, and Taylor, 1994; Appelbaum and Henderson, 1992; Cumings, 1997; Evans, 1995; World Bank, 1997). More recently, the government of China has shown how massive public investment can propel a poor country into upper-middle-income status, raising, as we have seen, hundreds of millions of people out of rural poverty. The Chinese government has spent trillions of dollars on economic development, including national networks of high-speed highways and 200 mph trains, large-scale investments in science and technology, and building entire cities and science parks (Appelbaum et al, 2018).

Although the world system changes very slowly, once-powerful countries in the core eventually lose their economic power over others. According to world-systems theory, some five centuries ago the Italian city-states of Venice and Genoa dominated the world capitalist economy, but eventually, they were superseded by the Dutch, who were then superseded by the British, who were then, in turn, superseded by the United States. Today, American dominance may be giving way to a more "multipolar" world where economic power will be shared among the United States, Europe, and Asia—or perhaps will yield to a rising China (Arrighi, 1994).

The Theory of Global Capitalism

The emergence of giant transnational firms that operate in many countries and are loyal to none has given rise to a fourth theory, one that emphasizes the rising power of stateless corporations. The theory of **global capitalism** argues that a transnational capitalist class is increasingly the major player in the global economy today, rather than the nationally oriented capitalists of major countries. According to this theory, we have entered a truly transnational phase of capitalism, characterized not only by global markets, production, and finance, but also by the emergence of a **transnational capitalist class** whose business concerns are global rather than national. The foremost proponent of this theory, sociologist William Robinson (2004, 2014, 2017, 2019), argues that global dominance is no longer exercised by states, but rather by the transnational capitalist class. According to Robinson's theory of global capitalism, the transnational capitalist class is more powerful than national capitalist classes; its global interests supersede any national loyalties. Its power is exerted in part through transnational organizations that oversee the global economy (for example, the World Trade Organization, the International Monetary Fund, the World Bank) and promote global business interests.

global capitalism The current transnational phase of capitalism, characterized by global markets, production, and finance; a transnational capitalist class whose business concerns are global rather than national; and transnational systems of governance (such as the World Trade Organization) that promote global business interests.

transnational capitalist class A social class whose economic interests are global rather than national, who share a globalizing perspective and similar lifestyles, and who see themselves as cosmopolitan citizens of the world.

What makes the transnational capitalist class transnational, according to Robinson? First, as previously noted, its *economic interests are global* rather than national: the firms it serves have global shareholders, workers, and markets, and provide goods and services that are sourced globally. Second, members of the transnational capitalist class share a *globalizing perspective*: They believe in neoliberalism and free trade and oppose efforts of governments to regulate their activities, arguing instead that they can be trusted to enforce corporate codes of conduct that call for responsible labor practices and environmental policies. Third, they share *similar lifestyles*: they send their children to the same (private) schools, they belong to exclusive clubs where they can play golf together and share business ideas; they have

Zhongguancun—a science park located in Beijing's Haidian District—is a major technological hub. It's home to 9,000 high tech firms and serves as an example of China's investment in economic development.

multiple homes in desirable areas around the world; they travel in private jets to their many homes, offices and workplaces in different countries, and attend global elite gatherings such as the annual World Economic Forum in Davos, Switzerland. Finally, they are *cosmopolitan*: Because of their similar lifestyles that span many countries, they see themselves as citizens of the world, rather than of any particular country.

Sociologist Leslie Sklair (2000) has divided the transnational capitalist class into four different (but overlapping) "class fractions:" a *corporate fraction* that owns and controls the major transnational corporations; a *state fraction* composed of the bureaucrats and politicians who staff transnational organizations; a *technical fraction* consisting of the lawyers, accountants, engineers, and other professionals who work for transnational corporations; and a *consumerist fraction* consisting of merchants, advertising media, and marketing specialists who sell the products. It is important to recognize that the transnational capitalist class operates not only in the economic sphere, but also politically (through its ability to shape national policies to better serve its global interests) and culturally (by fostering a global belief in the value of consumerism).

Evaluating Theories of Global Inequality

Each of the four sets of theories of global inequality has strengths and weaknesses. Together, they enable us to better understand the causes and cures for global inequality.

1. **Neoliberal theories recommend the adoption of modern capitalist institutions to promote economic development.** They further argue that countries can develop economically only if they open their borders to trade, and they cite evidence to support this argument. But neoliberal theories overlook economic ties between poor countries and wealthy ones—ties that can impede economic growth under some conditions and enhance it under others. They blame low-income countries for their poverty rather than acknowledge outside factors, such as the business operations of more powerful nations. Neoliberal theories also ignore the ways government can work with the private sector to spur

economic development. Finally, they fail to explain why some countries take off economically while others remain grounded in poverty and underdevelopment.

2. **Dependency theories emphasize how wealthy nations have exploited poor ones.** However, although these theories account for much of the economic poverty throughout the world, they cannot explain the occasional success stories, such as the rapidly expanding economies of China and East Asia. In fact, some formerly low-income countries have risen economically despite the presence of multinational corporations. Even some former colonies, such as Hong Kong and Singapore, are among the success stories.

3. **World-systems theory analyzes the world economy as a whole, looking at the complex global web of political and economic relationships that influence development and inequality in poor and rich nations alike.** Building on the notion of global commodity chains as well as dependency theory, it is well suited to understanding the global economy at a time when businesses are increasingly free to set up operations anywhere, acquiring an economic importance rivaling that of many countries, and where strong states often play a role in fostering economic growth. One challenge faced by world-systems theory lies in the difficulty of modeling a complex and interdependent world economy. It also has been criticized for emphasizing economic and political forces at the expense of cultural ones, such as the combination of nationalism and religious belief that is currently reshaping the Middle East. Finally, world-systems theory has been said to place too much emphasis on the role of nation-states in a world economy increasingly shaped by transnational corporations that operate independently of national borders (Robinson, 2004; Sklair, 2000).

CONCEPT CHECKS

1 Describe the main assumptions of neoliberal theories of global inequality.

2 Why are dependency theories of global inequality often criticized?

3 Compare and contrast core, peripheral, and semiperipheral nations.

4 How do world-systems theory and the theory of global capitalism differ in their view of the role of individual countries in the global economic system?

4. **The theory of global capitalism emphasizes the importance of an emerging and increasingly powerful transnational capitalist class, which is reshaping the world economy in its interests.** This class lacks national loyalty. Rather, its members see themselves as world citizens, sharing similar lifestyles, beliefs, and experiences. The theory of global capitalism argues that this class also dominates the global institutions that oversee and manage the world economy. The power of national capitalists, and the governments that serve their interests, has been severely weakened, as national capitalists are absorbed into the transnational capitalist class. One criticism of this approach is that it overemphasizes the economic and political power of global capitalism, pointing to the power of national business and non-business actors in such countries as China, which have developed a form of national capitalism in which the state plays a highly effective role. It also, like world-systems theory, downplays the ongoing importance of nationalism and religious belief in world politics.

Table 9.1

APPLYING SOCIOLOGY TO GLOBAL INEQUALITY

THEORY	APPROACH TO UNDERSTANDING GLOBAL INEQUALITY	CONTEMPORARY APPLICATION
Neoliberal Theories	Developing countries can improve their economies and lower inequality by opening their economies and markets to foreign investment, reducing the role of their governments, and adopting "western" institutions and cultural values	"Modernization theory," which called for U.S. investment in Latin America under the 1960s Alliance for Progress; most recently, free-market policies of the International Monetary Fund and the World Bank
Dependency Theories	Inequality and poverty in developing countries results from exploitation by rich countries; economic development can only occur if they control their own economies and—in extreme cases—engage in revolution	Bangladesh's economy is dependent on apparel factories that make clothing for foreign brands such as H&M and Gap; the result is low pay, dangerous working conditions, and lack of funds to invest in Bangladesh's development.
World-Systems Theory	The world economic system is comprised of core countries that extract wealth from poorer countries; a periphery that yields wealth to richer countries; and a semiperiphery that extracts wealth from the periphery and yields wealth to the core. Economic development requires a strong state that is committed to development.	The rapid economic growth of China, which has emerged as a world power in the twenty-first century, is evidence that a strong state dedicated to economic growth can be successful.
The Theory Of Global Capitalism	Global economic domination by core countries has been replaced by the growing power of giant transnational corporations, who increasingly control the global economy and shape the policies of national governments.	Giant corporations such as Walmart now have more economic power than most countries, whose economies (and therefore politicians and businesspeople) are beholden to them.

3 RESEARCH ON GLOBAL INEQUALITY TODAY

Wealth and poverty make life different in a host of ways. The Food and Agriculture Organization (2019b) estimates that 822 million people, roughly one in nine people in the world, suffer from chronic hunger, up from 785 million in 2015—the vast majority of whom live in developing countries. More than half of the world's hungry are found in Asia and the Pacific; approximately one-quarter are in sub-Saharan Africa. In Southern Asia alone, nearly 272 million people are undernourished, representing 15 percent of the population; 23 percent of the population of sub-Saharan Africa is undernourished. Almost all of them are illiterate, and many lack access to even primary school education. By mid-century, when the world population is projected to grow from its present level (roughly 7.7 billion) to nearly 9.7 billion people, there will be 2 billion more mouths to feed. That number increases to 3.2 billion more by the next century—most of them in the poorest countries (UN DESA, 2019). And under worst-case projections—if birth rates don't fall throughout the world as predicted—there may be as many as 13.2 billion people by the end of the century, an additional 5.5 billion people (UN DESA, 2017). More than half of the world's population (55 percent) lived in urban areas in 2018, a figure that is predicted to increase to 68 percent by 2050, when an estimated 2.5 billion additional people will swell the world's cities. The overwhelming majority of this increase will be in Asia (especially China and India) and Africa (UN DESA, 2019). Giant cities in poorer countries bring with them their own problems: Overcrowding, squalid slums, large homeless populations, and the need to supply fuel, food, and water over long distances.

Future population growth will have an enormous impact on global resources and the world ecosystem. We take up these issues in greater detail in Chapter 19. Here we look at the differences among high- and low-income countries in terms of health, hunger, and education.

Health

People in high-income countries are far healthier than their counterparts in low-income countries. Low-income countries generally suffer from inadequate health facilities, and the few hospitals or clinics seldom serve the poorest people. Residents of low-income countries also lack proper sanitation, drink polluted water, and risk contracting infectious diseases. They are more likely to suffer malnourishment, starvation, and famine (World Bank, 2019d). All of these factors contribute to physical weakness and poor health. Poor countries also often become dumping grounds for discarded consumer electronics and other toxic waste from high-income countries, and suffer environmental pollution from the factories that are manufacturing goods for high-income country corporations and consumers (see Chapter 19 for further discussion).

Because of such poor health conditions, people in low-income countries are more likely to die in infancy and less likely to live to old age than people in high-income countries. Children in low-income countries are 26 times more likely to die before they reach the age of five than children in high-income countries. Children often die of illnesses that are readily treated in wealthier countries, such as measles or diarrhea. People in low-income countries have an average life expectancy of 63 years, compared to 81 years in high-income countries. Still, conditions are improving somewhat. Over the 20-year period from 1998–2018, the child mortality rate dropped by nearly half, from 94 (per 1,000 live births) to 48 in low-income countries (World Bank, 2019m). In addition, over the same period average life expectancy at birth increased from 53 to 63 as a result of the wider availability of modern medical technology, improved sanitation, and rising incomes.

One interesting caveat is that in the United States and other countries, illnesses that had been all but eradicated are starting to resurface, due in large part to the fact that many parents are electing not to immunize their children over fears of a link between immunization and autism—a fear most scientific researchers believe is unfounded. Immunization rates in the United States have declined slightly in recent years, and outbreaks of whooping cough and measles in other countries are believed to have resulted from people who refused vaccines (Hviid et al., 2019; DeStefano and Shimabukuro,

2019; NIH, 2019). This is especially of concern in a highly globalized world, where people with communicable illnesses can easily cross borders. Over the past decade, a number of measles outbreaks have spread throughout Western Europe among unvaccinated populations (World Health Organization, 2019b).

One chilling example of the relationship between global poverty and disease is the Ebola epidemic that broke out in West Africa in 2014. Ebola—also called haemorrhagic fever because one of its symptoms is internal and external bleeding—is a deadly disease that is spread through contact with the blood or bodily fluids of infected persons who are showing symptoms. Because transmission requires direct physical contact, treatment requires that patients be isolated, and caregivers wear protective suits that cover their entire bodies. When Ebola victims are not completely quarantined, the disease can spread exponentially: One infected person can infect all who come in close bodily contact (such as family members who are unaware of the seriousness of the disease), and they, in turn, can infect everyone with whom they have physical contact. According to the U.S. Centers for Disease Control and Prevention (2016b), this was the largest outbreak of Ebola in history; two of five people who contracted the disease died. By the end of 2016, two years after Ebola first broke out in Liberia, Sierra Leone, and Guinea, nearly 29,000 cases had been reported in those countries and more than 11,000 people had died. The illness spread rapidly partly because it was new to this region of Africa and therefore went unrecognized. Caregivers, from family members to professional health workers, initially believed it to be malaria or some other disease transmitted by mosquitoes rather than human contact. It is worth noting that in another poor African country, the Democratic Republic of Congo, the disease was quickly recognized because it had broken out several times before; health care workers moved quickly to contain it, with the result that only 50 people died. Ebola also spread rapidly in West Africa because there were no health care facilities capable of dealing with the large and growing number of Ebola patients, facilities that required patients to be completely isolated and treated by trained medical personnel wearing special (and costly) protective suits.

Many victims were in remote rural areas that lacked usable roads or other infrastructure, making it difficult to identify, isolate, and treat them; when they flooded into crowded cities in search of treatment, the disease quickly spread. The borders between Liberia, Sierra Leone, and Guinea, drawn by colonial powers in the nineteenth century, are in many places open. Today, people freely cross them, making containment of the disease difficult. And years of war and corrupt governments in this region meant that a concerted state led response was unlikely (Fox, 2014). As a result, during the first months of the outbreak, as many as three-quarters of infected victims died. When Ebola is diagnosed early and treated adequately, even in impoverished areas of West Africa, some two-thirds survive (National Public Radio, 2014). Of the first 10 Ebola patients treated in the United States, most of whom were health care workers who had contracted the disease while treating patients in West Africa, eight recovered—an 80 percent recovery rate reflects what can be accomplished with modern health care facilities (*New York Times*, 2014).

When the deadly coronavirus broke out in the Chinese city of Wuhan at the end of December 2019, Chinese officials quarantined the city of 11 million people, imposed severe travel restrictions within China, and cooperated with the World Health Organization to stem its spread elsewhere. Yet at the same time, while the Ebola epidemic

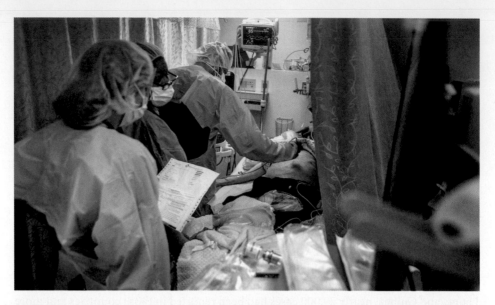

Medical staff at the Brooklyn Hospital Center in New York treat one of many patients in a COVID-19 ward.

was largely isolated within remote African villages, the coronavirus was far more readily spread to other countries: Wuhan is a cosmopolitan Chinese center of industry and commerce, and by the time the disease was identified and restrictive measures were put in place, unknowingly infected persons had traveled elsewhere in China as well as to other countries. As of August 2020, only eight months after the disease was first identified, the World Health Organization reported that the disease had spread to nearly every country in the world, resulting in nearly 126 million confirmed cases and 640,000 deaths—both numbers rapidly increasing. The United States alone, by September 2020, had accounted for over 6 million confirmed cases and 200,000 deaths (WHO, 2020e). The coronavirus also shuttered businesses around the world, as concerns over widespread contagion and massive numbers of deaths led many countries to adopt strict measures limiting or even prohibiting most retail activities. This, in turn, disrupted global supply chains, as factories around the world—themselves often sites of the pandemic—lost their customers. The result of today's highly interconnected world was therefore not only the global spread of a deadly disease, but the deepest global recession since World War II (World Bank, 2020a).

The coronavirus also shuttered businesses around the world, as concerns over widespread contagion and massive numbers of deaths led many countries to adopt strict measures limiting or even prohibiting most retail activities. This, in turn, disrupted global supply chains, as factories around the world—themselves often sites of the pandemic—lost their customers. The result of today's highly interconnected world was therefore not only the global spread of a deadly disease, but the deepest global recession since World War II (World Bank, 2020a).

Hunger and Malnutrition

Hunger and malnutrition are major global sources of poor health. Problems of inadequate food are nothing new. What seems to be new is their pervasiveness—the fact that so many people in the world today are on the brink of starvation (Global Map 9.2). As previously noted, The United Nations Food and Agriculture Organization (FAO) estimates that 822 million people worldwide, or roughly one in nine, are chronically undernourished, virtually all of them in developing countries. FAO defines undernourishment as a diet of 1,800 calories or less a day, the minimal number of calories (on average) required to provide adults with the nutrients required for active, healthy lives. (Of course, what is eaten is also a key determinant of health; one can have a high-calorie diet that lacks the required nutrients for good health.) The good news is that the number of chronically undernourished people has declined by 35 million over the past decade. The bad news is that all of the decline (72 million people) had occurred by 2015; since then the number has increased by 37 million (UN FAO, 2020b).

Most hunger today is the result of a combination of natural and social forces. As of 2018, the UN Food and Agriculture Organization had listed 33 countries in Africa, the Middle East, Central and South Asia, the Pacific, and the Caribbean as in need of external food assistance due to severe weather and conflict-related food shortages. More than half of the world's hungry are found in Asia and the Pacific; about a quarter are in sub-Saharan Africa. In 21 of these countries, conflict is the major problem: In Syria, for example, a long and violent civil war has left 85 percent of the population in poverty; nearly 7 million people are "acutely food insecure" and in need of urgent assistance (UN FAO, 2019b). Moreover, conditions are predicted to worsen considerably as a result of global climate change, which will significantly impact agricultural production, especially in the world's poorest countries. Absent a concerted effort by all countries to limit greenhouse gas production, the worst-case scenario estimates that an additional 165 million people would be plunged into extreme poverty by 2030 (UN FAO, 2016).

The countries affected by malnutrition are too poor to pay for new technologies that would increase food production. Nor can they afford sufficient food imports. As world hunger grows, the largest increases in food production occur where hunger is not a pervasive problem, while the poorest countries—those most in need of food—suffer from the lowest food production gains (Bjerga, 2017). In much of Africa, for example, food production per person has declined. Surplus food produced in high-income countries such as the United States is seldom affordable to the countries that need it most.

The HIV/AIDS epidemic has also contributed to food shortages and hunger, killing many working-age adults. There is evidence that the high rates of HIV infection in many African countries reflect the weakened health of impoverished people, especially children. UNAIDS estimates that since the beginning of the epidemic, some 75 million people around the world have been infected and 32 million have died. Roughly 38 million people are currently living with HIV/AIDS, the majority in sub-Saharan Africa. Two-thirds of new HIV infections occur in sub-Saharan Africa. Still, as devastating as HIV/AIDS can be, there is good news as well. Better understanding of the causes and prevention of the disease, along with the development of antiviral medications that enable people to live with the infection, have reduced both the incidence of new cases as well as deaths among HIV-positive people. Globally, new HIV infections have fallen by nearly 40 percent since 2000, and the number of AIDS-related deaths has dropped by 56 percent since the disease's peak in 2005 (UNAIDS, 2019a).

HUNGER IS A GLOBAL PROBLEM

Hunger is a global problem, although it is disproportionately found in the poorest regions of the world. It is estimated that 822 million people worldwide are chronically undernourished, the vast majority of which were in developing countries. In sub-Saharan Africa, which suffers from the highest rates of undernourishment, almost one in four people are hungry.

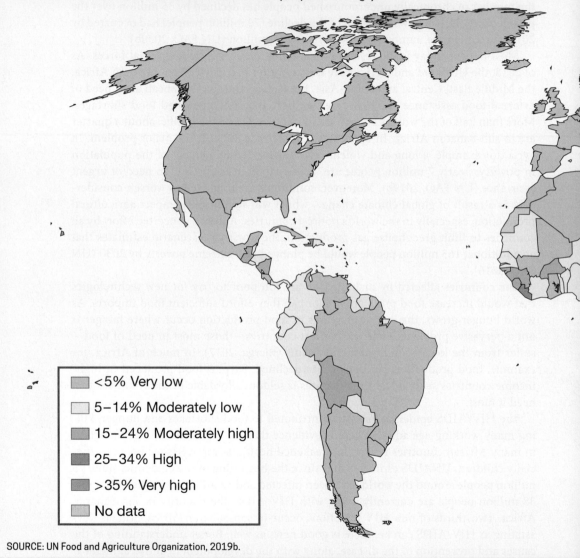

- <5% Very low
- 5–14% Moderately low
- 15–24% Moderately high
- 25–34% High
- >35% Very high
- No data

SOURCE: UN Food and Agriculture Organization, 2019b.

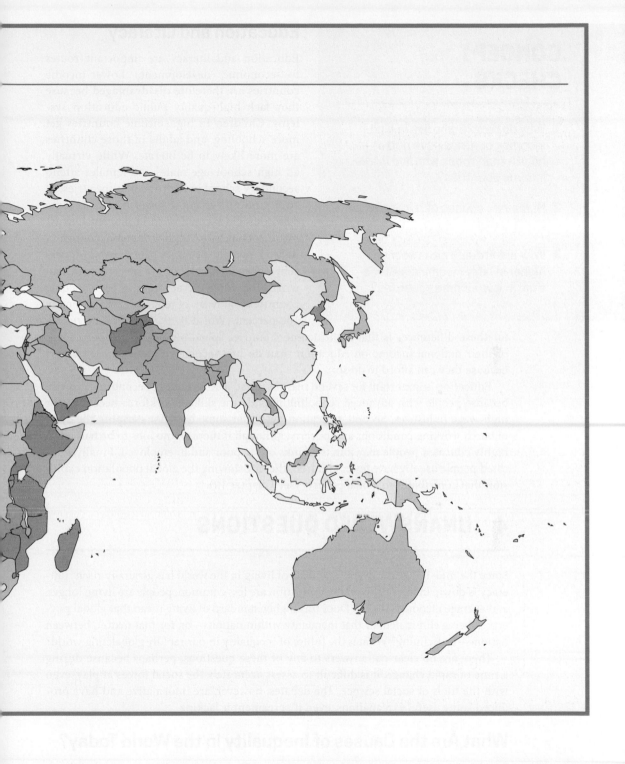

1   Why do people who live in high-income countries have better health than those who live in low-income countries?

2   Name two causes of hunger in the world today.

3   Why are literacy rates so much higher in high-income countries than in low-income countries?

Education and Literacy

Education and literacy are important routes to economic development. Lower-income countries are therefore disadvantaged because they lack high-quality public education systems. Children in high-income countries get more schooling, and adults in those countries are more likely to be literate. While virtually all high school–age males and females attend secondary school in high-income countries, in 2018, only 60 percent in lower-middle-income countries did so, and only 34 percent in low-income countries. In low-income countries, only 71 percent of males over 15 and 56 percent of females over 15 are able to read and write. The adult literacy rate in high-income countries, by way of comparison, is nearly 100 percent (World Bank, 2019d). One reason for these differences is that high-income countries spend a much larger percentage of their national income on education than do low-income countries, in large part because they can afford to do so.

Education is important for several reasons. First, it contributes to economic growth, because people with advanced schooling provide the skilled workforce necessary for high-wage industries. Second, education may offer some hope for escaping the cycle of harsh working conditions and poverty, although if there are no jobs to be had, even highly educated people may join the ranks of the poor and unemployed. Finally, educated people usually have fewer children, thereby slowing the global population explosion that contributes to global poverty (see Chapter 19).

4   UNANSWERED QUESTIONS

Since the mid-1970s, the overall standard of living in the world has generally risen. Illiteracy is down, infant deaths and malnutrition are less common, people are living longer, and average income is higher. Does this higher standard of living mean that global poverty is being eliminated, or that inequality within nations—or, for that matter, between nations—is declining? What is the future of inequality in our rapidly globalizing world?

There are no clear-cut answers to any of these questions, perhaps because during a time of rapid change, it is difficult to assess accurately the social forces at play, even with the tools of social science. The debates, however, are informative and have produced some useful explanations, even if agreement is lacking.

What Are the Causes of Inequality in the World Today?

Sociologists Roberto Patricio Korzeniewicz and Timothy Patrick Moran, in their book *Unveiling Inequality* (2012), provide a new and imaginative approach to answer an old question: What are the underlying causes of persistent inequality in the world today? Drawing on a world-systems approach, they analyze inequality between and within countries. By using statistical techniques for estimating inequality—including the Gini index, which measures the extent to which the distribution of income deviates from a perfectly equal distribution—they examine both forms of inequality over the past two centuries.

With regard to inequality within countries, Korzeniewicz and Moran show that many countries are trapped for decades (some for centuries) in a vicious cycle of persistently high levels of inequality, while others enjoy a virtuous cycle resulting in long-term low levels of inequality. One reason some countries are trapped in a cycle of long-term inequality is the central role played by discrimination on the basis of race, ethnicity, and nationality, which systematically excludes people from economic, social, and political opportunity. Slavery and the legacies of colonialism are key examples.

With regard to inequality between countries, they find that inequality has increased since the nineteenth century, which suggests that the global system itself is trapped in a vicious cycle of self-perpetuating inequality. Even though some countries move up—Japan, the emerging economies of East Asia, China, India—high levels of inequality persist. Although they do acknowledge that global inequality has actually declined somewhat during the past decade or so, they attribute this drop primarily to the economic rise of China.

A main reason for the persistence of inequality between countries, Korzeniewicz and Moran argue, is that the high-income countries in the world economy have been very effective in developing institutions that assure they remain on top. One such institution is restricting the ability of people from low-income countries to immigrate. While capital can move freely across borders, people cannot. The result is that poor people are largely trapped in poor countries, reinforcing the cycle of poverty in those countries. They conclude that a more open global migration system would help reduce inequality between countries.

While *Unveiling Inequality* provides an important explanation for the persistence of long-term inequalities both within and between countries, it arguably overstates the inevitability of long-term inequality in the global system. As global corporations move into lower-income countries in search of low-cost production, they provide jobs for millions of people. As we have seen, these jobs are often under terrible conditions. Yet, in some cases, they have lifted many people into middle-class status. In East Asia and China, this has enabled entire economies to move up in the global stratification system.

The question remains: Whatever the lessons of the past, will the forces reshaping the world economy today increase inequality within and between countries—or do they represent a new dynamic that, in the long run, will result in some form of global economic convergence?

Is Global Poverty Increasing or Decreasing?

Before we turn to the question of whether global poverty is increasing or decreasing, let's first consider a different question: Who are the global poor? The World Bank defines extreme poverty as those living on less than $1.90 a day. Four out of five of the world's poor live in rural areas; nearly two-thirds work in agriculture. Roughly two out of five are 14 or younger and lack formal education. About half (51 percent) of the global poor live in sub-Saharan Africa, while a third live in South Asia (World Bank, 2016b).

The number of people living in extreme poverty is declining. According to the World Bank, 734 million people lived in extreme poverty in 2015, about 10 percent of the world population; in 1993, the number was nearly two and a half times that amount, 1.8 billion people or roughly 34 percent of the world population at that time. This means that since 1993, more than 1.1 billion people have escaped extreme poverty (World Bank, 2019d). But these positive trends mask some disturbing differences between regions and countries (see Figure 9.2). Sub-Saharan Africa, the poorest region in the world, did experience a slight decline in the percentage living in extreme poverty, from 47 percent in 2010 to 42 percent in 2015. Because of overall population growth, however, the number of extremely poor people actually increased, from 394 million to 408 million during the same period (World Bank, 2020b).

In fact, a good part of the global reduction in extreme poverty can be attributed to a single region: East Asia and the Pacific. The dynamic economic growth of that region has reduced its extreme poverty rate from 81 percent in 1981 to 2 percent in 2015. And within that region, because of its giant size, China alone has accounted for the lion's share of the global reduction in number of extremely poor people. Between 1981 and 2015 (the most recent year for which the World Bank has Chinese poverty data), the number of Chinese subsisting on less than $1.90 a day declined from 800 million to 10 million (World Bank, 2019d). China's economic boom has lifted hundreds of millions of people out of extreme poverty in the past 30 or so years—roughly the same number as for the world as a whole, where declines in extreme poverty in East Asia, Europe, and Latin America have been more than offset by increases in the Middle East, Africa, and South Asia.

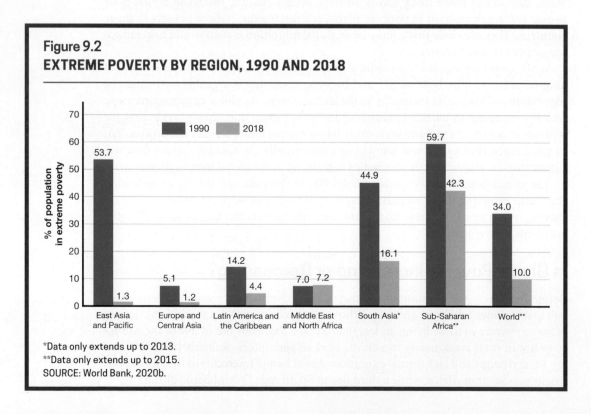

Figure 9.2
EXTREME POVERTY BY REGION, 1990 AND 2018

*Data only extends up to 2013.
**Data only extends up to 2015.
SOURCE: World Bank, 2020b.

Hong Kong (pictured above), along with Taiwan, South Korea, and Singapore, has become one of the most rapidly growing economies on earth.

What About Inequality Within Countries?

As we noted earlier in this chapter, export-oriented industrialization—the relocation of industrial manufacturing from high-wage to lower-wage countries—has enabled some of the latter to industrialize, resulting in their economic growth. This "rise of the rest" (Zakaria, 2009) has lowered the economic gap between high-income and middle-income countries, reducing global inequality, at least among those middle-income countries that have been able to benefit from these changes. This process began with Japan in the 1950s, but it quickly extended to what were called the newly industrializing economies (NIEs) in East Asia. Today, the more widely used term is **emerging economies**, or the rapidly growing economies of the world, particularly in East Asia but also in Latin America. The East Asian emerging economies included Hong Kong in the 1960s and Singapore, South Korea, and Taiwan in the 1970s and 1980s. Other Asian countries followed in the 1980s and the early 1990s, most notably China, but also Indonesia, Malaysia, and Thailand. Today, most of these countries are in the middle-income category, and some—such as Hong Kong, Singapore, South Korea, and Taiwan—have reached the high-income category.

China, the world's most populous country, has one of the most rapidly growing economies on the planet. At an average annual compound growth rate of 12 percent between 1980 and 2010 (World Bank, 2019d), the Chinese economy more than doubled, and is today the world's second-largest economy behind the United States, having surpassed Japan in 2010. Although China's rate of growth has slowed in the last few years (and plummeted in 2020, as a result of the COVID-19 pandemic), it remains the premier example of how export-oriented industrialization can reduce inequality between wealthy and once-poor nations.

emerging economies Developing countries, such as India and Singapore, that over the past two or three decades have begun to develop a strong industrial base.

Within countries, however, the story is somewhat different. Among high-income countries, inequality generally declined during much of the twentieth century, as policies were adopted (such as progressive income taxes, retirement systems, health care, and social welfare programs) that enabled a growing number of citizens to enjoy the fruits of expanding economies. But beginning in the 1970s, when the globalization of manufacturing began to take off, inequality once again began to increase in high-income countries.

One measure, the share of total national income going to the richest 1 percent of the population, suggests that at least in the United States, the level of inequality, which declined until the 1960s, has returned to what it was a century ago (Roser and Ortiz-Ospina, 2017). In 1913, the top 1 percent of U.S. households accounted for 18 percent of total U.S. income. By the 1960s, that share had dropped by more than half, to only about 9 percent; today, it has rebounded to higher levels than a century ago (22 percent in 2015). The pattern in the share going to the top tenth of 1 percent (the superrich) has been even more dramatic: It dropped from nearly 9 percent to 2 percent by the 1970s, but by 2018 it had grown to 11 percent, more than a five-fold increase (Saez, 2016; Inequality.org, 2020).

Although the growth of inequality in the United States is extreme among high-income countries, Britain and Canada have experienced similar patterns (Figure 9.3). In Europe, the pattern is different: While there has been a slight uptick in inequality

Figure 9.3
SHARE OF TOTAL INCOME GOING TO THE TOP 1%, 1900–2015

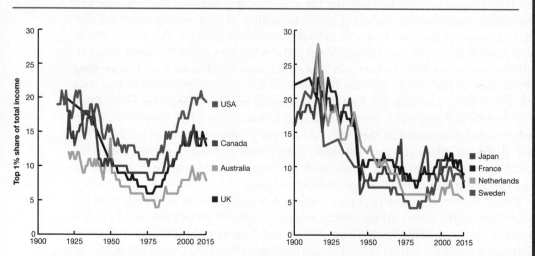

Inequality within some high-income countries has followed a U-shaped pattern over the past century, declining sharply until the 1960s and 1970s, then increasing, partly as a result of globalization. But other factors, such as national economic policies, are also important. Contrast the United States with European countries such as France and the Netherlands, as well as Japan, where national policies have muted the impact of globalization.

SOURCE: Atkinson et al., 2017.

since the 1970s, levels of inequality do not approach what they were a century ago. There are many reasons for this pattern, one of which is that the United States, Britain, and even Canada have pursued economic policies that are far more neoliberal than most European countries. As a result, the impact of globalization has been more severe.

What Does Rapid Globalization Mean for the Future of Global Inequality?

Today, the social and economic forces leading to a single global capitalist economy appear to be irreversible. State-driven socialism, which was the principal challenge to this outcome, came to an end with the collapse of the Soviet Union in 1991.

Many future scenarios are possible. In one, our world might be dominated by large global corporations, with falling wages for many people in high-income countries and rising wages for a few in low-income countries (see again Robinson, 2004, 2014, 2019; Sklair, 2000). Average income worldwide might level out, although at a level much lower than that currently enjoyed in the United States and other industrialized nations. In this scenario, the polarization between the haves and the have-nots within countries would grow, as the whole world would be divided into those who benefit from the global economy and those who do not. Such polarization could fuel conflict among ethnic groups, and even among nations, if those suffering from economic globalization blame others for their plight.

In another, more hopeful scenario, a global economy could mean greater opportunity for everyone as the benefits of modern technology stimulate worldwide economic growth. The republics of the former Soviet Union and the formerly socialist countries of Eastern Europe will eventually become high-income countries. Economic growth will spread to Latin America, Africa, and the rest of the world. Because capitalism requires that workers be mobile, the remaining caste societies will be replaced by class-based societies, which will experience enhanced opportunities for upward mobility. Indeed, the most successful countries in Asia and South America might be a sign of things to come. China and India, the world's two most populous countries, together have middle-class populations totaling as many as several hundred million people, while Brazil, the world's fifth most populous country, is also growing rapidly. Of course, the global environmental impacts of such a scenario could be catastrophic (see Chapter 19).

What is the future of global inequality? It is difficult to be entirely optimistic. Global economic growth has slowed, and while environmental challenges resulting from global warming will affect all countries, the poorest countries will be the hardest hit. The Russian economy, in its move from state-driven socialism to capitalism, has encountered many pitfalls, leaving many Russians poorer than ever. The European Union (EU), once thought to be a pillar of the global economy, is facing numerous challenges. While many countries have experienced economic growth, many have not; the gap between rich and poor remains large—and within many countries, this gap is growing.

The world is experiencing a significant pushback against what many see as the destructive effects of globalization. In June 2016, British voters narrowly approved

In June 2016, British voters approved a referendum, known as Brexit, to leave the EU. Britain formally left the EU on February 1, 2020.

"Brexit," a referendum on leaving the EU. Although it took an additional three years of often contentious parliamentary debate to decide how best to manage this radical change (or, indeed, whether to rethink leaving entirely), Britain and the EU officially parted company on February 1, 2020. The decision to leave the EU was driven in large part by concerns among many working- and middle-class voters that EU membership was hurting them economically, opening Britain's borders to immigrants who were seen as competing for jobs and, for some voters, as culturally "different" and therefore threatening. The EU, whose 28 members make it the world's second-largest economy (the United States is the largest), had been widely regarded as a reasonably successful example of globalization—a trading bloc whose open borders permitted businesses and workers alike to move freely for mutual benefit. Brexit made it clear that such benefits were not universally shared.

Brexit was but one example of how globalization is being challenged throughout the world. In countries as diverse as Turkey, China, Russia, India, Hungary, Poland, the Philippines, and even the United States, populist leaders have emerged whose appeal is strongest among those who believe they have been damaged by globalization. The emergence of far-right nationalist parties throughout Europe, many of which have achieved electoral success in recent years, suggests that Britain may not be the only country to consider such an action. In March 2018, the party that received the largest number of votes in Italy's national elections was the Five Star Party, a youthful party that is strongly environmentalist, populist, critical of what it sees as the destructive aspects of globalization, and skeptical of the EU. Strongly nationalist parties also earned a large percentage of the votes, leading observers to conclude that the elections may result in Italy also rethinking its relationship to the EU (Monti, 2018).

A survey of nearly 50,000 respondents in 44 countries found significant differences between those who lived in advanced economies and those who lived in developing ones in the perceived benefits of trade. When asked whether or not trade creates jobs, only 20 percent of respondents in the United States answered yes, while fully half believed that trade destroyed jobs. Among respondents in all advanced economies, only 44 percent believed trade created jobs, in comparison with 66 percent of those in developing economies (Pew Research Center, 2014f). There is clearly a widely shared belief that globalization has shifted jobs from more economically developed (higher-wage) countries to less economically developed (lower-wage) ones, with growing inequality one result. But are such perceptions correct? Is globalization the principal cause of job loss and growing inequality in the United States?

A growing body of research suggests that the answer to this question is no. One highly cited study found that even though the demand for goods manufactured in the United States has increased in recent years, the number of workers required to produce those goods has plummeted, the result of technological changes that have greatly increased worker productivity. By analyzing employment, trade, and productivity in all U.S. manufacturing jobs over the first decade of the twenty-first century, the study concluded that 88 percent of 6.5 million lost manufacturing jobs resulted from productivity increases rather than globalization. Thanks to technological advances, it simply takes fewer workers to manufacture the goods we all consume (Hicks and Devaraj, 2015).

Robotics—machines powered by information technology and artificial intelligence—are beginning to revolutionize production in the United States and around the globe. While China is often faulted for "stealing" American jobs, most of the U.S. jobs that have disappeared are now being performed digitally, from electronic cash registers that scan your purchases to automobile factories where huge computer-driven robotic arms perform welding and assembly. Three-dimensional printing, visual and voice recognition, and advances in information technology are rapidly claiming jobs that once led to a middle-class lifestyle; growing inequality is one result (Brynjolfsson and McAfee, 2014).

Nor is this process limited to advanced industrial countries like the United States, where workers once enjoyed relatively high wages. China's giant Foxconn factories, where worker suicides created a public outcry, are beginning to replace human labor with robots as well. In 2015, Foxconn CEO Terry Gou announced plans to introduce a million robots (dubbed "Foxbots"), replacing workers who engage in such tasks as spraying, welding, and assembling. Some 60,000 workers had reportedly been replaced by 2016 (Fox, 2015; Wakefield, 2016). Gou himself was heard to comment, on a visit to a zoo in Taiwan, that Foxconn "has a workforce of over one million worldwide, and as human beings are also animals, to manage one million animals gives me a headache" (reported in Kwong, 2012). Robots require less management than human workers, and they are not prone to committing suicide when overworked. Even in China, where wages are still far below wages in the United States, machines now perform many routine operations more cheaply than people could.

The pushback against globalization will not slow the technological revolution that is reshaping work and contributing to inequality. The future of global inequality remains an open question—one whose answer will depend, in large part, on whether globalization can be managed more equitably, and whether new jobs can be found for those displaced by technological innovation.

CONCEPT CHECKS

1 To what extent is the pushback against globalization likely to solve the problem of growing inequality?

2 What is the contribution of technology and globalization in deepening existing global inequalities?

THE BIG PICTURE

Chapter 9
Global Inequality

1 **Basic Concepts**

p. 289

2 **Theories of Global Inequality**

p. 296

LEARNING OBJECTIVES

Understand the systematic differences in wealth and power among countries.

Learn several sociological theories for why some societies are wealthier than others, and understand the strengths and weaknesses of each.

TERMS TO KNOW

globalization • global inequality • GNI • absolute poverty • relative poverty • Capabilities Approach

neoliberalism • modernization theory • dependency theories • core • periphery • colonialism • dependent development • global commodity chains • semiperiphery • world-systems theory • global capitalism • transnational capitalist class

CONCEPT CHECKS

1. Explain how the World Bank measures global inequality, and discuss some of the problems associated with measuring inequality.

2. Compare and contrast high-income, middle-income, and low-income countries.

3. What is the Capabilities Approach to measuring well-being, and how does it provide a more sociological understanding of development than purely economic measures?

1. Describe the main assumptions of neoliberal theories of global inequality.

2. Why are dependency theories of global inequality often criticized?

3. Compare and contrast core, peripheral, and semiperipheral nations.

4. How do world-systems theory and the theory of global capitalism differ in their view of the role of the individual countries in the global economic system?

Exercises: Thinking Sociologically

1. Summarize the four types of theories that explain why there are gaps between nations' economic development and resulting global inequality: neoliberal theories, dependency theories, world-systems theory, and global commodity chains theories. Briefly discuss the distinctive characteristics of each type of theory and how it differs from the others. Which theory do you feel best explains economic developmental gaps?

2. This chapter states that global economic inequality has personal relevance and importance to people in advanced, affluent economies. Briefly review this argument. Explain whether you were persuaded by it, or not.

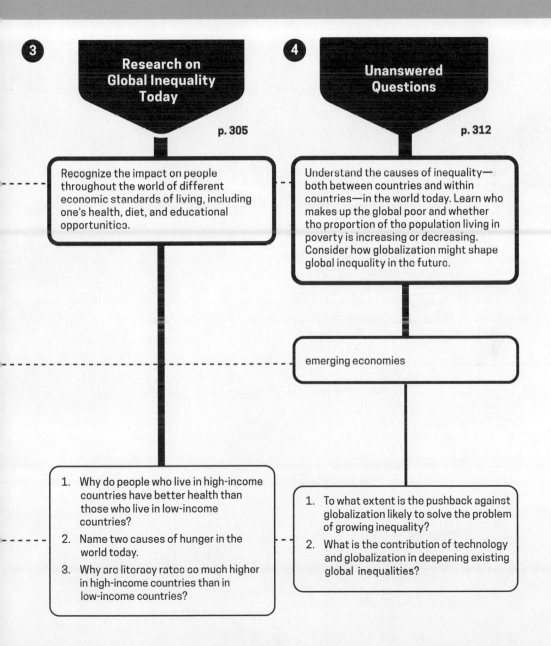

3

Research on Global Inequality Today

p. 305

Recognize the impact on people throughout the world of different economic standards of living, including one's health, diet, and educational opportunities.

1. Why do people who live in high-income countries have better health than those who live in low-income countries?
2. Name two causes of hunger in the world today.
3. Why are literacy rates so much higher in high-income countries than in low-income countries?

4

Unanswered Questions

p. 312

Understand the causes of inequality—both between countries and within countries—in the world today. Learn who makes up the global poor and whether the proportion of the population living in poverty is increasing or decreasing. Consider how globalization might shape global inequality in the future.

emerging economies

1. To what extent is the pushback against globalization likely to solve the problem of growing inequality?
2. What is the contribution of technology and globalization in deepening existing global inequalities?

10

Gender Inequality

In 2017, what proportion of all CEOs of Fortune 500 companies were women?

- **A** 5 percent
- **B** 10 percent
- **C** 25 percent
- **D** 50 percent

TURN THE PAGE FOR THE CORRECT ANSWER.

Most of us know that far fewer women than men hold leadership positions in business and politics today, yet we also know that women have made tremendous strides in education, politics, and the workplace over the past century. Business magazines regularly tout the accomplishments of women such as Safra Catz, who was named chief executive officer (CEO) of Oracle in 2014, and Mary Barra, who became CEO of General Motors the same year (that's her at the start of the chapter). In 2017, four out of eight Ivy League universities were led by women presidents: Christina Paxson (Brown University), Martha Pollack (Cornell University), Drew Gilpin Faust (Harvard University), and Amy Gutmann (University of Pennsylvania). Given these highly visible accomplishments of women in business and technology, we might think that at least one-tenth (answer *b*) or one-quarter (answer *c*) is the correct answer. Yet, according to *Fortune* magazine, which tracks the CEOs of the nation's top revenue-generating companies, women held just 27 of all Fortune 500 CEO positions in 2017. Stated otherwise, women held just 5.4 percent of all Fortune 500 CEO slots in 2017, although they account for roughly half of the total workforce (Brown, 2017). By 2019, these numbers had increased slightly, with 33 women holding CEO positions in Fortune 500 companies, a rate of 6.6 percent (Zillman, 2019).

Why do so few women hold leadership positions in business? This question is important because women are dramatically underrepresented in the upper echelons of business and industry, no matter the metric used. For instance, women account for 45 percent of all employees at Standard & Poor's (S&P) 500 firms, yet they hold just 27 percent of all board seats and just 11 percent of top-earner positions (Catalyst, 2020b; Fitzgerald, 2019). Few would point to outright discrimination as the culprit, yet most experts say that discrimination often takes place in subtle and hard-to-prove ways. Climbing to the top-tier positions at competitive Wall Street and Silicon Valley firms requires round-the-clock work along with "really macho kinds of behavior," including aggressiveness and even ruthlessness, according to Ilene Lang, president of Catalyst, a research organization focused on gender and work. These traits are at odds with traditional gender role socialization; "it is behavior that's admired in men but despised in women," Lang observes. Others point to lack of female mentors in corporate upper echelons and the tendency of some male decision makers to hold stereotypical and incorrect beliefs

LEARNING OBJECTIVES

1 Basic Concepts

Understand the ways that differences between women and men reflect biological factors, sociocultural influences, and the complex interplay between the two.

2 Sociological Theories of Gender Inequalities

Recognize and contrast competing explanations for gender inequality. Learn some feminist theories about gender equality.

THE ANSWER IS A.

about what women are capable of doing. Others say that women are kicked off the corporate "fast track" when they start having children and their colleagues view them as unfit for competitive and time-consuming work.

Women are striking back against both overt and subtle forms of gender discrimination at major Wall Street firms. In the past decade, banks including Goldman Sachs, Wells Fargo, Deutsche Bank, Citigroup, and others have been targets of sex discrimination lawsuits. Kelley Voelker, a former vice president with Deutsche Bank's securities lending desk, filed a sex-discrimination lawsuit against her employer in September 2011. Voelker claimed that despite consistently high performance reviews, Deutsche Bank denied her a promotion and eventually demoted her, one of its few female vice presidents, solely because of her gender and recent childbirth. Voelker said that shortly before she took her maternity leave for her first child, in 2003, her supervisor aired his doubts that she would return to work. In her lawsuit, Voelker accused the bank of "mommy-tracking" female employees, claiming that her supervisors "never took her seriously because she was a woman starting a family, and this was seen as a huge negative within the company." She also pointed to excessively "macho" behavior from some of her male colleagues—including vulgar language in the office and taking clients to strip clubs—as further evidence that her work climate was not friendly to women.

LEARNING OBJECTIVES

3 Research on Gender Today: Documenting and Understanding Gender Inequalities

Learn how gender differences are a part of our social structure and create inequalities between men and women. Learn the forms these inequalities take in social institutions such as the workplace, the family, the educational system, and the political system in the United States and globally.

4 Unanswered Questions: Why Do Gender Inequalities Persist?

Understand how sex segregation contributes to the gender gap in pay, learn about family-leave policies in other countries, explore the effects of gender inequality on men, and evaluate the competing explanations for the persistence of gender-based violence.

Wall Street banking firms are not alone in discriminating against their women executives. In April 2017, media giant Fox News was besieged with multiple gender-discrimination lawsuits, while the U.S. Department of Labor charged Google with "systemic compensation disparities" on the basis of gender (Lam, 2017; Steel and Chokshi, 2017). The Google allegations were just the latest outcry against both subtle and blatant sexism in the male-dominated high-tech industry in California's Silicon Valley. In July 2014, Whitney Wolfe, a cofounder and former executive at the dating app Tinder, filed a lawsuit against the company and its majority owner, the corporation IAC/InterActive Corp. According to the lawsuit, Wolfe said that she was subjected to "a barrage of horrendously sexist, racist, and otherwise inappropriate comments, emails and text messages" sent by Tinder's chief executive and chief marketing officer. Yet her lawsuit also cited more subtle slights; Wolfe said that although she played an essential role in launching the app, her colleagues often omitted her name from media coverage about the firm. Wolfe recalled that her senior male colleagues said that a 24-year-old "girl founder" would undermine the company's value (Wortham, 2014).

It's not only female corporate executives and high-tech wizards who experience obstacles to their career advancement. One of the largest and most famous gender-discrimination lawsuits in recent history was filed against Walmart by Betty Dukes, a cashier. When Dukes started her job at Walmart in 1994, she had more than 20 years' experience in retail and was eager to advance her career. When she approached her store manager about her desire to work her way up the ladder, she was brusquely dismissed. Dukes was undeterred. She performed well as a cashier, earning regular raises in her hourly wage. She repeatedly asked her manager for a promotion, and she requested opportunities to learn more about the store and take on more challenging assignments. She continued to be denied promotions and was not informed of postings for available positions or management training programs at the retailer. All the while, she watched her male associates get promoted, and she later learned that they were paid more than she was for the same job—although she had more years of work experience in retail and greater seniority at the company (U.S. Supreme Court, 2011).

The final straw came when Dukes was demoted from cashier to greeter. She contacted a lawyer and subsequently sued Walmart on the grounds that the retailer was violating the 1964 Civil Rights Act, which makes it illegal for employers to discriminate on the basis of gender, race, or religion. Dukes alleged that Walmart systematically paid women less than men who did the same jobs and promoted men to higher ranks at faster rates than women. When Dukes filed her case, her lawyer told her she wasn't alone, and that many other women had also complained that they weren't getting ahead with the multinational firm. The class-action lawsuit that was filed on behalf of roughly 1 million "similarly situated" plaintiffs eventually made its way to the Supreme Court.

Dukes and her fellow female Walmart employees were disappointed and angry when the Supreme Court threw out their case in June 2011. Observers say the verdict does not mean that discrimination did not happen in Dukes's case. Rather, all nine Supreme Court justices thought there was not "significant proof" that Walmart "operated under a general policy of discrimination" against each and every one of the million or so women who filed the suit. Nor did they find proof that all the women were systematically victimized by a discriminatory "corporate culture" at Walmart (Toobin, 2011).

These far-ranging cases, which affect professional and working-class women alike, raise awareness about the overt and subtle ways that gender shapes all aspects of our lives. Many people who encounter someone such as Betty Dukes might make certain assumptions about her life. They might assume, for example, that a disproportionate number of women become cashiers because it is "natural" for women to have certain kinds of occupations, including retail or secretarial jobs. People who hear the story of Kelley Voelker might assume that women prefer to work part time, or they do so because part-time work is compatible with child-rearing, while full-time work on Wall Street might be "bad for the children." Others might think that women's underrepresentation in high-tech start-ups reflects a lack of scientific aptitude or entrepreneurial risk-taking among women. It is the job of sociologists to analyze these assumptions and to adopt a much wider view of our society. Sociology allows us to understand why women make up only a minuscule proportion of all top CEOs in the United States, why women are more likely than men to work in low-paying clerical and retail jobs, why women are likely to spend more time on child care, and why women as a whole have less economic and political power than men.

In this chapter, we will take a sociological approach to the exploration of gender differences and gender inequality. Gender is a way for society to divide people into two categories: "men" and "women." According to this socially created division, men and women have different identities and social roles. Men and women are expected to think and act in different

(From right) Betty Dukes, Patricia Surgenson, Stephanie Odle, and Christine Kwapnoski charged that Walmart systematically discriminated against its hourly and salaried female employees by denying them promotions and equal pay.

ways across most life domains. Gender also serves as a social status, since in almost all societies, men's roles are valued more than women's roles are (Bem, 1993). At the same time, the cultural expectation that men must be strong, silent breadwinners creates tremendous pressure, with some researchers going so far as to argue that these pressures can be physically and emotionally dangerous to men, especially those who do not live up to this expectation (Springer, 2010).

Sociologists are interested in explaining how society differentiates between women and men, and how these differences serve as the basis for social inequalities (Chafetz, 1990). Yet sociologists recognize that gender alone does not shape our life experiences. Rather, there are pronounced differences in women's and men's lives on the basis of race, social class, age, birth cohort, religion, nation of origin, and even one's marital or parental status (Choo and Ferree, 2010). This recognition that gender intersects with other traits, such as race or social class, to affect our life chances is referred to by sociologists as the study of **intersectionality** (McCall, 2005). The distinctive challenges women and men face in wealthy Western nations also vary markedly from those experienced by individuals in the global south (Mohanty, 2013).

We will first identify core concepts related to sex and gender. Next, we will provide an overview of influential sociological and feminist theories that guide our understanding of gender. We will then review cutting-edge research on the ways that gender shapes our lives in the United States and throughout the world. In this section, we will focus on major social institutions such as the educational system, the workplace, the family, and the government. We will conclude by addressing several unanswered and controversial questions about the importance of gender in contemporary society.

intersectionality A sociological perspective that holds that our multiple group memberships affect our lives in ways that are distinct from single group memberships. For example, the experience of a Black female may be distinct from that of a White female or a Black male.

1 BASIC CONCEPTS

Before we explore the origins of differences between men and women, boys and girls, it is important that we define and differentiate those attributes and processes that make us male or female. One critical distinction is between sex and gender. **Sex** refers to physical differences of the body, whereas **gender** concerns the psychological, social, and cultural differences between males and females, such as personality, goals, and social roles. The distinction between sex and gender is fundamental because many of the most important differences between males and females are not biological. While sex is something we are born with, gender is something that we both learn and do. Sex and gender historically have been viewed as a binary, meaning the two categories of male and female, or masculine and feminine, are seen as distinctive and nonoverlapping—even opposing (Lorber, 1996). However, as we shall soon see, sex and gender can be fuzzy and overlapping categories, and the boundaries demarcating "male" and "female" behaviors, traits, and even bodies are fluid and evolving.

Gender role socialization is the process through which we learn about male- and female-typed roles and practices from socializing agents such as the family, peers, schools, and the media (as discussed in Chapter 4). For example, boys may learn how to engage in rambunctious and aggressive play by watching their favorite male superheroes on TV, while young girls may learn how to nurture their younger siblings by following the model set by their mothers or grandmothers. Through contact with primary and secondary agents of socialization, children internalize the social norms and expectations that correspond with their sex. Gender differences are not biologically determined; they are culturally produced.

How do children's toys contribute to gender role socialization?

We also learn how to "do" gender in our daily interactions with others (West and Zimmerman, 1987). Our clothing choices, how we wear our hair, even the pitch and intonation of our voice are all indications of how we "do gender" each day. This process of doing gender underscores the notion that gender is "socially constructed." Theorists who believe in the **social construction of gender** reject biological bases for gender differences. Gender identities emerge, they argue, in relation to perceived sex differences in societies and cultures, which in turn shape and even perpetuate those differences. For example, a society in which cultural ideas of masculinity are characterized by physical strength and tough attitudes will encourage men to cultivate a specific body image and set of mannerisms (Butler, 1989; Connell, 1987; Scott and Morgan, 1993). Men who fail to comply with what scholars call **"hegemonic masculinity"**—the social norms dictating that men should be strong, self-reliant, and unemotional—may be subtly sanctioned for not enacting gender roles in a way that is consistent with prevailing cultural norms (Connell and Messerschmidt, 2005). We will elaborate on these four concepts—sex, gender, gender role socialization, and social construction of gender—in the following sections. As you will soon see, our identities as "male" or "female" are not as simple as they seem.

Understanding Sex Differences: The Role of Biology

How much are differences in the behavior of women and men the result of sex—that is, biological differences—rather than gender? Some researchers assert that innate behavioral differences between the sexes appear in some form in all cultures; studies of sociobiology (Goldberg, 1999) and evolutionary behavior strongly support this idea (Eagly and Wood, 2011). For example, the fact that in almost all cultures, men rather than women take part in hunting and warfare suggests that men possess biologically based tendencies toward aggression that women lack. Scholars who endorse this perspective might also look at current occupational patterns and attribute them to biology. According to data from the U.S. Bureau of Labor Statistics (BLS), in 2019, 96 percent of dental hygienists, 93 percent of all secretaries, and 90 percent of registered nurses in the United States were women, whereas 98 percent of auto mechanics and 95 percent of welders were male (BLS, 2019). Supporters of the "nature" perspective might point out that women are "wired" to choose jobs that are supportive and nurturing, whereas men opt for jobs that require more physical strength or mechanical ability.

Most social scientists are unconvinced by these arguments, and even view them as potentially dangerous. In her classic book *The Lenses of Gender*, Sandra Lipsitz Bem (1993) notes that this kind of **biological essentialism** rationalizes and legitimizes gender differences as the natural and inevitable consequences of the intrinsic biological natures of women and men. As such, social influences are neglected or minimized. For example, social scientists who denounce biological essentialism would argue that the level of aggressiveness in men varies widely across cultures, and women are expected to be more passive or gentle in some cultures than in others (Elshtain, 1981).

sex The biological and anatomical differences distinguishing females and males.

gender Social expectations about behavior regarded as appropriate for the members of each sex. Gender refers not to the physical attributes distinguishing men and women but to socially formed traits of masculinity and femininity.

gender role socialization The learning of gender roles through social factors such as schooling, the media, and family.

social construction of gender The learning of gender roles through socialization and interaction with others.

hegemonic masculinity Social norms dictating that men should be strong, self-reliant, and unemotional.

biological essentialism The view that differences between men and women are natural and inevitable consequences of the intrinsic biological natures of men and women.

Further, some argue that women are just as aggressive as men; however, women use strategies that are consistent with gender role socialization. One meta-analysis of aggression in "real-world" (rather than laboratory) settings found that men generally show higher levels of aggression than women at all ages, yet among children and teens, women were more likely to use "indirect aggression" (Archer, 2004). For instance, adolescent girls will use "interpersonal aggression," such as malicious gossip or "bad-mouthing," rather than physical fights (Bjorkqvist, Lagerspetz, and Osterman, 2006). Other data suggest that as gender roles change over time, girls may become more physically aggressive. A national study conducted by the Substance Abuse and Mental Health Services Administration (SAMHSA, 2010) found that 19 percent of adolescent females got into a serious fight at school or work in the past year, 14 percent participated in a group-against-group fight, and nearly 6 percent attacked another person with the intent to cause serious harm.

Theories of "natural difference" are often grounded in data on animal behavior, critics say, rather than in anthropological or historical evidence about human behavior, which reveals variation over time and place. Despite critiques of the "nature" perspective, the hypothesis that biological factors determine behavior patterns cannot be wholly dismissed. Studies document persuasively that biological factors—including genetics, hormones, and brain physiology—differ by gender, and that these biological differences are associated with some social behaviors, including language skills, interpersonal interactions, and physical strength. However, nearly all social scientists agree that theories based solely on an innate predisposition neglect the vital role of social interaction in shaping human behavior.

What does the evidence show? One group of studies investigates gender differences in hormonal makeup. Some have claimed that the male sex hormone, testosterone, is associated with a propensity for violence (Archer, 1991). Research has indicated, for instance, that male monkeys castrated at birth become less aggressive than noncastrated monkeys; conversely, female monkeys given testosterone become more aggressive than normal females. However, it has also been found that providing monkeys with opportunities to dominate others actually increases testosterone levels. It is not the case that the hormone causes increased aggression; instead, aggressive behavior may affect production of the hormone (Steklis et al., 1985). In other words, there might be slight biological differences between men and women, but these small differences may be exacerbated and amplified by social contexts that promote behaviors that are consistent with gendered stereotypes and expectations.

Another source of evidence is direct observation of animal behavior. Researchers who connect male aggression with biological influences often emphasize male aggressiveness among the higher animals. Among chimpanzees, they say, males are consistently more aggressive than females. Yet critics note that there are large differences among types of animals. Gibbons, for instance, show few sex differences in aggression. Moreover, many female apes or monkeys are highly aggressive in some situations, such as when their young are threatened.

Other evidence comes from studies of identical twins, who derive from a single egg and have exactly the same genetic makeup. In one anomalous but particularly high-profile case, one identical male twin was seriously injured while being circumcised, and the decision was made by his physician and parents to reconstruct his genitals as female. He was thereafter raised as a girl. At age six, the twins demonstrated typical male and female traits as found in Western culture. The little girl enjoyed playing with other girls, helped with the housework, and wanted to get married when she grew up. The boy preferred the company of other boys, his favorite toys were cars and trucks, and he wanted to become a firefighter or police officer (Colapinto, 2001).

For some time, this case was treated as conclusive evidence of the overriding influence of social learning on gender differences. However, when the girl was a teenager, she was interviewed during a television program and revealed some unease about her gender identity, even wondering if perhaps she was "really" a boy after all. She had by then learned of her unusual background, and this knowledge may have led to an altered perception of herself (Colapinto, 2001).

Technological advances in the last two decades have provided a new source of evidence: brain-imaging research, which has identified several key differences between men's and women's brains (Brizendine, 2007, 2010). For example, Burman and colleagues (2007) found that the brains of school-age girls were more highly "activated," or worked harder, than the brains of school-age boys when presented with spelling and writing tasks. This greater level of activation has been associated with greater accuracy in performing such tasks. The authors do not conclude that girls' language skills are superior to those of boys, yet they do argue that their data show that girls and boys learn language in different ways. A mounting body of research concludes that gender differences in brain functioning may contribute, in part, to a wide range of social outcomes, including communication style, empathy, depression, anxiety, and fear. However, most scholars conducting this research are careful to point out that biological differences are almost always exacerbated or fostered by social contexts and norms (McCarthy, 2015).

Gender Socialization: How Gender Differences Are Learned

As we noted earlier, gender role socialization describes the processes through which we learn what it means to be "male" or "female" in our society. This approach distinguishes between biological sex and social gender—an infant is born with a sex and develops a gender. Children are guided in this process by positive and negative sanctions, that is, socially applied forces that reward or restrain behavior. For example, a young boy could be positively sanctioned for complying with masculine expectations ("What a brave boy you are!") or negatively sanctioned for violating these expectations ("Boys don't play with dolls. What are you, a sissy?"). Historically, if an individual developed gender practices that did not correspond with his or her biological sex, the explanation given was inadequate socialization. According to functionalist perspectives, socializing agents help maintain the smooth continuation of the existing social order by overseeing the smooth gender socialization of new generations. (See Chapter 1 for a review of the core themes of functionalism.)

Functionalist perspectives prevailed during the mid-twentieth century, yet in the late twentieth and early twenty-first centuries, this rigid interpretation of sex roles and socialization has been criticized on a number of fronts. Many writers argue that gender socialization is not an inherently smooth process; different agents, such as families, schools, and peer groups, may be at odds with one another. Moreover, socialization theories ignore individuals' ability to reject or modify the social expectations surrounding sex roles. Humans are not passive objects or unquestioning recipients of gender programming, as some sociologists have suggested. People actively create and modify roles for themselves. Gender is a product of individual choices and preferences, as well as social, contextual, and biological influences.

Consider the following two scenes. Two newborns, a few hours old, lie in the nursery of a hospital maternity ward. One, a male, is wrapped in a blue blanket; the other, a female, is in a pink blanket. Their respective grandparents are seeing them for the first time. The conversation between one pair of grandparents runs along these lines:

Grandma A: There he is—our first grandchild, and a boy.

Grandpa A: Hey, isn't he a hefty little fellow? Look at that fist he's making. He's going to be a regular little fighter, that guy is. (Grandpa A smiles and throws out a boxing jab to his grandson.) Atta boy! [. . .]

Grandma A: Let's go and congratulate the parents. I know they're thrilled about little Fred. They wanted a boy first.

Grandpa A: Yeah, and they were sure it would be a boy, too, what with all that kicking and thumping going on even before he got here.

When they depart to congratulate the parents, the grandparents of the other child arrive. The dialogue between them goes like this:

Grandma B: There she is . . . the only one with a pink bow taped to her head. Isn't she darling.

Grandpa B: Yeah—isn't she little. Look at how tiny her fingers are. Oh, look—she's trying to make a fist.

Grandma B: Isn't she sweet . . . You know, I think she looks a little like me.

Grandpa B: Yeah, she sorta does. She has your chin.

Grandma B: Oh, look, she's starting to cry . . . Poor little girl. (To the baby) There, there, we'll try to help you.

Grandpa B: Let's find the nurse. I don't like to see her cry . . .

Grandma B: Hmm. I wonder when they will have their next one. I know Fred would like a son, but little Fredericka is well and healthy. After all, that's what really matters.

Grandpa B: They're young yet. They have time for more kids. I'm thankful too that she's healthy. (Walum, 1977)

The contrast between the two conversations sounds so exaggerated that it's tempting to think they were made up. In fact, they are transcripts of actual dialogue recorded in a maternity ward. The first question usually asked of a new parent—in Western culture, at least—is "Is it a boy or a girl?" In fact, expectant parents today can buy over-the-counter tests to determine the sex of their fetus, and a recent trend is "gender reveal" parties, where expectant parents share pink or blue cakes with their friends as a celebratory way to announce the sex (O'Connor, 2012). The implication is that sex

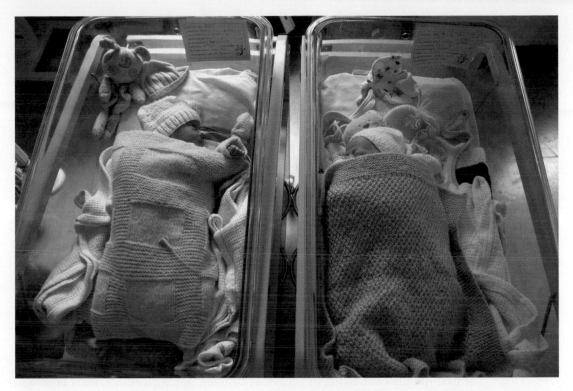
From the moment a child is born, we mark the baby as a boy or a girl, affirming the gender binary.

matters, because parents will raise boys and girls in different ways (Nugent, 2012). Once the infant is born and is marked as male or female, everyone who interacts with the child will treat it in accordance with its gender. They do so on the basis of the society's assumptions, which lead people to treat women and men differently, even as opposites, affirming the gender binary (Zosuls et al., 2009).

Clearly, gender socialization is very powerful, and challenges to it can be upsetting. Take the case of Baby Storm, for example. When Storm was born in 2011, the baby's parents did not want to place a "male" or "female" label on their infant, recognizing that such an assignment would virtually guarantee that their baby would be treated in highly gender-typed ways. For the first few years of Storm's life, the parents kept the baby's sex a secret from everyone except their very closest family members. Their goal was to allow their child to express his or her gender freely and creatively. However, Storm's parents, Kathy Witterick and David Stocker, found themselves at the center of an angry international debate and were accused of being psychologically abusive to their child and using Storm as part of an ill-advised social experiment. Two years later, Storm was reported to be a happily adjusted toddler; when a journalist asked about Storm's gender, Witterick replied, "Sometimes Storm says, 'I'm a girl,' and sometimes Storm says, 'I'm a boy'" (Poisson, 2013). Another three years later, when Storm was six, the child had "picked a pronoun—her gender identity is she," according to her father. Storm's parents thought that their unconventional approach to child-rearing was necessary to free their child from constraining and stifling gender expectations (Ostroff, 2016). As sociological studies repeatedly show, once a gender is "assigned," society expects individuals to act like "females" and "males." These expectations are fulfilled and reproduced in the practices of everyday life (Bourdieu, 1990; Lorber, 1994).

The Social Construction of Gender: How We Learn to "Do Gender"

Recently, a growing number of sociologists have criticized socialization and gender role socialization theories. Rather than seeing sex as biologically determined and gender as culturally learned, they argue that both sex and gender are socially constructed products. Not only is gender a purely social creation that lacks a fixed essence, but the human body itself is subject to social forces that shape and alter it in various ways.

Scholars who focus on gender roles and role learning accept that there is a biological basis for some gender differences. Adherents to socialization perspectives believe that the biological distinction between the sexes is the starting point for differences that become culturally elaborated and amplified in society. In contrast, theorists who believe in the social construction of gender reject all biological bases for gender differences.

Proponents of this view argue that gender is more than learning to act like a girl or boy; rather, it is something that we continually "do" in our daily interactions with others (West and Zimmerman, 1987). We learn how to present ourselves as "male" or "female" through our choice of behaviors, clothing, hairstyle, stance, body language, and even tone of voice. For example, a number of scholars have uncovered the discouraging finding that some young heterosexual women "play dumb" both because they believe it is consistent with gendered expectations for how girls should act and because they believe that doing so may help bolster the feelings of masculinity among the boys they are hoping to attract as romantic partners (Gove, Hughes, and Geerken, 1980). At the same time, young men feel great pressure to be strong, confident, and funny to attract a partner. As sociologist Maria do Mar Pereira discovered in her 2014 qualitative study of 14-year-old boys and girls, "Young people try to adapt their behavior according to these pressures to fit into society. One of the pressures is that young men must be more dominant—cleverer, stronger, taller, funnier—than young women, and that being in a relationship with a woman who is more intelligent will undermine their masculinity" (University of Warwick, 2014).

But precisely how we "do gender" varies widely by race, social class, and social context. We selectively choose to enact different aspects of gender expectations based on what we think will work best in a particular setting. For example, sociologist Nikki Jones (2009) found that young inner-city African American women would adjust their voice, stance, walk, and style of speaking in different situations, thus giving off the impressions of being "aggressive," "good," or "pretty" when they thought a particular type of femininity would "pay off." Jones described the ways that 22-year-old Kiara would "do gender." Kiara was hoping to collect signatures for a petition to stop a new development in a poor neighborhood adjacent to her own. As Jones (2009) describes:

> [Kiara] confidently, assertively, even aggressively approaches men on the street to sign her petition and then draws on normative expectations of manhood and

femininity to encourage them to add their names to the list: Babies and women are in danger, she tells them, letting the implication that real men would sign up to protect babies and women hang in the air. She switches from aggressive to demure just long enough to flirt with a man passing by on the street and then to defiant when she passes the police station on the corner. "They don't give a fuck!" she declares loudly.

Kiara's behavior shows the complexities of gendered expectations in contemporary social life.

Social Construction of Gender in Other Cultures

The subtle ways in which we do gender are so much a part of our lives that we don't notice them until they are missing or radically altered. Cross-cultural research conducted by anthropologists, in particular, helps us recognize how deeply entrenched gendered categories are in the United States and shows us strong evidence that gender is fluid and socially constructed. After all, if gender differences were mostly the result of biology, then we could expect that gender roles would not vary much from culture to culture.

New Guinea

In her classic New Guinea study, *Sex and Temperament in Three Primitive Societies,* Margaret Mead (1963; orig. 1935) observed wide variability among gender role prescriptions—and such marked differences from those in the United States—that any claims to the universality of gender roles had to be rejected. Mead studied three separate tribes in New Guinea: In Arapesh society, both males and females generally exhibited characteristics and behaviors that would typically be associated with the Western female role. Both sexes among the Arapesh were passive, gentle, unaggressive, and emotionally responsive to the needs of others. In contrast, Mead found that in another New Guinea group, the Mundugumor, both the males and females were characteristically aggressive, suspicious, and, from a Western observer's perspective, excessively cruel, especially toward children. In both cultures, however, men and women were expected to behave very similarly. In a third group, the Tchambuli tribe of New Guinea, gender roles of the males and females were almost exactly reversed from the roles traditionally assigned to males and females in Western society. Women "managed the business affairs of life" while "the men . . . painted, gossiped and had temper tantrums" (Mead, 1972).

The !Kung

The !Kung of the Kalahari Desert have specific gender roles, but it is very common for both men and women to engage in child care. Due to the nonconfrontational parenting practices of the !Kung, who oppose violent conflict and physical punishment, children learn that aggressive behavior will not be tolerated by either men or women. Although the !Kung abide by the seeming traditional arrangement where "men hunt and women gather," the vast majority of the tribe's food actually comes from the gathering activities of women (Draper, 1975). Women return from their gathering expeditions armed not only with food for the community but also with valuable information for hunters.

The *Bacha Posh* in Afghanistan

Formerly called Manoush, Mehran Rafaat, left, with her twin sisters, is regarded as a boy by her family. As a *bacha posh*, Mehran can work outside the home and appear in public without an escort.

In contemporary Afghanistan, boys are so highly prized that families with only daughters often experience shame and pity; as a result, some transform one young daughter into a son. The parents cut the girl's hair short, dress her in boy's clothes, change her name to a boy's name, and encourage her to participate in "boys' activities" such as bicycling and playing cricket. These children are called *bacha posh*, which translates into "dressed up as a boy."

Parents of bacha posh believe that boys are afforded so many advantages in Afghan culture that it is helpful, rather than cruel, to transform their girls into boys. A bacha posh can more easily receive an education, work outside the home, even escort her sisters in public, allowing freedoms that are unheard of for girls in a society that strictly segregates men and women. In most cases, a return to womanhood takes place when the child enters puberty, a decision almost always made by her parents (Nordberg, 2010).

Blurring the Boundaries Between the Genders

Adherence to the gender binary, or the belief that only two genders (i.e., male and female) exist, is not universal. The Spaniards who came to both North and South America in the seventeenth century noticed men in the native tribes who had taken on the mannerisms of women, as well as women who occupied male roles.

Several Native American cultures hold a special honor for persons of "integrated genders." For example, the Navajo term *nádleehí* literally means "one who constantly transforms" and refers to a male-bodied person with a feminine nature, a special gift according to Navajo culture. The Navajo believe that to maintain harmony, there must be a balanced interrelationship between the feminine and the masculine within a single individual. Native activists working to renew their cultural heritage adopted the English term *two-spirit* as useful shorthand to describe the entire spectrum of gender and sexual expression that is better and more completely described in their own languages (Nibley, 2011).

In the contemporary United States, growing numbers of young adults are challenging the male-female dichotomy and embracing both genders—or switching between the two. Eschewing labels such as "male" or "female," a small but growing community of college-age adults in particular are instead choosing to identify as "androgyne," "genderqueer," "genderfluid," "bigender," "agender," or "non-cis" (Schulman, 2013). "Non-cis" is shorthand for "non-cisgender." The term *cis* is Latin for "on the same side as," thus **cisgender** refers to a person whose gender identity matches his or her biological sex: for example, a person born male who identifies as a man. "Non-cis," by contrast, refers to a person whose gender identity does not align with the sex the person was assigned at birth. Some choose to identify as a gender different from the one assigned at birth; these people, broadly described as **transgender**, may encompass those who move between genders, who live as a person of the opposite gender, or who use medical assistance to physically transition from one category to the other. Celebrities like Olympic athlete Caitlyn (formerly Bruce) Jenner and Jazz Jennings, the young transgender girl who is the focus of the reality show *I Am Jazz,* have drawn national and international attention to the experiences of transgender persons.

Although sociologists do not know for certain precisely how many individuals define their gender in ways beyond the male/female dichotomy, it soon may be possible to calculate a number in some parts of the world. Several nations have begun to collect official statistics on persons who identify as "third gender" or "third sex," terms that encompass diverse experiences such as identifying as transgender or being born **intersex**. Intersex, like transgender, is a broad and diverse category may encompass those possessing both male and female genitalia or those with ambiguous genitalia. In 2011, Nepal became the first country to include a third gender category in its national census; India soon followed (Bochenek and Knight, 2012). By the end of 2013, a third sex option was available on passports in New Zealand and all "personal documents" in Australia. In Germany, parents now have the option of not specifying a child's sex in birth registries. The intention is to allow babies born with biological characteristics of both sexes to make a choice about who they are once they get older. Under this new law, "individuals can . . . opt to remain outside the gender binary altogether" (Heine, 2013).

Taken together, anthropological and sociological studies of gender reveal that culture, not biology, underlies gender differences. Sociologists have noted that while society teaches "masculine" and "feminine" gender roles, such an approach does not explain where these roles come from or how they can be changed. For this, we need to delve into classic and contemporary theoretical perspectives that shed light on how gender roles and gendered inequalities are built into social institutions (Lorber, 1994).

cisgender Individuals whose gender identity matches his or her biological sex. Statistically, this is the most common gender. It would include persons who are born female who identify as female and persons born male who identify as male.

transgender A person who identifies as or expresses a gender identity that differs from their sex at birth.

intersex An individual possessing both male and female genitalia. Although statistically rare, this subpopulation is of great interest to gender scholars.

CONCEPT CHECKS

1 What is the difference between sex and gender?

2 How do both biology and gender socialization contribute to differences between men and women?

3 What does it mean to say that gender is something we "do"? Give an example of a way you do gender in your daily life.

4 How can studies of other cultures contribute to the argument that gender is socially constructed?

2 SOCIOLOGICAL THEORIES OF GENDER INEQUALITIES

Investigating and accounting for gender inequality has become a central concern of sociologists. Explanations vary widely, from functionalist approaches, which view such differences as key to societal stability, to radical feminist approaches, which view gender inequalities as a product of male oppression. These perspectives have been advanced to explain men's enduring dominance over women—in the realm of economics, politics, the family, and elsewhere. In this section, we review the main theoretical approaches to explaining gender inequality in society.

Functionalist Approaches

Functionalist approaches see society as a system of interlinked parts that, when in balance, operate smoothly to produce social solidarity. Thus, functionalist and functionalist-inspired perspectives on gender argue that gender differences, and, specifically, men's and women's specialization in different tasks, contribute to social stability and integration. Though popular in the 1950s and 1960s, these perspectives have been heavily criticized for neglecting social tensions at the expense of consensus and for perpetuating a conservative view of the social world.

Scholars who support the concept of natural differences argue that women and men perform those tasks for which they are biologically best suited. The anthropologist George Murdock (1949) saw it as practical and convenient that women should concentrate on domestic and family responsibilities while men worked outside the home. On the basis of a cross-cultural study of more than 200 societies, Murdock concluded that the sexual division of labor is present in all cultures and that, although not the result of biological programming, it is the most logical and efficient basis for the organization of society.

Sociologist Talcott Parsons studied the role of the family in industrial societies (Parsons and Bales, 1955). He was particularly interested in the socialization of children and believed that stable, supportive families were the key to successful socialization. He saw the family as operating most efficiently with a clear-cut sexual division of labor in which women carry out *expressive* roles, providing care and security to children and offering them emotional support, and men perform an *instrumental* role—namely, being the breadwinner. Because of the stressful nature of men's role, women's expressive and nurturing tendencies should also be used to comfort and care for men. This complementary division of labor, springing from a biological distinction between the sexes, would ensure the solidarity and stability of the family, according to Parsons.

Another perspective on gender differences that is consistent with core themes of functionalist theories is attachment theory, advanced by psychologist John Bowlby (1953). Bowlby argued that the mother is crucial to the primary socialization of children. If the mother is absent or if a child is separated from the mother at a young age, the child may be inadequately socialized. This can lead to serious social and psychological difficulties later in life, including antisocial and psychopathic tendencies. Bowlby argued that a child's well-being and mental health require a close, personal, and continuous relationship with the mother or a female mother substitute. Some have used Bowlby's maternal deprivation thesis to argue that working mothers are neglectful of their children.

Feminists have sharply criticized claims of a biological basis for the sexual division of labor, arguing that there is nothing natural or inevitable about the allocation of tasks in society. Women are not prevented from pursuing occupations on the basis of biological features; rather, humans are socialized into roles that are culturally expected. Further, a steady stream of evidence suggests that the maternal deprivation thesis is questionable; studies have shown that children's educational performance and personal development are in fact enhanced when both parents work outside the home at least part of the time (e.g., Brooks-Gunn, Han, and Waldfogel, 2010).

Parsons's notion of the "expressive" female has also been attacked for implicitly condoning the subordination of women in the home. There is no basis for the belief that the "expressive" female is necessary for the smooth operation of the family—rather, the role is promoted largely for the convenience of men.

The degree to which a society is open to women performing stereotypically male activities changes across time and by context. For example, during World War II many women took jobs in aircraft factories.

In addition, cross-cultural studies show that societies vary greatly in terms of the degree to which they differentiate and assign tasks as being exclusively men's or women's (Baxter, 1997; Gornick and Meyers, 2003). The extent to which certain tasks can be shared, and even how open groups and societies are to women performing men's activities and roles, differs across cultures, across time, and in different political and economic contexts. Finally, cultures differ in the degree to which men are seen as "naturally" dominant over women. Thus, gender inequalities do not seem to be fixed or static.

Biological determinists see gender inequalities and differences based on gender as inevitable and unchangeable because they are consequences of biological necessities, not of social processes. Feminist scholars do not deny that men and women have distinctive biological characteristics, yet they argue that physical differences alone cannot explain the stark gender differences in men's and women's social and economic roles (e.g., Grosz, 1994). Sociological approaches, in general, hold that society, more than biology, guides gendered roles, interactions, and status differences today. Sociologists also emphasize that gender inequality is tied to issues of race and class. Women—rich and poor, Black and White, immigrant and native born—may share similar biological characteristics, yet their social experiences are vastly different (Rothenberg, 2007).

Feminist Theories

The feminist movement has given rise to a large body of **feminist theory** that attempts to explain gender inequalities and set forth agendas for overcoming those inequalities. While feminist writers are all concerned with women's unequal position in society, their explanations for it vary substantially. There is no one "feminism." Rather, different schools cite a variety of deeply embedded social processes such as sexism, patriarchy, capitalism, and racism. The following sections look at the arguments behind five main feminist perspectives—liberal, radical, socialist, Black, and postmodern feminism.

Liberal Feminism

Liberal feminism sees gender inequalities as rooted largely in social and cultural attitudes. Unlike radical feminists, liberal feminists do not see women's subordination as part of a larger system or structure. Instead, they identify many separate factors that contribute to inequalities—for example, sexism and discrimination in the workplace, in educational institutions, and in the media. They focus on establishing and protecting equal opportunities for women through legislation and other democratic means. Liberal feminists actively supported legal advances such as the Equal Pay Act of 1963 and the Civil Rights Act of 1964 arguing that mandating equality in law is essential to eliminating discrimination against women. Because liberal feminists seek to work through and within the existing political and economic systems to bring about reforms in a gradual way, they are more moderate in their aims and methods than radical feminists, who call for an overthrow of the existing system (Tong, 2009).

While liberal feminists have contributed greatly to the advancement of women over the past century, critics charge that they have been unsuccessful in dealing with the root cause of gender inequality and do not acknowledge the systemic nature of women's oppression in society (Bryson, 1999). Critics say that by focusing too much on the independent deprivations women suffer—sexism, discrimination, the glass ceiling, unequal pay—liberal feminists draw only a partial picture of gender inequality. Radical feminists accuse liberal feminists of encouraging women to accept an unequal society and its competitive character.

Radical Feminism

At the heart of **radical feminism** is the belief that men are responsible for, and benefit from, the exploitation of women. The analysis of **patriarchy**—the systematic domination of females by males—is of central concern, being viewed as a universal phenomenon that has existed across time and cultures. Radical feminists identify the family as one of the primary sources of women's oppression. They argue that men both exploit women by relying on their unpaid domestic labor in the home and, as a group, deny women access to positions of power and influence in society (Tong, 2009).

Radical feminists differ in their interpretations of the basis of patriarchy, but most agree that it involves some form of appropriation of women's bodies and sexuality. Shulamith Firestone (1970) argued that because men control women's roles in reproduction and child-rearing, women become dependent materially on men for protection and livelihood. This "biological inequality" is socially organized in the nuclear family. Firestone argued that women can be emancipated only through the abolition of the family and the power relations that characterize it.

Other radical feminists point to male violence against women as central to male supremacy. In this view, intimate partner violence, rape, and sexual harassment are all part of the systematic oppression of women, rather than isolated cases of pathological or criminal perpetrators. Even interactions in daily life—such as nonverbal communication, patterns of listening and interrupting, and women's sense of comfort in public—contribute to gender inequality. Moreover, popular conceptions of beauty and sexuality are imposed on women by men to produce a certain type of femininity. For example, social and cultural norms emphasizing a slim body, youthful face, and caring, nurturing attitude toward men perpetuate women's subordination. The objectification of women through the media, fashion, and advertising turns women into sexual objects whose main role is to please and entertain men (Kilbourne, 2010).

Radical feminists do not believe that women can be liberated from sexual oppression through legislative reforms or gradual attitudinal change. Because patriarchy is a systemic phenomenon, they argue, gender equality can be attained only by overthrowing the patriarchal order.

feminist theory A sociological perspective that emphasizes the centrality of gender in analyzing the social world and particularly the uniqueness of the experience of women. There are many strands of feminist theory, but they all share the desire to explain gender inequalities in society and to work to overcome them.

liberal feminism The form of feminist theory that posits that gender inequality is produced by unequal access to civil rights and certain social resources, such as education and employment, based on sex. Liberal feminists tend to seek solutions through changes in legislation that ensure that the rights of individuals are protected.

radical feminism The form of feminist theory that posits that gender inequality is the result of male domination in all aspects of social and economic life.

patriarchy The dominance of men over women. All known societies are patriarchal, although there are variations in the degree and nature of the power that men exercise as compared with women. One of the prime objectives of women's movements in modern societies is to combat existing patriarchal institutions.

In asserting that "the personal is political," radical feminists have drawn attention to the many linked dimensions of women's oppression. Their emphasis on male violence and the objectification of women has brought these issues into the heart of mainstream debates about women's subordination.

Many objections can be raised to radical feminist views. A key objection is that the concept of patriarchy is inadequate as a general explanation for women's oppression (Tong, 2009). Radical feminists have tended to claim that patriarchy has existed throughout history and across cultures—that it is a universal phenomenon. Critics argue, however, that the concept of patriarchy as a universal phenomenon does not leave room for historical or cultural variations. It also ignores the important influence of race, class, and ethnicity on the nature of women's subordination; in short, it fails to recognize that not all men have equal power to act as oppressors, and not all women are equally subjugated. In fact, seeing patriarchy as a universal phenomenon risks biological reductionism—attributing all the complexities of gender inequality to a simple distinction between men and women.

Socialist Feminism

Developed in the 1970s, socialist feminism incorporates key themes of Marxist theory, which we introduced in Chapter 1. Like Marxist theory, socialist feminism argues that capitalist society is oppressive toward ethnic minorities, the working class, and the poor. Like radical feminism, it also recognizes the fundamental oppression of women in patriarchal societies. Bringing these two themes together, socialist feminism focuses on the ways that gender and social class intersect. Importantly, adherents of this perspective depart from Marxist theorists because they believe that dismantling the capitalist hierarchical system is not sufficient to eradicate inequalities; gendered systems of stratification also must be eradicated (Martin, 1986).

Socialist feminists depart from other types of feminists in important ways. They challenge liberal feminists' vision that equality for women in all institutions of society, including government, law, and education, is possible through policy reforms. Socialist feminists reject the notion that true equality is possible in a society whose social and economic structures are fundamentally flawed. They depart from radical feminists, however, because socialist feminists believe that women should work with men to fight class

Radical feminism maintains that the objectification of women in advertising contributes to gender inequality by turning women into sexual objects for men's pleasure.

oppression. Socialist feminists do not generally believe that sex and the patriarchy are the sole roots of oppression; rather, gender is just one of several axes of oppression (Holmstrom et al., 2002).

Black Feminism and Transnational Feminism

Do the versions of feminism just described apply equally to the experiences of both White women and women of color? Many Black feminists and feminists from the global south claim they do not. They argue that the main feminist schools of thought address the dilemmas of White, predominantly middle-class women living in industrialized societies and in traditional two-parent families, and that it is not valid to generalize theories about women's subordination from the experience of a specific group. Moreover, the very idea of a unified form of gender oppression that all women experience equally is problematic (Collins, 2008) and neglects the concept of intersectionality, or the recognition that challenges facing women of color are often distinct from those facing White (and especially White middle-class) women (McCall, 2005).

Dissatisfaction with existing forms of feminism has led to the emergence of **Black feminism**, which concentrates on the problems facing Black women. Black feminist writings emphasize aspects of the past that inform current gender inequalities in the Black community: the legacy of slavery, segregation, and the civil rights movement. They point out that early Black suffragettes supported the campaign for women's rights but realized that the question of race could not be ignored because Black women were discriminated against on the basis of both race and gender. In recent years, Black women have not been central to the women's liberation movement in part because their race informed their identities and political allegiances more than their gender did (Collins, 2008).

Gloria Jean Watkins, better known as bell hooks, has written extensively on the distinct challenges facing women of color.

Author, feminist, and social activist bell hooks argues that explanatory frameworks favored by White feminists—for example, the view of the family as a mainstay of patriarchy—may not apply in Black communities, where the family often is headed by a woman and provides a safe, supportive haven against racism. In other words, the oppression of Black women may be found in different locations than that of White women.

Black feminists contend that any theory of gender equality that does not take racism into account cannot adequately explain Black women's oppression. Likewise, social class cannot be neglected. Some Black feminists hold that the strength of Black feminist theory is its focus on the interplay among race, class, and gender concerns. When these three factors interact, they reinforce and intensify one another (Brewer, 1993).

Transnational feminism, by contrast, focuses primarily on intersections among nationhood, race, gender, sexuality, and economic exploitation against the contemporary backdrop of global capitalism. This perspective recognizes that global processes, including colonialism, racism, and imperialism, shape gender relations and hierarchies in powerful ways (Mohanty, 2003). Pioneers of transnational feminism recognized that the key themes of liberal feminism, such as concerns about equal pay for equal work or the division of household labor, were not relevant for many women in the global south. Scholars working in this tradition often have a strong human rights orientation and see research as integral to social change. For instance, by understanding the processes through which female agricultural workers in Brazil are subordinated, transnational feminists can work to increase these women's bargaining power (Thayer, 2010).

Black feminism A strand of feminist theory that highlights the multiple disadvantages of gender, class, and race that shape the experiences of non-White women. Black feminists reject the idea of a single, unified gender oppression that is experienced evenly by all women, and argue that early feminist analysis reflected the specific concerns of White, middle-class women.

transnational feminism A branch of feminist theory that highlights the way that global processes—including colonialism, racism, and imperialism—shape gender relations and hierarchies.

postmodern feminism The feminist perspective that challenges the idea of a unitary basis of identity and experience shared by all women. Postmodern feminists reject the claim that a grand theory can explain the position of women in society, or that there is any single, universal essence or category of "woman." Instead, postmodern feminism encourages the acceptance of many different standpoints as equally valid.

CONCEPT CHECKS

1 Contrast functionalist and feminist approaches to understanding gender inequality.

2 What are the key ideas of liberal feminism? What are criticisms of this perspective?

3 What are the key ideas of radical feminism? What are criticisms of this perspective?

4 How do the key ideas of socialist feminism challenge the main themes of liberal and radical feminism?

5 Do you think that postmodern feminism is incompatible with liberal, radical, and Black feminist perspectives? Why or why not?

Postmodern Feminism

Like Black feminism, **postmodern feminism** challenges the idea that all women share a single basis of identity and experience. (Postmodern approaches in sociology were introduced in Chapter 1, and it may be helpful to review that section.) This strand of feminism draws on the cultural phenomenon of postmodernism in the arts, architecture, philosophy, and economics. Postmodern feminists reject the claim that there is a grand theory that can explain the position of women in society or that there is any universal category of "woman." Consequently, these feminists reject the accounts others give to explain gender inequality—such as patriarchy, race, or class—as "essentialist" (Beasley, 1999).

Instead, postmodern feminism encourages the acceptance of many different standpoints, representing very different experiences (heterosexuals, lesbians, Black women, working-class women, and so on). The "otherness" of different groups and individuals is celebrated in all its diverse forms. Emphasis on the positive side of otherness is a major theme in postmodern feminism and symbolizes plurality, diversity, difference, and openness: There are many truths, roles, and constructions of reality (Tong, 2009).

Postmodern feminism is said to have the most difficult relationship with the strands of feminism just discussed (Tong, 2009). This is largely because of its belief that many feminists are mistaken in assuming that it is possible to provide overarching explanations for women's oppression and to find steps toward its resolution.

Table 10.1
APPLYING SOCIOLOGY TO GENDER

CONCEPT	APPROACH TO UNDERSTANDING GENDER	CONTEMPORARY APPLICATION
Social Constructionist Approaches	Gender identities are not predetermined but emerge in relation to perceived sex differences in societies and cultures, which in turn shape and even perpetuate those differences.	A husband who loses his job may refuse to do housework as a way to "do gender" and reassert his masculine identity. This places a burden on his wife and perpetuates gendered social roles.
Socialization Approaches	Gendered identities and behaviors are learned, via processes of reinforcement and imitation—similar to other forms of learning.	A young girl who likes to play football is admonished to "act more ladylike." She may learn to stop playing in traditionally masculine sports and seek out more traditionally feminine ones.
Functionalist Approaches	Gender differences and, specifically, men's and women's specialization in different tasks, contribute to social stability and integration.	In the mid-twentieth century, many Americans believed it was "best" for the family and an efficient division of labor if the husband was the primary breadwinner and women were the primary caregiver.
Feminist Approaches	Everyday gender differences have their roots in men's and women's unequal positions in society. Social changes must focus on eradicating women's disadvantages. Precisely how these differences can be remedied, and other intersecting sources of differences like race, are emphasized in subtypes of feminist approaches including liberal, radical, socialist, Black, transnational, and postmodernist.	Feminist social policies hold that paying men and women equally for equal work, paying women for care work, and promoting equity in the workplace and education are ways to move toward gender equality in society.

3 RESEARCH ON GENDER TODAY: DOCUMENTING AND UNDERSTANDING GENDER INEQUALITIES

As we have learned so far, gender is one of the main dimensions along which we differentiate humans in society. Yet men and women are not merely viewed as different in most societies; in many domains, men and women experience unequal treatment, with men consistently holding more political, economic, and social power. Male dominance in a society is patriarchy. Although men are favored in almost all societies, the degree of patriarchy varies. In the United States, women have made tremendous progress in education, work, politics, and economics, but several forms of gender inequality persist.

Sociologists define **gender inequality** as the difference in the status, power, and prestige that women and men have in groups, collectives, and societies. In the following sections, we will review contemporary research that documents both the magnitude of, and the explanations for, gendered inequalities across multiple domains, including education, the workplace, the family, and politics. We will focus primarily on the United States but will also demonstrate that the disparities in the United States pale in comparison to those in other nations, where the cultural devaluation of women is widespread.

Gendered Inequalities in Education: Unequal Treatment in the Classroom

Sociologists have found that schools help foster gender differences in outlook and behavior. In the past, school regulations compelling girls to wear dresses or skirts served as an obvious means of gender typing. The consequences went beyond mere appearance. As a result of their clothes, girls lacked the freedom to sit casually, to join in rough-and-tumble games, or to run as fast as they were able. Although strict enforcement of school dress has become rare, differences in informal styles of dress persist, still influencing gender behavior in school.

School reading texts also perpetuate gender images. Although this, too, is changing, storybooks and coloring books used in elementary school often portray boys showing initiative and independence, and girls being more passive and watching their brothers. Stories written especially for girls often have an element of adventure, but usually in a domestic or school setting. Boys' adventure stories are more wide-ranging, with heroes who travel to distant places or who, in other ways, are sturdily independent (Fitzpatrick and McPherson, 2010; Statham, 1986).

In general, people interact differently with men and women, and boys and girls (Lorber, 1994)—even in elementary schools. Studies document that teachers interact differently, and often inequitably, with male and female students in terms of the frequency and content of teacher-student interactions. Such patterns are based on, and perpetuate, traditional assumptions about male and female behavior and traits. One study showed that, regardless of the sex of the teacher, male students interact more with their teachers than female students do. Boys receive more teacher attention and instructional time than girls do. This is partly because boys are more demanding than girls (American Association of University Women [AAUW], 1992). Another study reported that boys are eight times more likely to call out answers in class, thus grabbing their teachers' attention, and that even when boys do not voluntarily participate in class, teachers are more likely to solicit information from them than from girls. However, when girls try to bring attention to themselves by calling out in class without raising their hands, they are reprimanded (Sadker and Sadker, 1994).

In addition, the content of teacher-student interactions differs depending on the sex of the students. For example, the assumption that girls are bad at math may lead teachers to shy away from engaging girls in discussion during math class, ultimately perpetuating girls' insecurity about

gender inequality The inequality between men and women in terms of wealth, income, and status.

How does gender affect teacher-student interactions in the classroom?

their ability to succeed at this subject (Gunderson et al., 2011). After observing elementary school teachers and students over many years, researchers found that teachers helped boys in working out the correct answers, whereas they simply gave girls the correct answers and did not engage them in the problem-solving process. In addition, teachers posed more academic challenges to boys, encouraging them to think through their answers to find the best possible response (Sadker and Sadker, 1994).

Boys were also disadvantaged in important ways, however. Because of their rowdy behavior, they were more often scolded and punished than the female students. Moreover, boys outnumber girls in special education programs by startling percentages. Sociologists have argued that school personnel may be mislabeling boys' behavioral problems as learning disabilities. These patterns can have long-term effects; punishment, especially the most severe forms, such as school suspension, are linked with poorer grades, lower graduation rates, and ultimately poorer prospects for gainful employment (e.g., Shollenberger, 2014).

The ways that gendered stereotypes and expectations hurt boys and girls are even more harmful for African American children, underscoring the importance of intersectionality. A study of what it was like to be a Black female pupil in a White school reported that while the Black girls were, like the boys, initially enthusiastic about school, they altered their attitudes because of the difficulties they encountered. Even when the girls were young, age seven or eight, teachers would disperse them if they were chatting in a group on the playground, while tolerating similar behavior among White children. Once treated as "troublemakers," the Black girls rapidly became so (Bryan et al., 1987). Other work shows that Black girls were reprimanded more than Black boys or White girls for talking loudly, as such behavior was not considered appropriately feminine. As sociologist Edward Morris (2007) found in his study of elementary school classrooms, Black girls' manners were occasionally criticized by teachers, who would refer to outspoken girls as "loudies" rather than "ladies." Racial differences in how girls are treated emerge as young as preschool. A recent Department of Education (2014) study found that Black girls are suspended or expelled at a rate six times higher than that of White girls: Fully 12 percent of Black preschool-age girls (but just 2 percent of their White peers) received an out-of-school suspension.

Similar racial gaps emerge among boys, albeit for different reasons. Black boys are more likely than White boys to be disciplined harshly, consistent with stereotypes that equate Black masculinity with aggression. As with girls, these Black-White disparities start in preschool. The Department of Education study found that 20 percent of Black preschool-age boys (but just 6 percent of White preschool boys) received an out-of-school suspension. Black boys in elementary, middle, and high school also are more likely than any other subgroup of students to be physically restrained and even referred to law enforcement for misbehavior. Experts attribute these strong disciplinary reactions to stereotypes about race and masculinity, and to the fact that young Black boys are viewed as older than they actually are. One fascinating study concluded that "Black boys [are] seen as responsible for their actions at an age when White boys still benefit from the assumption that children are essentially innocent" (Goff et al., 2014).

The Gendering of College Majors

College is a time of exploration, when students take both general-education classes and specialized classes within their chosen major that prepare them for a career after graduation. Men and women differ starkly in the majors they choose, opting for fields that are consistent with gender-typed socialization; women focus on fields associated with caring and nurturing, whereas men tend to pursue fields that emphasize logic and analysis. Yet the majors women tend to choose are precisely those fields that garner the lowest earnings after graduation, whereas men are channeled into majors with high economic returns.

A research study by Glassdoor (2017) that spanned a seven-year time period, from 2010 to 2017, found that women dominated college majors such as social work (85 percent), healthcare administration (84 percent), nursing (80 percent), and education (66 percent). By contrast, men dominated engineering fields such as mechanical engineering (89 percent), civil engineering (83 percent), and computer science and engineering (74 percent).

Feminist scholars note that this stark gender segregation among college majors is one important reason for the persistent gender gap in pay. Glassdoor (2018) ranked college majors based on median base salary and found that social work (median annual salary $41,656), health care administration ($42,000), and education ($43,000) were among the lowest-ranked. Comparatively, engineering fields dominated heavily by men drew a median base salary of between $61,000 (civil engineering) and $68,438 (electrical engineering).

Research on how young people choose their majors consistently shows that subtle forces, including input from parents, friends, and guidance counselors; a lack of same-sex role models; active encouragement (or discouragement) from teachers; and limited exposure to particular fields of study tend to channel women into "female-typed" majors and men into "male-typed" majors (Morgan et al., 2013; Porter and Umbach, 2006).

Gendered Inequalities in the Workplace

Gender plays a powerful role in shaping workplace experiences. Everything from the jobs we hold, to how much we earn, to even our treatment at the hands of coworkers, is powerfully shaped by gender. Although women have seen tremendous progress in both rates of labor force participation and entry to a wide variety of occupations over the past century, as we shall see, stark inequities persist.

Women currently account for roughly half (47 percent) of the total workforce. This proportion is a stark increase from 1950, when women represented just 30 percent of the paid workforce. Nearly 57 percent of women are now employed outside the home, up from just 34 percent of women in 1950 (BLS, 2017h; BLS, 2019e). Although women's entry into the paid labor force is a fairly contemporary phenomenon, dating back only to the early 1970s, some women have always worked for pay. Poor, immigrant, and ethnic minority women have always had relatively high rates of employment. For example, in the United States in the early twentieth century, the female labor force consisted mainly of young, single women and children. More than a third of gainfully employed women were maids or house servants. When women or girls worked in factories or offices, employers often sent their wages to their parents. When young women married, they typically withdrew from the labor force.

Since then, women's participation in the paid labor force has risen more or less continuously, especially since the 1950s (Figure 10.1). However, since peaking at 60 percent in 2009, women's labor force participation has declined slightly. Men's rates of labor force participation declined over this period, from 86 percent in 1950 to 80 percent in 1970 to roughly 69 percent in 2018. These patterns largely reflect the fact that more younger men are in college and more older men are exiting the labor force in their fifties and sixties, due either to the early onset of work-related disabilities, or the fact that Social Security benefits enable them to retire comfortably—a benefit that was not available in the 1950s and 1960s (BLS, 2017d; BLS, 2019e). A more telling number may be the proportion of men in their prime working years, ages 25 to 54, who are currently working. In 2000, fully 92 percent of men in that age group were working, although the figure had dipped slightly to 89 percent by 2018 (Fox, 2017; BLS, 2019e).

Macroeconomic conditions are an important influence on the gender composition of the paid labor force. For instance, during the Great Recession of the late 2000s and early 2010s, men's employment rates dropped more steeply than women's employment rates because the types of jobs men work in were affected more severely (Mulligan, 2010). Men are more likely than women to work in the industries of finance, insurance,

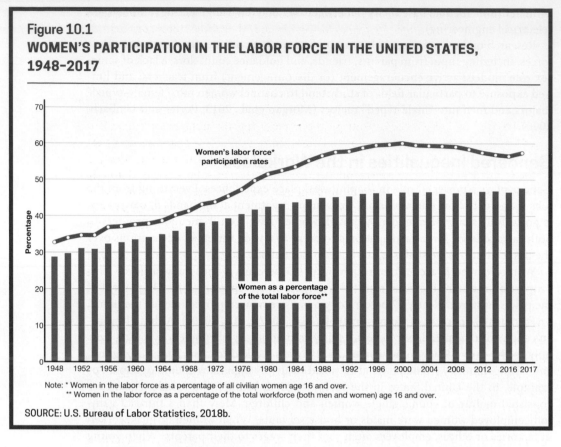

Figure 10.1
**WOMEN'S PARTICIPATION IN THE LABOR FORCE IN THE UNITED STATES,
1948–2017**

Women's labor force*
participation rates

Women as a percentage
of the total labor force**

Note: * Women in the labor force as a percentage of all civilian women age 16 and over.
** Women in the labor force as a percentage of the total workforce (both men and women) age 16 and over.

SOURCE: U.S. Bureau of Labor Statistics, 2018b.

real estate, and construction, which were particularly hard hit during the recession. Some pundits went so far as to dub the economic downturn a "he-cession" or "man-cession" to reflect the fact that 80 percent of the jobs lost were jobs held by men. Some would argue further that women's employment was essential for families' financial well-being during this difficult economic period.

Perhaps an even greater change in labor force participation has occurred among married mothers of young children. In 1978, only 14 percent of married women with preschool-age children worked full time year-round, yet this figure had increased to 59.6 percent by 2018; three-quarters (76.4 percent) of women with children between the ages of 6 and 17 were in the labor force in 2015 (BLS, 2019g). One impetus behind women's increased entry into the labor force was the increasing demand for cleri-cal and service workers in the mid-twentieth century, as the U.S. economy expanded and changed (Oppenheimer, 1970). From 1940 until the late 1960s, labor force activ-ity increased among women who were past their prime child-rearing years, such as "empty nest" women whose children had left the family home. During the 1970s and 1980s, as the marriage age rose, fertility declined, and women's educational attainment increased, the growth in labor force participation spread to younger women. Many women now postpone marriage and child-rearing to complete their education and establish themselves in the labor force. Despite family obligations, today, a majority of women of all educational levels work outside the home during their child-rearing years (Padavic and Reskin, 2002). Unmarried mothers are even more likely than married mothers to work during their child-rearing years. In 2018, 76.7 percent of unmarried mothers with children under 18 years old were in the labor force, compared with 69 percent of married mothers (BLS, 2019g).

Occupational Segregation

Until recently, women were overwhelmingly concentrated in routine, poorly paid occupations. The clerk (office worker) provides a good illustration. In 1850 in the United States, clerks held responsible positions requiring accountancy skills and carrying managerial responsibilities; fewer than 1 percent were women. The twentieth century saw a general mechanization of office work (starting with the introduction of the typewriter in the late nineteenth century), accompanied by a downgrading of the clerk's status—in tandem with an analogous occupation, secretary—into a routine, low-paid occupation. Women filled these occupations as the pay and prestige of such jobs declined (Reskin and Roos, 1990). In 2016, 94 percent of all secretaries and administrative assistants in the United States were women (BLS, 2018a).

Studies of certain occupations reveal how **gender typing** occurs in the workplace. Expanding areas of lower-level work, such as secretarial or retail sales positions, attract a substantial proportion of women. These jobs are poorly paid and hold few career prospects. Men with good educational qualifications aspire to something higher, whereas others choose blue-collar work. Once an occupation has become gender typed, inertia sets in: Job hierarchies are built around the assumption that men will occupy superior positions, while a stream of women will flow through subordinate jobs. Employers are guided in future hiring decisions by gender labels. And the very conditions of most female jobs lead to adaptive responses on the part of women— low job commitment, few career ambitions, high turnover, the seeking of alternative rewards in social relations—which fortify the image of women as suitable for only lower-level jobs (Lowe, 1987). These social conditions reinforce outlooks produced by early gender socialization, as women may grow up believing that they should put their husbands' careers before their own. (Men also are frequently brought up to believe the same thing.)

Women have recently made inroads into occupations once defined as "men's jobs." By the 1990s, women constituted a majority of workers in previously male-dominated professions such as accounting, journalism, psychology, and public service. In fields such as law, medicine, and engineering, the proportion of women rose substantially between 1970 and 2019 (Figure 10.2). Women now account for more than one-third of all lawyers and physicians. Further, for the first time ever, in the 2008–2009 academic year, American women earned more doctoral degrees than men. In 2017, women earned 54 percent of all doctoral degrees. However, men continue to earn a majority of doctorates in traditionally male-dominated fields such as engineering (76 percent) and mathematics and statistics (71 percent) (National Center for Education Statistics, 2018f; Okahana and Zhou, 2018; Glazer, 2019).

Recent evidence also suggests that the influx of women into particular fields may wax and wane over time. For example, women made tremendous inroads in

gender typing Women holding occupations of lower status and pay, such as secretarial and retail positions, and men holding jobs of higher status and pay, such as managerial and professional positions.

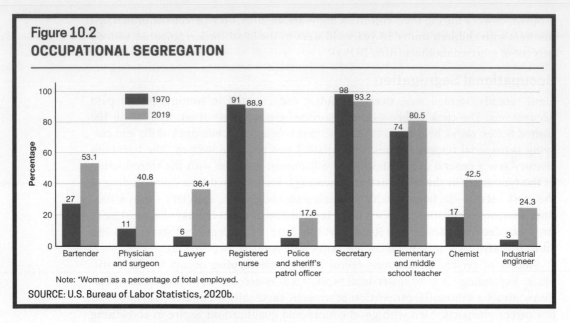

Figure 10.2
OCCUPATIONAL SEGREGATION

Legend:
- 1970
- 2019

Occupation	1970	2019
Bartender	27	53.1
Physician and surgeon	11	40.8
Lawyer	6	36.4
Registered nurse	91	88.9
Police and sheriff's patrol officer	5	17.6
Secretary	98	93.2
Elementary and middle school teacher	74	80.5
Chemist	17	42.5
Industrial engineer	3	24.3

Percentage (y-axis)

Note: *Women as a percentage of total employed.
SOURCE: U.S. Bureau of Labor Statistics, 2020b.

computer programming in the 1970s and 1980s. The proportion of young women majoring in computer science tripled from roughly 13 percent to 36 percent between 1970 and 1985, yet these numbers have inched downward steadily over the past three decades. Today, just slightly more than 15 percent of college women are majoring in computer science, a trend that experts attribute to a fascinating and counterintuitive phenomenon: the proliferation of home computers in the 1980s and forward (Hinn, 2014). As more and more homes would acquire PCs (and computer games), the perception spread that computer games and video games were "for boys." A content analysis of video games would certainly reinforce that assumption, where male characters outnumber women characters by roughly six to one (Williams et al., 2009). Popular films in the 1980s like *War Games* and *Weird Science* underscored the notion that boys, but not girls, could use computers for fun, adventure, and both professional and social advancement. As a result, parents, peers, and school teachers may have subtly conveyed the messages to young women that computer science wasn't for them, thus contributing to the plummeting numbers of female computer science majors in the late twentieth and early twenty-first centuries (Hinn, 2014). However, national educational initiatives like Girls Who Code, events like Girls in Tech Hackathons, and even the recent popularity of the film *Hidden Figures* may be instrumental in encouraging girls, and especially African American girls, to consider pursuing computer programming or other high-tech professions (Hatch, 2017; Leckart, 2015).

The "Glass Ceiling"

Although women are increasingly entering traditionally male jobs, they may not be seeing increases in pay—or increases in occupational mobility—because of the **glass ceiling**, a promotion barrier that prevents women's upward mobility. The glass ceiling is particularly problematic in male-dominated occupations and professions, such as investment banking, as we learned

glass ceiling A promotion barrier that prevents a woman's upward mobility within an organization.

earlier in this chapter. Women's progress is blocked not by virtue of innate inability or lack of basic qualifications but by lack of the sponsorship of powerful senior colleagues to articulate the women's value to the organization or profession (Alvarez et al., 1996). As a result, women progress into middle-management positions but do not, in proportionate numbers, move beyond them. The example of Kelley Voelker shows that, even today, women are subtly blocked access to high-level positions such as managing director (Lattman, 2010). One explanation for women's blocked mobility is that dated gender stereotypes persist. Research shows that college-educated White males in professional jobs identify potential leaders as people who are like them. Women are thus assessed negatively because they deviate from this norm (Cleveland, 1996).

Ironically, men who work in female-dominated professions do not face similar obstacles to promotion. To the contrary, they enjoy a boost up the corporate ladder. In 1992, sociologist Christine Williams coined the term "glass escalator" (1992) to reflect men's rapid ascent up the hierarchy when they work in female-dominated professions. She found that employers singled out male workers in traditionally female jobs—such as nurse, librarian, elementary school teacher, and social worker—and promoted them to top administrative jobs in disproportionately high numbers. These men often "face invisible pressures to move up in their professions. Like being on a moving escalator, they have to work to stay in place," writes Williams (1992). These pressures may take positive forms, such as close mentoring and encouragement from supervisors, or they may be the result of prejudicial attitudes of those outside the profession, such as clients who prefer to work with male rather than female executives.

In 2013, however, Williams updated her theory to more fully reflect the concept of intersectionality. She now argues that the glass escalator is most beneficial and relevant

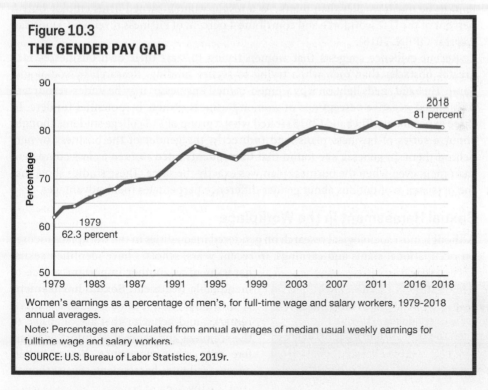

Figure 10.3
THE GENDER PAY GAP

Women's earnings as a percentage of men's, for full-time wage and salary workers, 1979-2018 annual averages.

Note: Percentages are calculated from annual averages of median usual weekly earnings for fulltime wage and salary workers.

SOURCE: U.S. Bureau of Labor Statistics, 2019r.

to White men who hold stable middle-class jobs, noting that "gay men and racial/ethnic minority men, in particular, seemed to be excluded from the benefits of the glass escalator" (Williams, 2013). She further notes that not all workplaces have a glass escalator; rather, the escalator operates only in organizations with stable employment, clear-cut job hierarchies, and career ladders—all aspects of the workplace that have changed dramatically over the past two decades.

The glass ceiling is one of several reasons women continue to earn less than men, although the gender pay gap has narrowed considerably in recent years (Figure 10.3). Between 1960 and 2018, the ratio of women's to men's earnings among full-time, year-round workers increased from 61 to 81 percent. Moreover, this ratio increased among all races and ethnic groups, yet gaps remain. For example, in 2018, White women earned 82 percent as much as their male counterparts, compared with 89 percent for Black women, 86 percent for Hispanic women, and 76 percent for Asian women (BLS, 2019r). Scholars disagree about why the gender gap persists; we will delve more deeply into these competing perspectives later in the chapter.

Gender Inequities in Entrepreneurship

Entrepreneurship, or starting one's own business, has long been considered a pathway through which disadvantaged groups, typically immigrants, could circumvent workplace barriers and succeed on their own. But what about women? Can they break through the glass ceiling by breaking out on their own? The answer is mixed. The number of women with their own business has increased steadily over the past several decades. Women-owned firms now account for 38 percent of all enterprises and are growing faster in number than most other types of businesses. Yet women's businesses tend to be much smaller than men's. As a result, women-owned firms employ only 8 percent of the U.S. workforce and contribute 4 percent of business revenues (American Express OPEN, 2016).

Recent evidence suggests that women trying to start their own businesses face greater obstacles than men when trying to secure funding. Research by sociologist Sarah Thébaud sheds light on why women-owned businesses may be under-resourced: unfounded negative perceptions of women business owners by potential funders. In three experiments, Thébaud (2015) tested what a group of 178 college students thought about a series of business plans, and indirectly, the gender of the business owners behind them. In general, she found that the students rated women as less competent than men, even when the business plan was exactly the same. These studies show that the persistence of notions about gender difference perpetuates men's advantages.

Sexual Harassment in the Workplace

Although most sociological research on gendered inequalities in the workplace focuses on occupational status and earnings, in recent years, scholars have identified sexual harassment as another important source of inequitable treatment. **Sexual harassment** is unwanted or repeated sexual advances, remarks, and behavior that are offensive to the recipient and cause discomfort or interfere with job performance. Power imbalances facilitate harassment; even though

sexual harassment The making of unwanted sexual advances by one individual toward another, with which the first person persists even though it is clear that the other party is resistant.

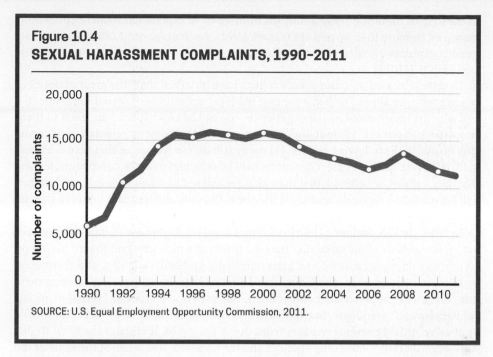

Figure 10.4

SEXUAL HARASSMENT COMPLAINTS, 1990–2011

Number of complaints (y-axis): 0, 5,000, 10,000, 15,000, 20,000

Years (x-axis): 1990 1992 1994 1996 1998 2000 2002 2004 2006 2008 2010

SOURCE: U.S. Equal Employment Opportunity Commission, 2011.

women can and do sexually harass subordinates, it is more common for men to harass women because men usually hold positions of authority (Uggen and Blackstone, 2004).

One of the most high-visibility cases of sexual harassment in recent years is the 2017 debacle at Fox News. In a single year, Fox News chairman Roger Ailes and talk show host Bill O'Reilly were ousted following multiple charges of harassing women reporters and producers for more than a decade; the company's copresident, Bill Shine, also resigned amid the turmoil. The Fox case garnered international attention because of the high profiles of the men involved, yet similar conditions happen at small firms every day. The U.S. courts have identified two types of sexual harassment. One is the quid pro quo, in which a supervisor demands sexual acts from a worker as a job condition or promises work-related benefits in exchange for sexual acts. The other is the "hostile work environment," in which a pattern of sexual language, sexual advances, or even sexually explicit or demeaning posters makes a worker so uncomfortable that it is difficult for the worker to do their job (Padavic and Reskin, 2002).

In recent years, an increasing number of women working in the male-dominated high-tech industries of Silicon Valley have spoken up about the hostile work climates they have faced. For example, Whitney Wolfe, whom we met earlier in this chapter, filed a sexual harassment suit against Tinder. In the suit, Wolfe alleged that company cofounder Justin Mateen had stripped her of a cofounder title because she was a young "girl" who "makes the company look like a joke"—and that he called her a "whore," "gold-digger," and a "disease" (Valenti, 2014).

Recognition of sexual harassment and women's willingness to report it have increased substantially since the testimony of Anita Hill to the Senate Judiciary Committee during the confirmation hearings for Clarence Thomas's 1991 nomination to the U.S. Supreme Court. Hill's recounting of Thomas's harassment raised public awareness of the problem and encouraged more women to report incidents (Figure 10.4).

In the first six months of 1992 alone, the number of workplace harassment complaints increased by more than 50 percent (Gross, 1992). An average of 12,000 sexual harassment complaints are filed each year (U.S. Equal Employment Opportunity Commission [EEOC], 2012).

Despite increased awareness, sociologists have observed that "the great majority of women who are abused by behavior that fits legal definitions of sexual harassment—and who are traumatized by the experience—do not label what has happened to them as sexual harassment" (Paludi and Barickman, 1991). Women's reluctance to report may be due to the following factors: (1) many still do not recognize that sexual harassment is an actionable offense; (2) victims may be reluctant to make complaints, fearing that they will not be believed, that their charges will not be taken seriously, or that they will be subject to reprisals; and (3) it may be difficult to differentiate between harassment and joking on the job (Giuffre and Williams, 1994).

In 1998, the U.S. Supreme Court ruled that the Civil Rights Act outlaws harassment between members of the same sex. The case involved a man who had to quit his job on an offshore oil rig because he had been repeatedly grabbed, ridiculed, and threatened by two male supervisors. The Court ruled that neither "roughhousing" among men, nor "flirtations" between men and women, nor even some types of "verbal or physical harassment" are illegal, but that when sexual harassment is so "severely hostile or abusive" that it prevents workers from doing their jobs, it violates the Civil Rights Act—regardless of whether the offender and the harassed person are of the same or the opposite sex (Savage, 1998).

Global Gendered Inequalities in Economic Well-Being

The United States is not alone in having a history of gender inequality in the workplace. Across the globe, men outpace women in most workplace and economic indicators. Women around the world work in the lowest-wage jobs and are likely to make less than men doing similar work—although there is some evidence that the wage gap is slowly decreasing, at least in industrialized countries (OECD, 2012). As in the United States, most nations have witnessed tremendous strides in women's economic progress in recent decades.

Globally, 50 percent of women participate in the labor force, compared to 76 percent of men. The International Labour Organization (2016) found that the gap between the labor force participation rates of men and women decreased only slightly between 1995 and 2015, mainly because both women's and men's participation rates have fallen. Women have high labor force participation rates in high-income countries, such as most European nations, where over two-thirds of the female adult population participate in the labor market and the male-female gap in labor force participation rates is less than 15 percent on average. This is especially true in nations with extensive social benefits (such as paid maternity leave) and where part-time work is possible. In North Africa and South Asia, by contrast, the gender gap in labor force participation is nearly 50 percent. Gender gaps are due largely to variations in women's labor force participation rates, from a high of 86 percent of women in Rwanda to 16 percent in Jordan. In contrast, men's participation rates are relatively stable across countries in different income strata.

Because women throughout the world also perform a greater share of housework and child care at the end of the paid workday than men, often dubbed the "second shift," women work longer hours than men in most developed countries, including the United States. On average, working women in developed nations work 32 minutes more per day than working men (8 hours and 9 minutes, compared to 7 hours and 36 minutes). This gap is even worse in developing nations: 9 hours and 20 minutes for women versus 8 hours and 7 minutes for men (ILO, 2016).

Women remain in the poorest-paying industrial and service-sector jobs in all countries, and in the less industrialized nations, they are concentrated in the declining agricultural sector. The feminization of the global workforce has brought with it the increased exploitation of young, uneducated, largely rural women around the world. These women labor under conditions that are often unsafe and unhealthy, at low pay and with nonexistent job security. As noted in Chapter 9, one of the most tragic examples of unsafe work environments was the April 2013 collapse of the eight-story Rana Plaza building in Bangladesh's capital city of Dhaka. More than 1,100 people working in garment and apparel factories housed in the building—most of whom were women   died in the collapse, and another 2,500 injured workers were pulled from the wreckage (Fitch, 2014).

Despite such tragedies and often unsafe conditions, even poor-paying factory jobs may enable some women to achieve a measure of economic independence and power. Some scholars and activists argue further that women's economic empowerment has contributed in large part to China's meteoric rise as an economic power. An estimated 80 percent of the factory workers in China's Guangdong province are female, and 6 of the 10 richest self-made women in the world are Chinese (Sorvino, 2017).

At the other end of the occupational spectrum, a recent study by the ILO concluded that women throughout the world still encounter a "glass ceiling" that restricts their movement into the top positions. Even though women have made progress in moving into managerial and professional positions, globally, 6 percent or less of the CEOs of the largest corporations are women, and those who do make it to the top typically earn less than their male counterparts (ILO, 2015; Catalyst, 2020a).

Recognition of these inequities is sparking state-level policies and initiatives to promote greater gender equity. In Japan, for example, women have been particularly likely to face barriers to career advancement, especially in professional and managerial positions. Only 13 percent of such positions are now held by women, due both to discriminatory hiring practices and the fact that fully 70 percent of Japanese women exit the workforce when they have their first child (Cunningham, 2013; Simms, 2013; Smith, 2019). However, policy makers in Japan recognize that this is a tremendous loss of worker potential, especially when low birthrates mean that the nation may soon face a dearth of young workers. In 2013, the government issued a mandate that by 2020, women should hold 30 percent of all upper-management positions in major corporations (Cunningham, 2013). Similar quota-based policies have already been passed in France, Iceland, the Netherlands, and Spain (ILO, 2011).

Female participation in senior management is rising, with women filling 18 percent of senior leadership roles in 2019. Women make up 27 percent of board members of major companies in the European Union (Eurostat, 2018). In many developing countries, greater progress has been made than in developed ones: In the Philippines and Indonesia, for example, more than 40 percent of senior managers are women. Regionally, women's share of senior management jobs is highest in Eastern Europe and the former Soviet Union, where 38 percent of senior roles are held by women, including

47 percent in Russia and 40 percent in Poland. The reason for these countries' high proportion of women in professional jobs is their long-standing policies supporting working mothers (Grant Thornton, 2017).

Gendered Inequalities in Families: Division of Household Labor

Early in this chapter, we saw how the career of Kelley Voelker was derailed after she returned from maternity leave. One key reason women face compromised labor force prospects relative to men is that household duties, ranging from child care to elder care to daily housework, are disproportionately borne by women. Over the past three decades, sociologists have documented that work and family are competing social roles, and women's family lives often impede their career and professional prospects.

Although there have been revolutionary changes in women's status in the United States in recent decades, including the entry of women into male-dominated professions, one area of work has lagged far behind: housework. Because of the increase of married women in the workforce and the resulting change in status, it was presumed that men would contribute more to housework. On the whole, this has not been the case. Although men now do more housework than they did three decades ago, a large gender gap persists. In 1965, women performed 32 hours of housework per week; this figure had dropped to 18 hours by 2011, and down to an average of 15 hours by 2018. By contrast, men's housework increased from 4 to 10 hours per week between 1965 and 2011, and have remained unchanged as of 2018. However, these statistics indicate that women still put in significantly more time than their spouses (Parker and Wang, 2013; BLS, 2019d).

The American Time Use Survey (ATUS) provides further insights into the ways men and women spend their time each day. On the typical day, 21 percent of men reported doing any housework—such as cleaning or doing laundry—compared with 50 percent of women. Forty-six percent of men did food preparation or cleanup activities, compared to 69 percent of women. Men were slightly more likely to engage in lawn and garden care than were women—11 percent compared with 7 percent. On those days when they performed any of these activities, women spent an average of 2.6 hours per day while men spent 2 hours (BLS, 2019c).

Further investigation shows that it is the intersection of gender, marital status, and parental status that most powerfully shapes housework. A recent study demonstrated that whereas women save their husbands an hour of housework a week, husbands create an additional 8 hours of housework for wives every week. Childless women do an average of 10 hours of housework a week before marriage and 17 hours after marriage. Childless men, by contrast, do 8 hours before marriage and 7 hours afterward. Married women with more than three kids are the most overworked, reporting an average of about 28 hours, while married men with more than three kids logged only 10 hours of housework a week (University of Michigan Institute for Social Research, 2008).

One reason that wives—even full-time employed, high-earning women—perform more hours of housework than their husbands is that women and men specialize in different chores. The chores that women typically perform are more time-consuming and happen on a daily rather than a sporadic basis. Wives do most of the daily chores, such as cooking and routine cleaning, while husbands take on more occasional tasks,

Thanks to the feminization of the global workforce, many women have achieved a degree of economic independence—but often at the price of unsafe labor conditions, low pay, and nonexistent job security.

such as mowing the lawn and doing home repairs. The major difference is the amount of control the individual has over when the work gets done. Women's household jobs bind them to a fixed schedule, whereas men's are more discretionary.

Women also spend more time on child-rearing responsibilities, which reflects pervasive assumptions that women are "naturally" the primary caregiver (Shelton, 1992). Sociologists argue that underlying this inequitable distribution of tasks is the implicit understanding that men and women are responsible for different spheres. Men are expected to be providers, women to be caretakers—even if they are breadwinners as well as mothers. By reproducing in everyday life these roles learned during childhood socialization, men and women "do gender" and reinforce it as a means for society to differentiate between the sexes.

Some sociologists have further suggested that women's greater burden at home is best explained as a result of economic forces: Household work is exchanged for economic support. Because women earn less than men, they are more likely to remain economically dependent on their husbands and thus perform the bulk of the housework. Until the earnings gap is narrowed, women will likely remain in their dependent position. Yet, ironically, the gender gap in housework and child care contributes to women's inferior economic position. Part of the reason that family responsibilities create obstacles for women is that their employers and colleagues may hold stereotypical ideas about women workers—especially the belief that mothers are less committed to their careers and thus less appropriate candidates for promotion than non-mothers. Research by Stanford University sociologist Shelley Correll and colleagues (Correll,

Benard, and Paik, 2007) found that mothers are 44 percent less likely to be hired than non-mothers who have the same work experience and qualifications; and mothers are offered significantly lower starting pay than equally qualified non-mothers (an average of $11,000 lower in this study) for the same job.

Women's struggles with the work-family balance illustrate the powerful ways that gender shapes our daily lives. As long as most of the population takes it for granted that parenting cannot be shared on an equal basis by both women and men, the problems facing women employees such as Kelley Voelker will persist. It will remain a fact of life, as one of the managers stated, that women are disadvantaged compared with men in their career opportunities. Yet the same forces that conspire to limit women's employment opportunities also may limit men's engagement with child rearing, carrying long-term implications for father-child relations. The expectation that men should be bread-winners prevents men from taking parental leave, even when the benefit is available to them. Sociologists have observed a "flexibility stigma," where men face a stigma if they take parental leave, cut back on their hours, or take family-friendly work in order to balance child care with paid employment (Coltrane et al., 2013). The persistent gender-typed expectations whereby women privilege child care and men privilege paid work has set the stage for women's economic disadvantage relative to men's and fathers' more tenuous ties with their children relative to mothers' (Lamb and Lewis, 2013).

Yet public policies may be effective in counteracting the obstacles imposed by employers' stereotypical views of mothers in the workplace. A team of sociologists led by Michelle Budig (2012) explored the ways that attitudes toward working mothers and public policies such as parental leave or public child care affected the earnings of women workers in 22 countries. They found that the "motherhood penalty" (or the earnings gap between mothers and childless women) varied across countries, rang-ing from just 4.5 percent to a whopping 33 percent. The gaps were smallest in nations where the cultural attitudes supported maternal employment and the government provided job-protected parental leave and publicly funded child care.

In the coming decades, experts anticipate that we may see greater gender equity in housework and child care. A recent study of young adults ages 18 to 32 in the United States found that the majority of respondents—regardless of gender or edu-cation level—aspired to a romantic relationship in which they would share earnings and household/caregiving responsibilities equally with their partners (Pedulla and Thébaud, 2015). A report by the Pew Research Center reported that 56 percent of adults state that sharing chores is very important to a successful marriage (Geiger, 2016).

Gender Inequality in Politics

Women are playing an increasingly important role in U.S. politics, although they are still far from achieving full equality. Before 1993, there were only 2 women in the U.S. Senate (out of 100 Senate members), and 29 in the U.S. House of Representatives (out of 435). In 2020, there were 131 women in Congress—26 women in the Senate and 105 women in the House—representing just 26 percent of the 535 members. Forty-seven are women of color (Manning and Brudnick, 2020; Rutgers, 2020).

Women are continuing to make strides in other elected offices, although at a slow pace. In 2020, just 9 of the nation's 50 governors were women. The U.S. Supreme Court had its first woman justice appointed in 1981 and its second 12 years later. Three women currently occupy seats on the Supreme Court—Ruth Bader Ginsburg, Elena Kagan, and Sonya Sotomayor—marking an all-time high. It was not until 1984 that a woman was nominated as the vice-presidential candidate of either major party. It would be more than another 30 years before Hillary Clinton would be named the 2016 Democratic nominee for president, becoming the first woman nominee for a major political party.

Women politicians are overwhelmingly affiliated with the Democratic Party. In the U.S. Congress, over three-quarters of women are Democrats, and in state legislatures, over 60 percent are Democrats (Manning and Brudnick, 2020; Rutgers, 2020). However, over the past decade, the Republican Party—and especially the "Tea Party" movement—has prominently featured women leaders, including former Alaska governor Sarah Palin, Minnesota congresswoman Michele Bachmann, and South Carolina governor Nikki Haley; in 2017, Haley took on the position of United States Ambassador to the United Nations under President Donald Trump.

Typically, the more local the political office, the more likely it is to be occupied by a woman. One reason is that local politics is often part-time work, especially in smaller cities and towns. Local politics can thus be good "women's work," offering low pay, part-time employment, flexible hours, and the absence of a clear career path (Carr, 2008). The farther from home the political office, the more likely it is to be regarded as "men's work," providing a living wage, full-time employment, and a lifetime career.

American women are not alone in their recent strides in elected politics. Women are playing an increasingly major role in politics throughout the world. Yet, of the 193 countries that belong to the United Nations, only 19 are presently headed by women. More than 87 countries have chosen a female head

In January 2017, Kamala Harris was sworn in as senator of California, becoming the state's first Black senator and only the second Black woman to ever serve in the Senate. The daughter of immigrants from India and Jamaica, Harris is also the first Indian American to serve in Congress and to be nominated as a vice presidential candidate for a major party.

CONCEPT CHECKS

1 Do you believe that girls or boys are more disadvantaged in the classroom? Why?

2 Describe at least three examples of how gender inequalities emerge in the workplace. How would a sociologist explain these inequities?

3 How do inequalities in the home, especially with regard to housework and child care, reflect larger gender inequities in society?

4 What are some important differences between men's and women's political participation?

of state or government at some point in their history; the United States is not among them (Women's Power Index, 2020). As of 2019, women made up less than a quarter (24 percent) of the combined membership of the national legislatures throughout the world (Atske, Geiger, and Scheller, 2019). Regionally, Nordic countries had the highest percentage of women in national legislatures (42.5 percent), while Arab states and Pacific Island nations trailed with only 19 percent and 16.3 percent, respectively (UN Women, 2019). Despite very low ratings on the UN's Human Development Index, Rwanda has the highest share of women in parliament in the world. The U.S. Congress ranks 78th out of 193 countries for which data exist (UN Women, 2019). Women are most likely to hold seats in national legislatures in countries in which women's rights are a strong cultural value—where women have long had the right to vote and are well represented in the professions (Kenworthy and Malami, 1999).

4   UNANSWERED QUESTIONS: WHY DO GENDER INEQUALITIES PERSIST?

We have demonstrated the many forms that gender inequalities take in society, in the workplace, in the family, in politics, and throughout the globe. Yet many readers of this textbook may wonder why gender inequalities still persist, especially during an era when young women outnumber young men in college classrooms, women make up nearly half the workforce, and a woman was nominated for president by a major political party. How and why do we see so much progress in some domains, but so little in others?

There are no easy answers to questions of why gender inequalities persist in the United States and throughout the world. In this section, we will delve into three particularly vexing questions about inequality, and we will provide competing insights into why the gender pay gap persists, why men continue to abide so closely to harmful components of masculine social roles and behaviors, and why women are disproportionately the target of sexual violence, whether on college campuses in the United States or in the war-torn deserts in parts of Africa.

The Gender Pay Gap: Why Do Women Earn Less Than Men?

The gender gap in pay is widely recognized. As we learned earlier in this chapter, women currently earn around 81 cents for every dollar earned by a man (BLS, 2019r). While the gender gap is now at its narrowest in history, experts believe that much of the recent convergence reflects the fact that men's wages took a hard hit during the 2008 recession. In other words, men are losing ground relative to women, and women are not necessarily seeing an objective improvement in their economic standing. What factors account for women's persistent disadvantage?

Many sociologists view **sex segregation**—the concentration of men and women in different occupations—as a cause of the gender gap in earnings. For instance,

sex segregation The concentration of men and women in different occupations.

according to data from the Bureau of Labor Statistics, occupations with the highest proportion of women include secretary, child-care worker, hairdresser, payroll clerk, receptionist, dental hygienist, speech-language pathologist, elementary and middle school teacher, maids and household cleaners, and nurse. Occupations with the highest proportion of male workers include construction worker, truck driver, pilot, plumber, electrician, carpenter, firefighter, auto mechanic, and machinist (BLS, 2019k; IWPR, 2019).

Sex segregation is problematic because the gender composition of a job is associated with the pay received for that job. This finding has emerged in numerous studies.

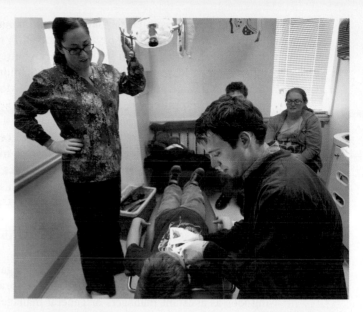

Sociologists point to sex segregation as a key component of the gender pay gap. Women are disproportionately represented in positions that put them in a subordinate position, such as dental hygienist.

An analysis of 1980 Census data (England, 1992) showed that both women and men are disadvantaged by employment in an occupation that is predominantly female. Even "after adjusting for cognitive, social, and physical skill demands, amenities, disamenities, demands for effort, and industrial and organization characteristics, jobs pay less if they contain a higher proportion of females" (England, 1992). More recent analyses show that these patterns have not changed over time, and jobs predominantly held by women have considerably lower wages than jobs largely held by men (Hegewisch and Hartmann, 2014). Ironically, though, as noted in our earlier discussion of the glass escalator, the gender gap persists even among female-dominated occupations. For example, even though women accounted for the vast majority of social workers and elementary/secondary school teachers, women in these jobs earned just 94 percent and 86 percent, respectively, of what their male colleagues earned (IWPR, 2019).

Economists and sociologists differ in explaining how occupational segregation leads to a gender gap in pay. Economists focus on women's occupational choices, while sociologists focus on the constraints women face. Many economists—as well as employers and public policy makers—endorse a **human capital theory** explanation. Developed by Gary Becker (1964), the theory argues that individuals make investments in their own "human capital" (such as formal schooling, on-the-job training, and work experience) to increase their productivity and earnings. Those who invest more in their own skills and knowledge are considered more productive and consequently are paid higher wages.

Human capital theorists reason that women select occupations that are easy to move in and out of and that offer flexible or part-time hours while still providing moderately good incomes. Central to this

human capital theory The argument that individuals make investments in their own "human capital" to increase their productivity and earnings.

argument is the assumption that women's primary allegiance is to home and family; they seek undemanding or flexible jobs that require little personal investment in training or skills acquisition so that they can better tend to household responsibilities. When women leave the labor force to rear children, their job skills deteriorate, and they suffer a wage penalty when they reenter. Moreover, employers may "invest" less in women workers because they believe women will work less continuously than men.

Feminist sociologists criticize human capital theory on several grounds. For example, they dispute the claim that women "choose" certain occupations. In fact, the forces blocking women from freely choosing a career may be indirect or direct. Childhood socialization promoting traditional gender roles may lead young women to choose occupations that are viewed as compatible with feminine traits such as warmth and nurturance—for example, teaching or nursing. More direct obstacles include discouragement from guidance counselors and college advisers, and discrimination on the part of bosses, coworkers, and customers. Also, workplace "gatekeepers" prohibit women from entering certain occupations.

For example, a class-action case was brought against Costco by more than 700 women workers on the grounds that store management practices prevented women from securing jobs as assistant managers or general managers (Greenhouse and Barbaro, 2007). In January 2014, as part of their settlement, Costco agreed to distribute $8 million in compensation to current and former employees who were incorrectly denied promotions. The company also agreed to evaluate its procedures for promoting assistant general managers and general managers to ensure fairer and less gender-biased practices.

Sociologists further argue that human capital theory neglects power differentials between men and women in the workplace and society. Numerous studies reveal that even when men and women are in the same job, men are paid more (Institute for Women's Policy Research, 2019). Because women's work is devalued by society and by employers, women are rewarded less for their work. Moreover, women's relative powerlessness prevents them from redefining the work they do as "skilled." As long as jobs predominantly filled by women, such as caring for children and the elderly, are viewed as "unskilled" or even "intuitive," and thus requiring little training, wages in women's jobs will remain low.

These competing explanations have very different implications for the future. According to human capital theory, the gender gap in pay could disappear if women and men received equal amounts of education and workplace training and if they took equal responsibility for family commitments such as child care. If feminist sociologists are correct in arguing that women's work is devalued, a drastic change in gender ideology must occur if men and women are to become equally rewarded for their participation in the workplace.

Increasing Gender Pay Equity: Lessons from Sweden

Gender and family scholars believe that the United States could follow the lead of other nations that have established effective policies to help achieve greater gender equity in the home and the labor force (Blau and Kahn, 2013). Swedish parents receive 480 days of paid parental leave, which they can take at any time until their child turns eight. And, recognizing that some parents do not want to return to full-time work after their 480 days have run out, the Swedish government gives workers the legal right to hold onto their jobs and cut back their hours by 25 percent until their child turns eight, although their pay reflects only those hours they work. Parents have state-supported flexibility even after they go back to work; if they need to pick up their child from school or take a few days off to care for a sick child, workers still receive 80 percent of their pay.

Similar policies are available in most other European nations and Australia. Current policies in the United States are far less generous, and they are available only to a small fraction of workers. The Family & Medical Leave Act (FMLA), passed during the Clinton administration, allows eligible employees to take up to 12 weeks of *unpaid* leave during any one-year period to care for a new infant

In Sweden, new parents—both mothers and fathers—receive 480 days of paid parental leave. The United States is the only industrialized country without federally mandated paid parental leave.

or unhealthy family member. However, the benefit extends only to those who have worked for their present company for at least 12 months and worked at least 1,250 hours during that period. Moreover, the FMLA applies only to companies that employ 50 or more workers. Given these rigid restrictions, a study by the Center for American Progress found that only 12 percent of all American employees work for companies that are eligible for FMLA (Glynn, 2015).

The payoff of more generous policies, like those in Sweden, is well documented. Family-friendly policies help boost parents' (and especially mothers') rates of employment and their lifetime earnings. Workers who are offered paid parental leave are more likely to return to the same firm, which in turn increases the firm's profitability by improving productivity and reducing turnover and absenteeism (Livingston, 2016).

How Does Gender Inequality Affect Men?

Discussions of gender inequality typically focus on women, given stark and persistent gender gaps in earnings and women's much higher rates of sexual victimization relative to men, as we will discuss next. Yet traditional gender role beliefs and practices exert a profound toll on men as well, undermining the quality of their personal relationships, their freedom to choose professions that mesh with their own interests, their physical and mental health, and, ultimately, their life spans. Pressures for men to abide by the expectations of hegemonic masculinity—or the cultural beliefs that men should be strong, forceful, and independent—also are linked with men's much higher rates of aggressive behavior, where men both perpetuate and are the victims of physical violence.

For instance, as we saw in Chapter 7, men make up the vast majority of persons arrested for violent crimes. Data from the Federal Bureau of Investigation (FBI) show that men account for 98 percent of all arrests for forcible rape, 90 percent of those

On average, women live about five years longer than men. This gender gap in life expectancy is due in part to the fact that traditional ideas about masculinity keep men from engaging in preventative health care such as getting a flu shot.

arrested for robbery, and 80 to 85 percent of those arrested for vandalism, arson, and motor vehicle theft. Given that aggression begets retaliative aggression, men also are more likely than women to die of a range of violent causes. For instance, men make up more than 90 percent of all drug- and gang-related homicides (FBI, 2016b). Men, especially young men, also are more likely than women to die from risky and reckless behaviors, including motor vehicle deaths (Centers for Disease Control and Prevention [CDC], 2017c).

Men also are more likely than women to die of suicide, at every point in the life course; as Chapter 18 will show, women are more likely than men to become depressed, but they are also more likely to turn to others for support and, as a result, are less likely to turn to a violent act like killing themselves. Men also tend to die younger than women; this partly reflects the fact that men, especially those who cling tightly to traditional notions about masculinity, are less likely to go to the doctor for regular checkups, or seek medical attention—acts which might be considered signs of vulnerability or weakness (Springer and Mouzon, 2011).

Adherence to traditional gender-typed behaviors and attitudes affects men's daily lives in far less dramatic ways. Men, especially men raised in the mid-twentieth century, often found that their career choices were constrained by the need to be a family's main breadwinner. One study of men and women who graduated Wisconsin high schools in 1957 found that by the time the men reached their thirties, they had abandoned any hopes of pursuing careers that they found personally rewarding, instead focusing on jobs that paid the bills (Carr, 2005). For instance, one man recounted that he could not pursue his dream of starting his own used car business because it was too risky for a sole breadwinner. Ed explained: "I had a wife and three kids, so it's pretty hard to make a career change without some sort of guarantee. And you don't get any guarantee in sales." Other men explicitly noted that they felt trapped in jobs they found blatantly unpleasant. Bob, a stock handler at a warehouse, described his job: "I couldn't stand it. It was so repetitious, the same thing every day. I knew I was going nowhere, and I couldn't do much about it. You have to just keep on working and keep up with the obligations day to day."

Constraints of the "good provider" role not only limited men's ability to leave undesirable jobs and pursue their personal career goals; these pressures also kept them from being as involved in child care as they would have liked. Nearly every father interviewed in the study said that his work responsibilities impeded the development of close family relationships. Al, a farm foreman with four children, recalled, "When we first bought [our] house, I worked a [second] part-time job. I used to work until 5, and I'd come home, grab lunch, and then I worked for a contractor driving trucks until 10 at night. When the kids were 6 and 7, I didn't have much home life with them. I look back now and I wish I had spent more time with them. But, I wanted to get the house paid off." Don, a heavy machinery mechanic at a paper mill, regretted that he regularly worked nights and weekends. He explained, "I had four children and changing jobs wasn't an option. . . . The [long] hours I put in helped the family out. But everything has a price. I would have liked to have been with my family more. All four kids now have good educations and good homes in good neighborhoods. I just wish that I could have been around more when they were little" (Carr, 2005).

The pressure on men to make sacrifices so that they can provide for their families takes a long- and short-term toll on their personal relationships. At every age, from childhood to later life, children report more close-knit and supportive relationships with their mothers than their fathers (Rossi and Rossi, 1990). Fathers' more tenuous ties with their children dissolve even further upon divorce (e.g., Kalmijn, 2013), creating a situation whereby older unmarried men have few sources of support in later life (Steptoe et al., 2013). For these reasons, the call for gender equality does not benefit women only; rather, equal opportunities for men and women are critical for the health, well-being, and quality of life for all.

Why Are Women So Often the Targets of Violence?

One of the most disturbing trends documented by gender scholars is the high rate of violence, including sexual violence, against women. From sexual assault on college campuses to the systematic use of rape during wartime, sexual violence remains a pressing concern for scholars and policy makers alike. Why does such violence persist?

Sexual Violence: Concepts and Patterns

Before discussing the reasons why gender-based violence persists, it is important that we first review data describing the magnitude and pervasiveness of such violence. Violence directed against women is found in many societies and takes multiple forms, including physical and sexual abuse, mutilation, and murder. A 2013 study by the World Health Organization indicated that more than a third of all women around the world have been abused in some way by intimate partners and that abuse from intimate partners is the most prevalent type of violence against women (World Health Organization, 2013).

Rape is an all-too-common subtype of violence against women and refers to the forcing of nonconsensual vaginal, oral, or anal intercourse. One in five women worldwide will be a victim of rape or attempted rape in her lifetime; this rate is the same for women in the United States (CDC, 2010). The vast majority of rapes are committed by men against women, although mounting evidence suggests that men also are victims of sexual assault, and gay and transgender men are particularly vulnerable. Early research documented cases where women take sexual advantage of young men who may be insecure, intoxicated, or of a lower status (Anderson and Struckman-Johnson, 1998). More recent data from the Centers for Disease Control (2005) found that 16 percent of men have experienced sexual assault by age 18, often at the hands

rape The forcing of nonconsensual vaginal, oral, or anal intercourse.

of a relative or acquaintance. Although all sexual assault is taboo, young men are particularly reluctant to come forward and report their experiences. Many feel stifled because they have internalized the belief that men should be strong, stoic, and able to defend themselves, while those assaulted by other men fear the stigma associated with sex between two men (Kassie, 2015).

Rape is an act of violence committed to wield power and control over its victim. Sexual assault often is carefully planned, rather than performed on the spur of the moment to satisfy some uncontrollable sexual desire. Many rapes involve beatings, knifings, and even murder. In some instances, sexual assault is facilitated by alcohol or women having their drinks spiked with the sedative Rohypnol (i.e., a "roofie") or drugs referred to as "date-rape drugs" (Michigan Department of Community Health, 2010). Even when rape leaves no physical wounds, it is a highly traumatic violation of the victim's person that leaves long-lasting psychological scars. This devastation was recounted in vivid and heart-breaking terms by a young woman who was sexually assaulted while unconscious by a Stanford University student-athlete. At the assailant's sentencing, the woman read a letter in which she shared, "I can't sleep alone at night without having a light on, like a five year old, because I have nightmares of being touched where I cannot wake up. I did this thing where I waited until the sun came up and I felt safe enough to sleep. . . . It is embarrassing how feeble I feel, how timidly I move through life, always guarded, ready to defend myself, ready to be angry."

It is difficult to know how many rapes actually occur because many rapes go unreported. In one comprehensive study of American sexual behavior, 22 percent of the women surveyed reported having been forced into a sexual encounter. Yet the same study found that only 3 percent of the men admitted to having forced a woman into sex, a discrepancy that the study's authors attribute to different perceptions between men and women regarding what constitutes forced sex (Laumann et al., 1994). The U.S. Department of Justice estimated that over the past 18 years, nearly 100,000 women between the ages of 18 and 24 were victims of sexual assault every year (U.S. Bureau of Justice Statistics, 2017).

Although media reports sensationalize "stranger rapes," most rapes are committed by relatives (fathers or stepfathers, brothers, uncles), partners, or acquaintances. Among college students, most rapes are committed by boyfriends, former boyfriends, or classmates (U.S. Department of Justice, 2017). The National Institute of Campus Sexual Assault study presents a chilling picture of violence against women on campuses across the country (Krebs et al., 2007). The study, conducted during the winter of 2006, asked college women about their experience with rape, attempted rape, coerced sex, and unwanted sexual contact. More than 3 percent (3.4 percent) of female students surveyed reported having been raped since entering college. A previous study conducted by the same organization found that for both completed and attempted rapes, 9 out of 10 offenders were known to the victim.

The incidence of other forms of victimization reported in the study was substantially higher than that of rape. Overall, 29 percent of female students reported having experienced attempted or completed sexual assault (Krebs et al., 2007). Moreover, nearly 16 percent of the women reported being victimized by attempted or completed sexual assault before they entered college (19 percent since the beginning of their college career).

Emma Sulkowicz, a student at Columbia University, carried a 50-pound mattress around campus in protest of the university's handling of her sexual assault case.

Why Does Violence Persist? Competing Perspectives

Some radical feminist scholars claim that men are socialized to regard women as sex objects and that this partly explains the high levels of victimization of women (Dworkin, 1987; Griffin, 1979). Susan Brownmiller (1975), for example, claims that the constant threat of rape contributes to a "rape culture" in which male domination fosters a state of continual fear in women. One aspect of a rape culture is male socialization to a sense of sexual entitlement, which may encourage sexual conquest and promote insensitivity to the difference between consensual and nonconsensual sex (Scully, 1990). From seemingly innocent high school locker room jokes, to television commercials and magazine ads depicting women as sexually inviting, to television and movie images equating masculinity with the conquest of women, many men learn to believe that women exist for their pleasure. Under such circumstances, rape is all too "normal" (Wolf, 1992).

Moreover, female victims of sexual assault often are victimized again by judges, community members, and a mass media that subtly or overtly holds women "responsible" for their sexual victimization. In her victim impact letter, the woman at the center of what came to be called the "Stanford rape case" recounted, "I was pummeled with narrowed, pointed questions that dissected my personal life, love life, past life, family life, inane questions, accumulating trivial details to try and find an excuse for this guy who had me half naked before even bothering to ask for my name."

The fact that "acquaintance rapes" occur suggests that some men feel entitled to sexual access if they already know the woman. In a survey of nearly 270,000 first-year college students, 55 percent of male students agreed with the following statement: "If two people really like each other, it's all right for them to have sex even if they've known each other only for a very short time." Only 31 percent of female students agreed (American Council on Education [ACE], 2001). Another national survey reported that 43 percent of all men believed that a woman is partly to blame if she is raped after changing her mind about having sex (Yankelovich, 1991).

Because some men are socialized to feel sexual entitlement, rape is most common when men believe that norms condemning rape do not apply—for example, in times of war. Indeed, war-related rapes are as old as human history. Followers of Rome's legendary founder, Romulus, were reputed to have captured and raped Sabine women to populate Rome. Japanese soldiers raped as many as 20,000 women when they conquered the city of Nanking in China in 1937 (Chang and Kirby, 1997). American soldiers committed rapes during the U.S. Civil War and the Vietnam War.

Rape is an especially potent instrument of war, since it dehumanizes the victims and—where sexual mores are highly restrictive—can break apart families and weaken the resolve of victims to resist their aggressors. David Rosen, professor of sociology and anthropology who has long studied war crimes in Africa, argues that the systematic rape of women by armed militias in Darfur is intended to destroy their communities and ultimately serve as a means of ethnic cleansing (Rosen, 2008). A study of rape in ethno-national conflicts supports this conclusion; it reports that rape is far more likely when the future existence of the state is threatened (Hayden, 2000).

During World War II, for example, Japanese soldiers forced as many as 200,000 young women and girls to serve as "comfort women" for Japanese troops. These women—mainly Korean but also taken from other Asian countries conquered by the Japanese—were forced to work as sex slaves in military brothels throughout the Pacific. Many died in captivity; others committed suicide (Stetz and Oh, 2001). Rape was widely used as a Serbian strategy in the wars in Kosovo and Bosnia in the 1990s. By systematically raping and impregnating Muslim women, the Serbian forces hoped to humiliate the Muslim population into fleeing their homelands (Allen, 1996). Similarly, rape is used as a weapon of war in the Congo, where groups of armed rebels rape women and children to humiliate them and their families—a context that journalist Nicholas Kristof (2010) has called "the world capital of rape, torture, and mutilation."

Sexual assault is devastating to its victims, yet the consequences are particularly dire for those living in cultures that devalue women and women's sexuality. For example, in their book *Half the Sky*, journalists Nicholas Kristof and Sheryl WuDunn (2009) recount the harrowing experience of Hawa, a young student living in a refugee camp in Sudan's Darfur region. Hawa was attacked and gang-raped by members of the government-sponsored Janjaweed militia. When her friends attempted to get her medical treatment for her injuries in a small clinic staffed by foreign doctors, local police arrested her. Premarital sexual intercourse is a crime in Sudan. For the police, the act of seeking medical attention constituted proof of Hawa's sexual engagement, and without the required four male witnesses to testify to the rape, she was presumed to be guilty.

Sexual violence and partner violence remain critical global health issues. However, policy makers are making incremental strides in both drawing attention to and devising policies to fight such violence. In March 2013, former president Barack Obama reauthorized the Violence Against Women Act (VAWA). VAWA creates and expands federal programs to assist local communities with law enforcement and helps victims of domestic/partner and sexual abuse. Important revisions to the reauthorized act include expanded protection of gay men, lesbian women, transgender individuals, Native Americans, and immigrants—all groups particularly vulnerable to victimization (Parker, 2013). This reauthorized act underscores the importance of recognizing intersectionality in public policies as well as in scholarship, where the intersections of race, class, sexual orientation, and immigrant status may render a person more or less vulnerable to gender-based mistreatment.

At a global level, the United Nations has been instrumental in raising awareness of sexual violence. In July 2012, the secretary-general's UNiTE to End Violence against Women campaign rolled out a series of public awareness and education events, which relied on artists and social media to help ensure that schools, workplaces, and cyberspace are safe spaces for women and girls. On the twenty-fifth day of each month, awareness campaigns, public service announcements, and public art exhibits draw attention to violence against women.

Feminist scholars are pessimistic that gendered inequalities, whether pay inequalities or sexual violence, will be eradicated anytime soon. However, Kristof and WuDunn (2009) provide insights into ways that these problems might be attacked, slowly and gradually. They describe the eradication of gendered inequalities as "the paramount moral challenge" of this century, and they believe that the education and financial empowerment of women is a first essential step. A similar recommendation is offered by the United Nations. On July 2, 2010, in a historic moment, the UN General Assembly voted unanimously to establish the UN Entity for Gender Equality and Empowerment, to be known as UN Women. With the establishment of UN Women, UN Secretary-General Ban Ki-moon said, "UN Women is recognition of a simple truth: Equality for women and girls is not only a basic human right, it is a social and economic imperative. Where women are educated and empowered, economies are more productive and strong. Where women are fully represented, societies are more peaceful and stable" (Fifth World Conference on Women, 2010).

CONCEPT CHECKS

1 Name three possible explanations for the gender pay gap.

2 Describe three ways that traditional expectations associated with male gender roles harm men and their families.

3 Discuss at least two reasons why women are so often the targets of sexual violence.

THE BIG PICTURE

Chapter 10
Gender Inequality

1 **Basic Concepts**

p. 328

2 **Sociological Theories of Gender Inequalites**

p. 338

LEARNING OBJECTIVES

Understand the ways that differences between women and men reflect biological factors, sociocultural influences, and the complex interplay between the two.

Recognize and contrast competing explanations for gender inequality. Learn some feminist theories about gender equality.

TERMS TO KNOW

intersectionality • sex • gender • gender role socialization • social construction of gender • hegemonic masculinity • biological essentialism • cisgender • transgender • intersex

feminist theory • liberal feminism • radical feminism • patriarchy • Black feminism • transnational feminism • postmodern feminism

CONCEPT CHECKS

1. What is the difference between sex and gender?
2. How do both biology and gender socialization contribute to differences between men and women?
3. What does it mean to say that gender is something we "do"? Give an example of a way you do gender in your daily life.
4. How can studies of other cultures contribute to the argument that gender is socially constructed?

1. Contrast functionalist and feminist approaches to understanding gender inequality.
2. What are the key ideas of liberal feminism? What are criticisms of this perspective?
3. What are the key ideas of radical feminism? What are criticisms of this perspective?
4. How do the key ideas of socialist feminism challenge the main themes of liberal and radical feminism?
5. Do you think that postmodern feminism is incompatible with liberal, radical, and Black feminist perspectives? Why or why not?

Exercises: Thinking Sociologically

1. What does cross-cultural evidence from tribal societies in New Guinea, Afghanistan, and North America suggest about the differences in gender roles? Explain.

2. Why are women of color likely to think very differently about gender inequality than White women? Explain.

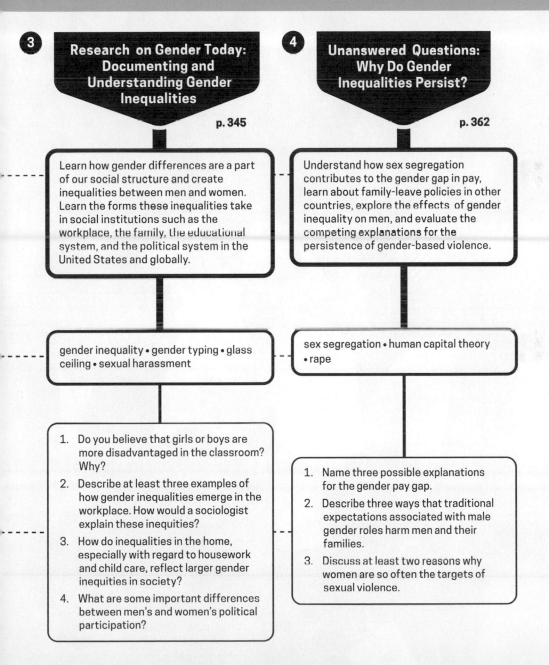

3 **Research on Gender Today: Documenting and Understanding Gender Inequalities**

p. 345

Learn how gender differences are a part of our social structure and create inequalities between men and women. Learn the forms these inequalities take in social institutions such as the workplace, the family, the educational system, and the political system in the United States and globally.

gender inequality • gender typing • glass ceiling • sexual harassment

1. Do you believe that girls or boys are more disadvantaged in the classroom? Why?
2. Describe at least three examples of how gender inequalities emerge in the workplace. How would a sociologist explain these inequities?
3. How do inequalities in the home, especially with regard to housework and child care, reflect larger gender inequities in society?
4. What are some important differences between men's and women's political participation?

4 **Unanswered Questions: Why Do Gender Inequalities Persist?**

p. 362

Understand how sex segregation contributes to the gender gap in pay, learn about family-leave policies in other countries, explore the effects of gender inequality on men, and evaluate the competing explanations for the persistence of gender-based violence.

sex segregation • human capital theory • rape

1. Name three possible explanations for the gender pay gap.
2. Describe three ways that traditional expectations associated with male gender roles harm men and their families.
3. Discuss at least two reasons why women are so often the targets of sexual violence.

11

Race, Ethnicity, and Racism

Projections by the U.S. Census Bureau suggest that:

A   Latinos will be in the majority in the United States by 2044.

B   Whites will no longer be a majority in the United States by 2044.

C   Whites will remain in the majority after 2044.

TURN THE PAGE FOR THE CORRECT ANSWER.

LEARNING OBJECTIVES

1 Basic Concepts

Understand the differing meanings of the terms *race* and *ethnicity*. Understand why race is a highly contested concept.

2 Thinking About Racism

Learn several key concepts that are important for understanding racism in the contemporary United States: color-blind racism, White privilege, institutional racism, overt racism, and microaggressions.

3 Race and Racism in Historical and Comparative Perspective

Familiarize yourself with the history and social dimensions of ethnic relations in the United States. Recognize the importance of the historical roots of ethnic conflict, particularly in the expansion of Western colonialism. Understand the different models for a multiethnic society.

4 Unanswered Questions

Understand the current state of immigration to the United States. Learn the forms of inequality experienced by different racial and ethnic groups in the United States.

D onald Trump was elected into office in part by working-class White voters who were largely victims of an economy that had outsourced millions of jobs and lost others to computerization. Many of these voters did not blame their troubles on economic transformations, however, but instead on the idea that non-Whites were increasingly taking their jobs and controlling the country.

You have no doubt heard the same message that many of these anxious White voters heard in the years leading up to the presidential election—that America is moving in the direction of what is called a "majority-minority" nation. By this, sociologists mean a country in which non-Hispanic Whites will no longer be in the majority; a nation in which non-Whites will be in the majority. The conventional wisdom, including projections by the U.S. Census Bureau, suggests that this is what is happening. Thus, the answer is *b*: According to the U.S. Census, Whites will no longer be a majority in the United States by 2044.

The Census Bureau is the official U.S. government agency for counting Americans. Ever since 1790, the Census Bureau has classified the population by race, and the way it has done so powerfully illustrates that race is not a biological reality, but rather a social and political construction. For the first century and a half of the census, these classifications were done by census workers who determined the race of a person by sight. Such classifications, no doubt, were quite arbitrary and often inaccurate. In 1960, the census moved to a system in which the people being counted self-reported their own race by choosing among predetermined categories.

Over the history of the census, the specific racial categories used have undergone major changes, illustrating that categories we take to be natural in one era are actually socially constructed. This concept is illustrated by the way in which categories vary over time. People from South Asia were long classified as White in the census, for example, but by the 1980s, were reclassified as Asian. Mexicans

THE ANSWER IS B.

were classified as White in the nineteenth century, as non-White in the 1930s, again as White in the 1940s, and then as Hispanic in the 1970s, all depending on demands for labor and the amount of prejudice in the country at a given moment. Today, there are ongoing debates about whether people from parts of the Middle East should continue to be classified as White since many are not seen by themselves or others in that way.

Racial categories themselves also go in and out of fashion. In the 1890 census, "quadroon" was the racial category for people who were a quarter Black, and "octoroon" was the racial category for people who were one-eighth Black. Ten years later, those categories were eliminated, and a new all-encompassing "Negro" category was added to the census. In 1970, "Negro or Black" was added to the census, and by 2000, the category was "Black, African American, or Negro." In 2013, the Census Bureau stopped using the category "Negro" because many respondents found it offensive; an older generation that identified with that term has largely passed on.

In 2016, sociologist Richard Alba published an article that challenged conventional wisdom on census classifications of White and non-White. He pointed out that the Census Bureau's way of classifying individuals by ethnicity and race yields the lowest possible estimate of the non-Hispanic White population. This is because children with one parent who is Asian, Hispanic, or Black are always counted as a minority. This, according to Alba, is basically an extension of the "one drop" rule that has always classified people as Black if they have some Black ancestry (Alba, 2016).

Consider the example of Senator Ted Cruz of Texas, who is classified as Hispanic since his ancestors came from Cuba. His wife, Heidi Nelson Cruz, is White and blond, and their two children also appear White and blond. Nevertheless, the only person in the Cruz household who would be classified as White by the Census Bureau is Heidi. But what if the United States were to move to the other extreme: to count anyone with one White parent as White? Under that assumption, Whites would remain three-

(left) The Census Bureau classifies individuals with one parent who is Asian, Black, or Hispanic as a member of that minority group. (right) According to the U.S. Census, Heidi Nelson Cruz is the only White person in the Cruz household. Some sociologists question whether this reflects the lived experiences of mixed-race families.

Four schoolboys represent the "racial scale" in South Africa: Black, Indian, half-caste, and White.

quarters of the U.S. population by mid-century. The interesting sociological question is, Which assumption fits better with the lived experience of mixed-race people?

According to Alba, the household incomes of mixed-race people tend to be closer to the White median income than to that of minorities. Likewise, many mixed-race people—such as those who are both Asian and White—tend to self-identify as White. While this tends not to be the case for those with Black ancestry, it is indeed the direction of identification to be found in many other partially White people. Alba also argues that for people who are partly minority and partly White, there is a greater tendency to choose a White marriage partner, which means that their children will tend to live in White neighborhoods and identify as White. For all these reasons, Alba argues, many mixed-race people will self-identify with the majority. It is, therefore, a mistake to take it for granted that America is becoming a "majority-minority" country.

Alba's ideas are consistent with the sociological understanding of the term *minority* as not simply a numerical category. There are many minorities in a numerical or statistical sense, such as people with red hair or people who weigh more than 250 pounds, but these are not minorities according to the sociological concept. In sociology, members of a **minority group** are disadvantaged as compared to the dominant group (a group possessing more wealth, power, and prestige) and thus have some sense of group solidarity. Subjection to prejudice and discrimination usually heightens feelings of common loyalty and interests.

Members of minority groups, such as Spanish speakers in the United States, often see themselves as distinct from the majority. Although members of minority groups tend to live in certain neighborhoods, cities, or regions of a country, their children often intermarry with members of the dominant group. Thus, future generations that the Census Bureau assumes will identify as minority may not experience the cultural distinctiveness or disadvantages that are today associated with the very idea of a minority group.

1 BASIC CONCEPTS

Race

In your daily life, you have no doubt used the terms *race* and *ethnicity* many times, but do you know what they mean? In fact, defining these terms is very difficult, not least because of the contradiction between their everyday usage and their scientific basis (or absence thereof).

When the Census Bureau asks people to classify themselves, many respondents mistakenly think that humans can be readily separated into biologically different races. Yet, in biological terms, there are no clear-cut races. We therefore define **race** as a socially constructed category rooted in the belief that there are fundamental differences among humans, associated with phenotype and ancestry (Monk, 2016).

Differences in physical type between groups of human beings arise from population inbreeding, which varies according to the degree of contact between different cultural or social groups. Human population groups are a continuum. The genetic diversity within populations that share visible physical traits is as great as the diversity between them. Thus, the racial differences the Census Bureau recognizes (Black, White, Hispanic) should be understood as physical variations singled out by the members of a community or society as socially significant and meaningful. Differences in skin color are treated as significant, for example, whereas differences in eye color and height are not. Racial categories are always nationally and historically specific (Fredrickson, 2002), and they can vary significantly from place to place.

Some social scientists argue that race is nothing more than an ideological construct whose use in academic circles perpetuates the commonly held belief that it has a basis in reality (Miles, 1993). For this reason, they argue, it should be abandoned. Others disagree, claiming that "race" still has meaning for many people and cannot be ignored. In historical terms, "race" has been an extremely important concept used by powerful social groups as part of strategies of domination (Spencer, 2014). For example, the contemporary situation of African Americans in the United States cannot be understood without reference to the slave trade, racial segregation, and persistent racial ideologies (Wacquant, 2010). Racial distinctions are more than ways of describing differences; they are also important factors in the reproduction of patterns of power and inequality.

Hence, "race" remains a vital, if highly contested, concept, which sociologists have to explore wherever it is in use. For this reason, you sometimes will come across sociological papers and books that put the word "race" in quotation marks to reflect its unscientific, problematic, but still commonplace usage in society.

Ethnicity

While the idea of race implies something fixed and biological, ethnicity is a source of identity based on society and culture. **Ethnicity** refers to a type of social identity related to ancestry (perceived or real) and cultural differences, which become effective or active in certain contexts. Members of ethnic groups see themselves as culturally distinct from other groups in a society, and are seen by those other groups to be so in return. Different characteristics may serve to distinguish ethnic groups from one another,

minority group A group of people in a given society who, because of their distinct physical or cultural characteristics, find themselves in situations of inequality compared with the dominant group within that society.

race A socially constructed category rooted in the belief that there are fundamental differences among humans, associated with phenotype and ancestry.

ethnicity Cultural values and norms that distinguish the members of a given group from others. An ethnic group is one whose members share a distinct awareness of a common cultural identity, separating them from other groups. In virtually all societies, ethnic differences are associated with variations in power and material wealth. Where ethnic differences are also racial, such divisions are sometimes especially pronounced.

The United States is home to a multitude of different ethnic groups. In midtown Manhattan, members of the city's Persian community participate in the annual Persian Parade. In Brooklyn, the West Indian Day Parade is a colorful celebration of Caribbean culture.

but the most common are language, history or ancestry (real or imagined), religion, and styles of dress or adornment.

In the United States, some of the first sociological research took place on ethnic groups such as Italian Americans, Irish Americans, Polish Americans, and German Americans, though the Irish and the Italians were also sometimes thought of as a race as well. As the United States has become more diverse, many other races see themselves as composed of distinct ethnicities. East Asians encompass Chinese, Koreans, and Japanese, among many other ethnic groups, while Blacks include West Indians and West Africans, among many others.

Ethnic differences are wholly learned, a point that seems self-evident until we remember how often some groups have been regarded as "born to rule" or "shiftless," "unintelligent," and so forth. Indeed, when people use the term "ethnicity," very often they do so (as with "race") when referring to inherent characteristics such as skin color or blood ties. Yet there is nothing innate about ethnicity; it is a purely social phenomenon that is produced and reproduced over time.

For many people, ethnicity is central to their individual and group identity, but for others,

CONCEPT CHECKS

1 How do the changing racial categories used on the Census help demonstrate that race is socially constructed?

2 Explain the difference between ethnicity and race.

3 Why are Hispanics and African Americans considered to be minority groups in American society?

it is irrelevant, and for still others, it seems significant only during times of conflict or social unrest. Ethnicity can provide an important thread of continuity with the past and is often kept alive through the practice of cultural traditions. For instance, third-generation Americans of Irish descent may proudly identify themselves as Irish American despite having lived their entire lives in the United States.

2   THINKING ABOUT RACISM

Defining Racism

Racism can be defined in many ways. Just as there are different understandings of what constitutes racism in different national and subnational contexts and historical periods, so there are similar variations in the understanding of racism. Racism can refer to explicit beliefs in racial supremacy, such as the systems established in Nazi Germany, before the civil rights movement in the United States, and under apartheid in South Africa. It can also refer to practices such as stereotyping that keep racial minorities in inferior positions, despite apparent good will and beliefs in equality. Two main components of racism are prejudice and discrimination.

Prejudice and Discrimination

Prejudice refers to opinions or attitudes held by members of one group toward another. These preconceived views are often based on hearsay and are resistant to change even in the face of direct evidence or new information. People may harbor favorable prejudices toward groups with which they identify and negative prejudices against others. Prejudice operates mainly through **stereotyping**, which means thinking in terms of fixed and inflexible categories. Stereotyping is often closely linked to the psychological mechanism of displacement, in which feelings of hostility or anger are directed against objects that are not at the root of those feelings. Stereotyping leads people to blame **scapegoats** for problems that are not their fault. Scapegoating is common when two deprived ethnic groups compete with one another for economic rewards. People who direct racial attacks against poor Mexicans or African Americans, for example, are often in a similar economic position to them. They blame Blacks or Mexicans for grievances whose real causes lie elsewhere.

Scapegoating is normally directed against groups that are relatively powerless because they make for easy targets. Protestants, Catholics, Jews, Italians, racial minorities, and

racism The attribution of characteristics of superiority or inferiority to a population sharing certain physically inherited characteristics. Racism is one specific form of prejudice, focusing on physical variations among people. Racist attitudes became entrenched during the period of Western colonial expansion, but seem also to rest on mechanisms of prejudice and discrimination found in human societies today.

prejudice The holding of preconceived ideas about an individual or group, ideas that are resistant to change even in the face of new information. Prejudice may be either positive or negative.

stereotyping Thinking in terms of fixed and inflexible categories.

scapegoats Individuals or groups blamed for wrongs that were not of their doing.

others have played the unwilling role of scapegoat at various times throughout Western history. Scapegoating frequently involves *projection*, the unconscious attribution to others of one's own desires or characteristics. For example, research has consistently demonstrated that when members of a dominant group practice violence against a minority and exploit it sexually, they are likely to believe that the minority group itself displays traits of sexual violence. In the United States, before the civil rights movement, for instance, some White men's ideas about the lustful nature of African American men probably originated in their own frustrations, since sexual access to White women was limited by the formal nature of courtship. Similarly, in apartheid South Africa, Black males were thought to be sexually dangerous to White women—but, in fact, virtually all criminal sexual contact was initiated by White men against Black women (Simpson and Yinger, 1986).

In contrast to prejudice, **discrimination** refers to actual behavior that denies to members of a particular group resources or rewards that others can obtain. College admissions officers have been known to discriminate against members of ethnic or racial groups when those members do not conform with stereotypes of those groups. One investigation of the Princeton University admissions office, for example, uncovered a rejected Hispanic applicant with this comment written on her file: "Tough to see putting her ahead of others. No cultural flavor in app." Such attitudes are racist when they function to keep Hispanics out of college or ensure that only certain "kinds" of Hispanics will gain access to institutions of higher learning.

Racism in the United States Today

Some people see racism as a system of domination operating in official social institutions like admissions offices or police departments, while others see it as operating through the actions of racist individuals. In this section, we detail several particular concepts that are important for understanding racism in the United States today: color-blind racism, White privilege, institutional racism, overt racism, and microaggressions.

Color-Blind Racism: Racism without Racists

Over the past several decades, some sociologists have argued that racial inequality is maintained less by overt acts of racial hatred than by color blindness itself. Sociologist Eduardo Bonilla-Silva (2006) defines color blindness as a means of maintaining racial inequality without appearing racist.

First, many Whites believe they are above racism and incapable of perpetuating discrimination. They are thus unaware of the ways in which their insensitivity is psychologically damaging to racial minorities. Second, by attempting to act as if race does not exist, they perpetuate inequalities that can only be addressed by explicit attention to racial differences. Third, many Whites who do make subtle or even explicitly racial distinctions have become adept at maintaining an appearance of neutrality. In all of these ways, much of racial inequality is maintained through the appearance of color-blind processes.

White Privilege One significant aspect of color blindness is how much Whites can take for granted. Many of those who profess to be "color-blind," for example, don't recognize the many ways that they benefit from their Whiteness. Just as many Blacks must take it for granted that racism pervades all actions in a systemic way, so it is that many Whites can take for granted that they will benefit from White privilege. **White privilege** refers to the unacknowledged and unearned assets that benefit Whites in their everyday lives. It manifests itself in the most taken-for-granted conditions of everyday life.

In a powerful metaphor, women's studies scholar Peggy McIntosh likens White privilege to "an invisible weightless knapsack of special provisions, assurances, tools, maps, guides, codebooks, passports, visas, clothes, compass, emergency gear, and blank checks" (1988). McIntosh then goes on to unpack this invisible knapsack by detailing more than 40 "special circumstances and provisions" she experiences as a White person that her African American counterparts cannot similarly expect in their day-to-day lives:

1. Make arrangements to hang out with people of one's own race most of the time.
2. Rent or purchase housing in an area one can afford and where one wants to live.
3. Assume that the people living next door will treat one with respect.
4. Go shopping alone without being followed around the store or harassed.
5. Turn on the TV and expect to see other people of one's race most of the time (1988).

Institutional Racism

The idea of **institutional racism** was developed in the United States in the late 1960s by Black Power activists Stokely Carmichael and Charles Hamilton before it was taken up and developed by sociologists in the 1970s. It is defined as the idea that racism occurs through the respected and established institutions of society rather than through the hateful actions of some bad people—that racism pervades all of society's structures in a systematic way. Those who focus on institutional racism study how social institutions, such as schools, hospitals, police departments, and businesses, have practices supporting White supremacy built into the very fabric of their operations. These institutions structure social relations in ways that are less obvious than overt discrimination.

The concept of institutional racism is well illustrated by the case of George Floyd. His death at the hands of a police officer on

discrimination Behavior that denies to the members of a particular group resources or rewards that can be obtained by others. Discrimination must be distinguished from prejudice: Individuals who are prejudiced against others may not engage in discriminatory practices against them; conversely, people may act in a discriminatory fashion toward a group even though they are not prejudiced against that group.

White privilege The unacknowledged and unearned assets that benefit Whites in their everyday lives.

institutional racism The idea that racism occurs through the respected and established institutions of society rather than through hateful actions of some bad people.

May 26, 2020, led to massive protests, riots, and calls for justice and police reform not only in Minneapolis, the site of the incident, but across the United States and even the world. The tragedy occurred after Floyd, a 46-year-old African American and frequent patron of Cup Foods, a local grocery store, paid for cigarettes with what was allegedly a fake twenty-dollar bill. Realizing that the bill was counterfeit, the cashier on duty followed him to his car and demanded that he return the cigarettes. Floyd, who was heavily intoxicated, refused, and the employee called 911. When the first police car arrived seven minutes later, Floyd was still outside the store, sitting in his blue van with two other passengers.

Upon reaching the car, one of the officers put a gun to Floyd's head until he lay both hands on the car's steering wheel. The officer then pulled Floyd out of his car and met with some resistance as he was handcuffing him. Once the officer explained to Floyd that he was arresting him for possible counterfeit, Floyd became compliant. On their way to the police car, however, Floyd stiffened up and fell, claiming to be claustrophobic. At this point, two additional officers showed up at the scene and helped force Floyd into the car. Videos made by witnesses then show one of the newly arrived officers, Derek Chauvin, dragging a handcuffed Floyd out of the passenger seat and back on the ground, belly down. At 8:19 pm Chauvin set his knee over Floyd's head and neck while two other officers held his back and legs, while the fourth one, Thomas Lane, watched.

Hundreds of Brooklyn residents gathered downtown to protest the killing of George Floyd by a Minneapolis police officer. Over 2,000 American cities joined in protest in the weeks following Floyd's murder.

Though Floyd repeatedly cried out "please!" "Mama!" and "I can't breathe," the officers replied that he was "talking fine." When several minutes had passed, Lane suggested to Chauvin that Floyd be turned on his side because he was concerned about "excited delirium," a term used to designate "a sudden cessation of struggle, respiratory arrest, and death." To this, Chauvin replied, "That's why we have him on his stomach." By 8:24 pm, George had stopped moving; a minute later he stopped speaking, at which point one of the cops holding Floyd down checked his pulse but "couldn't find one." Nonetheless, Chauvin kept his knee in place for nearly another two minutes. Eventually an ambulance arrived, and Floyd's body was removed. An hour later he was pronounced dead at the Hennepin County Medical Center.

The autopsy report issued by the Hennepin County medical examiner on the following day stated that the findings did not support "a diagnosis of traumatic asphyxia or strangulation." The complaint filed by the district court concluded that the combined effects of Floyd's "being restrained by the police, his underlying health conditions, and any potential intoxicants in his system [had] likely contributed to his death." It also noted, however, that "police are trained that this type of restraint with a subject in a prone position is inherently dangerous."

A second, independent autopsy report ordered by Floyd's family claimed that he had been asphyxiated by the pressure applied on his neck. Although both reports ultimately identified the cause of death as homicide, the one issued by the official medical examiner implied that Floyd may not have died at the hands of the police had he been in better medical shape.

Although Chauvin and all three fellow police officers will be prosecuted, the weight of their penalty will be determined by the way in which the jury chooses to understand the cause of Floyd's death and define "excessive force." As law enforcement officers, they may well receive a lighter sentence than civilians guilty of a similar crime. Data consistently shows not only that Blacks are far more likely to be maltreated by police, but that the public actually perceives this to be the case. Even though the murder of George Floyd was the direct result of the acts of a few police officers, the episode is unfortunately far from unique. Several other high-profile incidents in recent years have brought attention to inequalities in policing and a criminal justice system that places an unjust burden on Black people.

What we can see in George Floyd's killing and others like it is that discrimination often occurs through the practices of respected institutions. We find this not only in policing, but in other institutions as well. One of the best ways to understand how race and ethnicity operate in the United States through institutional racism is to recall that, until the late 1970s, most Black Americans lived in either urban ghettos or southern states that were still marked by the remnants of Jim Crow segregation. In the urban areas marked by ghettos, it was very difficult for Blacks to find housing outside these neighborhoods, either due to racial discrimination or violence against those Blacks who tried to move into White neighborhoods. In the South, long after the Civil War, there was still a sharp "color line" that separated the races in schools, housing, and public facilities. In both the North and the South, Blacks of all socio-economic classes led lives that were separate from Whites. Black Americans in the middle- and upper-classes were relegated to the same neighborhoods as those in the lower-class. In other words, if you were Black then you were Black, and that largely defined your life chances.

When we refer to the ghetto of the United States, or to southern Jim Crow, we are recognizing that racism is embedded in the structures of our political, economic, and social institutions. Even though there are many individual acts of discrimination, the racial system is not first and foremost kept alive by these individual acts. It is kept alive and perpetuated by a larger system of segregation that was established long before those currently affected were even born and that exists independently of individual acts of hatred or prejudice. In fact, once people live in a highly segregated society, it is possible for them to suffer great disadvantage based on their race without ever personally experiencing discrimination on a one-to-one basis.

Although an individual act, George Floyd's murder brought attention to systemic inequalities and discrimination that exist on an institutional level, and it resulted in an outpouring of protests in cities around the world. The impact of these protests was not merely to bring attention to institutional racism in the criminal justice system, but in all realms of life including education, housing, and the workplace. Indeed, the murder of George Floyd had the effect of taking a concept developed in the discipline of sociology and making it a part of mainstream discourse about racial inequality around the world.

Overt Racism: Racism with Racists

Though color-blind racism and White privilege are useful concepts for explaining racial inequality in an age when people are good at keeping their racist thoughts to themselves, it would be a mistake to conclude that overt racist acts have disappeared or that large numbers of people are not victimized by them. In everyday life, racism can be expressed in the ideas held by bigoted individuals. It is expressed overtly through individual attitudes, perceptions, and beliefs, and it is also sustained by the ideological racist statements of political leaders.

Overt racism, which was highly unusual in American politics after the Civil Rights era, saw a resurgence during the campaign and 2016–2020 term of President Donald Trump, as is evident from the examples below.

1. Trump began his presidential campaign on June 16, 2015, by attacking Mexican migrants to the United States as "rapists and criminals," saying, "When Mexico sends its people, they're not sending their best. They're not sending you. They're sending people that have lots of problems, and they're bringing those problems with [them]. They're bringing drugs. They're bringing crime. They're rapists. And some, I assume, are good people." Trump's rhetoric was aimed at painting Mexicans with one broad brush and suggesting that most of the migrants were dangerous. These claims were the basis of his arguments for building a giant border wall between the United States and Mexico.

2. Trump's attacks were focused not only on poor Mexican immigrants but also members of the Mexican American elite. In May 2016, Trump attacked Judge Gonzalo Curiel, who had ruled against his company on some legal issues. "He is a Mexican," Trump said. "We're building a wall between here and Mexico. The answer is, he is giving us very unfair rulings—rulings that people can't even believe."

In August 2017, members of the White nationalist groups participated in a "Unite the Right" rally in Charlottesville, Virginia. The rally, which was met by counterprotesters, erupted in violence and ended with one woman dead and nineteen others injured.

3. After the Democratic National Convention, Donald Trump attacked Khizr and Ghazala Khan, the Pakistani American parents of a Muslim U.S. Army officer who died in the Iraq War. The parents spoke at the Democratic Convention, accusing Trump of not understanding the U.S. Constitution: "Have you ever been to Arlington Cemetery? Go look at the graves of brave patriots who died defending the United States of America," said the soldier's father. "You will see all faiths, genders, and ethnicities. You have sacrificed nothing—and no one." Later Trump lashed out at the couple, suggesting that Mrs. Khan had been silent during the speech because Pakistani women are held in an inferior position. Trump's adviser Roger Stone claimed that Khizr Khan wants to enact sharia law in the United States.

4. Trump refused to disavow White supremacists when they made complimentary comments about him and his campaign. David Duke, the former leader of the KKK, stated on his radio show that not voting for Trump is "really treason to your heritage." After a "Unite the Right" rally in Charlottesville, Virginia, in August 2017 left one woman dead and nineteen others injured, Trump again failed to condemn White supremacists, instead asserting that the counterprotesters were as much to blame for the violence as the alt-right crowd.

Although President Trump claimed to be "the least racist person that you have ever met," he has continually made one bigoted statement after another, both during the campaign and then during his presidency. Usually these statements tended to paint one or another racial group with a broad brush.

Racial Microaggressions

In everyday life, racial minorities often experience brief interactions that send demeaning messages and appear to the victims to be based on their race. Unlike acts of overt racism, these interactions are perpetuated by Whites who are well meaning and well intentioned. Whereas the racial minority member experiences the interaction as an insult, the White perpetrator can be shocked to discover there has been any incident at all. At times, the perpetrator will claim that the minority has misunderstood an "innocent" comment or is making a "mountain out of a molehill." Often these interactions are experienced silently, with the victim never expressing the outrage they silently feel.

The idea of microaggression was originally proposed in the 1970s by Chester M. Pierce, an African American psychiatrist at Harvard (Pierce and Dimsdale, 1986). In recent years, it has caught on due to the further work of Derald Wing Sue, an Asian American psychologist at Columbia. **Racial microaggressions** are small slights, indignities, or acts of disrespect that are hurtful to people of color, even though they are often perpetrated by well-meaning Whites. Among the kinds of incidents cited by Sue as examples of microaggressions are people asking Asian Americans where they were born or telling them that they "speak good English." Such comments suggest that these Americans are immigrants, even when they and their families have been in this country for generations (Sue, 2010).

While the idea of microaggression has become very popular, it has also been widely criticized. Some believe the idea of microaggression is itself damaging because it encourages a victim mentality, spurs anger, and encourages people to jump to negative conclusions in ambiguous situations. As such, the debate over microaggression has become part of the phenomenon itself, an essential component to thinking about the phenomenon of racism in contemporary society.

CONCEPT CHECKS

1 In what ways does the killing of George Floyd at the hands of a Minneapolis police officer provide evidence of institutional racism?

2 How does color blindness maintain racial inequality?

3 Provide one example of White privilege. What does McIntosh mean by "an invisible weightless knapsack"?

4 What is microaggression? Why is this idea problematic to some?

Table 11.1

APPLYING SOCIOLOGY TO RACE AND ETHNICITY

CONCEPT	APPROACH TO RACE AND ETHNICITY	CURRENT APPLICATION
White Privilege	Unacknowledged and unmerited assets that benefit Whites in their everyday lives.	Whites can typically expect to go shopping without being followed around a store or harassed.
Institutional Racism	Racism that occurs under the auspices of respected civic and social institutions such as courts and police, rather than through the hateful or biased actions of particular prejudiced people.	Police stopping and searching Black drivers at stop signs twice as often as they do White ones, though Blacks are 26 percent less likely to be found in possession of contraband goods.
Overt Racism	Racism that is manifest in individual attitudes, perceptions, and beliefs, including statements made by political leaders.	Donald Trump initiating his 2016 presidential campaign with the accusation that Mexican migrants to the United States are "rapists and criminals."
Racial Microaggressions	Subtle, slight indignities and disrespectful actions that are hurtful to people of another race even though they are often perpetrated by well-meaning individuals.	Asking members of ethnic and racial minority groups where they are born under the assumption that they and their families have not been in the United States for long.

3 RACE AND RACISM IN HISTORICAL AND COMPARATIVE PERSPECTIVE

It is impossible to understand ethnic and racial divisions today without considering the effect of Western colonialism on the rest of the world (Global Map 11.1); global migratory movements resulting from colonialism helped create ethnic divisions by placing peoples in close proximity.

From the fifteenth century onward, Europeans ventured into seas previously uncharted and unexplored by them, pursuing exploration and trade but also conquering native peoples and settling in new areas. Europeans also occasioned a large-scale movement of people from Africa to the Americas via the slave trade. The following extraordinary shifts in population have occurred in the past 350 years or so:

1. **Europe to North America.** Since the seventeenth century, some 45 million people have emigrated from Europe to what are now the United States and Canada. About 200 million people in North America today trace their ancestry to this migration.

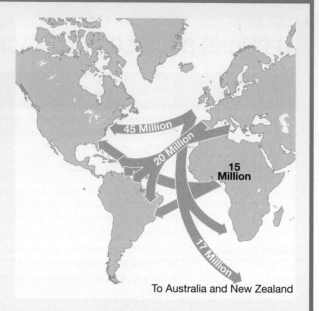

This map shows the massive movement of peoples from Europe who colonized the Americas, South Africa, Australia, and New Zealand, resulting in the ethnic composition of populations there today. People from Africa were brought to the Americas to be slaves.

45 Million

20 Million

15 Million

17 Million

To Australia and New Zealand

2. **Europe to Central and South America.** About 20 million people, mostly from Spain, Portugal, and Italy, have migrated to Central and South America. Some 50 million people in these areas today are of European ancestry.

3. **Europe to Africa and Australasia.** Approximately 17 million people in Africa and Australasia are of European ancestry. In Africa, the majority of emigrants went to the state of South Africa, which was colonized mainly by the British and the Dutch.

4. **Africa to the Americas.** Starting in the sixteenth century, about 10 million Blacks were unwillingly transported to the North and South American continents. Fewer than 1 million arrived in the sixteenth century; some 1.3 million in the seventeenth century; 6 million in the eighteenth century; and 2 million in the nineteenth century.

These population flows underlie the current ethnic composition of the United States, Canada, the countries of Central and South America, South Africa, Australia, and New Zealand. In all these societies, the indigenous populations were decimated by disease, war, and genocide, and subjected to European rule. They are now impoverished ethnic minorities. Because the Europeans themselves had diverse national and ethnic origins, they transplanted ethnic hierarchies and divisions to their new homelands. At the height of the colonial era, Europeans also ruled over native populations in South Asia, East Asia, the South Pacific, and the Middle East.

Throughout European expansion, ethnocentric attitudes caused many colonists to believe that, as Christians, they were on a civilizing mission to the rest of the world. Europeans of all political persuasions believed themselves superior to the peoples they colonized and conquered. The fact that many of those peoples possessed technologies, agricultural skills, and knowledge that the Europeans embraced and incorporated (for example, the civil service system in India) seemed irrelevant, because the Europeans possessed the power to institutionalize their interpretation of the relationship between themselves and the rest of the world. The early period of colonization coincided with the rise of **scientific racism**, or the misuse of science to support racist assumptions, and ever since then, the legacy of colonization has generated ethnic divisions that have affected regional and global conflicts. In particular, racist views distinguishing the descendants of Europeans from those of Africans became central to European racist attitudes.

The Rise of Racism

Why has racism flourished? There are several reasons. The first reason lies in the exploitative relations that Europeans established with the peoples they conquered. The slave trade could not have persisted had Europeans not constructed a belief system that allowed them to justify their actions by claiming that Africans belonged to an inferior race. Racism helped justify colonial rule over non-Whites and denied them the rights of political participation being won by Whites in the colonists' European homelands. The relations between Whites and non-Whites varied according to different patterns of colonial settlement

A young girl joins members of the Ku Klux Klan at a demonstration against the Martin Luther King Day holiday in Pulaski, Tennessee.

and were influenced by cultural differences among Europeans themselves.

Second, an opposition between the colors White and Black as cultural symbols was deeply rooted in European culture. White had long been associated with purity and Black with evil. (There is nothing natural about this symbolism; in some other cultures, it is reversed.) The symbol of Blackness held negative meanings *before* the West came into extensive contact with Black peoples. These symbolic meanings influenced the Europeans' reactions to Blacks when they first encountered them on African shores. The sense that there was a radical difference between Black and White peoples, combined with the "heathenism" of the Africans, led many Europeans to regard Blacks with disdain and fear.

A third factor was the invention and diffusion of the concept of race itself. Racist attitudes have existed for thousands of years. In China in 300 B.C.E., for example, we find descriptions of barbarian peoples "who greatly resemble monkeys from whom they are descended." But the notion of race as a cluster of inherited characteristics comes from European thought. Count Joseph Arthur de Gobineau (1816–1882), sometimes called the father of modern racism, proposed that three races exist: White, Black, and yellow. The White race possessed

scientific racism The use of scientific research or data to justify or reify beliefs about the superiority or inferiority of particular racial groups. Much of the "data" used to justify such claims are flawed or biased.

superior intelligence, morality, and willpower, and these inherited qualities underlay the spread of Western influence across the world. Blacks were the least capable, marked by an animal nature, a lack of morality, and emotional instability.

The ideas of Gobineau and other similar views were presented as supposedly scientific theories. Although completely without factual value, the notion of the superiority of the White race remains a key element of White racism—in the ideology of the Ku Klux Klan, for example—and was the basis of **apartheid** in South Africa.

Blacks in the United States

By 1780, there were nearly 4 million slaves in the American South. Slaves had no legal rights whatsoever. But they did not passively accept the conditions their masters imposed on them. The struggles of slaves sometimes took the form of direct opposition or disobedience to orders, and occasionally rebellion, though collective slave revolts were more common in the Caribbean than in the United States. On a more subtle level, their response involved a cultural creativity—a mixing of aspects of African cultures, Christian ideals, and cultural threads from their new environments. Some of the art forms they developed—for example, jazz—were genuinely new.

Hostility toward Blacks on the part of Whites was in some respects stronger in states where slavery had never existed than in the South itself. As the French political observer Alexis de Tocqueville noted in 1835, "The prejudice of race appears to be stronger in the states that have abolished slavery than in those where it still exists; and nowhere is it so intolerant as in those states where servitude has never been known." Moral rejection of slavery was confined to a few more educated groups. The main factors underlying the Civil War were political and economic; most Northern leaders were more interested in sustaining the Union than in abolishing slavery, although the abolition of slavery was an eventual outcome of the conflict. The formal abolition of slavery barely changed the real conditions of life for African Americans in the South. The "Black codes"—laws limiting the rights of Blacks—restricted the behavior of the former slaves and punished their transgressions in much the same way they had suffered under slavery. Acts legalizing segregation of Blacks from Whites in public places were passed. One kind of slavery was thus replaced by another: that of social, political, and economic discrimination.

Internal Migration from South to North

Industrial development in the North combined with the mechanization of agriculture in the South produced a progressive movement of African Americans northward. In 1900, more than 90 percent of African Americans lived in the South, mostly in rural areas. Today, three-quarters of the Black population live in Northern urban areas. African Americans used to be farm laborers and domestic servants, but in the course of little more than two generations, they have become mainly urban, industrial, and service-economy workers. But African Americans have not assimilated into the wider society in the way White immigrants did. They still face conditions of neighborhood segregation and poverty that other immigrants faced only upon arrival. Together with those of Anglo-Saxon origin, African Americans have lived in the United States far longer than most other immigrant groups. What was a transitional experience for most of the later White immigrants has become a seemingly permanent experience for Blacks.

The Civil Rights Movement

In contrast to other racial and ethnic minorities, Blacks and Native Americans have largely been denied opportunities for self-advancement. The National Association for the Advancement of Colored People (NAACP) and the National Urban League were founded in 1909 and 1910, respectively, to promote Black civil rights. However, they did not have a significant effect until after World War II, when the NAACP instituted a campaign against segregated public education. This struggle came to a head when the organization sued five school boards, challenging the concept of separate but equal schooling. In 1954, in *Brown v. Board of Education of Topeka, Kansas*, the U.S. Supreme Court unanimously ruled that "separate educational facilities are inherently unequal."

This decision underpinned struggles for civil rights from the 1950s to the 1970s. The strength of the resistance from many Whites persuaded Black leaders that mass militancy was necessary. In 1955, a Black woman, Rosa Parks, was arrested in Montgomery, Alabama, for declining to give up her seat on a bus to a White man. As a result, nearly the entire African American population of the city, led by a Baptist minister, Martin Luther King Jr., boycotted the transportation system for 381 days. Eventually, the city was forced to abolish segregation on public transportation.

Further boycotts and sit-ins followed, with the objective of desegregating other public facilities. The marches and demonstrations began to achieve a mass following from Blacks and from White sympathizers. In 1963, a quarter of a million civil rights supporters staged a march on Washington and cheered as King announced, "We will not be satisfied until justice rolls down like the waters and righteousness like a mighty stream." In 1964, the Civil Rights Act was passed by Congress and signed into law by President Lyndon B. Johnson, banning discrimination in public facilities, education, employment, and any agency receiving government funds. Subsequent bills outlawed discrimination in housing and ensured that African Americans became fully registered voters.

Although civil rights marchers were beaten up and some lost their lives, and in spite of some barriers to full realization of the Civil Rights Act's provisions, the law was fundamentally important. Its principles applied

Martin Luther King Jr. addresses a large crowd at civil rights march on Washington in 1963.

not just to African Americans but also to anyone subject to discrimination, including other ethnic groups and women. It spurred a range of movements asserting the rights of oppressed groups.

How successful has the civil rights movement been? On one hand, a substantial Black middle class has emerged. Many African Americans—such as the writer Toni Morrison, the literary scholar Henry Louis Gates Jr., former secretary of state Condoleezza Rice, media moguls Oprah Winfrey and Jay-Z, and President Barack Obama—have achieved positions of power and influence. On the other hand, a significant African American underclass remains trapped in the ghettos. Scholars have debated whether this underclass has resulted primarily from economic disadvantage or from dependency on the welfare system. Later in this chapter, we will examine the forms of inequality still experienced by African Americans and other minority groups.

Hispanics and Latinos in the United States

The wars of conquest that created the boundaries of the contemporary United States were directed not only against the Native American population but also against Mexico. The territory that later became California, Nevada, Arizona, New Mexico, and Utah—along with its quarter of a million Mexicans—was taken by the United States in 1848 as a result of the American war with Mexico. The terms *Mexican American* and *Chicano* refer to the descendants of these people, together with subsequent immigrants from Mexico. The term *Latino* refers to people descended from Latin America, while *Hispanic* tends to refer to anyone living in the United States descended from Spanish-speaking regions.

The four main groups of Hispanics in the United States come from Mexico (around 36.6 million), Puerto Rico (5.3 million), El Salvador (3.8 million), and Cuba (3.7 million). A further 10.4 million Spanish-speaking residents are from countries in Central and South America and other Hispanic or Latino regions (Stepler and Brown, 2016). California, Texas, Florida, New York, and Illinois have the largest Hispanic populations, accounting for nearly two-thirds of all Hispanics (Stepler and Lopez, 2016). In 2016, the more than 60 million Hispanics in the United States represented nearly 18.3 percent of the population—up from 4.7 percent in 1970 and 12.5 percent in 2000. However, the growth of the Hispanic population has slowed in recent years due to a decrease in immigration as well as declining birth rates among Hispanic women in the United States (Krogstad, 2016).

Mexican Americans

Mexican Americans reside mainly in California, Texas, and other southwestern states, although there are substantial groups in the Midwest and Northern cities as well. The majority work at low-paying jobs. In the post–World War II period up to the early 1960s, Mexican workers were admitted without much restriction. This period was succeeded by a phase of quotas on legal immigrants and deportations of undocumented immigrants. Today, undocumented immigrants continue to cross the border illegally. In 2016, there were an estimated 5.6 million unauthorized Mexican immigrants living in the United States, accounting for about half of all unauthorized immigrants

(Krogstad, Passel, and Cohn, 2017). Large numbers are intercepted and sent back each year, but most simply try again.

Because Mexico is a relatively poor neighbor of the wealthy United States, this flow of people northward is unlikely to cease. Undocumented immigrants can be employed more cheaply than indigenous workers, and they perform jobs that most of the rest of the population would not accept. Legislation passed by Congress in 1986 has enabled unauthorized immigrants living in the United States for at least five years to claim legal residence. In the past decade, however, immigration from Mexico has decreased. More Mexicans have left the United States than entered the country since the Great Recession ended (Gonzalez-Barrera, 2015).

Mexicans in the United States typically have levels of economic well-being and educational attainment far below that of native-born Americans. In 2017, 20 percent of Mexicans lived in poverty. More than two-thirds (71 percent) of Mexicans in the United States are proficient in English; however, only 12 percent hold bachelor's

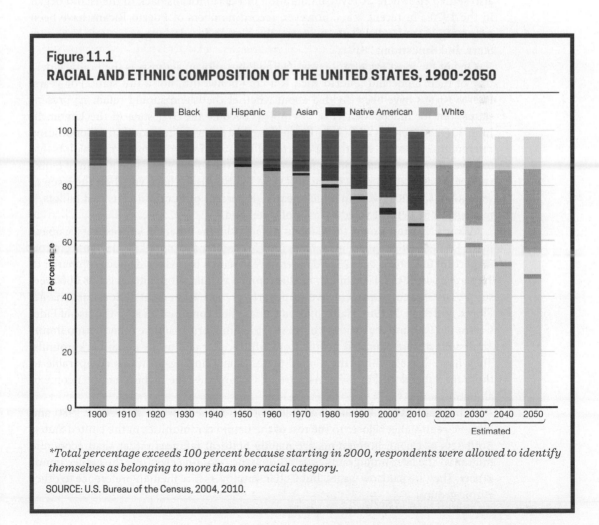

Figure 11.1
RACIAL AND ETHNIC COMPOSITION OF THE UNITED STATES, 1900-2050

Total percentage exceeds 100 percent because starting in 2000, respondents were allowed to identify themselves as belonging to more than one racial category.

SOURCE: U.S. Bureau of the Census, 2004, 2010.

degrees (Noe-Bustamante, Flores, and Shah, 2019b). Many Mexican Americans resist assimilation into the dominant English-speaking culture and increasingly display pride in their own cultural identity within the United States. Social scientists estimate that Mexican immigrants and their children may become increasingly assimilated into life in the United States in coming decades, due in part to policies that help them obtain an affordable college education. Given that about half of undocumented immigrants in the United States hail from Mexico, these policies will have a major impact on the lives of young Mexican immigrants.

Puerto Ricans and Cubans

Puerto Rico was acquired by the United States through war, and Puerto Ricans have been American citizens since 1917. The island is poor, and many of its inhabitants have migrated to the mainland United States to seek a better life. Puerto Ricans who emigrated originally settled primarily in New York City, but since the 1960s, they have also settled elsewhere. A reverse migration of Puerto Ricans back to the island began in the 1970s. In recent years, however, record numbers of Puerto Ricans have been migrating to the United States to escape the island's decade-long recession (Krogstad, Starr, and Sandstrom, 2017).

One of the most important issues facing Puerto Rican activists is the political destiny of their homeland. Puerto Rico is a commonwealth, not a full state. For years, Puerto Ricans have been divided about whether the island should retain its present status, opt for independence, or attempt to become the 51st state of the Union. In June 2017, 97 percent of Puerto Ricans voted in favor of statehood in a nonbinding referendum; however, less than a quarter of registered voters actually cast ballots due to boycotts. The vote came just a few weeks after the country declared a form of bankruptcy (Robles, 2017). This is the fifth time Puerto Ricans have voted on the issue of statehood. In a 2012 vote in which nearly 78 percent of Puerto Ricans cast ballots, a majority of 54 percent voted in favor of statehood.

A third Hispanic group, the Cubans, differs from the others in key respects. Cubans in the United States tend to be more successful compared to other U.S. Hispanic groups: 27 percent of Cubans ages 25 and older have at least a bachelor's degree (compared to 16 percent of all U.S. Hispanics), median annual earnings for Cubans is $28,000 (versus $25,000), and 16 percent live in poverty (versus 19 percent) (Noe-Bustamante, Flores, and Shah, 2019b). Half a million Cubans fled communism after the rise of Fidel Castro in 1959, and the majority of these settled in Florida. Unlike other Latino immigrants, most were educated people from white-collar and professional backgrounds. They have thrived within the United States, many finding positions comparable to those they abandoned in Cuba. As a group, Cubans have the highest family income of all Latinos.

A further wave of Cuban immigrants of less-affluent origin arrived in 1980 and live in circumstances closer to the rest of the Latino communities in the United States. Both sets of Cuban immigrants are mainly political refugees rather than economic migrants. The later immigrants have become the "working class" for the earlier immigrants. They are paid low wages, but Cuban employers hire them in preference to other ethnic groups.

Asian Americans

About 6 percent of the population of the United States is of Asian origin. Chinese Americans, Filipino Americans, and Indian Americans form the largest groups, but now there are also significant numbers of Vietnamese, Koreans, Japanese, and Pakistanis. As a result of the war in Vietnam, some 350,000 refugees from that country alone entered the United States in the 1970s.

Most of the early Chinese immigrants settled in California and worked in heavy industries, such as mining and railroad construction. The retreat of the Chinese into distinct Chinatowns was a response to the hostility they faced. Since Chinese immigration was legally banned in 1882, the Chinese remained isolated from the wider society, at least until recently.

The early Japanese immigrants also settled in California and the other Pacific states. During World War II, after the attack on Pearl Harbor by Japan, Japanese Americans in the United States were taken to remote "relocation centers" surrounded by barbed

Young Japanese Americans wait for the baggage inspection upon arrival at a World War II Assembly Center in Turlock, California, 1942. From here, they were transported to one of several internment camps for Japanese Americans.

wire and gun turrets. Even though most were American citizens, they were compelled to live in the hastily established camps for the duration of the war. Paradoxically, this situation promoted their greater integration within the wider society because, after the war, Japanese Americans did not return to their previously separate neighborhoods. Since then, they have attained high levels of education and income, marginally outstripping Whites. Japanese Americans have the highest rate of intermarriage of U.S. Asian groups: More than half of Japanese newlyweds married a non-Asian partner (Pew Research Center, 2013c).

Following the passage of a new immigration act in 1965, large-scale immigration of Asians again took place. Foreign-born Chinese Americans today outnumber those brought up in the United States. The newly arrived Chinese have avoided the Chinatowns in which the long-established Chinese remain.

Models of Ethnic Integration

In today's age of globalization and rapid social change, the rich benefits and complex challenges of ethnic diversity are confronting a growing number of states. As international migration accelerates along with the global economy, the mixing of populations will intensify. Meanwhile, ethnic tensions and conflicts continue, threatening the existence of some multiethnic states and hinting at protracted violence in others. How can ethnic diversity be accommodated and ethnic conflict be averted? Within

assimilation The acceptance of a minority group by a majority population, in which the new group takes on the values and norms of the dominant culture.

melting pot The idea that ethnic differences can be combined to create new patterns of behavior drawing on diverse cultural sources.

pluralism A model for ethnic relations in which all ethnic groups in the United States retain their independent and separate identities yet share equally in the rights and powers of citizenship.

multiculturalism A condition in which ethnic groups exist separately and share equally in economic and political life.

multiethnic societies, what should be the relationship between ethnic minority groups and the majority population? Four primary models of ethnic integration address these challenges: assimilation, the "melting pot," pluralism, and multiculturalism. These will be discussed shortly.

For many years, the two most common positive models of political ethnic harmony in the United States were those of assimilation and the melting pot. **Assimilation** meant that new immigrant groups would assume the attitudes and language of the dominant White community. The idea of the **melting pot** was different and involved merging different cultures and outlooks by stirring them all together. A newer model of ethnic relations is **pluralism**, in which ethnic cultures exist separately yet participate in the larger society's economic and political life. A recent outgrowth of pluralism is **multiculturalism**, in which ethnic groups exist separately and equally. It seems possible to create a society in which ethnic groups are separate and equal, as in Switzerland, where French, German, and Italian groups coexist in the same society. But this situation is unusual, and it is unlikely that the United States will mirror this achievement in the near future.

Global Migration

Today, floods of refugees and emigrants move restlessly across different regions of the globe, either escaping conflicts or fleeing poverty in search of a better life. Often they reach a new country only to face resentment from people whose forebears were immigrants themselves. Sometimes there are reversals, as in some areas of the United States along the Mexican border. Much of what is now California was once part of Mexico. Today, some Mexican Americans might say the new waves of Mexican immigrants are reclaiming what used to be their heritage—except that most of the existing groups in California don't quite see things this way.

Migratory Movements

Migration is accelerating as part of the process of global integration. Worldwide migration patterns reflect the rapidly changing economic, political, and cultural ties among countries (Global Map 11.2). It has been estimated that the world's migrant population in 1990 was more than 150 million people. In 2015, the number of migrants was estimated at nearly 244 million. Europe and Asia are home to nearly two-thirds of all international migrants (UN Population Division, 2015). The number will likely continue to increase in the twenty-first century, prompting some scholars to label this the "age of migration" (Castles and Miller, 1993). In fact, the Census Bureau projects that nearly one in five Americans will be foreign-born by 2060 (Trevelyan et al., 2016).

GLOBAL MIGRATORY MOVEMENTS SINCE 1973

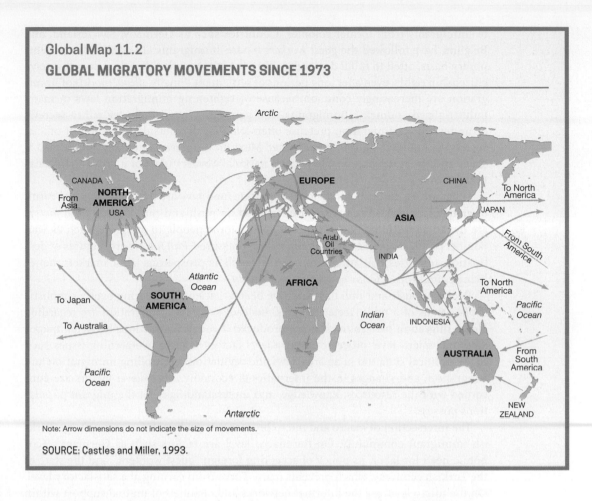

Note: Arrow dimensions do not indicate the size of movements.

SOURCE: Castles and Miller, 1993.

Immigration, the movement of people into a country to settle, and **emigration**, the process by which people leave a country to settle in another, combine to produce global migration patterns linking countries of origin and countries of destination. Migratory movements add to ethnic and cultural diversity and affect demographic, economic, and social dynamics. Rising immigration rates in many Western societies have challenged commonly held notions of national identity and have forced a reexamination of concepts of citizenship.

Scholars offer four models of migration to describe the main global population movements since 1945. The *classic model* applies to countries such as Canada, the United States, and Australia, which developed as nations of immigrants. These countries have encouraged immigration and promised citizenship to newcomers, although restrictions and quotas limit the annual intake. The *colonial model* of immigration, pursued by countries such as France and the United Kingdom, grants preferences

immigration The movement of people into one country from another for the purpose of settlement.

emigration The movement of people out of one country to settle in another.

to immigrants from former colonies. Countries such as Germany, Switzerland, and Belgium have followed the *guest workers model*: Immigrants are admitted on a temporary basis, often to fulfill demands within the labor market, but they do not receive citizenship rights, even after long periods of settlement. Finally, *illegal models* of immigration are increasingly common because of tightening immigration laws in many industrialized countries. Immigrants who gain entry into a country either secretly or under a nonimmigration pretense often live illegally, outside the realm of official society. Examples include undocumented Mexican immigrants in many Southern U.S. states and the refugees smuggled across national borders (part of a growing international business).

What are the forces behind global migration, and how are they changing as a result of globalization? Many early theories focused on push-and-pull factors. *Push factors* are dynamics within a country of origin that force people to emigrate, such as war, famine, political oppression, and population pressures. *Pull factors* are features of destination countries that attract immigrants, such as prosperous labor markets, better living conditions, and lower population density.

Recently, push-and-pull theories have been criticized for offering overly simplistic explanations of a multifaceted process. Instead, scholars of migration are regarding global migration patterns as systems produced through interactions between macro-level and micro-level processes. *Macro-level* factors refer to overarching issues such as the political situation in an area, laws and regulations controlling immigration and emigration, and changes in the international economy. *Micro-level* factors are concerned with the resources, knowledge, and understandings that the migrant populations possess.

The intersection of macro and micro processes is evident in Germany's large Turkish immigrant community. On the macro level are factors such as Germany's economic need for labor, its policy of accepting foreign "guest workers," and the state of the Turkish economy, which prevents many Turks from earning at a satisfactory level. On the micro level are the informal networks and channels of mutual support within the Turkish community in Germany and the strong links to family and friends in Turkey. Among potential Turkish migrants, knowledge about Germany and its "social capital"—its human or community resources—makes Germany one of the most popular destination countries. Supporters of the migration systems approach emphasize that no single factor can explain the process of migration. Rather, each migratory movement, like that between Turkey and Germany, is the product of an interaction between macro- and micro-level processes.

Stephen Castles and Mark Miller (1993) identified four tendencies that they claim will characterize migration patterns in the coming years:

1. **Acceleration**: Migration across borders is occurring in greater numbers than ever before.
2. **Diversification**: Most countries now receive immigrants of many different types—in contrast with earlier times, when particular forms of immigration, such as labor immigration or refugees, were predominant.
3. **Globalization**: Migration has become more global, involving a greater number of countries as both senders and recipients.

4. **Feminization**: A growing number of migrants are women, making contemporary migration much less male-dominated than previously. The increase reflects changes in the global labor market, including the growing demand for domestic workers, the expansion of sex tourism, "trafficking" in women, and the "mail-order brides" phenomenon.

> **diaspora** The dispersal of an ethnic population from an original homeland into foreign areas, often in a forced manner or under traumatic circumstances.

Global Diasporas

The term **diaspora** refers to the dispersal of an ethnic population from a homeland into foreign areas, often in a forced manner or under traumatic circumstances. Although members of a diaspora are scattered geographically, they are held together by factors such as a shared history, a collective memory of the homeland, or a common ethnic identity that is nurtured and preserved.

Robin Cohen has argued that diasporas occur in various forms, although the most commonly cited examples are those that result from persecution and violence. In *Global Diasporas* (1997), Cohen adopts a historical approach and identifies five categories of diasporas: *victim* (e.g., African, Jewish, and Armenian), *imperial* (British), *labor* (Indian), *trade* (Chinese), and *cultural* (Caribbean). In certain cases, such as that of the Chinese, large-scale population movements have occurred on a voluntary basis.

Despite the diversity of forms, all diasporas share certain key features (Cohen, 1997):

- a forced or voluntary movement from a homeland to a new region or regions
- a shared memory about the homeland, a commitment to its preservation, and a belief in the possibility of eventual return
- a strong ethnic identity sustained over time and distance
- a sense of solidarity with members of the same ethnic group also living in areas of the diaspora
- a degree of tension in relation to the host societies
- the potential for valuable and creative contributions to pluralistic host societies

Some scholars have accused Cohen of simplifying complex and distinctive migration experiences into a narrow typology by associating categories of diasporas with particular ethnic groups. Others argue that his conceptualization of diaspora is not sufficiently precise. Yet Cohen's study is valuable for demonstrating that diasporas are nonstatic, ongoing processes of maintaining collective identity and preserving ethnic culture in a rapidly globalizing world.

CONCEPT CHECKS

1 What are three reasons racism has flourished in the United States?

2 How did the civil rights movement help minority groups achieve equal rights and opportunities?

3 According to Castles and Miller, which four trends are likely to characterize migration in the near future?

4 What is a diaspora? Explain the role diasporas play in preserving ethnic culture in contemporary societies.

Do New Immigrants Help or Hinder the Nation's Economy?

The cultural and social landscape of the United States is viewed as an amalgam of diverse cultures, largely because of our nation's history as a refuge for immigrants. Today, however, policy makers and social scientists disagree over the social and economic costs of immigration.

Before discussing this debate, it is important to understand the current state of immigration to the United States. There are more than 44.4 million foreign-born individuals in the United States, comprising 13.6 percent of the total population (Radford, 2019). This represents a fourfold increase since 1960, when there were 9.7 million immigrants in the United States (Brown and Stepler, 2016). Each year about a million immigrants enter the United States (Lopez and Bialik, 2017). In contrast to the major wave of immigration in the 1880s and 1890s, just 12 percent of immigrants admitted into the United States since 1965 were of European origin. In fact, 51 percent have come from Latin America, including 25 percent from Mexico, and another 27 percent have come from South/East Asia (Radford, 2019). This change is attributed to two government acts: the 1965 Immigration and Nationality Act Amendments, which abolished preference for northern and western European immigrants and gave preference to "family reunification"—rather than occupational skills—as a reason for accepting immigrants; and the 1986 Immigration Reform and Control Act, which provided amnesty for many illegal immigrants. Since 2010, more Asian immigrants have come to the United States than Hispanic immigrants (Brown and Stepler, 2016). Immigration from Mexico

Hundreds of thousands of people marched in Los Angeles on April 15, 2006, to demand basic rights for immigrants.

People participate in a "We're Here to Stay" event in Washington, D.C., to protest President Trump's immigration policies.

has dropped precipitously in recent years, from 369,000 immigrants in 2005 to just 124,000 in 2017 (Migration Policy Institute, 2017; Radford, 2019).

Much of the debate focuses on new immigrants' ability to secure employment and achieve economic self-sufficiency. In his 1994 essay "The Economics of Immigration," economist George Borjas argued that since the 1980s, the United States has attracted "lower quality" immigrants with less education and few marketable job skills. Moreover, they are less skilled than both natives (i.e., people born in the United States) and earlier migrants; thus, they are more reliant on government assistance. Borjas estimates that recent immigrants will likely earn 20 percent less than native-born Americans for most of their working lives. In terms of the effect of immigrants on natives' economic prospects, Borjas argues that large-scale migration of less-skilled workers harms the economic opportunities of less-skilled natives—particularly African Americans. This occurs because immigrants increase the number of workers in the economy; as they create additional competition in the labor market, wages of the least-skilled workers fall.

Other economists and policy analysts claim that recent immigration has had either a positive effect or no influence on the U.S. economy. Economist Julian Simon (1981, 1989) has argued that immigrants benefit the U.S. economy by joining the labor force and paying into the federal revenue system for their whole lives. By the time they retire and collect government benefits such as Social Security and Medicare, their children will be covering these costs by working and paying into the tax system. Simon's arguments, however, assume that immigrants earn the same wages and are as employable as natives—an assumption refuted by Borjas's research.

Simon also holds that immigrants are a cultural asset to the United States. In fact, he claims that "the notion of wanting to keep out immigrants to keep our institutions and our values pure is prejudice" (quoted in Brimelow, 1995). He argues, moreover, that because human beings have the intelligence to adapt to their surroundings, the more immigrants that come to the United States, the larger the pool of potential innovators and problem solvers our nation will have.

Studies conducted by Simon and the Urban Institute, a nonprofit research organization, acknowledge that although some recent immigrants may benefit from federally funded programs such as welfare, these costs to the government are often quite short-term. Immigrant children who benefit from the U.S. educational system go on to become productive, taxpaying workers.

The National Immigration Forum has estimated that immigrant workers contribute significantly to the national economy. In 2017, immigrants represented 17 percent of the U.S. workforce; this includes about 4.6 percent of the workforce who are illegal immigrants (Radford, 2019). Even though most immigrants work in low-wage and hard-labor jobs, without them, the gross domestic product of the United States would be far less. Assessing the fiscal costs of immigration proves difficult, however. Although much of the public debate focuses on the costs of providing services to unauthorized immigrants, actual statistics documenting the number of unauthorized immigrants are difficult to obtain and verify. The Pew Research Center puts the population of unauthorized immigrants in the United States at 10.5 million in 2017. Furthermore, few policy analysts can predict whether U.S. immigration policy—or the characteristics of immigrants themselves—will change drastically in the future (Radford, 2019).

Has Real Progress Been Made Since the Civil Rights Movement of the 1960s?

On the one hand, an increasing number of Blacks joined the middle class by acquiring college degrees, professional jobs, and new homes. On the other hand, Blacks are far more likely than Whites to live in poverty and be socially isolated from good schools and economic opportunity. Also, many immigrants came to the United States throughout the 1980s and 1990s to find new economic opportunity. Yet some of these groups, particularly Mexicans, have among the lowest levels of educational achievement and live in dire poverty. Most sociologists agree on the facts about racial and ethnic inequality but disagree on how to interpret them. Is racial and ethnic inequality primarily the result of a person's racial or ethnic background, or does it reflect a person's class position? In this section, we examine how racial and ethnic inequality is reflected in educational and occupational attainment, income, health, residential segregation, and political power.

Educational Attainment

Differences between Blacks and Whites in levels of educational attainment have decreased, but these seem more the result of long-established trends than the direct outcome of the struggles of the 1960s. The U.S. high school graduation rate reached an all-time high of 85 percent in 2016–2017. Asian/Pacific Islander students had the highest graduation rate at 91 percent, compared to 89 percent for White students, 80 percent for Hispanic students, and 78 percent for Black students (National Center for Education Statistics [NCES], 2019b). The proportion of Blacks over the age of 25 with high school diplomas increased from about 20 percent in 1960 to 87 percent in 2016. By contrast, 90.1 percent of non-Hispanic Whites have completed high school (Figure 11.2A) (U.S. Bureau of the Census, 2020).

While more Blacks are attending college now than in the 1960s, a much higher proportion of Whites than Blacks have bachelor's degrees (Figure 11.2B). In today's global economy and job market, which value college degrees, the result is a wide disparity in incomes between Whites and Blacks (see the next section, "Employment and

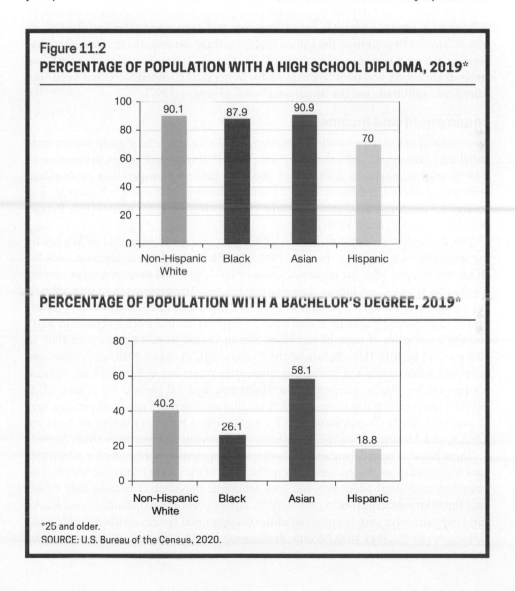

Figure 11.2

PERCENTAGE OF POPULATION WITH A HIGH SCHOOL DIPLOMA, 2019*

PERCENTAGE OF POPULATION WITH A BACHELOR'S DEGREE, 2019*

*25 and older.
SOURCE: U.S. Bureau of the Census, 2020.

Income"). Still, the number of bachelor's degrees awarded to Blacks each year nearly tripled between 1990 and 2015 (NCES, 2016b).

Another trend is the large gap in educational attainment between Hispanics and both Whites and Blacks. While the dropout rate for Hispanic students has decreased considerably in recent years, Hispanics still have the highest high school dropout rate of any group in the United States (9.5 percent, compared to 5.7 percent for Blacks and 4.6 percent for Whites) (NCES, 2018b). While rates of college attendance and graduation have improved for other groups, the rate for Hispanics has held relatively steady since the mid-1980s. Only about 18.8 percent hold a bachelor's degree, compared with 40.2 percent of non-Hispanic Whites (U.S. Bureau of the Census, 2020).

It is possible that these poor results reflect the large number of poorly educated immigrants from Latin America who have come to the United States since the 1980s, many of whom have limited English-language skills and whose children encounter difficulties in school. One study found, however, that even among Mexican Americans whose families have lived in the United States for three generations or more, there has been a decline in educational attainment (Bean et al., 1994). For Hispanics with low levels of education and poor language skills, living in the United States has been "the American nightmare, not the American dream" (Holmes, 1997).

Employment and Income

As a result of increased educational attainment, Blacks now hold slightly more managerial and professional jobs than they did in 1960, though still not in proportion to their overall numbers. In 2019, out of about 59 million managerial or professional positions in the United States, Blacks held 9.6 percent; Hispanics, 9.7 percent; and Asians, 8.5 percent; the other nearly three-quarters were held by Whites (U.S. Bureau of Labor Statistics [BLS], 2019i).

The unemployment rate of Black and Hispanic men outstrips that of Whites by the same degree today as in the early 1960s. While the total unemployment rates for all groups jumped after the economic crisis of 2007, the total unemployment rate for Blacks and Hispanics is higher than that for Whites. The proportion of unemployed Whites increased from 3.5 percent in 2005 to 7.5 percent in 2010, while the proportion of unemployed Blacks increased from 7.5 percent in 2005 to 13.4 percent in 2010, and the proportion of unemployed Hispanics increased from 4.8 percent in 2005 to 10.8 percent in 2010 (U.S. Bureau of the Census, 2012c). As of 2018, unemployment rates had fallen across the board, but disparities remained: 3.5 percent for Whites, 6.5 percent for Blacks, 4.7 percent for Hispanics, and 3.0 percent for Asians (BLS, 2019i). However, this gap is considerably smaller among more educated persons ages 25 and over. The unemployment rates for adults with a bachelor's degree or more are 2.0, 2.9, and 2.9 percent for Whites, Blacks, and Hispanics, respectively (BLS, 2019h).

There has also been debate about whether employment opportunities for minorities have improved or worsened, especially in the wake of the recent recession. Statistics on unemployment don't adequately measure economic opportunity because they reflect only those known to be looking for work. A higher proportion of disillusioned Blacks and Hispanics have simply opted out of the occupational system, neither working nor looking for work. They have become disillusioned by the frustration of searching for employment that is not there. Unemployment figures also do not reflect the increasing numbers of young minority men in prison (see also Chapter 7).

While the disparities between the earnings of Blacks and Whites have diminished, significant gaps in earnings and income remain (Figure 11.3). As measured in terms of median weekly earnings, Black men earned 74.9 percent of the level of pay of White men in 2019 (BLS, 2019q). In 1959, the proportion was 49 percent. Black women fare relatively better but still lag behind White women today, earning 81 percent as much as their White counterparts. The Black-White gap in household income has remained relatively unchanged since the early 1970s. In 2018, median household income for Blacks was $40,258, less than 60 percent of median household income for Whites that year ($68,145) (U.S Census Bureau, 2017l). Even more stark in the recent recessionary era is the Black-White gap in wealth: The median household net worth among Whites is 14 times that of Blacks ($132,483 versus $9,211 in 2013) (U.S. Bureau of the Census, 2017o).

Though the economic status of Blacks appears to have improved, prospects for Hispanics stagnated or worsened over the same time period. Between 2000 and 2012, Hispanic household incomes (adjusted for inflation) decreased significantly. Yet the rate of Hispanic household poverty has remained very similar to that of Blacks. In 2017, the poverty rate was 18.3 percent for Hispanics and 21.2 percent for Blacks (U.S. Census Bureau, 2018c). The large influx of poor immigrants explains some of the decline in average income, but even among Hispanics born in the United States, income levels have declined. As one Latino group leader commented, "Most Hispanic residents are caught in jobs like gardener, nanny, and restaurant worker that will never pay well and from which they will never advance" (quoted in Goldberg, 1997). As a result, Hispanic households lagged far behind White households. In 2017, median household

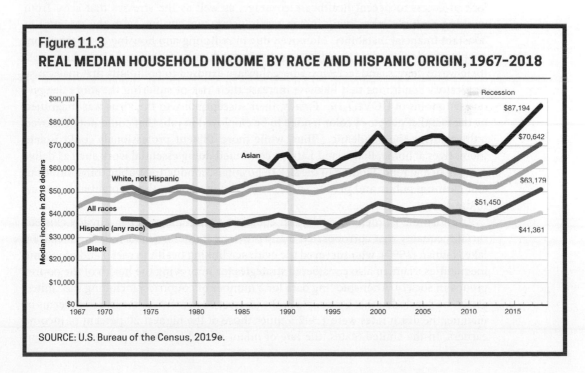

Figure 11.3
REAL MEDIAN HOUSEHOLD INCOME BY RACE AND HISPANIC ORIGIN, 1967-2018

SOURCE: U.S. Bureau of the Census, 2019e.

income of Hispanics was 74 percent that of non-Hispanic Whites (U.S. Census Bureau, 2017l). The median White household wealth was more than 10 times that of Hispanics ($139,300 versus $19,990) (Eggleston & Hays, 2019).

Health

Race not only affects our life chances in the form of education, employment, and income; it also has an impact on our health. The 2020 COVID-19 pandemic is a perfect case in point. Though the virus was dubbed the great equalizer—one that struck rich and poor alike—the statistics indicate otherwise. The rate of infection, hospitalization, and fatality was, in fact, far higher among Blacks and Latinos than it was among Whites and Asians. Although scientists and the media reported that the greatest risk factor for those infected was age, the number of fatalities among Blacks and Latinos ages 18 to 49 belied that claim. Indeed, by April 2020 it became clear that Blacks were bearing the brunt of the pandemic. Constituting a mere 13 percent of the U.S. population, they accounted for 30 percent of the deaths. In some states the disparity was even worse; in Wisconsin, for example, where Blacks amount to only 6 percent of the population, they accounted for 40 percent of the fatalities. As there is no evidence that people of color are more susceptible to coronavirus, how can this difference be explained?

The answer seems to lie primarily in preexisting medical issues caused by social inequality. Studies by the CDC indicate that Blacks and Latinos have significantly higher rates of obesity, high blood pressure, and diabetes—all conditions that exacerbate the effects of the coronavirus and increase the possibility of hospitalization and death. The vulnerability of these populations to these pre-conditions is due to a combination of factors, most notably their lower socioeconomic status within society, their lack of access to decent healthcare coverage, as well as the stresses that arise from working multiple jobs, living in sub-par housing, and dealing with the pressure of constant financial instability. Moreover, due to redlining and housing discrimination, people of color are also more likely to live in neighborhoods close to large highways, toxic waste dumps, and factories, where they are exposed to pollutants that may cause respiratory conditions that likewise increase their risk of suffering the more dangerous symptoms of COVID-19. Finally, their susceptibility to the virus was magnified by the fact that people of color tended to be employed in jobs that could not be moved online during the pandemic. Thus, while more affluent professionals could isolate themselves at home, Blacks and Latinos continued doing essential work such as delivering mail and food, tending to the sick in hospitals, conducting public transportation, and cleaning public and private spaces—thereby increasing their potential exposure to the disease.

In short, the pandemic was less an equalizer than a magnifier of already existent racial inequality that corroborated many previous studies, such as that conducted by Jake Najman (1993), who surveyed the evidence linking health to racial and economic inequalities. Najman also considered strategies for improving the health of the poorer groups in society. After studying data for a number of countries, including the United States, he concluded that for people in the poorest 20 percent, as measured in terms of income, the death rates were 1.5–2.5 times those of the highest 20 percent of income earners. In the United States, the rate of infant mortality for the poorest 20 percent was four times higher than for the wealthiest 20 percent. When differences were measured between the wealthiest Whites and the poorest African Americans in the United States, rather than only in terms of income, the contrast in infant mortality rates was even higher—five times higher for Blacks than for Whites. We have, however, seen some improvement in recent years: Between 1995 and 2017, the infant mortality rate for Blacks dropped from 14.6 to 11 deaths per 1,000 births, narrowing the Black-White gap in infant mortality by 30 percent.

While there remains a Black-White gap in life expectancy—the average age to which an individual at birth can expect to live—this gap has also decreased in recent years, from 7 years in 1990 to 3.5 years in 2017; this decrease is due in part to greater decreases in death rates for Blacks for heart disease, cancer, and HIV (Arias and Xu, 2019). The homicide death rate for Blacks has also gone down, though the peak rate for Black men is still nearly nine times higher than for White men (Smith and Cooper, 2013).

How might the influence of poverty and race on health be countered? Extensive programs of health education and disease prevention are one possibility. But such programs work better among prosperous, well-educated groups and usually produce only small changes in behavior. Increased accessibility to health services would help, but probably to a limited degree. The only truly effective policy option, it is argued, would be to attack poverty itself, so as to reduce the income gap between rich and poor (Najman, 1993).

Residential Segregation

Neighborhood segregation seems to have declined little over the past quarter century. Studies show that discriminatory practices between Black and White clients in the housing market continue (Pager and Shepard, 2008). Black and White children now attend the same schools in most rural areas of the South and in many smaller and medium-size cities throughout the country. Most Black college students now also attend the same colleges and universities as Whites, instead of all-Black institutions (Bullock, 1984; U.S. Department of Education, 2016). Yet, in the larger cities, a high level of educational segregation persists as a result of the continuing movement of Whites to suburbs or rural areas. A recent report out of UCLA on educational segregation found that the average Black student attends a school that is 49 percent Black while the average White student attends a school with just 8 percent Black students. In central cities, nearly 90 percent of students are non-White. Importantly, schools that serve majority Black and Latino students are also predominantly low income, amounting to what the study authors refer to as "double segregation"—segregation by both race and class (Orfield and Frankenberg, 2014).

In *American Apartheid* (1993), Douglas S. Massey and Nancy A. Denton argue that the history of racial segregation and its urban form, the Black ghetto, are responsible for the perpetuation of Black poverty and the continued polarization of Black and White people. Even many middle-class Blacks still find themselves segregated from White society. For them, as for poor Blacks, this becomes a self-perpetuating cycle. Affluent Blacks who could afford to live in predominantly White neighborhoods may choose not to because of the struggle for acceptance they might face. The Black ghetto, the authors conclude, was constructed through a series of well-defined institutional practices of racial discrimination—private behavior and public policies by which Whites sought to contain growing urban Black populations. Until policy makers, social scientists, and private citizens recognize the crucial role of such institutional discrimination in perpetuating urban poverty and racial injustice, the United States will remain a deeply divided and troubled society.

Political Power

Barack Obama made history when he was elected the first Black president of the United States in 2008. His election is part of a larger trend of Blacks making tremendous gains in holding elective offices; the number of Black public officials increased from 40 in 1960 to 9,101 in 2000 and more than 10,500 in 2010 (Bositis, 2001; Joint Center for Political and Economic Studies, 2011). In spite of high-profile victories such as Obama's, most elected Black officials hold relatively minor local positions, although they do include quite a few mayors and judges.

The share of representation that Latinos and African Americans have in Congress is still not proportionate to their percentage of the population; however, racial minorities now represent nearly a quarter of Congress. In 2019, there were 52 Black members and 42 Hispanic members of Congress (Brown and Atske, 2019). Most of this diversity is found in the House of Representatives. As of 2019, there were still only three Black senators—Kamala Harris from California, Cory Booker from New Jersey, and Tim

Barack Obama became the first African American president of the United States in the historic election of 2008.

Scott from South Carolina—and four Hispanic senators: Catherine Cortez Masto from Nevada, Bob Menendez from New Jersey, Marco Rubio from Florida, and Ted Cruz from Texas.

How Can Ethnic Conflict Be Reduced?

The most extreme and devastating form of group relations involves **genocide**—the systematic destruction of a racial, political, or cultural group. The most horrific recent instance of brutal destruction of such a group was the massacre of 6 million Jews in the German concentration camps during World War II. Other examples of mass genocide in the twentieth century span the globe. Between 1915 and 1923, more than a million Armenians were killed by the Ottoman Turkish government. In the late 1970s, 2 million Cambodians died under the Khmer Rouge. During the 1990s, in the African country of Rwanda, hundreds of thousands of the minority Tutsi were massacred by the dominant Hutu group. In the former Yugoslavia, Bosnian and Kosovar Muslims were executed by the Serb majority. And in the Darfur region of Sudan, the conflict between the Arabic-speaking, nomadic Janjaweed and the non-Arab Sudanese who speak African languages escalated to genocide, with hundreds of thousands of people killed and approximately 2 million forced to flee their homes.

The conflicts in the former Yugoslavia involved **ethnic cleansing**—the creation of ethnically homogeneous areas through the mass expulsion of other ethnic populations via targeted violence, harassment, threats, and campaigns of terror. Croatia, for example, became a "monoethnic" state after a costly war in which thousands of Serbs were expelled from the country. The war—which broke out in Bosnia in 1992 between Orthodox Serbs, Catholic Croats, and Bosnian Muslims—involved the ethnic cleansing of the Bosnian Muslim population at the hands of the Serbs. Thousands of Muslim men were forced into internment camps, and Muslim women were systematically raped. The war in Kosovo in 1999 was prompted by charges that Serbian forces were ethnically cleansing the Kosovar Albanian (Muslim) population from the province.

In Bosnia and Kosovo, ethnic conflict became internationalized. Hundreds of thousands of refugees fled to neighboring areas, further destabilizing the region. Western states intervened diplomatically and militarily to protect the human rights of targeted ethnic groups. In the short term, such interventions succeeded, yet they had unintended consequences as well. The fragile peace in Bosnia has persisted only through the presence of peacekeeping troops and the partitioning of the country into separate ethnic enclaves. In Kosovo, reverse ethnic cleansing ensued after the North Atlantic Treaty Organization (NATO) bombing campaign. Ethnic Albanian Kosovars began to drive the local Serb population out of Kosovo; the presence of NATO-led Kosovo Force troops was inadequate to prevent ethnic tensions from reigniting.

Violent conflicts worldwide are increasingly civil wars with ethnic dimensions. In a world of growing interdependence and competition, international factors become even

genocide The systematic, planned destruction of a racial, political, or cultural group.

ethnic cleansing The creation of ethnically homogeneous territories through the mass expulsion of other ethnic populations.

segregation The practice of keeping racial and ethnic groups physically separate, thereby maintaining the superior position of the dominant group.

more important in shaping ethnic relations, while the effects of internal ethnic conflicts are felt well outside national borders—sometimes provoking military intervention and sometimes requiring international war crimes tribunals. Responding to and preventing ethnic conflicts have become key challenges facing individual states and international political structures.

In some areas of the world, the concept of group closure has been institutionalized in the form of **segregation**—a practice whereby racial and ethnic groups are kept physically separate by law, thereby maintaining the superior position of the dominant group. For instance, in apartheid-era South Africa, laws forced Blacks to live separately from Whites and forbade sexual relations between races. In the United States, African Americans experienced numerous legal forms of segregation, including, until 1967, the prohibition of interracial marriage, which had been criminalized for more than 270 years in every state except Alaska and Hawaii. Even today, segregated residential areas still exist in many cities, leading some to claim that an American system of apartheid has developed (Massey and Denton, 1993).

Conflict and Economic Power

Many commentators have argued that the best way to reduce ethnic conflicts is to establish democracy and a free market; this would promote peace by giving everyone a say in running the country and giving all people access to the prosperity that comes from trade. In *World on Fire: How Exporting Free Market Democracy Breeds Ethnic Hatred and Global Instability* (2003), Amy Chua, a professor at Yale University, contests this view.

Chua's starting point is that in many developing countries, a small ethnic minority enjoys disproportionate economic power. One example is the White minority that exploited non-White ethnic groups in apartheid South Africa. Chua argues that the massacre of Tutsi by Hutu in Rwanda in 1994 and the hatred felt by Serbs toward Croats in the former Yugoslavia were partly related to the economic advantage enjoyed by the Tutsi and the Croats in their respective countries.

Chua often mentions the Chinese ethnic minority in Indonesia, where the free-market policies of the former dictator General Suharto enriched the country's tiny Chinese minority. In turn, Chinese Indonesians supported the Suharto dictatorship. By 1998, the year that mass pro-democracy demonstrations forced Suharto to resign, Chinese Indonesians controlled 70 percent of Indonesia's private economy but made up just 3 percent of its population. The end of Suharto's regime was accompanied by violent attacks against the Chinese minority. Chua (2003) writes, "The prevailing view among the pribumi [ethnic] majority was that it was 'worthwhile to lose 10 years of growth to get rid of the Chinese problem once and for all.'"

As Suharto's dictatorship collapsed, the United States and other Western countries called for the introduction of democratic elections. Yet Chua argues that introducing democracy to countries with what she calls "market dominant minorities," such as the Chinese in Indonesia, is not likely to bring peace but, instead, a backlash from the country's ethnic majority. Political leaders will emerge who scapegoat the resented minority and encourage the ethnic majority to reclaim the country's wealth for the "true" owners of the nation, as the pribumi majority in Indonesia did against the Chinese minority.

Chua's account illustrates that although democracy and the market economy are in principle beneficent forces, they must be grounded in an effective system of law and civil society. Where they are not, new and acute ethnic conflicts can emerge.

CONCEPT CHECKS

1 What are some of the main reasons there is a large gap in educational attainment between Hispanics and Blacks in the United States?

2 How do Massey and Denton explain the persistence of residential segregation?

3 Compare and contrast three forms of ethnic conflict.

THE BIG PICTURE

Chapter 11
Race, Ethnicity, and Racism

---

1 Basic Concepts — p. 378

2 Thinking About Racism — p. 381

LEARNING OBJECTIVES

1 Understand the differing meanings of the terms *race* and *ethnicity*. Understand why race is a highly contested topic.

2 Learn several key concepts that are important for understanding racism in the contemporary United States: color-blind racism, White privilege, institutional racism, overt racism, and microaggressions.

TERMS TO KNOW

1 minority group • race • ethnicity

2 racism • prejudice • stereotyping • scapegoats • discrimination • White privilege • institutional racism • racial microaggressions

CONCEPT CHECKS

1
1. How do the changing racial categories used on the Census help demonstrate that race is socially constructed?
2. Explain the difference between ethnicity and race.
3. Why are Hispanics and African Americans considered to be minority groups in American society?

2
1. In what ways does the killing of George Floyd at the hands of a Minneapolis police officer provide evidence of institutional racism?
2. How does color blindness maintain racial inequality?
3. Provide one example of White privilege. What does McIntosh mean by "an invisible weightless knapsack"?
4. What is a microaggression? Why is this idea problematic to some?

Exercises: Thinking Sociologically

1. Review the discussion of the assimilation of different American minorities. Then write a short essay comparing the assimilation experiences of Asians and Latinos. In your essay, identify the criteria for assimilation and discuss which group has assimilated most readily. Then explain the sociological reasons for the difference in assimilation between the two groups.

2. Does affirmative action still have a future in the United States? On the one hand, increasing numbers of African Americans have joined the middle class by acquiring college degrees, professional jobs, and new homes. On the other hand, Blacks are still far more likely than Whites to live in poverty, attend poor schools, and lack economic opportunity. Given these differences and other contrasts mentioned in the text, do we still need affirmative action?

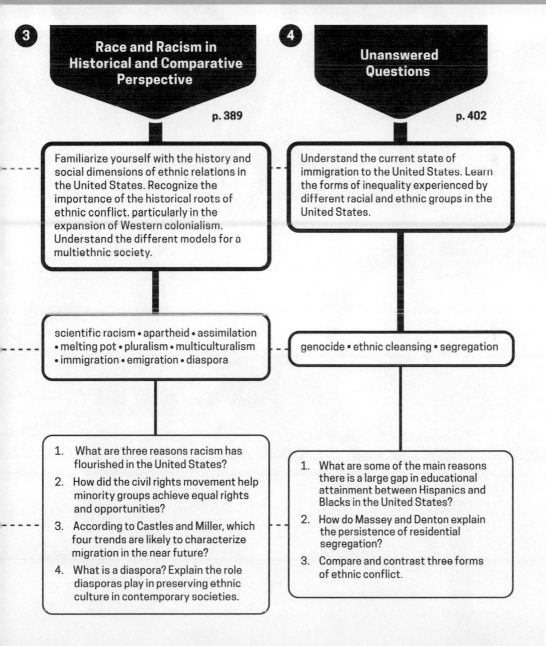

3

Race and Racism in Historical and Comparative Perspective

p. 389

Familiarize yourself with the history and social dimensions of ethnic relations in the United States. Recognize the importance of the historical roots of ethnic conflict, particularly in the expansion of Western colonialism. Understand the different models for a multiethnic society.

scientific racism • apartheid • assimilation • melting pot • pluralism • multiculturalism • immigration • emigration • diaspora

1. What are three reasons racism has flourished in the United States?

2. How did the civil rights movement help minority groups achieve equal rights and opportunities?

3. According to Castles and Miller, which four trends are likely to characterize migration in the near future?

4. What is a diaspora? Explain the role diasporas play in preserving ethnic culture in contemporary societies.

4

Unanswered Questions

p. 402

Understand the current state of immigration to the United States. Learn the forms of inequality experienced by different racial and ethnic groups in the United States.

genocide ▪ ethnic cleansing ▪ segregation

1. What are some of the main reasons there is a large gap in educational attainment between Hispanics and Blacks in the United States?

2. How do Massey and Denton explain the persistence of residential segregation?

3. Compare and contrast three forms of ethnic conflict.

12

Aging

Which of the following is true about older adults (persons age 65+) in the United States today?

A   Physical illness and senility are inevitable aspects of aging.

B   Older adults are economically well off because benefits such as Social Security and Medicare provide a stable income and free health insurance.

C   The most common residence for older adults is a nursing home.

D   Older adults are a highly diverse population, with their health and well-being varying widely by age, race, gender, and social class.

TURN THE PAGE FOR THE CORRECT ANSWER.

1 Basic Concepts

Learn some basic facts about the increase in the proportion of the U.S. population that is age 65 and older. Recognize that aging is a combination of biological, psychological, and social processes. Understand how technological advances affect each of the three aging processes.

2 Growing Old: Theories of Aging

Understand key theories of aging, particularly those that focus on how society shapes the social roles of older adults and that emphasize aspects of age stratification.

3 Research on Aging in the United States Today

Evaluate the experience of growing old in the United States and how this experience is shaped by race, social class, gender, and birth cohort.

4 Unanswered Questions: The Political and Economic Impact of Population Aging

Understand and analyze the politics of generational equity. Assess the social issues of graying on a global level.

What do the terms *senior citizen, elderly*, or *old age* conjure up in your mind? For many Americans, old age is viewed as a time of senility, poverty, poor health, loneliness, and celibacy. Others view old age as a "golden" time, when cash-flush retirees sell their homes, move to Florida, and live the good life, surrounded by their golf buddies and devoted grandchildren (Carr, 2019). The truth is somewhere in between. Older adults—persons ages 65 and older—are a highly diverse group, with some enjoying good health, wealth, and happiness, and others suffering from poverty, illness, physical disability, and loneliness. This divide was especially apparent during the COVID-19 crisis of 2020; older adults were dying in large numbers, with those in poor health even prior to the pandemic the most vulnerable. Often, the trajectories that set one on the path toward a rewarding or distressing later life begin decades earlier, sometimes as early as childhood.

Witness the cases of Judy Hofstadter and Alice Garvin. Judy Hofstadter, 81, lives in New York City and works full time as a financial planner at a large firm. She keeps up a vigorous exercise regimen, shops weekly at the local farmers' market for healthy food, devotes time to organizations promoting peace in the Middle East, and donates her time and money to political candidates she believes in. In 2006, while going door to door before midterm elections, she tripped and broke her wrist. "I sacrificed my hand in service to my country," Hofstadter says, laughing. Although she now suffers from breast cancer, significant hearing loss, a serious case of glaucoma, and excruciating neck and back pain, "she has learned to make lemonade from everything," according to her son David Tuller (2009).

Hofstadter learned at a young age how to overcome challenges with her sense of humor

THE ANSWER IS D.

intact. Born into a middle-class Jewish family that promoted academic achievement, Hofstadter entered Harvard Law School in 1951, joining only the second class to admit women. She married a physician who was physically abusive, so she gathered up the courage to take her two children and leave him. To preserve her spirit during those difficult years after she left, as her son David notes, "She funneled her energy and passion into political and social causes. She fought for integrated housing and civil liberties and infused [her children] with her progressive spirit" (Tuller, 2009).

Her fighting spirit hasn't waned in later life. When she was first diagnosed with breast cancer, David said that she "investigated the issue like a lawyer. . . . She scoured the literature, interrogated researchers at medical conferences, and joined the boards of breast cancer advocacy groups." Her son proudly describes her as "my model . . . for how to age with grace, compassion and vitality." According to Hofstadter, "I think having passions takes you outside of yourself and animates your life. . . . It makes you want to take care of yourself so you can keep on going. I still look forward to the next adventure."

Hofstadter is fortunate to have had a prestigious education, an intellectually challenging and well-paying career, two emotionally supportive and financially secure children—one a professor, the other a therapist—and a well-honed sense of problem solving. Not all older adults are so lucky. Just a few miles away, in Brooklyn, 77-year-old Alice Garvin has been dealt a much worse hand.

Alice Garvin is now fighting foreclosure, while also struggling to support her children, grandchildren, great-grandson, and grandnephew. Garvin, a retired home health aide, first faced foreclosure four years ago when she found an eviction notice on the front door of her apartment building (Mascia, 2009). The second time, the loss of her apartment was a blessing in disguise; she was evicted from a rundown apartment in a dangerous neighborhood "she couldn't wait to leave" because of gunshots outside and "bugs falling from the ceiling" (Mascia, 2009). In both cases, Mascia notes, "Foreclosure was beyond her control: she is not a homeowner, but a tenant." Garvin was saved by a local charity that provided her with money so she could move into a new apartment big enough for her and her large extended family.

Now in her new apartment, Garvin continues to struggle financially. Her family "survives on a patchwork of welfare," including Social Security for Garvin, disability payments for her children and grandchildren, and an occasional visit to a food pantry. Foreclosure and economic struggles are difficult for anyone, but for Garvin, "it is just the latest blow in a lifetime filled with difficulty." Born in South Carolina, Garvin was "an orphan by the time she was 14; she was 36 when her husband died from an alcohol-related illness. Four of her six children have died"—one from the effects of Agent Orange exposure in the Vietnam War, two from pneumonia, and one from AIDS.

Garvin is caregiver and financial provider to her two surviving sons; one cannot work because of a congenital heart problem, and the other was nearly beaten to death in a mugging 20 years ago and cannot work due to frequent seizures. Her two teenage grandsons and grandnephew were born addicted to cocaine and have lingering behavioral problems. And this past spring, Garvin became a great-grandmother. Despite her seemingly insurmountable responsibilities, she keeps a positive attitude: "I try to look forward, not back. I have a lot to keep me going now."

Growing old can be a fulfilling and rewarding experience, as Judy Hofstadter knows. Or it can be filled with adversity and stress, as Alice Garvin has discovered. For most older Americans, the experience of aging lies somewhere in between. How we experience old age is shaped by our gender, race, social class, and historical context. Yet aging also is a cumulative process and is molded by our experiences, resources, and struggles in earlier life. How older adults navigate their later years reflects not only their personal resources, such as optimism, problem-solving skills, and energy, but also structural factors, such as economic opportunities and public policies.

Although old age is often accompanied by physical and cognitive declines and economic and psychological distress—as the lives of Hofstadter and Garvin reveal—more Americans are leading longer, healthier, and more productive lives than ever before. In 2020, more than 56 million Americans were age 65 or older, comprising 17 percent of the U.S. population, including more than 6.7 million adults over 85 years old (Mather and Kilduff, 2020). In this chapter, we examine the nature of aging in U.S. society, exploring what it means to grow old in a world that is rapidly changing.

We first review the core concepts of aging, including the graying of the U.S. population and biological, psychological, and social aspects of aging. We next look at sociological theories that describe how people adapt to growing old. This will lead us to a discussion of contemporary research on aging in the United States, focusing on some of the special challenges facing older adults, including social isolation, health declines, and elder abuse. We next delve into important, although unresolved, questions regarding political and economic issues surrounding the aging of the American population, including Social Security and Medicare. The future of these programs affects the lives of all Americans and will gain increasing significance given the growing numbers of older people. We conclude with a discussion of the graying of the world population and what this means for individuals, governments, and societies.

1 BASIC CONCEPTS

The Graying of Society

The United States and other industrial societies are said to be **graying**—that is, experiencing an increase in the proportion of the population classified as **older adults**. Older adults are generally considered to be persons ages 65 and older, although, as we will see later in this chapter, aging is a multifaceted process. Graying is the result of two long-term trends in industrial societies: the tendency of families to have fewer children (discussed in Chapter 15) and the fact that people are living longer.

For most of human history, the average life expectancy at birth was less than 20 years; the main reason was that many people died in infancy or during early childhood. As such, the "average" age at which a person died was very low. About 2,000 years ago, the average newborn baby in Rome could expect to live to just age 22. In 1900 in the United States, the average baby boy could expect to live to about age 46 and the average baby girl to about 48. Today, by contrast, the average baby boy born in the United States has a life expectancy of 76.2 years, while life expectancy for the average baby girl is 81.2 years (Figure 12.1) (World

graying A term used to indicate that an increasing proportion of a society's population is older.

older adults Adults ages 65 and older.

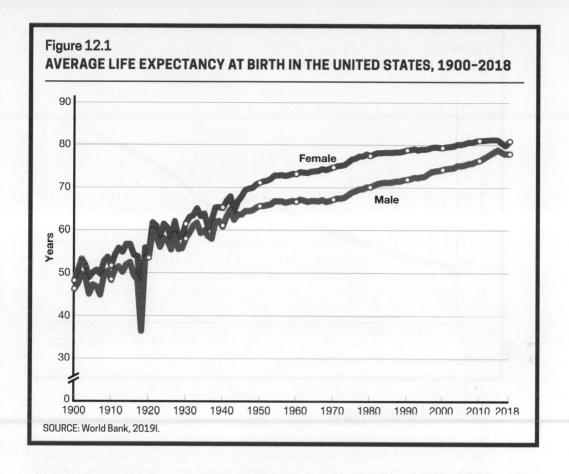

Figure 12.1
AVERAGE LIFE EXPECTANCY AT BIRTH IN THE UNITED STATES, 1900–2018

SOURCE: World Bank, 2019l.

Bank, 2019l). However, there is enormous variation in life expectancy depending on where a baby is born—from 84 years in Japan to 53 years in Sierra Leone (World Health Organization, 2018). Even within the United States, life expectancy varies widely; a Black baby boy born today can expect to live until about 71, whereas a White baby girl will live an average of 10 years longer—until age 81 (Kochanek et al., 2020).

What explains the aging of the United States and other societies? Modern agriculture, sanitation systems, epidemic control, improved nutrition, and medicine have all contributed to a decline in mortality and an increase in life expectancy throughout the world. In most societies today, fewer children die in infancy and more adults survive until their seventies, eighties, and even older. The U.S. population, like that of other industrial societies, is aging even faster than that of less industrialized nations. The number of older adults in the United States is expected to nearly double, from 52 million in 2018 to more than 95 million by 2060 (Mather et al., 2019).

Given the growing numbers of older adults and the declining numbers of younger persons, the median age of the population is rising. In 1850, half the U.S. population was older than 19. Today, half is over 38; by 2050, half will be over 42 (Figure 12.2). These trends have enormous importance for the future of U.S. society. In a culture that often worships eternal youth, what will happen when a quarter of the population is over 65?

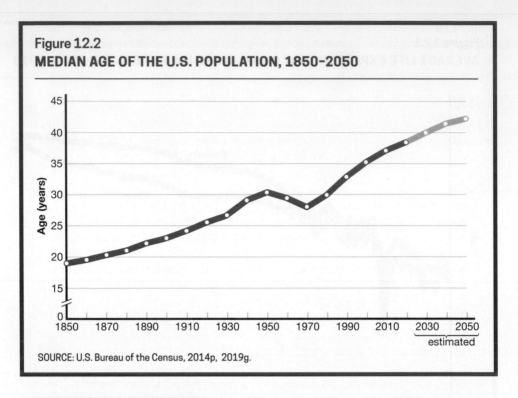

Figure 12.2
MEDIAN AGE OF THE U.S. POPULATION, 1850–2050

SOURCE: U.S. Bureau of the Census, 2014p, 2019g.

How Do People Age?

In examining the nature of aging, we will draw on studies of **social gerontology**, a discipline concerned with the study of the social aspects of aging. Studying aging requires a sociological imagination. How people experience old age is shaped by social and historical context (Riley, Foner, and Waring, 1988). For Americans born in the first quarter of the twentieth century, a high school education was regarded as more than sufficient for most available jobs, and most people did not expect to live much past their sixties—and then only at the cost of suffering a variety of disabilities. Today, those very same people find themselves in their seventies and eighties; many are relatively healthy, unwilling to disengage from work or social life, and in need of more schooling than they ever dreamed would be necessary to compete in today's information-based economy.

What does it mean to age? **Aging** can be defined as the combination of biological, psychological, and social processes that affect people as they grow older (Abeles and Riley, 1987; Atchley, 2000; Riley, Foner, and Waring, 1988). These processes can be thought of as three different, although interrelated, developmental clocks: (1) biological, which refers to the physical body; (2) psychological, which refers to the mind, including one's mental, emotional, and cognitive capabilities; and (3) social, which refers to cultural norms, values, and role expectations related to age. There is an enormous

social gerontology The study of aging and older adults.

aging The combination of biological, psychological, and social processes that affect people as they grow older.

range of variation in all three of these processes. The very meaning of old age is changing rapidly, both because research is dispelling many outdated notions about aging and because advances in nutrition, health, and medical technology now enable many people to live longer, healthier lives than ever before.

Biological Aging

The biological effects of aging are well established, although the exact chronological age at which they occur varies greatly depending on one's genes, lifestyle, and luck. In general, for men and women alike, biological aging typically means:

- Declining vision, as the eye lens loses its elasticity
- Hearing loss, first of higher-pitched tones, then of lower-pitched ones
- Wrinkles, as the skin's underlying structure becomes more and more brittle
- A decline in muscle mass and an accompanying accumulation of fat, especially around the abdomen
- A drop in cardiovascular efficiency, as less oxygen can be inhaled and used during exercise
- Declining immune function, and less capacity to fight viruses

The latter condition, in particular, is one reason why older adults have been particularly vulnerable to both contracting and dying of COVID-19. Older adults make up just 16 percent of the U.S. population, but they accounted for one-third of all cases, 45 percent of all hospitalizations, and 80 percent of deaths associated with COVID-19. This risk of death increased steadily with age, with persons ages 85+ three times more likely than those ages 65 to 84 from die from COVID-19 (CDC COVID-19 Response Team, 2020a). However, it is important to once again point out the vast diversity among older adults. Those persons most vulnerable to COVID-19 are those with underlying health conditions, a factor that is related to old age but not synonymous with it. Many older adults have no underlying conditions, and as such are not particularly vulnerable to the virus.

Yet despite troubling media images of older adults' deaths from COVID-19, many older adults fared safely during the pandemic. Biological aspects of aging are inevitable, but they can be partly delayed by good health, low to modest levels of stress, proper diet and nutrition, and regular participation in vigorous exercise (Butler, 2010). Lifestyle can make a significant health difference for people of all ages. Some scientists have even argued that with a healthy lifestyle and advances in medical technology, more and more people will be able to live relatively illness-free lives until they reach their biological maximum, experiencing only a brief period of sickness just before death (Fries, 1980; Vaupel et al., 1998). Eventually, of course, the biological clock runs out for everyone. About 90 to 100 years seems to be the upper end of the genetically determined age distribution for most human beings, although some have argued that it may be as high as 120 (Fries, 1980; Olshansky, Carnes, and Grahn, 2003).

Gerontologists agree that senescence, or physical decline that accompanies aging, is inevitable. However, today's older adults now have unprecedented access to many assistive technologies that enable them to live full and active lives. These are products that increase, maintain, or improve the functional capabilities of individuals with disabilities. Such products range from hearing aids and eyeglasses to canes, walkers,

What are some of the assistive technologies that allow us to live full, active lives as we age?

and "grabbers" (which help frail older adults reach a box of cereal on a high shelf in their kitchen), to computer-screen magnifiers and oversize kitchen utensils. Gerontologists also consider household modifications, such as chair lifts, wheelchair ramps, and grab bars in the shower, as assistive devices.

A recent study found that about 30 percent of older adults had used a mobility device, including a cane, walker, wheelchair, or scooter, in the last month (Freedman et al., 2013). One of the most important benefits of such devices is that they enable older adults to maintain their independence, keep up daily routines, and stay in their own homes (rather than move to an assisted-living facility) for as long as possible. These devices are particularly helpful for preventing falls; one-third of persons over age 65 report a fall each year, making falls the leading cause of accidents and a common trigger of hospitalizations among older adults (Center for Technology and Aging, 2010). In this way, technological advances have altered the impact of biological aging on older adults' lives.

Psychological Aging

The psychological effects of aging are less well established than the physical effects. Even though memory, intelligence, reasoning skills, and both the capacity and motivation to learn are widely assumed to decline with age, research into the psychology of aging suggests a much more complicated process (Schaie and Willis, 2010). For most people, memory and learning ability, for example, do not decline significantly until very late in life, although the speed with which one recalls or analyzes information may slow somewhat, giving the false impression of mental impairment. For most older adults whose lives are stimulating and rich, such mental abilities as motivation to learn, clarity of thought, creativity, and problem-solving capacity do not decline significantly until the late eighties (Cohen, 2005; Atchley, 2000).

Even **Alzheimer's disease**—the progressive deterioration of brain cells that is the primary cause of dementia in old age—is relatively rare in noninstitutionalized persons under 75, although it afflicts about one-third (32 percent) of all people over 85 and is the sixth leading cause of death in the United States (Alzheimer's Association, 2017). Given the projected steep growth in the number of persons 85 and older in the coming decades, caring for and treating Alzheimer's patients will be an important challenge. An estimated 5.6 million older

Alzheimer's disease A degenerative disease of the brain resulting in progressive loss of mental capacity.

social aging The norms, values, and roles that are culturally associated with a particular chronological age.

adults currently suffer from Alzheimer's disease. This number is expected to increase by almost 35 percent, to 7.1 million older adults, by 2025 and may nearly triple by 2050.

Scientists have recently developed new technologies that enable an earlier and more accurate detection of dementia and Alzheimer's. This advance holds great promise for treating patients before the disease progresses too far (Alzheimer's Association, 2017). Former president Ronald Reagan is perhaps the most famous example of someone who suffered from Alzheimer's; his wife Nancy Reagan spoke out publicly about the profound physical and emotional challenges of providing care to an Alzheimer's patient and called for the use of stem-cell research to find a cure (Collins, 2004). Gerontologists are cautiously optimistic about the promise of science to help fight the ravages of Alzheimer's disease.

Social Aging

Social aging refers to the norms, values, and roles that are culturally associated with a particular chronological age. Historically, social roles in the United States have been closely tied to one's age. The role of "student" was held by young people, while the roles of "worker" (typically for men) and "parent" (typically for women) were held by young adults and middle-aged persons, and the role of "retiree" was reserved for older adults. Social roles also were highly age segregated; the only "old" person in a college classroom was typically the professor.

Throughout the twentieth century, however, links between age and social roles have grown more tenuous, and social roles have become less segregated by age. For example, as young people stay in school longer and graduate from school later, they delay the traditional markers of "adulthood"—full-time employment, marriage, childbearing, and home ownership—until their thirties, forties, and even later. Young people in their twenties and thirties are living with their parents, unable to afford their own apartments against the backdrop of the Great Recession (Parker, 2012). People who become new parents for the first time in their forties are parents to young adults at age 65, while in prior generations, most people aged 65 were happily settled into the role of grandparent or even great-grandparent.

Similarly, changes in the labor force mean that adults are working into late life and many need to retrain or retool their skills. "Nontraditional age" students now represent nearly 50 percent of college enrollment. Many older adults saw their pensions, home values, and savings evaporate in the recession that began in 2007, forcing them to delay their retirement past age 65. Some remain in their lifelong jobs, while others cut back to part-time hours or take "bridge" (transitional) jobs between their full-time lifelong job and retirement (Sackmann and Wingens, 2003). Yet, retirement is no longer the exclusive domain of older adults. Some middle-aged adults, especially those in high-paying jobs, may be forced to retire early

CONCEPT CHECKS

1 What is the "graying" of the U.S. population?

2 Compare and contrast biological, psychological, and social aging processes.

3 How has technology affected the processes of biological, psychological, and social aging?

if their companies can no longer afford to employ them—instead hiring less skilled, less costly younger workers.

Social aging, like biological and psychological aging, has been transformed by technology. In earlier decades, older adults (especially women) were considered physically undesirable because they defied the cultural standard of youthful beauty. Today, cosmetic surgery helps older women (and men, to a lesser extent) maintain a taut, dewy complexion via processes such as Botox injections and face lifts, and a svelte physique via procedures such as tummy tucks and liposuction (Brooks, 2017). The cultural belief that older adults are uninterested in sex or incapable of maintaining a healthy sex life has been shattered by the development of impotence drugs such as Viagra (Loe, 2004). In the United States today, virility drugs top $5 billion in annual sales. Social scientists agree that, more than ever before, age is "just a number."

2   GROWING OLD: THEORIES OF AGING

Social gerontologists have developed several influential theories of aging in Western society. Some of the earliest theories emphasized individual adaptation to changing social roles as a person grows older. Later theories focused on how society shapes the social roles of older adults, often in inequitable ways, and emphasized various aspects of age stratification. The most recent theories emphasize micro-macro links and focus on how persons ages 65+ actively create their lives within specific institutional and historical contexts (Bengston, Putney, and Johnson, 2005).

The First Generation of Theories: Functionalism

The earliest theories of aging reflected the functionalist approach that was dominant in sociology during the 1950s and 1960s. These early theories often assumed that aging brings with it physical and psychological decline and that changing social roles should take into account this decline (Hendricks, 1992). Functionalist theories, in particular, emphasized how individuals adjusted to changing social roles as they aged and how the roles older adults fulfilled were useful to society.

Talcott Parsons (1960), one of the most influential functionalist theorists of the 1950s, argued that U.S. society needs to find roles for older persons that are compatible with their advanced age. He expressed concern that the United States, with its emphasis on youth and its denial of death, had failed to provide roles that adequately drew on the potential wisdom and maturity of its older citizens. This failure could lead to older people becoming discouraged and alienated from society. To achieve a "healthy maturity," Parsons (1960) argued, older adults need to adjust psychologically to their changed circumstances, while society needs to redefine the social roles of the older population.

disengagement theory A functionalist theory of aging that holds that it is functional for society to remove people from their traditional roles when they become older adults, thereby freeing up those roles for others.

socioemotional selectivity theory The theory that adults maintain fewer relationships as they age, but that those relationships are of higher quality.

Disengagement Theory

Parsons's ideas set the stage for the development of **disengagement theory**, which asserts that it is functional for society to relieve people of their traditional roles when they become old, thereby freeing up those roles for other, younger persons (Cumming and Henry, 1961; Estes, Binney, and Culbertson, 1992). According to this perspective, given the increasing frailty, illness, and dependency of older persons, it becomes increasingly dysfunctional for them to occupy roles they are no longer capable of adequately fulfilling. Older adults should therefore retire from their jobs, pull back from civic life, and eventually withdraw from their other activities and relationships. Disengagement is assumed to be functional for society because it opens up roles formerly filled by the older adults for younger people, who presumably will carry them out with fresh energy and new skills. Disengagement also is assumed to be functional for older adults because it enables them to abandon potentially taxing social roles and instead invest their energies in more private introspective activities as they prepare for their eventual demise.

Although there is some empirical support and ample anecdotal evidence for the validity of disengagement theory, the idea that old people should completely disengage from the larger society presumes that old age necessarily involves frailty and dependence. This is an incorrect assumption; one in five older adults lives disease-free (Schafer and Ferraro, 2011), and 7 percent of deaths in old age occur suddenly, meaning the older person had no illness prior to death (Lunney et al. 2003). Recent studies suggest that selective disengagement from some roles—rather than complete disengagement from all roles—can be healthy if the older adult chooses which roles to drop and which to maintain. For example, most retirees report quite high levels of life satisfaction; however, the happiest retirees are those in good health, with strong social ties, adequate financial resources, and engagement in other productive activities, such as volunteering or part-time work (Atchley, 2000; Barnes and Parry, 2004).

Scholars also have found that older adults may cut back on the number of social relationships they maintain, often dropping those relationships that are not a source of great joy or support. **Socioemotional selectivity theory** states that older adults selectively choose to maintain fewer, but higher-quality, relationships as they age and experience declines in health. Casual, less rewarding ties may lapse, while only the most meaningful relationships are maintained (Carstensen, Isaacowitz, and Charles, 1999).

Activity Theory

Given this strong evidence that disengagement from all social roles is rare, and such disengagement does not ease the aging process, the very assumptions of disengagement theory have been challenged, often by some of the theory's original proponents (Cumming, 1963, 1975; Hendricks, 1992; Henry,

Activity theory holds that older adults who stay busy and engaged can be functional for society.

1965; Hochschild, 1975; Maddox, 1965, 1970). These challenges gave rise to another functionalist theory of aging, which drew conclusions quite opposite to those of disengagement theory: activity theory.

According to **activity theory**, people who are busy and engaged, leading fulfilling and productive lives, can be functional for society. The guiding assumption is that an active individual is much more likely to remain healthy, alert, and socially useful. In this view, people should remain engaged in their work and other social roles as long as they are capable of doing so. If a time comes when a particular role becomes too difficult or taxing, then other roles can be sought—for example, volunteer work in the community.

Activity theory is supported by research showing that continued activity well into old age—whether it's volunteer work, paid employment, hobbies, or visits with friends and family—is associated with enhanced mental and physical health (Birren and Bengston, 1988; Rowe and Kahn, 1987; Schaie, 1983). Yet critics observe that not all activities are equally valuable, giving rise to the development of **continuity theory**. This theory specifies that older adults' well-being is enhanced when they participate in activities that are consistent with their personality, preferences, and activities earlier in life (Atchley, 1989). For instance, a retired elementary school teacher may find volunteering at a local elementary school to be much more satisfying than taking bus trips to Atlantic City or playing bingo at a local community center.

Critics of functionalist theories of aging argue that these theories emphasize the need for older persons to adapt to existing conditions, by either disengaging from socially useful roles or actively pursuing them, but that they do not question whether the circumstances older adults face are just. In response to this criticism, another group of theorists arose—those growing out of the social-conflict tradition (Hendricks, 1992).

The Second Generation of Theories: Social Conflict

Unlike their predecessors, who emphasized the ways older adults could be integrated into society, the second generation of theorists focused on sources of social conflict between retirement-age persons and the larger society (Hendricks, 1992). Like other theorists who were studying social conflict in U.S. society during the 1970s and early 1980s, these theorists stressed the ways in which the larger social structure helped shape the opportunities available to older adults; unequal opportunities were seen as creating the potential for conflict.

According to this view, many of the problems of aging—such as poverty, poor health, or inadequate health care—are systematically produced by the routine operation of social institutions. A capitalist society, the reasoning goes, favors those who are most economically powerful. While some older people certainly have "made it" and are set

activity theory A functionalist theory of aging that holds that busy, engaged people are more likely to lead fulfilling and productive lives.

continuity theory The theory that older adults' well-being is enhanced when their activities are consistent with their personality, preferences, and activities earlier in life.

conflict theories of aging Arguments that emphasize the ways in which the larger social structure helps to shape the opportunities available to older adults. Unequal opportunities are seen as creating the potential for conflict.

life course The various transitions and stages people experience during their lives.

for life, many have not—and these people must fight to get even a meager share of society's scarce resources.

Conflict theories of aging flourished during the 1980s, when a shrinking job base and cutbacks in federal spending threatened to pit different social groups against each other in the competition for scarce resources. Older persons were seen as competing with the young for increasingly scarce jobs and dwindling federal dollars. Conflict theorists further pointed out that even among older adults, those who fared worst were women, low-income people, and ethnic minorities (Atchley, 2000; Estes, 2011; Hendricks, 1992; Hendricks and Hendricks, 1986).

As we will see later in this chapter, the concerns articulated by conflict theorists persist today. For example, while poverty rates among older adults have plummeted over the past 60 years, with less than 10 percent of older adults now living in poverty, this figure is as high as 40 percent among unmarried Black and Hispanic older women (Carr, 2019).

Life course theorists maintain that the aging process is shaped by historical time and place and that early life experiences can have a significant effect on later life.

The Third Generation of Theories: Life Course

Life course theorists reject what they regard as the one-sided emphases of both functionalism and conflict theories, where older adults are viewed either as merely adapting to the larger society (functionalism) or as victims of the stratification system (social conflict). Rather, life course theorists view older persons as playing an active role in determining their own physical and mental well-being, yet recognize the constraints imposed by social structural factors.

According to the life course perspective, the aging process is shaped by historical time and place; factors such as wars, economic shifts, the development of new technologies, and the emergence of new infectious diseases like COVID-19 shape how people age. Yet this perspective also emphasizes agency, where individuals make choices that reflect both the opportunities and the constraints facing them. The most important theme of the life course perspective is that aging is a lifelong process; relationships, events, and experiences of early life have consequences for later life.

CONCEPT CHECKS

1 Summarize the three theoretical frameworks used to describe the nature of aging in U.S. society.

2 What are the main criticisms of functionalism and conflict theory?

3 What are three themes of the life course perspective?

4 Describe the processes of cumulative adversity and advantage over the life course.

Mounting research shows that our physical and mental health in later life is closely linked to the advantages and disadvantages we faced early in life, dating back as far as childhood and infancy. People who begin life in a position of social advantage generally are better positioned to acquire additional resources than those who begin life at the bottom of the stratification system. Those born into well-off families enjoy richer economic resources, better health, and more educational opportunities in early life—all of which set the stage for rewarding jobs, good health, and emotional well-being in later life.

Those with adversities earlier in life, like Alice Garvin, who we introduced earlier in this chapter, often are denied access to the opportunities that ensure a happy and healthy old age. Researchers have found that childhood and adolescent experiences—including parental death (Slavich, Monroe, and Gotlib, 2011), parental divorce (Amato, 2000), child-abuse victimization (Slopen et al., 2010), poverty (Duncan, Ziol-Guest, and Kalil, 2010), and living in an unsafe neighborhood (Vartanian and Houser, 2010)—have harmful implications for health among older adults. Often, these early adversities put young people at risk of poor health behaviors, economic strains, marital troubles, and other difficulties in young adulthood that may contribute to lifelong health problems (Carr, 2019). In other words, adversities in early life give rise to various challenges in adulthood, which accumulate to make the aging process very difficult for the disadvantaged.

Table 12.1
APPLYING SOCIOLOGY TO AGING

THEORY	APPROACH TO UNDERSTANDING AGING	CONTEMPORARY APPLICATION
Disengagement Theory	It is functional for societies to relieve older people of their social roles, thereby freeing up those positions for younger persons.	Forced retirement policies that push older adults out of the workforce to make room for younger employees.
Activity Theory	Keeping older people busy and engaged allows them to lead productive lives, which can be functional for society.	Social programs like bingo and movie nights for older adults, regardless of their interests and skills.
Continuity Theory	Older adults' well-being is enhanced when they are in social contexts that are consistent with their personality, preferences, and activities earlier in life	Efforts by assisted living facilities to decorate and arrange residents' rooms similar to their long-time homes.
Conflict Theories	Many of the problems of aging—such as poverty, poor health, or inadequate health care—are systematically produced by the routine operation of social institutions.	Rates of poverty among older adults differ dramatically by race and gender, reflecting systems of race and gender stratification.
Life Course Perspectives	Aging processes are shaped by structural factors like economic shifts, and aspects of personal agency, like aspirations.	Boys and girls in the early twentieth century may have held similar career aspirations, but men received more structural support than women.

3 RESEARCH ON AGING IN THE UNITED STATES TODAY

Who Are America's Older Adults?

Older adults reflect the diversity of U.S. society that we've noted elsewhere in this textbook: They are rich, poor, and in between; they belong to all racial and ethnic groups; they live alone and in families of various sorts; they vary in their political views; and they are gay and lesbian as well as heterosexual. Furthermore, like other Americans, they are diverse with respect to health: Although some suffer from mental and physical disabilities, most lead active, independent lives.

A portrait of older Americans reveals that Whites are overrepresented among persons age 65 and older. Fully 77 percent of Americans age 65 and older in 2016 were non-Hispanic White, just 9 percent were Black, 8 percent Hispanic (of any race), 4 percent Asian/Pacific Islander, and 0.5 percent Native American (U.S. Bureau of the Census, 2017j). These statistics reflect both Whites' longer life expectancy relative to Blacks and the fact that many older Latino immigrants return to their home countries in later life so that they can spend their final years with their families.

Currently, over 13.9 percent of the age 65+ population in the United States are foreign born (Mizoguchi et al., 2019). In California, New York, Hawaii, and other states that receive large numbers of immigrants, as many as one-fifth of the older population were born outside the United States (Shin and Kominski, 2010). Most older immigrants either do not speak English well or do not speak it at all. Integrating older immigrants into U.S. society poses special challenges: Some are highly educated, but most are not. Most lack a retirement income, so they depend on their families or public assistance for support. Linguistic isolation also is a concern, for those who live with family members or in neighborhoods where few people share their language (Gubernskaya and Treas, 2020).

Finally, as people live to increasingly older ages, the age 65+ population is becoming diverse in terms of age itself. It is useful to distinguish among different age categories of the old, such as the **young old** (ages 65 to 74), the **old old** (ages 75 to 84), and the **oldest old** (ages 85 and older). The young old are most likely to be economically independent, healthy, active, and engaged; the oldest old, the fastest-growing segment of the older population, are most likely to encounter difficulties such as poor health, financial insecurity, isolation, and loneliness. As the COVID-19 pandemic revealed, oldest old adults accounted for a vastly disproportionate share of deaths, a function not solely of biological aging, but due to the fact that they were more likely to live in congregate living situations like long-term care facilities (Gardner, States, and Bagley, 2020).

Social, economic, and psychological differences among the young, old, and oldest old are not due only to the effects of aging; they may also reflect one's birth cohort. The young old came of age during the

young old Sociological term for persons age 65 to 74.

old old Sociological term for persons age 75 to 84.

oldest old Sociological term for persons age 85 and older.

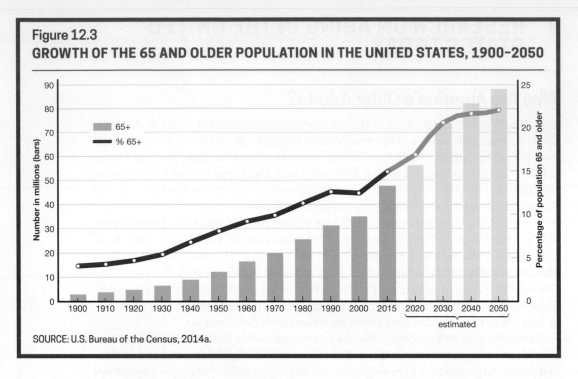

Figure 12.3

GROWTH OF THE 65 AND OLDER POPULATION IN THE UNITED STATES, 1900–2050

Legend:
- 65+
- % 65+

(Y-axis left: Number in millions (bars); Y-axis right: Percentage of population 65 and older; X-axis: 1900 through 2050, with 2020–2050 marked as estimated)

SOURCE: U.S. Bureau of the Census, 2014a.

post–World War II period of strong economic growth and benefited as a result: They are more likely to be educated; to have acquired wealth in the form of a home, savings, or investments; and to have had many years of stable employment. These advantages are much less likely to be enjoyed by the oldest old, partly because their education and careers began at an earlier time, when economic conditions were not so favorable and medical technologies were less well developed (Alwin, 2008; Idler, 1993; Manton et al., 2008).

What is the experience of growing old in the United States today? Although older adults do face some special challenges, especially in the face of pandemic, many lead healthy, satisfying, and socially engaged lives (Carr, 2019). In this section, we describe contemporary sociological studies that document differences among aged population in the United States, and we investigate some of the common problems that they confront. In the next section, we delve into several debates about the impact of aging on society, and the ways that older persons, governments, and societies can adjust and adapt to the challenges of population aging.

Social Security A government program that provides economic assistance to persons faced with unemployment, disability, or agedness.

Medicare A program under the U.S. Social Security Administration that reimburses hospitals and physicians for medical care provided to qualifying people over 65 years old.

Poverty

Just over 9 percent of persons age 65 and older currently live in poverty, although some of the very poorest Americans are older adults, particularly among Blacks and Latino persons, women, and those living in rural areas (Li and Dalaker, 2019). Because most older people have retired from full-time work, their income is based primarily on **Social Security** and private retirement programs, for those fortunate enough to have a private pension. Social Security and **Medicare** have been especially important in lifting many retirement-age people out of poverty. Yet people who depend solely on these two programs for income and health care coverage are likely to live modestly at best.

Nearly 9 out of 10 older adults receive Social Security benefits. In 2015, Social Security provided 33 percent of the average older adult's income, earnings provided 34 percent, pensions provided 20 percent, and asset income accounted for 9 percent (Administration for Community Living, 2018). Low-income households in particular are likely to rely heavily on Social Security. Among older adults in the lowest fifth of the income distribution, Social Security accounts for 81 percent of aggregate income and cash public assistance for another 10 percent. By contrast, for those whose income is in the highest income category, Social Security accounts for 15 percent, pensions for 22 percent, and asset income for 14 percent; earnings account for 45 percent (Social Security Administration, 2016c). Yet even the combination of Social Security and private pensions results in modest retirement incomes for most people; in 2017, the median income of households headed by a person age 65+ was about $45,000 (Gusman, 2019).

The economic conditions of older adults have improved steadily since the 1970s due to major expansions of the Social Security program. In 1959, 35 percent of all people 65 or older lived in poverty. That figure began to drop during President Lyndon B. Johnson's War on Poverty in the mid-1960s, when Medicare was enacted and Social Security benefits increased. By the early 1970s, poverty rates among those ages 65+ had dropped to below 15 percent, and today, the rate is less than 9 percent. Contrast this with the rate of poverty among children under 18 years, 16.2 percent of whom were poor in 2018 (Semega et al., 2019). However, the low overall poverty rate among older adults conceals two serious problems: the economic strains facing persons in late midlife—those ages 55 to 64—and tremendous race and gender gaps in late-life poverty rates.

Poverty Among Persons Ages 55–64

The Great Recession of 2008 took a very severe toll on persons on the brink of retirement, those ages 55 to 64. As of September 2020, it was clear that millions of Americans had lost their jobs due to the economic downturns and business shutdowns that resulted from the COVID-19 pandemic. Many near-retirement age adults whose businesses were shuttered also struggled to find new work, facing the added obstacle of ageism. These "nearly old or late-midlife" persons are among the older members of the large baby boom cohort, the 75 million babies born between roughly 1945 and 1964. The unemployment rates for workers between the ages of 55 and 64 more than doubled during the recession, from 3.1 percent in 2007 to 7.1 percent in 2010 (and decreased back down to 3.2% in 2016). According to a recent U.S. government study, unemployed older workers have more difficulty finding new jobs and remain unemployed for a longer period than their younger counterparts (U.S. Government Accountability Office [GAO], 2011). Some face discrimination by potential employers, who believe that older workers may be less able to acquire new skills. Others may have early onset health problems that limit the kind of work they can do. Due to the cohort's large size, unemployed persons in their late fifties and early sixties may face stiff competition from their peers who are also seeking work.

To make matters worse, many older Americans saw their retirement savings and home values plummet due to volatility in the stock and housing markets. The average income for adults age 55 to 64 fell by 6 percent during the recessionary period of 2007 to 2010, and their median household net worth dropped nearly 14 percent between 2007 and 2009. Due in part to their long spells of unemployment and evaporating assets, many near-old adults were pushed into poverty during the Great Recession. Poverty rates for adults age 55 to 64 rose from 8.6 percent in 2007 to 10.1 percent in 2010. As older Americans lost their employer-provided health insurance or exhausted their savings, many were forced to delay their medical care or receive Social Security early, at the age of 62, with a resulting 25 percent reduction in benefits.

It's not surprising, then, that these aging baby boomers are very pessimistic about their financial situation. According to a 2012 poll conducted by the American Association of Retired Persons (AARP), only 54 percent of adults ages 50 to 64 are satisfied with their financial situation. As such, fully two-thirds say that they will delay their retirement, while one-half say they may never retire (Kiger, 2012). These strains and anxieties may set the stage for a difficult transition to old age; only future research will tell whether the well-being of older adults declines for future cohorts (GAO, 2011).

Subgroup Differences in Late-Life Poverty Rates

The low overall poverty rate also conceals stark race, gender, and marital status differences in poverty among persons age 65+. In 2017, the poverty rate for older women was 10.5 percent compared to 7.5 percent for older men. Older Blacks and Hispanics experience the highest poverty rates at 19.1 percent and 17 percent, respectively, compared to 7 percent of older Whites and 10.9 percent of older Asians (Figure 12.4). We see the highest poverty rates among older women living alone: 41 percent of Hispanic women who live alone and 29 percent of Black women who live alone are in poverty (U.S. Bureau of the Census, 2016a).

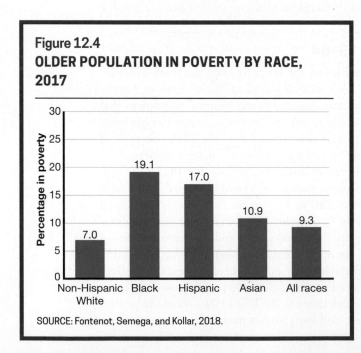

Figure 12.4
OLDER POPULATION IN POVERTY BY RACE, 2017

SOURCE: Fontenot, Semega, and Kollar, 2018.

Despite tremendous improvements in overall economic well-being among older adults during the past half century, the future looks uncertain—at least for some older persons. Some policy experts argue that the current government indicator of poverty (see Chapter 8) does not adequately capture the economic realities of late life. The federal government has proposed a new calculation that takes into account rising health care costs. Under this new formula, the proportion of older adults living in poverty would jump to 18.6 percent (Carr, 2019). Although some older adults may find their retirement years to be "golden," others may need to continue working far past age 65 just to maintain a minimum standard of living (Carr, 2019).

Social Isolation

Old age historically has been considered a time of social isolation. Disengagement theory proposed that it was beneficial for both the older adult and society if the older person gradually withdrew from their social roles and relationships (Cumming and Henry, 1961). Similarly, classic role theories held that the loss of the work role for men (via retirement) and loss of the wife role for women (via widowhood) would leave older adults socially isolated and despondent (Biddle, 1986). More recent research counters, however, that while loneliness and social isolation are problematic, they are neither inevitable nor universal features of aging.

Most older adults have family members and friends they can turn to. Four out of five older people have living children, and the vast majority of them can rely on their children for support if necessary. More than 9 out of 10 adult children say that maintaining parental contact is important to them, including the provision of financial support if it is needed (Suitor et al., 2011). The reverse is also true: Many studies have found that aged parents continue to provide support for their adult children, particularly during times of difficulty, such as divorce. Most older parents and adult children report feeling that the amount of support they receive from the other is fair, and that their relationship is close and loving (Birditt, Jackey, and Antonucci, 2009). Most older adults have regular contact with their children and live near them; about 85 percent of older persons live within an hour of one of their children. However, relatively few live with their children. This arrangement is exactly what they want; studies repeatedly show that older adults—even those with serious physical health limitations—prefer to remain independent and reside in their own homes. They want "intimacy at a distance" (Gans and Silverstein, 2006).

However, in spring 2020 when the COVID-19 pandemic raged, most older adults were advised to quarantine in their homes, to minimize their risk of contracting the virus through social contact. This isolation was mandated for residents of long-term care facilities like nursing homes and hospitalized persons, who were prohibited from having visitors. Although educated older adults who were computer-savvy could remain engaged with their friends and family through videoconferencing platforms, the well-documented "digital divide" meant that those who lacked computers and smartphones were the most isolated (Morrow-Howell et al., 2020).

As tragic as this isolation was, isolation and loneliness are not necessarily synonymous. Over the past three decades, researchers have discovered that loneliness is not triggered by a quantitative lack of relationships, but rather by a lack of satisfaction with the number or quality of one's relationships. Contemporary researchers have identified distinct types of loneliness: **Emotional loneliness** refers to the absence of an intimate confidant, while **social loneliness** refers to the absence of a broader social network. The two types often overlap; widowed persons, those living alone, or those living far away from their friends and families consistently report higher levels of both types of loneliness than persons who are more socially integrated, such as married persons or those who live with their adult children (de Jong Gierveld and Havens, 2004).

emotional loneliness The absence of an intimate confidant.

social loneliness The absence of a broader social network.

The mere presence of personal relationships does not ward off loneliness, however. An estimated 25 percent of older married persons report emotional and social loneliness; this pattern is particularly common among persons whose spouses are ill, who have a dissatisfying (or nonexistent) sexual relationship, and who have infrequent or conflicted conversations (de Jong Gierveld et al., 2009). As de Jong Gierveld and Havens (2004) noted, loneliness depends on one's "standards as to what constitutes an optimal network of relationships." That is, it's getting less support than we want rather than the objective number of social ties that matters when it comes to loneliness.

Despite its subjective nature, loneliness is a serious problem for many older adults; it is linked to sleep problems, poor cardiovascular health, and elevated blood pressure, each of which carries long-term consequences for mortality risk (Cacioppo et al., 2002). Loneliness also may be a particularly serious social problem for older adults in future generations. Smaller families and increased rates of divorce and childlessness among future cohorts of older adults may create a context where older persons maintain objectively fewer relationships, thus triggering social loneliness (Manning and Brown, 2011). More important, however, some have argued that current cohorts of midlife adults have unrealistically high expectations for what their social relationships should provide (e.g., one's partner should be their "soul mate"); if these lofty expectations go unfulfilled, then older adults may report higher levels of emotional loneliness as well (Carr and Moorman, 2011).

Who Suffers More: Women or Men?

Researchers continue to debate whether men or women are more socially isolated in later life. Women are less likely than men to be married, yet they tend to have richer social and emotional ties to children and friends. These ties reflect patterns of lifelong

Why might future generations face more social isolation as they age?

gender socialization, where women are raised to emphasize social relationships and men are raised to be independent and autonomous (Carr and Moorman, 2011).

Statistics confirm that older women are far less likely than men to be married. Because men die younger than women, women are more likely than men to become widowed. Women also are more likely than men to remain widowed; a dearth of eligible male partners prevents most older women from remarrying. Among people 65 and older in the United States, there are about 1.25 women per man (125 women for every 100 men), and this gap increases to nearly 2.0 women for every man by age 85 (189 women for every 100 men). As a result, only 11 percent of men ages 65 and older were widowers in 2018; by contrast, 32 percent of older women were widowed. Given the stark gender gap in widowhood, women are much more likely than men to live alone (34 percent versus 21 percent). By age 75, nearly half of women (44 percent) live alone (Administration for Community Living, 2018).

However, as we have just learned, being single and living alone does not necessarily mean loneliness. Many older women report that they have little interest in dating and remarrying. Carr (2004) estimated that 18 months after becoming widowed, only 10 percent of older women (yet 20 percent of men) were dating, and just 15 percent of women (yet nearly 40 percent of men) said that they would like to date. Some older women report that they do not want to remarry because they do not want to take on the homemaking and caregiving responsibilities that often accompany marriage to an older man (van den Hoonard, 2002).

Women's more emotionally intimate social relations over the life course are an important resource as they adjust to spousal loss and social isolation. Older widows receive more practical and emotional support from their children than do widowers, given mothers' closer relationships with their children throughout the life course. Women also are more likely to have larger and more varied friendship networks than men, and these friendships provide an important source of support to women as they cope with the strains of late life (Ha, 2008).

Men, by contrast, are more likely than women to experience physical health declines, increased disability, and heightened risk of mortality after their spouses die. While popular lore claims that widowers may "die of a broken heart," research shows that the loss of a helpmate and caretaker is actually the culprit. Wives typically monitor their husbands' diets, remind them to take their daily medications, and urge them to give up vices such as smoking and drinking (Umberson, Wortman, and Kessler, 1992). For many older men, wives often are their primary (or only) source of social support and integration; when a man loses his wife, he also loses an important connection to his social networks.

Prejudice

Discrimination on the basis of age, or **ageism**, is prohibited by federal law. The Age Discrimination in Employment Act of 1967 (ADEA) protects job applicants and employees 40 years of age and older from discrimination on the basis of age in hiring, firing, promotion, and pay. Nonetheless, prejudices based on false stereotypes are common. Older adults are frequently seen

> **ageism** Discrimination or prejudice against a person on the grounds of age.

as lonely, sad, frail, forgetful, dependent, senile, old-fashioned, inflexible, and embittered (Palmore, 2015). Ageism intensified during the COVID-19 pandemic, as "old age" became viewed as synonymous with sickness and death. However, epidemiologists and medical professionals are quick to point out that the most serious risk factor for the virus is underlying conditions. A 45-year-old who suffers from high blood pressure, asthma, and type 2 diabetes may be at greater risk than a healthy 72-year-old.

There are a number of reasons for such prejudice. Americans' obsession with youthful beauty and vigor, reflected in popular entertainment and advertising, leads many younger people to disparage their elders, frequently dismissing them as irrelevant. Associated with the emphasis on youthfulness is a fear-filled avoidance of reminders of death and dying. Such fear carries over into negative attitudes toward older persons, who serve as a constant reminder of one's mortality (Fry, 1980). The information-technology culture undoubtedly reinforces these prejudices because youthfulness and computer abilities seem to go hand in hand. In the fast-paced world of Twitter and Snapchat, young people may come to view older persons as anachronistic. Over the past decade, a new stereotype has emerged; that older adults are "greedy geezers" who are relying on Social Security benefits they don't need, and in the process robbing Generation X of a secure financial future (Street and Cossman, 2006).

These stereotypes are false, yet they can also do harm in several ways. First, merely believing negative stereotypes about aging can take a toll on the health and longevity of older adults. Becca Levy (2002) and her colleagues asked a sample of older adults how much they agreed or disagreed with statements such as "As you get older, you are less useful." When researchers followed up with the study participants 10 years later, they found that 87 percent of those with positive attitudes, yet just 66 percent of those with negative attitudes, were still alive. The pattern was even more pronounced at the 22-year follow-up, when 50 percent of those with positive attitudes, yet just 27 percent of those with negative attitudes, were still alive. Even after statistically controlling for possible explanatory pathways, such as health, socioeconomic status, and health behaviors, these patterns persisted, suggesting that harmful beliefs can exact a physical toll, although researchers are not certain as to why.

Second, older adults can be harmed if other people's ageist beliefs are translated into discriminatory treatment. For example, one recent study found that nearly two-thirds of older adults reported that they had been the victim of ageism, with their experiences ranging from minor slights, such as being treated as if they were not smart or receiving poor service at a restaurant, to more serious experiences, such as job or health care discrimination. Moreover, those persons who had experienced such mistreatment later experienced poorer physical and mental health than their peers who had not been victimized (Luo et al., 2011).

If ageist stereotypes are so harmful, why do they persist? Age-based stereotypes, like all stereotypes, have a kernel of truth (LeVine and Campbell, 1972). Prior cohorts of older adults often were less vigorous, healthy, financially well-off, integrated into society, and technologically savvy than both their younger counterparts and current cohorts of older adults. These patterns are less a reflection of older persons themselves than of society's failure to afford equal opportunities to older adults. Current cohorts of older adults, by contrast, are healthier, more integrated into society, and technologically savvier than ever before. These patterns, in turn, may start to chip away at outdated and inaccurate notions of what old age is. Consider that Oscar-winner actor Tom Hanks graced the cover of *AARP* magazine in 2019, the year he turned 63. Hanks is three years younger than 66-year-old luminary Oprah Winfrey, who is four years younger than septuagenarian Bruce Springsteen, who turned 71 in 2020.

Just as older adults are a vital part of popular culture, they are becoming an increasingly large presence online. In 2016, 64 percent of older Americans were using the Internet and more than a third were using social media (Pew Research Center, 2017a). Experts agree that baby boomers may play a critical role in further helping to dissolve stereotypes of the frail, out-of-it older adult.

Elder Abuse

The National Research Council (NRC) report *Elder Mistreatment: Abuse, Neglect, and Exploitation* (Bonnic and Wallace, 2003) defines elder abuse as "(a) intentional actions that cause harm or create a serious risk of harm, whether or not intended, to a vulnerable elder by a caregiver or other person who stands in a trust relationship to the elder, or (b) failure by a caregiver to satisfy the elder's basic needs or to protect the elder from harm." Mistreatment may take many forms, including physical, sexual, emotional, or financial abuse, neglect, or abandonment.

Elder mistreatment is very difficult to measure and document. Older adults who are embarrassed, ashamed, or fearful of retaliation by their abusers may be reluctant to report such experiences. As a result, official prevalence rates are low. Worldwide, it is estimated that 15.7 percent of persons age 65+ experience some form of abuse in community setting (Yon et al., 2017; WHO, 2018). In the United States, the prevalence of elder abuse is estimated to be about 10 percent (Lachs and Pillemer, 2015). The most recent study of elder abuse, of more than 4,000 older adults in New York, found that 7.6 percent of participants had experienced some form of abuse in the last year (Burnes et al., 2015). A national survey (2008) found that 9 percent of older adults reported verbal mistreatment, 3.5 percent reported financial mistreatment, and less than 1 percent reported physical mistreatment by a family member. Women and persons with physical disabilities were most likely to report abuse. Elder abuse is likely grossly underreported: One study found that only about 7 percent of cases of elder abuse are reported to authorities (National Center on Elder Abuse, 2012).

It is widely believed that abuse results from the anger and resentment that adult children feel when confronted with the need to care for their infirm parents (King, 1984; Steinmetz, 1983). Most studies, however, have found this assumption to be false. In the aforementioned national survey, most mistreatment was perpetrated by someone other than a member of the elder's immediate family. Of those who reported verbal mistreatment, 26 percent named their spouse or romantic partner as the perpetrator, 15 percent named their child, and 57 percent named someone other than a spouse, parent, or child. Similarly, 56 percent of elders who reported financial mistreatment said that someone other than a family member was responsible; of family members, though, children were mentioned most often, while spouses were rarely named (Laumann, Leitsch, and Waite, 2008).

Health Problems

The prevalence of chronic disabilities among older adults has declined in recent years, and most older people rate their health as reasonably good and free of major disabilities. Still, older people obviously suffer from more health problems than most younger people, and the number and intrusiveness of health difficulties often increase with advancing age. Of adults 75 and older, more than half suffer from arthritis and about a third from heart disease (35 percent) and cancer (32 percent); hypertension is the most frequently occurring condition, afflicting 72 percent of men age 75 and over and 80 percent of women 75 and over (AOA, 2017).

More than three-quarters (82 percent) of older adults between the ages of 65 and 74 consider their health to be "excellent," "very good," or "good"; about three out of four adults 75 and older reported the same (Graham, 2019). It is not surprising that the percentage of people needing help with personal care increases with age: Only 4 percent of adults between the ages of 65 and 74 report needing help with personal care, yet this figure rises to 9 percent for people between 75 and 84 and to 20 percent for people over 85 (Administration for Community Living, 2018).

The oldest old, or persons ages 85+, make up the fastest-growing group of older adults. Because advanced old age is associated with greater use of health care, an aging population is accompanied by rising health-care expenditures. Medicare expenditures, or public health-care expenditures, on retirement-age older adults increase with age; per capita spending for older adults in 2011 was more than twice as high among

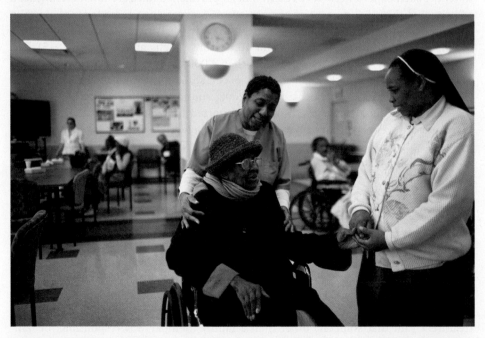

An alternative to nursing homes, PACE (Programs for All-Inclusive Care for the Elderly) is a Medicare program that allows older adults to stay in their homes while receiving the care they need.

persons age 96 ($16,145) versus age 70 ($7,566). This increase is due in large part to the high costs of medical care at the end of life (Neuman et al., 2015).

Evidence suggests that the most disadvantaged members of the baby boom cohort may fare particularly poorly as they reach later life; a recent analysis of National Health and Nutrition Examination Survey data shows that persons between 60 and 69 are more disabled than prior generations of young old adults (Seeman et al., 2009); the authors attribute this increase to rising rates of obesity among young and middle-aged Americans, especially Blacks and Latinos. According to the Administration for Community Living (2018), more than twice as many (44.3 percent) of people 75 years and older report having difficulty in physical functioning as those 45 to 64 years of age (19.7 percent).

Health insurance is essential for older adults, given the high and rising costs of medical care. Almost all (93 percent) older Americans are covered to some extent by Medicare. But because Medicare covers about half the total health care expenses of older adults, half of older adults supplement this coverage with private insurance. The rising costs of private insurance, unfortunately, have made this option impossible for a growing number of older adults. In 2016, older adults spent an average of $5,994 on out-of-pocket health care expenditures—an increase of 38% since 2006. Despite Medicare, health care costs still comprise 13.1 percent of older adults' total expenses (Administration for Community Living, 2018).

When older adults become physically unable to care for themselves, they may move into assisted-living facilities, long-term care facilities, or nursing homes. Only 3 percent of the 65+ population in 2015 lived in institutional settings such as nursing homes; however, this percentage increases dramatically with age. While only 1 percent of older adults ages 65 to 74 and 3 percent of adults ages 75 to 84 live in institutional settings, 9 percent of older adults ages 85+ do (AOA, 2017).

The average cost of a semiprivate room in a nursing home is now over $82,000 a year, while the annual cost of a room at an assisted-living facility averages $43,500 (Genworth Financial, 2016). As a result of these high costs, many reasonably well-off older adults who require such institutionalization may see their lifetime savings quickly depleted (a process dubbed "spending down"). Some receive Medicaid coverage; Medicaid is the government program that provides health insurance for the poor. It covers long-term supervision and nursing costs, although only when most of one's assets (except for one's home) have been used up.

Nursing homes have long had a reputation for austerity and loneliness. Living in a nursing home was cited as a concern about growing old by over half of respondents, according to a survey (Table 12.2). However, the quality of care in most homes has improved in recent years because federal programs such as Medicaid help cover the cost of care and because of federal quality regulations. Further, long-term care offers diverse options to older adults, ranging from apartments with partial nursing care and meals to units that provide round-the-clock medical assistance. Many also offer a wide array of cultural, social, and recreational programs for their residents.

However, the reputation of nursing homes and long-term care facilities was tarnished in 2020, as they were the seat of many COVID-19 outbreaks. However, these outbreaks were not a function of low-quality care or facilities. Rather, viruses spread

Table 12.2

WHAT IS YOUR BIGGEST FEAR ABOUT GROWING OLD?

When it comes to growing old, most Americans fear losing their health and independence far more than being alone or living in a nursing home.

Losing memory	73%
Losing your health	72%
Running out of money	65%
Losing ability to care for yourself	62%
Winding up in a nursing home	59%

SOURCE: NORC at the University of Chicago, 2017.

rapidly in congregate housing, especially when the residents already had compromised health. Nursing home staff, many of whom lived in crowded homes or who relied on public transit, were at particular risk of not only contracting the virus, but bringing it to the homes in which they work (Barnett and Grabowski, 2020). As a result, the future of nursing homes and Americans' faith in them is uncertain.

Lifelong Learning

As more and more people live well beyond the age of retirement, they enter a new stage of life for which there are few socially prescribed roles (Moen, 1995). Many people can look forward to 10 or 20 years of relatively healthy living, free from the obligations of paid work and raising a family. Furthermore, the older population will be increasingly well educated because young people today are much more likely than their parents or grandparents to have gone to college. While only 28 percent of older adults had high school diplomas in 1970, 86 percent of older adults in 2016 were high school graduates (Administration for Community Living, 2018).

These trends suggest that older persons are much more likely to remain a part of mainstream society rather than to become isolated (Jarvis, 2007). It is important for older adults to maintain a readiness to learn, stimulated by participation in a wide variety of learning activities; this engagement can contribute to mental alertness, a positive psychological attitude, and even improved physical health (Findsen and Formosa, 2011).

Many two-year and four-year colleges today recognize the importance of lifelong learning and offer tuition waivers for older adults. For example, 51 universities in the United States are classified as "age-friendly," meaning that they abide by 10 principles focused on encouraging the participation of older adults in all the core activities of the university, including educational and research programs (Eisenberg, 2019). Community colleges also play an important role in lifelong learning. As noted by the

CONCEPT CHECKS

1 Contrast young old, old old, and oldest old persons.

2 Describe four common problems older Americans often confront.

3 What characteristics differentiate those older adults who are emotionally and physically well from those who face great distress in later life?

American Council on Education (2008), about half of college-going adults age 50 and older attend community colleges, primarily for fun, to connect with other people, and to retool for a new career.

4 UNANSWERED QUESTIONS: THE POLITICAL AND ECONOMIC IMPACT OF POPULATION AGING

Older adults are a potent voice in Washington, due both to their large and rapidly growing numbers and to their high levels of political engagement. **AARP** (formerly the American Association of Retired Persons) is a highly effective advocate for the aged population. AARP is a nonprofit organization that boasts a membership of nearly 38 million Americans age 50 and older—reportedly the largest member-based organization in the world next to the Roman Catholic Church and approximately 8 times larger than the National Rifle Association (AARP, 2017; Birnbaum, 2005; Kessler, 2014).

Those 60 and older have high voter turnout rates—71 percent in the 2016 presidential election—compared to just 43 percent of those 18 to 24 years old (U.S. Bureau of the Census, 2017n). This is not to suggest that all older adults hold the same political views; on the contrary, they are as politically heterogeneous as the other age groups. But on issues they perceive as affecting their interests, such as retirement pensions and health care reform, they are likely to have strong opinions. Moreover, because cuts in programs for older adults would shift the burden of supporting them to their families, opposition to significant reductions in these programs is likely to be widespread.

Because there is "strength in numbers," some observers have argued that older adults have undue political influence and may benefit from government programs more than younger persons. Others counter, however, that older adults are entitled to programs such as Social Security and Medicare on the grounds of both equity and social justice (Kotlikoff and Burns, 2012). Yet as the large baby boom cohort, 75 million strong, enters later life, social scientists and policy makers are in heated debates over whether the federal government can afford to provide these benefits to older adults in coming years (Urban Institute, 2010). Such debates extend beyond the borders of the United States; throughout the globe, social scientists and policy makers wrestle with whether and how the planet can fairly provide services to an unprecedented number of older adults, sometimes dubbed the "gray tsunami" (O'Neill, 2009).

Do Older Americans Get an Unfair Amount of Government Support?

The costs of providing for older adults come largely out of taxes paid by working people. In the United States, the growing ratio of older adults to the working-age population has alarmed policy makers. They point out that for every 100 people of working age (20 to 64 years old) there are roughly 25 persons 65 and older; this figure will increase to 38 by 2050. A rapidly aging population will

AARP U.S. advocacy group for people age 50 and over, formerly the American Association of Retired Persons.

pose serious challenges to public policy throughout this century (He, Goodkind, and Kowal, 2016).

Do government programs adequately promote **generational equity**—the striking of a balance between the needs and interests of members of different generations? The issue of generational equity was first raised by an organization called Americans for Generational Equity (AGE), created in 1984 by David Durenberger, a U.S. senator from Minnesota, to challenge the notion that older adults are entitled to Social Security benefits (Quadagno, 1989).

AGE argued that as the U.S. population ages, those who are working will bear an increasing burden for those who are not. AGE also argued that Social Security unfairly favors retirees over other needy groups in society. For example, AGE pointed out that retirees are sometimes wealthier than the working people whose taxes fund Social Security. To illustrate, in 2015, 17.5 percent of persons under age 18 (12.8 million) and 11.2 percent of adults age 18 to 64 (24.2 million) lived at or below the poverty line, while less than 9.2 percent of persons age 65 and older (4.7 million) did so (Fontenot, Semega, and Kollar, 2018). The difficulty arises from the fact that there are fewer and fewer working-age people to shoulder the tax burden necessary to support more and more retirees.

In practice, however, there is limited evidence that the average American is concerned about generational equity and the potential threat of older adults disproportionately benefiting from public programs. For example, opinion poll data show that younger Americans report greater support for increased spending on Social Security than do older persons, while older adults are most likely to favor increased spending on education (Street and Cossman, 2006). Further, most Americans support Medicare and Social Security; a 2011 survey found that nearly 90 percent feel that both programs are "good for the country." However, a 2015 Gallup poll found that two-thirds of Americans say Social Security is in a state of crisis or has major problems (Newport, 2015).

Americans may recognize that the old and young generations are not in competition; rather, benefits provided to one generation may help the other. At the same time, Americans' anxieties about how to fund such benefits are well founded, as we will see in the next section.

Can Medicare and Social Security Survive the "Graying" of America?

The two principal governmental programs that provide financial support for the retirement-age population are Medicare, which was instituted in 1965, and Social Security, whose benefits were increased at about the same time. (The program itself was begun in 1935.) The full benefits of Medicare and Social Security are available at age 65 for current cohorts of older adults, although partial benefits are available to some people a few years earlier. For birth cohorts born in 1960 and later, however, Social Security benefits will start for most people at age 67.

generational equity The striking of a balance between the needs and interests of members of different generations.

Social Security and Medicare are financed by workers' payroll deductions, employer contributions, and taxes on those who are self-employed. Working Americans pay into these programs today so they can be eligible for benefits when they are no longer able to earn a living. By providing a degree of economic support for older adults, such programs also make it economically possible to retire; in the absence of the economic security such programs provide, older adults would be under greater economic pressure to continue working as long as they are physically capable. In 2020, about 65 million Americans will received over one trillion dollars in Social Security benefits. About 71 percent of benefits went to retired workers and their dependents; the remainder went to disabled workers and their dependents and to survivors of deceased workers (Social Security Administration, 2020). Although the program was not initially designed to be the sole financial resource for retirees, more than one-third of older adults rely on Social Security for 90 percent or more of their income (Social Security Administration, 2016c).

The monthly benefit one receives under Social Security depends in part on earnings before retirement. The average monthly benefit in December 2019 was $1,503 for retired workers and $1,258 for disabled workers (Social Security Administration, 2019). Because retired women are less likely than men to have had continuous paid employment throughout their lives, their average retirement income is typically lower than men's. As these figures suggest, Social Security provides a minimal level of support for older adults—by itself, barely enough to keep recipients out of poverty (Sullivan, 2012). Still, without such benefits, an estimated three-quarters of all older adults would live in poverty (Carr, 2019).

Protestors at a rally in Olympia, Washington, ask lawmakers not to cut the budgets for long-term health care facilities such as nursing homes and assisted-living facilities.

Medicare is the nation's largest health insurer, providing health insurance to 55 million Americans. Spending on Medicare totaled $582 billion in 2018, accounting for about 14 percent of the federal budget (Peter G. Peterson Foundation, 2019). Because it reaches so many people, Medicare has made an enormous difference in the aged population's access to adequate health care—although at a high cost.

Programs such as Social Security and Medicare will become increasingly costly as more and more Americans retire and live long lives after they retire; further, the share of the population funding Social Security is shrinking. As a result, the worker-to-beneficiary ratio has fallen, from 16.5 to 1 in 1950 to 2.8 to 1 in 2015. By 2037, it will be 2.1:1 (Social Security Administration, 2016b; Urban Institute, 2010). There is particular concern over whether the Social Security system will remain financially sound as retiring baby boomers collect their pensions. It is currently expected to have sufficient assets to pay full benefits until at least 2033, although if it is to avoid running out of money in the long run, changes will have to be made in the way the system works.

A variety of solutions have been proposed, including charging co-payments for home health care services, requiring beneficiaries to pay higher premiums, and requiring drug companies to provide discounts (Pear, 2011). One controversial proposal would involve "means testing," or allocating benefits based on an older person's financial means and needs. In the past decade, there also have been calls to privatize at least part of Social Security—that is, to enable workers to invest part of their Social Security withholdings in the stock market, rather than simply paying it all into a government fund. The effectiveness of this approach depends, of course, on how well the stock market performs in the future. The future of Social Security and Medicare will likely remain at the center of one of the major political debates of this century.

How Will Nations of the World Cope with Global Aging?

A "gray tsunami" is sweeping the world today. According to the United Nations, in 1950, there were 129 million persons age 65 and older on the planet, or 5 percent of the world population; by 2018, this number had jumped to 673 million—8.87 percent of the world population (World Bank, 2019d). The United Nations projects that the older population will more than double by 2050 to 1.5 billion, comprising nearly 16 percent of the global population (UN DESA, 2017). The world's average life expectancy grew from age 47 in 1950 to age 72 in 2016 and will reach age 77 by 2050 (He, Goodkind, and Kowal, 2016; World Health Organization, 2016).

The extent to which nations are "graying" varies widely. Older adults made up 18 percent of the population in more developed countries in 2015; this proportion is projected to reach 27 percent by 2050 (UN DESA, 2017). The percentage of people age 65 and older in less developed nations is considerably lower due to three important factors that suppress life expectancy: poverty, disease, and malnutrition. In 1950, less than 4 percent of the population in less developed countries was age 65+. As of 2018, that proportion had risen slightly to 4 percent and is projected to reach 14 percent by mid-century (UN DESA, 2017; World Bank, 2019d).

Global aging, such as the graying of the U.S. population, is largely a women's issue worldwide. In 2017, for every 100 women age 65 and older, there were 80 men, and only 54 men for every 100 women age 80 and over. These patterns are due primarily to women's life expectancy advantage in most nations of the world. The Central Intelligence Agency (2013) has identified just 12 nations where older men outnumber older women: These generally are places that have higher maternal mortality rates, lower levels of schooling among women, and higher levels of gender oppression.

Just as population composition varies starkly worldwide, the experiences of older adults in less developed nations differ tremendously from those of their peers in wealthier nations. Retirement is "an unaffordable luxury" for most older adults in Africa, and many in Latin America and parts of Asia (Bremner et al., 2010). Four out of five older adults worldwide receive no retirement income from pensions or government entitlement programs. Many must continue to work or rely on their families for financial support. Some work in the informal economy, such as selling products in street markets or working on farms with no benefits or health protection.

Although children and grandchildren historically have cared for their aging parents and grandparents, this support is eroding in some parts of the world. For example, in many parts of Africa, young people are moving to urban areas to work, while others are dying prematurely due to HIV/AIDS, and others still are grappling with their own poverty and cannot support their parents. As a result, many older adults are left to take care of themselves. These challenges are compounded by the fact that many frail older adults unexpectedly find themselves as caretakers to their grandchildren, when their own children (that is, the grandchildren's parents) have died due to ravages such as the AIDS epidemic (Bremner et al., 2010).

Worldwide, the "gray tsunami" (O'Neill, 2009) has enormous implications for social policy. As we learned earlier, when a large share of the population enters into older age, there are fewer working-age people to support them. In 1950, there were 10 working-age persons for every person age 65 and older worldwide. That number will drop steeply between 2015 and 2050, from 7 to less than 4. By 2050, demographers predict that there will be just 2 working-age adults per older adult in more developed nations, 4 in less developed nations, and 8 in the least-developed nations (UN DESA, 2017).

With fewer people working and paying into the system and more taking out, policy makers are concerned about the solvency of social programs. Countries vary widely in what they are doing to cope with their growing numbers of older people. More than 150 nations currently provide public assistance for people who are older or disabled, or for their survivors when they die. As we have seen already, the United States relies primarily on Social Security and Medicare to serve the financial and health needs of the older adults. Other industrial nations provide a much broader array of services.

In Japan, one of the oldest nations in the world, 23 percent of men and 29 percent of women are now 65 and older (UN DESA, 2017). Many older adults remain active well into old age because the Japanese culture encourages this activity and because business policies often support post-retirement work with the same company one worked for before retirement. A number of national laws in Japan support the employment and training of older workers, and private businesses also support retraining (Statistics Bureau Japan, 2015).

Societies that have large extended families and practice ancestor worship historically have been more likely to treasure their elders, honoring them at public events

In China, the constitution stipulates that "children who have come of age have the duty to support and assist their parents." In a recent case, a judge ordered a woman to visit her mother (pictured) at least once every two months.

and seeking their counsel in political matters. East Asian nations, in particular, have a tradition of following the Confucian teaching of filial piety. Children care for their parents in old age out of gratitude for the care they received when young (Sung, 2000). As a result, parents historically have lived with, and are cared for by, their children when they are no longer able to care for themselves (Cowgill, 1968; Falk, Falk, and Tomashevich, 1981).

This pattern of parent-child co-residence in Asia is starting to fade, however, due to economic development and globalization. Economic development in wealthier Asian nations now enables older adults to live on their own, if they choose to do so. For example, improvements in the health and financial status of older persons now enable Japanese older adults to maintain their own homes and the desirable status of "intimacy at a distance" (Kumagai, 2010).

Globalization also has altered the treatment and status of the aged population throughout the world (Cowgill, 1986; Foner, 1984; Fry, 1980; Holmes, 1983). As previously agrarian societies become part of the emerging global economy, traditional ways of thinking and behaving are likely to change. For example, adult children in China are now abandoning their rural villages to seek jobs in urban regions. Yet these moves often mean leaving behind their aging parents, who are responsible for supporting themselves, often by working in arduous agricultural jobs. Although economic conditions require that children move, cultural beliefs still condemn such moves. In one high-visibility case from 2006, a 60-year-old Chinese widow successfully sued her son and daughter for abandonment. The courts ruled that she was allowed to live with her daughter and obliged her son to pay her monthly support (French, 2006).

The combination of graying and globalization will shape the lives of older people throughout the world well into this century. Traditional patterns of family care will be challenged as family-based economies continue to give way to labor on the farms and in the offices and factories of global businesses. Like the industrial nations earlier in the twentieth century, all societies will be challenged to find roles for their aging citizens. This challenge will include identifying new means of economic support, often financed by government programs. It will also entail identifying ways to incorporate rather than isolate older persons, by drawing on their considerable reserves of experience and talent.

CONCEPT CHECKS

1 What is generational equity?

2 Describe the debate surrounding the future of Social Security and Medicare programs in the United States.

3 What is the feminization of global aging?

4 What are the implications of the graying world population for social policy?

THE BIG PICTURE

Chapter 12
Aging

1 Basic Concepts

p. 420

2 Growing Old: Theories of Aging

p. 426

LEARNING OBJECTIVES

Learn some basic facts about the increase in the proportion of the U.S. population that is age 65 and older. Recognize that aging is a combination of biological, psychological, and social processes. Understand how technological advances affect each of the three aging processes.

Understand key theories of aging, particularly those that focus on how society shapes the social roles of older adults and that emphasize aspects of age stratification.

TERMS TO KNOW

graying • older adults • social gerontology • aging • Alzheimer's disease • social aging

disengagement theory • socioemotional selectivity theory • activity theory • continuity theory • conflict theories of aging • life course

1. What is the "graying" of the U.S. population?
2. Compare and contrast biological, psychological, and social aging processes.
3. How has technology affected the processes of biological, psychological, and social aging?

1. Summarize the three theoretical frameworks used to describe the nature of aging in U.S. society.
2. What are the main criticisms of functionalism and conflict theory?
3. What are three themes of the life course perspective?
4. Describe the processes of cumulative adversity and advantage over the life course.

Exercises: Thinking Sociologically

1. Briefly discuss the competing theories about growing old that are presented in this chapter. How do these theories compare with each other? Which theory do you feel is most appropriate to explain aging, and why do you feel this way about that theory?

2. What do you think the United States could do socially and politically to alleviate the problems of aging for its older citizens? How likely is it that your suggestions for alleviating the problems of age could be adopted into the American political process, and why?

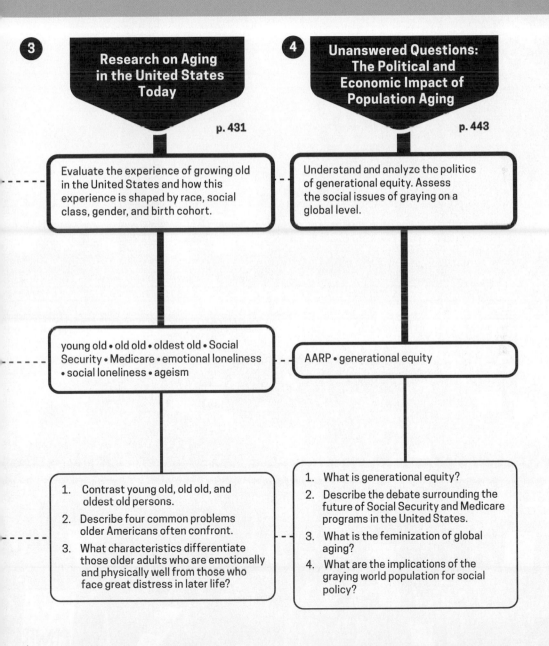

3

Research on Aging in the United States Today

p. 431

Evaluate the experience of growing old in the United States and how this experience is shaped by race, social class, gender, and birth cohort.

young old • old old • oldest old • Social Security • Medicare • emotional loneliness • social loneliness • ageism

1. Contrast young old, old old, and oldest old persons.
2. Describe four common problems older Americans often confront.
3. What characteristics differentiate those older adults who are emotionally and physically well from those who face great distress in later life?

4

Unanswered Questions: The Political and Economic Impact of Population Aging

p. 443

Understand and analyze the politics of generational equity. Assess the social issues of graying on a global level.

AARP • generational equity

1. What is generational equity?
2. Describe the debate surrounding the future of Social Security and Medicare programs in the United States.
3. What is the feminization of global aging?
4. What are the implications of the graying world population for social policy?

13

Government, Political Power, and Social Movements

Approximately what percentage of the world's population lives in countries that enjoy the following rights: freedom to participate freely in politics, including voting in fair and open elections for accountable representatives; freedom of expression and belief, including the right to freely assemble; a just and equitable legal system; and access to economic opportunity, including the right to own property?

A   35 percent

B   44 percent

C   54 percent

D   64 percent

E   75 percent

TURN THE PAGE FOR THE CORRECT ANSWER.

Every year, an organization called Freedom House (2019) classifies countries as either "free," "partly free," or "not free" based on a country-by-country survey of political rights (including open and fair elections, a multiparty system, and the absence of governmental corruption) and civil liberties (including freedom of expression and association, the rule of law, and individual rights). By these measures, in 2019, less than half the world's population (44 percent) lived in countries that were classified as "free"; 30 percent of the global population lived in countries that were classified as "partly free," while the rest of the population—numbering some 1.9 billion people living in 49 countries, or 26 percent of the world's total—was classified as "not free." Freedom House reports that on some measures, the percentage of people who would be classified as "free" has increased in recent years. For example, in 1986, only 34 percent of the countries surveyed were classified as free; by 2019, as noted, the figure had increased to 44 percent. But the major gains resulted when India was reclassified from "partly free" to "free," which added nearly a billion people to the "free" category.

This points out one of the principal limitations of such broad-stroke classifications: Although India now formally enjoys a wide range of political rights and civil liberties and a growing economy and middle class, as many as a half billion people in India still live in grinding poverty. Freedom House also classifies India's press and Internet as only "partly free." Whatever freedoms Indians may have on paper are severely limited by economic hardship and corrupt or indifferent local officials, a situation that has contributed to widespread discontent, protests, and an increasingly authoritarian government (Chandra, 2016).

To take an example closer to home, candidates for the 2016 U.S. elections and their supporters are estimated to have spent nearly $6.5 billion on the presidential race and congressional campaigns, suggesting that extremely wealthy individuals, large corporations, organized labor, and lobbying groups have an enormous ability to shape electoral outcomes to reflect their interests (Link, 2017). Moreover,

LEARNING OBJECTIVES

1 Basic Concepts

Understand basic ideas underlying modern nation-states and social movements. Learn about different types of democracy.

2 Who Rules? Theories of Democracy

Learn the key theories about power in a democracy.

3 Recent Research on U.S. Politics and Social Movements

Learn about some of the trends associated with modern-day democracy. Assess the effect of globalization and technology on social movements today. Learn about nationalism and the importance of nationalist movements.

4 Unanswered Questions

Understand why voter turnout in the United States is low and consider the role that the Internet played in the 2016 election. Evaluate whether democracy is in trouble.

THE ANSWER IS B.

any trend toward greater freedom is not irreversible: Since 2004, freedom has significantly declined in Russia and the former Soviet states in Central Europe (Freedom House, 2019; Shkolnikov, 2010).

What difference does it make whether a country is free? The answer is that it clearly matters how the decisions are made that affect its citizens' lives. Furthermore, most people (and their governments) at least profess to believe that people should enjoy basic political and social freedoms. The second paragraph of the Declaration of Independence famously says, "We hold these truths to be self-evident, that all men are created equal, that they are endowed by their Creator with certain unalienable Rights, that among these are Life, Liberty and the pursuit of Happiness . . . That to secure these rights, Governments are instituted among Men, deriving their just powers from the consent of the governed."

Is greater freedom spreading around the world? Is the idea of freedom contagious, as some have suggested? Before turning to theories and research that address this issue, it is first necessary to define some basic concepts.

1 BASIC CONCEPTS

Democracy

The terms *freedom* and **democracy** are sometimes used interchangeably, since the latter is intended to guarantee the former. The word democracy has its roots in the Greek term *demokratia*, from *demos* (people) and *kratos* (rule). It refers to a political system in which the people rule. But what does it mean to be "ruled by the people"? Many questions can be raised about this seemingly obvious phrase (Held, 2006).

Regarding the "people," who exactly are they? Everyone? Only people who are affected by the decisions? What should be the proper voting age? What about people who are currently in jail or once were? What about people who are not citizens but who have lived in the country for years and have a strong stake in any decisions that might affect them? What if there are strong differences of opinion among "the people"—how are the rights of the minority protected? What about people who choose not to participate or who find it difficult to participate, because of work or family obligations or lack of understanding of complex issues?

Regarding "rule," how, exactly, is it exercised? By periodic voting? Actual participation in all decisions that might affect one's life? Does "rule" refer only to government decisions or to other spheres of life as well, such as the economy? Does it encompass the daily administrative decisions of governments, or should it refer only to major policy decisions? Are all rules equally binding? Should rule-breaking be punished, and, if so, how severely? How much (and what forms of) dissent should be tolerated? If some people believe that the rules are unjust, do they have the right to disobey them?

Answers to these questions have varied over time and in different societies. For example, during U.S. history, "the people" have been variously understood as owners of

> **democracy** A political system that allows the citizens to participate in political decision making or to elect representatives to government bodies.

property, White men, educated men, men, and adult men and women. In some societies, democracy is limited to the political sphere; in others, it extends to other areas of social life. Moreover, in modern societies, it is not really feasible to have everybody "rule." This reality has led to at least two different forms of democracy: participatory democracy and liberal democracy.

Participatory Democracy

Participatory democracy exists when decisions are made communally by those affected by them. This was the original type of democracy practiced in ancient Athens, where the citizens, constituting a small minority of Athenian society (women and slaves were excluded), regularly assembled to consider policies and make major decisions. Participatory democracy has limited importance in modern societies, where the mass of the population has political rights, rendering it impossible for everyone to participate actively in the making of all the decisions that affect them.

In modern societies, **direct democracy** is a much more realistic approach to engaging citizens in decisions. A direct democracy is a form of participatory democracy in which citizens vote directly on laws and policies; however, they do not need to convene in one setting to do so. For example, Americans can visit voting booths in their hometowns to vote directly on legislation that affects their lives.

Yet some facets of participatory democracy do play a part in modern societies. Some New England towns still hold annual town hall meetings that are a form of participatory democracy. The holding of a referendum, whereby the majority expresses its views on a particular issue, is another form of participatory democracy. Direct consultation of large numbers of people is made possible by simplifying the issue to one or two questions to be answered. Referenda are employed frequently on a state level in the United States to decide controversial issues, such as the legalization of marijuana.

Many states have held referenda, a form of participatory democracy whereby the entire electorate votes on a particular proposal, on hot-button issues such as marijuana legalization and the death penalty.

participatory democracy A system of democracy in which all members of a group or community participate collectively in making major decisions.

direct democracy A form of participatory democracy that allows citizens to vote directly on laws and policies.

monarchies Systems of government in which unelected kings or queens rule.

Monarchies and Liberal Democracies

Not all countries today claim to be democratic. In a handful of countries (e.g., Saudi Arabia, Jordan, and some small Middle Eastern emirates), **monarchies** (rule by unelected kings or queens) still exist. While this was a common form of government well into the nineteenth century, true monarchies are rare today. **Constitutional monarchs** are still found (the queen of England, the king of Sweden, the emperor of Japan), but they are monarchs in name only. Their actual power is severely restricted by their respective countries' constitutions, which vest authority in the elected representatives of the people.

Countries in which voters can choose between two or more political parties and in which the majority of the adult population has the right to vote are usually called **liberal democracies**. The United States, the Western European countries, Japan, Australia, and New Zealand all fall into this category. Some developing countries, such as India, also have liberal democratic systems.

Populist Authoritarianism

In recent years, there has been a turn toward what has been described as "populist authoritarianism" in many countries, including European countries and the United States. Populist authoritarianism is both a philosophy and a style of governance characterized by assertive leadership that values security over civil liberties. It is typically coupled with a strong nationalism that is anti-immigrant and—in its current form—strongly anti-globalization. As the term suggests, it combines two ideas: **populism** (the belief in "popular sovereignty and direct democracy at any cost, if necessary overriding minority rights, elite expertise, constitutional checks-and-balances, conventional practices, and decision-making by elected representatives . . . [in which leaders] maintain direct links with their followers, through public rallies, television studios, and social media") and **authoritarianism** ("policy positions which endorse the values of tough security against threats from outsiders, xenophobic nationalism, strict adherence to conventional moral norms, and intolerance of multiculturalism"). Populist authoritarianism can become a challenge to liberal democracy (Norris and Inglehart, 2018).

The Concept of the State

When we say "the people rule," we are typically referring such a right to an entity called a **nation-state**—an entity composed of a **nation** (people with a common identity that ideally includes shared culture, language, and feelings of belonging) and a **state** (a political apparatus or government that rules over a territory). A modern state claims a specific territory and includes institutions such as a congress or parliament, a president or prime minister, judges, and other public

constitutional monarchs Kings or queens who are largely figureheads. Real power rests in the hands of other political leaders.

liberal democracies A type of representative democracy in which elected representatives hold power.

populism The belief that politics should reflect the needs and interests of ordinary people rather than those of elite individuals or groups.

authoritarianism A political system in which the governing bodies or leaders use force to maintain control.

nation-state Particular types of states, characteristic of the modern world, in which governments have sovereign power within defined territorial areas, and populations are citizens who know themselves to be part of single nations.

nation People with a common identity that ideally includes shared culture, language, and feelings of belonging.

state A political apparatus (government institutions plus civil service officials) ruling over a given territorial order, whose authority is backed by law and the ability to use force.

officials; its authority is often backed by a legal system and the ability to use military force to implement its policies.

Characteristics of the State

Sovereignty The territories ruled by traditional states were poorly defined, the level of control wielded by the central government being quite weak. The notion of national **sovereignty**—that a government possesses authority over an area with clear-cut borders, within which it is the supreme power—is a relatively modern one. All modern nation-states are sovereign states. **Failed states** exist when the central government has lost authority over large parts of its national territory and resorts to the use of deadly force, often against civilian populations, in an effort to retain some degree of power. Examples today include Chad, the Democratic Republic of the Congo, Somalia, Sudan, and Yemen (*Foreign Policy*, 2013).

Nationalism Nation-states are associated with the rise of **nationalism**, which can be defined as a set of symbols and beliefs that creates a sense of membership in a single political community—such as being American, Canadian, or Russian. Although people may have always identified with their family, village, or religious community, nationalism appeared only with the development of the modern state. It is the main expression of identity with a distinct political community.

Nationalistic loyalties do not always fit the physical borders marking nations' territories. Because all nation-states comprise communities of diverse backgrounds, **local nationalism** frequently arises in opposition to that fostered by the state—such as nationalist feelings among the French-speaking population in Québec, Canada. While the relation between the nation-state and nationalism is complicated, the two are part of the same process. (We will return to nationalism when we explore its effect on international politics.)

Power and Authority For states to operate effectively, they must have **power**—the ability of individuals or groups to make their own interests or concerns count, even when others resist. Power, therefore, sometimes involves the use of force. Power is present in almost all social relationships: between parent and child, professor and student, employer and employee. The exercise of power is, in turn, almost always accompanied by belief systems that justify its use. **Authority** is a form of power that is seen as rightfully exercised, or (to use a term preferred by sociologists and political scientists) "legitimate." Those who are subject to a government's authority voluntarily consent to it. Contrary to what many

sovereignty The undisputed political rule of a state over a given territorial area.

failed states States in which the central government has lost authority and resorts to deadly force to retain power.

nationalism A set of beliefs and symbols expressing identification with a national community.

local nationalism The belief that communities that share a cultural identity should have political autonomy, even within smaller units of nation-states.

power The ability of individuals or the members of a group to achieve aims or further the interests they hold. Power is a pervasive element in all human relationships.

authority A government's legitimate use of power.

believe, democracy is not the only type of legitimate government. Dictatorships can have legitimacy as well, as can states governed by religious leaders.

Citizenship Before the emergence of modern societies, most people lacked awareness or even interest in those who governed them; moreover, they had no political rights or influence. Normally, only the dominant classes or richest groups felt a sense of belonging to a political community. In modern societies, by contrast, most people living within the borders of the political system are **citizens**, individuals having common rights and duties, who know they are members of a common national community (Brubaker, 1992). Although some people are political refugees or are "stateless," almost everyone in the world today identifies as a member of some national political order.

Citizenship Rights Three types of rights are associated with citizenship (Marshall, 1973). First, **civil rights** are rights of the individual as established by law; these include privileges that took a long time to achieve and are not fully recognized in all countries. Examples are the freedom of individuals to live where they choose, freedom of speech and religion, the right to own property, and the right to equal justice before the law. These rights were not fully established in most European countries until the early nineteenth century, and not all groups were allowed the same privileges. Although the U.S. Constitution granted such rights to Americans well before most European states had them, African Americans were excluded until the mid-nineteenth century. Even after the Civil War, when Blacks legally obtained these rights, they were unable to exercise them. Blacks were assured full legal equality only with the passage of

Civil rights demonstrators march in 1964 in St. Augustine, Florida. Civil rights include the right to own property and the right to a fair trial.

the Civil Rights Act of 1964—and then only because of more than a decade of marches, demonstrations, and nonviolent civil disobedience led by Dr. Martin Luther King Jr. and countless others in the civil rights movement (Branch, 1989).

Women also were denied many civil rights; at the turn of the nineteenth century in the United States, women had few rights independent of their husbands. They could not own property, write wills, collect an inheritance, or even earn a salary. Throughout the nineteenth century, states slowly and gradually began affording such rights to women, regardless of their marital status (Speth, 2011).

The second type of citizenship rights consists of **political rights**, especially the right to participate in elections and run for public office. Again, these rights were not won easily or quickly. In the United States, the achievement of full voting rights even for all men is relatively recent; it occurred only after the African American struggle for civil rights. In most European countries, the vote was at first limited to male citizens owning a certain amount of property—in other words, an affluent minority. In most Western countries, the vote for women was achieved partly through the efforts of women's movements and partly as a consequence of women entering the formal economy early in the twentieth century, during World War I. As recently as September 2011, Saudi Arabia's King Abdullah officially granted women the right to vote and run in local elections.

The third type of citizenship rights consists of **social rights**—the right of every individual to enjoy a minimum standard of economic welfare and security. Social rights include sickness benefits, unemployment benefits, and a guaranteed minimum wage—in other words, welfare provisions. In most societies, social rights developed last because the establishment of civil and political rights underpinned the fight for social rights. Social rights have been won largely as a result of the political strength that poorer groups have been able to develop after obtaining the vote.

Social rights are typically achieved through a **welfare state**, which exists when government organizations provide material benefits for citizens. Some of these benefits are intended to help those who cannot support themselves adequately through paid employment—the unemployed, the sick, the disabled, and the elderly. Many benefits go to the middle class as well: free or low-cost public education from kindergarten through state colleges and universities (although the cost of the latter is rapidly rising in many states), freeways, and Social Security, to

political rights Rights of political participation, such as the right to vote in local and national elections, held by citizens of a national community.

social rights Rights of social and welfare provision held by all citizens in a national community, including, for example, the right to claim unemployment benefits and sickness payments provided by the state.

welfare state A political system that provides a wide range of welfare benefits for its citizens.

revolutions Processes of political change involving the mobilizing of a mass social movement, which, by the use of violence, successfully overthrows an existing regime and forms a new government.

social movements Large groups of people who seek to accomplish, or to block, a process of social change. Social movements normally exist in conflict with organizations whose objectives and outlook they oppose. However, movements that successfully challenge power, once they become institutionalized, can develop into organizations.

name a few examples. In Western countries, an extensive welfare state has been considered the ideal expression of citizenship rights for more than half a century; however, in many poorer countries, welfare benefits, especially for the poor, are virtually nonexistent.

Although an extensive welfare state was seen as the culmination of the development of citizenship rights, in recent years, welfare states have come under pressure from increasing global economic competition and the movement of people from poorer, often war-torn, countries to richer ones. As a result, the United States and some European countries have sought to reduce benefits to noncitizens and to prevent new immigrants from entering their borders. For example, for many years the U.S. government has patrolled its border with Mexico and constructed walls of concrete and barbed wire in an attempt to keep undocumented immigrants out of the country—an issue that resurfaced during the 2016 presidential campaign. In 2015, more than a million refugees from civil war and religious violence in Syria, Afghanistan, Iraq, and other countries fled their homelands and sought asylum in Europe, straining resources and provoking an anti-immigrant backlash among some segments of the European population. Citizenship, and the bundle of rights and privileges accompanying it, serves as a powerful instrument of social closure (Brubaker, 1992), whereby prosperous nation-states have attempted to exclude the migrant poor from the status and the benefits that citizenship confers. Concern over immigrants was one of the driving forces behind the 2016 British vote to leave the European Union (the so-called "Brexit"), and contributed to Donald Trump's electoral victory in the U.S. 2016 presidential race (during the campaign, one of Trump's promises was to "build a wall" between the United States and Mexico and make Mexico pay for it).

Social change sometimes occurs outside the established political system. **Revolutions** occur when an existing political order is overthrown by means of a mass movement that emerges when desired changes cannot be achieved within the system, often using violence (Foran, 1997, 2005). Yet for all their high drama, revolutions occur relatively infrequently. More commonly, political change is achieved through **social movements**—collective attempts to further a common interest or secure a common goal through action outside the sphere of established institutions. Social movements are as evident in the contemporary world as are the formal, bureaucratic organizations they often oppose. Many contemporary social movements are international and utilize information technology in linking local campaigners to global issues.

CONCEPT CHECKS

1 Why is participatory democracy not a viable option for most modern states?

2 Describe three characteristics of the state.

3 What is the welfare state? Can the United States be classified as a welfare state? Why?

2 WHO RULES? THEORIES OF DEMOCRACY

Classical sociology offers three different ideas of how modern democracies actually function: through rule by elites who possess the necessary expertise but are accountable to the electorate; through interest groups that compete for influence, providing a form of checks and balances against one another; and through an elite of the wealthy and powerful that operates in the background, thereby shaping policy in their interest.

Democratic Elitism

One of the most influential views of the nature and limits of modern democracy was set out by Max Weber and, in modified form, by economist Joseph Schumpeter (1983; orig. 1942). Their ideas are called the theory of **democratic elitism**.

Weber held that direct democracy is impossible as a means of regular government in large-scale societies—not only for the logistical reason that millions of people cannot meet to make political decisions, but also because running a complex society demands expertise. Participatory democracy, Weber believed, can succeed only in small organizations where the work is straightforward. When complicated decisions or policies are involved, even in modest-sized groups, such as small business firms, specialized knowledge and skills are necessary. Because experts carry out their jobs on a continuous basis, positions requiring expertise cannot be subject to regular election by people with vague knowledge of the necessary skills and information. Although higher officials, responsible for overall policy decisions, are elected, a large substratum of full-time bureaucratic officials must play a large part in running a country (Weber, 1979; orig. 1921). In Weber's view, the development of mass citizenship, which is closely connected with the idea of general democratic participation, greatly expands the need for bureaucratic officialdom. For example, provision for welfare, health, and education requires permanent, large-scale administrative systems.

Representative multiparty democracy, according to Weber, helps defend against both arbitrary decision making on the part of political leaders (because they are subject to popular elections) and power being completely usurped by bureaucrats (because elected officials set overall policy). But under these circumstances, the contribution of democratic institutions falls short of achieving pure democracy. "Rule by the people" is possible in only a very limited sense. To achieve power, political parties must become organized in a systematic way—they must become bureaucratized. "Party machines" then develop that threaten the autonomy of parliaments or congresses in discussing and formulating policies. If a party with a majority representation can dictate policy, and if that party is run by officials who are permanently in control, then the level of democracy is low.

democratic elitism A theory of the limits of democracy. It holds that in large-scale societies democratic participation is necessarily limited to the regular election of political leaders.

pluralist theories of modern democracy Theories that emphasize the role of diverse and potentially competing interest groups, none of which dominates the political process.

For democratic systems to be effective, Weber argued, two conditions must be met. First, there must be parties that represent different interests and have different outlooks. If the policies of competing parties are basically the same, voters lack any effective choice. Weber held that one-party systems cannot be democratic in any meaningful way. Second, there must be political leaders with imagination and the courage to escape the inertia of bureaucracy. Weber emphasized the importance of leadership in democracy, which is why his view is known as democratic elitism: Rule by elites is inevitable; ideally, they will represent our interests in an innovative and insightful fashion. Parliaments and congresses give

As this closed-off section of the Capitol suggests, individual citizens have limited ways of participating in a representative democracy.

rise to political leaders who can counter the influence of bureaucracy and command mass support. Weber valued multiparty democracy more for the quality of leadership it generates than for the mass participation in politics it makes possible.

Joseph Schumpeter (1983) agreed with Weber about the limits of mass political participation and about democracy being important as a method of generating effective and responsible government. For Schumpeter, as for Weber, democracy is more important as a method of generating effective and responsible government than as a means of providing significant power for the majority. Democracy, Schumpeter stated, is the rule of the politician, not the people. To achieve voting support, however, politicians must be minimally responsive to the demands and interests of the electorate. Only if there is competition to secure votes can arbitrary rule be avoided.

Pluralist Theories

While pluralists accept that individual citizens can have little or no direct influence on political decision making, they argue that the presence of interest groups can limit the centralization of power in the hands of government officials. According to **pluralist theories of modern democracy**, government policies in a democracy are influenced by the continual processes of bargaining among numerous groups representing different interests—business organizations, trade unions, ethnic groups, environmental organizations, religious groups, and so forth. Competing interest groups or factions are vital to democracy because they divide up power, reducing the exclusive influence of any one group or class (Truman, 1981). A democratic political order involves a balance among competing interests, all having some effect on policy but none dominating the mechanisms of government. Elections are also influenced by this situation; to achieve a majority of votes, the parties must be responsive to diverse interest groups. In the view of pluralist theorists, the United States is one of the most pluralistic of industrialized societies and, therefore, the most democratic. Competition among diverse interest groups occurs not only at the national level but also within the states and in local communities.

The Power Elite

C. Wright Mills's celebrated work *The Power Elite* (1956) takes a view different from that of pluralist theories. According to Mills, early in its history, American society did show flexibility and diversity at all levels; however, this has since changed. Mills argued that during the twentieth century, a process of institutional centralization occurred in the political order, the economy, and the military. On the political side, individual state governments used to be very powerful and were loosely coordinated by the federal government. But by the mid-twentieth century, Mills argued, political power had become tightly coordinated at the federal level. Similarly, the economy once comprised many small units, businesses, banks, and farms, but now was dominated by a cluster of very large corporations. Finally, since World War II, the military, once restricted in size, had grown to a giant establishment at the heart of the country's institutions.

Not only had each sphere become more centralized, according to Mills, but all had increasingly merged into a unified system of power. Those holding the highest positions in all three institutional areas had similar social backgrounds, enjoyed parallel interests, and often knew one another personally. They had become a **power elite** that ran the country and, given the international position of the United States, influenced much of the rest of the world. Today, this elite group is sometimes called the "deep state"—entrenched government officials and bureaucrats, often linked to global business interests, who are unresponsive to the electorate, even in liberal democracies. Widespread dissatisfaction with governments considered unresponsive has fueled the rise of anti-government movements on both the right and left throughout the world, as we will discuss later in this chapter.

According to Mills, the power elite is composed mainly of White Anglo-Saxon Protestants (WASPs) who are from wealthy families, attend the same prestigious universities, belong to the same clubs, and sit on government committees with one another. They have closely connected concerns. Business and political leaders work together, and both have close relationships with the military through weapons contracting and the supply of goods for the armed forces. There is considerable movement among top positions in the three spheres. Politicians have business interests; business leaders often run for public office; high-ranking military

power elite Small networks of individuals who, according to C. Wright Mills, hold concentrated power in modern societies.

personnel sit on the boards of the large companies. The Trump cabinet, for example, included two former investment bankers (Treasury Secretary Steven Mnuchin and Commerce Secretary Wilbur Ross), two from business (Secretary of State Rex Tillerson, since replaced by Mike Pompeo, and Education Secretary Betsy DeVos), and originally included two former U.S. Marine Corps generals (Defense Secretary James Mattis and White House Chief of Staff John F. Kelly) who have since been replaced by Defense Secretary Mark Esper (a top lobbyist for U.S. defense contractor Raytheon) and standing White House Chief of Staff Mick Mulvaney. The net worth of the entire Trump administration is estimated at more than $12 billion, believed to be the highest in history (Martel, 2017).

In opposition to pluralist interpretations, Mills saw three distinct levels of power in the United States. The power elite occupies the highest level, formally and informally making key decisions affecting both domestic and foreign policy. Interest groups operate at the middle levels of power, together with local government agencies. Their influence over major policy decisions is limited. At the bottom is the mass of the population, who have virtually no influence on policy decisions because these are made within closed settings by the power elite. Because the power elite spans the top of both party organizations, the choices open to voters in presidential and congressional elections are so small as to be of little consequence.

Since Mills published his study, other researchers have analyzed the social background and interconnections of leading figures in American society. All studies find that the social backgrounds of those in leading positions are highly unrepresentative of the population as a whole (Domhoff, 1971, 1979, 1983, 1998, 2013).

The main argument among sociologists about the distribution of power in the United States now focuses on the relative power of government officials and of the business leaders who run large corporations. Some scholars argue that true power lies with politicians in government and that business leaders are much less powerful (Amenta, 1998; Orloff, 1993; Skocpol, 1992). Other scholars hold that corporate business executives and families of great wealth form a capitalist class that greatly influences government officials and experts through lobbying, campaign contributions, the sponsorship of think tanks, and the appointment of top corporate leaders to important government positions (Domhoff, 1998, 2013); some argue that a transnational capitalist class increasingly dominates national politics (Robinson, 2004, 2014). Both sides agree, however, that it is not inevitable for business leaders or government officials always to be dominant. Although an elite class—whether elected, expert, or corporate—rules America, the power of groups can change over time, leaving open the possibility that those who are now powerless could be dominant in the future.

The Role of the Military

Mills's argument that the military plays a central role in the power elite was buttressed by a well-known warning from a former military hero and U.S. president, Dwight David Eisenhower. In his farewell address in 1961, Eisenhower warned, "In the councils of government, we must guard against the acquisition of unwarranted influence,

Table 13.1

APPLYING SOCIOLOGY TO GOVERNMENT, POLITICAL POWER, AND SOCIAL MOVEMENTS

CONCEPT	APPROACH TO UNDERSTANDING GOVERNMENT, POLITICAL POWER, AND SOCIAL MOVEMENTS	CONTEMPORARY APPLICATION
Democratic Elitism	In societies with large populations, direct democracy (in which everybody participates in making policy) is not possible. What is possible is government by elected representatives, although such representative democracy may be weakened when political parties emerge that establish elite control over public policies.	In the United States, two political parties (Democrat and Republican) dominate politics. The degree to which either represents the interest of the majority is often debated, and voter turnout tends to be lower than in other industrialized countries.
Pluralist Theories	Although direct democracy may not be possible in large-scale societies, it can be achieved nonetheless, since interest groups emerge that represent competing interests in society, such that each group ultimately has a voice that is heard. Examples of such competing interests are business organizations, trade unions, ethnic groups, environmental organizations, and religious groups.	During the latter part of the twentieth century, big unions (such as the United Automobile Workers) were seen as countervailing powers against the economic might of companies like General Motors (then the world's largest corporation). Unions have declined in membership and power over the past half century, however.
The Power Elite	Democracy is thwarted by small groups of rich and powerful individuals whose interests ultimately shape government policy.	General Dwight David Eisenhower, U.S. president (1953–1961) and Supreme Commander of the Allied forces in Europe during World War II, warned during his farewell presidential address that "we must guard against the acquisition of unwarranted influence, whether sought or unsought, by the military-industrial complex. The potential for the disastrous rise of misplaced power exists and will persist."

whether sought or unsought, by the military-industrial complex. The potential for the disastrous rise of misplaced power exists and will persist" (Eisenhower, 1961). Eisenhower's experience lent considerable credence to his assertion: He served for eight years as president (1953–1961), held the top rank of five-star army general, and had been Supreme Commander of the Allied forces in Europe during World War II. In 1989, at the end of the Cold War, U.S. defense spending—which had reached

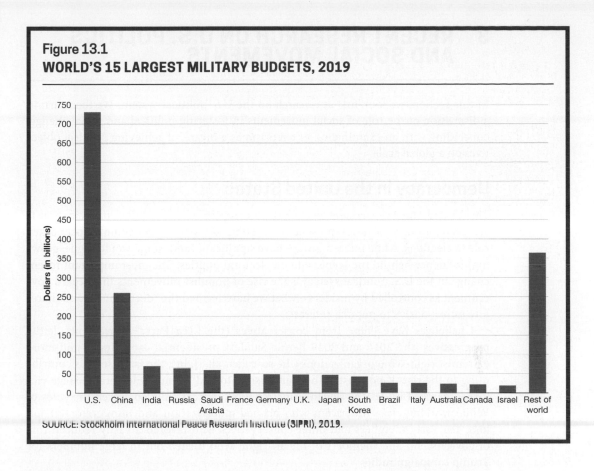

Figure 13.1
WORLD'S 15 LARGEST MILITARY BUDGETS, 2019

Dollars (in billions)

U.S. China India Russia Saudi Arabia France Germany U.K. Japan South Korea Brazil Italy Australia Canada Israel Rest of world

SOURCE: Stockholm International Peace Research Institute (SIPRI), 2019.

$300 billion in that year—began to decline slightly. With the collapse of the Soviet Union in 1991, the United States became the world's unrivaled military superpower; there was even talk of a "peace dividend" to spend on improving schools, repairing highways, or other domestic needs. But the decline proved to be short lived. The global war on terrorism triggered another cycle of military spending, which surpassed $700 billion in 2010 (Shah, 2011). U.S. military spending in 2019 was $732 billion (SIPRI, 2019). However, other studies estimate that the United States has spent $5.4 trillion on the war on terror as of 2020, and has over $1 trillion in obligations to veterans through 2059 (Crawford, 2019). Total military spending in the United States is greater than that for nearly all other countries in the world combined (see Figure 13.1). Eisenhower's dire warning seems no less true today than when he uttered it half a century ago.

3 RECENT RESEARCH ON U.S. POLITICS AND SOCIAL MOVEMENTS

In this section, we look first at research on the U.S. political system. We then turn to a discussion of the role of social movements in fostering political and social change, concluding with an examination of terrorism as a means of achieving political objectives on a global scale.

Democracy in the United States

The United States is a representative democracy in which political participation is achieved through elected representatives. Political parties have come to play a key role in elections, while interest groups have significant (and, some would argue, growing) influence behind the scenes and on electoral politics. The most important recent change in the U.S. political system is the rise of populist movements that regard government as controlled by insiders—what we have termed the "deep state"—and therefore unresponsive to popular interests.

Challenges have come from conservatives (the "Tea Party" movement), leftist progressives (the 2016 and 2020 Bernie Sanders presidential campaigns), and more extremist right-wing organizations (the so-called alt-right), the latter seen as contributing to the rise of populist authoritarianism. Donald Trump's Electoral College victory, organized under the slogan "America First," successfully coalesced the votes of White working-class Americans who blamed globalization and immigrants for job loss; Tea Party members and other conservatives who favored a vastly reduced role of government; and members of the alt-right, who turned out in large numbers for Trump campaign rallies.

Elections

A political party is an organization of individuals with broadly similar political aims, oriented toward achieving legitimate control of government through an electoral process. Two parties dominate political systems where elections are based on the principle of winner take all, as in the United States. The candidate who gains the most votes wins the election, no matter what proportion of the overall vote they gain. Exceptions to this general rule in the United States involve presidential elections, which are decided by the Electoral College. Under this system, each state has a number of electors equal to its total congressional representation: the number of seats it holds in the House of Representatives (which is proportional to its population), plus its two senators. Whichever candidate gets the largest number of votes in a state gets all the state's electoral votes.

As a result, a tiny margin of victory in a populous state such as California, New York, or Florida can swing a close election. At three times in American history, one candidate won the majority of votes from citizens (the popular vote) but still lost the Electoral College vote. This occurred in 2000, when Al Gore outpolled George W. Bush by about 500,000 votes but still lost the electoral vote by 271 to 267, and again in 2016, when Hillary Clinton outpolled Donald Trump by 2.9 million votes but lost the electoral vote by 306 to 232. Although Clinton won large margins of victory in populous states such as California and New York, she failed to carry crucial states such as Florida, Michigan, North Carolina, Ohio, Pennsylvania, and Wisconsin—so-called "swing" states that the Clinton campaign was initially favored to win. In three of those states, accounting for 46 electoral votes (Michigan, Pennsylvania, and Wisconsin), Clinton lost by a combined total of 80,000 votes; a shift of 1 percent of the vote in each of those states would have resulted in her winning the Electoral College (Bump, 2016b).

Where elections are based on different principles, such as proportional representation (in which seats in a representative assembly are allocated according to the proportions of the vote attained), five or six or more parties may be represented in the assembly. When no single party has a majority, some of the parties have to form a coalition, an alliance with one another, to form a government.

As a consequence of the winner-take-all electoral system, the United States effectively has only two significant political parties, Republicans and Democrats, since it is virtually impossible for minor parties to garner sufficient electoral votes to win presidential elections. Two-party systems often lead to a concentration on the middle ground, where most votes are found, although in recent years, the two parties in the United States have become increasingly polarized. While the Democratic Party remains divided between its left-liberal, centrist, and more conservative members (the so-called "Blue Dog Democrats"), the Republican Party has become much more consistently conservative.

Multiparty systems, on the other hand, allow more direct expression of divergent interests and provide scope for the representation of radical alternatives. Green Party representatives and representatives of far right or far left parties, found in some European parliaments, are cases in point. However, often no single party can achieve an overall majority, and the resulting government by coalition may lead either to a stalemate (if compromises can't be made) or to a rapid succession of elections and new governments, none remaining in power for long. The rise of populist authoritarianism in Europe—largely in reaction to unfavorable economic conditions and the influx of millions of refugees from war-torn countries in the

U.S. politics is dominated by two major parties. In the 2016 election, younger voters and Black and Hispanic voters overwhelmingly favored Clinton while Trump drew older voters as well as voters from small towns and rural areas.

Middle East and North Africa—has resulted in the resurgence of right-wing nationalist parties in Hungary, France, the Netherlands, Greece, Austria, Germany, and even liberal Sweden.

Some writers have studied the connection between voting patterns and class differences. Liberal and leftist parties historically have gained the most votes from lower-class voters, whereas conservative and rightist parties often win the vote of the affluent (see, for example, Bartels, 2008; Pew Research Center for the People and the Press, 2005; Stonecash, 2000). Although the Democratic Party has tended to appeal more to lower-class groups, and the Republicans have drawn support from the more affluent sectors, the connections are not absolute. In 2012, 63 percent of voters making less than $30,000 supported Obama, but that percentage dropped to 57 percent for voters making between $30,000 and $49,000. For those making $50,000 or more, a majority—53 percent—supported Romney (*New York Times*, 2012).

By 2016, however, the relationship between income and voting preference had weakened. The percentage of those earning less than $30,000 who voted for the Democratic candidate (Clinton) dropped from 63 to 53 percent; for those making between $30,000 and $49,000, it dropped from 57 to 51 percent. Unlike four years earlier, however, less than a majority of those earning more than $50,000 (29 percent) voted for the Republican candidate (Trump). "Third party" candidates Jill Stein (Green Party) and Gary Johnson (Libertarian Party) drew roughly 6 percent of the national vote away from both major party candidates, denying either a majority of the votes.

The largest differences in voting preferences, however, had to do with age, race, and education. Younger voters (especially those under 30) overwhelmingly favored Clinton; older voters (over 40) preferred Trump. Only 37 percent of all White voters favored Clinton, compared with 88 percent of Black voters and 65 percent of Latino voters. More highly educated voters strongly favored Clinton, while voters from small towns and rural areas voted strongly for Trump (Gould and Harrington, 2016). Trump, running as an insurgent candidate outside the Republican Party mainstream, was able to tap into many of the same themes that have contributed to the rise of populist authoritarianism in Europe, in particular, the eroding economic fortunes of many working-class Whites, anger over job losses blamed on the offshoring of manufacturing and undocumented immigrant labor, and fear of terrorism.

The reasons that support for Democrats has eroded have been much debated (Bartels, 2006, 2008; Frank, 2004, 2005, 2016). Several factors, however, seem especially important. In all income groups except the poorest, White voters tend to identify as Republican—with the exception of those who belong to **unions**, who remain more likely to call themselves Democrats. As union membership has declined, so has support for Democrats, and even among households with union members, support for Clinton was considerably lower than it had been for Obama four years earlier (Rosenfeld, 2014; Minchin, 2016; Bump, 2016a). The Democratic Party's support for free trade and liberal policies on immigration have also resulted in an erosion of support among working-class Whites, many of whom no longer see the Democratic Party as supportive of their interests (Frank, 2016).

unions Organizations that advance and protect the interests of workers with respect to working conditions, wages, and benefits.

The 2016 elections signalled a major political realignment in the United States that has carried over to the 2020 election cycle. Bernie Sanders's strength in the 2016 Democratic primaries, with his strong support among young people—and Donald Trump's victory in the 2016 Republican primaries and the general election—clearly signal among many voters a concern with the status quo in American politics. One national survey of nearly 2,700 people age 18–29 found that three out of five wanted to "help unite, not further divide" America; half believe that the news they get on Facebook is "fake news" (four out of five have Facebook accounts); and 48 percent identify or lean Democratic (compared with 28 percent Republican and 22 percent independent) (Harvard Kennedy School Institute of Politics, 2017).

Political Parties

The founders of the American governmental system did not foresee a role for parties in the political order. George Washington recognized that interest groups would develop, but he warned against "the harmful effects of the spirit of party." Thomas Jefferson echoed these sentiments, but he in fact became the leader of one of the earliest party organizations. The early parties endorsed candidates for Congress, and the subsequent national division of parties spread to the state legislatures. Soon the parties developed into state organizations representing specific interests and points of view. A two-party system was well established by the 1830s, and its fundamental nature has not altered greatly to this day. Building mass support for a party in the United States is difficult because the country is so large and includes so many regional, cultural, and ethnic groups. The parties have all cultivated electoral strength by forging broad regional bases of support and campaigning for very general political ideals.

As measured by levels of membership, party identification, and voting support, both of the major American parties are in decline. In 2002, roughly equal proportions of registered voters identified as Democrats (34 percent) and Republicans (33 percent), with significantly fewer identifying as Independents (26 percent). As of December 2019, the number of self-identified Democrats had dropped to 28 percent. Twenty-eight percent identified as Republicans, while the largest percentage of people (41 percent) described themselves as independents (Gallup, 2019).

The decline in party identification reflects a steadily growing distrust of politics among American voters. According to one survey conducted in 2016, only 19 percent of adults reported they could trust the government "always or most of the time." The reasons for this are many: an economic recession in 2008 that left 1 out of every 10 American workers jobless, followed by a recovery that was widely perceived as mainly benefitting the most affluent Americans; partisan fighting in a strongly divided Congress; growing polarization between the Democratic and Republican parties; and a general decline in the public's confidence that elected officials are able to represent their interests (Toedtman, 2016).

Although trust in government has been declining for years (it briefly peaked after 9/11, before continuing its long-term decline), distrust in government achieved force with the rise of the "Tea Party," a conservative movement strongly identified with the Republican Party that first appeared on the scene in 2009. The Tea Party is not actually a political party; its name comes from the Boston Tea Party protests of 1773, in which the colonists dumped tea into Boston Harbor, protesting British taxes on tea exported to the colonies. The Tea Party is a well-organized social movement opposed to what its adherents viewed as the Obama administration's excessive interference in the economy, as seen in its efforts to end the recession through federal spending, its partial takeover of failing corporations, and its push for universal health care coverage. According to the Gallup poll, popular support for the Tea Party peaked early in the Obama administration, reached 32 percent in 2010, but, five years later, had fallen to 17 percent (Norman, 2015).

In the 2016 elections, the Tea Party played a less prominent role than did the alt-right, a loose organization of far-right groups and individuals who reject mainstream conservative ideas in favor of a belief in economic populism combined with White nationalism—the belief that the economy should be made to work for "ordinary" people, coupled with White supremacy, anti-Semitism, and anti-Islamic beliefs. The alt-right made effective use of social media to advance its ideas and appeal, and it found a home in *Breitbart News*, described as "the platform for the alt-right" by its CEO Stephen Bannon (Posner, 2016). Bannon left *Breitbart News* to run the Trump campaign in August 2016 and was named a senior adviser to the president following the election. Although he eventually fell out of favor with President Trump, his role in the presidential campaign brought many supporters of the alt-right to Trump campaign rallies, and Bannon is credited with helping to write Trump's inaugural address, which claimed that "from this day forward, it's going to be only America first. America first" (Calamur, 2017). The presence of the alt-right reinforced a strong note of populism in the Republican presidential campaign—just as the Bernie Sanders campaign had done during the 2016 Democratic primaries. It also raised concerns about the rise of populist authoritarianism, given its strong right-wing views.

Given the openly racist views of some alt-right groups and members, it is arguable that racism also played an important role in the election, and one widely cited post-election analysis of American National Election Study data bears this out (Wood, 2017). Racism was evident in the two previous presidential elections as well. In 2008, Barack Obama became the first African American to be elected president, winning by a decisive margin (52 to 46 percent) over Republican John McCain. While Obama received 95 percent of the Black vote and 66 percent of the Latino vote, he lost decisively among White voters, 55 percent of whom voted for McCain (Keeter, 2008; Kohut, 2008). The 2012 election between Barack Obama and Republican challenger Mitt Romney revealed an even more polarized electorate. Black, Hispanic, and Asian voters chose Obama by 93 percent, 71 percent, and 73 percent, respectively, but White voters chose Romney by 59 percent (*Washington Post*, 2012).

Whether these divisions portend a longer-term shift in American political identifications remains to be seen, although at least one trend would seem to favor Democrats: The United States is predicted to become majority-minority by 2044, at which point non-Hispanic Whites will comprise less than half (47 percent) of the population. This change will result almost entirely from a substantial increase in the historically Democrat-identified Latino population, whose share is projected to increase from less than 18 percent in 2017 to 29 percent in 2060 (Colby and Ortman, 2015). The strong support of young people for Bernie Sanders (and, although to a lesser degree, for Hillary Clinton when she emerged as the Democratic Party candidate) also suggests that the party may become stronger in future national elections, particularly if it can appeal to the strong populist currents that seem to be reshaping American politics.

Interest Groups

Interest groups and lobbying play a distinctive part in American politics. An **interest group** is any organization that attempts to persuade elected officials to consider its aims when deciding on legislation. The American

> **interest group** A group organized to pursue specific interests in the political arena, operating primarily by lobbying the members of legislative bodies.

Medical Association, the National Organization for Women, and the National Rifle Association are three examples. Some interest groups are national; others are statewide. Some are permanently organized; others are short-lived. *Lobbying* is the act of persuading influential officials to vote in favor of a cause or otherwise lend support to the aims of an interest group. The word *lobby* originated in the British parliamentary system: In days past, members of Parliament did not have offices, so their business was conducted in the lobbies of the Parliament buildings.

The U.S. Lobbying Disclosure Act of 1995 requires all organizations employing lobbyists to register with Congress and to disclose whom they represent, whom they lobby, what they are lobbying for, and how much they are paid. In 2019, more than 11,000 different lobbyists were registered (Center for Responsive Politics [CRP], 2020b). To run as a political candidate is enormously expensive, and interest groups

The National Rifle Association, an interest group that advocates for gun rights, holds an annual meeting for members.

provide much of the funding at all levels of political office. Donald Trump, the 2016 Republican candidate for president, raised roughly $398 million, while Hillary Clinton, the Democratic candidate, raised nearly twice as much ($768 million). On the other hand, Trump received far greater media coverage throughout the campaign; such "free media" exposure was estimated as worth more than $5.9 billion for Trump, more than twice the $2.8 billion in free media estimated for Clinton. When "outside money" is factored in, including money from political action committees (PACs) that are set up by interest groups to raise and distribute campaign funds, total spending on the 2016 presidential and congressional campaigns is estimated to have exceeded $6.4 billion: nearly $2.4 billion for the presidency, and more than $4 billion for House and Senate seats (Sultan, 2017). It clearly costs a great deal of money to run for office, with the result that national officeholders spend a great deal of their time raising money (in the case of House representatives, who are up for election every two years, fund-raising for the next campaign cycle often begins immediately after the last election).

Incumbents have an enormous advantage in soliciting money. In the 2018 House and Senate elections, incumbents raised one and a half times as much money as their challengers—$1.3 billion compared with $898 million (Center for Responsive Politics, 2020a). Incumbents are preferred as fundraisers partly because they can curry favor with special interests and other contributors, since they are in a position to ensure favorable votes and obtain spending on their contributors' pet projects and other "pork" for their districts. Incumbency also provides familiarity—a formidable (and costly) obstacle for most challengers to overcome. The cost of elections has increased significantly in the last few decades (see Figure 13.2).

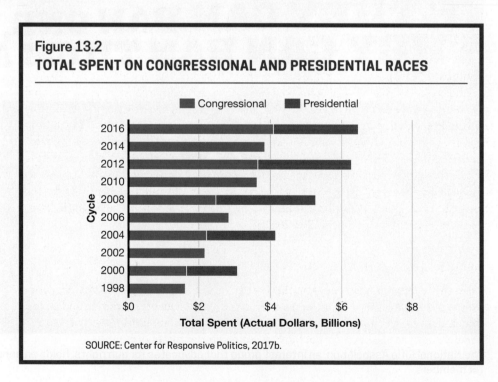

Figure 13.2
TOTAL SPENT ON CONGRESSIONAL AND PRESIDENTIAL RACES

SOURCE: Center for Responsive Politics, 2017b.

In 2010, the U.S. Supreme Court, in a narrow 5–4 decision (*Citizens United v. Federal Election Commission*), overturned a 63-year-old law that limited corporate and union spending in elections. The conservative majority on the Court reasoned that corporations and unions were protected under First Amendment free-speech rights, and so were free to spend as much as they chose to express their independent opinions on candidates—so long as these were not coordinated with candidates' campaigns (Liptak, 2010). This decision has raised concern among liberals that businesses will now be able to saturate the airwaves with political ads during elections, thereby exerting undue influence on voters. This, they reason, will further tip the balance of political influence toward those corporations that have deep pockets. Instead of "one person, one vote," it will more likely be "one dollar, one vote," with those having the most dollars able to garner the largest number of votes (Johnson, 2010).

Corporations, which have a strong stake in getting favorable legislation and government contracts, are the largest contributors to campaigns, outspending organized labor by as much as 17 to 1. In the 2016 election cycle, donations from businesses totaled $3.3 billion; donations from organized labor reached only $194 million. While these numbers may somewhat overstate the relative influence of corporations as opposed to labor unions, the overall trend is clear. Business donations narrowly favored Republican candidates over Democrats (51 to 49 percent), while the much smaller donations from organized labor strongly favored Democrats (87 to 13 percent).

Two other sources of funding played a role in the 2016 elections: So-called ideological organizations (mainly single-issue organizations such as the National Rifle Association, EMILY's List, and Environment for America) donated $460 million, with nearly two-thirds going to Democrats, while a large category of "other" donors (including educators, government employees, nonprofits, religious groups, and retired individuals) accounted for $699 million, with 58 percent going to Democrats (CRP, 2017a). PAC donations accounted for $542 million of total funding, 58 percent going to Republican candidates. The top 20 PACs included 17 corporations and 3 labor unions (CRP, 2017e).

Paid lobbyists play a significant role in influencing the outcome of congressional votes and presidential decisions. The Center for Responsive Politics (CRP, 2017d) reported that businesses, unions, and other advocacy groups spent some $3.1 billion in 2016, employing more than 11,000 lobbyists. The largest sector, health, was the target of $510 million in lobbying efforts, with the pharmaceutical industry accounting for nearly half of that amount. The U.S. Chamber of Commerce, broadly representing business interests, was the top spender in 2016 ($104 million), followed by the National Association of Realtors ($65 million). All of the top 20 lobbyists in 2016 represented business interests (CRP, 2017d).

The Political Participation of Women

The early women's movements saw the vote as both the symbol of political freedom and the means of achieving greater economic and social equality. In the United States, women did not get the right to vote until 1920; in France, not until 1944. Even today, in many countries, women do not have the same voting rights as men.

Women obtaining the vote has not greatly altered the nature of politics, although women's votes did contribute significantly to Obama's victory in 2008 and again in 2012. Women's voting patterns, like those of men, are shaped by party preferences, policy options, and the choice of candidates. In the 2016 election, 54 percent of women voted for Clinton compared to 42 percent for Trump. The reverse was true for men, with 53 percent voting for Trump and 41 percent for Clinton (Pew Research Center, 2016a), suggesting a strong gender gap in the first U.S. election in which a major party presidential candidate was female. The overall female preference for Clinton reflects the fact that Black and Latino women overwhelmingly voted Democrat; a majority of White women (53 percent) voted for Trump, including 62 percent of White women without a college degree (Puglise, 2016; Malone, 2016). Clearly race, education, and party affiliation intersected with gender in determining the outcome of the election.

There has been much debate—most of it informed by speculation rather than systematic analysis of data—over the reasons that Clinton, who had been heavily favored by statisticians and pollsters right up to the election, lost to Trump. While the unwillingness of some voters to elect a woman president may have played a role, most likely the results reflected the fact that many voters were tired of both parties' policies and wanted a change. Clinton, who had a long resume as an "insider" (the politically engaged wife of former President Bill Clinton, New York State senator, secretary of state under Obama) lost to Trump, the ultimate "outsider" candidate.

Women such as Nancy Pelosi, Elizabeth Warren, Kirsten Gillibrand, Kamala Harris, and Nikki Haley now play central roles in American politics. Still, women remain

While women such as Elizabeth Warren have made inroads, women still remain underrepresented in government, especially in statewide and national offices.

underrepresented in government. In 2019, there were only 25 women in the Senate (out of 100 members) and only 106 in the House of Representatives, comprising almost 25 percent of total seats in Congress (Center for American Women and Politics, 2018). While these percentages might seem low, from a historical perspective, they represent a sea change in women's roles in politics. Just 40 years ago, in 1970, there was only a single woman in the Senate and just 10 in the House.

Since 1990, female candidates have been successful when they have run for office. The critical factor seems to be that political parties (which are run largely by men) have not recruited as many women to run for office. The factors that impede women's advancement in the economy also operate in the realm of politics. Rising within a political organization requires considerable effort and time, which women shouldering major domestic burdens can rarely generate. That is perhaps why women are more likely to run for local elected positions, such as city council or mayor, rather than for statewide or national offices, which would require them to relocate far from their families. But there may be an additional influence in political life, where a high level of power is concentrated: Perhaps men are especially reluctant to abandon their dominance in such a sphere.

The influence of women on U.S. politics cannot be assessed solely through voting patterns and elected officials. Feminist groups have influenced political life independently of the franchise, particularly in recent decades. Since the early 1960s, the National Organization for Women (NOW) and other women's groups in the United States have been instrumental in the passing of equal opportunity acts and in getting a range of issues directly affecting women on the political agenda. Such issues include equal rights at work, the availability of abortion, changes in family and divorce laws, and lesbian rights. In 1973, women achieved a legal victory when the Supreme Court ruled in *Roe v. Wade* that women had a legal right to abortion. The 1989 Court ruling in *Webster v. Reproductive Health Services*, which placed restrictions on that right, caused a resurgence of involvement in the women's movement.

Although women in the United States may have achieved increased political power in recent decades, in terms of global comparisons, the country still has a long way to go. The Inter-Parliamentary Union (IPU) compiles a ranking of 193 countries, based on the percentage of women in each country's lower legislative house (comparable with the U.S. House of Representatives). As of February 2019, the United States ranked 76th, with almost 25 percent of combined House and Senate seats occupied by women. Rwanda—an African country where intertribal genocide claimed more than 800,000 lives in 1994—ranked first, with 56 percent of all seats held by women (IPU, 2019).

Some 70 women have served as heads of state (as presidents or prime ministers) during the twentieth and twenty first centuries (Geiger and Kent, 2017). Bangladesh—a predominantly Muslim country with 156 million people—has had female heads of state for more than half of its 46 years, the longest period of any modern country. The current prime minister, Sheikh Hasina, first served from 1996 to 2001, and has again been serving since 2009; her political rival, Khaleda Zia, served from 1991 to 1996, and again from 2001 to 2006. Other predominantly Muslim nations that have had a female head of state include Pakistan, Turkey, Indonesia, Senegal, Kosovo, Kyrgyzstan, and Mauritius (Dalia G, 2015). As of December 2019, 22 countries had female leaders, including Germany (Angela Merkel), Norway (Erna Solberg), Jacinda Ardern (New Zealand), and Mette Frederiksen (Denmark).

Political Participation in the United States

The Internet transcends national and cultural borders, facilitating the global spread of ideas. More and more people worldwide access the Internet regularly and consider it important to their lifestyles. According to one service that tracks global Internet usage, as of 2019, more than 4.3 billion people were using the Internet in some form—approximately 56 percent of the world's population. Internet use, of course, reflects global inequalities as well: 86 percent of people living in developed countries are Internet users, compared with 47 percent in developing countries, and 19 percent in least developed countries. Still, this picture is rapidly changing: Internet usage in Africa has grown to 28 percent, more than two and half times the rate of Internet usage in 2010—by far the highest rate of increase in the world (International Telecommunications Union [ITU], 2019).

While a January 2017 survey by the Pew Research Center found that 88 percent of Americans report using the Internet, those most likely to do so are young (100 percent of people between the ages of 18 and 29, compared with only 73 percent of people 65 and older), relatively wealthy (98 percent of those earning over $75,000, compared with 82 percent of those earning less than $30,000), and educated (98 percent of those with a college education, compared with only 71 percent of those without a high school diploma). Racial differences were almost nonexistent, with 92 percent of Whites using the Internet, compared with 86 percent of Hispanics, and 85 percent of African Americans (Pew Research Center, 2019b). Americans increasingly use the Internet on an array of devices and gadgets. In 2019, 81 percent of adults in the United States owned a smartphone. Younger people—those ages 18 to 29—are much more likely to use smartphones (96 percent) than people 65 and older (53 percent) (Pew Research Center, 2019e).

The Internet is replacing television and newspapers as the principal source for news for a growing number of people. Nearly half of all Americans with access to the Internet report getting news about government and politics from Facebook (43 percent)—roughly the same number as do from local TV (49 percent), and more than from CNN (44 percent), Fox News (39 percent), or NBC News (37 percent) (Pew Research Center, 2016f; Geiger, 2019). Does this easy access to the world's information result in greater open-mindedness—an ability to find information that challenges one's pet beliefs, thereby contributing to the free exchange of ideas ideally associated with democracy? This answer is far from clear-cut. While the Internet may democratize access to wide-ranging sources, most people get their news and information from Internet sources that reinforce their beliefs. On Facebook, for example, politically related postings are likely to come from like-minded friends (Pew Research Center, 2016f).

While the Internet (especially social media) played a major role in the 2016 presidential election, television still proved to be a more important source of information. During the presidential primaries, 62 percent of Trump supporters reported that they got most of their election news from television, compared with only 28 percent who relied on news websites and social media. For those supporting Clinton, the corresponding figures were similar: 56 percent and 28 percent. Yet nearly half (48 percent) of all Democrats who supported someone other than Clinton relied on news websites and social media, as opposed to television (37 percent)—a result that most likely reflected young persons' support for Sanders (Gottfried, Barthel, and Mitchell, 2017). Perhaps not surprisingly, the percentage of adults who report they often get their news online decreases with age: For Americans 18–49, the figure is roughly half; it drops to 29 percent for those 50–64, and 20 percent for those over 65 (Mitchell at al., 2016).

Both as candidate and now as president, Trump has used Twitter to mobilize his supporters. During the primaries, one study found that during one three-week period, Trump, Clinton, and Sanders posted roughly the same number of times on both Facebook and Twitter, but that Trump's postings produced by far the greatest response. His tweets, for example, were retweeted on average 6,000 times; Sanders was retweeted 2,500 times, and Clinton 1,500 times. At the time, Trump had roughly 10 million followers on Twitter and nearly as many on Facebook, both greatly exceeding the numbers for Clinton and Sanders (Pew Research Center, 2016b). After he was elected president, his number of Twitter followers rapidly increased, once it became clear that he was not abandoning his favorite medium as a principal means of communication. President Trump now has more than 32 million Twitter followers on his personal account and another 18 million on his presidential account (although many are likely on both) (Presto, Gingras, and Welch, 2017).

Trump's use of Twitter, which clearly outstrips any president (and most likely any other U.S. political figure), provided him with direct access to his strongest supporters, bypassing the more mainstream print and television news outlets. Because his tweets were often provocative and controversial, they were frequently covered by the mainstream media, enabling Trump to reach an even wider audience. One study of Trump's speeches and tweets during the presidential primaries, a time when he and his rival Republican candidates were vying for the support of the conservative Republican base, partly attributed his primary win to the fact that he used Twitter more than the other candidates. The study also flagged his communication style as key: grandiose pronouncements about himself, his plans, and his ability to make sweeping changes; his use of first-person pronouns; and the dynamic, nonverbal aspects of his speeches (Ahmadian, Azarshahi, and Paulhus, 2017). Twitter limits its posts to 140 characters, encouraging the use of short words and simple statements, roughly the length of this sentence. While this limitation clearly does not favor complex political analyses of challenging issues, it is well adapted to simplicity, impulsiveness, and—all too often—incivility: debasing attacks rather than reasoned discourse (Ott, 2017).

Political and Social Change through Social Movements

Political life is by no means carried out only within the framework of political parties, voting, and representation in legislative and governmental bodies. When groups' objectives or ideals cannot be achieved within, or are blocked by, this framework (as under authoritarian regimes), political and social change may require other forms of political action. Social movements, which operate outside the established political system, have been an important source of social change throughout U.S. history. Terrorism can be seen as an extreme form of social movement—one that is willing to use violence, often directed against civilian populations, to achieve its goals.

Why Do Social Movements Occur?

Because mass social movements have been so important around the world over the past two centuries, many theories try to account for them. Some theories were formulated early in the history of the social sciences; the most important were those of Karl Marx. He intended his views not just to analyze the conditions of revolutionary change but to actually promote such change. Indeed, Marx's ideas had an immense practical effect on twentieth-century social change.

We examine four frameworks for the study of social movements, many of which were developed in the context of revolution: Economic deprivation, resource mobilization, structural strain, and fields of action.

Economic Deprivation Marx's view of social movements arises from his interpretation of human history (see Chapter 1). According to Marx (1983; 2008, orig. 1867; see also Marx and Engels, 2008, orig. 1848), the development of societies involves periodic class conflicts that lead to revolutionary change. Class struggles derive from the contradictions—irresolvable tensions—in societies. In any stable society, there is a balance among the economic structure, social relationships, and the political system.

Deprivation of the peasantry compared to the elite in France led to the overthrow of the monarchy.

As the forces of production change, contradictions intensify, leading to open clashes between classes—and ultimately to revolution.

Industrial capitalism, according to Marx, sets up contradictions, which in his view would lead to revolutions prompted by Communist ideals (Appelbaum, 1988). Industrial capitalism, an economic order based on the private pursuit of profit and on competition among firms to sell their products, requires individual capitalists to cut costs continually in order to remain competitive. This cost-cutting is accomplished in two principal ways: Firms reduce wages at home, often by replacing workers with the latest "labor-saving" technologies, and they move their production to low-wage countries overseas. Both these strategies, while enabling businesses to survive, create a gulf between a rich minority that controls the industrial resources and an increasingly impoverished majority of waged workers. The resulting wealth disparity not only is seen as unjust by workers, fueling their revolutionary fervor, but also creates a fatal economic contradiction: Even though businesses produce an ever-increasing supply of goods, the growing masses of workers become too poor to buy them. This results, in the long run, in declining profits and economic stagnation. Capitalism, in other words, is the first economic system in history to suffer from producing too many goods rather than too few. The resulting economic crises, Marx predicted, would eventually lead the workers to overthrow the capitalist system and set up an alternative one in which they could better enjoy the fruits of their own labor. When a dominant class is particularly entrenched, Marx believed, violence is necessary to achieve the required transition. In other circumstances, this process might happen peacefully through parliamentary action; a violent revolution would not be necessary.

Contrary to Marx's expectations, revolutions failed to occur in the advanced industrialized societies of the West. Why? One reason is that capitalism proved to be more resilient than Marx had predicted, finding ways to resolve the economic contradictions Marx believed would eventually lead to its collapse. The welfare state, enacted throughout Europe and North America in response to the Great Depression of the 1930s, was one solution: Raise taxes, especially upon wealthier individuals, to provide a "social safety net" for those who are less well off. Examples include government-funded retirement programs such as Social Security, unemployment compensation, welfare payments to the poor, and universal health care. Globalization provides another solution: While the loss of jobs to low-wage countries hurts many workers, it also results in ever-cheaper commodities, enabling people to buy products they otherwise might not be able to afford. A third solution is the credit economy: Even when their incomes are stagnant or declining, people are able to consume goods (at least for a while). Whether these approaches will suffice in the long run is currently being challenged by the rise of populist movements around the world.

Sociologist James Davies (1962), a critic of Marx, offered another explanation for the absence of revolutions in industrialized societies. Davies identified periods in history when people lived in dire poverty but did not rise up in protest. Constant poverty or deprivation does not make people into revolutionaries; rather, they usually endure such conditions with resignation or mute despair. Social protest, and ultimately revolution, is more likely when people's living conditions improve. Then their expectations also go up. If improvement in actual conditions subsequently slows down, propensities to revolt develop because rising expectations are frustrated.

relative deprivation Deprivation a person feels by comparing himself with a group.

collective action Action undertaken in a relatively spontaneous way by a large number of people assembled together.

Thus, it is not absolute deprivation that leads to protest but **relative deprivation**—the discrepancy between people's actual lives and what they think could realistically be achieved. Davies's theory illuminates the connections between revolution and modern social and economic development. The ideals of progress, together with expectations of economic growth, induce rising hopes, which, if frustrated, spark protest. Such protest gains strength from the ideas of equality and democratic political participation, which were key not only in the American Revolution of 1776 and the Russian Revolution of 1917 but also in the revolutions of 1989 in Europe.

As Charles Tilly (1978) has pointed out, however, Davies's theory does not explain how and why different groups mobilize to seek revolutionary change. Protest might often occur against a backdrop of rising expectations; to understand how it becomes a mass social movement, we need to identify how groups collectively organize to make effective political challenges.

Resource Mobilization In *From Mobilization to Revolution*, Tilly (1978) analyzed processes of revolutionary change in the context of broader forms of protest and violence. He distinguished four main components of **collective action** taken to contest or overthrow an existing social order:

1. The *organization* of the group or groups involved. Protest movements are organized in many ways, varying from the spontaneous formation of crowds to tightly disciplined revolutionary groups. The Russian Revolution, for example, began as a small group of activists.
2. *Mobilization*, the ways in which a group acquires resources to make collective action possible. Such resources may include material goods, political support, and weaponry. Lenin acquired material and moral support from a sympathetic peasantry, together with many townspeople.
3. The *common interests* of those engaging in collective action, what they see as the gains and losses resulting from their policies. Common goals always underlie mobilization to collective action. Lenin built a broad coalition of support because many people had a common interest in removing the existing government.
4. *Opportunity*. Chance events may provide opportunities to pursue revolutionary aims. Numerous forms of collective action, including revolution, are influenced by such incidental events. Lenin's success depended on contingent factors, including success in battle. If Lenin had been killed, would there have been a revolution?

Collective action can be defined as people acting together in pursuit of shared interests—for example, gathering to demonstrate in support of their cause. Some of the people may be intensely involved; others may lend more passive or irregular support. Effective collective action, such as action that culminates in revolution, usually moves through all four stages.

Social movements, in Tilly's view, develop as a way of mobilizing group resources either when people have no institutionalized means of voicing their concerns or when the state authorities repress their needs. Although collective action at some point involves open confrontation with the political authorities, it is not likely to affect established patterns of power unless groups who are systematically organized support it.

Modes of collective action and protest vary with historical and cultural circumstances. In the United States today, for example, most people are familiar with mass marches, large assemblies, and street riots. Other types of collective protest (such as fights between villages, machine breaking, or lynching) have become less common or have disappeared. Protesters can also build on examples taken from other places; for instance, guerrilla movements proliferated in various parts of the world once disaffected groups learned how successful guerrilla actions could be against regular armies. And new forms of social protest are now being accomplished via the Internet, as exemplified during the 2016 election, including the greater influence of the alt-right and the increasingly effective use of social media such as Facebook and Twitter to mobilize support. Another example is the January 21, 2017, women's march, a worldwide protest in support of women's rights and other human rights issues. Globally, some 700 marches mobilized an estimated 5 million people, including 3–4 million in the United States, a half million of whom marched in Washington (Darrow, 2017; Hamilton, 2017; Stein, Hendrix, and Hauslohner, 2017; Women's March, 2017).

When and why does collective action become violent? After studying many incidents in Western Europe since 1800, Tilly concluded that most collective violence develops from action that is not initially violent. Whether violence occurs depends

On January 21, 2017, hundreds of thousands of protesters descended on the nation's capital for the Women's March on Washington. Across the globe, an estimated 5 million people participated in the march.

not so much on the nature of the activity as on other factors—in particular, how the authorities respond. Consider the street demonstration: The vast majority of such demonstrations occur without damage to people or property. A few lead to violence and are then labeled as riots. Sometimes the authorities step in when violence has already occurred; more often, the historical record shows, the authorities are the originators of violence and, in fact, are responsible for most deaths and injuries. This is not surprising given their special access to arms and military discipline. The groups they attempt to control, conversely, do greater damage to objects and property.

Tilly's concepts have wide application, and his use of them is sensitive to the variability of historical time and place. How social movements are organized, the resources they mobilize, the common interests of groups contending for power, and chance opportunities are all important facets of social transformation. According to Theda Skocpol (1979), Tilly assumes that social movements are guided by the deliberate pursuit of interests and that successful revolutionary change occurs when people realize these interests. Skocpol, in contrast, sees social movements as more ambiguous and indecisive in their objectives. Revolutions, she emphasizes, emerge largely as unintended consequences of more partial aims:

> In fact, in historical revolutions, differently situated and motivated groups have become participants in complex unfoldings of multiple conflicts. These conflicts have been powerfully shaped and limited by existing social, economic and international conditions. And they have proceeded in different ways depending upon how each revolutionary situation emerged in the first place. (Skocpol, 1979)

Skocpol's argument seems correct when we analyze the revolutionary changes that occurred in Eastern European societies in 1989, compared with earlier revolutionary episodes.

Structural Strain Neil Smelser (1963) distinguished six conditions underlying the origins of collective action in general and social movements in particular: structural conduciveness, structural strain in society, generalized beliefs, precipitating factors, effective leadership, and the nature of social control directed against the social movement.

1. *Structural conduciveness* refers to the social conditions promoting or inhibiting the formation of social movements. In Smelser's view, the sociopolitical system of the United States leaves open certain avenues of mobilization for protest because there is little or no state regulation in those areas. For example, there is no state-sponsored religion. People are free to exercise their religious beliefs. This creates a conducive environment in which religious movements might compete for individuals, so long as they do not transgress criminal or civil law.
2. Conducive conditions are not enough to bring a social movement into being. There must be **structural strain**—tensions (in Marx's terminology, contradictions) that produce conflicting interests. Uncertainties, anxieties, ambiguities, and direct clashes

structural strain Tension that produces conflicting interests within societies.

of goals are expressions of such strains. Sources of strain may be general or specific. Thus, sustained inequalities between ethnic groups create overall tensions; these may become focused in specific conflicts when, say, Blacks begin to move into a previously all-White area.

3. Social movements do not develop simply as responses to vaguely felt anxieties or hostilities. They are shaped by the influence of *generalized beliefs*—definite ideologies—that crystallize grievances and suggest courses of action to remedy those grievances. Revolutionary movements, for instance, are based on ideas about why injustice occurs and how it can be alleviated by political struggle.

4. *Precipitating factors* are events that trigger direct action by those involved in the movement. In 1955, when a Black woman named Rosa Parks refused to give up her seat to a White man on a bus in Montgomery, Alabama, her action helped spark the civil rights movement (see Chapter 11).

Rosa Parks's refusal to give up her seat to a White man on a bus in 1955 sparked the civil rights movement and is an example of a precipitating factor.

5. The first four conditions combined might occasionally lead to street disturbances or outbreaks of violence, but such incidents do not promote the development of social movements unless a coordinated group mobilizes for action. *Leadership* and some means of *regular communication* among participants, together with funding and material resources, are necessary for a social movement to exist.

6. Finally, the manner in which a social movement develops is influenced by the *operation of social control*. The governing authorities may respond initially by intervening in the conditions of conduciveness that gave rise to the movement. For instance, steps might be taken to reduce the ethnic inequality that generates resentment and conflict. Other important aspects of social control concern the responses of the police or armed forces. A harsh response might spark further protest and help solidify the movement. Also, doubt and divisions within the police and military can be crucial in deciding the outcome of confrontations with revolutionary movements.

Smelser's model is useful for analyzing the sequences in the development of social movements and collective action in general. Each stage "adds value" to the overall outcome; also, each stage is a necessary condition for the next one. But Smelser's theory bears some criticism as well. For example, some social movements become strong without precipitating incidents. Conversely, a series of incidents might highlight the need to establish a movement to change the circumstances that gave rise to the incidents. Also, a movement itself might create strains, rather than develop in response to them. For example, the women's movement has sought to identify and combat gender inequalities where they had previously gone unquestioned. Smelser's theory treats social movements as responses to situations, rather than acknowledging that members might spontaneously organize to achieve desired social changes. In this respect, his ideas contrast with the approach developed by Alain Touraine.

Fields of Action Alain Touraine (1977, 1981) developed his analysis of social movements on the basis of four main ideas. The first, which he called **historicity**, explains why there are many more social movements in the modern world than in earlier times. In modern societies, individuals and groups know that social activism can achieve social goals and reshape society.

Second, Touraine focused on the rational objectives of social movements. Such movements are not irrational responses to social divisions or injustices; rather, they develop from specific views and rational strategies for overcoming injustices.

Third, Touraine saw a process of interaction in the shaping of social movements. Movements develop in deliberate antagonism with established organizations and sometimes with rival social movements. According to Touraine, other theories of social movements have not adequately considered how the objectives of a social movement are shaped by encounters with others holding divergent positions and by the ways in which they themselves influence their opponents' outlooks and actions. For instance, the objectives and outlook of the women's movement were shaped in opposition to the male-dominated institutions the women's movement seeks to alter. The movement's goals and outlook have shifted in relation to its successes and failures and have influenced men's perspectives. These changed perspectives, in turn, have stimulated a reorientation in the women's movement.

Fourth, social movements and change occur in the context of "fields of action." A **field of action** comprises the connections between a social movement and the forces or influences against it. Mutual negotiation among antagonists in a field of action may produce the social changes sought by the movement, as well as changes in the movement itself and in its antagonists. In either circumstance, the movement may evaporate or become institutionalized as a permanent organization. For example, labor union movements became formal organizations when they achieved the right to strike and to engage in types of bargaining acceptable to both workers and employers. These changes were forged out of earlier processes involving widespread violent confrontation on both sides. Where there are continuing sources of conflict (as in the relation between unions and employers), new movements still tend to emerge.

Touraine's analysis can also be applied to movements concerned with individual change. For instance, Alcoholics Anonymous is a movement based on medical findings about the harmful effects of alcohol on people's health and social activities. The movement has been shaped by its own opposition to advertising that encourages alcoholic drinking and by its attempt to confront the pressures alcoholics face in a society that readily tolerates drinking.

historicity The use of an understanding of history as a basis for trying to change history—that is, producing informed processes of social change.

field of action The arena within which social movements interact with established organizations, often producing a modification of the ideas and outlook of the members of both.

Technology and Social Movements

Recently, two of the most influential forces in late modern societies—information technology and social movements—have come together with astonishing results. Social movements worldwide can now join in huge regional and international networks, including nongovernmental organizations, religious and humanitarian groups, human rights associations, consumer protection advocates, environmental activists, and others campaigning in the public interest. These electronic networks can respond immediately to events as they occur; gain access to and share sources of information; and put pressure on corporations, governments, and international bodies as part of their campaigning strategies. The Internet has been at the forefront of these changes, although cell phones, fax machines, and satellite broadcasting also hastened their evolution.

The ability to electronically coordinate international political campaigns is worrisome for governments and inspiring to participants in social movements. Indeed, the number of international social movements has grown steadily with the spread of the Internet. From global protests in favor of canceling developing world debt to the international campaign to ban land mines (which culminated in a Nobel Peace Prize), the Internet has united campaigners across national and cultural borders. Some observers argue that the information age is witnessing a migration of power away from government and toward new nongovernmental alliances and coalitions. Unlike revolutions and protests at earlier points in history, the Internet and social media now facilitate revolutionary movements. Through the use of Twitter, Facebook, Internet chat rooms, and other forms of social media, protesters and refugees (as well as jihadists) can now report in "real time" what they did and saw. Social movements now use social media to transmit messages and images to their peers and fellow protesters, and to viewers worldwide as well.

The original 2011 Arab Spring protests, for example, had far-reaching effects on protests worldwide. Images and video of young people's activism—and the political changes it forged—instantly traveled the world through social media, inspiring large protests across the globe (Kulish, 2011). In India, hundreds of thousands of

Antigovernment bloggers in Egypt gather in a Cairo café in Tahrir Square.

disillusioned young people supported rural activist Kisan Baburao "Anna" Hazare in his hunger strike. Hazare starved himself for 12 days until the Indian Parliament met some of his demands to implement an anticorruption measure. In Israel, an estimated 430,000 people gathered in Tel Aviv, Jerusalem, and Haifa to protest high unemployment, high costs of living, and other social injustices. In London, violence erupted at a protest march organized by the Trades Union Congress (TUC); an estimated 250,000 to 500,000 people marched from the Thames Embankment to the Houses of Parliament to Hyde Park to show their opposition to planned public spending cuts. "Occupy Wall Street" and "Black Lives Matter" protests have been held throughout the United States. All these movements inspired one another through social media.

Yet the power of social media–generated protests does not always lead to the desired social change. While the overthrow of Egyptian president Mubarak did produce the first democratic election in Egyptian history, the winner of the election—Mohamed Morsi, a leading member of the Muslim Brotherhood—soon issued a constitutional declaration giving himself virtually unlimited power. This triggered another wave of popular protests, resulting, unfortunately, not in a peaceful return to greater democracy. Instead, the Egyptian military staged a coup. Morsi was imprisoned (and eventually sentenced to death); thousands of his followers were killed or imprisoned by the Egyptian military; and Egypt returned to the autocratic rule that had prompted its "Arab Spring" uprisings in the first place. Yemen and Libya descended into civil war, with armed factions—often supported by outside powers—laying waste to cities and villages. Protests in Syria were brutally suppressed by the Assad regime, drawing the United States and Russia into opposite sides in a civil war that forced millions of refugees to flee into Europe.

These unfortunate developments, in turn, resulted in a rise of anti-immigrant political movements throughout Europe and have threatened the European Union's open-border policy—one of the key components of European unity. Social media also played a role in Brexit: One study found that Brexit supporters were twice as numerous on Instagram (and five times more active) than "Remain" activists (Polonski, 2016). It has also played a role in the rise of nationalist parties elsewhere in Europe that are calling for an end to the European Union (Polakow-Suransky, 2016). Social media, such as Facebook, Twitter, and WhatsApp, which had prompted protests and calls for democracy across the world in 2011, has been effectively used by Islamic extremists to recruit jihadists and suicide bombers from Europe and North America, facilitating the efforts to create the so-called Islamic State across a vast swath of the Middle East (Blaker, 2015). Social media clearly cuts both ways: It can be used to promote either democracy or violent social movements.

Globalization and Social Movements

Social movements vary widely. Some have only a few dozen members; others include thousands or millions of people. Although some social movements operate within the law, others are illegal or underground groups. Protest movements operate near the margins of what is legally permissible.

Social movements often seek change on a public issue, such as expanding civil rights for a segment of the population. In response, counter movements sometimes arise in defense of the status quo. The campaign for women's right to abortion, for example, has been challenged by anti-abortion ("pro-life") activists, who believe that abortion should be illegal.

Black Lives Matter is a social movement calling for an end to racial profiling, police brutality, and the mass incarceration of Black people.

Often, laws or policies are altered as a result of the action of social movements. These changes can have far-ranging effects. For example, it used to be illegal for workers' groups to call their members out on strike, and striking was punished with varying degrees of severity in different countries. Eventually, however, the laws were amended, making the strike a permissible tactic of industrial conflict.

The last few decades have seen an explosion of social movements around the globe. These movements—ranging from the civil rights and feminist movements of the 1960s and 1970s, respectively, to the antinuclear and ecological movements of the 1980s, to the gay rights campaign of the 1990s, to today's Black Lives Matter—are called **new social movements**. They are often concerned with the quality of private life as much as with political and economic issues, calling for changes in the way people think and act.

What makes new social movements "new" is that, unlike conventional social movements, they are not based on single-issue objectives related to the distribution of economic resources or power. Rather, they seek collective identities based on entire lifestyles, often calling for sweeping cultural changes. New social movements have emerged around issues such as ecology, peace, gender and sexual identity, gay and lesbian rights, women's rights, alternative medicine, and opposition to globalization.

Because new social movements involve new collective identities, they can provide a

> **new social movements** A set of social movements that have arisen in Western societies since the 1960s in response to the changing risks facing human societies. New social movements differ from earlier social movements in that they focus on a range of human rights as opposed to economic concerns, and thus draw support from across class lines.

strong incentive for action. Participation is viewed as a moral obligation (and even a pleasure), rather than a calculated effort to achieve some specific goal. Moreover, the forms of protest new social movements choose constitute an "expressive logic" whereby participants make a statement about who they are: Protest is an end in itself, a way of affirming one's identity, as well as a means of achieving concrete objectives (Polletta and Jasper, 2001).

The rise of new social movements is a reflection of the changing risks facing human societies. Traditional political institutions are increasingly unable to cope with the challenges before them, such as threats to the natural environment, the potential dangers of nuclear energy and genetically modified organisms, and the powerful effects of information technology. Because existing democratic political institutions cannot fix these problems, they go ignored or avoided until a full-blown crisis occurs.

As a cumulative effect of these new challenges and risks, people feel less secure and more isolated—a combination that leads to a sense of powerlessness. By contrast, corporations, governments, and the media appear to be dominating more aspects of people's lives, heightening the sensation of a runaway world. There is a growing sense that globalization presents ever-greater risks to citizens' lives.

Although faith in traditional politics seems to be waning, the growth of new social movements is evidence that citizens in late-modern societies are not apathetic or uninterested in politics. Rather, there is a belief that direct action and participation are more useful than reliance on politicians and political systems. More than ever before, people are supporting social movements as a way of putting complex moral issues at the center of social life. In this respect, new social movements are helping revitalize civic culture and **civil society**—the sphere between the state and the marketplace occupied by family, community associations, and other noneconomic institutions.

Nationalist Movements

Some of the most important social movements today are nationalist movements. Although the countries of the world have become more interdependent, especially since the 1970s, this interdependence has not spelled the end of nationalism. It may even have helped intensify it. Recent thinkers have contrasting ideas about why this is so. There are also disagreements about the stage of history at which nationalism, the nation, and the nation-state came into being.

Nationalism and Modern Society Different nations have followed divergent patterns of development in relation to ethnic communities. In some, including most of the nations of Western Europe, a single ethnic community expanded and pushed out earlier rivals. Thus, in seventeenth-century France, several other languages were spoken and different ethnic histories were linked to them. As French became the dominant language, most of these rivals disappeared. Yet remnants persist in a few areas. One is in the Basque country overlapping the French and Spanish frontiers. The Basque language is different from either French or Spanish, and the Basques claim a separate cultural history. Some Basques want their own nation-state. Although there has been nothing like the level of violence seen in other areas—such as East Timor, or Chechnya in southern Russia—separatist groups in the Basque country have sporadically used bombing campaigns to further their goal of independence.

Forty years ago, in a work that has shaped our understanding of the rise of modern nation-states, Benedict Anderson argued that modern nation-states were actually (to use his terms) "imagined communities" that were largely the result of the rise of capitalism, abetted by the printing press, which facilitated the widespread dissemination of the notion that the "nation" was composed of people with shared ethnic and cultural identity (Anderson, 2016; orig. 1983). National identities, he argued, were socially constructed—a process that began in Western Europe and then spread around the globe. Nations might be socially constructed, he argued, but their adherents do not see them this way: Nationalism, and national identity, are experiences sufficiently real that people are often willing to kill (and be killed) for their countries. Nationalism, as we have noted previously in this chapter, is resurgent at this time: Increasing numbers of people across Europe see themselves as British (and sometimes even Scottish or English before British) or French or some other nationality, rather than as European. Anderson's notion of "imagined community" can even apply to groups of individuals without national borders. These range from the so-called Islamic State, whose violent efforts to create a homeland in Syria and Iraq have largely been thwarted; online communities of like-minded people; diasporic groups such as Palestinians (Al-Hardan, 2016), Jews (Abramson, 2017), and Kurds (Ross and Mohammadpur, 2016); groups based on sexual identity (Alm and Martinsson, 2017); and even transnational corporations (Buckler, 2016).

civil society The realm of activity that lies between the state and the market, including the family, schools, community associations, and noneconomic institutions. Civil society, or civic culture, is essential to vibrant democratic societies.

nations without states Instances in which the members of a nation lack political sovereignty over the area they claim as their own.

Nations without States The persistence of well-defined ethnic communities within established nations contributes to the phenomenon of **nations without states**—imagined communities, to use Anderson's phrase, that exist in other states but lack a territorial state of their own. Kurds, Palestinians, and Tibetans are current examples of nations who aspire to their own state. This has been a significant source of conflict in the world today.

Several types of nations without states can be recognized, depending on the relationship between the ethnic community and the nation-state in which it exists (Guibernau, 1999):

- In some situations, a nation-state may accept the cultural differences among its minorities and allow them a certain amount of active development. Thus, in Great Britain, Scotland and Wales are recognized as having histories and cultural features partly divergent from the rest of the United Kingdom, and, to some extent, they have their own institutions. The majority of Scots, for instance, are Presbyterians, and Scotland has long had a separate educational system from that of England and Wales. Scotland and Wales achieved further autonomy within the United Kingdom with the creation of a Scottish Parliament and a Welsh Assembly in 1999.

- Some nations without states have a higher degree of autonomy. In Québec (the French-speaking province of Canada) and Flanders (the Dutch-speaking area in northern Belgium), regional political bodies have the power to make major decisions even though they are not fully independent. They also contain nationalist movements agitating for complete independence.
- Some nations completely lack recognition from the state that contains them. In such cases, the larger nation-state uses force to deny recognition to the minority. Palestinians are an example. Others include the Tibetans in China, and the Kurds, whose homeland overlaps parts of Iran, Iraq, Syria, and Turkey.

States without Nations Recall the definition of nation-state: "particular types of states, characteristic of the modern world, in which governments have sovereign power within defined territorial areas, and populations are citizens who know themselves to be part of single nations." What happens when significant sectors of the population come from different ethnic or tribal groups, and they do not believe that they are a part of the imagined community that comprises the nation-state?

This has proven to be a problem in many African and Middle Eastern countries, often with violent results. The borders of these countries were the result of European colonialism, drawn up by the major European powers at the Berlin Conference of 1884–1885. The borders reflected the negotiated interests of Germany, France, Britain, Belgium, Portugal, Spain, and other European countries; they had little or nothing to do with the tribal identities of the people who actually lived there. In many of these countries, boundaries between colonial administrations that were set arbitrarily in Europe ignored economic, cultural, or ethnic divisions among the population being colonized. As a consequence, most colonized areas contained a mosaic of ethnic communities and other groups (Figure 13.3).

Nationalist movements promoting independence in Africa following World War II sought to free the colonized areas from European domination. Once this had been achieved, the new leaders faced enormous problems trying to create national unity. Many of the leaders in the 1950s and 1960s had been educated in Europe or the United States, and there was a vast gulf between them and their citizens, most of whom were illiterate, poor, and unfamiliar with the rights and obligations of democracy. Under colonialism, some ethnic groups had prospered more than others; these groups had different interests and goals, and they legitimately saw each other as enemies. When the former colonies finally achieved independence in the second half of the twentieth century, it was hard to create a sense of nationhood. Although nationalism had played a great part in securing the independence of colonized areas, it was confined to small groups of activists and did not reflect the majority of the population. As a result, many postcolonial states were threatened by internal rivalries and competing claims to political authority. Civil wars broke out in several postcolonial states in Africa, such as Nigeria, Sudan, and Zaire; ethnic rivalries and antagonisms characterized many others in both Africa and Asia.

To take one example, in Sudan—the third-largest country in Africa—about 40 percent of the population speaks Arabic and claims Arabic ethnic origins. Elsewhere in the country, particularly in the south, Arabic is barely spoken at all. Once the nationalists took power, they set up a program for national integration, with Arabic as the

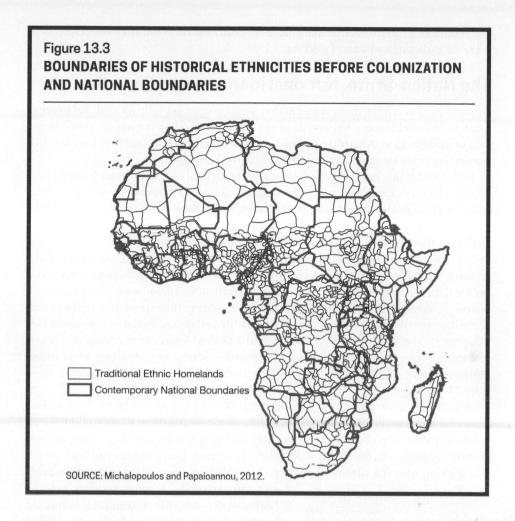

Figure 13.3
BOUNDARIES OF HISTORICAL ETHNICITIES BEFORE COLONIZATION AND NATIONAL BOUNDARIES

☐ Traditional Ethnic Homelands
☐ Contemporary National Boundaries

SOURCE: Michalopoulos and Papaioannou, 2012.

national language. The attempt was only partly successful, and the stresses it produced are still visible. In January 2011, a referendum was held in South Sudan, with nearly 100 percent of those voting supporting independence. South Sudan became an independent country as a result, although conflicts and open fighting between the two countries remain. Civil war erupted in South Sudan two years after the country gained independence, the result of conflict between the country's two largest ethnic groups: the Dinka and Nuer. As of January 2018, the United Nations reported that more than five million people lacked adequate food, with an additional 2 million people in danger of extreme food shortage, and 155,000 people in danger of starving to death; 1.3 million children were said to be malnourished (World Food Programme, 2018). Nor is South Sudan alone: Somalia, Nigeria, and Yemen all face conflict and famine, their challenges worsened by drought (Gettleman, 2017).

In summary, most states in the developing world underwent different processes of nation formation from those in the industrialized world. States were imposed externally on areas that often had no prior cultural or ethnic unity, leading to problems that are very difficult to overcome. Many of these newly formed countries are examples of what we earlier described as failed states.

The Nation-State, National Identity, and Globalization

In some parts of Africa, nations and nation-states are not yet fully formed. Yet in other areas of the world, some writers are speaking of the "end of the nation-state" in the face of globalization. According to Japanese writer Kenichi Ohmae (1995), we live in a borderless world in which national identity is weakening.

How valid is this point of view? All states are certainly affected by globalizing processes. The very rise of "nations without states" is probably bound up with globalization. As globalization progresses, people often revive local identities to achieve security in the rapidly changing world. Nations have less economic power of their own than they used to have, as a result of the spreading global marketplace.

Yet it wouldn't be accurate to say that we are witnessing the end of the nation-state. In some ways, the opposite is the case. Today, the nation-state has become a universal political form. Until quite recently, it still had rivals; after all, for most of the twentieth century, colonized areas and empires existed alongside nation-states. It is arguable that the last empire disappeared only in 1990, with the collapse of Soviet communism (see Chapter 8). The satellite states constituting the Soviet Union's former empire in Eastern Europe now have become independent nation-states, as have many areas inside the former Soviet Union itself. There are far more sovereign nations today than there were 25 years ago.

A more accurate way of framing the current situation would be to think of two powerful forces at play today—the international world of nation-states and the transnational forces of globalization that are challenging the nation-state. Nation-states remain important in the world today; they alone have governments and legal structures, along with the means to enforce laws—both internally (through police powers) and externally (through military means). Nation-states are the recognized actors in international organizations, such as the United Nations and the World Trade Organization; they form economic and military alliances with one another, and all too often wage wars to achieve their objectives.

Yet the economic, political, environmental, and cultural power of nation-states is everywhere being challenged by globalizing forces that show little regard for national borders. Trillions of dollars cross borders with the click of a mouse, while products that are designed in one country give jobs to workers half a world away. As we discuss in the next section, military force seems to be of limited value against stateless enemies such as al Qaeda and ISIS, which operate in many countries yet pledge allegiance to none. Global warming and environmental degradation threaten everyone on

CONCEPT CHECKS

1 How does the two-party system in the United States affect political involvement?

2 Describe the role that interest groups play in American politics.

3 What role has technology played in social movements?

4 Describe the arguments given for the persistence of the nation-state.

the planet, regardless of which country is the immediate source of the problem. YouTube, the Internet, and popular culture generally flow freely around the world, despite the efforts of authoritarian regimes to control them.

Whether the outcome of this titanic conflict between nation-states and globalization will ultimately favor one or the other is uncertain—which is one reason globalization has become such a fascinating topic for sociologists and other social scientists to study.

4 UNANSWERED QUESTIONS

In this final section, we focus on four of the many unanswered questions concerning politics and social movements. Three have to do with some challenges faced by democracies in the United States and elsewhere: low voter turnout, the impact of the Internet, and the future of democracy.

Why Is Voter Turnout So Low in the United States?

Since the early 1960s, voter turnout in the United States has generally decreased, although recent elections suggest a possible reversal of that trend. In the 1960 presidential election, 64 percent of the eligible voting-age population turned out to vote; by the year 2000, that figure had dropped to 56 percent. In the 2016 presidential elections, voter turnout was slightly higher, at around 60 percent. The reasons for these small increases are not clear, although higher-than-usual youth turnout, mobilized by Rock the Vote and other organizations, and (in 2008 and 2012, the appeal of Barack Obama to young voters) undoubtedly accounts for part. The turnout for midterm congressional elections is usually only around 40 percent (U.S. Elections Project, 2017).

There are significant differences in voter turnout by race and ethnicity, age, educational attainment, and income. In the 2016 election, only 61 percent of the citizen voting-age population bothered to vote. Turnout was highest among non-Hispanic Whites (65 percent), somewhat lower for Blacks (60 percent), and considerably lower for Hispanics (48 percent). Turnout also varied considerably with age, with older citizens voting at much higher rates than younger adults: 71 percent of eligible citizens 65 and older turned out to vote, compared with 67 percent of adults between the ages of 45 and 64, 59 percent of adults ages 30 to 44, and only 46 percent of adults ages 18 to 29 (File, 2017). Education also influences voting behavior: In the 2016 presidential election, 35 percent of persons who lacked a high school diploma turned out to vote, compared with 76 percent of those with bachelor's degrees or higher. Turnout was just 48 percent among voters whose family income was less than $30,000, rising to 78 percent among voters whose family income was over $100,000 (U.S. Bureau of the Census, 2017n).

Voter turnout in the United States is among the world's lowest. Many studies have found that countries with high rates of literacy, high average incomes, and well-established political freedoms and civil liberties have high voter turnout (International Institute for Democracy and Electoral Assistance [IIDEA], 2004). Even though the United States ranks high on all these measures, it fails to motivate people to vote.

At a polling place in Allenstown, N.H., voters show identification before voting in the New Hampshire presidential primary election on Feb. 9, 2016

The United States ranks 31st in voter turnout among the 35 advanced industrial countries that belong to the Organisation for Economic Cooperation and Development (OECD), which includes the United States, Japan, Israel, most European countries, and such emerging economies as Chile, Turkey, and Korea. Voting is compulsory for six OECD countries, but that alone cannot account for the United States' low ranking (25 OECD countries that do not legally require people to vote still outrank the United States; Desilver, 2016).

Why is voter turnout so low in the United States? While there are no clear-cut answers to this question, a number of factors undoubtedly play a role. First, in the United States—unlike in many other countries—voter registration is not automatic. Many people find the process of registering to vote burdensome, and so don't bother. While 15 states permit people to register the same day they vote, most do not. One study found that same-day registration resulted in somewhat higher voter turnout (Burden et al., 2013). Education also makes a difference—as we have seen, more highly educated people are more likely to vote.

Another factor is winner-take-all elections, which discourage the formation of third parties. As a result, voters may feel a lack of viable choices; a large (and growing) number of people clearly feel that the current system is unresponsive to their needs. This was an important factor in the rise of populism in the 2016 presidential campaigns, with Sanders and Trump—both rejecting "business as usual"—attracting the most enthusiastic support among dedicated followers. In many countries, including most European countries, some system of proportional representation is practiced, under which parties receive seats in proportion to the vote they get in electoral districts. Thus, for example, if a district has 10 seats in parliament, and the Conservative Party gets 30 percent of the vote, that district would send three Conservative representatives to parliament. Under this system, even small parties can often muster sufficient support to elect one or two representatives. When voters have a wider range of choices, they are more likely to vote.

Finally, in some states, significant barriers have been raised to make it more difficult for some people to vote, including so-called voter ID laws, which require a driver's license, a birth certificate, or some other form of photo identification to vote. Voter ID laws have proliferated in recent years, and as of 2020 (as well as for the 2016 election cycle), 10 states required photo identification in order to vote. These laws are most likely to affect low-income and minority voters (Hajnal, Lajevardi, and Nielson, 2017; Highton, 2017; NCLS, 2020).

Did the Internet Shape the Outcome of the 2016 Presidential Election?

The Internet is a potentially democratizing force, although it can also have the opposite effect—for example, when governments control what is acceptable on the Internet, or when extremists use their websites to mobilize support for acts of violence. The Internet fosters social networking: It allows like-minded people to find one another in cyberspace. While this may contribute to increased dialogue and debate on political issues, it can also create an "echo chamber" in which people seek out only information that confirms, and therefore reinforces, their existing beliefs or prejudices. In the 2016 election, the Internet also provided a way for groups and candidates to appeal directly to voters—and for foreign governments to play a role as well.

As we have previously noted, the 2016 election witnessed an unprecedented—and highly effective—use of the Internet. We also noted that Trump's use of social media, particularly Twitter, was far more effective than Clinton's. Not only did Trump have far more followers than Clinton, but his tweets were retweeted far more frequently and, importantly, were much more likely to be discussed in the mainstream news, providing a layer of free media coverage estimated to be worth as much as $4 billion. According to some estimates, half the Trump campaign media budget went to digital media, which included a Facebook Live broadcast of the third presidential debate. The campaign hired Cambridge Analytica, a big data firm that had worked on the Brexit campaign, which used massive amounts of data (derived from social media and other sources) to psychologically target 13.5 million voters in six battleground states that it believed could be won over (Persily, 2017). The Trump campaign, as well as the candidate himself, was acutely aware that in order for tweets or any social media to go viral, they had to be provocative, even outrageous. Trump's tweets famously created "twitterstorms" that energized his base, outraged his opponents, and assured widespread television and newspaper coverage.

The 2016 election also saw the appearance of truly "fake news"—made-up news stories treated as authentic that originated from extremist groups and websites. In perhaps the most frightening example, one right-wing conspiracy theory claimed that a Washington, D.C., pizza shop, Comet Ping Pong, was actually the headquarters of a child sex-trafficking and pornography ring run by Hillary Clinton and John Podesta, her campaign manager. When Alex Jones, the host of the far-right website Infowars, publicized this claim, it made the rounds of the alt-right; one person followed up by firing a shot into the restaurant. Although no one was hurt—and Jones later removed his post and apologized—this event (dubbed "Pizzagate" by the mainstream media) showed how even demonstrably false claims can have potentially disastrous consequences when the Internet permits them to reach millions of people (Shelbourne, 2017; Miller, 2017).

Such "fake news" was also deliberately created by foreign and domestic individuals and organizations in an effort to discredit Clinton. Teenagers in Macedonia, realizing that they could make money by publishing anti-Clinton stories that were sufficiently outrageous to attract large numbers of viewers (some of whom would click on the banner ads that would appear), posted made-up stories on some 140 websites. Such stories claimed (among other things) that Tom Hanks and Pope Francis had endorsed Trump, or that an FBI agent who had leaked Clinton's emails had been killed. Such fake news generated more engagement than mainstream news toward the close of the election. Some of these stories were retweeted by the Trump campaign—for example, a story from a fake-news website claiming that protesters disrupting Trump's rallies had been sent by Clinton (Persily, 2017).

Anti-Clinton messages were also traced to Russia, which effectively hacked into Clinton campaign emails, using bots (automated accounts that are difficult to trace) to spread information and fake news Russian operatives deemed harmful to Clinton or favorable to Trump. According to an official U.S. report from the Director of National Intelligence (DNI),

> We assess Russian President Vladimir Putin ordered an influence campaign in 2016 aimed at the U.S. presidential election. Russia's goals were to undermine public faith in the U.S. democratic process, denigrate Secretary Clinton, and harm her electability and potential presidency. We further assess Putin and the Russian Government developed a clear preference for President-elect Trump. . . . Moscow's influence campaign followed a Russian messaging strategy that blends covert intelligence operations—such as cyber activity—with overt efforts by Russian Government agencies, state-funded media, third-party intermediaries, and paid social media users or "trolls" (U.S. DNI, 2017).

While the Internet has the ability to foster democracy by encouraging widespread engagement in politics, information sharing, and the building of social movements, it also invites the participation of demagogues, extremists, Internet trolls seeking to create conflict, and foreign governments in domestic politics. The Internet can appeal to our best—and worst—impulses. The declining influence (and financial fortunes) of mainstream media has created an opening for the more direct communication that is made possible by the Internet—a world in which anyone with a smartphone or laptop computer can become a blogger, a source of information, a potential player in a presidential election. Yet, while anyone can post a message, not every message gets read. One study of the top 10 bloggers (the heads of liberal websites such as Daily Kos or conservative websites such as Instapundit) found that half were professional journalists from mainstream news organizations; eight were educated at elite institutions of higher education (seven had a PhD, one a JD); and only one was a woman (Hindman, 2008).

To the extent that established institutions lose their power, the Internet can fill the political void in a way that favors populist movements: It enables the leaders of such movements to directly reach their followers, without the need for established political parties or mainstream media. Will this encourage the rise of pro-democracy movements—as it did briefly in the "Arab Spring" of 2010–2012? Or will it fuel the rise of populist authoritarian social movements, as it has in Turkey, India, and in European countries such as Hungary, France, the Netherlands, Greece, Austria, Germany, and Sweden?

Is Democracy in Trouble?

Democracy almost everywhere is in some peril. This is not only because it is hard to set up a stable democratic order in places such as Russia and other formerly Communist societies. Democracy is in trouble even in its countries of origin—such as the United States. For example, as just noted, voter turnout in presidential and other elections has generally declined. In surveys, many people say they don't trust politicians.

In 1964, confidence in government was fairly high: Nearly four out of five people answered "most of the time" or "just about always" when asked, "How much of the time do you trust the government in Washington to do the right thing?" This level of confidence dropped steadily for the following 20 years, rose somewhat in the 1980s, then dropped to a low of one in five in 1994. Following the terrorist attacks of September 11, 2001, a solid majority (55 percent) of Americans reported that they trusted the government "most of the time" or "just about always." Recently, however, trust in the government has declined as a result of disillusionment over the wars in Iraq and Afghanistan, the economic collapse of 2008, the tepid recovery that followed, and government paralysis in Washington. By 2019, just 17 percent of Americans said they could trust the government in Washington almost always or most of the time (Pew Research Center, 2019f).

Roughly half of all Americans believe that government is too large, a perception that in part reflects this low level of trust (Pew Research Center, 2019d). Yet among the 27 industrial democracies in the OECD, the United States ranks 24th in terms of total federal, state, and local government spending as a proportion of its total economy. Nine OECD countries spend more than half of their GDP on government at all levels, with France and Finland topping the list at 57 percent of GDP. The United States, by way of comparison, spends only 37 percent (OECD, 2015). There are, however, significant differences among those who believe that government is too big. One obvious difference is partisanship: While roughly three-quarters of Republicans and Republican-leaning independents prefer a smaller government providing fewer services, two-thirds of Democrats and Democratic-leaning independents prefer a large government that provides more services. There are significant differences by age as well: While 50 percent of younger Americans (30 and under) favor larger government, only 43 percent of those over 65 share this opinion (Pew Research Center, 2019d).

Americans may have lower taxes than other industrial democracies, but they also receive lower levels of support for health care, housing, education, unemployment, and social services in general. This may be another reason for low levels of confidence in government and poor voter turnout: Americans expect less, and get less, from their government.

Finally, for the past quarter century, there has been a steady stream of well-financed criticism from conservative think tanks, news media, and politicians who share the belief that government is part of the problem, rather than part of the solution. This has been highly effective in changing the national discourse on the role of government (Gonzales and Delgado, 2006).

Why are so many people dissatisfied with democracy, a political system that not long ago seemed to be sweeping across the world? The answers may be bound up with the very factors that help spread democracy—the effect of capitalism and the globalizing of social life. For instance, while capitalist economies generate more wealth than any other type of economic system, the wealth is unequally distributed (see Chapter 8). And economic inequalities influence who votes, joins parties, and gets elected. Wealthy individuals and corporations back interest groups that lobby elected officials to support their aims when deciding on legislation. Not being subject to election, interest groups are not accountable to the majority of the electorate (Lessig, 2011).

Economic inequalities also create an underclass of people living in poverty—about 20 percent of the population of liberal democracies. Most Western liberal democracies establish policies to reduce poverty levels, but they vary in spending to achieve that aim. Societies that implement a complex welfare system require a higher level of taxation and a larger nonelected government bureaucracy. The question arises as to how much of an economic and political price a society is willing to pay to reduce poverty, who pays for it, and what the effect is of this cost.

In the modern welfare state, government was expected to provide a wide range of services to be funded by taxes on individuals and corporations. During much of the twentieth century, when the economies of the advanced industrial nations were to a large extent based within national borders, this strategy met with some success—at least during times of economic growth, when businesses were thriving, personal incomes were rising, and government revenues were strong. Political parties tried to woo voters by promising many benefits and services; as a result, governments acquired more responsibilities than they could easily fund and manage, from establishing public ownership of industries, utilities, and transportation to creating extensive welfare programs.

A half century ago, sociologist James O'Connor's *Fiscal Crisis of the State* (1973) predicted that a gap would occur between state expenditures and revenues. Globalization, which facilitated the easy movement of capital, has contributed to this crisis. The offshoring of manufacturing to low-wage countries contributed to the decline of manufacturing in the United States, and with it, the loss of millions of jobs that once paid middle-class wages. This both reduced personal income available for taxation and contributed to an increase in the cost of such government-funded services as unemployment compensation and welfare payments. During the twenty-first century, automation has arguably claimed as many, or many more, jobs than the offshoring of manufacturing, a trend that is likely to increase in coming years (Hicks and Devaraj, 2015). Taxes on corporations, as a portion of federal revenues, have also declined: In 1970, corporate income taxes accounted for 25 percent of federal government revenue, while in 2018, the corporate share had dropped to only 6 percent (CBPP, 2019).

The 2016 election, with its strong populist appeal, highlighted the fact that the Democratic Party in the United States has lost some of its traditional support from working-class voters, who needed the promised (but undelivered) services. The rise of alt-right politics reflects an attempt to cope with this situation by trimming back the state and encouraging private enterprise—a trend seen in Europe as well as the United States.

Jürgen Habermas (1975) argued that this situation should be understood as a **legitimation crisis** (Offe, 1984, 1985), since modern governments lack the legitimacy to carry out tasks they are required to undertake, such as providing highways, public housing, and health care. People who feel that they pay most for these services through higher taxes—the more affluent—may believe they gain the least from them. On the one hand, governments must take more responsibility for reducing poverty and homelessness; on the other, taxpayers either resist increases in taxation or want taxes reduced. Governments cannot cope with the contradictory demands of lower taxes and more responsibilities, leading to decreased public support and general disillusionment about government's capabilities. According to Habermas, legitimation crises could probably be overcome if the electorate were persuaded to accept high taxation in return for a wide range of government services.

legitimation crisis The failure of a political order to be able to govern properly because it did not generate a sufficient level of commitment and involvement on the part of its citizens.

As sociologist Daniel Bell (1976) observed a half century ago, national government is too small to address the big questions, such as the influence of global economic competition or the destruction of the world's environment, but it has become too big to address the small questions, such as issues affecting cities or regions. Governments have little power, for instance, over giant business corporations, the main actors within the global economy. A U.S. corporation may shut down its production plants in America and set up a new factory in Mexico in order to lower costs and compete with other corporations. The result is that thousands of American workers lose their jobs and expect the government to do something, but national governments cannot control processes bound up with the world economy. All a government can do is soften the blow—for example, by providing unemployment benefits or job retraining.

At the same time that governments have shrunk in relation to global issues, they have become more remote from the lives of most citizens. Many Americans resent that "power brokers" in Washington—party officials, interest groups, lobbyists, and bureaucratic officials—make decisions affecting their lives. They also believe that government is unable to address important local issues, such as crime and homelessness. Thus, Americans' faith in government has dropped substantially, which affects Americans' willingness to participate in the political process.

CONCEPT CHECKS

1 What are the reasons that voter turnout is so low? How could it be improved?

2 How might the Internet be used to stifle movements for democracy?

3 Provide two explanations for the current tide of dissatisfaction with democracy.

THE BIG PICTURE

Chapter 13
Government, Political Power, and Social Movements

1
Basic Concepts
p. 455

2
Who Rules? Theories of Democracy
p. 462

LEARNING OBJECTIVES

Understand basic ideas underlying modern nation-states and social movements. Learn about different types of democracy.

Learn the key theories about power in a democracy.

TERMS TO KNOW

democracy • participatory democracy • direct democracy • monarchies • constitutional monarchs • liberal democracies • populism • authoritarianism • nation-state • nation • state • sovereignty • failed states • nationalism • local nationalism • power • authority • citizens • civil rights • political rights • social rights • welfare state • revolutions • social movements

democratic elitism • pluralist theories of modern democracy • power elite

CONCEPT CHECKS

1. Why is participatory democracy not a viable option for most modern states?
2. Describe three characteristics of the state.
3. What is the welfare state? Can the United States be classified as a welfare state? Why?

1. According to Weber, what are the necessary conditions for democratic systems to be effective?
2. Compare and contrast pluralist theories of modern democracy and the power elite model.

Exercises: Thinking Sociologically

1. Discuss the differences between the pluralistic and the power elite theories of democratic political processes. Which theory do you find most appropriate to describe U.S. politics in recent years?

2. Your textbook offers a variety of explanations on the formation of social movements. Briefly review the predisposing conditions for social movements, and then discuss their relevance to the rise of nationalist movements in the developing world.

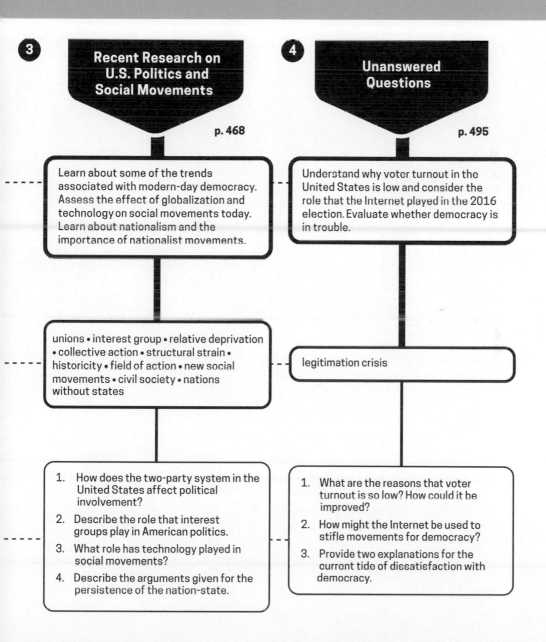

3 **Recent Research on U.S. Politics and Social Movements**

p. 468

Learn about some of the trends associated with modern-day democracy. Assess the effect of globalization and technology on social movements today. Learn about nationalism and the importance of nationalist movements.

unions • interest group • relative deprivation • collective action • structural strain • historicity • field of action • new social movements • civil society • nations without states

1. How does the two-party system in the United States affect political involvement?
2. Describe the role that interest groups play in American politics.
3. What role has technology played in social movements?
4. Describe the arguments given for the persistence of the nation-state.

4 **Unanswered Questions**

p. 495

Understand why voter turnout in the United States is low and consider the role that the Internet played in the 2016 election. Evaluate whether democracy is in trouble.

legitimation crisis

1. What are the reasons that voter turnout is so low? How could it be improved?
2. How might the Internet be used to stifle movements for democracy?
3. Provide two explanations for the current tide of dissatisfaction with democracy.

Social Institutions

Social institutions are the cement of social life. They are the basic living arrangements that human beings work out with one another, by means of which continuity is achieved across the generations.

We begin in Chapter 14 with work and economic life. Although the nature of work varies widely both within and across societies, work is one of the most pervasively important of all human pursuits. In Chapter 15, we look at the institutions of kinship, marriage, and the family. Although the social obligations associated with kinship vary depending on the type of society, in each, families are the context within which the young are provided with care and protection. Marriage is more or less universally connected to the family because it is a means of establishing new kin connections and forming a household in which children

are brought up. In traditional cultures, much of the direct learning a child receives occurs within the family context. In modern societies, children spend many years of their lives in special places of instruction outside the family—schools and colleges. They also are constantly fed images and information from the mass media.

Chapter 16 looks at the ways in which formal education is organized, concentrating particularly on the relationship between education and inequality. The subject of Chapter 17 is religion. Although religious beliefs and practices are found in all cultures, the changes affecting religion in modern societies have been particularly acute. We analyze the nature of these changes, considering in what ways traditional types of religion still maintain their influence.

14

Work and Economic Life

Which company makes your favorite athletic shoe?

A Nike

B Reebok

C Asics

D Adidas

E Puma

F New Balance

G Converse

H Under Armour

I Timberland

J Rockport

K Pou Chen

TURN THE PAGE FOR THE CORRECT ANSWER.

LEARNING OBJECTIVES

1 Basic Concepts

Understand that modern economies are based on the division of labor and economic interdependence.

2 Theories of Work and Economic Life

Consider the different forms that capitalism has taken, and understand how a shift in the predominant form of industrial organization in modern society has shaped the kinds of jobs people are likely to find.

3 Current Research on Work and Economic Life

Recognize the importance of the rise of large corporations; consider particularly the global effect of transnational corporations. Learn about the challenges facing workers today, including growing unemployment, the decline of labor unions, the rise of low-wage work, and the global trading system.

4 Unanswered Questions

Learn about the effect of automation on employment. Consider how work will change in the future.

You may suspect that this is a trick question—but it isn't! Nor is it an infomercial for leading athletic shoe brands. Whatever your preferred brand, one thing is certain: Your favorite brand did not actually make the shoe you are wearing. Whether you buy a branded athletic shoe for running, walking, or cycling, or whether you prefer basketball, tennis, or soccer, your favorite brand's job was to design the shoe, launch an effective marketing campaign, and eventually convince you—and millions of others—that this particular shoe, in this particular style, and most likely at this (often seemingly outrageous) price, is the key to your athletic success, whether you are a weekend walker or a national track star.

The company that actually made your favorite athletic shoe has a one-in-five chance of bearing a name that you most likely have never heard of: Yue Yuen, the Hong Kong subsidiary of a Taiwanese firm, Pou Chen, which specializes in footwear manufacture. Pou Chen is a transnational corporation and the largest manufacturer of branded athletic footwear in the world. Its nearly 360,000 workers in China, Vietnam, Indonesia, Bangladesh, Myanmar, Cambodia, and Taiwan turn out 300 million pairs of shoes every year, reportedly accounting for approximately 20 percent of branded athletic and casual footwear sold in the world today (Wu, 2019). Pou Chen's sprawling factory in Dongguan, in southern China, produces nearly a million pairs of athletic shoes a month for Nike, Adidas, Reebok, and practically every other major brand. (In fact, Usain Bolt wore a pair of Puma shoes made entirely at a Pou Chen facility while competing in the 2016 Rio Olympics.) Working with these numerous brands, Pou Chen engages in research to develop the best materials to use in its products; has developed its own advanced manufacturing technology; and is engaged in high-tech logistics, coordinating its global supply chain to ensure that all the components required in shoe manufacture are acquired in a timely fashion (Appelbaum and Lichtenstein, 2006; Yue Yuen, 2014; *Fortune*, 2016).

THE ANSWER IS K.

Yet all is not rosy in Yue Yuen factories. On April 14, 2014, some 45,000 workers in the company's Dongguan factories went on strike. The 10-day strike occurred when it was discovered that Yue Yuen had been systematically underpaying its state-mandated social insurance and housing benefits to its workers. The workers demanded complete restitution of the missing payments, as well as a higher living allowance. The strike, which shuttered factories and cost Yue Yuen $27 million in lost business, ended when the Chinese government ordered Yue Yuen to pay up. The settlement reportedly increased yearly employee costs some $31 million (Wong, 2014), which apparently did not sit well with the company and was one reason it decided to open its Myanmar factory. And although Yue Yuen's profits reached nearly a half billion dollars in 2017, the firm refused to comply with a Cambodian Arbitration Council ruling that the company compensate 478 workers who were entitled to severance pay when Yue Yuen closed the factory—a payout that would have cost Yue Yuen less than a million dollars.

Pou Chen/Yue Yuen is an example of an important development in the global economy, one that is reshaping the nature of work throughout the world. Countries once referred to as "developing economies"—now frequently termed "emerging economies"—are playing an increasingly important role as suppliers and assemblers of the products consumed throughout the world. Design and marketing may remain centered in the United States, Europe, Japan, and a few other advanced economies, but the actual goods are produced by independently owned factories throughout the world. Giant transnational corporations—owned by individuals from China, Hong Kong, South Korea, and Taiwan—operate apparel, electronic assembly, and other consumer goods factories around the world.

Global supply chains today dominate the world economy, shaping the nature of work and economic life. While they have provided an enormous array of low-cost consumer goods, they have also resulted in many jobs being relocated to low-wage countries where the goods are produced—countries in which labor laws and environmental protections are either nonexistent or poorly enforced. There are benefits and costs to global production systems, both in the advanced industrial economies and in the emerging economies. In this chapter we will examine both sides of global production, in order to gain a better understanding of its effects on American workers.

When you buy a pair of jeans, whatever its brand might be, it may well have been made in Mexico, Nicaragua, or the African country of Lesotho, in a factory owned by Nien Hsing, a Taiwanese textile firm that makes clothing for such well-known brands and retailers as Target, Gap, and Levi's (Nien Hsing, 2012). The sweatshirt or hoodie sold in your campus bookstore—the one that bears your college's logo or name—was certainly not made by your college, nor was it made by Nike, Russell Athletic, or Knights Apparel, three of the leading brands that design products specifically for the college market. It, too, was made in a factory overseas, anywhere from the Caribbean to China.

The Pou Chen/Yue Yuen case illustrates another important point: Workers are becoming more militant everywhere. Even in China, where the government has never approved of labor unrest, workers until fairly recently were able to engage in unauthorized strikes to protest low wages and poor working conditions. Today, the Chinese government has taken an increasingly hard line position on worker unrest, severely punishing workers who even speak out against factory conditions. Businesses

Countries such as China have played a central role as suppliers and assemblers of the products consumed across the globe. Rising wages in China, however, have led some firms to relocate production to lower-wage countries such as Vietnam and Cambodia.

also respond to worker militancy, and the rising wages it often produces, by moving to lower-cost areas such as Vietnam and Myanmar, where the government is more likely to quickly repress strikes. This dynamic greatly affects work and economic life in the United States, as many manufacturing jobs—and increasingly service-sector jobs, from accounting to software engineering—are moving to low-wage countries. What kinds of jobs are replacing them back home? What does it mean for the nature of work when brands such as Nike or retailers such as Walmart rely on foreign firms halfway around the world to actually manufacture the products that bear their names or are sold on their shelves?

Most adults in capitalist economies spend the better part of their waking hours at work. The jobs they do determine their economic prospects, shape their lifestyles, and provide them with friends and acquaintances. Yet the nature of work is often determined by forces far beyond their control, and sometimes even beyond their understanding. In this chapter, we analyze the nature of work in modern societies and look at the major changes affecting economic life today. We investigate the changing nature of industrial production, the ownership structure of large business corporations, and the changing nature of work itself. We then turn to some important unresolved questions about our economic future.

1 BASIC CONCEPTS

Work can be defined as the carrying out of tasks that require the expenditure of mental and physical effort; it has as its objective the production of goods and services that cater to human needs. An **occupation**, or job, is work that is done in exchange for a regular wage, or salary. In all cultures, work is the basis of the economic system, or **economy**. The economy consists of institutions that provide for the production and distribution of goods and services.

Modern societies are capitalistic. **Capitalism** is an economic system based on the private ownership of wealth, which is invested and reinvested in order to produce profit. It is distinguished by the following important features: Private ownership of the means of production; profit as incentive; competition for markets to sell goods, acquire cheap materials, and use cheap labor; and restless expansion and investment to accumulate capital. Capitalism, which began to spread with the growth of the Industrial Revolution in the early nineteenth century, is a vastly more dynamic economic system than any other that preceded it in history. Although the system has had many critics, such as Karl Marx, it is now the most widespread form of economic organization in the world.

Modern industry differs in a fundamental way from premodern systems of production, which were primarily based on agriculture. In modern societies, in contrast, most people no longer work on farms or in fields. In economically advanced economies such as the United States, large numbers no longer work in factories, as was the case for much of the twentieth century. Rather, in such countries today's jobs involve providing services to others—services that range from those contributed by high-paid professionals, such as managers of giant corporations, to those administered by low-paid workers requiring limited skills and training, such as salesclerks at Walmart.

The study of economic institutions is of major importance in sociology because the economy influences all segments of society and, therefore, social life in general. And economic institutions are themselves always changing. One reason for such change is **technology**, which harnesses science to machinery, electronics, and even biology to produce an ever-increasing variety of goods more cheaply. Another reason is globalization, which creates global competition among not only firms but also workers: Whether you are an autoworker in a Detroit factory, an engineer in Silicon Valley, or a graphic designer in New York City, someone half a world away likely has the skill, talent, and drive to challenge you for your job.

We often associate the notion of work with drudgery—a set of tasks that we want to minimize and, if possible, escape altogether. (You may have this very thought in mind as you set out to read this chapter!) Is

work The activity by which people produce from the natural world and so ensure their survival. Work should not be thought of exclusively as paid employment. In traditional cultures, there was only a rudimentary monetary system, and few people worked for money. In modern societies, there remain types of work that do not involve direct payment (e.g., housework).

occupation Any form of paid employment in which an individual regularly works.

economy The system of production and exchange that provides for the material needs of individuals living in a given society. Economic institutions are of key importance in all social orders. What goes on in the economy usually influences other areas of social life. Modern economies differ substantially from traditional ones because the majority of the population is no longer engaged in agricultural production.

capitalism An economic system based on the private ownership of wealth, which is invested and reinvested in order to produce profit.

technology The application of scientific knowledge of the material world to production, involving the creation of material instruments (such as machines) used in human interaction with nature.

this most people's attitude toward their work, and, if so, why? We will try to find out in the following pages.

Work is more than just drudgery, or people would not feel so lost and disoriented when they become unemployed. How would you feel if you thought you would never get a job? In modern societies, having a paid job is important for maintaining self-esteem, as well as paying the bills. Even where work conditions are relatively unpleasant, and the tasks involved are dull, work tends to be a structuring element in people's psychological makeup and the cycle of their daily activities. Several characteristics of work are relevant here.

- *Money.* A wage or salary is the main resource many people depend on to meet their needs. Without such an income, anxieties about coping with day-to-day life tend to multiply.
- *Activity level.* Work often provides a basis for the acquisition and exercise of skills and capacities. Even where work is routine, it offers a structured environment in which a person's energies may be absorbed. Without it, the opportunity to exercise such skills and capacities may be reduced.
- *Variety.* Work provides access to contexts that contrast with domestic surroundings. In the working environment, even when the tasks are relatively dull, individuals may enjoy doing something different from home chores.
- *Structuring one's time.* For people in regular employment, the day is usually organized around the rhythm of work. Although work may sometimes be oppressive, it provides a sense of direction in daily activities. Those who are out of work frequently find boredom a major problem and may develop a sense of apathy about time.
- *Social contacts.* The work environment often provides friendships and opportunities to participate in shared activities with others. Separated from the work setting, a person's circle of possible friends and acquaintances is likely to dwindle.
- *Personal identity.* Work is usually valued for the sense of stable social identity it offers. For men in particular, self-esteem is often bound up with the economic contribution they make to maintaining the household. In addition, job conditions—such as the opportunity to work in jobs that are challenging, not routinized, and not subject to close supervision—are known to have a positive effect on a person's sense of self-worth (Crowley, 2014).

Against the backdrop of this formidable list, it is not difficult to see why being without paid employment may undermine individuals' confidence in their social value. Yet even though we often think of work as equivalent to having a paid job, in fact, this is an oversimplified view. **Housework**, which has traditionally been carried out mostly by women, is usually unpaid. But it is work nonetheless, sometimes satisfying, often difficult and exhausting. Unpaid housework includes such things as having primary responsibility for raising children, cleaning, shopping, and attending to countless (and unending) household chores. It typically involves one of the most important tasks of any society: the socialization of children, a crucial step in preparing them for adulthood.

One study found that in 1965, women put in an average of 40 hours per week on household work. Today, as an increasing number of women have joined the paid workforce, it is estimated that women spend approximately half that amount of time each week on household labor. Men have not exactly taken up the slack: Their weekly contribution in 1965 was 14 hours; today it is roughly the same. On an average day, one out of every five men did housework such as cleaning or laundry, compared with half of all women (BLS, 2019b). When men do household work, the work they do tends to be gendered: men are more likely to do outdoor work or repairs that can fit into their schedules, while women are more likely to do such routine daily work as shopping, house cleaning, laundry, and child care (Quadlin and Doan, 2018). According to one estimate, if housework were monetized—that is, paid according to its true value—it would have increased the U.S. GNI (gross national income) by nearly $1.5 trillion (Wezerek and Ghodsee, 2020).

When the New York City Marathon got canceled after Superstorm Sandy, many runners who had planned to race turned to volunteer cleanup efforts instead. What social role does such unpaid labor play?

Another form of unpaid labor that has an important social role involves volunteer work for charities or other organizations. According to one estimate, in 2018, about 63 million Americans—over one-fifth of all adults—contributed 8 billion hours of volunteer service, estimated as worth $203 billion (Independent Sector, 2019).

One of the most distinctive characteristics of the economic system of modern societies is the existence of a highly complex **division of labor**: Work has become divided into an enormous number of different occupations in which people specialize. In traditional societies, nonagricultural work entailed the mastery of a craft. Workers learned craft skills through a lengthy period of apprenticeship, with the worker normally carrying out all aspects of the production process from beginning to end. For example, a metalworker making a plow would forge the iron, shape it, and assemble the implement itself. With the rise of modern industrial production, most traditional crafts have disappeared altogether, replaced by skills that form part of more large-scale production processes. An electrician working in an industrial setting today, for instance, may inspect and repair only a few parts of one type of machine; different people will deal with the other parts and other machines.

The contrast in the division of labor between traditional and modern societies is truly extraordinary. Even in the largest traditional societies, there usually existed no more than 20 or 30 major craft trades, together with such specialized pursuits as merchant,

housework Unpaid work carried out in the home, usually by women; domestic chores such as cooking, cleaning, and shopping. Also called domestic labor.

division of labor The specialization of work tasks by means of which different occupations are combined within a production system. All societies have at least some rudimentary form of division of labor, especially between the tasks allocated to men and those performed by women. With the development of industrialism, the division of labor became vastly more complex than in any prior type of production system. In the modern world, the division of labor is international in scope.

CONCEPT CHECKS

1 Describe six characteristics that shape one's everyday experiences at work.

2 Name two forms of unpaid labor.

3 Contrast the division of labor in traditional and modern societies.

soldier, and priest. A modern industrial system has literally thousands of occupations. The U.S. Census Bureau lists more than 31,000 different jobs in the American economy (U.S. Bureau of the Census, 2016i). In traditional communities, most of the population worked on farms and were economically self-sufficient. They produced their own food, clothes, and other necessities of life. One of the main features of modern societies, by contrast, is an enormous expansion of **economic interdependence**. We all depend on an immense number of other workers—today stretching right across the world—for the products and services that sustain our lives. With few exceptions, the vast majority of people in modern societies do not grow the food they eat, build the houses in which they live, or produce the material goods they consume. Moreover, as you learned from the chapter opener, the division of labor is now truly global, since the components of virtually all products are sourced from many factories in different countries.

2 THEORIES OF WORK AND ECONOMIC LIFE

To better understand the social organization of work, we first consider the different forms that capitalism has taken, before turning to a discussion of two broad types of economic organization in modern society that play a central role in shaping the kinds of jobs people are likely to find: Fordism and post-Fordism.

Types of Capitalism

There have been at least four general stages in the development of business **corporations**, although each overlaps with the others and all continue to coexist today. Some sociologists see a fifth stage emerging as well.

The first stage, characteristic of the nineteenth and early twentieth centuries, was dominated by **family capitalism**. Large firms were run either by individual **entrepreneurs** or by members of the same family, and then passed on to their descendants. The famous corporate dynasties, such as the Rockefellers and Fords, belong in this category. These individuals and families did not just own a single large corporation but held a diversity of economic interests and stood at the apex of economic empires.

Most of the big firms founded by entrepreneurial families have since become public companies—that is, shares of their stock are traded on the open market—and have passed into managerial control. But important elements of family capitalism remain, even within some of the largest corporations, such as 21st Century Fox, which in 2015 was the world's fourth-largest media conglomerate until it was acquired by the Walt Disney Corporation in 2019. 21st Century Fox had been the owner of Fox News, FX, Hulu, and a host of worldwide cable networks and satellite broadcasters (Fox Corporation held on to its television networks after the sale). Australian-born founder, Rupert Murdoch, who turned 88 in 2019, took over his father's struggling media business in 1953, building it into a global media empire and then passing control to his two sons, Lachlan and James Murdoch, in 2015 (Hagey, 2015).

Among small firms, such as local owner-run shops, small plumbing and house-painting businesses, and so forth, family capitalism continues to dominate. Some of these firms, such as shops that remain in the hands of the same family for two or

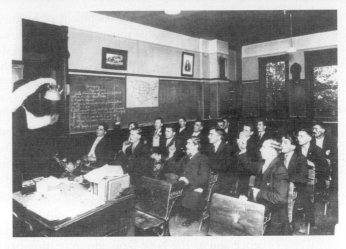

English classes were one of the services offered by large firms practicing welfare capitalism in the late nineteenth and early twentieth centuries.

more generations, are also dynasties, albeit on a minor scale. However, the small-business sector is highly unstable, and economic failure is common; the proportion of firms owned by members of the same family for extended periods is minuscule.

In the large corporate sector, family capitalism was increasingly succeeded by **managerial capitalism**. As managers came to have more and more influence through the growth of very large firms, the entrepreneurial families were displaced. The result has been described as the replacement of the family in the company by the company itself. The company is no longer privately owned by the founding family, but rather is publicly traded on the stock market, in theory giving everyone an opportunity to buy shares and become an owner. The corporation thus emerged as a more defined economic entity, with professional management—although as we shall see later in this chapter, ownership (and therefore a degree of control) is likely concentrated in a relatively small number of shareholders.

There is no question that managerial capitalism has left an indelible imprint on modern society. The large corporation drives not only patterns of consumption but also the experience of employment in contemporary society—as large corporations have moved much of their production overseas, the work lives of many Americans have changed. Those changes have often involved the loss of higher-paying jobs in large, unionized factories, and their replacement with lower-paying service jobs, from serving food in restaurants to driving for Lyft or Uber.

Sociologists have identified another area in which the large corporation has left a mark on modern institutions. Representing

economic interdependence The fact that in the division of labor, individuals depend on others to produce many or most of the goods they need to sustain their lives.

corporations Business firms or companies.

family capitalism Capitalistic enterprise owned and administered by entrepreneurial families.

entrepreneur The owner/founder of a business firm.

managerial capitalism Capitalistic enterprises administered by managerial executives rather than by owners.

the third stage in the development of business corporations, **welfare capitalism** refers to a practice that sought to make the corporation—rather than the state or trade unions—the primary shelter from the uncertainties of the market in modern industrial life. Beginning at the end of the nineteenth century, large firms began to provide certain services to their employees, including childcare, recreational facilities, profit-sharing plans, paid vacations, and life and unemployment insurance. By the end of World War II, many corporations, as well as public employers such as governments and educational institutions, also began to offset much of the cost of purchasing private medical insurance for their employees. These programs often had a paternalistic bent, such as sponsoring "home visits" for the "moral education" of employees. Viewed in less benevolent terms, welfare capitalism had as one of its major objectives coercion, as employers deployed all manner of tactics, including violence, to avoid unionization. As such, conventional histories typically suggest that welfare capitalism met its demise in the Great Depression years, as labor unions achieved unprecedented levels of influence and as the New Deal administration began to guarantee many of the benefits provided by firms.

In contrast to this standard interpretation, others argue that welfare capitalism did not die but instead went underground during the height of the labor movement (Jacoby, 1998). In firms that avoided unionization during the period between the 1930s and 1960s—such as Kodak, Sears, and Thompson Products—welfare capitalism was modernized, shedding blatantly paternalistic aspects and routinizing benefit programs. When the union movement began to weaken after 1970, these companies offered a model to other firms such as Walmart, which were then able to press their advantage against unions, reasserting the role of the firm as "industrial manor" and workers as "industrial serfs."

Many scholars now see the contours of a fourth phase emerging in the evolution of the corporation. They argue that managerial capitalism has today partly ceded place to **institutional capitalism**. This term refers to the emergence of a consolidated network of business leadership, concerned not only with decision making within single firms but also with the development of corporate power beyond them. Institutional capitalism is based on the practice of corporations holding stock shares in other firms. In effect, **interlocking directorates**—linkages among corporations created by individuals who sit on two or more corporate boards—exercise control over much of the corporate landscape (Calazza et al., 2018). This system reverses the process of increasing managerial control because the large blocks of shares other corporations own dwarf the managers' shareholdings. For example, JPMorgan Chase, one of the world's largest financial services and banking corporations, is itself owned in large part by a half dozen other financial service companies that control more than a quarter of the company's stock. The two largest individual shareholders—one the CEO of JPMorgan Chase, the other one a member of its board of directors—together account for less than 1 percent of the total stock (Downie, 2020).

One of the main reasons for the spread of institutional capitalism is the shift in patterns of investment that has occurred since the 1970s. Rather than investing directly by buying shares in a business, individuals now invest in money market, trust, insurance, and pension funds that are controlled by large financial organizations, which in turn invest these grouped savings in industrial corporations.

Finally, some sociologists argue that we have now entered a fifth stage in the development of business corporations—a form of institutional capitalism they see as **global capitalism**. According to this view, corporations are increasingly stateless: giant transnational entities that roam freely around the planet in search of lower costs and higher profits, loyal to no country regardless of where they might be headquartered. The major corporations today are global not only in the sense that they operate transnationally, but also because their shareholders, directors, and top officers are drawn from many countries (Chapter 9) (Robinson, 2004, 2014, 2018, 2019; Sklair, 2000).

Fordism and Scientific Management (Taylorism)

Alongside these changes in the nature of capitalist economic systems, there has also been a change in the predominant type of industrial organization in capitalist economies. This change involves a shift from mass production in large bureaucratic organizations for a mass consumer market to more flexible forms of production through global networks of suppliers, tailored to more individualized consumer tastes. Because the former emerged with the modern automobile industry, it is sometimes called "Fordism." **Fordism**, therefore, is the name given to designate the system of mass production tied to the cultivation of mass markets. Affixing the prefix *post* to *Fordism* (post-Fordism) suggests that Fordism is being replaced by something entirely new, signaling the end of the Fordist era. This view is misleading, since both forms of industrial organization are found throughout the world today, although these new forms are becoming increasingly important, as we shall see.

Writing more than two centuries ago, Adam Smith, one of the founders of modern economics, identified advantages that the division of labor provides in terms of increasing productivity. His most famous work, *The Wealth of Nations* (1776), opens with a description of the division of labor in a pin factory. A person working alone could perhaps make 20 pins per day. By breaking down that worker's task into a number of simple operations, however, 10 workers carrying out specialized jobs in collaboration with one another could collectively produce 48,000 pins per day. The rate of production per worker, in other words, is increased from 20 to 4,800, with each specialist operator producing 240 times more than he or she could if working alone.

More than a century later, these ideas reached their most developed expression in the writings of Frederick Winslow Taylor, an American management consultant. Taylor's approach to what he called "scientific

welfare capitalism The practice by which large corporations protect their employees from the fluctuations of the economy.

institutional capitalism Consolidated networks of business leadership in which corporations hold stock shares in one another, resulting in increased concentration of corporate power.

interlocking directorates Linkages among corporations created by individuals who sit on two or more corporate boards.

global capitalism The current transnational phase of capitalism, characterized by global markets, production, finances; a transnational capitalist class whose business concerns are global rather than national; and transnational systems of governance (such as the World Trade Organization) that promote global business interests.

Fordism The system of production pioneered by Henry Ford, in which the assembly line was introduced.

management" involved the detailed study of industrial processes to break them down into simple operations that could be precisely timed and organized. **Taylorism**, as scientific management came to be called, was not merely an academic study. It was also a system of production designed to maximize industrial output, and it had a widespread effect not only on the organization of industrial production and technology but also on workplace politics. In particular, Taylor's time and motion studies wrested control over knowledge of the production process from the worker and placed such knowledge firmly in the hands of management, eroding the basis on which craft workers maintained autonomy from their employers (Braverman, 1974). As such, Taylorism has been widely associated with the de-skilling, degradation, and control of labor.

The industrialist Henry Ford adopted the principles of Taylorism. In 1908, Ford designed his first auto plant in Highland Park, Michigan, to manufacture only one product, the Model T, thereby allowing the introduction of specialized tools and machinery designed for speed, precision, and simplicity of operation. One of Ford's most significant innovations was the introduction of the assembly line, said to have been inspired by Chicago slaughterhouses in which animals were disassembled section by section on a moving conveyor belt. Each worker on Ford's assembly line was assigned a specialized task, such as fitting the left-side door handles as the car bodies moved along the line. By 1929, when production of the Model T ceased, more than 15 million cars had been assembled.

Ford was among the first to realize that mass production requires mass markets. He reasoned that if standardized commodities such as the automobile were to be produced on an ever-greater scale, the presence of consumers who were able to buy those commodities must also be ensured. In 1914, Ford took the unprecedented step of unilaterally raising wages at his Dearborn, Michigan, plant to $5 for an eight-hour day—a very generous wage at the time and one that ensured a working-class lifestyle that included owning an automobile. As David Harvey (1990) remarks, "The purpose of

One of Henry Ford's most significant innovations was the introduction of the assembly line, which allowed for mass production of the Model T.

the five-dollar, eight-hour day was only in part to secure worker compliance with the discipline required to work the highly productive assembly-line system. It was coincidentally meant to provide workers with sufficient income and leisure time to consume the mass-produced products the corporations were about to turn out in ever vaster quantities." Ford also enlisted the services of a small army of social workers, who were sent into the homes of workers to educate them in the proper habits of consumption.

"Fordism" is also sometimes used to refer to a historical period in the development of post–World War II capitalism in which mass production was associated with relative stability in labor relations and a high degree of unionization. Under Fordism, firms made long-term commitments to workers, and wages were tightly linked to productivity growth. Collective-bargaining agreements—formal agreements negotiated between firms and unions—provided for rising wages, seniority rights, and benefits in exchange for worker consent to increasingly automated systems of production. The rising wages also helped to ensure that there was sufficient demand for the mass-produced commodities. Worker strife was not absent from this system, and the heyday of Fordism—the period from the end of World War II (1945) to the early 1970s, when the American economy was rapidly expanding—was marked by dozens of major strikes and countless lesser ones. Workers in industries large and small walked off the job to demand their share of the growing economic pie. From the Great Strike Wave of 1946, which cut across many industries and utilities, to the automobile workers' strikes of the early 1970s, workers—backed by strong unions—fought hard for rising wages and fair working conditions.

The system is generally understood to have broken down in the 1970s, giving rise to greater "post-Fordist" flexibility, with resulting insecurity in working conditions. The reasons for the declining importance of Fordism are complex and intensely debated. As firms in a variety of industries adopted Fordist production methods, the system encountered certain limitations. Fordism was not suitable for all industries; it could be applied successfully only to industries that produced standardized commodities for large markets. At one time, it looked as though Fordism represented the likely future of industrial production as a whole. This has not proven to be the case. Setting up mechanized production lines is enormously expensive, and once a Fordist system is established, it is quite rigid; to alter a product, for example, requires substantial reinvestment. Fordist production is easy to copy if sufficient funding is available to set up the plant. But firms in countries in which labor power is expensive find it difficult to compete with those where wages are cheaper. This was one of the factors originally leading to the rise of the car industry in Japan (although Japanese wage levels today are no longer low), followed by South Korea, and more recently China.

Work and Alienation

Fordism and Taylorism involve what some industrial sociologists call **low-trust systems**. Jobs are set by management and are geared to machines. Those who carry out the work tasks are closely supervised and are allowed little autonomy of action. Where there are many low-trust positions, the level of worker dissatisfaction and absenteeism

Taylorism A set of ideas, also referred to as "scientific management," developed by Frederick Winslow Taylor, involving simple, coordinated operations in industry.

low-trust systems Organizational or work settings in which people are allowed little responsibility for, or control over, the work task.

is high, and industrial conflict is common. **High-trust systems** are those in which workers are permitted to control the pace and even the content of their work, within overall guidelines. Such systems are usually concentrated at the higher levels of industrial organizations.

Karl Marx was one of the first writers to grasp that the development of modern industry would reduce many people's work to dull, uninteresting tasks, resulting—to use today's language—in low-trust systems. According to Marx, the division of labor alienates human beings from their work. For Marx, **alienation** refers to feelings of estrangement and even hostility—initially to one's job and eventually to the overall framework of capitalist-industrial production. In Marx's view, workers in a capitalist society lack ownership of the products they make, which they often cannot even afford to buy; they are dehumanized by tedious and demeaning labor processes over which they have no control; and they find themselves in competition with their fellow workers for scarce jobs. Marx saw this situation as counter to human nature, which he believed involved creativity, control over one's activities, and cooperation with others (Marx, 2000; orig. 1844; Appelbaum, 1988). In traditional societies, he pointed out, work was often exhausting—peasant farmers sometimes had to toil from dawn to dusk. Yet peasants held a real measure of control over their work, which required considerable knowledge and skill. Many industrial workers, by contrast, have little control over their jobs, contribute only a fraction to the creation of the overall product, and have no influence over how or to whom it is eventually sold. Work thus appears as something alien, a task that the worker must carry out to earn an income but that is in itself unsatisfying.

Post-Fordism

Globalization, as we saw in the opening to this chapter, has created global supply chains, giving corporations still greater flexibility in terms of hiring workers: whether a firm is in the business of selling shoes or computers, it can now outsource its production to independently owned factories, called contractors, around the world. If costs go up in one factory—or if workers decide to go on strike for higher wages or better working conditions—the firm can shift its production to another factory, perhaps even in another country. Developments in artificial intelligence, discussed later in this chapter, further increase firm flexibility, to the extent that workers can be replaced by robots, other electronic devices, or software applications.

Since the 1970s, flexible practices have been introduced in a number of spheres. Increasingly, global supply chains involving not only independent contract factories, but also group production, problem-solving teams, multitasking, niche marketing, and

high-trust systems Organizational or work settings in which individuals are permitted a great deal of autonomy and control over the work task.

alienation The sense that our own abilities as human beings are taken over by others. The term was originally used by Karl Marx to refer to the projection of human powers onto gods. Subsequently he used the term to refer to the loss of workers' control over the nature and products of their labor.

post-Fordism The period characterized by the transition from mass industrial production, using Fordist methods, to more flexible forms of production favoring innovation and aimed at meeting market demands for customized products.

even the so-called gig-economy (involving temporary workers on short-term contracts) are just some of the strategies adopted by companies attempting to restructure themselves under shifting conditions. Some commentators have suggested that, taken collectively, these changes represent a radical departure from the principles of Fordism; they contend that we are now operating in a period that can best be understood as **post-Fordism** (Table 14.1). *Post-Fordism*, a term initially popularized by Michael Piore and Charles Sabel in *The Second Industrial Divide* (1984), describes a new era of capitalist-economic production in which flexibility and innovation are maximized to meet market demands for diverse customized products—albeit often with adverse effects on the workforce.

Table 14.1

FORDIST VERSUS POST-FORDIST PRODUCTION SYSTEMS

FORDISM	POST-FORDISM
Bureaucratic/vertical	Flexible/horizontal
Mass production	Mass customization
Most work in-house (local)	Most work outsourced (global)
Job security (high wage, long term, full time, high career advancement)	Job insecurity (low wage, short term, part time, low career advancement)

The idea of post-Fordism is somewhat problematic, however. The term is used to refer to a set of overlapping changes that are occurring not only in the realm of work and economic life but also throughout society as a whole. Some writers argue that the tendency toward post-Fordism can be seen in spheres as diverse as party politics, welfare programs, and consumer and lifestyle choices. While observers of late modern societies often point to many of the same changes, there is no consensus about the precise meaning of post-Fordism or, indeed, if this term is even the best way of understanding the phenomenon we are witnessing.

Regardless of the confusion surrounding the term *post-Fordism*, several distinctive trends within the world of work have emerged in recent decades that seem to represent a clear departure from earlier Fordist practices. These include the replacement of highly bureaucratic, vertically organized business structures with more flexible, horizontally organized networked approaches; the transition from mass production to mass customization; a shift from in-house production to global outsourcing; and the resulting severe erosion in job security for employees. We now consider each of these in turn. We will consider a fifth trend, the decline of labor union power, later in this chapter.

Flexible Business Structures

One of the most important changes in worldwide production processes over the past few years has been an increase in the organizational flexibility of many large firms. For much of the twentieth century, the most important business organizations were large manufacturing firms that controlled both the making of goods and their final sales. Giant automobile companies, such as Ford and General Motors (GM), typified this approach. These companies employed tens of thousands of factory workers to make everything from components to the final cars, which were then sold in the manufacturers' showrooms. Such manufacture-dominated production processes were organized as large bureaucracies, often controlled by a single firm.

If General Motors, a highly bureaucratic organization, represented the prototypical corporation of the twentieth century, Walmart may well prove to be symbolic of the twenty-first (Lichtenstein, 2010, 2011; Appelbaum, 2019). Sociologist Gary Hamilton has described a world in which "big buyers"—global retailers—are becoming increasingly dominant in the global economy, not only reshaping business structures but also driving economic development in those regions (such as East Asia) that supply their products (Petrovic and Hamilton, 2006). While both General Motors and Walmart are giant transnational corporations, GM is organized vertically: Most of its production is still done under its own roof, controlled by its own management structure in a highly bureaucratized fashion. GM still designs, produces, and markets the cars that it sells. Control, in other words, is highly centralized.

Walmart is the world's largest corporation, with 2018 revenues of more than $514 billion and 2.2 million employees worldwide. Although it is a publicly traded company on the stock market, more than half of all shares are owned by the descendants of founder Sam Walton, making it a family-owned company. Unlike GM, Walmart designs very little of what it sells and produces next to nothing. Walmart sells products designed by others—the thousands of brands and labels available in its stores. Those brands and labels, in turn, seldom actually make the products they design: That task falls to factories around the world. Like GM, Walmart exerts control over its suppliers—but in this case, the suppliers are outside the firm rather than part of it. The resulting horizontal network of retailers, brands, and factories enables each to respond quickly to changes in market conditions, in a way that the more vertically organized GM never could hope to do. If an economic slowdown or changing buyer tastes causes a drop in sales for GM, the corporation still has to cover the cost of expensive plants and equipment, as well as meet the payroll of hundreds of thousands of employees, from management to the factory floor. While Walmart has plenty of stores to maintain (some 5,400 in the United States and an additional 6,200 worldwide)(Walmart, 2020), its situation is markedly different from GM's: If Sony flat-panel TVs are not moving, Walmart can simply tell Sony it is reducing its orders and shift to Panasonic. Sony, in turn, can respond by canceling orders in some of the contract factories that are its suppliers. Those factories then either switch to other labels (perhaps Panasonic) or else lay off workers.

Walmart controls its suppliers through the information technology (IT) that has revolutionized the field of supply chain management. Today's world of flexible production involves complex networks of buyers and suppliers: A clothing company such as the Gap may have hundreds or even thousands of independently owned factories supplying its stores, while each of those factories may in turn be making clothing for many competing brands. Coordinating these activities requires sophisticated computer technology—electronic data interchange (EDI) software systems that enable firms to share relevant data, beginning with the information on the bar code attached to each product that is scanned at the time of purchase. The most advanced systems, such as those pioneered by Walmart, enable firms to order just the right number of products to meet demand, shift their orders among different suppliers, and respond "nimbly"—a favored term of business—to changing market conditions. Today, even large automobile manufacturers such as GM have moved down the post-Fordist path, outsourcing as much work as possible and using advanced information systems to manage their supply chains.

Mass Customization

Controlling such far-flung networks of suppliers is only part of the challenge modern businesses face. They must also cater to their customers' changing demands—demands that are shaped, in turn, by a constant flow of advertising in magazines, newspapers, television, radio, and movies. Film franchises such as *The Avengers, Star Wars, Spiderman,* and *Transformers* are always accompanied by a deluge of toys based on the movie. Although Taylorism and Fordism successfully produced mass products (that were all the same) for mass markets, they were completely unable to produce small orders of goods, let alone goods specifically made for an individual customer. GM or Ford changed the overall design of its cars every couple of years, and the changes were often largely cosmetic: Large tail fins adorned cars in the 1950s, marketed as providing "greater stability on the nation's highways."

Mass customization has changed all this (Pine, 1999). It combines the large-volume production associated with Fordism with the flexibility required to tailor products to consumers' needs. Computer-aided design, coupled with other types of computer-based technology such as EDI, now permits factories to alter their assembly lines for small-batch production, serving (and creating) particular market niches. Information can be solicited about individual consumers and analyzed to determine the key types of consumer preferences for particular products, which are then manufactured to those specifications. In a modern car factory, several different models can even be built on the same assembly line. The latest development in mass customization is additive manufacturing, or 3D printing, a technology that dates back to the 1980s but only became commercially available (and increasingly affordable) in recent years. This printing process involves the ability, using computerized technology, to add layers of materials that result in physical objects such as fashion accessories, car parts, artificial organs, weapons, and even component parts for the Mars land rover. Nike, Adidas, and Reebok, for example, have developed the ability to scan a customer's foot and print out a custom-designed athletic shoe—or eventually, as 3D printers come down in cost, perhaps even in the customer's home (Matisons, 2015). Nike's "Zoom Vaporfly Elite Flyprint 3D" was designed with the help of Eliud Kipichoge, winner of the 2018 Berlin Marathon. Nike claims that the Vaporfly' light-weight 3D-tailored construction can reduce a runner's energy output by 4 percent, presumably increasing their performance by a comparable amount (Iftikhar, 2018).

Dell was one of the first major computer companies to carry mass customization to a high level, although it is now commonplace for consumers of all major brands to custom design their computer online, charge the purchase to their credit card, and, within a week, receive the custom-made computer at their door. Dell is often thought of as a computer-manufacturing company, but in fact, the company does not make any significant computer components. Instead, it assembles components others produce, controlling its supply chains through EDI. In effect, Dell has turned traditional ways of doing business upside down. Firms used to build a product first, then worry about selling it. Now mass customizers such as Dell sell first and build second. Such a shift has important consequences for industry. The need to hold stock of parts on hand, a major cost for manufacturers, has been dramatically reduced. In addition, an

Current technology allows factories to respond to specific market and consumer needs. Companies like Dell sell first and build second.

increasing share of production is outsourced. Thus, the rapid transfer of information between manufacturers and suppliers is essential to the successful implementation of mass customization.

One form of mass customization is the smartphone app, which gives users access to countless different sources of products, services, games, and information. Today, one can use an app (once a shortened version of "application," now a word in itself) to custom design a computer, find a taco stand or gas station nearby, determine whether a product is environmentally friendly, turn a photo of a best friend's face into an aging zombie, or do millions of other things: as of mid-2019, there were 2.5 million Android apps and 2 million Apple apps (Statista, 2019).

Global Outsourcing

Changes in industrial production include not only how products are manufactured but also where they are manufactured. In **flexible production** systems, there is truly a global assembly line: The companies that design and sell products seldom make them in their own factories, instead **outsourcing** production to factories around the world. As we saw in Chapter 9, none of the 185 million iPhones sold in 2019 (Graham, 2020) were assembled in the United States; with few exceptions, the production of almost all the iPhone's components were done in virtually a United Nations catalogue of countries.

As we learned in the chapter opener, few, if any, industries are as globalized as the industry that makes the clothing and footwear that fill your closet. Almost no major U.S. companies today make their own apparel or footwear; rather, they outsource to independently owned factories that do the work for them. These factories are found in more than 100 different countries and range from tiny sweatshops to giant plants owned by transnational corporations. Most so-called garment manufacturers actually employ no garment workers at all. Instead, they rely on thousands of factories around the world to make their apparel, which they then sell in department stores and other retail outlets. Clothing manufacturers do not own any of these factories and are therefore free to use them or not, depending on their needs. While this system provides the manufacturers with the flexibility previously discussed, it creates great uncertainty both for the factories, which must compete with one another for orders, and for the workers in those factories, who may lose their jobs if their factory loses business (Bonacich and Appelbaum, 2000).

Bonacich and Appelbaum (2000) argue that such flexible production, driven by global competition, has resulted in a global "race to the bottom," in which retailers and manufacturers will go anyplace on earth where they can find the lowest wages, the fewest environmental restrictions, and the most lax governmental regulations. This system invites abuses—as evidenced by the well-publicized cases of toxic toys made in Chinese factories under contract to leading U.S. brands such as Mattel.

Job Insecurity

Flexible production has produced some benefits for consumers and the economy as a whole, but the effect on workers has not been wholly positive. Though some workers undoubtedly do learn new skills and have less monotonous jobs, the majority find their work lives less secure than before. For many workers inside the United States, the long-term employment, rising wages, career advancement, and health and retirement benefits once associated with a job at a General Motors or Ford plant have become a thing of the past. To keep their jobs, U.S. workers have had to accept pay cuts and reduced benefits packages. And, of course, many have lost their jobs to overseas competition.

The Informal Economy

Many types of work do not conform to orthodox categories of paid employment; they cannot be classified as either Fordist or post-Fordist. Much of the work done in all societies, for example, is performed outside formal business firms, and indeed, outside the formal economy itself. The term **informal economy** refers to transactions outside the sphere of regular employment, sometimes involving the exchange of cash for goods and services provided, for which no official records are kept, and which therefore escape government notice. Your child's babysitter might be paid in cash, "off the books," without any receipt being given or details of the job recorded; the same may be true of the person who cleans your house or does your gardening, if you have such services.

In poor countries, a significant part of the national economy consists of such informal work. One study estimates that the informal economy may account for 70 percent of employment in sub-Saharan Africa and contribute about 55 percent of the region's GNI (UN Economic Commission for Africa, 2015). The informal economy in the developing world has a high presence of women, involving as many as 60 percent of working women (Mbaye and Benjamin, 2014). The high prevalence of informal economy work in developing countries has both positive and negative effects. Among the former, such work provides employment and earnings, and, in many cases, can make the difference between absolute poverty and subsistence-level survival. While much informal-sector work involves self-employment, in some cases, it also enables people to form small businesses. On the negative side, because such work is by definition "off the books," the informal sector is unregulated, unreported,

flexible production A manufacturing system involving a complex network of contract factories that enable both the process of production, and the product itself, to be quickly modified in order to meet changing demand and market conditions.

outsourcing A business practice that sends production of materials to factories around the world. The components of one final product often originate from many different countries and then are sent elsewhere to be put together and sold. Factories from different countries must compete with one another to obtain business.

informal economy Economic transactions carried on outside the sphere of orthodox paid employment.

unprotected by the state, and prone to abuse. Since informal-sector work is officially unknown to the state, it does not contribute to taxes or pension funds, which deprives the state of revenues (although where governments are corrupt, this may actually be a benefit) (Benjamin, 2014).

In the United States, the informal economy was estimated to add only 9 percent to the GNI in the year 2000—which, given the large size of the American economy, amounted to nearly $1 trillion in goods and services exchanged that never appeared in any official government accounts (Schneider and Enste, 2002; Barnes, 2009). Another study doubles that amount, concluding that income-tax evasion annually involves some $2 trillion in unreported income (Cebula and Feige, 2011). This includes illegal goods and services, from drugs to prostitution, which can now be purchased on the so-called "dark web" with a high degree of anonymity. "Darknet markets," such as the Dream Market—which shut down in 2019 following government crackdowns on web drug trafficking and cyber ransom demands (Cimpanu, 2019)—operate through such legal websites as the Tor Network, an open-source website that assures anonymity by relaying messages to a secret distributed network of servers around the world.

One study estimated that as of April 2015, there were 15 darknet marketplaces listing over 43,000 illicit drugs (Digital Citizens Alliance [DCA], 2015). Illegal drugs

It is estimated that the majority of female workers in developing countries work in the informal economy. Women in Madagascar sell fish on the street.

constitute a major part of the informal economy in some countries: In Afghanistan, opiate trade brought in an estimated $1–2 billion in 2019 representing 6–11 percent of the country's GNI (UN Office on Drugs and Crime, 2019). There is widespread disagreement over the size of the global drug trade—not surprising, perhaps, given its illicit and secretive nature. Moreover, drug enforcement agencies have an interest in showing that there is a significant need for their services, which may result in inflated estimates of the problem (Blickman, 2003; Thoumi, 2003; Reuter and Greenfield, 2001).

The informal economy includes not only "hidden" cash transactions but also many forms of self-provisioning, which people carry on inside and outside the home. Do-it-yourself activities and household appliances and tools, for instance, provide goods and services that would otherwise have to be purchased. And it also often includes the labor of possibly millions of undocumented immigrant workers who toil in factories and restaurants or clean houses and do yard work. Such work often goes unreported, which means the wages are often below the legal minimum, and workers have no recourse if they are underpaid (or indeed, not paid at all).

Globally, it is estimated that there are nearly 70 million domestic workers, the vast majority of whom are women. Nearly one out of six are migrants in the countries where they work, which means they are especially vulnerable to all forms of economic, physical and sexual abuse (ILO, 2016). In the United States, some 2 million domestic workers play a critical economic role, doing work such as housecleaning, caring for children, and serving as caregivers for the infirm and elderly. Home health care is one of the fastest-growing jobs in the U.S. economy, as aging baby boomers, many with declining health, choose to stay at home rather than move into nursing homes (there are currently 55 million Americans over 70, and 20 million over 80). An estimated 2 million home health care workers, mainly women, earn poverty-level wages providing emotionally stressful and physically demanding work (the 2017 median income for home health care workers was only $16,200). Turnover in this field is understandably high, and an additional million new jobs will be needed by 2026 to serve the growing number of elderly who need care (PHI, 2019; Newman, 2019; US Census, 2018e).

Most domestic workers are women; most are non-White; and many are immigrants (including many who are undocumented). Because domestic workers are typically socially isolated as well as "off the books," their lack of access to legal protection invites exploitation and abuse. There is a large demand for domestic workers, both because in two-person households both members are likely to be working, and because there is an abundant supply of people who are desperate for work (Wallis, 2019; Burnham, Theodore, and Ehrenreich, 2012).

CONCEPT CHECKS

1 Describe five forms that capitalism has taken.

2 What are two key differences between Fordism and post-Fordism?

3 Define and provide an example of an informal economy.

3 CURRENT RESEARCH ON WORK AND ECONOMIC LIFE

The changes we have just described affect many aspects of work and economic life. These changes have generally favored the growing power of corporations relative to their workers. We first look at the growth of transnational corporations and how this is reshaping the nature of economic organization in the twenty-first century, before turning to a discussion of workers, unions, and the challenges they face. We conclude the discussion of current research by looking at some forms of industrial conflict that occur when labor and management fail to agree.

Corporations and Corporate Power

Since the turn of the twentieth century, modern capitalist economies have been more and more influenced by the rise of large business corporations, particularly those in financial services such as banks, stock brokerages, and investment funds. While manufacturing remains important in the U.S. economy, representing about 9 percent of the U.S. workforce and 13 percent of U.S. GNI, the corporations with the largest assets are now banks (Scott, 2015).

The world economy is increasingly influenced by the rise of large business corporations. In 2019, the 2,000 largest corporations in the world had total annual revenues of more than $40 trillion, and assets valued at $186 trillion. According to one estimate, this represents half the value of all officially measured assets on the world combined. The two largest economic sectors, banking and finance, account for nearly three-fifths of total assets. The largest bank in the world is the Industrial and Commercial Bank of China, with more than $4 trillion in assets (Ponciano and Hansen, 2019; *Fortune*, 2019b; Shorrocks, Davies, and Lluberas, 2019b; Desjardins, 2019). The power of the financial services sector was seen in the financial collapse of 2007–2008, when large financial institutions paid the price for making risky (so-called "subprime") loans in housing and other sectors. When this financial bubble collapsed because the loans could not be repaid, it threatened to take down the entire U.S. economy—a crisis that was averted only when the government stepped in and provided bailout loans for major banks and corporations that were deemed "too big to fail" in terms of their widespread economic impact.

Of course, there still exist thousands of smaller firms and enterprises within the American economy. In these companies, the image of the entrepreneur—the boss who owns and runs the firm—is by no means obsolete. The large corporations are a different matter. Ever since Adolf Berle and Gardiner Means published their celebrated study *The Modern Corporation and Private Property* (1982; orig. 1932), it has been accepted that those who own most of the largest firms do not actually run them. In theory, large corporations are the property of their shareholders, who have the right to make all important decisions. But Berle and Means argue that because share ownership is so dispersed, actual control has passed into the hands of the managers who run the firms on a day-to-day basis. Ownership of corporations is thus separated from their control.

Whether owners or managers run them, major corporations have extensive power. When one or a handful of firms dominate in a given industry, they often cooperate in setting prices rather than freely competing with one another. Thus, the giant oil companies normally follow one another's lead in the price charged for gasoline. When one firm occupies a commanding position in a given industry, it is said to be in a **monopoly** position. More common is a situation of **oligopoly**, in which a small group of giant corporations predominates. In situations of oligopoly, firms are able more or less to dictate the terms on which they buy goods and services from the smaller firms that are their suppliers.

The emergence of the global economy has contributed to a wave of corporate mergers and acquisitions on an unprecedented scale, exceeding $3.3 trillion in 2018. Three of the largest mergers and acquisitions involved pharmaceuticals (Cigna acquired Express Scripts for $68.5 billion) and telecommunications (AT&T acquired Time Warner for $85 billion, and T-Mobile acquired Sprint for $58.7 billion) (Stebbins, 2018a; Gold and Schneider, 2018). The previous year, the drug store chain CVS's merger with health insurer Aetna was valued at $69 billion, while Amazon's acquisition of Whole Foods (for $13.7 billion) signaled that the online retail giant was moving into the grocery business (Stebbins, 2018b). The resulting giants are seen as oligopolies that critics predict will restrict consumer choice and ultimately raise prices. AT&T, Comcast, Verizon, Walt Disney Corporation, 21st Century Fox, and CBS Corporation are among the world's biggest media and communication corporations; all are based in the United States (although the largest telecom company, in terms of subscribers, is China Telecom) (Parietti, 2019).

Chinese firms are rapidly getting into the mergers and acquisitions game (Shepard, 2016). At first, Chinese state-owned firms were the primary players, buying up energy and commodities companies to power the country's factories: Two state-owned Chinese energy firms—Sinopec (the world's second-largest corporation in 2019, based on revenues) and China National Petroleum (the fourth largest)—had gone on a global shopping spree in 2014, acquiring part or complete ownership of Chesapeake Energy (U.S.), Petrobras Energia (Peru), Apache Corporation (U.S.), ENI East Africa (Mozambique), and the Kashagan oilfields (Kazakhstan) (China.org.cn, 2014). Since then, Chinese firms, including private entrepreneurs, have shifted their focus from raw materials to brands and technology, purchasing the Finnish game maker behind *Clash of Clans* and *Boom Beach*, as well as Italian football team AC Milan (*Bloomberg*, 2017).

A number of factors have contributed to this trend, including technological advances, which have lowered global transportation and communications costs; a relaxation of regulation of corporate business activities; and new and efficient ways of financing and pooling the large sums of capital needed to conduct a merger or acquisition. One of the primary aims of the recent wave of business consolidations has been to eliminate direct competition and productive overcapacity. Overcapacity is a problem that occurs when businesses produce more goods than the market will consume. Following the logic of supply and demand, overcapacity leads to a decline in the value of the goods produced and to a decline in profits. Consolidation of firms is an attempt to avoid this problem.

monopoly The domination by a single firm in a given industry.

oligopoly The domination by a small number of firms in a given industry.

Transnational Corporations

With the intensifying of globalization, most large corporations now operate in an international economic context. When they establish branches in two or more countries, they are referred to as **transnational corporations**. Swiss researchers identified more than 43,000 transnational corporations networked together across the globe in 2007 (although the study has not been replicated with more recent data, its findings would most likely be similar today). They found that only 147 of these corporations controlled almost 40 percent of the total monetary value of the entire network; 737 firms accounted for 80 percent. The top 50 firms were primarily financial institutions such as Barclays, JPMorgan Chase, and Merrill Lynch, which strongly suggests that the financial services industry has a great deal of power and influence in the global economy (Vitali, Glattfelder, and Battiston, 2011).

The largest transnationals are gigantic; their wealth outstrips that of many countries (Table 14.2). The scope of these companies' operations is staggering. The combined revenues of the world's 500 largest transnational corporations totaled $32.7 trillion in 2018 (*Fortune*, 2019a). Walmart alone, the world's largest corporation, had 2018 revenues of more than a half trillion dollars ($514 billion). To give an idea of the magnitude of that number, in 2018, $86 trillion in goods and services was produced by the *entire world* (World Bank, 2020c).

The United States is home to the largest number of firms among the top 500 transnational corporations, although the share of American-based companies has fallen sharply in recent years as the number of transnational corporations based in other countries—especially Asian countries such as China and Japan—has increased. In 2005, the United States had 176 companies among the Global 500; in 2018, the number had declined to 121. China has moved in the opposite direction: It had only 16 companies among the top in 2005, and none among the top 10. Today, it boasts 119, including 3 among the top 10 (DuBois, 2011; Colvin, 2019).

Transnational corporations have assumed an increasingly important place in the world economy over this century. They are of key importance in the **international division of labor**—the specialization in producing goods for the world market that divides regions into zones of industrial or agricultural production or high- or low-skilled labor (Fröbel, Heinrichs, and Kreye, 1979; McMichael, 1996). Just as national economies have become increasingly concentrated—dominated by a limited number of very large companies—so has the world economy. In the case of the United States and several of the other leading industrialized countries, the firms that dominate nationally also have a wide-ranging international presence. Many sectors of world production (such as agribusiness) are oligopolies. Over the past two or three decades, international oligopolies have developed in the automobile, microprocessor, and electronics industries and in the production of some other goods marketed worldwide.

The reach of the transnationals since the mid-1970s would not have been possible without advances in transportation and communications. Air travel now allows people to

transnational (or multinational) corporations Business corporations located in two or more countries.

international division of labor The specialization in producing goods for the world market that divides regions into zones of industrial or agricultural production or high- or low-skilled labor.

Table 14.2
CORPORATE GLOBALIZATION: THE WORLD'S 50 LARGEST ECONOMIES (IN BILLIONS OF DOLLARS) (2018)*

1	United States	$20,494.1	26	Thailand	$505.0
2	China	$13,608.2	27	Austria	$455.7
3	Japan	$4,970.9	28	Norway	$434.8
4	Germany	$3,996.8	29	**Sinopec**	**$414.6**
5	United Kingdom	$2,825.2	30	United Arab Emirates	$414.2
6	France	$2,777.5	31	Nigeria	$397.3
7	India	$2,726.3	32	**Royal Dutch Shell**	**$396.6**
8	Italy	$2,073.9	33	**China National Petroleum**	**$393.0**
9	Brazil	$1,868.6	34	**State Grid**	**$387.1**
10	Canada	$1,709.3	35	Ireland	$375.9
11	Russian Federation	$1,657.6	36	Israel	$369.7
12	Korea, Rep.	$1,619.4	37	South Africa	$366.3
13	Australia	$1,432.2	38	Singapore	$364.2
14	Spain	$1,426.2	39	Hong Kong SAR, China	$363.0
15	Mexico	$1,223.8	40	**Saudi Aramco**	**$355.9**
16	Indonesia	$1,042.2	41	Malaysia	$354.3
17	Netherlands	$912.9	42	**BP (British Petroleum)**	**$303.7**
18	Saudi Arabia	$782.5	43	**Exxon Mobil**	**$290.2**
19	Turkey	$766.5	44	**Volkswagen**	**$278.3**
20	Switzerland	$705.5	45	**Toyota Motor**	**$272.6**
21	Poland	$585.8	46	**Apple**	**$265.6**
22	Sweden	$551.0	47	**Berkshire Hathaway**	**$247.8**
23	Belgium	$531.8	48	**Amazon.com**	**$232.9**
24	Argentina	$518.5	49	**United Health Group**	**$226.2**
25	**Walmart**	**$514.4**	50	**Samsung Electronics**	**$221.6**

*The European Union (EU) is actually the world's second-largest economy, with combined GNI totaling $18.7 trillion in comparison with the United States' $20.6 trillion. In this table, however, we consider the European countries separately, since the EU does not function entirely as a single economy. The world economy as a whole has a combined GNI of $85.8 trillion. By this measure (GNI), the US, European Union, and China account for more than three-fifths (62%) of total world GNI.

SOURCES: *Fortune*, 2019a; World Bank, 2020c.

A major force behind globalization, containerization allows for the rapid movement of goods around the world.

move around the world at a speed that would have seemed inconceivable even 60 years ago. Technological innovations allowing containerization have permitted the rapid movement and distribution of bulk goods around the world. The best example of containerization is the development of intermodal transport, which involves moving huge containers around the world by means of a combination of truck, rail, ship, and sometimes air. The containers, which are typically 40 feet in length and may carry as much as 30 tons of goods, are loaded at the factory (for example, in China) where the goods are produced. They are then lifted onto the beds of trains or 18-wheeler trucks and hauled to a modern container port (for example, Shanghai, the world's busiest container port), where they are stacked like Legos by electronically controlled robot cranes, until they are ready to be loaded onto giant container ships. The world's largest container ship, the MSC Gülsün, was launched in August 2019. It is a quarter mile long, slightly more than 200 feet wide, approximately 20 stories high, and can carry 23,800 20-foot containers—enough to stretch nearly 90 miles if placed end to end. This ship, built for the Swiss-owned Mediterranean Shipping Company by Hyundai Heavy Industries, a Korean transnational corporation, might take a little over two weeks to cross the Pacific from Shanghai to Los Angeles, where the containers would be unloaded, placed on a truck or train, and hauled to Walmart or some other retail outlet.

The global corporations have become the first organizations able to plan on a truly world scale. Apple, McDonald's, and Coca-Cola ads reach billions. A few companies with developed global networks are able to shape the commercial activities of diverse nations. One useful way to think about this is through a typology developed by Richard Barnet and John Cavanagh (1994). In their view, there are four webs of interconnecting commercial activity in the new world economy. These are what they call the global cultural bazaar, the global shopping mall, the global workplace, and the global financial network.

The global cultural bazaar is the newest of the four but already the most extensive. Global images and global dreams are diffused through movies, TV programs, music, videos, games, toys, and T-shirts, sold on a worldwide basis. All over the earth, even in the poorest developing countries, people use the same electronic devices to see or listen to the same commercially produced songs and shows. When Apple releases a new iPhone, crowds form at Apple stores from Beijing to Baltimore.

The global shopping mall is a "planetary supermarket with a dazzling spread of things to eat, drink, wear and enjoy," according to Barnet and Cavanagh. It is more exclusive than the global cultural bazaar because the poor do not have the resources to participate—they have the status only of window shoppers. Of the nearly 7.7 billion people who make up the world's population, nearly three out of five lack the cash or credit to purchase any consumer goods.

The third global web, the global workplace, is the increasingly complex global division of labor that affects all of us. It consists of the massive array of offices, factories, restaurants, and millions of other places where goods are produced and consumed or information is exchanged.

This web is closely bound up with the fourth web—the global financial network, which it fuels and is financed by. The global financial network consists of billions of bits of financial information stored in computers and portrayed on computer screens. It entails almost endless currency exchanges, credit card transactions, insurance plans, and buying and selling of stocks and shares.

The Twenty-First-Century Corporation: Different from Its Twentieth-Century Counterpart

There are considerable differences between the large corporation of the early twenty-first century and its mid-twentieth-century counterpart. Many of the names are the same—General Electric, General Motors, Ford, IBM, AT&T—but these have been joined by other giant firms, largely or completely unknown in the 1950s, such as Walmart, Microsoft, Apple, Google, Facebook, and Intel. They all wield great power, and their top executives typically still inhabit the large buildings that dominate so many cities.

But below the surface similarities between today

Bringing in more than $2.81 billion in worldwide ticket sales, *Avengers: Endgame* became one of the highest grossing films of all time, due in large part to its strong international appeal: the film grossed nearly $2 billion internationally, especially in China, where it broke all records for its first five days ($331 million).

and half a century ago, some profound transformations have taken place. The origin of these transformations lies in a process we have encountered often in this book: globalization. Since the 1950s, the giant corporations have become more and more caught up in global competition; as a result, both their internal composition and, in a way, their very nature have altered. Nearly thirty years ago, former U.S. labor secretary (now University of California-Berkeley economics professor) Robert Reich (1991) wrote:

> Underneath, all is changing. America's core corporation no longer plans and implements the production of a large volume of goods and services; it no longer invests in a vast array of factories, machinery, laboratories, inventories, and other tangible assets; it no longer employs armies of production workers and middle-level managers. . . . In fact, the core corporation is no longer even American. It is, increasingly, a façade, behind which teems an array of decentralized groups and subgroups continuously contracting with similarly diffuse working units all over the world.

The large corporation is less a big business than an "enterprise web"—a central organization that links together smaller firms. IBM, for example, which used to be one of the most jealously self-sufficient of all large corporations, joined with dozens of U.S.-based companies and more than 80 foreign-based firms in the 1980s and early 1990s to share strategic planning and cope with production problems. Nelson Lichtenstein (2006), a labor historian who spent many years studying Walmart, has characterized this as a shift from General Motors to Walmart, which he describes as "a template for twenty-first-century capitalism":

> GM workers were often life-time employees so factory turnover was exceedingly low: these were the best jobs around, and they were jobs that rewarded longevity.... At Wal-Mart, in contrast, employee turnover approaches 50 percent a year, which means it must be even higher for those hired at an entry level wage.... The hours of labor, the very definition of a full work day, constitutes the other great contrast dividing America's old industrial economy from that of its retail future.... At Wal-Mart a 32 hour work week is considered "full time" employment. This gives managers great flexibility and power, enabling them to parcel out the extra hours to fill in the schedule, reward favored employees, and gear up for the holiday rush. But the social consequences of this policy are profound: Unlike General Motors, Wal-Mart is not afraid to hire thousands of new workers each year, but employee attachment to their new job is low, and millions of Americans find it necessary, and possible, to moonlight with two part time jobs.

Walmart, Lichtenstein points out, provides us with a steady stream of low-cost products, making it possible for millions of Americans of limited means to feed and clothe their families. Walmart thus permits many Americans to enjoy a lifestyle of consumption that would otherwise not be possible. The giant retailer also provides jobs, although most are not nearly as well paying as the millions of manufacturing jobs that have been lost in recent years.

The one place where jobs have been gained, and in large numbers, is in the emerging economies of the developing world. Manufacturing has boomed in China, where 250 to 300 million workers labor under harsh conditions, in millions of factories that turn out everything from running shoes to flat-panel TVs to smartphones. China's factories provide the goods that are sold in Walmart's thousands of U.S. stores, linking the economies of both countries tightly together. In turn, Walmart's global supply chains, along with those of all corporations that design, make, and sell products today, link the world in a web of production networks that now reach every place on the planet. For better or worse, the personal lives and work lives of all of us—indeed, of all people everywhere—are increasingly intertwined.

Some corporations remain strongly bureaucratic and centered in the United States. However, most are no longer so clearly located anywhere. The old transnational corporation used to work mainly from its American headquarters, from where its overseas production plants and subsidiaries were controlled. Now, with the transformation of space and time noted earlier (Chapter 5), groups situated in any region of the world are able, via telecommunications and computer, to work with others. Nations still try to influence the flow of information, resources, and money across their borders, but modern communication technologies make this more and more difficult, if not impossible. Knowledge and finances can be transferred across the world as electronic blips moving at nearly the speed of light.

Even the production of the technology that makes the global activities of transnational corporations possible is spread out over the globe. With revenues of $71 billion in 2018, the California-based computer chip manufacturer Intel dominates the global personal computer microchip industry, boasting a global workforce of 107,400 employees, slightly more than half of them outside the United States (Intel, 2019). Its six wafer-fabrication plants (so-called *fabs*) and three assembly-test facilities are found in the United States, China, Ireland, Israel, Malaysia, and Vietnam, although its most advanced facilities—the ones working with the smallest chips—are in the United States and Israel (Intel, 2019). Intel is especially interested in China, where it has been operating laboratories, manufacturing facilities, and testing facilities for more than 20 years. Its chip fabrication plant in Dalian, China, was the first such plant the company has located in an emerging economy. The reason China was selected? Not low labor costs (chip fabrication depends on expensive equipment rather than cheap labor), but rather China's growing supply of talented engineers, along with generous financial incentives provided by the Chinese government (Parker and Appelbaum, 2012; Appelbaum et al., 2018).

Workers and Their Challenges

The idea of work is actually a complex one. All of us work in many ways besides in paid employment. Cleaning the house, planting a garden, and going shopping are plainly all work. But for two centuries or more, Western society has been built around the central importance of paid work. The experience of unemployment—being unable to find a job when one wants it—is still a largely negative one. Unemployment clearly brings with it unfortunate effects, including, sometimes, falling into poverty.

An individual's quality of life depends on their position in the labor market. Arguably this is truer in the United States than in any other comparably developed economy. Americans spend more time at work than do citizens of other advanced industrial countries. U.S. living standards also reflect income and employment-related benefits more directly than do living standards in other comparably developed countries where governments universally guarantee paid vacation, job training, and health insurance. There is also more variability in terms of pay and work conditions in the U.S. labor market than elsewhere. Yet, in spite of the overwhelming importance of the labor market for the life conditions of working Americans, there has been relatively little investigation of how workers view the framework through which the U.S. labor market is governed.

For this reason, Richard Freeman of Harvard University and Joel Rogers of the University of Wisconsin set out to find out what workers want in regard to the conditions under which they labor. Freeman and Rogers (1999) designed the Worker Representation and Participation Survey (WRPS) to canvass workers systematically in a wide variety of professions for their opinions on their employment and how their workplaces could be improved. Freeman and Rogers's findings are based on a national telephone survey of 2,400 workers in private-sector establishments that employ 25 or more people. They excluded top managers, the self-employed, owners of firms or their relatives, public-sector workers, and employees in small firms. Overall, the population from which survey respondents were selected covers approximately 75 percent of all

Fast-food workers protest outside a McDonald's restaurant in Richmond, Virginia, as part of a nationwide strike calling for a higher minimum wage.

private-sector workers. The findings range across a wide variety of aspects of people's work lives, including causes of worker dissatisfaction, attitudes toward unionization, views of management, and worker knowledge of protective labor legislation. In-depth, follow-up interviews were conducted with 801 workers, who were asked about their views of alternative institutional designs for American workplaces.

The overwhelming finding of Freeman and Rogers's study is that what workers want is more influence at work. American workers believe that if they had more say over how production is carried out, not only would they enjoy work more, but also their firms would be more competitive, and problems would be solved more effectively. Furthermore, influence is associated with a wide range of attitudes about work: Workers satisfied with their degree of influence report that they enjoy going to work, grade employee-management relations as excellent, and trust their employers. In contrast, workers who are dissatisfied with their degree of influence tend to dislike going to work, report poor relations with management, and distrust their employers.

One of the most surprising findings of the WRPS concerns the kind of institutional arrangement workers consider ideal for achieving greater say. Contrary to what Freeman and Rogers expected, workers prefer an organization run jointly by workers and management to one run by employees alone. Workers were also asked to choose between two hypothetical employee organizations, "one that management cooperated with in discussing issues, but had no power to make decisions," and "one that had more power, but management opposed." Sixty-three percent of all employees chose the former organization, whereas only 22 percent stated that they would prefer the latter. These results—in which workers effectively indicated that they would prefer weaker to stronger organizations, in spite of the fact that they also reported wanting more say at work—make sense in light of another question on Freeman and Rogers's survey. When asked if they thought an organization could be effective without managerial support, nearly three-quarters (73 percent) of all respondents indicated that they believed an employee organization could function only with management cooperation.

Industrial Conflict

There have long been conflicts between workers and those who have economic and political authority over them. Riots against conscription and high taxes and food riots at periods of harvest failure were common in urban areas of Europe in the eighteenth century. These "pre-modern" forms of labor conflict continued up until not much more than a century ago in some countries. For example, there were food riots in several large Italian towns in 1868 (Geary, 1981). Such traditional forms of confrontation were not just sporadic, irrational outbursts of violence: The threat or use of violence had the effect of lowering the price of grain and other essential foodstuffs (Booth, 1977; Rudé, 1964; Thompson, 1971).

Industrial conflict between workers and employers at first tended to follow these older patterns. In situations of confrontation, workers would quite often leave their places of employment and form crowds in the streets; they would make their grievances known through their unruly behavior or by engaging in acts of violence against the authorities. Workers in some parts of France in the late nineteenth century would threaten disliked employers with hanging (Holton, 1978). Use of the strike as a weapon, today commonly associated with organized bargaining between workers and management, developed only slowly and sporadically.

Strikes A **strike** is a temporary stoppage of work by a group of employees to express a grievance or enforce a demand. All the components of this definition are important in separating strikes from other forms of opposition and conflict. A strike is temporary because workers intend to return to the same job with the same employer; when workers quit altogether, the term *strike* is not appropriate. As a stoppage of work, a strike is distinguishable from an overtime ban or "slowdown." A group of workers has to be involved, because a strike is a collective action, not the response of one individual worker. That those involved are employees serves to separate strikes from protests that tenants or students may conduct. Finally, a strike involves seeking to make known a grievance or to press a demand; workers who miss work to go to a ball game could not be said to be on strike.

Workers choose to go on strike for many specific reasons. For much of the twentieth century, U.S. workers typically went on strike to secure higher wages, better hours, safer working conditions, and security of employment, and occasionally to protest against technological changes that would make their work duller or lead to layoffs. In all these circumstances, the strike is essentially a mechanism of power: a weapon of people who are relatively powerless in the workplace and whose working lives are affected by managerial decisions over which they have little or no control. It is usually a weapon of last resort, to be used when other negotiations have failed, because workers on strike either receive no income or depend on union funds, which might be limited.

> **strike** A temporary stoppage of work by a group of employees in order to express a grievance or enforce a demand.

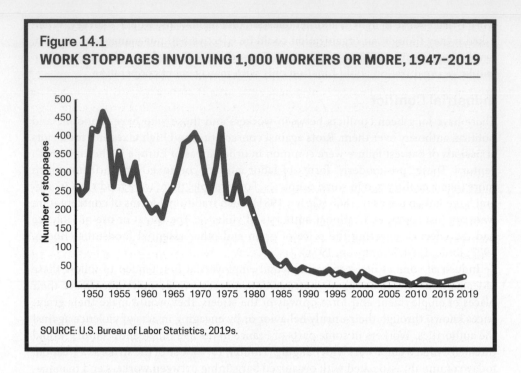

Figure 14.1

WORK STOPPAGES INVOLVING 1,000 WORKERS OR MORE, 1947-2019

SOURCE: U.S. Bureau of Labor Statistics, 2019s.

Throughout much of the latter half of the twentieth century, at least in the automobile, steel, and other industries where labor unions were strong, strikes were usually successful. An expanding economy, coupled with well-organized labor militancy, ensured that workers would share in economic growth. During the past quarter century, however, globalization has eroded many of these gains. Competition with low-wage labor elsewhere in the world has resulted in factory closures and layoffs, undermining the effectiveness of strikes and other militant forms of labor action. As Figure 14.1 shows, the number of strikes peaked in the early 1950s: There were 470 strikes in 1952, involving 2.7 million workers. The number of strikes then declined through the early 1960s, peaked once again in the late 1960s, and then generally plummeted. Today, strikes are increasingly rare, although recent years have seen a bit of an upturn. In 2016, there were only 15 strikes with a thousand or more workers, involving a total of 99,000 workers; three years later the number of strikes had increased to 25, involving 425,500 workers (U.S. Bureau of Labor Statistics [BLS], 2017e, 2019l). Workers in many industries have had to accept pay cuts in the hope of keeping their jobs, and as we will discuss later, labor union membership has declined significantly.

Lockouts and "Work to Rule" Strikes represent only one aspect or type of conflict in which workers and management may become involved. Other closely related expressions of organized conflict are lockouts, in which the employers, rather than the workers, bring about a stoppage of work to force workers to accept a particular contract. "Work to rule" is a form of organized labor action in which workers do the minimum work that is legally required of them, carefully following health, safety, and other regulations. Work to rule usually results in costly slowdowns for the firm because workers routinely exceed the requirements of their contracts and often may even violate health, safety, and wage-and-hour regulations to get the job done. Work to rule is typically done in situations where strikes may be illegal, such as among schoolteachers, whose contracts often forbid strikes. Less-organized expressions of conflict may include high labor turnover, absenteeism, and interference with production machinery.

Unequal Pay

There are significant differences in how people are compensated for their work throughout the U.S. economy. To begin at the top, in 2018 the average CEO of the largest 350 corporations took home $17.2 million, including salary and stock options—278 times more than the wages and benefits realized by the average worker (excluding managers) in the same industries. This gap has grown dramatically over the past half century. In 1965, the CEO-to-worker gap was only 20-to-1; in 1989, 58-to-1 (Mishel and Wolfe, 2019). While it can be difficult to make comparisons between countries, the gap is far higher in the United States than it is in other advanced industrial economies (Kotnick, Sakinc, and Guduras, 2018; Statista, 2016). While there are many reasons for this, one is that workers have more power in many other countries: Germany, for example, has a policy of "co-determination," including worker representation on corporate boards (Derousseau, 2014; Fox, 2018).

CEO-worker pay gaps notwithstanding, aren't U.S. workers doing much better than they were a half century ago, sharing in a long period of economic growth? In 1964, private-sector workers (excluding managers) on average made only $2.50 an hour; in 2018 their hourly earnings had grown ninefold, to $22.65.

These seeming gains mask the fact that wages have barely kept pace with inflation: $2.50 in 1964 had the same purchasing power as $20.27 today—meaning that after taking inflation into account, average wages today are only 12% higher than they were a half century ago (Desilver, 2018; see Figure 14.2). Significantly, the wage gains that have occurred have gone mainly to the top wage earners: according to one study, since the year 2000 the lowest tenth of wage earners have seen an increase of only 3 percent in real (inflation-adjusted) terms, while the top tenth increase was 16 percent (Desilver, 2018).

There are also significant wage differences by race, ethnicity, and gender. For full-time workers, the gender wage gap has come down significantly over the past forty years. In 1979, the annual earnings of women who worked full time were only 65 percent of their male counterparts; today, the difference is roughly 82 percent. This is a major improvement, reflecting years of women's struggle for equal pay. Yet it does not tell the whole story. Far fewer women work full time year round (63.0 percent) compared with men (75.4 percent), both because women are more likely to work in occupations characterized by part-time work, and because women are more likely than men to take time off—whether it be a few weeks, a month, or a year or more—for child-rearing and other forms of caregiving (Hegewisch, 2018). One study looked at total earnings, by gender, for all men and women who had worked at least one year between 2001 and 2015. While nearly three out of five men worked persistently

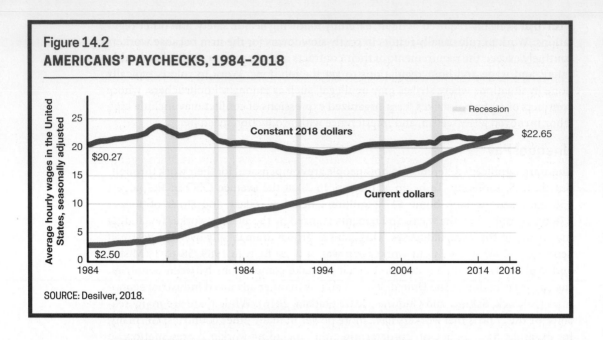

Figure 14.2
AMERICANS' PAYCHECKS, 1984–2018

SOURCE: Desilver, 2018.

full time for all fifteen years, only slightly more than one out of four women did so. These differences had a striking impact on labor market outcomes: the study found that women earned less than half (49 percent) than men over the fifteen-year period (Rose and Hartmann, 2018).

Racial and ethnic wage differences also persist, with only small improvements over time. In 2018, the median weekly earnings for Black women were 75.5 percent that of White women; Hispanic/Latina women earned 80.0 percent as much as White women. Among men, the differences were slightly larger: relative to White men, Black men earned 73.4 percent; Hispanic/Latino men, 71.9 percent (Hegewisch and Hartmann, 2019). While racial and ethnic earnings gaps have narrowed slightly for Black and Hispanic/Latina women over the past several decades, they have remained largely unchanged for Hispanic/Latino men (Patten, 2016).

The reasons for these persistent earnings gaps are much debated by sociologists and labor market economists. Some research has found that minority wage earners typically have fewer years of formal education, work in lower-paying occupations, and often have less consistent workforce experience (Blau and Kahn, 2016; Grodsky and Pager, 2001; Fryer, 2010). Discrimination also plays a role: one survey of nearly 3,800 adults found that 62 percent of Black respondents said Blacks were treated less fairly than Whites in the workplace, and 70 percent felt that racial discrimination made it harder for Blacks to get ahead. White respondents had a very different perception of these issues: only 22 percent believed that Blacks were treated less fairly than Whites at work, and 36 percent felt racial discrimination to be an impediment for Blacks (Patten, 2016).

Unemployment

Rates of unemployment fluctuated considerably over the course of the twentieth century. In Western countries, unemployment reached a peak during the Great Depression in the early 1930s, when as many as a quarter of the U.S. labor force was out of work. Economist John Maynard Keynes, who strongly influenced public policy in Europe and the United States during the post–World War II period, believed that unemployment results from consumers' lack of sufficient resources to buy goods. Governments can intervene to increase the level of demand in an economy, for example by investing in public work projects or cutting income taxes (both put more money into the economy), leading to the creation of new jobs; the newly employed then have the income with which to buy more goods, thus creating yet more jobs for people who produce them (and, according to Keynes, paying off the government spending that was needed to stimulate economic growth). State management of economic life, most people came to believe, meant that high rates of unemployment were a thing of the past. Commitment to full employment became part of government policy in virtually all Western societies. Until the 1970s, these policies seemed successful, and economic growth was more or less continuous.

During the 1970s and 1980s, however, Keynesianism was largely abandoned. In the face of economic globalization, governments lost the capability to control economic life as they once did. At the same time, there was a growing belief, particularly among economists, that the "free market" by itself, rather than the government, was best equipped to ensure economic prosperity. These ideas were especially appealing to conservative politicians, initially in the United States and Britain in the 1980s and, to a lesser extent, in other Western industrialized economies. During the same period, **unemployment rates** increased in many countries.

In the United States, unemployment rates have fluctuated greatly since World War II, although they have generally trended upward. Unemployment fell as low as 2.5 percent during the boom years of the early 1950s, and it peaked at nearly 10 percent during the depths of the bust years of 1982–1983 and 2009–2010 (see Figure 14.3). Despite some ups and downs, during the 1950s and 1960s, unemployment averaged under 5 percent. During the 1980s, it jumped to more than 7 percent, dropping to slightly under 6 percent during the 1990s and the first decade of the twentieth century. Unemployment rates among Blacks, Hispanics, and Latinos are significantly higher than those among Whites. During the ten-year period 2009–2019, which spanned the 2008–2009 economic recession and subsequent recovery, unemployment averaged 5.9 percent for Whites, 11.4 percent for Blacks, and 8.3 percent for Hispanics and Latinos (BLS, 2019e). Structural and institutional discrimination, from differences in educational and training opportunities to outright discrimination when it comes to hiring, account for such labor market differences (see Chapter 11).

The economic recession, not surprisingly, resulted in a steep jump in unemployment: The unemployment rate was 5 percent in 2007; two years later, it had doubled to close to 10 percent. While the recession affected

unemployment rate The proportion of the population sixteen and older that is actively seeking work but is unable to find employment.

everyone, minorities were hardest hit: at the height of the recession, in July 2009, 15 percent of Blacks and 13 percent of Hispanics and Latinos were out of work, compared with 9 percent of Whites. Although the economic recovery took many years, by February 2020 only 3.5 percent were out of work—a figure economists consider acceptable, in that there is always turnover as people transition between jobs, or look for work after finishing school. Again, however, differences persisted by race and ethnicity: unemployment among Whites had dropped to 3.1 percent; for Blacks, 5.8 percent, and Hispanics and Latinos, 4.4 percent (BLS, 2020d).

While the economic recovery accounted for most of the decline in joblessness, other factors also played a role—for example, a decline in the number of people looking for work. In July 2009, for example, 66 percent of persons 20 and older were working or looking for work; by July 2019, the number had declined to 63 percent (BLS, 2019h). This decline occurred in part for demographic reasons, such as the aging of the population, with many post-war baby boomers (the large cohort of children born during the two decades following World War II) now reaching retirement age. It was also due, in part, to the lingering effects of the recession, which may have discouraged some from actively seeking a job (CBO, 2018).

By May 2020, however, the employment picture had changed dramatically. Within the span of barely two months, as the highly contagious and deadly COVID-19

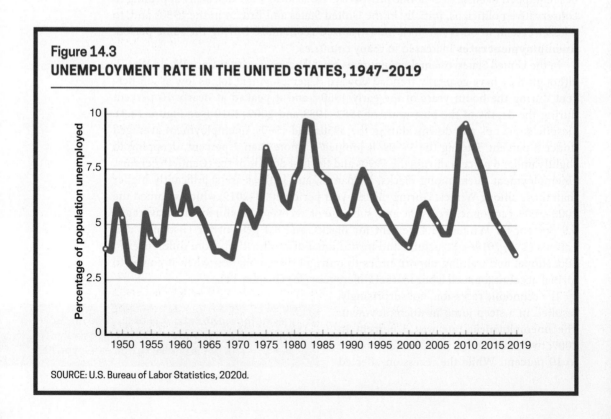

Figure 14.3
UNEMPLOYMENT RATE IN THE UNITED STATES, 1947–2019

SOURCE: U.S. Bureau of Labor Statistics, 2020d.

pandemic spread across the United States, governments at all levels issued stay-at-home and shelter-in-place orders, requiring people to avoid close physical contact. This effectively closed all businesses considered "non-essential," including schools and universities. While many professionals were able to work remotely from their homes, most of the U.S. economy was effectively shuttered, leading to massive unemployment. By the end of May 2020, as the number of confirmed U.S. COVID-19 cases approached two million and 100,000 people had died of the disease (John Hopkins, 2020), 40 million workers had filed jobless claims. Since not all U.S. workers are covered by unemployment insurance, it was estimated at the time that the national unemployment rate could be as high as 23 percent—comparable to the 1930s Great Depression (*New York Times*, 2020). Racial minorities were the hardest hit: a survey in early April found that 45 percent of Black workers had lost their jobs or experienced reduced hours, compared with 31 percent of White workers (Kurtzleben, 2020; Weller, 2020; Data for Progress, 2020). While such disparities are partly due to the fact the minority groups have also been hardest hit by the pandemic, they are also because minorities are much less likely to work at home. According to the U.S. Department of Labor, while 30 percent of Whites have worked from home in recent years, this was true for only 20 percent of Blacks and 16 percent of Latinos (BLS, 2019t).

This rapid downturn of the U.S. economy, and resulting joblessness, are hopefully short-term: they are the result of a viral pandemic rather than underlying economic weaknesses. Only time will tell how long it takes for economic recovery—something that will partly depend on how long the pandemic lasts, and whether an effective vaccine is found. It does illustrate, however, just how vulnerable the U.S economy is to an aspect of globalization that up until now has been largely overlooked: the spread of new, untreatable pandemic diseases that are carried from country to country by as many as 2 billion international tourist and business travelers each year.

Labor Unions: Once a Source of Strength; Now Struggling to Be Effective

Although their levels of membership and the extent of their power vary widely, union organizations exist in all Western countries, which also all legally recognize the right of workers to strike in pursuit of economic objectives. Why have unions become a basic feature of Western societies? Why does union-management conflict seem to be a more or less ever-present possibility in industrial settings?

In the early development of modern industry, workers in most countries had no political rights and little influence over the conditions of work in which they found themselves. Unions developed as a means of redressing the imbalance of power between workers and employers. Whereas workers had virtually no power as individuals, through collective organization, their influence was considerably increased. An employer can do without the labor of any particular worker but not without that of all or most of the workers in a factory or plant. Unions originally were mainly "defensive" organizations, providing the means whereby workers could counter the overwhelming power that employers wielded over their lives.

In most developed countries, the period from 1950 to 1980 was a time of steady growth in **union density**—a statistic that represents the number of union members as a percentage of the number of people who could potentially be union members. Countries that reached the highest levels of union density—Belgium, Denmark, Finland, and Sweden, with more than 80 percent of all workers belonging to labor unions in 1985—had three features in common (Western, 1997). First, strong working-class political parties created favorable conditions for labor organizing. Second, bargaining between firms and labor unions was coordinated at the national level rather than occurring separately in different industries, or at the local level. Third, unions, rather than the state, directly administered unemployment insurance, ensuring that workers who lost their jobs did not leave the labor movement. Countries lacking one or more of these factors had lower rates of union density, ranging between two-fifths and two-thirds of the working population.

Workers today have voting rights in the political sphere, and there are established forms of negotiation with employers, by means of which economic benefits can be pressed for and grievances expressed. However, union influence, both at the level of the local plant and nationally, still remains primarily veto power. In other words, using the resources at their disposal, including the right to strike, unions can only block employers' policies or initiatives, not help formulate them in the first place. There are exceptions to this—for instance, when unions and employers negotiate periodic contracts covering conditions of work.

Earnings tend to be higher in those industries that are more heavily unionized. In 2018, the median weekly earnings of nonunion workers ($860) were four-fifths that of union workers ($1,051) (BLS, 2019p). Unionization rates are highest in the government sector, resulting in significant differences in weekly earnings between unionized and nonunionized workers, especially at the state ($1,011 vs. $883) and local ($1,071 vs. $817) levels (BLS, 2017g).

After 1980, unions suffered declines across the advanced industrial countries. In the United States, where unions clearly face a crisis of greater dimensions than their counterparts in most European countries, the decline began even earlier: Unionization peaked at more than a third of the workforce during the 1950s, and it has been declining steadily since then, to only 11 percent in 2018. The decline has been steepest among private-sector wage and salary workers, where only 6.4 percent (7.6 million workers) are unionized. There is, however, considerable variation in U.S. union membership by occupation and industry. For example, compared with the private sector as a whole, the unionization rate was more than three times higher among utility workers (20 percent) and twice as high in construction (13 percent). Among public-sector (government) workers, fully 34 percent (7.2 million workers) remain unionized. The highest rates of unionization are in local government (40.3 percent), since police officers, firefighters, and teachers are often unionized (BLS, 2019o, 2019p).

Union-protected working conditions and wages have eroded in major industries over the past 30 years. Workers in the trucking, steel, and car industries have all accepted lower wages than those previously negotiated. The unions came out second

The Services Employees International Union (SEIU), which includes health care workers, is the fastest growing U.S. labor union.

best in several major strikes, beginning with the crushing of the air traffic controllers' union in the early 1980s. In recent years, the United Auto Workers (UAW) has been forced to reach agreements with Ford, Chrysler, and General Motors that conceded wage cuts, in exchange for a freeze on outsourcing jobs, along with promises of employer support for retired workers' health care.

One thing to bear in mind is that not all workers who are protected by union contracts necessarily belong to unions. Some workers are able to get a "free ride" because their wages reflect union-management agreements, even though they are not union members. Among private-sector workers, for example, while 7.6 million workers belong to unions, 8.5 million workers are covered by union contracts; the comparable figures for public-sector workers are 7.2 million union members, with 7.9 million covered by union contracts (BLS, 2019o).

The rapid fall in private-sector union membership in the United States is due to a combination of factors associated with post-Fordism. Manufacturing has traditionally been a stronghold for organized labor, while jobs in such services as wholesale and retail trade, health services, and leisure and hospitality have historically been more resistant to unionization. One major factor, therefore, is the loss of once-unionized manufacturing jobs to low-wage countries around the world, particularly in East Asia, and most notably China—a country where independent labor unions are illegal. Such job loss, real or threatened, has greatly weakened the bargaining power of unions in the manufacturing sector, and as a result, has lowered their appeal to workers. Why join a union and pay union dues if the union cannot deliver wage increases or job security? Unionization efforts in the United States have also been hampered in recent years by decisions of the National Labor Relations Board (NLRB), the government agency responsible for protecting the right of workers to form unions and engage in collective bargaining. The NLRB has proven ineffective at protecting efforts to unionize workplaces, failing to take aggressive action when businesses harass or fire union organizers (Estlund, 2006; Clawson and Clawson, 1999).

Even though service-sector jobs have generally been difficult to unionize, the fastest-growing U.S. labor union is the Service Employees International Union (SEIU), whose 2 million-plus members include more than 1.1 million health care workers and more than 1 million local and state government workers, public school employees, bus drivers, and child-care providers (SEIU, n.d.). Relatively high union densities are still found in protective services (34 percent) and in education, training, and library occupations (34 percent) (BLS, 2019o). And even unions traditionally tied to manufacturing have recognized that service workers, especially those whose jobs cannot be exported, are fertile grounds for unionization drives. The United Auto Workers, for example, has branched out to organize technical, office, and professional workers, including graduate students and other academic workers at the University of California and many other colleges and universities (UAW, 2014). Yet one of the largest employers of the growing number of service workers has been highly effective at stifling all efforts of their workforce to unionize: Walmart, the world's largest corporation. Walmart's 1.5 million U.S. workers, which Walmart prefers to call "associates," have been effectively prevented from forming unions through a variety of harassment techniques (Lichtenstein, 2012a, 2012b; Greenhouse, 2015). Walmart workers have not been acquiescent; in July 2019, after a Walmart employee was fired for posting an internal document on Reddit, Walmart workers flooded a subreddit with pro-union memes (Ongweso, 2019).

One consequence of the erosion of workers' power has been a revolt within the labor movement itself. As the U.S. organized labor movement has shrunk, it has also splintered, which has greatly hampered its effectiveness (Early, 2011). A number of unions challenged the dominance of the once-powerful American Federation of Labor and Congress of Industrial Organizations (AFL-CIO), a confederation of 55 unions representing 12.5 million workers (AFL-CIO, 2017). Frustrated with the AFL-CIO's inability to organize more workers or achieve significant gains, in 2005, seven leading unions broke off to form Change to Win, a more militant 5.5-million-person federation, including many women and minority service-sector workers. The unions that made up this new organization at the time represented more than a third of the original membership of the AFL-CIO. The revolt was led by the Service Employees International Union (SEIU) and its charismatic leader Andy Stern and originally included the SEIU, Teamsters, and five other unions, although internal divisions within the new federation have led some of its original member unions to pull out.

Change to Win concentrated its initial organizing in areas where the jobs could not be sent overseas: For example, they focused on Walmart employees, hotel workers, and truckers who move goods from U.S. container ports. Among their demands was the passage of the Employee Free Choice Act, which would require employers to recognize a union if the majority of its workers signed cards saying they were in favor. This "card check" approach to union membership would bypass elections, as currently required by law. Proponents claim that elections are seldom democratic because companies often harass or fire union organizers, threaten workers who support the union, and coerce workers into voting against union formation. Since its formation, however, Change to Win has lowered its expectations, now describing itself as a "strategic organizing center" rather than a new federation of labor unions.

Low-Wage Work

Scholars associated with the Russell Sage Foundation's Program on the Future of Work have produced numerous studies on "the causes and consequences of the deteriorating quality of low-wage jobs in the United States." The results of their studies are not encouraging:

> In the thirty years after World War II, incomes grew rapidly for most Americans and unprecedented numbers were able to join the middle class. Beginning in the early 1970s, however, the real wages of male workers without a college degree began to fall, and today these workers earn real wages markedly lower than those of their counterparts thirty years ago. (Russell Sage, 2014)

Increasingly intense economic competition, now global, has led many firms to attempt to cut labor costs through wage freezes, cuts in benefits, increasing part-time or temp labor, offshoring, and other strategies that have had a negative impact on workers. But the hopeful news is that there are major differences in how advanced industrial nations have responded, suggesting that political decisions, rather than economic necessity, lie at the root of the problem.

The Russell Sage Foundation has sponsored a series of studies that have examined an important question: Are these trends inevitable, or are there government policies in some advanced industrial economies that have proven more beneficial to workers? By comparing policies and outcomes in the 19 wealthy industrial economies that are members of the Organization for Economic Co-operation and Development (OECD), the answer seems to be clear: Policies by more pro-labor governments have made a difference. Low-wage labor, for example, varies from a low of 8 percent in Denmark to a high of 25 percent in the United States. Moreover, what these studies term the "inclusiveness" of a country's approach to labor-capital relations (collective-bargaining agreements, minimum-wage laws, enforcement of national labor laws, health insurance, pensions, family leave, paid vacation time) can significantly influence workers' quality of life, even for low-wage workers (Gautié and Schmitt, 2010).

One follow-up study found that while low-wage work is sometimes thought to be a stepping-stone to higher-wage jobs, this is seldom the case. By comparing the OECD countries, John Schmitt (2012) found that economic growth, even when measured by average per-person income, is not necessarily associated with a decline in the percentage of low-wage workers. On the other hand, he did find that a more "inclusive" governmental approach again does make a difference, both in the number of low-wage workers and their quality of life. While these are benefits that are widely shared among the OECD economies, they are weakest in the United States:

1 What are three defining characteristics of transnational corporations?

2 According to Freeman and Rogers's research, how can workplaces be changed to better meet the desires of modern workers?

3 Provide three explanations for growing unemployment in the United States.

4 What is a labor union? Why have unions in the United States suffered from a decline in membership since the 1980s?

[L]ow pay is often among the least of the labor-market problems facing low-wage workers, especially in the United States. . . . U.S. labor law offers workers remarkably few protections. U.S. workers, for example, have the lowest level of employment security in the OECD and no legal right to paid vacations, paid sick days, or paid parental leave. (Schmitt, 2012)

These studies clearly show that there may be some lessons about work and economic life to be learned from other wealthy industrial nations. And some governmental bodies seem to be adopting more pro-labor strategies: During 2019, 13 states (and the District of Columbia) raised their minimum wage through legislation, while another 8 had routine increases, since their minimum wages increase with the rate of inflation (NCSL, 2019). These increases have put billions of dollars into the hands of millions of low-wage workers. In total, 29 states (and the District of Columbia) now have minimum wages above the federal level (Economic Policy Institute, 2019). And municipalities have also gotten into the act: As of 2019, 44 localities have adopted minimum wages above their state minimum, with Santa Monica mandating increases that when reached (by 2020) will be $15 an hour, more than double the current federal minimum of $7.25 wage (Economic Policy Institute, 2019).

4 UNANSWERED QUESTIONS

The nature of work and economic life in the United States—indeed, throughout the world—is rapidly changing. Advances in technology, global supply chains, the information revolution, a revolution in shipping—all these are transforming the world at a pace unprecedented since the Industrial Revolution of the eighteenth and nineteenth centuries. As a result, the occupational structure in all industrialized countries has changed substantially since the beginning of the twentieth century, and the United States is no exception (Figure 14.4).

In 1900, about three-quarters of the employed American population were in manual work, either farming or blue-collar work such as manufacturing. White-collar professional and service jobs were much fewer in number. By 1960, however, more people worked in white-collar professional and service jobs than in manual labor. By 1993, the occupational system had basically reversed its structure from 1900. Almost three-quarters of the employed population worked in white-collar professional and

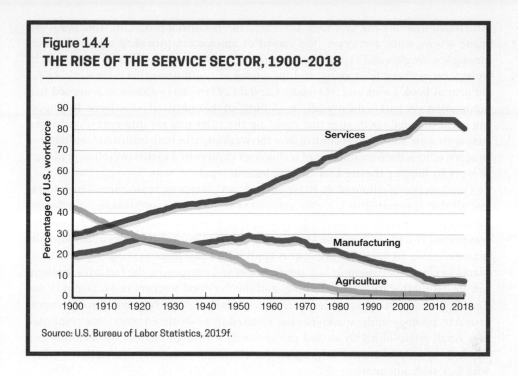

Figure 14.4

THE RISE OF THE SERVICE SECTOR, 1900–2018

Services

Manufacturing

Agriculture

Percentage of U.S. workforce

0 10 20 30 40 50 60 70 80 90

1900 1910 1920 1930 1940 1950 1960 1970 1980 1990 2000 2010 2018

Source: U.S. Bureau of Labor Statistics, 2019f.

service jobs, while the rest worked in blue-collar and farming jobs. These trends have continued; in 2019, less than 9 percent of the U.S. workforce worked in manufacturing, while white-collar professional and service employment accounted for more than 80 percent (BLS, 2019f).

The reasons for this shift, and how it will play out in terms of job opportunities for young people today, remain poorly understood. Perhaps because we are in the midst of such a significant transformation, there are disagreements over its causes and consequences.

Will Automation Make Things Better or Worse for Workers?

The relationship between technology and work has long been of interest to sociologists. How is our experience of work affected by the type of technology involved? As industrialization has progressed, technology has assumed an ever-greater role at the workplace—from factory automation to the computerization of office work. The current information-technology revolution has attracted renewed interest in this question. Technology can lead to greater efficiency and productivity, but how does it affect the way work is experienced by those who carry it out? For sociologists, one of the main questions is how the move to more complex systems influences the nature of work and the institutions in which it is performed.

The concept of **automation**, or programmable machinery, was introduced in the mid-1800s, when Christopher Spencer, an

automation Production processes monitored and controlled by machines with only minimal supervision from people.

American, invented the first fully automatic turret lathe, a programmable lathe that made screws, nuts, and gears. The spread of automation provoked a heated debate among sociologists and experts in industrial relations over the effect of the new technology on workers, their skills, and their level of commitment to their work. In his influential book *Labor and Monopoly Capital* (1974), Harry Braverman argued that automation was part of the overall "de-skilling" of the industrial labor force. By imposing organizational techniques that broke up the labor process into specialized tasks, managers were able to exert control over the workforce. In both industrial settings and modern offices, the introduction of technology contributed to this overall degradation of work by limiting the need for creative human input.

One function of automation, Braverman argued, was to increase control over workers; all that is required in a highly automated factory is an unthinking, unreflective body capable of endlessly carrying out the same unskilled task. Although Braverman was primarily writing about the kind of assembly line work that occurs in automobile-manufacturing facilities, his arguments apply with equal force to the giant electronics plants in China that assemble our smartphones and computers, the factories throughout the world that make our clothing, and the fast-food workers in McDonald's and Taco Bell who serve up our orders in a matter of minutes. The introduction of computerized technology in the workplace has resulted in a two-tiered workforce composed of a small group of highly skilled professionals with high degrees of flexibility and freedom in their jobs and a larger group of clerical, service, and production workers who lack such autonomy.

Technology has also led to the offshoring of manufacturing and service-sector jobs to countries where wages are lower. Those firms that remain in the United States often employ fewer workers, thanks also to advances in technology (Sherk, 2010): automobile plants where robots assemble cars, banks that use ATMs, supermarkets with automatic checkout services. While much has been made of "twenty-first-century onshoring"— the return of some manufacturing jobs to the United States—these jobs often pay low wages, and, thanks to automation, also require fewer workers (Semuels, 2015).

A little more than ten years ago, the Princeton economist Alan Blinder conducted a detailed analysis of the U.S. occupational structure, classifying hundreds of different jobs in terms of the likelihood they would be offshored. In a widely cited paper, he concluded that between 22 and 29 percent of all jobs, involving between 29 million and 38 million U.S. workers, were potentially offshorable. Many of the most highly vulnerable jobs, he argued, were not in manufacturing, but rather were white-collar jobs such as computer programmers, accountants, statisticians, or film editors (Blinder, 2007).

How well did Blinder's predictions stand the test of time? The answer is, not very well. A recent study (Ozimek, 2019) looked again at jobs supposedly threatened by offshoring and concluded that instead of going to countries like India or China, many of these jobs were going to—the homes of U.S. workers! According to this recent study, at least 5 percent of the U.S. workforce now work remotely, thanks to advances in information technology—and this doesn't include workers who do at least part of their work from home. In fact, some of these workers are even working remotely for non-U.S. clients. It turns out that U.S. knowledge workers often have a competitive advantage over foreign workers: they share a common language and culture with their employers, not to mention eliminating the challenge of coordinating work a half a world (and twelve time zones) away. Blinder himself, in acknowledging the new study, admitted that "Where in retrospect I missed the boat is in thinking that the gigantic gap in labor costs between here and India would push it to India rather than to South Dakota. . . . There were other aspects of the costs to moving the activities that we weren't thinking about very much back then when people were worrying about off-shoring" (Casselman, 2019)

If offshoring has not created a "white-collar job apocalypse" (Casselman, 2019), what about artificial intelligence, rapid advances in such areas as business intelligence, decision making, and "big data" analysis, which hold the promise of automating occupations that currently require college degrees? The services provided by professionals such as lawyers, accountants, radiologists, and many middle managers can increasingly be performed by artificial intelligence software. One estimate is that as many as two-fifths of all jobs in the United States could be replaced by software (Brynjolfsson and McAfee, 2014; Ford, 2009, 2010). As one technology writer has noted, "The evidence is irrefutable that computerized automation, networks and artificial intelligence (AI)—including machine-learning, language-translation, and speech- and pattern-recognition software—are beginning to render many jobs simply obsolete" (*Economist*, 2011). Some commentators predict that robotics will result in a jobless future in which machines do most of our labor: "Robots will drive our cars, manufacture our goods, and do our chores" (Wadwha, 2014).

Yet automation has also created a host of new services, from ride-sharing services, to the marketing giant Amazon, which has put many small (and some large) retailers out of business. Why wait to hail down a taxi, when you can hail an Uber or Lyft on your phone, have one arrive usually within a few minutes thanks to GPS location services, and have your credit card automatically charged with no cash or even physical credit card needed? Why trudge down to the local bookstore, appliance store, furniture store, or perhaps even grocery store (now that Amazon has bought Whole Foods), looking for an item that may or may not be there, and wait in line to pay, when with a click on your smart phone Amazon can usually deliver pretty much anything to your home within a couple of days, often at bargain basement prices?

Automation has made all this possible. Whether the seeming benefits to consumers will be outweighed by the cost to workers and small business remains to be seen. Uber and Lyft drivers—like others in the Gig Economy—may enjoy the freedom to operate out of their homes (or cars), but they are also notoriously underpaid, and lack basic benefits such as health insurance or retirement packages (Zoepf et al., 2014; Rao, 2019). Amazon has resulted in the demise of chains that specialized in selling books, toys, and sporting goods, leading to a loss of jobs in those industries (Pandey, 2018). Yet Amazon employs hundreds of thousands of workers in its warehouses, and recently announced that it was spending $700 million to retrain a third of its workforce to do high-tech tasks needed to run its physical operation (Casselman and Satariano, 2019).

Automation and artificial intelligence are disruptive technologies, much like the steam engine once was, that ushered in the Industrial Revolution. How this will play out over your lifetimes will shape not only your world of consumption, but perhaps more importantly, your world of work.

Table 14.3

APPLYING SOCIOLOGY TO WORK AND ECONOMIC LIFE

CONCEPT	APPROACH TO UNDERSTANDING WORK AND ECONOMIC LIFE	CONTEMPORARY APPLICATION
Fordism	A dominant form of production in the twentieth century, pioneered by Henry Ford (for whom it is named). Characterized by large, bureaucratic corporations that design, market, and mass produce products on assembly lines that require workers to repeatedly perform the same task. While this greatly increases productivity, it also results in a high degree of management control over factory workers.	General Motors, whose revenues made it the largest corporation in the mid-twentieth century, typifies this process.
Post-Fordism	A dominant form of production in the twenty-first century, characterized by flexible business structures in which large corporations specialize in the most profitable activities (designing and marketing their products), with actual manufacturing outsourced to independent contract factories who compete with one another by lowering their costs in order to get the work.	Giant retailers such as Walmart, whose revenues made it the largest corporation in the early twenty-first century, typifies this process.
Global Outsourcing	The principal way that flexible production is achieved in the early twenty-first century, in which factory production is outsourced to low-wage countries around the world. This often results in low wages, harsh and unsafe working conditions, and the absence of environmental regulations, as factories around the world compete with one another for manufacturing.	The apparel and electronic assembly industries, in which our clothing and computer electronics are made in factories in China, India, or in developing countries in Asia and Africa.
The Informal Economy	That sector of the economy that is outside the sphere of regular employment ("off the books"), and therefore unreported to the government. Common in wealthy countries, and often a major part of the economy in poor countries. Since it is unregulated, workers lack legal protections.	Includes many activities that would be legal if reported (such as housecleaning, yardwork, babysitting), as well as illegal activities (such as drug dealing, criminal behavior in general).
The Gig Economy	A recently emerging sector of the economy that involves extreme flexibility: temporary or freelance workers on short-term contracts, often operating on their own, with low pay, the absence of benefits such as health insurance or retirement packages, and few or no legal protections.	Lyft and Uber drivers; Instacart; TaskRabbit; Handy; Thumbtack; Fiverr.

Robots weld car frames at the Hyundai factory in Beijing.

What Will the Economy of the Future Look Like?

As we have seen, there has been significant job loss in manufacturing, with a corresponding growth in service-sector jobs. Unlike the jobs that have been lost in manufacturing, service-sector jobs tend to be nonunionized and low-wage. Some observers suggest that what is occurring today is a transition to a new type of society no longer based primarily on manufacturing or low-paying service work. We are entering, they claim, a phase of development beyond the industrial era altogether. A variety of terms have been coined to describe this new social order, such as the *postindustrial society*, the *information age*, and the *"new" economy*. The term that has come into most common usage, however, is **knowledge economy**.

A precise definition of the knowledge economy is difficult to formulate, but in general, it refers to an economy in which ideas, information, and forms of knowledge underpin innovation and economic growth. In a knowledge economy, much of the workforce is involved in research and development; advanced technologies; and the design, marketing, sales, and service of innovative products, rather than in their physical production. Employees in this economy can be termed "knowledge workers." The knowledge economy is dominated

> **knowledge economy** A society no longer based primarily on the production of material goods but instead on the production of knowledge. Its emergence has been linked to the development of a broad base of consumers who are technologically literate and have made new advances in the computing, entertainment, and telecommunications part of their lives.

by the constant flow of information and opinions and by the powerful potential of science and technology.

How widespread is the knowledge economy at the start of the twenty-first century? The World Bank (2012) created a Knowledge Economy Index (KEI), which rates countries based on their overall preparedness to compete in the knowledge economy. Knowledge-based industries are understood broadly to include high technology, education and training, research and development, and the financial and investment sector. Knowledge-economy jobs are typically said to include scientists and engineers engaged in innovative research and development, and research scholars more generally; highly skilled occupations that involve the use of advanced technology; financial management and services; and, in general, any occupation or profession that requires the ability to think symbolically and analytically (and that typically involves higher education and specialized skills) (Castells, 2000).

The current, expanded version of the KEI (see, for example, Pospisil et al., 2019) uses four "pillars" to gauge a country's knowledge-economy performance. To rank high on the index, a country must have

1. A high degree of educational attainment at the secondary, college, and technical levels, providing the skills needed for innovation;
2. Access to advanced communications, including widely accessible broadband networks;
3. Scientific accomplishments, as measured by high levels of spending on research and development, publications in scientific journals, and number and quality of patents; and
4. An open political and economic environment, including adherence to the rule of law, an effective regulatory environment; and openness to free trade with other countries.

Based on these measures, one study (Ojanperä, Graham, and Zook, 2019), using 2012 data, ranked the Scandinavian nations (Sweden, Finland, Denmark, and Norway) at the top of list, since they score high on all these measures. The United States is not far behind. China, on the other hand—partly because it lacks the open political and economic environment that makes up one of the four "pillars" of the index—ranks far behind, roughly in the same category as Russia, Mexico, and much of Latin America.

While no one can deny that innovation is an important driver of economic competitiveness, nor that knowledge is a key component of innovation, it is not clear that all four "pillars" of the knowledge economy must be satisfied for a country to succeed economically.

China, for example, ranks poorly on the KEI index—yet has rapidly advanced technologically over the past decade, to the point where in a number of areas it appears to be rivalling the United States. One study of 17.2 million scientific papers in the hottest technology fields, published between 2013 and 2018, found that China dominated 23 of the 30 fields (the United States dominated the remaining seven). Some key fields where China had the largest number of scientific papers included batteries (examples: organic thin-film solar and lithium-ion batteries); semiconductors; new and advanced materials (examples: photocatalysts and carbon quantum dots); and biotech (examples: nucleic acid-targeted cancer treatment). China tripled its spending on research and development between 2010 and 2016, and currently spends as much as the United States (Okoshi, 2019). China now leads the world in the sheer volume of Internet retail transactions; a Chinese company, Huawei, is globally dominant in the development and sales of 5G Internet equipment; and China's space program has landed a vehicle on the far side of the moon.

The Chinese government has played a key role in these achievements. In 2006, it developed a 15-year national science and technology plan intended to end China's reliance on other countries for advanced technologies. The plan identified key areas for large-scale public investment, in the belief that the state should play a key role—alongside the market—in determining (and funding) which areas would drive innovation. Other 5- and 15-year plans have followed. This state-centered approach to development runs counter to the more market-driven approach championed by the United States and other advanced industrial countries and reflected in the KEI measures that give China poor marks despite the country's obvious achievements. (It should be noted that China's success is not only due to state development plans and public investment in key fields; China has also derived some of its technological gains by requiring foreign firms that operate in China to share their technology, as well as by outright technological theft; see Appelbaum et al., 2018).

China is offering the world another model, and it remains an open question whether or not it will succeed in its efforts to create a knowledge economy in which the government plays a key role at all levels. Will China's heavy-handed state-led approach encourage knowledge economy innovation—or stifle it?

What does this portend for the United States? No one can say for sure, but it seems unlikely that the American nonfarm workforce—which in July 2019 included more than 164 million employed people, along with another 6.1 million people (3.7 percent of the labor force) looking for work (BLS, 2019h)—will all somehow become knowledge-economy workers. Will current economic changes produce another period of sustained economic growth, in which workers at all levels become a scarcity, with wages and salaries steadily rising, as they did in the post–World War II period? Or will the American workforce increasingly be split into two categories: those with the educational background, skills, and good fortune to thrive as knowledge workers, and everyone else, who may find themselves chasing after a dwindling number of manufacturing jobs and lower-paying service work?

How Permanent Is Your Job Likely to Be?

This leads to another question: Does the future of work mean the end of the full-time, lifelong career with one or at best a few employers?

Since the mid-1980s, in all the industrialized countries except the United States, the average length of the working week has become shorter. Workers still undertake long stretches of overtime, but some governments are beginning to introduce new limits on permissible working hours. In France, for example, annual overtime is restricted to a maximum of 130 hours a year. In most countries, there is a general tendency toward shortening the average working career. More people would probably quit the labor force at age 60 or earlier if they could afford to do so.

Another important employment trend of the past decade has been the replacement of full-time workers by part-time workers and contingency workers, or workers who are hired on a contract or "freelance" basis often for a short-term task. Most temporary or contingent workers are hired for the least-skilled, lowest-paying jobs. But, increasingly, contingent work is making its way into professional occupations as well, including higher education. Contingent faculty now comprise three-fourths of higher education faculty (House Committee on Education and the Workforce, 2014). As a general rule, part-time and contract jobs do not include the benefits associated with full-time work, such as medical insurance, paid vacation time, or retirement benefits. Because employers can save on the costs of wages and benefits, the use of part-time and contingent workers has become increasingly common. A 2015 survey found that the proportion of the U.S. workforce engaged in alternative work arrangements, defined as temp workers, contract workers, on-call workers, and freelancers, increased over 50 percent between 2005 and 2015, from 10 percent in 2005 to nearly 16 percent in 2015 (Katz and Kreuger, 2016). According to the General Accountability Office (2015), if you expand alternative work to include part-time employees, the proportion rises to more than 40 percent.

The temporary employment agency Manpower Group, Inc., founded in Milwaukee, Wisconsin, in 1948, has become a global leader in the provision of temporary workers. This company placed 3.4 million temps in 80 countries and territories in 2014, claiming 400,000 clients worldwide (Manpower Group, 2014). But Manpower has been surpassed in size by Kelly Services, founded in Detroit in 1946. Kelly Services was previously known as "Kelly Girls," but it was renamed in 1966 "to reflect the growing services of the company" (including the fact that it placed men as well

Contingent faculty, including graduate student instructors, at New York University protest for better pay, benefits, and job security.

as women). Kelly Services found jobs for more than 540,000 workers in 2013; it was ranked 490th among the Fortune 500 in 2017. Temp agencies like Manpower Group and Kelly Services provide labor on a flexible basis around the world, in blue-collar manufacturing as well as services (Grabell, 2013). Clearly, temporary labor has become a critical component of the worldwide organization of work and occupations.

How will work change in the future? It appears very likely that people will take a more active look at their lives than in the past, moving in and out of paid work at different points. These are positive options, however, only when they are deliberately chosen. The reality for most is that regular paid work remains the key to day-to-day survival and that part-time work is experienced as a hardship rather than an opportunity.

CONCEPT CHECKS

1 Why does automation lead to worker alienation?

2 What are the fastest-growing job sectors? Based on these trends, what are the implications for careers in the future?

3 In your opinion, how will globalization change the nature of work?

THE BIG PICTURE

Chapter 14
Work and Economic Life

1 Basic Concepts
p. 510

2 Theories of Work and Economic Life
p. 514

LEARNING OBJECTIVES

Understand that modern economies are based on the division of labor and economic interdependence.

Consider the different forms that capitalism has taken, and understand how a shift in the predominant form of industrial organization in modern society has shaped the kinds of jobs people are likely to find.

TERMS TO KNOW

work • occupation • economy • capitalism • technology • housework • division of labor • economic interdependence

corporations • family capitalism • entrepreneur • managerial capitalism • welfare capitalism • institutional capitalism • interlocking directorates • global capitalism • Fordism • Taylorism • low-trust systems • high-trust systems • alienation • post-Fordism • flexible production • outsourcing • informal economy

CONCEPT CHECKS

1. Describe six characteristics that shape one's everyday experiences at work.
2. Name two forms of unpaid labor.
3. Contrast the division of labor in traditional and modern societies.

1. Describe five forms capitalism has taken.
2. What are two key differences between Fordism and post-Fordism?
3. Define and provide an example of an informal economy.

Exercises: Thinking Sociologically

1. Explain the meaning of globalization of the modern economy. Explain how this textbook sees globalization affecting workers in third world countries and in advanced industrial societies.

2. Discuss some of the important ways that the nature of work will change for the contemporary worker as companies apply more automation and larger-scale production processes and as oligopolies become more pervasive. Explain each of these trends and how they affect workers, both now and in the future.

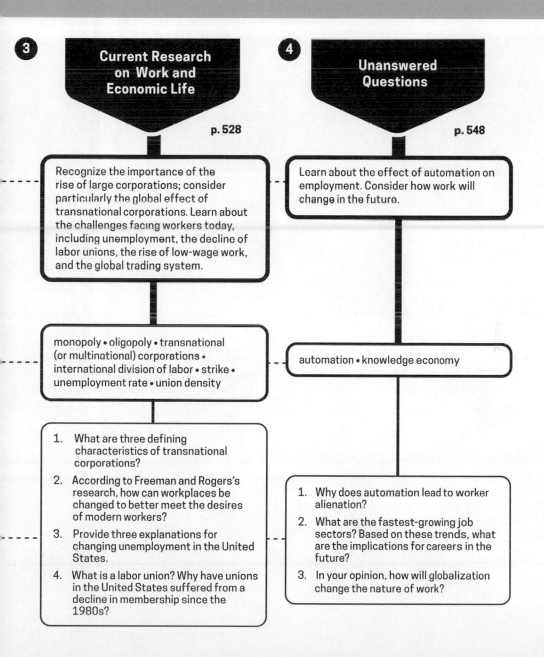

3 **Current Research on Work and Economic Life**

p. 528

Recognize the importance of the rise of large corporations; consider particularly the global effect of transnational corporations. Learn about the challenges facing workers today, including unemployment, the decline of labor unions, the rise of low-wage work, and the global trading system.

monopoly • oligopoly • transnational (or multinational) corporations • international division of labor • strike • unemployment rate • union density

1. What are three defining characteristics of transnational corporations?

2. According to Freeman and Rogers's research, how can workplaces be changed to better meet the desires of modern workers?

3. Provide three explanations for changing unemployment in the United States.

4. What is a labor union? Why have unions in the United States suffered from a decline in membership since the 1980s?

4 **Unanswered Questions**

p. 548

Learn about the effect of automation on employment. Consider how work will change in the future.

automation • knowledge economy

1. Why does automation lead to worker alienation?

2. What are the fastest-growing job sectors? Based on these trends, what are the implications for careers in the future?

3. In your opinion, how will globalization change the nature of work?

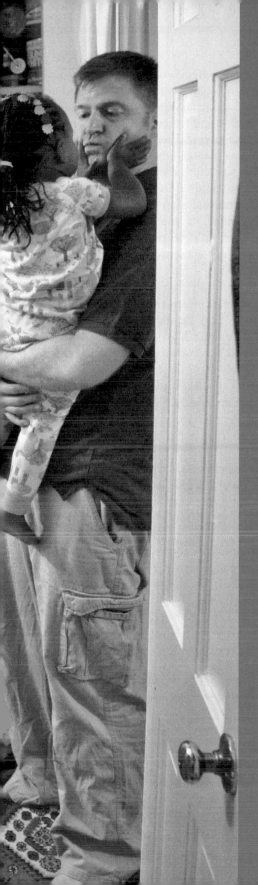

15

Families and Intimate Relationships

What proportion of children in the United States currently live in a "typical" American family made up of a mother, father, and their children?

- **A**   25 percent
- **B**   50 percent
- **C**   70 percent
- **D**   90 percent

TURN THE PAGE FOR THE CORRECT ANSWER.

f you answered *b* (50 percent), you would be correct. But if you answered *c* (70 percent), you would also be correct. How is that possible? This is a bit of a trick question because it depends on precisely how you think about families. Roughly half of all children currently live in households with a mother and father who are in their first marriage. But then another 7 percent of children live with two parents who are cohabiting but not legally married to each other. And another 15 percent of children live with a mother and father who married each other after their first marriages ended. If you add these numbers together, then fully 68 percent live with two parents, although these two-parent families are a highly diverse group (Federal Interagency Forum on Child and Family Statistics, 2019).

Most scholars agree that there is no such thing as a "typical" family in the United States today. As popular television shows such as *Modern Family*, *Blackish*, and *This is Us* reveal, no one family form or structure accounts for the majority of U.S. households today. Families today include people who live alone, single parents with children, stepfamilies, grandparents who share a home with their grandchildren, same-sex couples both with and without children, cohabiters both with and without children, divorced spouses who share a home because they can't afford two separate homes, and married spouses who live miles apart due to their jobs. The notion that the "typical" household includes a breadwinner dad, a stay-at-home mom, and two perfect children is even more dated. Just 14 percent of children under 18 live in a household with a breadwinner father and stay-at-home mother in their first marriage (Livingston, 2015). Families today also are more dynamic than ever, meaning that marriages end in divorce, divorced people remarry or form new cohabiting unions, and single parents may find a new partner. These partnership transitions mean that children may live with multiple different parents or parent-like figures during the first 18 years of life; these changes bring challenges (as well as benefits) that shape child well-being (Fomby and Cherlin, 2007).

LEARNING OBJECTIVES

1 Basic Concepts

Learn how sociologists define and describe families.

2 Theoretical and Historical Perspectives on Families

Review the development of sociological thinking about families. Learn how families have changed over the last 500 years, and the social and economic factors underlying these changes.

3 Research on Families Today

Learn about patterns of dating, cohabitation, marriage, same-sex unions, childbearing, divorce, remarriage, and child-free families. Analyze how these patterns today differ from those of other periods. Understand race, ethnic, and social class differences in contemporary families.

4 Unanswered Questions

Understand the ways that cohabitation differs from marriage, how parents' sexual orientation affects their children, and the linkage between marital status and happiness.

THE ANSWER IS B OR C.

Census data can tell us what the "statistical" norm is, or those behaviors that are objectively more or less common in the United States today. Sociologists, by contrast, help shed light on what the "cultural" norm is—and why. Are certain family forms considered "best" for the health and well-being of American society? Or do all family forms confer their own distinctive benefits? And, if so, why do so many Americans still hold on to the belief that some family forms are superior to others, often couching their arguments in terms of "what's best for the children"?

Sociologists David Popenoe and Judith Stacey have been engaged in a decades-long debate over this very question. Popenoe (1993, 1996) argues that families have changed for the worse since 1960. Over the past six or seven decades, divorce, non-marital births, and cohabitation rates have increased, while marriage and marital fertility rates have decreased. He claims these trends underlie social problems such as child poverty, adolescent pregnancy, substance abuse, and juvenile crime. Increasing rates of divorce and nonmarital births throughout the latter half of the twentieth century created millions of female-headed households and have removed men from the child-rearing process—a situation that is harmful to children, Popenoe argues.

Stacey (1998, 2011) counters that the "traditional" American family of the 1950s—praised by Popenoe, conservative politicians, conservative media sources like Fox News, and online communities like OneMillionMoms as the panacea for all social problems—is a dated and oppressive institution. According to Stacey, the "modern family" with "breadwinner father and child-rearing mother" perpetuated the "segregation of the sexes by extracting men from, and consigning White married women to, an increasingly privatized domestic domain." The modern family has been replaced by the "postmodern family"—single mothers, blended families, cohabiting couples, same-sex unions, dual-career families, and families with a breadwinning mother and stay-at-home dad. The postmodern family is well suited to meet the challenges of the current economy and is an appropriate setting for raising children, who need capable, loving caretakers—regardless of their gender, marital status, employment status, or sexual orientation, argues Stacey.

Popenoe agrees that children need capable, loving caretakers, yet he maintains that "two parents—a father and a mother—are better for a child than one parent." He claims that biological fathers make "distinctive, irreplaceable contributions" to their children's welfare. Fathers offer a strong male role model to sons, act as disciplinarian for trouble-prone children, provide daughters with a male perspective on heterosexual relationships, and, through their unique play styles, teach their children about teamwork, competition, independence, self-fulfillment, self-control, and regulation of emotions. Mothers, on the other hand, teach their children about nurturance and communion, the feeling of being connected to others. Both needs can be met only through the gender-differentiated parenting of a mother and father, Popenoe argues.

Stacey retorts that the postmodern family is better suited to the postmodern economy, in which employment has shifted from unionized heavy industries to nonunionized clerical, service, and new industrial and high-tech sectors. The loss of union-protected jobs means that many men no longer earn enough to support a wife and children. And, during the recessionary years of the early twenty-first century, men who suffered long-term unemployment often relied on their wives to fully support their families. At the same time, demand for clerical and service labor, escalating consumption standards, increases in women's educational attainment, and high and steady divorce rates have led most women, including mothers of young children, to work for pay outside the home.

Stacey also disagrees with media rhetoric and claims by conservatives, such as Popenoe, who elevate the married, two-parent family as the "ideal" family form. Rather than condemning contemporary family forms, Stacey reasons, family sociologists and policy makers should develop strategies to mitigate the harmful effects of family instability on children. She suggests restructuring work schedules and benefit policies to accommodate familial responsibilities; redistributing work opportunities to reduce unemployment rates; enacting comparable worth standards of pay equity to enable women as well as men to earn a family wage; providing universal health care, prenatal and child care, and sex education; and rectifying the economic inequities of divorce (Biblarz and Stacey, 2010).

Claiming that "marriage must be re-established as a strong social institution," Popenoe argues that employers should stop relocating married couples with children and should provide more generous parental leave. He also supports a two-tiered system of divorce law. Marriages without minor children would be relatively easy to dissolve, but marriages with young children would be dissolvable only by mutual agreement or on grounds involving a wrong by one party against the other. The proposal has been met with skepticism among feminist scholars, who address the costs for children and adults alike of reinstating grounds of fault for divorce.

Where does the "truth" lie—with Stacey, with Popenoe, or somewhere in between? In this chapter, we will learn what families actually look like in the twenty-first century, how families have changed through history, the wide range of forms that families take, and some of the challenges family members face today. We will see that the postmodern family is clearly the statistical norm in the United States in the twenty-first

Television shows such as *The Fosters* and *This is Us,* advertising campaigns, and major retailers are embracing more inclusive images and ideas of families.

century. Although cultural norms tend to lag slightly behind statistical realities, in recent years, the number of television shows, films, and advertising campaigns upholding a broad and inclusive image of "family" has flourished.

For instance, an ad for Google Home features gay dads Ross and Alex asking the device for information on local traffic so that they can decide which parent should drive their children to school (Rook, 2017), while a TV spot for Honey Maid features a young boy whose parents have divorced and each remarried. When Isaac talks about his blended family, he casually mentions that his stepdad has Black hair and his dad has brown hair, but he doesn't see other differences. Both men are his "dads." Starting nearly a decade ago, department stores like Target and JC Penney began actively marketing their wedding registries to same-sex couples, who could identify as "bride," "groom," or "partner" as they registered for wedding gifts (Maxwell, 2012). These cultural images and practices have helped to contribute to more expansive attitudes about what constitutes a "normal American family." In this chapter we will show how common such patterns are and discuss the implications of shifting families for the well-being of children and their parents.

family A group of individuals related to one another by blood ties, marriage, or adoption, who form an economic unit, the adult members of which are responsible for the upbringing of children. All known societies involve some form of family system, although the nature of family relationships varies widely. While the main family form in modern societies is the nuclear family, extended family relationships are also found.

kinship A relation that links individuals through blood ties, marriage, or adoption. Kinship relations are by definition part of marriage and family, but they extend much more broadly. While in most modern societies few social obligations are involved in kinship relations extending beyond the immediate family, in other cultures, kinship is of vital importance to social life.

marriage A socially approved sexual relationship between two individuals. Marriage historically has involved two persons of opposite sexes, but in the past decade, marriage between same-sex partners was ruled legal in the United States in 2015, and in a growing number of nations throughout the world. Marriage normally forms the basis of a family of procreation—that is, it is expected that the married couple will produce and bring up children.

nuclear family A family group consisting of two adults and dependent children.

1   BASIC CONCEPTS

A **family** is a group of people directly linked by kin connections, the adult members of which take care of the children. **Kinship** ties are connections among individuals, established either through marriage, the lines of descent that connect blood relatives (mothers, fathers, children, grandparents, etc.), or adoption. **Marriage** can be defined as a socially acknowledged and approved sexual union between two adult individuals. When two people marry, they become kin to each other; however, the marriage bond also connects a wider range of kinspeople. Parents, brothers, sisters, and other blood relatives become relatives of the partner, or "in-laws," through marriage.

Virtually all societies contain what sociologists and anthropologists call the **nuclear family**, two adults living together in a household with their own or adopted

extended family A family group consisting of more than two generations of relatives living either within the same household or very close to one another.

families of orientation The families into which individuals are born. Also known as families of origin.

families of procreation The families individuals initiate through marriage, cohabitation, or by having children.

matrilocal A family system in which the husband is expected to live near the wife's parents.

patrilocal A family system in which the wife is expected to live near the husband's parents.

monogamy A form of marriage in which each married partner is allowed only one spouse at any given time.

polygamy A form of marriage in which a person may have two or more spouses simultaneously.

polygyny A form of marriage in which a man may simultaneously have two or more wives.

polyandry A form of marriage in which a woman may simultaneously have two or more husbands.

children. In most traditional societies, the nuclear family was part of a larger kinship network. When close relatives, in addition to a married couple and children, live either in the same household or in a close and continuous relationship with one another, we speak of an **extended family**. An extended family may include grandparents, brothers and their wives, sisters and their husbands, aunts, nephews, and so on.

Whether nuclear or extended, families can be divided into **families of orientation**, or families of origin, and **families of procreation**. The first is the family into which a person is born or adopted. The second is the family into which one enters as an adult; for those who have children, it is the context in which a new generation of children is brought up. A further distinction concerns place of residence. In the United States, when two people marry, they do not necessarily set up their own household in the same area where either spouse's parents live, although they often do so. In some other societies, however, married couples live close to or within the same dwelling as the parents of either or both spouses. When the couple lives near or with the female spouse's parents, the arrangement is **matrilocal**. In

(left) The Kazaks in Mongolia usually live in extended families and collectively herd their livestock. The youngest son will inherit the father's house, and the elder sons will build their own houses close by when they get married. (right) Parents wait for the metro with their child. How is a nuclear family different from an extended family?

a **patrilocal** pattern, the couple lives near or with the male spouse's parents.

In Western societies, marriage, and therefore family, is associated with **monogamy**. It is illegal for a person to be married to more than one individual at any one time. But in several parts of the world, monogamy is far less common than it is in Western nations. In his classic research, George Murdock (1967, 1981) compared several hundred societies from 1960 through 1980 and found that **polygamy**, a marriage that allows a person to have more than one spouse, was permitted in over 80 percent of them (see also Gray, 1998). There are two types of polygamy: **polygyny**, in which a man may be married to more than one woman at the same time, and **polyandry**, much less common, in which a woman may have two or more husbands simultaneously. Of the 1,231 societies tracked, Murdock found that just 15 percent of societies were monogamous, 37 percent had occasional polygyny, 48 percent had more frequent polygyny, and less than 1 percent had polyandry (Murdock, 1981). In contemporary society, polygamy rates have been particularly high in Africa's "polygamy belt" reaching from Senegal to Tanzania, where as many as one-third of women are in polygamous unions (Jacoby, 1995).

Yet recent work suggests that polygamy has grown less common over time due to social and economic conditions, including increasing levels of democracy, a declining acceptance of arranged marriage, an increase in marriages based on a desire for love and companionship, and strides in the education and human rights protections afforded to women. Polygyny is disadvantageous to women, and as such, has declined as women gain more rights and power in many parts of the world (Bailey and Kaufman, 2010).

> ## CONCEPT CHECKS
>
> 1 Contrast a family of orientation and a family of procreation.
>
> 2 Provide an example of a nuclear versus an extended family.
>
> 3 What are several alternatives to monogamy?
>
> 4 Why have rates of polygamy declined in contemporary society?

2 THEORETICAL AND HISTORICAL PERSPECTIVES ON FAMILIES

The study of families and family life encompasses contrasting approaches. Many perspectives adopted even a few decades ago now seem dated and unconvincing in light of recent research and changes in the social world, including the 2015 legalization of same-sex marriage in the United States. Nevertheless, it is valuable to trace the evolution of sociological thinking before discussing contemporary approaches to the study of families. We discuss three of the main theories used to understand the contemporary family and then provide a historical context for understanding contemporary families.

Sociological Theories of Families

Functionalism

The functionalist perspective sees society as a set of social institutions that perform specific functions to ensure continuity and consensus. According to this perspective, families perform important tasks that contribute to society's basic needs and help perpetuate social order. Sociologists in the functionalist tradition regard the nuclear family as fulfilling specialized roles in modern societies. With the advent of industrialization in the late nineteenth century, families became less important as a unit of economic production and more focused on bearing, rearing, and socializing children.

According to U.S. sociologist Talcott Parsons, the two main functions of families are primary socialization and personality stabilization (Parsons and Bales, 1955). **Primary socialization** is the process by which children learn their society's cultural norms and expectations for behavior. Because this process happens during early childhood, the family is the most important site for the development of the human personality. **Personality stabilization** refers to the role of the family in assisting adult family members emotionally. Marriage between two adults is the arrangement through which personalities are supported and kept healthy. In industrial societies, families may play a critical role in stabilizing adult personalities because the nuclear family is often geographically distant from its extended kin and cannot draw on larger kinship ties.

Parsons regarded the nuclear family as best equipped to handle the demands of industrial society. In the "conventional" family, one adult can work outside the home for pay while the second adult cares for the home and children. In practical terms, this specialization of roles has historically meant the husband adopts the "instrumental" role as breadwinner and the wife assumes the "affective," or emotional support, role in the home.

Functionalist theories emphasize how the family helps meet society's needs and maintain order. Functionalism viewed a strict division of labor—with men in an instrumental role and women in an affective role—as rational and functional for society.

Today, Parsons's view of families seems inadequate and outdated. Functionalist theories of families have come under heavy criticism for justifying the domestic division of labor between men and women as something natural and unproblematic. Moreover, functionalist perspectives presume that a male-female married couple is essential for the successful rearing of children and the efficient operation of households; Parsons failed to consider that same-sex and single-parent families may run efficiently and effectively parent and socialize their children. He also failed to recognize that in many families, wives may be better suited to breadwinning and their husbands better suited to child-rearing, or that the two would share both tasks equally. Many of these critiques are similar to those that sociologist Judith Stacey levied against conservative sociologist David Popenoe. Yet Parsons' theories are more understandable when we consider the broader historical backdrop. The immediate post–World War II years (when Parsons proposed his theories) saw men reassuming positions as sole breadwinners after returning from the war overseas; this arrangement was rational for the family because men typically earned far more than women (Becker, 2009). Because women were no longer needed in the labor force in large numbers, they returned to their traditional roles of wives, mothers, and homemakers after having worked in offices, factories, shipyards, and stores during the war when the men were away.

Assessing Parsons's view in light of contemporary society, however, we can criticize functionalist views on other grounds. In emphasizing the importance of the family, such theories neglect the role of other social institutions—such as government, media, peers, and schools—in socializing children. The theories also neglect family forms that do not reflect the nuclear family. Families that did not conform to the White, suburban, middle-class ideal were considered deviant, including same-sex, child-free, and single-parent families, as well as families in which husbands were not primary breadwinners.

Symbolic Interactionist Approaches

Symbolic interactionist approaches to studying the family stand in stark contrast with functionalist perspectives. Whereas functionalist approaches emphasize stability and maintaining the current social order, symbolic interactionism emphasizes the contextual, subjective, and even ephemeral nature of family interactions, power relations, and interpersonal communication (LaRossa and Reitzes, 1993). Sociologist Ernest Burgess (1926) was one of the earliest scholars to apply symbolic interactionist approaches to the family, which he described as "a unity of interacting personalities" in which the behavior or identities of individual family members mutually shaped one another over time.

Symbolic interactionist approaches do not take power differentials for granted, and they do not necessarily assume that men have more power than women or that adults have more power than children. For example, Willard Waller (1938) developed the principle of least interest to show that the partner who is least committed to, or interested in, their romantic relationship has more power and might often exploit that power. Think about some of the couples you know; your friend might be an independent and assertive person, but if he or she is very intent on making a relationship work with a partner who is slightly less excited about the relationship, your friend might cede the upper hand to the partner in an effort to keep the relationship going.

More contemporary work emphasizes the ways that family members continually negotiate, define, and redefine their roles. Recall from Chapter 10 the concept of

primary socialization The process by which children learn the cultural norms and expectations for behavior of the society into which they are born. Primary socialization occurs largely in the family.

personality stabilization According to functionalist theory, the family plays a crucial role in assisting its adult members emotionally. Marriage is the arrangement through which personalities are supported and kept healthy.

"doing gender" (West and Zimmerman, 1987). In this view, the ways that men and women behave are neither biological nor static; rather, these roles are socially constructed based on the immediate social context. Marriage and romantic relationships are a particularly important site of doing gender. Studies have explored the ways that couples negotiate housework and how they "do gender," even when no longer performing the household tasks typically associated with their sex. Emslie and colleagues (2009) studied the ways that colorectal cancer patients "did gender" when their illness prevented them from carrying out the gender-typed household roles they previously performed. The couples developed narratives to maintain their gendered identities, where women organized "cover" for housework and child care when they were ill, and men focused on making sure that their families were financially secure and spouses were "protected" from the stress of the men's cancer battles. "Doing gender" is not limited to different-sex married couples, however. In his study of same-sex couples, Christopher Carrington (1999) found that men in same-sex couples often "covered up" their role in serving nightly meals, as a way to reinforce their masculinity, whereas female partners claimed responsibility for meals, and in doing so reinforced their appearance of femininity.

Symbolic interactionist approaches have been applied to parent-child relationships as well. Whereas scholarship on functionalist traditions took a "top down" approach to socialization and presumed that parents taught and socialized their children, symbolic interactionist studies find that children often shape, influence, and guide their parents in particular social situations. Several recent studies of immigrant and refugee families, for instance, show that parents and children often must renegotiate their roles when they inhabit unfamiliar contexts (Katz, 2014). Children may have relatively higher status than their parents, especially if they have a better understanding of the language and practices in the United States. This knowledge allows them to serve as the family's liaison to schoolteachers and health care providers.

Symbolic interactionist scholars offer provocative insights into family dynamics, but this perspective is critiqued on the grounds that it places too much emphasis on cooperation and consensus. Other critics find that the perspective is overly descriptive; it tells us what is happening, but it does not tell us why. Finally, some scholars, especially those working in the feminist tradition, find fault with the perspective's lack of explicit attention to social structure and deeply embedded gender differences in social and interpersonal power.

Feminist Approaches

For most people, families provide solace, practical support, comfort, love and companionship. Yet families can also be sites of exploitation, loneliness, and profound inequality. In this regard, feminism has challenged the vision of families as harmonious and protective. In 1963, the American feminist Betty Friedan wrote in *The Feminine Mystique* of "the problem with no name"—the isolation and boredom of many suburban American housewives trapped in an endless cycle of child care and housework. Other writers followed, exploring the phenomenon of the "captive wife" (Gavron, 1966) and the damaging effects of "suffocating" family settings on interpersonal relationships (Laing, 1971).

During the 1970s and 1980s, feminist perspectives dominated debates and research on families. Where, previously, family sociology had focused on family structures, the historical development of the nuclear and extended family, and the importance of kinship ties, feminism directed attention inside family dynamics to examine women's experiences in the domestic sphere. Many feminist writers questioned the vision of families as cooperative units based on common interests and mutual support, arguing instead that unequal power relationships within families meant that certain family members benefited more than others (Ferree, 2010).

Feminist approaches to understanding families focus on a broad range of topics, yet three are particularly important. The first is the division of household labor—the way in which tasks are allocated, where women often specialize in homemaking and child rearing and men specialize in breadwinning. Feminists disagree about the historical emergence of this division. Some see it as an outcome of industrial capitalism, where factory work would take men out of the home to work for pay (unlike earlier agricultural economies) and women would be left to manage the home front. Others link it to patriarchy and thus see it as predating industrialization. Although a domestic division of labor probably did exist before industrialization, capitalist production caused a sharper distinction between the domestic and work realms. This process resulted in the crystallization of "male spheres" and "female spheres" and the power relationships that persist today. Some have argued that the gendered allocation of household roles also is a byproduct of economic factors; men's earnings historically have outpaced women's, so the opportunity costs—or family wages lost—are lower when women reduce or abandon paid work for unpaid household labor (Stratton, 2012). Until recently, the male breadwinner model has been widespread in most industrialized societies.

Feminist sociologists have studied the way men and women share domestic tasks, such as child care and housework. They have investigated the validity of claims such as that of the "symmetrical family" (Young and Willmott, 1973)—the belief that, over historical time, family roles and responsibilities are becoming more egalitarian. Findings have shown that women still bear the main responsibility for domestic tasks and enjoy less leisure time than men, even though more women are working in paid employment outside the home than before (Bianchi et al., 2012). Data from the 2016 American Time Use Study showed that, on an average day, 21 percent of men did housework, such as cleaning or doing laundry, compared with 50 percent of women. Not only are men less likely to do housework, but when they do, they spend less time doing it, only about 30 percent as much time on average as women in 2016 (U.S. Bureau of Labor Statistics [BLS], 2017a). Interestingly, in same-sex couples, partners tend to share housework more equally than do heterosexual couples, revealing the complex ways that gender shapes household arrangements (Goldberg, Smith, and Perry-Jenkin, 2012).

A second theme is the unequal power relationships within many families, especially the phenomenon of domestic violence, including intimate partner violence. Spousal abuse, marital rape, incest, and the sexual victimization of children have all received more public attention as a result of feminists' claims that the violent and abusive sides of family life have long been ignored in both academic contexts and legal and policy circles. Feminist sociologists consider how the family serves as an arena for gender oppression and physical abuse. For example, through much of U.S. history, a husband had the legal right to engage his wife in coerced or forced sex. For most of the twentieth century, marital rape was considered an exemption to rape laws, although the exemption was repealed in all states as of 1993. Yet, a dozen states still maintain laws that handle marital rape in quite different ways from rape outside of marriage.

Sociologists today are interested in transformations in family forms, including the rise in remarriage and emergence of blended families such as the Trumps.

Depending on the state, marital rape might be charged under a different section of the criminal code, restricted to a shorter reporting period, and held up to different standards and definitions of force and coercion; assailants are even given slightly different punishments (Byrne, 2015).

Carework constitutes a third theme that feminists address. This broad realm encompasses a variety of processes, from attending to a family member who is ill to looking after an older relative over a long period. Sometimes caregiving means simply being attuned to someone else's psychological well-being. Not only do women shoulder concrete tasks such as cleaning and child care, but they also invest significant emotional labor in maintaining personal relationships (Pinquart and Sorensen, 2006). While caring activities may be grounded in love and deep emotion, they also require an ability and willingness to listen, perceive, negotiate, and act creatively. Caring activities often involve long spells of unpaid labor, and these responsibilities often limit women's ability to work for pay outside the home. In these ways, caregiving indirectly contributes to women's relative economic disadvantage in society. Research shows persuasively that women's economic disadvantage relative to men, especially among older adults, is due in part to their tendency to cut back on paid work when caring for their families, thus reducing the pensions that they are entitled to in old age (Harrington, Meyer, and Herd, 2007). Critiques of feminist theory emphasize that the focus on gender draws attention away from social-class influences, race differences, and other important sources of intersectionality.

Table 15.1

APPLYING SOCIOLOGY TO FAMILIES

CONCEPT	APPROACH TO UNDERSTANDING FAMILIES	CONTEMPORARY APPLICATION
Functionalism	Social institutions like families perform specific functions to ensure continuity and stability.	Conservative scholar David Popenoe's argument that families function best when husband works for pay and wives raise and socialize children.
Symbolic Interactionism	Family relationships are contextual, subjective, and continually renegotiated.	Spouses develop narratives to maintain their gendered identities, even when illness prevents them from carrying out household tasks historically associated with one's gender.
Feminist Theories	Families are distinguished by unequal power relationships, such that some family members benefit more than others.	Because women historically earn less than men, they are often burdened with emotion- and time-intensive unpaid caregiving labor in the home.

Contemporary Perspectives in the Sociology of Families

Recent theoretical and empirical studies conducted from a feminist perspective have generated increased interest in the family among both academics and the general population. Terms such as the *second shift*—referring to women's dual roles at work and at home—have entered our vocabulary. But because feminist studies often focused on issues within the domestic realm, they did not always address trends and influences outside the home.

Since the 1990s, an important body of sociological literature on the family has emerged that draws on feminist perspectives but is not strictly informed by them. Of primary concern are the larger transformations in family forms—the formation and dissolution of families and households and the evolving expectations within personal relationships. The rise in divorce and single parenting, the emergence of "reconstituted families" (i.e., remarriages), same-sex families, the popularity of cohabitation and child-free families, and the diverse and dynamic nature of the households in which children are raised are all topics of inquiry.

In the years following the recession of the early 2000s, scholars have intensified their focus on shifting gender roles within families, where men's and women's "traditional" roles have converged or even crossed over. As the recession disproportionately struck "male" industries such as finance and manufacturing, an increasing number of households now have breadwinner wives and dads who either stay at home with children or juggle part-time work with child-rearing (Livingston, 2018). However, attitudes lag far behind. A 2017 national survey found that 71 percent of adults said it's "very important" for men to be able to support their families financially to be considered good partners. By contrast, only 32 percent of respondents believed the same about women (Parker and Stepler, 2017).

Historical Perspectives on Families

Historical lore and nostalgia tend to romanticize the ways families were in the past, erroneously characterizing highly interdependent extended families as the norm. However, the notion that the extended family was the predominant form of family in premodern eras has been disproved. Historical research shows that the nuclear family has long been preeminent. Throughout the seventeenth, eighteenth, and nineteenth centuries in the United States, the average household size was just 4.75 persons, often including domestic servants. The current average is 2.5, which isn't dramatically lower than the average household size several centuries ago (U.S. Bureau of the Census, 2017c). The smaller size today is largely due to the high proportion of Americans who live alone, especially older widowed women and young professionals who maintain their own homes (Klinenberg, 2012a).

Other historical research also challenges the idyllic image some hold of families in the days of yore. In the premodern United States and Europe, children as young as seven or eight often worked, helping their parents on the farm. Most who did not remain in the family enterprise left the parental household at an early age to do domestic work for others or to follow apprenticeships. Children who went away to work rarely saw their parents again. Families also were unstable and impermanent then, as they are today (a theme we revisit later in this chapter). High mortality rates (numbers of deaths per 1,000 of the population in any one year) meant that a quarter or more of all infants in early modern Europe died within the first year of life, and women frequently died in childbirth. The notion of staying married until "old age" often was not realized due to mortality. The death of children or of one or both spouses often shattered family relations. Instability and severed ties are permanent functions of family life throughout history, although the reasons may differ.

The Historical Development of Family Life

The emotional and interpersonal nature of families also has shifted over time. Historical sociologist Lawrence Stone (1980) distinguished three phases in the development of the family from the 1500s to the 1800s. First, from the fifteenth century to the early seventeenth century, the main form was a type of nuclear family that lived in fairly small households but maintained deeply embedded relationships within the community, including with other kin. According to Stone (although some historians have challenged this idea), the family was

CONCEPT CHECKS

1 According to the functionalist perspective, what are the two main functions of the family?

2 How do symbolic interactionist approaches to studying family differ from functionalist approaches? What are two critiques of the symbolic interactionist perspective?

3 According to feminist perspectives, what three aspects of family life are sources of concern? Why are these three aspects troubling to feminists?

4 What characteristics distinguished the three historical stages of family development, as articulated by historical sociologist Lawrence Stone?

not a major focus of emotional attachment or dependence for its members, as it is today. Individual freedom of choice in courtship, marriage, and other matters of family life were subordinated to the interests of par-

ents, other kin, or the community. Sex within marriage was not regarded as a source of pleasure but as a necessity to produce children. Outside of aristocratic circles, where it was sometimes actively encouraged, passionate or romantic love was regarded by moralists and theologians as a sickness. As Stone (1980) put it, the family during this period "was an open-ended, low-keyed, unemotional, authoritarian institution. . . . It was also very short-lived, being frequently dissolved by the death of the husband or wife or the death or very early departure from the home of the children."

Next came a transitional form of family that lasted from the early seventeenth century to the beginning of the eighteenth. Although largely a feature of the upper classes of society, this form was very important because from it spread attitudes that have since become almost universal. The nuclear family became a more separate entity, distinct from other kin and the local community. There was a growing emphasis on marital and parental love, although the authoritarian power of fathers also increased.

The third phase, which emerged in the mid-eighteenth century and persisted through the mid-twentieth century, gave rise to the type of family system currently widespread in the West. This family is a group tied by close emotional bonds, domestic privacy, and child-rearing. It is marked by **affective individualism**, courtship and marriage based on personal choice, and sexual attraction or romantic love. Sexual aspects of love became glorified within marriage instead of in extramarital relationships. The family became geared to consumption rather than production, as a result of workplaces being separate from the home. Women became associated with domesticity and men with being the breadwinners. Originating among affluent groups, this family type became fairly universal in Western countries with the spread of industrialization.

In premodern Europe, marriage usually began as a property arrangement. In the middle years of marriage, the couple focused mainly on raising children, whereas in the later stages, marriage was about love. Few couples married for love, but many grew to love each other as they jointly managed their household, raised their children, and shared a lifetime of experiences together. By contrast, in most of the modern West, marriage begins with a couple in love; in its middle, it is mostly about raising children (if there are children), and marital quality wanes. By later life, those couples whose marriages survive are typically marked by high levels of love, affection, and companionship (Karney and Bradbury, 1995; Umberson et al., 2005).

3 RESEARCH ON FAMILIES TODAY

Contemporary research on family formation and family life, both in the United States and worldwide, is unified by four key themes. First, family structure continues to change and evolve. Second, there is tremendous variation in what families look like; our family experiences are powerfully shaped by our social group memberships, including race, social class, religion, sexual orientation, and age. Third, families are an important influence on the health and well-being of both adults and children. And,

A mural in Guangzhou, China, advertises the country's one-child policy—a population control policy instituted in the late 1970s. As of 2016, couples can now have two children.

finally, while families have been historically thought of as a safe haven, they also have a dangerous side where family members may inflict abuse and pain on one another. We review recent research on the current state of families and suggest ways they may change in future decades.

Changes in Family Patterns Worldwide

Many family forms exist today. In some areas, such as remote regions in Asia, Africa, and the Pacific Rim, traditional family systems are changing slowly, with most still maintaining or aspiring to one lifelong marriage with children. In most wealthy countries, however, changes are occurring rapidly. In some nations in Western and Northern Europe, for instance, only a minority will ever marry, with most preferring to cohabit with their romantic partner. Among the complex origins of these changes is the spread of Western ideals of romantic love. Another is the development of centralized government in areas previously comprising autonomous smaller societies. People's lives become influenced by their involvement in a national political system; moreover, governments attempt to alter traditional ways of behavior. Because of rapid population growth, states frequently introduce programs advocating smaller families, the use of contraception, and so forth.

Finally, and perhaps most importantly, employment opportunities away from the land and in organizations such as government bureaucracies, mines, plantations, and industrial firms disrupt family systems previously centered on landed production in the local community.

These changes have created worldwide movement toward the predominance of the nuclear family, breaking down extended-family systems and other types of kinship groups. This movement was first documented by William J. Goode in his book *World Revolution in Family Patterns* (1963) and has been borne out by subsequent research. Building on Goode's work, sociologists have identified seven important changes that have characterized global family change over the past half-century:

1. Clans and other kin groups are declining in influence.
2. There is a general trend toward the free choice of a spouse or romantic partner.
3. The rights of women are more widely recognized, with respect both to initiating marriage and to making decisions within families.
4. Kin marriages are less common.
5. Higher levels of sexual freedom are developing in societies that were formerly very restrictive.

6. Birth rates are declining, meaning that women are giving birth to fewer babies.
7. There is a general trend toward extending children's rights.

In many countries, especially Western industrial societies, five additional trends have occurred within the past four decades:

1. An increase in the number of births that occur outside of marriage.
2. A liberalization of laws and norms regarding divorce.
3. An increase in nonmarital cohabitation among romantic partners.
4. An increasing age at first marriage and first birth.
5. A growing number of and cultural and legal acceptance for same-sex couples.

Countries vary widely in how rapidly these changes are occurring (Ng, 2016). For instance, most nations in Asia are witnessing a rapid transition in family life, with divorce rates rising, family size decreasing, and multigenerational families declining in number, a function of young adults' desire for autonomy and independence, and turning away from Confucian values (Ng, 2016). For instance, the divorce rate in Japan increased 66 percent between 1980 and 2012, while the rate in the United States decreased by roughly 25 percent during that period (OECD, 2019). Currently, divorce rates in the United States are higher than in Japan (2.9 vs. 1.7 per 1,000 population). Other nations are witnessing dramatic shifts in the types of unions young adults enter. Only a minority of young adults ultimately marry in Scandinavian nations; they instead form long-term cohabiting relationships in which they bear and rear children. In 2014, fully 70 percent of births in Iceland were to unmarried parents; rates were just slightly lower in Sweden and Norway. However, nearly all these births were to cohabiting partners in committed long-term relationships (Chamie, 2016). Though, cohabiting unions are more likely than marital unions to dissolve—both in Europe and the United States—lending some instability to the lives of children born or adopted into those unions (Wilcox and DeRose, 2017).

Dating and Courtship

"Reality" TV shows like "Married at First Sight" and "90 Day Fiance" would have us believe that people jump into marriage shortly after meeting, perhaps after a brief and passionate whirlwind romance. Yet most couples take the leap into cohabitation or marriage after a lengthy period of dating or courtship, in which they get to know each other before committing to a lifetime together. Courtship might include activities like dating where couples or groups get together for shared activities like dinner, movies, parties, or

Dating apps like Tinder allow people to develop romantic relationships without having face-to-face contact.

sporting events. But dating is more than just recreation; this is the process through which romantic partners learn about each other's personalities, values, goals, and foibles, and become acquainted with their partners' family members who may eventually become in-laws (Weigel, 2017). Modern romantic relationships can begin and develop without face-to-face contact, thanks to apps like Tinder and Bumble, which allow singles to find a partner whom they find attractive without having to rely on traditional means like parties, bars, or blind dates. Virtual dating, sending text messages, instant messaging, writing emails, or video-chatting through Skype or FaceTime are modern ways that partners use to get to know each other (Rosenfeld, 2018). Online dating and even online dates became the only option for young singles when stay-at-home orders were in place during the 2020 pandemic (Vinopal, 2020).

Dating and courtship are taken-for-granted experiences for young people today, but the romantic notion of choosing one's own life partner based on physical attraction, personality compatibility, and the feeling of having found one's "soulmate" is a very modern and Western phenomenon (Weigel, 2017). Arranged marriages were the norm in most parts of the world until the eighteenth century and largely disappeared from Western industrialized nations as the values of individualism and personal autonomy flourished (Coontz, 2006). However, arranged unions are still the norm in many parts of the world, especially South Asia. Family members, typically one's parents, select the young person's romantic partner, occasionally with the assistance of a professional matchmaker. The reasons for arranged marriage vary across time and place, but some of the most common reasons are wealth and inheritance concerns, cultural or religious tradition, and ensuring that one's child marries a person of their own ethnic, racial, or religious group.

Scholars have asked the important question of whether arranged versus autonomous ("love") marriages are more successful, and they do not have definitive answers. The evidence generally shows that in arranged marriages, love and friendship can emerge over time, and that autonomous marriages have no guarantee that the love and romance will persist—as evidenced by high rates of divorce in wealthy Western nations. In other words, there's no guarantee that any type of romantic union will be happy and harmonious forever, regardless of one's pathway into that union (Epstein, Pandit, and Thakar, 2013). Feminist scholars have also pointed out that young women manage to exert some choice and creatively navigate the process of arranged meetings with potential spouses (Pande, 2015).

Even in the contemporary United States, the ways that young people meet and interact with romantic partners has shifted dramatically over the past century. It was only in the early twentieth century that dating emerged as a "fun" activity that was considered a normal stage of adolescence and early adulthood. However, dating in the 1920s and 1930s was more chaste than it is today; premarital sex was frowned upon so couples progressed very quickly from dating to marriage. Following the sexual revolution of the 1960s and 1970s, premarital sex became more widely accepted, so dating couples could enjoy sexual relationships without rushing into marriage as a way to consummate their relationship (Coontz, 2006). In the late twentieth and early twenty-first centuries, young people may "hook up" with a sexual partner or "hang out" with large groups of friends rather than go on traditional "dates" like dinner and a movie (Garcia et al., 2012). Although some scholars and conservative pundits have argued that casual sexual relationships or "hookups" are demeaning and demoralizing to young people (especially heterosexual women), other researchers suggest that these relationships allow young people to focus on their career goals, without concerns that they will be tied down by a partner (Armstrong and Hamilton, 2015). Moreover, "hook up" or "friends with benefits" relationships often do progress into more long-lasting unions. One study found that fully half of all college students' committed dating relationships began as a "hookup" (Bogle, 2007).

An additional consequence of rising levels of individualism over the past century is that young people feel less constrained to date partners who share the same ethnic, racial, or religious background as their parents or grandparents. Adolescents and young adults also are more likely than past generations to try same-sex dating; one recent study of 24,000 college students found that 25 percent of women and 12 percent of men who identified as "heterosexual" had their most recent hook-up with a partner of the same-sex (Kuperberg and Walker, 2018). However, sociologists are careful to point out that young people's latitude in choosing whom to date is shaped by social context, such that LGBTQ youth are more comfortable "coming out" and dating same-sex partners in schools with more accepting climates and fewer practices that uphold heteronormativity, like a strong "football culture" (Wilkinson and Pearson, 2009).

Similarly, interracial dating is more common in schools that are racially and ethnically diverse (Kao, Joyner, and Ballisteri, 2019). Kao and colleagues (2019) analyzed data from the National Longitudinal Study of Adolescent to Adult Health, a survey of more than 15,000 middle and high school students in the mid-1990s and tracked them over the next 15 years. They concluded that "giving young people the opportunity to interact with individuals of different races is essential to promoting interracial friendships and romantic relationships. A lot of sociologists … believe that individual characteristics—education, income level, etc.—make people more likely to have interracial … romances, but we found that the positive association of simply attending a diverse school outweighs those other factors" (Cummings, 2019). Taken together, these studies powerfully show that our dating lives, something we think of as being guided solely by our own romantic tastes, are highly structured by the environments in which we live and interact.

Family Formation and Dissolution Trends in the Contemporary United States

Given the ethnic, racial, and cultural diversity of the United States, there are considerable variations in family and marriage within our country. Most research on families in the United States compares broad racial groups as defined by the U.S. Census: White, Black, Asian, and Native American, as well as persons with Hispanic ethnicity, regardless of race (see Chapter 11). However, as we shall see below, intermarriage, or marriage between two persons of different racial backgrounds, has grown increasingly common over the past two decades. Most research shows quite striking differences in the marriage and childbearing patterns of White and U.S.-born Black families; Asian American families resemble Whites in many ways, while patterns among persons of Hispanic-origin and Black immigrants are highly varied based on their particular culture or country of origin. These differences reflect long-standing economic and historical factors that shape family formation. After considering these differences, we

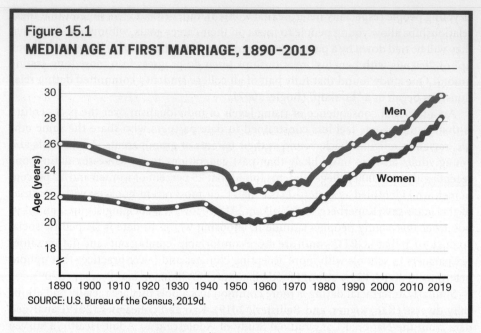

Figure 15.1

MEDIAN AGE AT FIRST MARRIAGE, 1890–2019

SOURCE: U.S. Bureau of the Census, 2019d.

will examine divorce, remarriage, stepparenting, and childbearing in relation to contemporary patterns of family life.

The United States has long had high marriage rates; nearly 90 percent of adults in their mid-fifties and early sixties today are married or have previously been married (U.S. Bureau of the Census, 2017b). However, recent evidence shows that the age at which Americans marry for the first time has risen sharply in recent decades, leading researchers to debate whether marriage is simply being delayed or is being forgone all together. In 2019, the median age at first marriage in the United States was 28 for women and 29.8 for men; this marks a dramatic increase from 1960, when the median ages were 20.3 and 22.8, respectively (see Figure 15.1) (U.S. Bureau of the Census, 2019d). Sociologists offer several explanations for this trend.

First, some researchers contend that increases in cohabitation among younger people account for the decrease (or delay) in marriage among this group. In past decades, young people who wanted to live with their romantic partner typically got married, given the stigma associated with "living in sin" and having sexual relations with a person to whom one was not legally married. Within the past four decades, however, cohabitation has grown exponentially in popularity among young adults, alongside the disappearing stigma of premarital sexual relations. Cohabitation is also increasingly popular among older adults, and nonmarital cohabitation is replacing remarriage as the main way that midlife and older adults repartner following divorce (Brown and Wright, 2017). In 2007, the Current Population Survey (CPS), a national survey of U.S. adults, introduced a measure that identifies all cohabiting partners in a household (Kennedy and Fitch, 2012). Because the practice and formal measurement of cohabitation is relatively new, it is not easy to make direct comparisons with much earlier time periods. Nonetheless, we can estimate that the number of younger-age couples who have ever lived together without being married has risen steeply from half a million couples around 1970 to almost 3 million in 1990. By 2016, more than 8 million couples were cohabiting in the United States (U.S. Bureau of the Census,

2017h). Among young adults ages 18–24, cohabitation is now more common than living with a spouse: 9 percent lived with an unmarried partner in 2018, compared to 7 percent who lived with a spouse (Gurrentz, 2018).

Others argue that increases in postsecondary school enrollment, especially among women, are partially responsible. Most couples prefer to delay marriage until they have completed their formal schooling (Wang and Parker, 2014). That's part of the reason why marriage has become an institution of social and economic advantage; young adults with higher levels of education and income are more likely than those with fewer economic advantages to transition from cohabitation to marriage (Gurrentz, 2018). Not only does it cost money to have a wedding, but young people believe that economic security is a prerequisite for marrying and may wait until they graduate, find a secure job, and pay off college loans (Sassler, Michelmore, and Qian, 2018). Similarly, women's increased participation in the labor force means many women establish careers before getting married and starting a family (Copen et al., 2012).

Finally, some researchers believe that modernization and a secular change in attitudes promote individualism and downplay the importance of marriage. According to this perspective, young people are not just delaying marriage but may forgo marriage altogether. As we will see later in this chapter, cohabitation has surpassed marriage in popularity in some Western and Northern European nations. Sociologists do not predict a parallel trend in the United States, where well over half of unmarried young adults say that they do want to marry someday (Wang and Parker, 2014). However, according to Census Bureau predictions, a sizeable proportion of Generation Y and Millennials will remain unmarried for life, with this pattern especially common among those with fewer financial advantages (Wang and Parker, 2014).

The actual reason for the delay in marriage and accompanying decline in marriage rates is likely a combination of economic, social, and cultural factors. Still, we must be careful in drawing the conclusion that Americans are turning their back on marriage. Although some social critics have argued that the trend toward marriage later in life is a break from tradition, the age of first marriage in the United States is now more similar to what it was between 1890 and 1940 and departs markedly only from the very low ages of first marriage in the mid-twentieth century. In 1890, the median age at first marriage for men was 26, lower than the median age of 30 today, but still a far cry from the 1950s, when marriage happened in one's very early twenties (U.S. Bureau of the Census, 2017i). To say that people today are postponing marriage dramatically is true only if we compare ourselves with Americans in the 1950s. It might be more accurate to say that the 1950s generation married at an unusually young age.

No one knows how the trend toward cohabitation will develop in the future, but we can get useful information from other industrial countries. In France, Sweden, and other nations where cohabitation is as widespread as marriage, many people, especially younger adults, view the two as interchangeable (Treas et al., 2014). By contrast, in the United States, only two-thirds of those cohabiting say that their relationship is a precursor to marriage (Pew Research Center, 2011d). And plans to marry don't always lead to a walk down the aisle; sociologist Karen Guzzo (2009) found that one-quarter of cohabitors who were engaged or planned to marry ended up changing their minds or ending their unions. We return to the topic of cohabitation as an alternative to marriage later in this chapter.

An extraordinary increase in the proportion of people living alone in the United States has taken place recently—a phenomenon that partly reflects the high levels of marital separation and divorce. More than one in every four households (28 percent) in 2016 consisted of one person, more than twice the proportion (13.1 percent) in 1960 (U.S. Bureau of the Census, 2017e). There has been a particularly sharp rise for individuals living alone in the 24 to 44 age bracket.

As we noted in this chapter's introduction, some people still think the "average" American family consists of a husband who works in paid employment and a wife who looks after the home and their two children. However, less than a quarter of married couples with children under 15 fit this picture (U.S. Bureau of the Census, 2016b). One reason is the high and stable divorce rate: A substantial proportion of the population lives either in single-parent households or in stepfamilies, or both. Another is the high proportion of women who work. Dual-career marriages and single-parent families are now the norm. Although men historically were the only breadwinner or the higher earner in the marriage, this pattern is rapidly changing; women outearn their husbands in 29 percent of households today (Bureau of the Census, 2019b).

There are also significant differences in patterns of childbearing between parents in the 1950s and later generations. The birth rate rose sharply just after World War II and again during the 1950s. Women in the 1950s had their first child earlier than later generations did, and subsequent children were born closer together. Since the late 1960s, the average age at which women have their first child has risen steadily. In 2015, the average age of first-time moms was 26.4, up from 22.1 in 1970. The proportion of women giving birth in their 30s and 40s also has increased sharply. In 1976, only 20 percent of births were to women over age 30. By 2015, this proportion had grown to 44 percent (Martin et al., 2017). Specifically, the first birth rates for women between the ages of 35 and 39 have increased dramatically since the early 1970s, jumping more than six-fold (Mathews and Hamilton, 2014). Delayed childbearing, like delayed marriage, is due largely to rising levels of education and greater career opportunities for women today, relative to five decades ago.

Family structures and patterns are powerfully shaped by both structural and cultural factors. Structural factors—including shifts in educational attainment, economic prospects of young adults, widening levels of income inequality, and whether one has the legal right to marry—have a powerful influence on the ways families are formed. At the same time, cultural factors, ranging from attitudes toward marriage, sexuality, and cohabitation to beliefs about the appropriate context for raising children, shape family lives. For these reasons, American families vary widely based on factors such as social class, race, ethnicity, religion, and even the geographic region where one lives. We briefly focus on the ways that race and social class shape family life in the contemporary United States.

Race, Ethnicity, and American Families

Sociologists have documented stark differences in family structure among White, Black, Native American, Asian, and Hispanic-origin families. Early studies failed to consider distinctions between race and ethnicity, lumping together, for instance, U.S.-born and non-U.S.-born Blacks, and attributed Black-White differences in family structure to "cultural" differences, including beliefs about the importance of marriage and about the importance of being economically self-sufficient (Lewis, 1969). However, in recent decades, scholars have moved away from "cultural" approaches and instead recognize the critical importance of structural factors, recognizing that socioeconomic resources, including education, the opportunity to work in jobs that

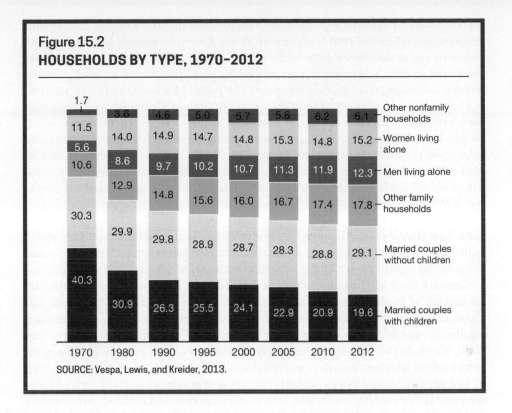

Figure 15.2
HOUSEHOLDS BY TYPE, 1970–2012

	1970	1980	1990	1995	2000	2005	2010	2012
Other nonfamily households	1.7	3.6	4.6	5.0	5.7	5.6	6.2	6.1
Women living alone	11.5	14.0	14.9	14.7	14.8	15.3	14.8	15.2
Men living alone	5.6 / 10.6	8.6	9.7	10.2	10.7	11.3	11.9	12.3
Other family households	30.3	12.9 / 14.8						
			14.8	15.6	16.0	16.7	17.4	17.8
Married couples without children		29.9	29.8	28.9	28.7	28.3	28.8	29.1
Married couples with children	40.3	30.9	26.3	25.5	24.1	22.9	20.9	19.6

SOURCE: Vespa, Lewis, and Kreider, 2013.

provide a living wage and enable people to amass savings, are among the key factors that contribute to differences in family structure—most notably, the greater tendency of Whites and Asians (relative to Blacks, Hispanic-origin persons, and Native Americans) to marry, to remain married, and to have children within marriage. However, as we have seen elsewhere in this book, race and socioeconomic status are so closely intertwined in the United States that it is difficult to parse the distinctive effects of one over the other. Another advance in recent years is attention to multiracial families; younger cohorts are far more likely than their parents to date and marry persons of a different race. One in six recent newlyweds married persons of a race different from theirs, shedding light on the increasingly complex ways that race shapes family experiences in the United States (Livingston and Brown, 2017).

Native American Families Kinship ties are very important in Native American families. As family scholar Andrew Cherlin (1999) notes, "Kinship networks constitute tribal organization; kinship ties confer identity" for Native Americans. However, for those who live in cities or away from reservations, kinship ties may be less prominent. Furthermore, Native Americans have higher rates of intermarriage than any other racial or ethnic group. According to 2013 American Community Survey data, fully 58 percent of all newlywed Native Americans married non-natives. By way of comparison, just 11 percent of Whites, 18 percent of Blacks, 29 percent of Asians and 27 percent of Hispanics who married in 2015 wed a partner of a different racial background (Bialik, 2017).

Native American women have a low overall birth rate, but a high percentage of these births occur outside of marriage. At 9.7 babies per 1,000 women ages 15 to 44, it was the lowest of any ethnic group in the United States in 2015, a drastic change from 25 years ago, when the 1990 birth rate of Native American women was 19 per 1,000 women—one of the highest rates in the United States (Martin et al., 2017). However, compared to all U.S. women, a high proportion of Native American births were to women under age 20 (11 percent compared to 6 percent for women of all ethnicities). Native American women also have their first children at a younger age; as a group, they have the youngest mean age at first birth at just over 23. Furthermore, nearly 66 percent of all Native American women giving birth in 2015 were not married (Martin et al., 2017). Sandefur and Liebler (1997) also report a high divorce rate for Native Americans, who, in addition, are at particularly high risk of domestic violence. Yet, as we will see later in this chapter, family violence can afflict persons of any ethnicity (T. Williams, 2012).

Hispanic and Latinx-Origin Families Persons of Hispanic and Latinx origin vary widely with respect to culture, history, and socioeconomic status, and consequently also are heterogeneous when it comes to family patterns. Mexicans, Puerto Ricans, and Cubans are three of the largest Hispanic subgroups. In 2017, Mexicans constituted 62 percent of the Hispanic population, Puerto Ricans constituted 10 percent, and Cubans were just 4 percent; the rest of the Hispanic population was made up of much smaller groups from many Latin American nations (Noe-Bustamante, Flores, and Shah, 2019b, 2019c, 2019a). Overall, recent cohorts of Latinx persons are among the most likely of all ethnic groups to marry someone of a different ethnicity. In 2015, fully 27 percent of Hispanic-origin persons (regardless of ethnicity) married someone who does not identify as Hispanic origin, with men and women equally likely to out-marry.

Mexican American families often live in multigenerational households and have a high birth rate. Economically, Mexican American families are more successful than Puerto Rican families but less so than Cuban families. Defying cultural stereotypes

of a Mexican American home with a male breadwinner and female homemaker, almost 60 percent of all Mexican American women are in the labor force (BLS, 2020b). However, this situation is due to necessity rather than desire. Many Mexican American families would prefer the breadwinner-homemaker model but are constrained by finances (Hurtado, 1995).

Family members from Mexico and other Central American nations, including Guatemala and El Salvador, often must grapple with separation from one another. Often, family members will migrate to the United States sequentially, where one person (usually the

Like many Mexican American families, the Camargo household contains multiple generations, including Beatriz Camargo and her husband and three kids, Beatriz's parents, two brothers, and her sister.

father) secures a job and sends money, or "remittances," back to his family. The plans for the rest of the family to move to the United States and reunite are often delayed or halted due to immigration laws (Smokowski and Bacallao, 2011). Even after family members arrive, those who are undocumented may risk deportation, again causing family separation (Chang-Muy, 2009). Undocumented families have faced particular uncertainty and turmoil under the Trump administration; during just a two-month period in 2019, Immigration and Customs Enforcement (ICE) removed roughly 1,000 migrant children from their families, often for reasons as minor as a parent having a traffic citation (Jordan, 2019). The short- and long-term effects of separation and parental deportation for a child's emotional, physical, and cognitive well-being are dire (Allen, Cisneros, and Tellez, 2013; Capps et al., 2007).

The case is very different for Puerto Ricans, because Puerto Rico is a U.S. commonwealth. Because of their status as U.S. citizens, Puerto Ricans move freely between Puerto Rico and the mainland without the difficulties immigrants encounter. When barriers to immigration are high, only the most able (physically, financially, and so on) members of a society can move to another country; because Puerto Ricans face fewer barriers, even the least able can manage the migration process. Thus, they are the most economically disadvantaged of all the major Hispanic groups in the United States. Puerto Rican families have a higher percentage of children born to unmarried mothers than any other Hispanic group—69.2 percent in 2018 (CDC, 2019). Only African Americans (71 percent) and Native Americans (66 percent) have higher rates of births to unmarried women (Martin et al., 2017). However, consensual unions—cohabiting relationships in which couples consider themselves married but are not legally married—are often the context for births to unmarried mothers. Nancy Landale and Kelly Fennelly (1992) studied the marital experiences of Puerto Rican women and found that many lived in consensual unions. They suggest that Puerto Ricans may respond to tough economic times by forming consensual unions as the next best option to a more expensive legal marriage.

Cuban American families are the most prosperous of all the Hispanic groups but are less prosperous than Whites. Cuban Americans historically have settled in the Miami area, forming enclaves in which they rely on other Cubans for their business and social needs (such as banking, schools, and shopping). The relative wealth of Cuban Americans is driven largely by family business ownership. In terms of childbearing, Cuban Americans have lower levels of fertility than non-Hispanic Whites and equally low levels of nonmarital fertility, suggesting that economic factors are equally if not more important than cultural factors in shaping family lives in the United States.

Black Families Black Americans are a diverse group, including those who have lived in the United States for generations, as well as more recent migrants from Africa, the Caribbean, and Latin America (Anderson, 2015). Most of what we know about Black families in the contemporary United States is based on U.S.-born Blacks whose family lives have been shaped by the legacy of slavery (Wilson, 1987). However, in recent years scholars have pointed out stark differences in the marriage and family formation patterns of U.S.-born versus immigrant Blacks. We highlight several examples later in this section, to reveal how race, migration, culture and economic factors shape the family experiences of Americans.

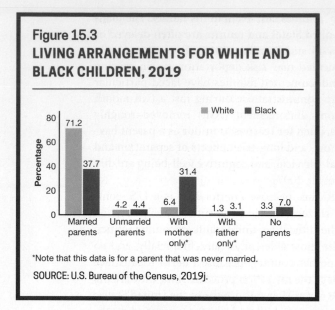

Figure 15.3

LIVING ARRANGEMENTS FOR WHITE AND BLACK CHILDREN, 2019

	White	Black
Married parents	71.2	37.7
Unmarried parents	4.2	4.4
With mother only*	6.4	31.4
With father only*	1.3	3.1
No parents	3.3	7.0

*Note that this data is for a parent that was never married.

SOURCE: U.S. Bureau of the Census, 2019j.

U.S.-born Black and White families differ dramatically in terms of family structure, although these differences are largely attributable to structural factors, including economic resources that facilitate marriage and marital stability. Blacks have higher rates of childbearing outside marriage, are less likely ever to marry, and are less likely to marry after having a nonmarital birth (Figure 15.3). These differences are of particular interest to sociologists because single parenthood in the United States is both a cause and consequence of poverty (Harknett and McLanahan, 2004).

The contemporary state of U.S.-born Black families has deep historical roots. One of the first sociological analyses was carried out by E. Franklin Frazier, in his 1939 book *The Negro Family in the United States*. Frazier examined how historical factors such as slavery, racism, urban migration, and economic adversities affected families. Frazier's work has been critiqued by feminist scholars, among others, who believe he subtly blames problems facing U.S.-born Blacks (e.g., youth crime) on female-headed households, absentee fathers, and nonmarital births, and that he suggests that the two-parent nuclear family is the ideal. Yet other contemporary scholars laud his work for showing that Black families are highly diverse and are resilient against a historical backdrop of deeply entrenched and systemic racism (e.g., Semmes, 2001).

Three decades after Frazier published his trailblazing work, Senator Daniel Patrick Moynihan (1965) described Black families as "disorganized" and caught up in a "tangle of pathology." Moynihan, too, referenced historical factors shaping experiences of Black families. For instance, he noted that the circumstances of slavery prevented Blacks from maintaining the cultural customs of their societies of origin. Slave owners often regarded them as little better than livestock and as inherently promiscuous and, therefore, unworthy of marriage. After emancipation, new cultural experiences and structural factors threatened Black families. Among these were new forms of racial discrimination, changes in the economy such as the development of sharecropping in the South after the Civil War, and the migration of Black families to Northern cities early in the twentieth century (Jones, 1986).

A persistent puzzle facing researchers is the question of why Black and White family patterns have diverged even further since the 1960s, when Moynihan's study was published and public benefits for poor families were expanded dramatically as part of President Lyndon B. Johnson's Great Society program with the goal of minimizing poverty and eradicating racial injustice. We focus on contemporary factors that have contributed to the increasingly large gap in the structure of Black and White families. In 1970, 33 percent of African American families with children under age 18 were headed by single mothers; the comparable rate among White families was 9 percent.

By 2016, the proportion of Black families with children under 18 headed by single mothers had risen to 55 percent, while the comparable proportion for White families was 21 percent. In addition, fewer Black families are maintained by a married couple: In 2016, 34 percent of Black families included a married couple, compared to 69 percent of White families (U.S. Bureau of the Census, 2017g).

One social condition that contributes to high rates of nonmarital childbearing (and, consequently, female-headed households) is what sociologist William Julius Wilson calls a shortage of "marriageable" Black men (1987), a function of Black men's high rates of incarceration, unemployment, and underemployment. Marriage opportunities for women are constrained if there are not enough men employed in the formal labor market. A woman is less inclined to marry a man who is not earning a living wage and may instead opt to have and raise a child on her own, rather than enter a marital union marked by financial instability. Wilson's argument rests on the assumption that Black heterosexual women exclusively marry Black heterosexual men, an assumption that has become less defensible over time. In 1980, just five percent of Black newlyweds were married to a person of a different race; by 2015, this proportion jumped to 18 percent (Livingston and Brown, 2017). However, there is a vast gender disparity such that Black men are more than twice as likely as Black women to out-marry; in 2015, just 12 percent of Black women but fully 24 percent of Black men who were newlyweds married a partner of a different racial background. Taken together, these trends have been cited for Black women's low rates of marriage relative to their White peers; one analysis found that just 7 percent of White but 34 percent of Black women had yet to be married by age 40 (Raley, Sweeney and Wondra, 2015).

Contemporary research provides some support for Wilson's "marriageable male" hypothesis. Recent research confirms that one of the best predictors of whether parents marry after a nonmarital birth is the availability of eligible partners in a geographic area (Harknett and McLanahan, 2004), demonstrating the continued importance of marriage markets even after the birth of a child. However, as we shall see in the section that follows, the patterns that Wilson documented are largely limited to lower-income African Americans; middle-class Blacks reveal family patterns that are very similar to Whites.

African Americans are often embedded in larger and more complex family networks than Whites, but these ties are a source of both support and strain. Anthropologist Carol Stack (1997) lived in a low-income Black community in Illinois to study the support systems that poor Black families formed. Getting to know the kinship system from the inside, she demonstrated that families adapted to poverty by forming large, complex support networks. Thus, a mother heading a one-parent family is likely to have a close and supportive network of relatives to depend on. Yet, these family ties often come with demands—especially on older African American women, who are more likely than any other group to live with and raise their grandchildren. They step into this role when their own children can no longer adequately fulfill their parenting role (Hughes et al., 2007).

Most research on Black families to date focuses on U.S.-born African Americans. However, emerging research shows vast differences in the experiences of U.S.-born versus immigrant Blacks in the United States. For instance, among Black adults ages 18 and older in 2013, just 28 percent of U.S.-born but 48 percent of foreign-born Blacks were currently married (Anderson, 2015). The latter is nearly identical to the overall U.S. average of 50 percent. More fine-grained analyses show only slight differences in rates of marriage among immigrant Blacks from different parts of the world: 52 percent of African immigrants, 45 percent of Caribbean immigrants, and 48 percent of Black immigrants from Latin America were married. These patterns are largely due to the higher levels of education and earnings of immigrant Blacks relative to their U.S.-born counterparts; 26 percent of immigrant Blacks (vs. 19 percent of U.S.-born Blacks) have a college degree, and immigrant Blacks reported a median household income of $43,800 in 2013 (vs. just $33,500 among U.S.-born Blacks). Thus, any discussion of Black-White differences in family structure needs to consider the distinctive background and socioeconomic resources among the large and heterogeneous population of Blacks in the United States.

Asian American Families Asian American families historically have been characterized by interdependence among members of the extended family. In many Asian cultures, family concerns take priority over individual concerns. Family interdependence also helps Asian Americans prosper financially. In fact, family and friend networks often pool money to help their members start a business or buy a house; this help is reciprocated through contributions to the others. The result is a median family income for Asian Americans that is higher than that for non-Hispanic Whites. As each generation of Asian Americans grows increasingly acculturated to life in the United States, however, scholars predict that they will come to resemble White families more and more (Pew Research Center for the People and the Press, 2012). This process may be further hastened by outmarriage. In 2015, 17 percent of all newlywed couples were interracial; however, 29 percent of Asians married that year wed a person from a different race (Livingston and Brown, 2017).

Although there is less research on the differences among various Asian American subgroups than among Hispanic-origin subgroups, some fertility differences have been established. Chinese American and Japanese American women have much lower fertility rates than any other racial or ethnic group, due partly to their high levels of educational attainment. These differences in educational attainment reflect a range of economic factors, including the type of jobs their parents held, the conditions under which their families emigrated to the United States, and their language skills. As women remain in school and delay marriage and childbearing, they typically go on to have fewer children. Chinese, Japanese, and Filipino families have lower levels of nonmarital fertility than all other racial or ethnic groups, including non-Hispanic Whites. Low levels of nonmarital fertility combined with low levels of divorce for most Asian American groups demonstrate the emphasis on marriage as the appropriate forum for family formation and maintenance (Pew Research Center, 2013c).

Multiracial Families Young adults today are more likely than ever to date, cohabit with, and ultimately marry a partner from a different ethnic or racial background. College students may find this increase in intermarriage and interracial dating unsurprising; many of their political leaders and cultural icons like President Barack Obama, American-born British royal Meghan Markle, rapper Drake, and singer Halsey are proudly bi- or multiracial. Yet this change has been dramatic over the past six decades.

In 2015, 17% of all U.S. newlyweds had a spouse of a different race or ethnicity, a dramatic jump since 1967, when just 3% of newlyweds were intermarried. In that pivotal year, the U.S. Supreme Court ruled in *Loving v. Virginia* that marriage across racial lines was legal throughout the country. Until this ruling, interracial marriage was illegal in many states (Livingston and Brown, 2017).

Given how recent these changes have been, the sociological study of multiracial families is still in its nascent forms. Some studies find no differences in the stability of same-race versus interracial marriages, whereas others find that intermarriages are more likely to end in divorce (Guzzo and Hayford, 2011; Zhang and Van Hook, 2009). More fine-grained explorations suggest that interracial marriages vary based on the race and gender of each partner. For instance, recent evidence suggests that marriage between a Black husband and White wife, and White husband and Latinx wife are slightly more likely than White-White marriages to divorce (Bratter and King 2009; Fu and Wolfinger, 2011). Studies also yield inconsistent findings regarding childbearing, with some studies showing that intermarried couples have fewer children than same-race White or Black couples (Qian and Lichter, 2017) and others showing no difference (Choi and Goldberg, 2018). Intermarried couples also are similar to same-race couples with respect to unintended pregnancy, with interracial couples mirroring that of same-race couples from the husband's racial or ethnic group.

Cultural values are slow to change, and as a result, some studies suggest that spouses in intermarriages (especially women) may be vulnerable to discrimination and microaggressions that undermine their well-being and the well-being of their children. For instance, White–Black couples report negative reactions from strangers as well as less support from family and friends (Childs, 2005). Some White mothers face discrimination if they marry persons of a different ethnicity or race, as they may experience the stigma of being perceived as unqualified to raise and nurture children who are not White (Twine, 1999). Consistent with this finding, Bratter and Eschbach (2006) found White women in intermarriages reported higher rates of distress, relative to their Black female and White male counterparts in intermarriages. However, as multiracial families become more common with each subsequent generation, discriminatory treatment and its consequences may diminish. In 1990, an astonishing 63 percent of White U.S. adults in the General Social Survey said they were "very" or "somewhat" opposed to a close relative marrying a Black person. By 2016, this share plummeted to just 14 percent (Livingston and Brown, 2017). More accepting attitudes may create a more supportive climate for parents and children alike in multiracial families.

Social Class and American Families

Sociologists studying racial and ethnic differences in American families are always keenly aware of the role that social class plays. As we learned in Chapter 11, Whites, Blacks, Native Americans, Latinos, and Asians differ starkly with respect to their levels of education, the kinds of jobs they hold, their income, their savings, and whether they own homes. Economic and occupational stability is a powerful influence on families, where those with richer resources are more likely to marry and to have children within (rather than outside of) marriage. Even studies that focus primarily on race are essentially studies of social class, because race, ethnicity, immigration status, and class have historically been so closely intertwined. Contemporary researchers now largely agree that "the differences between [U.S.-born] Black and White extended family relationships are mainly due to contemporary differences in social and economic class positions of group members. Cultural differences are less significant" (Sarkisian and Gerstel, 2004).

This finding leads us to a thought-provoking and policy-relevant question: Are racial differences in family formation due primarily to economic or to cultural factors? Consider an example of four individuals, all women, who are the heads of their households: (1) a Black doctor, (2) a White doctor, (3) a Black nurse's aide, and (4) a White nurse's aide. The cultural argument suggests that Blacks and Whites are different, which means that the Black doctor and Black nurse's aide should have family lives that are more similar to each other than they are to the family lives of the White doctor or White nurse's aide. The class argument argues the opposite: that the two nurse's aides and the two doctors will be more similar to each other than they will be to people of the same race but from a different class position.

Recent studies show that race and class each have distinctive and often complicated influences on family behavior. For instance, while Whites from working-class and poor, often rural, backgrounds—often residing in the southern United States—report very strong ideological support for marriage and bearing children within marriage, their behaviors often depart from these conservative ideals. White young adults of lower- and working-class backgrounds are much more likely than their wealthier peers to get pregnant prior to marriage, marry young, and subsequently divorce (Cahn and Carbone, 2010). Because they often do not attend college, they marry young and bear children young—often before they are financially or emotionally prepared. As a result, they often struggle unsuccessfully with the challenges of marriage and babies, and ultimately divorce. In the past decade, White working-class families have been particularly vulnerable to the opioid crisis, where a young adult's addiction can derail their life chances and destabilize family well-being. For young adult addicts with small children, addiction and death by overdose often means that older adults become custodial grandparents to their orphaned grandchildren (Whalen, 2016).

Middle-class young adults, by contrast, show much more stable family formation patterns. Many cohabit while in school or working in their first jobs, so they marry later and bear children later. Delaying marriage until they are emotionally and financially ready is one of the key reasons college-educated young Whites have lower rates of divorce than their more economically disadvantaged counterparts (Cahn and Carbone, 2010).

Research comparing middle-class Blacks with their less-advantaged counterparts was scarce until the past decade or two, when scholars began to explore middle-class Black families in depth (Lacy, 2007; Landry and Marsh, 2011; Pattillo, 2013). Although middle-class Black families are much more likely than their less economically advantaged peers to live in married-couple households, recent studies detect a new form of middle-class Black family, especially among young adults—the single-person household. Due in part to the shortage of marriageable men and Black men's fairly high rate of intermarrying described earlier, college-educated Black women often live on their own without a romantic partner (Marsh et al., 2007). Studies of intersectionality, or the complex interplay between race and class, provide important insights into the ways both culture and structure shape family lives.

Nonmarital Childbearing Nonmarital childbearing continues to be one of the most hotly debated and well-researched areas of family sociology. This intense interest is driven, in part, by the fact that the number of children born outside of a marital union today is more than six times higher than it was in the 1950s (see Figure 15.4). Nonmarital childbearing rates peaked in 2008 and have since declined, but they remain high—especially for ethnic minorities. In 2015, 71 percent of all births to Black women, 66 percent of births to American Indian or Alaska Native women, and 53 percent of births to Hispanic women occurred outside marriage, compared with 29 percent for non-Hispanic White women and 16 percent for Asian or Pacific Islander women (Martin et al., 2017). Yet these numbers can be misleading because they suggest that babies are being born to women without male partners, thus denying the children a "father figure." Recent studies show that the majority (63 percent) of all nonmarital births take place in cohabiting unions (Wildsmith, Manlove, and Cook, 2018), meaning that many of these children are raised by two parents who just happen not to be legally married to each other.

A key question sociologists address is, why do women have children out of wedlock? This is an important concern to policy makers because children born to unmarried mothers are more likely to grow up in a single-parent household, experience instability in living arrangements, and live in poverty. As these children reach adolescence, they are more likely to have low educational attainment, engage in sex at younger ages, and have a premarital birth. As young adults, children born outside marriage are more

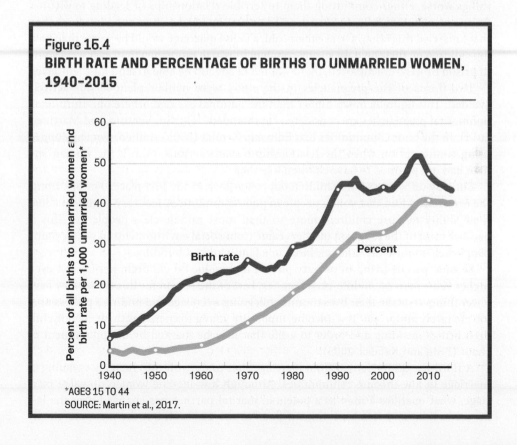

Figure 15.4
BIRTH RATE AND PERCENTAGE OF BIRTHS TO UNMARRIED WOMEN, 1940–2015

*AGES 15 TO 44
SOURCE: Martin et al., 2017.

likely to be idle (neither in school nor employed), have lower occupational status and income, and have more troubled marriages and more divorces than those born to married parents. Studies of children born into unmarried cohabiting unions generally show that they fare better on average than those children born to mothers without a coresidential partner, yet they still fare worse on average than those born into marital unions (Manning, 2015).

Of course, most studies conclude that it is not single or cohabiting mothers who are the problem, but rather, the economically disadvantaged conditions that both give rise to and follow from nonmarital childbearing (Child Trends, 2012). For children of cohabiting parents, instability in the parents' relationship statuses—such as break-ups and new partnerships—also is a source of children's disadvantage regarding school outcomes and health (Fomby and Cherlin, 2007; Manning, 2015). We revisit this topic in our consideration of family structure and child well-being.

Kathryn Edin and Maria Kefalas (2005) ask why low-income women continue to have children out of wedlock when they can hardly afford to do so. Following in the tradition of scholars such as Carol Stack and Elijah Anderson, Edin and Kefalas lived with their subjects—among poor Blacks, Whites, and Puerto Ricans in Philadelphia and in Camden, New Jersey. Their interviews with 165 low-income single mothers in Black and White neighborhoods led them to argue that single mothers were not eschewing marriage. To the contrary, women of all ethnicities whom they interviewed highly valued marriage but believed that getting married at that time would make things worse, either committing them to terrible relationships or leading to divorce. As one woman told Edin and Kefalas, "I'd rather say I had a child out of wedlock than that I married this idiot." Or, as others said, a failed marriage would be worse than having children on their own. In an environment in which more men than ever were going to prison or were unemployed, these women needed to be able to fend for themselves.

Two-thirds of the pregnancies in the study were neither planned nor actively avoided. This figure is much higher than the national average, where one-third of all nonmarital pregnancies are considered "unintended" (Curtin, Ventura, and Martinez, 2014). In the poor communities that Edin and Kefalas (2005) studied, women stopped using contraception when the relationship became serious, even if the woman and man had not planned to have children together.

But why do women have children out of wedlock in the first place? For one thing, the researchers find that young people in poor communities feel very confident about their ability to raise children, more so than most middle-class people do. This is because most of the pregnant mothers came from social environments in which young people helped raise the other children in a family or in a building.

Second, people living in poverty place a high value on children, perhaps an even higher value than do middle-class families. Part of the reason for this is that they have fewer things to make their lives meaningful; going to college and finding a professional job are rarely options for low-income, inner-city young women. For them, having children brings meaning and order to a life that may be marked by disappointment or chaos (Edin and Kefalas, 2005).

A third reason to "retreat from marriage" has to do with the changing meaning of marriage in low-income communities. Although low-income women do value marriage, what qualifies a man as a potential marital partner has changed over the last 50 years. Edin and Kefalas comment that "in the 1950s all but the most marginally employed men found women who were willing to marry them. Now, however, even men who are stably employed at relatively good jobs at the time of the child's birth . . . aren't automatically deemed marriageable." This view is consistent with the work of sociologist William Julius Wilson (1987), who theorized that a lack of "marriageable" men contributed to low rates of marriage among poor African Americans.

Taken together, this research suggests that women have become more selective. When women who value motherhood highly also set the bar higher for marriage, higher rates of nonmarital fertility follow. Through Edin and Kefalas's (2005) work, we can understand the worldviews of Black, White, and Puerto Rican young people who are having children out of wedlock.

Class-Based Cultural Practices Social class shapes more than just whether one marries or cohabits, and whether or when one has children. Many sociological studies have found that child-rearing practices also are powerfully shaped by social class (Sherman and Harris, 2012). In her classic book *Worlds of Pain,* sociologist Lillian Rubin (1977) proposed that children raised in low-income or working-class families were socialized to feel powerless, which would render them vulnerable to anger, and a limited capacity to plan for the future in adulthood. Rubin's work set the stage for contemporary scholars like Annette Lareau, whose work reveals how cultural differences in values and beliefs can result in divergent child-rearing, parenting, and disciplinary practices.

Annette Lareau (2011) concluded that middle-class parents engage in "concerted cultivation," working hard to cultivate their children's talents through many nonschool-based activities, as well as continuous linguistic interaction. Working-class and low-income parents, by contrast, focus their childrearing on the "accomplishment of natural growth": Talk is brief and instrumental, children learn to be more compliant with adult directives, and they participate in few organized activities outside school. They learn to occupy themselves, often playing with neighborhood friends. Lareau drew these conclusions by closely observing 12 families—6 White, 5 Black, and 1 interracial.

As a result of these child-rearing strategies, Lareau claims, middle-class children develop a sense of entitlement and value an individualized sense of self. They become comfortable questioning authority and making demands on adults and institutions. In contrast, the working-class child-rearing strategy promotes a sense of constraint in children, who become more cautious in dealing with adults, bureaucratic institutions, and authority. Like anthropologist Carol Stack, Lareau also finds that working-class and low-income parents place great importance on close kin ties; thus, these children develop closer

According to Annette Lareau, middle-class parents and working-class parents adopt different child-rearing strategies: Middle-class parents engage in "concerted cultivation," keeping their children busy with nonschool-based activities such as organized sports. Working-class parents undertake the "accomplishment of natural growth."

relationships with their siblings, cousins, and other relatives. Recognizing the possible dangers of attributing differences to "culture," Lareau carefully points out that the differences between working-class and middle-class child-rearing practices do not reflect radically different values and priorities but, instead, vastly different levels of income and wealth. Her evidence suggests that if economically disadvantaged parents had more money, their child-rearing strategies would change.

Divorce and Separation

Divorce rates increased steadily through the latter half of the twentieth century, yet they have leveled off in recent years. Attitudes have changed in tandem, with a stark decline in the proportion of Americans who disapprove of divorce. Whereas for centuries in the West, marriage was regarded as indissoluble, today, most countries are making divorce more easily available. Divorce rates (based on the number of divorces per 1,000 married men or women per year) have fluctuated in the United States in different periods (Figure 15.5). They rose, for example, after World War II, then dropped off to very low levels in the 1950s before increasing steeply from the 1960s to 1980 (thereafter tapering off and declining somewhat). It used to be common for divorced women to move back to their parents' homes; today, most set up their own households.

Divorce has a substantial impact on children. Since 1970, more than 1 million American children per year have been affected by divorce. In one calculation, about half of children born in 1980 became members of a one-parent family. Since two-thirds of women and three-fourths of men who are divorced eventually remarry, most of these children nonetheless grew up in a family environment, often acquiring new stepsiblings in the process. In 2016, less than 4 percent of children under 18 in the United States were not living with either parent. Remarriage rates are substantially lower for African Americans. Only 32 percent of Black women and 55 percent of Black

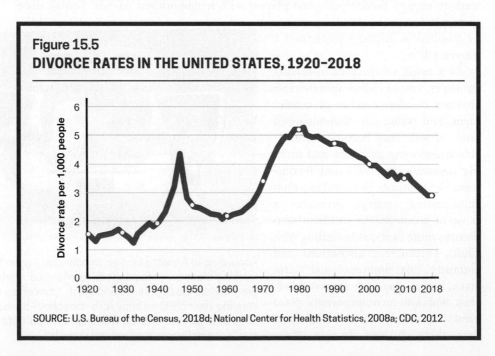

Figure 15.5
DIVORCE RATES IN THE UNITED STATES, 1920–2018

SOURCE: U.S. Bureau of the Census, 2018d; National Center for Health Statistics, 2008a; CDC, 2012.

men who divorce remarry within 10 years. White children are more than twice as likely as Black children (71 percent versus 34 percent) to reside in a home with two married parents (U.S. Bureau of the Census, 2017d).

Divorce also takes a significant toll on the spouses, although the financial toll is much more severe for women than men. According to one study, the living standards of divorced women and their children fell by 27 percent in the first year following the divorce settlement. The average standard of living of divorced men, by contrast, rose by 10 percent. However, more in-depth investigations find that the economic toll on men varies widely based on the spouses' financial arrangements prior to divorce and custody arrangements following divorce. For instance, one study found that men who were contributing more than 80 percent to family income prior to divorce improved their living standards after divorce by approximately 10 percent at the median, but that for men who contributed a smaller share to family income, divorce resulted in a reduction in living standards (McManus and DiPrete, 2001).

The psychological consequences of divorce, by contrast, are less profound than previously thought. Although divorced women may report heightened symptoms of depression and divorced men may experience increases in depressive symptoms and drinking behavior in the first year or two after divorce, most fare well in the longer term. Remarriage provides significant psychological benefits to men and both psychological and economic benefits to women. However, divorces marked by high levels of acrimony and conflicts regarding child support and child-rearing, for example, often bring psychological strain and distress to the ex-spouses even several years after their marriages have ended (Carr and Springer, 2010; Carr, Springer, and Williams, 2014).

Reasons for Divorce Divorce rates are not a direct indicator of marital unhappiness. For example, they do not include separated people who are not legally divorced. Moreover, unhappily married people may stay together because they believe in the sanctity of marriage, worry about the consequences of breaking up, decide to remain together for the sake of the children, or can't afford the costs of divorce proceedings and maintaining two separate residences.

Why did divorce become increasingly common throughout the latter half of the twentieth century? There are several reasons, which involve the wider changes in modern societies and social institutions. First, changes in the law have made divorce easier. Today, individuals may file for a "no-fault" divorce, where one or both parties want the marriage to end and there is no need to present evidence that one spouse is at "fault." Through the first six decades of the twentieth century, by contrast, one party had to prove that the other was at "fault," necessitating compelling evidence of abuse, neglect, infidelity, or other forms of mistreatment that could be difficult to prove from a legal standpoint (Marvell, 1989).

Second, except for a few wealthy people, marriage no longer reflects the desire to perpetuate property and status across generations. As women become more economically independent, it is easier for them to establish a separate household (Lee, 1982). The fact that little stigma is now attached to divorce is partly the result of these developments but also adds momentum to them. Third, there is a growing tendency to evaluate marriage in terms of personal satisfaction. Rising divorce rates do not indicate dissatisfaction with marriage as such, but an increased determination to make it a rewarding and satisfying relationship for the individual spouses, with a reduced desire to stay (unhappily) married "for the sake of the children" (Cherlin, 2009).

Divorce and Children The effects of divorce on children are difficult to gauge, and both public sentiment and scholarly research have evolved dramatically over the past four decades. Scholarly interest has shifted as well, with researchers moving away from the very specific question of how divorce affects children, and instead exploring how family instability—including parental divorces and cohabitation break-ups, repartnering, and other changes in the household—affect children's emotional, physical, and cognitive development. As we shall see in the sections below, social selection—or the factors that give rise to parental relationship instability—also may take a toll on child well-being.

Researchers also recognize that not all relationship dissolutions are the same. The conditions under which a parent dissolved their union also bear on child outcomes. For instance, how contentious the relationship is between the parents before separation; the ages of the children; whether there are siblings, grandparents, and other relatives; the children's relationship with their individual parents; and how frequently the children continue to see both parents—all affect the adjustment process.

Early studies of divorce found that children may suffer emotional anxiety right after their parents' separation, yet these effects are relatively short-lived. In a classic study, Judith Wallerstein and Joan Kelly (1980) tracked 131 children of 60 families in Marin County, California, after the separation of their parents. They contacted the children at the time of the divorce, a year and a half after, and five years after. Almost all the children experienced intense emotional disturbance at the time of the divorce. Preschool-age children were confused and frightened, blaming themselves for the separation. Older children better understood their parents' motives for the split but worried about its effects on their future and expressed anger over it. At the end of the five-year period, however, two-thirds were coping reasonably well with their home lives and their outside commitments. One-third remained dissatisfied, and expressed feelings of sadness and loneliness, even when the parent they were living with had remarried.

Wallerstein continued studying 116 of the original 131 subjects at the end of 10-year and 15-year periods (1980, 1989, 2000). She found that these children brought memories and feelings of their parents' divorce into their own romantic relationships. Almost all felt they had suffered from their parents' mistakes. Most of them shared a hope for something their parents had failed to achieve—a good, committed marriage based on love and faithfulness. Although many of them got married, the legacy of their parents' divorce lived with them. Those who appeared to manage the best had supportive relationships with one or both parents.

Can we reasonably conclude, then, that divorce is bad for children? Despite the many strengths of the Wallerstein study, including an unusually long follow-up period, it also had many limitations that undermine its generalizability. The parents and children studied all came from an affluent White area and might or might not have been representative of the wider population. Moreover, the families were self-selected: They had approached counselors. Those who actively seek counseling might be less (or more) able to cope with separation than those who do not. In general, studies based on "clinical" or help-seeking samples tend to overstate problems; by definition, the study participants were troubled enough that they had sought professional help.

More recent studies based on population samples found that people with divorced parents had slightly worse mental health, on average, than those whose parents stayed together but much of the difference had been identified in the children at age seven, before the families experienced divorce (Cherlin, Chase-Lansdale, and McRae, 1998). Recent syntheses of decades of research have identified several common consequences of divorce for children (Amato and Keith, 1991; Amato, 2001):

- Almost all children experience an initial period of intense emotional upset after their parents separate.
- Most resume normal development without serious problems within two years of the separation.
- A minority of children experience some long-term problems as a result of the breakup that may persist into adulthood.

Repartnering and Stepparenting

Before 1900, almost all marriages in the United States were first marriages. Most remarriages involved at least one widowed person. With the progressive rise in the divorce rate, the level of remarriage also began to climb, and in an increasing proportion of remarriages at least one person was divorced. Today, fully 40 percent of marriages involve at least one previously married person and 20 percent involve two previously married persons (Livingston, 2014b). Up to age 35, the majority of remarriages are between divorced people. After that age, the proportion of remarriages with widows or widowers rises (Sweeney, 2010). Over the past two decades, however, some divorced and widowed persons are turning their back on marriage, instead preferring to cohabit or to date steadily without living together, a relationship referred to as living apart together (LAT) (Brown and Wright, 2017).

While repartnering—whether through marriage or cohabitation—has become the norm for formerly married people, men are more likely than women to repartner, and more highly educated, financially secure people are more likely than their less advantaged peers to form new unions (Livingston, 2014). While remarriages provide many of the same benefits as first marriages, including love, companionship, and the economies of scale that come from sharing a household, they also are more likely to result in divorce (Cherlin, 2009). This statistic does not mean that second marriages are doomed to fail. Divorced people may have higher expectations of marriage than those who remain with their first spouses; hence, they may be more ready to dissolve new marriages. The second marriages that endure are usually more satisfying than the first.

The rise in rates of remarriage and cohabitations after one's first union dissolved has been accompanied by a rising number of stepfamilies. A **stepfamily** refers to a family in which at least one of the adults is a stepparent. Many who repartner become stepparents of children who regularly visit rather than live in the same household. By this definition, the number of stepfamilies is much greater than official statistics indicate because the statistics usually refer only to families with whom stepchildren live. Stepfamilies give rise to kin ties resembling those of some traditional societies in non-Western countries. Children may now have

> **stepfamily** A family in which at least one partner has children from a previous marriage, living either in the home or nearby.

four parents involved in their lives: their natural parents and their stepparents. Some stepfamilies regard all the children and close relatives (including grandparents) from previous marriages as part of the family.

Certain difficulties arise in stepfamilies. First, there is usually a biological parent living elsewhere whose influence over the child or children remains powerful. Cooperative relations between ex-partners often become strained when one or both remarry or enter a new cohabiting union. Consider a woman with two children who marries a man with two children, all six living together. If the "outside" parents demand the same times of visitation as previously, the pressures on the newly established family will likely be intense. It may prove impossible to have the new family all together on weekends.

Second, since most stepchildren belong to two households, the possibilities of clashes of habits and outlooks are considerable (Fine, Coleman, and Ganong, 1998). There are few established norms defining the relationship between stepparent and stepchild. Should a child call a new stepparent by name, or is "Dad" or "Mom" more appropriate? Should the stepparent play the same part in disciplining the children as the natural parent? How should a stepparent treat the new spouse of his or her previous partner when picking up the children? The difficulties in negotiating these decisions often intensify in later life as aging parents need to turn to their children for caregiving, and stepchildren may not willingly oblige (Sherman, Webster, and Antonucci, 2013).

Single-Parent Households

As a result of increasing divorce rates and births outside of marriage, more than half of all children will spend at least some time in a single-parent family. In 2016, 20.2 million children under the age of 18, representing about a quarter of all children, lived with one parent: 17.2 million with their mother and 3 million with their father. More than 80 percent of such families are headed by women because the mother usually obtains custody of the children after a divorce (in a few single-parent households, the individual, again almost always a woman, has never been married). There were 11 million single-parent households with children under age 18 in the United States in 2018, 8.8 million single-mother and 2.1 million single-father families (Figure 15.6), constituting about 30 percent of all families with children under 18 (U.S. Bureau of the Census, 2019a). They are among the poorest groups in contemporary society.

The category of single-parent households is internally diverse. For instance, more than half of widowed mothers are homeowners, but the majority of never-married single mothers live in rented accommodations. Single parenthood tends to be a changing state. For a person who is widowed, the break is clear-cut—although they have been living alone for some while if the partner was hospitalized before death. About 60 percent of single-parent households today, however,

The vast majority of the more than 20 million children living with one parent live with their mother.

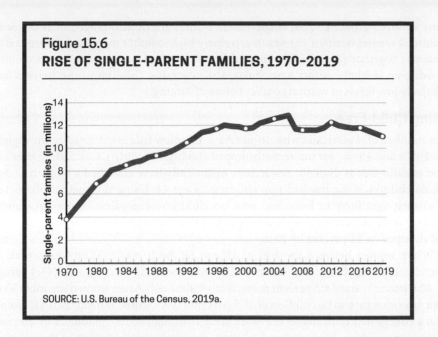

Figure 15.6
RISE OF SINGLE-PARENT FAMILIES, 1970–2019

SOURCE: U.S. Bureau of the Census, 2019a.

are the result of separation or divorce. In such cases, individuals may live together sporadically over a lengthy period.

Most people do not wish to be single parents, but a growing minority choose to
have a child or children without the support of a spouse or partner. "Single mothers
by choice" aptly describes some parents who possess sufficient resources to manage
as a single-parent household. According to the National Center for Health Statistics,
the most rapidly increasing rates of nonmarital births between the years 2007 and
2012 were to unmarried women ages 35 and older. During the same period, rates of
nonmarital births among younger women either declined or stayed stable. Women in
their late thirties and forties today recognize that they can have a child on their own
without facing the stigma that plagued single mothers in earlier generations. Many
also have the financial means to support a child on their own (Curtin, Ventura, and
Martinez, 2014).

For the majority of unmarried or never-married mothers, however, the reality is
different: There is a high correlation between the rate of births outside marriage and
indicators of poverty and social deprivation. These are key influences underlying the
high proportion of single-parent households among families of African American
background in the United States.

Sociologists debate the effect on children of growing up with a single parent. A
highly influential study by Sara McLanahan and Gary Sandefur (1994) rejects the
claim that children raised by only one parent do just as well as children raised by both
parents. A large part of the reason is economic: the sudden drop in income associated with divorce. Other reasons include inadequate parental attention and lack of
social ties. Separation or divorce weakens the connection between child and father,
and the link between the child and the father's network of friends and acquaintances.
The authors conclude it is a myth that strong support networks or extended family
ties are usually available to single mothers. Others have also pointed out that although

most children growing up in single-parent homes are disadvantaged, it is better for children's mental health if parents in extremely high-conflict marriages divorce rather than stay together (Amato, Loomis, and Booth, 1995). Divorce may benefit children growing up in high-conflict households while harming children whose parents have relatively low levels of marital conflict before divorcing.

Being Child-Free

The number of Americans who do not have children increased steadily throughout the 1980s and 1990s, yet has recently dipped (Livingston, 2015). Calculating precisely who is child-free is difficult; researchers historically have classified a woman as having no children if she has had zero children by age 44. Using this metric, proportion of women ages forty to forty-four with no children—regardless of marital status—climbed from 10 percent in 1986 to 15 percent in 1986 to 20 percent in 2006; the share had dropped to 14 percent by 2016.

White women between the ages of 15 and 50, both married and unmarried, are considerably more likely than Black or Hispanic women to be child-free (44.4 percent vs. 40.8 percent, and 44.2 percent respectively), although Asian women are more likely than any other race to be childless at 45.5 percent (U.S. Census Bureau, 2018a). Women with a college degree or higher are more likely than high school graduates or dropouts to have no children. Most studies find that a relatively small fraction of these women are involuntarily childless; with advances in health and technology, the proportion who cannot physically bear children is modest. Rather, the reasons are often social and psychological, including not having a partner with whom one would want to have a child, a preference for a child-free lifestyle, concerns about the environment and bringing a child into an unsafe world, and concerns about whether one has the financial and emotional wherewithal to have a child (Connidis and McMullin, 1996; Jacobson and Heaton, 1991).

Childlessness was historically viewed as a stigmatized identity, a mark of a "barren" woman or a woman who was "selfish" and prioritized her own career pursuits over motherhood (May, 1997). However, in recent decades, being child-free has been increasingly recognized as a status that is desirable and even preferable for many women and men. Those who do not have children have myriad opportunities to "give back" to the next generation by volunteering or caring for nieces or nephews, should they choose to do so (Sandler, 2013).

Same-Sex Couples

Many lesbian, gay, bisexual, transgender and queer (LGBTQ)-identified persons live in stable relationships as couples today. According to estimates from the 2010 Census, there are 131,729 same-sex married-couple households and 514,735 same-sex unmarried-partner households in the United States (U.S. Bureau of the Census Bureau, 2011p). Same-sex couples account for roughly 1 percent of households in the United States today (Lofquist, 2011).

The number of same-sex partners who are legally married is expected to skyrocket in the next decade. One of the most profound and rapid social changes of the twenty-first century has been the legalization of gay marriage. One important turning point occurred in June 2013, when the U.S. Supreme Court declared the Defense of Marriage Act (DOMA) to be unconstitutional in the landmark *Windsor v. United States of America*. DOMA, passed by Congress and signed by President Bill Clinton in 1996,

In June 2015, the U.S. Supreme Court legalized same-sex marriage, guaranteeing all same-sex married couples the same benefits as opposite-sex married couples at both the state and federal level.

had defined marriage as "a legal union between one man and one woman." Yet an even more important and path-breaking Supreme Court decision was handed down on June 26, 2015, when the Court ruled by a 5 to 4 vote that the U.S. Constitution guarantees individuals the right to same-sex marriage. Technically, the ruling says that states cannot prohibit the issuing of marriage licenses to same-sex couples or deny recognition of lawfully performed out-of-state marriage licenses to same-sex couples. This ruling invalidated same-sex marriage bans and effectively made same-sex marriage legal in every state in the nation (Liptak, 2015).

The United States is not alone in its rapidly growing acceptance of same-sex unions. A growing number of countries have legalized same-sex marriage, including Argentina, Canada, Ireland, Norway, Spain, Denmark, Uruguay, New Zealand, South Africa, Germany, and France, and, most recently, Northern Ireland, Ecuador, and Austria. Other parts of the world are slower to adapt; South Africa is the only nation in Africa where same-sex marriage is legally recognized (Human Rights Campaign, 2017). Similarly, Taiwan became the first country in Asia to legalize same-sex marriage nationwide in May 2019 and in 2020 Costa Rica became the first nation in Central America to legalize gay marriage.

The Bleak Side of Families

Family life encompasses the whole range of emotional experience. Family relationships—between spouses or cohabiting romantic partners, parents and children, brothers and sisters, or more distant relatives—can be warm and fulfilling. But they can equally be extremely tense, driving people to despair or imbuing them with anxiety and guilt. The dark side of family life belies the rosy images of family harmony frequently depicted in TV shows and commercials. It can take many forms. Among the most devastating are the incestuous abuse of children and domestic violence.

Family Violence

Violence within families is perpetuated primarily by men. The two broad categories of family violence are child abuse and intimate partner violence (IPV). Because of the sensitive and private nature of violence within families, it is difficult to obtain national data on levels of domestic violence. Data on child abuse are particularly sparse because of the cognitive development and ethical issues involved in studying child subjects. While family violence has been a concern throughout history, it was particularly acute during the COVID-19 pandemic, when stay-at-home orders meant that victims were essentially trapped at home with their abuser (Humphreys et al., 2020).

Child Abuse The most common definition of child abuse is serious physical harm (trauma, sexual abuse with injury, or willful malnutrition) with intent to injure. One national study of married or cohabiting adults indicated that about 3 percent of respondents abused their children, though cohabiting adults were no more or less likely to abuse their children than married couples (Brown, 2004; Sedlak and Broadhurst, 1996).

More recent statistics are based on national surveys of child-welfare professionals. However, these surveys miss children who are not seen by professionals or who are not reported to state agencies. Researchers estimate that as many as 50 to 60 percent of child deaths from abuse or neglect are not recorded (U.S. Department of Health and Human Services [DHHS], 2008). Statistics based on the National Child Abuse and Neglect Data System indicate that in 2018, an estimated 678,000 children were victims of abuse or neglect. Of these, 60.8 percent suffered neglect, 10.7 percent suffered physical abuse, and 7 percent were sexually abused; 77.5 percent of victims were maltreated by their parents. American Indian or Alaska Native children suffered the highest rate of abuse at 15.2 per 1,000 children in the population of the same race or ethnicity. Black children experienced the second highest rate at 14.0 per 1,000 children of the same race or ethnicity (Children's Bureau, 2020).

The effects of child abuse can linger for years, if not decades, after the child escapes the abusive situation. Recent studies show that adult men and women who suffered physical or sexual abuse in childhood are at elevated risk of multiple health conditions in midlife, including depression, chronic pain (Goldberg, 1994), sleep problems (Greenfield et al., 2011), and metabolic syndrome (Lee, Tsenkova, and Carr, 2014). Some evidence also suggests that victims of child abuse are more likely to commit abuse against partners and their own children, thus amplifying and perpetuating the cycle of abuse for future generations (Widom, Czaja, and DuMont, 2015).

Intimate Partner Violence Abuse of one's spouse or romantic partner is widespread in the United States. A 1985 study by Murray Straus and his colleagues found that IPV had occurred at least once in the past year in 16 percent of all marriages and at some point in the marriage in 28 percent of all marriages. This study does not, however, distinguish between severe acts, such as beating up and threatening with

CONCEPT CHECKS

1 What are four conditions that have contributed to changing family forms throughout the world?

2 Briefly describe changes in family structure in the United States since 1960.

3 Name two ways that Black and White families differ from each other.

4 What are the main reasons divorce rates increased sharply during the latter half of the twentieth century?

or using a gun or knife, and less severe acts, such as slapping, pushing, grabbing, or shoving. When the authors disaggregated this number, they found that approximately 3 percent of all husbands admitted perpetrating at least one act of severe violence on their spouse in the previous year; this figure is likely an underestimate.

More recent data, based on the National Intimate Partner and Sexual Violence Survey (NISVS), found even higher rates of severe violence, although these data refer to abuse among both married and nonmarried romantic partners. For instance, these data from 2011 show that 16 percent of women and 10 percent of men had experienced sexual violence by an intimate partner during their lifetimes. Severe physical violence by an intimate partner (including acts such as being hit with something hard, being kicked or beaten, or being burned on purpose) was reported by 22 percent of women and 14 percent of men during their lifetimes (Breiding et al., 2014).

Trend data can tell us about the prevalence of IPV, but not the nature of or context giving rise to abuse. Michael Johnson (1995) has identified two broad types of IPV: "patriarchal terrorism," which is perpetuated by feelings of power and control, versus "common couple violence," which generally relates to a specific incident and is not rooted in power or control. Sociological studies show that IPV is closely related to structural factors, including low levels of power among women, and cultural factors, including widespread acceptance of violence and beliefs that male power is equated with violence (Jewkes, 2002). Violence is particularly likely to occur among couples whose relationships are marked by conflict, especially conflicts about finances, jealousy, substance use, and the husband's belief that his wife is violating traditional gender roles. Women who are more empowered educationally, economically, and socially are most protected from IPV (Jewkes, 2002).

4   CONTEMPORARY QUESTIONS

As you have learned so far, family is an ever-evolving institution. As families change and new questions arise about these new forms, sociologists face the challenge of developing rigorous research to address these questions. Some of the most pressing questions facing family sociologists today focus on family forms that were once considered "nontraditional" or even "deviant," such as cohabiting families, same-sex couples with children, and persons who choose to forgo marriage and live life on their own. Each of these fascinating groups has grown rapidly in number over the past half-decade, prompting sociologists to explore new and evolving questions.

Is Cohabitation a Substitute for Marriage?

If current statistics are any indicator, roughly half of all students reading this textbook will live with their romantic partner before marrying. **Cohabitation**—in which a couple lives together in a sexual relationship without being married—has become increasingly widespread in most Western societies. Until a few decades ago, cohabitation was regarded as somewhat scandalous,

cohabitation Two people living together in a sexual relationship of some permanence without being married to one another.

but during the 1980s, the number of unmarried men and women sharing a household went up sharply. The proportion of young couples who cohabit has risen from 11 percent in the early 1970s to 44 percent in the early 1980s and slightly below 50 percent by 2013 (Copen, Daniels, and Mosher, 2013). Cohabitation has become widespread among college and university students, although they did not initiate this trend. Larry Bumpass and coworkers (Bumpass, Sweet, and Cherlin, 1991) found that the cohabitation phenomenon started with lower-educated groups in the 1950s—probably as a substitute for marriage, which may involve economic constraints.

While, for some, cohabitation today may be a substitute for marriage, for many, it is a stage in the process of relationship building that precedes marriage. Young people usually come to live together by drifting into it, rather than through calculated planning. A couple having a sexual relationship spend increasing time together, eventually giving up one of their individual homes. While in the 1980s and 1990s, cohabiting couples said their main reason for cohabiting was to "be sure they are compatible before marriage" (Bumpass, Sweet, and Cherlin, 1991), very different reasons are given by cohabiters in the early twenty-first century. One study of cohabiters found that the main reasons a couple moved in together were because the partners "loved spending time together" and to share love, intimacy, and space (see Table 15.2) (Rhoades, Stanley, and Markman, 2009).

Gender differences have been found when it comes to the reasons cited for cohabiting. One recent study conducted focus group interviews with cohabiting men and women and found that both genders said their primary motives for cohabiting included spending time together and evaluating compatibility. Men, however, were concerned about the loss of freedom that would come with marriage whereas women worried that cohabitation would further delay marriage. One of the most important factors for lower-income young adults is money; sharing an apartment helps save money, and cohabiting pushes off the expenses of a wedding (Huang et al., 2011; Sassler and Miller, 2018).

For most couples, cohabitation is a temporary state—leading either to marriage or a breakup. The likelihood that cohabitation leads to marriage has diminished for recent cohorts, while the chances that a cohabiting union breaks up has increased. Mernitz (2018) studied two cohorts of cohabitors, one born in the early 1980s and the other born in the late 1950s through early 1960s. Only one-third of the younger cohort of cohabiters married within five years of entering their union, compared to 41 percent among the older cohort. Similarly, younger cohorts are more likely to see their cohabiting union breakup (Guzzo, 2014; Kuo and Raley, 2016).

The chances of a cohabiting union transitioning to a first marriage are related to several socioeconomic factors. For instance, White cohabiting couples are more likely than their Black or Latinx counterparts to marry within three years. The likelihood of a first marriage resulting from cohabitation is positively associated with higher education, the absence of children during cohabitation, and higher family income. It is also more likely in communities with low male unemployment rates (Copen, Daniels, and Mosher, 2013; Bramlett and Mosher, 2002). These data are consistent with the claim that marriage vis à vis cohabitation has become an institution of economic and racial privilege (Cherlin, 2009; Sassler and Miller, 2018)

Increasingly, evidence shows that rather than being a "stage in the process" between dating and marriage, cohabitation may be an end in itself. For a very small subset, cohabitation is preferable to marriage. Long-time cohabiters with no plans to marry say

Table 15.2
REASONS FOR COHABITING

Researchers interviewed 123 heterosexual cohabiting couples and asked them how strongly they agreed or disagreed with each of 29 reasons for cohabiting with their partners. A score of 1 meant "strongly disagree," and a score of 7 meant "strongly agree." Here are the top five and bottom five reasons listed.

TOP FIVE REASONS

Because I love spending time with him/her.

Because I wanted to spend more time with him/her.

So that we could have more daily intimacy and sharing.

Because I want us to have a future together.

Because we were spending most nights together anyway.

BOTTOM FIVE REASONS

Because I had doubts about how well I could handle being in a serious relationship.

Because I was concerned that he/she might not make a good husband/wife and thought living together would be a good way to find out.

Because it was inconvenient to have some of my stuff at my place and some at my partner's.

Because I wanted to find out how much work he/she would do around the house before deciding about marriage.

Because I was concerned about how my partner handles money and wanted time to test out my concerns before marriage.

SOURCE: Rhoades et al., 2009.

that they prefer cohabitation due to their unease about the meanings associated with marriage and concerns about what marriage does to the relationship (Hatch, 2015).

For a rapidly growing number of couples, cohabitation is "marriage-like" in that it is a context for bearing and rearing children. In the early 1980s, 29 percent of all nonmarital births were to those in cohabiting unions. Recent estimates suggest that 62 percent of births to never-married women are to women in a cohabiting union (Lamidi, 2016). However, White and Latinx women are much more likely than Black women to have a birth in the context of a cohabiting relationship (Payne et al., 2012). Part of the reason more babies are born into cohabiting unions is that pregnant women today don't feel the same social pressure to marry their partner as they would have in past years. In the past, couples who got pregnant before they were married might have had a "shotgun"

Cohabitation has grown in popularity in the United States and other Western countries. For most couples, cohabitation is a temporary state.

marriage before the birth of the baby. Currently, however, only 11 percent of single women who have a pregnancy that results in a live birth are married by the time the child is born. Fewer unmarried couples—whether cohabiting or not—are marrying before the birth of their child. There has, however, been an increase in the rate at which unmarried women begin cohabiting with their partner once they find out they are pregnant: Currently, 11 percent of single women who have a pregnancy that results in a live birth begin cohabiting by the time the baby is born—the same number as marry to "legitimate" a pregnancy.

Although cohabitation is increasingly like marriage in that couples enter into it for love, companionship, support, and child-rearing, it does differ from marriage in one important way: Cohabitation is less stable than marriage. Whereas the likelihood of a first marriage ending in separation or divorce within 5 years is 20 percent, there is a 49 percent chance that a premarital cohabitation will break up within 5 years. Similarly, after 10 years, the probability of a first marriage ending is 33 percent, compared with 62 percent for cohabitations (Bramlett and Mosher, 2002). Because cohabiting unions tend to be less stable than marriage, children born to cohabiting parents experience family instability which can undermine their emotional and cognitive well-being (Manning, 2015). Part of this association is due to social selection; as we noted earlier, cohabiting families are more likely than married families to be poor, and poverty harms children in many ways. Cohabiting parents also tend to have less formal education—a key indicator of both economic and social resources—than married parents do. And cohabiting parent families don't have the same legal protections that married parent families have. However, more fine-grained analyses show that stable cohabiting families with two biological parents offer many of the same health, cognitive, and behavioral benefits that stable married biological parent families provide. Overall, scholars tend to believe that cohabitation is a highly varied experience, with some enjoying long-term satisfying unions that are "marriage-like" and provide a stable environment for their children, whereas with others living together as a trial, treating cohabitation as a more serious form of "dating."

Do Children Raised by Same-Sex Parents Fare Differently than Children Raised by Opposite-Sex Parents?

Alongside the increase in same-sex marriage, same-sex couples are forming families with children in unprecedented numbers. Sixteen percent of same-sex-couple households include children, out of which, 8.1 percent of same-sex male couples and over 24 percent of same-sex female couples raised children between 2014 and 2016 (Goldberg and Conron, 2018). According to the Williams Institute, an estimated 37 percent of LGBTQ-identified persons have been a parent, and an estimated 6 million children in the United States have lived with a gay parent at some point in their lives (Gates, 2013).

The legal, cultural, and technological landscapes facing gay parents and their children have changed dramatically in recent years. Increasingly tolerant attitudes toward LGBTQ persons have been accompanied by a growing tendency for courts to allocate custody of children to mothers living in lesbian relationships. All 50 states now allow LGBTQ individuals to adopt a child, although states vary in their policies regarding second-parent adoption (where one partner adopts a child and the partner applies to be a second or co-parent) and joint adoption (where the partners adopt a child together) (Family Equality Council, 2014). Although lesbian couples may have a child by donor insemination and gay men may rely on a surrogate to carry a biological child, same-sex couples are four times as likely as different-sex married or cohabiting couples to have an adopted child or stepchild (22 percent versus 5 percent). Just 73 percent of same-sex couples have biological children only (compared to roughly 90 percent of different-sex married or cohabiting couples). Roughly similar shares of same-sex and different-sex couples have both biological and adopted children or stepchildren (4 to 6 percent) (Gates, 2013).

Popular media images in recent years, such as the film *The Kids Are All Right* and TV show *Modern Family*, depict same-sex parents as providing the same love and guidance as heterosexual parents. But what do sociological studies show? Does parental sexual orientation shape how children turn out? This question continues to generate heated political debates today, although a strong consensus has emerged among scholars that the ability to parent effectively is not related to sexual orientation. Although one controversial study argued that children of parents who had ever had a same-sex relationship would go on to face greater adversity, this study has since been discredited for its serious methodological limitations (Regnerus, 2012).

The most persuasive and comprehensive studies to date, including the American Psychological Association's (2005) review of 60 studies and the American Academy of Pediatrics' (2013) seminal report, have concluded that "not a single study has found children of lesbian or gay parents to be disadvantaged in any significant respect relative to children of heterosexual parents" (Perrin, Cohen, and Caren, 2013). The 60 studies considered a range of outcomes, including school performance, social adjustment, and emotional well-being, concluding that children's well-being is much more closely tied to their parents'

Most sociological research finds that children raised by same-sex parents fare no better or worse than children raised by different-sex parents.

"sense of competence and security"—and the "social and economic support" parents provided their children—than sexual orientation.

For example, Rosenfeld (2010) finds that children of gay parents are just as likely as the children of straight parents to progress successfully throughout their school grades without being left back. Part of the reason children fare equally well regardless of parental sexual orientation is that sexual orientation has no bearing on one's capacity to be a loving parent. Moreover, children of same-sex couples usually share a common peer and school environment with children of heterosexual couples. As such, their experiences at school and with peers are very similar regardless of their parents' romantic preferences (Rosenfeld, 2010). Most studies also show no differences in the psychological adjustment of children raised by same-sex or opposite-sex parents; for example, several studies of teenagers show no differences in their depressive symptoms, anxiety, self-esteem, or risk of ADHD (attention deficit hyperactivity disorder) (Baiocco et al., 2018; Adams and Light, 2015; Gattrell and Bos, 2010; Lamb, 2012).

Although children of either gay or straight parents are not significantly advantaged or disadvantaged, some studies point out a small number of differences. For example, sociologists Judith Stacey and Timothy Biblarz (2001) reviewed 21 studies dating back to the 1980s and found that children in gay households are more likely to buck stereotypical male-female behavior. For example, boys raised by lesbians appear to be less aggressive and more nurturing than boys raised in heterosexual families. Daughters of lesbians are more likely to aspire to become doctors, lawyers, engineers, and astronauts. The balance of evidence shows that children of gay parents are just as happy, healthy, and academically successful as their peers raised by heterosexual parents, and they may have more flexible views of gender and gender-typed behaviors.

Are Single People Less Happy than Married People?

The broad category of "single" encompasses both people who have never married and those who have married but are now single due to divorce, separation, or widowhood. The number of people living alone in U.S. society has increased dramatically in recent decades. Several factors have combined to create this trend. First, people are marrying later than ever. That means that more people in their twenties, thirties, and even forties are living alone, waiting for the "right one" to come along. Second, the rise and stabilization of divorce rates over the past half century mean that many more people are living on their own when their marriage ends. Third, the "graying" of the U.S. population (see Chapter 12) is accompanied by growing numbers of older adults whose partners have died and who now live alone as widows and widowers, as well as rising numbers of persons who divorce in later life and prefer not to repartner. Fourth, the "stigma" of being single has diminished, due in part to television shows such as *Sex and the City*, which glamorized the lifestyles of "single and fabulous" women. As such, many more Americans are happily choosing to live their lives on their own (Byrne and Carr, 2005; Klinenberg, 2012a).

Yet are people really happy on their own, or are they better off being married? A large body of literature dating back to Émile Durkheim's classic *Suicide* (1966; orig. 1897) argues that social ties, especially marriage and parenthood, are essential to one's physical, social, and emotional well-being. Recent contemporary studies also show that divorced and widowed people report more sickness, depression, and anxiety compared with their married counterparts, although much of this disadvantage reflects the strains that precede a marital transition (such as a spouse's illness or marital strife), as well as the strains that follow from the dissolution, such as financial worries or legal battles (Carr and Springer, 2010).

But what about people who are long-term singles or who choose to live alone without a spouse or partner? To date, these individuals are relatively rare; more than 90 percent of American adults do ultimately marry. However, researchers have projected that as many as one in five Millennials will never marry. Many reasons are given, including the four reasons cited in this section's opening paragraph. Millennials (those born in the 1980s and thereafter) are particularly likely to face financial obstacles to marry, given their high levels of unemployment, school debt, and tendency to live with their parents rather than on their own when in their twenties (Wang and Parker, 2014).

Yet is life-long singlehood a bad thing? Are singles' lives marked by loneliness and desolate evenings at home eating frozen dinners alone? Research by sociologist Eric Klinenberg (2012a) and others finds that living alone can "promote freedom, personal control, and self-realization—all prized aspects of contemporary life" (Klinenberg, 2012b). After interviewing more than 300 people who live alone, he found that they had more rather than less social interaction than their married counterparts, and much of their social interactions were those they sought out by choice: encounters with friends, volunteering, arts events, classes, and other meetings that rounded out their lives. These patterns hold among older adults and younger adults alike. As Klinenberg observed, for many people, living alone and being able to choose how and with whom they spend their time is a sought-after luxury.

Taken together, research showing that people who live alone (by choice) are no better or worse off than their partnered peers underscores one of the core themes of sociology of families: There is no one "best" or "typical" way in which Americans arrange their social lives. Rather, the freedom to choose one's relationships is essential to one's happiness.

CONCEPT CHECKS

1 What differences have researchers detected when comparing the children of gay versus straight parents?

2 Contrast the social lives and well-being of persons who live alone versus those who live with a spouse or partner.

THE BIG PICTURE

Chapter 15
Families and Intimate Relationships

1 **Basic Concepts**

p. 565

2 **Theoretical and Historical Perspectives on Families**

p. 567

p. 565
p. 567

LEARNING OBJECTIVES

Learn how sociologists define and describe families.

Review the development of sociological thinking about families. Learn how the family has changed over the last 500 years, and the social and economic factors underlying these changes.

TERMS TO KNOW

family • kinship • marriage • nuclear family • extended family • families of orientation • families of procreation • matrilocal • patrilocal • monogamy • polygamy • polygyny • polyandry

primary socialization • personality stabilization • affective individualism

CONCEPT CHECKS

1. Contrast a family of orientation and a family of procreation.
2. Provide an example of a nuclear versus an extended family.
3. What are several alternatives to monogamy?
4. Why have rates of polygamy declined in contemporary society?

1. According to the functionalist perspective, what are the two main functions of the family?
2. How do symbolic interactionist approaches to studying family differ from functionalist approaches? What are two critiques of the symbolic interactionist perspective?
3. According to feminist perspectives, what three aspects of family life are sources of concern? Why are these three aspects troubling to feminists?
4. What characteristics distinguished the three historical stages of family development, as articulated by historical sociologist Lawrence Stone?

Exercises: Thinking Sociologically

1. Compare the structures and lifestyles among contemporary White non-Hispanic, Asian American, Hispanic, and African American families using the text's presentation.

2. Increases in cohabitation and single-parent households suggest that marriage may be losing ground in contemporary society. However, this chapter claims that marriage and the family remain firmly established social institutions. Explain the rising patterns of cohabitation and single-parent households, and show how these seemingly paradoxical trends can be reconciled with the claims offered by this textbook.

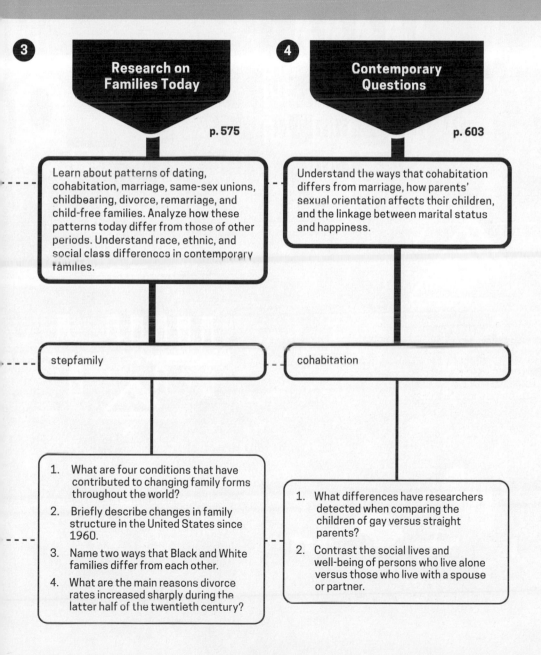

3

Research on Families Today

p. 575

Learn about patterns of dating, cohabitation, marriage, same-sex unions, childbearing, divorce, remarriage, and child-free families. Analyze how these patterns today differ from those of other periods. Understand race, ethnic, and social class differences in contemporary families.

stepfamily

1. What are four conditions that have contributed to changing family forms throughout the world?
2. Briefly describe changes in family structure in the United States since 1960.
3. Name two ways that Black and White families differ from each other.
4. What are the main reasons divorce rates increased sharply during the latter half of the twentieth century?

4

Contemporary Questions

p. 603

Understand the ways that cohabitation differs from marriage, how parents' sexual orientation affects their children, and the linkage between marital status and happiness.

cohabitation

1. What differences have researchers detected when comparing the children of gay versus straight parents?
2. Contrast the social lives and well-being of persons who live alone versus those who live with a spouse or partner.

16

Education

The admissions process at major American universities has

A — always favored prettier or more handsome people.

B — always favored minorities.

C — always favored athletes.

D — undergone serious revision over time.

TURN THE PAGE FOR THE CORRECT ANSWER.

The correct answer is *d*, because the criteria for admission to universities have changed over time. In the early twentieth century, college admissions began to undergo a series of major transformations, for reasons that were kept discreetly out of the public eye (Karabel, 2005; Gladwell, 2005). In 1905, the SAT was instituted, and for the first time, people started getting into college on the basis of standardized tests. Within a few years, the Harvard class had become 15 percent Jewish, as Jews (not unlike Asians today) excelled at the standardized test in disproportionate numbers. Sociologists to this day disagree about whether this success can be explained by cultural characteristics or economic advantages that even some relatively poor ethnic and religious minorities experience in comparison with many other minority groups that don't do as well.

Nevertheless, reflecting the wider anti-Semitism of the era, the people who were running Harvard looked at this outcome as a very undesirable turn of events. The administrators drew an analogy between the university and hotels in upstate New York—first the Jews would arrive, then the Gentiles would leave, and then the Jews would leave and nobody would be left or want to attend the school anymore (Zimmerman, 2010). So, Harvard determined that it needed to find another way of conducting admissions. Rather than putting quotas on Jews, they decided to change to a system of admissions very much like the one we know today. They would start to look at "the whole person," rather than give advantages to people simply because they'd done well on a standardized test. In recent years, these institutions have generally transitioned to looking for "best graduates" rather than "best students"; that is, not students who will excel academically in college, but instead, those who will become successful after college (Gladwell, 2005). Excellent high school students compete for a limited number of spots at elite American colleges, with many able candidates being rejected in favor of athletes or student leaders in lower academic standing.

LEARNING OBJECTIVES

1 Basic Concepts

Learn sociologists' explanations for achievement gaps among different groups of students.

2 Sociological Theories of Education

Understand the social functions of schooling. Learn three major sociological perspectives on the role of schooling in society.

3 Research on Education Today

Become familiar with the most important research on whether education reduces or perpetuates inequality. Learn the social and cultural influences on educational achievement.

4 Unanswered Questions

Learn about some of the current educational issues that concern sociologists, including the debate over the sources of IQ, the merits of homeschooling, and the benefits of international education.

THE ANSWER IS D.

Today, it seems natural that a college would want to get to know a student as a whole person. In your college application, you had to write an essay that helped define you as a total human being. You may have tried to show what an interesting person you are by discussing the clubs you were a part of and the sports you participated in. While answer *c* is not entirely correct, athletes may experience an advantage in admissions over their peers, even when their GPAs and SAT scores are lower, particularly when they are seen as contributing to the college's extramural sports programs (in many universities, competitive sports teams can produce significant revenues). When Ivy League schools switched to the new system, they would also send representatives to various schools around the country to interview prospective students. They didn't want too many "nerds." They wanted well-rounded, good-looking people—future leaders who would have an impact on the country and who would make these schools look good in return. And so they would conduct interviews and keep notes on whether an applicant was tall, handsome, or pretty (by whatever standard that was determined).

There were things the admissions office simply didn't like: people with big ears, for example. Short people were also undesirable, as recommendation files from that time indicate. In the mid-1950s, Harvard, Princeton, and Yale were actually keeping records on the number of men who entered the freshman class who were over six feet tall. Today, all schools release records about their incoming freshman classes, but they are more likely to keep track of race, class, and gender variables than height or ear size. Thus, answer choice *a* is incorrect if we are considering the present day; though physical appearance was at one time a salient aspect of college admissions criteria, it is generally no longer a consideration. Moreover, even the use of SATs is now being reconsidered by many colleges and universities, since there is evidence that performance on such tests is closely linked to family income, education, and race, as discussed below. Some 50 accredited higher education institutions announced in 2018 and 2019 that they were dropping SAT requirements, bringing the total to more than a thousand, including more than half of the highest-rated colleges in US News & World Report, and resulting in greater student body diversity (Strauss, 2019). All in all, the trend at universities has been toward creating a level playing field for applicants of all income levels, races, and educational background and thus reducing inequalities in society at large.

1 BASIC CONCEPTS

Before we delve into complex theories of the ways that education shapes our everyday lives, we first define several key concepts that are essential to our understanding of this major social institution.

Achievement Gap: Components, Patterns, and Explanations

One of the core concepts in the sociology of education is the notion of educational inequalities, or **achievement gap** among different groups of students. This gap refers to the fact that certain groups, such as poor or working-class students, and certain minority groups, tend to receive lower scores on standardized tests and other measures of academic success (e.g., high school graduation rates and college admission rates) than do their more privileged counterparts. Sociologists have sought to explain achievement gaps in a variety of ways and have highlighted the importance of influences such as social background—particularly the educational and economic resources of one's parents—as well as intelligence.

Sociologist Sean Reardon has done extensive research on the achievement gap, identifying its sources and how it has changed over time. Throughout the second half of the twentieth century, the achievement gap between the richest and poorest children—those living in households in the 10th and 90th percentile of income distribution, respectively—increased dramatically. For children born in 2001, the class-based achievement gap is 30 to 40 percent greater than it was for children born in the 1970s. Today, the gap between rich and poor students is nearly twice as large as the well-documented achievement gap between Black and White ones (Reardon, 2011, 2012).

Four explanations have been offered for the stark and growing socioeconomic gap in achievement (Reardon, 2012). First, middle- and upper-middle-class parents tend to invest more heavily in their children's cognitive development (by reading stories, playing word games, and consciously engaging them in activities explicitly related to intellectual development) than in their health, nutrition, or safety. Sociologist Julia Wrigley's analysis of parenting magazine articles throughout the twentieth century found that in recent decades, children's cognitive development has become a major concern of middle-class parents, who see success in school as essential to a successful career (Wrigley, 1989). Second, income inequality has increased sharply throughout the late twentieth century, as we learned in Chapter 8. Reardon (2012) argues that those with greater income can buy the goods and services needed to help their child thrive in school. The benefits accrued to the "haves" versus "have-nots" have

Parents with greater income are able to buy goods and services, such as expensive test-prep courses, that help their children succeed in school.

thus escalated considerably. Third, income is related to a range of other social resources that enable parents to support their children's intellectual development. Parents with education possess the specific skills and knowledge needed to help their children's performance in school. Income, too, is related to family structure, as we saw in Chapter 15. Co-residential married parents may have more time to engage children in activities such as reading or writing (Reardon, 2012). Finally, residential segregation on the basis of income rose throughout the late twentieth century. Today's wealthier families can afford homes in safer neighborhoods with higher-quality schools and more enrichment activities. As we shall see later in this chapter, neighborhoods and schools have the power to shape what, how, and how successfully children learn.

intelligence Level of intellectual ability, particularly as measured by IQ (intelligence quotient) tests.

emotional intelligence The ability to identify, assess, and control the emotions of oneself or others.

IQ (intelligence quotient) A score attained on tests of symbolic or reasoning abilities.

Cognitive and Noncognitive Resources

Standardized and IQ tests may seem like simple concepts, but both are complex and potentially controversial. For years, psychologists, geneticists, statisticians, and others have debated whether any single human capability can be called **intelligence**, and if so, whether it rests on innately determined differences. The term intelligence as it is usually employed is difficult to define because it covers qualities that may be unrelated to each other. We might suppose, for example, that the "purest" form of intelligence is the ability to solve abstract mathematical puzzles. However, people who are very good at such puzzles sometimes show low capabilities in other areas, such as history or art. Scholars today increasingly believe in the existence of multiple forms of intelligence that pertain to different areas, such as art, music, language, interpersonal relations, and spatial skills, to name a few. Some scholars have also argued that **emotional intelligence**—generally defined as the ability to identify, assess, and control the emotions of oneself or others (Goleman, 1996)—is as important to professional and personal success as is the more intellect-based type (Gardner and Hatch, 1989).

Because the concept of intelligence has proven so resistant to definition, some psychologists have proposed (and many educators have by default accepted) that it should simply be regarded as "what the **IQ (intelligence quotient)** tests measure." Most IQ tests consist of a mixture of conceptual and computational problems. The tests are constructed in a way that the average score falls at 100 points: Thus anyone scoring below that number is labeled

CONCEPT CHECKS

1 Name at least three factors that contribute to the high school dropout rate.

2 What is the "achievement gap"?

3 Define and contrast different types of intelligence.

"below-average intelligence," while anyone scoring above it is viewed as "above-average intelligence." Despite the fundamental difficulty of measuring intelligence, IQ tests are widely used in research studies as well as in schools and businesses. Nonetheless, sociologists remain critical and wary of the concept. Researchers have found that IQ is powerfully affected by the socioeconomic resources of one's parents, thus calling into question the belief that intelligence is "innate" or "inborn" (Fischer et al., 1996). Later in this chapter, we will delve further into the debates surrounding the meaning of, and influences on, intelligence.

2 SOCIOLOGICAL THEORIES OF EDUCATION

When we think of education, we tend to see it from an individual perspective. We may think of our own reasons for attending college: to cultivate our intelligence, enjoy a fun and social "college experience," or prepare for a career. We also tend to think of education as a means of upward mobility. But sociologists look beyond the individual student and his or her goals to connect these to the larger social functions of schools. We discuss three major sociological theories of the role schooling plays in the larger society: schooling as a process of assimilation or acculturation; schooling as a credentialing mechanism; and schooling as a process of social, or cultural, reproduction.

Assimilation

The first perspective, schooling as a process of assimilation, focuses on what might be called the "official" curriculum and looks at questions such as how learning a common language and the facts of a common history and geography create a sense of "affinity" among members of society, which is something less than full consensus (Shils, 1972). The official curriculum promotes feelings of nationalism and is instrumental in the development of national societies, constituted of citizens from different regions who would then know the same history and speak a common language (Ramirez and Boli, 1987; Shils, 1972). In this approach, the content of education is particularly important in creating a common culture. For example, public schools historically have taught the children of immigrants about "American" foods, holidays, legends, and heroes to help them (and their immigrant parents) become fully steeped in our nation's culture. But even children whose parents are part of the country's dominant culture depend on the official curriculum to develop an image of themselves as Americans with a common history.

Credentialism

A second influential perspective is credentialism. Adherents to this way of thinking place less emphasis on the content of an official curriculum. They argue that the specific skills and information that students learn in the classroom are much less relevant to their later achievements than the actual diploma. The primary social function of mass education derives from the need for degrees to determine one's credentials for a job, even if the work involved has nothing to do with the education one has received (Collins, 1979). Over time, the practice of credentialism results in demands for higher credentials, which require higher levels of educational attainment. Jobs that 30 years ago would have required a high school diploma, such as that of a sales representative, now require a college degree. Since educational attainment is closely related to class position, credentialism reinforces the class structure within a society.

Hidden Curriculum

A third perspective, described as "critical" or Marxist, places the emphasis on social reproduction. In the context of education, social reproduction refers to the ways in which schools help perpetuate social and economic inequalities across the generations. A number of sociologists have argued that the hidden curriculum is the mechanism through which social reproduction occurs. The **hidden curriculum** refers to the idea that students from different social class

Practices such as the Pledge of Allegiance help promote feelings of nationalism among students.

backgrounds are provided different types of education, in terms of both curricular materials and the kinds of interactions in which their teachers engage them. More specifically, the notion of the hidden curriculum suggests that the expansion of education was brought about by employers' needs for certain personality characteristics in their workers—self-discipline, dependability, punctuality, obedience, and the like—which are all taught in schools.

In their classic study of social reproduction, Samuel Bowles and Herbert Gintis (1976) provide an example of how the hidden curriculum works. They argue that modern education is a response to the economic needs of industrial capitalism. Schools help provide the technical and social skills industrial enterprise requires, and they instill discipline and respect for authority in the labor force. Schools also socialize children to get along with one another. Being able to "play well with others" is, after all, an important characteristic of a good worker.

hidden curriculum Traits of behavior or attitudes that are learned at school but not included in the formal curriculum—for example, gender differences.

Some sociologists view schooling as a response to the need for disciplined and obedient workers.

Authority relations in school, which are hierarchical and place strong emphasis on obedience, directly parallel those dominating the workplace. The rewards and punishments held out in school also replicate those found in the world of work. Schools help motivate some individuals toward "achievement" and "success" while discouraging others, who find their way into low-paying jobs. You might even have noticed this in your own high school, where students from wealthier backgrounds took college-prep courses, while their classmates from more disadvantaged backgrounds were tracked into vocational programs. As noted earlier, institutions of higher learning tend to favor applicants whom they believe are most likely to have successful careers after graduation.

A cruder way of putting this idea is that schools facilitate the ruling class's need to exploit a docile or cooperative workforce. Here the emphasis is on the fact that much of what students learn in school has nothing directly to do with the formal content of lessons. Schools, by the nature of the discipline and regimentation they entail, tend to teach students an uncritical acceptance of the existing social order. These lessons are not consciously taught; they are implicit in school procedures and organization. Thus, the hidden curriculum teaches children from underprivileged backgrounds that their role in life is "to know their place and to sit still with it" (Illich, 1983). Children spend long hours in school, and they learn a great deal more in the school context than is contained in the lessons they are actually taught. Children get an early taste of what the world of work will be like, learning that they are expected to be punctual and to apply themselves diligently to the tasks that those in authority set for them. From this perspective, even if a student in a poor inner-city school learned very little in her classes, the basic training she received in arriving on time for class would end up serving her well as a worker at a fast-food restaurant. Such an analysis can be quite depressing, but it may be a realistic way of understanding the place of education in the lives of such people.

Adherents to this perspective don't completely dismiss the content of the official curriculum. They accept that the development of mass education has had many beneficial consequences. Illiteracy rates are low compared with premodern times, and schooling provides access to learning experiences that are intrinsically self-fulfilling. Yet because education has expanded mainly as a response to economic needs, the school system falls far short of what enlightened reformers had hoped it would achieve. That is, according to this perspective, schooling has not become the "great equalizer"; rather, within the current economic and political system, schooling reproduces social-class stratification.

Pierre Bourdieu and Cultural Capital

cultural capital The advantages that well-to-do parents usually provide their children.

Another seminal figure who wrote about education and reproduction is French sociologist Pierre Bourdieu, who argued that schools reproduce social-class inequality by rewarding certain cultural norms over others (1984, 1988). Bourdieu's focus on the role of culture in the process of reproduction distinguished his theory from a strict Marxist analysis that focused on how schools mirrored and reproduced economic-class structures. For this reason, he used the term *cultural reproduction.* In relation to his theory of cultural reproduction, Bourdieu argued that people could possess many kinds of capital other than financial capital. Specifically, he was concerned with the existence of what he called **cultural capital**. That is, his theory of cultural reproduction proposes that middle- and upper-class children come to schools with a certain kind of cultural capital—speech patterns, demeanors, tastes, and so on—that the school values, and thus rewards. Bourdieu argues that children from low-income or working-class homes do not possess these same cultural characteristics and thus are placed at a disadvantage in schools.

Another important concept Bourdieu offers is the notion of habitus, which refers to a class-based set of dispositions, such as taste, language use, and demeanor. For Bourdieu, these dispositions are internalized unconsciously through social practices within one's social group. Put simply, poor and working-class children are socialized into a particular habitus—one that is not valued within the school system. In arguing that working-class individuals are unconsciously socialized into a working-class culture (and therefore are not likely to obtain the dispositions required for school success), Bourdieu, like Bowles and Gintis, ultimately proposes a theory of reproduction in which the cycle of domination seems unbreakable.

These kinds of theories have been challenged by the notion of schools as contested spaces (Aronowitz and Giroux, 1985; Willis, 1977). It has been proposed that social reproduction does not happen without struggle or opposition from oppressed groups. Written over 40 years ago but still important today, Paul Willis's influential ethnographic study of working-class British youth known as "the lads" shows how working-class students exhibit an implicit understanding that schooling is not structured to benefit their group (industrial factory workers) as a whole. The lads express their understanding that schooling is not designed to better their own conditions as members of the working class by embracing a working-class culture that valorizes manual labor and a counter-school culture. In doing so, they participate in the reproduction of

Two students at a vocational high school in Florida learn how to wire a light switch. Career academies such as this one encourage students to work toward national industry certifications.

Table 16.1
APPLYING SOCIOLOGY TO EDUCATION

CONCEPT	APPROACH TO EDUCATION	CURRENT APPLICATION
Assimilation	Education is important in creating a common culture.	The use of curricula in high schools across the country that instill a common set of values in students regardless of their racial, ethnic, and religious differences.
Credentialism	The diploma one gets at graduation is more important than what a person learns in school.	Parents going to exorbitant lengths and costs to hire consultants who will help their children get into elite undergraduate schools despite the fact that they can learn as much at a local state school.
Hidden Curriculum	Unspoken academic, social, and cultural messages that are communicated to students while they are in school.	Popular fashions and trends in minority communities that are forbidden by school authorities, thereby implying that they are inferior to those of mainstream culture (e.g., bans on baggy pants).
Cultural Capital	Knowledge and tastes possessed by the elites that are mainly learned at home and not taught in school. These can include highbrow culture like classical music or a rich vocabulary, or superior knowledge of how institutions work.	Parents' knowledge of the college admissions process can give their children a significant edge over less advantaged children of equal ability.

CONCEPT CHECKS

1 Contrast credentialism and social-reproduction perspectives on education.

2 How does the hidden curriculum serve to perpetuate social and economic inequalities?

3 What did Pierre Bourdieu mean by "cultural capital"?

their own class subordination. Willis suggests that these insights demonstrate that working-class youth are not passive dupes in the process of reproduction. Willis also suggests that the emphasis on the lads being in control of their destiny points to possibilities for organized resistance. A number of subsequent studies of resistance in schooling in the United States (Foley, 1994; McLaren, 1985; McLeod, 1995; Solomon, 1992; Valenzuela, 1999) have expanded our understanding of schools as contested spaces.

3   RESEARCH ON EDUCATION TODAY

In the previous sections, we learned that the purpose and function of schooling have been viewed from a variety of perspectives. On the one hand, education has consistently been seen as a means of equalization. Access to universal education, it has been argued, could help reduce disparities in wealth and power. On the other hand, some theorists have argued that schools serve to perpetuate, or reproduce, inequalities. Are educational opportunities equal for everyone? Has education in fact proven to be a great equalizer?

There is a vast amount of research that examines these questions. Next, we outline some of the important research related to educational equality and differential outcomes (when one group consistently outperforms another group in terms of educational achievement). The concepts offered here help to frame recent debates surrounding education in the United States. We also report on recent studies that help us understand the development and proliferation of the Internet, and "digital gaps," or disparities in its access and use.

Macrosocial Influences on Student Outcomes: Do Schools and Neighborhoods Matter?

Many of us believe that if we are intelligent and hardworking, and receive encouragement from our teachers, parents, and peers, we can succeed in school. This belief is true—to a point—but the types of schools we attend, the types of classes we take, and the experiences we have within those schools also may affect our lives. The notion that schools may matter dates back to the classic studies of sociologist James Coleman in the 1960s. The ways that schools shape our daily lives both today and in our futures have been documented dramatically by author Jonathan Kozol. Yet a large and controversial body of research on school tracking emphasizes that even within a single school, one's outcomes are powerfully shaped by the types of classes to which one is assigned.

Coleman's Study of Between-School Effects in American Education

The study of "between-school effects," or the ways students' experiences at School A differ from those at School B, has been the focus of sociological research for more than five decades. One of the classic investigations of educational inequality was undertaken in the United States in the 1960s. The Civil Rights Act of 1964 required the commissioner of education to prepare a report on educational inequalities resulting from differences in ethnic background, religion, and national origin. James Coleman, a sociologist, was appointed director of the research program. The outcome was a study based on one of the most extensive research projects ever carried out in sociology (Coleman et al., 1966).

Information was collected on more than half a million pupils who were given a range of achievement tests assessing verbal and nonverbal abilities, reading levels, and mathematical skills. Sixty thousand teachers also completed forms providing data for about 4,000 schools. The report found that a large majority of children went to schools that effectively segregated Black students from White students. Almost 80 percent of schools attended by White students contained only 10 percent or fewer African American students. White and Asian American students scored higher on achievement tests than did Blacks and other ethnic minority students. Coleman had supposed his results would also show that predominantly African American schools had worse facilities, larger classes, and more inferior buildings than predominantly White schools. But, surprisingly, the results showed far fewer differences of this type than had been anticipated.

Coleman, therefore, concluded that the material resources provided in schools made little difference to educational performance; the decisive influence was the children's backgrounds. The report stated, "Inequalities imposed on children by their home, neighborhood, and peer environment are carried along to become the inequalities with which they confront adult life at the end of school" (Coleman et al., 1966). However, some evidence suggested that students from deprived backgrounds who formed close friendships with those from more favorable circumstances were likely to be more successful educationally.

Not long after Coleman's study, Christopher Jencks and coworkers (1972) produced an equally celebrated work that reviewed empirical evidence accumulated on education and inequality up to the end of the 1960s. Jencks reaffirmed two of the earlier study's conclusions: First, educational and occupational attainment are governed mainly by family background and non-school factors, and second, on their own, educational reforms can produce only minor effects on existing inequalities. Jencks's work has been criticized on methodological grounds, but the study's overall conclusions remain persuasive. Subsequent research has tended to confirm them.

Children Left Behind

Between 1988 and 1990, the journalist Jonathan Kozol studied schools in about 30 neighborhoods around the United States. He used no special logic in choosing the schools, except that he went where he happened to know teachers, principals, or ministers. What startled him most was the segregation within these schools and the inequalities among them. Kozol brought these terrible conditions to the attention of the American people in his books, including *Savage Inequalities* (1991) and *Amazing Grace* (1995).

In his passionate opening chapter of *Savage Inequalities*, Kozol first took readers to East St. Louis, Illinois, a city that was 98 percent Black, had no regular trash collection, and had few jobs. Three-quarters of its residents were living on welfare at the time. City residents were forced to use their backyards as garbage dumps, which attracted a plague of flies and rats during the hot summer months. One resident told Kozol about "rats as big as puppies" that lived in his mother's yard. City residents also contended with fumes from two major chemical plants in the city. Another public health problem resulted from raw sewage, which regularly backed up into people's homes. East St. Louis had some of the sickest children in the United States, with extremely high rates of infant death, asthma, and poor nutrition and extremely low rates of immunization. Only 55 percent of the children had been fully immunized for polio, diphtheria, measles, and whooping cough. Among the city's other social problems were crime, dilapidated housing, poor health care, and lack of education.

Kozol showed how the problems of the city often spilled over into the schools—in this case, literally. Over the course of two weeks, raw sewage backed up into the school on three occasions, each time requiring the evacuation of students and the cancellation of classes. Kozol documented other problems, which he argued stemmed from inadequate and disparate funding. Teachers often had to hold classes without chalk or paper. One teacher commented, "Our problems are severe. I don't even know where to begin. I have no materials with the exception of a single textbook given to each child. If I bring in anything else—books or tapes or magazines—I bring it in myself. The high school has no VCRs. They are such a crucial tool. So many good things run on public television. I can't make use of anything I see unless I unhook my VCR and bring it into school. The AV equipment in the school is so old that we are pressured not to use it." Comments from students reflected the same concerns. "I don't go to physics class, because my lab has no equipment," one student said. Another added, "The typewriters in my typing class don't work." Only 55 percent of the students in this high school ultimately graduate, about one-third of whom go on to college.

Kozol also wrote about the other end of the inequality spectrum, taking readers into a wealthy suburban school in Westchester County, outside New York City. This school had 96 computers for the 546 students. Most students studied a foreign language for four or five years. Two-thirds of the senior class were enrolled in an advanced placement (AP) class. Kozol visited an AP class to ask students about their perceptions of inequalities within the educational system. Students at this school were well aware of the economic advantages that they enjoyed at both home and school. In regard to their views about less-privileged students, the general consensus was that equal spending among schools was a worthy goal, but it would probably make little difference because poor students lacked motivation and would fail because of other problems. These students also realized that equalizing spending could have adverse effects on their school. As one student said, "If you equalize the money, someone's got to be short-changed. I don't doubt that [poor] children are getting a bad deal. But do we want *everyone* to get a mediocre education?"

More than two decades later, Kozol went back and revisited the neighborhoods and children he studied to find out what had happened to them. His portraits are often depressing, with many of the children growing up to be troubled adults. Their lives often were derailed by alcohol abuse, unwanted pregnancies, murders, prison time, and even death by suicide. Yet Kozol did find that a handful of the students succeeded despite the odds. Most of these resilient children had been fortunate to have especially devoted parents, support from their religious community, or a serendipitous scholarship opportunity. As Kozol noted, "These children had unusual advantages: someone intervened in every case." For example, one young girl named Pineapple, whom Kozol met when she was a kindergartner, went on to graduate from college and become a social worker. Pineapple had attended a school that Kozol described as "almost always in a state of chaos because so many teachers did not stay for long." A local minister helped her get scholarships to private schools. The daughter of Spanish-speaking immigrants, Pineapple had to work hard to overcome deficits in reading, writing, and basic study skills, but she and her older sister both went on to become the first generation of their family to finish high school and attend college (Kozol, 2012).

School funding typically comes from local property taxes, which means schools in poorer areas receive less money.

While the personal tales of Pineapple and her sister are inspiring, Kozol's analyses reveal that very little has improved in the past two decades. For example, there remain vast disparities in educational spending in largely Black and Latino central cities versus largely White well-to-do suburbs. He reported that in 2002–2003, New York City spent $11,627 on each public school child, while in Nassau County, the towns of Manhasset and Great Neck spent $22,311 and $19,705, respectively. These patterns weren't limited to the New York area but rather were found throughout the United States. Because school funding tends to come from local property taxes, wealthier areas generate more funding for schools, while poorer neighborhoods with few lavish private homes have far less money for schools. As with his earlier studies of East St. Louis, Kozol visited schools that were just a few miles apart geographically but that offered vastly different educational opportunities. While suburban White schools would offer advanced math, literature, and an array of arts electives, the nearby primarily Black school would offer classes like hairdressing, typing, and auto shop. Ten years later, the situation hadn't changed: In 2019, the Chicago Ridge School District, where two-thirds of students come from low-income families, spent $10,987 per child. Less than an hour north, in a wealthy Chicago suburb, the Rondout District spent $31,491 per student (Illinois State Board of Education, 2019).

Kozol's poignant journalistic account of educational inequality has become part of our nation's conventional wisdom on the subject of educational inequality. But many sociologists have argued that although Kozol's book (1991) is a moving portrait, it provides an inaccurate and incomplete view of educational inequality. Why would Kozol's research not be compelling? There are several reasons, including the unsystematic way in which he chose the schools he studied. Other sociologists have proposed a variety of theories and identified myriad factors contributing to inequality and differential outcomes.

> **tracking** Dividing students into groups that receive different instruction on the basis of assumed similarities in ability or attainment.

Tracking and Within-School Effects

Kozol's work vividly revealed the vast disparities between schools found in wealthy versus impoverished school districts. Yet sociologists are also interested in inequalities even within a single school. The practice of **tracking**, also known as ability grouping—dividing students into groups that receive different instruction on the basis of assumed similarities in ability or attainment—is common in American schools. In some schools, students are tracked only for certain subjects; in others, for all subjects. Sociologists have long believed that tracking is entirely negative in its effects and that its use partly explains why schooling seems to have little effect on existing social inequalities, since being placed in a particular track labels a student as either able or otherwise. As we have seen in the case of labeling and deviance, once attached, such labels are hard to break away from. Children from more privileged backgrounds, in which academic work is encouraged, are likely to find themselves in the higher tracks early on—and by and large stay there.

A now-classic study by Jeannie Oakes (1985) examined tracking in 25 junior and senior high schools, both large and small and in both urban and rural areas. She concentrated on differences within schools rather than between them. She found that although several schools claimed they did not track students, virtually all of them had mechanisms for sorting students into groups that seemed to be alike in ability and achievement, to make teaching easier. In other words, they employed tracking but did not choose to use the term *tracking*. Even where tracking existed only in this informal fashion, Oakes found strong labels developing—"high ability," "low-achieving," "slow," "average," and so on. Individual students in these groups came to be defined by teachers, other students, and themselves in terms of such labels. A student in a "high-achieving" group was considered a high-achieving person—smart and quick. Pupils in a "low-achieving" group came to be seen as slow, below average—or, in more colloquial terms, as "dummies." What was the effect of tracking on students in the low group? A subsequent study by Oakes (1990) found that these students received a poorer education in terms of the quality of the courses, teachers, and textbooks made available to them. Moreover, the negative effect of tracking affected mostly African American, Latino, and poor students.

The usual reason given for tracking is that bright children learn more quickly and effectively in a group of others who are equally able and that clever students are held back if placed in mixed groups. Surveying the evidence, Oakes attempted to show that these assumptions are wrong. The results of later research investigations are not wholly consistent, but a path-breaking study by sociologist Adam Gamoran and his colleagues (1995) concluded that Oakes was partially correct in her arguments. They agreed with Oakes's conclusions that tracking reinforces previously existing inequalities for average or poor students but countered her argument by asserting that tracking does have positive benefits for "advanced" students. The debate about the effects of tracking is sure to continue as scholars analyze more data.

School Discipline

In the past two decades, scholars and educators have been increasingly interested in another aspect of school culture that may affect student outcomes: school discipline. Some sociologists have noted that there has been a shift in school discipline toward more punitive policies that mirror current trends in our nation's criminal justice system. Moreover, this shift has been most acute among schools located in poor areas and attended largely by members of ethnic minority groups.

One of the major changes in school discipline came in 1995, when Congress amended the Gun-Free School Zones Act. This act, and subsequent federal mandates, established a "zero-tolerance" policy for weapons and drugs in schools. Zero tolerance was initially meant to address school violence by mandating suspension or expulsion for possession of drugs or weapons in school. However, as it was implemented nationwide, it was expanded to include a broad range of misbehavior. Critics of the policy argue that it has led to unnecessary police intervention in schools and has increased racial bias. For example, data from the U.S. Department of Education Office for Civil Rights (2018) show that while Black students represent only 15 percent of total enrollment, they account for 31 percent of students referred to law enforcement or subjected to a school-related arrest. Activists and educators opposed to zero tolerance have coined the term *school-to-prison pipeline* as a way of emphasizing the negative impact of the policy.

Disciplinary practices in schools, it has been argued, also appear to be influenced by media representations and negative images of Black and Latino youth. Ann Arnett Ferguson's ethnographic study of middle school children (2000), for example, shows how institutional discourses (such as the use of prison metaphors), the subjective views of teachers, and the treatment Black boys receive in school influence the ways in which Black boys see themselves— that is, as criminally oriented.

A police officer walks a drug-sniffing dog through the halls of a school in Indianapolis. Opponents of punitive school-discipline policies claim they create a school-to-prison pipeline.

Other researchers have noted that punitive school-discipline policies appear to be, in part, a response to low performance in inner-city schools populated by low-income, minority students. Based on ethnographic research in an urban school, Kathleen Nolan and Jean Anyon (2004) theorize that, within our current economy, criminalizing school-discipline policies are a means to manage an economically and educationally marginalized group. They also contend that when students embrace an oppositional culture, they may no longer be participating in the reproduction of their status as manual laborers, as Paul Willis argued (1977). Instead, as misbehavior comes to be managed by the police in schools, students may be participating in the reproduction of themselves as "criminalized subjects," or as individuals who will spend a lifetime entangled in one way or another (incarceration, parole, probation) with the criminal justice system.

Cultural and Social-Psychological Influences on Student Outcomes

Sociologists are not only interested in the ways schools and socioeconomic factors affect children's educational backgrounds; some are interested also in the ways cultural and psychological factors affect children's educational opportunities and outcomes. These explanations are typically invoked to explain race and gender differences in students' academic outcomes. In general, these theories propose that ethnic minorities and women are more likely than Whites and men to be socialized in a way that may disadvantage them in education (and in the workplace). Although race and gender disparities in many important educational outcomes have narrowed over the past half century, a number of gaps persist; sociologists are intent on figuring out why.

Race and the "Acting White" Thesis

Black and Latino students lag behind White and Asian students in their rates of graduating from high school. Yet even at younger ages, an achievement gap has been documented. For example, analyses by the National Center for Education Statistics (NCES) in 2017 showed that Black and Hispanic students trailed their White peers by an average of more than 20 test-score points on the standardized math and reading assessments in the fourth and eighth grades, a difference of about two grade levels (NCES, 2019d). These achievement gaps persisted even though the score differentials between Black and White students narrowed between 1992 and 2007 in fourth-grade math and reading and eighth-grade math (NCES, 2009, 2011). Between 1992 and 2017, score differentials for reading assessments narrowed between Hispanic and White students, but the achievement gap remained constant between Black and White students. Meanwhile, scores in math assessment narrowed between Black and White students, yet remained constant between Hispanic and White students (NCES, 2019d). There are also significant racial achievement gaps in SAT scores: In 2018, the average scores on the math section for Blacks (463) and Hispanics (489) were significantly lower than the average score of Whites (557) (NCES, 2018e).

In attempting to explain these declining yet persistent racial achievement gaps in education, anthropologists John Ogbu and Signithia Fordham (1986) proposed the **"acting White" thesis**. Based on ethnographic research of the educational experiences of Black students, Ogbu and Fordham concluded that the achievement gap can be partially explained by Black students' reluctance to embrace school norms, which Black students associate with White culture. In subsequent years, however, a number of researchers have challenged the "acting White" thesis. For example, Roslyn Mickelson's research (1990) on the achievement attitudes of African American students

> **"acting White" thesis** The thesis that Black students do not aspire to or strive to get good grades because it is perceived as "acting White."

abstract and concrete attitudes Abstract attitudes are ideas that are consistent with mainstream societal views, while concrete attitudes are ideas that are based on actual experience.

cultural navigators People who draw from both their home culture and mainstream culture to create an attitude that allows them to succeed.

gender gap The differences between women and men, especially as reflected in social, political, intellectual, cultural, or economic attainments or attitudes.

revealed that students held both **abstract and concrete attitudes** toward schooling. Their abstract attitudes were consistent with mainstream attitudes that placed a high value on education and the attainment of academic credentials for future success. However, these students also held concrete anti-achievement attitudes based on their experiences in school and their perception that they had few options in terms of entrance into higher education or lucrative careers even if they were to obtain a high school diploma.

More recently, sociologist Prudence Carter's study (2005) of the experiences of high school students in New York City revealed that Black and Latino students overwhelmingly believe in the importance of school and the need for educational credentials. Carter notes that Black and Latino students' academic and social experiences are heterogeneous, and the most successful students are not necessarily the ones who assimilate to White, mainstream speech patterns, styles, and tastes. Instead, students whom she calls **cultural navigators**—those who draw from resources from both their home culture and the mainstream culture—tend to be highly successful in school. Ultimately, Carter argues, schools must promote intercultural communication and understanding to mitigate unequal academic outcomes.

Gender and Achievement

For many years, girls performed better on average than boys on standardized tests until they reached the middle years of secondary education. They then fell behind: Boys did better than girls, particularly in math and science. However, in recent years, we have seen a convergence and, in some cases, a reversal in the gender gap (College Board, 2016). In 2018, boys and girls scored roughly the same on the critical reading section of the SAT, while boys outpaced girls by 30 points on math (542 versus 522), and girls slightly outpaced boys on the writing component of the test (539 versus 534) (NCES, 2018e). Moreover, girls are more likely than boys to attend a four-year college immediately following high school graduation, and this gap is particularly pronounced among African Americans. For example, in 2017, 50.3 percent of girls who completed high school enrolled in a four-year school compared to 37.2 percent of boys (NCES, 2018c). Since the mid-1990s, a higher proportion of women than men have graduated from four-year colleges each year (Pollard, 2011).

Given this evidence, most scholars concur that today's **gender gap** places girls ahead of boys. Sociologists have attempted to explain the reversal in the gender gap in a variety of ways. Some have argued that girls are doing better in schools today because the new service economy has created more opportunities for women, while factory jobs, traditionally a male terrain, have decreased in number because of new technologies and the relocation of manufacturing industries to developing countries. Other studies focus on the achievements made within the women's movement and its effect on women's self-esteem and expectations. Another important impact of the women's movement is that teachers have become more aware of gender discrimination in the classroom and have taken steps to avoid gender stereotyping. Many teachers now incorporate learning materials that are free of gender bias, and they encourage girls to explore traditionally "male" subjects.

Some sociologists today are wary of all the attention directed at underachieving boys. They contend that, although girls have forged ahead, they are still less likely than boys to choose subjects in school that lead to careers in science, technology, engineering, and mathematics (STEM). In 2016, women accounted for 36 percent of degrees in STEM fields (NCES, 2019a). Boys pull away from girls by about age 11 in science and continue to outperform girls through college. And women continue to be disadvantaged in the job market despite the fact that they are entering college at higher rates than young men. The question of "Who fares worse, boys or girls?" will continue to challenge social scientists and educators in future generations as they strive to develop programs and policies to enhance gender equity.

Stereotype Threat

Differential outcomes between White students and minority students and between girls and boys have also been explained in social psychological terms. Claude Steele and Joshua Aronson's influential work (Steele and Aronson, 1995, 2004) on **stereotype threat** suggests that when African American students (or female students) believe they are being judged not as individuals but as members of a negatively stereotyped social group, they will do worse on tests. Conversely, students who believe they are judged as members of a positively stereotyped group have been found to do better on tests. Sociologist Jennifer Lee refers to this as **stereotype promise**, a phenomenon she detected among Asian American students. The Chinese American and Vietnamese American students she tracked talked about how their teachers assumed that they were smart, hard-working achievers. These perceptions affected the way their teachers treated them, the grades they received, and their chances of securing slots in their schools' most competitive programs, like AP classes (Lee and Zhou, 2014).

Public Policy Influences on Student Outcomes

We have described the ways in which macrosocial factors such as social class and school organization, as well as microsocial processes such as stereotype threat and stereotype promise, may account for educational inequalities. However, a third set of factors also has a powerful influence on student outcomes: public policies.

stereotype threat The idea that when African American students believe they are being judged not as individuals but as members of a negatively stereotyped social group, they will do worse on tests.

stereotype promise A phenomenon where being viewed through the lens of a positive stereotype may lead one to perform in such a way that confirms the positive stereotype, thereby enhancing performance.

Educational Reform in the United States

Sociological research has played a major role in reforming the educational system. These reforms, in turn, have had a powerful impact on the lives of children who are affected by such policies. The object of James Coleman's research, commissioned as part of the 1964 Civil Rights Act, was not solely academic; it was undertaken to influence policy—and it succeeded. On the basis of the act, the courts decided that segregated schools violated the rights of minority pupils. But rather than attacking the origins of educational inequalities directly, as Christopher Jencks's later work suggested was necessary, the courts decided that the schools in each district should achieve a similar racial balance. Thus began the practice of busing students to other schools.

In 1970, a U.S. judge in North Carolina ordered that Black students be bused to White schools and that White students be bused to Black schools. It was hoped that this crosstown school busing would end the de facto segregation of public schools caused by White students living in predominantly White neighborhoods and Black students living in predominantly Black neighborhoods.

functional literacy Reading and writing skills that are beyond a basic level and are sufficient to manage one's everyday activities and employment tasks.

Busing provoked a great deal of opposition, particularly from parents and children in White areas, and led to episodes of violence at the gates of schools where the children were bused in from other neighborhoods. White children paraded with placards reading, "We don't want them!" Still, busing met with a good deal of success, reducing levels of school segregation quite steeply, particularly in the South. But busing also produced a number of unintended consequences. Some White parents reacted to busing either by putting their children into private schools or moving to mainly White suburbs where busing wasn't practiced. As a result, in the cities, some schools are virtually as segregated as the old schools had been in the past. Busing, however, was only one factor prompting the "White flight" to the suburbs. Whites also left as a reaction to urban decay: to escape city crowding, housing problems, and rising crime rates.

One important target of educational policy today is improving levels of **functional literacy**. Literacy is more than the ability to read and write; literacy is also the ability to process complex information in our

Secretary of Education Betsy DeVos is a vocal advocate of school choice. This movement seeks to use federal funds to expand options outside the traditional public school system, including charter schools such as this one in New York City.

increasingly technology-focused society. The National Center for Education Statistics breaks literacy into three components: prose literacy, document literacy, and quantitative literacy. Prose literacy means that a person can look at a short piece of text to get a small piece of uncomplicated information. Document literacy refers to a person's ability to locate and use information in forms, schedules, charts, graphs, and other informational tables. Quantitative literacy is the ability to do simple addition. In the United States today, only 13 percent of the population is proficient in these three areas (Kutner et al., 2007). Of course, the United States is a country of immigrants, who, when they arrive, may not be able to read and write, and who may also have trouble with English. But this doesn't explain why the United States has higher levels of functional illiteracy than most other industrial countries; many functionally illiterate people are not recent immigrants at all.

What is to be done? Some educators have argued that the most important change that needs to be made is to improve the quality of teaching, either by increasing teachers' pay or introducing performance-related pay scales, with higher salaries going to the teachers who are most effective in the classroom. Others have proposed giving schools more control over their budgets (a reform that Britain has implemented). The idea is that more responsibility for, and control over, budgeting decisions will create a greater drive to improve the school. Further proposals include the re-funding of federal programs such as Head Start to ensure healthy early-child development and thus save millions of dollars in later costs. Others have called for the privatization of public education, a proposal that has gained numerous supporters in recent years, including President Trump's Secretary of Education, Betsy DeVos.

Education Policy Today

Education has long been a political battleground. In the 1960s, some politicians, educators, and community activists pushed for greater equality and universal access to education through such initiatives as bilingual education programs, multicultural education, open admissions to college, the establishment of ethnic studies programs on campuses, and more equitable funding schemes. Such initiatives were seen as supporting civil rights and equality. Educational policies in the twenty-first century have similarly intended to provide quality education for all children and to close the achievement gap. However, scholars disagree about how successful recent policies have been in meeting this goal.

The most significant piece of federal legislation influencing education in the past two decades is the No Child Left Behind (NCLB) Act enacted by Congress in 2001 and signed into law by President George W. Bush in 2002. NCLB reauthorized the 1965 Elementary and Secondary Education Act but also expanded it by implementing a host of policies meant to improve academic outcomes for all children and close the achievement gap. Indeed, NCLB is the most expansive and comprehensive piece of education legislation passed since 1965, addressing virtually every aspect of education—including, for example, testing, school choice, teacher quality, the education of English language learners, military recruitment in schools, and school discipline. At the top of its agenda is instituting standardized testing as a means of measuring students' academic performance. The Act also provides a strong push for school choice—that is, in the spirit of competition, parents are to be given choices about where to send their children to school. Low-performing schools, at risk of losing students, thus jeopardize their funding and risk being closed. Another significant implication of NCLB is that, for the first time since 1968, states are not required to offer non-English-speaking students bilingual education. Instead, the Act emphasizes learning English over using students' native language and favors English-only program models. NCLB also provides support for a zero-tolerance approach to school discipline that was first mandated in the 1990 Gun-Free School Zone Act.

The NCLB has been widely criticized because teachers must "teach to the test." Critics have argued that the emphasis on **standardized testing**—that is, where all students in a state take the same test under the same conditions—as the means of assessment encourages teachers to teach a narrow set of skills that will increase students' test performance, rather than help them acquire an in-depth understanding of important concepts and skills (Hursh, 2007). Others have condemned the program as a punitive model of school reform (i.e., teachers and principals at underperforming schools risk job loss) and note that achievement gaps have not changed and that the policy neglects the important fact that the broader socioeconomic context affects school functioning.

In 2012, recognizing that NCLB may not be effective for all school systems, President Barack Obama granted waivers from NCLB requirements to 32 states, allowing them to develop their own standards and exempting them from the 2014 targets set by the law. In exchange for that flexibility, those states "have agreed to raise standards, improve accountability, and undertake essential reforms to improve teacher effectiveness," the White House said in a statement. The Obama administration also implemented its own program, called Race

standardized testing A situation in which all students take the same test under the same conditions.

to the Top, a competitive grant program designed to spur innovation and reform in K-12 education. The program rewards states that demonstrate improvements in student outcomes, including closing achievement gaps, increasing graduation rates, and better preparing students for college. States competing for the more than $4 billion in grant money had to outline plans for developing and adopting common standards and assessments; building data systems that track student growth; recruiting and retaining high-quality teachers and administrators; and improving the lowest-achieving schools.

Like NCLB, however, Race to the Top has been roundly criticized for relying too heavily on high-stakes testing and also failing to address the true causes of low student achievement, namely poverty and lack of opportunity. Teachers' unions and educators have also complained that the tests are an inaccurate way to measure teachers, and that such measures haven't worked in the past. Political conservatives say that Race to the Top imposes federal control on state schools. Critics say that high-stakes testing is unreliable, that charter schools weaken public education, or that the federal government should not influence local schools (Dillon, 2010).

The crisis in American schools won't be solved in the short term, and it won't be solved by educational reforms alone, no matter how expansive. In fact, a 2006 study by the U.S. Department of Education found that schools identified for improvement were disproportionately urban, high-poverty schools, and that "school poverty and district size better predicted existing improvement status than the improvement strategies undertaken by the schools." A further unintended consequence of the current emphasis on testing is that schools have narrowed their course offerings to focus much more heavily on tested subject areas while cutting time in science, social studies, music, art, and physical education (McMurrer, 2007).

Programs like No Child Left Behind and Race to the Top have been criticized for relying too heavily on standardized testing, which encourages teachers to "teach to the test."

The lesson of sociological research is that inequalities and barriers in educational opportunity reflect wider social divisions and tensions. While the United States remains wracked by racial tensions, and the polarization between decaying cities and affluent suburbs persists, the crisis in the school system is likely to prove difficult to turn around. Jean Anyon's (2006) analysis of how political and economic forces influence schooling helps clarify these challenges. Anyon argues that not until educational reform is linked to more sweeping economic reforms, such as job creation and training programs and corporate tax reform, will schools improve.

Global Perspectives: Education and Literacy in the Developing World

You have already learned about vast educational inequalities in the United States. However, from a global perspective, another disparity is of tremendous concern: cross-national disparities in literacy. Without literacy, schooling cannot proceed; it is the "baseline" of education. We take it for granted in the West that the majority of people are literate, but this is only a recent development in Western history, and in previous times, no more than a tiny proportion of the population had any literacy skills.

Today, roughly 14 percent of the world population over the age of 15, or 786 million persons, is illiterate—two-thirds of whom are women (World Bank, 2018c). However, younger generations are faring better than their parents; youth literacy rates in nearly every region of the world are higher than adult literacy rates—although these generational gaps vary widely by region. Youth literacy rates refer to persons ages 15 to 24, while adult literacy rates apply to the population age 15 and older. Worldwide, the lowest literacy rates are observed in sub-Saharan Africa (65 percent of adults and 77 percent of youth) and in South and West Asia (74 percent of adults and 91 percent of youth) (Global Map 16.1) (UNICEF, 2019a). However, even within regions, there is great heterogeneity; for example, adult literacy rates range from just 30 percent in Guinea to 95 percent in Equatorial Guinea. By contrast, East Asia, Central Asia, and Central and Eastern Europe enjoy literacy rates of nearly 100 percent (UNESCO, 2017b).

What accounts for these marked gaps in global literacy rates? Sociologists believe that these patterns are best understood in a historical perspective and reflect enduring consequences of colonialism. During the period of colonialism, governments regarded education with some trepidation. Until the twentieth century, most colonial governments believed indigenous populations were too primitive to be worth educating. Later, education was seen as a way of making local elites responsive to European interests and ways of life. But, to some extent, the result was to spark discontent and rebellion. The majority of those who led anticolonial and nationalist movements were educated elites who had attended schools or colleges in Europe; they were able to compare firsthand the democratic institutions of the European countries with the absence of democracy in their lands of origin.

The education that the colonizers introduced usually pertained to Europe, not the colonial areas themselves. Educated Africans in the British colonies knew about the kings and queens of England and read Shakespeare and Milton, but they knew next to nothing about their own countries' histories or past cultural achievements. Policies of educational reform since the end of colonialism have not completely altered the situation, even today.

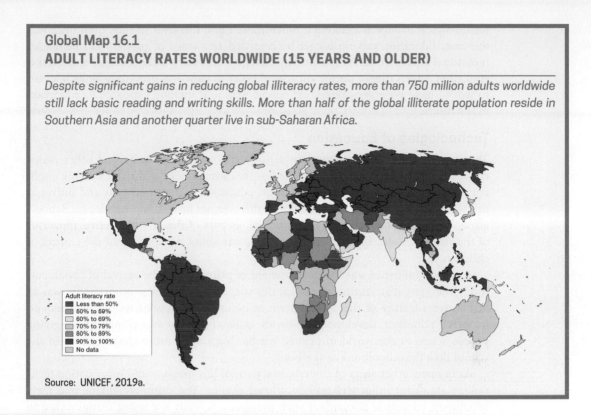

Global Map 16.1
ADULT LITERACY RATES WORLDWIDE (15 YEARS AND OLDER)

Despite significant gains in reducing global illiteracy rates, more than 750 million adults worldwide still lack basic reading and writing skills. More than half of the global illiterate population reside in Southern Asia and another quarter live in sub-Saharan Africa.

Adult literacy rate
- Less than 50%
- 50% to 59%
- 60% to 69%
- 70% to 79%
- 80% to 89%
- 90% to 100%
- No data

Source: UNICEF, 2019a.

Partly as a result of the legacy of colonial education, which was not directed toward the majority of the population, the educational system in many developing countries is top-heavy: Higher education is disproportionately developed relative to primary and secondary education. The result is a correspondingly overqualified group who, having attended colleges and universities, cannot find White-collar or professional jobs. Given the low level of industrial development, most of the better paid positions are in government, and there are not enough of those to go around.

In recent years, some developing countries, recognizing the shortcomings of the curricula inherited from colonialism, have tried to redirect their educational programs toward the rural poor in an effort to raise literacy rates. They have had limited success because usually there is insufficient funding to pay for the scale of the necessary innovations. As a result, countries such as India have begun programs of self-help education. Communities draw on existing resources without creating demands for high levels of finance. Those who can read and write and who perhaps possess job skills are encouraged to take others on as apprentices, whom they coach in their spare time.

The Impact of the Media and Educational Technology on Everyday Life

While we spend hours a day using technology for fun and for socializing, technology also has shaped where, how, and with whom we learn. The spread of information technology looks set to influence education in several different ways, humans with machines in some types of work. New technologies are already affecting the nature of work, replacing humans with machines in some types of work. The sheer pace of technological change is creating a much more rapid turnover of jobs than once was the case. Education can no longer be regarded as a stage of preparation before an individual enters work. As technology changes, necessary skills change, and even if education is seen from a purely vocational point of view—as providing skills relevant to work—most observers agree that people will need lifelong exposure to education in the future.

Technologies of Education

The rise of education in its modern sense was connected with several other major changes in the nineteenth century. One was the development of the school. One might naïvely think that there was a demand for education and that schools and universities were set up to meet that demand. But that was not how things happened. Schools arose, as Michel Foucault (1975) has shown, as part of the administrative apparatus of the modern state. The hidden curriculum was about discipline and the control of children.

A second influence was the development of printing and the arrival of "book culture." The mass distribution of books, newspapers, and other printed media was as distinctive a feature of the development of industrial society as were machines and factories. Education developed to provide skills of literacy and computation, giving people access to the world of printed media. Nothing is more characteristic of the school than the schoolbook or textbook.

As in many other areas of contemporary social life, markets and information technology are major influences on educational change. The commercializing and marketizing of education also reflect such pressures. Schools are being reengineered to resemble business corporations. Many of those likely to enter the education field will be organizations whose relation to schooling was previously marginal or nonexistent. These include cable companies, software houses, telecommunication groups, filmmakers, and equipment suppliers. Their influence will not be limited to schools or universities. They are already forming part of what has been called "edutainment"—a sort of parallel education industry linked to the software industry in general and to museums, science parks, and heritage areas.

Education and the Technology Gap

Whether these new technologies will have the radical implications for education that some claim is still an open question. Critics have pointed out that, even if they do have major effects, these technologies may act to reinforce educational inequalities. **Information poverty** might be added to the material deprivations that currently have such an effect on schooling. The sheer pace of technological change and the demand of employers for computer-literate workers may mean that those who are technologically competent "leapfrog" over people who have little experience with computers.

Some already fear the emergence of a "computer underclass" within Western societies. Although developed countries have the highest levels of computer and Internet usage in the world, there are stark inequalities in computer use within those societies. Many schools and colleges are suffering

information poverty The state of people who have little or no access to information technology, such as computers.

from underfunding and long-standing neglect; even if these institutions become beneficiaries of schemes that distribute secondhand computer hardware to schools, they must gain the technical expertise and ability to teach information technology skills to pupils. Because the market for computer specialists is so strong, many schools are struggling to attract and keep information-technology teachers, who can earn far greater incomes in the private sector.

Such inequalities came to the fore during the 2020 pandemic, when K-12 schools across the nation were forced to switch to remote learning and the advantages of well-funded public schools became far more obvious. Since many of the students in such schools already resided in households with electronic devices, administrators could afford to provide the small number of needy students with the equipment required to participate in remote learning. But many heavily populated or financially strapped districts could not afford to do so. The public school system in New York City—the epicenter of the pandemic when schools initially transitioned to remote learning— employs 75,000 educators and administrators and accommodates 1 million K-12 students. It was able to supply 175,000 children with laptops, iPads, and Chromebooks but left thousands of others with nothing more than paper packets.

Moreover, access to a device was not necessarily a solution to the problem since 6 to 7 million schoolchildren across the country lived in households with no Internet connection. As all libraries and institutions with public WiFi were on lockdown, such students were incapable of making the switch from live to virtual classroom. For this reason, school districts with large numbers of needy students too poor to afford computers, tablets or broadband service, were forced to resort to other options. In Memphis, Tennessee, for example, where two-thirds of students lacked any type of digital device (including cellphones) and one-third had no Internet access, classes were broadcast over a local TV channel.

Though serious, the technology gap in Western societies seems minor when compared to the digital divide separating Western classrooms from their counterparts in the developing world. As the global economy becomes increasingly knowledge based, there is a real danger that poorer countries will become even more marginalized because of the gap between the information rich and the information poor. Internet access has become a new line of demarcation between the rich and the poor. Information-technology enthusiasts argue that computers need not result in greater national and global inequalities—that their very strength lies in their ability to draw people together and to open up new opportunities. Schools in Asia and Africa that lack textbooks and qualified teachers can benefit from the Internet, it is claimed. Distance-learning programs and collaboration with colleagues overseas could be the key to overcoming poverty and disadvantage. When technology is put in the hands of smart, creative people, they argue, the potential is limitless.

Technology can be breathtaking and can open important doors, but there is no such thing as an easy "techno-fix." Underdeveloped regions that struggle with mass illiteracy and lack telephone lines and electricity need an improved educational infrastructure before they can truly benefit from distance-learning programs. The Internet cannot be substituted for direct contact between teachers and pupils under these conditions.

Students in a school in the remote Thai highlands use tablets to practice English. While technology is transforming classrooms across the globe, there remains a significant digital divide.

Lifelong Learning

New technologies and the rise of the knowledge economy are transforming traditional ideas about work and education. Training and the attainment of qualifications now occur throughout people's lives, rather than just early in life. Mid-career professionals are choosing to update their skills through continuing-education programs and online courses. Many employers now allow workers to participate in on-the-job training as a way of enhancing loyalty and improving the company's skill base.

As our society continues to transform, the traditional beliefs and institutions that underpin it are also undergoing change. The idea of education—implying the structured transmission of knowledge within a formal institution—is giving way to a broader notion of learning that takes place in diverse settings. The shift from education to learning is not an inconsequential one. Learners are active, curious social actors who can derive insights from a multiplicity of sources, not just within an institutional setting. An emphasis on learning acknowledges that skills and knowledge can be gained through all types of encounters—with friends and neighbors, at seminars and museums, in conversations at the local coffee shop, via the Internet and other media, and so forth.

The shift in emphasis toward lifelong learning can already be seen within schools themselves, where there is a growing number of opportunities for pupils to learn outside the confines of the classroom. The boundaries between schools and the outside world are breaking down, not only via **cyberspace**, but in the physical world as well. "Service learning," for example, has

cyberspace Electronic networks of interaction between individuals at different computer terminals.

become a mainstay of many American secondary schools. As part of their graduation requirements, pupils devote a certain amount of time to volunteer work in the community. Partnerships with local businesses have also become commonplace in the United States, fostering interaction and mentor relationships between adult professionals and pupils.

Lifelong learning should and must play a role in the move toward a knowledge society. Not only is learning essential to a well-trained, motivated workforce, but it should also be seen in relation to wider human values. Learning is both a means and an end to the development of a well-rounded and autonomous self-education in the service of self-development and self-understanding. There is nothing utopian in this idea; indeed, it reflects the humanistic ideals of education developed by educational philosophers. An example already in existence is lifelong-learning programs for the age 65+ population, which provide retired people with the opportunity to educate themselves as they choose, developing whatever interests they care to follow.

CONCEPT CHECKS

1 How do Coleman's findings differ from the results of Kozol's research? Whose theory, in your opinion, can better explain race and class gaps in educational achievement?

2 What effect does tracking have on academic achievement?

3 Explain two theories that sociologists have developed to account for the ways that cultural and psychological factors affect educational outcomes.

4 What are the goals of No Child Left Behind and Race to the Top? What are criticisms of these policies?

5 What are some of the reasons there are high rates of illiteracy in developing nations?

4   UNANSWERED QUESTIONS

As you have learned in this chapter, the sociological study of education and the media is a rapidly evolving field. With each new technological development or the implementation of a new public policy, new issues and challenges arise. Sociologists continue to grapple with important questions about the media and education, and answers to these questions are often challenging and contested. We focus here on three "unanswered" questions: Is intelligence shaped by genes or the environment? Is home-schooling a substitute for formal education? And who benefits from international education?

Is Intelligence Shaped by Genes or Environment?

What social or biological factors shape how "intelligent" we are? This question has been at the center of hotly contested debates for nearly five decades. Understanding the sources of IQ is an important goal for educational researchers, because scores on IQ tests correlate highly with academic performance (which is not surprising, given that IQ tests were originally developed to predict success in school). They therefore also correlate closely with social, economic, and ethnic differences because these are associated with variations in levels of educational attainment. Another reason scholars are interested in factors that shape IQ is because answers to this question may help remedy the achievement gap we learned about earlier in this chapter. White students score better, on average, than African Americans or members of other disadvantaged minorities. An article published by Arthur Jensen in 1969 caused a furor by attributing IQ differences between Blacks and Whites in part to genetic variations (see also Jensen, 1979). Most sociologists argue that such attributions are incomplete and misleading.

Later, Richard J. Herrnstein, a psychologist, and Charles Murray, a sociologist, reopened the debate about IQ in a controversial way. They argued in their book *The Bell Curve* (1994) that the accumulated evidence linking IQ to genetic inheritance was now overwhelming. The significant differences in intelligence among various racial and ethnic groups, they said, must in part be explained in terms of heredity. According to Herrnstein and Murray, the available evidence strongly indicated that some ethnic groups on average had higher IQs than other groups. Asian Americans, particularly Japanese Americans and Chinese Americans, on average possessed higher IQs than Whites, although the difference was not large. The average IQs of Asians and Whites, however, were substantially higher than those of Blacks. Summarizing the findings of 156 studies, Herrnstein and Murray found an average difference of 16 IQ points between these two racial groups. The authors argued that such differences in inherited intelligence contributed in an important way to social divisions in American society. The smarter an individual is, the greater the chance they will rise in the social scale. Those at the top are there partly because they are smarter than the rest of the population—from which it follows that those at the bottom remain there because, on average, they are not as smart.

Herrnstein and Murray's claim created a great deal of controversy and raised the ire and indignation of countless liberals, social scientists, and members of the African American community. Although Herrnstein and Murray's claims may be seen as racist and reprehensible, are these sufficient reasons to attack their work? Or are their conclusions based on faulty social research? The answer to both questions is a resounding yes. A team of sociologists at the University of California at Berkeley later reanalyzed much of the data that Herrnstein and Murray had based their conclusions on and came up with quite different findings.

In the original analysis, Herrnstein and Murray analyzed data from the National Longitudinal Study of Youth (NLSY), a survey of more than 10,000 young Americans who were interviewed multiple times over a period of more than a decade. As part of this study, subjects were given the Armed Forces Qualifying Test (AFQT), a short test that assesses IQ. Herrnstein and Murray then conducted statistical analyses, which used the AFQT score to predict a variety of outcomes. They concluded that having a high IQ was the best predictor of later economic success and that low IQ was the best predictor of poverty later in life. The Berkeley sociologists, in their 1996 book *Inequality by Design* (Fischer et al., 1996), countered that the AFQT does not necessarily measure intelligence, but only how much a person has learned in school. Moreover, they found that intelligence is only one factor among several that predicts how well people do in life. Social factors, including education, gender, community conditions, marital status, current economic conditions, and (perhaps most important) parents' socioeconomic status, better predict one's occupational and economic success.

In the original analysis, Herrnstein and Murray measured parents' socioeconomic status by taking an average of mother's education, father's education, father's occupation, and family income. The Berkeley sociologists recognized that each of these four factors matters differently in predicting a child's occupational outcomes and thus weighted the four components differently. Their analysis showed that the effects of socioeconomic background on a young adult's risk of later poverty were substantially greater than Herrnstein and Murray originally found. The Berkeley sociologists also recognized that IQ is closely associated with one's level of education. They reanalyzed the NLSY data, taking into consideration the individual's level of education, and found that Herrnstein and Murray had drastically overestimated the effects of IQ on a person's later achievements.

The relationship between race and intelligence is also best explained by social rather than biological causes, according to the Berkeley sociologists. All societies have oppressed ethnic groups. Low status, often coupled with discrimination and mistreatment, leads to socioeconomic deprivation, group segregation, and a stigma of inferiority. The combination of these forces often prevents racial minorities from obtaining a quality education, and, consequently, their scores on standardized intelligence tests are lower.

The average lower IQ score of African Americans in the United States is remarkably similar to that of deprived ethnic minorities in other countries—such as the "untouchables" in India (who are at the very bottom of the caste system), the Maori in New Zealand, and the *burakumin* of Japan. Children in these groups score an average of 10 to 15 IQ points below children belonging to the ethnic majority. The *burakumin*—descendants of people who, in the eighteenth century, as a result of local wars, were dispossessed from their land and became outcasts and vagrants—are a particularly interesting example. They are not in any way physically distinct from other Japanese, although they have suffered from prejudice and discrimination for centuries. In this case, the difference in average IQ results cannot derive from genetic variations because there are no genetic differences between them and the majority population; yet the IQ difference is as thoroughly fixed as that between Blacks and Whites. *Burakumin* children in the United States, where they are treated like other Japanese, do as well on IQ tests as other Japanese children.

Such observations strongly suggest that the IQ variations between African Americans and Whites in the United States result from social and cultural differences. This conclusion receives further support from a comparative study of 14 nations (including the United States) showing that average IQ scores have risen substantially over the past half century for the population as a whole (Coleman, 1987). IQ tests are regularly updated. When old and new versions of the tests are given to the same group of people, they score significantly higher on the old tests. Present-day children taking IQ tests from the 1930s outscored 1930s groups by an average of 15 points—just the kind of average difference that currently separates Blacks and Whites. Children today are not innately superior in intelligence to their parents or grandparents; the shift presumably derives from increasing prosperity and social advantages. The average social and economic gap between Whites and African Americans is at least as great as that between the different generations and is sufficient to explain the variation in IQ scores. Although genetic variations between individuals may influence scores on IQ tests, these have no overall connection to racial differences.

Is Homeschooling a Substitute for Traditional Schooling?

Homeschooling has increased dramatically in popularity in recent decades. An estimated 1.8 million (or 3.4 percent of all) children are currently homeschooled, up from 850,000 children (1.7 percent) in 1999 (Murphy, 2012; Redford, Battle, and Bielick, 2017). Homeschooling means that a child is taught by his or her parents, guardians, or a team of adults who oversee the child's educational development. The curricula that homeschooled children follow vary widely from state to state, with some states mandating quite strict ones and others far more lax ones, offering parents greater leeway.

A recent survey conducted by the U.S. Department of Education queried parents about their motivation for homeschooling their children. The most frequently cited reasons were a concern about the school environment (91 percent), a desire to provide moral instruction (77 percent), and dissatisfaction with the academic instruction at other schools (74 percent) (Redford, Battle, and Bielick, 2017). It remains to be seen how well homeschooling prepares young adults for the future challenges of college or employment in the United States. Some studies suggest that homeschooled children are just as well prepared for college as their traditionally educated counterparts, while others say that homeschooling deprives children of important life lessons.

Before we can ascertain whether homeschooling is beneficial, we need to consider that homeschooling is a "selective" process, and the traits that "select" people into homeschooling may also affect their later prospects. White students have a higher homeschooling rate than Blacks and Hispanics; fully 59 percent of homeschooled students in 2016 were White (NCES, 2018a). In addition, students in two-parent households make up 80 percent of the homeschooled population, and those in two-parent households with one parent in the labor force make up 55 percent of the homeschooled population (NCES, 2018a). Students in households earning between $25,001 and $75,000 per year had higher rates of homeschooling than their peers in households earning $25,000 or less a year. Thus, many children who are homeschooled have several social advantages, including wealthier or more stable families.

The impossibility of homeschooling a larger segment of the population became evident during the 2020 COVID-19 epidemic, when parents across the United States were unexpectedly forced to play a far more significant role in their children's education after K-12 schools closed their doors for an undetermined period. Although classes were conducted remotely, via online platforms, television broadcasts, and paper pamphlets, parents were called on to supervise their children's progress and assume many of the responsibilities of teachers. Those with the homeschooling experience suddenly became wellsprings of information and advice (Kamenetz and Turner, 2020; Rummel, 2020; Willen, 2020), which, however well-intentioned, was often irrelevant or useless to parents without the knowledge, temperament, and vocation of professional educators (Long, 2020). Those able to hold on to their jobs by working remotely had to find ways to juggle their professional responsibilities, the regular duties of parenting, and their children's education. Those laid off from their jobs had the stress of dealing with financial hardship, job hunting, and an uncertain future. This is not to mention the many households affected by the virus itself, who were forced into collective quarantine or flung into mourning for a victim of the pandemic.

Although the situation was difficult for most working parents, those of comfortable means generally had the educational background, the resources, and physical space to provide proper supervisions for their children and cope with homeschooling for an extended time. Those without these luxuries were often at a loss: How could they teach a subject of which they had no knowledge? How could they find a quiet place for their children to study in a crowded inner-city apartment shared by extended family? How could they maintain discipline at home and ensure that each child got equal time to do their work on a shared device? How did one deal with disruptions by other family members, emotionally unstable neighbors,

The most commonly cited reason parents opt to homeschool their children is a concern about the school environment.

noise in the corridors, etc.? Homeschooling, even on a part-time basis, was not a viable option for households struggling with these problems.

Parents who were called on to homeschool students with disabilities were especially hard hit as teachers were not required to provide them with Individualized Educational Plans (IEPs) once schools shut their doors. Even when they did, many parents lacked the proper training or time to provide or keep up with the special needs of their children, whose conditions were in danger of rapid regression if their carefully structured schedules unraveled (Chlavaroli, 2020). In other cases, it was the parent who suffered from a disability or debilitating illness, and who now faced the challenge of supplementing their child's (or children's) education all day long for weeks on end (Panico and Duhart, 2020).

The frustration, even exasperation voiced by parents throughout the pandemic bore witness to the fact that homeschooling, however successful for a small minority, is not an effective alternative for the population at large.

It is much harder to ascertain whether homeschooled children fare better on outcomes such as standardized test scores or success in college because little data are available on these topics. Most studies concluding that homeschoolers outperform traditional students are criticized on the grounds that they are focused on biased samples (e.g., Oplinger and Willard, 2004; Rudner, 1999). Experts also argue that it is hard to describe definitively the experience of homeschoolers because they are such a diverse group, representing every possible religious, political, and spiritual orientation (Murphy, 2012).

Who Benefits from "International Education"?

How many international students are enrolled in your sociology course? How many international students attend your university? In 1943, approximately 8,000 foreign students were enrolled in American colleges and universities. In the 2015–2016 academic year, the number of international students surpassed 1 million for the first time, representing 5 percent of the total student population at U.S. colleges and universities (Institute of International Education [IIE], 2016). Most foreign students today come from Asia; China, India, South Korea, Vietnam, Taiwan, and Japan all send sizeable contingents of students abroad. However, in 2015–2016, Saudi Arabia became the third-largest sender of international students to the United States (after China and India). The United States takes in more foreign students than any other country: New York University and the University of Southern California are the top two destinations. What do foreign students in the United States study? About half in 2018–2019 pursued STEM fields. More than one-fifth study engineering, 16.6 percent study business and management, 18.5 percent concentrate on math and computer sciences, and 7.6 percent study the social sciences (IIE, 2019a).

Some scholars regard the exchange of international students as a vital component of globalization. Foreign students, in addition to serving as global "carriers" of specialized technical and scientific knowledge, play an important cultural role in the globalizing process. Cross-national understandings are enhanced, and xenophobic and isolationist attitudes are minimized as native students in host countries develop social ties to their foreign classmates and as foreign students return to their countries of origin with an appreciation for the cultural mores of the nation in which they have studied.

Yet there is considerable debate in the United States about what is sometimes called the "internationalization of education." On most college and university campuses, it is not hard to find disgruntled students who complain that the influx of foreign students deprives deserving Americans of educational opportunities—especially given the increasingly competitive nature of the U.S. higher education system. Moreover, although more than two-thirds of foreign students receive nothing in the way of scholarships, some top-notch foreign students *are* given financial inducements to attend American schools. The outcry against this practice has been loudest at public universities, which receive support from tax revenues. Critics charge that U.S. taxpayers

Chinese students explore their options at the China International Exhibition Tour college fair. In the 2018–2019 academic year, China accounted for 34 percent of all international students in the United States (IEE, 2019b).

should not shoulder the financial burden of educating foreign students whose families have not paid U.S. taxes and who are likely to return home after earning their degrees.

Supporters of international education find such arguments unconvincing. Some Americans may lose out to foreign students in the competition for slots at prestigious universities, but this is a small price to pay for the economic, political, and cultural benefits the United States receives from having educated millions of foreign business executives, policy makers, scientists, and professionals over the years—many of whom became sympathetically disposed to the United States as a result of their experiences here. And although some foreign students receive scholarships from American universities, most are supported by their parents. In fact, it is estimated that foreign students pump billions of dollars each year into the U.S. economy—more than $41 billion in 2018–2019, including tuition, housing, and related purchases (NAFSA, 2019a). Rather than curtail the number of foreign students admitted to American universities, supporters of international education suggest that even more should be done to encourage the exchange of students.

On the one hand, greater effort should be made to recruit foreign students, help them select the university and program that will best meet their needs, and provide them with a positive social and educational experience while they are in the United States. On the other hand, more Americans should be encouraged to study abroad. American students are notorious for having poor or no foreign-language skills and for knowing little about global geography, much less about the cultures of other nations. This cultural and linguistic ignorance puts the United States at a disadvantage relative to other countries as the world becomes increasingly globalized; encouraging Americans to study overseas may be the best way to inculcate a global worldview.

Should there be a greater focus on international education in American colleges and universities? Should the international exchange of students be expanded? These are among the issues that educational institutions are forced to confront in the context of globalization. Still, more and more U.S. students are studying abroad—more than 332,727 U.S. students studied abroad for credit during the 2017–2018 academic year. While this figure represents an increase of nearly 2.7 percent over the year before, still only about 10 percent of college students study abroad (NAFSA, 2019b). Of those who do study abroad, more than half (53 percent as of 2017–2018) study in Europe, with about one-third studying in the United Kingdom, Italy, or Spain (IIE, 2016). There is a gender gap in who studies abroad, with women accounting for two-thirds of American students studying abroad. Most scholars agree that in our increasingly global society, international education is essential to having a well-informed, open-minded, and forward-looking population.

CONCEPT CHECKS

1 Explain the relationship between race and intelligence. Do you find the evidence compelling?

2 What are three reasons parents decide to homeschool their children?

3 Describe several characteristics of the "typical" international student enrolled at a U.S. college or university.

THE BIG PICTURE

Chapter 16
Education

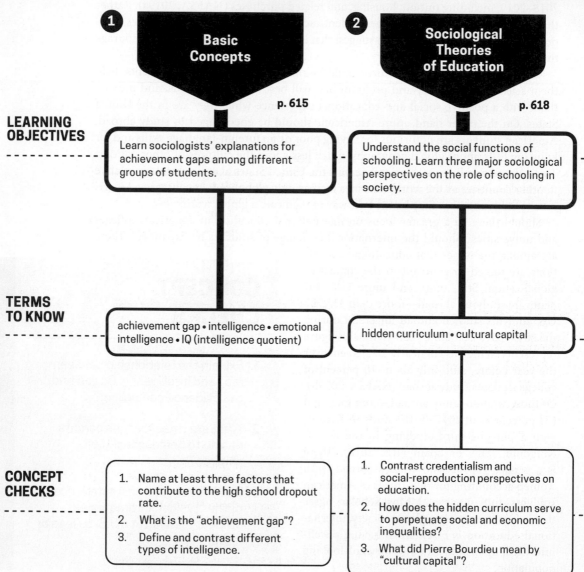

1 **Basic Concepts**

p. 615

2 **Sociological Theories of Education**

p. 618

LEARNING OBJECTIVES

Learn sociologists' explanations for achievement gaps among different groups of students.

Understand the social functions of schooling. Learn three major sociological perspectives on the role of schooling in society.

TERMS TO KNOW

achievement gap • intelligence • emotional intelligence • IQ (intelligence quotient)

hidden curriculum • cultural capital

CONCEPT CHECKS

1. Name at least three factors that contribute to the high school dropout rate.
2. What is the "achievement gap"?
3. Define and contrast different types of intelligence.

1. Contrast credentialism and social-reproduction perspectives on education.
2. How does the hidden curriculum serve to perpetuate social and economic inequalities?
3. What did Pierre Bourdieu mean by "cultural capital"?

Exercises: Thinking Sociologically

1. From your reading of this chapter and your own educational experiences, describe what might be the principal advantages and disadvantages of having children go to private versus public schools in the United States at this time. Assess whether privatization of our public schools would help improve them.

2. Back in 1964, Marshall McLuhan argued that radio and television helped to produce a global village—that is, a world linked by instantaneous media coverage of worldwide events and news. Explain how the advent of the Internet and cell phones is extending the concept of the global village even further and faster.

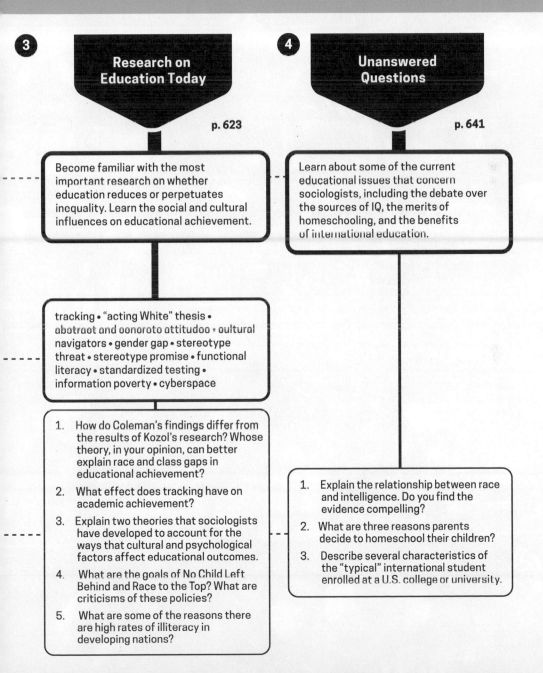

3

Research on Education Today

p. 623

Become familiar with the most important research on whether education reduces or perpetuates inequality. Learn the social and cultural influences on educational achievement.

tracking • "acting White" thesis • abstract and concrete attitudes • cultural navigators • gender gap • stereotype threat • stereotype promise • functional literacy • standardized testing • information poverty • cyberspace

1. How do Coleman's findings differ from the results of Kozol's research? Whose theory, in your opinion, can better explain race and class gaps in educational achievement?

2. What effect does tracking have on academic achievement?

3. Explain two theories that sociologists have developed to account for the ways that cultural and psychological factors affect educational outcomes.

4. What are the goals of No Child Left Behind and Race to the Top? What are criticisms of these policies?

5. What are some of the reasons there are high rates of illiteracy in developing nations?

4

Unanswered Questions

p. 641

Learn about some of the current educational issues that concern sociologists, including the debate over the sources of IQ, the merits of homeschooling, and the benefits of international education.

1. Explain the relationship between race and intelligence. Do you find the evidence compelling?

2. What are three reasons parents decide to homeschool their children?

3. Describe several characteristics of the "typical" international student enrolled at a U.S. college or university.

17

Religion in Modern Society

Can you rank the following list of some of the world's major religions from fastest growing to slowest growing?

A   Christianity

B   Islam

C   Judaism

D   Hinduism

E   Buddhism

TURN THE PAGE FOR THE CORRECT ANSWER.

This is a difficult question, and if you failed to answer it correctly, you are in good company. Very few Americans would get this question right. The correct order is Islam, Christianity, Hinduism, Judaism, and Buddhism. Islam is the world's second-largest religion, with an estimated 1.8 billion adherents—nearly a quarter of the global population; from 2015 to 2060, the Muslim population is projected to grow by a whopping 70 percent—more than twice as fast as the global population—due primarily to the religion's young population and high fertility rate. In contrast, Christianity, currently the world's largest religion with some 2.3 billion adherents, is projected to rise by 34 percent by 2060. This means that Muslims will likely outnumber Christians in the second half of this century (Lipka and Hackett, 2017).

While Hinduism and Judaism are both projected to increase in number of adherents, they are growing more slowly than the global population itself, so they will actually account for smaller percentages of the global population in 2060 than they did in 2015. The third-largest religious group in 2015, Hinduism has nearly 1.1 billion adherents and is projected to grow 27 percent by 2060. Judaism, with 14.3 million adherents, is projected to grow by only 15 percent by 2060. Lastly, Buddhism, which currently has nearly 500 million adherents, is projected to decline by 7 percent between 2015 and 2060 due to an aging population and low fertility rates (Pew Research Center, 2017c).

Christianity, Islam, and Judaism are all most likely familiar to you—they are called the "Abrahamic faiths" because they all trace their origins to Abraham and all accept the Old Testament of the Bible as an authoritative religious source (although Christianity, unlike Judaism, is founded on the New Testament of the Bible as well, and Islam looks to the Qur'an as authoritative). Hinduism is less likely to be familiar, although yoga and meditation—practices associated with Hinduism and popularized in the United States—may provide at least superficial familiarity with the 4,000-year-old religion that originated in ancient India. The same can be

LEARNING OBJECTIVES

1 Basic Concepts

Understand how sociologists define and study religion. Learn about the different types of religious organizations: churches and sects, denominations, and cults.

2 Sociological Theories of Religion

Understand the sociological approaches to religion developed by Marx, Durkheim, and Weber; the contemporary debate over secularization; and the religious economy approach.

3 The Sociology of Religion: Current Research

Understand current trends in global religious affiliation and religious affiliation in the United States. Explore the interrelations of gender and religion, as well as the global rise of religious nationalism.

4 Unanswered Questions

Learn about the sociological debates surrounding trends such as fundamentalism, secularization, and religious violence.

THE ANSWER IS B, A, D, C, E.

said of Buddhism, a religion that also comes from India and includes contemplative practices such as meditation.

Toward the end of the nineteenth century, the German philosopher Friedrich Nietzsche announced, "God is dead." Religions, he argued, used to be a point of reference for our sense of purpose and meaning. Henceforth, we would have to live without this security. Living in a world without God would mean creating our own values and getting used to what Nietzsche called "the loneliness of being"—understanding that our lives are without purpose and that no superior entities watch over our fate. Nietzsche believed that with the rise of science and technology, **secularization**—the movement of a society away from religious beliefs and institutions—would triumph.

Nietzsche was clearly wrong in his prediction. Religion is one of the most truly global of all social institutions, affecting many aspects of life. Throughout the world today, there is a religious revival. While religious revival is not limited to any particular socioeconomic group, it has especially taken root among those who are the most dispossessed. While globalization has brought benefits to many, it has brought hardship to many as well. Grinding poverty, in combination with the erosion of long-standing cultural values and traditions, is fertile ground for religious revival—especially among young people, who comprise a large part of the population in countries in the global south. One major study of secularization and religious revival in nearly 200 societies around the world concluded that religious revival is likely to win out over secularization among people who lack what the authors term "existential security"—"the feeling that survival is secure enough that it can be taken for granted" (Norris and Inglehart, 2004).

Why is it important to have better knowledge of the world's religions? One reason is that it provides a better understanding of the global social changes of recent decades, in which religion has played a central role. For instance, in Vietnam in the 1960s, Buddhist priests burned themselves alive to protest the policies of the South Vietnamese government, contributing to the emergence of an antiwar movement in the United States, where the self-immolations were viewed on television. Today, Buddhist monks living in exile in India have set themselves on fire to protest Chinese rule over Tibet, while Buddhist monks in Thailand are protesting deforestation and inadequate care for AIDS victims.

During the latter part of the twentieth century, an activist form of Catholicism, **liberation theology**, combined Catholic beliefs with a passion for social justice for the poor, particularly in Central and South America and in Africa. Catholic priests and nuns organized farming cooperatives, built health clinics and schools, and challenged government policies that impoverished the peasantry; many paid with their lives for their activism, which government and military leaders often regard as subversive. Islamic socialists in Pakistan and Buddhist socialists in Sri Lanka have played a similar role (Berryman, 1987; Juergensmeyer, 1993;

secularization A process of decline in the influence of religion. Although modern societies have become increasingly secularized, tracing the extent of secularization is a complex matter. Secularization can refer to levels of involvement with religious organizations (such as rates of church attendance), the social and material influence wielded by religious organizations, and the degree to which people hold religious beliefs.

liberation theology An activist Catholic religious movement that combines Catholic beliefs with a passion for social justice for the poor.

Sigmund, 1990). In some Central and Eastern European countries once dominated by the former Soviet Union, long-suppressed religious organizations helped to overturn socialist regimes during the early 1990s. In Poland, for example, the Catholic Church was allied with the Solidarity movement, which toppled the socialist government in 1989. Churches and religious leaders played a key role in the abolition of slavery in the United States in the nineteenth century and the civil rights movement in the twentieth century.

Religion has also been central in reviving ancient ethnic and tribal hatreds. In Bosnia and elsewhere in the former Yugoslavia, for example, religious differences helped justify "ethnic cleansing," with Christian Serbs and Croats engaging in the mass murder, rape, and deportation of Muslims from communities and farmlands where the Muslims had lived for centuries. When religious beliefs align with strong national feelings, violence can result. And as we shall see, religious violence is not limited to any particular religion. While all major religions profess love and compassion, all have also given rise to offshoots that justify the use of violence (Juergensmeyer, 2001, 2008). Another reason it is important to better understand the world's religions is that ignorance can fuel suspicion, prejudice, and hatred.

On August 5, 2012, Wade Michael Page, a 40-year-old guitarist associated with hate-rock bands, walked into a Sikh temple in Oak Creek, Wisconsin, and opened fire on the worshippers. Before police respondents arrived and shot him, he had killed six people and wounded others. Page's reasons for shooting innocent worshippers may never be fully known; he died at the scene. But it is known that he was a White supremacist who hated Muslims and had reportedly called for massive bombing of the Middle East after September 11, 2001 (Goffard and Hennessy-Fiske, 2012). It seems likely that Page went on his shooting rampage intending to kill Muslims, not realizing that Sikhism is unrelated to Islam. Sikhism, a relatively new religious tradition some 500 years old, is unlikely to be familiar to most Americans, even though an estimated quarter million Sikhs live in the United States. To Page's bigoted eye, the turbaned Sikh men, with their long black beards, were likely indistinguishable from Muslims.

If Page indeed had been venting his anger against people he believed to be Muslims, he was not alone in harboring negative stereotypes. A nationwide survey in 2014 found that Americans viewed Islam more negatively than any other major religion (Pew Research Center, 2014m). Just three years earlier, a similar survey had found that only 57 percent of Americans had a favorable opinion of Muslims, compared with 89 percent for Christians and 82 percent for Jews. Among those polled, roughly half believed that some religions are

Anti-Islamic protestors gather outside an event for Texas Muslim Capitol Day. A 2014 survey found that Americans view Islam more negatively than any other major religion.

more prone to violence than others; fully 70 percent of those with such beliefs also claimed that Islam is the most violent religion, compared with 9 percent for Christianity and 2 percent for Judaism. In fact, nearly half (45 percent) of all Americans polled stereotyped Islam as violent, with 7 out of 10 reporting being concerned about Muslim extremism in the United States (Pew Research Center, 2011a).

Religion plays a key role in the world today. Religious groups were a major force in the Arab Spring that began with the self-immolation of Mohamed Bouazizi, a poor Tunisian street vendor who set himself on fire to protest harassment by corrupt local officials who had made it impossible for him to eke out a living selling produce from a cart. Bouazizi's sacrifice, seen around the world on YouTube and other social media, sparked revolutions in the Middle East and North Africa that overturned dictatorships in Egypt, Libya, and Yemen and sparked a civil war in Syria.

The popular 2011 uprising in Cairo's Tahrir Square toppled then-president Hosni Mubarak, a military leader who had run the country for 30 years. Egypt held its first free elections the following year, and the Muslim Brotherhood's candidate, Mohamed Morsi, was elected president with 52 percent of the popular vote. A large and influential religious organization throughout the Arab world, the Muslim Brotherhood had been kept mainly underground until then. Morsi came to be seen by many Egyptians, including the still-powerful military, as moving to consolidate power and shift Egypt in a strong Islamist direction. In 2013, he was arrested by the military, which launched a brutal crackdown against the Muslim Brotherhood and its perceived supporters. Tens of thousands were arrested as terrorists, and hundreds were sentenced to death. Abdel Fattah el-Sisi, the general who led the military coup, was elected president in 2014.

The Arab Spring proved to be equally fleeting elsewhere in the Middle East. Syria, Yemen, and Libya were ravaged by internal strife and civil wars that had, at least in part, a religious dimension. Conflicts spilled over into Jordan and Lebanon, as well as parts of North Africa. With the exception of Egypt, where it was repressed, there was a resurgence of Islamic fundamentalism throughout the region. The only country to remain democratic, among all the countries that had participated in the Arab Spring, was Tunisia—the country where it began. We will return to the role of religion in the Middle East later in this chapter.

1 BASIC CONCEPTS

Religion is one of the oldest human institutions. According to anthropologists, there have probably been about 100,000 religions throughout human history (Hadden, 1997a). When sociologists study religion, they hope to better understand its historical and contemporary role in shaping society and, conversely, the historical and contemporary social forces that shape religion itself (Hamilton, 2001).

Sociologists define **religion** as a cultural system of commonly shared beliefs and rituals that provides a sense of ultimate meaning and purpose by creating an idea of reality

> **religion** A set of beliefs adhered to by the members of a community, incorporating symbols regarded with a sense of awe or wonder together with ritual practices. Religions do not universally involve a belief in supernatural entities.

theism A belief in one or more supernatural deities.

that is sacred, all-encompassing, and supernatural (Berger, 1967; Durkheim, 1965, orig. 1912; Wuthnow, 1988). There are three key elements in this definition:

1. Religion is a form of culture, which consists of the shared beliefs, values, norms, and material conditions that create a common identity among a group of people. Religion has all these characteristics.
2. Religion involves beliefs that take the form of ritualized practices—special activities in which believers take part and that identify them as members of the religious community.
3. Religion provides a feeling that life is ultimately meaningful. It does so by explaining coherently and compellingly what transcends or overshadows everyday life, in ways that other aspects of culture (such as an educational system or a belief in democracy) cannot (Geertz, 1973; Wuthnow, 1988).

What is absent from the sociological definition of religion is just as important as what is included: Nowhere is there mention of a god. We often think of **theism**—a belief in one or more supernatural deities—as basic to religion, but this is not necessarily the case. As we shall see, some religions, such as Buddhism, believe in spiritual forces rather than a singular god.

How Sociologists Think about Religion

When sociologists study religion, they do so as unbiased scientists and not as believers (or disbelievers) in any particular faith. This stance has a number of implications:

- **Sociologists are not concerned with whether religious beliefs are true or false.** The sociological perspective regards religions as socially constructed by human beings. Thus, sociologists put aside their personal beliefs and address the human, rather than the divine, aspects of religion. Sociologists ask: How is the religion organized? What are its principal beliefs and values? How is it related to the larger society? What explains its success or failure in recruiting and retaining believers? The question of whether a particular belief is "good" or "true" is not something that sociologists can address. (As individuals, they may have strong opinions on the matter, but as sociologists, they must keep these opinions from biasing their research.)
- **Sociologists are especially concerned with the social organization of religion.** Not only are religions a primary source of the deepest-seated norms and values, but they are practiced through an enormous variety of social forms. Within Christianity and Judaism, for example, religious practice often occurs in formal organizations, such as churches or synagogues. Yet within Hinduism and Buddhism, religious practices occur in the home as well as in temples or other natural settings. The sociology of religion considers how different religious institutions and organizations actually function. The earliest European religions were often indistinguishable from the larger society since beliefs and practices were incorporated into daily life. In modern industrial society, however, some religions have become established in separate, often bureaucratic, organizations (Hammond, 1992). This institutionalization has led some

sociologists to view religions in the United States and Europe as similar to business organizations, competing with one another for members (Warner, 1993).

- **Sociologists have often viewed religions as a major source of social solidarity in that they offer believers a common set of norms and values.** Religious beliefs, rituals, and bonds create a "moral community" in which all members know how to behave (Wuthnow, 1988). If a single religion dominates a society, the religion may be an important source of social solidarity—although it may also be oppressive if, like the Taliban, it requires absolute conformity to a particular set of beliefs and punishes those who deviate.

- **If a society's members adhere to competing religions, religious differences may lead to destabilizing social conflicts.** Recent examples of religious conflict within a society include struggles among Sikhs, Hindus, and Muslims in India; clashes between Muslims and Christians in Bosnia and other parts of the former Yugoslavia; conflicts between Shiite and Sunni Muslims in Iraq; and hate crimes against Jews, Muslims, and other religious minorities in the United States.

- **Sociologists explain the appeal of religion in terms of social forces rather than personal, spiritual, or psychological factors.** Sociologists do not question the depth of believers' transcendent feelings and experiences, yet they also do not limit themselves to a purely spiritual explanation of religious commitment. In fact, some researchers argue that people often turn to, or "get," religion when their fundamental sense of social order is threatened by economic hardship, loneliness, loss or grief, physical suffering, or poor health (Berger, 1967; Glock, 1976; Schwartz, 1970; Stark and Bainbridge, 1980). In explaining the appeal of religious movements, sociologists are more likely to focus on problems in the social order than on the individual's psychological response.

What Do Sociologists of Religion Study?

Several types of social forces are of special interest to sociologists of religion. First, sociologists study the ways in which a crisis in prevailing beliefs promotes religious fervor. Such a crisis occurred in the United States during the 1960s as a result of the civil rights movement, opposition to the Vietnam War, social movements among racial and ethnic minorities, and the youth-oriented counterculture. Large numbers of people were attracted to religious teachers, ranging from Indian gurus to fundamentalist preachers, who offered everything from meditation and yoga to astrology and New Age religions (Wuthnow, 1988, 1998).

There is currently a resurgence of religious fervor throughout the world among Christians, Muslims, and Jews; while the reasons for this resurgence are not fully understood, part of the explanation has to do with the global changes sweeping the world today (Juergensmeyer, 2009). These include the failure of nonreligious institutions, particularly governments, to promote political and economic security in many parts of the world; the global spread of cultural norms and values and their perceived threat to traditional beliefs and values; and the explosion of new forms of media, especially the Internet, which has made it easier for religiously like-minded people to share their beliefs and build their religious institutions.

Second, sociologists study how competition among religious organizations leads some to thrive and others to perish. This study has sparked an increased interest in the organizational dynamics of religious groups (Finke and Stark, 1988, 2005; Hammond, 1992; Roof and McKinney, 1990; Stark and Bainbridge, 1987).

Third, sociologists address the relationship among religion, ethnic identity, and politics. This interconnection is seen in the resurgence of ethnically based religion in pluralist societies such as the United States and in the rise of religious nationalism worldwide (Juergensmeyer, 1993, 2008; Lawrence, 1989; Merkyl and Smart, 1983; Sahliyeh, 1990; see later discussion of religious nationalism).

Although the sociology of religion has long included non-European religions, there has been a tendency to view all religions through concepts based in the European experience. For example, notions such as *denomination*, *sect*, and *cult* (defined in the next section) presuppose formally organized religious institutions; they are of questionable utility in studying religions that emphasize spiritual practice as a part of daily life or that pursue the complete integration of religion with civic and political life. Recently, there has been an effort to create a comparative sociology of religion that examines religious traditions from within their own frames of reference (Juergensmeyer, 1993; Smart, 1989; van der Veer, 1994; Wilson, 1982).

Types of Religious Organizations

Early theorists such as Max Weber (1963; orig. 1922), Ernst Troeltsch (1931), and Richard Niebuhr (1929) described religious organizations according to the degree to which they were well established and conventional: In their view, churches are conventional and well established, cults are neither, and sects fall somewhere in the middle. These distinctions were based on a study of European and U.S. religions. There is much debate over how well they apply to the non-Christian world.

Churches and Sects

Churches are large, established religious bodies; one example is the Roman Catholic Church. They normally have a formal, bureaucratic structure with a hierarchy of officials. Churches often represent the conservative face of religion, because they are integrated within the existing institutional order. Most of their adherents are born into, and grow up within, the church.

A **sect** is typically described as a religious subgroup that breaks away from the larger organization and consequently follows its own unique set of rules and principles. Sects are smaller, less organized groups of committed believers, usually set up in protest of an established church. Sects aim to discover or follow the "true way" and try to either change the surrounding society or withdraw into communities of their own, a process known as *revival*. The members of sects often regard established churches as corrupt. Many sects have few or no officials, and all members are equal participants. For the most part, people are not born into sects but join them to further personal beliefs.

churches Large bodies of people belonging to an established religious organization. The term is also used to refer to the place in which religious ceremonies are carried out.

sects Religious movements that break away from orthodoxy.

Denominations

A **denomination** is a sect that has become an institutionalized body rather than an activist protest group. Sects that survive over time become denominations. Calvinism, Methodism, and Mormonism were sects during their early period, when they generated great fervor among their members; but, over the years, they became established denominations. (Calvinists today are called Presbyterians.) Denominations are recognized as legitimate by churches, often cooperating harmoniously with them. Other examples of Christian denominations include Baptists, Lutherans, and many of the evangelical Christian groups that have gained adherents and become more mainstream during recent decades.

denomination A religious sect that has lost its revivalist dynamism and become an institutionalized body, commanding the adherence of significant numbers of people.

cults Fragmentary religious groupings to which individuals are loosely affiliated but that lack any permanent structure.

Cults

Cults resemble sects, but their emphases are different. The most loosely knit and transient of all religious organizations, cults comprise individuals who reject the values of the outside society. They are a form of religious innovation rather than revival. Their focus is on individual experience, bringing like-minded people together. Cults often form around the influence of an inspirational leader.

Cults are often in a high degree of tension with the larger society. In 1997, 39 members of Heaven's Gate, a cult whose members believed they were destined for a "higher level," took their lives to ascend to a spaceship they believed lurked behind the Hale-Bopp Comet. The Japanese cult Aum Shinrikyo ("Om Supreme Truth"), which once claimed as many as 20,000 members, combined elements of Buddhism and Christianity, including Christian predictions about a pending global apocalypse derived from the Book of Revelations and the writings of the sixteenth-century Christian Nostradamus. (Such doomsday predictions are not uncommon in Christian cults as well.) Aum Shinrikyo's members regarded the group's founder and leader, Shoko Asahara, as Christ. In 1995, cult members released the deadly nerve gas sarin on five Tokyo subway trains; 12 people died and thousands were injured, some seriously. Investigations revealed that the cult had previously spread germs at numerous locations in Japan, although without any toxic effects. A large number of the cult members were subsequently tried and convicted in Japan for the subway gassing and other crimes; some, including Asahara, were sentenced to death. In 2000, Aum Shinrikyo changed its name to Aleph, reportedly moderated its teachings, and now claims 1,000 or so members (Juergensmeyer, 2008).

Like sects, cults flourish when there is a breakdown in well-established societal belief systems. This breakdown is happening worldwide today, in places as diverse as Japan, India, and the United States. When such a breakdown occurs, cults may either originate within the society itself or be "imported" from outside. In the United States, examples of homegrown, or indigenous, cults include New Age religions based on spiritualism, astrology, and religious practices adapted from Asian or Native American cultures. Examples of imported cults include the Reverend Sun Myung Moon's Unification Church (whose members are popularly, if derogatively, known

Members of the Unification Church, founded by Reverend Sun Myung Moon, participate in a mass wedding. The Holy Marriage Blessing Ceremony strengthens participants' dedication to the church.

as "Moonies"), which originated in South Korea, and the Transcendental Meditation movement, which was promoted by the Maharishi Mahesh Yogi in India. A cult arising out of the Siddha Yoga tradition was brought to the United States in the 1970s by Swami Muktananda; since his death in 1982, the global spiritual movement—it has centers in nearly three dozen countries—has been led by his female disciple Gurumayi Chidvilasananda.

A cult in one country may be an established religious practice in another. When Indian gurus practice in the United States, what might be considered an established religion in India is regarded as a cult in the United States. Christianity began as an indigenous cult in ancient Jerusalem, and in many Asian countries today, evangelical Protestantism is regarded as a cult imported from the United States. A leading sociologist of religion, Jeffrey K. Hadden (1997a), points out that all the approximately 100,000 religions that humans have devised were once new; most were initially despised cults from the standpoint of respectable religious belief of the times. For example, Jesus was crucified because his ideas threatened the established order of the Roman-dominated religious establishment of ancient Judaea.

CONCEPT CHECKS

1 What are the three main components of religion as a social institution?

2 How do sociologists differ from other scholars in their approach to studying religion?

3 Describe four types of religious organizations.

2 SOCIOLOGICAL THEORIES OF RELIGION

Sociological approaches to religion are strongly influenced by the ideas of Marx, Durkheim, and Weber. None of the three theorists was religious himself, and each argued that religion was fundamentally an illusion: The very diversity of religions and their obvious connection to different societies and regions made their advocates' claims inherently implausible, according to these early theorists.

The Classical View

Marx, Weber, and Durkheim all wrote about religion but drew radically different conclusions. For Marx, religion was a form of false consciousness, blinding people to the underlying causes of inequality. Durkheim viewed religion as an important source of social solidarity, while Weber analyzed the relationship between religion and the emergence of capitalism.

Marx: Religion and Inequality

Karl Marx never studied religion in any detail. His thinking on religion was derived mostly from the writings of Ludwig Feuerbach, who believed that through a process he called **alienation**, human beings attribute their own culturally created values and norms to alien, or separate, beings (i.e., divine forces or gods) because they do not understand their own history. Thus, the story of the Ten Commandments given to Moses by God is a mythical version of the origins of moral precepts that govern the lives of Jewish and Christian believers.

Marx accepted Feuerbach's view that religion represents human self-alienation. In a famous phrase, he declared that religion was the "opium of the people":

> Religion is the sigh of the oppressed creature, the heart of a heartless world, just as it is the spirit of a spiritless situation. It is the opium of the people. The abolition of religion as the illusory happiness of the people is required for their real happiness. (Marx, 1994; orig. 1843–1844)

Religion defers happiness and rewards to the afterlife, Marx argued, teaching a resigned acceptance of conditions in the earthly life—including inequalities and injustices. Religion contains a strong ideological element: Religious belief can provide justifications for those in power. For example, "The meek shall inherit the earth" suggests humility and nonresistance to oppression. In Marx's view, people had to shed their religious beliefs to better understand the social forces that were oppressing them. Only then, he argued, would people rise up, overthrow the oppressive order, and create a society that truly served their interests.

> **alienation** The sense that our own abilities as human beings are taken over by other entities. The term was originally used by Karl Marx to refer to the projection of human powers onto gods. Subsequently, he used the term to refer to the loss of workers' control over the nature and products of their labor.

Durkheim: Religion and Functionalism

In contrast to Marx, Émile Durkheim extensively studied religion and connected religion not with social inequalities or power but with the overall nature of a society's institutions. In *The Elementary Forms of the Religious Life* (1965; orig. 1912), Durkheim concentrated on *totemism*, the worship of objects such as animals or plants believed to embody mystical spirits. Durkheim studied totemism as practiced by Australian aboriginal societies, arguing that such totemism represented religion in its most "elementary" form.

Durkheim defined religion in terms of a distinction between the sacred and the profane. **Sacred** objects and symbols, he held, are treated as apart from routine aspects of day-to-day existence—the realm of the **profane**. A totem (an animal or plant believed to have symbolic significance), Durkheim argued, is a sacred object, regarded with veneration and surrounded by ritual activities. These ceremonies and rituals, in Durkheim's view, are essential to unifying the members of groups.

Durkheim's theory of religion is a good example of the functionalist tradition. To analyze the function of a social behavior or social institution such as religion is to study its contribution to the continuation of a group, community, or society. According to Durkheim, religion promotes a stable society by ensuring that people meet regularly to affirm common beliefs and values.

Weber: World Religions and Social Change

Whereas Durkheim based his arguments on a restricted range of examples, Max Weber conducted a massive study of religions worldwide. No scholar before or since has undertaken a task of the scope Weber attempted. His writings on religion differ from those of Durkheim because they concentrate on the connection between religion and social change, and they contrast with those of Marx because Weber argued that religion was not necessarily a conservative force; on the contrary, religiously inspired movements have often produced dramatic social transformations. Thus, Protestantism, particularly Puritanism, according to Weber, was the source of the capitalist outlook found in the modern West. The early entrepreneurs were mostly Calvinists. Their drive to succeed, which helped initiate Western economic development, was originally prompted

Max Weber categorized Eastern religions as "otherworldly" and Christianity as a "salvation religion." Weber believed that Hinduism stressed escaping material existence to a higher plane of being, which cultivated an attitude of passivity. In contrast, he argued that Christianity and its emphasis on salvation could stimulate revolt against the existing order.

by a desire to serve God. Material success was considered a sign of divine favor. But because Calvinists also believed that one should not ostentatiously flaunt one's wealth, Calvinist entrepreneurs were likely to reinvest their wealth in their enterprises, rather than spend it on personal consumption. Such "worldly asceticism," as Weber called it, resulted in capital accumulation—the hallmark of a successful capitalist system.

Weber's discussion of the effect of Protestantism on the development of the West was connected to a comprehensive attempt to understand the influence of religion on social and economic life in various cultures. After analyzing the Eastern religions, Weber concluded that they prevented the widespread development of industrial capitalism because they were oriented toward different values, such as escape from the toils of the material world. In traditional India and China, Weber held, periodic development of commerce, manufacturing, and urbanism did not generate the radical patterns of social change that led to industrial capitalism in the West. In his view, Indian and Chinese belief systems significantly inhibited such change. Hinduism in India, he argued, sees material reality as a veil hiding the true spiritual concerns to which humankind should be oriented; one should focus on spiritual development rather than the material world.

In China, according to Weber, Confucianism also directs activity away from economic "progress" because it emphasizes harmony with the world rather than promoting an active mastery of it. Although China was long the most powerful and most culturally developed civilization in the world, its dominant religious values acted as a brake on a stronger commitment to economic development. It is interesting to note that a century later, sociologists have attributed the current economic growth of China and other East Asian countries, at least in part, to the same set of beliefs that Weber saw as a deterrent, drawing parallels between certain aspects of Confucianism and the Protestant ethic (Tu, 1989; Berger, 1988).

Weber regarded Christianity as a *salvation religion*—one in which human beings can be "saved" if they accept the beliefs of the religion and follow its moral tenets. The notions of sin and of being rescued from sinfulness by God's grace generate an emotional dynamism absent from the Eastern religions. Whereas Eastern religions cultivate an attitude of passivity or acceptance, Christianity demands a constant struggle against sin and thereby can stimulate revolt against the existing order. Religious leaders—such as Luther or Calvin—have arisen who reinterpret doctrines in such a way as to challenge the existing power structure.

Critical Assessment of the Classical View

Marx, Durkheim, and Weber each identified some important general characteristics of religions, and, in some ways, their views complement one another. Marx was right to claim that religion often has ideological implications, serving to justify the interests of ruling groups at the expense of others. There are innumerable examples in history. Consider the European missionaries who sought to convert "heathen" peoples to Christian beliefs; their motivations may have been sincere, yet their teachings reinforced the destruction of traditional cultures and the imposition of White domination. Also, almost all Christian denominations tolerated or endorsed slavery in the United States and other parts of the world into the nineteenth century. Doctrines were developed proclaiming slavery to be based on divine law, with disobedient slaves being considered guilty of an offense against God as well as their masters (Stampp, 1956).

secular thinking Worldly thinking, particularly as seen in the rise of science, technology, and rational thought in general.

But Weber was also correct in stressing the unsettling and often revolutionary effect of religious ideals on the established social order. In spite of the churches' early support for slavery in the United States, church leaders later played a key role in fighting to abolish the institution. Religious beliefs have at times prompted social movements against unjust systems of authority. Religious sentiments were prominent in the civil rights movements of the 1960s, where Black churches played the key role. Dr. Martin Luther King Jr., a Baptist minister, was a cofounder of the Southern Christian Leadership Conference, an organization of Southern Black churches dedicated to ending racial segregation through nonviolent protests (Branch, 1989, 1999, 2007).

The divisive influences of religion find little mention in Durkheim's work, which emphasized the role of religion in promoting social cohesion. Yet it is not difficult to redirect his ideas toward explaining religious division, conflict, and change, as well as solidarity. After all, much of the strength of feeling generated against other religious groups derives from the commitment to religious values that binds each community of believers. Among the most valuable points of Durkheim's writings is his emphasis on ritual and ceremony. All religions hold regular assemblies of believers, at which ritual prescriptions are observed. As Durkheim rightly points out, ritual activities also mark the major transitions of life—birth, entry to adulthood, marriage, and death (van Gennep, 1977; orig. 1908).

Marx, Durkheim, and Weber based their theories of religion on their studies of societies in which a single religion predominated. Consequently, it seemed reasonable to examine the relationship between a predominant religion and the society as a whole. However, since the 1950s, some U.S. sociologists have challenged this classical view. Living in a society that is highly tolerant of religious diversity, contemporary theorists have focused on religious pluralism rather than on religious domination. Not surprisingly, their conclusions differ substantially from the views of Marx, Durkheim, and Weber, each of whom regarded religion as closely bound with the larger society. Religion was believed to reflect and reinforce society's values, or at least the values of those who are most powerful; provide solidarity and social stability; and serve as an engine of social change. According to this view, religion is threatened by **secular thinking**, particularly as seen in the rise of science, technology, and rational thought.

Secularization, as we have noted previously, involves a decrease in religious belief and involvement, and therefore results in a weakening of the social and political power of religious organizations. Peter Berger (1967) has described religion in premodern societies as a "sacred canopy" that covers all aspects of life and is seldom questioned. In modern society, however, the sacred canopy is more like a quilt, a patchwork of different religious and secular belief systems. When beliefs are compared, it becomes increasingly difficult to sustain the idea that there is any single true faith.

Contemporary Approaches: Religious Economy

One influential recent approach to the sociology of religion is tailored to societies, such as the United States, that encompass many different faiths. Taking their cue from economic theory, sociologists who favor the **religious economy** approach argue that religions can be understood as organizations in competition with one another for followers (Finke and Stark, 1988, 2005; Hammond, 1992; Moore, 1994; Roof and McKinney, 1990; Stark and Bainbridge, 1980, 1985, 1987; Warner, 1993). These sociologists argue that competition is preferable to monopoly when it comes to ensuring religious vitality. Whereas the classical theorists Marx, Durkheim, and Weber assumed that religion was weakened when challenged by different religious or secular viewpoints, the advocates of the religious economy perspective argue that competition increases the overall level of religious involvement in society. First, the competition makes each religious group try that much harder to win followers. Second, the presence of numerous religions means there is likely something for everyone. In a culturally diverse society, a single religion will probably appeal to a limited range of followers, whereas the presence of, say, Hindu gurus and fundamentalist preachers, in addition to mainline churches, will likely encourage a high level of religious participation.

> **religious economy** A theoretical framework within the sociology of religion that argues that religions can be fruitfully understood as organizations in competition with one another for followers.

This analysis is adapted from the business world, in which competition presumably encourages the emergence of specialized products appealing to specific markets. In fact, religious economists borrow the language of business in describing the conditions that lead to the success or failure of a particular religious organization. According to Finke and Stark (2005), a successful religious group must be well organized for competition, have eloquent preachers who are effective "sales reps" in spreading the word, offer beliefs and rituals that are packaged as an appealing product, and develop effective marketing techniques. Television evangelists, or televangelists, have been especially good businesspeople in selling religious products. As Finke and Stark (2005) put it, "The churching of America was accomplished by aggressive churches committed to vivid otherworldliness." Religious economy scholars thus do not see competition as undermining religious beliefs and contributing to secularization. Rather, they argue that modern religion constantly renews itself through active marketing and recruitment.

Religious economy scholars argue that successful religious groups must have effective representatives spreading their beliefs. For example, the fall of communism in Mongolia brought religious freedom to this sparsely populated country located between China and Russia. It also brought foreigners eager for converts, such as Mormon missionaries.

Although a large body of research supports the notion that competition is good for religion, not all studies come to this same conclusion (Land, Deane, and Blau, 1991). Some have argued that the religious economy approach overestimates the extent to which people rationally choose a religion. According to this view, among deeply committed believers, even in societies where people can choose among religions, most practice their childhood religion without considering alternatives. Wade Clark Roof's 1993 study of 1,400 baby boomers found that a third remained loyal to their childhood faith, while another third continued to profess their childhood beliefs although they no longer belonged to a religious organization. Thus, only a third were actively seeking a new religion, making the sorts of choices the religious economy approach presumes.

A study by the Pew Research Center, however, found Americans to be more religiously fickle than was previously believed. The study, based on thousands of interviews, concluded, "Americans change religious affiliation early and often" (Pew Research Center, 2009). A more recent 2015 study from Pew found that a third of American adults (34 percent) practice a different religion than the one they were born into, not including switching among different Protestant denominations (Pew Research Center, 2015c). Americans—especially young people—more than ever seem to be a nation of seekers.

Secularization: The Sociological Debate

The debate over secularization is one of the most complex areas in the sociology of religion. Basically, the disagreement is between supporters of the secularization thesis (who see religion as diminishing in power and importance in the modern world) and opponents (who argue that religion remains a significant force, albeit often in new and unfamiliar forms).

There is little consensus about how to measure secularization or even how to define religion. Some argue that religion is best understood in terms of the world's traditional faiths; others seek a much broader view to include dimensions such as personal spirituality and deep commitment to certain values. We can evaluate secularization according to a number of dimensions. Some are objective, such as the level of membership of religious organizations—how many people belong to a church or other religious body and attend services or other ceremonies. With the exception of the United States, the industrialized countries have all experienced considerable secularization according to this index.

The pattern of religious decline seen in Britain is found in most of Western Europe, including predominantly Catholic countries such as France and Italy. More Italians than French attend church regularly and participate in the major rituals (such as Easter Communion), but the overall pattern of declining religious observance is similar in both cases. In France and Germany, less than 10 percent attend weekly religious services; in Belgium, the Netherlands, the United Kingdom, and Luxembourg, 10–15 percent are regular churchgoers. Regular attendance is only marginally higher in Spain (21 percent), Portugal (29 percent), and Italy (31 percent) (Manchin, 2004).

The United States is by far the most religious country among the advanced industrialized nations. Indeed, when sociologists Pippa Norris and Ronald Inglehart (2004) examined data from four World Values Surveys conducted over a 20-year period in 80 societies, they concluded that the United States was one of the most religious nations in the world. A recent survey found that 51 percent of Americans say that religion is very important in their lives, compared to 29 percent in Canada, 21 percent in Italy, 22 percent in Spain, 11 percent in Germany, 11 percent in France, and 10 percent in Japan (Brenan, 2018; Evans and Baronavski, 2018; Lipka, 2019; Pew Research Center, 2018).

In the global south, the story is quite different. In the poorest countries, where people are most vulnerable, religiosity is thriving. This is especially true in parts of the Islamic world, but it can also be seen in the growing strength of Christianity, especially in Africa. In sub-Saharan Africa, the regional average is 89 percent of people who say religion is very important in their lives (Pew Research Center, 2018). A recent report by the Pew Research Center on the future of world religions estimated that 4 out of every 10 Christians in the world will live in sub-Saharan Africa by 2050 (Pew Research Center, 2015a). People who live in the poorest nations are not only more religious than people who live in industrialized ones; they also have much higher fertility rates, so their population is growing more rapidly. As Norris and Inglehart (2004) succinctly put it, "The world as a whole now has more people with traditional religious views than ever before—and they constitute a growing proportion of the world's population."

A second dimension of secularization concerns how far churches and other religious organizations maintain their social influence, wealth, and prestige. In earlier times, religious organizations wielded considerable power over governments and social agencies and commanded high respect in the community. How much is this still the case? By the twenty-first century, religious organizations had lost much of their former social and political influence, particularly in the advanced industrial nations. Church leaders could no longer expect to be as influential with the powerful. Although some established churches remain very wealthy and some new religious movements have rapidly built up fortunes, the material circumstances of many long-standing

Muslims pray at the Grand Mosque in Senegal. Religion is thriving in the global south, particularly in countries in sub-Saharan Africa, which is projected to be home to a growing share of the world's Muslims.

CONCEPT CHECKS

1 Why did Karl Marx call religion "the opium of the people"?

2 What are the differences between classical and contemporary approaches to understanding religion?

3 Does the Pew study provide support for the religious economy approach? Why or why not?

religious organizations have become insecure. In the United States, however, since the 1970s, there has been a resurgence in the power of churches, particularly from what has come to be known as the Christian Right. We shall discuss this resurgence later in this chapter.

A third dimension of secularization concerns beliefs and values—the dimension of religiosity. As in the other dimensions, we need an accurate understanding of the past to see how far religiosity has declined today. Supporters of the secularization thesis argue that in the past, religion was far more important to daily life than it is now. The church was at the heart of local affairs and strongly influenced family and personal life. Yet critics of this thesis argue that just because people attended church more regularly does not prove that they were more religious. As two leading sociologists of religion have noted, most Americans during Colonial times were far from puritanical, even though American schoolchildren are raised on images of pious Pilgrims bowed in prayer over Thanksgiving turkey. According to Roger Finke and Rodney Stark (2005), "Boston's taverns were probably fuller on Saturday night than were its churches on Sunday morning." Finke and Stark go on to argue that Americans are in fact more religious today on the whole than they were in Colonial times—largely because there are more religions to choose from, as we shall see in the following section of this chapter.

On balance, it does seem that the hold of religious ideas today is weaker than in the traditional world—particularly if we include the range of the supernatural. Most of us no longer experience our environment as permeated by divine or spiritual entities that need to be worshipped and placated, lest they do us harm. It is certainly true that some of the major tensions in the world today—such as those afflicting the Middle East or the violence perpetrated by ISIS—derive from religious differences. But the majority of conflicts and wars remain secular, concerned with divergent political goals or material interests, although these may coincide with ethnic and religious differences.

3 THE SOCIOLOGY OF RELIGION: CURRENT RESEARCH

If classical theorists believed that religious beliefs were giving way to scientific thought and secularization, today it is clear that a religious revival has been occurring, both globally and in the United States. In our review of current research, we first present a current picture of trends in world religions and religion in the United States, before turning to two topics that are of particular interest to many sociologists of religion: gender and religion, and the global rise of religious nationalism.

World Religions

monotheism Belief in a single god.

Although there are thousands of religions worldwide, three of them—Christianity, Islam, and Hinduism—are embraced by nearly three-quarters of the people on earth (Global Map 17.1).

Christianity

With its estimated 2.4 billion followers—roughly a third of the world's population—Christianity encompasses enormously divergent denominations, sects, and cults (CIA, 2020c). Common to all is the belief that Jesus of Nazareth was the Christ (Messiah, or "anointed one") foretold in the Hebrew Bible. Christianity is a form of **monotheism**—belief in a single all-knowing, all-powerful God—although in most Christian faiths, God is also regarded as a trinity embracing a heavenly Father, His Son the Savior, and His sustaining Holy Spirit.

When Christianity emerged in ancient Palestine some 2,000 years ago, it was a persecuted sect outside mainstream Jewish and Roman religious practices. Yet within four centuries, Christianity had become the official religion of the Roman Empire. In the eleventh century, Christianity divided into the Eastern Orthodox Church (based in Constantinople, now Istanbul) and the Catholic Church (based in Rome). A second great split occurred within the Catholic branch in the sixteenth century, when the Protestant Reformation gave rise to numerous Protestant denominations, sects, and cults. Protestants emphasize a direct relationship between the individual and God,

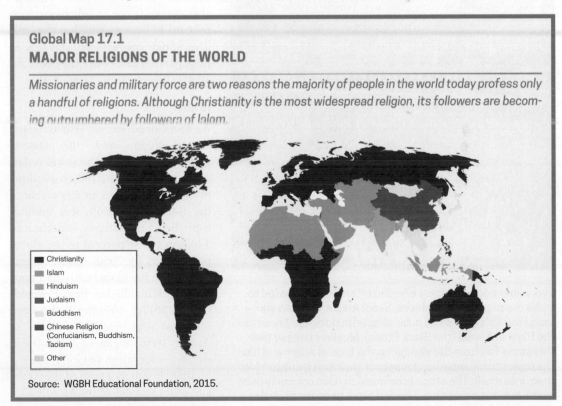

Global Map 17.1
MAJOR RELIGIONS OF THE WORLD

Missionaries and military force are two reasons the majority of people in the world today profess only a handful of religions. Although Christianity is the most widespread religion, its followers are becoming outnumbered by followers of Islam.

- Christianity
- Islam
- Hinduism
- Judaism
- Buddhism
- Chinese Religion (Confucianism, Buddhism, Taoism)
- Other

Source: WGBH Educational Foundation, 2015.

with each person being responsible for his or her own salvation. Catholics, in contrast, emphasize the importance of the Church hierarchy as the means to salvation, with the pope in Rome being the highest earthly authority.

Christianity was spread through conquest and missionary work. The European colonization of much of Africa, Asia, and North and South America that began in the fifteenth century brought Christian teachings, churches, and large-scale conversion of native peoples. In some places, converts were people from the impoverished classes, for whom Christianity was a means of social mobility. Only in Asia are Christians a small minority, largely because countries such as Japan and China successfully resisted most colonization and its accompanying Christianization.

Recently, Protestant evangelical groups have increased their efforts to convert people throughout the world, making significant inroads in traditionally Catholic countries. Protestant missionaries from the United States not only "spread the Word," but they also build homes and orphanages, help local people start small businesses, and engage in a variety of relief and development projects in the global south (Wuthnow, 2010). Local Protestant missionaries also play a key role. In Mexico, for example, the number of evangelical Protestants grew from 900,000 to 6.1 million between 1970 and 2000, owing to the efforts of local (Mexican) missionaries. Most of this increase has been in rural areas, including those areas where indigenous people predominate. The growth of evangelical Christianity may prove difficult to sustain. It makes considerable demands on its followers, so it remains to be seen whether the children of new converts will stay true to their parents' faith once they become adults (Bowen, 1996; Dow, 2005).

Every able-bodied Muslim who can afford to is obligated to make the pilgrimage to Mecca, Saudi Arabia. Pilgrims surround the Ka'aba, a small cube-shaped building that houses the Hajar al Aswad (the Black Stone). Muslims believe that this stone fell from the sky during the time of Adam and has the power to cleanse worshippers of their sins by absorbing them into itself. The stone is believed to have originally been white, but it is said to have turned black because of all the sins it has absorbed.

Islam

As mentioned earlier, Islam is the second-largest, and the fastest-growing, religion in the world today. There were about 1.8 billion Muslims in the world in 2015, or 23 percent of the global population; that number is predicted to increase 70 percent to 3 billion (or 31 percent of the global population) by 2050, reaching near parity with the global Christian population (CIA, 2020c; Pew Research Center, 2017c). (*Muslim* is the word for those who practice *al-islam*, an Arabic term meaning submission without reservation to God's will.)

Islam began as a faith of the Arabs and other peoples of the Middle East and has spread into Africa, Central

Asia, China, Europe, India, Indonesia, Pakistan, and Russia. Today, some 50 countries have Muslim-majority populations, while more than 60 different ethnic groups of a million or more people practice Islam. In fact, far more non-Arabs than Arabs identify as Muslims. Indonesia, for example, is by far the largest Muslim country in the world. With 232 million adherents, it is home to 13 percent of the global Muslim population (CIA, 2020b). A number of non-Muslim countries have large Muslim minorities, among them Hindu-majority India, with 188 million Muslims (14.2 percent of the population), Ethiopia (36.6 million, or 34 percent), and Russia (14.3 million, or 10 percent). Although less than 2 percent of China's population is Muslim, the numbers are nonetheless large (25.1 million) (CIA Factbook, 2020c). In 2010, there were 43.5 million Muslims living in Europe, about 6 percent of the total European population (Pew Research Center, 2015c), mostly immigrants seeking better economic opportunities.

Home to an estimated 13 percent of the global Muslim population, Indonesia is the largest Muslim country in the world.

Muslims believe in absolute, unquestioning, positive devotion to Allah (God) (Aslan, 2006). Although modern Islam dates to the Arab prophet Muhammad (c. 570–632), Muslims trace their religion to the ancient Hebrew prophet Abraham, also regarded as the founder of Judaism. The precepts of Islam are believed to have been revealed to Muhammad and are contained in a sacred book dictated to his followers, called the Qur'an (the common English form of the book's name, which means "recitation"). Muhammad's ideas were not accepted in his birthplace of Mecca, so in 622, he and his followers moved to Medina (both in what is today Saudi Arabia). This migration, called the *hegira*, marks the beginning of Islam, which soon spread throughout Arabia. Muslims do not worship Muhammad but regard him as a great teacher and prophet, the last in a line that includes Abraham, Noah, Moses, and Jesus.

Islam is an all-encompassing religion. The sacred *sharia* ("way") includes prescriptions for worship, daily life, ethics, and government. Although U.S. standards might find Muslim beliefs to be extremely restrictive, Muslims frequently view American life as spiritually undisciplined, corrupt, and immoral (Abdul-Rauf, 1975; Arjomand, 1988; Esposito, 1984; Kedouri, 1992; MacEnoin and al-Shahi, 1983; Martin, 1982).

Islam, like Christianity, comprises different religious groups. The principal division is between Sunnis (about 87–90 percent of all Muslims) and Shiites (about 10–13 percent) (Pew Research Center, 2015a). Sunni Muslims follow a series of traditions deriving from the Qur'an that tolerate a diversity of opinion, in contrast to the more rigid views of Shiites. Shiism split from the main body of orthodox Islam early in its history and has remained influential ever since. Iran (once known as Persia) is the only major Islamic country that is overwhelmingly Shiite, although there are Shiite majorities in several other countries, including Iraq. Large numbers of Shiites are found in other Middle Eastern countries and in Turkey, Afghanistan, India, and Pakistan. A sect known as Sufism encompasses more mysticism and rituals than the practice by Sunnis and Shiites (Pew Research Center, 2012b).

Shiism has been the official religion of Iran since the sixteenth century and was fundamental to the religiously conservative Iranian Revolution of 1978–1979. The Shiites trace their beginnings to Imam Ali, a seventh-century religious and political leader who showed outstanding virtue and personal devotion to God. Ali's descendants were considered the rightful leaders of Islam because they were held to belong to the prophet Muhammad's family, unlike the dynasties actually in power. The Shiites believed that the rule of Muhammad's rightful heir would eventually be instituted, doing away with the tyrannies and injustices associated with existing regimes. Muhammad's heir would be a leader directly guided by God, governing in accordance with the Qur'an.

There is no separation of church and state in a few highly religious Islamic societies, such as Iran. In most Muslim countries, however, religious leaders live in uneasy alliance with secular governments. Algeria, Egypt, Indonesia, and Turkey, for example, are all predominantly Muslim societies in which mosque and state are separate. As we noted in Chapter 13, even countries such as Jordan, Morocco, and Turkey, where more religiously traditional Islamist parties have won recent elections, have not lost basic democratic values or the fundamental separation of mosque and state.

Judaism

With 15.3 million followers worldwide, Judaism is by far the smallest of the world's major religions. Jews were among the first people to practice monotheism. According to Jewish beliefs, some 3,500 years ago, God entered into a covenant with Abraham, a descendant of Noah: Abraham was to spread the word of God, and he in turn would father a "great nation" (Genesis 12:2) in the land that now includes Israel. As a symbol of this covenant, all the male descendants of Abraham were to be circumcised in a ritual ceremony eight days after birth.

The story of Abraham and his descendants is told in the first five books of the Bible, called the Torah ("teachings" or "law"), which provides a foundation for Jewish religious beliefs (as well as those of the other "Abrahamic" traditions, Christianity and Islam). These teachings include the Ten Commandments, which, according to the Torah, were among the laws God revealed to Moses during the 40 years the Jews were wandering in the Sinai Desert after escaping from Egyptian slavery. According to Jewish tradition, the entire Torah is read in an annual cycle during religious services. The Jewish Bible is made up of 24 books: the Torah, the writings of the prophets, philosophical works (for example, the Book of Job), and poetry (such as the Psalms). In the Christian tradition, these books are collectively known as the Old Testament, to distinguish them from the New Testament, which focuses on the story and teachings of Jesus. Later texts that are central to Jewish beliefs include the Talmud, a compendium of the debates and teachings of Jewish rabbis (religious teachers) over many centuries.

After their desert wanderings, the Jews eventually conquered the land promised by God to Abraham, encompassing what is today Israel, Lebanon, and the west bank of the Jordan River, along with coastal parts of Jordan, Egypt, and Syria. Jerusalem became the religious center and political capital of the Jewish nation some 3,000 years ago, although it was conquered numerous times by various empires during the next thousand years. During times of conquest, some Jews began to flee to other countries, in what later became known as the Diaspora (exile or "scattering"). During the first century after Jesus, the Diaspora became complete: Following an unsuccessful revolt against their Roman conquerors, the remaining Jews were forced to settle throughout Europe and parts of North Africa and the Middle East. Throughout this period, religious Jews lamented the loss of Jerusalem; every year, after recounting the escape of the Jews from Egyptian slavery during the ritual Passover meal called the *seder* ("order"), the vow was made: "next year in Jerusalem."

Judaism has exerted an influence greater than its limited numbers would suggest. First, as noted, it is the source of the world's two largest religions, Christianity and Islam. Second, in European and U.S. culture, Jews have played a role disproportionate to their numbers in such diverse fields as music, literature, science, education, and business. Third, the existence of Israel as a Jewish state since 1948 has given the Jewish faith international prominence. Israel has existed in nearly constant tension with many of its neighboring Arab countries since its founding and has seldom been out of the news.

Jews have often suffered persecution. From the twelfth century on, European and Russian Jews were often forced to live in special districts termed "ghettos," where they lacked full rights as citizens and were sometimes the target of harassment, attacks, and murders. Partly in reaction to these conditions, and partly because the Torah identifies the city of Jerusalem as the center of the Jewish homeland, some Jews embraced *Zionism*, a movement calling for the return of Jews to ancient Palestine and the creation of a Jewish state. (Zion is a biblical name for the ancient city of Jerusalem.) Although secular Zionists viewed Israel as a country where persecuted Jews could seek refuge, religious Zionists saw it as the one Jewish homeland and saw returning to it as fulfilling biblical prophecies. Zionists established settlements in Palestine early in the twentieth century, living relatively peacefully with their Arab and Palestinian neighbors. However, after World War II and the Nazi extermination of 6 million Jews during the Holocaust, the League of Nations, and subsequently the United Nations, approved the creation of the state of Israel as a homeland for the survivors. This action ended the once relatively peaceful relationship between Zionists and their neighbors.

Hinduism

Hinduism, which dates to about 2000 B.C.E., is one of the world's oldest religions. It is not based on the teachings of any individual, and its followers do not trace their national origins to a single god. Hinduism is an ethical religion that calls for an ideal way of life. There were just over 1 billion Hindus worldwide in 2020, comprising 15 percent of the global population; 94 percent of the world's Hindu population (974 million) lives in India, comprising 80 percent of India's population (Pew Research Center, 2017c). Nepal and Bangladesh follow far behind with 24.6 and 16.2 million Hindus, respectively (CIA, 2020c).

As we saw in Chapter 8, India's social structure is characterized by a caste system in which people are believed to be born into a certain status that they occupy for life. Although the caste system was officially abolished in 1949, it remains powerful. The caste system has its origins in Hindu beliefs that hold that an ideal life is partly achieved by performing the duties appropriate to one's caste.

Perhaps because Hinduism does not have a central organization or leader, its philosophy and practice are extremely diverse. Religious teachings direct all aspects of life, but in a variety of ways—ranging from promoting the enjoyment of sensual pleasures to advising the renunciation of earthly pursuits. Mohandas Gandhi was a modern example of a man who devoted his life to the Hindu virtues of "honesty, courage, service, faith, self-control, purity, and non-violence" (Potter, 1992).

Despite the teaching that life is *maya*, or "illusion," Hindu religious beliefs have an earthly quality. For example, although temples and pilgrimage centers are located on sacred sites, any location may be a place of devotion. Hindus believe in the godlike unity of all things, yet their religion also has aspects of **polytheism**—the belief that different gods represent various categories of natural forces. For example, Hindus worship gods representing aspects of the whole, such as the divine dimension of a spiritual teacher (Basham, 1989; Kinsley, 1982; Potter, 1992; Schmidt, 1980).

Religion in the United States

As we noted earlier, in comparison with citizens of other industrial nations, Americans are highly religious. Even though secularization may have weakened the power of religious institutions in the United States, it has not significantly diminished the strength of religious beliefs. In 2017, more than half (53 percent) of all American adults said religion is "very important" in their lives, a slight decline from 2007 (when it was 56 percent); 89 percent reported believing in God (down from 92 percent), while 55 percent said they pray daily (down from 58 percent) (Pew Research Center, 2018).

Yet one long-term measure of religiosity, based on indicators such as belief in God, religious membership, and attendance at religious services, found that the index reached its highest levels in the 1950s and has declined ever since—in part because post–World War II baby boomers were less religious, at least in the traditional sense, than their predecessors (Roof, 1999). In one national survey, overwhelming majorities of Catholics, liberal Protestants, and conservative Protestants reported attending church weekly while they were children, although their attendance had dropped sharply by the time they reached their early twenties. Among the three groups, attendance had declined the most among liberal Protestants and the least among conservative Protestants (Roof, 1999).

Another survey of nearly 114,000 adults in 1990 and more than 50,000 adults in 2007 found that religious identification had declined sharply during the 17-year period. In 1990, 90 percent of all respondents identified with some religious group; in 2007, the figure was 83 percent. By 2014, the proportion of American adults who were religiously affiliated had dropped even further, to 77 percent. The principal decline has been among self-identified Christians (from 78 percent in 2007 to 71 percent in 2014), specifically mainline Protestants and Catholics. In contrast, the number of adults who report no religious affiliation is growing, referred to as the "rise of the nones." In 2019, religious "nones"—people who identify as atheists or agnostics or who say their religion is "nothing in particular"—comprised nearly a quarter (26 percent) of the U.S. adult population, up from 16 percent in 2007. Much of this growth can be tied to generational replacement: 40 percent of millennials are religiously unaffiliated (Pew Research Center, 2019c).

Civil Religion

Although there is a constitutional separation of church and state in the United States, all U.S. presidents have attended church, and some have been deeply and publicly religious. In fact, sociologists have argued that the United States has a **civil religion**— a set of religious beliefs through which a society interprets its own history in light of some conception of ultimate reality (Bellah, 1968, 1975). Civil religion usually consists

civil religion A set of religious beliefs through which a society interprets its own history in light of some conception of ultimate reality.

of "god-language used in reference to the nation," including "historical myths about the society's divine origins, beliefs about its sacred historical purpose, and occasionally religious restrictions on societal membership" (Wuthnow, 1988). The notion that westward expansion in the nineteenth century was America's "Manifest Destiny" is one example.

The importance of civil religion in the United States is seen in the Pledge of Allegiance. By referring to "one nation, under God," the pledge infuses civic life with a religious belief derived from the Judeo-Christian heritage. Congress added the phrase "under God" in 1954, during the height of Cold War fears about "godless communism." Even though the Bill of Rights of the U.S. Constitution calls for a separation of church and state, the Pledge posits a theistic religious belief as central to U.S. citizenship. Every president of the United States, whether religious or not, professes to be so and regularly attends church.

Constitutional separation of church and state notwithstanding, many Americans believe that the United States is fundamentally a Christian nation. Growing religious diversity is challenging this assumption. While Americans often pride themselves on the right of everyone to freely pursue their own faiths, they seldom actually interact

Evidence of a civil religion can be seen in the singing of "God Bless America" at sporting events such as Major League Baseball games.

with people who do not share the same beliefs and so have little understanding of religious differences. Sociologist Robert Wuthnow (2007), whose research focuses on the effects of religious diversity, calls for a strategy of "reflective pluralism" as a means to promote greater religious understanding.

Trends in Religious Affiliation

One reason so many Americans are religiously affiliated is that religious organizations are an important source of social ties and friendship networks. Churches, synagogues, and mosques are communities of people with shared beliefs and values who support one another during times of need. Religious communities thus often play a family-like role. About 67.3 percent of Americans identify as Christian (including 21 percent who identify as Catholic), 1.9 percent as Jewish, 0.9 percent as Muslim, 0.7 percent as Buddhist, and 0.7 percent as Hindu (CIA, 2020c).

Protestantism: The Growing Strength of Conservative Denominations A clearer picture of trends in American religion emerges if we break down the Protestant category into major subgroups. According to the U.S. Religious Landscape Survey of more than 35,000 adults in 2014, Baptist households account for 33 percent of all Protestants. There were far fewer Methodists (10 percent), Pentecostals (10 percent), Lutherans (8 percent), Presbyterians (5 percent), and Episcopalians (3 percent). More than half of all Protestants (55 percent) describe themselves as evangelical (Pew Research Center, 2015c). These figures indicate the growing strength of conservative Protestants, who emphasize a literal interpretation of the Bible, morality in daily life, and conversion through evangelizing. In contrast are the more historically established liberal (or mainline) Protestants, who adopt a more flexible, humanistic approach to religious practice. Somewhere in between are moderate Protestants.

Since the 1960s, the more liberal Protestant churches have experienced declining membership, whereas the number of evangelical Protestants has increased: The more evangelical denominations inspire deep loyalty and commitment, and are highly effective at recruiting new members, particularly young people. Today, 25 percent of all American adults belong to evangelical Protestant churches, compared with only 15 percent belonging to more liberal ones (Pew Research Center, 2015c).

Liberal Protestantism in particular has suffered. The aging members of the liberal Protestant denominations have not been replaced, commitment is low, and some current members are switching to other faiths. From 1965 to 1989—a time when mainline Protestant denominations began to decline in favor of evangelical churches—losses were substantial for Lutherans, United Methodists, the United Church of Christ, Episcopalians, Presbyterians, and Disciples of Christ. Together, these six denominations lost nearly 23 million members—almost the same number that was gained by such conservative Protestant denominations as the Southern Baptists, the Church of the Nazarene, the Seventh-Day Adventists, the Assemblies of God, the Church of God, and the Church of Jesus Christ of Latter-Day Saints. Between 1990 and 2008, the four largest mainline denominations—Methodists, Lutherans, Presbyterians, and Episcopalians—lost an additional 4 million members, a decline of 13 percent from 1990 (U.S. Bureau of the Census, 2012b). At the same time, Black Protestant churches have thrived in the United States, as their members move into the middle class and achieve economic and political prominence (Finke and Stark, 2005; Roof and McKinney, 1990).

Catholicism Catholics make up about a fifth of the U.S. population. The number of Catholics appears to be declining, in part because more people are leaving Catholicism for another faith than are joining the Church: Of the nearly one-third of Americans who were born Catholic, 41 percent no longer identify with the Catholic Church (Pew Research Center, 2015c). Church attendance among Catholics has also declined. In 1975, 47 percent of Catholics reported attending Mass at least once a week. By 2017, that figure had dropped to 39 percent (Saad, 2018). While church attendance has declined for Catholics of all ages, the drop has been sharpest for young Catholics (ages 18 to 29); currently, only about 30 percent of young Catholics attend church every week. A 2018 Gallup Poll found that 25 percent of young Catholics (21–29 years of age) attended church in the last 7 days. While the reasons for such declines are unclear, one reason likely has to do with the 1968 papal encyclical *Of Human Life* (*Humane Vitae*), which reaffirmed the ban on all forms of artificial contraception by Catholics. People whose conscience allowed for the use of contraceptives were faced with disobeying the Church, and many did just that. According to a 2015 Pew survey, three-quarters (76 percent) of U.S. Catholics say the Church should allow the use of birth control (Pew Research Center, 2015d).

Other Religious Groups Judaism in the United States has historically been divided into three major movements: Orthodox Judaism, which believes in the divine origins of the Jewish Bible (as previously noted, called the Old Testament by Christians) and follows highly traditional religious practices; Conservative Judaism, which is a blend of traditional and more contemporary beliefs and practices; and Reform Judaism, which rejects most traditional practices and is progressive in its ritual practices (services, for example, are more likely to be conducted in English than in Hebrew). Both Conservative and Reform Judaism reflect efforts by Jewish immigrants (or their descendants) to develop beliefs and rituals that turned away from "Old World" ones, developing forms more consistent with their new homeland. Reform Judaism is the largest Jewish denominational movement in the United States, comprising 38 percent of all American Jews (Berkley Center, 2020).

Despite (or perhaps partly because of) these efforts to modernize Judaism, the number of Jews in the United States has declined as a result of low birthrates, intermarriage, and assimilation. According to a 2016 Gallup Poll survey, the percent of U.S. adults who identify as Jewish has declined from about 10 percent of the U.S. population to about 2 percent since the late 1950s. Intermarriage rates are also on the rise; nearly 60 percent of Jews who have gotten married since 2000 have a non-Jewish spouse (Pew Research Center, 2013a). Estimates of the number of Jewish Americans in the United States today vary widely, which may reflect precisely how Jews are identified and counted. Some Americans identify as Jewish if they have a Jewish mother—even if they have never practiced their religion. Some may self-identify as Jewish only if they participate actively in the religion, whereas others still may identify as "culturally Jewish," meaning they celebrate their heritage and culture but do not actively practice the religion. Survey data from the Pew Research Center reports that in 2014, just 1.9 percent of the U.S. population was Jewish (Pew Research Center, 2015c). This percent has not changed as of 2020 (CIA, 2020c).

Among Muslims, growing emigration from Asia and Africa may change the U.S. religious profile. CIA World Factbook estimates that in 2015, there were approximately

2.9 million Muslims in the United States, accounting for almost 1 percent of the population (CIA, 2020c). It is projected that this share will double by 2050 (Mohamed, 2016). A majority of Muslim Americans are first-generation immigrants to the United States (63 percent), with many coming from the Asia-Pacific region, the Middle East, North Africa, and sub-Saharan Africa (Lipka, 2017).

New Religious Movements

Today, sociologists are aware that the terms *sect* and *cult* have negative connotations, so instead, they sometimes use the phrase *new religious movements* to characterize novel religious organizations lacking the respectability that comes with being well established for a long period (Hadden, 1997b; Hexham and Poewe, 1997). **New religious movements** encompass an enormously diverse range of religious and spiritual groups, cults, and sects that have emerged in Western countries, including the United States, alongside mainstream religions. One example is the Unification Church, founded by the Korean Sun Myung Moon. The cult boasts a membership of 50,000 in the United States and 3 million worldwide (Melton, 1996). Other new religious movements include Scientology, Wicca, Eckankar, Druidism, Lukumi (also called Santería), and Rastafarianism. Their beliefs might seem unusual mixtures of traditional and modern religious ideas, but in fact, all long-established religions mix elements from diverse cultural sources.

This change in characterization has proven to be controversial, however. A loosely knit "anti-cult movement" composed of academics, church groups, families of cult members, and some former cult members themselves argues that regarding cults simply as "new religious movements" masks their identity as fringe organizations that can be dangerous and even deadly. Janja Lalich, a sociologist who at one time belonged to a political organization she now views as a cult, argues that cults can be distinguished from new religious movements by the virtually total control they exert over members' daily lives and thinking. Cult members, she argues, exist in a situation of "bounded choice": However seemingly irrational, harmful, or even fatal their acts (as in the examples of Heaven's Gate and Aum Shinrikyo), they are done "in a context that makes perfect sense at the time to those who [perform the acts] and are, in fact, consistent with an ideology or belief system that [the members] trust represents their highest aspirations" (Lalich, 2004). Cult members are socialized into a way of thinking that is all-encompassing; they are not permitted to question the authority of the cult leader and so come to view the cult's beliefs, however bizarre or dangerous, as normal.

From the new religious movement perspective, cults—like all **religious movements**—can be best understood sociologically as a subtype of social movements. A religious movement is an association of people who spread a new religion or promote a new interpretation of an existing religion. From this perspective, all sects and cults can be classified as religious

new religious movements The broad range of religious and spiritual groups, cults, and sects that have emerged alongside mainstream religions. New religious movements range from spiritual and self-help groups within the New Age movement to exclusive sects such as the Hare Krishnas.

religious movements Associations of people who join together to seek to spread a new religion or to promote a new interpretation of an existing religion.

movements. Examples of religious movements include the groups that originally founded and spread Christianity in the first century, the Lutheran movement that split Christianity in Europe about 1,500 years afterward, and the groups involved in the more recent Islamic Revolution (discussed later in the chapter).

Religious movements pass through phases of development. In the first phase, the movement derives life and cohesion from a powerful leader. Max Weber classified such leaders as **charismatic**—that is, having inspirational qualities capable of capturing the imagination and devotion of a mass of followers. (Charismatic leaders in Weber's formulation could include political as well as religious figures—revolutionary China's Mao Zedong, for example, as well as Jesus and Muhammad.) The leaders of religious movements usually criticize the religious establishment and proclaim a new message. In their early years, religious movements are fluid; they do not have an established authority system. Their members are normally in direct contact with the charismatic leader, and together they spread the new teachings.

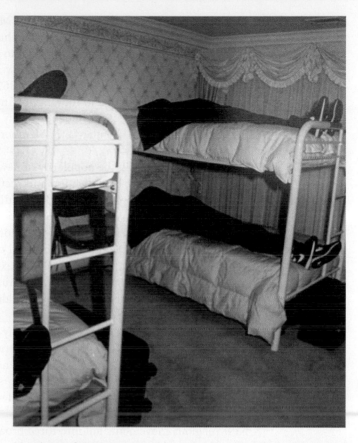

Members of the Heaven's Gate cult, who killed themselves in a mass suicide in 1997.

The second phase occurs following the death of the charismatic leader, when the movement must face what Weber termed the "routinization of charisma." To survive, the movement has to create formalized rules and procedures because it can no longer depend on the central role of the original leader in organizing the followers. Many movements fade away when their leaders die or lose influence. A movement that takes on a permanent character becomes a church—a formal organization of believers with an established power structure and established symbols and rituals. The church itself might later become the source of other movements that question its teachings and either set themselves up in opposition to the church or break away.

Many new religious movements are derived from mainstream religious traditions, such as Hinduism, Christianity, and Buddhism, whereas others have emerged from traditions that were almost unknown in the West until recently. Some new religious movements are creations of the charismatic leaders who head their activities. This is the case with the previously mentioned

> **charismatic** The inspirational quality of leaders that makes them capable of capturing the imagination and devotion of a mass of followers.

Unification Church, led by the Reverend Sun Myung Moon until his death in 2012, when his widow, Hak Ja Han, became the church's spiritual leader. Members are expected to fraternize only with one another, to donate their property to the church, and to obey the church's commands. This new religious movement was introduced into the United States at the beginning of the 1960s, and it appealed to many who were rejecting traditional religion and looking for insight in Eastern religious teachings. Membership in new religious movements mostly consists of converts rather than individuals brought up in a particular faith. Members are usually well educated and from middle-class backgrounds.

Various theories explain the popularity of new religious movements. Some observers argue that they reflect liberalization and secularization within society and within traditional churches. People who feel that traditional religions have become ritualistic and devoid of spiritual meaning may find comfort and a greater sense of community in smaller, less impersonal new religious movements. Others see new religious movements as an outcome of rapid social change (Wilson, 1982). As traditional social norms are disrupted, people search for explanations and reassurance. The rise of groups and sects emphasizing personal spirituality, for example, suggests that many individuals need to reconnect with their own values or beliefs in the face of instability and uncertainty.

Furthermore, new religious movements may appeal to people who feel alienated from mainstream society. The collective, communal approaches of sects and cults, some authors argue, can offer support and a sense of belonging. For example, today's middle-class youth are not marginalized from society in a material sense, but they may feel isolated emotionally and spiritually. Membership in a cult can overcome this alienation (Wallis, 1984).

New religious movements fall into three broad categories: *world-affirming*, *world-rejecting*, and *world-accommodating* movements. Each category is based on the relationship of the group to the larger social world. The enduring popularity of new religious movements presents another challenge to the secularization thesis. Opponents point to the diversity and dynamism of new religious movements and argue that religion and spirituality remain central facets of modern life. As traditional religions lose their hold, they claim, religion is not disappearing but is heading in new directions. Not all scholars agree, however. Proponents of secularization hold that these movements remain peripheral to society, even if they profoundly affect the lives of their followers. New religious movements are fragmented and relatively unorganized; they also suffer from high turnover rates. Compared to a serious religious commitment, proponents argue, participation in a new religious movement appears to be little more than a hobby or lifestyle choice.

World-affirming Movements

World-affirming movements are more like self-help or therapy groups than conventional religious groups. These movements often lack rituals, churches, or formal theologies, focusing instead on members' spiritual well-being. World-affirming movements do not reject the outside world or its

world-affirming movements Religious movements that seek to enhance followers' ability to succeed in the outside world by helping them unlock their human potential.

World-affirming movements such as the Church of Scientology, which was established by science fiction writer L. Ron Hubbard in 1954, are inclusive and focus on members' spiritual well-being.

values. Rather, they seek to enhance their followers' abilities to perform and succeed in that world by unlocking human potential.

The Church of Scientology is one such group. Founded by L. Ron Hubbard, it has grown from its original base in California to include a large membership worldwide. Scientologists believe that all people are spiritual beings but have neglected their spiritual nature. Through training that makes them aware of their real spiritual capacities, people can recover forgotten supernatural powers, clear their minds, and reveal their full potential.

Many strands of the so-called **New Age movement** are world-affirming movements. The New Age movement emerged from the counterculture of the 1960s and 1970s and encompasses a broad spectrum of beliefs, practices, and ways of life. Pagan teachings (Celtic, Druidic, Native American, and others), shamanism, forms of Asian mysticism, Wiccan rituals, and Zen meditation are among activities thought of as New Age.

The mysticism of the New Age movement appears to contrast with the modern societies in which it is favored. Followers of New Age movements develop alternative ways of life to cope with the challenges of modernity. Yet New Age activities should not be interpreted as simply a radical break with the present. They are also part of a larger

> **New Age movement** A general term to describe the diverse spectrum of beliefs and practices oriented on inner spirituality. Paganism, Eastern mysticism, shamanism, alternative forms of healing, and astrology are all examples of New Age activities.

cultural trajectory exemplifying mainstream culture. In modern societies, individuals possess unparalleled degrees of autonomy and freedom to chart their own lives. The aims of the New Age movement thus coincide closely with those of the modern age: People are encouraged to move beyond traditional values and expectations and to live actively and reflectively.

World-rejecting Movements

World-rejecting movements are highly critical of the outside world and often demand significant lifestyle changes from their followers—such as living ascetically, changing their dress or hairstyle, or following a certain diet. World-rejecting movements are frequently exclusive, in contrast to world-affirming movements, which are inclusive. Some world-rejecting movements display characteristics of **total institutions**; members subsume their individual identities into that of the group, follow strict ethical codes or rules, and withdraw from activity in the outside world.

Most world-rejecting movements demand more of their members, in terms of time and commitment, than do older established religions. Some groups use the technique of "love bombing" to gain the individual's total adherence. A potential convert is overwhelmed by attention and constant displays of affection until he or she is drawn emotionally into the group. The Unification Church reportedly employs this technique. Some new movements, in fact, have been accused of brainwashing their adherents—robbing them of the capacity for independent decision making (Lalich, 2004).

Many world-rejecting cults and sects have come under the intense scrutiny of state authorities, the media, and the public. Certain extreme cases have attracted much concern. The Branch Davidian cult, based in Waco, Texas, became embroiled in a deadly confrontation with federal authorities in 1993 after accusations of child abuse and weapons stockpiling. Eighty members of the cult (including 19 children) burned to death in their compound during an assault by federal officials that ended a lengthy armed standoff. Federal officials maintain that the cult members were virtual prisoners of their charismatic leader, David Koresh, who was allegedly stockpiling illegal weapons, had numerous wives, and was having sex with some of the children. Controversy remains over whether the fire was ordered by Koresh, who reportedly preferred mass suicide to surrender, or whether the actions of the federal authorities caused the tragedy (Tabor and Gallagher, 1995).

World-accommodating Movements

World-accommodating movements emphasize the importance of inner religious life over more worldly concerns. Members of such groups seek to reclaim the spiritual purity that they believe has been lost in traditional religious settings. Whereas followers of world-rejecting and world-affirming groups may alter their lifestyles in accordance with their religious activity, many adherents of world-accommodating movements carry on their lives and careers with little visible change. One example is Pentecostalism, a Christian renewal movement that emphasizes the direct, ecstatic experience of God that its adherents believe existed at the time of Christ. Pentecostals believe that the Holy Spirit can be heard through individuals who are granted the gift of "speaking in tongues."

Religious Affiliation and Socioeconomic Status

Substantial socioeconomic and regional differences exist among the principal religious groupings in the United States. Liberal Protestants are well educated, somewhat upper income, and middle or upper class. Ethnically, they comprise White Anglo-Saxon Protestants (WASPs) of British or German origins. Moderate Protestants have a lower level of education, income, and social class. In fact, they are typical of the national average on these measures. Moderate Protestants are from a variety of European ethnic backgrounds, including British, German, Scandinavian, Irish, and Dutch. Black Protestants are the least educated and poorest of any of the religious groups listed. Conservative Protestants have a similar profile, although they are at a slightly higher level on all these measures. They comprise a diverse profile of European ethnicities, although some are African American as well. Nearly half of all Protestants live in the South (Pew Research Center, 2015g).

Catholics strongly resemble moderate Protestants in terms of their socioeconomic profile. The largest ethnic group is European in origin (primarily German, Italian, Slavic, and Irish, and, to a lesser extent, English and French), followed by Latinos from Mexico and Central and South America. Catholics are pretty evenly distributed across the United States, though we are witnessing a shift from the Northeast and Midwest to the South and West (Pew Research Center, 2015c).

Jews have the highest socioeconomic profile. Most are college graduates in middle- or upper-income categories. One study found that Jewish educational and occupational attainment was significantly higher than that of other Whites. Jews are largely European in origin, particularly Eastern European and German, although some are from northern Africa. Whereas the large majority of Jews once lived in the Northeast, today, less than half do. One recent study suggests that their high degree of geographical mobility is associated with lowered involvement in Jewish institutions. Jews who move throughout the country are less likely to belong to synagogues or temples, have Jewish friends, or be married to Jewish spouses (Goldstein and Goldstein, 1996; Hartman and Hartman, 1996; Pew Research Center, 2008; Roof and McKinney, 1990).

In sum, Jews and liberal Protestants are the most heavily middle and upper class; moderate Protestants and Catholics are somewhat in the middle (although the growing number of poor Catholic Latino immigrants may be changing this position); conservative and Black Protestants are overwhelmingly lower class. These groupings correspond roughly with social and political liberalism and conservatism as well. In terms of civil liberties, racial justice, and women's rights, Jews are, by far, the most tolerant. Liberal Protestants and Catholics are somewhat more tolerant than the average American, while moderate Protestants and Black Protestants are somewhat less tolerant. Conservative Protestants are the least tolerant of all religious groupings (Roof and McKinney, 1990). For example, according to a 2015 poll put on by the Pew Research Center, while three-quarters of Jews strongly favor same-sex marriage, the same is true of less than half (45 percent) of all Christians and drops to just a quarter (28 percent) of evangelical Protestants (Pew Research Center, 2015c).

There are political differences across religious groups as well. Jews are the most heavily Democratic; fundamentalist and evangelical Christians, the most Republican. The more moderate Protestant denominations are somewhere in between (Kosmin, Mayer, and Keysar, 2001).

Gender and Religion

Like other social institutions, churches and denominations have, on the whole, excluded women from power. The following sections examine some of the interrelations of religion and gender. This is an area in which significant changes are occurring.

Religious Images

In Christianity, although Mary, the mother of Jesus, is sometimes treated as having divine qualities, God is "the Father," a male figure, and Jesus took the human shape of a man. Genesis, the first book of the Bible, teaches that woman was created from a man's rib. These facts have not gone unnoticed by women's movements. Over a hundred years ago, Elizabeth Cady Stanton published a series of commentaries on the Scriptures, titled *The Woman's Bible.* In her view, the deity had created women and men as beings of equal value, and the Bible should fully reflect this fact. The "masculinist" character of the Bible reflected the fact that it was written by men. In 1870, the Church of England established a Revision Committee to revise and update the biblical texts, but the committee contained no women. Stanton asserted that there was no reason to suppose that God is a man, because it was clear in the Scriptures that all human beings were fashioned in the image of God. She subsequently organized the Women's Revision Committee in America, composed of 23 women, to advise her in preparing *The Woman's Bible,* which was published in 1895.

In some Buddhist orders, especially Mahayana Buddhism, women are represented in a favorable light. But, on the whole, Buddhism is "an overwhelmingly male-created institution dominated by a patriarchal power structure," in which the feminine is mostly "associated with the secular, powerless, profane, and imperfect" (Paul, 1985). The contrasting pictures of women that appear in Buddhist texts no doubt mirror the ambiguous attitudes of men toward women in the secular world: Women are portrayed as wise, maternal, and gentle, yet also as mysterious, polluting, and destructive, threatening evil.

The Role of Women in Religious Organizations

In both Buddhism and (later) Christianity, women were allowed to express strong religious convictions by becoming nuns. Although the first orders for women were probably established in the twelfth century, their membership remained small until the 1800s. At that time, many women took religious vows to become teachers and nurses because these occupations were largely controlled by the religious orders. Nonetheless, female religious orders remained subject to a male hierarchy, and elaborate rituals reinforced this subjugation. For example, all nuns were regarded as "brides of Christ." Until some orders made changes in the 1950s and 1960s, "marriage" ceremonies were carried out, during which the novice would cut her hair, receive her religious name, and sometimes be given a wedding ring. After several years, a novice would take a vow of perpetual profession, after which she was required to receive dispensation if she chose to leave.

Women's orders today show considerable diversity. In some convents, nuns still dress in traditional habits and live in communities removed from the secular world. In other convents, nuns wear ordinary dress and live in apartments or houses. Traditional restrictions, such as not talking to others during certain periods of the day or walking with hands folded and hidden under the habit, are rarely evident.

Today, women play an increasingly important role as religious leaders. The Reverend Amy Butler is the first woman to hold the job of senior minister at Riverside Church in New York.

Despite such liberalization, women have filled only lower-status positions in religious organizations. This situation is changing, in line with changes affecting women in society generally. In recent years, women's groups have pressed for equal status in religious orders. Increasingly, the Catholic and Episcopalian churches are under strong pressure to allow women an equal voice in their hierarchies. Yet in 1977, the Sacred Congregation for the Doctrine of the Faith in Rome declared that women could not be admitted to the Catholic priesthood; the reason was that Jesus had not called a woman to be one of his disciples. Ten years later, 1987 was officially designated the "Year of the Madonna," during which the Congregation advised women to recall their traditional role as wives and mothers.

The barriers to Catholic women in the hierarchy of the church thus remain formidable. In a letter published in May 1994, Pope John Paul II reaffirmed the Roman Catholic Church's ban on the ordination of women. And in July 2010, in response to widely publicized scandals involving priests who had sexually abused children, the Vatican strengthened its rules on such abuses, characterizing them as "grave crimes"— but the same decree also extended the list of "grave crimes" to include any priest who ordained a woman. Catholic organizations that favored the ordination of women priests complained that the decree implied that female ordination and pedophilia were equally grave offenses (Bates, 2010; Catholic Women's Ordination, 2010).

The Episcopal Church has allowed women into its priesthood since 1976. Altogether, women have been ordained as ministers in about half the Protestant denominations in the United States, including the Presbyterian Church (U.S.A.), the Evangelical Lutheran Church in America, the African Methodist Episcopal Church, and the United Methodist Church. And, except within Orthodox Judaism, women in the United States can become rabbis as well.

Women and Islam

Despite the resurgence of traditional Islamist views in some parts of the Muslim world in recent years, Muslim women in most countries continue to experience a high degree of freedom and equality. As noted in Chapter 13, women have served as heads of state in such predominantly Muslim nations as Bangladesh, Pakistan, and Turkey. The first person to found a university was reportedly a Muslim woman, Fatima al-Fihri, who founded a Moroccan university in the ninth century. In Afghanistan, before the militant Islamic nationalists known as the Taliban took over in 1996, women played prominent roles: Shafiqa Habibi was the country's most popular television news anchor, her face (uncovered) known throughout the country. During the Taliban's rule, she spent her time at home, hidden from public view. When she ventured out, her body had to be covered by a *burka*, a traditional tentlike garment with a screen sewn into the fabric over her face to hide her eyes but allow some ability to see (Filkins, 1998).

Habibi's experience was shared by all Afghan women. The Taliban's extreme Islamic beliefs forbade women from working outside the home, attending school, or appearing in public without covering their bodies from head to toe. Women seen in public with any man who was not their husband or relative were brutally beaten or killed. Since the overthrow of the Taliban in 2001, women have begun to regain their rights in Afghanistan, at least in the capital city of Kabul. But throughout much of the rest of the country, local religious leaders, including the Taliban, have begun to make a comeback, and women are afraid to exercise their legal rights for fear of retribution.

There is a debate among Muslim scholars as to whether Islam in fact requires severe restrictions on the role of women. At one extreme, the highly conservative interpretation sometimes known as Wahhabism (after the name of its nineteenth-century founder) has led to the severe treatment of women practiced by the Taliban. This strict version of Islam is strongly practiced in oil-rich Saudi Arabia, which has funded *madrassas* ("schools") throughout the Muslim world, where Wahhabism is taught. A more moderate view of women's roles—which still calls for restrictions such as veiling—was advanced by the prominent Iranian philosopher Ali Shariati. In his view, women should be veiled both because this reflects the chastity and piety of Muhammad's daughter Fatima, and because it represents defiance of the Western view of women (Aslan, 2006; Shariati, 1971). Many Muslim women voluntarily choose to veil themselves, out of religious belief or as a cultural rejection of Western attitudes toward what is proper for women; a feminist case for wearing the veil can also be made (Francois-Cerrah, 2014; Elver, 2012).

A feminist view is offered by Amina Wadud in her book *Qur'an and Woman: Rereading the Sacred Text from a Woman's Perspective* (1999). Wadud argues that women's inferior status in some Muslim-majority countries results partly from Islam's seventh-century Arabian origins, when women were relegated to an inferior status, and partly from the hostility toward women that has characterized centuries of male-centered interpretations of the Qur'an. Reza Aslan (2006), an Iranian-born American sociologist who has written extensively on Islam, states the feminist position succinctly:

> As Shirin Ebadi proudly declared while accepting the 2003 Nobel Peace Prize for her tireless work in defending the rights of women in Iran, "God created us all as equals. . . . By fighting for equal status, we are doing what God *wants* us to do." . . .

The so-called Muslim women's movement is predicated on the idea that Muslim men, not Islam, have been responsible for the suppression of women's rights. For this reason, Muslim feminists throughout the world are advocating a return to the society Muhammad originally envisioned for his followers.

The Bible, like the Qur'an, provides a range of moral teachings, many in conflict with one another, that were rooted in the moral beliefs of the time. Some of these teachings would be regarded by most Christians and Jews today as completely unacceptable. Examples include:

"If . . . no proof of the girl's virginity can be found, she shall be brought to the door of her father's house and there the men of her town shall stone her to death." (Deuteronomy 22:20–21)
"Women should remain silent in the churches. They are not allowed to speak, but must be in submission, as the Law says." (1 Corinthians 14:34)
"I do not permit a woman to teach or to have authority over a man, but to be in silence." (Timothy 2:12)

From a sociological perspective, it is important to ask not only how such beliefs arose a thousand or more years ago, but also how they are being interpreted today— and how these interpretations find their way into new religious movements and social practices.

The Global Rise of Religious Nationalism

Religious nationalism involves the linking of deep religious convictions with beliefs about a people's social and political destiny. In countries around the world, religious nationalist movements reject the notion that religion, government, and politics should be separate and instead call for a revival of traditional religious beliefs that are directly embodied in the nation and its leadership (Beyer, 1994). These nationalist movements represent a strong reaction against the impact of technological and economic modernization on local religious beliefs. In particular, religious nationalists oppose what they regard as the destructive aspects of Western influence on local culture and religion, ranging from U.S. television, movies, and social media to the missionary efforts of foreign evangelicals.

Religious nationalist movements accept many aspects of modern life, including modern technology, politics, and economics. They effectively use social media to reach millions of new recruits worldwide. Yet, at the same time, they require a strict interpretation of religious values, rejecting altogether the notion of secularization. Religious nationalist movements do not simply revive ancient religious beliefs. Rather, they partly "invent" the past, drawing on different traditions and reinterpreting events to serve their current beliefs and interests. Violent conflicts between religious groups sometimes result from their differing interpretations of the same historical event (Anderson, 1991; Juergensmeyer, 1993, 2001, 2009; van der Veer, 1994).

religious nationalism The linking of strongly held religious convictions with beliefs about a people's social and political destiny.

Table 17.1
APPLYING SOCIOLOGY TO RELIGION IN MODERN SOCIETY

CONCEPT	APPROACH TO UNDERSTANDING RELIGION IN MODERN SOCIETY	CONTEMPORARY APPLICATION
New Religious Movements	A phrase used to characterize new or unusual religious organizations that lack the respectability that comes with being well established for a long period. Preferred by many sociologists of religion over terms such as "cult" or "sect," which often have negative connotations.	Unification Church, Scientology, Wicca, Eckankar, Druidism, Lukumi (also called Santería), and Rastafarianism
World-Affirming Movements	A subcategory of New Religious Movements that focuses on practices that affirm members' ability to overcome personal limitations and unlock their human potential, and thereby achieve success in the outside world.	Self-help and therapy groups; "New Age" Movements such as paganism, shamanism, astrology; Scientology
World-Rejecting Movements	A subcategory of New Religious Movements that is highly critical, and therefore rejecting, of the outside world. Tend to be extremely demanding of members, requiring them to subsume their individual identities to that of the group, adhere to strict rules and behaviors, and often withdraw from activity in the outside world.	Branch Davidians, People's Temple; Krishna Consciousness; the Manson family; Heaven's Gate
World-Accommodating Movements	A subcategory of New Religious Movements, they are often offshoots of existing religious denominations that emphasize the importance of an inner religious life and spiritual purity believed to have been lost in traditional religious settings. Adherents accommodate to the outside world, carrying on their lives and careers with little visible change, while practicing inner religious devotion.	Neo-Pentecostalism; Subud (Susila Budhi Dharma); Charismatic Renewal (within Catholicism)
Religious Nationalism	The linking of strongly held religious convictions with beliefs about a people's social and political destiny, involving a revival of traditional religious beliefs that are directly embodied in the nation and its leadership. Often oppose what are seen as the destructive aspects of Western influence on local culture and religion.	Islamic Nationalism (Taliban, Islamic State, Boko Haram); Hindu Nationalism (Hindutva, Sangha Parivar); Buddhist Nationalism (Sinhalese Bodu Bala Sena Buddhist Power Force); Christian Nationalism (National Reform Association, Christian Identity Movement)

Religious nationalism is rising because in times of rapid social change, unshakable ideas have strong appeal. The collapse of the Soviet Union, the end of the Cold War, and today's sweeping global economic and political changes have led many nations to reject the secular solutions offered by the United States and its former socialist enemies and to look instead to their own past and cultures (Juergensmeyer, 1995). In the Middle East, for example, many Palestinian Muslims as well as Israeli Orthodox Jews renounce the notion of a secular democratic state, arguing for a religious nation purged of nonbelievers. In India, Hindus, Muslims, and Sikhs face off against one another.

Islamic Nationalism

Islamic nationalism has triumphed in Iran, Sudan, and, until 2001, Afghanistan; today, it is making a resurgence in that country. It has also made significant inroads in Algeria, Egypt, Malaysia, Pakistan, Palestine, Turkey, and elsewhere. Since the 1970s, Islamic nationalism has shaped the contours of both national and international politics. To understand this phenomenon, we must look both to aspects of Islam as a traditional religion and to secular changes affecting countries where its influence is pervasive.

Islam, like Christianity, has continually stimulated activism. The Qur'an is full of instructions to believers to "struggle in the way of God" against both unbelievers and those within the Muslim community who introduce corruption. Over the centuries, there have been successive generations of Muslim reformers, and Islam has become as internally divided as Christianity.

During the Middle Ages, there was a continuous struggle between Christian Europe and the Muslim states. During the height of Islamic power, the *caliphs* (Islamic rulers) ruled over an area extending from what later became Spain, Greece, the former Yugoslavia, Bulgaria, and Romania to India, Pakistan, and Bangladesh. Europeans eventually reclaimed most of these lands, and many Muslim areas in North Africa were colonized by European powers in the eighteenth and nineteenth centuries. These reversals were catastrophic for Islam and Muslim civilization, which Islamic believers held to be the highest and most advanced possible. In the late nineteenth century, the inability of the Muslim world to resist the spread of Western culture led to reform movements seeking to restore Islam to its original purity and strength. A key idea was that Islam should respond to the Western challenge by affirming the identity of its beliefs and practices.

This idea developed in various ways in the twentieth century and underlay Iran's Islamic Revolution of 1978–1979, which was fueled initially by internal opposition to the shah ("the king"), Mohammad Reza Pahlavi (1941–1979). When the shah's premier, Mohammad Mossadeq, nationalized the oil industry in 1951, a conflict ensued between the pro-West shah and the supporters of the nationalistic Mossadeq. The shah eventually fled the country but returned in 1953, when a U.S.- and British-led coup overthrew Mossadeq. The shah tried to promote forms of modernization modeled on the West—for example, land reform, extending the vote to women, and developing secular education. He also used the army and secret police to brutally suppress those who opposed his regime. The fact that he had been installed by Western powers helped fuel nationalist sentiments that eventually led to the revolution that overthrew him. A dominant figure in the revolution was Ayatollah Ruhollah Khomeini, a religious leader

Protestors in Tehran hold up a poster of Ayatollah Ruhollah Khomeini in January 1979. The Islamic Revolution led to the ouster of the shah and the creation of a new Islamic republic under Ayatollah Khomeini.

exiled in France during the shah's reign, who provided a radical reinterpretation of Shiite ideas.

Khomeini established a government in strict accordance with traditional Islamic law, fusing religion and the state. The government initially made its extremist version of Shiite Islam the basis of all social, political, and economic life in Iran. Men and women were kept rigorously segregated, women had to cover their heads in public, homosexuals could be shot by a firing squad, and women accused of adultery were stoned to death. The strict code reflected a pronounced nationalistic outlook, strongly rejecting Western influences. It should be noted that these practices are not condoned throughout the Muslim world, and, in the view of leading Islamic scholars, are contrary to Islamic beliefs (Oakford, 2014).

The aim of the Islamic republic in Iran was to organize government and society so that Islamic teachings would dominate all spheres. The Guardian Council of religious leaders determines whether laws, policies, and candidates for parliament conform to Islamic beliefs, even though Iran has a U.S.-style constitution providing for elected officials and the separation of powers.

Although recent years have seen some hopeful signs that Iran is liberalizing, such hopes have proved to be short lived in the past. A reform-minded president, Mohammad Khatami, captured control of parliament in the 2000 elections, but Iran's Guardian Council reversed that victory in elections four years later by disqualifying 2,400 liberal candidates (nearly a third of all candidates). Mahmoud Ahmadinejad, a conservative candidate close to Iran's religious leaders, won the presidency in that year, and Iran's relations with Europe and the United States rapidly deteriorated. The pro-democracy Green Movement mobilized millions of people in peaceful protests against the Ahmadinejad government during the 2009 presidential elections but was brutally repressed as a consequence.

The most recent elections (2013) saw a swing in the liberal direction, with the election of Hassan Rouhani as president. Rouhani has sought to improve relations with the West, and one of his chief goals has been to ease the West's economic sanctions, initially imposed on Iran by the United States in 1979, following the Iranian Revolution. Many other countries joined the United States in imposing sanctions after 2006, when the UN Security Council passed a resolution calling for sanctions in an effort to stop Iran's nuclear enrichment program, seen as a key step in developing nuclear weapons. An agreement to ease sanctions, in exchange for a verifiable cessation of Iran's nuclear weapons program, was reached in July 2015. Whether this effort will succeed—and, more broadly, whether Iran will continue its current liberalizing trend—remains to be seen.

The Spread of Islamic Revivalism

Although the ideas underlying the Iranian Revolution were supposed to unite the whole Islamic world against the West, governments of Sunni-majority countries where Shiites are in a minority have not aligned themselves with the Islamic Revolution in Iran. Yet Islamic fundamentalism (often called "Islamism," the complete adherence to Islamic law along with rejection of most non-Islamic influences) has become popular in most of these states, and various forms of Islamic revivalism elsewhere have been stimulated by it.

Although Islamic fundamentalist movements have grown in many countries in North Africa, the Middle East, and South Asia, they have won power in only two states: Sudan and Afghanistan. Sudan has been ruled since a 1989 military coup by Omar al-Bashir, who heads the National Congress Party. The fundamentalist Taliban regime consolidated its hold on the fragmented state of Afghanistan in 1996 but was ousted at the end of 2001 by Afghan opposition forces and the U.S. military, although the Taliban still commands significant power in many parts of the country and in the neighboring border areas of Pakistan as well. Islamist movements also exist in states such as Malaysia, Bangladesh, and Indonesia, and several provinces in Nigeria have implemented sharia courts, which enforce a strict interpretation of Islamic religious law, operating in parallel with civil courts.

Al Qaeda was an early example of a loosely knit transnational network of militant religious fundamentalists with a global vision. Founded by Osama bin Laden, al Qaeda sought to overthrow what it regarded as corrupt Muslim governments, drive Western influence from the Middle East, and eventually establish a religiously based government that would encompass a billion Muslims throughout Europe, Africa, and Asia. Islamic rule would be subject to strict religious discipline, as it currently is in those parts of Afghanistan ruled by the Taliban.

In 2012, a U.S. Navy Seal unit helicoptered into the Pakistan compound where bin Laden had long been hiding, killing bin Laden and raising hopes that al Qaeda would be seriously weakened by the death of its founder. But by then, events in the Middle East had significantly changed the political landscape. The 2003 U.S. invasion of Iraq succeeded in toppling Saddam Hussein, but it also resulted in escalating violence, suicide bombings, and growing sectarian conflict. Some Iraqis mobilized against the U.S. occupation, which lasted until 2011; others were caught up in conflicts between Iraq's Shiite majority and Sunni minority. Tens of thousands of Iraqi civilians died during this period. Sunnis, who had ruled Iraq under Saddam, now found themselves under the control of Shiite governments believed to be aligned with Shiite Iran.

One result was an Islamist revival among fundamentalist Sunnis, who saw the chaos in Iraq and neighboring Syria as providing an opportunity to create an Islamic state. Shiite governments ruled both Iraq and Syria; both countries were wracked by sectarian violence and civil war. Islamist Sunnis called for the creation of a caliphate across a broad swath of Iraq and Syria. This was to be an Islamic state governed by strict religious principles and ruled over by a *caliph*, a religious and political successor to the prophet himself. It would enforce—by violent means if necessary—a return to the strict seventh-century religious beliefs attributed to the prophet Muhammad. Following significant military victories over the Iraqi army, the Islamic State of Iraq and Syria (ISIS) was proclaimed to be a global caliphate in 2014. (ISIS is sometimes simply referred to as IS—Islamic State—and sometimes as ISIL, Islamic State of Iraq and the Levant. "Levant" is a term that has been used for centuries to refer to the area in the eastern Mediterranean.)

Syrians cross the border into Turkey in June 2015, fleeing heavy fighting between ISIS and Kurdish forces.

By 2017, however, ISIS had lost much of its territory in Iraq, including control over its key cities, thanks to military efforts by the Iraqi government, supported by the presence of U.S.-led NATO military ground forces and airstrikes. The situation in Syria has been less clear, since the fight against ISIS involves complex alliances among numerous military groups (some labeled as terrorist by the United States) attempting to overthrow Syrian president Bashar al-Assad. The Syrian conflict has also been caught up in a geopolitical struggle between the United States (which favored Bashad's ouster) and Russia (which supported Bashad) (Lister, 2017; Baron, 2017). The defeat of ISIS as a territory-holding state does not, however, necessarily mean its defeat as a potent religious and political force. Rather, its adherents may spread out, becoming a global jihadist movement that seeks control elsewhere or, failing that, continues to engage in acts of terrorism elsewhere in the world (Juergensmeyer, 2016).

ISIS was the creation of Abu Bakr al-Baghdadi, who became its founding caliph. Under his rule, unbelievers—Shiites, Christians, foreigners—were either driven from the caliphate or killed. Beheadings, crucifixions, and mass shootings of civilians were filmed and went viral on social media. ISIS has engaged in an expensive, professional, and effective social media campaign to recruit young people worldwide, including young women as potential brides. The group has a strong presence on Facebook and Twitter and has posted graphic execution videos on YouTube to disseminate its message and attract new followers to its extremist cause.

Such Islamic revivalism cannot be understood wholly in religious terms. It largely represents a reaction against what Iranian writer Jalal Al Ahmad (1997; orig. 1962) called "Weststruckedness" or "Westoxification"—the seductive (and, in his view, corrupting) power of Western cultural beliefs and practices. In countries where as much as half the population is under age 15, where poverty is widespread, and where many well-educated young men and women face a life of marginal employment and uncertainty, such beliefs find fertile ground.

The strong Western presence in the Middle East has provided additional fuel for anti-Western sentiments. In his *fatwas* (opinions that he claimed to be grounded in Islamic law), bin Laden repeatedly condemned U.S. troop presence in Saudi Arabia (which, as the land of Muhammad, is regarded by Islam as its most sacred place), U.S. support for Israel in its conflict with the Palestinians, the first Gulf War against Iraq, and what bin Laden claimed were a million deaths resulting from the postwar

CONCEPT CHECKS

1 What are the three largest religious groups in the world?

2 What are the reasons so many Americans belong to religious organizations?

3 To what extent does the treatment of women reflect social conditions, and to what extent does it derive from holy writings such as the Bible and the Qur'an?

4 What is religious nationalism? Why can't it be viewed as a reaction to economic modernization of local religious beliefs and Westernization?

economic sanctions against Iraq. Al-Baghdadi called on his followers to "explode the volcanoes of jihad [holy war] everywhere."

Muslim religious leaders throughout the world have condemned ISIS, whose violent methods are abhorrent to the vast majority of Muslims, who view its teachings as contrary to Islamic beliefs. But it still has appeal to thousands of young Muslim men—and some young Muslim women—in Europe and the United States, as well as parts of Asia and Africa. The result has been heightened security and surveillance in many countries and coordinated military attacks on ISIS strongholds. Only time will tell if current efforts to destroy ISIS will be successful.

4 UNANSWERED QUESTIONS

The resurgence of religion throughout the world has posed some challenges to the sociological study of religion. For much of the early twentieth century, it was widely argued that the rise of science, technology, and the critical thinking associated with modernity would prove a decisive challenge to religious thought, which is based in large part on faith rather than scientifically acceptable standards of evidence. Yet religious beliefs, in all religions, have proven to be remarkably durable. This raises a number of important questions that have yet to be conclusively answered by the sociology of religion.

Is America Experiencing Secularization or Religious Revival?

According to Philip Hammond (1992), there have been three historical periods in the United States when religion has undergone **disestablishment**—that is, when the political influence of established religions has been successfully challenged. The first such disestablishment occurred with the 1791 ratification of the Bill of Rights, which calls for the separation of church and state. Some sociologists see this separation as characteristic of the industrial societies of Europe and North America, in which different institutions specialize in different functions—from economics to medicine and from education to politics. Religion is no exception (Chaves, 1993, 1994; Parsons, 1964; orig. 1951, 1960).

The second disestablishment occurred between the 1890s and the 1920s, fed by an influx of about 17 million immigrants (mainly European), many of whom were Catholic. The long-standing notion of a predominantly Protestant United States was challenged, and the mainstream Protestant churches never fully regained their influence in politics or in defining national values.

The third disestablishment occurred during the 1960s and 1970s, when the anti–Vietnam War movement, the fight for racial equality, and experimentation with alternative lifestyles eroded core religious beliefs and values. Fundamental challenges arose in areas such as sexuality, family authority, sexual and lifestyle preferences, women's rights,

disestablishment A period during which the political influence of established religions is successfully challenged.

and birth control (Glock, 1976; Hammond, 1992; Hunter, 1987; Roof and McKinney, 1990; Wuthnow, 1976, 1978, 1990).

> **evangelicalism** A form of Protestantism characterized by a belief in spiritual rebirth (being "born again").

This disestablishment of religion challenged the political influence of religion. Did it also mean that religion was less important to individuals or that secular influences were on the rise? Even during the 1960s and 1970s, when the third disestablishment was at its peak, the religious beliefs of many Americans appeared to be stronger than ever (Roof, Carroll, and Roozen, 1995). For many people, religious beliefs became increasingly private as more people sought spiritual experiences outside of established religious organizations (Roof, 1993; Wuthnow, 1998). In fact, the third religious disestablishment arguably contributed to the growing strength of conservative religious denominations, whose adherents reacted strongly to what they perceived as the bankruptcy of liberal theology. Conservative evangelicals effectively helped shape public debate, bringing moral issues such as abortion, sexuality, and lifestyle into political discourse. While liberal theology dominated the mainline churches, conservative theology became increasingly influential in politics (Wuthnow, 1990). Beginning with the Reverend Jerry Falwell's Moral Majority in the 1970s, evangelical groups, especially those with fundamentalist values, have become increasingly involved in the Christian Right in national politics, particularly in the conservative wing of the Republican Party (Kiecolt and Nelson, 1991; Simpson, 1985; Woodrum, 1988). The Christian Right has emerged as a significant force in politics, waging what it views as the "culture wars" between liberalism and traditional religious values.

How Resurgent Is Evangelicalism?

Evangelicalism, a belief in spiritual rebirth (being "born again"), is a response to growing secularism, religious diversity, and the decline of once-core Protestant values in public life (Wuthnow, 1988, 1990). The late-twentieth-century growth in evangelical denominations in the United States appears to have slowed or even declined slightly; while the number of evangelical Christians has expanded with the U.S. population, it has declined slightly as a percentage of the total population, although mainstream Protestant religious affiliations have experienced more significant declines (Pew Research Center, 2015g). Some Protestants are seeking the more direct, personal, and emotional religious experience evangelical denominations promise.

Although some evangelicals combine a modern lifestyle with traditional religious beliefs, others strongly reject many aspects of

Members of the Korean American Presbyterian Church worship together in Queens, New York. Recent years have witnessed the tremendous growth of evangelical denominations in the United States.

fundamentalists Evangelicals who are highly antimodern in many of their beliefs and adhere to strict codes of morality and conduct.

contemporary life. **Fundamentalists** are evangelicals who are antimodern, calling for strict codes of morality and conduct. These frequently include taboos against drinking, smoking, and other "worldly evils," a belief in biblical infallibility, and a strong emphasis on Christ's impending return to earth (Balmer, 1989).

Evangelical organizations have been especially effective at mobilizing resources to achieve their religious and political objectives. They have become extremely competitive "spiritual entrepreneurs" in the "religious marketplace" (Hatch, 1989). Some evangelicals use radio and television as marketing technologies to reach a wider audience, although the heyday of "televangelists"—preachers with huge television audiences who preached a "gospel of prosperity"—appears to have peaked. Still, the current large

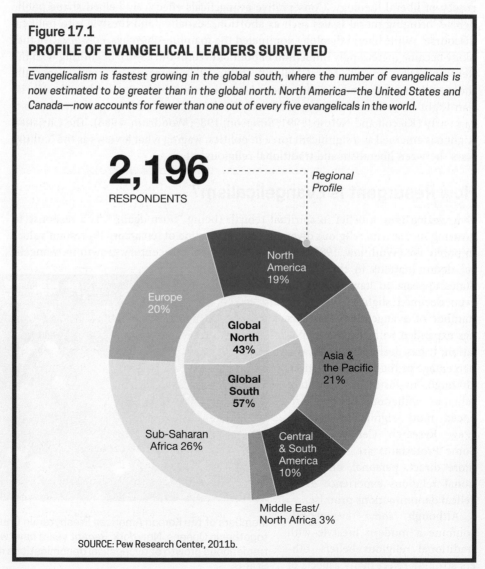

Figure 17.1
PROFILE OF EVANGELICAL LEADERS SURVEYED

Evangelicalism is fastest growing in the global south, where the number of evangelicals is now estimated to be greater than in the global north. North America—the United States and Canada—now accounts for fewer than one out of every five evangelicals in the world.

2,196
RESPONDENTS

Regional Profile

North America 19%

Europe 20%

Global North 43%

Asia & the Pacific 21%

Global South 57%

Sub-Saharan Africa 26%

Central & South America 10%

Middle East/ North Africa 3%

SOURCE: Pew Research Center, 2011b.

number of religious television networks includes the Christian Broadcasting Network, the Eternal Word Television Network, the Trinity Broadcasting Network, Sky Angel Faith and Family Television, and FamilyNet. Some scholars argue that these ministries are stronger today than ever before (Hadden, 2004). The 2010 U.S. Census reported that the number of people who self-identify as belonging to denominations that would be classified as evangelical grew from roughly 42 million in 1990 to 45 million in 2001, to 49 million in 2008. The Pew Research Center puts the current number of evangelical Protestants at around 54 million, or one in five U.S. adults (Pew Research Center, 2015c).

The growth of evangelicalism may have peaked in the United States, but it is growing rapidly throughout the world, spurred by evangelical missionary zeal (Figure 17.1). In a 2011 survey of nearly 2,200 evangelical leaders throughout the world, only 44 percent of those who lived in the United States, Europe, and other advanced industrial countries expected that the state of evangelical Christianity in their countries would be better in five years than it is today; 33 percent expected it to be worse. U.S. evangelical leaders are the most pessimistic, with nearly half (48 percent) expecting things to be worse in five years, compared with only 31 percent who expected things to be better. By way of contrast, those who lived in Africa, the Middle East, Latin America, and parts of Asia were overwhelmingly optimistic about the future: 71 percent expected the state of evangelical Christianity to be better, while only 12 percent expected it to be worse. When asked about the principal threats to evangelical Christianity, 71 percent of the global evangelical leaders—including 92 percent of U.S. leaders—cited the influence of secularism (Pew Research Center, 2011b).

In 2010, 8 out of 10 White evangelical Protestants believed that religion's influence on U.S. politics and government leaders was declining. Almost all saw this decline as a bad thing—and while fewer than 1 in 5 viewed the Democratic Party as friendly to religion, slightly more than half viewed the Republican Party favorably (Pew Research Center, 2011b). The Tea Party movement, discussed in Chapter 13, represents an effort by political conservatives, many with strong religious roots, to exert influence through a Republican Party that more closely reflects their views. White evangelical Protestants have become a core constituency of the Republican Party, whose program reflects fundamentalist religious beliefs on such topics as opposition to abortion and a reduced role for government in the economy. As of 2016, White evangelical Protestants tied most to the Republican Party than any other religious group. Forty-nine percent of White evangelical Protestants identify with the Republican Party, another 31 percent identify as independent, and 14 percent identify with the Democratic Party (Cox, 2017).

Is Religious Violence on the Rise?

It is important to remember that before the September 11, 2001, attack on the World Trade Center and the Pentagon by Islamist fanatics associated with Osama bin Laden and al Qaeda, the worst terrorist attack on U.S. soil occurred at the hands of a Christian fanatic. On April 19, 1995, Timothy McVeigh, a former U.S. Army soldier who believed the United States was dominated by an anti-Christian conspiracy, ignited a truck laden with explosives in front of the Alfred P. Murrah Federal Building in downtown Oklahoma City. One hundred and sixty-eight people died in the enormous blast, including 19 children under six years old in the building's day-care center. Nearly 700 additional people were injured in the blast, which also damaged hundreds of other nearby buildings. McVeigh, who was later executed for the attack, believed he was waging a "cosmic war" against his version of the unfaithful (Juergensmeyer, 2008).

Understandably, since 9/11, many Americans have been concerned about the global spread of Islamic violence, a concern that contributes to false stereotypes about a relationship between Islam and violence. The rise of ISIS, suicide bombings, the Islamist attack that claimed 12 lives at the French satirical magazine *Charlie Hebdo* because it had caricatured the Prophet Muhammad—all these understandably raise the question, How could Islamic religious views—or any religious views—give rise to such a culture of violence? Sociologist Mark Juergensmeyer (2001, 2009; see also Aslan, 2009) has come to a startling conclusion: Even though all major religious traditions call for compassion and understanding, violence and religion nonetheless go hand in hand. Juergensmeyer, who has studied religious violence among Muslims, Sikhs, Jews, Hindus, Christians, and Buddhists, argues that under the right conditions, ordinary conflicts can become recast as religious "cosmic wars" between good and evil that must be won at all costs. He argues that a violent conflict is most likely to seek religious justification as a cosmic war when (1) the conflict is regarded as decisive for defending one's basic identity and dignity—for example, when one's culture is seen as threatened—and (2) when losing the conflict is unthinkable, although (3) winning the conflict is unlikely.

> If any of these conditions is present, Juergensmeyer says, it is more likely that a real-world struggle may be perceived in cosmic terms as a sacred war. The occurrence of all three simultaneously strongly suggests it. A struggle that begins on worldly terms may gradually take on the characteristics of a cosmic war as solutions become unlikely and awareness grows of how devastating it would be to lose.

In such instances, the proponents of cosmic warfare justify the loss of innocent lives as serving God's larger purpose. Juergensmeyer also argues that responding to violence with still greater violence runs the risk of showing the Islamic world that the conflict is indeed cosmic, particularly if the most powerful nations on earth become embroiled. Based on interviews with proponents of terrorism, Juergensmeyer concludes that this is just what al Qaeda wants—to be elevated from the status of a minor criminal terrorist organization to a worthy opponent in a global war against the West. This will increase the appeal of al Qaeda to a wider group of young Islamic men who blame the West for declining Islamic influence and growing hardships many Muslims worldwide face.

To what extent are bin Laden's views about "Westoxification" shared in the Muslim world? The Pew Research Center (2003) polled 50,000 people worldwide in 2002 and 2003, not long after the 9/11 attacks. Large majorities, including Muslims, reported that such things as television, the Internet, and cell phones were making their lives better. (Pakistan, one of the world's largest Islamic countries, was a notable exception.)

Most people, including most Muslims, felt that foreign TV, movies, and music were a "good thing" (again, except in Pakistan). At the same time, large majorities of Muslims and others also believed that their traditional ways of life were being lost and needed protection against foreign influence.

Although expressing concern that "there are serious threats to Islam today," the vast majority of Muslims reject suicide bombings and other forms of violence against civilians as a legitimate means of "defending Islam against its enemies." Recent surveys have found that the vast majority of respondents in Muslim-majority countries have unfavorable views of ISIS, including nearly all respondents in Lebanon and 94 percent in Jordan (Lipka, 2017). A 2017 survey by the Pew Research Center found that ISIS is globally considered the top threat to national security, closely followed by global climate change (Poushter and Manevich, 2017). By 2018, the Global Attitudes Survey found that climate change was considered globally as the top threat to national security, followed by ISIS, and cyberattacks (Poushter and Huang, 2019).

Bin Laden's belief that "Westoxification" is a serious problem calling for a violent solution is clearly not widely shared among ordinary Muslims.

CONCEPT CHECKS

1 During what three periods did the United States experience disestablishment? How did disestablishment contribute to the growing strength of conservative religious denominations?

2 How do sociologists explain the resurgence of evangelicalism in the United States in the late twentieth century?

THE BIG PICTURE

Chapter 17
Religion in
Modern Society

1 **Basic Concepts**

p. 655

2 **Sociological Theories of Religion**

p. 661

LEARNING OBJECTIVES

Understand how sociologists define and study religion. Learn about the different types of religious organizations: churches and sects, denominations, and cults.

Understand the sociological approaches to religion developed by Marx, Durkheim, and Weber; the contemporary debate over secularization; and the religious economy approach.

TERMS TO KNOW

secularization • liberation theology • religion • theism • churches • sects • denomination • cults

alienation • sacred • profane • secular thinking • religious economy

CONCEPT CHECKS

1. What are the three main components of religion as a social institution?
2. How do sociologists differ from other scholars in their approach to studying religion?
3. Describe four types of religious organizations.

1. Why did Karl Marx call religion "the opium of the people"?
2. What are the differences between classical and contemporary approaches to understanding religion?
3. Does the Pew study provide support for the religious economy approach? Why or why not?

Exercises: Thinking Sociologically

1. Karl Marx, Émile Durkheim, and Max Weber had different viewpoints on the nature of religion and its social significance. Briefly explain the viewpoints of each. Which theorist's views have the most to offer in explaining the rise of national and international fundamentalism today? Why?

2. Drawing on this textbook's discussion, summarize the role of religion for most Americans today and assess whether religion is increasing or decreasing in importance for most people. Explain what it means for people to become more secular or fundamentalist in their religious practices. Are Americans becoming more secular or fundamentalist in their religious observances?

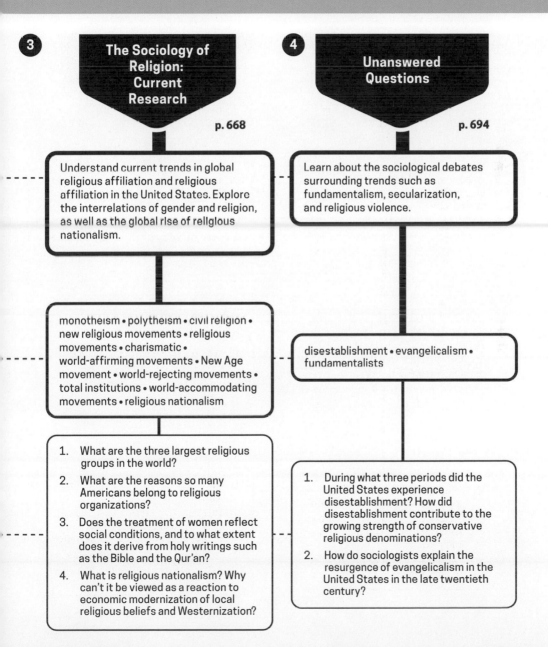

3

The Sociology of Religion: Current Research

p. 668

Understand current trends in global religious affiliation and religious affiliation in the United States. Explore the interrelations of gender and religion, as well as the global rise of religious nationalism.

monotheism • polytheism • civil religion • new religious movements • religious movements • charismatic • world-affirming movements • New Age movement • world-rejecting movements • total institutions • world-accommodating movements • religious nationalism

1. What are the three largest religious groups in the world?

2. What are the reasons so many Americans belong to religious organizations?

3. Does the treatment of women reflect social conditions, and to what extent does it derive from holy writings such as the Bible and the Qur'an?

4. What is religious nationalism? Why can't it be viewed as a reaction to economic modernization of local religious beliefs and Westernization?

4

Unanswered Questions

p. 694

Learn about the sociological debates surrounding trends such as fundamentalism, secularization, and religious violence.

disestablishment • evangelicalism • fundamentalists

1. During what three periods did the United States experience disestablishment? How did disestablishment contribute to the growing strength of conservative religious denominations?

2. How do sociologists explain the resurgence of evangelicalism in the United States in the late twentieth century?

Social Change in the Modern World

Throughout much of human history, the pace of social change was slow; most people followed ways of life similar to those of their forebears. By contrast, today's world is subject to dramatic and continuous transformation. In the remaining chapters, we consider some of the major areas of change.

The growing field known as sociology of the body addresses one of the most far-reaching influences of globalization. Chapter 18 examines how global processes affect our bodies, including diet, health, disease, and sexual behavior.

In turn, the globalizing of social life both influences and is influenced by changing patterns of urbanization, which is the subject of Chapter 19. This chapter also analyzes the tremendous growth in world population and the increasing threat of environmental problems.

The concluding chapter explores some of the major processes of social change from the eighteenth century to the present, offers general interpretations of the nature of social change, and considers where global change is likely to lead us in the twenty-first century.

18

The Sociology of the Body: Health, Illness, and Sexuality

Physical and mental health aspects of our body, such as our body weight, how long we live, and the diseases we suffer from are

A   due to our genetic makeup.

B   a consequence of our personal choices.

C   due to whether one can afford resources such as a healthy diet, medicine, and health insurance.

D   all of the above.

TURN THE PAGE FOR THE CORRECT ANSWER.

LEARNING OBJECTIVES

1 Basic Concepts

Understand how social, cultural, and historical contexts shape attitudes toward health, illness, and sexual behavior.

2 Theories and Historical Approaches to Understanding Health, Illness, and Sexuality

Learn about theoretical perspectives on physical and mental health and illness in contemporary society, as well as the approaches to studying sexuality throughout history.

3 Research on Health, Illness, and Sexuality Today

Learn about health patterns in the United States according to social class, gender, and race, and understand the competing explanations for the persistence of these patterns. Understand how society and culture influence sexual practices and attitudes.

4 Unanswered Questions

Understand the state of current research on the link between health and income inequality. Learn about the growth of complementary and alternative medicine (CAM), gendered patterns of body-image concerns, and the debate about the influence of biological factors versus social learning on human sexual orientation.

If you answered *d*, you would be correct. Some of us might have answered *a*, thinking that our bodies and minds are handed down to us through our genes; you might have a friend who says that she gets her slender physique from "her mom's side of the family," while another friend may say that he was "just born big-boned." Others might think the answer is *b*—that our physical and mental health reflect our personal choices about what to eat and drink, our willpower in getting up and going to the gym every morning, or the ways that we choose to cope with stress. Students who have taken many sociology courses might think that *c* is correct—that social class, including where we live, the foods we can afford, and whether we have access to a doctor or therapist, affects our health and well-being. Each of these answers is partly correct in that each and every one of these things contributes to our physical and emotional health, leading us to the correct response of *d*.

Aspects of our physical body, including how much we weigh, the diseases we suffer from, and how long we live; our mental health, such as whether we are prone to depression or substance use; and even aspects of our sexuality and sexual behavior reflect a range of social, biological, and economic factors, including our genetic makeup, the activities that fill our day, and even our beliefs about what constitutes a "beautiful" body.

To illustrate this point, let's think about a social phenomenon that many observers refer to as the "obesity epidemic" in the United States. Obesity is considered the top public health problem facing Americans today. **Obesity**, or excessive body weight, increases an individual's risk for a wide range of health problems, including heart disease and diabetes (Haslam and James, 2005; Wang et al., 2011). Yet excessive body weight may also take a social and psychological toll. Overweight and obese Americans are more likely than their thinner

THE ANSWER IS D.

peers to experience employment discrimination, discrimination by health care providers, and daily experiences of teasing, insults, and shame (Carr and Friedman, 2005). Negative attitudes toward overweight and obese persons develop as early as elementary school (Puhl and Latner, 2007). In one classic sociological study (Richardson et al., 1961), a sample of 10- and 11-year-old boys and girls were given six images of children and asked to report how much they liked each child. The six drawings included an obese child and children with various physical disabilities and disfigurements. The obese child was ranked dead last—a finding that has been replicated many times in more recent studies (e.g., Latner and Stunkard, 2003; Puhl and Latner, 2007).

obesity Excessive body weight, indicated by a body mass index (BMI) over 30.

Part of the reason why overweight and obese Americans are the targets of teasing and discrimination is that a thin ideal prevails today. Simply pick up a fashion magazine or turn on a television and it will be clear that, today, beauty is equated with slenderness. But this has not always been the case. In most premodern societies, the ideal female shape was a fleshy one. Thinness was not desirable, partly because it was associated with poverty, starvation, and illness. Even in Europe in the 1600s and 1700s, the ideal female shape was curvaceous—as evident in paintings by Rubens, for example. The notion of slimness as the desirable feminine shape originated among some middle-class groups in the late nineteenth century, but it became generalized as an ideal for most women only recently. A historical examination of the physiques of Miss America winners between 1922 and 1999, for example, shows that for much of the twentieth century, pageant winners had a body weight that would be classified as "normal," yet in recent years, the majority of winners would be classified as "underweight" using medical guidelines (Rubinstein and Caballero, 2000). As a result, even young girls who are genetically disposed to a fuller figure may work very hard to fight their biology as they strive to achieve a thin ideal (Haberstick et al., 2010). Recent evidence suggests that boys, too, increasingly struggle to maintain a lean and muscular physique (Field et al., 2014).

Soda and other sugary drinks are blamed for contributing to the obesity epidemic, especially among children and teenagers. Currently, 17 percent of children and 21 percent of teens are obese.

Sociologists are fascinated with the puzzle facing our nation today. Negative attitudes toward overweight and obese persons persist, yet at the same time, these individuals currently make up the statistical majority of all Americans. According to the Centers for Dis-

Table 18.1
WHAT IS YOUR BODY MASS INDEX?

People are classified into one of four standard weight categories based on their body mass index (BMI), which reflects one's current height and weight. BMI can be calculated using the following formula:

$$BMI = 703 \times \frac{\text{weight (lb)}}{\text{height}^2 \text{ (in}^2)}$$

WEIGHT	BODY MASS CATEGORY INDEX (BMI)
Underweight	less than 18.5
Normal	from 18.5 to 24.9
Overweight	from 25.0 to 29.9
Obese	30.0 or higher

Source: National Heart, Lung, and Blood Institute, 2015.

ease Control and Prevention (CDC), roughly 70 percent of adults are now overweight (see Table 18.1 for technical definitions of weight categories). More than 40 percent of American adults (43 percent of men and 42 percent of women) are currently obese. This proportion varies widely by race; for example, 57 percent of Black women and 44 percent of Hispanic women are now obese, compared with 40 percent of non-Hispanic White women (Hales et al., 2020).

An even more troubling trend is the increase in the proportion of American children and adolescents who are obese. Between 1976 and 1980, just 6.5 percent of children (ages 6 to 11) and 5 percent of teens (ages 12 to 19) were obese. By contrast, in 2014, 18.4 percent of children and 20.6 percent of adolescents were obese (Hales et al., 2017). If body weight reflected biology alone, then we would expect that the rates of overweight and obese people would be fairly constant across history—because human physiology has changed little throughout the millennia.

The reasons behind the obesity crisis are widely debated. Some argue that the apparent increase in the overweight and obese population is a statistical artifact. The proportion of the U.S. population who are middle-aged has increased rapidly since the mid-1980s as the large baby boom cohort grew older. Middle-aged persons, due to slowing metabolism, are at greater risk of excessive body weight. Others attribute the pattern—especially the childhood obesity increase—to compositional factors. The proportion of children in the United States who are Black or Hispanic is higher today than in earlier decades, and both these ethnic groups are at a much greater risk of becoming overweight than their White peers. Still others argue that the measures used to count and classify obese persons have shifted, thus leading to an excessively high count. Finally, some observers believe that public concern over obesity is blown out of proportion and reflects more of a "moral panic" than a "public health crisis" (Campos et al., 2006; Saguy, 2012).

Most public health experts, however, believe that obesity is a very real problem caused by what Kelly Brownell calls the "obesogenic environment"—or a social environment that unwittingly contributes to weight gain. Among adults today, sedentary desk jobs have replaced physical work such as farming. Children are more likely to spend their after-school hours sitting in front of a computer or television than playing tag or riding bikes around the neighborhood. Parents are pressed for time, given their hectic work and family schedules, and turn to unhealthy fast food rather than home-cooked meals. Restaurants, eager to lure bargain-seeking patrons, provide enormous serving sizes at low prices. A Big Mac is less expensive than a healthy salad in most parts of the country (Brownell and Horgen, 2004).

The social forces that promote high fat and sugar consumption and that restrict the opportunity to exercise are particularly acute for poor persons and ethnic minorities. Small grocery stores in poor neighborhoods rarely sell fresh or low-cost produce. Large grocery stores are scarce in poor inner-city neighborhoods and rural areas, as well as in predominantly African American neighborhoods (Morland et al., 2002). Given the scarcity of high-quality healthy foods in poor neighborhoods, scholars have dubbed these areas "**food deserts**" (Walker, Keane, and Burke, 2010). Additionally, high crime rates and high levels of traffic in inner-city neighborhoods make exercise in public parks or jogging on city streets potentially dangerous (Brownell and Horgen, 2004).

Policy makers and public health professionals have proposed a broad range of solutions to the obesity crisis. Some have (unsuccessfully) proposed practices that place the burden directly on the individual. For example, some schools have considered having a "weight report card," where children and parents would be told the child's **body mass index (BMI)**, in an effort to trigger healthy behaviors at home (Dogloff, 2010). Yet most experts endorse solutions that attack the problem at a more macro level, such as making healthy low-cost produce more widely available; providing safe public places for fitness, free exercise classes, and instruction in health and nutrition to poor children and their families; and requiring restaurants and food manufacturers to note clearly the fat and calorie content of their products.

Former First Lady Michelle Obama's *Let's Move!* program is held up as an outstanding initiative because it includes programs to help children and their families maintain healthy lifestyles (White House, 2014). *Let's Move!* provides parents with the tools and information they need to make healthier food choices for their children; for instance, an updated food pyramid and new food-package labels will help point consumers to healthy

Why do many parents turn to fast food to feed their families? What are the consequences?

food choices. Increased funding for school lunch and breakfast programs, encouraging school food suppliers to deliver healthy low-fat and low-salt meals to schools, funding inner-city farmers' markets, and implementing programs to increase children's fitness levels are all steps that may help eradicate the childhood obesity epidemic. Only in attacking the "public issue" of the obesogenic environment will the private trouble of excessive weight be resolved (Brownell and Horgen, 2004).

Taken together, the "obesity epidemic" debate and its proposed solutions illustrate many core themes of sociology. First, they illustrate the ways in which a "personal trouble," such as suffering from obesity-related health problems, also reflects "public issues," such as a social context that prevents poor individuals from buying costly low-fat foods or accessing public parks and other spaces that allow for regular exercise. Second, they reveal that social inequalities based on race, class, and geographic region can shape our bodies. Third, they reveal that no "single-bullet" explanation can account for major social and public health issues; rather, the source of the problem often encompasses a range of biological, social, economic, and technological factors. In fact, in 2014, the Medical College Admissions Test (MCAT) introduced a social-science module, recognizing that future physicians must "consider how income and social status, education, home and work environments and other factors shape health outcomes" (Tran, 2014).

The study of body weight is just one topic investigated by sociologists specializing in the subfield known as **sociology of the body**. These scholars investigate how and

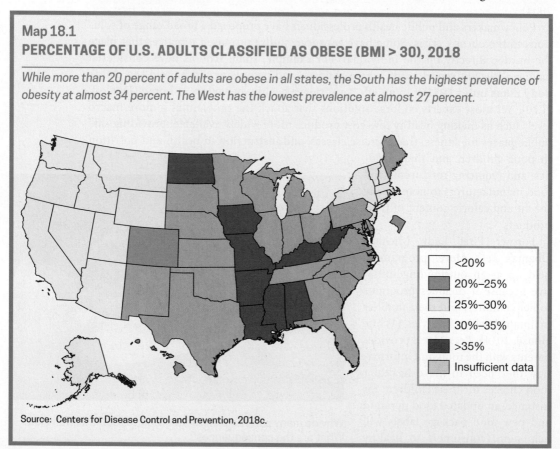

Map 18.1
PERCENTAGE OF U.S. ADULTS CLASSIFIED AS OBESE (BMI > 30), 2018

While more than 20 percent of adults are obese in all states, the South has the highest prevalence of obesity at almost 34 percent. The West has the lowest prevalence at almost 27 percent.

Legend:
- <20%
- 20%–25%
- 25%–30%
- 30%–35%
- >35%
- Insufficient data

Source: Centers for Disease Control and Prevention, 2018c.

why our bodies and minds are affected by our social experiences and the norms and values of the groups to which we belong. The ways that social factors affect our health was painfully illustrated when the COVID-19 crisis devastated populations worldwide, with low-wage workers like grocery store clerks and nursing home aids and those living in overcrowded housing particularly vulnerable.

sociology of the body A field that focuses on how our bodies are affected by social influences. Health and illness, for instance, are determined by social and cultural influences.

sociology of sexuality A field that explores and debates the importance of biological versus social and cultural influences on human sexual behavior.

health "A state of complete physical, mental, and social well-being and not merely the absence of disease or infirmity."

Another central theme in the sweeping field of sociology of the body is the increasing separation of the body from "nature." Our bodies are affected by science and technology in diverse ways, ranging from life-sustaining machines, to the chemicals in our food, to reproductive technologies. A closely related subfield, **sociology of sexuality**, explores and debates the importance of biological versus social and cultural influences on human sexual behavior, an important facet of sociology of the body. Only recently have sociologists recognized the profound interconnections between social life and the body. Therefore, this field is quite new and exciting. Using these two interrelated frameworks, in this chapter, we analyze the social dimensions of health and illness in the United States and worldwide and examine social and cultural influences on our sexual behavior, identities, and practices.

1 BASIC CONCEPTS

Before we can delve into theories describing the social and biological influences on health, illness, and sexuality, it is important that we first identify key terms and concepts.

Changing Conceptions of Health, Illness, and Medicine

What does it mean to be "healthy"? The simplest and most widely accepted definition is the one provided by the World Health Organization (1948): "**Health** is a state of complete physical, mental and social well-being and not merely the absence of disease or infirmity." In practice, however, cultures differ in what they consider healthy and in what they see as appropriate "treatment" for ill health. All cultures have known concepts of physical and mental health and illness, but most of what we now recognize as medicine is a consequence of developments in Western society over the past three centuries.

In premodern cultures, the family was the main institution for coping with sickness or affliction. There have always been individuals who specialized as healers, using a mixture of physical and magical remedies, and many such traditional systems survive today in non-Western cultures. For instance, Ayurvedic medicine (traditional healing) has been practiced in India for nearly 2,000 years. It is founded on a theory of the equilibrium of psychological and physical facets of the personality, imbalances of which are treated by nutritional and herbal remedies. Chinese folk medicine similarly aims to restore harmony among aspects of the personality and bodily systems and involves the use of herbs and acupuncture for treatment.

Modern medicine sees the origins and treatment of disease as physical and explicable in scientific terms. Indeed, the application of science to medical diagnosis and cure underlay the development of modern health care systems. Sociologists have argued that in contemporary Western societies, conditions that were previously viewed as having their roots in social, cultural, or religious causes are now "medicalized," or viewed as biomedical in their roots. Medicalization, according to sociologist Peter Conrad, is the process by which conditions and problems of social life become defined and treated as medical conditions, and thus become the subject of medical study, diagnosis, prevention, or treatment (Conrad, 2007). The medicalization of pregnancy and childbirth, for example, developed slowly as obstetric specialists replaced local physicians and midwives. In industrialized societies, most births today occur in a hospital, with the help of a specialized medical team.

It's not just physical health conditions that are medicalized; our emotions and mental health also are medicalized. Sociologist Allan Horwitz has argued that in the United States, the emotion of "sadness," a normal response to stressors like loss, failure, and disappointment, has now been transformed into the medical disorder of "depression," which is believed to have its roots in biological causes such as brain chemistry or genetics (Horwitz and Wakefield, 2007). As such, depressed persons today are much more likely to be treated with medications, such as antidepressants, rather than "talk therapy," in which a therapist would focus on the social or emotional roots of the sad feelings. Medicalization is tightly linked to the economic organization of medical care. Patients are reimbursed by their health insurers for treatments only when they have a

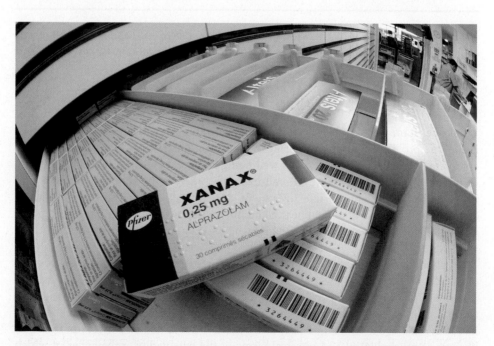

Today, depressed people are much more likely to be treated with medication. Sociologist Allan Horwitz argues that we have experienced a "loss of sadness" in the United States.

definable medical condition; as Horwitz and Wakefield (2007) note, a physician could not easily find a reimbursable "code" for sadness, but many options are available for a patient presenting at a doctor's office with "depression" (Moore, 2004).

Other features of modern medicine are the acceptance of the hospital as the setting within which to treat serious illnesses and the development of the medical profession as a body with codes of ethics and significant social power. The scientific view of disease is linked to the requirement that medical training be systematic and long-term; self-taught healers are typically excluded. Although professional medical practice is not limited to hospitals, the hospital has provided an environment in which doctors can treat and study large numbers of patients in circumstances permitting the concentration of medical technology.

On rare occasions, tensions may arise when physicians adhere to modern medical models and their patients adhere to folk or spiritual models of health. These cultural tensions are portrayed poignantly in the book *The Spirit Catches You and You Fall Down: A Hmong Child, Her American Doctors, and the Collision of Two Cultures* (Fadiman, 1997). The book recounts the experience of the Lee family, ethnic Hmong immigrants from Laos, whose infant daughter had epilepsy. The Lees believed their daughter's illness stemmed from spiritual causes, while doctors believed the condition was biological and could be alleviated with anticonvulsive drugs. After trying to comply with a difficult medication regimen, the Lees stopped administering the drugs, and their daughter was placed in foster care, with tragic results.

Just as cultural beliefs about health and illness change across time and place, the very illnesses from which individuals suffer, and the causes and cures of these illnesses, vary widely by sociohistorical context. In medieval times, the major illnesses were infectious diseases such as tuberculosis, cholera, malaria, and bubonic plague. In the fourteenth century, the epidemic of the plague, also referred to as the Black Death, killed a quarter of the population of England and devastated large areas of Europe. Since that time, rates of infectious diseases declined dramatically and were a minor cause of death in

A tragic clash between spiritual beliefs and modern medicine is the focus of Anne Fadiman's account of an epileptic Hmong girl in *The Spirit Catches You and You Fall Down.*

industrialized countries, accounting for just 6 percent of deaths annually in the 2010s (Xu et al., 2020). Infectious diseases had given way to noninfectious diseases such as cancer and heart disease as the leading causes of death. However, the assumption that infectious diseases were a thing of the past was challenged in early 2020, when the coronavirus struck China and Italy, and the United States shortly thereafter. As of July 2020, over 130,000 persons in the United States and over 560,000 worldwide had died of the virus (CDC COVID-19 Response Team, 2020b; WHO, 2020d).

Although in premodern societies the highest rates of death were among infants and young children, death rates today (the proportion of the population who die each year) rise with increasing age. The leading causes of death today, heart disease and cancer, disproportionately strike persons age 65 and older. While infectious diseases can strike anyone today, just as they did during past centuries, older adults are especially vulnerable to coronavirus. According to estimates from the Centers for Disease Control, roughly 80 percent of all people who died of the COVID-19 virus in early 2020 were age 65 and over (CDC COVID-19 Response Team, 2020b).

When sociologists take a long-term view of health, they have found that improvements in medical care accounted for only a minor part of the decline in death rates before the twentieth century. Effective sanitation, better nutrition, water purification, milk pasteurization, control of sewage, and improved hygiene were more consequential (Dowling, 1977). Drugs, advances in surgery, and antibiotics did not significantly decrease death rates until well into the twentieth century. Antibiotics used to treat bacterial infections first became available in the 1930s and 1940s; most immunizations (against diseases such as polio) were developed later.

Diverse Conceptions of Human Sexuality

Just as notions of health, illness, and medicine are shaped by sociohistorical and cultural contexts, human sexuality is a complex concept, tightly tied to cultural beliefs and contexts. Judith Lorber (1994) distinguished as many as 10 different sexual identities: straight (heterosexual) woman, straight man, lesbian woman, gay man, bisexual woman, bisexual man, transvestite woman (a woman who regularly dresses as a man), transvestite man (a man who regularly dresses as a woman), transsexual woman (a man who becomes a woman), and transsexual man (a woman who becomes a man). The terminology used to describe people's sexualities has evolved since that time, with terms like transgender and noncisgender replacing the terms transsexual and transvestite, and the introduction of terms like gender fluid, genderqueer, gender nonconforming, and non-binary to reflect the fact that gender and sexuality do not sit neatly in the old boxes of male versus female, or gay versus straight (GLAAD, 2020). As we saw in Chapter 10, people today are more likely than ever before to define themselves in ways that may or may not match the body they were born into, blend these categories, or even move fluidly among the categories set forth by Lorber (GLAAD, 2020; Padawer, 2014; Schulman, 2013).

Sexual practices themselves are even more diverse. Sigmund Freud argued that human beings are born with a wide range of sexual tastes that are ordinarily curbed through socialization—although some adults may follow these tastes even when, in a given society, these practices are regarded as immoral or illegal. Freud began his research during the Victorian period, when many people were sexually prudish, yet his patients still revealed an amazing diversity of sexual pursuits. Freud's work underscores the complex ways that biology and social contexts shape human sexuality.

Among possible sexual practices are the following: A man or woman can have sexual relations with women, men, or both. This can happen with one partner at a time or with two or more partners participating. One can have sex with oneself (masturbation) or with no one (celibacy). One can have sexual relations with people who erotically cross-dress, use pornography or sexual devices, practice sadomasochism (the erotic use of bondage and the inflicting of pain), and so on (Lorber, 1994). In most societies, sexual norms encourage some practices and discourage or condemn others. Such norms, however, vary across cultures. Same-sex sexual relations is an example. As we will discuss later, some cultures have actively encouraged such relations in certain contexts. Among the ancient Greeks, for instance, the love of men for boys was idealized as the highest form of sexual love.

Accepted types of sexual behavior also vary between cultures, which indicates that most sexual responses are learned and not a product of solely biological forces. The most extensive cross-cultural study was carried out by Clellan Ford and Frank Beach (1951), using anthropological evidence from more than 200 societies. Striking variations were found in what was regarded as "natural" sexual behavior and in norms of sexual attractiveness. For example, in some cultures, extended foreplay is desirable and even necessary before intercourse; in others, foreplay is nonexistent. Some societies believe that overly frequent intercourse leads to physical debilitation or illness.

In most cultures, norms of sexual attractiveness (held by both females and males) focus more on physical looks for women than for men, a situation that may be changing worldwide as women become active in spheres outside the home. The traits seen as most important in female beauty, however, differ greatly. In wealthy industrialized nations, a slim, small physique is admired, while in other cultures, a more generous shape is attractive. Some societies consider the breasts a source of sexual stimulus, whereas other societies do not attach erotic significance to them. Some societies value the shape of the face, whereas others emphasize the shape and color of the eyes or the size and form of the nose and lips. Although anthropologists and sociologists focus on cross-cultural differences in mate-selection processes, evolutionary theorists emphasize universals since these purportedly universal practices contribute to the continuation of the human species. For instance, research by David Buss reveals widespread male preference for a relatively low waist-to-hip ratio in women (i.e., an "hourglass" figure) because it can be seen as an indicator of a woman's reproductive fitness, or her ability to bear healthy offspring. Women, by contrast, are drawn to men with ambition and economic stability, which are considered indications of an ability to adequately provide for offspring (Buss, 2003).

Sexual Orientation

Sexual orientation is an important component of human sexuality because it involves the direction of one's sexual or romantic attraction. The term *sexual preference*, which is sometimes incorrectly used instead of *sexual orientation*, is misleading and should be avoided because it implies that one's sexual or romantic attraction is entirely a matter of personal choice. As you will see, sexual orientation results from a complex interplay of biological and social factors not yet fully understood.

The most commonly found sexual orientation in all cultures, including the United States, is *heterosexuality*, a sexual or romantic attraction for persons of the opposite sex. In the United States, heterosexuals are also sometimes called "straight." It is important to note that although heterosexuality may be the prevailing norm in most cultures, it is not "normal" in the sense of being dictated by some universal moral or religious standard. Like all behavior, heterosexual behavior is socially learned within a particular culture.

Homosexuality is the term historically used to describe a sexual or romantic attraction for persons of one's own sex. However, that term is now considered offensive and new terms are widely used to describe those attracted to persons of the same sex. The term *gay* is used to refer to men who experience sexual desire toward other men, *lesbian* for women who experience sexual desire for other women, and *bi* as shorthand for *bisexual*, which is used to describe people who are sexually attracted to both men and women. Young people increasingly use the term *queer* to describe a person whose sexual orientation is not exclusively heterosexual, as they find the gender-specific terms gay and lesbian to be too limiting (GLAAD, 2020). Researchers estimate that approximately 3.5 to 8 percent of the population in the United States identifies as LGB (lesbian, gay, or bisexual), although these numbers may be underestimates because of the stigma that sexual minorities still face in some communities (Gates, 2013; Laumann et al., 1994). According to the latest General Social Survey, 3.3 percent of Americans identify as bisexual, and 1.7 percent identify as gay or lesbian as of 2018 (Burkholder, 2019).

The term *homosexuality* has a troubled history. It was first used by the medical community in 1869 to characterize what was then regarded as a personality disorder. The American Psychiatric Association did not remove homosexuality from its list of mental illnesses until 1973, or from its influential *Diagnostic and Statistical Manual of Mental Disorders* (DSM) until 1980. These long-overdue steps were taken only after prolonged lobbying and pressure by gay rights organizations. The medical community was belatedly forced to acknowledge that no scientific research had ever found gays and lesbians as a group to be psychologically unhealthier than heterosexuals (Burr, 1993). However, the DSM-IV continues to classify other aspects of sexuality as "disorders," including disorders of desire (e.g., low interest in sex), disorders of sexual arousal (e.g., lubrication and erectile problems), and orgasmic disorders (American Psychiatric Association, 2000). Even the updated DSM-V, published in 2013, defines individuals as possessing gender dysphoria if they are intensely uncomfortable with their assigned gender and strongly identify with, and want to become, the opposite gender (American Psychiatric Association, 2013). This diagnosis does not accurately represent the experiences of transgender or noncisgender people who are comfortable with their gender identity differing from the sex they were assigned at birth.

CONCEPT CHECKS

---

1 Define the term *health*.

2 Define and provide an example of medicalization.

3 Describe three features of modern medicine.

4 Why is the term *sexual preference* problematic?

In a small number of cultures, same-sex relationships are the norm in certain contexts and do not necessarily signify what today is termed LGBTQ identities. For example, the anthropologist Gilbert Herdt (1981, 1984, 1986) reported that among more than 20 tribes in Melanesia and New Guinea, ritually prescribed same-sex encounters among young men and boys were considered necessary for subsequent masculine virility (Herdt and Davidson, 1988). Ritualized male-male sexual encounters also occurred among the Azande of Africa's Sudan and Congo (Evans-Pritchard, 1970), Japanese samurai warriors in the nineteenth century (Leupp, 1995), and highly educated Greek men and boys in the time of Plato (Rousselle, 1999). These examples underscore the importance of social and historical contexts in shaping sexuality.

2 THEORIES AND HISTORICAL APPROACHES TO UNDERSTANDING HEALTH, ILLNESS, AND SEXUALITY

To best understand the issues of health, illness, and sexuality in contemporary society, it is essential that we step back and look at both the history of these topics as well as the changing theoretical approaches to understanding them.

Colonialism and the Spread of Disease

The types of illnesses from which individuals suffer, the treatments available for these conditions, and the very ways we think about "causes" of illness have changed dramatically throughout human history. The hunting and gathering communities of the Americas, before the arrival of the Europeans, were not as susceptible to infectious disease as the European societies of the period. Many infectious organisms thrive only when human populations live above the density level that is characteristic of hunting and gathering life. The highest population density among hunter-gatherer communities was 22 people per square mile among the Chumash people; to put this in perspective, in 2019 there were 929 people per every square mile in the United States overall, and more than 27,000 in New York City (Erlandson et al., 2001; World Population Review, 2020). Permanently settled communities, particularly large cities, risk the contamination of water supplies by waste products. Hunters and gatherers were less vulnerable in this respect because they moved continuously across the countryside.

During the colonial era, efforts to bring Western ideals to developing societies also brought certain diseases into other parts of the world. Smallpox, measles, and typhus, among other major maladies, were unknown to the indigenous populations of Central and South America before the Spanish conquest in the early sixteenth century. English and French colonists brought the same diseases to North America (Dubos, 1959). Some of these illnesses produced epidemics that ravaged or completely wiped out native populations, which had little or no resistance to them.

In Africa and subtropical parts of Asia, infectious diseases have been rife for a long time. Tropical and subtropical conditions are especially conducive to diseases such as malaria, carried by mosquitoes, and sleeping sickness, carried by the tsetse fly. Historians believe that risk from infectious diseases was lower in Africa and Asia before

Europeans tried to colonize these regions, since colonists often brought with them practices that negatively affected the health of local natives. The threat of epidemics, drought, or natural disaster always loomed, but colonialism led to major unforeseen changes in the relation between populations and their environments, producing harmful effects on health patterns. The Europeans introduced new farming methods, upsetting the ecology of whole regions. For example, before the Europeans' arrival, Africans successfully maintained large herds of cattle in East Africa. Changes introduced by the intruders allowed for the multiplication and uncontrolled spread of the tsetse fly, which carries illnesses that are fatal to both humans and livestock. Today, large areas of East Africa are completely devoid of cattle (Kjekshus, 1977).

The most significant consequence of the colonial system was its effect on nutrition and, therefore, on levels of resistance to illness as a result of the changed economic conditions involved in producing for world markets. In many parts of Africa, the nutritional quality of native diets became substantially depressed as cash crop production supplanted the production of native foods.

This was not a one-way process, however. Indeed, early colonialism also radically changed Western diets, having a paradoxical impact in terms of health. On the one hand, Western diets benefited from the addition of new foods, such as bananas, pineapples, and grapefruit. On the other hand, the importation of tobacco, together with raw sugar (which found uses in all manner of foods), has had harmful consequences. Thus, the diseases from which we suffer are shaped by not only human biology but also complex macrosocial influences such as globalization, colonialism, and the development of technologies that foster the growth of particular crops.

Sociological Theories of Health and Illness

One of contemporary sociologists' main concerns is the experience of physical and mental disease or illness—how individuals experience being sick, chronically ill, or disabled and how these experiences are shaped by one's social interactions with others. If you have ever been ill, even for a short period, you know that patterns of daily life are temporarily modified and your interactions with others change. This is because the normal functioning of the body is a vital, but often taken-for-granted, part of our daily lives. Our sense of self is predicated on the expectation that our bodies will facilitate, not impede, our social interactions and daily activities.

Illness has both personal and public dimensions. When we become ill, not only do we experience pain, discomfort, confusion, and other challenges, but others are affected as well. In the case of infectious diseases like COVID-19, we can infect other people with whom we live, work, and interact. When we ail from other conditions, our friends, families, and coworkers may extend sympathy, care, support, and assistance with practical tasks. They may struggle to understand our illness or to adjust the patterns of their own lives to accommodate it. Many try to make sense of the illness or figure out the cause of the health problem. Those we encounter react to our illness; their reactions, in turn, shape our own interpretations and can pose challenges to our sense of self. For instance, a long-time smoker who develops lung disease may be made to feel guilt or shame by family members.

Two sociological perspectives on the experience of illness have been particularly influential. The first perspective, associated with the functionalist school, proposes

Infectious diseases were introduced to entirely new populations during the era of colonialism. In this 1884 engraving, European ship passengers are held at a smallpox quarantine camp in Egypt to prevent the spread of the disease. At the same time, they try to keep malaria at bay with mosquito netting.

that "being sick" is a social role, just as "worker" or "mother" is a social role. As such, unhealthy persons are expected to comply with a widely agreed-upon set of behavioral expectations. The second perspective, favored by symbolic interactionists, explores how the meanings of illness are socially constructed and how these meanings influence people's behavior.

Functionalist Perspectives: Sick Role Theory

The functionalist theorist Talcott Parsons (1951) developed the notion of the **sick role** to describe patterns of behavior that the sick person adopts to minimize the disruptive impact of illness. Functionalist thought holds that society usually operates in a smooth and consensual manner. Illness is, therefore, seen as a dysfunction that can disrupt the flow of this normal state. A sick individual, for example, might be unable to perform standard responsibilities or be less reliable and efficient than usual. Because sick people cannot carry out their normal roles, the lives of people around them are disrupted: Assignments at work go unfinished and cause stress for coworkers, responsibilities at home are not fulfilled, and so forth.

> **sick role** A term associated with the functionalist Talcott Parsons to describe the patterns of behavior that a sick person adopts to minimize the disruptive impact of their illness on others.

According to Parsons, people learn the sick role through socialization and enact it, with the cooperation of others, when they fall ill. As with other social roles, such as gender roles, sick persons face societal expectations for how to behave; at the same time, other members of society abide by a generally agreed-upon set of expectations for how they will treat the sick individual. The sick role is distinguished by three sets of normative expectations:

1. The sick person is not held personally responsible for his or her poor health. Illness is seen as the result of physical causes beyond the individual's control.
2. The sick person is entitled to certain rights and privileges, including a release from normal responsibilities. Since the sick person bears no responsibility for the illness, he or she is exempted from certain duties, roles, and behaviors. For example, a sick adult might be released from normal household duties; a sick child, excused from attending school. Behavior that is not as polite or thoughtful as usual or an unkempt appearance might be excused. The sick person gains the right to stay in bed, for example, or to take time off from work. A person with mental illness who allegedly commits a crime may be found "not guilty by reason of insanity."
3. The sick person is expected to take sensible steps to regain his or her health, such as consulting a medical expert and agreeing to become a patient. To occupy the sick role, the sick person's claim of illness should be corroborated by a medical professional who legitimates the claim. Such confirmation allows those surrounding the sick person to accept the validity of his or her claims. Without such confirmation, the sick person may be viewed as a malingerer, or one who feigns health problems to avoid his or her obligations. A sick person who refuses to consult a doctor or who does not heed the advice of a medical authority puts his or her sick role status in jeopardy. To revisit an earlier example, a mentally ill person on trial for committing a crime may be ordered by the court to take psychotropic medications to treat his or her symptoms.

Over the past six decades, sociologists have refined Parsons's sick role theory. They argue that the experience of the sick role varies with the type of illness, since people's reactions to a sick person vary according to the severity of the illness and their perception of its nature and cause. Thus, not all people will uniformly experience the rights and privileges that accompany the sick role. Eliot Freidson (1970) identified three versions of the sick role that correspond with different types of illness. The conditional sick role applies to individuals suffering from a temporary condition that ultimately will be cured. The sick person is expected to get well and receives some rights and privileges according to the severity of the illness. For example, someone with a serious and potentially life-threatening condition like coronavirus would reap more benefits than someone with a common cold.

The unconditionally legitimate sick role refers to individuals who are suffering from incurable or terminal illnesses. Because the sick person cannot do anything to get well, he or she is automatically entitled to occupy the sick role. The expectation that one will seek timely medical care may be relaxed, because care-seeking may be futile for some health conditions. The unconditionally legitimate role might apply to individuals with alopecia (total hair loss) or severe acne (in both cases, there are no special privileges but rather an acknowledgment that the individual is not responsible for the illness), or with cancer or Parkinson's disease, which result in important privileges and the right to abandon many duties.

The third sick role is the *illegitimate* role, which applies when an individual suffers from a disease or condition that is stigmatized by others. In such cases, there is a sense that the individual might be partially responsible for his or her illness; additional rights and privileges are not necessarily granted. HIV/AIDS is perhaps the most vivid example of a historically stigmatized illness that affects a sufferer's perceived right to assume the sick role. Some HIV/AIDS patients may be held "responsible" for their condition and may be judged negatively for having engaged in high-risk behaviors such as unprotected sex or the use of unclean needles. Pediatric AIDS patients, those who contracted AIDS through a tainted blood transfusion, or other persons perceived to be "innocent" victims, by contrast, may be spared stigmatization.

Critiques of Sick Role Theory Although the sick role model reveals how the ill person is an integral part of a larger social context, a number of criticisms can be leveled against it. Some argue that the sick role formula does not adequately capture the *lived experience* of illness. Others point out that it cannot be applied across all contexts, cultures, and historical periods. For example, it does not account for instances when doctors and patients disagree about a diagnosis or have opposing interests. It also fails to explain illnesses that do not necessarily lead to a suspension of normal activity, such as alcoholism, certain disabilities, and some chronic diseases. Furthermore, adopting the sick role is not always a straightforward process. Some individuals who suffer for years from chronic pain or from misdiagnosed symptoms are denied the sick role until they get a clear diagnosis. Other sick people, such as young adults with autoimmune diseases, often appear physically healthy despite constant physical pain and exhaustion; because of their "healthy" outward appearance, they may not be readily granted sick role status. In other cases, social factors such as race, class, and gender can affect whether and how readily the sick role is granted. The sick role cannot be divorced from the social, cultural, and economic influences that surround it.

The realities of life and illness are more complex than the sick role suggests. The leading causes of death in the twenty-first century are heart disease and cancer, two diseases that are associated with unhealthy behaviors such as smoking, a high-fat diet, and a sedentary lifestyle. Given the emphasis on taking control over one's health and lifestyle in our modern age, individuals bear ever-greater responsibility for their own well-being. This sense of responsibility contradicts the first premise of the sick role—that the individual is not to blame for his or her illness. Moreover, sick role theory is less useful for understanding chronic illness (versus infectious disease) because there is no single formula for chronically ill or disabled people to follow. Moreover, chronically ill persons often find that their symptoms fluctuate, so that they feel and appear healthy on some days, yet experience debilitating symptoms on other days. Living with illness is experienced and interpreted in multiple ways.

Symbolic Interactionist Approaches: Illness as "Lived Experience"

Symbolic interactionists study the ways people interpret the social world and the meanings they ascribe to it. Many sociologists have applied this approach to health and illness and view this perspective as a partial corrective to the limitations of functionalist approaches to health. Symbolic interactionists are not concerned with identifying risk factors for specific illnesses. Rather, they address questions such as: How do people react and adjust to news about a serious illness? How does illness shape individuals' daily lives? How does living with a chronic illness affect an individual's self-identity?

One theme that sociologists address is how chronically ill individuals cope with the practical and emotional implications of their illness. Certain illnesses require regular treatments or maintenance that can affect daily routines. Undergoing dialysis or insulin injections or taking large numbers of pills requires individuals to adjust their schedules. Some illnesses have unpredictable effects, such as violent nausea or sudden loss of bowel or bladder control. People suffering from such conditions often develop strategies for managing their illness in daily life. These include practical considerations—such as noting the location of the restrooms when in an unfamiliar place—as well as skills for managing interpersonal relations, both intimate and commonplace. Although symptoms can be embarrassing and disruptive, people develop coping strategies to live as normally as possible (Kelly, 1992).

At the same time, the experience of illness can pose challenges to and changes in people's sense of self. These develop not only through the reactions of other people but also through the ill person's perception of those reactions. For the chronically ill or disabled, routine social interactions become tinged with risk or uncertainty, and interpretations of common situations may differ substantially. An ill person may need assistance but not want to appear dependent, for example. A healthy individual may feel sympathy for someone diagnosed with an illness but might be unsure whether to address the subject directly. The changed context of social interactions can precipitate transformations in self-identity.

Some sociologists have investigated how individuals with chronic physical or mental illness manage their symptoms and treatments within the overall context of their lives (Jobling, 1988; Williams, 1993). Illness can place enormous demands on people's time, energy, strength, and emotional reserves. Serious illness can also tax the emotional resources of loved ones. Corbin and Strauss (1985) identified three types of "work" incorporated into the everyday strategies of the chronically ill. *Illness work* refers to activities involved in managing the condition, such as taking medications, doing diagnostic tests, or undergoing physical therapy. *Everyday work* pertains to the management of daily life, such as maintaining relationships with others, running household affairs, and pursuing professional or personal interests. *Biographical work* involves the process of incorporating the illness into one's life, making sense of it, and developing ways of explaining it to others. Such a process can help people with mental and physical illness restore meaning and order to their lives.

Each of these processes of adaptation may be particularly difficult for those who suffer from a stigmatized health condition, such as extreme obesity, alcoholism, schizophrenia, HIV/AIDS, or lung cancer. Sociologist Erving Goffman (1963) developed the concept of **stigma**, which refers to any personal characteristic that is devalued in a particular social context. Stigmas typically come in one of three forms: "abominations of the body" (such as disfigurement, disability, or obesity), "tribal stigma of race, nation, or religion" (such as belonging to a historically denigrated racial or ethnic group), and "blemishes of individual character" (such as laziness, lack of personal

stigma Any physical or social characteristic that is labeled by society as undesirable.

control, or immorality). Stigmatized individuals and groups often are treated with suspicion, hostility, or discrimination.

Some ill persons, particularly those marked by "abominations of the body," may arouse feelings of sympathy or compassion, especially if they are not held responsible for their illness. They may even receive special privileges. For example, one study showed that adolescents offered much less critical appraisals of overweight persons when they believed that the weight was caused by a thyroid problem, and thus was due to a biological factor rather than to a character flaw such as laziness or lack of self-control (Dejong, 1993). Studies are less conclusive regarding mental illness; some find that diagnosing mental illness as a "brain disease" (and thus beyond one's control) diminishes the stigma, whereas others show that attributing mental illness to genetic factors does not minimize society's negative views (e.g., Corrigan and Watson, 2004; Phelan et al., 2005).

By contrast, when a health condition is viewed as indicative of a "character blemish," such as sexual promiscuity or gluttony, then the healthy population may reject the sufferers. Similarly, throughout history, many infectious diseases, especially those contracted by the poor, were often stigmatized and viewed as indicators of shame and dishonor. This occurred in the Middle Ages with leprosy, when people were isolated in leper colonies. HIV/AIDS often provokes such stigmatization today—in spite of the fact that, as with leprosy, the risk of contracting the disease in ordinary situations is almost nonexistent. The Joint United Nations Programme on HIV/AIDS reports incidences in Kerala, India, when children infected with HIV have been barred from schools and denied any interaction with other children (U.N. Joint Programme on HIV/AIDS [UNAIDS], 2003).

Stigmas are, however, rarely based on valid understandings or scientific data. They spring from stereotypes or perceptions that may be false or only partially correct. Further, the nature of a stigma

Symbolic interactionists are interested in how illnesses shape individuals' daily lives. For example, people with diabetes must constantly monitor their blood sugar levels.

Table 18.2
APPLYING SOCIOLOGY TO THE BODY

CONCEPT	APPROACH TO UNDERSTANDING BODIES	CONTEMPORARY APPLICATION
Functionalist perspectives argue that society operates in a smooth and consensual manner. Illness is, therefore, seen as a dysfunction that can disrupt the flow of this normal state.	Sick role theory describes how sick persons work to minimize the disruptive impact of illness on institutions like work and family.	When an employee takes a sick day from work, they are expected to stay home and focus on healing, to facilitate their return to work.
Symbolic interactionists study the ways people interpret the social world and the meanings they ascribe to it.	Symbolic interactionists focus on meaning-making and everyday experiences of health, like how living with a chronic illness affects one's identity, behavior, and interactions with others.	A person who is diagnosed with a health condition like autoimmune disease may consider that a major part of their identity, talk about regularly, join Facebook support groups, and adjust their daily activities accordingly.
Stigma theory holds that some personal traits are devalued in a particular social context, and elicit unkind or discriminatory treatment from others.	Physical visible health conditions may be stigmatized because they are visually unappealing to others, while other conditions are stigmatized because others incorrectly view them as indicative of a character flaw.	Medical and public health experts emphasize that substance use disorders like opioid addiction are diseases rather than matters of choice or personal character, to fight the stigmatization of persons with such conditions.

varies widely across sociocultural contexts: The extent to which a trait is devalued depends on the values and beliefs of those who do the stigmatizing. For instance, in the United States, obese persons are much more likely to be stigmatized by White upper-middle-class persons than they are to be stigmatized by African Americans or working-class Whites (Carr and Friedman, 2005). By contrast, other health conditions, including major mental illness and HIV/AIDS (as we will read about later in this chapter), are much more widely stigmatized. One recent study of 16 countries, including the United States and nations in Europe, Africa, and Asia, found that even in the most liberal, tolerant countries, the majority of the public held stigmatizing attitudes and a willingness to exclude people with schizophrenia from close, personal relationships and positions of authority, seeing them as unpredictable and potentially dangerous (Pescosolido et al., 2013).

History of Sexuality in Western Culture

Just as particular diseases have been subject to (or spared from) stigmatization throughout history, sexual behavior has also been judged as "normal" or not across differential sociohistorical contexts. Western attitudes toward sexual behavior were for nearly 2,000 years molded primarily by Christianity, whose dominant view was that all sexual behavior is suspect except that needed for reproduction. During some periods, this view produced an extreme prudishness, but at other times, many people ignored the church's teachings and engaged in practices such as adultery. The idea that sexual fulfillment can and should be sought through marriage was rare.

In the nineteenth century, religious presumptions about sexuality were partly replaced by medical ones. Most early writings by doctors about sexual behavior, however, were as stern as the views of the church. Some argued that any type of sexual activity unconnected with reproduction would cause serious physical harm. Masturbation was said to cause blindness, insanity, heart disease, and other ailments, while oral sex was claimed to cause cancer.

In Victorian times, sexual hypocrisy abounded. Many Victorian men—who appeared to be sober, well-behaved citizens, devoted to their wives—regularly

Sexual hypocrisy abounded in the Victorian era. Virtuous women were said to be indifferent to sexuality, while it was acceptable for their husbands to visit prostitutes or keep mistresses. This 1878 illustration of the St. Louis red-light district shows that prostitution was openly tolerated.

visited prostitutes or kept mistresses. Such behavior was accepted, whereas "respectable" women who took lovers were regarded as scandalous and shunned in polite society. Virtuous women were believed to be indifferent to sexuality, accepting their husbands' advances only as a duty. The differing attitudes toward the sexual activities of men and women formed a double standard, which persists today.

Currently, traditional attitudes exist alongside much more permissive attitudes, which developed especially rapidly in the 1960s. Some people, particularly those influenced by Christian teachings, believe that premarital sex is wrong; they frown on all forms of sexual behavior except heterosexual activity within marriage—although it is now more commonly accepted that sexual pleasure is an important feature of marriage. Others approve of premarital sex and tolerate different sexual practices.

Sexual attitudes have undoubtedly become more permissive over recent decades in most parts of the world, although some behaviors remain consistently more acceptable than others. For example, the proportion of Americans saying that premarital sex is "always wrong" dropped from 34 percent in 1972 to 20 percent in 2016. By contrast, disapproval of extramarital sex has remained consistently high and even increased during that same period. The proportion of Americans saying that extramarital sex is "always wrong" increased from 69 to 75 percent between 1973 and 2016 (Smith et al., 1972–2016).

Early Research on Sexual Behavior: Kinsey's Study

Much of what we know about human sexuality in the twentieth century is due to the pathbreaking research of pioneering scientist Alfred Kinsey. When Kinsey began his research in the United States in the 1940s and 1950s, it was the first major scientific investigation of sexual behavior. Kinsey and his collaborators (1948, 1953) faced condemnation from religious organizations, and his work was denounced in the newspapers and in Congress as immoral. But he persisted, thus making his study the largest rigorous study of sexuality at that time, although his sample was not representative of the overall American population.

Kinsey's results were surprising because they revealed a tremendous discrepancy between prevailing public expectations of sexual behavior and actual sexual conduct. He found that almost 70 percent of men in his study had visited a prostitute and 84 percent had had premarital sexual experience. Yet, following the double standard, 40 percent of men expected their wives to be virgins at the time of marriage. More than 90 percent of men had engaged in masturbation and nearly 60 percent in oral sexual activity—activities that were frowned upon (and never discussed publicly) at that time. Among women, about 50 percent had had premarital sexual experiences, although mostly with the man whom they eventually married. Some 60 percent had masturbated, and the same percentage had engaged in oral-genital contact.

Dr. Kinsey's (center) pathbreaking research into sexual behavior in the 1940s and 1950s revealed a large discrepancy between publicly accepted attitudes and actual sexual conduct.

The gap between publicly accepted attitudes and actual behavior was probably especially pronounced just after World War II, the time of Kinsey's study. A phase of sexual liberalization had begun in the 1920s, when many younger people felt freed from the strict moral codes that had governed earlier generations. Sexual behavior probably changed, but issues concerning sexuality were not openly discussed. People participating in sexual activities that were still strongly disapproved of on a public level concealed them, not realizing that others were engaging in similar practices behind closed doors. The more permissive 1960s brought openly declared attitudes more into line with the realities of behavior. As we will see in subsequent sections, as research methods have improved, social scientists have been able to get a more accurate handle on adult sexual behavior. Yet, as we will also see, the more things change, the more they stay the same. Even in the twenty-first century, some sexual behaviors continue to be judged harshly as "not normal," and some individuals continue to face stigmatization and discrimination due to their sexual behavior and preferences.

CONCEPT CHECKS

1 Describe how the primary causes of death have changed between colonial times and the present day.

2 How do functionalist theorists and symbolic interactionists differ in their perspectives on health and illness?

3 Describe several changes in sexual practices over the past two centuries.

4 What are the most important contributions of Alfred Kinsey's research on sexuality?

3 RESEARCH ON HEALTH, ILLNESS, AND SEXUALITY TODAY

Life expectancy for people in most parts of the world increased steadily over the twentieth and early twenty-first centuries. Infectious diseases such as polio, scarlet fever, and diphtheria have been largely eradicated. In wealthy and industrialized nations infant mortality rates have dropped precipitously, leading to an increase in the average age of death in the developed world. Compared with other parts of the world, standards of physical health and well-being are high. Many advances in public health have been attributed to the power of modern medicine. It is commonly assumed that medical research has been, and will continue to be, successful in uncovering the biological causes of disease and developing effective treatments. At the same time, however, the proportion reporting mental health conditions, including depression and anxiety disorders, has increased steeply through the twentieth and twenty-first centuries, raising new questions about how we define, detect, and diagnose mental health conditions (Greenberg, 2010; Horwitz, 2013).

While sociologists recognize that, on average, physical health and risk of mortality have improved and mental health has, by some accounts, declined in the past century,

epidemiology The study of the distribution and incidence of disease and illness within a population.

these patterns vary widely throughout the population both within the United States and across the globe. Research has shown that certain groups of people enjoy much better health than others. These health inequalities appear to reflect larger systems of social stratification, including race, gender, and social class stratification. From 2015 to 2017, the United States witnessed three consecutive years of declining life expectancy, a stunning development after a half century of improvements in life expectancy. A close look at the data show that shortening life spans overall were a function of health conditions that were particularly devastating to economically disadvantaged adults, most notably middle-aged high school dropouts who had high rates of "deaths of despair" including suicides and deaths related to opioid addiction (Case and Deaton, 2020).

Deaths from COVID-19 also follow stark social patterns. As of July 2020, it was too soon to tell how the pandemic would affect overall life expectancy in the United States, but one fact is clear: COVID-19 deaths, like deaths of despair, disproportionately strike economically disadvantaged persons who live in crowded housing and work in jobs that place them at risk, like bus drivers or grocery store clerks. One examination of New York City found that the Bronx—the borough with the highest proportion of racial and ethnic minorities, the most persons living in poverty, and lowest levels of educational attainment—had higher rates of hospitalization and death related to COVID-19 than all other boroughs (Wadhera et al., 2020).

Understanding the distribution and incidence of disease and illness within a population is the primary goal of the field of **epidemiology**—the science that studies the distribution and incidence of disease and illness within the population. Epidemiologists attempt to explain the link between physical and mental health and variables such as social class, gender, race, age, and geography. While most scholars acknowledge the strong positive correlation between socioeconomic resources and good health, they do not agree about the nature of the connection or how to address health inequalities. One of the main areas of debate involves the relative importance of individual variables (e.g., lifestyle, behavior, diet, stress, and cultural patterns) versus environmental or structural factors (e.g., income distribution, poverty, and access to health care).

In this section, we examine cutting-edge research on health patterns in the United States according to social class, gender, and race, and we review some competing explanations for the persistence of those patterns. We also discuss current research on how society and culture influence sexual practices and attitudes, with a particular focus on the changing acceptance of same-sex sexual relations. We conclude by highlighting the ways our bodies—something we think of as "natural"—are increasingly shaped and affected by a further aspect of the macrosocial context: science and technology.

Social Patterning of Health and Illness in the United States

One of the most enduring patterns social epidemiologists have documented is the persistence of health inequalities, where members of those social groups with more status, prestige, power, and economic resources typically enjoy better physical and mental health. Although we see some exceptions to this rule—for example, women currently live longer than men in the United States, despite persistent earnings differences between the two groups—the social class and Black-White gaps have endured, and even widened, over the last several decades. We now provide evidence of these patterns and offer explanations for why they persist.

Social Class–Based Inequalities in Health

In Chapter 8, we defined *social class* as a concept that encompasses education, income, occupation, and assets. In U.S. society, people with more education, higher incomes, and more prestigious occupations have better health. What is fascinating is that each of these dimensions of social class may be related to health and mortality for different reasons.

Income is the most obvious dimension. In countries such as the United States, where medical care is expensive and many people have historically lacked insurance, those with the richest financial resources have better access to physicians and medicine. But inequalities in health also persist in countries that have national health insurance, such as Great Britain. The landmark *Black Report* revealed that social inequalities in health and mortality in the United Kingdom had not diminished since the implementation of the National Health Service (NHS) but had instead increased (Townsend and Davidson, 1982). Yet, part of this growing gap was due to improvements in mortality among the wealthier classes and not due to declines among the lower socioeconomic groups. This suggested that the upper classes were making greater (or somehow "better") use of the improved access to medical resources. Thus, we must think beyond income and consider the other dimensions of social class: occupational status and education.

Differences in occupational status may lead to inequalities in health and illness even when medical care is fairly evenly distributed. One study of health inequalities in Great Britain (Townsend and Davidson, 1982) found that manual workers had substantially higher mortality rates than professional workers, even though Britain's health service had made great strides in equalizing the distribution of health care.

Indeed, different occupations are associated with different levels of health risks. Those who work in offices or domestic settings have less risk of injury or exposure to hazardous materials. Jobs can be dangerous in one of two ways: conditions that increase one's risk of on-the-job accidents, and continuous exposure to dangerous or stressful conditions that eventually hasten one's death.

According to the U.S. Bureau of Labor Statistics (2019m), 9 of the 10 most "fatal" jobs in 2018 due to occupational injuries were manual labor jobs, including logger, fisherman, aircraft pilots and flight

Type 2 diabetes is a chronic condition that typically develops in adults and disproportionately affects the poor and minority groups.

engineers, roofer, refuse and recyclable material collector, drivers/sales workers, and truck drivers, farmer, rancher, and other agricultural worker, steel worker, first-line supervisors of construction trades and extraction workers, and groundskeeper. Public-service jobs such as police officer, firefighter, and military personnel also placed their workers at heightened risk of accidental or sudden death (BLS, 2014). Other jobs are hazardous because they expose their workers to dangerous conditions over time, ultimately leading to disease and death. Other work settings are hazardous because they expose their employees to infectious diseases. Workers in long-term care settings like nursing homes are particularly susceptible to COVID-19 because their workplaces them in confined spaces with older adults suffering from the disease. Nursing home workers need to move from room to room assisting patients and serving them meals, heightening their own risk (Yourish et al., 2020). In general, industrial-based disease is difficult to calculate because it is hard to determine whether an illness is acquired from working conditions or from other sources. However, some work-related diseases are well documented: Lung disease is widespread in mining, as a result of dust inhalation; work with asbestos has been shown to produce certain types of cancer (BLS, 2012).

Education is also a powerful predictor of health, where those with higher levels of education have longer life spans than persons with fewer years of schooling. In recent years, the least-educated Americans—especially women—have actually experienced a decrease in life expectancy, while all other groups have experienced gains (Cockerham, 2014). Not only do high school dropouts die younger than persons with higher levels of education, but they also have experienced an absolute decline in life expectancy, or the number of years they live, since the 1990s (Olshansky, Antonucci, and Berkman et al., 2012). A recent study found that life expectancy increased for college-educated people and declined for persons without a four-year college degree. Closer inspection of these differences found that rates of "deaths of despair" from suicide and drug abuse are particularly high among those with less education (Case and Deaton, 2020; Sasson and Hayward, 2019).

What accounts for the steep educational gradient in life span today? Numerous studies find a positive correlation between education and a broad array of preventive health behaviors. Better-educated people are significantly more likely to engage in aerobic exercise and to know their blood pressure (Shea et al., 1991) and less likely to smoke (Kenkel, Lillard, and Mathios, 2006) or be overweight (Himes, 1999). By contrast, poorly educated people engage in more cigarette smoking; they also have more problems with cholesterol and body weight (Winkleby et al., 1992). People with low levels of education also are less likely to have health insurance and are more likely to misuse and even overdose on prescription medications (Tavernise, 2012). More highly educated people also respond differently to health threats. One study of smokers found that after suffering a heart attack, highly educated persons were much more likely than poorly educated persons to quit smoking (Wray et al., 1998). Lest we jump to the conclusion that persons with less education make "bad choices," sociologists have acknowledged that access to safe places to exercise, grocery stores with healthy foods, and other heath-enhancing amenities are more common in higher-income neighborhoods (Althschuler et al., 2004).

Mental health is similarly affected by social class–based inequalities. In general, persons with lower levels of education and income fare worse along most mental health outcomes, including risk of depression, anxiety, and suicidal ideation. The stressors related to economic adversity, including unsatisfying jobs, strained marriages, and worries about money and one's personal safety, may overwhelm one's ability

health literacy One's capacity to obtain, process, and understand basic health information and services needed to make appropriate health decisions.

to cope. The COVID-19 crisis is a case in point; stay-at-home orders, rampant business shut-downs, and job loss are stressful for everyone, but are most overwhelming for low-income persons who live paycheck to paycheck and don't have ample savings to sustain them during periods of layoff or furlough. Depressive symptoms (feelings of profound sadness and hopelessness) and anxiety (nervousness about one's daily experiences) are emotional consequences of living under persistently stressful circumstances (Carr, 2014).

Most social epidemiologists view education as the most important of the three dimensions of socioeconomic status in predicting health. This is because education is associated with a broad range of traits that promote positive health behaviors, including high levels of perceived control over one's environment (Mirowsky and Ross, 2005) and **health literacy**, which refers to one's capacity to obtain, process, and understand the basic health information and services needed to make appropriate health decisions (Zarcadoolas et al., 2006). Understanding one's health risks and having the means to do something about them are core components of the health-belief model (Becker, 1974; Rosenstock, 1974), which provides a framework for understanding why some individuals participate in positive health behaviors while others do not. The model proposes that individuals' decisions to engage in positive health behaviors (or to change their health behaviors) are based on their evaluation of the possible threat a health condition poses and the perceived benefits of, and barriers to, taking action to prevent getting the health condition. Both evaluating one's level of threat and developing a strategy to minimize risk are clearly shaped by social-structural factors.

Race-Based Inequalities in Health

Blacks fare worse than Whites in the United States on nearly all health indicators, ranging from body weight to mortality rates to risk of major illnesses like diabetes and cancer. Life expectancy at birth in 2015 was about 81 years for White females but 78.5 years for Black females. Likewise, life expectancy at birth in 2015 was about 76 years for White males yet less than 72 years for Black males (Figure 18.1). An even more startling gap emerges when early life mortality is considered: Black infants have more than twice the mortality rate of White infants. Roughly 11 Black infants per every 1,000 born in 2014 died in their first year of life, compared to about 5 deaths per 1,000 for White and Hispanic infants (Arias et al., 2019).

Racial differences in health reveal the complex interplay among race, social class, and culture. A powerful example of the multiple ways that race affects health is the Hispanic health paradox: Although Hispanics in the United States have poorer socioeconomic resources than Whites, on average, their health—and especially the health of their infants—is just as good as, if not better than, that of Whites. Blacks, by contrast, face economic disadvantages that are similar to those of Hispanics, yet Blacks do not enjoy the health benefits Hispanics experience. Experts attribute Hispanics' health advantage relative to Blacks' to cultural factors such as social cohesion but also to methodological factors. Studies of Hispanic health in the United States focus on those Hispanics who successfully migrated to the United States; as such, they are believed to be in better health, or more robust, than those who remained in their native countries (Perea, 2012).

A closer inspection of Blacks' health and mortality disadvantage further reveals the multiple ways that race matters for health. One of the main reasons for Blacks' health disadvantage is that Blacks as a group have less money than Whites. The median wealth of White households is roughly 14 times that of Black households and 10 times that of Hispanic households (U.S. Bureau of the Census, 2017l). And the median income of a Black man is less than 59 percent that of a White man (Proctor, Semega, and Kollar, 2016). In 2016, the median wealth of Black and Hispanic households was $17,600 and $20,700, respectively. Meanwhile, the median wealth of White families was $171,000 (Hanks, Solomon, and Weller, 2018). Yet the differences in Black and White health go beyond economic causes and reflect other important aspects of the social and cultural landscape. Consider racial gaps in mortality. The rise in violent crime in the late 1980s accompanied the rise of widespread crack cocaine addiction, mainly affecting poor African American neighborhoods that were plagued by high levels of unemployment (Wilson, 1996). Homicide victimization rates for all races have declined considerably over the past 20 years, yet the stark racial gap persists: The murder rate for young Black males is ten times higher than for their White peers (Widra, 2018).

Other race-based inequalities in health status, health behaviors, and health care are also stark. There is a higher prevalence of hypertension among Blacks, especially Black men—a difference that may be partly biological. Early evidence also suggests that Blacks are more likely than Whites to contract and die from COVID-19. There are many reasons why, including the jobs they work in, greater use of public transit, less access to health care, higher rates of underlying health conditions, living in crowded housing with extended family members, and higher rates of living in institutions like prisons where infection rates are very high (CDC, 2020).

Despite the persistence of Black-White disparities in health and health behaviors, some progress has been made in eradicating them. According to the Centers for Disease Control and Prevention, racial differences in cigarette smoking have decreased (CDC, 2017a). In 1965, half of White men and 60 percent of Black men age 18 and over smoked cigarettes. By 2015, 16.8 percent of White men and 20.3 percent of Black men smoked. In 1965, roughly equal proportions of Black and White women age 18 and older smoked (33 and 34 percent, respectively). This equivalence was preserved in 2015, with 13.2 percent of Black women and 14.8 percent of White women smoking.

Hypertension among Blacks also has been greatly reduced, yet rates remain high. In the early 1970s, half of Black adults between the ages of 20 and 74 suffered from hypertension. During 2015–2016, roughly 40 percent of Black adults, compared to 28 percent of White adults, suffered from hypertension (Fryar et al., 2017). Despite the overall decline, this rate is still high and may reflect the currently high and rising rates of obesity among Black women. Eighty-two percent of Black women are considered overweight or obese, as compared to almost 64 percent of White women (CDC, 2017a). Black women also are far less likely than White women to exercise regularly, a pattern that most social scientists attribute to their hectic schedules of juggling work

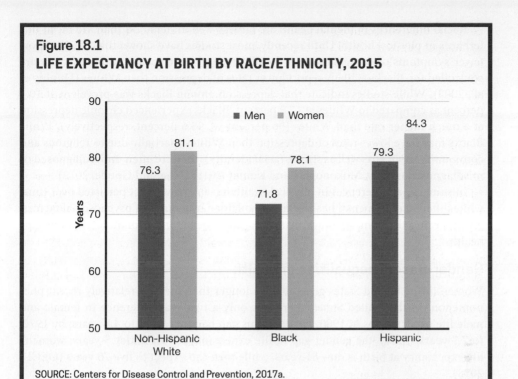

Figure 18.1
LIFE EXPECTANCY AT BIRTH BY RACE/ETHNICITY, 2015

SOURCE: Centers for Disease Control and Prevention, 2017a.

and family and the high costs of fitness programs and gym memberships (August and Sorkin, 2010). However, in 2011, then-U.S. surgeon general Regina M. Benjamin drew attention and some ridicule by suggesting that Black women avoid exercise because it may ruin their hair; Black women often spend considerable time and money on treatments such as hair relaxers (Versey, 2014). A recent study by the University of Ohio found that while many clinicians engage Black women in conversations regarding exercise and weight, only about 25 percent ever discuss practical implications of hair maintenance. The study highlighted hair maintenance as a barrier to regular exercise (Tolliver et al., 2019).

Patterns of physician visitation, hospitalization, and preventive medicine also have improved, yet racial equity remains elusive. For example, Black women historically have been less likely than White women to receive mammograms. This gap has narrowed in recent years. In fact, in 2015, a higher proportion of Black women (72 percent) than White women (68 percent) had had a mammogram within the past two years (CDC, 2017a). However, some studies suggest that Black women delay receiving mammograms, and thus, those with breast cancer have their condition detected at a later—and more dangerous—stage of the disease's progression. Tumors in more advanced stages increase one's mortality risk and impede the effectiveness of potential treatments (Smith-Bindman et al., 2006). Studies show that while the rates of cancer are about the same in Black women and White women, the likelihood of death for Black women is 19 percent higher than for White women (Monticciolo et al., 2019).

Racial differences in mental health are far less well understood than are racial differences in physical health. Until recently, most studies have shown that Blacks report fewer symptoms of depression than do Whites, and once socioeconomic factors are controlled for, Blacks actually report lower rates of depression than Whites (Dunlop et al., 2003). While studies indicate that depression among Blacks was prevalent at 10.4 percent as compared to Whites at 17.9 percent, Blacks experienced chronic depression at a much higher rate than Whites (56 percent vs. 38.6 percent, respectively). While Blacks may have lower rates of depression then Whites (partially due to religious and community support as well as strong racial identity), they are often underdiagnosed or misdiagnosed (Bailey, Mokonogho, and Kumar, 2019; Oates and Goode, 2012).

In sum, racial differences in physical health have narrowed yet persisted over time, while differences in mental health can be explained by a range of psychosocial factors, underscoring the complex ways that biological, social, and economic factors shape health.

Gender-Based Inequalities in Health

Women in the United States generally live longer than men—a relatively recent phenomenon. In the United States, there was only a two-year difference in female and male life expectancies in 1900. By 1940, this gap had increased to 4.4 years; by 1970, to 7.7 years. Today, the gender gap in life expectancy is just under 5 years; women's life expectancy at birth is now 81 years, while men can expect to live 76 years (OECD, 2018).

The main reason for the gender gap in life expectancy is that the leading causes of death have changed since the turn of the century—and the main causes of death today disproportionately strike men. In 1900, the leading cause of death was infectious disease, which struck men, women, and children equally. However, emerging evidence suggests that COVID-19 is distinct among infectious disease for disproportionately affecting men, although scientists do not fully understand why (Gupta, 2020). Chronic diseases like heart disease and cancer, which are the leading causes of death today, also disproportionately strike men. These conditions are heavily influenced by lifestyle, diet, and behavior—all of which are shaped by the distinctive experiences of women and men in contemporary society. The World Health Organization also notes that newborn girls are more likely to survive to their first birthday as compared to newborn boys. This inherent biological advantage continues through life and women are expected to live six to eight years more than men in many regions of the world (WHO, 2020a).

Social explanations for women's mortality advantage focus on behavioral differences between men and women. Men historically have been socialized to equate risk with masculinity (Mahalik et al., 2007). Men are more likely than women to smoke cigarettes. Likewise, higher proportions of men drink alcoholic beverages, binge drink, and smoke marijuana (CDC, 2017a). However, in recent years, female high school dropouts have experienced a decrease in life expectancy, due to poor health behaviors such as smoking, drinking, and prescription drug misuse (Olshansky, Antonucci, and Berkman et al., 2012). As a result, the gender gap in life expectancy has narrowed for those with the least education, yet this change is due to declines in women's health rather than improvement in men's.

While sociologists generally focus on societal factors in explaining the gender gap in life expectancy, biological factors may also pertain. Disentangling the effects of biology from social context is very difficult, however, given that gender shapes one's social experiences from the moment of birth (see Chapter 10). One study from the 1950s used an innovative design in its attempts to identify the distinctive effects of biology versus social environment on mortality risk. The researchers focused on a subpopulation of men and women who were believed to have identical lifestyles, diets, and levels of stress: nuns and monks (Madigan, 1957). The nuns lived longer than the monks, and both had life expectancies essentially the same as that for the rest of the population. Because the living environments were equalized for the two groups, lifestyle elements such as diet, drinking, and stress could be ruled out as explanatory factors (Madigan, 1957). However, critics noted that the monks smoked more than the nuns did, so the study did not entirely account for lifestyle differences. Further, the study could not account for the gender-related lifestyle factors that existed before persons entered the religious order.

Numerous studies spanning the fields of biology and epidemiology provide suggestive evidence that women have a biological advantage. Recent studies suggest that estrogen helps protect women against heart disease by reducing circulatory levels of harmful cholesterol, whereas testosterone increases low-density lipoprotein. Women also have stronger immune systems, in part because testosterone causes immunosuppression (Ness and Kuller, 1999). Emerging evidence also suggests that women with COVID-19 have a higher level of antibodies than men, which are a protective factor (Gupta, 2020).

Biologists have also cited genetic factors. Humans have 23 pairs of chromosomes, one of which determines sex. Males have XY sex chromosomes, while females have two X chromosomes. The X chromosome carries more genetic information than the Y, including some defects that can lead to physical abnormalities. Instead of making females more vulnerable to X-linked disorders, this seems to give females a genetic advantage. A female typically needs two defective X chromosomes for most genetically linked disorders to manifest themselves; otherwise, one healthy X chromosome can override the abnormal one. A male who has a defective X chromosome will have a genetically linked disease because there is no other X chromosome to cancel it out. This fact may account for the higher numbers of miscarriages of male fetuses, male infant deaths, and deaths at all ages due to congenital abnormalities and weaker cardiopulmonary systems (Hayflick, 1994; Hill and Upchurch, 1995). However, biology alone cannot explain gender difference in mortality, especially because this relationship differs substantially over time and across nations.

One of the apparent ironies of health research is that women have an advantage in mortality, yet they appear to fare worse than men on nearly every indicator of self-reported health problems on surveys. For instance, women report higher rates of illness from acute conditions and nonfatal chronic conditions, including arthritis, osteoporosis, and depressive and anxiety disorders. Women are slightly more likely to report their health as fair to poor, they spend about 40 percent more days in bed each year, and their activities are restricted due to health problems about 25 percent more than are men's. In addition, they make more physician visits each year and undergo twice the number of surgical procedures as do men (National Center for Health Statistics, 2008). Women also are twice as likely as men to report symptoms of depression

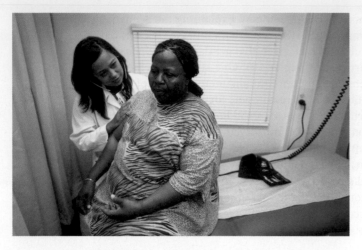

One of the explanations for women's mortality advantage is that women engage in more preventive care.

and to be diagnosed with a major depressive disorder (Van de Velde, Bracke, and Leveque, 2010).

What would explain this paradox, that men die younger but women report more health problems? Sociologists offer two main explanations: (1) Advancing age brings poorer health, and women are older than men on average due to their greater life expectancy and (2) women make greater use of medical services, including preventive care, and thus are more cognizant of their health symptoms (National Center for Health Statistics, 2008). Men may experience as many, or more, health symptoms as women, but they may ignore their symptoms, underestimate the extent of their illness, or utilize preventive services less often (Waldron, 1986). Further, men who are socialized to believe that men should be "traditionally masculine," strong, and self-sufficient are less likely to seek out annual checkups (Springer and Mouzon, 2011).

Explanations for the gender gap in depression are less clear, yet scholars typically attribute women's greater level of depression to measurement issues and differences in stress exposure. First, standard instruments used to measure depression typically emphasize symptoms that are more likely to be endorsed by women, as these symptoms are more closely linked to stereotypical female behavior such as "I felt sad" or "I cried a lot" (Stommel et al., 1993). Men are less likely to endorse such items, leading some scholars to question whether depression in men goes underdetected. Second, given the strains that women increasingly face in juggling work and family roles, compounded by other stressors that disproportionately strike women, such as single parenthood or workplace discrimination, women may be more likely than men to be depleted and depressed by the daunting demands they face (Nolen-Hoeksema, 1993).

A major question for sociologists is whether the gender gap in life expectancy will continue to close in coming years. Many researchers believe that it will, yet for an unfortunate reason: Women's life expectancies may erode and thus become more similar to men's. As men's and women's gender roles have converged over the past several decades, women have increasingly taken on unhealthy "male-typed" behaviors such as smoking and alcohol use, as well as emotional and physical stress in the workplace. These patterns are particularly pronounced for women of low socioeconomic status. One recent study found that American women have lost ground with respect to life expectancy compared with women from other nations. In the early 1980s, the life expectancy of women in the United States ranked 14th in the world, yet by 2010, American women had fallen to 41st place (Karas-Montez and Zajacova, 2013). Currently, the United States is ranked last in life expectancy for both men and women in comparable large and wealthy countries (Kamal, 2017). These disheartening findings reveal that gender differences in health and mortality are not a function of biology alone but of the social advantages and adversities men and women experience in particular sociohistorical contexts.

Global Health Inequalities

We've just documented stark disparities in health and mortality in the United States. Yet when we step back and look at health through a global lens, we see even bleaker disparities. Some economically disadvantaged societies struggle to maintain basic living standards that are necessary for good health, such as adequate food, basic medical supplies, and clean water. Although major strides have occurred in reducing and, in some cases, eliminating infectious diseases worldwide, these strides have stalled in the era of the COVID-19 pandemic. Although Italy, China, and the United States have received the most media coverage, there is hardly a country untouched. Lower-income countries also face greater struggles in providing medical care to those infected with the virus.

Basic medical resources are still lacking in many low-income nations. The relatively few hospitals and trained doctors are concentrated in urban areas, where the affluent minority monopolizes their services. Most developing countries have introduced some form of national health service, organized by the central government, but the medical services are limited. The wealthy use private health care, sometimes traveling to the West for sophisticated medical treatment. Conditions in many developing world cities, particularly in the shantytowns, make the control of infectious diseases very difficult: Many shantytowns lack basic services such as water, sewage systems, and garbage disposal.

Water and sanitation are critical factors for public health, yet many nations fall short on both dimensions. The World Health Organization and UNICEF (2019a) reported that in 2017, 2.2 billion people

Progress has slowed in the battle to eradicate malaria. Fully 90 percent of new malaria cases occur in Africa.

lacked safe water. Further, in 2017, 2 billion people lacked access to basic sanitation facilities such as toilets or latrines; 673 million people still practiced open defecation. The vast majority of those without basic sanitation live in Asia and sub-Saharan Africa. These conditions are breeding grounds for diseases such as diarrhea, malaria, and trachoma, although the means of transmission varies based on the disease. For example, trachoma—an infectious eye disease that can cause blindness—is strongly related to lack of face washing, given the lack of water supply. This example vividly and sadly illustrates the powerful and varied ways that poverty affects health.

Human Immunodeficiency Virus (HIV) and Acquired Immunodeficiency Syndrome (AIDS)

COVID-19 is not the only infectious disease to ravage populations in the United States and worldwide in contemporary times: HIV/AIDS is a devastating global epidemic. Since the start of the epidemic in the early 1980s, 32 million people have died from AIDS-related illnesses as of the end of 2018. More than 37.9 million people worldwide were living with HIV in 2018 (Global Map 18.2). In 2018 alone, 1.7 million people became newly infected with HIV and another 770,000 people died from AIDS-related illnesses (UNAIDS, 2019b). The majority of people affected in the world today are heterosexual and about half are women.

Although the spread of HIV/AIDS in Western societies has slowed, the illness is still a source of crisis, especially in the developing world, where health education is limited and the medical establishment is poor. Fully 25 percent of new HIV infections occur in Eastern and Southern Africa, where 20.6 million people are currently living with HIV/AIDS. But progress is being made: New infections declined in that region by 28 percent overall between 2010 and 2018 and new infections among children dropped by 92.4 percent; AIDS-related deaths dropped by 4 percent during the same period (UNAIDS, 2019a; Avert, 2020).

In high-income countries, the rate of new infections has declined, yet the demographics are striking. Just as we reported on racial gaps in infant mortality and life expectancy earlier in this chapter, we now highlight stark Black-White differences in rates of HIV infection and treatment effectiveness. In the United States, approximately 38,500 people become infected with HIV each year, and roughly 1.1 million people are living with HIV. The incidence of infection, however, is not proportionately represented throughout the United States. In 2018, 50 percent of new AIDS diagnoses were made in the South. Although African Americans represent just 12 percent of the U.S. population, they accounted for 43 percent of HIV diagnoses in 2017. Hispanics are also disproportionately affected: They account for about 18 percent of the population but 26 percent of HIV diagnoses. In 2015, the rate of HIV infection among Blacks was nearly 9 times as high as that among Whites and more than 2 times as high as that among Hispanics. Heterosexuals accounted for 24 percent of new infections in 2015, while men who have sex with men accounted for another 66 percent. Another 6 percent of cases were attributed to intravenous drug use (CDC, 2016a; 2017b; Avert, 2019).

Although there was a steep drop in AIDS-related deaths after the introduction of antiretroviral therapy, African Americans are less likely than Whites to benefit from such life-prolonging treatments. African Americans have the highest death rate of people with HIV, more than seven times higher than that of their White counterparts and nearly three times the rate for Hispanics (CDC, 2016a).

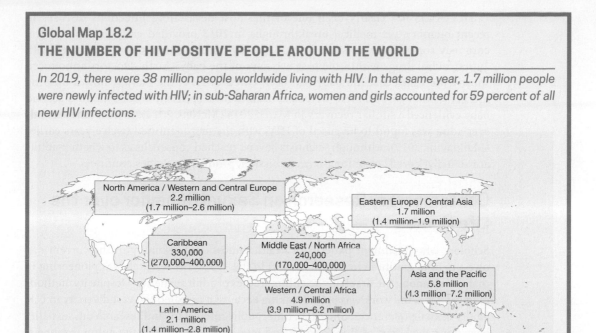

Global Map 18.2

THE NUMBER OF HIV-POSITIVE PEOPLE AROUND THE WORLD

In 2019, there were 38 million people worldwide living with HIV. In that same year, 1.7 million people were newly infected with HIV; in sub-Saharan Africa, women and girls accounted for 59 percent of all new HIV infections.

North America / Western and Central Europe
2.2 million
(1.7 million–2.6 million)

Eastern Europe / Central Asia
1.7 million
(1.4 million–1.9 million)

Caribbean
330,000
(270,000–400,000)

Middle East / North Africa
240,000
(170,000–400,000)

Asia and the Pacific
5.8 million
(1.3 million–7.2 million)

Western / Central Africa
4.9 million
(3.9 million–6.2 million)

Latin America
2.1 million
(1.4 million–2.8 million)

Eastern / Southern Africa
20.7 million
(18.4 million–23.0 million)

Source: UNAIDS, 2019a.

Stigmatization of people with HIV/AIDS remains a major barrier to successful treatment. The stigma that associates HIV-positive status with sexual promiscuity, same-sex sexual relations, and IV drug use results in avoidance of HIV/AIDS prevention and treatment programs. In the United States, one in seven people living with HIV/AIDS do not know they are infected (CDC, 2017b). Part of the reason is the high level of fear and denial associated with being diagnosed as HIV positive. The stigma of having HIV/AIDS and the discrimination against people living with these infections are major barriers to the treatment of the epidemic worldwide. A recent study of 1,450 HIV-positive patients seeking care in India found that two-thirds of them reported authoritarian behavior from doctors, and 55 percent felt they were not treated in a dignified manner (Mehta, 2013).

Besides the devastation to individuals who suffer from it, the AIDS epidemic is creating severe social consequences, including sharply rising numbers of orphaned children. Frail older adults are increasingly called on to provide physical care to their adult children who suffer from AIDS, or to care for their grandchildren who were orphaned by their parents' death from AIDS (Knodel, 2006). The decimated population of working adults combined with the surging population of orphans sets the stage for massive social instability; economies break down, and governments cannot provide for the social needs of orphans, who become targets for recruitment into gangs and armies.

HIV/AIDS has clearly been one of the most devastating infectious diseases in recent memory, yet medical breakthroughs in 2013 provided early evidence that a cure may someday be possible. In 2013, a baby born in Mississippi was treated with antiretroviral drugs within the first two days of the baby's birth. Doctors announced shortly thereafter that the baby had been cured of HIV; the baby is now a thriving toddler. Although observers were skeptical, their skepticism eroded when a second baby evidenced a similar recovery in March 2014 (McNeil, 2014). In 2019, the second-ever adult was found to be cured of HIV, with the first identified twelve years earlier (Mandavilli, 2019). Although scientists haven't reached consensus as to whether adults are actually "cured" or in long-term remission, productive strides continue.

Contemporary Research on Sexual Behavior over the Life Course

Scholars who document patterns of health, illness, and sexuality in the current day owe a debt of gratitude to Alfred Kinsey; in the 1950s, his research was pioneering in that it was among the first truly scientific studies of adult sexuality. Despite its methodological flaws, the work was path-breaking because it revealed the vast diversity in U.S. adults' sexual preferences. Since that time, public interest in, and research on, sexuality have flourished. Part of this research and interest was driven by the cultural zeitgeist at the time. In the 1960s, social movements that challenged the existing order, such as those associated with countercultural lifestyles, broke with existing sexual norms. These movements preached sexual freedom, and the introduction of the contraceptive pill allowed sexual pleasure to be separated from reproduction. Women's groups also started pressing for greater independence from male sexual values, rejection of the double standard, and the need for women to achieve greater sexual satisfaction in their relationships. Until relatively recently, it was unclear to what extent sexual behavior had changed since the time of Kinsey's research.

In the late 1980s, Lillian Rubin (1990) interviewed 1,000 Americans between the ages of 13 and 48 to identify changes in sexual behavior and attitudes over the previous 30 years or so. Her findings indicated significant changes. Sexual activity begins at a younger age; moreover, teenagers' sexual practices are as varied and comprehensive as those of adults. There is still a double standard, but it is not as powerful as before. Contemporary scholarship confirms this finding. Studies of high school–age students find that sexual permissiveness is much greater today than it was in the 1970s. According to the CDC (2016a; Abma and Martinez, 2017), a study conducted between 2011 and 2015 found that about 42 percent of all high school students reported having sexual intercourse by age 18, and 12 percent reported having had four or more partners. Both figures represent declines from 1991, when more than 54 percent of high school students had had sex and nearly 19 percent had had four or more partners. Still, U.S. rates are far higher than those in Japan and China (Tang and Zuo, 2000; Toufexis, 1993).

Recent research on the sexual lives of college students shows that a "hookup" culture dominates college campuses, where both male and female students will have one-night stands, short-lived sexual relationships, or "friends with benefits" relationships where friends will occasionally have sexual relations, without the expectation that their friendship will transform into a full-blown romance (Wade, 2017; Garcia et al., 2012; Hamilton and Armstrong, 2009). However, when a team of sociologists delved more closely into the sexual lives of college students, they found that while casual sexual encounters were relatively common, men and women were fairly selective in such encounters.

Sociologist Paula England and colleagues interviewed more than 14,000 undergraduate students at 19 universities and colleges about their romantic and sexual lives. Nearly three-quarters (72 percent) of both women and men said that they had at least one "hookup" during their senior year. But, for most, hookups were relatively rare. Of those students who said that they ever "hooked up," equal proportions said that they had fewer than three (40 percent) or between four and nine (40 percent) hookups. Just one in five reported 10 or more hookups in their lifetimes. Moreover, not all of these hookups involved sexual intercourse. When asked about their most recent hookup, roughly one-third each said they had participated in sexual intercourse, oral or manual stimulation of the genitals, or kissing and touching. And while TV shows and movies would lead us to believe that all college students are having sex, England and her collaborators found that fully 20 percent of college seniors had never had sexual intercourse (England, Shafer, and Fogarty, 2012).

Studies of the sexual lives of adults beyond college age also reveal that Americans report relatively few sexual partners and less frequent sex than their counterparts in other nations. For example, in 1994, a team of researchers led by Edward Laumann published *The Social Organization of Sexuality: Sexual Practices in the United States*, the most comprehensive study of sexual behavior since Kinsey. Their findings reflect an essential sexual conservatism among Americans. For instance, 83 percent of their subjects had had only one partner (or no partner at all) in the preceding year, and among married people, the figure was fully 96 percent, suggesting that only a tiny share of married people have been unfaithful to their spouse in the past year. Fidelity to one's spouse was also quite common: Only 10 percent of women and less than 25 percent of men reported having an extramarital affair during their lifetime. According to the study, Americans average only three partners during their entire lifetime. Despite the apparent ordinariness of sexual behavior, some distinct historical changes were revealed in this study, the most significant being a progressive increase in the level of premarital sexual experience, particularly among women.

Although documenting and monitoring the sexual behavior of young people remains a widespread concern even in the twenty-first century, researchers are increasingly documenting sexual activity among older persons (Karraker, Delamater, and Schwartz, 2011). Older persons, once considered either uninterested in, or physically incapable of having satisfying sexual relations, reveal high levels of both sexual activity and satisfaction. The National Social Life, Health, and Aging Project (NSHAP), a study of sexuality among American women and men ages 57 to 85, reports that most married older persons have had sex in the last year. Although sexual problems do arise, they were reported by a minority of respondents. Women tended to report more sexual problems than men; commonly reported problems included lack of sexual interest, inability to climax, pain, and lack of pleasure during intercourse. Among men, by contrast, sexual problems included climaxing too early and performance anxiety (Lindau et al., 2007). However, older adults may adjust their sexual practices so that they can accommodate their physical declines, often substituting touching and other forms of closeness for sexual intercourse (Ginsberg, Pomerantz, and Kramer-Feeley, 2005).

Methodological Advances in Studying Sexual Behavior in the United States

Sociologists frequently use survey questionnaires to gain information on human behavior. However, obtaining detailed information on sexual behavior and attitudes is difficult. The two most comprehensive studies of sexuality in the United States—the Kinsey studies (1948, 1953) and the Laumann study (1994)—offer very different portraits of sexual preferences and behaviors. Do these conflicting results reflect historical changes in sexual mores, or are the differences an outcome of methodological approaches?

In stark contrast to Kinsey's results, which found that a high proportion of men had premarital or extramarital sex, in the Laumann study, 83 percent of survey respondents said they had had only one or no sexual partners in the year prior to the study. Moreover, only 10 percent of women and less than 25 percent of men reported ever having had an extramarital affair. It's possible that Americans have become more sexually conservative—perhaps from fear of AIDS and other sexually transmitted diseases.

An alternative explanation for the discrepant findings is the researchers' different methodological approaches. Kinsey, an evolutionary biologist, first gave a questionnaire about sexual practices to students in his zoology classes. Finding this method unsatisfactory, he next conducted face-to-face interviews and then focused on specific social groups. He and his colleagues eventually interviewed nearly 18,000 people. Kinsey recognized that the ideal survey would be random, and that the results would, therefore, represent the general population. However, he did not believe it was possible to persuade a randomly selected group of Americans to answer deeply personal questions about their sexual behavior. Consequently, his survey respondents were primarily college students living in sorority and fraternity houses, prisoners, psychiatric patients, and friends. To make his data more credible, Kinsey made every effort to interview 100 percent of the members of each group, such as all students living in a given fraternity house. Because Kinsey's data are based on a convenience sample, they are not representative of the American public. Moreover, many of his survey respondents volunteered to participate in the study. Thus, they may have been different from nonvolunteers in having wider sexual experiences or a greater interest in sexuality. Further, many of his study questions asked about "lifetime" behavior or whether one had ever engaged in a particular practice; such a question will necessarily yield a greater number of positive responses than a question that focuses on a limited time frame, such as the past 12 months.

The Laumann study, in contrast, is based on data from the National Health and Social Life Survey (NHSLS). The NHSLS data were obtained from a nationally representative random sample of more than 3,000 American men and women between the ages of 18 and 59 who spoke English. In addition, Laumann's team purposely oversampled among Blacks and Hispanics so that they would have enough members of these minority groups to analyze their survey responses separately with confidence that findings were statistically reliable and valid. Recognizing that people are often hesitant to discuss sexuality, Laumann's team paid particular attention to choosing nonjudgmental language in their questionnaire. The team also built several "checks" into their questionnaire to ensure the veracity of responses. Several questions were redundant but were asked in different ways throughout the interview to gauge whether respondents were answering truthfully. The team also included 11 questions that had been asked previously on another national random sample survey of Americans. Comparisons of responses to the two sets of questions provided Laumann's researchers with assurance that their results were consistent with others' findings.

Although the Kinsey and Laumann studies are influential works on human sexuality, they also demonstrate that the process through which sociological knowledge is obtained can be as important as the actual research findings.

heterosexism The greater status, prestige, and benefits afforded to heterosexual people.

homophobia An irrational fear of or disdain for gays and lesbians.

The Persistence of Heterosexism

The research we have reviewed so far reveals that Americans' attitudes toward human sexuality have grown increasingly expansive and open-minded throughout much of the twentieth and twenty-first centuries. Yet does this open-mindedness extend to all groups? Some contend that anti-gay prejudice persists, and that gay, lesbian, bisexual, and transgender (LGBT) Americans still do not enjoy the same rights and privileges as their heterosexual and cisgender peers. The greater status, prestige, and benefits afforded to heterosexual people is called **heterosexism**. It is closely related to the concept of **homophobia**, a term coined in the late 1960s that refers to attitudes and behaviors marked by an aversion to, or hatred of, LGBTQ persons and their practices. It is a form of prejudice reflected not only in overt acts of hostility and violence toward lesbian, gay, and bisexual persons but also in forms of verbal abuse that are widespread in American culture; for example, using words such as *fag* or *homo* to insult heterosexual males or using female-related offensive terms such as *sissy* or *pansy* to insult gay men (Pascoe, 2011).

A 2017 survey found that in the United States, 33 percent of students who self-identified as gay, lesbian, or bisexual have been bullied on school property. Another 27 percent experienced cyberbullying. Comparatively, heterosexual peers experienced 17.1 percent and 13.3 percent, respectively (Kann

A recent survey of LGBT students found that nearly 6 in 10 felt unsafe at school due to their sexual orientation.

et al., 2018). Another national study from 2015 of more than 10,500 LGBT students between the ages of 13 and 21 found that 85 percent reported that they had been verbally harassed at school, 27 percent were physically harassed, and 49 percent had been victims of cyberbullying. Fully 58 percent felt "unsafe" at school (Kosciw et al., 2016).

Although some may discount teasing as harmless, this is a faulty assumption. LGBTQ youth have much higher rates of suicide, suicidal thoughts, depression, and substance use than straight youth, due in large part to the victimization and teasing they suffer at the hands of their classmates and to the failure, at times, of their families and teachers to protect them (Espelage, Aragon, and Birkett, 2008; Ryan et al., 2009; Russell and Joyner, 2001).

Sexual prejudice is widespread in U.S. culture, although it is slowly starting to erode. It was only in the recent past (2003) that the Supreme Court ruled in *Lawrence v. Texas* that the state of Texas's prohibition on same-sex sexual relations was a violation of the constitutional right to privacy; in many states, same-sex relations was still a legally punishable crime. Same-sex couples couldn't marry nationwide until 2015, when the Supreme Court ruled in favor of marriage equality in *Obergefell v. Hodges*. Public figures who use homophobic language are publicly upbraided. In 2011, for the first time in its history, the Gallup Poll found that the majority of Americans (53 percent) supported gay marriage (Newport, 2011). In 2019, 61 percent of the population reported supporting gay marriage (Pew Research Center, 2019a).

The Movement for LGBTQ Civil Rights

Until recently, most gay, lesbian, and queer persons hid their sexual orientation for fear that "coming out of the closet"—publicly revealing one's sexual orientation—would cost them their jobs, families, and friends, and leave them open to verbal and physical abuse. Yet, since the late 1960s, many LGBTQ persons have acknowledged their sexual orientation openly, and, in some cities, the lives of lesbian and gay Americans have become quite normalized (Saguy, 2020). Celebrities—ranging from pop singers Halsey and Adam Lambert to news anchor Anderson Cooper—are "out" publicly, with little fanfare. Major league sports, long considered a bastion of heterosexism, embraced Jason Collins, who came out as gay before he played his last season for the NBA's Brooklyn Nets. With his announcement, Collins became the first active player in one of the four major American professional team sports to announce that he was gay (ESPN, 2013). In 2014, Michael Sam attracted national attention as the first openly gay member of the NFL, although he was cut from the Dallas Cowboys during his first year of play (Belson, 2014). New York City, San Francisco, London, and other large metropolitan areas worldwide have thriving gay and lesbian communities. Coming out may be important not only for the person who does so but also for others in the larger society: Previously closeted lesbians and gays discover they are not alone, while heterosexuals recognize that people whom they admire and respect are gay.

The current global wave of gay and lesbian civil rights movements began partly as an outgrowth of the social movements of the 1960s, which emphasized pride in racial and ethnic identity. One pivotal event was the Stonewall riots in June 1969, when New York City's gay community, angered by continual police harassment, fought the New York Police Department for two days (D'Emilio, 1983; Weeks, 1977). The Stonewall riots became a symbol of gay pride. In 1994, on the 25th anniversary of the Stonewall riots, 100,000 people attended the International March on the United Nations to Affirm the Human Rights of Lesbian and Gay People. In May 2005, the International Day against Homophobia (IDAHO) was first celebrated, with events held in more than 40 countries. Clearly, significant strides have been made, although discrimination and homophobia remain serious problems for many LGBT Americans.

Today, there is a growing movement worldwide for the civil rights of gays and lesbians. The International Lesbian, Gay, Bisexual, Trans and Intersex Association (2020), which was founded in 1978, has more than 1,600 member organizations in some 150 countries and territories. It holds international conferences, supports lesbian and gay social movement organizations, and lobbies international organizations. For example, it persuaded the Council of Europe to require all its member nations to repeal laws banning same-sex relations. In general, active lesbian and gay social movements thrive in countries that emphasize individual rights and liberal state policies (Frank and McEneaney, 1999).

Yet many other nations still ban same-sex relations. In Africa, gay male sex acts have been legalized in only a handful of countries, whereas lesbian relations are seldom mentioned in the law at all. In South Africa, the official policy of the former White government was to regard homosexuality as a psychiatric problem that threatened national security. Once the Black government took power, however, it legislated full equality. In Asia and the Middle East, male same-sex relations are banned in most countries, including all those that are predominantly Islamic. For example, as recently as 2012, four Iranian men were found guilty of sodomy and were sentenced to death. Taiwan is considered among the most liberal nations in Asia, yet it legalized same-sex marriages only as recently as 2019. In contrast, Europe has some of the most liberal laws in the world: Same-sex relations has been legalized in nearly all countries, and many European nations legally recognize same-sex marriages. As of 2020, 30 out of 194 countries for which data are available allow same-sex couples to marry: Northern Ireland (2019), Ecuador (2019), Taiwan (2019), Austria (2019), Australia (2017), the Netherlands (2000), Belgium (2003), Canada (2005), Spain (2005), South Africa (2006), Norway (2009), Sweden (2009), Argentina (2010), Iceland (2010), Portugal (2010), Denmark (2012), Brazil (2013), France (2013), New Zealand (2013), Uruguay (2013), England and Wales (2013), Luxembourg (2014), Scotland (2014), Finland (2015), Greenland (2015), Ireland (2015), the United States (2015), Colombia (2016), Germany

The Stonewall Inn nightclub raid in 1969 is regarded as the first shot fired in the battle for gay rights in the United States.

In June 2017, Germany legalized gay marriage. As of 2019, 30 countries have legalized gay marriage.

(2017), and Malta (2017). Same-sex couples are allowed to wed in parts of Mexico (Pew Research Center, 2019g). (See Chapter 15 for further information on the legalization of gay marriage.)

Social change is occurring, slowly but steadily, even in countries that historically have had cruel and oppressive policies toward gays and lesbians. For example, in 2014, the Constitutional Court in Uganda invalidated a previously passed "anti-gay" bill, which allowed for jail terms up to life for persons convicted of having gay sex, and stipulated lengthy jail terms for persons convicted of "attempted homosexuality" or the "promotion of homosexuality" (Gettleman, 2014). This marked a significant change in a nation where, just three years earlier, the outspoken gay rights activist David Kato was beaten to death with a hammer.

Reproduction in the Twenty-First Century: Pushing the Limits of Technology

Another area of research among contemporary scholars is the ways that science and technology shape experiences of the body. The development of technologies—ranging from reproductive technologies to the development of medications that help our mental health, physical health, and even sexual performance—has created a context where we have much more control over our bodies today than in the past. Yet this "control" presents us with both exciting possibilities and new anxieties and problems. All this development is part of what sociologists call the **socialization of nature**—a process in which phenomena that used to be "natural," or given in nature, become social, in that they depend on our personal decisions.

> **socialization of nature** A process by which phenomena that used to be considered "natural," or given in nature, become social, in that they depend on our personal decisions.
>
> **procreative technology** Techniques for influencing the human reproductive process.

Childbirth

Giving birth is often described as a "natural" and "beautiful" part of life. For hundreds of years, most women's lives were dominated by childbirth and child-rearing. In premodern times, contraception was ineffective or unknown. Even as late as the eighteenth century in Europe and the United States, women commonly experienced as many as 20 pregnancies (often involving miscarriages and infant deaths). Today, owing to improved methods of contraception, women in industrialized countries no longer have so many pregnancies. Advances in contraceptive technology enable most women and men to control whether and when to have children.

Contraception is only one **procreative technology**. Prospective parents also are turning to technologies that increase their chances of conceiving a child. Fertility drugs, in vitro fertilization (IVF), artificial insemination, and hormone treatments are among the technologies that are assisting reproductively challenged couples in their desire to start a family (Franklin, 2013). The use of such technologies also is altering the nature of family life; the number of twins born in the United States increased by roughly 50 percent, and the number of triplet or higher-number births soared by 404 percent between 1980 and 1997 (Martin and Park, 1999). From 1980 to 2004, increases in the number of twin births averaged nearly 3 percent a year (peaking at more than 4 percent from 1995 to 1998). From 2005 to 2011, however, the pace of increase slowed to one-half percent annually (Martin et al., 2013). Between 2014 and 2018, the National Center for Health Statistics reported that the birth rate of twins has decreased on average 1 percent annually, or 4 percent during the time period (Martin and Osterman, 2019). This rise and plateauing in multiple births is partially explained by the growing popularity of fertility drugs such as clomiphene and procedures such as in vitro fertilization, which result in multiple births more frequently than unassisted fertilizations do.

Genetic Engineering: Designer Babies

In the past, new parents had to wait until the birth to learn the sex of their baby and whether it would be healthy. Today, prenatal tests such as the sonogram (an image of the fetus produced by ultrasonic waves) and amniocentesis (which samples amniotic fluid from around the fetus) can reveal structural or chromosomal abnormalities before birth.

Considerable scientific resources are being devoted to intervening in the genetic makeup of the fetus to influence its subsequent development. The likely social effect of such genetic engineering is provoking debates almost as intense as those over abortion. According to supporters, genetic engineering will bring many benefits—for example, identifying the genetic factors that make some people vulnerable to certain diseases. Genetic reprogramming would ensure that these illnesses are no longer passed from generation to generation. It would be possible to "design" our children's bodies before birth in terms of skin color, hair and eye color, weight, and so forth.

This issue is a prime example of the opportunities and problems that the increasing socialization of nature creates. What choices will parents make if they can design their babies, and what limits should be placed on those choices? Genetic engineering is unlikely to be cheap. Will this mean that those who can afford to pay will program out from their children any traits they see as socially undesirable? What will happen to the children of more deprived groups, who will continue to be born unaltered? Some sociologists argue that differential access to genetic engineering might lead to the emergence of a "biological underclass." Those who don't have the physical advantages that genetic engineering can bring might be subject to prejudice and discrimination and might have difficulty finding employment and life or health insurance (Duster, 1990).

The medical community also continues to grapple with the ethical implications of designing a baby (Murray, 2014). The core question is, how much discretion should parents be granted in determining what sort of child they have? A consensus has yet to be reached, as most major medical societies, such as the American Society for Reproductive Medicine (ASRM) and the American Congress of Obstetricians and Gynecologists (ACOG) vary widely in their recommendations about when and where these techniques should be allowed (Murray, 2014). For example, the ASRM typically honors a client's wishes on issues such as sex selection, while the ACOG calls for the prohibition of sex selection because it may perpetuate gender discrimination in society. The Food and Drug Administration (FDA), by contrast, regulates only the safety and effectiveness of genetic-engineering techniques and leaves ethical issues unaddressed. Debates over designer babies may lead to a reformulation of how we as a society think about reproduction and parenthood (Murray, 2014).

CONCEPT CHECKS

1 In what ways does race matter for health?

2 What are the two main explanations for the gender gap in health? Why do experts think this gap may decrease in the future?

3 Why are infectious diseases more common in developing nations than in the United States today?

4 Describe patterns of adolescent sexual behavior in contemporary U.S. society.

5 Describe two ways that the development of new technologies has led to the "socialization of nature."

4 UNANSWERED QUESTIONS

As you have learned throughout this chapter, the sociological study of the body and sexuality is a fascinating and rapidly evolving field. Each day, social scientists struggle with new and vexing questions about the ways that social, biological, technological, economic, and cultural forces transpire to promote (or constrain) physical and sexual well-being. We briefly describe here four unanswered questions that sociologists are now investigating, using the most sophisticated data, methods, and conceptual models.

Does Income Inequality Threaten Health?

As we learned in Chapter 8, the distribution of income in the United States is highly unequal, and this gap is widening. In 2018, the top 5 percent of households in the United States received 23.1 percent of total income, the highest 20 percent obtained 52 percent, while the bottom 20 percent received only slightly more than 3.1 percent (U.S. Census Bureau, 2019e). Some researchers have argued that societies with a vastly unequal distribution of economic resources are unhealthy societies, and that disparities take a toll on all.

British researcher Richard Wilkinson (1996) is one of the most vocal advocates of the argument that the healthiest societies are not necessarily the richest ones but those in which income is distributed most evenly and levels of social integration are highest. In surveying empirical data from countries worldwide, Wilkinson notes a clear relationship between mortality rates and patterns of income distribution. Inhabitants of countries such as Japan and Sweden, which are among the most egalitarian societies in the world, enjoy better levels of health than do citizens of countries with a more pronounced gap between rich and poor, such as the United States. In Wilkinson's view, growing income inequality undermines social cohesion and makes it more difficult for people to manage risks and challenges. Wilkinson argues that social factors—the strength of social contacts, ties within communities, a sense of security—are the main determinants of the health of a society.

Wilkinson's thesis—that income inequality harms health—has provoked energetic responses. Some claim that his work should become required reading for policy makers and politicians. They agree that the drive toward prosperity has failed many members of society and that it is time to consider more humane and socially responsible policies to support those who are disadvantaged (Kawachi and Kennedy, 1997). Others criticize his study on methodological grounds and argue that he has not demonstrated a clear causal relationship between income inequality and poor health (Judge, 1995). Illness, critics contend, could be caused by any number of other factors. They argue that the empirical evidence for Wilkinson's claims remains suggestive at best.

Two recent studies may help to successfully resolve this debate. Zheng (2012) tracked income inequality in the United States from 1986 through 2004 and then examined whether these trends predicted increases in poor health and mortality several years into the future. This approach allowed him to address the main concern Wilkinson's critics raised—that he had not effectively established causal ordering. Zheng found that for every .01 increase in the **Gini coefficient**—a standard measure of a country's economic disparity, where 0 represents perfect equality and 1 represents maximum inequality—an average person's cumulative risk of death increased by 112 percent over the next 12 years. Zheng (2009) also found that a dramatic increase in income inequality between 1972 and 2004 increased Americans' perceptions that their health was suffering.

Gini coefficient A standard measure of a country's economic disparity, where 0 represents perfect equality (everyone has the same income) and 1 represents maximum inequality.

Although scholars and policy makers may find Zheng's research to be compelling evidence that income inequality undermines health, we still don't fully understand the reasons for this. Some scholars have hypothesized that in countries with rising income inequality, the interests of the wealthy tend to diverge from those of the rest of society. The wealthiest people may push government for more services for themselves, rather than invest in public goods such as education or affordable medical services—services that can affect health for the majority of people (Zheng, 2009, 2012). Others argue that inequality may create a culture of upward comparison, where many people see the lifestyles of the rich and feel they can't live up to expectations. Upward comparison can lead to negative views of oneself, frustration, and depression, which have been linked to sickness and mortality (Kawachi and Kennedy, 1997; Pickett and Wilkinson, 2011). Consistent with this notion, recent cross-national studies show that levels of depression are higher in countries with high levels of income inequality, and a feeling of "status anxiety" partially accounts for this linkage (Layte, 2011).

Is Alternative Medicine as Effective as "Mainstream" Medicine?

Actress and television host Jenny McCarthy made headlines when she refused doctors' advice for how to treat her autistic son. Instead, she worked with nutritionists and placed her son, Evan, on a strict gluten- and casein-free diet, in the hope that it would minimize his symptoms. Alternative therapies, such as the one McCarthy followed, are being explored by a record high number of people today and are slowly gaining acceptance by the mainstream medical community.

Medical sociologists refer to such unorthodox medical practices as **complementary and alternative medicine (CAM)**. CAM encompasses a diverse set of approaches and therapies for treating illness and promoting well-being that generally fall outside standard medical practices. These approaches are usually not taught in medical schools and not practiced by physicians or other professionals trained in medical programs. However, in recent years, medical and nursing schools have started offering courses in alternative medicine (Fenton and Morris, 2003). Examples of common CAM therapies include chiropractic, massage, deep-breathing techniques, homeopathy, reflexology, herbal remedies, and acupuncture. Complementary medicine is distinct from alternative medicine in that the former is meant to be used in conjunction with medical procedures to increase their efficacy or reduce side effects, while the latter is meant to be used in place of standard medical procedures (Saks, 1992). Some alternative approaches, such as homeopathy, reject the basis of orthodox medicine entirely.

Industrialized countries have some of the best-developed, best-resourced medical facilities in the world. Why, then, are a growing number of people exploring treatments that have not yet proven effective in controlled clinical trials, such as aromatherapy and hypnotherapy? It has been estimated that as many as 1 in 10 Americans has at some time consulted an alternative practitioner. An even larger proportion of Americans have sought out CAM treatments on their own. A recent survey conducted by the CDC and the National Center for Health Statistics (NCHS)

complementary and alternative medicine (CAM) A diverse set of approaches and therapies for treating illness and promoting well-being that generally fall outside standard medical practices.

found that 33 percent of American adults had used some form of CAM in the past year (Clarke et al., 2015). CAM use is more frequent among women and individuals with higher levels of educational attainment. Furthermore, Whites are more likely to use CAM than their Black and Asian counterparts. The most common reasons people use such treatments are back, neck, and joint pain (Barnes, Bloom, and Nahin, 2008).

> **biomedical model of health** The set of principles underpinning Western medical systems and practices. The biomedical model of health defines diseases objectively, in accordance with the presence of recognized symptoms, and believes that the healthy body can be restored through scientifically based medical treatment. The human body is likened to a machine that can be returned to working order with the proper repairs.

There are many reasons for seeking the services of an alternative-medicine practitioner or pursuing CAM regimens on one's own. Some people perceive orthodox medicine to be deficient or ineffective in relieving chronic pain or symptoms of stress and anxiety. Others are dissatisfied with features of modern health care systems such as long waits, referrals through chains of specialists, and financial restrictions. Connected to this dissatisfaction are concerns about the harmful side effects of medication and the intrusiveness of surgery, both staples of modern Western medicine. The asymmetrical power relationship between doctors and patients also drives some people to seek alternative medicine. Those people feel that the role of the passive patient does not grant them enough input into their own treatment and healing. Finally, some individuals profess religious or philosophical objections to orthodox medicine, which treats the mind and body separately. They believe that orthodox medicine often overlooks the spiritual and psychological dimensions of health and illness. All these concerns are critiques of the **biomedical model of health** (the foundation of the Western medical establishment), which defines disease in objective terms and believes that scientifically based medical treatment can restore the body to health (Beyerstein, 1999).

The growth of alternative medicine is a fascinating reflection of the transformations occurring within modern societies. We are living in an age where much more information is available to draw on when making choices. The proliferation of health-related websites such as WebMD and MedicineNet and fitness trackers such as Fitbit provide instant access to information on health symptoms and treatments. Thus, individuals are increasingly becoming health consumers, adopting an active stance toward their own health and well-being. Not only are we choosing the type of practitioners to consult, but we are also demanding more involvement in our own care and treatment.

Members of the mainstream medical community, once viewed as completely resistant to the notion of alternative medicine,

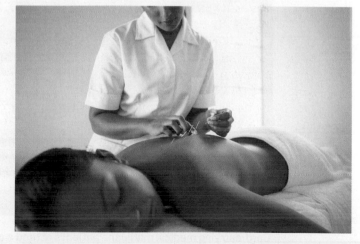

Acupuncture is a popular CAM therapy. Women and those with higher levels of education are more likely to use CAM.

are increasingly taking a more open-minded approach to such therapies. Many now cautiously endorse patients' desires to consult an ever-expanding array of medical information. However, medical leaders believe that CAM should be given the same level of scientific scrutiny as mainstream medicine: It should be held up to rigorous scientific evaluation. Former editors of *The New England Journal of Medicine* Marcia Angell and Jerome Kassirer (1998) have observed that "many alternative remedies have recently found their way into the medical mainstream. . . . There cannot be two kinds of medicine—conventional and alternative. There is only medicine that has been adequately tested and medicine that has not, medicine that works and medicine that may or may not work. Once a treatment has been tested rigorously, it no longer matters whether it was considered alternative at the outset. If it is found to be reasonably safe and effective, it will be accepted." Most experts conclude that alternative medicine is unlikely to overtake mainstream health care altogether, but that its usage will continue to grow.

One hotly contested alternative treatment today is medical marijuana. As of 2020, 32 of the 50 U.S. states and the District of Columbia had legalized marijuana for medical use, and seven states and the District of Columbia had legalized marijuana for recreational use. According to national surveys, 91 percent of Americans support the legal use of marijuana for medical and recreational purposes (Daniller, 2019). Advocates of medical marijuana cite clinical trial data to show that it helps soothe pain and allay nausea, especially for patients of fibromyalgia, glaucoma, multiple sclerosis, some

Card-carrying medical marijuana patients attend a cannabis farmers' market in Los Angeles. As of 2020, 32 states and the District of Columbia had legalized marijuana for medical use.

cancers, and neuropathy (e.g., Campbell et al., 2001). By contrast, opponents question such findings, challenging the researchers' methods, and arguing that some conditions, such as schizophrenia, may be exacerbated by smoking pot. Further, some argue that marijuana is less effective in treating symptoms than medications, which patients may eschew if they have easy access to pot. Others argue that enhanced access to marijuana will increase drug use, especially among teens (Jacobson, 2014). However, the majority of doctors agree with the general conclusion of Angell and Kassirer (1998), that mainstream and alternative remedies are best used in tandem.

Are Eating Disorders Primarily a "Women's" Problem?

We learned earlier in this chapter that one of the most serious concerns threatening the health of Americans today is the obesity epidemic. Yet as college students, you may notice that some of your classmates are dieting or exercising excessively, striving to look like the models gracing the covers of fashion magazines such as *Vogue* or *Men's Health*. You may think that another equally important body-weight issue faces our nation: excessive slenderness and eating disorders such as anorexia nervosa and bulimia. These are serious social problems, and ones that disproportionately strike women—but why? And why are young men increasingly monitoring their calorie intake, upping their time at the gym, or even turning to steroids in the hopes of having "Adonis"-like physiques (Pope, Phillips, and Olivardia, 2002)?

It's important first to step back and consider the history of such conditions. Anorexia, an eating disorder characterized by extreme food restriction and an irrational fear of gaining weight, is thought of as a contemporary social problem, but the condition was first identified as a disorder in France in 1874. It remained obscure until the past 30 or 40 years and has since become increasingly common among young women (Brown and Jasper, 1993). So has bulimia—bingeing on large portions of food, followed by self-induced vomiting. Anorexia and bulimia often occur in the same individual. A recent study estimates that 1.3 million women and 450,000 men suffer from anorexia, 2.25 million women and 750,000 men suffer from bulimia, and 5.25 million women and 3 million men suffer from binge eating. A total of 30 million Americans, or about 9 percent of the population, suffer from one or more forms of eating disorders (Eating Disorders Coalition [EDC], 2009; National Association of Anorexia Nervosa and Associated Disorders, 2020).

Anorexia has the highest mortality rate of any psychological disorder; 20 percent of anorexics will die from it (EDC, 2009). Once a young person starts to diet and exercise compulsively, she can become locked into a pattern of refusing food or vomiting up what she has eaten. As the body loses muscle mass, it loses heart muscle, so the heart gets smaller and weaker, which ultimately leads to heart failure. About half of all anorexics also have low white blood cell counts, and about a third are anemic. Both conditions can lower the immune system's resistance to disease, leaving an anorexic vulnerable to infections. However, these harmful patterns may be broken through psychotherapy and medical treatment.

These harmful consequences are particularly devastating when one considers that the occurrence of eating disorders in the United States has doubled since 1960 (EDC, 2009). Over 80 percent of 10-year-old children are afraid of being fat (EDC, 2003). About 95 percent of U.S. college women say they want to lose weight, and up

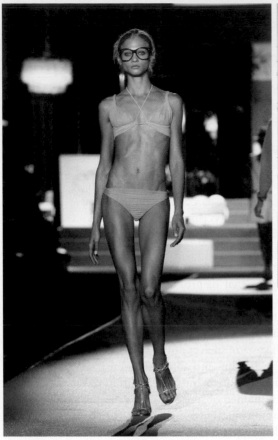

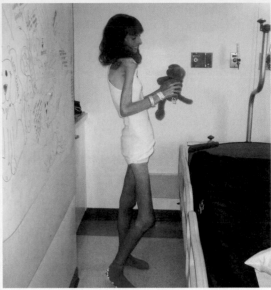

An anorexic woman (right) has starved herself thin; people suffering from anorexia feel compelled to lose weight by a variety of social and personal pressures, often continuing to view themselves as overweight even when they have reached a state of emaciation. Eating disorders are unlikely to disappear as long as severely underweight fashion models and actresses (left) are upheld as paragons of beauty.

to 85 percent suffer serious problems with eating disorders during their college years. Around 25 percent experience bulimic episodes or anorexia. In American society, 60 percent of girls age 13 have already begun to diet; this proportion rises to over 80 percent for women age 18. College men suffer similar experiences, but to a lesser extent. About 50 percent of American male college students want to lose weight, while about 30 percent are on diets (Hesse-Biber, 1997).

Obsession with slenderness—and the resulting eating disorders—extends beyond the United States and Europe. Fashion magazines today regularly feature images of models who are severely underweight, yet are upheld as paragons of beauty. The average fashion model today is 23 percent thinner than the average American woman; 25 years ago, that number was 8 percent (Derenne and Beresin, 2006). As Western images of feminine beauty have spread to the rest of the world, so have associated illnesses. Eating problems also have surfaced among young, primarily affluent women in Hong Kong and Singapore, and in urban areas in China, India, Pakistan, the Philippines, and Taiwan (Efron, 1997).

Given how harmful eating disorders are, why do they persist, and why do they affect young women more than either young men or older women? Although roughly 10 percent of those with eating disorders are men, they don't suffer from anorexia or bulimia as often as women—partly because social norms stress the importance of physical attractiveness more for women than for men, and partly because desirable body images of men differ from those of women. Anorexia and other eating disorders reflect the fact that women now play a larger part in the wider society but are still judged as much by their appearance as by their accomplishments. Eating disorders are rooted in feelings of shame and a desire to have control over one's body. The individual feels inadequate and imperfect, and her anxieties about how others perceive her become focused through feelings about her body. At that point, shedding weight becomes the means of making everything right in her world. Sociologists believe that as long as young women are raised to equate their self-worth with their physical appearance, eating disorders will persist.

Just as young women often struggle to maintain a slender physique, young men increasingly struggle to maintain a taut, muscular body, a phenomenon called the Adonis complex (Pope et al., 2002). A small yet significant number of young men may limit their calories, become addicted to exercise, especially weight-lifting, or may turn to anabolic-androgenic steroids to achieve a physique equated with the cultural "ideal" image of masculinity. One recent study of more than 2,000 high school students found that boys who considered themselves "small" or "skinny" were more likely to use steroids and to suffer from poor body image (e.g., Blashill and Wilhelm, 2014; Blashill, 2014).

Cultural pressures to comply with gender-typed body ideals have potential lethal consequences since both anorexia and steroid use are linked with heart problems, even among adolescents (Achar, Rostamanian, and Narayan, 2010). In this way, our bodies are powerfully shaped by gendered cultural expectations (Wienke, 1998).

Is Sexual Orientation Inborn or Learned?

Most sociologists believe that sexual orientation—whether LGBTQ, heterosexual, bisexual, or asexual—results from a complex interplay between biological factors and social learning. Since heterosexuality is the norm for most people in U.S. culture, considerable research has focused on why some people are gay. Some scholars argue that biological influences predispose certain people to become gay from birth (Bell, Weinberg, and Hammersmith, 1981; Green, 1987). Biological explanations have included differences in brain characteristics of gays and lesbians (LeVay, 1996; Maugh and Zamichow, 1991), genetic influences on sexual orientation (Hamer et al., 1993), and the effect on fetal development of the mother's hormone production during pregnancy (Blanchard and Bogaert, 1996; Manning, Koukourakis, and Brodie, 1997; McFadden and Champlin, 2000). Such studies, which are based on small numbers of cases, give highly inconclusive (and highly controversial) results (Healy, 2001). It is virtually impossible to separate biological factors from early social influences in determining a person's sexual orientation (LeVay, 2011).

Studies of twins may shed light on any genetic basis for sexual orientation since identical twins share identical genes. In two related studies, Bailey and Pillard (1991) examined 167 pairs of brothers and 143 pairs of sisters, with each pair of siblings raised in the same family, in which at least one sibling defined himself or herself as gay. Some of these pairs were identical twins (who share all genes), some were fraternal twins (who share some genes), and some were adoptive brothers or sisters (who share no genes). The researchers reasoned that if sexual orientation is determined entirely by biology, then since in each case at least one of the identical twins identified as gay, all the study's identical twins, having the identical genetic makeup, should also identify as gay. Among the fraternal twins, some pairs would identify as gay, since some genes are shared. The lowest rates of LGBTQ orientation were predicted for the adoptive brothers and sisters.

The results seem to show that preferences for a same-sex sexual partner, like preferences for an opposite-sex sexual partner, result from a combination of biological and social factors. Among the men and the women studied, in roughly one out of every two identical twin pairs, the second twin also identified as gay, compared with 1 out of every 5 fraternal twins and 1 out of every 10 adoptive brothers and sisters (Bailey and Pillard, 1991; see also Burr, 1993; Maugh, 1991, 1993). In other words, a woman or man is five times as likely to be gay if her or his identical twin is gay than if her or his sibling is gay but related only through adoption. These results offer some support for the importance of biological factors, since the higher the percentage of shared genes, the greater the percentage of cases in which both siblings identified as gay. However, because approximately half of the identical twin brothers and sisters of individuals who identified as gay did not themselves identify as gay, social learning must also be involved; otherwise, one would expect all identical twin siblings of individuals who identify as gay to also identify as gay.

Clearly, even studies of identical twins cannot fully isolate biological from social factors. It is often the case that even in infancy, identical twins are treated more like one another by parents, peers, and teachers than are fraternal twins, who in turn are treated more like one another than are adoptive siblings. Thus, identical twins may have more than genes in common: They may also share a higher proportion of similar socializing experiences.

Sociologist Peter Bearman (2002) has shown the intricate ways that genetics and social experience are intertwined. Bearman found that males with a female twin are twice as likely to report same-sex attractions. He theorized that parents of opposite-sex twins are more likely to give them unisex treatment, leading to a less traditionally masculine influence on the males. Having an older brother decreases the rate of homosexuality. Bearman hypothesized that an older brother establishes gender-socializing mechanisms for the younger brother to follow, which allows him to compensate for unisex treatment. Bearman's work is consistent with the statements offered by professional organizations such as the American Academy of Pediatrics, which concludes that "sexual orientation probably is not determined by any one factor but by a combination of genetic, hormonal, and environmental influences" (American Academy of Pediatrics, 2004).

Scholarly debates over the "cause" of sexual orientation underscore the very themes that have provided the foundation for this chapter and for the sociological study of the body and sexuality more generally. It is simplistic to think that there is a "single-bullet" explanation for phenomena as complex as health, sexuality, and illness; rather, a complex array of cultural, biological, technological, social, and economic factors play a dynamic and essential role.

The sociology of health, illness, and the body is a fascinating and ever-evolving field. As sociologists look to the new decade, they will learn much more about how and why diseases like COVID-19 spread so quickly, why some populations are especially vulnerable, and the ways that everyday life is affected by the disease's spread. As new health conditions arise, some will be stigmatized and others will not, and medical sociologists will develop insights, policies, and practices to help people manage their illness and the challenges that accompany it.

CONCEPT CHECKS

1 What are two possible reasons income inequality affects health?

2 Name three reasons a person might turn to complementary and alternative medicine.

3 Why are young women at the greatest risk of suffering from an eating disorder?

4 Contrast biological and social explanations as possible "causes" of same-sex versus opposite-sex sexual attraction.

Chapter 18
The Sociology of the
Body: Health, Illness,
and Sexuality

1 **Basic Concepts**

p. 711

2 **Theories and Historical Approaches to Understanding Health, Illness, and Sexuality**

p. 717

LEARNING OBJECTIVES

Understand how social, cultural, and historical contexts shape attitudes toward health, illness, and sexual behavior.

Learn about theoretical perspectives on physical and mental health and illness in contemporary society, as well as the approaches to studying sexuality throughout history.

TERMS TO KNOW

obesity • food deserts • body mass index (BMI) • sociology of the body • sociology of sexuality • health

sick role • stigma

CONCEPT CHECKS

1. Define the term *health*.
2. Define and provide an example of medicalization.
3. Describe three features of modern medicine.
4. Why is the term *sexual preference* problematic?

1. Describe how the primary causes of death have changed between colonial times and the present day.
2. How do functionalist theorists and symbolic interactionists differ in their perspectives on health and illness?
3. Describe several changes in sexual practices over the past two centuries.
4. What are the most important contributions of Alfred Kinsey's research on sexuality?

Exercises: Thinking Sociologically

1. Statistical studies of our national health show a gap in life expectancies between the rich and the poor. Review all the major factors that would explain why rich people live about eight years longer than poor people.

2. This text discusses the biological and sociocultural factors associated with sexual orientation. Why are twin studies the most promising type of research on the genetic basis of sexual orientation? Summarize the analysis of these studies, and show whether it presently appears that sexual orientation results from genetic differences, sociocultural practices and experiences, or both.

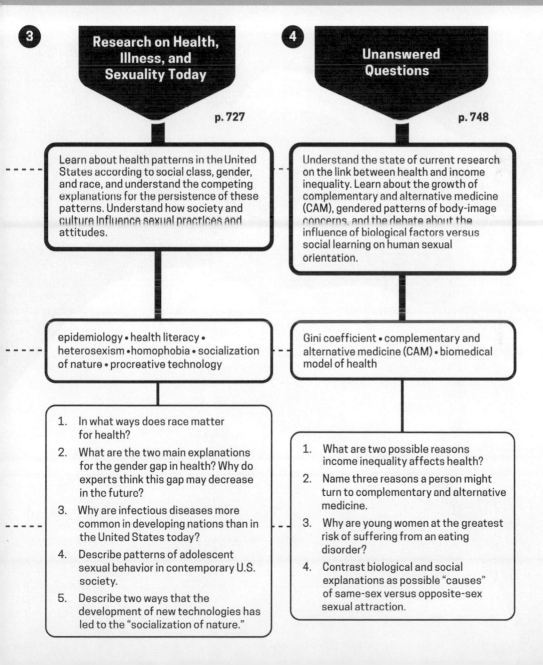

3

Research on Health, Illness, and Sexuality Today

p. 727

Learn about health patterns in the United States according to social class, gender, and race, and understand the competing explanations for the persistence of these patterns. Understand how society and culture influence sexual practices and attitudes.

epidemiology • health literacy • heterosexism •homophobia • socialization of nature • procreative technology

1. In what ways does race matter for health?

2. What are the two main explanations for the gender gap in health? Why do experts think this gap may decrease in the future?

3. Why are infectious diseases more common in developing nations than in the United States today?

4. Describe patterns of adolescent sexual behavior in contemporary U.S. society.

5. Describe two ways that the development of new technologies has led to the "socialization of nature."

4

Unanswered Questions

p. 748

Understand the state of current research on the link between health and income inequality. Learn about the growth of complementary and alternative medicine (CAM), gendered patterns of body-image concerns, and the debate about the influence of biological factors versus social learning on human sexual orientation.

Gini coefficient • complementary and alternative medicine (CAM) • biomedical model of health

1. What are two possible reasons income inequality affects health?

2. Name three reasons a person might turn to complementary and alternative medicine.

3. Why are young women at the greatest risk of suffering from an eating disorder?

4. Contrast biological and social explanations as possible "causes" of same-sex versus opposite-sex sexual attraction.

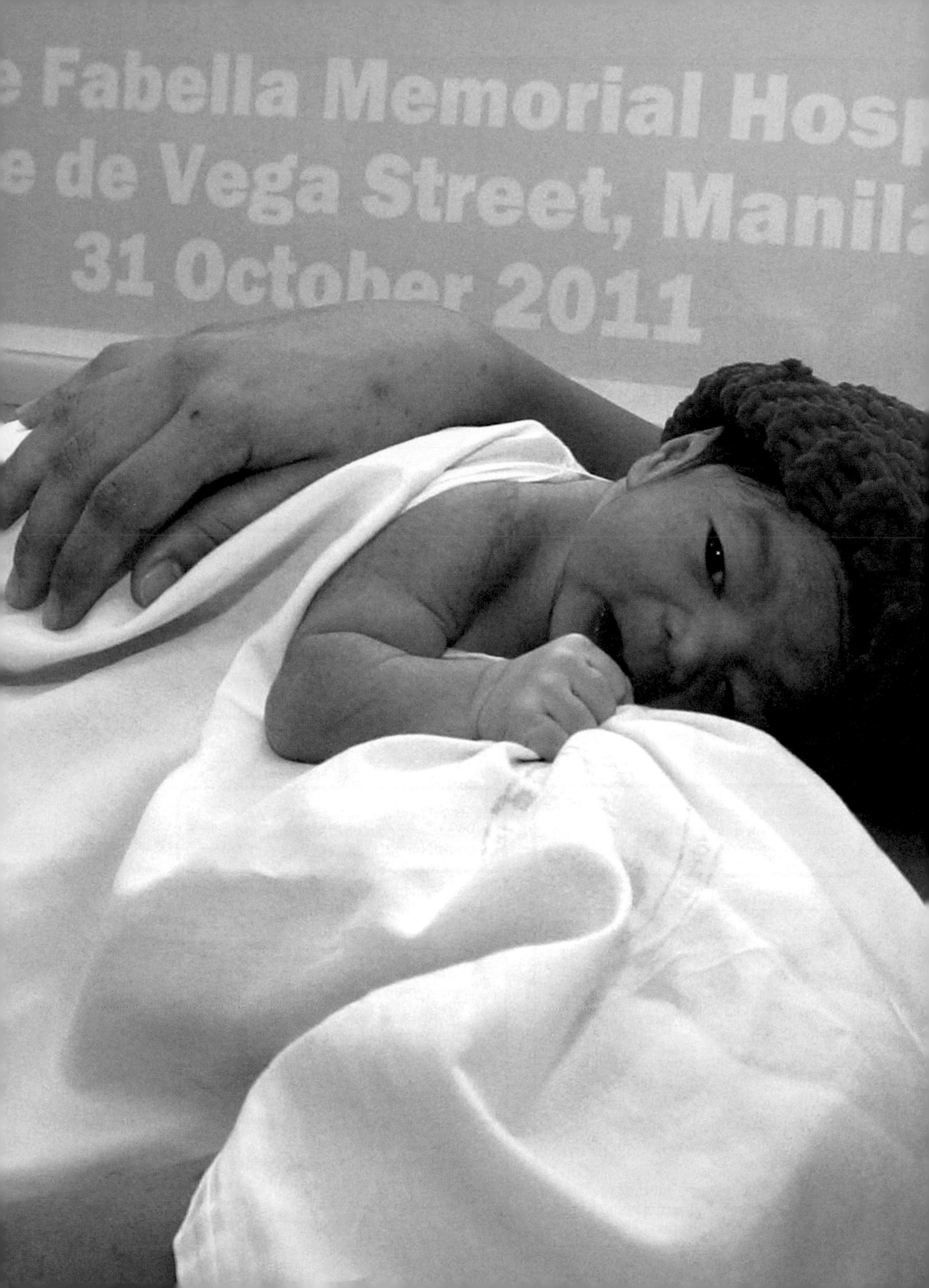
Fabella Memorial Hosp
de Vega Street, Manil
31 October 2011

19

Population, Urbanization, and the Environment

What do you think is the most widely accepted official prediction for the global population in 2050?

- **A** 9–10 billion
- **B** 14–15 billion
- **C** 19–20 billion
- **D** 24–25 billion
- **E** 29–30 billion

TURN THE PAGE FOR THE CORRECT ANSWER.

At the time of Christ's birth roughly 2,000 years ago, there were roughly 300 million people in the entire world—fewer than the 330 million who live in the United States today (U.S. Census Bureau, 2018b). It took nearly all of human history to add the first billion people to our planet, a number that was reached only two centuries ago, around 1800. It took another 130 years (until 1930) to add the second billion, 30 years (until 1960) to add the third billion, 15 years (until 1975) to add the fourth billion. Since that time, every twelve years the world's population has added another billion people, reaching 7 billion in 2011 (to signal this momentous event, the United Nations designated Danica May Camacho, born in the Philippines on October 31, as "baby number 7 billion"). By the time you are reading this textbook, the global population will have grown to 7.7 billion. Such rapid growth has enormous implications for the way people live, for the quality of their lives. Indeed, as humans transform the earth's forests and savannahs into giant cities and farms, there is widespread agreement among climate scientists that the entire planet is under threat.

It is difficult to predict with any precision the rate at which the world population will rise, but United Nations researchers have produced several scenarios based on recent trends. Their most likely estimate assumes "medium" levels of fertility: roughly two children being born, on average, to women throughout the world. (Obviously, some women will have more children and some fewer; this is an estimated average.) According to this scenario, the world population will reach 9.7 billion people by 2050 before stabilizing at 10.9 billion by the end of the century. The correct answer, then, is 9–10 billion, at the low end of the choices in our opening quiz (UNDESA, 2019). This may seem like good news: The rate of population growth appears to have slowed quite a bit. Instead of adding a billion people every 12 years, over the next three decades a billion will be added every fifteen years.

Unfortunately, this slowdown is not as hopeful as it seems. Unless there are changes in the way humans live, even current population levels—much less adding billions more people to the planet—may prove unsustainable. In this

LEARNING OBJECTIVES

1 Basic Concepts

Learn the key concepts demographers use to understand world population growth and the changes in cities.

2 Urban Sociology: Some Influential Theories

Understand how theories of urbanism have placed an increasing emphasis on the influence of socioeconomic factors on city life.

3 Population Growth, Urbanization, and Environmental Challenges: Recent Research

See how the environment is a sociological issue related to industrialization, urbanization, and population growth.

4 Unanswered Questions

Consider that global population growth will outstrip our resources, and what might be the best sociologically informed approach to environmental change.

THE ANSWER IS A.

chapter, we will examine the ways in which people are affecting the planet. We will begin by looking at population growth, since more people mean additional demands on planetary resources. We will then examine urbanization, the "built environment" in which rapidly growing populations live, and which has significant impacts on the natural environment. The combined forces of urbanization, industrialization (previously discussed in Chapter 14), and population growth now threaten to result in major environmental changes throughout the planet—changes that will be most strongly felt throughout your lives after college.

We will examine these changes in detail, and how they might be best addressed through the lens of sociology. We conclude with two unanswered questions—one concerning the likely relationship between global population growth and global food production, the other asking whether current efforts to address the major environmental changes that are occurring are likely to be successful, or if some other radically different approaches are needed.

1   BASIC CONCEPTS

Population Analysis: Demography

As we saw in the opening discussion, the human population has exploded over the last few centuries. It is important to understand the dynamics of population growth because when it comes to the effect of humans on the planet, numbers matter.

Given the importance of understanding the dynamics and effects of human population growth, an entire field has emerged to study it scientifically: **demography**. The term has its roots in ancient Greek: *demos* (the people) and *graphos* (writing, recording). It was invented about a century and a half ago, at a time when nations were beginning to keep official statistics on the size of their populations, in an effort to explain population growth, decline, and geographical distribution. As we shall see, such population dynamics are governed by three factors: births, deaths, and migrations. Demography is therefore often treated as a branch of sociology because these factors are largely social and cultural in nature.

Much demographic work tends to be statistical, relying on large-sample surveys as well as on official birth and death records. Virtually all countries in the world today gather and analyze basic statistics on their entire populations by carrying out systematic surveys called censuses. Although every effort is made to count each and every person, censuses still are not 100 percent accurate, nor is every individual adequately represented. In the United States, for example, a comprehensive population census every 10 years (the decennial census) is mandated by the Constitution, and sample surveys are also regularly conducted. Yet many people are not counted in the official population statistics, including undocumented immigrants, homeless people, transients, and others who, for one reason or another, either did not complete their surveys or were not located by census takers. In many countries in the global south, particularly those with recent high rates of population growth, demographic statistics are much more unreliable.

demography The study of populations.

crude birthrates Statistical measures representing the number of births within a given population per year, normally calculated in terms of the number of births per 1,000 members.

age-specific birthrates Statistical measures representing the number of births within a given population per year in relation to age distribution.

fertility The average number of live-born children produced by women of childbearing age in a particular society.

crude death rates Statistical measures representing the number of deaths that occur annually in a given population, normally calculated as the ratio of deaths per 1,000 members. Crude death rates give a general indication of the mortality levels of a community or society, but they are limited in their usefulness because they do not take into account the age distribution.

Among the basic concepts demographers use, the most important are crude birthrates, fertility, and crude death rates. **Crude birthrates** are expressed as the number of live births per year per 1,000 persons in the entire population. They are called "crude" rates because they do not focus on women of childbearing age, which is a much better predictor of population growth: A population with a high percentage of young women can be expected to have a much higher birthrate than one in which older men predominate. **Age-specific birth rates** take into account such differences: for instance, the number of births per 1,000 women in the 25- to 34-year-old age group.

Crude birthrates are useful for making overall comparisons among different groups, societies, and regions. The crude birthrate for the world as a whole in 2019 was 19 per 1,000. For the United States, it was far lower, at 13 per 1,000. Other industrialized countries had even lower rates: for example, 9 per 1,000 in Germany and Italy, and 8 per 1,000 in Japan. In many other parts of the world, crude birthrates were much higher. In India, for instance, the crude birthrate was 18 per 1,000, and in many African nations, it was more than 40 per 1,000. The crude birth rates in Angola, Niger, and Mali—44 per 1,000—were the world's highest in 2019 (World Population Review, 2019a). In fact, the crude birth rate for low-income countries as a whole (35 per 1,000) is more than three times that of high-income countries (11 per 1,000), making the poorest countries the fastest-growing, with the youngest populations (World Bank, 2019a).

It is important to note that for the world as a whole, the crude birthrate has declined considerably over the past half century—from 36 per 1,000 in 1963 to 19 today. While fewer births suggests lower population growth and therefore reduced pressure on the environment, as we shall see below, declining global birthrates by themselves will not solve our environmental problems. **Fertility** refers to how many live-born children the average woman actually has, in contrast to the number that are biologically possible. (Social and cultural factors, including birth control practices, play a role in determining actual fertility.) A fertility rate is usually calculated as the average number of births per 1,000 women of childbearing age.

Crude death rates (also called "mortality rates") are calculated in the same way as birthrates—the number of deaths per 1,000 of the population per year. Again, there are major variations among countries, but death rates in many societies in the global south are falling to levels comparable to those of the West. The crude death rate for the world as a whole was 8 per 1,000 in 2019—a rate shared by many countries throughout the world, including Canada, Argentina, and some African countries such as Burundi and Zimbabwe. (Perhaps surprisingly, the United States crude death rate, 9 per 1,000, is slightly higher than the world average.) Both India and China had slightly lower crude death rates (7 per 1,000). At the other extreme, Bulgaria, Lesotho, and Serbia have the highest crude death rates, at 15 to 16 per 1,000. A high crude death rate can result from many factors, with poverty—and the poor health care that often goes along with it—being a major cause. But HIV/AIDS, warfare, drugs (such as opioids in the United States) and natural disasters also play a role. Crude death rates globally have fallen even more significantly than crude birth rates over the past half century, from 18 per 1,000 in 1960 to 8 per 1,000 today (World Bank, 2019b). While declining global mortality is obviously good news from the standpoint of public health (and personal suffering), there is one downside: Since global population growth necessarily results from the difference between births and deaths, the fact that the number of deaths has declined even more than the number of births is the reason that the world's population continues to grow, with resulting pressures on the environment.

Like crude birthrates, crude death rates provide only a very general index of **mortality** (the number of deaths in a population), and can be very misleading, since they do not reflect the age structure of a country: A country with an aging population will obviously have a higher mortality rate than a country with a younger population. For example, mortality rates in the European Union (10 per 1,000) are twice that in the Middle East and North Africa (5 per 1,000), even though the former is wealthier (and therefore healthier) than the latter. The reason: Europe has four times as many people over 65 (20 percent) than the Middle East and North Africa (5 percent) (World Bank, 2019b, 2019i).

A particularly important specific death rate is the **infant mortality rate**—the number of babies per 1,000 births in any year who die before reaching age one. One of the key factors underlying the population explosion has been the reduction in infant mortality rates. For the world as a whole, in 2018, out of every 1,000 births, 29 babies died in infancy, a significant drop over barely three decades (as recently as 1990 the rate was 65). Infant mortality ranged from a low of 1to 2 per 1,000 in countries such as Norway, Sweden, and Finland, three Scandinavian countries with strong public health care systems, to a high of 85 in war-torn Central African Republic. The infant mortality rate in the United States—6 per 1,000—is at the low end, but not as low as high-income countries as a whole, or, for that matter, Cuba (both are 4 per 1,000) (World Bank, 2019f). Although Cuba is a poor (and undemocratic) country, its government has made preventive medicine, including a strong primary health care system, one of its top priorities (MEDICC, 2016).

Declining rates of infant mortality are the most important influence on increasing **life expectancy**—that is, the number of years the average person can expect to live. In 1900, life expectancy at birth in the United States was about 40 years. Today, it has increased to nearly 79 years (World Population Review, 2019b). This does not mean, however, that most people at the turn of the century died when they were about 40 years of age. If we look at the life expectancy of those people who survive the first year of life, we find that in 1900, the average person could expect to live to age 58. Illness, nutrition, and natural disasters are the other factors influencing life expectancy. Life expectancy has to be distinguished from **life span**, which is the maximum number of years that an individual could live. Although

mortality The number of deaths in a population.

infant mortality rate The number of infants who die during the first year of life, per 1,000 live births.

life expectancy The number of years the average person can expect to live.

life span The maximum length of life that is biologically possible for a member of a given species.

life expectancy has increased in most societies in the world, life span has remained unaltered. Only a small proportion of people live to be 100 or more.

Dynamics of Population Change

Rates of population growth or decline are measured by subtracting the yearly number of deaths per 1,000 from the number of births per 1,000. (Actual population growth or decline also requires taking into account the number of people who have migrated into the country, as well as the number who have emigrated out of the country.) For the world as a whole, population is increasing 1.1 percent each year, which is half the rate of fifty years ago (World Bank, 2019j). While this trend is certainly promising—the population explosion is clearly slowing—as we have seen it will still result in several billion more people by the end of the century, if the predicted trends prove to be correct.

How can such a tiny rate of growth (1.1 percent each year) produce billions of more people over the next seventy or so years? The answer is that population growth is **exponential**: People born today add to the total population, creating a larger base for future growth. Since today there are approximately 7.7 billion people in the world, and the annual growth rate is currently 1.1 percent, then next year there will be 84.7 million more people (7,700,000,000 × 1.1 percent = 84,700,000), bringing the total to 7,784,700,000. If this larger population base continues to grow at 1.1 percent each year, then two years from now 85,631,700 more people will be added, and so on into the future. Each year, the number of people added will grow. We can measure this effect by means of the **doubling time**—the period of time it takes for the population to double. The formula used to calculate doubling time is 70 divided by the current growth rate. For example, a population growth of 1 percent will produce a doubling of numbers in 70 years. At 2 percent growth, a population will double in 35 years, while at 3 percent, it will double in 23 years.

Virtually all industrialized countries have growth rates of less than 0.6 percent. For example, the rate of population growth for the European Union in 2018 was only 0.2 percent (doubling in 350 years); for the United States, 0.6 percent (doubling in 117 years). While some countries have experienced population decline because of war or economic collapse (Syria and Venezuela are current examples), this also is true of such advanced industrial countries as Japan, Portugal and Italy (all –0.2 percent) (World Bank, 2019j). In these countries, fertility has declined relative to mortality sufficiently that births (and net migration) no longer outnumber deaths. As we shall see, economic success appears to go hand-in-hand with declining population growth (and, at the extreme, even population decline).

On the other hand, as previously noted, the poorest countries in the world have the highest crude birth rates and therefore the fastest-growing populations. The number of people in low-income countries grew 2.6 percent in 2018, meaning their

rates of population growth or decline A measurement of population change calculated by subtracting the yearly number of deaths per 1,000 from the number of births per 1,000.

exponential A geometric, rather than linear, rate of progression; producing a fast rise in the numbers of a population experiencing such growth.

doubling time The time it takes for a particular level of population to double.

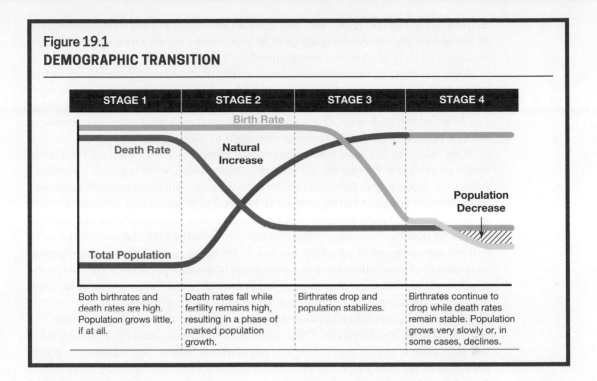

Figure 19.1
DEMOGRAPHIC TRANSITION

STAGE 1	STAGE 2	STAGE 3	STAGE 4

Birth Rate

Death Rate

Natural Increase

Population Decrease

Total Population

Both birthrates and death rates are high. Population grows little, if at all.	Death rates fall while fertility remains high, resulting in a phase of marked population growth.	Birthrates drop and population stabilizes.	Birthrates continue to drop while death rates remain stable. Population grows very slowly or, in some cases, declines.

populations will double in only 27 years (World Bank, 2019j). High birth rates also mean a youthful population: 42 percent of people living in low-income countries are under 14, compared with only 17 percent in high-income countries. In Niger, the world's "youngest country," fully half the population is under 14 (World Bank, 2019h). A young, poor population creates numerous social and economic challenges: Educational opportunities are often nonexistent, and many children must work full time, while others eke out a living as street children, begging for whatever they can. Large numbers of unemployed or underemployed young people, especially young men, are often a prescription for unrest, providing a recruiting ground for organizations that advocate for radical (and sometimes violent) change (Darden, 2019).

While poor countries consume far less than rich countries (and in that sense have less of an environmental impact), their more rapidly growing populations require additional resources. And to the extent that they successfully industrialize and improve their living standards, their environmental impacts will only increase, at least in the short run (in the long run, successful industrialization may also result in slower population growth).

The Demographic Transition

During the nineteenth century, successful industrialization and economic development in Europe and the United States did in fact result in slower population growth. This has been termed the **demographic transition**, a notion first worked out by

demographic transition A theory that shows how birth and death rates are related to stages of industrial development, with high birth and death rates transitioning to low birth and death rates as a country transitions from a preindustrial to an industrialized economy.

Warren S. Thompson (1929), who described a three-stage process in which one type of population stability would eventually be replaced by another, as a society reached an advanced level of economic development.

Stage one refers to the conditions characteristic of most pre-industrial societies, in which both birthrates and death rates are high and the infant mortality rate is especially high. Population grows little, if at all, as the high number of births is more or less offset by the large number of deaths. Although there were sometimes periods of marked population increase, these were followed by increases in death rates.

Stage two, which began with industrial development in Europe and the United States in the early part of the nineteenth century (with wide regional variations), occurs when death rates fall while fertility remains high. The death rates fell because of improved agriculture, resulting in more stable food supplies, as well as some advances in public health (such as water supplies, sewage and sanitation controls, and the growth of medical knowledge). Fertility initially remains high, however, because of cultural lag—long-standing beliefs and practices that supported having large families were slow to change. This was, therefore, a phase of marked population growth. (Some scholars divide this stage into two phases, one in which birth rates remain high but death rates drop, and a second in which death rates also begin to decline).

Stage three occurs when cultural norms change from favoring high birthrates to instead favoring low birthrates. Once again, birthrates and death rates are aligned—this time both at low levels. Once again, population is stable. This transition is partly the result of the changing economics of having many children. As economies transitioned from agricultural to industrial, parents no longer required many children to help maintain their farms, although at least initially children could work in factories. But as industrial economies matured, child labor was made illegal; instead, compulsory schooling meant that parents were expected to support their children throughout their school years—and sometimes even throughout their college years. Instead of being seen as an economic asset, children came to be viewed as an economic cost. Parents became increasingly concerned with "child quality" and providing resources to ensure the best possible life for their offspring, rather than "child quantity," or having many children.

Industrial development also was accompanied by technologies that allowed women to control their own fertility, as well as a cultural change regarding people's views toward childbearing. How many children a woman would have was now viewed as under her own control, rather than as a "gift from God." In contemporary society, as women have achieved higher levels of education and higher earnings in the labor market, the incentive to have fewer children has increased. Higher education among both men and women also is linked to delayed marriage and, consequently, delayed (and thus diminished) childbearing (Caldwell et al., 2010).

Demographers do not fully agree about how to interpret this sequence of change or how long-lasting stage three is likely to be. Fertility in the Western countries has not been completely stable over the past century or so; considerable differences in fertility remain among the industrialized nations, and among classes or regions within them.

Nevertheless, it is generally accepted that this sequence accurately describes a major transformation in the demographic character of modern societies.

In recent decades, demographers have debated whether a "**second demographic transition**" has begun in the most developed industrial countries. Under this new model, fertility rates continue to fall because of shifts in family structure. Key influences on the second demographic transition include delayed marriage, delayed childbearing, rising rates of cohabitation, high, steady rates of divorce, and the relative ease of obtaining effective means of birth control. All of these factors arguably lead to lower birthrates, because under these circumstances many people may prefer not to have children (van de Kaa, 2003). This may account for the extremely low birthrates among advanced industrial societies. In fact, as we have previously seen, some appear to have moved into a fourth stage, in which birthrates decline below replacement levels; that is, mortality rates (which remain low) outstrip fertility rates (which drop even lower than mortality rates), resulting in population decline.

The shift to still lower birthrates, and even population decline, has been the recent experience of many European countries as well as Japan and Singapore. A process of aging has resulted, in which the proportion of young people declines while the proportion of the elderly markedly increases. If this trend continues, it can have widespread economic and social implications for economically developed countries. First, there will be an increase in the **dependency ratio**, the ratio of economically dependent members (the older population) to economically productive members (younger working members) of the population. Economically dependent persons are those considered too young or too old to work, typically those under age 15 and over age 65. As the dependency ratio increases, pressure will mount on health care and social services—with relatively fewer persons working (and therefore able to pay the taxes) needed to finance them.

second demographic transition A new demographic model that calls for fertility rates that may continue to fall because of shifts in family structure.

dependency ratio The ratio of people of dependent ages (children and the older population) to people of economically active ages.

CONCEPT CHECKS

1 Why is demography considered a branch of sociology?

2 How does the age structure of a society affect fertility, mortality, and thereby population growth?

3 What are the stages of a demographic transition, and why do some demographers believe that we've now entered a fourth stage?

2 URBAN SOCIOLOGY: SOME INFLUENTIAL THEORIES

Urbanization—the movement of the population into towns and cities, away from rural farmland—results when cities grow in population, perhaps partly through natural increase but mainly through migration from rural areas by people in search of the economic opportunities associated with urban life. During the twentieth century and for the first time in history, humans have opted for large-scale urban living rather than rural life. This change has had enormous consequences not only for individuals, but for the planetary environment as well. Before we turn to some of these consequences, however, it is important to understand how sociologists have viewed urban life, since such understanding played a major role in the emergence of the discipline during the twentieth century. We begin with scholars associated with the University of Chicago's so-called "Chicago School" from the 1920s to the 1940s—especially Robert Park, Ernest Burgess, and Louis Wirth—who developed ideas that were, for many years, the chief basis of theory and research in urban sociology. Some important ideas, however, came from outside universities—for example, in the work of Jane Jacobs, whom we will also consider. We will also examine some other leading theories of urban sociology, before examining city life throughout the world today.

The Chicago School

Two concepts developed by the "Chicago School" are worthy of special attention. One is the so-called **ecological approach** to urban analysis (Park, 1952); the other is the characterization of urbanism as a *way of life*, developed by Wirth (1938). It is important to understand these ideas as the Chicago School initially conceived of them and to see how sociologists in more recent decades have revised and even replaced them.

Urban Ecology

Ecology—the study of the adaptation of plant and animal organisms to their environment—is a term taken from the physical sciences. The Chicago School believed that cities grew and took shape by adapting to their environments, much as is the case with plants and animals. Large urban areas initially tend to develop along the shores of rivers, in fertile plains, or at the intersection of trading routes or railways. They then become ordered into "natural areas" through such seemingly natural processes as competition, invasion, and succession—a set of concepts taken directly from biological ecology. Much like plants and animals in a natural environment, different neighborhoods develop through the adjustments inhabitants make as they struggle to gain their livelihoods. The Chicago School sought to show that cities grew outward in

urbanization The movement of the population into towns and cities and away from rural areas.

ecological approach In the field of urban analysis, a perspective emphasizing the "natural" distribution of city neighborhoods into areas having contrasting characteristics.

concentric rings: In the center are the **inner-city** areas, a mixture of big-business prosperity and decaying private homes; beyond these are older established neighborhoods, housing workers employed in stable manual occupations; farther out still are the suburbs, in which higher-income groups tend to live. Processes of invasion and succession occur within the segments of the concentric rings. Thus, as property decays in a central or near-central area, ethnic minority groups might start to move into it. As they do so, more of the preexisting population starts to leave, precipitating a wholesale flight to neighborhoods elsewhere in the city or out to the suburbs. Within this larger framework, *differentiation* occurs—different groups will compete for space. For example, groups on which many others depend (banks, corporate headquarters, insurance companies) will have a dominant role, often reflected in their central geographical position; members of different ethnic groups may all live in certain neighborhoods, ranging from poor to wealthy depending on the fortunes of the group (Hawley, 1950, 1968).

inner city The areas composing the central neighborhoods of a city, as distinct from the suburbs. In many modern urban settings in the developed world, inner-city areas are subject to dilapidation and decay, with the more affluent residents having moved to outlying areas.

ghetto A place where a racial or ethnic group initially comes to live as a consequence of systematic exclusion from more desirable places.

These processes were treated as immutable as the laws of nature, an assumption which might have provided some scientific credence to sociological reasoning, but which, as we shall see, often proved to be incorrect.

Cities are human-made and are therefore shaped by human—and not natural—forces. The assumptions of human ecology were challenged when two Black graduate students, drawing on extensive historical and ethnographic data, published the book *Black Metropolis* (Drake and Cayton, 1945). Their research showed that Chicago's Black residential neighborhoods were **ghettos**, places where a racial or ethnic group initially comes to live as a consequence of systematic exclusion from more desirable places. Chicago's ghettos, they argued, were by no means the result of "natural forces" but were instead shaped by unnatural social forces: Blacks had been given no

Robert Park of the Chicago School applied an ecological approach to urban analysis arguing that, like natural organisms, cities such as Chicago sprout up in response to advantageous features of the environment.

urbanism A term used by Louis Wirth to denote distinctive characteristics of urban social life, such as its impersonality.

choice but to live in the worst areas of the city. There was nothing natural about this placement, and it would not have occurred if not for social forces such as exclusion, violence, and restrictive covenants where neighborhood "improvement" associations passed laws making it illegal to sell land in a community to Blacks. After the publication of Drake and Cayton's *Black Metropolis*, it was harder for sociologists to think of the distributions of populations in urban areas as natural.

Urbanism as a Way of Life

Wirth's thesis of **urbanism** as a *way of life* (1938) focuses on the ways that life in cities is different from life elsewhere, but also helps to shape life outside cities—for example, by influencing styles of dress and behavior. As a "way of life," however, cities are unique in that large numbers of people live in close proximity to one another in virtual anonymity, without knowing one another personally—a fundamental contrast to small, traditional villages. As a result, within cities most contact (for example, with sales clerks, baristas, passengers on trains) is fleeting and partial, serving as a means to other ends, rather than being a satisfying relationship in itself. Given the fast pace of life, the bonds that unite people tend to be weak; competition prevails over cooperation. Yet at the same time, some neighborhoods may preserve the characteristics of small communities—for example, among immigrant communities. The more such areas are absorbed into wider patterns of city life, however, the less these characteristics survive.

Whether listening to music on portable devices or texting on their phones, many people have strategies for distancing themselves and managing social boundaries in busy urban environments.

Wirth was among the first to address the "urban interaction problem" (Duneier and Molotch, 1999), the necessity for city dwellers to respect social boundaries when so many people are in close physical proximity all the time. Wirth elaborates that "the reserve, the indifference, and the blasé outlook that urbanites manifest in their relationships may thus be regarded as devices for immunizing themselves against the personal claims and expectations of others." Many people walk down the street in cities acting unconcerned about the others near them, often talking on cell phones or listening to music that blocks out the sounds of urban life. Through such appearance of apathy, they can avoid unwanted transgression of social boundaries.

Wirth's ideas have deservedly enjoyed wide currency. The impersonal nature of many day-to-day contacts in modern cities is undeniable, but to some degree, this is true of social life in general in modern societies: Even in rural areas, people must manage social boundaries in their face-to-face interactions with others, as has been found as far afield as in western Samoa (Duranti, 1994) or among the African Poro people (Bellman, 1984). Furthermore, neighborhoods marked by close kinship and personal ties are not only the result of immigrant groups seeking to preserve their ethnic ties or previous ways of living; they can also result from the interaction among people who share common interests, whether it be religion, politics, language, or art and culture. A small town or village does not easily allow the development of such subcultural diversity (Fischer, 1984). An artist might find few others in a village or small town with whom to associate but may find a community of like-minded artistic or intellectual peers in neighborhoods such as Williamsburg in Brooklyn, New York. Likewise, some gay and lesbian young people may find more hospitable communities in cities that have large gay subcultures, such as San Francisco, compared to the small towns where they may have grown up.

A large city may be a world of strangers, yet it supports and creates personal relationships. It may be difficult to meet people when one first moves to a large city, but given the diversity of people in large cities, opportunities exist to seek out and befriend like-minded individuals. By contrast, anyone moving to a small, established rural community may find one's neighbors to be friendly and polite, but it may take years to become truly accepted when one is "new" in town. Wirth's ideas retain some validity, but in light of subsequent contributions, they clearly are overgeneralized. Modern cities frequently involve impersonal, anonymous social relationships, but they are also sources of diversity—and, sometimes, intimacy.

Jane Jacobs: "Eyes and Ears upon the Street"

Like most sociologists in the twentieth century, the Chicago School researchers were professors who saw their mission as contributing to a scholarly literature and advancing the field of social science. At certain moments in the history of sociology, however, advances have also come from thinkers working outside universities without formal training in sociology. One such person was Jane Jacobs, who published *The Death and Life of Great American Cities* in 1961, and who emerged as a highly influential public intellectual who helped shape the field of urban studies.

Jacobs, like Wirth, noted that "cities are, by definition, full of strangers," some of whom are dangerous. She then tried to explain what makes it possible for cities to meet the challenge of "assimilating strangers" in such a way that strangers can feel comfortable together. She argued that cities are most habitable when they feature a diversity of uses, thereby ensuring that many people will be coming and going on the streets at any time. When enough people are out and about, Jacobs wrote, "respectable" eyes and ears dominate the street and are fixed on strangers, who will thus not get out of hand. Underneath the seeming disorder of a busy street is the very basis for order in "the intricacy of sidewalk use, bringing with it a constant succession of eyes." The more people who are out, or looking from their windows at the people who are out, the more their gazes will safeguard the street.

More than five decades after her book was published, Jacobs's ideas remain extremely influential. Yet times have changed since Jacobs's writing, and a great diversity of people are now found on city sidewalks, often representing economic inequalities, cultural differences, and extremes of behavior. From the homeless seeking a few dollars, to the mentally ill who have no other place to go, sidewalk life can often seem unpredictable and threatening (Duneier, 1999). Under these conditions, strangers do not necessarily feel the kind of solidarity and mutual assurance she described. Sociologists today must ask: What happens to urban life when "the eyes and ears upon the street" represent vast inequalities and cultural differences? Under what conditions do the assumptions Jacobs made still hold up?

Urbanism and the Created Environment

Whereas the earlier Chicago School of sociology emphasized that the distribution of people in cities occurs naturally, scholars such as Drake and Cayton (1945) showed that there was nothing "natural" about the formation of ghettos, and more recent theories of the city have stressed that urbanism has to be analyzed in relation to larger patterns of political and economic change. This focus on the political economy of cities, and increasingly in a global context, represented a new and critical direction for urban sociology.

Harvey: The Restructuring of Space

Urbanism is one aspect of the **created environment** brought about by the spread of industrial capitalism, according to David Harvey (1973, 1982, 1985, 2009). In traditional societies, city and countryside were clearly differentiated. In the modern world, industry blurs the division between city and countryside. Agriculture becomes mechanized and is run according to considerations of price and profit, just like industrial work, and this process lessens the differences in modes of social life between urban and rural people.

Harvey points out that in modern urbanism, space is continually *restructured*. The process is determined by decisions of large firms (where they choose to place their home offices, research and development centers, and factories); the controls that governments operate over both land and industrial production; and the activities of private investors who buy and sell houses and land. Business firms, for example, are constantly

created environment An environment made up of constructions established by human beings to serve their needs, derived from the use of human-made technology—including, for example, roads, railways, factories, offices, private homes, and other buildings.

weighing the relative advantages of new locations against existing ones. As production becomes cheaper in one area than another, or as the firm moves from one product to another, offices and factories will be closed down in one place and opened up elsewhere. Once the offices or factories have been built and the area redeveloped, investors look for the potential for further speculative building elsewhere. What is profitable in one period will not necessarily be so in another, when the financial climate changes.

The activities of private home buyers are strongly influenced by how far, and where, business interests buy up land, and by rates of loans and taxes fixed by local and central government. After World War II, for instance, there was vast expansion of suburban development outside major U.S. cities. This expansion was due partly to ethnic discrimination and the tendency of Whites to move away from inner-city areas. However, it was made possible, Harvey argues, only because of government tax breaks to home buyers and construction firms and because financial organizations set up special credit arrangements. These provided the basis for the building and buying of new homes on the peripheries of cities and, at the same time, promoted demand for industrial products such as the automobile.

Castells: Urbanism and Social Movements

Like Harvey, Manuel Castells (1977, 1983) argues that cities are almost wholly artificial environments, constructed by people, rather than the natural forces emphasized by the Chicago School. Both also stress that the spatial form of a society is closely linked to the larger political economy. Castells, however, also focuses on the **collective consumption** that cities make possible, such as the buying and selling of property. Homes, schools, transport services, and leisure amenities are ways in which people consume the products of modern industry. Large corporations, banks, and insurance companies, which provide capital for building projects, have a great deal of power over these processes; government agencies also directly affect many aspects of city life, by building roads and public housing, planning parks, and through tax policies and development subsidies. The physical shape of cities is thus a product of both market forces and the power of government.

But the nature of the created environment is not just the result of the activities of wealthy and powerful people. Castells stresses the importance of the struggles of underprivileged groups to alter their living conditions. Urban problems stimulate a range of social movements concerned with improving housing conditions, protesting against air pollution, defending parks, and combating building development that changes the nature of an area. For example, Castells studied the 1970s gay movement in San Francisco, which succeeded in restructuring neighborhoods around its own cultural values—allowing many gay organizations, clubs, and bars to flourish—and gained influence over local politics.

John Logan and Harvey Molotch (1987) have suggested an approach that directly connects the perspectives of authors such as Harvey and Castells with some features of the ecological standpoint. They agree with Harvey and Castells that broad features of economic development, stretching nationally and internationally, affect urban life in

collective consumption A concept used by Manuel Castells to refer to processes of urban consumption—such as the buying and selling of property.

The Castro district in San Francisco is not only open but celebratory about its thriving gay and lesbian population.

a quite direct way. But these wide-ranging economic factors, they argue, are focused through local organizations, including neighborhood businesses, banks, and government agencies, together with the activities of individual home buyers. Places (land and buildings) are bought and sold, according to Logan and Molotch, just like other goods in modern societies, but the markets that structure city environments are influenced by how different groups of people want to use the property they buy and sell. Many tensions and conflicts arise as a result of this process—and these are the key factors structuring city neighborhoods. For instance, an apartment house is seen as a home by its residents but as a source of income by its landlord. Businesses are most interested in buying and selling property in an area to obtain the best production sites or to make profits in land speculation. Their interests and concerns are quite different from those of residents, for whom the neighborhood is a place to live.

Saskia Sassen: Global Cities

Saskia Sassen has been one of the leading contributors to theoretical debates on cities and globalization. She shows how globalization is transforming cities into vital hubs within the global economy. Urban centers have become critical in coordinating information flows, managing business activities, and innovating new services and technologies. As business, production, advertising, and marketing assume a global scale, an enormous amount of organizational activity must be performed to maintain and develop these global networks. Power has been dispersed around the globe, concentrated in what Sassen (1991, 1998) terms **global cities**. These are urban centers that are home to the headquarters of large transnational corporations and a superabundance of financial, technological, and consulting services. In her early work, Sassen (1991) focuses on three such cities:

global city A city, such as London, New York, or Tokyo, that has become an organizing center of the new global economy.

New York, London, and Tokyo. The contemporary development of the world economy, she argued, has created a novel, strategic role for major cities. Most such cities have long been centers of international trade, but they now have four new traits:

1. They have developed into command posts—centers of direction and policy making—for the global economy.
2. They are the key locations for financial and specialized service firms, which have become more important than manufacturing in influencing economic development.
3. They are the sites of production and innovation in these newly expanded industries.
4. They are markets in which the "products" of financial and service industries are bought, sold, or otherwise disposed of.

Within the highly dispersed world economy of today, cities such as these provide for central control of the specialized services business organizations require for administering offices and factories scattered across the world, and of financial innovations and markets. Services and financial goods are the "things" the global city makes. In the downtown areas of global cities, local firms mingle with national and multinational organizations, including a multiplicity of foreign companies. Global cities compete with one another, but they also constitute an interdependent system, partly separate from the nations in which they are located. Sassen (1998) further argues that global cities have produced a new, interrelated dynamic of inequality: a prosperous central business district interlinked with a nearby impoverished area. The growth sectors of the new economy—financial services, marketing, high technology—are reaping profits far greater than any found within traditional economic sectors. As the salaries and bonuses of the very affluent continue to climb, the wages of those employed to clean and guard their offices are dropping. Sassen argues that we are witnessing the "valorization" of work located at the forefront of the new global economy, along with the "devalorization" of work that occurs behind the scenes. A geography of "centrality and marginality" is taking shape, as Mitch Duneier's (1999) study in New York's Greenwich Village revealed. Alongside resplendent affluence there is acute poverty. Yet although these two worlds coexist side by side, the actual contact between them can be

CONCEPT CHECKS

1 How does urban ecology use language from the physical sciences to explain life in modern cities? How did Drake and Cayton's study challenge the ideas of urban ecology?

2 What is the urban interaction problem?

3 According to Jane Jacobs, the more people there are on the streets, the safer the streets will be. Do you agree with Jacobs's hypothesis and her explanation for this proposed pattern?

4 What are the four main characteristics of global cities?

surprisingly minimal. As Mike Davis (1990) noted in his study of Los Angeles, there has been a "conscious 'hardening' of the city surface against the poor." Walled compounds, neighborhoods guarded by electronic surveillance, and "corporate citadels" have replaced accessible public spaces.

Sassen and others have built on her earlier work, noting that as globalization progresses, more and more cities are joining New York, London, and Tokyo in the ranks of the global cities, with places such as Chicago, Frankfurt, Hong Kong, Los Angeles, Milan, Osaka, Singapore, and Zurich serving as major global centers for business and financial services. Beneath these, new sets of regional centers are developing as key nodes within the global economy. Cities such as Buenos Aires, Jakarta, Madrid, Moscow, São Paulo, and Seoul are becoming important hubs for activity within the so-called emerging markets.

3   POPULATION GROWTH, URBANIZATION, AND ENVIRONMENTAL CHALLENGES: RECENT RESEARCH

Since the beginning of the practice of agriculture thousands of years ago, human beings have left an imprint on nature. Hunting and gathering societies lived mainly in nature; they existed on what the natural environment provided and made little attempt to change the world around them. With the advent of agriculture, this situation was altered. For crops to grow, land must be cleared, trees cut down, and encroaching weeds and wild foliage kept at bay. Even primitive farming methods can lead to soil erosion. Once natural forests are cut down and clearings made, the wind may blow away the topsoil. The farming community then clears some fresh plots of land, and so the process goes on. Some landscapes that we today think of as natural, such as the rocky areas and scrubland in southwestern Greece, are actually the result of soil erosion farmers created 5,000 years ago.

Yet before the development of modern industry and its associated urbanization, nature dominated human life far more than human activities influenced nature. Today, the human onslaught on the environment is so intense that few natural processes are uninfluenced by human activity. Nearly all cultivable land is under agricultural production. What used to be almost inaccessible wildernesses are now often nature reserves, visited routinely by thousands of tourists. Modern industry, still expanding worldwide, has led to steeply climbing demands for sources of energy and raw materials. Yet the world's supply of such energy sources and raw materials is limited, and some key resources are bound to run out if global consumption is not restricted. Even the world's climate, as we shall see, has been affected by global industrialization and economic growth—and the world's wealthiest countries have had the largest impact.

In this section we provide a brief history of urbanization across the globe, followed by an examination of recent urbanization in the United States and the Global South. We then turn to the major theme in this chapter: the effect of population growth, urbanization, and industrialization on our shared environment—the planet Earth.

A Brief History of Urbanization

At the beginning of the twentieth century, fewer than one out of every seven people on the planet lived in cities. In 2018, more than half of the world's population (55 percent) lived in cities (World Bank, 2019l); by mid-century, more than two-thirds may be urban, with 90 percent of the increase taking place in Asia and Africa (UNDESA, 2018a). As population growth continues and globalization results in the spread of manufacturing throughout the world, we can expect the growth of cities, many of them gigantic in size, to continue.

Premodern Cities

In premodern times, cities were self-contained entities that stood apart from the predominantly rural areas in which they were located. Road systems sometimes linked major urban areas, but travel was a specialized affair for merchants, soldiers, and others who needed to cross distances with some regularity. Communication among cities was limited.

The world's first cities appeared at around 3500 B.C.E., in the river valleys of the Nile in Egypt, the Tigris and Euphrates in what is now Iraq, and the Indus in what is today Pakistan. Cities in traditional societies were very small by modern standards. Babylon, for example, one of the largest ancient Near Eastern cities, extended over an area of only 3.2 square miles and, at its height, around 2000 B.C.E., probably numbered no more than 15,000 to 20,000 people. Rome under Emperor Augustus in the first century B.C.E. was easily the largest premodern city outside China, with some 300,000 inhabitants—the population of Stockton, California, or Cincinnati, Ohio, today. Most cities of the ancient world shared certain features. They were surrounded by walls for the purposes of military defense. Their centers, often protected by a second inner wall, typically featured a religious temple, royal palace, government buildings, a public square, and a market (Fox, 1964; Sjoberg, 1960, 1963; Wheatley, 1971). The dwellings of the ruling class or elite tended to be concentrated in or near the center, while less-privileged groups lived closer to the city walls or sometimes outside them, moving inside if the city came under attack. Different ethnic and religious communities were often segregated in separate neighborhoods, where their members lived and worked; sometimes even these neighborhoods were walled. Lacking any form of mass printing, public officials had to shout at the tops of their voices to deliver pronouncements. "Streets" were usually strips of land on which no one had yet built. A few traditional civilizations boasted sophisticated road systems linking particular cities, but these existed mainly for military purposes, and transportation for the most part was slow and limited. Merchants and soldiers were the only people who regularly traveled over long distances. Sanitary conditions were rudimentary at best, with open sewers and animal excrement likely to be everywhere.

Although cities became the main centers for science, the arts, and cosmopolitan culture, their influence over the rest of the country was always weak. No more than a tiny proportion of the population lived in the cities, and the division between cities and the countryside was pronounced. By far the majority of people lived in small rural communities and rarely came into contact with more than the occasional state official or merchant from the towns.

The Rise of the Megalopolis

Britain was the first society to undergo industrialization, beginning in the mid-eighteenth century. The process of industrialization generated increasing urbanization. In 1800, less than 20 percent of the British population lived in towns or cities with more than 10,000 inhabitants. By 1900, this proportion had risen to 74 percent. London held about 1.1 million people in 1800; by the beginning of the twentieth century, it had increased in size to a population of more than 7 million, at that date the largest city ever seen in the world. It was a vast manufacturing, commercial, and financial center at the heart of the still-expanding British Empire.

The urbanization of most other European countries and the United States took place somewhat later. When the American colonies declared independence in 1776, the largest city was Philadelphia, with a population of only 40,000. By 1800, the United States was more of a rural society than were the leading European countries; fewer than 10 percent of Americans lived in communities with populations of more than 2,500 people. Between 1800 and 1900, as industrialization grew in the United States, the population of New York City leapt from 60,000 people to 4.8 million. It is currently the largest city in the United States at 8.6 million.

The contrast in size between the largest modern cities today and those of premodern civilizations is extraordinary. The most populous cities in the industrialized countries—sometimes termed "megacities"—number more than 10 million inhabitants. A **conurbation**—a cluster of cities and towns forming a continuous network—may include even larger numbers of people. The peak of urban life today is represented by what is called the **megalopolis**, the "city of cities." The term was first used in modern times to refer to the Northeast Corridor of the United States, an area covering some 450 miles from north of Boston to south of Washington, D.C. In this region, some 56 million people live at a density of more than 800 persons per square mile. Large, dense urban populations can also be found in the lower Great Lakes region surrounding Chicago.

Manuel Castells (1996) refers to **megacities** as one of the main features of third-millennium urbanization. They are global cities, functioning as population magnets for the countries or regions in which they are located. People are drawn to large urban areas for various reasons, including somehow benefitting from their global role, and there is evidence that at least some succeed: Average urban incomes are higher than those in rural areas, and there is usually better access to public services such as education, health, transportation, communication, water supply, and sanitation. Because of economies of scale, cities are better equipped to provide such services efficiently and cheaply to large, concentrated populations (UNDP, 2007). Yet at the same time, densely populated urban areas have proven to be fertile grounds for the spread of disease, as the deadly COVID-19 pandemic revealed: by the end of May 2020, of the approximately 100,000 known COVID-related deaths that had occurred in the

conurbation An agglomeration of towns or cities into an unbroken urban environment.

megalopolis The "city of all cities" in ancient Greece; used in modern times to refer to very large conurbations.

megacities A term favored by Manuel Castells to describe large, intensely concentrated urban spaces that serve as connection points for the global economy.

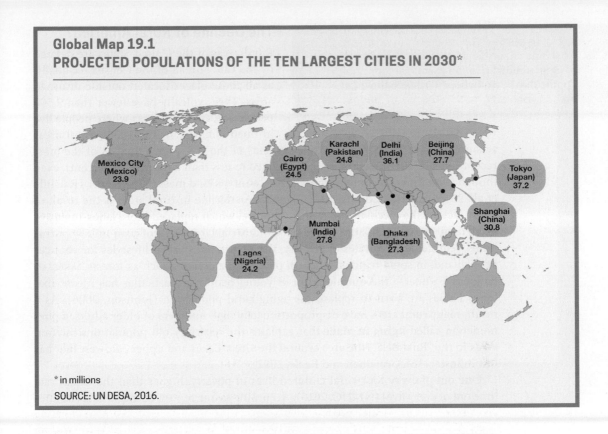

Global Map 19.1
PROJECTED POPULATIONS OF THE TEN LARGEST CITIES IN 2030*

Mexico City (Mexico) 23.9

Cairo (Egypt) 24.5

Karachi (Pakistan) 24.8

Delhi (India) 36.1

Beijing (China) 27.7

Tokyo (Japan) 37.2

Shanghai (China) 30.8

Mumbai (India) 27.8

Dhaka (Bangladesh) 27.3

Lagos (Nigeria) 24.2

* in millions
SOURCE: UN DESA, 2016.

entire United States, over a quarter of which (20,000) were in New York City (CDC COVID-19 Response Team, 2020b).

Although there are exceptions, urbanization generally goes hand in hand with economic growth. The least urbanized countries are also low-income countries (where only 33 percent live in urban areas); next come the more urbanized middle-income countries (with 53 percent urban); high-income countries are the most urbanized (81 percent). With the exception of some small island nations (such as Gibraltar or Bermuda) and city-states (such as Monaco or Singapore), the most urbanized countries are Belgium (98 percent); Uruguay (95 percent); and Israel, Argentina, and Japan (92 percent). The United States, 82 percent urban, is somewhat more urbanized than the European Union (76 percent). The least urbanized countries are those in South Asia (34 percent), which is also one of the poorest regions in the world (World Bank, 2019l).

Urbanization in the United States

One of the major changes in U.S. population distribution in the period since World War II is the movement of large parts of city populations to urban areas, both large cities and newly constructed suburbs. At the same time, rural populations have continued to decline as young people seek richer professional and personal opportunities in our nation's large and small cities. We therefore begin with a discussion of rural America and suburbia before moving on to look at larger metropolitan areas.

The Decline of Rural America?

Rural areas of the United States are defined by the U.S. Bureau of the Census residually, as all those places located outside of urban areas. They typically have fewer than 2,500 people and are often areas where people live in open country. In the 1950s, rural areas accounted for more than a third (36 percent) of the U.S. population; as of the most recent Census (2010), that figure has declined to less than a fourth (19 percent), even though rural America contains most of the country's land mass (97 percent), (Ratcliffe et al., 2016; America Counts, 2017). Population decline in rural areas is the result of many factors: the mechanization of agriculture, which replaced more labor-intensive small family farms with large mechanized industrial farms; lack of economic opportunities, reflected in high rates of poverty; the attraction of urban lifestyles for younger people; and, in some regions, a dearth of natural amenities such as forests, lakes, or temperate winters. The outmigration of young people in particular has meant that fewer babies are born to replace the aging rural population (Johnson, 2006). As a result, many rural areas have disproportionately high numbers of older adults, a phenomenon called **aging in place** that explains the relatively old populations in rural areas in the "Rust Belt" (the area around the Great Lakes and upper Midwest that has lost industry) (McGranahan and Beale, 2002).

One out of every four rural children lives in poverty, higher than the urban rate (one out of every five) (NLIHC, 2015). According to one report, of the 50 U.S. counties

About 19 percent of Americans live in rural areas, such as Hensley, West Virginia. According to the U.S. Census, rural areas are those with fewer than 2,500 people.

with the highest rates of poverty, 48 are rural (*The Atlantic*, 2016). Race also shapes rural poverty, just as it shapes urban poverty. Rural counties with the highest child-poverty rates often have majority non-White populations. These areas include Black-majority counties in the Mississippi Delta and counties in the Midwest and West that have large Native American populations, often dwelling on Indian reservations (O'Hare and Mather, 2008).

High rates of poverty in rural areas are associated with a host of other social problems. A large body of research has found that people who live in rural areas are beset with numerous health-related issues, such as disease and disability, obesity, injury, and chronic pain (Monnat and Beeler Pickett, 2011; Schiller et al., 2012). Partly as a result, life expectancies are shorter (Singh and Siahpush, 2014); rates of alcohol- and drug-related mortality and suicide are higher (Hedegaard et al., 2018). Opioid addiction and abuse, a growing problem throughout the United States, were once thought to be especially prevalent in rural areas, although the most detailed study to date found that opioid-related deaths among non-Hispanic Whites were actually highest in large metropolitan counties, partly because opioids were more readily available there. While opioid deaths varied across rural counties, some of the highest rates in all U.S. counties were found in rural counties where mines had closed or other jobs were lost. The economic distress of those who remained behind, often coupled with family breakdown, went hand-in-hand with psychological distress; anxiety, despair, and hopelessness resulted in alcohol abuse, drug addiction, and suicide. It is important to emphasize that all rural life is not bleak; there are enormous variations between rural areas (Monnat, 2019).

One indication that many rural areas still have strong appeal is that the decline in rural population appears to have leveled off in 2011–2012 and has since begun a slight uptick (USDA, 2018). And some of the most rapidly growing counties in the United States are rural: North Dakota's Williams County, for example, was the fastest-growing county in the United States between 2010 and 2018. Its 22,400 people grew to 35,350 (a three-fifths increase), driven in part by oil and agriculture (US Census, 2019f; Williams County, 2019). The economic recovery of the past decade may be part of the reason, although some surveys show that many Americans would prefer to live in rural areas rather than large cities, if they had a choice. A recent poll (Gallup, 2018), for example, found that more than a quarter of all respondents (27 percent) said they would choose a rural area. The preference for rural living, however, was strongest (31 percent) among respondents over 50; respondents 18–29 overwhelmingly chose big cities (17 percent) and their suburbs (28 percent). While city lights still hold their allure for younger people, this may change, as information technology increasingly provides the flexibility to work at home, even when that home is distant from the office.

Suburbanization

In the United States, **suburbanization**—the massive development and inhabiting of towns surrounding a city—rapidly increased during the 1950s and 1960s, a time of great economic growth. During the postwar decade, the population in cities increased by 10 percent, whereas in the suburban areas, it grew by nearly half. A series of federal

> **suburbanization** The development of suburbia; areas of housing outside inner cities.

policies after World War II encouraged Americans to pursue the "American dream": owning a house and a piece of land. The Federal Housing Administration (FHA) provided assistance in obtaining mortgage loans, making it possible in the early postwar period for families to buy housing in the suburbs for less than they would have paid for rent in the cities. The FHA did not offer financial assistance to improve older homes or to build new homes in the central areas of ethnically mixed cities; its large-scale aid went only to the builders and buyers of suburban housing. The FHA, together with the Veterans Administration, which provided assistance to returning soldiers, funded almost half of all suburban housing built during the 1950s and 1960s.

President Eisenhower oversaw the passage of the Federal-Aid Highway Act in 1956, authorizing $32 billion ($300 billion in today's dollars) to be used for building the National System of Interstate and Defense Highways. Gasoline taxes were also used to fund the emerging interstate highway system, which launched today's network of freeways and toll roads. The interstate highway system both resulted from—and contributed to—the expansion of the automobile industry, as the two-car family became common. High-speed highways and the rapidly growing number of cars that came to rely on them provided a boost in the postwar economy. At the same time, they enabled families to move to lower-tax, less expensive suburbs, and drive to work in neighboring cities. As industries and services followed people to the suburbs, commuting between suburbs also became common. Suburbs eventually became more racially and ethnically diverse; by 2010, minorities had come to comprise 35 percent of all suburban residents—close to their proportion of the overall U.S. population—although the fastest-growing, low-density, distant suburbs (so-called "exurbs") remained largely White (Brookings Institution, 2011). Members of minority groups move to the suburbs for reasons similar to those who preceded them: better housing, schools, and amenities. Like the people who began the exodus to suburbia in the 1950s, they are mostly middle-class professionals.

Today, scholars debate whether the divide between "suburb" and "city" is meaningful, as many older suburbs, often on the fringes of major cities, share many characteristics that were once hallmarks of city life—pockets of poverty, an aging housing stock (occupied by aging residents), old infrastructure, growing immigrant populations, and little land left for new development that will generate property-tax revenue. These inner suburbs stand in stark contrast to outer suburbs that have new housing stock, expanses of open land, and populations that tend to be more racially and ethnically homogeneous. As a result, researchers increasingly use the terms *urban area* or *metropolitan area* to describe regions that encompass central cities and their immediate outskirts. Between 2010 and 2018, metropolitan areas—encompassing center cities and their surrounding suburbs—grew by 19 million people (7.1 percent). Roughly 86 percent of the U.S. population now lives in metropolitan areas (some 281 million people) (U.S. Bureau of the Census, 2019f).

While the last several decades saw a movement from the cities to the suburbs, they also witnessed a shift in the regional distribution of the U.S. population from north to south and east to west. Between 2010 and 2018, regional growth was much more rapid in the South (8.6 percent) and West (8.2 percent) than in the Northeast (1.3 percent) and Midwest (2.0 percent). Overall, the South and West accounted for 88.4 percent of the total U.S. population growth between 2000 and 2010 (U.S. Bureau of the Census, 2019i).

Suburban Levittown, New York, in the 1950s (left). A new housing development in the exurb of Highland, California (right).

Urban Problems: Gentrification, Urban Renewal, and Racial Segregation

Beginning in the 1950s, many major U.S. cities—particularly in the Northwest and Midwest—began losing businesses, jobs, and middle-class residents, who fled to the suburbs. Millions of blue-collar jobs disappeared, which particularly affected the poorly educated, who were drawn mostly from minority groups. By the 1990s, an urban underclass had emerged, partly as the result of an economic transformation that was replacing manufacturing jobs with information economy jobs requiring new skills, or low-wage service sector employment (Kasarda, 1993). William Julius Wilson (1991, 1996) has argued that the problems of the urban underclass grew out of this economic transformation (see Chapter 8).

More recently, there has been a revival of many central cities, as wealthier professionals in some regions have moved back into downtown areas. This revival has resulted in a process of **gentrification** whereby older, deteriorated housing and other buildings are renovated as more affluent groups move into an area. Such a renewal process is called *gentrification* because those areas or buildings become upgraded and return to the control of the urban "gentry"—high-income dwellers—rather than remain in the hands of the poor. Gentrification sometimes results from market forces, as when wealthier newcomers buy up cheap, run-down properties and fix them up, resulting in neighborhood changes that attract other affluent buyers, in a cycle that eventually drives up housing prices and rents, forcing out the poor who can no longer afford housing costs. Gentrification is nothing new—30 years ago sociologist Elijah Anderson (1990) analyzed the effect of gentrification in a Philadelphia neighborhood. He found that many Black residences were condemned, forcing more than a thousand

> **gentrification** A process in which older, deteriorated housing and other buildings are renovated as more affluent groups move into an area.

people to leave in search of more affordable neighborhoods. The White newcomers had come in search of cheap "antique" housing, closer access to their city-based jobs, and a trendy urban lifestyle. Over time, the neighborhood was gradually transformed into a White middle-class enclave.

Often gentrification results not purely from market forces but is the result of government policies that put public funds into poor areas. **Urban renewal** (sometimes called **urban redevelopment**) is the process of renovating deteriorating neighborhoods by using public funds to renew old buildings and construct new ones, often through large-scale demolition of slum housing. While the twin processes of gentrification and urban renewal are not new, they gained force after World War II, in large part when the 1949 and 1954 Federal Housing Acts pumped billions of federal dollars into urban renewal programs in run-down urban areas, leading Black novelist James Baldwin to describe urban renewal as "Negro removal." The Federal Highway-Aid Act resulted in another form of slum clearance, since it enabled federal and state governments to build expressways through urban areas that were almost always occupied by low-income African Americans. Gentrification and urban renewal may have made downtown areas more desirable for affluent professionals, but they have driven out those who are unable to afford the higher housing costs, including many middle-class households. Areas that were especially hard-hit included several major urban areas in California: San Francisco/Oakland/San Jose (home to Silicon Valley), Orange County, and San Diego (Uh, 2016).

These economic changes and public policies also contributed to increased residential segregation of different racial and ethnic groups and social classes, as we saw in Chapter 11. Discriminatory practices by home sellers, real estate agents, and mortgage lending institutions further added to this pattern of segregation. One-quarter of the roughly 29 million African Americans living in the largest metropolitan areas are found in segregated neighborhoods, defined as neighborhoods where more than four out of every five residents are Black (24/7 Wall St., 2016). How can this be the case, when racial segregation was outlawed more than a half century ago by the 1968 Fair Housing Act?

While some may argue that this is because most people prefer to live in racially homogeneous neighborhoods populated by people similar to themselves, it turns out that racial segregation today is in large part the result of government housing policies that began during the Great Depression of the 1930s and continued for several decades after World War II. Richard Rothstein (2017) argues that housing built under the federal Public Works Administration was deliberately segregated, with most going to Whites. After World War II, the 1949 Housing Act provided Federal Housing Administration (FHA) guarantees for bank loans, enabling the construction of large-scale White-only housing developments, with deeds that prohibited resale to African Americans (so-called restrictive covenants). At the local level, African American neighborhoods were frequently rezoned to allow industrial (and often toxic) uses, effectively turning them into slums. These and other government policies enabled White working-class Americans to buy homes in decent neighborhoods at affordable prices, while consigning most African Americans to rental housing in substandard areas.

Over many decades, home ownership became the principal source of wealth for White Americans as their homes appreciated in value over time. Rothstein argues that this historical race-based denial of equal home-ownership opportunities resulted in an enormous racial wealth gap that persists today. While Black income is currently around 60 percent of White income, Black wealth is only 5 percent to 7 percent of White wealth, making it more difficult for Blacks to buy homes at today's prices or afford to send their children to college. These challenges are especially severe for low-income (and disproportionately minority)

For his Pulitzer Prize–winning ethnography *Evicted: Power and Profit in the American City*, sociologist Matthew Desmond conducted participant observation research of the private housing market, illuminating the often exploitative relationship between landlords and their poor tenants.

households, since there is an acute shortage of affordable rental units (NLIHC, 2017). Moreover, the landlord-tenant relationship is often exploitative: In the absence of rent and eviction controls, landlords will charge whatever the market will bear, and can legally evict tenants for any (or no) reason—for example, to find tenants who can afford significant rent increases. Frequent evictions, requiring moves to new neighborhoods, can serve to undermine long-term relations in low-income communities. The ties among the urban poor become weaker; the social ties that contribute to a health community become what sociologist Matthew Desmond (2016) has termed "disposable." Evictions can be highly destructive of individuals and communities; Desmond's work points to the central importance of affordable housing programs in a broad range of antipoverty policies.

The Ghetto as a Social and Historical Problem

Many Americans mistakenly believe that *ghetto* means a place where African Americans or Latinos live, but the word originated in sixteenth-century Italy and applied to areas of Rome and Venice where Jews were forced to live by official decree, as a way of isolating them from mainstream Christian society.

Sociologists originally drew a distinction between ghettos on the one hand and slums on the other. Ghettos were residential zones where particular groups were forced to live, not necessarily because they were poor, but because they belonged to a particular ethnic or racial group viewed as inferior and therefore in need of being forcibly cordoned off by the wider society. Slums, on the other hand, were zones inhabited by poor people who couldn't afford to live elsewhere, including members of a dominant, nonstigmatized group, such as poor Whites in the United States. In recent years, many sociologists have started using the terms *ghetto* and *slum* interchangeably, but it is better to retain the analytical clarity inherent in the former distinction.

A crucial criterion for the definition of the ghetto is that the people who live there must have been forced to do so. Indeed, this was the situation of Blacks in the United States and Jews in Rome. In the United States, Blacks were forced to live in certain parts of the northern cities because of restrictive covenants that made it illegal to sell them land in particular neighborhoods. Jews were forced to live in ghettos because of decrees by the popes. During the fourteenth century, most Jews were also forced to wear insignias when they traveled outside the zones where they lived, to indicate that they were Jews.

Whereas the inhabitants of the original ghettos were given little choice of where they could live, inhabitants of today's ghettos may feel that they live in their highly segregated and impoverished neighborhoods by choice. Sociological studies have demonstrated over and again that when poor people have an opportunity to move, they will often resist every chance to do so. This is not because they do not want to improve their life chances, but because they do not believe their lives would be better independent of the social networks and neighborhood institutions that sustain them, even in their poor and segregated neighborhoods.

Are ghettos necessarily zones for the economically marginalized and exploited populations of stigmatized people? Whereas the U.S. ghetto was used to warehouse a significant labor supply for growing factories during the two world wars, the Jewish ghetto of Venice did not originally seem to have such a mission. Jews were very successful, and they continued to have significant economic ties to the wider society long after they were ghettoized (Stow, 2000). Ultimately, laws were enacted that made it difficult for Jews to carry on their occupations, but these were not intrinsic to ghettoization.

There have been many ghettos in the history of the world, but there are no sociological studies that compare ghettos in more than a few societies. For this reason, there is still much to know about the characteristics that would define the ghetto concept. From what we know, a ghetto is a residential zone in which stigmatized racial or religious groups are compelled to live by the wider society.

This takes us to an example in the contemporary United States. When Hurricane Katrina struck New Orleans, Louisiana, in August 2005, the victims of the floods that ravaged the city in the storm's aftermath were mainly poor Blacks who lived in the most impoverished ghettos of the city. Why were these poor people disproportionately affected by the extreme weather conditions? The answer has mainly to do with the social and political history of these particular residential zones, which were always given fewer resources for drainage and pumping systems after past storms. It also has to do with the limited resources that poor people have to evacuate and the limited networks they have outside the zones where they live. By contrast with the poor Blacks who were trapped inside the ghettos as they flooded, many middle-class Whites had the resources and social connections to leave the city when warnings first appeared on the national news. The effect of Hurricane Katrina followed the fault lines of the larger urban problems that are associated with racial segregation and ghettoization in the inner cities today.

Explosive Urbanization in the Global South

Most urban growth is now occurring in cities in the global south, in regions with large populations. Africa remains mostly rural, with 57 percent of its 1.3 billion people still living in rural areas—a figure that rises to 72 percent in eastern Africa. Parts of Asia also remain highly rural: Nearly two-thirds (64 percent) of South Asia's 1.9 billion people still live outside of urban areas (a region that includes India, Bangladesh, Nepal, and Pakistan) (UN DESA, 2018c). By mid-century, this is predicted to change dramatically. By 2050, 59 percent of all Africans and 54 percent of southern Asians will be living in urban areas—a rural-urban shift involving some 1.5 billion people in these two regions alone. For the less developed regions of the world as a whole (excluding China), the rural-urban shift is predicted to involve more than 2 billion people. These shifts are likely due to two factors: The previously noted higher birthrates in poor countries, in urban as well as rural areas, and widespread *internal migration* from rural areas to urban ones, as rural poverty prompts many people to try their hand at city life: According to the World Bank (2017b), urban areas account for roughly four-fifths of the world's gross domestic product. China is a case in point: Over the past three decades, as China transitioned from a largely impoverished country to the world's second largest economy, it also transitioned from being 26 percent to 61 percent urban. In what is likely the largest internal migration in history, hundreds of millions of Chinese moved from farms and villages to giant cities, where jobs in factories and supporting services could be found (UNDESA, 2018b, 2018c).

There are currently 31 megacities with 10 million or more inhabitants, 24 of which are in the global south, including Lagos, Nigeria. It is predicted that by 2030 there will be 43 megacities, each with more than 10 million people.

Residents of South New Delhi, India, collect water from a government water tank. Access to safe water supplies is a chronic problem in urban areas of the global south.

Rapid urbanization in the global south may provide the promise of work and a better life for many, but it has brought many problems as well. Factory jobs turn out to require endless hours, provide low pay, are completely lacking in basic workers' rights, and involve extremely hazardous working conditions. To take one example, over the past couple decades more than 2,000 factory workers have perished in fires and building collapses in Bangladesh, a country that has emerged as a major source of garment manufacturing (Appelbaum and Lichtenstein, 2016). Because the migration to cities often exceeds the available jobs, an informal economy emerges consisting of unregulated work done for cash "off the books" that is barely a step above poverty (Chapter 14). In India, for example, the informal economy accounts for 84 percent of nonagricultural employment (ILO, 2013). While such work may be important for helping thousands of families (and women especially) to survive in urban conditions, it is often harsh and exploitative. And since it is off the books, it is also untaxed, denying the state badly needed revenues.

Another problem of rapid urbanization in the global south is housing: As many as a billion people are now forced to live in makeshift shantytowns and squatter settlements on the fringes of megacities, resulting in what urban historian Mike Davis (2007) has graphically described as a "planet of slums." Brazil's two largest cities, Rio de Janeiro and São Paulo, house millions of people in makeshift hillside shantytowns called *favelas*; it is estimated that in Rio alone, nearly a quarter of the city's 6 million residents live in roughly a thousand such communities. While some *favelas* are notorious for being dangerous, crime-ridden places that lack adequate water, sanitation, and basic urban services, many serve as functioning communities for the city's urban poor, the only housing that they can afford (Catalytic Communities, 2015). Living in even crime-ridden shantytowns is preferable to the only alternative that many urban poor face: living on the streets.

The Environment: A Sociological Issue

The environment is a central concern for sociology. Growing human population, industrialization, and the concentration of people in enormous metropolitan areas have resulted in environmental challenges that play out on a planetary scale. Earth system scientists now agree: Humans play a starring role in global warming and climate change. Sociologists therefore have a role to play in understanding how social behavior may determine the environmental fate of the planet.

The New Ecological Paradigm in Sociology

A change in thinking about human–environmental relations emerged in the 1970s. Classical sociology had tended to minimize, if not completely ignore, the importance of human impacts on the environment. This was partly because the negative impacts were less pervasive (recall that by 1900 there were still fewer than 2 billion people in the world), but primarily because sociology, like much of social science thought, generally took for granted human domination of nature (Leiss, 1994).

As we saw in Chapter 1, sociology emerged during the late nineteenth and early twentieth centuries, a period that reflected what has been termed "optimistic ethnocentrism" during an "age of exuberance" (Catton and Dunlap, 1980). This refers to the belief that science, technology, and industrial development, fueled by vast lands and resources in North and South America, as well as a seemingly endless supply of fossil fuel, would provide for limitless opportunity and endless progress. This view has been termed the *Human Exceptionalism Paradigm* (HEP), reflecting the belief that humans are unique among all creatures: We dominate all species and can remake the world to serve our needs, since human destiny is shaped by social and cultural factors and not the physical environment (Catton and Dunlap, 1980).

This view held sway until the early 1970s, when it was seriously challenged by a growing number of sociologists and ecologists. This was a period during which social movements were already questioning prevailing worldviews, including the taken-for-granted assumption that human life could somehow be divorced from the natural world. The HEP was further challenged when an offshore oil-drilling platform in the Santa Barbara Channel in California blew out in early 1969, covering miles of pristine coastline with oil, killing thousands of birds and creating the largest ecological disaster in U.S. history. The oil spill received widespread media attention; President Nixon even paid a visit. It inspired the first Earth Day, as well as one of the country's first environmental studies programs, at UC Santa Barbara. The oil spill also highlighted the tensions between the petroleum industry and local residents, raising questions about the nature of power in America (Molotch, 1970). Popular books such as Rachel Carson's *Silent Spring* (1962), which exposed the effects of pesticides on water, had already raised public awareness about environmental issues. The Club of Rome's *Limits to Growth* study (Meadows et al., 1972), which used computer modeling to analyze the complex interaction among such factors as population, food production, industrialization, capital flows, pollution, and natural resources, predicted global economic and demographic collapse before the year 2100.

The change in thinking about human–environmental relations that emerged in the 1970s was labeled the New Ecological Paradigm (NEP), a framework that emphasized the complex interactions involved in global ecosystems. Humans, it argued, are not somehow exempt from the "web of nature," and our biophysical environment is not limitless. On the contrary, the carrying capacity of our planet is limited, and we must come to understand and respect these limits, or we will pay a price (Catton and Dunlap, 1980; Schnaiberg, 1980; Dunlap, 2002; Buttel, 1987; Freudenberg, Frickel, and Gramling, 1995).

Sociologist Allen Schnaiberg's influential book, *The Environment: From Surplus to Scarcity* (1980), argued that in the post–World War II period, capitalism's profit-driven need to produce and sell more and more products had resulted in an ever-expanding global demand for natural resources and cheap labor. The resulting adverse environmental impacts were seen as especially felt in developing countries, where natural resources and cheap labor are found and extracted by firms in wealthy industrial countries. Rich countries therefore export their pollution and natural resource depletion to poor, less developed ones. Economics trumps ecology; labor, capital, and states all share an interest in economic expansion that interact in a system bent on ecological degradation. As technological innovation speeds the process, natural resources are depleted and environmental destruction becomes widespread in Schnaiberg's phrase a "treadmill of production" that increases in speed with ever diminished returns, resulting in toxic planetary ecological effects.

Schnaiberg's work is credited with creating the field of environmental sociology (Islam, 2015; Gould, Pellow, and Schnaiberg, 2004, 2008), which is concerned with examining the relationships between social systems and the ecosphere. Environmental sociologists study such areas as the origins and impacts of technology, the relationship between social change and environmental change, and the role of social inequality and power relationships in shaping human interactions with the environment (American Sociological Association, 2019). The once-radical ideas of the early environmental sociologists have by now become mainstream in environmental sociology (Pellow and Brehm, 2013, 2015).

The New Ecological Paradigm challenged another sociological theory about human–environmental relations that emerged at roughly the same time, Ecological Modernization Theory. Just as classical Modernization Theory (discussed in Chapter 8) argued that when poor countries pursue certain economic and technological policies they can find a path to economic development, Ecological Modernization Theory argued that when poor countries develop economically, they also turn a corner and reduce their environmental impact. This notion is embodied in the so-called Environmental Kuznets Curve, which predicts that during early stages of economic development, economic growth (measured, for example, by a country's per-capita income) results in environmental degradation; but that when a certain level of development is reached, policies and technologies are adopted that reduce environmental impact. The Environmental Kuznets Curve, like the original Kuznets Curve (also discussed in Chapter 8), thus argues that a form of inequality increases during early stages of capitalist economic development, then declines at later stages—in this case, environmental inequality rather than income inequality (Dinda, 2004). If the New Ecological Paradigm viewed economic degradation as a largely inevitable result of capitalism, Ecological Modernization Theory argued that a combination of scientific and technological advances, market reforms, new forms of governance, and social movements could make a difference (Jänicke, 1991; Spaargare and Mol, 1992; Jänicke and Weidner, 1995; Neale, 1997; Mol and Sonnenfeld, 2000). The former called for radical changes in existing economic systems; the latter favored reforms, possibly in part because the early scholars were largely European, where national policies tended to be more disposed toward environmental protection than those of the United States.

Global Environmental Threats

The spread of industrial production may already have done irreparable damage to the environment. Ecological questions concern not only how we can best cope with and contain environmental damage but also the very ways of life within industrialized societies. Economic development in many countries has meant that more people are living under better conditions than a half century ago, thanks to rising levels of consumption: As living standards rise, people are able to afford more food, clothing, personal items, leisure time, vacations, cars, travel, and all the goods and services associated with middle-class life. But rapidly expanding global consumption requires energy to produce and transport goods, which pollutes the environment. During the twenty-year period from 1997 to 2017, per-person income, one measure of consumption, in the world as a whole increased by nearly 40 percent. In China, now the world's second largest economy, per-person income increased more than fourfold during the same period (World Bank, 2019k). If China, with nearly a fifth of the world population, reaches its understandable goal of achieving economic parity with the United States and other advanced industrial countries, the environmental impact of such massive consumption could be extreme.

According to one popular website, Global Footprint Network, if all people on earth were somehow to achieve the standard of living of the average American, it would require seven planets to feed, clothe, shelter, and provide the countless consumer items that make up what most of us consider a decent life. While such calculations are perhaps somewhat fanciful, the overall message is not: Our current path, whether as a nation or as all humanity, is no longer sustainable. Technological progress is, of course, unpredictable, and it may be that the earth will, in fact, yield sufficient resources to permit global industrialization without it resulting in irreversible ecological changes to the planet. At the moment, however, this does not seem feasible, and if the countries in the global south are to achieve living standards comparable to those currently enjoyed in the West, global readjustments will be necessary.

Global environmental threats are of several basic sorts: global warming and climate change, the loss of biodiversity, food insecurity, and environmental injustice. We will look at each of these in turn, before turning to a consideration of what is being done to address them.

Global Warming and Climate Change: Welcome to the Anthropocene

There is consensus in the scientific community that the earth is getting warmer, even more quickly than was believed to be the case a decade ago, and that the human use of energy—coal, oil, and gas—is largely responsible. Global warming occurs because carbon dioxide, methane, and other greenhouse gases are released into the atmosphere by the burning of fuels such as oil and coal in cars and power stations, as well as gases released into the air by the use of such things as aerosols, material for insulation, and air-conditioning units. This buildup of greenhouse gases in the earth's atmosphere functions like the glass of a greenhouse. The atmosphere allows the sun's rays to pass through but acts as a barrier to prevent the rays from passing back, causing the Earth to heat up. For this reason, global warming is sometimes termed the "greenhouse effect." Atmospheric carbon dioxide, which has been increasing since the Industrial Revolution, has risen steeply in the last half century, and now exceeds 400 parts per million (climate scientists believe that once carbon dioxide levels reach 450 parts per million, it will be extremely difficult, if not impossible, to keep global temperatures from increasing more than 2 degrees Centigrade). It is estimated that nearly half (47 percent) of atmospheric carbon dioxide has resulted from human activities since the Industrial Revolution, with more than half of all industrial emissions reportedly occurring in the last 30 years (Friedlingstein et al., 2019; Frumhoff, 2014).

The U.S. Energy Information Administration (2016) projected that worldwide energy use will increase by nearly 50 percent between 2012 and 2040, and more than half of that increase will occur in China and India. In 2010, those two countries accounted for 24 percent of the total growth in energy use. If current trends continue, the EIA predicts that by 2040, China will be using more than twice the energy of the United States (Figure 19.2). Despite breakthroughs in renewable energy, it is predicted that fossil fuels will still comprise more than three-quarters of global energy consumption.

Most of America's energy currently comes from nonrenewable fossil fuels—mainly petroleum and, to a lesser degree, coal and natural gas. According to U.S. government figures, the United States consumes 21 percent of the world's petroleum, 22 percent of its natural gas, and 11 percent of its coal, and produces 16 percent of all carbon emissions that result from fossil-fuel consumption (U.S. EIA, 2017). Since the United States has less than 5 percent of the world's population, it is clearly consuming a greatly enlarged share of global energy reserves. This is what sociologist Bill Freudenberg termed the *disproportionality thesis*, according to which a vastly disproportionate amount of environmental harm is being done by a small number of countries, in which the United States is a principal actor (Freudenberg, 2006).

While China's growth is predicted to greatly increase its use of energy, it is currently second to the United States, consuming 13 percent of the world's petroleum (US EIA, 2019c). Unlike the United States, China relies heavily on coal, which produces more carbon dioxide than petroleum to produce the same amount of energy, although it is in the process of shutting down its most polluting coal plants and switching to "clean coal" as well as renewables. When all greenhouse gases are taken into account, China surpassed the United States as the world's largest emitter in 2005, and currently accounts for 27 percent of the world total, twice the share of the United States (13 percent). Yet when making comparisons it is important to bear in mind that China is an industrializing country with four times the U.S. population. On a per person basis, the United States is by far the world's largest producer of greenhouse gases: It currently emits twice as much carbon dioxide per person as China (Oliver and Peters, 2018). Also recall that China's greenhouse gas emissions come in large part from factories that are making products that we all consume, for firms that are headquartered in the United States, Europe, and Japan. In an important sense, therefore, the production of greenhouse gases has been outsourced to firms in China as well as other industrializing countries.

In 2007, the Intergovernmental Panel on Climate Change (IPCC), a blue-ribbon group of scientists from 195 countries created by the United Nations Development Programme (UNDP) and the United Nations' World Meteorological Organization in 1988, took the planet's temperature and found it had already increased by 1 degree Celsius (1.8 degrees Fahrenheit) since pre-industrial times (the period 1850–1900 is used as an approximation) and has been rising steeply since the mid-twentieth century. Rising temperatures result in the rapid shrinking of Arctic ice caps, along with mountain glaciers; long-term droughts in some regions, with greater rainfall in others; an increase in hurricane activity in the North

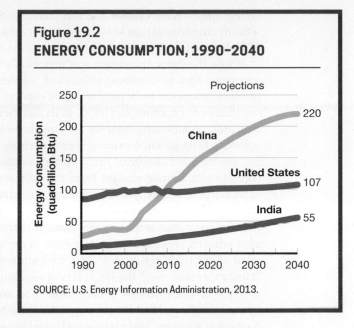

Figure 19.2
ENERGY CONSUMPTION, 1990–2040

SOURCE: U.S. Energy Information Administration, 2013.

Atlantic; and, in general, more turbulence in global weather. Most significantly, the 2007 IPCC report stated unequivocally that human activity was the principal source of global warming, very likely causing most of the temperature increase over the last century.

By 2014, when the IPCC issued its synthesis report based on the most recent research, the experts warned of "severe, pervasive, and irreversible impacts for people and ecosystems," including continued global warming to 2 degrees Celsius (3.6 degrees Fahrenheit) by the end of the century, more frequent and longer-lasting heat waves, and more extreme weather such as tropical storms, cyclones, and hurricanes. The best hope was to limit the total increase to no more than 1.5 degrees Celsius (2.7 degrees Fahrenheit) from pre-industrial levels, which meant only another 0.5 degree Celsius (0.9 degree Fahrenheit) from current levels (Intergovernmental Panel on Climate Change, 2015). The 2014 IPCC report suggested ways to mitigate the worst consequences of global warming. The first and most important step would be for the countries of the world to adopt conservation measures that would limit global warming to no more than 2 degrees Celsius (and, as noted above, 1.5 degrees Celsius is necessary if major climate changes are to be avoided). This would require national policies that reduce greenhouse gas emissions, which in turn would require massive conversion from economies based on fossil fuels to economies based on clean energy. In December 2015, 195 nations met in Paris and reached an agreement to limit temperature increase to no more than 1.5 degrees Celsius (2.7 degrees Fahrenheit). Each country agreed to submit a climate plan. The United States, for example, committed to a 2025 goal of greenhouse-gas emissions 26 percent to 28 percent lower than they were in 2005. China took a somewhat different approach, pledging to lower emissions per unit of GDP by 60 to 65 percent (which would mean total emissions would continue to rise at least until 2030, since China hopes to continue building its rapidly growing

GDP). The Paris Agreement also included a "loss and damage" principle, under which wealthy countries agreed to create a fund to help poorer countries cope with the effects of global warming (UNFCC, 2015).

While the Paris Agreement was historically significant and was seen by many as a hopeful sign, it is unclear whether it will be honored. There are no enforcement mechanisms, apart from regular public reports that may shame countries into fulfilling their commitments. The IPCC, in its October 2018 Special Report, expressed grave concerns, commenting "that we are already seeing the consequences of 1°C of global warming through more extreme weather, rising sea levels and diminishing Arctic sea ice, among other changes." The report also noted that greenhouse gas emissions continue to rise, despite pledges from virtually every country to lower them, and that substantial action by governments and the private sector are required if the goal of limiting temperature increase to 1.5 degrees Celsius is to be realized. The report gave the world less than a dozen years (until 2030) to achieve the 1.5 degree Celsius goal, after which it predicted far greater risks of droughts, floods, and extreme heat waves, all of which could result in poverty for hundreds of millions of people (Watts, 2018). "Now more than ever," the IPCC report concludes, "unprecedented and urgent action is required of all nations" if the world is to avoid extreme hot days, an increase in heavy rainfalls and flooding in some areas and prolonged droughts in others, stronger melting of ice sheets and glaciers and a resulting increased sea level rise (IPCC, 2018).

A separate IPCC report on the oceans, glaciers, and permafrost, published a year later, noted a significant shrinkage of the earth's glaciers, snow cover, and Arctic sea ice, a warming of the oceans, and a melting of northern permafrost in recent decades (IPCC, 2019b). According to the report, melting glaciers have resulted in sea levels that have risen more in the past century than at any time during the past several thousand years, and resulted in coastal flooding. The predicted increase in average global temperature was sufficient, in the eyes of some scientists, to destabilize the ice sheets that cover Greenland and the western part of Antarctica; were they to melt in their entirety, sea levels would rise an estimated 30 feet or more. While such a catastrophic event seems unlikely in the foreseeable future, in 2019 the Greenland ice sheet lost 300 billion tons of ice, far more than normal, the result of record hot weather during the summer months (Tutton, 2019; NSIDC, 2019).

The report also noted an increase in tropical cyclones, rainfall, and winds from warming oceans; threats to ecologically (and economically) important animal plant species; wildfires in many regions; and negative impacts on food security and water. For the first time, the IPCC also emphasized the negative effects on indigenous peoples, who depend most heavily on their natural surroundings for sustenance (IPCC, 2019b). The period 2001–2018 saw 17 of the 18 hottest years ever recorded; July 2019 was the hottest month since records have been kept. In the United States, wildfires now afflict large regions of the western United States, while storm surges and river flooding have plagued Houston and the Midwest. While specific weather events cannot be definitively tied to global climate change, it seems increasingly likely that warmer weather is a major cause.

Such global warming, in combination with population growth and urbanization, can have deadly consequences. One study predicts that heat-related deaths in India will double by 2080, the direct result of global warming (*Economic Times*, 2015);

another study drew similar conclusions for New York City (Freedman, 2013). In Pakistan, 1,250 people died during a heat wave in June 2015, and during spring 2016, Karachi—Pakistan's largest city, with more than 22 million people—began to run out of water, with people queuing up for hours for potable water that had to be brought in on trucks (Awaz.TV, 2016). Nor is Pakistan alone; currently, two-thirds of the global population "live in areas that experience water scarcity for at least one month a year" (UNESCO, 2017c). A November 2019 report in the prestigious medical journal *Lancet*, that drew on the findings of 35 leading academic institutions and UN agencies from every continent, concluded that if present trends continue, "a child born today will experience a world that is more than four degrees warmer than the pre-industrial average, with climate change impacting human health from infancy and adolescence to adulthood and old age," noting that children and the 65+ population will suffer the greatest risks (Watts et al., 2019).

While climate skeptics claim that climate scientists overstate the case for climate change, in fact the opposite is more likely: Advances in scientific knowledge and measurement have made it clear that the earliest scientific studies of climate change in fact underestimated the rate of change (Oreskes, Oppenheimer, and Jamieson, 2019; Oppenheimer et al., 2019; Linden, 2019). Debra Roberts, co-chair of the IPCC working group on impacts, warns that "it's a line in the sand and what it says to our species is that this is the moment and we must act now. . . . This is the largest clarion bell from the science community, and I hope it mobilizes people and dents the mood of complacency" (Watts, 2018). Such changes have led to the claim that we are now experiencing a "climate emergency" that must be urgently addressed (Gills and Morgan, 2019; IPCC, 2018; Watts, 2018).

Such dramatic climate change, and the scientific consensus that they are the result of human activities, has led earth-system scientists to argue that we are now in a newly identified geological era: the **Anthropocene** (Oldfield et al., 2018). At the turn of the twenty-first century, Paul Crutzen, an atmospheric chemist and recipient of the Nobel Prize in chemistry, popularized the term *Anthropocene* ("human epoch") to characterize the current geological period, a time when human activities have become the main agent of change in our planetary ecosystem (Crutzen and Stoermer, 2000). This label has caught on: The term has appeared in hundreds of scientific publications, and the International Union of Geological Sciences, the organization charged with identifying geological periods, has convened scholars to decide whether the Holocene (the period that began after the last ice age, some 12,000 years ago, providing the conditions under which modern human societies developed) has been officially superseded by the Anthropocene (Stromberg, 2013). The term is significant, because it reflects the overwhelming scientific consensus that humans have become the driving force behind global ecological change, and that global warming has significantly altered the conditions that gave rise to the agricultural revolution and modern societies. It recognizes that an understanding of the Anthropocene requires that many different disciplines work together, "from engineering and environmental science to the social sciences and humanities" (Oldfield et al., 2018).

Anthropocene A term used to denote the current geological epoch, in which many geologically significant conditions and processes are profoundly altered by human activities.

Loss of Biodiversity

Environmental ecology, the scientific study of the distribution and abundance of life and the interactions between organisms and their natural environment, highlights another challenge that results in part from global climate change: the planetary loss of biodiversity. According to a May 2019 UN report, "nature is declining globally at rates unprecedented in human history—and the rate of species extinctions is accelerating, with grave impacts on people around the world now likely" (IPBES, 2019). The report, which drew on 15,000 scientific and government sources, concluded that up to a million animal and plant species are threatened with extinction, out of a total eight million currently existing species—a threat it says is unprecedented in human history. Among land-based, freshwater, and sea-based species that have been studied in detail, an estimated one out of every four is believed to be threatened. A third of all coral reefs are imperiled, threatening the loss of a key habitat for many ocean species, as well as jeopardizing the welfare of those who depend on coral reefs for seafood, commercial fishing, and tourism. Even insects, which are vital for pollination of crops and plants, are in peril; as much as a tenth of all insect species are threatened (IPBES, 2019).

There are many causes of biodiversity loss. Growing global population and urbanization have altered three-quarters of our planet's land and two-thirds of its marine environments, with more than a third of all land and three-quarters of all freshwater resources now being used for crops or livestock. Deforestation, the result of timber harvesting, agricultural expansion, and fires, has increased significantly. Pollution from toxic industrial waste, runoff from fertilizers, and plastics has contributed to extensive ocean "dead zones"; plastic pollution alone has increased tenfold over the past 40 years. Global warming has made its own direct contribution to biodiversity loss, playing a role in massive forest fires, droughts, and flooding. As ocean temperatures have risen, and as the oceans absorb increasing amounts of atmospheric carbon dioxide, they also lose oxygen and become increasing acidic, destroying coral reefs and threatening the sea life that depends on them. Global warming has also meant the extinction of existing species ill-suited to the rising temperatures, and their replacement by other "invasive" species that are better suited, further reducing biodiversity (NOAA, 2019; IPBES, 2019; IPCC, 2019b).

Industrialized countries have become "throwaway societies," polluting the environment by routinely discarding a staggering volume of items: When we buy food in grocery stores it is often wrapped in packages that are immediately discarded; products bought online arrive in cardboard or plastic, which winds up in garbage dumps (and often the ocean); electronic waste—computers, cell phones, and the host of toys and gadgets that contain electronic circuits—are routinely "recycled" to landfills in poor countries, where there are few, if any, safeguards against contaminating local watersheds, farmlands, and communities.

The loss of biodiversity means more to humans than the loss of natural habitat, although many would agree with the nineteenth-century American writer Henry David Thoreau's spiritual musing, "In wilderness lies the preservation of the world." Biodiversity also provides humans with new medicines and sources and varieties of food, and it plays a role in regulating

environmental ecology The scientific study of the distribution and abundance of life and the interactions between organisms and their natural environment.

atmospheric and oceanic chemistry. The recent UN report concludes that "ecosystems, species, wild populations, local varieties and breeds of domesticated plants and animals are shrinking, deteriorating or vanishing. The essential, interconnected web of life on Earth is getting smaller and increasingly frayed. This loss is a direct result of human activity and constitutes a direct threat to human well-being in all regions of the world" (IPBES, 2019).

Food Security

Global warming, climate change, and the resulting losses of biodiversity already have had significant impacts on **food security**—access to sufficient, safe, and nutritious food that meets the need for an active and healthy life. A recent report by the Intergovernmental Panel on Climate Change noted that global food production is already challenged by increased population and rising incomes, the latter causing an increased demand for animal-sourced products that require additional land for livestock feed. Climate change is projected to worsen these stressors, with food insecurity found almost entirely in the developing world.

Recently, the human exceptionalism paradigm has been challenged by the new ecological paradigm, which emphasizes the complex interactions involved in global ecosystems. Some believe we have even entered a new geological era, the Anthropocene, in which humans are the main drivers of change in our ecosystems.

Persistent warming and long drought cycles, coupled with deforestation and land degradation, will have strong negative impacts on food production, the nutritional quality of the food that is produced, and increased damage from invasive pests and resulting crop diseases. Extreme climate change–related weather events, such as flooding, extreme heat, and associated droughts, will worsen food security still further. The result is "immediate and long-term impacts on livelihoods of poor and vulnerable communities, contributing to greater risks of food insecurity that can be a stress multiplier for internal and external migration" (IPCC, 2019a).

According to a report by the UN special rapporteur on the right to food, an estimated 821 million people were already undernourished in 2017, especially in parts of sub-Saharan Africa, Southeastern and Western Asia, and Latin America—a figure that, if current global warming trends continue, could rise to nearly a billion people by mid-century. The number at risk of hunger is predicted to increase by as much as 20 percent over the same period, with two-thirds located in sub-Saharan Africa.

Most of the world's poor live in rural areas; some 2.5 billion people depend on agriculture for their survival, providing food as well as household income. The UN report concludes that "climate change is undermining

> **food security** Having access to sufficient, safe, and nutritious food that meets the need for an active and healthy life.

the right to food, with disproportionate impacts on those who have contributed least to global warming and are most vulnerable to its harmful effects" (Elver, 2015a).

Environmental Injustice

Although the rich are the world's main consumers, the environmental damage that is caused by growing consumption has the greatest effect on the poor. The wealthy are in a better position to enjoy the many benefits of consumption without having to deal with its negative effects. The poor are the most vulnerable, since they lack access to the resources that might enable them to adjust to climate change. Sociologist Robert Bullard (1996) pioneered the concept of environmental justice, based on the principle that all people and communities are entitled to equal protection of a country's environmental and public health laws and regulations. Bullard studied the ways in which toxic environments in the United States, such as the location of highly polluting industrial plants, fell most heavily on the poor and racial minorities. Chemical plants, power stations, major roads, railways, and airports are often sited close to low-income areas. As Bullard succinctly summarizes his four decades of research, "Individuals who physically live on the 'wrong side of the tracks' are subjected to elevated environmental health threats and more than their fair share of preventable diseases" (Bullard, 2020).

> **environmental injustice** The harms suffered by ecosystems today are closely linked to and mirror the harms experienced by the most marginalized human beings across the planet.

With increased attention to the global environmental implications of climate change, Bullard's arguments have been extended globally (Agyeman, Bullard, and Edwards, 2003; Bullard, 2005; Bullard et al., 2016; Elver, 2015b) The notion of **environmental injustice**—that the harms suffered by ecosystems today are closely linked to and mirror the harms experienced by the most marginalized human beings across the planet—links the effects of climate change to the world's most vulnerable people (Pellow,

Kids play on a merry-go-round near an oil refinery at the Carver Terrace housing project playground in West Port Arthur, Texas. West Port Arthur sits squarely on a two-state corridor routinely ranked as one of the country's most polluted regions.

2017). On a global level, as we have already seen, soil degradation, deforestation, water shortages, and toxic emissions of all sorts are most heavily concentrated in the global south. Apart from severe droughts, which are turning once-fertile lands into deserts, global warming threatens the water supplies of hundreds of millions of people, increases the danger of flooding for others, adversely affects agriculture in parts of the world, and further reduces the planetary biodiversity on which many depend.

This alerts us to another aspect of global environmental injustice: the fact that the most toxic industries are located in the poorest nations with the fewest enforced

In Mexico City, a newspaper salesman uses a mask to protect himself from air pollution. Behind him a screen indicates the day's pollution levels.

protections for vulnerable workers and communities. If, as Bullard comments, living on the "wrong side of the tracks" in the United States means one is more likely to get the toxic dump, living on the "wrong side of the world" means getting the factory that dumps pollutants into the neighborhood water supply, or pumps them into the air that is breathed by local residents. Bangladesh and Pakistan, two countries where factories make clothing and textile for U.S. and European firms, are among the countries with the worst atmospheric pollution (World Population Review, 2019c).

Sadly, even efforts to be ecologically responsible in the United States can contribute to environmental injustice in poor countries. In the Indonesian village of Tropodo, a village of 5,000 people that makes much of the tofu that is part of the regional diet, the air is foul with acrid black smoke that results from burning paper and plastic waste, a major fuel in the tofu industrial process. The paper and plastic, in turn, originates with U.S. and other industrial countries' recycling efforts. Much of this material had previously gone to China for recycling, but in recent years, citing health and environmental concerns, China placed severe restrictions on receiving waste paper, discarded plastic and unwanted metals. Such "foreign garbage" (as China described it) wound up in other, poorer countries in the region, including Indonesia. While most of the recycled plastic was supposed to be repurposed in fleece jackets and athletic shoes, in fact much of it turned out to be unusable or intermixed with paper. Tofu manufacturers prefer burning the paper-plastic mix to burning wood, since it is far cheaper; yet this exacts a significant environmental health toll on the workers and the entire community. Plastic fumes contain a number of toxic substances, including dioxin, a highly toxic chemical that causes cancer, birth defects, and Parkinson's disease. It also gets into the soil, where it is ingested by local hens and winds up in the eggs that are consumed throughout the village (Ives, 2019; Paddock, 2019; IPEN, 2019).

Addressing Climate Change—What Is Being Done?

Given the scientific consensus that global warming and climate change require urgent attention if we are to avoid a "climate emergency" in the future, some steps have been taken to address its primary cause: greenhouse gas emissions. Governments, businesses, and ordinary citizens have all gotten in on the action. Are the actions that are currently being taken sufficient?

The Politics of Climate Change: National Action to Stop Global Warming

The Paris Agreement, as we have seen, has thus far failed to get countries to comply with the necessary greenhouse gas reductions that would limit post-industrial global warming to 1.5 degrees Celsius, or even 2.0 degrees. It was further weakened in 2017, when President Trump announced that the United States would no longer honor it. Following nearly two years of negotiations, formal withdrawal was announced in November 2019, to become effective late 2020. The United States' official reasons for withdrawal, as stated by Secretary of State Mike Pompeo, were that compliance with the Paris Agreement would hamper economic growth, and that the United States' current approach "incorporates the reality of the global energy mix and uses all energy sources and technologies cleanly and efficiently, including fossils fuels, nuclear energy, and renewable energy" (quoted in Friedman, 2019). U.S. withdrawal also reflected the official climate skepticism of the Trump administration, including that of President Trump himself, who on numerous occasions had either described climate change as a "hoax," or had argued that climates always change, while denying the scientific consensus that current changes are human-caused (Schulman, 2019).

The United States' withdrawal was unique, since by the time of the announcement every other country had signed on. Although newly elected members of Congress in 2016 called for a "green new deal," as of early 2020 it remains to be seen whether current U.S. climate policies will change, or whether China and the other world signatories will eventually take leadership and significantly reduce their dependency on fossil fuels. China currently accounts for 29 percent of the world's human-made carbon emissions, although it is now investing heavily in green technology. According to a recent report by the International Renewable Energy Agency, in 2017 China accounted for nearly half of all global expenditures on renewable energy investment, leading to the conclusion that "no country has put itself in a better position to become the world's renewable energy superpower than China" (IRENA, 2019). China's president, Xi Jinping, has called on China to play a leadership role in clean-energy investment and addressing the issue of climate change, even as the United States appears to be retreating from such a leadership position (Associated Press, 2018).

Yet even if all other countries meet their Paris Agreement commitments to reduce greenhouse gases, and the United States reverses its decision to formally pull out in late 2020, will these actions be sufficient to halt global warming? The UN Environmental Programme's 2019 Emissions Gap Report was not hopeful, noting that despite the Paris Agreement, greenhouse gas emissions continued to rise, with the world's 20 wealthiest economies accounting for four-fifths of the total. The largest emitters, according to the report, remained the United States and China. Unless drastic actions were taken, the report predicted, global temperatures were on pace to rise by as much as 3.9 degrees Celsius (7 degrees Fahrenheit) by 2100. In order to achieve the optimal Paris goal of a 1.5 degrees Celsius increase, global emissions would have to decline by 7.6 percent a year over the next decade. "The size of these annual cuts may seem shocking," the report concluded, "particularly for 1.5°C. They may also seem impossible, at least for next year. But we have to try" (UNEP, 2019).

Sustainable Development

Stopping—or even slowing—the environmental effects of climate change will therefore require significant actions on the part of individuals as well as nations. If the impoverished nations of the world are to catch up with the richer ones, a new path to development is needed. Such a path must couple scarce resource conservation with the reduction of greenhouse gases and other pollutants. This path has been called **sustainable development**, a term that was first used in a report by the World Commission on Environment and Development (1987), popularly known as the Brundtland Report, after former Norwegian prime minister Gro Harlem Brundtland, who chaired the commission. The report defined sustainable development simply as "development that meets the needs of the present without compromising the ability of future generations to meet their own needs." This definition sought to reconcile two seemingly intractably opposed communities: environmentalists, who were often seen as anti-growth, and business people, who were often seen as anti-environment. Environmentalists could now argue that, at least in wealthy industrial nations, environmentally harmful economic development should be limited, while conceding that economic growth might be necessary to lift people out of poverty in the global south.

The notion of sustainable development, while popular, remains unclear: What are the needs of the present? How much development can occur without compromising the future, particularly since we don't know what the future effects of technological change may be (Giddens, 2009)? However imprecise the term, "sustainable development" is generally taken to mean that growth should, at least minimally, be carried on in such a way as to preserve and recycle physical resources rather than deplete them, to maintain biodiversity, and to keep pollution to a minimum by protecting clean air, water, and land. Stated most simply, sustainable development means that today's business and political leaders should leave our planet's future in good health for their children and grandchildren.

One way sustainable development is to be achieved is by switching from a carbon-based economy to one based on renewable energy that emits fewer greenhouse gases. This involves moving from coal, petroleum, and gas to clean technologies (so-called "greentech"), such as solar and wind power, the use of biofuels, more fuel-efficient transportation, advanced storage batteries, and hi-tech power grids. As the cost of greentech has come down, global greentech investments have gone up, with $332 billion invested in clean energy in 2018. China, as noted previously, is the largest investor in greentech, followed by Europe and the United States (Bloomberg, 2019). While $332 billion may seem like a large investment, by way of comparison, total global

sustainable development Development that meets the needs of the present without compromising the ability of future generations to meet their own needs.

investment in conventional, nonrenewable energy was four times as great in 2018 ($1.5 trillion) (International Energy Agency, 2019). In that year the world's governments provided roughly the same amount in tax breaks and other forms of subsidies in support of oil extraction as was being invested in clean energy (Meyer, 2018).

There was initially some hopeful evidence that economies could grow sustainably without producing increased greenhouse gases. Even though global GDP grew by 3 percent during the two-year period of 2014–2015, carbon emissions remained flat (International Energy Agency, 2016). But according to the World Meteorological Association, between 2015 and 2019 carbon dioxide emissions actually increased, resulting in an accelerated increase in the atmospheric concentration of major greenhouse gases (WMO, 2019). One detailed study of leading fossil fuel–producing countries found that rather than curbing fossil fuel production as sought by the Paris Agreement, "governments are planning to produce about 50 percent more fossil fuels by 2030 than would be consistent with a 2°C pathway and 120 percent more than would be consistent with a 1.5°C pathway" (SEI et al., 2019). So far, the efforts of the world's leading economies to meet Paris goals and stop (or even slow) global warming have not been encouraging.

A case can be made that nuclear energy is a clean alternative to petroleum, since nuclear plants do not emit greenhouse gases. Although widely used in Europe—more than a quarter of Europe's energy comes from nuclear power plants—nuclear energy also has a number of potential drawbacks. One problem is the possibility of a nuclear plant accident that releases deadly radiation, such as the one that occurred in Chernobyl, Ukraine, in 1986, exposing more than 6 million people and requiring the resettlement of some 300,000. There are also problems with disposing of radioactive waste from spent nuclear fuel, which remains highly toxic for thousands of years. There is the danger that nuclear fuel could be stolen and used to make nuclear weapons. Even unrelated natural disasters can create serious safety concerns: It is estimated that a fifth of the world's 460 reactors are in areas vulnerable to earthquakes, while a quarter are located on coastlines where flooding—increasingly likely with sea level rise—is a danger (World Nuclear Association, 2019; Vidal, 2018). In 2011, a 9.0 magnitude earthquake and resulting tsunami caused three nuclear reactors to experience meltdown at the Fukushima Daiichi nuclear power plant in Japan, requiring the evacuation of some 63,000 people; seven years later, less than half had returned home (Harding, 2018). As a result of the Japan disaster, several European countries planned to phase out nuclear power. Germany, for example, took the dramatic step of pledging to shutter its nuclear reactors by 2022, although it is not clear that goal will be reached on time (Huggler, 2019).

Environmental Social Movements

Individual actions, such as recycling or buying sustainable products, are important steps that signal a personal commitment to make a difference. But such actions, by themselves, are unlikely to have a significant effect on global warming. To be truly effective, individual actions have to be mobilized into large-scale social movements, which we defined (in Chapter 13) as "collective attempts to further a common interest or secure a common goal through action outside the sphere of established institutions."

Table 19.1

APPLYING SOCIOLOGY TO POPULATION, URBANIZATION, AND THE ENVIRONMENT

CONCEPT	APPROACH TO UNDERSTANDING POPULATION, URBANIZATION, AND THE ENVIRONMENT	CONTEMPORARY APPLICATION
Second Demographic Transition	In a few industrial economies, birth rates have become lower than death rates, as families choose to have fewer children. This results in an aging population, along with population decline.	Greece, Japan, Italy, and Portugal have all lost population from natural increase—a fate that may await other countries as they become wealthier.
The New Ecological Paradigm	An increasingly influential way of thinking, emerging in the 1970s, that emphasizes the complex human and natural interactions involved in global ecosystems, and recognizing that the biophysical environment is not limitless.	Environmental sociology—a branch of sociology that examines the relationships between social systems and the ecosphere, studying such areas as the origins and impacts of technology, the relationship between social change and environmental change, and the role of social inequality and power relationships in shaping human interactions with the environment.
Anthropocene	A term meaning "human epoch" used to denote the current geological period, in which many geologically significant conditions and processes are profoundly altered by human activities.	Understanding the role of carbon emissions and the greenhouse effect; global warming and climate change; and the need for concerted international action to avoid increasingly catastrophic climate emergencies.
Food Security	People's access to sufficient, safe, and nutritious food that meets the need for an active and healthy life.	Global warming, climate change, and drought threaten food security for a significant portion of the world population; even today, more than 800 million people are undernourished.
Environmental Injustice	Damaged ecosystems are closely linked to the harms experienced by the most marginalized human beings across the planet. Pollution, climate change, and other ecological challenges do the most damage to the world's poorest people.	Deforestation in the Amazon further impoverishes the indigenous peoples who live there and depend on the forests; the most toxic industries are found in the poorest communities and nations.
Sustainable Development	Economic development that meets the needs of the present without compromising the ability of future generations to meet their own needs.	Switching from carbon-based economy to renewable energy; balancing economic development with ecological considerations; studying social movements in support of sustainable development.

There is evidence that a social movement may be emerging around climate change. During the September 2019 "Global Week for the Future" (also called the Climate Strike), an estimated 4 million people took to the streets in 150 countries around the world to demand that their governments take action to halt global warming. Massive peaceful demonstrations, drawing hundreds of thousands of participants, many of whom were school age, occurred in major metropolitan areas such as New York City, London, Berlin, Melbourne, Manila, Nairobi, and Rio de Janeiro, as well as towns on every continent (even scientists in Antarctica joined in). The demonstrations were timed to coincide with the United Nations Climate Action Summit, which brought world leaders together to address climate change (Sengupta, 2019).

The global demonstrations were the direct result of actions a year earlier by a 15-year-old Swedish schoolgirl. In August 2018, Greta Thunberg stopped going to school, deciding it was more important to protest Swedish government inaction on the climate crisis. So instead of attending classes, Thunberg protested outside of the Swedish Parliament, holding a sign that read "*Skolstrejk för klimatet*" ("school strike for the climate"). Her ideas quickly caught on, creating an international movement of school students who were willing to miss classes to protest government inaction on climate change, even if it meant being disciplined for absenteeism. Thunberg became a global symbol of the urgency felt by a growing number of high school and college students, who had come to the conclusion that they would be paying the price for their parents' generation's inaction on climate change. When she addressed the UN Summit, Thunberg pulled no punches:

> This is all wrong. I shouldn't be up here. I should be back in school on the other side of the ocean. Yet you all come to us young people for hope. How dare you! You have stolen my dreams and my childhood with your empty words. And yet I'm one of the lucky ones. People are suffering. People are dying. Entire ecosystems are collapsing. We are in the beginning of a mass extinction, and all you can talk about is money and fairy tales of eternal economic growth. How dare you! (Thunberg, 2019)

Students gather on Jungfernstieg, a main boulevard in Hamburg, Germany, as part of a global demonstration to demand action against climate change.

By early 2020 Thunberg had amassed some 3 million followers on Twitter and Facebook, and more than 8 million followers on Instagram. Her efforts clearly show that all it takes is one young girl to inspire massive demonstrations, if the issue is seen as urgent and the timing is right. Thunberg's success is also the result of social media's ability to go viral, communicating direct actions (such as Thunberg's solitary protest outside the Swedish Parliament) to a large and receptive youthful audience.

But do large-scale protests, even involving millions of people, constitute an effective social movement that will lead to change? There is evidence that a large majority of people around the planet are now deeply concerned about climate change. A 2018 Pew Research Center survey of nearly 28,000 people in 26 countries found that 68 percent viewed climate change as a "major threat," up from 56 percent only five years earlier. For the United States, the figure was somewhat lower (58 percent), although still significantly higher than five years earlier (40 percent). The survey did find that there were strong partisan differences in the United States: 83 percent of respondents who reported being or leaning Democrat reported seeing climate change as a major threat, compared with only 27 percent of respondents who reported being or leaning Republican (Fagan and Huang, 2019). Perhaps most significant, there appear to be significant differences by age in the United States—not surprising, perhaps, given the youth-driven protests inspired by Thunberg. A 2018 Gallup survey found that 70 percent of Millennials (ages 18–34) were worried either "a great deal" or "fair amount" about global warming, compared with only 56 percent of Boomers (ages 55 and older) (Reinhart, 2018).

There are numerous social movement organizations concerned with climate change, global warming, and climate justice. One of the largest, 350.org, links hundreds of organizations around the globe, has been involved in more than a dozen campaigns, and supports grassroots efforts by organizations in communities that are directly impacted by climate change. (The name 350 is taken from 350 parts per million of carbon dioxide, identified more than a decade ago as one climate "tipping point" for atmospheric carbon dioxide concentration.) Founder Bill McKibben argues that "If we don't solve it soon, we will never solve it, because we will pass a series of irrevocable tipping points and we're clearly now approaching those deadlines" (McKibben, 2019). While he is hopeful that there are growing and increasingly effective global environmental social movements, Doug McAdam, one of sociology's leading social movement theorists, has pointed out that there have historically been a number of barriers that have thwarted their success in the United States: the influence of well-funded and politically powerful climate change deniers in shaping public opinion; congressional gridlock; the fact that the worst impacts are in the future and are therefore intangible, relative to more pressing problems; and the absence of what he termed "ownership" by any significant segment of the public, unlike African Americans mobilizing around police shootings, or women around sexual assault (McAdam, 2017; Martinovich, 2017). With the increased involvement of youth around the world, McAdam does offer some guarded optimism, noting that "In the

CONCEPT CHECKS

1 What is urbanization? How is it related to globalization?

2 How do population growth, urbanization, and industrialization affect the global environment?

3 What are the principal causes of global climate change, and what is being done to address them?

4 Define sustainable development and provide at least one criticism of the concept.

'60s, it was civil rights and then the Vietnam War. Climate change absolutely has that kind of emotional resonance for people, particularly for young people, because they're going to have to deal with it." But McAdam also points out that in the 1960s, youth activism was reinforced by broader progressive trends in U.S. politics, leading him to wonder how much staying power today's young activists will have, if their efforts do not lead to immediate results (quoted in Weise, 2019). Social movement scholars debate whether such movements are more effective when they focus on grassroots action, such as mass mobilizations and nonviolent protests or when they become more institutionalized, focusing on lobbying, legislation, and working within established governance frameworks (Ogrodnik and Staggenborg, 2016).

4 UNANSWERED QUESTIONS

Population growth, industrialization, urbanization, and the resulting environmental disruptions provide many challenges for sociological research. In this final section, we consider two questions whose answers remain contested—one asking whether global population growth will outstrip global food production, resulting in widespread famine; the other asking whether avoiding climate change through sustainable development is even possible, or if far more drastic measures need to be taken?

Will Global Population Growth Outstrip Resources?

During the rise of industrialism, many looked forward to a new age in which food scarcity would be a phenomenon of the past. The development of modern industry, it was widely supposed, would create a new era of abundance. In his celebrated work *Essay on the Principle of Population* (2003; orig. 1798), Thomas Malthus criticized these ideas and initiated a debate about the connection between population and food resources that continues to this day.

At the time Malthus wrote, the population of Europe was growing rapidly. Malthus pointed out that whereas population growth is exponential, food supply depends on fixed resources that can be expanded only by developing new land for cultivation. Population growth therefore tends to outstrip the means of support available. The inevitable outcome is famine, which, combined with the influence of war and plagues, acts as a natural limit to population increase. Malthus predicted that human beings would always live in circumstances of misery and starvation, unless they practiced what he called "moral restraint." His cure for excessive population growth was for people to delay marriage and to strictly limit their frequency of sexual intercourse. (The use of contraception, he proclaimed to be a "vice.")

For a while, **Malthusianism** was ignored. The population development of the Western countries followed a quite different pattern from that which he had anticipated. Rates of population growth trailed off in the nineteenth and twentieth centuries. Indeed, in the 1930s, there were major worries about population decline in many industrialized

Malthusianism A doctrine about population dynamics developed by Thomas Malthus, according to which population increase comes up against "natural limits," represented by famine and war.

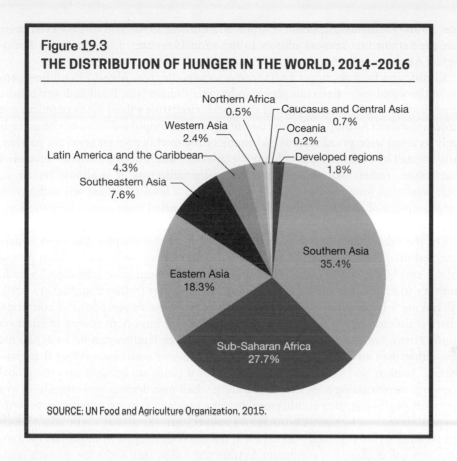

Figure 19.3

THE DISTRIBUTION OF HUNGER IN THE WORLD, 2014–2016

Northern Africa
0.5%

Caucasus and Central Asia
0.7%

Western Asia
2.4%

Oceania
0.2%

Latin America and the Caribbean—
4.3%

Developed regions
1.8%

Southeastern Asia
7.6%

Southern Asia
35.4%

Eastern Asia
18.3%

Sub-Saharan Africa
27.7%

SOURCE: UN Food and Agriculture Organization, 2015.

countries, including the United States. Malthus also failed to consider that technology that fostered increases in food production would be developed in the modern era. However, the upsurge in world population growth in the twentieth century has again lent some credence to Malthus's views. Population expansion in the global south seemed to be outstripping the resources that those countries could generate to feed their citizenry—especially in nations that suffered from such natural disasters as droughts and floods that hurt local food supplies.

Malthusian arguments got a boost when the biologist Paul Ehrlich published his best-selling book *The Population Bomb* in 1968. Ehrlich (1968) predicted a catastrophic global collapse, as an exploding world population vastly outstripped global food production. Famine would overtake India and other populous countries, and hundreds of millions of people would perish in the coming decades. His arguments received support from another study published a few years later. The authors of *The Limits to Growth* (Meadows et al., 1972) used advanced (for the time) computer-simulation modeling to project the complex interaction of five factors they believed to be key to understanding the earth–human system interrelationship: population, industrialization, pollution, food production, and resource depletion. Their predictions were dire: a high likelihood of global agricultural and economic collapse by the mid- to late-twenty-first century. Ehrlich updated (and reaffirmed) his arguments some 20 years later in *The Population Explosion* (Ehrlich and Ehrlich, 1990), and he gave even more dire predictions in a keynote address to the annual meeting of the American Sociological Association in 2012.

Famine and food shortages are indeed a serious concern. About 795 million people in the world suffer from hunger or undernourishment (UN Food and Agriculture Organization, 2015). In some parts of the world, more than a third of the population is undernourished. As the population rises, levels of food output will need to rise accordingly to avoid widespread scarcity. Yet many of the world's poorest areas are particularly affected by water shortages, shrinking farmland, and soil degradation—processes that reduce, rather than enhance, agricultural productivity. It is almost certain in such areas that food production will not occur at a level to ensure self-sufficiency. Large amounts of food and grain will need to be imported from areas where there are surpluses.

On the other hand, as noted at the beginning of this chapter, the most widely accepted prediction of global population sees a leveling off at 10–12.5 billion people by the end of the century, the result of a "second demographic transition," which, contrary to Malthusian predictions, would result in lower (rather than higher) fertility. Having a large number of children may make sense in preindustrial countries, where child mortality is high and children provide an important source of labor on family farms, but in modern industrial societies, large families can be an economic cost rather than an asset: Children tend to be economic consumers rather than producers. As more and more countries in the global south are brought into the global economy, the reasoning goes, they will undergo their own demographic transition to a low mortality/low fertility equilibrium, thereby radically slowing population growth. Population may in fact initially surge: As countries in the global south adopt modern farming technology and public health measures developed in industrial nations, mortality will decline. But eventually, fertility will follow suit, and a low-growth equilibrium will result. Among industrial economies, such as Germany, Italy, Japan, and Russia, fertility has dropped below replacement levels, resulting in a declining population, at least among the native-born population. (Growth in such cases can occur only through immigration.)

Moreover, doomsday predictions have long underestimated global increases in food production, which, thanks in part to advances in farming technology, have so far managed to keep pace with population growth. According to the UN Food and Agricultural Organization, even the projected population growth to 2050 can be accommodated by increased food supply—if certain conditions are met: drawing on additional (but available) land and water resources, higher crop yields, and preserving biodiversity. The study concludes:

> According to FAO's baseline projections, it should be possible to meet the future food and feed demand of the projected world population in 2050 within realistic rates for land and water use expansion and yield development. However, achieving this will not at all be automatic and several significant challenges will have to be met. . . . The conditions under which this can be achieved are strong economic growth, global expansion of food supplies by about 70 percent, relatively high production growth in many developing countries achievable through growing capital

stock, higher productivity and global trade helping the low income food deficit countries to close their import gaps for cereals and other food products at affordable prices. (UN Food and Agriculture Organization, 2011)

The key problem, according to this view, is not that population growth is outstripping food production, as Malthus predicted more than 200 years ago; it is that the results of increased agricultural productivity are not equitably distributed. The counterargument to Malthusian pessimism, simply stated, lies neither with the biological food-producing capacity of the planet nor with the failure of agricultural technology to keep pace. It lies with the fact that a small proportion of the world's population consumes a vastly unequal proportion of the world's natural resources. The solutions, in other words, are to be found in societal terms, not a biological imperative. Karl Marx (1977, 1993), in his criticism of Malthus, argued that starvation results not from overpopulation, but rather an economic system that enables the capitalist class to enjoy the fruits of production (including food) at the expense of everyone else. The solution, in Marx's view, was neither war, pestilence, nor famine, but rather communism, an economic system that he thought would provide adequate food for workers and farmers, and also enable them to self-regulate their population growth rate.

What will be the consequences of these changes? Some observers see the makings of widespread social upheaval—particularly in countries in the global south undergoing demographic transition. The rapid growth of cities will be likely to lead to environmental damage, new public health risks, overloaded infrastructures, rising crime, and impoverished squatter settlements. Changes in the economy and labor markets may prompt widespread internal migration as people in rural areas search for work. Warfare and civic violence also cause people to migrate. Civil war in Syria, along with the rise of radical Islamist movements in the Middle East and North Africa, have laid waste to entire cities. Millions of refugees have fled war-torn countries as a result. In 2015 alone, it is estimated that 1.3 million migrants fled to Europe seeking asylum, with Germany the destination of choice (BBC, 2016). Many paid large sums of money to risk a hazardous crossing of the Mediterranean in flimsy, greatly overloaded rafts; more than 7,000 paid with their lives by the end of 2015 (Hume, 2016).

Refugees, like all migrants, seek out major cities, where the possibility of finding work is the greatest. This enormous movement of people has placed significant strains on the resources of the destination countries. While Germany was initially among the most generous of countries in opening its doors to refugees, by 2016, even Germany began to close its borders. Other countries responded far more harshly: Those bordering on Greece—a destination of choice for many migrants since the water crossing from Turkey to the Greek island of Samos is only five miles—closed their borders in 2015, stranding many migrants in one of Europe's poorest countries.

Technological advances in agriculture and industry are unpredictable, so no one can be sure how large a population the world might eventually be able to support. Even if technological solutions are found, will they be used to benefit those in the poorest regions of the world, who face the most dire Malthusian prospects—or to increase the consumption of those in relatively wealthy countries, who are most likely to be insulated from catastrophic collapse?

Sustainable Development, or Adaptation to the Inevitable?

As we have seen, sustainable development requires governments to take immediate actions to reduce their countries' carbon emissions, in part by switching to more renewable forms of energy, commitments that are reflected in the Paris Agreements. Apart from state-led efforts, many environmental advocates argue that if global ecological disaster is to be avoided, people in rich countries should consume more sustainably: recycle, carpool, use public transportation, buy fewer items. Consumers are urged to buy eco-friendly products, which is now possible since virtually all major corporations claim to be fully committed to ecological sustainability. To take but two examples, Walmart, whose revenues make it the world's largest corporation, promises over the next 5 to 10 years to have reduced its greenhouse gas emissions by a billion metric tons while deriving half of its energy from renewable sources (Walmart, 2019). The Sustainable Apparel Coalition comprises more than a hundred major apparel, footwear, and textile companies that promise "no unnecessary environmental harm" in manufacturing their products. To achieve this goal, the member firms self-report environmental and workplace conditions throughout their supply chains, which are then compiled into a sustainability index (SAC, 2019; Kibbey, 2016).

Critics counter that while government and individual sustainable development efforts are laudable and should be pursued, by themselves they are unlikely to solve our climate problems. They point out that whatever governments may have agreed to in Paris, in fact fossil fuel production remains heavily subsidized and has actually increased in recent years. In terms of individual actions, critics claim that eco-friendly shopping is certainly a worthy goal that may make a small difference, but in terms of significantly affecting climate change is unlikely to be effective unless billions of people join in. Furthermore, they argue, it relies on businesses to truthfully report their ecological impacts—claims that must be treated skeptically, since such claims are almost never independently verified. Business efforts to trumpet their sustainability are seen as all too often a form of "greenwashing," an effort to boost sales by convincing consumers that the products they buy are eco-friendly (Appelbaum, 2016; Appelbaum and Lichtenstein, 2016).

Because some amount of global warming seems inevitable, the recent IPCC report emphasized measures that might be taken to offset some of the predicted consequences. These included recommendations for such things as early warning systems, flood and cyclone shelters, sea walls and levees, desalinization plants to convert sea water to drinking water, and programs to educate people about the dangers of global warming. But will such actions prove sufficient? In the view of some scientists, even with such limited measures, rising temperatures and associated destructive climate events are inevitable, unless truly drastic steps are taken. Another, more drastic solution is **geoengineering**, large-scale interventions in the earth's natural systems to counteract climate change. Some geoengineering proposals are global in scope, but do not seek to dramatically alter existing ecosystems—for example, massive reforestation to remove carbon dioxide from the atmosphere. Other

geoengineering Large-scale interventions in the earth's natural systems to counteract climate change.

proposals involve novel interventions with unknown long-term ecological effects: building giant "space mirrors" or releasing reflective particles in the upper atmosphere to deflect the warming rays of the sun; converting seawater into droplets that can be used to seed clouds and increase cloud cover; building huge machines to remove and bury atmospheric carbon dioxide; seeding the ocean with nutrients that will grow plants that absorb carbon dioxide (Oxford Engineering Programme, 2019; Pierce, 2019). Critics worry that such large-scale efforts to re-engineer the earth's ocean, land, and atmosphere may divert attention from the need to reduce greenhouse gas emissions, while potentially resulting in disastrous ecological consequences (NAS, 2015; Vaughan, 2019).

One final approach involves simply accepting the inevitability of climate change and learning to live with it. According to this view, climate-induced social collapse is inevitable, requiring a *deep adaptation agenda* in response. Such an agenda has three components: recognizing that individuals and societies have proven remarkably resilient in bouncing back from trauma and disaster, so things will eventually work themselves out; letting go of past expectations about the possibility of endless but sustainable growth; and adapting to the "new normal" by rediscovering a simpler way of life—the beliefs and lifestyles that preceded our current carbon-driven economies. The new lifestyle involves such things as restoring the original wildland environments; dieting with locally produced seasonal foods, rather than importing food grown half a world away; and replacing our electronically-mediated forms of virtual interaction with a return to actual face-to-face local communities. Deep adaptation will clearly be psychologically and spiritually challenging for many, since it means adapting to a very different world than the one most of us were born into (Slater and Bendel, 2019; Verlie, 2019).

Where do you stand personally on this debate? How might a sociological understanding help you make an informed decision?

CONCEPT CHECKS

1 How does the new ecological paradigm differ from the human exceptionalism paradigm?

2 Explain Malthus's position on the relationship between population growth and the food supply.

3 Is sustainable development possible—or is it now necessary to find ways to adapt to global warming and extreme climate change?

THE BIG PICTURE

Chapter 19
Population, Urbanization, and the Environment

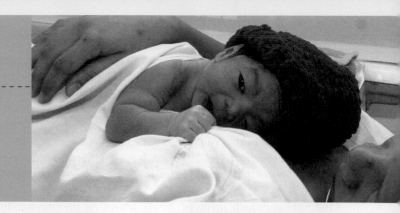

1 Basic Concepts
p. 763

2 Urban Sociology: Some Influential Theories
p. 770

LEARNING OBJECTIVES

Learn the key concepts demographers use to understand world population growth and the changes in cities.

Understand how theories of urbanism have placed an increasing emphasis on the influence of socioeconomic factors on city life.

TERMS TO KNOW

demography • crude birthrates • age-specific birth rates • fertility • crude death rates • mortality • infant mortality rate • life expectancy • life span • rates of population growth or decline • exponential • doubling time • demographic transition • second demographic transition • dependency ratio

urbanization • ecological approach • inner city • ghetto • urbanism • created environment • collective consumption • global city

CONCEPT CHECKS

1. Why is demography considered a branch of sociology?
2. How does the age structure of a society affect fertility, mortality, and therefore population growth?
3. What are the stages of a demographic transition, and why do some demographers believe that we've now entered a fourth stage?

1. How does urban ecology use language from the physical sciences to explain life in modern cities? How did Drake and Cayton's study challenge the ideas of urban ecology?
2. What is the urban interaction problem?
3. According to Jane Jacobs, the more people there are on the streets, the safer the streets will be. Do you agree with Jacobs's hypothesis and her explanation for this proposed pattern?
4. What are the four main characteristics of global cities?

Exercises: Thinking Sociologically

1. Explain what makes the urbanization now occurring in developing countries, such as Brazil and India, different from and more problematic than the urbanization that took place a century ago in New York, London, Tokyo, and Berlin.

2. Following analysis presented in this chapter, concisely explain how the expanded quest for cheap energy and raw materials and present-day dangers of environmental pollution and resource depletion threaten not only the survival of people in developed countries but also that of people in less developed countries.

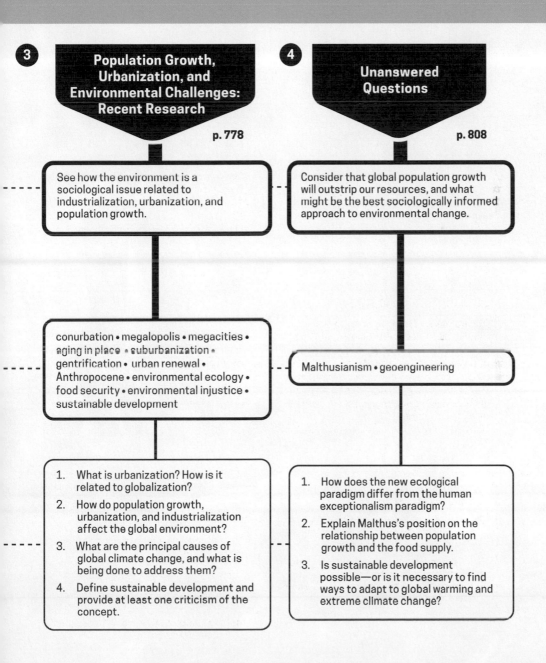

3

Population Growth, Urbanization, and Environmental Challenges: Recent Research

p. 778

See how the environment is a sociological issue related to industrialization, urbanization, and population growth.

conurbation • megalopolis • megacities • aging in place • suburbanization • gentrification • urban renewal • Anthropocene • environmental ecology • food security • environmental injustice • sustainable development

1. What is urbanization? How is it related to globalization?
2. How do population growth, urbanization, and industrialization affect the global environment?
3. What are the principal causes of global climate change, and what is being done to address them?
4. Define sustainable development and provide at least one criticism of the concept.

4

Unanswered Questions

p. 808

Consider that global population growth will outstrip our resources, and what might be the best sociologically informed approach to environmental change.

Malthusianism • geoengineering

1. How does the new ecological paradigm differ from the human exceptionalism paradigm?
2. Explain Malthus's position on the relationship between population growth and the food supply.
3. Is sustainable development possible—or is it necessary to find ways to adapt to global warming and extreme climate change?

20

Globalization in a Changing World

Which of these countries has the largest movie industry, as measured by the number of major films produced each year? (For extra credit, rank them in descending order of the size of the film industry.)

- **A** United States
- **B** China
- **C** Japan
- **D** India
- **E** Nigeria

TURN THE PAGE FOR THE CORRECT ANSWER.

LEARNING OBJECTIVES

1 Basic Concepts

Recognize that numerous factors influence social change, including the physical environment, political organization, culture, and economic factors.

2 Current Theories: Is Globalization Today Something New—or Have We Seen It All Before?

Understand the debates among skeptics, hyperglobalizers, and transformationalists over whether globalization differs radically from anything in human history.

3 Recent Research on Globalization and Social Change

Recognize that globalization is not solely an economic phenomenon but rather the combined effect of technological, political, and economic changes. Understand how globalization has contributed to the rise of individualism, reshaped work patterns, influenced pop culture, and created new forms of risk and inequality.

4 Unanswered Questions

Evaluate the notion that social change is ushering us into a postindustrial or postmodern stage of social organization. Understand why new forms of global governance are needed to address the risks, challenges, and inequalities produced by globalization.

If you guessed the United States and Hollywood, you are not even close! India tops the list by far. In 2000, India produced more than 2,000 films, and by 2019 it had produced 2,446 feature films, resulting in nearly 2 billion admissions (UNESCO, 2017a; India Central Board of Film Certification, 2020). India's film industry produces films in more than a dozen different languages, reflecting the extraordinary cultural and linguistic diversity of a country that is well known locally and globally for its Hindi-language "Bollywood" films, based in the city of Mumbai (Bombay).

Bollywood films are truly global in origin: They draw from such wide-ranging sources as twentieth-century Hollywood musicals, ancient Sanskrit dramas that combine lavish music and dance, Indian folk theater, and even MTV. The results are rich, elaborate films with romantic characters, numerous plots and subplots, lavish costuming, highly theatrical performances, and lots of dancing. Indian films have had widespread impact outside India: Satyajit Ray's *Apu Trilogy* was released in the 1950s to critical acclaim and was ranked among the top 100 movies ever made by *Time* magazine. More recently, British filmmaker Danny Boyle's Academy Award–winning film *Slumdog Millionaire*, based on an Indian novel, was filmed in Mumbai; Boyle—who also orchestrated the opening ceremony for the 2012 Olympics in London—credits Indian film as a major influence.

Nigeria comes in second, with more than 1,000 films in 2017, and by 2019, 2,000 film and TV productions. Unlike in India, many films in Nigeria are low budget: They are usually shot using digital handheld cameras, burned onto CDs, and sold inexpensively throughout Africa. A Nigerian online platform for on-demand films, called iRokoTV, streams these homegrown movies across the globe; even Netflix has a dedicated section for Nigerian films (Veselinovic, 2015; Saliu and Jun, 2019). The country's burgeoning film industry, sometimes

THE ANSWER IS D.

dubbed "Nollywood," provides significant employment in the job-starved country: Nigeria's film industry employs more than 1 million people and is the second-largest employer in the country after agriculture. It has its own Academy Awards, enlivened with

> **hybridity** The fact that cultures are neither wholly isolated nor entirely distinct, but instead constantly borrow from one another.

visits from Hollywood movie stars such as Danny Glover and Forest Whitaker. While the films deal with a range of topics, they often draw on local themes and are shot on location, rather than in studios. According to the U.S. International Trade Commission (2016), Nigeria's film industry is a $600 million business. Currently, it accounts for 0.27 percent of the Nigerian GDP (*The Guardian*, 2019). China came in fourth with 850 films in 2017. In the global sweepstakes of feature films, the United States ranked only fourth in 2017, producing 660 feature films—although its blockbuster, high-budget (and high-special-effects) films are popular throughout the world, accounting for the highest revenues. Japan came in fifth place with 594 films (UNESCO, 2017).

Films around the world draw on one another for themes, cinematographic techniques, and technology. While Hollywood remains an important influence, each country (indeed, in many countries, each region) has developed its own style and approach. The global film industry is an example of **hybridity**—a notion borrowed from biology to capture the fact that cultures are neither isolated nor wholly distinct but in fact borrow from one another. This has been true historically and arguably has accelerated in recent years. Globalization today brings people, and their cultures, into intimate contact with one another, whether through travel or migration, economic interdependence, mass media, or popular culture. Social media play a key role in connecting people, films, and popular music across a global space.

Fairly recent on the horizon, after Latino rock, is Mandarin pop, a Cantonese and Pacific American combination of styles. One of its original inspirations is Hong Kong crooners doing Mandarin cover versions of Japanese popular ballads. The Japanese ballads were already a mixture of Japanese and American styles that featured, for instance, saxophone backgrounds. Mandarin pop (or Mandopop) is part of the soundscape of the Pacific Chinese diaspora. Its audience ranges from youngsters in China, Hong Kong, and Taiwan, to prosperous second-generation Chinese immigrants in the United States (Nederveen Pieterse, 2001).

In this chapter, we go beyond our earlier discussions of globalization, examining the ways global processes affect our lives on many levels. We explore how globalization has contributed to the profound social changes that are sweeping the world today and consider what the future is likely to bring.

1 BASIC CONCEPTS

Imagine standing before a clock that measures time on a cosmic scale, in which each second represents 60,000 years. On such a clock, it would take 24 hours for the 5-billion-year history of our planet to unfold. Humanlike apes would not even appear until the last two minutes, and human beings only in the last four seconds. Compared to us, even the dinosaurs would look like long-term residents of the planet; they roamed the earth for nearly three-quarters of an hour on our 24-hour clock, before disappearing forever. Will human beings—whose great civilizations appeared only in the last quarter second—do nearly as well?

Human beings are very recent residents of planet Earth, yet we have unquestionably made our presence known. Our numbers have exploded to some 7.6 billion people and will probably reach 9 billion to 10 billion by 2050. We have spread to every nook and cranny on the planet. Thanks to modern science and industry, each of us uses up a vastly greater amount of the planet's limited resources than did our apelike ancestors. Indeed, the combination of population explosion and modern industrial expansion threatens both our planet and human civilization.

Humans have demonstrated a unique ability to create massive problems—and then find ways to solve them. Today our problems are global, requiring global solutions. Globalization has contributed to such challenges as global warming and climate change, the worldwide spread of HIV/AIDS, as well as conflict among nations, terrorism, and global poverty. Yet globalization can also contribute to their solution. All human beings share a common home and, therefore, a common interest in its preservation.

Social Change

During a period of only two or three centuries—a sliver of time in the context of human history—human social life has been wrenched away from the types of social order in which people lived for thousands of years. **Social change** can be defined as the transformation over time of the institutions and culture of a society. Globalization has accelerated these processes of social change, affecting virtually all of humanity. As a result, far more than any generation before us, we face an uncertain future. To be sure, previous generations were at the mercy of natural disasters, plagues, and famines. And while these problems still trouble much of the world, today we must also deal with the social forces that we ourselves have unleashed.

Social theorists have tried for the past two centuries to develop a single grand theory that explains social change. Marx, for example, emphasized the importance of economic factors in shaping social life, including politics and culture. But no single-factor theory can account for the diversity of human social development from hunting and gathering and pastoral societies, to traditional civilizations, to the highly complex social systems of today. In analyzing social change, we can accomplish two tasks: We can identify major factors that have consistently influenced social change, such as the physical environment, political organization, culture, and economics; and we can develop theories that explain particular periods of change, such as modern times.

social change Alteration in basic structures of a social group or society. Social change is an ever-present phenomenon in social life but has become especially intense in the modern era. The origins of modern sociology can be traced to attempts to understand the dramatic changes shattering the traditional world and promoting new forms of social order.

The Physical Environment

The physical environment often affects the development of human social organization. This is clearest in extreme environmental conditions, where people must organize their ways of life in relation to the weather. For example, people in polar regions develop different practices from those living in subtropical areas. Residents of Alaska, where the winters are long and cold and winter days very short, follow different patterns of social life than residents of the much warmer U.S. South. Most Alaskans spend more of their lives indoors and, except in summer months, plan outdoor activities carefully, given the inhospitable environment.

Less extreme physical conditions can also affect society. The indigenous population of Australia has remained hunters and gatherers because the continent has hardly any indigenous plants suitable for cultivation or animals suitable for pastoral production. Most of the world's early civilizations originated in areas with rich agricultural land—for instance, in river deltas. The ease of communication across land and the availability of sea routes are also important: Societies cut off from others by mountain ranges, impassable jungles, or deserts often remain relatively unchanged over long periods.

Jared Diamond (2005) makes a strong case for the importance of environment in his book *Collapse: How Societies Choose to Fail or Succeed*. Diamond, a physiologist, biologist, and geographer, examines more than a dozen past and present societies, some of which collapsed (past examples include Easter Island and the Anasazi of the southwestern United States; more recent examples include Rwanda and Haiti) and some of which overcame serious challenges to succeed. Diamond identifies five factors contributing to a society's collapse: the presence of hostile neighbors, the absence (or collapse) of trading partners for essential goods, climate change, environmental problems, and an inadequate response to environmental problems. Three of these factors involve environmental conditions. The first four factors are often outside a society's control and need not always result in collapse. The final factor, however, is always crucial: As the subtitle of his book suggests, success or failure depends on the choices made by a society and its leaders.

The collapse of Rwanda, for example, is typically attributed to ethnic rivalries between Hutu and Tutsi, fueled by Rwanda's colonial past. According to some explanations of the genocide that left more than 800,000 Tutsi dead after a few horrific months in 1994, much of the cause lay in the legacy of colonialism. During the first part of the twentieth century, Belgium ran Rwanda through Tutsi administrators because, according to prevailing European racial theories, the Belgians considered the Tutsi—who tended on average to be somewhat taller and lighter skinned than the Hutu and, therefore, closer in resemblance to Europeans—to be more "civilized." This belief led to resentment and hatred, which boiled over in 1994, fueled by Hutu demagogues urging the killing of all Tutsi.

Diamond holds that this explanation is only part of the story. Through careful analysis of patterns of landholding, population, and killing, he argues that the root causes are found in overpopulation and the resulting environmental destruction. The population of Rwanda, he shows, was one of the fastest growing on earth, with disastrous consequences for the country's land and people, who had become one of the planet's most impoverished populations. Faced with starvation—and the absence of land to share among the growing number of (male) children—Rwanda was ripe for violence and collapse. Although ethnic rivalries may have fueled the fires of rage, Diamond also shows that in some hard-hit provinces, Hutu killed other Hutu, as young men sought to acquire scarce farmland by any means.

Some have criticized Diamond for overemphasizing the environment at the expense of other factors. By itself—except perhaps for extreme circumstances, such as the extended drought that doomed the Anasazi early in the fourteenth century—the environment does not necessarily determine how a society develops. Today especially, when humans can control much of their immediate living conditions, environment seems less important: Modern cities have sprung up in the arctic cold and the harshest deserts.

Political Organization

Another factor influencing social change is the type of political organization that operates in a society. In hunter-gatherer societies, this influence is minimal because no political authorities can mobilize the community. In other types of society, however, distinct political agents—chiefs, lords, monarchs, and governments—strongly influence the course of social development. How a people respond to a crisis can determine whether they thrive or fail, and leadership is crucial to success. A leader capable of pursuing dynamic policies and generating a mass following or radically altering pre-existing modes of thought can overturn a previously established order. However, individuals can reach positions of leadership and become effective only under favorable social conditions. Mohandas Gandhi, the famous pacifist leader in India, succeeded in securing his country's independence from Britain because World War II and other events had unsettled the existing colonial institutions in India.

Japan illustrates how effective leadership can avert possible ecological and economic collapse (Diamond, 2005). Political and military stability under the Tokugawa *shoguns* (military rulers from 1603 to 1867) ushered in a period of prosperity. This economic growth, however, contributed to massive deforestation of the island country. Its leaders (the celebrated *samurai* warriors) instituted programs of conservation and reforestation, and today—despite having one of the highest population densities of any industrial country—nearly three-quarters of Japan is covered with forests (Diamond, 2005).

Military strength played a fundamental part in the establishment of most traditional states, but the connections between level

Rwandan refugees try to reach the UN camp in Tanzania. According to the United Nations, approximately 800,000 Tutsi and moderate Hutu were killed during a period of 100 days in 1994. Hundreds of thousands of Rwandans fled to neighboring countries to escape the bloodshed.

of production and military strength are indirect. A ruler may channel resources into building up the military, for example, even when this impoverishes the rest of the population—as happened in Iraq in the 1980s under the rule of Saddam Hussein and in North Korea during the 1990s under Kim Jong Il.

The most important political factor that has promoted change in the modern era is the emergence of the modern state, a vastly more efficient mechanism of government than those of premodern societies. Government plays a much bigger role in our lives, for better or worse, than it did before modern industrial societies arose.

Globalization today may be challenging national governments' ability effectively to exert leadership. A number of theorists argue that political power is becoming increasingly uncoupled from geography (Sassen, 1996; Shaw, 2000). Sociologist William Robinson (2001, 2004, 2014), for example, claims that as economic power has become deterritorialized, so, too, has political power: Just as transnational corporations operate across borders, with few or no national allegiances, transnational political organizations are becoming stronger as national governments are becoming weaker. The World Trade Organization (WTO) has the power to punish countries that violate its principles of free trade (Conti, 2011). European countries have opened their borders to one another, established a common currency, and given up substantial political power to the European Union (EU), a regional form of governance.

Will the twenty-first century see new forms of political organization better suited to a world in which people, products, knowledge, religious beliefs, pop culture, and pollution all cross borders easily? Although it is too soon to tell, most likely, the most important forms of political organization of this century will bear little resemblance to those of the twentieth.

Culture

The third main influence on social change is culture, including communications systems, religious and other belief systems, and popular culture. Communications systems, in particular, affect the character and pace of social change. The invention of writing, for instance, allowed for effective record keeping, making possible the development of large-scale organizations. In addition, writing altered people's perception of the relationship among past, present, and future. Societies that write keep a record of past events, through which they gain a sense of their evolution. The existence of a written constitution and laws enables a country to have a legal system based on the interpretation of legal precedents—just as written scriptures enable religious leaders to justify their beliefs by citing chapters and verses from religious texts, such as the Bible or the Qur'an.

We saw in Chapters 5, 6, 13, and 16 how the Internet and the proliferation of smartphones have transformed our personal relationships, our forms of recreation, the ways in which we learn and work, the nature of politics and social movements—in fact, almost every aspect of modern life. These changes, among the most rapid in human history, have caused what geographer David Harvey (1989) calls the "time-space compression." And they have all occurred within a single generation.

Religion, as we have seen, may be either a conservative or an innovative force in social life. Some forms of religious belief and practice have acted as a brake on change,

An Egyptian girl walks next to the Muslim Fulla dolls at a kids' shop in Cairo. Two years after she first came on the market, Fulla is now thought to be the best-selling girls' toy in the Arab world, displacing her Western rival, Barbie.

emphasizing traditional values and rituals. Yet, as Max Weber held, religious convictions frequently mobilize pressures for social change. For instance, many American church leaders promote attempts to reduce poverty or diminish inequalities in society. Religious leaders such as Dr. Martin Luther King Jr. were at the forefront of the American civil rights movement, and adherents of liberation theology fought for better schools, water supplies, health services, and democracy in Latin America—often at the cost of their lives.

Yet, at the same time, certain religious communities today have resisted many of the cultural aspects of globalization. Islamic fundamentalists, fundamentalist Christians, and ultra-Orthodox Jewish *Haredim* all reject what they regard as the corrupting influences of modern secular culture, now spreading globally through mass media and the Internet (Juergensmeyer, 1993, 2008; Juergensmeyer, Griego, and Soboslai, 2015). Islamic fundamentalists call this "Westoxification"—literally, getting drunk on the temptations of modern Western culture. While such religious communities usually embrace modern technology, which they sometimes use to disseminate their ideas, they reject what they view as the "McWorld" corruptions that go along with it.

Political scientist Samuel Huntington (1993, 1998) advanced the controversial thesis that such differences are part of seismic fault lines between entire civilizations. According to his "clash of civilizations" thesis,

> The great divisions among humankind and the dominating source of conflict will be cultural. Nation states will remain the most powerful actors in world affairs, but the principal conflicts of global politics will occur between nations and groups of different civilizations. The clash of civilizations will dominate global politics. The fault lines between civilizations will be the battle lines of the future. (1993)

Huntington identified several major civilizations as having great potential for future conflict: Christianity, subdivided into Western Christianity and Eastern Orthodox; Islam; Hindu; Chinese; African; Buddhist; and Japanese. Although his thesis seems especially plausible after the events of September 11, 2001, it has been criticized as overly simplistic. Each of his so-called civilizations encompasses enormous differences in beliefs and practices, while old-fashioned geopolitical interests (for example, involving scarce resources such as oil and water) will likely shape international conflicts well into the twenty-first century. Moreover, to the extent that national policies are influenced by a belief in the clash of civilizations, Huntington's thesis may become a self-fulfilling prophecy, as different sides square off for a cosmic war against what each believes to be the forces of unmitigated evil (Juergensmeyer, 1993).

In fact, the principal cultural clashes of the twenty-first century may not be between so-called civilizations but between those who believe that truthful understanding derives from religious faith and those who find such understanding in science, critical thinking, and secular thought (Juergensmeyer, 1993). Secular ideals, such as self-betterment, freedom, equality, and democratic participation, are largely creations of the past two or three centuries. In the United States, political debates rage between right-wing Republicans who promote teaching creationism (versus evolution) in schools and oppose abortion, and liberal Democrats whose politics are guided by scientific evidence and preservation of civil rights. Not surprisingly, creationism is much more likely to be taught in public school systems in politically conservative districts in the South than more liberal regions of the North (Kirk, 2014).

Economic Factors

Of economic influences, the farthest reaching is industrial capitalism. Capitalism differs fundamentally from previous production systems because it involves the constant expansion of production and the ever-increasing accumulation of wealth. In traditional production systems, levels of production were fairly unchanging because they were geared to customary needs. Capitalism requires the constant revision of the technology of production, a process that increasingly involves science. The rate of technological innovation fostered in modern industry is vastly greater than that in any previous type of economic order. And such technological innovation has helped create a global economy whose production lines draw on a worldwide workforce.

Economic changes help shape other changes as well. Science and technology, for example, are driven in part by economic factors. Corporations, to remain competitive, must spend large sums on research and development to commercialize scientific insights. Governments often spend far more money than individual businesses can afford in an effort to ensure that their countries don't fall behind militarily or economically. For instance, when the Soviet Union launched the world's first satellite, *Sputnik*, in 1957, the United States responded with a massive and costly space program, inspired by fear that the Russians were winning the "space race." During the 1960 presidential campaign, John F. Kennedy heightened that fear by repeatedly accusing the Republicans of being lax on Russian missile technology, suggesting that a "missile gap" made the United States vulnerable to nuclear attack. The arms race, fueled by government contracts with corporations, has provided major economic support for scientific research and more general support for the U.S. economy.

Most recently, governments worldwide are spending vast sums to win the next technological race, whether it be information technology, biotechnology, or nanotechnology—the latest area that promises solutions to a wide range of problems that all societies confront today. *Nanotechnology* involves working with matter at the atomic, or "nano," scale (a billionth of a meter), creating new materials that have novel properties: tiny particles that can enter the bloodstream and "search and destroy" particular cancer cells, replacing much more toxic chemotherapy; ultra-strong, lightweight carbon fibers, which have already found their way into golf clubs, tennis rackets, and bicycle frames, and which promise to revolutionize aircraft; data storage devices that can store a hundred times as much data as the most powerful electronics currently available; and highly efficient nanoscale filtration devices that can remove major industrial contaminants from groundwater. Countries are investing significant public funds in support of research, development, and commercialization of advanced technologies, hoping to profit while solving some of the world's most vexing problems.

2 CURRENT THEORIES: IS GLOBALIZATION TODAY SOMETHING NEW—OR HAVE WE SEEN IT ALL BEFORE?

In recent years, globalization has become a hotly debated topic. Most people accept that important transformations are occurring, but the extent to which one can attribute them to "globalization" is contested. This disagreement is not surprising, given the unpredictable and turbulent process that globalization involves. David Held and his colleagues (1999) have identified three schools of thought: skeptics, hyperglobalizers, and transformationalists. These approaches to the globalization debate are summarized in Table 20.1.

The Skeptics

Skeptics in the globalization controversy believe that present levels of economic interdependence are not unprecedented. Pointing to nineteenth-century statistics on world trade and investment, they contend that modern globalization differs from the past only in the intensity of interaction among nations. While they agree that countries today may have more contact than in previous eras, in their eyes, the current world economy is not sufficiently integrated to constitute a truly globalized economy. This is because the bulk of trade occurs within three regional groups: Europe, Asia-Pacific, and North America. The countries of the EU, for example, trade predominantly among themselves. The same is true of the other regional groups, thereby invalidating the notion of a single global economy (Hirst, 1997).

Many skeptics focus on *regionalization* within the world economy—such as the emergence of major financial and trading blocs—as evidence that the world economy has become less integrated rather than more (Boyer and Drache, 1996; Hirst and Thompson, 1999). Compared with the patterns of trade that prevailed a century ago, they argue, the world economy is less global in its geographical scope and more concentrated on intense pockets of activity. They strongly reject the view held by some, such as the hyperglobalizers, that globalization is producing a world order in which national governments are less central. According to the skeptics, national governments continue to be key players because of their involvement in regulating and coordinating economic activity. Governments, for example, are the driving force behind many trade agreements and policies of economic liberalization.

The Hyperglobalizers

The hyperglobalizers argue that globalization is a very real phenomenon, the consequences of which can be felt almost everywhere. They see globalization as a process that is indifferent to national borders. In their view, globalization is producing a new global order, swept along by powerful flows of cross-border trade and production. They argue that individual countries no longer control their economies because of the vast growth in world trade. National governments and the politicians within them have decreasing control over the issues that cross their borders, such as volatile financial markets and environmental threats. Citizens recognize that politicians' ability to address these problems is limited and, as a result, lose faith in existing systems of governance. Some hyperglobalizers believe that the power of national governments is also being challenged from above—by new regional and international institutions, such as the EU and the WTO. These shifts signal the dawning of a global age (Albrow, 1997) in which national governments decline in importance and influence.

Sociologists such as William Robinson (2001, 2004), Leslie Sklair (2002a, 2002b, 2003), and Saskia Sassen (1996, 2005) tend to reject the label of *hyperglobalist*, a term they associate with such popular writers or journalists as Thomas Friedman, whose best-selling books *The Lexus and the Olive Tree* (2000) and *The World Is Flat* (2005) paint a picture of globalization as a juggernaut that sweeps up everything in its path. Nonetheless, they do argue that transnational economic actors and political institutions are challenging the dominance of national ones. Robinson has studied these changes throughout the world, with a special focus on Latin America. He argues that the most powerful economic actors today are not bound by national boundaries; they are transnational. For example, the "transnational capitalist class" is emerging out of (and is transforming) the capitalist classes of individual countries, because the transnational corporations they manage are global rather than national. By the same token, he argues that nation-states are becoming "component elements" of a transnational state—exemplified, for example, by the WTO, which serves the interests of global businesses as a whole by ensuring that individual countries adhere to the principles of free trade. Robinson (2001) concludes that "the nation-state is a historically specific form of world social organization in the process of becoming transcended by globalization."

Table 20.1

CONCEPTUALIZING GLOBALIZATION: THREE TENDENCIES

CHARACTERISTIC	SKEPTICS	TRANSFORMA-TIONALISTS	HYPERGLOBAL-IZERS
What's New?	Trading blocs, weaker geogovernance than in earlier periods	Historically unprecedented levels of global interconnectedness	A global age
Dominant Features	World less interdependent than in 1890s	"Thick" (intensive and extensive) globalization	Global capitalism, global governance, global civil society
Power of National Government	Reinforced or enhanced	Reconstituted, restructured	Declining or eroding
Driving Forces of Globalization	Governments and markets	Combined forces of modernity	Capitalism and technology
Pattern of Stratification	Increased marginalization of global south	New architecture of world order	Erosion of old hierarchies
Dominant Motif	National interest	Transformation of political community	McDonald's, Apple, etc.
Conceptualization of Globalization	As internationalization and regionalization	As the reordering of interregional relations and action at a distance	As a reordering of the framework of human action
Historical Trajectory	Regional blocs/clash of civilizations	Indeterminate: global integration and fragmentation	Global civilization
Summary Argument	Internationalization depends on government acquiescence and support	Globalization transforming government power and world politics	The end of the nation-state

Source: Adapted from Held et al., 1999.

The Transformationalists

The transformationalists take more of a middle position. Writers such as David Held and Anthony G. McGrew (Held et al., 1999) and Anthony Giddens, one of the authors of this textbook (1990), see globalization as the central force behind a broad spectrum of change. According to them, the global order is being transformed, but many of the old patterns remain. Governments, for instance, still retain a good deal of power in spite of global interdependence. These transformations are not restricted to economics but are equally prominent within politics, culture, and personal life. Transformationalists contend that the current level of globalization is breaking down established boundaries between internal and external, international and domestic. In adjusting to this new order, societies, institutions, and individuals must navigate contexts where previous structures have been shaken up.

Unlike hyperglobalizers, transformationalists see globalization as a dynamic and open process that is subject to influence and change. It is developing in a contradictory fashion, encompassing tendencies that frequently operate in opposition to one another. Globalization is a two-way flow of images, information, and influences. Global migration, media, and telecommunications are contributing to the diffusion of cultural influences. According to transformationalists, globalization is a decentered process characterized by links and cultural flows that work in a multidirectional way. Because globalization is the product of numerous intertwined global networks, it is not driven from one particular part of the world.

Rather than losing sovereignty, as the hyperglobalizers argue, countries are restructuring in response to new, nonterritorial forms of economic and social organization (e.g., corporations, social movements, and international bodies). Transformationalists argue that we are no longer living in a state-centric world; instead, governments must adopt a more active, outward-looking stance under the complex conditions of globalization (Cerny, 2005; Rosenau, 1997). In other words, nation-states remain relevant actors, but their function is changing. Globalization can perhaps be best understood as a tension between *inter*national (among nation-states) and *trans*national (borderless) social forces.

Whose View Is Most Nearly Correct?

There are elements of truth in all three views, although those of the transformationalists are perhaps the most balanced. The skeptics underestimate how much the world is changing; world finance markets, for example, are organized on a global level much more than ever before. Yet, at the same time, the world has undergone periods of globalization before—only to withdraw into periods when countries protected their markets and closed their borders to trade. Although the march of globalization seems inevitable, it may not continue unabated: Countries that find themselves losing out may attempt to stem the tide, as indicated by Brexit as well as recent elections in Germany, Poland, and the United States.

On the one hand, the hyperglobalizers are correct in pointing to the current strength of globalization as dissolving many national barriers, changing the nature of state power, and creating powerful transnational social classes. On the other hand, they often see globalization too much in economic terms and too much as a one-way process. In reality, globalization is much more complex. World-systems theorists such as Immanuel Wallerstein (2004) and Giovanni Arrighi (1994) argue that while countries remain important actors on the global field, so, too, are transnational corporations. National governments will neither dissolve under the weight of a globalized

CONCEPT CHECKS

1 Compare and contrast how the skeptics, the hyperglobalizers, and the transformationalists explain the phenomenon of globalization.

2 How might skeptics, hyperglobalizers, and transformationalists interpret differently the growing global prominence of China?

economy (as some hyperglobalizers argue) nor reassert themselves as the dominant political force (as some skeptics argue), but rather will seek to steer global capitalism to their own advantage. The world economy of the future may be much more globalized than today's, with multinational corporations and global institutions playing increasingly important roles. But some countries in the world economy may still be more powerful than even the most powerful transnational actors.

The world is in the midst of a highly dynamic and turbulent transformation. It is not surprising, perhaps, that scholars cannot agree on the social forces that are reshaping it.

3   RECENT RESEARCH ON GLOBALIZATION AND SOCIAL CHANGE

As we have emphasized throughout this textbook, *globalization* refers to the fact that we increasingly live in one world, so that individuals, groups, and nations become more *interdependent*—that is, what happens 12,000 miles away is likely to have enormous consequence for our daily lives. In this section, we examine how advances in technology, coupled with political and economic changes, including the rise of transnational corporations, have contributed to globalization. We then consider the impact of globalization on both our personal lives and the wider social world, examining how globalization has introduced new forms of risk and exacerbated global wealth inequality.

Factors Contributing to Globalization

Although globalization is often portrayed solely as an economic phenomenon, it is in fact created by the coming together of technological, political, and economic factors. It has been driven above all by the development of information and communications technologies that have intensified the speed and scope of interaction among people worldwide.

Information Flows

Important advances in technology and the world's telecommunications infrastructure have facilitated the explosion in global communications. The post–World War II era has seen a transformation in the scope and intensity of telecommunications flows. Traditional telephone communication, which depended on analog signals sent through wires and cables, has been replaced by integrated systems in which vast amounts of information are compressed and transferred digitally. Cable technology has become more efficient and less expensive. The development of fiber-optic cables, for example, has dramatically expanded the number of channels that can be carried, and even this recent technology has achieved significant advances. The spread of communications satellites has also helped expand international communications. As of 2019, the United Nations Office for Outer Space Affairs stated that there were 4,987 satellites revolving around the earth (Chaturvedi, 2019).

The effect of these communications systems has been staggering. In countries with highly developed telecommunications infrastructures, homes and offices have multiple

Workers man a call center in Gurgaon, India.

links to the outside world, including telephones (both land lines and cell phones), digital and cable television, and the Internet. The Internet is the fastest-growing communication tool ever developed. More than 4.1 billion people worldwide (over half of the world's population) were estimated to be using the Internet at the end of 2019, representing more than 273 percent growth in usage since 2005 (International Tele-communication Union, 2020).

These forms of technology facilitate the compression of time and space: Two individuals located on opposite sides of the planet can not only hold a conversation in real time, they can send documents and images or tweet their ideas to each other with the help of satellite technology. Widespread use of the Internet and smartphones is accelerating processes of globalization; more people are becoming interconnected through these technologies in places that have previously been isolated or poorly served by traditional communications. Although the telecommunications infrastructure is not evenly developed around the world, a growing number of countries now have access to international communications networks.

Globalization is also being driven forward by the electronic integration of the world economy. The global economy increasingly involves activity that is weightless and intangible (Quah, 1999), because so many products have their base in information, as with computer software, media and entertainment products, and Internet-based services. A variety of new terms describe this new social order, such as *information society*, *service society*, and *knowledge society*. The emergence of this "knowledge society" reflects a broad base of consumers who are technologically literate and who eagerly integrate new advances in computing, entertainment, and telecommunications into their everyday lives.

The very operation of the global economy reflects the changes characteristic of the information age. Many aspects of the economy now require networks that cross national boundaries (Castells, 1996). To be competitive in globalizing conditions, businesses and corporations have become more flexible and less hierarchical. Production practices and organizational patterns have become more flexible, partnering arrangements with other firms have become commonplace, and participation in worldwide distribution networks has become essential.

Whether a job is in a factory or a call center, it can be done more cheaply in China, India, or some other country in the global south. The same is true for software engineering, graphic design, and financial advice. Of course, to the extent that global competition for labor reduces the cost of goods and services, it also provides for a wealth of cheaper products (Roach, 2005). As consumers, we all benefit from low-cost flat-panel TVs made in China or inexpensive computer games programmed in India. It is an open question, however, whether the declining cost of consumption will balance out wage and job losses due to globalization.

Political Changes

Political changes are driving forces behind contemporary globalization. One of the most significant was the collapse of Soviet-style communism, which occurred in Eastern Europe in 1989 and in the Soviet Union itself in 1991. Since then, countries in the former Soviet bloc—including Russia, Ukraine, Poland, Hungary, the Czech Republic, the Baltic states, and the states of the Caucasus and Central Asia—have been moving toward Western-style political and economic systems and are increasingly integrated into the global community. In fact, the collapse of communism not only hastened processes of globalization but also was a result of it. The centrally planned Communist economies and the ideological and cultural control of Communist political authority ultimately could not survive in an era of global media and an electronically integrated world economy.

A second political factor leading to intensifying globalization is the growth of international and regional mechanisms of government. The UN and the EU are two prominent examples of international organizations that bring together nation-states into a common political forum. Whereas the UN does this as an association of individual nation-states, the EU is a form of transnational governance in which member states relinquish some national sovereignty. The governments of EU states are bound by directives, regulations, and court judgments from common EU bodies, but they also reap

The proliferation of smartphones is accelerating the process of globalization.

economic, social, and political benefits from their participation in the regional union.

Yet both the UN and the EU have been challenged in recent years. The UN, unfortunately, has proven to be a weak actor. One of the reasons is that significant UN actions require the consent of its Security Council, which in turn requires the agreement of at least 9 of its 15 members, including all 5 of its permanent members (the United States, France, England, Russia, and China). Another reason is that member nations are

international governmental organizations (IGOs) International organizations established by treaties between governments for purposes of conducting business between the nations making up their membership.

international nongovernmental organizations (INGOs) International organizations established by agreements between the individuals or private organizations making up their membership.

not willing to give up their sovereignty to the UN, which consequently lacks the means to enforce its actions. The EU has had difficulty managing the economic slowdown of its member nations, including the near-insolvency of debt-ridden countries such as Greece. The influx of refugees from war-torn Syria and other countries has created seemingly insurmountable challenges, particularly since once they are in any European country, migrants can freely cross borders into any other. Antimigrant sentiments have grown, leading some to question the "open borders" policies that have thus far created a strongly unified Europe.

One result was the so-called "Brexit" vote in Britain, a June 2016 referendum in which slightly more than half of all voters (52 percent) called for Britain to withdraw from the EU. The vote passed because of voters' concerns about immigration and the belief that Britain was surrendering too much national sovereignty to the EU governance system in Brussels. While opponents of Brexit argued that such concerns were greatly overblown, they could not assuage the fears of a majority of voters. The Brexit vote sent shock waves throughout the EU, since it raised fears that other countries may eventually follow suit.

A third political factor is the growing importance of **international governmental organizations (IGOs)** and **international nongovernmental organizations** (**INGOs**; see also Chapter 6). An international governmental organization is a body that is established by participating governments and given responsibility for regulating or overseeing a domain of activity that is transnational in scope. Such bodies regulate issues ranging from civil aviation to broadcasting to the disposal of hazardous waste. In 1909, 37 IGOs were in existence to regulate transnational affairs; by 2005, there were more than 7,000 (Union of International Associations, 2005). Prominent examples

Brexit, a June 2016 referendum in which a majority of voters called for Britain to exit the European Union, was fueled in part by concerns about immigration. Most EU member countries share open borders.

include the International Monetary Fund, the World Bank, the World Trade Organization, and the UN.

INGOs differ from IGOs in that they are not affiliated with government institutions. Rather, they are independent organizations that work alongside governmental bodies in making policy decisions and addressing international issues. Some of the best-known INGOs—such as Greenpeace, Médecins Sans Frontières (Doctors Without Borders), the International Committee of the Red Cross, and Amnesty International—are involved in environmental protection and humanitarian relief efforts. But the activities of the nearly 40,000 lesser-known groups also link countries and communities (United States Institute of Peace, 2013).

Finally, the spread of information technology has expanded the possibilities for contact among people worldwide, while also facilitating the flow of information about people and events in distant places. Some of the most gripping events of recent decades—such as the fall of the Berlin Wall; the violent crackdown on democratic protesters in China's Tiananmen Square; the terrorist attacks of September 11, 2001, Paris in 2015, Brussels in 2016, Manchester and London in 2017; and the Arab Spring protests—unfolded through the media before a truly global audience. Such events, along with less dramatic ones, have caused a reorientation in people's thinking from the level of the nation-state to the global stage.

This shift to a global outlook has two significant consequences. First, as members of a global community, people increasingly perceive that social responsibility extends beyond national borders. There is a growing assumption that the international community has an obligation to act in crisis situations to protect the physical well-being or human rights of people whose lives are under threat. In the case of natural disasters, such interventions take the form of humanitarian relief and technical assistance. In recent years, earthquakes in Haiti, floods in Mozambique, famine in Africa, hurricanes in Central America, the tsunami that hit Asia and Africa, and the 2015 earthquake in Nepal that claimed more than 8,000 lives and injured another 23,000 have been rallying points for global assistance. Today, with a growing awareness of the scientific consensus on the possible ramifications of global warming, environmental movements—united by social media—have mushroomed from the Marshall Islands to Miami.

There have also been stronger calls for interventions in the case of war, ethnic conflict, and the violation of human rights, although such mobilizations are more problematic than with natural disasters. In the case of the Gulf War in 1991 and the violent conflicts in Bosnia and Kosovo (in the former Yugoslavia), many people saw military intervention as justified in the interest of defending human rights and national sovereignty.

Second, a global outlook means that people increasingly look to sources other than the nation-state in formulating their own sense of identity. This phenomenon is produced by and further accelerates processes of globalization. Local cultural identities in various parts of the world are experiencing powerful revivals at a time when the traditional hold of the nation-state is undergoing profound transformation. In Europe, for example, inhabitants of Scotland and the Basque region of Spain might be more likely to identify themselves as Scottish or Basque (or simply as Europeans) rather than as British or Spanish. The nation-state as a source of identity is waning in many areas as political shifts at the regional and global levels loosen people's orientations toward the states in which they live. A form of nationalism based on ethnicity, religion, or culture—rather than nation-state—is reflected in growing persecution in many countries, and sometimes outright violence, against those perceived as non-native, such as immigrants or members of religious minorities.

Economic Changes: The Growing Importance of Transnational Corporations

Among the many economic factors driving globalization, the role of transnational corporations is particularly important. **Transnational corporations** are companies that produce goods or market services in more than one country. These may be small firms with one or two factories outside the country where they are based or gigantic international ventures whose operations crisscross the globe. Some of the biggest transnational corporations are Apple, Disney, ExxonMobil, Volkswagen, General Motors, Google, McDonald's, Nike, Starbucks, Toyota, and Walmart. Even when transnational corporations have a clear national base, they are oriented toward global markets and global profits.

Transnational corporations account for some two-thirds of all world trade, are instrumental in diffusing new technology around the globe, and are major actors in international financial markets. As one group of writers has noted, they are "the linchpins of the contemporary world economy" (Held et al., 1999). A Swiss study of more than 43,000 transnational corporations found that a mere 737 firms—less than 2 percent of the total—accounted for four-fifths of their combined monetary value. The financial services industry is a power player in the global economy: The top 50 firms were primarily financial organizations such as banks and giant investment firms (Vitali, Glattfelder, and Battiston, 2011). The world's 500 largest transnational corporations had combined revenues of more than $32.7 trillion in 2018 (*Fortune*, 2019); in the same year, $75.6 trillion in goods and services were produced by the entire world (World Bank, 2017c). While the United States remains home to the largest number of giant transnational corporations, its share has slipped considerably in recent years, particularly with the rise of Asian countries such as Japan, South Korea, and especially China.

Transnational corporations became a global phenomenon after World War II. Expansion initially came from firms based in the United States, but by the 1970s, European and Japanese firms also began to invest abroad. In the late 1980s and 1990s, transnational corporations expanded dramatically with the establishment of three powerful regional markets: Europe (the Single European Market), Asia-Pacific (the Osaka Declaration, which guaranteed free and open trade by 2010), and North America (the North American Free Trade Agreement, or NAFTA). Since the early 1990s, countries in other areas have also eased restrictions on foreign investment. By the turn of the twenty-first century, few economies were beyond the reach of transnational corporations. Over the past decade, transnational corporations based in industrialized economies have been expanding their operations in countries in the global south, as well as in countries in Eastern Europe and countries that were part of the former Soviet Union.

The "electronic economy" also underpins economic globalization. Banks, corporations, fund managers, and individual investors can now shift funds internationally with

transnational corporations Business corporations located in two or more countries.

Transnational corporations such as Coca-Cola are eager to tap growing markets in countries such as China and India. Corporate leaders break ground on a new plant in the Gansu province of China. Coca-Cola has opened 45 production facilities in mainland China, an investment of over $13 billion, since it entered the market in 1979.

the click of a mouse. This new ability carries great risks, however. Transfers of vast amounts of capital can destabilize economies and trigger international financial crises. As the global economy becomes increasingly integrated, a financial collapse in one part of the world can have an enormous effect on distant economies. This fact became painfully evident when the once-venerable financial services firm Lehman Brothers filed for bankruptcy in 2008. The collapse of Lehman Brothers, which held an estimated $600 billion in assets, caused financial shockwaves throughout the United States and global economies. The Dow Jones dropped by more than 4 percentage points immediately following Lehman's filing for Chapter 11 bankruptcy. Banks and insurers throughout the world, from Scotland to Japan, registered devastating losses as a result (Council on Foreign Relations, 2013). The Dow's drop following Lehman Brothers' collapse was only recently topped in 2020 when the rise of coronavirus infections in the United States led the Dow Jones to drop over 12 percentage points, making it the largest single drop since the 9/11 attacks in 2001 (Imbert, 2020).

The Effect of Globalization on Our Lives

Although globalization is often associated with changes within big systems—such as world financial markets, production and trade, and telecommunications—its effects are felt equally strongly in the private realm. Inevitably, our personal lives have been altered as globalizing forces enter into our local contexts, our homes, and our communities through impersonal sources—such as the media, the Internet, and popular culture—as well as through personal contact with individuals from other countries and cultures.

As the societies in which we live undergo profound transformations, the institutions that underpin them have become outdated, which is, in turn, forcing a redefinition of the family, gender roles, sexuality, personal identity, our interactions with others, and our relationships to work. The political, economic, social, and technological factors just described are producing a phenomenon without parallel in terms of intensity and scope.

The Rise of Individualism

In the current age, individuals have much more opportunity to shape their own lives than once was the case. At one time, tradition and custom strongly influenced the path of people's lives. Factors such as social class, gender, ethnicity, and religious affiliation could close off certain avenues for individuals or open up others. The values, lifestyles, and ethics prevailing in one's community provided fixed guidelines for living.

Conditions of globalization, however, bring a new individualism in which people actively construct their own identities. The weight of tradition and established values is lessening as local communities interact with a new global order. The social codes that formerly guided people's choices and activities have significantly loosened. Traditional frameworks of identity are dissolving; new patterns of identity are emerging. Globalization is forcing people constantly to respond and adjust to the changing environment; as individuals, we now evolve within the larger context. Even small choices in daily life—what to wear, how to spend leisure time, and how to care for our health and our bodies—are part of an ongoing process of creating and re-creating our self-identities.

Work Patterns

Although we may regard work as a chore or a necessary evil, it is undeniably a crucial element in our lives. Not only our jobs but also many other aspects of our existence—from our friends to our leisure pursuits—are shaped by our work patterns.

Globalization has unleashed profound transformations within the world of work. New patterns of international trade and the move to a knowledge economy have significantly altered long-standing employment patterns. Many traditional industries have become obsolete or are losing their share of the market to competitors abroad whose labor costs are lower than in industrialized countries. Global trade and new forms of technology have affected traditional manufacturing communities, where industrial workers have been left unemployed and without the skills required by the knowledge-based economy. These communities are facing new social problems, including long-term unemployment and rising crime rates, as a result of economic globalization.

If at one time people's working lives were dominated by employment with one employer over several decades—the so-called job-for-life framework—today, more individuals are creating their own career paths. Often this process involves changing jobs several times over the course of a career, building up new skills and abilities, and transferring them to diverse work contexts. Standard patterns of full-time work are dissolving into more flexible arrangements: working from home via information technology, job sharing, short-term consulting projects, flextime, and so forth (Kalleberg, 2003). While flexibility affords new opportunities for some, for most it means greater uncertainty. Job security and attendant health care and retirement benefits have largely become things of the past.

Women having entered the workforce in large numbers has strongly affected the personal lives of people of both sexes. Expanded professional and educational opportunities have led many women to put off marriage and children until after they have begun a career. Also, many women return to work shortly after having children, instead of remaining at home. These shifts have required important adjustments within families, in terms of the domestic division of labor, the role of men in child-rearing, and the emergence of more family-friendly work policies to accommodate the needs of dual-earner households. Tech companies such as Facebook, Amazon, Microsoft, Snap, and Netflix all recently expanded their parental leave policies, and as of 2017, IKEA now offers all 13,000 of its employees—men and women, part-time workers and full-time workers—up to four months of paid parental leave.

Popular Culture

The cultural effects of globalization have received much attention. Images, ideas, goods, and styles are now disseminated worldwide more rapidly than ever. Trade, new information technologies, the international media, and global migration have all promoted the free movement of culture across national borders. Many people believe that we now live in a single information order—a massive global network where information is shared quickly and in great volumes. A simple example illustrates this point.

The 2009 film *Avatar* is a 3D science-fiction epic in which a greedy Earth-based corporation threatens to destroy a lush forest on the habitable moon Pandora, along with the humanlike Na'vi who live there in peaceful harmony with nature, to obtain the precious mineral called (appropriately) "unobtainium." *Avatar* quickly became the highest-grossing film in history, garnering $2.8 billion at the box office, three-quarters of which came from outside the United States. The film is one of many cultural products that has succeeded in cutting across national boundaries and creating a truly international phenomenon. More recently, films like *Star Wars: The Rise of Skywalker* and *Wonder Woman* have enjoyed worldwide success.

What accounts for the enormous popularity of a film such as *Avatar*? And what does its success tell us about globalization? At one level, *Avatar* was popular for straightforward reasons: It combined romance (one of the humans who assumed the bodily shape—avatar—of a Na'vi to infiltrate their community predictably falls in love with a beautiful Na'vi woman) and drama (will the avatar go native and side with the Na'vi? Will the primitive weaponry of the Na'vi triumph over the high-tech weaponry of the humans?). The film was also lavishly produced and included dazzling state-of-the-art special effects.

But another reason for *Avatar*'s popularity is that it reflected ideas and values that resonated with audiences worldwide. One of the film's central themes is the possibility of romantic love prevailing over vast cultural (indeed, racial) differences and community traditions. Can a human male, even occupying the body of an avatar, truly find love with a 10-foot-tall blue-skinned Na'vi woman? The film, happily in the eyes of its many viewers, shows that true love can indeed conquer all, including a galactic version of racial prejudice and the power of transgalactic corporations that will stop at nothing to satisfy their greed.

These themes undoubtedly resonated with both widely shared romantic yearnings and growing environmentalist concerns. The success of a film such as *Avatar* reflects changing values and may also contribute to this shift in values. Western-made films and television programs, which dominate the global media, advance political, social, and economic agendas that reflect a specifically Western worldview. Some people worry that globalization is fostering a global culture in which the values of the most powerful and affluent—in this instance, Hollywood filmmakers—overwhelm local customs and tradition. According to this view, globalization is a form of cultural imperialism in which Western values, styles, and outlooks smother individual national cultures.

Others, by contrast, have linked globalization to a growing differentiation in cultural traditions and forms, as is seen in the Indian Bollywood and Nigerian Nollywood film industries discussed at the beginning of this chapter. Global society is characterized by an enormous diversity of cultures existing side by side. Local traditions are joined by a host of additional cultural forms from abroad, presenting a bewildering array of lifestyle options. Rather than a unified global culture, what we are witnessing is the fragmentation of cultural forms (Friedman, 1994). Established identities and ways of life grounded in local communities and cultures are giving way to hybrid identities composed of elements from contrasting cultural sources (Hall, 1992). For example, while *bhangra* melodies hail from the Punjab region of India, U.S. music fans may recognize bhangra harmonies and rhythms from hip-hop artists such as Beyoncé and Jay-Z. India's film industry sells twice as many tickets as Hollywood—although revenues from U.S. films eclipse those from Bollywood.

Globalization and Risk

The consequences of globalization are far-reaching, affecting virtually all aspects of the social world. Yet, because globalization is an open-ended and internally contradictory process, it produces outcomes that are difficult to predict and control. Another way of thinking of this dynamic is in terms of risk. Many of the changes wrought by globalization present new forms of risk. Unlike risks from the past, which had established causes and known effects, today's risks are incalculable in origin and indeterminate in their consequences.

American films such as *Star Wars: The Rise of Skywalker* dominate the global box office. Does this amount to cultural imperialism?

The Spread of "Manufactured Risk"

Humans have always had to face risks, but today's risks are qualitatively different from those of earlier times. Until recently, human societies were threatened by **external risk** from the natural world—dangers such as drought, earthquakes, famines, and storms. Today, however, we increasingly face various types of **manufactured risk**—risks created by the effect of our own knowledge and technology on the natural world. Many current environmental and health risks are the outcomes of our own interventions into nature.

Environmental Risks One of the clearest illustrations of manufactured risk involves threats posed to the natural environment (see Chapter 19). A consequence of accelerating industrial and technological development has been the steady spread of human intervention in nature—for example, through urbanization, industrial production and pollution, large-scale agricultural projects, the construction of dams and hydroelectric plants, and nuclear power. The collective outcome of such processes has been widespread environmental destruction whose precise cause is indeterminate and whose consequences are difficult to calculate.

In the globalizing world, ecological risk takes many forms. One example of ecological risk is global warming. Concern over global warming has been mounting in the scientific community; it is now generally accepted that Earth's temperature has been increasing due to the buildup within the atmosphere of greenhouse gases—a by-product of human-made processes such as deforestation and the burning of fossil fuels. The potential consequences of global warming are devastating: If polar ice caps continue to melt at the current rate, sea levels will rise and may threaten low-lying land masses and their human populations. Changes in climate patterns have been cited as possible causes of the severe floods that afflicted Mozambique in 2000, the record number of hurricanes that swept through the Atlantic and Gulf of Mexico in the fall of 2005, as well as Hurricane Katrina, which devastated New Orleans, and Hurricane Sandy, which leveled entire neighborhoods in New Jersey and New York in 2012. Most recently, the brushfires in Australia, also linked to climate change, destroyed 27.2 million acres, and are estimated to have killed over 1 billion animals (Zaveri and Rueb, 2020; Woodward, 2020).

Because environmental risks are diffuse in origin, it is unclear how to address them or determine who bears responsibility for remedying them. For example, although scientists have found that chemical pollution levels have harmed Antarctic penguin colonies, it is impossible to identify either the exact origins of the pollution or its possible consequences for the penguins in the future. In such an instance—and in hundreds of similar cases—action to address the risk is unlikely because the extent of both the cause and the outcome is unknown (Beck, 1995).

external risk Dangers that spring from the natural world and are unrelated to the actions of humans. Examples of external risk include droughts, earthquakes, famines, and storms.

manufactured risk Dangers that are created by the impact of human knowledge and technology on the natural world. Examples of manufactured risk include global warming and genetically modified foods.

Health Risks Lately, the dangers posed to human health by manufactured risks have attracted great attention. The media and public health campaigns, for example, urge people to limit their exposure to harmful ultraviolet rays and apply sunscreen to prevent burning. Sun exposure has been linked to a heightened risk of skin cancer, possibly due to the depletion of the ozone layer—the layer of Earth's atmosphere that normally filters out ultraviolet light. Because of the high volume of chemical emissions produced by human activities and industry, the concentration of ozone in the atmosphere has been diminishing, and, in some cases, ozone holes have opened up.

Many examples of manufactured risk are linked to food, because advances in science and technology have heavily influenced modern farming and food production techniques. For example, chemical pesticides and herbicides are widely used in commercial agriculture, and chickens, pigs, and many other animals raised for food are pumped full of hormones and antibiotics. Some people have suggested that such farming techniques compromise food safety and could adversely affect humans. Two particular controversies have raised widespread public concern: the debate over genetically modified foods and the outbreak of mad cow disease.

The saga of genetically modified foods began 20 years ago, when some of the world's leading chemical and agricultural firms decided that new knowledge about genes could transform the world's food supply. These companies had been making pesticides and herbicides but wanted to develop a major market for the future. The American firm Monsanto was the leader in developing much of the new technology. Monsanto bought up seed companies, sold off its chemical division, worked to bring the new crops to market, and launched a gigantic advertising campaign promoting the benefits of its genetically modified crops to farmers and consumers. The early responses were just as the company had confidently anticipated. By early 1999, 55 percent of the soybeans and 35 percent of the corn produced in the United States contained genetic alterations. From 1996 to 2016, genetically modified foods experienced an unprecedented 110-fold increase in worldwide production (International Service for the Acquisition of Agri-biotech Applications, 2016).

It is currently estimated that upward of 75 percent of all processed foods sold in grocery stores contain some genetically modified components (Center for Food Safety, 2017). In addition to North America, genetically modified crops are being widely grown in China. Since genetically modified crops are relatively new, no one can be certain about their effects once they are introduced into the environment. Many ecological and consumer groups are concerned about the potential risks involved with the adoption of this largely untested technology.

Bovine spongiform encephalopathy (BSE), known popularly as mad cow disease, was first detected in British cattle in 1986. Scientists have linked BSE infection to the practice of raising cattle, normally herbivores, on feed containing traces of the parts of other animals. After the outbreak, the British government took steps to control the disease among cattle, but it claimed that eating beef was safe for humans. Only in the mid-1990s was it admitted that several human deaths from Creutzfeldt-Jakob disease, a degenerative brain condition, had been linked to the consumption of beef from infected cattle. Thousands of British cattle were killed, and strict new legislation was passed to regulate cattle farming and the sale of beef products. Most recently, cattle infected with BSE have been discovered in Canada and the United States, sparking widespread fears about the safety of the food supply.

Although extensive scientific research has explored the risks to humans from BSE, the findings remain inconclusive. There is a risk that individuals who consumed British beef in the years preceding the discovery of BSE may have been exposed to infection. Calculating the risks to humans from BSE is an example of the complexity of risk assessment in the contemporary world. It is necessary to know if and when infected cattle were part of a certain food chain, the level and distribution of the infection present in the cattle, how the beef was processed, and many other details. The sheer quantity of unknown factors has complicated the task.

The Global "Risk Society"

Global warming, the debate over genetically modified foods, the BSE crisis, and other manufactured risks present new choices and challenges. Individuals, countries, and transnational organizations must negotiate risks as they make choices about how to live and conduct business. Because there are no definitive answers about the causes and outcomes of such risks, this endeavor can be bewildering. Should we use food and raw materials if their production or consumption might harm our health and the natural environment?

German sociologist Ulrich Beck (1992) sees these risks contributing to a global "risk society." As technological change progresses and produces new forms of risk, we must constantly respond and adjust to these changes. The risk society, he argues, is not limited to environmental and health risks; it includes a series of interrelated changes within contemporary social life: shifting employment patterns, heightened job insecurity, the declining influence of tradition and custom on self-identity, the erosion of traditional family patterns, and the democratization of personal relationships. Because personal futures are much less fixed than they were in traditional societies, decisions of all kinds present risks. Getting married, for example, is a riskier endeavor today than when marriage was a lifelong institution. Decisions about educational qualifications and career paths can also feel risky: It is difficult to predict what skills will be valuable in an economy that is changing so rapidly.

According to Beck (1995), an important aspect of the risk society is that its hazards are not restricted spatially, temporally, or socially. Today's risks have global, not merely personal, consequences. Many forms of manufactured risk, such as those concerning human health and the environment, cross national boundaries. Consider the disaster at the Fukushima Daiichi nuclear power plant in Japan in 2011. Everyone living in the immediate vicinity—regardless of age, class, gender, or status—was exposed to dangerous levels of radiation.

Globalization and Inequality

Beck and other scholars have identified risk as one of the main outcomes of globalization and technological advance. Yet globalization is generating other important challenges because its effect is differential—and some of its consequences are not benign. Next to mounting ecological problems, the expansion of inequalities within and between societies is one of the most serious challenges facing the world today.

The majority of the world's wealth is concentrated in the industrialized countries of the global north, whereas countries in the global south suffer from widespread poverty, overpopulation, inadequate educational and health care systems, and crippling

Demonstrators march in the streets of Portland, Oregon, as part of an international protest against Monsanto and the use of GMOs.

foreign debt. The disparity between the global north and the global south widened steadily over the course of the twentieth century and is now the largest it has ever been. A recent report on global wealth shows that global inequality is at extreme levels. Taken together, the bottom half of the global population own less than 1 percent of total wealth. In sharp contrast, the richest 10 percent hold 82 percent of the world's wealth, and the top 1 percent alone account for 45 percent of global assets (Shorrocks et al., 2019). Thought of another way, in 2019, just 26 people owned the same wealth as the 3.8 billion people who make up the poorest half of humanity (Oxfam, 2019).

These vast disparities in economic well-being are all the more jarring when daily income is considered. A recent study from the Brookings Institute shows that at the end of 2019, approximately 600 million people are living in extreme poverty; that is, they live on less than $1.90 per day. This is largely due to reduction of poverty in India. Although the proportion of persons who live under such dire circumstances has decreased markedly over the last three decades—from 44 percent in 1981 to 10.7 percent in 2013—the absolute numbers living in abject poverty remain high because the populations in these poor nations are so large. Further, about 70 percent of the world's poor live in Africa. Extreme poverty is clustered in sub-Saharan Africa, which accounts for half of the world's extreme poor (Brookings, 2019).

In much of the global south, levels of economic growth and output over the past century have not kept up with the rate of population growth, whereas the level of economic development in industrialized countries has far outpaced it. These opposing tendencies have caused a marked divergence between the richest and poorest countries. North America has the largest share of global wealth (31 percent). China, on the other hand, accounts for more than 21 percent of the global adult population but only 17 percent of total wealth. And for Africa and India, the population share surpasses the wealth share by multiples greater than 10 and 5, respectively (Shorrocks et al., 2019).

Globalization seems to be exacerbating these trends by further concentrating income, wealth, and resources within a small core of countries. The expansion of global trade has been central to this process. Global trade in goods and services has increased by nearly 60 percent in the last decade, from $13 trillion in 2005 to nearly $19.5 trillion in 2016 (UNCTAD, 2019). The volume of merchandise exports in 2018 exceeded $19.5 trillion—up from $10.6 trillion in 2005. The volume of service exports in 2018 was nearly $5.8 trillion, or 6.4 percent of total global output—up from $2.6 trillion in 2005 (World Bank, 2017e; UNCTAD, 2019). Only a handful of countries in the global south have managed to benefit from the overall rapid growth, and the process of integration into the global economy has been uneven. Some countries—such as the East Asian economies, Chile, India, and Poland—have fared well, with significant growth in exports. Other countries—such as Algeria, Russia, Venezuela, and most of sub-Saharan Africa—have seen few benefits from expanding trade and globalization (UNDP, 2006). There is a danger that many of the countries most in need of economic growth will be left further behind as globalization progresses.

Many scholars see free trade as the key to economic development and poverty relief. Organizations such as the WTO work to liberalize trade regulations and reduce trade barriers. Free trade across borders is viewed as a win-win proposition for countries in both the global north and south. While the industrialized economies are able to export their products to markets worldwide, it is claimed that countries in the global south will benefit by gaining access to world markets. This, in turn, would improve their prospects for integration into the global economy. But many are now challenging this belief, since free trade has also resulted in the loss of millions of U.S. jobs to low-wage countries.

The Campaign for Global Justice

Not everyone agrees that free trade is the solution to poverty and global inequality. In fact, many critics argue that free trade is a one-sided affair that benefits those who are already well off, leads to massive job loss of industrial workers in advanced economies, and exacerbates poverty and dependency within the global south. During the 2016 presidential primary campaigns, Democrat Bernie Sanders and Republican Donald Trump seemed to agree on just one thing: Free trade agreements such as the proposed Trans Pacific Partnership (TPP) were costing Americans their jobs. President Trump since doubled down on his campaign pledge to rethink all trade agreements: He pulled the United States out of the TPP and renegotiated the North American Free Trade Agreement (NAFTA) with Mexico and Canada. The new agreement was named the United States-Mexico-Canada Agreement (USMCA) and was signed by leaders of the three countries in November 2018 (Office of the U.S. Trade Representative, 2020).

Recently, much of this criticism has focused around the WTO, which is at the fore-front of efforts to increase global trade. In 1999, more than 50,000 people from around the world took to the streets of Seattle to protest during the WTO's Millennium Round of trade talks. Trade unionists, environmentalists, human rights campaign-ers, antinuclear activists, farmers, and representatives from hundreds of local and international nongovernmental organizations joined forces to voice their frustration with the WTO—an organization many see as favoring economic imperatives over all other concerns, including human rights, labor rights, the environment, and sustain-able development. Negotiators from the WTO's 134 member states—the number of members has since risen to 164—had come together to discuss measures to liberalize conditions for global trade and investment in agriculture and forest products, among other issues. Yet the talks broke off early with no agreements reached. The organizers of the protests were triumphant—not only had the demonstrations succeeded in dis-rupting the talks, but internal disputes among delegates had also surfaced. The Seattle protests were heralded as the biggest victory to date for campaigners for global justice. Since that time, every ministerial meeting of the WTO has faced massive demonstra-tions by those excluded from the processes of setting the rules for global trade.

Does this campaign represent the emergence of a powerful anti-globalization movement, as some commentators have suggested? Protesters in other cities, such as London and Washington, D.C., argue that free trade and economic globalization fur-ther concentrate wealth in the hands of a few, while increasing poverty for the majority of the world's population. Most of these activists agree that global trade is necessary and potentially beneficial for national economies, but they claim that it needs to be regulated by different rules: trade rules oriented toward protecting human rights, the environment, labor rights, and local economies—not toward ensuring larger profits for already rich corporations.

The protesters claim that the WTO is an undemocratic organization dominated by the interests of the world's richest nations, particularly the United States. Although the members of the WTO include many countries in the global south, many have no influ-ence over the organization's policies because the richest nations set the agenda. Poorer nations have fewer resources, in terms of money and trained personnel, to confront the highly complex issues related to international trade. The president of the World Bank has pointed out that 19 of the 42 African states that are members of the WTO have little or no representation at its headquarters in Geneva (World Bank, 2000).

Such imbalances have very real consequences. For example, although the WTO has insisted that countries in the global south open their markets to imports from industrialized countries, it has allowed industrialized countries to maintain high bar-riers to agricultural imports and provide vast subsidies for their domestic agriculture production to protect their own agricultural sectors. Between 1995 and 2014, the U.S. government spent $322 billion on subsidies to boost the income of crop and livestock farmers (Environmental Working Group, 2016). In 2019 alone, the USDA gave $19 billion in subsidies to farmers (NPR, 2019). For certain crops, like sugar and rice, agricultural subsidies amount to as much as 80 percent of farm income (Stiglitz, 2007). The EU spends $65 billion each year on their farmers, and the farm budget takes up to 40 percent of the EU's yearly expenditure (*New York Times*, 2019). In fact, the average European cow gets a subsidy of approximately $2 a day; more than half of the people

Workers in New Delhi participate in an anti-WTO protest. What are some of the criticisms leveled at the WTO?

in the global south live on less than that amount (Stiglitz, 2007). This means that the world's poorest (and predominantly agricultural) countries do not have access to the large markets for agricultural goods in industrialized countries.

This issue has confounded the expansion of WTO rules covering trade in services, foreign investment, government procurement, and other areas. Beginning with the 2003 WTO ministerial meeting in Mexico, the "Group of 21" countries in the global south, led by Brazil and India, have refused to consider the expansion of WTO rules until the United States and the EU eliminate subsidies for agriculture production and allow greater access to other agriculture markets, such as cotton. The issue of agriculture subsidies still has not been resolved. A group of countries in the global south, again led by Brazil, won two major disputes at the WTO over subsidies for European sugar and American cotton. Despite these rulings, the issue of illegal subsidies Europe and the United States use to support their farmers continues to hamper WTO ministerial meetings.

A similar divide exists over the protection of intellectual property rights—an issue monitored by a WTO multilateral agreement called TRIPS (Trade-Related Aspects of Intellectual Property Rights). In 2016, high-income countries accounted for more than 50 percent of patent applications. Just five patent offices (United States, China, Japan, South Korea, and the European patent office) accounted for nearly 84.5 percent of patent applications (World Intellectual Property Organization, 2018). The concept of intellectual property rights, however, is alien to the global south. Recently, there has been a significant increase in the number of patent claims as biotechnology companies and research institutes push to control and "own" more forms of knowledge, technology, and biodiversity. Many samples of plant material, for example, have been taken from biodiverse areas such as rain forests and developed by pharmaceutical companies into profitable—and patented—medicines. Local knowledge about the medicinal uses of the plants is often used in developing and marketing the medicines, yet the indigenous people receive no compensation for their contribution. As industrialized countries within the WTO push to strengthen intellectual property laws, many people in the global south argue that such a move works against the needs of their countries. Research agendas are dictated by profit interests, not human interests, and valuable forms of technology may end up inaccessible to poorer countries that could benefit from their use.

Another criticism of the WTO is that it operates in secret and is not accountable to citizens who are affected by its decisions. In many ways, this criticism is valid. Trade disputes between members of the WTO are decided behind closed doors by a committee of "experts" who are appointed rather than elected. When a decision is handed down, it is legally binding on all member states and enforceable through a mechanism that authorizes WTO member nations to enact punitive trade policies unless the losing nation complies with the decision.

The WTO can also challenge or override laws that are seen as barriers to trade. This includes national laws or bilateral agreements designed to protect the environment, conserve scarce resources, safeguard public health, or guarantee labor standards and human rights. For example, the WTO has ruled against the EU's ban on U.S. hormone-treated beef (because of its possible links to cancer) and has challenged a law passed in Massachusetts that prohibits companies from investing in Myanmar (Burma) because of its government's human rights violations. In another instance, the United States and the EU attempted to use the TRIPS provision to block the importation of inexpensive generic HIV/AIDS medication into countries in sub-Saharan Africa, whose populations are being devastated by this epidemic. This move produced worldwide public outrage, which forced the WTO to reconsider its rules that regulate patent rights when public health is at stake.

A final concern is the undue influence the United States wields over the activities of the WTO and other international bodies such as the World Bank and the International Monetary Fund. With its overwhelming economic, political, and military might, the United States is able to influence debates and decision making in many international institutions. The unevenness of globalization in part reflects the fact that political and economic power is concentrated in the hands of a few core states. Even as the United States influences the WTO, the United States is also subject to the WTO's rules and decisions. In fact, the United States almost always loses when it is forced to defend its trading practices before a WTO appellate panel (Conti, 2008). For example, in 2003, the WTO determined that high tariffs placed on imports of steel into the United States violated the rights of WTO member nations. Under heavy pressure from its trading partners, the United States eventually rescinded the tariffs and complied with WTO law. This example highlights a tension between the nature of power and the processes of globalization: Can we expect the world's sole superpower to play by the rules when the rules go against the interests of that superpower? What effect will this tension have on the creation of a just and equitable global legal and political system?

CONCEPT CHECKS

1 How has technology facilitated the compression of time and space?

2 What are the three causes of increasing globalization?

3 What effect does globalization have on our everyday lives?

4 Why is globalization associated with new forms of risk? What are the new forms of risk?

5 Briefly describe the debate over the role that free trade plays in global inequality.

4   UNANSWERED QUESTIONS

We are in the midst of a global transformation, so it is difficult to see where we are headed and how we can manage these changes. We face important sociological debates over what comes next and what steps we should take to best address the social, economic, and environmental challenges that have resulted from globalization. In this section, we consider differing views on what comes after modern industrialism and how globalization's rough edges might be best softened.

What Comes after Modern Industrial Society?

Where is social change leading us today? If social theorists do not agree on the nature of globalization, they also differ on where these changes are leading us. Here, we examine two competing perspectives: the notion that we are a postindustrial society and the idea that we have reached a postmodern period.

Some observers have suggested that what is occurring today is a transition to a new society, one that is no longer primarily based on industrialism. We are entering, they claim, a phase of development beyond the industrial era altogether. A variety of terms have been coined to describe this new social order, such as *information society*, *service society*, and *knowledge society*. The term that has come into most common use, however—first employed by Daniel Bell (1976) in the United States and Alain Touraine (1974) in France—is **postindustrial society**, the *post* (meaning "after") referring to the sense that we are moving beyond the old forms of industrial development.

The diversity of terms reflects the countless ideas put forward to interpret current social changes. But one consistent theme is the significance of information or knowledge in the society of the future. Our ways of life throughout the nineteenth and twentieth centuries, based largely on machine power (the manufacture of material goods in factories), is being displaced by one in which information underlies the production system.

In his now-classic *The Coming of Post-Industrial Society*, Bell (1976) argues that the postindustrial order is distinguished by a growth of service occupations at the expense of jobs that produce material goods. The blue-collar worker is no longer the most essential type of employee. White-collar (clerical and professional) workers outnumber blue-collar (factory) workers, with professional and technical occupations growing fastest of all. People working in higher-level white-collar occupations specialize in the production of information and knowledge. The production and control of what Bell calls "codified knowledge"—systematic, coordinated information—is society's main productive resource. Those who create and distribute this knowledge—scientists, computer specialists, economists, engineers, and professionals of all kinds—increasingly become the leading social groups, replacing industrialists and entrepreneurs. On the level of culture, there is a shift away from the work ethic characteristic of industrialism;

postindustrial society A notion advocated by those who believe that processes of social change are taking us beyond the industrialized order. A postindustrial society is based on the production of information rather than on material goods. According to postindustrialists, we are currently experiencing a series of social changes as profound as those that initiated the industrial era some 200 years ago.

We now live in an information society in which knowledge and information rather than manufactured goods are the chief output of the U.S. economy.

people are freer to innovate and enjoy themselves in both their work and their domestic lives.

Other scholars have gone as far as saying that the developments now occurring are even more profound than signaling the end of the era of industrialism. Postmodern scholars claim that we are witnessing a movement beyond modernity—the attitudes and ways of life associated with modern societies, such as our belief in progress, the benefits of science, and our capability to control the modern world. Advocates of post modernity claim that modern societies drew inspiration from the idea that history has a shape—it "goes somewhere" and leads to progress—and that now this notion has collapsed. There are no longer any overall conceptions of history that make sense (Lyotard, 1985). Not only is there no general notion of progress that can be defended, but there is no such thing as history. The TRIPS **postmodern society** is thus highly pluralistic and diverse. In countless films, videos, and TV programs, images circulate worldwide. We encounter many ideas and values, but these have little connection with the history of the areas we live in, or indeed with our own personal histories. Everything seems constantly in flux. According to one group of authors,

> Our world is being remade. Mass production, the mass consumer, the big city, big-brother state, the sprawling housing estate, and the nation-state are in decline: flexibility, diversity, differentiation, and mobility, communication, decentralization and internationalization are in the ascendant. In the process our own identities, our sense of self, our own subjectivities are being transformed. We are in transition to a new era. (Hall et al., 1988)

postmodern society A technologically sophisticated society that is preoccupied with consumer goods and media images.

While both the postindustrial and postmodern theorists provide important insights, each has shortcomings as well. Critics of the postindustrial argument claim that the trend toward service occupations began with the Industrial Revolution and that service workers have replaced not industrial workers so much as agricultural workers. Moreover, the notion that creative and challenging white-collar work is replacing highly routinized factory work is incorrect; much service-sector employment today is just as routinized and unsatisfying as factory work was in the past (and pays less). The postindustrial society thesis is also criticized for exaggerating the importance of economic factors in producing social change. Finally, critics point out that any attempt to divide history into before and after stages is bound to be proven wrong over time as new (and unanticipated) technological breakthroughs, and their associated social changes, occur.

Postmodern theorists agree with this final criticism, seeing societies as moving into a stage that is so radically different that any attempt to understand general processes

Table 20.2

APPLYING SOCIOLOGY TO GLOBALIZATION IN A CHANGING WORLD

CONCEPT	APPROACH TO UNDERSTANDING GLOBALIZATION IN A CHANGING WORLD	CONTEMPORARY APPLICATION
Time-Space Compression	Technological changes that reduce the time required to cover a given distance, thereby altering the experience of time, and increasing the possibility of human activity over ever-greater distances.	Advances in transportation and telecommunication, which have made it possible to cross the United States coast-to-coast in 5–6 hours by air (as opposed to 5–6 months by horse a century ago)—or to have a face-to-face conversation with a friend a half a world away by smartphone (something that would have been unthinkable a century ago).
Manufactured Risk	Risks that are created by the effects of our own knowledge and technology on the natural world (as opposed to external risks from the natural world that do not result from human activity). Many current environmental and health risks are the outcomes of our own interventions into nature.	Global warming and climate change; global pandemics such as SARS, MERS, and COVID-19; mad cow disease; genetically modified foods.
Postindustrial Society	Society is increasingly based on the production of information rather than on manufactured goods, resulting in social and cultural changes as profound as those that followed the Industrial Revolution some two centuries ago.	The Internet, social media, smartphones, virtual reality, artificial intelligence, virtual meetings (and relationships); the growth of the service economy.

in the social world is doomed, as is the notion that we can change the world for the better. Writers such as Ulrich Beck and Anthony Giddens have strongly criticized this position, arguing instead that, as much as ever, general theories of the social world allow us to intervene to shape it in a positive way. Such theories have considered how contemporary societies are becoming globalized, while everyday life is breaking free from tradition and custom. But these changes should not spell the end of social and political reform. Values, such as a belief in the importance of social community, equality, and caring for the weak and vulnerable, are still very much alive worldwide.

Is There a Need for Global Governance?

Globalization has brought with it violence, internal conflict, and chaotic transformations in many areas of the world. The existing political structures and models appear unequipped to manage the risks, inequalities, and challenges that transcend national borders. Individual governments cannot control the spread of HIV/AIDS or Zika, counter the effects of global warming, or regulate volatile financial markets. Critics of globalization see global organizations such as transnational corporations or the WTO as responsible. Others see opportunities to harness globalizing forces in the pursuit of greater equality, democracy, and prosperity.

Protesters against the WTO and other international financial institutions argue that exuberance over global economic integration and free trade is forcing people to live in an economy rather than a society. Many are convinced that such moves will further weaken the economic position of poor societies by allowing transnational corporations to operate with few or no safety and environmental regulations. Commercial interests, they claim, are increasingly taking precedence over concern for human well-being. Not only within countries in the global south, but in industrialized ones as well, the call is for greater investment in "human capital" (public health, education, and training) if global divisions are not to deepen. In their view, a key challenge for the twenty-first century is to ensure that globalization works for people everywhere, not only for those who are already well placed to benefit from it.

Walden Bello is a sociologist, member of the Philippine Parliament, and anti-globalization activist. Bello (2005) has called for **deglobalization**—reducing global interdependence by rendering economies less dependent on trade and global supply chains, instead making them as local as possible. Bello envisions democratically controlled local economies, where greater equality, rather than profit maximization, would be the goal. This goal would be achieved by subjecting key economic decisions to democratic choice rather than the marketplace. Bello's deglobalized world would boast income redistribution, community cooperatives, small and medium-size businesses, and state enterprises—but no transnational corporations.

Bello regards deglobalization as necessary on ecological as well as moral grounds. He argues that today's global economy, where products move thousands of miles, is in large part responsible for fossil fuel depletion, pollution, greenhouse gases, and global climate change. As he sees it,

We must no longer think simply in terms of neutralizing the multilateral agencies that form the outer trenches of the system

deglobalization The reduction of global interdependence by making economies as local as possible.

but of disabling the transnational corporations that are fortresses and the earth-works that constitute the core of the global economic system. I am talking about disabling not just the WTO, the IMF, and the World Bank but the transnational corporation itself. And I am not talking about a process of "reregulating" the TNCs but of eventually disabling or dismantling them as fundamental hazards to people, society, the environment, to everything we hold dear. (Bello, 2005)

Bello's views on deglobalization would be regarded as completely wrongheaded by those who argue that global capitalism is not only here to stay, but has resulted in higher living standards for hundreds of millions of people. Even those who share many of his criticisms of globalization would most likely regard his call for deglobalization as utopian. They would argue that the challenge is to make globalization work better for everyone—to establish institutions that would more effectively regulate the global economy, instead of leaving it to the marketplace. The Nobel Prize–winning economist Joseph Stiglitz (2003, 2007, 2010) and the philanthropist George Soros (2000, 2005, 2009) have both called for reforms of the current system, rather than overturning it completely.

New forms of global governance could help promote a cosmopolitan world order in which transparent rules and standards for international behavior, such as the defense of human rights, are established and observed. Yet the existing institutions of global governance hardly seem up to the task of reform: The UN and its affiliated organizations, such as the International Labor Organization, have little or no enforcement power, while the WTO, as presently constituted, seeks to promote free trade and economic deregulation (although Stiglitz and others have proposed reforms that could make it more responsive to social concerns).

Erik Olin Wright's 2012 presidential address to the American Sociological Association called for "envisioning real utopias"—nonreformist reforms that would move us incrementally toward a more egalitarian world. In his book *Envisioning Real Utopias* (2010), Wright critically evaluates the pros and cons of numerous proposals for reform, as well as specific organizations (such as worker-owned cooperatives or a guaranteed minimal income) that provide concrete examples of what might be possible. This is important, he argues, because

> most people in the world today, especially in the economically developed regions of the world, no longer believe in this possibility. Capitalism seems to most people part of the natural order of things. . . . This book hopes to contribute to rebuilding a sense of possibility for emancipatory social change by investigating the feasibility of radically different kinds of institutions and social relations that could potentially advance the democratic egalitarian goals historically associated with the idea of socialism. In part this investigation will be empirical, examining cases of institutional innovations that embody in one way or another emancipatory alternatives to the dominant forms of social organization. In part it will be more speculative, exploring theoretical proposals that have not yet been implemented but nevertheless are attentive to realistic problems of institutional design and social feasibility.

The idea is to provide empirical and theoretical grounding for radical democratic egalitarian visions of an alternative social world. (Wright, 2010)

The move toward global governance and more effective regulatory institutions, and the search for alternatives to the present system, are clearly warranted at a time when global interdependence and the rapid pace of change link all people together more than ever before. Whether such changes should take the form of a move toward less global interdependence, as Bello and the global justice movement envision, or reforming the current system, as Soros, Stiglitz, and Wright call for, is open for discussion and debate.

It is not beyond our abilities to reassert our will on the social world. Indeed, such a task appears to be both the greatest necessity and the greatest challenge facing human societies in the twenty-first century.

CONCEPT CHECKS

1 What is the "postindustrial society"?

2 What is the "postmodern era"? What is the main criticism of this concept?

3 What are some examples of a move toward a global democratic structure?

4 Summarize optimistic versus pessimistic views toward global governance.

THE BIG PICTURE

Chapter 20
Globalization in a
Changing World

1 **Basic
Concepts**

p. 819

2 **Current Theories:
Is Globalization Today
Something New—or
Have We Seen It All
Before?**

p. 826

**LEARNING
OBJECTIVES**

Recognize that numerous factors
influence social change, including
the physical environment, political
organization, culture, and
economic factors.

Understand the debates among
skeptics, hyperglobalizers, and
transformationalists over whether
globalization differs radically from
anything in human history.

**TERMS
TO KNOW**

hybridity • social change

**CONCEPT
CHECKS**

1. What are the most important
   political factors that influence social
   change?
2. Name two examples of cultural
   factors that may influence social
   change.
3. How does industrial capitalism affect
   social change?

1. Compare and contrast how the
   skeptics, the hyperglobalizers, and
   the transformationalists explain
   the phenomenon of globalization.
2. How might skeptics, hyperglobalizers,
   and transformationalists interpret
   differently the growing global
   prominence of China?

Exercises: Thinking Sociologically

1. Discuss the many influences on social change: environmental, political, and cultural factors. Summarize how each element can contribute to social change.

2. According to this chapter, we now live in a society where we increasingly face various types of manufactured risks. Briefly explain what these risks consist of. Do you think the last decade has brought us any closer to or further away from confronting the challenges of manufactured risks? Explain.

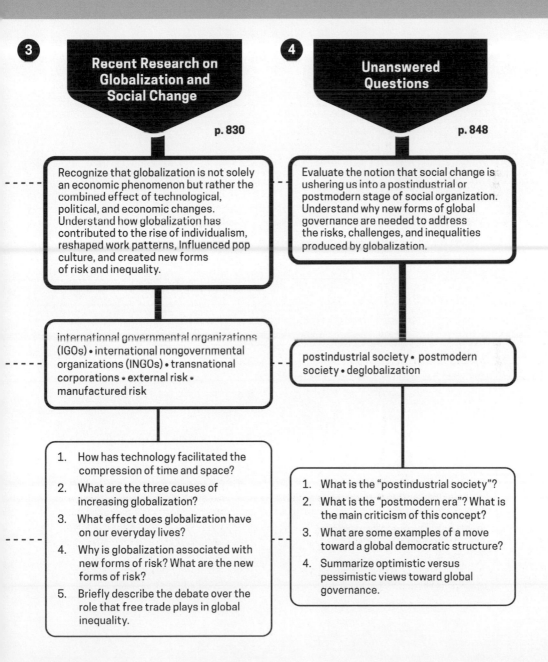

3 **Recent Research on Globalization and Social Change**

p. 830

Recognize that globalization is not solely an economic phenomenon but rather the combined effect of technological, political, and economic changes. Understand how globalization has contributed to the rise of individualism, reshaped work patterns, Influenced pop culture, and created new forms of risk and inequality.

international governmental organizations (IGOs) • international nongovernmental organizations (INGOs) • transnational corporations • external risk • manufactured risk

1. How has technology facilitated the compression of time and space?
2. What are the three causes of increasing globalization?
3. What effect does globalization have on our everyday lives?
4. Why is globalization associated with new forms of risk? What are the new forms of risk?
5. Briefly describe the debate over the role that free trade plays in global inequality.

4 **Unanswered Questions**

p. 848

Evaluate the notion that social change is ushering us into a postindustrial or postmodern stage of social organization. Understand why new forms of global governance are needed to address the risks, challenges, and inequalities produced by globalization.

postindustrial society • postmodern society • deglobalization

1. What is the "postindustrial society"?
2. What is the "postmodern era"? What is the main criticism of this concept?
3. What are some examples of a move toward a global democratic structure?
4. Summarize optimistic versus pessimistic views toward global governance.

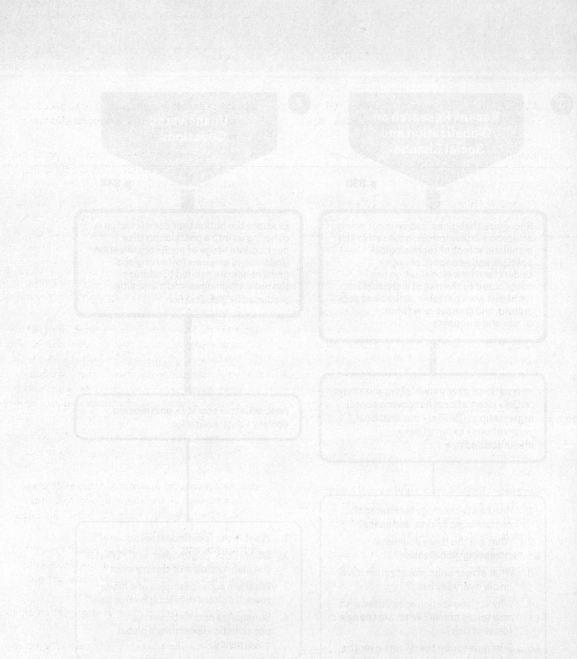

Glossary

Words in **bold** type within entries refer to terms found elsewhere in the glossary.

AARP: U.S. advocacy group for people age 50 and over; formerly the American Association of Retired Persons.

absolute poverty: Not meeting the minimal requirements necessary to sustain a healthy existence.

abstract and concrete attitudes: Abstract attitudes are ideas that are consistent with mainstream societal views, while concrete attitudes are ideas that are based on actual experience.

achievement gap: Disparity on a number of educational measures between the performance of groups of students, especially groups defined by **gender**, **race**, **ethnicity**, ability, and socioeconomic status.

"acting White" thesis: The thesis that Black students do not aspire to or strive to get good grades because it is perceived as "acting White."

activity theory: A functionalist theory of **aging** that holds that busy, engaged people are more likely to lead fulfilling and productive lives.

affective individualism: The belief in romantic attachment as a basis for contracting **marriage** ties.

age-grade: The system found in small traditional **cultures** by which people belonging to a similar age group are categorized together and hold similar rights and obligations.

age-specific birthrates: Statistical measures representing the number of births within a given population per year in relation to age distribution.

ageism: Discrimination or **prejudice** against a person on the grounds of age.

agency: The ability to think, act, and make choices independently.

agents of socialization: Groups or social contexts within which processes of **socialization** take place.

aging: The combination of biological, psychological, and social processes that affect people as they grow older.

aging in place: A phenomenon in which many rural areas have disproportionately high numbers of older adults because young persons seek opportunities elsewhere and leave the older persons behind.

agrarian societies: Societies whose means of subsistence are based on agricultural production (crop growing).

alienation: The sense that our own abilities as human beings are taken over by other entities. The term was originally used by Marx to refer to the projection of human powers onto gods. Subsequently, he used the term to refer to the loss of workers' control over the nature and products of their labor.

Alzheimer's disease: A degenerative disease of the brain resulting in progressive loss of mental capacity.

anomie: A concept first brought into wide usage in sociology by Durkheim to refer to a situation in which social **norms** lose their hold over individual behavior.

Anthropocene: A term used to denote the current geological epoch, in which many geologically significant conditions and processes are profoundly altered by human activities.

apartheid: The system of racial **segregation** established in South Africa.

assimilation: The acceptance of a **minority group** by a majority **population** in which the new group takes on the **values** and **norms** of the dominant **culture**.

authoritarianism: A political system in which the governing bodies or leaders use force to maintain control.

authority: A government's legitimate use of **power**.

automation: Production processes monitored and controlled by machines with only minimal supervision from people.

anticipatory socialization: The process whereby we learn about a **social role** in advance.

back region: Areas apart from **front region** performance, as specified by Erving Goffman, in which individuals are able to relax and behave informally.

biological essentialism: The view that differences between men and women are natural and inevitable consequences of the intrinsic biological natures of men and women.

biomedical model of health: The set of principles underpinning Western medical systems and practices. The biomedical model of health defines diseases objectively, in accordance with the presence of recognized symptoms, and believes that the healthy body can be restored through scientifically based medical treatment. The human body is likened to a machine that can be returned to working order with the proper repairs.

Black feminism: A strand of **feminist theory** that highlights the multiple disadvantages of **gender**, **class**, and **race** that shape the experiences of non-White women. Black feminists reject the idea of a single, unified gender oppression that is experienced evenly by all women, and argue that early feminist analysis reflected the specific concerns of White, **middle-class** women.

body mass index (BMI): A measure of body fat based on height and weight.

bourgeoisie: People who own companies, land, or stocks (shares) and use these to generate economic returns.

bureaucracy: A type of **organization** marked by a clear hierarchy of **authority** and the existence of written rules of procedure and staffed by full-time, salaried officials.

capabilities approach: An approach to development that uses social indicators to emphasize the degree to which people are capable of achieving a life they value, given the opportunities they face.

capitalism: An economic system based on the private ownership of **wealth**, which is invested and reinvested in order to produce profit.

caste: A social system in which one's social **status** is held for life.

charismatic: The inspirational quality of leaders that makes them capable of capturing the imagination and devotion of a mass of followers.

churches: Large bodies of people belonging to an established religious **organization**. The term is also used to refer to the place in which religious ceremonies are carried out.

cisgender: Individuals whose **gender** identity matches his or her biological sex. Statistically, this is the most common gender. It would include persons who are born female who identify as female and persons born male who identify as male.

citizens: Members of a political community, having both rights and duties associated with that membership.

civil inattention: The process whereby individuals in the same physical setting glance at each other and quickly look away to indicate awareness of each other but not intrusiveness.

civil rights: Legal rights held by all **citizens** in a given national community.

civil religion: A set of religious beliefs through which a **society** interprets its own history in light of some conception of ultimate reality.

civil society: The realm of activity that lies between the **state** and the market, including the **family**, schools, community associations, and noneconomic institutions. Civil society, or civic culture, is essential to vibrant democratic societies.

class: Although it is one of the most frequently used concepts in sociology, there is no clear agreement about how the notion should be defined. Most sociologists use the term to refer to socioeconomic variations between groups of individuals that create variations in their material prosperity and **power**.

class systems: A system of social hierarchy that allows individuals to move among classes. The four chief bases of class are ownership of wealth, occupation, income, and education.

clock time: Time as measured by the clock, in terms of hours, minutes, and seconds, as opposed to measuring it by the rising and setting of the sun.

cognition: Human thought processes involving perception, reasoning, and remembering.

cohabitation: Two people living together in a sexual relationship of some permanence without being married to one another.

collective action: Action undertaken in a relatively spontaneous way by a large number of people assembled together.

collective consumption: A concept used by Manuel Castells to refer to processes of urban consumption—such as the buying and selling of property.

colonialism: The process whereby Western nations established their rule in parts of the world away from their home territories.

communism: A social system based on everyone owning the means of production and sharing in the wealth it produces.

community policing: A renewed emphasis on crime prevention rather than law enforcement to reintegrate policing within the community.

comparative research: Research that compares one set of findings on one **society** with the same type of findings on other societies.

complementary and alternative medicine (CAM): A diverse set of approaches and therapies for treating illness and promoting well-being that generally fall outside standard medical practices.

compulsion of proximity: People's need to interact with others in their presence.

concrete operational stage: A stage of cognitive development, as formulated by Piaget, in which a child's thinking is based primarily on physical perception of the world. In this phase, the child is not yet capable of dealing with abstract concepts or hypothetical situations.

conflict theories of aging: Arguments that emphasize the ways in which the larger **social structure** helps to shape the opportunities available to the older adult population. Unequal opportunities are seen as creating the potential for conflict.

conflict theory: A sociological perspective that emphasizes the role of political and economic **power** and oppression as contributing to the existing social order.

constitutional monarchs: Kings or queens who are largely figureheads. Real **power** rests in the hands of other political leaders.

continuity theory: The theory that older adults' well-being is enhanced when their activities are consistent with their personality, preferences, and activities earlier in life.

contradictory class locations: Positions in the class structure, particularly routine white-collar and lower managerial jobs, that share characteristics of the class positions both above and below them.

control theory: The theory that views **crime** as the outcome of an imbalance between impulses toward criminal activity and controls that deter it. Control theorists hold that criminals are rational beings who will act to maximize their own reward unless they are rendered unable to do so through either social or physical controls.

conurbation: An agglomeration of towns or cities into an unbroken urban environment.

conversation analysis: The empirical study of conversations, employing techniques drawn from **ethnomethodology**. Conversation analysis examines details of naturally occurring conversations to reveal the organizational principles of talk and its role in the production and reproduction of social order.

core: According to **world-systems theory**, describes the most advanced industrial countries, which take the lion's share of profits in the world economic system.

corporate crime: Offenses committed by large **corporations** in **society**. Examples of corporate crime include pollution, false advertising, and violations of **health** and safety regulations.

corporations: Business firms or companies.

correlation coefficients: The measure of the degree of correlation between variables.

countercultures: Cultural groups within a wider **society** that largely reject the **values** and **norms** of the majority.

created environment: An environment made up of constructions established by human beings to serve their needs, derived from the use of man-made **technology**—including, for example, roads, railways, factories, offices, private homes, and other buildings.

crime: The result of any action that contravenes the **laws** established by a political **authority**.

crude birthrates: Statistical measures representing the number of births within a given **population** per year, normally calculated in terms of the number of births per 1,000 members. Although the crude birthrate is a useful index, it is only a general measure because it does not specify numbers of births in relation to age distribution.

crude death rates: Statistical measures representing the number of deaths that occur annually in a given **population**, normally calculated as the ratio of deaths per 1,000 members. Crude death rates give a general indication of the **mortality** levels of a community or **society**, but they beare limited in their usefulness because they do not take into account the age distribution.

cults: Fragmentary religious groupings to which individuals are loosely affiliated but that lack any permanent structure.

cultural appropriation: When members of one cultural group borrow elements of another group's **culture.**

cultural capital: The accumulated cultural knowledge within a **society** that confers **power** and **status**.

cultural lag: The idea, introduced by William Ogburn, that changes in cultural **values** and **norms** take time to catch up with technological developments.

cultural navigators: People who draw from both their home **culture** and mainstream culture to create an attitude that allows them to succeed.

cultural relativism: The practice of judging a **society** by its own standards.

cultural turn: Sociology's recent emphasis on the importance of understanding the role of **culture** in daily life.

cultural universals: Values or **modes** of behavior shared by all human **cultures**.

culture: The **values**, **norms**, and material goods characteristic of a given group. Like the concept of **society**, the notion of culture is widely used in sociology and the other social sciences (particularly anthropology). Culture is one of the most distinctive properties of human social association.

culture of poverty: The thesis, popularized by Oscar Lewis, that poverty is not a result of individual inadequacies but is instead the outcome of a larger social and cultural atmosphere into which successive generations of children are socialized. The culture of poverty refers to the **values**, beliefs, lifestyles, habits, and traditions that are common among people living under conditions of material deprivation.

cybercrime: Criminal activities by means of electronic **networks** or involving the use of new information **technologies**. Electronic money laundering, personal **identity** theft, electronic vandalism, and monitoring electronic correspondence are all emergent forms of cybercrime.

cyberspace: Electronic networks of interaction between individuals at different computer terminals.

deglobalization: The reduction of global interdependence by making economies as local as possible.

degree of dispersal: The range or distribution of a set of figures.

democratic elitism: A theory of the limits of democracy. It holds that in large-scale societies democratic participation is necessarily limited to the regular election of political leaders.

demographic transition: An interpretation of **population** change that holds that a stable ratio of births to deaths is achieved once a certain level of economic prosperity has been reached. According to this notion, in preindustrial societies there is a rough balance between births and deaths because population increase is kept in check by disease, war, or lack of available food. In modern societies, by contrast, population equilibrium is achieved because **families** are moved by economic incentives to limit the number of children.

demography: The study of **populations**.

denomination: A religious **sect** that has lost its revivalist dynamism and become an institutionalized body, commanding the adherence of significant numbers of people.

dependency culture: A term popularized by Charles Murray to describe individuals who rely on state welfare provision rather than entering the labor market. The dependency culture is seen as the outcome of the "paternalistic" **welfare state** that undermines individual ambition and people's capacity for self-help.

dependency ratio: The ratio of people of dependent ages (children and the **older adults**) to people of economically active ages.

dependency theories: Marxist theories of economic development that argue that the poverty of low-income countries stems directly from their exploitation by wealthy countries and by the **transnational** (or multinational) corporations that are based in wealthy countries.

dependent development: The theory that poor countries can still develop economically, but only in ways shaped by their reliance on wealthier countries.

desocialization: The process whereby people unlearn rules and **norms** upon exiting a particular social world.

deviance: Modes of action that do not conform to the **norms** or **values** held by most members of a group or **society**. What is regarded as deviant is as variable as the norms and values that distinguish different **cultures** and **subcultures** from one another. Forms of behavior that are highly esteemed by one group may be regarded negatively by others.

deviant subculture: A **subculture** whose members hold **values** that differ substantially from those of the majority.

diaspora: The dispersal of an ethnic **population** from an original homeland into foreign areas, often in a forced manner or under traumatic circumstances.

differential association: An interpretation of the development of criminal behavior proposed by Edwin H. Sutherland, according to whom criminal behavior is learned through association with others who regularly engage in **crime**.

direct democracy: A form of **participatory democracy** that allows **citizens** to vote directly on **laws** and policies.

discrimination: Behavior that denies to the members of a particular group resources or rewards that can be obtained by others. Discrimination must be distinguished from **prejudice**: Individuals who are prejudiced against others may not engage in discriminatory practices against them; conversely, people may act in a discriminatory fashion toward a group even though they are not prejudiced against that group.

disengagement theory: A functionalist theory of **aging** that holds that it is functional for **society** to remove people from their traditional **roles** when they become retirement age, thereby freeing up those roles for others.

disestablishment: A period during which the political influence of established **religions** is successfully challenged.

division of labor: The specialization of **work** tasks by means of which different **occupations** are combined within a production system. All **societies** have at least some rudimentary form of division of labor, especially between the tasks allocated to men and those performed by women. With the development of industrialism, the division of labor became vastly more complex than in any prior type of production system. In the modern world, the division of labor is international in scope.

doubling time: The time it takes for a particular level of **population** to double.

dyad: A group consisting of two persons.

ecological approach: In the field of urban analysis, a perspective emphasizing the "natural" distribution of city neighborhoods into areas having contrasting characteristics.

economic interdependence: The fact that in the **division of labor**, individuals depend on others to produce many or most of the goods they need to sustain their lives.

economy: The system of production and exchange that provides for the material needs of individuals living in a given **society**. Economic institutions are of key importance in all social orders. What goes on in the economy usually influences other areas of social life. Modern economies differ substantially from traditional ones because the majority of the **population** is no longer engaged in agricultural production.

egocentric: According to Jean Piaget, the characteristic quality of a child during the early years of his or her life. Egocentric thinking involves understanding objects and events in the environment solely in terms of one's own position.

emerging economies: Developing countries, such as India or Singapore, that over the past two or three decades have begun to develop a strong industrial base.

emigration: The movement of people out of one country in order to settle in another.

emotional intelligence: The ability to identify, assess, and control the emotions of oneself or others.

emotional loneliness: The absence of an intimate confidant.

empirical investigation: Factual inquiries carried out in any area of sociological study.

encounter: A meeting between two or more people in a situation of face-to-face interaction. Our daily lives can be seen as a series of different encounters spread out across the course of the day. In modern societies, many of these encounters are with strangers rather than with people we know.

entrepreneur: The owner/founder of a business firm.

environmental ecology: The scientific study of the distribution and abundance of life and the interactions between organisms and their natural environment.

environmental injustice: The harms suffered by ecosystems today are closely linked to and mirror the harms experienced by the most marginalized human beings across the planet.

epidemiology: The study of the distribution and incidence of disease and illness within a **population**.

ethnic cleansing: The creation of ethnically homogeneous territories through the mass expulsion of other ethnic **populations**.

ethnicity: Cultural **values** and **norms** that distinguish the members of a given group from others. An ethnic group is one whose members share a distinct awareness of a common cultural **identity**, separating them from other groups. In virtually all **societies**, ethnic differences are associated with variations in **power** and material **wealth**. Where ethnic differences are also racial, such divisions are sometimes especially pronounced.

ethnocentrism: The tendency to look at other **cultures** through the eyes of one's own culture, and thereby misrepresent them.

ethnography: The firsthand study of people using observation, in-depth interviewing, or both. Also called *fieldwork*.

ethnomethodology: The study of how people make sense of what others say and do in the course of day-to-day **social interaction**. Ethnomethodology is concerned with the "ethnomethods" by which people sustain meaningful interchanges with one another.

evangelicalism: A form of Protestantism characterized by a belief in spiritual rebirth (being "born again").

exchange mobility: The exchange of positions on the socioeconomic scale such that talented people move up the economic hierarchy while the less talented move down.

experiment: A **research method** by which variables can be analyzed in a controlled and systematic way, either in an artificial situation constructed by the researcher or in a naturally occurring setting.

exponential: A geometric, rather than linear, rate of progression, producing a fast rise in the numbers of a **population** experiencing such growth.

extended family: A **family** group consisting of more than two generations of relatives living either within the same household or very close to one another.

external risk: Dangers that spring from the natural world and are unrelated to the actions of humans. Examples of external risk include droughts, earthquakes, famines, and storms.

failed states: States in which the central government has lost authority and resorts to deadly force to retain power.

families of orientation: The families into which individuals are born. Also referred to as families of origin.

families of procreation: The families individuals initiate through **marriage**, **cohabitation**, or by having children.

family: A group of individuals related to one another by blood ties, **marriage**, or adoption, who form an economic unit, the adult members of which are responsible for the upbringing of children. All known **societies** involve some form of family system, although the nature of family relationships varies widely. While the main family form in modern societies is the **nuclear family**, **extended family** relationships are also found.

family capitalism: Capitalistic enterprise owned and administered by entrepreneurial **families**.

fecundity: A measure of the number of children that it is biologically possible for a woman to produce.

feminism: Advocacy of the rights of women to be equal with men in all spheres of life. Feminism dates from the late eighteenth century in Europe, and feminist movements exist in most countries today.

feminist theory: A sociological perspective that emphasizes the centrality of **gender** in analyzing the social world and particularly the uniqueness of the experience of women. There are many strands of feminist theory, but they all share the desire to explain **gender inequality** in **society** and to work to overcome it.

feminization of poverty: An increase in the proportion of the poor who are female.

fertility: The average number of live-born children produced by women of childbearing age in a particular **society**.

field of action: The arena within which **social movements** interact with established **organizations**, often producing a modification of the ideas and outlook of the members of both.

flexible production: Process in which computers design customized products for a mass market.

focused interaction: Interaction between individuals engaged in a common activity or in direct conversation with one another.

food deserts: Geographic areas in which residents do not have easy access to high-quality affordable food. These regions are concentrated in rural areas and poor urban neighborhoods.

food security: Having access to sufficient, safe, and nutritious food that meets the need for an active and healthy life.

Fordism: The system of production pioneered by Henry Ford, in which the assembly line was introduced.

formal operational stage: According to Piaget's theory, a stage of cognitive development at which the growing child becomes capable of handling abstract concepts and hypothetical situations.

formal organization: A group that is rationally designed to achieve its objectives, often by means of explicit rules, regulations, and procedures.

formal relations: Relations that exist in groups and **organizations**, as laid down by the **norms**, or rules, of the official system of **authority**.

front region: Settings of social activity in which people seek to put on a definite "performance" for others.

functionalism: A theoretical perspective based on the notion that social events can best be explained in terms of the functions they perform—that is, the contributions they make to the continuity of a **society**.

fundamentalists: Evangelists who are highly antimodern in many of their beliefs and adhere to strict codes of morality and conduct.

gender: Social expectations about behavior regarded as appropriate for the members of each **sex**. Gender refers not to the physical attributes distinguishing men and women but to socially formed traits of masculinity and femininity.

gender gap: The differences between women and men, especially as reflected in social, political, intellectual, cultural, or economic attainments or attitudes.

gender inequality: The inequality between men and women in terms of **wealth**, **income**, and **status**.

gender roles: Social roles assigned to each **sex** and labeled as masculine or feminine.

gender role socialization: The learning of **gender roles** through social factors such as schooling, the media, and **family**.

gender typing: Women holding **occupations** of lower **status** and pay, such as secretarial and retail positions, and men holding jobs of higher status and pay, such as managerial and professional positions.

generalized other: A concept described by G. H. Mead according to which the individual takes over the general **values** and moral rules of a given group or **society** during the **socialization** process.

generational equity: The striking of a balance between the needs and interests of members of different generations.

genocide: The systematic, planned destruction of a racial, political, or cultural group.

gentrification: A process of **urban renewal** in which older, deteriorated housing is refurbished by affluent people moving into the area.

geoengineering: Large-scale interventions in the earth's natural systems to counteract climate change.

ghetto: A place where a racial or ethnic group initially comes to live as a consequence of systematic exclusion from more desirable places.

Gini coefficient: A standard measure of a country's economic disparity, where 0 represents perfect equality (everyone has the same income) and 1 represents maximum inequality.

glass ceiling: A promotion barrier that prevents a woman's upward mobility within an **organization**.

global capitalism: The current transnational phase of capitalism, characterized by global markets, production, finances; a **transnational capitalist class** whose business concerns are global rather than national; and transnational systems of governance (such as the World Trade Organization) that promote global business interests.

global city: A city—such as London, New York, or Tokyo—that has become an organizing center of the new global **economy**.

global commodity chains: Worldwide **networks** of labor and production processes yielding a finished product.

global inequality: The systematic differences in **wealth** and **power** among countries.

globalization: The development of social and economic relationships stretching worldwide. In current times, we are all influenced by **organizations** and social **networks** located thousands of miles away. A key part of the study of globalization is the emergence of a world system—for some purposes, we need to regard the world as forming a single social order.

GNI: Gross National Income, a commonly used measure based on the monetary value of a country's yearly output of goods and services.

graying: A term used to indicate that an increasing proportion of a **society**'s **population** is 65+.

health: A state of complete physical, mental, and social well-being rather than merely the absence of disease or infirmity.

health literacy: One's capacity to obtain, process, and understand basic health information and services needed to make appropriate health decisions.

hegemonic masculinity: Social **norms** dictating that men should be strong, self-reliant, and unemotional.

hidden curriculum: Traits of behavior or attitudes that are learned at school but not included within the formal curriculum—for example, **gender** differences.

high-trust systems: Organizations or **work** settings in which individuals are permitted a great deal of autonomy and control over the work task.

historicity: The use of an understanding of history as a basis for trying to change history—that is, producing informed processes of **social change**.

homeless: People who have no place to sleep and either stay in free shelters or sleep in public places not meant for habitation.

homophobia: An irrational fear of or disdain for homosexuals.

housework: Unpaid work carried out in the home, usually by women; domestic chores such as cooking, cleaning, and shopping. Also called *domestic labor*.

human capital theory: The argument that individuals make investments in their own "human capital" in order to increase their productivity and earnings.

hunting and gathering societies: Societies whose mode of subsistence is gained from hunting animals, fishing, and gathering edible plants.

hybridity: The fact that cultures are neither wholly isolated nor entirely distinct, but instead constantly borrow from one another.

hypotheses: Ideas or educated guesses about a given state of affairs, put forward as bases for empirical testing.

ideal type: A "pure type," constructed by emphasizing certain traits of a social item that do not necessarily exist in reality. An example is Max Weber's ideal type of bureaucratic **organization**.

identity: The distinctive characteristics of a person's or group's character that relate to who he is and what is meaningful to him. Some of the main sources of identity include **gender**, sexual orientation, nationality or **ethnicity**, and social **class**.

ideologies: Shared ideas or beliefs that serve to justify the interests of dominant groups. Ideologies are found in all **societies** in which there are systematic and ingrained inequalities among groups. The concept of ideology connects closely with that of **power**, since ideological systems serve to legitimize the power that groups hold.

immigration: The movement of people into one country from another for the purpose of settlement.

impression management: Preparing for the presentation of one's **social role**.

income: Money received from paid wages and salaries or earned from investment.

industrialization: The process of the machine production of goods. See also **industrialized societies**.

industrialized societies: Strongly developed **nation-states** in which the majority of the **population** works in factories or offices rather than in agriculture, and most people live in urban areas.

infant mortality rate: The number of infants who die during the first year of life, per 1,000 live births.

informal economy: Economic transactions carried on outside the sphere of orthodox paid employment.

informal relations: Relations that exist in groups and **organizations** developed on the basis of personal connections; ways of doing things that depart from formally recognized modes of procedure.

information and communication technology: Forms of **technology** based on information processing and requiring microelectronic circuitry.

information poverty: The state of people who have little or no access to information **technology**, such as computers.

in-groups: Groups toward which one feels particular loyalty and respect—the groups to which "we" belong.

inner city: The areas composing the central neighborhoods of a city, as distinct from the suburbs. In many modern urban settings in the developed world, inner-city areas are subject to dilapidation and decay, with the more affluent residents having moved to outlying areas.

instincts: Fixed patterns of behavior that have genetic origins and that appear in all normal animals within a given species.

institutional capitalism: Capitalistic enterprise organized on the basis of institutional shareholding.

institutional racism: The idea that **racism** occurs through the respected and established institutions of **society** rather than through hateful actions of some bad people.

intelligence: Level of intellectual ability, particularly as measured by **IQ (intelligence quotient)** tests.

interactional vandalism: The deliberate subversion of the tacit rules of conversation.

interest group: A group organized to pursue specific interests in the political arena, operating primarily by lobbying the members of legislative bodies.

intergenerational mobility: Movement up or down a **social stratification** hierarchy from one generation to another.

interlocking directorates: Linkages among corporations created by individuals who sit on two or more boards.

international division of labor: The specialization in producing goods for the world market that divides regions into zones of industrial or agricultural production or high- or low-skilled labor.

international governmental organizations (IGOs): International organizations established by treaties between governments for purposes of conducting business between the nations making up their membership.

international nongovernmental organizations (INGOs): International organizations established by agreements between the individuals or private **organizations** making up their membership.

intersectionality: A sociological perspective that holds that our multiple group memberships affect our lives in ways that are distinct from single group memberships. For example, the experience of a Black female may be distinct from that of a White female or a Black male.

intersex: An individual possessing both male and female genitalia. Although statistically rare, this subpopulation is of great interest to gender scholars.

intragenerational mobility: Movement up or down a **social stratification** hierarchy within the course of a personal career.

IQ (intelligence quotient): A score attained on tests of symbolic or reasoning abilities.

iron law of oligarchy: A term coined by Weber's student Robert Michels meaning that large **organizations** tend toward centralization of **power**, making **democracy** difficult.

kinship: A relation that links individuals through blood ties, **marriage**, or adoption. Kinship relations are by definition part of marriage and the **family**, but they extend much more broadly. While in most modern societies few social obligations are involved in kinship relations extending beyond the immediate family, in other **cultures** kinship is of vital importance to social life.

knowledge economy: A **society** no longer based primarily on the production of material goods but instead on the production of knowledge. Its emergence has been linked to the development of a broad base of consumers who are technologically literate and have made new advances in computing, entertainment, and telecommunications part of their lives.

Kuznets curve: A formula showing that inequality increases during the early stages of capitalist development, then declines, and eventually stabilizes at a relatively low level; advanced by the economist Simon Kuznets.

labeling theory: An approach to the study of **deviance** that suggests that people become "deviant" because certain labels are attached to their behavior by political authorities and others.

language: The primary vehicle of meaning and communication in a **society**, language is a system of **symbols** that represent objects and abstract thoughts.

latent functions: Functional consequences that are not intended or recognized by the members of a social system in which they occur.

laws: Rules of behavior established by a political **authority** and backed by state **power**.

legitimation crisis: The failure of a political order to be able to govern properly because it did not generate a sufficient level of commitment and involvement on the part of its **citizens**.

liberal democracies: A type of representative democracy in which elected representatives hold power.

liberal feminism: The form of **feminist theory** that posits that **gender inequality** is produced by unequal access to **civil rights** and certain social resources, such as education and employment, based on **sex**. Liberal feminists tend to seek solutions through changes in legislation that ensure that the rights of individuals are protected.

liberation theology: An activist Catholic **religious movement** that combines Catholic beliefs with a passion for social justice for the poor.

life chances: A term introduced by Max Weber to signify a person's opportunities for achieving economic prosperity.

life course: The various transitions and stages people experience during their lives.

life expectancy: The number of years the average person can expect to live.

life span: The maximum length of life that is biologically possible for a member of a given species.

linguistic relativity hypothesis: A **hypothesis**, based on the **theories** of Sapir and Whorf, that perceptions are relative to **language**.

local nationalism: The belief that communities that share a cultural **identity** should have political autonomy, even within smaller units of **nation-states**.

looking-glass self: According to Cooley's **theory**, the reactions we elicit in social situations create a mirror in which we see ourselves.

lower class: A social class comprising those who work part time or not at all and whose household income is typically lower than $20,000 a year.

low-trust systems: Organizational or **work** settings in which people are allowed little responsibility for, or control over, the work task.

macrosociology: The study of large-scale groups, **organizations**, or social systems.

Malthusianism: A doctrine about **population** dynamics developed by Thomas Malthus, according to which population increase comes up against "natural limits, " represented by famine and war.

managerial capitalism: Capitalistic enterprise administered by managerial executives rather than by owners.

manifest functions: The functions of a type of social activity that are known to and intended by the individuals involved in the activity.

manufactured risk: Dangers that are created by the impact of human knowledge and **technology** on the natural world. Examples of manufactured risk include global warming and genetically modified foods.

market-oriented theories: Theories about economic development that assume that the best possible economic consequences will result if individuals are free to make their own economic decisions, uninhibited by governmental constraint.

marriage: A socially approved sexual relationship between two individuals. Marriage historically has involved two persons of opposite sexes, but in the past decade marriage between same-sex partners has been legalized in a growing number of states and nations throughout the world. Marriage normally forms the basis of a **family of procreation**—that is, it is expected that the married couple will produce and bring up children.

Marxism: A body of thought deriving its main elements from the ideas of Karl Marx.

mass media: Forms of communication, such as newspapers, magazines, radio, and television, designed to reach mass audiences.

master status: A single **identity** or **status** that overpowers all the other identities one holds.

material culture: The physical objects that a **society** creates that influence the ways in which people live.

materialist conception of history: The view developed by Karl Marx, according to which material, or economic, factors have a prime role in determining historical change.

matrilocal: A **family** system in which the husband is expected to live near the wife's parents.

mean: A statistical measure of central tendency, or average, based on dividing a total by the number of individual cases.

means of production: The means whereby the production of material goods is carried on in a **society**, including not just **technology** but also the social relations between producers.

measures of central tendency: The ways of calculating averages.

median: The number that falls halfway in a range of numbers—a way of calculating central tendency that is sometimes more useful than calculating a **mean**.

Medicare: A program under the U.S. **Social Security** Administration that reimburses hospitals and physicians for medical care provided to qualifying people over 65 years old.

megacities: A term favored by Manuel Castells to describe large, intensely concentrated urban spaces that serve as connection points for the global **economy**.

megalopolis: The "city of all cities" in ancient Greece—used in modern times to refer to very large **conurbations**.

melting pot: The idea that ethnic differences can be combined to create new patterns of behavior drawing on diverse cultural sources.

microsociology: The study of human behavior in the context of face-to-face interaction.

middle class: A social **class** composed broadly of those working in white-collar and lower managerial **occupations**.

minority group: A group of people in a given **society** who, because of their distinct physical or cultural characteristics, find themselves in situations of inequality compared with the dominant group within that society.

mode: The number that appears most often in a given set of data. This can sometimes be a helpful way of portraying central tendency.

modernization theory: A version of market-oriented development theory that argues that low-income societies develop economically only if they give up their traditional ways and adopt modern economic institutions, **technologies**, and cultural **values** that emphasize savings and productive investment.

monarchies: Systems of government in which unelected kings or queens rule.

monogamy: A form of **marriage** in which each married partner is allowed only one spouse at any given time.

monopoly: The domination by a single firm in a given industry.

monotheism: Belief in a single god.

mortality: The number of deaths in a **population**.

multiculturalism: A condition in which ethnic groups exist separately and share equally in economic and political life.

nation: People with a common identity that ideally includes shared culture, language, and feelings of belonging.

nationalism: A set of beliefs and **symbols** expressing identification with a national community.

nation-states: Particular types of **states**, characteristic of the modern world, in which governments have sovereign **power** within defined territorial areas, and **populations** are **citizens** who know themselves to be part of single nations.

nations without states: Instances in which the members of a nation lack political **sovereignty** over the area they claim as their own.

neoliberalism: The economic belief that free-market forces, achieved by minimizing government restrictions on business, provide the only route to economic growth.

networks: Sets of informal and formal social ties that link people to each other.

New Age movement: A general term to describe the diverse spectrum of beliefs and practices oriented on inner spirituality. Paganism, Eastern mysticism, shamanism, alternative forms of healing, and astrology are all examples of New Age activities.

new religious movements: The broad range of religious and spiritual groups, **cults**, and **sects** that have emerged alongside mainstream **religions**. New religious movements range from spiritual and self-help groups within the **New Age movement** to exclusive sects such as the Hare Krishnas.

new social movements: A set of **social movements** that have arisen in Western **societies** since the 1960s in response to the changing risks facing human societies. New social movements differ from earlier social movements in that they are single-issue campaigns oriented to nonmaterial ends and draw support from across class lines.

nonmaterial culture: Cultural ideas that are not themselves physical objects.

nonverbal communication: Communication between individuals based on facial expression or bodily gesture rather than on **language**.

norms: Rules of conduct that specify appropriate behavior in a given range of social situations. A norm either prescribes a given type of behavior or forbids it. All human groups follow definite norms, which are always backed by **sanctions** of one kind or another, varying from informal disapproval to physical punishment.

nuclear family: A **family** group consisting of two adults and dependent children.

obesity: Excessive body weight, indicated by a **body mass index (BMI)** over 30.

occupation: Any form of paid employment in which an individual regularly works.

older adults: Adults ages 65 and older.

oldest old: Sociological term for persons age 85 and older.

old old: Sociological term for persons age 75 to 84.

oligarchy: Rule by a small minority within an **organization** or **society**.

oligopoly: The domination by a small number of firms in a given industry.

organic solidarity: According to Durkheim, the social cohesion that results from the various parts of a **society** functioning as an integrated whole.

organization: A large group of individuals with a definite set of **authority** relations. Many types of organizations exist in **industrialized societies**, influencing most aspects of our lives. While not all organizations are bureaucratic, there are close links between the development of organizations and bureaucratic tendencies.

out-groups: Groups toward which one feels antagonism and contempt—"those people."

outsourcing: A business practice that sends production of materials to factories around the world. The components of one final product often originate from many different countries and then are sent elsewhere to be put together and sold. Factories from different countries must compete with one another to obtain business.

pariah groups: Groups who suffer from negative **status discrimination**—they are looked down on by most other members of **society**.

participant observation: A method of research widely used in sociology and anthropology in which the researcher takes part in the activities of the group or community being studied.

participatory democracy: A system of democracy in which all members of a group or community participate collectively in making major decisions.

pastoral societies: **Societies** whose subsistence derives from the rearing of domesticated animals.

patriarchy: The dominance of men over women. All known **societies** are patriarchal, although there are variations in the degree and nature of the **power** men exercise as compared with women. One of the prime objectives of women's movements in modern societies is to combat existing patriarchal institutions.

patrilocal: A **family** system in which the wife is expected to live near the husband's parents.

peer group: A friendship group composed of individuals of similar age and social **status**.

periphery: Describes countries that have a marginal role in the world **economy** and are thus dependent on the **core** producing societies for their trading relationships.

personality stabilization: According to the theory of **functionalism**, the **family** plays a crucial role in assisting its adult members emotionally. **Marriage** is the arrangement through which personalities are supported and kept healthy.

personal space: The physical space individuals maintain between themselves and others.

pilot study: A trial run in **survey** research.

pluralism: A model for ethnic relations in which all ethnic groups in the United States retain their independent and separate identities yet share equally in the rights and **powers** of citizenship.

pluralist theories of modern democracy: Theories that emphasize the role of diverse or potentially competing interest groups, none of which dominates the political process.

political rights: Rights of political participation, such as the right to vote in local and national elections, held by **citizens** of a national community.

polyandry: A form of **marriage** in which a woman may simultaneously have two or more husbands.

polygamy: A form of **marriage** in which a person may have two or more spouses simultaneously.

polygyny: A form of marriage in which a man may simultaneously have two or more wives.

polytheism: Belief in two or more gods.

population: The people who are the focus of social research.

populism: The belief that politics should reflect the needs and interests of ordinary people rather than those of elite individuals or groups.

portfolio workers: Workers who possess a diversity of skills or qualifications and are therefore able to move easily from job to job.

post-Fordism: The period characterized by the transition from mass industrial production, using Fordist methods, to more flexible forms of production favoring innovation and aimed at meeting market demands for customized products.

postindustrial society: A notion advocated by those who believe that processes of **social change** are taking us beyond the industrialized order. A postindustrial society is based on the production of information rather than on material goods. According to postindustrialists, we are currently experiencing a series of social changes as profound as those that initiated the industrial era some 200 years ago.

postmodern feminism: The feminist perspective that challenges the idea of a unitary basis of **identity** and experience shared by all women. Postmodern feminists reject the claim that there is a grand theory that can explain the position of women in **society,** or that there is any single,

universal essence or category of "woman." Instead, postmodern feminism encourages the acceptance of many different standpoints as equally valid.

postmodern society: A technologically sophisticated **society** that is preoccupied with consumer goods and media images.

postmodernism: The belief that **society** is no longer governed by history or progress. **Postmodern society** is highly pluralistic and diverse, with no "grand narrative" guiding its development.

poverty line: An official government measure to define those living in poverty in the United States.

power: The ability of individuals or the members of a group to achieve aims or further the interests they hold. Power is a pervasive element in all human relationships. Many conflicts in **society** are struggles over power, because how much power an individual or group is able to achieve governs how far they are able to put their wishes into practice.

power elite: Small **networks** of individuals who, according to C. Wright Mills, hold concentrated **power** in modern **societies**.

prejudice: The holding of preconceived ideas about an individual or group, ideas that are resistant to change even in the face of new information. Prejudice may be either positive or negative.

preoperational stage: A stage of cognitive development, in Jean Piaget's theory, in which a child has advanced sufficiently to master basic modes of logical thought.

primary deviation: According to Edwin Lemert, the actions that cause others to label one as a deviant.

primary groups: Groups that are characterized by intense emotional ties, face-to-face interaction, intimacy, and a strong, enduring sense of commitment.

primary socialization: The process by which children learn the cultural **norms** and expectations for behavior of the **society** into which they are born. Primary socialization occurs largely in the **family**.

procreative technology: Techniques for influencing the human reproductive process.

profane: That which belongs to the mundane, everyday world.

proletariat: People who sell their labor for wages, according to Marx.

qualitative methods: Approaches to sociological research that often rely on personal and/or collective interviews, accounts, or observations of a person or situation.

quantitative methods: Approaches to sociological research that draw on objective and statistical data and often focus on documenting trends, comparing subgroups, or exploring correlations.

race: A socially constructed category rooted in the belief that there are fundamental differences among humans, associated with phenotype and ancestry.

race socialization: The specific verbal and nonverbal messages that older generations transmit to younger generations regarding the meaning and significance of race.

racial microaggressions: Small slights, indignities, or acts of disrespect that are hurtful to people of color even though they are often perpetuated by well-meaning Whites.

racism: The attribution of characteristics of superiority or inferiority to a **population** sharing certain physically inherited characteristics. Racism is one specific form of **prejudice**, focusing on physical variations among people. Racist attitudes became entrenched during the period of Western colonial expansion, but seem also to rest on mechanisms of prejudice and **discrimination** found in human **societies** today.

radical feminism: The form of **feminist theory** that posits that **gender inequality** is the result of male domination in all aspects of social and economic life.

random sampling: Sampling method in which a sample is chosen so that every member of the **population** has the same probability of being included.

rape: The forcing of nonconsensual vaginal, oral, or anal intercourse.

rates of population growth or decline: A measurement of population change calculated by subtracting the yearly number of deaths per 1,000 from the number of births per 1,000.

rational choice approach: More broadly, the theory that an individual's behavior is purposive. Within the field of criminology, rational choice analysis argues that deviant behavior is a rational response to a specific social situation.

rationalization: A concept used by Max Weber to refer to the process by which modes of precise calculation and organization, involving abstract rules and procedures, increasingly come to dominate the social world.

reference group: A group that provides a standard for judging one's attitudes or behaviors.

regionalization: The division of social life into different regional settings or zones.

relative deprivation: Deprivation a person feels by comparing himself with a group.

relative poverty: Poverty defined according to the living standards of the majority in any given society.

religion: A set of beliefs adhered to by the members of a community, incorporating **symbols** regarded with a sense of awe or wonder together with ritual practices. Religions do not universally involve a belief in supernatural entities.

religious economy: A theoretical framework within the sociology of **religion** that argues that religions can be fruitfully understood as **organizations** in competition with one another for followers.

religious movements: Associations of people who join together to seek to spread a new **religion** or to promote a new interpretation of an existing religion.

religious nationalism: The linking of strongly held religious convictions with beliefs about a people's social and political destiny.

representative sample: A sample from a larger **population** that is statistically typical of that population.

research methods: The diverse methods of investigation used to gather empirical (factual) material. Different research methods exist in sociology, but the most commonly used are fieldwork (or **participant observation**) and **survey** methods. For many purposes, it is useful to combine two or more methods within a single research project.

resocialization: The process whereby people learn new rules and **norms** upon entering a new social world.

response cries: Seemingly involuntary exclamations individuals make when, for example, they are taken by surprise, drop something inadvertently, or want to express pleasure.

revolutions: Processes of political change involving the mobilizing of a mass **social movement**, which, by the use of violence, successfully overthrows an existing regime and forms a new government.

roles: The expected behaviors of people occupying particular **social positions**. The idea of **social role** originally comes from the theater, referring to the parts that actors play in a stage production. In every **society**, individuals play a number of **social roles**.

sacred: That which inspires attitudes of awe or reverence among believers in a given set of religious ideas.

sample: A small proportion of a larger **population**.

sampling: Studying a proportion of individuals or cases from a larger **population** as representative of that population as a whole.

sanction: A mode of reward or punishment that reinforces socially expected forms of behavior.

scapegoats: Individuals or groups blamed for wrongs that were not of their doing.

scientific racism: The use of scientific research or data to justify or reify beliefs about the superiority or inferiority of particular racial groups. Much of the "data" used to justify such claims are flawed or biased.

secondary deviation: According to Edwin Lemert, following the act of **primary deviation**, secondary deviation occurs when an individual accepts the label of deviant and acts accordingly.

secondary groups: Groups characterized by large size and by impersonal, fleeting relationships.

second demographic transition: A new demographic model that calls for **fertility** rates that may continue to fall because of shifts in **family** structure.

sects: Religious movements that break away from orthodoxy.

secularization: A process of decline in the influence of **religion**. Although modern **societies** have become increasingly secularized, tracing the extent of secularization is a complex matter. Secularization can refer to levels of involvement with religious **organizations** (such as rates of **church** attendance), the social and material influence wielded by religious organizations, and the degree to which people hold religious beliefs.

secular thinking: Worldly thinking, particularly as seen in the rise of **science**, **technology**, and rational thought in general.

segregation: The practice of keeping racial and ethnic groups physically separate, thereby maintaining the superior position of the dominant group.

self-consciousness: Awareness of one's distinct **social identity** as a person separate from others. Human beings are not born with self-consciousness but acquire an awareness of self as a result of early **socialization**. The learning of **language** is of vital importance to the processes by which a child learns to become a self conscious being.

self-identity: The ongoing process of self-development and definition of our personal **identity** through which we formulate a unique sense of ourselves and our relationship to the world around us.

semiotics: The study of the ways in which nonlinguistic phenomena can generate meaning—as in the example of a traffic light.

semiperiphery: Describes countries that supply sources of labor and raw materials to the **core** industrial countries and the world **economy** but are not themselves fully **industrialized societies**.

sensorimotor stage: According to Jean Piaget, a stage of human cognitive development in which the child's awareness of his or her environment is dominated by perception and touch.

sex: The biological and anatomical differences distinguishing females and males.

sex segregation: The concentration of men and women in different **occupations**.

sexual harassment: The making of unwanted sexual advances by one individual toward another, in which the first person persists even though it is clear that the other party is resistant.

shaming: A way of punishing criminal and deviant behavior based on rituals of public disapproval rather than incarceration. The goal of shaming is to maintain the ties of the offender to the community.

sick role: A term associated with the functionalist Talcott Parsons to describe the patterns of behavior that a sick person adopts in order to minimize the disruptive impact of their illness on others.

signifier: Any vehicle of meaning and communication.

slavery: A form of **social stratification** in which some people are owned by others as their property.

social aggregate: A simple collection of people who happen to be together in a particular place but do not significantly interact or identify with one another.

social aging: The **norms**, **values**, and **roles** that are culturally associated with a particular chronological age.

social category: People who share a common characteristic (such as **gender** or **occupation**) but do not necessarily interact or identify with one another.

social change: Alteration in basic structures of a **social group** or **society**. Social change is an ever-present phenomenon in social life, but has become especially intense in the modern era. The origins of modern sociology can be traced to attempts to understand the dramatic changes shattering the traditional world and promoting new forms of social order.

social constraint: The conditioning influence on our behavior of the groups and **societies** of which we are members. Social constraint was regarded by Émile Durkheim as one of the distinctive properties of **social facts**.

social construction: An idea or practice that a group of people agree exists. It is maintained over time by people taking its existence for granted.

social construction of gender: The learning of **gender roles** through **socialization** and interaction with others.

social facts: According to Émile Durkheim, the aspects of social life that shape our actions as individuals. Durkheim believed that social facts could be studied scientifically.

social gerontology: The study of **aging** and older adults.

social group: A collection of people who regularly interact with one another on the basis of shared expectations concerning behavior and who share a sense of common **identity**.

social identity: The characteristics that are attributed to an individual by others.

social interaction: The process by which we act and react to those around us.

socialization: The social processes through which children develop an awareness of social **norms** and **values** and achieve a distinct sense of self. Although socialization processes are particularly significant in infancy and childhood, they continue to some degree throughout life. No individuals are immune from the reactions of others around them, which influence and modify their behavior at all phases of the **life course**.

socialization of nature: The process by which we control phenomena regarded as "natural, " such as reproduction.

social loneliness: The absence of a broader social network.

social mobility: Movement of individuals or groups between different **social positions**.

social movements: Large groups of people who seek to accomplish, or to block, a process of **social change**. Social movements normally exist in conflict with **organizations** whose objectives and outlook they oppose. However, movements that successfully challenge **power**, once they become institutionalized, can develop into organizations.

social position: The **social identity** an individual has in a given group or **society**. Social positions may be general in nature (those associated with **gender roles**) or more specific (occupational positions).

social reproduction: The process of perpetuating **values**, **norms**, and social practices through **socialization**, which leads to structural continuity over time.

social rights: Rights of social and welfare provision held by all **citizens** in a national community, including, for example, the right to claim unemployment benefits and sickness payments provided by the **state**.

social roles: Socially defined expectations of an individual in a given **status** or **social position**.

Social Security: A government program that provides economic assistance to persons faced with unemployment, disability, or agedness.

social self: The basis of **self-consciousness** in human individuals, according to the theory of G. H. Mead. The social self is the **identity** conferred upon an individual by the reactions of others. A person achieves self-consciousness by becoming aware of this **social identity**.

social stratification: The existence of **structured inequalities** between groups in **society** in terms of their access to material or symbolic rewards. While all societies involve some forms of stratification, only with the development of state-based systems did wide differences in **wealth** and **power** arise. The most distinctive form of stratification in modern societies is **class** divisions.

social structure: The underlying regularities or patterns in how people behave in their relationships with one another.

society: A group of people who live in a particular territory, are subject to a common system of political **authority**, and are aware of having a distinct **identity** from other groups. Some societies, such as **hunting and gathering societies**, are small, numbering no more than a few dozen people. Others are large, numbering millions. Modern Chinese society, for instance, has a **population** of more than a billion people.

sociobiology: An approach that attempts to explain the behavior of both animals and human beings in terms of biological principles.

socioemotional selectivity theory: The theory that adults maintain fewer relationships as they age, but that those relationships are of higher quality.

sociological imagination: The application of imaginative thought to the asking and answering of sociological questions. Someone using the sociological imagination "thinks himself away" from the familiar routines of daily life.

sociology of sexuality: A field that explores and debates the importance of biological versus social and cultural influences on human sexual behavior.

sociology of the body: A field that focuses on how our **health** and illness are affected by social and cultural influences.

sovereignty: The undisputed political rule of a **state** over a given territorial area.

standard deviation: A way of calculating the spread of a group of numbers.

standardized testing: A situation in which all students take the same test under the same conditions.

state: A political apparatus (government institutions plus civil service officials) ruling over a given territorial order, whose **authority** is backed by **law** and the ability to use force.

status: The social honor or prestige that a particular group is accorded by other members of a **society**. Status groups normally display distinct

styles of life—patterns of behavior that the members of a group follow. Status privilege may be positive or negative.

stepfamily: A **family** in which at least one partner has children from a previous **marriage**, living either in the home or nearby.

stereotype promise: A phenomenon where being viewed through the lens of a positive stereotype may lead one to perform in such a way that confirms the positive stereotype, thereby enhancing performance.

stereotype threat: The idea that when African American students believe they are being judged not as individuals but as members of a negatively stereotyped **social group**, they will do worse on tests.

stereotyping: Thinking in terms of fixed and inflexible categories.

stigma: Any physical or social characteristic that is labeled by **society** as undesirable.

strike: A temporary stoppage of **work** by a group of employees in order to express a grievance or enforce a demand.

structural mobility: Mobility resulting from changes in the number and kinds of jobs available in a **society**.

structural strain: Tension that produces conflicting interests within **societies**.

structured inequalities: Social inequalities that result from patterns in the **social structure**.

subcultures: **Values** and **norms** distinct from those of the majority, held by a group within a wider **society**.

suburbanization: The development of suburbia, areas of housing outside **inner cities**.

surplus value: In Marxist theory, the value of a worker's labor **power** left over when an employer has repaid the cost of hiring the worker.

surveillance: The supervising of the activities of some individuals or groups by others in order to ensure compliant behavior.

survey: A method of sociological research in which questionnaires are administered to the **population** being studied.

sustainable development: Development that meets the needs of the present without compromising the ability of future generations to meet their own needs.

symbol: One item used to stand for or represent another—as in the case of a flag, which symbolizes a nation.

symbolic interactionism: A theoretical approach in sociology developed by George Herbert Mead that emphasizes the role of **symbols** and **language** as core elements of all human interaction.

Taylorism: A set of ideas, also referred to as "scientific management," developed by Frederick Winslow Taylor, involving simple, coordinated operations in industry.

technology: The application of knowledge of the material world to production; the creation of material instruments (such as machines) used in human interaction with nature.

theism: A belief in one or more supernatural deities.

time-space: When and where events occur.

timetables: The means by which **organizations** regularize activities across time and space.

total institutions: Groups who exercise control over their members by making them subsume their individual **identities** in that of the group, compelling them to adhere to strict ethical codes or rules, and sometimes forcing them to withdraw from activity in the outside world.

tracking: Dividing students into groups that receive different instruction on the basis of assumed similarities in ability or attainment.

transgender: A person who identifies as or expresses a **gender** identity that differs from their **sex** at birth.

transnational capitalist class: A social class whose economic interests are global rather than national, who share a globalizing perspective and similar lifestyles, and who see themselves as cosmopolitan citizens of the world.

transnational (or multinational) corporations: Business **corporations** located in two or more countries.

transnational feminism: A branch of **feminist theory** that highlights the way that global processes—including **colonialism**, **racism**, and imperialism—shape **gender** relations and hierarchies.

triad: A group consisting of three persons.

underclass: A **class** of individuals situated at the bottom of the class system, normally composed of people from **ethnic minority** backgrounds.

unemployment rate: The proportion of the **population** 16 and older that is actively seeking work but is unable to find employment.

unfocused interaction: Interaction occurring among people present in a particular setting but not engaged in direct face-to-face communication.

union density: A statistic that represents the number of union members as a percentage of the number of people who could potentially be union members.

upper class: A social **class** broadly composed of the more affluent members of **society**, especially those who have inherited **wealth**, own businesses, or hold large numbers of stocks (shares).

urban ecology: An approach to the study of urban life based on an analogy with the adjustment of plants and organisms to the physical environment. According to ecological theorists, the various neighborhoods and zones within cities are formed as a result of natural processes of adjustment on the part of **populations** as they compete for resources.

urbanism: A term used by Louis Wirth to denote distinctive characteristics of urban social life, such as its impersonality.

urbanization: The development of towns and cities.

urban renewal: The process of renovating deteriorating neighborhoods by using public funds to renew old buildings and construct new ones, often through large-scale demolition of slum housing.

values: Ideas held by individuals or groups about what is desirable, proper, good, and bad. What individuals value is strongly influenced by the specific **culture** in which they happen to live.

wealth: Money and material possessions held by an individual or group.

welfare capitalism: The practice by which large **corporations** protect their employees from the vicissitudes of the market.

welfare state: A political system that provides a wide range of welfare benefits for its **citizens**.

white-collar crime: Criminal activities carried out by those in white-collar, or professional, jobs.

White privilege: The unacknowledged and unearned assets that benefit Whites in their everyday lives.

work: The activity by which people produce from the natural world and so ensure their survival. Work should not be thought of exclusively as paid employment. In traditional **cultures**, there was only a rudimentary monetary system, and few people worked for money. In modern **societies**, there remain types of work that do not involve direct payment (e.g., housework).

working class: A social **class** broadly composed of people working in blue-collar, or manual, **occupations**.

working poor: People who work but whose earnings are not enough to lift them above the **poverty line**.

world-accommodating movements: Religious **movements** that emphasize the importance of inner religious life and spiritual purity over worldly concerns.

world-affirming movements: Religious movements that seek to enhance followers' ability to succeed in the outside world by helping them unlock their human potential.

world-rejecting movements: Religious movements that are exclusive in nature, highly critical of the outside world, and demanding of their members.

world-systems theory: Pioneered by Immanuel Wallerstein, this **theory** emphasizes the interconnections among countries based on the expansion of a capitalist world **economy**. This economy is made up of **core**, **semiperiphery**, and **periphery countries**.

young old: Sociological term for persons age 65 to 74.

Bibliography

Abdul-Rauf, M. (1975). *Islam: Creed and Worship*. Washington, DC: Islamic Center.

Abeles, R. P., and M. W. Riley. (1987). "Longevity, Social Structure, and Cognitive Aging." In C. Schooler and K. Warner Schaie, eds., *Cognitive Functioning and Social Structure over the Life Course*. Norwood, NJ: Ablex.

Abma, J. C., and F. L. Sonenstein. (2017). "Sexual Activity and Contraceptive Practices Among Teenagers in the United States, 2011–2015." *National Health Statistics Reports* 104: 1–23.

Abramson, Y. (2017). "Making a Homeland, Constructing a Diaspora: The Case of Taglit-Birthright Israel." *Political Geography* 58: 14–23.

Achar, S., A. Rostamian, S. M. Narayan. (2010). "Cardiac and metabolic effects of anabolic-androgenic steroid abuse on lipids, blood pressure, left ventricular dimensions, and rhythm." *American Journal of Cardiology* 106(6): 893–901

Acs, G. (2011). "Downward Mobility from the Middle Class: Waking Up from the American Dream." Washington, DC: The Pew Charitable Trusts, Economic Mobility Project (September 2011). Retrieved 6/18/12, from www.pewstates.org/uploadedFiles/PCS_Assets/2011/MiddleClassReport.pdf.

Adams, J., and R. Light. (2015). "Scientific consensus, the law, and same sex parenting outcomes." *Social Science Research* 53: 300–310.

Administration for Community Living. (2018a). "2017 Profile of Older Americans." Retrieved from https://acl.gov/sites/default/files/Aging%20and%20Disability%20in%20America/2017OlderAmericansProfile.pdf.

Administration for Community Living. (2018b). "2018 Profile of Older Americans." Retrieved from https://acl.gov/sites/default/files/Aging%20and%20Disability%20in%20America/2018OlderAmericansProfile.pdf.

Agyeman, J., R. D. Bullard, and B. Edwards, ed. (2003). *Just Sustainabilities: Development in an Unequal World (Urban and Industrial Environments)*. Cambridge, MA: MIT Press.

Ahmadian, S., S. Azarshahi, and D. L. Paulhus. (2017). "Explaining Donald Trump via Communication Style: Grandiosity, Informality, and Dynamism," *Personality and Individual Differences* 107 (March): 49–63.

Al Ahmad, J. (1997; orig. 1962). *Gharbzadegi: Weststruckedness*. Costa Mesa, CA: Mazda Publications.

Alba, R. (2016). "The Likely Persistence of a White Majority," *American Prospect*, January 11, 2016.

Albrow, M. (1997). *The Global Age: State and Society Beyond Modernity*. Stanford, CA: Stanford University Press.

Aldrich, H. E., and P. V. Marsden. (1988). "Environments and Organizations." In N. J. Smelser, ed., *Handbook of Sociology*. Newbury Park, CA: Sage.

Alemayehu, B., and K. E. Warner. (2004). "The lifetime distribution of health care costs." *Health Services Research* 39(3): 627–642.

Alexander, M. (2011). "The New Jim Crow: How Mass Incarceration Turns People of Color into Permanent Second-Class Citizens." *The American Prospect* 22(1).

Alexander, M. (2012). *The New Jim Crow*. New York: The New Press.

Al-Hardan, A. (2016). *Palestinians in Syria: Nakba Memories of Shattered Communities*. New York: Columbia University Press.

Allen, B., E. M. Cisneros, and A. Tellez. (2013). "The children left behind: The impact of parental deportation on mental health." *Journal of Child and Family Studies* 24(2): 386–392.

Allred, C. (2019). "Divorce Rate in the U.S.: Geographic Variation, 2018." *Family Profiles*, FP-19-23. National Center for Family & Marriage Research. Retrieved from https://www.bgsu.edu/content/dam/BGSU/college-of-arts-and-sciences/NCFMRdocuments/FP/fp-19-23-divorce-rate-geo-var-2018.pdf.

Alm, E., and L. Martinsson. (2017). "The Rainbow Flag as Friction: Transnational Imagined Communities of Belonging Among Pakistani LGBTQ Activists." *Culture Unbound* 8(3): 218–39.

Altshuler, A., C. P. Somkin, and N. E. Adler. (2004). "Local services and amenities, neighborhood social capital, and health." *Social Science & Medicine* 59(6): 1219–1229.

Alvaredo, F., A. B. Atkinson, T. Piketty, and E. Saez. (2013). "The Top 1 Percent in International and Historical Perspective. *Journal of Economic Perspectives* 27: 3–20. Retrieved 12/14, from http://eml.berkeley.edu/,saez/alvaredo-atkinson-piketty-saezJEP13top1percent.pdf.

Alvarez, R., L. Robin, M. Tuan, and S.-I. Huang. (1996). "Women in the Professions: Assessing Progress." In P. J. Dubeck and K. Borman, eds., *Women and Work: A Handbook*. New York: Garland.

Alwin, D. F. (2008). "History, Cohort, and Patterns of Cognitive Aging." In S. M. Hofer and D. F. Alwin, eds., *Handbook of Cognitive Aging: Interdisciplinary Perspectives*. Thousand Oaks, CA: Sage. 9–38.

Alzheimer's Association. (2017). "2017 Alzheimer's Disease Facts and Figures," Retrieved from http://www.alz.org/documents_custom/2017-facts-and-figures.pdf.

Alzheimer's Association. (2019). "Facts and Figures." Retrieved from https://www.alz.org/alzheimers-dementia/facts-figures.

Amato, P. (2000). "The Consequences of Divorce for Adults and Children." *Journal of Marriage and the Family* 62: 1269–87.

Amato, P., L. S. Loomis, and A. Booth. (1995). "Parental Divorce, Marital Conflict, and Offspring Well-Being during Early Adulthood." *Social Forces* 73: 895–915.

Amato, P. R., and B. Keith. (1991). "Parental divorce and the well-being of children: a meta analysis." *Psychological Bulletin* 110:1: 26.

Amenta, E. (1998). *Bold Relief: Institutional Politics and the Origins of Modern American Social Policy*. Princeton, NJ: Princeton University Press.

American Academy of Pediatrics. (2004). "Sexual Orientation and Adolescents." *Pediatrics* 113(6): 1827–32.

AARP. (2017). "AARP Fact Sheet." Retrieved from https://press.aarp.org/?intcmp=GLBNAV-FX-BTM-PRESS-CENTER.

American Association of University Women (AAUW). (1992). *How Schools Shortchange Girls*. Washington, DC: American Association of University Women Educational Foundation.

American Council on Education (ACE). (2001). "The American Freshman: National Norms for Fall 2000." Los Angeles, CA: UCLA Higher Education Research Institute and ACE. Results also published in "This Year's Freshmen at 4-Year Colleges: Their Opinions, Activities, and Goals." *Chronicle of Higher Education* (January 26): A49.

American Council on Education (ACE). (2008). "Mapping New Directions: Higher Education for Older Adults." Washington, DC: American Council on Education. Retrieved 9/08/12, from www.acenet.edu/Content/NavigationMenu/ProgramsServices/CLLL/Reinvesting/MapDirections.pdf.

American Express OPEN. (2014). *The 2014 State of Women-Owned Businesses Report*, Retrieved from http://www.womenable.com/content/userfiles/2014_State_of_Women-owned_Businesses_public.pdf.

American Psychiatric Association. (2000). *Diagnostic and Statistical Manual of Mental Disorders*, 4th ed., text rev. Washington, DC: American Psychiatric Association.

American Psychiatric Association. (2013). "Gender Dysphoria." Washington, DC: American Psychiatric Association. Retrieved 10/24/14, from "http://www.dsm5.org/documents/gender%20dysphoria%20fact%20sheet.pdf.

American Sociological Association. (2019). "Environmental Sociology." Retrieved from https://www.asanet.org/asa-communities/sections/environmental-sociology.

Amin, S. (1974). *Accumulation on a World Scale*. New York: Monthly Review Press.

Ammons, S. K., and W. T. Markham. (2004). "Working at Home: Experiences of Skilled White-Collar Workers." *Sociological Spectrum* 24(2): 191–238.

Amsden, A. H., J. Kochanowicz, and L. Taylor. (1994). *The Market Meets Its Match: Restructuring the Economies of Eastern Europe*. Cambridge, MA: Harvard University Press.

Anderson, B. (1991). *Imagined Communities: Reflections on the Origin and Spread of Nationalism*, rev. ed. New York: Routledge.

Anderson, B. (2016; orig. 1983). *Imagined Communities: Reflections on the Origin and Spread of Nationalism*. London: Verso Books.

Anderson, E. (1990). *Streetwise: Race, Class, and Change in an Urban Community*. Chicago: University of Chicago Press.

Anderson, E. (2011). *The Cosmopolitan Canopy: Race and Civility in Everyday Life*. New York: W. W. Norton.

Anderson, M. (2015). "A rising share of the US Black population is foreign born." Pew Research Center. Retrieved from https://www.pewsocialtrends.org/2015/04/09/a-rising-share-of-the-u-s-black-population-is-foreign-born/.

Anderson, M. (2018). "A Majority of Teens Have Experienced Some Form of Cyberbullying." Pew Research Center, Sept. 27. Retrieved from https://www.pewresearch.org/internet/2018/09/27/a-majority-of-teens-have-experienced-some-form-of-cyberbullying/.

Angell, M., and J. P. Kassirer. (1998). "Alternative Medicine: The Risks of Untested and Unregulated Remedies." *New England Journal of Medicine* 339: 839.

Angier, N. (1995). "If You're Really Ancient, You May Be Better Off." *New York Times*, June 11. Retrieved from http://www.nytimes.com/1995/06/11/weekinreview/the-nation-if-you-re-really-ancient-you-may-be-better-off.html.

Anyon, J. (2006). "Social Class, School Knowledge, and the Hidden Curriculum Revisited." In L. Weiss and G. Dimitriadis, eds., *The New Sociology of Knowledge*. New York: Routledge.

Anzaldúa, G. (1990). *Making Face, Making Soul: Haciendo Caras: Creative and Critical Perspectives by Feminists of Color*. San Francisco: Aunt Lute Foundation.

Appelbaum, R. (1988). *Karl Marx*. Thousand Oaks, CA: Sage.

Appelbaum, R. (1990). "Counting the Homeless." In J. A. Momeni, ed., *Homeless in the United States* (vol. 2). New York: Praeger.

Appelbaum, R. (2019). "Labor." in M. Juergensmeyer, S. Sassen, and M. Steger, eds., *The Oxford Handbook of Global Studies*, (pp. 291–308). New York: Oxford University Press.

Appelbaum, R. P. (1989). *Karl Marx*. Newbury Park, CA: Sage.

Appelbaum, R. P. (2016). "From Public Regulation to Private Enforcement: How CSR Became Managerial Orthodoxy." In R. P. Appelbaum and N. Lichtenstein, eds., *Achieving Workers' Rights in the Global Economy* (pp. 32–50). Ithaca, NY: Cornell University Press.

Appelbaum, R. P. (2017). "Mental Models of Economic Development." In P. Battersby and R. Roy, eds., *International Development: A Global Perspective on Theory and Practice* (pp. 23–49). London: Sage.

Appelbaum, R. P., and B. Christerson. (1997). "Cheap Labor Strategies and Export-Oriented Industrialization: Some Lessons from the East Asia/Los Angeles Apparel Connection." *International Journal of Urban and Regional Research* 21(2): 202–17.

Appelbaum, R. P., C. Cao, X. Han, R. Parker, and D. Simon. (2018). *Innovation in China: Challenging the Global Science and Technology System*. Cambridge, UK: Polity Press.

Appelbaum, R. P., and J. Henderson, eds. (1992). *States and Development in the Asian Pacific Rim*. Newbury Park, CA: Sage.

Appelbaum, R., and N. Lichtenstein. (2006). "A New Work of Retail Supremacy: Supply Chains and Workers' Chains in the Age of Wal-Mart." *International Labor and Working-Class History* 70: 106–25.

Appelbaum, R. P., and N. Lichtenstein, eds. (2016). *Achieving Workers' Rights in the Global Economy*. Ithaca, NY: Cornell University Press.

Appiah, Kwame Anthony. (2020). "The Case for Capitalizing the *B* in Black." *The Atlantic*. Retrieved from https://www.theatlantic.com/ideas/archive/2020/06/time-to-capitalize-blackand-white/613159/.

Apple. (2019). "Apple Supplier List." Retrieved from https://www.apple.com/supplier-responsibility/pdf/Apple-Supplier-List.pdf.

Archer, J. (2004). "Sex Differences in Aggression in Real-World Settings: A Meta-Analytic Review." *Review of General Psychology* 8(4): 291–322.

Arias, E., and J. Xu. (2019). "United States Life Tables, 2017." *National Vital Statistics Reports* 68(7). Retrieved from https://www.cdc.gov/nchs/data/nvsr/nvsr68/nvsr68_07-508.pdf.

Ariès, P. (1965). *Centuries of Childhood*. New York: Random House.

Arjomand, S. A. (1988). *The Turban for the Crown: The Islamic Revolution in Iran*. New York: Oxford University Press.

Armstrong, E., and L. Hamilton. (2015). *Paying for the Party: How College Maintains Inequality*. Cambridge, MA: Harvard University Press.

Arnett, J. J. (2000). "Emerging Adulthood: A Theory of Development from the Late Teens through the Twenties." *American Psychologist* 55(5): 469–80.

Aronowitz, S., and H. A. Giroux. (1985). *Education under Siege: The Conservative, Liberal and Radical Debate over Schooling*. London: Routledge.

Arrighi, G. (1994). *The Long Twentieth Century: Money, Power, and the Origin of Our Times*. New York: Verso.

Asch, S. (1952). *Social Psychology*. Englewood Cliffs, NJ: Prentice-Hall.

Aslan, R. (2006). *No God but God: The Origins, Evolution, and Future of Islam*. New York: Random House.

Aslan, R. (2009). *How to Win a Cosmic War: God, Globalization, and the End of the War on Terror*. New York: Random House.

Associated Press. (2018). "Trump says climate change not a hoax, not sure of its source." Retrieved from https://apnews.com/029c37e1c3b94f0490e8a84b2bd9f21f.

Atchley, R. (1989). "A Continuity Theory of Normal Aging." *Gerontologist* 29: 183–90.

Atchley, R. C. (2000). *Social Forces and Aging: An Introduction to Social Gerontology*, 9th ed. Belmont, CA: Wadsworth.

The Atlantic. (2016). "The Adversity of a Child's Life in Rural Kentucky," Sept. 22, Retrieved from https://www.theatlantic.com/video/index/500768/life-in-rural-kentucky/.

Atske, S., A. W. Geiger, and A. Scheller. (2019). "The share of women in legislatures around the world is growing, but they are still underrepresented." Pew Research Center, March 18. Retrieved from https://www.pewresearch.org/fact-tank/2019/03/18/the-share-of-women-in-legislatures-around-the-world-is-growing-but-they-are-still-underrepresented/.

Attaran, M. (2004). "Exploring the Relationship between Information Technology and Business Process Reengineering." *Information and Management* 41(5): 585–96.

August, K. J., and D. H. Sorkin. (2010). "Racial and Ethnic Disparities in Indicators of Physical Health Status: Do They Still Exist Throughout Late Life?" *Journal of the American Geriatrics Society* 58: 2009–2015.

Autor, D. (2014). "Skills, education, and the rise of earnings inequality among the 'other 99 percent.'" *Science*, May 23, 344(6186): 843–51.

Avert. (2019). "HIV and AIDS in the United States of America (USA)." Retrieved from https://www.avert.org/professionals/hiv-around-world/western-central-europe-north-america/usa.

Avert. (2020). "HIV and AIDS in East and Southern Africa Regional Overview." Retrieved from https://www.avert.org/professionals/hiv-around-world/sub-saharan-africa/overview.

Avery, R. B., G. B. Canner, and R. E. Cook. (2005). "New Information Reported under HMDA and Its Application in Fair Lending Enforcement." *Federal Reserve Bulletin* 91(2): 344–94. Retrieved spring 2006, from www.federalreserve.gov/pubs/bulletin/2005/3–05hmda.pdf (site discontinued).

Awaz.TV. (2016). "Pakistan's Largest City Is Running Out of Water." Retrieved from http://www.awaztoday.tv/News-Talk-Shows/113790/Pakistans-largest-city-is-running-out-of-water-Roshan-Pakistan.aspx.

Backstrom, L., and J. Kleinberg. (2013). "Romantic Partnerships and the Dispersion of Social Ties: A Network Analysis of Relationship Status on Facebook," Proc. 17th ACM Conference on Computer Supported Cooperative Work and Social Computing (CSCW), 2014.

Bailey, J. M., and R. C. Pillard. (1991). "A Genetic Study of Male Sexual Orientation." *Archives of General Psychiatry* 48: 1089–96.

Bailey, M., and A. J. Kaufman. (2010). Polygamy in the Monogamous World: Multicultural Challenges for Western Law and Policy. Santa Barbara, CA: Praeger.

Bailey, R., J. Mokonogho, and A. Kumar. (2009). "Racial and Ethnic Differences in Depression: Current Perspectives." *Neuropsychiatric Disease and Treatment* 15: 603–609.

Baiocco, R., N. Carone, S. Ioverno, L. Vittorio. (2018). "Same-Sex and Different-Sex Parent Families in Italy." *Journal of Developmental & Behavioral Pediatrics* 39(7): 555–63.

Bair, J., ed. (2009). *Frontiers of Commodity Chain Research*. Stanford, CA: Stanford University Press.

Bales, R. F. (1953). "The Egalitarian Problem in Small Groups." In T. Parsons, ed., *Working Papers in the Theory of Action*. Glencoe, IL: Free Press.

Bales, R. F. (1970). *Personality and Interpersonal Behavior*. New York: Holt, Rinehart, and Winston.

Balmer, R. (1989). *Mine Eyes Have Seen the Glory: A Journey into the Evangelical Subculture in America*. New York: Oxford University Press.

Balswick, J. O. (1983). "Male Inexpressiveness." In K. Soloman and N. B. Levy, eds., *Men in Transition: Theory and Therapy*. New York: Plenum Press.

Barker, C. (2004). *The SAGE Dictionary of Cultural Studies*. Thousand Oaks, CA: Sage.

Barnes, H., and J. Parry. (2004). "Renegotiating Identity and Relationships: Men's and Women's Adjustment to Retirement." *Ageing and Society* 24: 213–33.

Barnes, P. M., B. Bloom, and R. Nahin. (2008). "The Use of Complementary and Alternative Medicine in the United States." Figure 1. CAM Use by U.S. Adults and Children, 2007. *CDC National Health Statistics Report No. 12*, December. Retrieved 9/24/12, from http://nccam.nih.gov/sites/nccam.nih.gov/files/camuse.pdf.

Barnes, T. (2009). "America's 'Shadow Economy' Is Bigger Than You Think—and Growing." *Christian Science Monitor*, November 12. Retrieved spring 2013, from www.csmonitor.com/Business/2009/1112/americas-shadow-economy-is-bigger-than-you-think-and-growing.

Barnet, R. J., and J. Cavanagh. (1994). *Global Dreams: Imperial Corporations and the New World Order*. New York: Simon and Schuster.

Barnett, M. L., and D. C. Grabowski. (2020). "Nursing Homes Are Ground Zero for COVID-19 Pandemic." *Journal of the American Medical Association Health Forum* 1(3): e200369-e200369.

Baron, K. (2017). "How the U.S. Military Sees the Anti-ISIS Fight," *The Atlantic*, Jan. 18, Retrieved from https://www.theatlantic.com/international/archive/2017/01/obama-doctrine-military-trump/513470/.

Bartels, L. M. (2006). "What's the Matter with *What's the Matter with Kansas*?" *Quarterly Journal of Political Science* 1 (March): 201–26.

Bartels, L. M. (2008). *Unequal Democracy: The Political Economy of the New Gilded Age*. Princeton, NJ: Princeton University Press.

Barzilai-Nahon, K., and G. Barzilai. (2005). "Cultured Technology: Internet and Religious Fundamentalism." *The Information Society* 21 (1): 25–40.

Basham, A. L. (1989). *The Origins and Development of Classical Hinduism*. Boston: Beacon Press.

Basow, S. (2004). "The Hidden Curriculum: Gender in the Classroom." In M. A. Paludi (Ed.), *Praeger Guide to the Psychology of Gender* (pp. 117–131). Wesport, CT: Praeger.

Bates, T. (2010). "Vatican Angers Many with 'Grave Crimes' List." *AOL News*, July 16. Retrieved spring 2013, from www.aolnews.com/2010/07/16/vatican-puts-ordaining-women-priests-on-par-with-child-sex-abuse/.

Baxter, J. (1997). "Gender Inequality and Participation in Housework: A Cross-National Perspective." *Journal of Comparative Family Issues* 28: 220–28.

Bayer, P., F. Ferreira, and S. L. Ross. (2018). "What Drives Racial and Ethnic Differences in High-Cost Mortgages? The Role of High-Risk Lenders." *The Review of Financial Studies* 31(1):175–205.

BBC. (2016). "Migrant Crisis: Migration to Europe Explained in Seven Charts," March 4. Retrieved from http://www.bbc.com/news/worldeurope-34131911.

Bean, F. D., R. Chanove, R. Cushing, R. de la Garza, C. Haynes, G. Freeman, and D. Spener. (1994). *Illegal Mexican Migration and the United States/Mexico Border: Operation Hold-the-Line and El Paso/Juarez*. Washington, DC: U.S. Commission on Immigration Reform.

Bearman, P. (2002). "Opposite-Sex Twins and Adolescent Same-Sex Attraction." *American Journal of Sociology* 107: 1179–1205.

Bearman, P. (2008). "Exploring Genetics and Social Structure," *American Journal of Sociology*, 114 (S1): v–x.

Beasley, C. (1999). *What Is Feminism?* Thousand Oaks, CA: Sage.

Beck, U. (1992). *Risk Society*. London: Sage.

Beck, U. (1995). *Ecological Politics in an Age of Risk*. Cambridge, UK: Polity Press.

Becker, G. (1964). *Human Capital*. New York: National Bureau of Economic Research.

Becker, G. S. (2009). *A Treatise on the Family*. Cambridge, MA: Harvard University Press.

Becker, H. S. (1963). *Outsiders: Studies in the Sociology of Deviance*. New York: Macmillan.

Becker, M. H., ed. (1974). "The Health Belief Model and Personal Health Behavior." *Health Education Monographs* 2: 324–473.

Bell, A., M. Weinberg, and S. Hammersmith. (1981). *Sexual Preference: Its Development in Men and Women*. Bloomington, IN: Indiana University Press.

Bell, D. (1976). *The Coming of Post-Industrial Society: A Venture in Social Forecasting*. New York: Basic Books.

Bellah, R. N. (1968). "Civil Religion in America." In W. G. McLoughlin and R. N. Bellah, eds., *Religion in America*. Boston: Houghton Mifflin.

Bellah, R. N. (1975). *The Broken Covenant*. New York: Seabury Press.

Bellah, R. N., R. Madsen, W. Sullivan, A, Swidler, S. Tipton. (1985). *Habits of the Heart: Individualism and Commitment in American Life*. New York: Harper and Row.

Bellman, B. (1984). *The Language of Secrecy: Symbols and Metaphors in Poro Ritual*. New Brunswick, NJ: Rutgers University Press.

Bello, W. (2000). "From Melbourne to Prague: The Struggle for a Deglobalized World." International Network on Disarmament and Globalization. Vancouver, Canada. Retrieved spring 2013, from http://ratical.org/co-globalize/WB0900.html.

Bello, W. (2005). *Deglobalization: Ideas for a New World Economy*. London: Zed Book.

Belson, K. (2014). "Rams Cut Michael Sam, First Openly Gay Player Drafted in N.F.L." *New York Times*, August 30. Retrieved 10/26/14, from http://www.nytimes.com/2014/08/31/sports/football/rams-cut-michael-sam-first-openly-gay-nfl-draft-pick.html.

Bem, S. L. (1993). *The Lenses of Gender: Transforming the Debate on Sexual Inequality*. New Haven: Yale University Press.

Bendel, J. (2016). "Deep Adaptation: A Map for Navigating Climate Tragedy," IFLAS Occasional Paper 2. University of Cumbria, UK: Initiative for Leadership and Sustainability. Retrieved from https://mahb.stanford.edu/library-item/deep-adaptation-map-navigating-climate-tragedy.

Bendel, J. (2019a). "Will We Care Enough to Matter to Them? Climate Justice, Solidarity and Deep Adaptation." Retrieved from https://jembendell.com/2019/11/05/will-we-care-enough-to-matter-to-them-climate-justice-solidarity-and-deep-adaptation/.

Bendel, J. (2019b). "Hope in a time of climate chaos: A speech to psychotherapists." Retrieved from https://jembendell.com/2019/11/03/hope-in-a-time-of-climate-chaos-a-speech-to-psychotherapists/.

Bengston, V. L., N. M. Putney, and M. Johnson. (2005). "The Problem of Theory in Gerontology Today." In M. Johnson, V. Bengtson, P. G. Coleman, and T. B. L. Kirkwood, eds., *The Cambridge Handbook of Age and Ageing*. Cambridge, UK: Cambridge University Press.

Benjamin, N. (2014). "Informal Economy and the World Bank," World Bank Poverty Reduction and Economic Management Network Policy Research Working Paper 6888 (May). from http://papers.ssrn.com/sol3/Delivery.cfm/6888.pdf?abstractid=2440936&mirid=5.

Bennett, J. W. (1976). *The Ecological Transition: Cultural Anthropology and Human Adaptation*. New York: Pergamon Press.

Berger, P. L. (1967). *The Sacred Canopy: Elements of a Sociological Theory of Religion*. Garden City, NY: Anchor Books.

Berger, P. L. (1986). *The Capitalist Revolution: Fifty Propositions about Prosperity, Equality, and Liberty*. New York: Basic Books.

Berger, P. L. (1988). "An East Asian Development Model?" In P. L. Berger and H. M. Hsiao, eds., *In Search of an East Asian Development Model*. New Brunswick, NJ: Transaction Books.

Berkley Center. (2020). "Demographics of Judaism." Georgetown University. Retrieved from https://berkleycenter.georgetown.edu/essays/demographics-of-judaism.

Berle, A., and G. C. Means. (1982; orig. 1932). *The Modern Corporation and Private Property*. Buffalo, NY: Heim.

Berry, A. (2018). "50 Highest Paying College Majors." Glassdoor. Retrieved from https://www.glassdoor.com/blog/50-highest-paying-college-majors/.

Berryman, P. (1987). *Liberation Theology: Essential Facts about the Revolutionary Movement in Central America and Beyond*. Philadelphia: Temple University Press.

Beyer, P. (1994). *Religion and Globalization*. Thousand Oaks, CA: Sage.

Beyerstein, B. L. (1999). "Psychology and 'Alternative Medicine'. Social and Judgmental Biases That Make Inert Treatments Seem To Work." *Scientific Review of Alternative Medicine* 3(2)

Bialik, K. (2017). "Key facts about race and marriage, 50 years after Loving v. Virginia." Pew Research Center. Retrieved from https://www.pewresearch.org/fact-tank/2017/06/12/key-facts-about-race-and-marriage-50-years-after-loving-v-virginia/.

Bianchi, S. M., L. C. Sayer, M. A. Milkie, and J. P. Robinson. (2012). "Housework: Who Did, Does, or Will Do It and How Much Does It Matter?" *Social Forces* 91: 55–63.

Biblarz, T. J. and J. Stacey, (2010). Ideal Families and Social Science Ideals. *Journal of Marriage and Family,* 72: 41–44.

Bird, R., and F. Newport. (2017). "What Determines How Americans Perceive Their Social Class?" Gallup, Feb. 27. Retrieved from https://news.gallup.com/opinion/polling-matters/204497/determines-americans-perceive-social-class.aspx.

Biddle, B. J. (1986). "Recent Developments in Role Theory." *Annual Review of Sociology* 12: 67–92.

Birditt, K. S., L. M. H. Jackey, and T. C. Antonucci. (2009). "Longitudinal Patterns of Negative Relationship Quality Across Adulthood." *Journals of Gerontology* 64B: 55–64.

Birnbaum, J. H. (2005). "AARP Leads with Wallet in Fight over Social Security." *Washington Post,* March 30. Retrieved 12/06/05, from www.washingtonpost.com/wp-dyn/articles/A11076-2005Mar29.html.

Birren, J. E., and V. L. Bengston, eds. (1988). *Emerging Theories of Aging.* New York: Springer.

Bjorkqvist, K., K. M. Lagerspetz, and K. Osterman. (2006). "Sex Differences in Covert Aggression." *Aggressive Behavior* 202(December 6): 27–33.

Blaker, L. (2015). "The Islamic State's Effective Use of Online Social Media," *Military Cyber Affairs* 1: 1 Article 4, Retrieved from http://scholarcommons.usf.edu/cgi/viewcontent.cgi?article=1004&context=mca.

Blanchard, R., and A. F. Bogaert. (1996). "Homosexuality in Men and Number of Older Brothers." *American Journal of Psychiatry* 153: 27–31.

Blankfeld, K. (2016). "Forbes Billionaires: Full List Of The 500 Richest People In The World 2016." *Forbes.* Retrieved from https://www.forbes.com/sites/kerenblankfeld/2016/03/01/forbes-billionaires-full-list-of-the-500-richest-people-in-the-world-2016/#6fdb12491897.

Blashill, A. J. (2014). "A Dual Pathway Model of Steroid Use among Adolescent Boys: Results from a Nationally Representative Sample." *Psychology of Men and Masculinity* 15: 220–33.

Blashill, A. J., and S. Wilhelm. (2014). "Body Image Distortions, Weight, and Depression in Adolescent Boys: Longitudinal Trajectories into Adulthood." *Psychology of Men and Masculinity* 15: 445–51.

Blau, P. (1963). *Bureaucracy in Modern Society.* New York: Random House.

Blau, P. (1977). *Inequality and Heterogeneity: A Primitive Theory of Social Structure.* New York: Free Press.

Blau, F., and L. Kahn. (2016). "The Gender Wage Gap: Extent, Trends, and Explanations." NBER Working Paper no. 21913. Retrieved from https://www.nber.org/papers/w21913.pdf.

Blau, P., and O. D. Duncan. (1967). *The American Occupational Structure.* New York: Wiley.

Blickman, T. (2003). "The Economic Impact of the Illicit Drug Industry." The Transnational Institute. Retrieved spring 2013, from www.tni.org/archives/acts/impact.pdf.

Blinder, A. S. (2007). "How Many U.S. Jobs Might be Offshorable?" CEPS Working Paper no. 142. https://www.princeton.edu/~ceps/workingpapers/142blinder.pdf.

Bloomberg. (2017). "China Deal Watch," Accessed April 26, Retrieved from https://www.bloomberg.com/graphics/2016-china-deals/.

Bloomberg. (2020). "Bloomberg Billionaires Index." Retrieved from https://www.bloomberg.com/billionaires/.

BloombergNEF. (2019). "Clean Energy Investment Exceeded $300 Billion Once Again in 2018." Retrieved from https://about.bnef.com/blog/clean-energy-investment-exceeded-300-billion-2018/.

Board of Governors of the Federal Reserve System. (2020a). "Consumer Credit – G.19." Retrieved from https://www.federalreserve.gov/releases/g19/current/default.htm.

Board of Governors of the Federal Reserve System. (2020b). "Distributional Financial Accounts." Retrieved from https://www.federalreserve.gov/releases/efa/efa-distributional-financial-accounts.htm.

Bochenek, M., and K. Knight. (2012). "Establishing a Third Gender Category in Nepal." *Emory International Law Review* 26: 11–41.

Boden, D., and H. Molotch. (1994). "The Compulsion of Proximity." In D. Boden and R. Friedland, eds., *Nowhere: Space, Time, and Modernity.* Berkeley: University of California Press.

Bohan, S. (1999). "Bohemian Grove and Global Elite." *Sacramento Bee,* August 2. Retrieved 12/28/04, from www.mt.net/~watcher/bohemiangrove.html.

Bonacich, E., and R. P. Appelbaum. (2000). *Behind the Label: Inequality in the Los Angeles Garment Industry.* Berkeley, CA: University of California Press.

Bonilla-Silva, E. (2006). *Racism without Racists.* Oxford, UK: Rowman and Littlefield.

Bonnell, V. E., and L. Hunt, eds. (1999). *Beyond the Cultural Turn.* Berkeley, CA: University of California Press.

Bonnie, R., and R. Wallace, eds. (2003). "Elder Mistreatment: Abuse, Neglect, and Exploitation in an Aging America." *Panel to Review Risk and Prevalence of Elder Abuse and Neglect.* Washington, DC: National Academies Press.

Booth, A. (1977). "Food Riots in the North-West of England, 1770–1801." *Past and Present* 77: 90.

Borjas, G. (1994). "The Economics of Immigration." *Journal of Economic Literature* 30: 1667–1717.

Bositis, D. (2001). "Black Elected Officials: A Statistical Summary: 2001." *Joint Center for Political and Economic Studies.* Retrieved 1/08, from www.jointcenter.org/publications1/publication-PDFs/BEO-pdfs/2001-BEO.pdf (site discontinued).

Bourdieu, P. (1984). *Distinction: A Social Critique of Judgment of Taste.* Cambridge, MA: Harvard University Press.

Bourdieu, P. (1986). "The Forms of Capital." In J. Richardson (Ed.), *Handbook of Theory and Research for the Sociology of Education* (241-258). New York: Greenwood.

Bourdieu, P. (1988). *Language and Symbolic Power.* Cambridge, UK: Polity Press.

Bourdieu, P. (1990). *The Logic of Practice.* Palo Alto, CA: Stanford University Press.

Boushey, H., and A. S. Hersh. (2012). *The American Middle Class, Income Inequality, and the Strength of Our Economy: New Evidence in Economics.* Washington, DC: Center for American Progress. Retrieved 6/18/12, from www.americanprogress.org/issues/2012/05/pdf/middleclass_growth.pdf.

Bowen, K. (1996). *Evangelism and Apostasy: The Evolution and Impact of Evangelicals in Modern Mexico.* Montreal, Canada: McGill-Queens University Press.

Bowlby, J. (1953). *Child Care and the Growth of Love.* Baltimore, MD: Penguin.

Bowles, S., and H. Gintis. (1976). *Schooling in Capitalist America.* New York: Basic Books.

Boyer, R., and D. Drache, eds. (1996). *States against Markets: The Limits of Globalization.* New York: Routledge.

Braithwaite, J. (1996). "Crime, Shame, and Reintegration." In P. Cordella and L. Siegel, eds., *Readings in Contemporary Criminological Theory.* Boston: Northeastern University Press.

Bramlett, M. D., and W. D. Mosher. (2002). "Cohabitation, Marriage, Divorce, and Remarriage in the United States." National Center for Health Statistics (NCHS). *Vital Health Statistics* 23: 22.

Branch, T. (1989). *Parting the Waters: America in the King Years 1954–1963.* New York: Simon and Schuster.

Branch, T. (1999). *Pillar of Fire: America in the King Years 1963–1965.* New York: Simon and Schuster.

Branch, T. (2007). *At Canaan's Edge: America in the King Years 1965–1968.* New York: Simon and Schuster.

Brass, D. J. (1985). "Men's and Women's Networks: A Study of Interaction Patterns and Influence in an Organization." *Academy of Management Journal* 28: 327–43.

Bratter, J. L., and K. Eschbach. (2006). "'What about the couple?' Interracial marriage and psychological distress." *Social Science Research* 35(4): 1025–47.

Bratter, J. L., and R. B. King. (2008). "'But Will It Last?': Marital Instability Among Interracial and Same-Race Couples." *Family Relations* 57: 160–71.

Braverman, H. (1974). *Labor and Monopoly Capital: The Degradation of Work in the Twentieth Century.* New York: Monthly Review Press.

Breiding, M. J., S. G. Smith, K. C. Basile, M. L. Walters, J. Chen, and M. T. Merrick. (2014). "Prevalence and Characteristics of Sexual Violence, Stalking, and Intimate Partner Violence Victimization—National Intimate Partner and Sexual Violence Survey, United States, 2011." *Morbidity and Mortality Weekly Report* 63(8), September 5.

Bremner, J., A. Frost, C. Haub, M. Mather, K. Ringheim, and E. Zuehlke. (2010). "World Population Highlights: Key Findings from PRB's World Population Data Sheet." *Population Bulletin* 65(2). Retrieved 8/11/12 from www.prb.org/pdf10/65.2highlights.pdf.

Brenan, M. (2018). "Religion Considered Important to 72% of Americans." Gallup, December 24. Retrieved from https://news.gallup.com/poll/245651/religion-considered-important-americans.aspx.

Brennan, T. (1988). "Controversial Discussions and Feminist Debate." In N. Segal and E. Timms, eds., *The Origins and Evolution of Psychoanalysis.* New Haven: Yale University Press.

Bresnahan, T., E. Brynjolfsson, and L. Hitt. (2002). "Information Technology, Workplace Organization, and the Demand for Skilled Labor: Firm-Level Evidence." *Quarterly Journal of Economics* 117(1): 339–76.

Brewer, R. M. (1993). "Theorizing Race, Class and Gender: The New Scholarship of Black Feminist Intellectuals and Black Women's Labor." In S. M. James and A. P. A. Busia, eds., *Theorizing Black Feminisms: The Visionary Pragmatism of Black Women.* New York: Routledge.

Bricourt, J. C. (2004). "Using Telework to Enhance Return to Work Outcomes for Individuals with Spinal Cord Injuries." *Neurorehabilitation* 19(2): 147–59.

Bridgman, B. (2016). "Accounting for Household Production in the National Accounts: An Update, 1965–2014," Retrieved from https://www.bea.gov/scb/pdf/2016/2%20February/0216_accounting_for_household_production_in_the_national_accounts.pdf.

Brimelow, P. (1995). *Alien Nation: Common Sense about America's Immigration Disaster.* New York: Random House.

Brizendine, L. (2007). *The Female Brain.* New York: Broadway.

Brizendine, L. (2010). *The Male Brain.* New York: Broadway.

Bronson, J., and E. A. Carson. (2019). "Prisoners in 2017." U.S. Department of Justice, Bureau of Justice Statistics. Retrieved from https://bjs.gov/content/pub/pdf/p17.pdf.

Brookings Institution. (2011). "The Re-Emergence of Concentrated Poverty: Metropolitan Trends in the 2000s." *Metropolitan Opportunity Series.* Retrieved summer 2012, from www.brookings.edu/./media/research/files/papers/2011/11/03%20poverty%20kneebone%20nadeau%20berube/1103_poverty_kneebone_nadeau_berube.

Brooks, A. T. (2017). *The ways women age. Using and refusing cosmetic intervention.* New York: New York University Press, 2017.

Brooks, J., and K. Weidrich. (2012). "Assets and Opportunity Scorecard: A Portrait of Financial Insecurity and Policies to Rebuild Prosperity in America. Four-Year Degree by Income." *Corporation for Enterprise Development: 2010 American Community Survey.* Washington, DC: U.S. Department of Commerce, Census Bureau, 2010. Data calculated by the Bay Area Council Economic Institute. Retrieved 9/21/12, from http://scorecard.assetsandopportunity.org/2012/measure/four-year-degree-by-income.

Brooks-Gunn, J., W. Han, and J. Waldfogel. (2010). "First-Year Maternal Employment and Child Development in the First Seven Years." *Monographs of the Society for Research in Child Development* 75 (2).

Brown, A. (2017). *The Data on Women Leaders* (March 17, 2017). Pew Research Center. Retrieved from http://www.pewsocialtrends.org/2017/03/17/the-data-on-women-leaders/#ceos.

Brown, A., and R. Stepler. (2016). "Statistical Portrait of the Foreign-Born Population in the United States, 2014." Pew Research Center, April 19. Retrieved from http://www.pewhispanic.org/2016/04/19/statistical-portrait-of-the-foreign-born-population-in-the-united-states-2014-key-charts/.

Brown, A., and S. Atske. (2019). "Blacks have made gains in the U.S. political leadership, but gaps remain." Pew Research Center, Jan. 18. Retrieved from https://www.pewresearch.org/fact-tank/2019/01/18/blacks-have-made-gains-in-u-s-political-leadership-but-gaps-remain/.

Brown, C., and K. Jasper, eds. (1993). *Consuming Passions: Feminist Approaches to Eating Disorders and Weight Preoccupations.* Toronto, Canada: Second Story Press.

Brown, D. E. (1991). *Human Universals.* New York: McGraw-Hill.

Brown, S. L., and I. F. Lin. (2012). "The Gray Divorce Revolution: Rising Divorce Among Middle-Aged and Older Adults, 1990-2010." *Journals of Gerontology, Series B: Psychological Sciences and Social Sciences* 67(6): 731–41.

Brown, S. L., and M. R. Wright. (2017). "Marriage, cohabitation, and divorce in later life." *Innovation in Aging* 1(2): igx015.

Brown, T. N. and C. L. Lesane-Brown. (2006). "Race Socialization Messages Across Historical Time." *Social Psychology Quarterly* 69(2): 201-213.

Brown, T. N., E. E. Tanner-Smith, C. L. Lesane-Brown, and M. E. Ezell. (2006). "Child, Parent, and Situational Correlates of Family Ethnic/Racial Socialization." *Journal of Marriage and Family* 16: 14–25.

Brown, T. N., E. E. Tanner-Smith, and C. L. Lesane-Brown. (2009). "Investigating Whether and When Ethnic/Race Socialization Improves Academic Performance." *The Journal of Negro Education* 78(4): 385-404.

Brownell, K., and K. Horgen. (2004). *Food Fight: The Inside Story of the Food Industry, America's Obesity Crisis, and What We Can Do about It.* New York: McGraw-Hill.

Brownmiller, S. (1975). *Against Our Will: Men, Women, and Rape.* New York: Simon and Schuster.

Brubaker, R. (1992). *The Politics of Citizenship.* Cambridge, MA: Harvard University Press.

Bryan, B., S. Dadzie, and S. Scafe. (1987). "Learning to Resist: Black Women and Education." In G. Weiner and M. Arnot, eds., *Gender under Scrutiny: New Inquiries in Education.* London: Hutchinson.

Brynjolfsson, E., and A. McAfee. (2014). *The Second Machine Age: Work, Progress, and Prosperity in a Time of Brilliant Technologies*. New York: NY: W. W. Norton, Inc.

Bryson, V. (1999). *Feminist Debates: Issues of Theory and Political Practice*. Basingstoke: Macmillan.

Buckler, S. (2016). "Imagined Communities Incorporated: Corporate Social Responsibility and Value Creation in a Globalised World," from *Corporate Social Responsibility Academic Insights and Impacts*, ed. Vertigans, S. and Idowu, S. Switzerland: Springer International Publishing.

Burkholder, K. (2019). "Percentage of Bisexual Americans on the Rise, Survey Finds." *The Georgia Voice*, April 25. Retrieved from https://thegavoice.com/news/percentage-of-bisexual-americans-on-the-rise-survey-finds/.

Bull, P. (1983). *Body Movement and Interpersonal Communication*. New York: Wiley.

Bullard, R. D., ed. (2005). *The Quest for Environmental Justice: Human Rights and the Politics of Pollution*. Berkeley: Counterpoint Press.

Bullard, R. D. (2019) "Environmental Justice: It's More Than Waste Facility Siting." *Social Science Quarterly* 77(3): 493–499.

Bullard, R. D. (2020). "Learn About Environmental Justice" Retrieved from https://drrobertbullard.com/learn-about-environmental-justice/.

Bullard, R. D., M. Gardezi, C. Chennault, and H. Dankbar. (2016). "Climate Change and Environmental Justice: A Conversation with Dr. Robert Bullard." *Journal of Critical Thought and Praxis* 5(2).

Bullock, C., III. (1984). "Equal Education Opportunity." In C. S. Bullock III and C. M. Lamb, eds., *Implementation of Civil Rights Policy*. Monterey, CA: Brooks and Cole.

Bump, P. (2016a). "Donald Trump got Reagan-like support from union households," *Washington Post*, Nov. 10, Retrieved from https://www.washingtonpost.com/news/the-fix/wp/2016/11/10/donald-trump-got-reagan-like-support-from-union-households/?utm_term=.6c0aa3f2906f.

Bump, P. (2016b). "Donald Trump Will Be President Thanks to 80,000 People in Three States," *Washington Post*, Dec. 1, Retrieved from https://www.washingtonpost.com/news/the-fix/wp/2016/12/01/donald-trump-will-be-president-thanks-to-80000-people-in-three-states/?utm_term=.c470b9352104.

Bumpass, L., J. A. Sweet, and A. Cherlin. (1991). "The Role of Cohabitation in Declining Rates of Marriage." *Journal of Marriage and the Family* 53: 913–27.

Burden, B. C., D. T. Cannon, K. R. Mayer, and D. P. Moynihan. (2013). "Election Laws, Mobilization, and Turnout: The Unanticipated Consequences of Election Reform." *American Journal of Political Science* 58 (1): 95–109.

Burgess, E. W. (1926). *The Family as a Unity of Interacting Personalities*. American Association for Organizing Family Social Work.

Burke, J. (2010). "More of World's Poor Live in India Than in All Sub-Saharan Africa, Says Study." *Guardian,* July 13. Retrieved summer 2012, from www.guardian.co.uk/world/2010/jul/14/poverty-india-africa-oxford.

Burman, D. D. et al. (2007). "Sex Differences in Neural Processing of Language among Children." *Neuropsychologia* 46(5): 1349–62.

Burnes D, K. Pillemer, P. L. Caccamise, et al. (2015). "Prevalence of and Risk Factors for Elder Abuse and Neglect in the Community: A Population-Based Study." *Journal of the American Geriatrics Society* 63:1906-1912.

Burnham, L., N. Theodore, and B. Ehrenreich. (2012). *Home Economics: The Invisible and Unregulated World of Domestic Work*. New York: National Domestic Workers Alliance (NDWA). Retrieved from http://www.idwfed.org/en/resources/home-economics-the-invisible-and-unregulated-world-of-domestic-work/@@display-file/attachment_1.

Burr, C. (1993). "Homosexuality and Biology." *Atlantic Monthly* 271: 47–65.

Burris, B. H. (1993). *Technocracy at Work*. Albany, NY: State University of New York Press.

Burris, B. H. (1998). "Computerization of the Workplace." *Annual Review of Sociology* 24: 141–57.

Buss, D. M. (2003). *Evolution of Desire: Strategies of Human Mating*. New York: Basic Books.

Butler, J. (1989). *Gender Trouble: Feminism and the Subversion of Identity*. New York: Routledge.

Butler, R. (2010). *The Longevity Prescription: The 8 Proven Keys to a Long, Healthy Life*. New York: Avery.

Buttel, F. H. (1987). "New Directions in Environmental Sociology." *Annual Review of Sociology* 13: 465–88.

Butterfield, F. (1998). "Decline of Violent Crimes Is Linked To Crack Market." *New York Times*, December 28, p. A18.

Byrne, A., and D. Carr. (2005). "Caught in the Cultural Lag: The Stigma of Singlehood." *Psychological Inquiry* 16: 84–90.

Byrne, B. P. (2015). "These 13 States Still Make Exceptions For Marital Rape." *Vocativ* (July 28, 2015). Retrieved from fhttp://www.vocativ.com/215942/these-13-states-still-make-exceptions-for-marital-rape/.

Cacioppo, J. T., L. C. Hawkley, L. E. Crawford, J. M. Ernst, M. H. Burleson, R. B. Kowalewski, W. B. Malarkey, E. Van Cauter, and G. G. Berntson. (2002). "Loneliness and Health: Potential Mechanisms." *Psychosomatic Medicine* 64: 407–17.

Cahalan, M., L. Perna, M. Yamashita, R. Ruiz, and K. Franklin. (2016). "Indicators of Higher Education Equity in the United States: 2016 Historical Trend Report," Washington, DC: Pell Institute for the Study of Opportunity in Higher Education.

Cahn, N., and J. Carbone. (2010). *Red Families v. Blue Families: Legal Polarization and the Creation of Culture*. New York: Oxford University Press.

Caiazza, R., A. A. Cannella Jr., P. H. Phan, and M. Simoni. (2018). "An Institutional Contingency Perspective of Interlocking Directorates." *International Journal of Management Reviews* 21(3): 277–93.

Calamur, K. (2017). "A Short History of 'America First,'" *The Atlantic*, Jan. 21, Retrieved from https://www.theatlantic.com/politics/archive/2017/01/trump-america-first/514037/.

Caldwell, J., B. K. Caldwell, P. Caldwell, P. F. McDonald, and T. Schindlmayr. (2010). *Demographic Transition Theory*. New York, NY: Springer.

Cameron, S. V., and J. J. Heckman. (2001). "Dynamics of Educational Attainment for Black, Hispanic, and White Males." *Journal of Political Economy* 109(3): 455–98. Retrieved 12/14, from http://athens.src.uchicago.edu/jenni/Handout_archive/Cameron_Heckman/Cameron_Heckman_2001_JPE_109_3.pdf.

Campbell F. A., M. R. Tramer, D. Carroll, D. J. Reynolds, R. A. Moore, H. J. McQuay. (2001). "Are cannabinoids an effective and safe treatment option in the management of pain? A qualitative systematic review." *BMJ* 323(7303): 3–6.

Campos, P., A. Saguy, P. Ernsberger, E. Oliver, and G. Gaesser. (2006). "The Epidemiology of Overweight and Obesity: Public Health Crisis or Moral Panic?" *International Journal of Epidemiology* 35: 55–60.

Canedy, D. (2016). "Talking to Children About Race, Policing and Violence." *New York Times,* July 12. Retrieved from https://www.nytimes.com/interactive/2016/07/12/us/how-to-talk-to-your-kids-about-violence-and-race.html.

Caplow, T. (1956). "A Theory of Coalitions in the Triad." *American Sociological Review* 21: 489–93.

Caplow, T. (1959). "Further Development of a Theory of Coalitions in Triads." *American Journal of Sociology* 64: 488–93.

Caplow, T. (1969). *Two Against One: Coalitions in Triads.* Englewood Cliffs, NJ: Prentice Hall.

Capps, R., R. M. Castañeda, A. Chaudry, and R. Santos. (2007). *Paying the Price: The Impact of Immigration Raids on America's Children.* Washington, DC. Urban Institute for National Council of La Raza.

Cardoso, F. H., and E. Faletto. (1979). *Dependency and Development in Latin America.* Berkeley: University of California Press.

Carr, D. (2010). "Golden Years? Poverty among Older Americans." *Contexts* 9(1): 62–63.

Carr, D. (2019). *Golden Years? Social Inequality in Later Life.* New York: Russell Sage.

Carr, D., and K. Springer. (2010). "Advances in Families and Health Research in the 21st Century." *Journal of Marriage and Family* (Decade in Review Special Issue) 72: 744–62.

Carr, D., and S. M. Moorman. (2011). "Social Relations and Aging." In R. A. Settersten Jr., and J. L. Angel, eds., *Handbook of Sociology of Aging* (pp. 145–60). New York: Springer.

Carrington, C. (1999). *No Place Like Home: Relationships and Family Life among Lesbians and Gay Men.* Chicago: University of Chicago Press.

Carson, R. (1962). *Silent Spring.* New York, NY: Houghton Mifflin.

Carstensen, L. L., D. Isaacowitz, and S. T. Charles. (1999). "Taking Time Seriously: A Theory of Socioemotional Selectivity." *American Psychologist* 54: 165–81.

Carter, P. (2005). *Keepin' It Real: School Success Beyond Black and White.* New York: Oxford University Press.

Case, A., and A. Deaton. (2020). *Deaths of Despair and the Future of Capitalism.* Princeton, NJ: Princeton University Press.

Casey, N. (2020). "College Made Them Feel Equal. The Virus Exposed How Unequal Their Lives Are." *New York Times,* May 5. Retrieved from https://www.nytimes.com/2020/04/04/us/politics/coronavirus-zoom-college-classes.html.

Casselman, B. (2019). "The White-Collar Job Apocalypse That Didn't Happen." *New York Times,* Sept. 27. Retrieved from https://www.nytimes.com/2019/09/27/business/economy/jobs-offshoring.html.

Casselman, B., and A. Satariano. (2019). "Amazon's Latest Experiment: Retraining Its Work Force." *New York Times,* July 11. Retrieved from https://www.nytimes.com/2019/07/11/technology/amazon-workers-retraining-automation.html.

Castells, M. (1977). *The Urban Question: A Marxist Approach.* Cambridge, MA: MIT Press.

Castells, M. (1983). *The City and the Grass Roots: A Cross-Cultural Theory of Urban Social Movements.* Berkeley, CA: University of California Press.

Castells, M. (1996). *The Rise of the Network Society.* Malden, MA: Blackwell.

Castells, M. (2000). *The Rise of the Network Society* (vol. 1). New York: Wiley-Blackwell.

Castells, M. (2001). *The Internet Galaxy.* Oxford, UK: Oxford University Press.

Castles, S., and M. J. Miller. (1993). *The Age of Migration: International Population Movements in the Modern World.* London: Macmillan.

Catalyst. (2020a). "List: Women CEOs of the S&P 500." Retrieved from https://www.catalyst.org/research/women-ceos-of-the-sp-500/.

Catalyst. (2020b). "Pyramid: Women in S&P 500 Companies." Retrieved from https://www.catalyst.org/research/women-in-sp-500-companies/.

Catalytic Communities. (2015). "Rio Favela Facts," Retrieved from http://catcomm.org/favela-facts/.

Catholic Women's Ordination (CWO). (2010). CWO e-news. 28 (June). Retrieved spring 2010, from www.catholic-womens-ordination.org.uk/cutenews/data/upimages/Enews%201007.pdf.

Catton, W. R., Jr., and R. E. Dunlap. (1980). "A New Ecological Paradigm for Post-exuberant Sociology." *American Behavioral Scientist* 24(1): 15–47.

Cebula, R., and E. L. Feige. (2011). "America's Underground Economy: Measuring the Size, Growth, and Determinants of Income Tax Evasion in the U.S." MPRA (Munich Personal RePEc Archive (January). Retrieved from http://mpra.ub.uni-muenchen.de/29672/1/MPRA_paper_29672.pdf.

Center for Immigration Studies. (2016). "Immigrants in the United States: A profile of the foreign-born using 2014 and 2015 Census Bureau data." Retrieved from http://cis.org/sites/cis.org/files/immigrant-profile_0.pdf.

Center for Responsive Politics (CRP). (2017a). "Business-Labor-Ideology Split in PAC & Individual Donations to Candidates, Parties, Super PACs and Outside Spending Groups." Retrieved from https://www.opensecrets.org/overview/blio.php.

Center for Responsive Politics (CRP). (2017b). "Election 2016: Trump's free media helped keep cost down, but fewer donors provided more of the cash." Retrieved from: https://www.opensecrets.org/news/2017/04/election-2016-trump-fewer-donors-provided-more-of-the-cash/.

Center for Responsive Politics (CRP). (2017c). "Incumbent Advantage." Retrieved from https://www.opensecrets.org/overview/incumbs.php.

Center for Responsive Politics (CRP). (2017d). "Lobbying Database." Retrieved from https://www.opensecrets.org/lobby/.

Center for Responsive Politics (CRP). (2017e). "Top PACS." Retrieved from https://www.opensecrets.org/overview/toppacs.php?cycle=2016.

Center for Response Politics (CRP). (2020a). Incumbent Advantage: By Type of Candidate, Senate Races, 2017–2018. *OpenSecrets.org.* Retrieved from https://www.opensecrets.org/elections-overview/incumbent-advantage?cycle=2018&type=A.

Center for Responsive Politics (CRP). (2020b). "Lobbying Data Summary." Retrieved from https://www.opensecrets.org/federal-lobbying/summary.

Center for Technology and Aging. (2010). "Fact Sheet: Highlights from the Assistive Technologies for Functional Improvement Technology Review." Public Health Institute. Retrieved 8/07/12, from www.techandaging.org/ATfactsheet.pdf.

Center for American Women and Politics. (2018). "Women in elective office 2018." Retrieved from http://www.cawp.rutgers.edu/women-elective-office-2018.

Center on Budget and Policy Priorities. (2019). "Policy Basics: Where Do Federal Tax Revenues Come From?" Retrieved from https://www.cbpp.org/research/federal-tax/policy-basics-where-do-federal-tax-revenues-come-from.

Centers for Disease Control and Prevention (CDC). (2010). "National Intimate Partner and Sexual Violence Survey." Retrieved 12/14, from http://www.cdc.gov/ViolencePrevention/pdf/NISVS_Report2010-a.pdf.

Centers for Disease Control and Prevention (CDC). (2012). "Provisional Number of Marriages and Marriage Rate: United States, 2000–2010." National Center for Health Statistics. Last updated January 10, 2012. Retrieved from www.cdc.gov/nchs/nvss/marriage_divorce_tables.htm.

Centers for Disease Control and Prevention. (CDC). (2016a). "HIV Surveillance Report, 2015; vol. 27." Retrieved from http://www.cdc.gov/hiv/library/reports/hiv-surveillance.html.

Centers for Disease Control and Prevention. (CDC). (2016b). "2014–2016 Ebola Outbreak in West Africa." Retrieved from https://www.cdc.gov/vhf/ebola/outbreaks/2014-west-africa/.

Centers for Disease Control and Prevention. (CDC). (2016c). "Youth Risk Behavior Surveillance—United States, 2015." Morbidity and Mortality Weekly Report, 2016; vol. 65, No. 6. Retrieved from https://www.cdc.gov/healthyyouth/data/yrbs/pdf/2015/ss6506_updated.pdf.

Centers for Disease Control and Prevention. (CDC). (2017a). "Health, United States, 2016: With Chartbook on Long-term Trends in Health." Retrieved from https://www.cdc.gov/nchs/data/hus/hus16.pdf#053.

Centers for Disease Control and Prevention. (CDC). (2017b). "HIV in the United States: At A Glance." Retrieved from https://www.cdc.gov/nchhstp/newsroom/docs/factsheets/hiv-incidence-fact-sheet_508.pdf.

Centers for Disease Control and Prevention. (CDC). (2017c). "Injury Prevention & Control: Motor Vehicle Safety." [Online]. National Center for Injury Prevention and Control, Centers for Disease Control and Prevention. Available at http://www.cdc.gov/MotorVehicleSafety/Teen_Drivers/teendrivers_factsheet.html.

Centers for Disease Control and Prevention. (CDC). (2018a). Health, United States, 2018. Retrieved from

https://www.cdc.gov/nchs/data/hus/hus18.pdf?.

Centers for Disease Control and Prevention. (CDC). (2018b). "Summary Health Statistics: National Health Interview Survey, 2017. Table P-1a." Retrieved from https://ftp.cdc.gov/pub/Health_Statistics/NCHS/NHIS/SHS/2017_SHS_Table_P-1.pdf.

Centers for Disease Control and Prevention. (2018c). U.S. Adult Obesity Prevalence Maps. Retrieved from https://www.cdc.gov/obesity/data/prevalence-maps.html.

Centers for Disease Control and Prevention. (CDC). (2019). Births: Final Data for 2018. National Vital Statistics Reports, Vol. 68, No. 13, November 27, 2019. Retrieved from https://www.cdc.gov/nchs/data/nvsr/nvsr68/nvsr68_13-508.pdf.

Centers for Disease Control and Prevention. (CDC). (2020). "Health Equity Considerations and Racial and Ethnic Minority Groups." Retrieved from https://www.cdc.gov/coronavirus/2019-ncov/need-extra-precautions/racial-ethnic-minorities.html.

Centers for Disease Control (CDC) COVID-19 Response Team. (2020a). "Severe outcomes among patients with coronavirus disease 2019 (COVID-19)—United States, February 12–March 16, 2020." Morbidity and Mortality Weekly Report 69(12): 343–346.

Centers for Disease Control COVID-19 Response Team. (2020b). "Cases in the U.S." Retrieved from https://www.cdc.gov/coronavirus/2019-ncov/cases-updates/cases-in-us.html.

Central Board of Film Certification. (2020). "Indian Feature Films Certified from 1-4-2018 to 31-3-2019." Retrieved from http://www.filmfed.org/downloads/Language-wise-Region-2018-19-26062019.pdf.

Central Intelligence Agency. (2013). "Field Listing: Sex Ratio." CIA World Factbook. Retrieved spring 2013, from www.cia.gov/library/publications/the-world-factbook/fields/2018.html.

Central Intelligence Agency. (2020a). "China." The World Factbook. Retrieved from https://www.cia.gov/library/publications/the-world-factbook/geos/ch.html#field-anchor-people-and-society-religions.

Central Intelligence Agency. (2020b). "Indonesia." The World Factbook. Retrieved from https://www.cia.gov/library/publications/resources/the-world-factbook/geos/id.html.

Central Intelligence Agency. (2020c). The World Factbook. Retrieved from https://www.cia.gov/library/publications/resources/the-world-factbook/geos/xx.html.

Cerny, P. (2005). "Political Globalization and the Competition State." In R. Stubbs and G. Underhill, eds., The Political Economy of the Changing Global Order. Oxford: Oxford University Press.

Chafetz, J. S. (1990). Gender Equity: An Integrated Theory of Stability and Change. Newbury Park, CA: Sage.

Chamberlain, A., and J. Jayaraman (2017). "The pipeline problem: how college majors contribute to the gender pay gap." Glassdoor. Retrieved from https:// www.glassdoor.com/research/app/uploads/sites/2/2017/04/FULL-STUDY-PDF-Gender-Pay-Gap2FCollege-Major-1.pdf.

Chambliss, W. J. (1988). On the Take: From Petty Crooks to Presidents. Bloomington, IN: Indiana University Press.

Chamie, J. (2017). "Out-of-Wedlock Births Rise Worldwide." Yale Global Online, March 16, 2017.

Chandra, K. (2016). "Authoritarian India: The State of the World's Largest Democracy," Foreign Affairs, June 16, Retrieved from https://www.foreignaffairs.com/articles/india/2016-06-16/authoritarian-india.

Chaney, D. (1994). The Cultural Turn: Scene-Setting Essays in Contemporary Cultural History. New York: Routledge.

Chang, I., and W. C. Kirby. (1997). The Rape of Nanking: The Forgotten Holocaust of World War II. New York: Basic Books.

Chang-Muy, F. (2009). "Legal classifications of immigrants." In F. Chang Muy and E. P. Congress, eds., Social work with immigrants and refugees: Legal issues, clinical skills, and advocacy (pp. 39–62). New York: Springer Publishing Company.

Charles, D. (2019). "Farmers Got Billions from Taxpayers in 2019, and Hardly Anyone Objected." NPR, Dec. 31. Retrieved from https://www.npr.org/sections/thesalt/2019/12/31/790261705/farmers-got-billions-from-taxpayers-in-2019-and-hardly-anyone-objected.

Chaturvedi, A. (2019). "Do you know how many satellites are currently orbiting around the Earth?" Geospatial World, Jan. 20. Retrieved from https://www.geospatialworld.net/blogs/do-you-know-how-many-satellites-earth/.

Chaves, M. (1993). "Intraorganizational Power and Internal Secularization in Protestant Denominations." American Journal of Sociology 99: 1–48.

Chaves, M. (1994). "Secularization as Declining Religious Authority." Social Forces 72: 749–74.

Chen, B. X. (2014). "Apple's Tim Cook Talks of Retail Expansion in China." New York Times (October 23). Retrieved from http://bits.blogs.nytimes.com/2014/10/23/apples-tim-cook-talks-of-retail-expansion-in-china/?_r=0.

Cherlin, A. (1999). Public and Private Families: An Introduction, 2nd ed. New York: McGraw-Hill.

Cherlin, A. J. (2009). The Marriage-Go-Round: The State of Marriage and the Family in America Today. New York: Knopf.

Cherlin, A., P. Chase-Lansdale, and C. McRae. (1998). "Effects of Parental Divorce on Mental Health Throughout the Life Course." *American Sociological Review* 63: 239–49.

Chetty, R., D. Grusky, M. Hell, N. Hendren, R. Manduca, and J. Narang. (2016). "The Fading American Dream: Trends in Absolute Income Mobility Since 1940." Retrieved from: http://www.equality-of-opportunity.org/assets/documents/abs_mobility_summary.pdf.

Chetty, R., N. Hendren, P. Kline, E. Saez. and N. Turner. (2014). "Is the United States still the land of opportunity? Recent trends in intergenerational mobility." NBER working paper 19844, January. Retrieved 12/14, from http://www.nber.org/papers/w19844.pdf.

Chiavaroli, A. (2020). "School closures pose added challenges for parents of special needs children." *SouthCoastToday*, March 22. Retrieved from https://www.southcoasttoday.com/news/20200320/school-closures-pose-added-challenges-for-parents-of-special-needs-children.

Child Trends. (2012). "Percentage of Births to Unmarried Women." Retrieved 9/10/12, from www.childtrendsdatabank.org/?q=node/196.

Child Trends Databank. (2016). "Children in Poverty: Indicators of Child and Youth Well-being." Retrieved from https://www.childtrends.org/wp-content/uploads/2016/12/04_Poverty.pdf.

Child Trends Databank. (2019). "Children in poverty." Retrieved from https://www.childtrends.org/?indicators=children-in-poverty.

Children's Bureau. (2020). "Child Maltreatment 2018." U.S. Department of Health & Human Services, Administration for Children and Families; Administration for Children & Families. Retrieved from https://www.acf.hhs.gov/cb/research-data-technology/statistics-research/child-maltreatment.

Childs, E. C. (2005). *Navigating Interracial Borders: Black–White Couples and Their Social Worlds*. Piscataway, NJ: Rutgers University Press.

China.org.cn. (2014). "Top 10 overseas M&A by Chinese companies" (June 20). Retrieved from http://www.china.org.cn/business/2014-06/20/content_32721884.htm.

Chodorow, N. (1978). *The Reproduction of Mothering*. Berkeley, CA: University of California Press.

Chodorow, N. (1988). *Psychoanalytic Theory and Feminism*. Cambridge, UK: Polity Press.

Choi, K. H., and R. E. Goldberg. (2018). "Fertility behavior of interracial couples." *Journal of Marriage and Family* 80(4): 871–887.

Choo, H. Y., and M. M. Ferree. (2010). "Practicing Intersectionality in Sociological Research: A Critical Analysis of Inclusions, Interactions, and Institutions in the Study of Inequalities." *Sociological Theory* 28: 129–49.

Christakis, N. A., and J. H. Fowler. (2007). "The Spread of Obesity in a Large Social Network over 32 Years." *New England Journal of Medicine* 357: 370–79.

Chronicle of Higher Education. (2010). "China Begins to Reform Its Controversial College-Entrance Exam." July 7. Retrieved 7/23/12, from http://chronicle.com/article/China-Begins-to-BMREForm-Its/65804/.

Chua, A. (2003). *World on Fire: How Exporting Free Market Democracy Breeds Ethnic Hatred and Global Instability*. New York: Doubleday.

Cimpanu, C. (2019). "Top Dark Web Marketplace Will Shut Down Next Month." ZDNet, March 29. Retrieved from https://www.zdnet.com/article/top-dark-web-marketplace-will-shut-down-next-month/.

Cisco. (2009). "Cisco Study Finds Telecommuting Significantly Increases Employee Productivity, Work-Life Flexibility and Job Satisfaction." Press release, June 25. Retrieved fall 2010, from http://newsroom.cisco.com/dlls/2009/prod_062609.html.

Clarke, T. C., L. I. Black, B. J. Stussman, P. M. Barnes, and R. L. Nahin. (2015). "Trends in the use of complementary health approaches among adults: United States, 2002–2012." National health statistics reports, no. 79. Hyattsville, MD: National Center for Health Statistics.

Clawson, D., and M. A. Clawson. (1999). "What Has Happened to the U.S. Labor Movement? Union Decline and Renewal." *Annual Review of Sociology* 25: 95–119.

Cleveland, J. N. (1996). "Women in High-Status Nontraditional Occupations." In P. J. Dubeck and K. Borman, eds., *Women and Work: A Handbook*. New York: Garland.

Cloward, R. A., and L. E. Ohlin. (1960). *Delinquency and Opportunity*. New York: Free Press.

Coate, J. (1994). "Cyberspace Innkeeping: Building Online Community." Retrieved 12/29/04, from www.well.com:70/0/Community/Innkeeping.

Cockerham, W. C. (2014). "The emerging crisis in American female longevity." *Social Currents* 1: 220–27.

Cohen, A. (1955). *Delinquent Boys: The Culture of the Gang*. Glencoe, IL: Free Press.

Cohen, G. D. (2005). *The Mature Mind: The Positive Power of the Aging Brain*. New York: Basic Books.

Cohen, L. E., J. P. Broschak, and H. A. Haveman. (1998). "And Then There Were More? The Effect of Organizational Sex Composition on the Hiring and Promotion of Managers." *American Sociological Review* 63: 5.

Cohen, P. (2012). *In Our Prime: The Invention of Middle Age*. New York, NY: Scribner.

Cohen, R. (1997). *Global Diasporas: An Introduction*. London: UCL Press.

Colapinto, J. (2001). *As Nature Made Him: The Boy Who Was Raised as a Girl*. New York: Harper.

Colby, S. L., and J. M. Ortman. (2014). "Projections of the Size and Composition of the U.S. Population: 2014 to 2060," U.S. Census Bureau, Retrieved from https://www.census.gov/content/dam/Census/library/publications/2015/demo/p25-1143.pdf.

Coleman, J. S. (1987). "Families and Schools." *Educational Researcher* 16: 6.

Coleman, J. S., et al. (1966). *Equality of Educational Opportunity*. Washington, DC: U.S. Government Printing Office.

College Board. (2016). "2016 College-Bound Seniors: Total Group Profile Report," New York. College Board. Retrieved from https://secure-media.collegeboard.org/digitalServices/pdf/sat/total-group-2016.pdf.

Collins, D. (2004). "Strong Plea from a Strong Lady: Nancy Reagan Urges Expanded Stem Cell Research," CBS News, May 10. Retrieved 7/30/10, from www.cbsnews.com/stories/2004/05/10/health/main616473.shtml.

Collins, P. H. (2008). *Black Feminist Thought: Knowledge, Consciousness, and the Politics of Empowerment*. New York: Routledge Classics.

Collins, R. (1979). *The Credential Society: An Historical Sociology of Education*. New York: Academic Press.

Coltrane, S., E.C. Miller, T. DeHaan, and L. Stewart. (2013). "Fathers and the Flexibility Stigma." Journal of Social Issues 69, no. 2 (2013): 279–302.

Colvin, G. (2019). "It's China's World." *Fortune*, July 22. Retrieved from https://fortune.com/longform/fortune-global-500-china-companies/.

Combat 18. (1998). "Blood and Honour." Retrieved 1/10/05, from www.combat18.org.

Computer Security Institute. (2011). "2010/2011 Computer Crime and Security Survey." Retrieved winter

2014, from http://gatton.uky.edu/FACULTY/PAYNE/ACC324/CSISurvey2010.pdf.

Congressional Budget Office. (2018). "Factors Affecting the Labor Force Participation of People Ages 25 to 54." Feb. 7. Retrieved from https://www.cbo.gov/publication/53452.

Conley, D. (1999). *Being Black, Living in the Red: Race, Wealth, and Social Policy in America*. Berkeley and Los Angeles: University of California Press.

Connell, R. W. (1987). *Gender and Power: Society, the Person, and Sexual Politics*. Boston: Allen and Unwin.

Conrad, Peter. (2007). *The Medicalization of Society: On the Transformation of Human Conditions into Medical Disorders*. Baltimore: Johns Hopkins University Press.

Conti, J. (2008). "The Good Case: Decisions to Litigate at the World Trade Organization." *Law and Society Review* 42(1): 145–82.

Conti, J. (2011). *Between law and diplomacy: The social contexts of disputing at the World Trade Organization*. Palo Alto, CA: Stanford University Press.

Cook, C. R., K. R. Williams, N. G. Guerra, T. E. Kim, and S. Sadek. (2010). "Predictors of Bullying and Victimization in Childhood and Adolescence: a Meta-analytic Investigation." *School Psychology Quarterly*, 25, 65–83.

Cook, K. (2015). *Kitty Genovese: The Murder, the Bystanders, and the Crime that Changed America*. New York: W. W. Norton.

Cooley, C. H. (1964; orig. 1902). *Human Nature and the Social Order*. New York: Schocken Books.

Coontz, S. (2006). *Marriage, a History: How Love Conquered Marriage*. New York: Penguin.

Copen, C. E., K. Daniels, J. Vespa, and W. D. Mosher. (2012). "First Marriages in the United States: Data from the 2006–2010 National Survey of Family Growth." *National Health Statistics Report, No. 49*. National Center for Health Statistics, Hyattsville, MD.

Copen, C. E., K. Daniels, and W. D. Mosher. (2013). "First Premarital Cohabitation in the United States: 2006–2010 National Survey of Family Growth." *National Health Statistics Report*, April 4, 2013, http://www.cdc.gov/nchs/data/nhsr/nhsr064.pdf

Corbin, J., and A. Strauss. (1985). "Managing Chronic Illness at Home: Three Lines of Work." *Qualitative Sociology* 8: 224–47.

Correll, S. J., S. Benard, and I. Paik. (2007). "Getting a Job: Is There a Motherhood Penalty?" *American Journal of Sociology* 112: 1297–338.

Corrigan, P. W., and A. C. Watson. (2004). "At Issue: Stop the Stigma: Call Mental Illness a Brain Disease." *Schizophrenia Bulletin* 30: 477–79.

Corsaro, W. (1997). *The Sociology of Childhood*. Thousand Oaks, CA: Pine Forge Press.

Cosmides, L., and J. Tooby. (1997). "Evolutionary Psychology: A Primer." University of California at Santa Barbara: Institute for Social, Behavioral, and Economic Research Center for Evolutionary Psychology. Retrieved 1/11/05, from www.psych.ucsb.edu/research/cep/primer.html.

Costa, L., and A. Veloso. (2016). "Being (Grand) Players: Review of Digital Games and Their Potential to Enhance Intergenerational Interactions." *Journal of Intergenerational Relationships* 14(1): 43–59.

Council on Foreign Relations. (2013). "Reflecting on Lehman's Global Legacy" (September 13). Retrieved 2/08/14, from http://www.cfr.org/economics/reflecting-lehmans-global-legacy/p31391.

Council on Foreign Relations. (2020). "Women's Power Index." Retrieved from https://www.cfr.org/article/womens-power-index?utm_source=pressnote.

Coward, R. (1984). *Female Desire: Women's Sexuality Today*. London: Paladin.

Cowgill, D. O. (1968). "The Social Life of the Aged in Thailand." *Gerontologist* 8: 159–63.

Cowgill, D. O. (1986). *Aging around the World*. Belmont, CA: Wadsworth.

Crawford, N. (2019). "United States Budgetary Costs and Obligations of Post-9/11 Wars through FY2020: $6.4 Trillion." Watson Institute of International and Public Affairs. Brown University. Retrieved from https://watson.brown.edu/costsofwar/files/cow/imce/papers/2019/US%20Budgetary%20Costs%20of%20Wars%20November%202019.pdf.

Credit Suisse. (2016). "Global Wealth Report: 2016." Retrieved from http://publications.credit-suisse.com/tasks/render/file/index.cfm?fileid=AD783798-ED07-E8C2-4405996B5B02A32E.

Crowley, M. (2014). "Class, Control, and Relational Indignity: Labor Process Foundations for Workplace Humiliation, Conflict, and Shame." *American Behavioral Scientist* 58(3) 416–34. Retrieved from http://abs.sagepub.com/content/58/3/416.full.pdf.

Crutzen, P. J. and E. F. Stoermer (2000). "The "Anthropocene," International Geosphere-Biosphere Programme." *IGBP Newsletter* 41: 17–18. Retrieved

from http://www.igbp.net/download/18.316f18321323470177580001401/1376383088452/NL41.pdf.

Cubanski, J., W. Koma, A. Damico, and T. Neuman. (2020). "How Many Seniors Live in Poverty?" Kaiser Family Foundation, Nov. 19. Retrieved from https://www.kff.org/medicare/issue-brief/how-many-seniors-live-in-poverty/.

Cumings, B. (1997). *Korea's Place in the Sun: A Modern History*. New York: W.W. Norton.

Cumming, E. (1963). "Further Thoughts on the Theory of Disengagement." *International Social Science Journal* 15: 377–93.

Cumming, E. (1975). "Engagement with an Old Theory." *International Journal of Aging and Human Development* 6: 187–91.

Cumming, E., and W. E. Henry. (1961). *Growing Old: The Process of Disengagement*. New York: Basic Books.

Cummings, M. (2019). "Friendship, romance and race: What sociologist Grace Kao found." *Yale News*, Nov. 13. Retrieved from https://news.yale.edu/2019/11/13/friendship-romance-and-race-what-sociologist-grace-kao-found.

Curtin, S. C., S. J. Ventura, and G. M. Martinez. (2014.) "Recent declines in nonmarital childbearing in the United States." NCHS data brief, no 162. Hyattsville, MD: National Center for Health Statistics.

D'Andrade, R. (1995). *The Development of Cognitive Anthropology*. New York: Cambridge University Press.

Daniller, A. (2019). "Two-thirds of Americans support marijuana legalization." Pew Research Center. Retrieved from https://www.pewresearch.org/fact-tank/2019/11/14/americans-support-marijuana-legalization/.

Darden, J. T. (2019). "Tackling Terrorists' Exploitation of Youth." American Enterprise Institute. Retrieved from https://www.un.org/sexualviolenceinconflict/wp-content/uploads/2019/05/report/tackling-terrorists-exploitation-of-youth/Tackling-Terrorists-Exploitation-of-Youth.pdf.

Darrow, B. (2017). "Turns Out Attendance at Women's March Events Was Bigger Than Estimated," *Fortune*, Jan. 23, Retrieved from http://fortune.com/2017/01/23/womens-march-crowd-estimates/.

Davidson, P. (2020). "Unemployment soars to 14.7%, job losses reach 20.5 million in April as coronavirus pandemic spreads." *USA Today*, May 8. Retrieved from https://www.usatoday.com/

story/money/2020/05/08/april-jobs-reports-20-5-m-become-unemployed-covid-19-spreads/3090664001/.

Davies, J. C. (1962). "Towards a Theory of Revolution." *American Sociological Review* 27: 5–19.

Davis, D., and K. Polonko. (2001). "Tele-work America 2001 Summary." International Telework Association and Council. Retrieved 1/20/05, from www.telecommute.org/telework/twa2001.html.

Davis, K., and W. E. Moore. (1945). "Some Principles of Stratification." *American Sociological Review* 10: 242–49.

Davis, M. (1990). *City of Quartz: Excavating the Future in Los Angeles.* New York: Verso.

Davis, M. (2006). *Planet of Slums.* London: Verso.

Davis, S. (1988). *2001 Management: Managing the Future Now.* New York: Simon and Schuster.

Deacon, T. W. (1998). *The Symbolic Species: The Co-Evolution of Language and the Brain.* New York: W. W. Norton.

Death Penalty Information Center. (2018). "Execution List 2018." Retrieved from https://deathpenaltyinfo.org/executions/2018.

DeCarlo, S. and N. Rapp. (2016). "This Chart Shows the World's 500 Largest Companies," Retrieved from http://fortune.com/global-500-companies-chart/.

Defense of Marriage Act. (1996). H.R. 3396—Defense of Marriage Act (Enrolled Bill [Final as Passed Both House and Senate]—ENR). Library of Congress. Retrieved 7/01/13, from http://thomas.loc.gov/cgi-bin/query/z?c104:H.R.3396.ENR.

DeJong, W. (1993). "Obesity as a Characterological Stigma: The Issue of Responsibility and Judgments of Task Performance." *Psychological Reports* 73: 963–70.

de Jong Gierveld, J., M. Broese van Groenou, A. W. Hoogendoorn, and J. H. Smit. (2009). "Quality of Marriages in Later Life and Emotional and Social Loneliness." *Journals of Gerontology* 64B: 497–506.

de Jong Gierveld, J., and B. Havens. (2004). "Cross-National Comparisons of Social Isolation and Loneliness: Introduction and Overview." *Canadian Journal on Aging* 23: 109–13.

Deloitte. (2018). "2018 Global Mobile Consumer Survey: US Edition." Retrieved from https://www2.deloitte.com/us/en/pages/technology-media-and-telecommunications/articles/global-mobile-consumer-survey-us-edition.html

D'Emilio, J. (1983). *Sexual Politics, Sexual Communities: The Making of a Homosexual Minority in the United States, 1940–1970.* Chicago: University of Chicago Press.

Derenne, J. L., and E. Beresin. (2006). "Body Image, Media, and Eating Disorders." *Academic Psychiatry* 30: 257–61.

Desilver, D. (2016). "U.S. Voter Turnout Trails Most Developed Countries." Pew Research Center, Aug. 2. Retrieved from http://www.pewresearch.org/fact-tank/2016/08/02/u-s-voter-turnout-trails-most-developed-countries/.

Desilver, D. (2018). "For most U.S. workers, real wages have barely budged in decades." Pew Research Center, August 7. Retrieved from https://www.pewresearch.org/fact-tank/2018/08/07/for-most-us-workers-real-wages-have-barely-budged-for-decades/.

Desjardins, J. (2020). "All the World's Wealth in One Visualization." Visual Capitalist, Jan. 16. Retrieved from https://www.visualcapitalist.com/all-of-the-worlds-wealth-in-one-visualization/.

Desmond, M. (2016). *Evicted: Poverty and Profit in the American City.* New York: Crown Publishing Group.

DeStefano, F., and T. T. Shimabukuro. (2019). "The MMR Vaccine and Autism." *Annual Review of Virology* 6(1): 585–600.

Dettling, L. J., J. W. Hsu, L. Jacobs, K. B. Moore, and J. P. Thompson. (2017). "Recent Trends in Wealth-Holding by Race and Ethnicity: Evidence from the Survey of Consumer Finances." Board of Governors of the Federal Reserve System. September 27. Retrieved from https://www.federalreserve.gov/econres/notes/feds-notes/recent-trends-in-wealth-holding-by-race-and-ethnicity-evidence-from-the-survey-of-consumer-finances-20170927.htm.

de Tocqueville, A. (1969; orig. 1835). *Democracy in America.* New York: Doubleday.

Diamond, J. (1999). *Guns, Germs, and Steel: The Fates of Human Societies.* New York: W. W. Norton.

Diamond, J. (2005). *Collapse: How Societies Choose to Fail or Succeed.* New York: Penguin.

Digital Citizens Alliance. (2015). "Darknet Marketplace Watch – Monitoring Sales of Illegal Drugs on the Darknet (Q1)." Retrieved from http://www.digitalcitizensalliance/content.aspx?page=Darknet.

Dillon, S. (2010). "Formula to Grade Teachers' Skill Gains Acceptance, and Critics." *New York Times*, August 31. Re-

trieved 10/19/12, from www.nytimes.com/2010/09/01/education/01teacher.html.

DiMaggio, P. (1997). "Culture and Cognition." *Annual Review of Sociology* 23: 263–87.

Dimitrova, D. (2003). "Controlling Teleworkers: Supervision and Flexibility Revisited." *New Technology Work and Employment* 18(3): 181–95.

Dinda, S. (2004). "Environmental Kuznets Curve Hypothesis: A Survey." *Ecological Economics* 49: 431–45.

Dobash, R. E., and R. P. Dobash. (1992). *Women, Violence, and Social Change.* New York: Routledge.

Dogloff, Joanna. (2010). "Should Schools Send Home 'Weight Report Cards'?" *Huffington Post*, February 19. Retrieved 9/24/12, from www.huffingtonpost.com/joanna-dolgoff-md/should-schools-send-home_b_468848.html.

Dolan, K. A., ed. (2020). "World's Billionaires List: The Richest in 2020." *Forbes.* Retrieved from https://www.forbes.com/billionaires/.

Domhoff, G. W. (1971). *The Higher Circles: The Governing Class in America.* New York: Vintage Books.

Domhoff, G. W. (1974). *The Bohemian Grove and Other Retreats.* New York: Harper and Row.

Domhoff, G. W. (1979). *The Powers That Be: Processes of Ruling Class Domination in America.* New York: Vintage Books.

Domhoff, G. W. (1983). *Who Rules America Now? A View for the '80s.* New York: Prentice Hall.

Domhoff, G. W. (1998). *Who Rules America? Power and Politics in the Year 2000.* Belmont, CA: Mayfield.

Domhoff, G. W. (2005). "Power in America: Wealth, Income, and Power." Retrieved spring 2006, from http://sociology.ucsc.edu/whorulesamerica/power/wealth.html.

Domhoff, G. W. (2013). *Who Rules America? The Triumph of the Corporate Rich.* NY: McGraw Hill.

Dow, J. W. (2005). "The Expansion of Protestantism in Mexico: An Anthropological View." *Anthropological Quarterly* 78 (4): 827–51.

Dowling, H. (1977). *Fighting Infection: Conquests of the Twentieth Century.* Cambridge, MA: Harvard University Press.

Downie, R. (2020). "The Top 6 Shareholders of JP Morgan Chase (JPM)." Investopedia. Retrieved from https://www.investopedia.com/articles/insights/052416/top-5-jp-morgan-shareholders-jpm.asp.

Drake, S., and H. Cayton. (1945). *Black Metropolis: A Study of Negro Life in a Northern City*. New York: Harcourt, Brace.

Draper, P. (1975). "!Kung Women: Contrasts in Sexual Egalitarianism in Foraging and Sedentary Contexts. In R. R. Reiter, ed., *Toward an Anthropology of Women*. New York: Monthly Review Press.

Drentea, P. (1998). "Consequences of Women's Formal and Informal Job Search Methods for Employment in Female-Dominated Jobs." *Gender and Society* 12: 321–38.

DuBois, S. (2011). "U.S. Losing Grip on World's Largest Companies." http://archive.fortune.com/2011/07/14/news/companies/us_losing_grip_largest_companies.fortune/index.htm.

Du Bois, W. E. B. (1903). *The Souls of Black Folk*. New York: Dover.

Dubos, R. (1959). *Mirage of Health*. New York: Doubleday/Anchor.

Duffin, E. (2019). "Pay Gap between CEOs and Average Workers, by Country 2018." Statista, November 5. Retrieved from https://www.statista.com/statistics/424159/pay-gap-between-ceos-and-average-workers-in-world-by-country.

Duncan, G. J., K. M. Ziol-Guest, and A. Kalil. (2010). "Early-Childhood Poverty and Adult Attainment, Behavior, and Health." *Child Development* 81: 306–25.

Duneier, M. (1999). *Sidewalk*. New York: Farrar, Straus and Giroux.

Duneier, M., and H. Molotch. (1999). "Talking City Trouble: Interactional Vandalism, Social Inequality, and the Urban Interaction Problem." *American Journal of Sociology* 104: 1263–95.

Dunlap, R. (2002). "Environmental Sociology: A Personal Perspective on the First Quarter Century," *Organization and Environment*, 15:1 (March): 10–29.

Dunlop, D. D., J. Song, J. S. Lyons, L. M. Manheim, and R. W. Chang. (2003). "Racial and Ethnic Differences in Rates of Depression among Preretirement Adults," *American Journal of Public Health* 93: 1945–52.

Dunn, A. (2018). "Partisans are divided over the fairness of the U.S. economy–and why people are rich or poor." Pew Research Center, Oct. 4. Retrieved from https://www.pewresearch.org/fact-tank/2018/10/04/partisans-are-divided-over-the-fairness-of-the-u-s-economy-and-why-people-are-rich-or-poor/.

Duranti, A. (1994). *From Grammar to Politics: Linguistic Anthropology in a Western Samoan Village*. Berkeley: University of California Press.

Durkheim, É. (1964; orig. 1893). *The Division of Labor in Society*. New York: Free Press.

Durkheim, É. (1965; orig. 1912). *The Elementary Forms of the Religious Life*. New York: Free Press.

Durkheim, É. (1966; orig. 1897). *Suicide*. New York: Free Press.

Duster, T. (1990). *Backdoor to Eugenics*. New York: Routledge.

Dworkin, A. (1987). *Intercourse*. New York: Free Press.

Dye, T. R. (1986). *Who's Running America?* 4th ed. Englewood Cliffs, NJ: Prentice Hall.

Eagly, A., and W. Wood. (2011). "Feminism and the Evolution of Sex Differences and Similarities." *Sex Roles* 64: 758–67.

Early, S. (2011). *The Civil Wars in U.S. Labor*. Chicago: Haymarket Books.

Easterlin, R. A. (2001)."Income and Happiness: Towards a Unified Theory." *Economic Journal* 111: 465–84.

Easterlin, R. A. (2003). "Explaining Happiness." *Proceedings of the National Academy of Sciences* 100: 11176–83.

Easterlin, R. A. (2010). *Happiness, Growth, and the Life Cycle*. New York: Oxford University Press.

Easterlin, R. A., L. A. McVey, M. Switek, O. Sawangfa, and S. Zweig. (2010). "The Happiness–Income Paradox Revisited." *Proceedings of the National Academy of Sciences* 107: 22463–68.

Easterlin, R. A., R. Morgan, M. Switek, and F. Wang. (2012). "China's Life Satisfaction, 1990–2010." *Proceedings of the National Academy of Sciences* 109 (25): 9775–80.

Easterlin, R. A., and O. Sawangfa. (2010). "Happiness and Economic Growth: Does the Cross Section Predict Time Trends? Evidence from Developing Countries." In E. Diener, D. Kahneman, and J. Helliwell, eds., *International Differences in Well-Being* (pp. 166–216). New York: Oxford University Press.

Eating Disorders Coalition (EDC). (2003). "Statistics." Retrieved 12/29/04, from www.eatingdisorderscoalition.org/reports/statistics.html (site discontinued).

Eating Disorders Coalition (EDC). (2009). "Statistics." Retrieved 5/15/10, from www.eatingdisorderscoalition.org/reports/statistics (site discontinued).

Ebomoyi, E. (1987). "The Prevalence of Female Circumcision in Two Nigerian Communities." *Sex Roles* 17: 3–4.

Economic Policy Institute. (2019). "Minimum Wage Tracker." Retrieved from https://www.epi.org/minimum-wage-tracker/.

Economic Times. (2015). "Heat-related Deaths Will Double in Urban India by 2080," July 6. Retrieved from https://health.economictimes.indiatimes.com/news/industry/heat-related-deaths-will-double-in-urban-india-by-2080-iim/47957731.

Economist. (2011). "Difference Engine: Luddite Legacy," November 4. Retrieved from http://www.economist.com/blogs/babbage/2011/11/artificial-intelligence.

Edin, K., and M. Kefalas. (2005). *Promises I Can Keep: Why Poor Women Put Motherhood before Marriage*. Berkeley: University of California Press.

Edin, K., and L. Lein. (1997). "Work, Welfare, and Single Mothers' Economic Survival Strategies." *American Sociological Review* 62: 2.

Edmond, C. (2017). "These rich countries have high levels of child poverty." World Economic Forum, June 28. Retrieved from https://www.weforum.org/agenda/2017/06/these-rich-countries-have-high-levels-of-child-poverty/.

Efron, S. (1997). "Eating Disorders Go Global." *Los Angeles Times*, October 18, p. A-1.

Eggleston, J., and D. Hays. (2019). "Gaps in the Wealth of Americans by Household Type: Many U.S. Households Do Not Have Biggest Contributors to Wealth: Home Equity and Retirement Accounts." U.S. Bureau of the Census. Retrieved from https://www.census.gov/library/stories/2019/08/gaps-in-wealth-americans-by-household-type.html.

Ehrlich, P. (1968). *The Population Bomb*. New York: Ballantine Books.

Ehrlich, P., and A. H. Ehrlich. (1990). *The Population Explosion*. New York: Touchstone.

Eibl-Eibesfeldt, I. (1972). "Similarities and Differences between Cultures in Expressive Movements." In R. A. Hinde, ed., *Nonverbal Communication*. New York: Cambridge University Press.

Eisenberg, R. (2019). "Age-Friendly Universities Are Finally Here." *Forbes*, June 4. Retrieved from https://www.forbes.com/sites/nextavenue/2019/06/04/age-friendly-universities-are-finally-here/#158afb4670f5.

Eisenhower, D. D. (1961). "Military-Industrial Complex Speech, Dwight D. Eisenhower, 1961." *Public Papers of the Presidents*. Retrieved Fall 2010. www.h-net.org/,hst306/documents/indust.html.

Ekman, P., and W. V. Friesen. (1978). *Facial Action Coding System*. New York: Consulting Psychologists Press.

el Dareer, A. (1982). *Woman, Why Do You Weep? Circumcision and Its Consequences*. Westport, CT: Zed.

Elias, N. (1987). *Involvement and Detachment*. London: Oxford University Press.

Elias, N., and E. Dunning. (1987). *Quest for Excitement: Sport and Leisure in the Civilizing Process*. Oxford, UK: Blackwell.

Elliott, A. (2008). *Making the Cut: How Cosmetic Surgery Is Transforming Our Lives*. London: Reaktion Books.

El Issa, E. (2016). "2016 American Household Credit Card Debt Study," Nerd Wallet, Dec. 16, Retrieved from https://www.nerdwallet.com/blog/average-credit-card-debt-household/.

Elver, H. (2012). *The Headscarf Controversy: Secularism and Freedom of Religion*. New York: Oxford University Press.

Elver, H. (2015a). "Report of the Special Rapporteur on the impacts of climate change on the right to food (A/70/287)." United Nations Special Rapporteur on the Right to Food. Retrieved from https://hilalelver.org/resources/thematicreports/climatechange/.

Elver, H. (2015b). "Report of the Special Rapporteur on the justiciability of the right to food and barriers to accessing justice (A/HRC/28/65)." United Nations Special Rapporteur on the Right to Food. Retrieved from https://hilalelver.org/resources/thematicreports/access-to-justice/.

Elwell, C. K. (2014a). "The Distribution of Household Income and the Middle Class." Congressional Reference Service, March 10. Retrieved 12/14, from http://fas.org/sgp/crs/misc/RS20811.pdf.

Elwell, C. K. (2014b). "Inflation and the Real Minimum Wage: A Fact Sheet." Congressional Research Service, January 8. Retrieved 12/14, from http://fas.org/sgp/crs/misc/R42973.pdf.

Emirbayer, M., and A. Mische. (1998). "What is Agency?" *American Journal of Sociology, 103*, 962–1023.

Emmanuel, A. (1972). *Unequal Exchange: A Study of the Imperialism of Trade*. New York: Monthly Review Press.

Emslie, C., S. Browne, U. MacLeod, L. Rozmovits, E. Mitchell, and S. Ziebland. (2009). "'Getting Through' Not 'Going Under': A Qualitative Study of Gender and Spousal Support After Diagnosis with Colorectal Cancer." *Social Science & Medicine* 68, no. 6: 1169-1175.

England, P., E. Fitzgibbons Shafer, and A. C. K. Fogarty. (2012.) "Hooking Up and Forming Romantic Relationships on Today's College Campuses," in *The Gendered Society Reader*, 5th ed. (pp. 559–72), ed. M. Kimmel and A. Aronson. New York: Oxford University Press.

Entertainment Software Association. (2011). "Essential Facts about the Computer and Video Game Industry." Retrieved summer 2012, from www.theesa.com/facts/pdfs/ESA_EF_2011.pdf.

Entertainment Software Association. (2014). "Majority of Parents Say Video Games Are a Positive Part of Kids' Lives," Retrieved from http://www.theesa.com/article/majority-parents-say-video-games-positive-part-kids-lives/.

Environmental Protection Agency (EPA). (2015). "DDT—A Brief history and status." Retrieved from https://www.epa.gov/ingredients-used-pesticideproducts/ddt-brief-history-and-status.

Environmental Working Group. (2016). "EWG's farm subsidy database." Retrieved from https://farm.ewg.org/.

Epstein, R., M. Pandit, and M. Thakar. (2013). "How love emerges in arranged marriages: Two cross-cultural studies." *Journal of Comparative Family Studies* 44(3): 341–360.

Ericson, R., and K. Haggerty. (1997). *Policing the Risk Society*. Toronto: University of Toronto Press.

Erlandson, J. M., T. C. Rick, D. J. Kennett, and P. L. Walker. (2001). "Dates, demography, and disease: cultural contacts and possible evidence for Old World epidemics among the Protohistoric Island Chumash." *Pacific Coast Archaeological Society Quarterly* 37(3): 11–26.

Espelage, D. L., S. R. Aragon, and M. Birkett. (2008). "Homophobic teasing, psychological outcomes, and sexual orientation among high school students: What influence do parents and schools have?" *School Psychology Review* 37: 202–16.

ESPN. (2013). "Jason Collins Says He's Gay." *ESPN* (April 30, 2013). Retrieved from http://espn.go.com/nba/story/_/id/9223657/jasoncollins-first-openly-gay-active-player.

Esposito, J. L. (1984). *Islam and Politics*. Syracuse, NY: Syracuse University Press.

Estes, C. (2011). "Crises and Old Age Policy." In R. A. Settersten Jr., and J. L. Angel, *Handbook of Sociology of Aging* (pp. 297–320). New York: Springer.

Estes, C. L., E. A. Binney, and R. A. Culbertson. (1992). "The Gerontological Imagination: Social Influences on the Development of Gerontology, 1945–Present." *Journal of Aging and Human Development* 35: 49–67.

Estlund, C. L. (2006). "The Death of Labor Law?" *Annual Review of Law and Social Science* 2: 105–23.

Estrich, S. (1987). *Real Rape*. Cambridge, MA: Harvard University Press.

Eurostat. (2018). "Positions held by women in senior management positions." Retrieved from https://ec.europa.eu/eurostat/tgm/table.do?tab=table&init=1&language=en&pcode=sdg_05_60&plugin=1&tableSelection=2.

Evans, J., and C. Baronovski. (2018). "How do European countries differ in religious commitment?" Pew Research Center, Dec. 5. Retrieved from https://pewresearch.org/fact-tank/2018/12/05/how-do-european-countries-differ-in-religious-commitment/.

Evans, P. (1979). *Dependent Development*. Princeton, NJ: Princeton University Press.

Evans, P. (1995). *Embedded Autonomy: States and Industrial Transformation*. Princeton, NJ: Princeton University Press.

Evans-Pritchard, E. E. (1970). "Sexual Inversion among the Azande." *American Anthropologist* 72: 1428–34.

Facebook. (2019). "Facebook Reports Third Quarter 2019 Results." Retrieved from https://investor.fb.com/investor-news/press-release-details/2019/Facebook-Reports-Third-Quarter-2019-Results/default.aspx

Fadiman, A. (1997). *The Spirit Catches You and You Fall Down*. New York: Farrar, Straus and Giroux.

Fagan, M., and C. Huang. (2019). "A look at how people around the world view climate change." Pew Research Center, April 18. Retrieved from https://www.pewresearch.org/fact-tank/2019/04/18/a-look-at-how-people-around-the-world-view-climate-change/.

Falk, G., U. Falk, and V. Tomashevich. (1981). *Aging in America and Other Cultures*. Saratoga, CA: Century Twenty-One.

Family Equality Council. (2014.) Equality Maps. Retrieved 3/29/15, from http://www.familyequality.org/get_informed/equality_maps/joint_adoption_laws/.

Fardouly, J., and L. Vartanian. (2016). "Social Media and Body Image Concerns: Current Research and Future Directions." *Current Opinion in Psychology* 9: 1–5.

Federal Bureau of Investigation (FBI). (2014). "Crime in the United States: 2013: Offenses Known to Law Enforcement," Table 25: "Percent of Offenses Cleared by Arrest or

Exceptional Means, by Population Group, 2013." Retrieved 1/13/15, from http://www.fbi.gov/about-us/cjis/ucr/crime-in-the-u.s/2013/crime-in-the-u.s.-2013.

Federal Bureau of Investigation (FBI). (2016a). "Crime in the United States: 2015, CIUS Summary." Retrieved from https://ucr.fbi.gov/crime-in-the-u.s/2015/crime-in-the-u.s.-2015/resource-pages/2015-cius-summary_final.

Federal Bureau of Investigation (FBI). (2016b). "Crime in the United States: 2015, Table 33: Ten-Year Arrest Trends by Sex, 2006–2015." Retrieved from https://ucr.fbi.gov/crime-in-the-u.s/2015/crime-in-the-u.s.-2015/tables/table-33.

Federal Bureau of Investigation. (2018a). "Crime in the United States: 2018." Retrieved from https://ucr.fbi.gov/crime-in-the-u.s/2018/crime-in-the-u.s.-2018/.

Federal Bureau of Investigation. (2018b). "Hate Crime Statistics: 2018. Table 1: Incidents, Offenses, Victims, and Known Offenders by Bias Motivation, 2018." Retrieved from https://ucr.fbi.gov/hate-crime/2018/tables/table-1.xls.

Federal Interagency Forum on Child and Family Statistics. (2019). "America's Children: Key National Indicators of Well-Being, 2019." Washington, DC: U.S. Government Printing Office. Retrieved from https://www.childstats.gov/pdf/ac2019/ac_19.pdf.

Federal Reserve Bank of New York. (2020). "Quarterly Report on Household Debt and Credit." Retrieved from https://www.newyorkfed.org/microeconomics/hhdc/background.html.

Fenton M. V., and D. L. Morris. (2003). "The Integration of Holistic Nursing Practices and Complementary and Alternative Modalities into Curricula of Schools of Nursing." *Alternative Therapies in Health and Medicine* 9(4): 62–67.

Ferguson, A. A. (2000). *Bad Boys: Public Schools in the Making of Black Masculinity.* Ann Arbor: University of Michigan Press.

Ferree, M. M. (2010). "Filling the Glass: Gender Perspectives on Families." *Journal of Marriage and Family*, 72: 420–43.

Field, A. E., K. R. Sonneville, R. D. Crosby, S. A. Swanson, K. T. Eddy, C. A. Camargo Jr., N. J. Horton, and N. Micali. (2014). "Prospective associations of concerns about physique and the development of obesity, binge drinking, and drug use among adolescent boys and young

adult men." *JAMA Pediatrics* 168: 34–9. Retrieved 10/23/14, from http://archpedi.jamanetwork.com/article.aspx?articleid=1766495.

File, T. (2017). "Voting in America: A Look at the 2016 Presidential Election," U.S. Census Bureau, May 190, Retrieved from https://www.census.gov/newsroom/blogs/random-samplings/2017/05/voting_in_america.html.

Filkins, D. (1998). "Afghans Pay Dearly for Peace." *Los Angeles Times*, October 22: A-1.

Findsen, B., and M. Formosa. (2011). *Lifelong Learning in Later Life: A Handbook on Older Adult Learning.* Boston: Sense Publishers.

Fine, M. A., M. Coleman, and L. H. Ganong. (1998). "Consistency in perceptions of the step-parent role among step-parents, parents and stepchildren." *Journal of Social and Personal Relationships*, 15(6), 810–828.

Finke, R., and R. Stark. (1988). "Religious Economies and Sacred Canopies: Religious Mobilization in American Cities, 1906." *American Sociological Review* 53: 41–49.

Finke, R., and R. Stark. (2005). *The Churching of America, 1776–1990: Winners and Losers in Our Religious Economy.* New Brunswick, NJ: Rutgers University Press.

Finkel, Eli J. et al. (2012). "Online Dating: A Critical Analysis From the Perspective of Psychological Science," *Psychological Science in the Public Interest* 13(1): 3–66. Retrieved from http://psi.sagepub.com/content/13/1/3.full.pdf.

Fins, A. (2019). "National Snapshot: Poverty among Women & Families, 2019." National Women's Law Center. Retrieved from https://nwlc-ciw49tixgw5lbab.stackpathdns.com/wp-content/uploads/2019/10/PovertySnapshot2019.pdf.

Firestone, S. (1970). *The Dialectic of Sex: The Case for Feminist Revolution.* New York: William Morrow & Company.

Fischer, C. S. (1984). *The Urban Experience,* 2nd ed. New York: Harcourt Brace Jovanovich.

Fischer, C. S., M. Hout, M. Sánchez Jankowski, S. R. Lucas, A. Swidler, and K. Vos. (1996). *Inequality by Design: Cracking the Bell Curve Myth.* Princeton, NJ: Princeton University Press.

Fitch, N. (2014). "The Deadly Cost of Fashion." *New York Times*, April 14. Retrieved 10/14, from http://www.nytimes.com/2014/04/15/opinion/the-deadly-cost-of-fashion.html.

Fitzgerald, M. (2019). "There is now a woman board member at every S&P 500 company." CNBC, July 25.

Retrieved from https://www.cnbc.com/2019/07/25/there-is-now-a-woman-board-member-at-every-sp-500-company.html.

Fitzpatrick, M. J., and B. J. McPherson. (2010). "Coloring Within the Lines: Gender Stereotypes in Contemporary Coloring Books." *Sex Roles* 62: 127–37.

Foley, D. (1994). *Learning Capitalist Culture: Deep in the Heart of Tejas.* Philadelphia: University of Pennsylvania Press.

Fomby, P., and A. J. Cherlin. (2007). "Family Instability and Child Well-Being." *American Sociological Review* 72(2): 181–204.

Foner, N. (1984). *Ages in Conflict: A Cross-Cultural Perspective on Inequality between Old and Young.* New York: Columbia University Press.

Fontenot, K., J. Semega, and M. Kollar. (2018). "Income and Poverty in the United States: 2017." U.S. Bureau of the Census. Retrieved from https://census.gov/content/dam/Census/library/publications/2018/demo/p60-263.pdf.

Foran, J., ed. (1997). *Theorizing Revolutions.* New York: Routledge.

Forbes. (2012). "The World's Billionaires." July 23. Retrieved 3/4/13, from www.forbes.com/sites/luisakroll/2011/03/09/the-worlds-billionaires-2011-inside-the-list/.

Ford, M. (2009). *The Lights in the Tunnel: Automation, Accelerating Technology and the Economy of the Future.* Amazon CreateSpace Independent Publishing Platform.

Ford, M. (2010). "Your Job in 2020." *Forbes*, April 8. Retrieved from http://www.forbes.com/2010/04/08/unemployment-google-2020-technology-data-companies-10-economy.html.

Ford, C. S., and Beach, F. A. (1951). *Patterns of Sexual Behavior.* New York: Harper and Row.

Foreign Policy. (2013). "Failed States." *Foreign Policy.* Retrieved summer 2014, from http://www.foreignpolicy.com/failedstates2013.

Forest, Amanda L. and Joanne V. Wood. (2012). "When Social Networking Is Not Working: Individuals With Low Self-Esteem Recognize but Do Not Reap the Benefits of Self-Disclosure on Facebook," *Psychological Science* (March) 23: 295–302.

Forsberg, C., Thornberg, R., and Samuelsson, M. (2014). "Bystanders to Bullying: Fourth- to Seventh-grade Students' Perspectives on Their Reactions." *Research Papers in Education,* 29, 557–576.

Fortune. (2016). "Most Powerful Women International." Retrieved from http://fortune.com/most-powerful-women-international/tsai-patty-pei-chun-37/.

Fortune. (2017). "Global 500." Retrieved from http://beta.fortune.com/global500/.

Fortune. (2019a) "Global 500." Retrieved from https://fortune.com/global500/.

Fortune. (2019b). "Industrial & Commercial Bank of China." Retrieved from https://fortune.com/global500/2019/industrial-commercial-bank-of-china/.

Foucault, M. (1971). *The Order of Things: An Archaeology of the Human Sciences*. New York: Pantheon.

Foucault, M. (1975). *Discipline and Punish: The Birth of the Prison*. Paris: Gallimard.

Foucault, M. (1988). "Technologies of the Self." In L. H. Martin, H. Gutman, and P. H. Hutton, eds., *Technologies of the Self: A Seminar with Michel Foucault*. Amherst: University of Massachusetts Press.

Fox, J. (2017). "Men Slowly Return to the Labor Force." *Bloomberg View* (May 5, 2017). Retrieved from https://www.bloomberg.com/view/articles/2017-05-05/men-slowly-return-to-the-labor-force.

Fox, J. (2018). "Why German Corporate Boards Include Workers." *Bloomberg Opinion*, Aug. 24. Retrieved from https://www.bloomberg.com/opinion/articles/2018-08-24/why-german-corporate-boards-include-workers-for-co determination.

Fox, M. (2014). "A Tale of Two Outbreaks: Why Congo Conquered Ebola." NBC News, November 24. Retrieved 12/2014, from http://www.nbcnews.com/storyline/ebola-virus-outbreak/tale-two-outbreaks-why-congo-conquered-ebola-n253911.

Fox, O. C. (1964). "The Pre-Industrial City Reconsidered." *Sociological Quarterly* 5.

Francois-Cerrah, M. (2014). "The Feminist Case for the Veil," *New Statesman*, Dec. 12, Retrieved from http://www.newstatesman.com/religion/2014/12/feminist-case-veil.

Frank, A. G. (1966). "The Development of Underdevelopment." *Monthly Review* 18.

Frank, A. G. (1969a). *Capitalism and Underdevelopment in Latin America: Historical Studies of Chile and Brazil*. New York: Monthly Review Press.

Frank, A. G (1969b). *Latin America: Underdevelopment or Revolution*. New York: Monthly Review Press.

Frank, A. G. (1979). *Dependent Accumulation and Underdevelopment*. London: Macmillan.

Frank, D. J., and E. H. McEneaney. (1999). "The Individualization of Society and the Liberalization of State Policies on Same-Sex Sexual Relations, 1984–1995." *Social Forces* 7(3): 911–44.

Frank, T. (2004). *What's the Matter with Kansas? How Conservatives Won the Heart of America*. New York: Metropolitan Books.

Frank, T. (2005). "Class Is Dismissed." Retrieved fall 2010, from www.google.com/url?sa=t&source=web&cd=1&ved=0CBoQFjAA&url=http%3A%2F%2Fuserwave.service.emory.edu%2F,dlinzer%2FFrank-ClassDismissd.pdf&ei=52xhTOPfJ4uCsQOB4Y24CA&usg=AFQjCNF7H96XIOzUBnwojH9iI-sXrD4MCg&sig2=8XnbyZGOcf_eVGeKTFq3XA.

Frank, T. (2016). *Listen, Liberal: Or, What Ever Happened to the Party of the People?* New York: Metropolitan Books.

Franklin, S. (2013). *Biological Relatives: IVF, Stem Cells, and the Future of Kinship* (Experimental Futures). Durham, NC: Duke University Press.

Frazier, E. F. (1939). *The Negro Family in the United States*. Chicago: University of Chicago Press.

Fredrickson, G. (2002). *Racism: A Brief History*. Princeton: Princeton University Press.

Freedman, A. (2013). "Study Projects Steep Increase in NYC Heat-Related Deaths." Climate Central, May 19. http://www.climatecentral.org/news/study-projects-steep-increase in heat-related-deaths-in-new-york-16012.

Freedman, V. A., E. M. Agree, J. C. Cornman, B. C. Spillman, J. D. Kasper (2013). "Reliability and Validity of Self-Care and Mobility Accomodation Measures in the National Health and Aging Trends Study." *The Gerontologist*. September 19. http://gerontologist.oxfordjournals.org/content/early/2013/09/18/geront.gnt104

Freedom House. (2016). "Freedom on the Net 2016," Retrieved from https://freedomhouse.org/report/freedom-net/freedom-net-2016.

Freedom House. (2019). "Democracy in Retreat: Freedom in the World 2019." Retrieved from https://freedomhouse.org/report/freedom-world/freedom-world-2019/democracy-in-retreat.

Freeman, R. B., and J. Rogers. (1999). *What Workers Want*. Ithaca, NY: ILR Press and Russell Sage Foundation.

Freidson, E. (1970). *Profession of Medicine: A Study of the Sociology of Applied Knowledge*. New York: Dodd, Mead.

French, H. W. (2001). "Diploma at Hand, Japanese Women Find Glass Ceiling Reinforced with Iron." *New York Times*, January 1: A1.

French, H. W. (2006). "As Chinese Cities Boom, Old Are Left Behind." *New York Times*, November 3. Retrieved from http://www.nytimes.com/2006/11/03/world/asia/03iht-age.3383555.html?_r=0.

Freudenburg, W. R. (2006), "Environmental Degradation, Disproportionality, and the Double Diversion: Reaching Out, Reaching Ahead, and Reaching Beyond." *Rural Sociology* 71: 3–32.

Freudenberg, W. R., S. Frickel, and R. Gramling. (1995). "Beyond the Nature/Society Divide: Learning to Think about a Mountain." *Sociological Forum* 10(3): 361–92.

Fried, A., and D. B. Harris. (2001). "On Red Capes and Charging Bulls: How and Why Conservative Politicians and Interest Groups Promoted Public Anger." In J. R. Hibbing and E. Theiss-Morse, *What Is It about Government That Americans Dislike?* (pp. 157–74). New York: Cambridge University Press.

Friedlingstein, P. et al. (2019). "Global Carbon Budget 2019." *Earth System Science Data* 11(4): 1783–1838.

Friedman, L. (2019). "Trump Serves Notice to Quit Paris Climate Agreement," *New York Times*, Nov. 4. Retrieved from https://www.nytimes.com/2019/11/04/climate/trump-paris-agreement-climate.html.

Fries, J. F. (1980). "Aging, Natural Death, and the Compression of Morbidity." *New England Journal of Medicine* 303: 130–35.

Frobel, F., J. Heinrichs, and O. Kreye. (1979). *The New International Division of Labor*. New York: Cambridge University Press.

Frumhoff, P. (2014). "Global Warming Fact: More than Half of All Industrial CO2 Pollution Has Been Emitted Since 1988." Union of Concerned Scientists, Dec. 15. Retrieved from https://blog.ucsusa.org/peter-frumhoff/global-warming-fact-co2-emissions-since-1988-764.

Fry, C. L. (1980). *Aging in Culture and Society*. New York: Bergin.

Fry, R. (2012). "A Record One-in-Five Households Now Owe Student Loan Debt," Pew Research Center. September 26. Retrieved 1/13/15, from http://www.pewsocialtrends.org/2012/09/26/a-record-one-in-five-households-now-owe-student-loan-debt/.

Fry, R. and P. Taylor. (2013). "A Rise in Wealth for the Wealthy; Declines for the Lower 93%" Pew Research

Social & Demographic Trends, April 23. Retrieved 12/14, from http://www.pewsocialtrends.org/2013/04/23/a-rise-in-wealth-for-the-wealthydeclines-for-the-lower-93/.

Fryar, C. D., Y. Ostchega, C. M. Hales, G. Zhang, and D. Kruszon-Moran. (2017). "Hypertension prevalence and control among adults: United States, 2015–2016." NCHS data brief, no. 289. Hyattsville, MD: National Center for Health Statistics.

Fryer, Jr., R. G. (2010). "Racial Inequality in the 21st Century: The Declining Significance of Discrimination." NBER Working Paper no. 16256. Retrieved from https://www.nber.org/papers/w16256.pdf.

Fu, V. K., and N. H. Wolfinger. (2011). "Broken Boundaries or Broken Marriages? Racial Intermarriage and Divorce in the United States." *Social Science Quarterly* 92(4): 1096–1117.

Furstenberg Jr., F. F. (2010). "On a New Schedule: Transitions to Adulthood and Family Change." *The Future of Children* 20(1): 67–87.

G, Dalia. (2015). "Meet The Nine Muslim Women Who Have Ruled Nations," *Egyptian Streets,* June 9, Retrieved from https://egyptianstreets.com/2015/06/09/meet-the-nine-muslim-women-who-have-ruled-nations.

Gallup. (2013). "Tea Party Favorability Falls to Lowest Yet," December 11. Retrieved summer 2014, from http://www.gallup.com/poll/166217/tea-party-favorability-falls-lowest-yet.aspx.

Gallup. (2017). "The State of the American Workplace," Retrieved from http://www.gallup.com/reports/199961/state-american-workplace-report-2017.aspx.

Gallup. (2019). "Party Affiliation." Retrieved from https://news.gallup.com/poll/15370/party-affiliation.aspx.

Gamoran, A., and M. Nystrand. (1995). "An organizational analysis of the effects of ability grouping." *American Educational Research Journal* 32(4): 687–715.

Gans, D., and M. Silverstein. (2006). "Norms of Filial Responsibility for Aging Parents across Time and Generations." *Journal of Marriage and Family* 68(4): 961–76.

Garcia, J. R., C. Reiber, S. G. Massey, and A. M. Merriwether. (2012). "Sexual hookup culture: A review." *Review of General Psychology* 16: 161–76.

Gardner, W., D. States, and N. Bagley. (2020). "The Coronavirus and the Risks to the Elderly in Long-Term Care." *Journal of Aging & Social Policy* 32(4-5): 310–15.

Gardner, H., and T. Hatch. (1989). "Multiple Intelligences Go to School: Educational Implications of the Theory of Multiple Intelligences." *Educational Researcher* 18(8): 4–9.

Garfinkel, H. (1963). "A Conception of, and Experiments with, 'Trust' as a Condition of Stable Concerted Actions." In O. J. Harvey, ed., *Motivation and Social Interaction*. New York: Ronald Press.

Garland, D. (2010). *Peculiar Institution: America's Death Penalty in an Age of Abolition*. Cambridge, MA: Belknap Press.

Gates, G. J. (2012). "LGBT Identity: A Demographer's Perspective." *Loyola of Los Angeles Law Review* 45 (693). Retrieved 9/25/12, from http://digitalcommons.lmu.edu/llr/vol45/iss3/2.

Gates, G. J., and F. Newport. (2013). Gallup Special Report: New Estimates of the LGBT Population in the United States. Los Angeles, CA: The Williams Institute. Retrieved 10/24/14, from http://williamsinstitute.law.ucla.edu/research/census-lgbt-demographics-studies/gallup-lgbt-pop feb-2013/.

Gautié, J. and J. Schmitt (Eds.). (2010). *Low-Wage Work in the Wealthy World*. Russell Sage Foundation.

Gavin, L. A., and Furman, W. (1989). "Age Differences in Adolescents' Perceptions of Their Peer Groups." *Developmental Psychology,* 25, 827–834.

Gavron, H. (1966). *The Captive Wife: Conflicts of Housebound Mothers*. London: Routledge and Kegan Paul.

Geary, D. (1981). *European Labor Protest, 1848–1939*. New York: St. Martin's Press.

Gebrekidan, S., M. Apuzzo, and B. Novak. (2019). "The Money Farmers: How Oligarchs and Populists Milk the E.U. for Millions." *New York Times,* Nov. 3. Retrieved from https://www.nytimes.com/2019/11/03/world/europe/eu-farm-subsidy-hungary.html.

Geertz, C. (1973). *The Interpretation of Cultures*. New York: Basic Books.

Geiger, A. W. (2016). "Sharing chores a key to good marriage, say majority of married adults." Pew Research Center, Nov. 30. Retrieved from https://www.pewresearch.org/fact tank/2016/11/30/sharing-chores-a-key-to-good-marriage-say-majority-of-married-adults/.

Geiger, A.W. (2019). "Key findings about the online news landscape in America." Pew Research Center, Sept. 11. Retrieved from https://www.pewresearch.org/fact-tank/2019/09/11/key-findings-about-the-online-news-landscape-in-america/.

Geiger, A. W. and L. Kent. (2017). "Number of Women Leaders around the World Has Grown, but They're Still a Small Group." Pew Research Center, March 8. Retrieved from http://www.pewresearch.org/fact-tank/2017/03/08/women-leaders-around-the-world/.

Gelb, I. J. (1952). *A Study of Writing*. Chicago: University of Chicago Press.

General Accountability Office. (2015). "Contingent Workforce: Size, Characteristics, Earnings, and Benefits," Retrieved from https://www.gao.gov/assets/670/669766.pdf.

Genworth Financial. (2016). "Cost of Care." Retrieved from https://www.genworth.com/about-us/industry-expertise/cost-of-care.html.

Gerbner, G., L. Gross, M. Morgan, and N. Signorielli. (1986). "Television's Mean World: Violence Profile No. 14–15." Philadelphia: Annenberg School of Communication, University of Pennsylvania.

Gereffi, G. (1995). "Contending Paradigms for Cross-Regional Comparison: Development Strategies and Commodity Chains in East Asia and Latin America." In P. H. Smith, ed., *Latin America in Comparative Perspective: New Approaches to Methods and Analysis*. Boulder, CO: Westview Press.

Gereffi, G. (1996). "Commodity Chains and Regional Divisions of Labor in East Asia." *Journal of Asian Business* 1(1): 75–112.

Gereffi, G., K. Fernandez-Stark, and P. Psilos (Eds.). (2011). *Skills for Upgrading: Workforce Development and Global Value Chains in Developing Countries* (pp. 1-12). Durham, NC: Duke University, Center on Globalization, Governance, and Competitiveness.

Gettleman, J. (2014). "Uganda Anti-Gay Law Struck Down by Court. " *New York Times,* August 1. Retrieved 10/26/14, from http://www.nytimes.com/2014/08/02/world/africa/uganda-anti-gay-law-struck-down-by-court.html.

Gettleman, J. (2017). "Drought and War Heighten Threat of Not Just 1 Famine, but 4." *New York Times,* March 27, 2017. Retrieved from https://www.nytimes.com/2017/03/27/world/africa/famine-somalia-nigeria-south-sudan-yemen-water.html?_r=0.

GLAAD. (2020). "GLAAD Media Reference Guide - Lesbian / Gay / Bisexual Glossary of Terms." Retrieved from https://www.glaad.org/reference/lgbtq.

Giddens, A. (1990). *The Consequences of Modernity*. Cambridge, UK: Polity Press.

Giddens, A. (2009). *The Politics of Climate Change*. Cambridge, UK: Polity Press.

Gilligan, C. (1982). *In a Different Voice: Psychological Theory and Women's Development*. Cambridge, MA: Harvard University Press.

Gills, B. and J. Morgan. (2019). "Global Climate Emergency: after COP24, climate science, urgency, and the threat to humanity." *Globalizations* 17(6): 885–902.

Ginsberg, T. B., S. C. Pomerantz, and V. Kramer-Feeley. (2005). "Sexuality in older adults: behaviours and preferences." *Age and Ageing* 34(5): 475.

Giuffre, P. A., and C. L. Williams. (1994). "Boundary Lines: Labeling Sexual Harassment in Restaurants." *Gender and Society* 8: 378–401.

Gladwell, M. (2005). "Getting in: The Social Logic of Ivy League Admissions." *New Yorker*, October 15.

Gladwell, M. (2014). "The Crooked Ladder: The Criminal's Guide to Upward Mobility." *New Yorker*, August 11.

Glassner, B. (1999). *The Culture of Fear: Why Americans Are Afraid of the Wrong Things*. New York: Basic Books.

Glazer, A. (2019). "National Mathematics Survey." MIT Women in Mathematics. Retrieved from https://math.mit.edu/wim/2019/03/10/national-mathematics-survey/.

Glenza, J. (2011). "NYPD urged to step up body-worn camera pilot after chokehold death." *Guardian*, August 12. Retrieved 1/13/15, from http://www.theguardian.com/world/2014/aug/12/nypd-body-worn-camera-pilot-chokehold-death.

Global Workplace Analytics. (2014). "Latest Telecommuting Statistics." Retrieved summer 2014, from http://www.globalworkplaceanalytics.com/telecommuting-statistics.

Glock, C. Y. (1976). "On the Origin and Evolution of Religious Groups." In C. Y. Glock and R. N. Bellah, eds., *The New Religious Consciousness*. Berkeley, CA: University of California Press.

Glynn, S. J. (2015). "Administering Paid Family and Medical Leave Learning from International and Domestic Examples." Washington, DC: Center for American Progress (November 2015). Retrieved from https://cdn.americanprogress.org/wp-content/uploads/2015/11/19060022/PaidLeaveProposal-report-11.19.15.pdf.

Goff, P. A., M. C. Jackson, B. A. Lewis Di Leone, C. M. Culotta, and N. A. DiTomasso. (2014). "The Essence of Innocence: Consequences of Dehumanizing Black Children." *Journal of Personality and Social Psychology* 106, no. 4 (2014): 526.

Goffard, C., and M. Hennessy-Fiske. (2012). "The Nonthreatening Path of a Future Mass Murder." *Los Angeles Times*, August 9. Retrieved spring 2013. www.latimes.com/news/nationworld/nation/la-na-wisconsin-gunman-20120809,0,6250188,full.story (site discontinued).

Goffman, A. (2009). "On the Run." *American Sociological Review* 74 (3): 339–57.

Goffman, A. (2014). *On the Run: Fugitive Life in an American City*. Chicago: University of Chicago Press.

Goffman, E. (1963). *Stigma: Notes on the Management of Spoiled Identity*. Englewood Cliffs, NJ: Prentice-Hall.

Goffman, E. (1967). *Interaction Ritual*. New York: Doubleday/Anchor.

Goffman, E. (1971). *Relations in Public: Microstudies of the Public Order*. New York: Basic Books.

Goffman, E. (1973). *The Presentation of Self in Everyday Life*. New York: Overlook Press.

Goffman, E. (1981). *Forms of Talk*. Philadelphia: University of Pennsylvania Press.

Gold, H. R. (2017). "Never Mind the 1%, Let's Talk about the 0.1%." Chicago Booth Review. Retrieved from https://review.chicagobooth.edu/economics/2017/article/never-mind-1-percent-lets-talk-about-001-percent.

Gold, H., and J. Schneider. (2018). "AT&T Completes Acquisition of Time Warner." CNN Business, June 14. Retrieved from https://money.cnn.com/2018/06/14/media/att-time-warner-deal/index.html.

Goldberg, A. E., J. Z. Smith, and M. Perry-Jenkins. (2012). "The Division of Labor in Lesbian, Gay, and Heterosexual New Adoptive Parents." *Journal of Marriage and Family* 74(4): 812–28.

Goldberg, C. (1997). "Hispanic Households Struggle amid Broad Decline in Income." *New York Times*, January 30, pp. A1, A16.

Goldberg, S. (1999). "The Logic of Patriarchy." *Gender Issues* 17: 53–69.

Goldberg, S. K., and K. J. Conron. (2018). "How Many Same-Sex Couples in the U.S. are Raising Children?" UCLA School of Law. Retrieved from https://williamsinstitute.law.ucla.edu/publications/same-sex-parents-us/.

Goldstein, S., and A. Goldstein. (1996). *Jews on the Move: Implications for Jewish Identity*. Albany, NY: State University of New York Press.

Goleman, Daniel. (1996). *Emotional Intelligence: Why It Can Matter More Than IQ*. New York: Bantam Books.

Gonzales, M. G., and R. Delgado. (2006). *Politics of Fear: How Republicans Use Money, Race and the Media to Win*. Abingdon, UK: Routledge.

Gonzalez-Barrera, A. (2015). "More Mexicans leaving than coming to the U.S." Retrieved from http://www.pewhispanic.org/2015/11/19/moremexicans-leaving-than-coming-to-the-u-s/.

Goode, E. (2011). "Video, a New Tool for the Police, Poses New Legal Issues, Too." *New York Times*, October 11. Accessed winter 2014, from http://www.nytimes.com/2011/10/12/us/police-using-body-mounted-video-cameras.html?pagewanted=all.

Goode, W. J. (1963). *World Revolution in Family Patterns*. New York: Free Press.

Gornick, J. C., and M. K. Meyers. (2003). "Welfare Regimes in Relation to Paid Work and Care." In J. Z. Giele and E. Holst, eds., *Changing Life Patterns in Western Societies*. Netherlands: Elsevier.

Gottfredson, M. R., and T. Hirschi. (1990). *A General Theory of Crime*. Stanford, CA: Stanford University Press.

Gottfried, J., M. Barthel, and A. Mitchell. (2017). "Trump, Clinton Voters Divided in Their Main Source for Election News," Jan. 18, Retrieved from http://www.journalism.org/2017/01/18/trump-clinton-voters-divided-in-their-main-source-for-election-news/.

Gould, E. (2010). "The State of American Wages 2017." Economic Policy Institute. Retrieved from https://www.epi.org/publication/the-state-of-american-wages-2017-wages-have-finally-recovered-from-the-blow-of-the-great-recession-but-are-still-growing-too-slowly-and-unequally/.

Gould, K. A., D. N. Pellow, and A. Schnaiberg. (2004). "Interrogating the treadmill of production: Everything you wanted to know about the treadmill but were afraid to ask." *Organization & Environment* 17(3): 296–316.

Gould, K. A., D. N. Pellow, and A. Schnaiberg. (2008). *The Treadmill of Production: Injustice and Unsustainability in the Global Economy*. Abingdon, UK: Paradigm Publishers.

Gould, S., and R. Harrington. (2016). "7 Charts Show Who Propelled Trump to Victory," *Business Insider*, Nov. 10, 2016, Retrieved from http://www.businessinsider.com/exit-polls-who-voted-for-trump-clinton-2016-11/#more-women-voted-for-clinton-as-expected-but-trump-still-got-42-of-female-votes-1.

Gove, W. R., M. Hughes, and M. R. Geerken. (1980). "Playing Dumb: A Form of Impression Management with Undesirable Side Effects." *Social Psychology Quarterly*, 89–102.

Grabe, S., L. M. Ward, and J. S. Hyde. (2008). "The Role of the Media in Body Image Concerns among Women: A Meta-analysis of Experimental and Correlational Studies." *Psychological Bulletin,* 134, 460–476.

Grabell, M. (2013). "The Expendables: How the Temps Who Power Corporate Giants Are Getting Crushed," *Pro-Publica,* June 27, Retrieved from http://www.propublica.org/article/the-expendables-how-the-temps-who-power-corporate-giants-are-getting-crushe.

Graham, J. (2019). "Many Older Adults Feel Positive about Their Health. Here's why." *Washington Post,* June 28. Retrieved from https://www.washingtonpost.com/health/many-older-adults-feel-positive-about-their-health-heres-why/2019/06/28/36b8c564-9372-11e9-b58a-a6a9afaa0e3e_story.html.

Graham, J. (2020). "Once again, iPhones top tech seller of the year, but AirPods the hit." *USA Today,* Dec. 31. Retrieved from https://www.usatoday.com/story/tech/2019/12/31/iphone-sales-dip-but-still-no-1-2019-airpods-and-watch-rise/2775193001/.

Gramlich, J. (2019a). "5 facts about crime in the U.S." Pew Research Center, Oct. 17. Retrieved from https://www.pewresearch.org/fact-tank/2019/10/17/facts-about-crime-in-the-u-s/.

Gramlich, J. (2019b). "The gap between the number of blacks and whites in prison is shrinking." Pew Research Center, April 30. Retrieved from https://www.pewresearch.org/fact-tank/2019/04/30/shrinking-gap-between-number-of-blacks-and-whites-in-prison/.

Granic, I., A. Lobel, and R. C. Engels. (2014). "The Benefits of Playing Video Games." *American Psychologist,* 69, 66–78.

Granovetter, M. (1973). "The Strength of Weak Ties." *American Journal of Sociology* 78: 1360–80.

Grant Thornton. (2017). "Women in Business: New Perspectives on Risk and Reward," Retrieved from https://www.grantthornton.global/globalassets/1.-member-firms/global/insights/article-pdfs/2017/grant-thornton_women-in-business_2017-report.pdf.

Gray, P. (1998). "Ethnographic Atlas Codebook." *World Cultures* 10: 86–136.

Green, F. (1987). *The "Sissy Boy" Syndrome and the Development of Homosexuality.* New Haven, CT: Yale University Press.

Greenberg, G. (2010). "Inside the Battle to Define Mental Illness." *Wired,* December 27. Retrieved 6/15/15, from http://www.wired.com/2010/12/ff_dsmv/.

Greenberger, E., and L. D. Steinberg. (1981). "The Workplace as a Context for the Socialization of Youth," *Journal of Youth and Adolescence* 10: 185. Retrieved from https://doi.org/10.1007/BF02088970.

Greenfield, E. A., C. Lee, E. L. Friedman, and K. W. Springer. (2011.) "Childhood abuse as a risk factor for sleep problems in adulthood: evidence from a US national study." *Annals of Behavioral Medicine* 42(2): 245–56.

Greenhouse, G. (2015). "How Walmart Persuades Its Workers Not to Unionize," *Bloomberg,* June 8, Retrieved from https://www.theatlantic.com/business/archive/2015/06/how-walmart-convinces-its-employees-not-to-unionize/395051/.

Greenhouse, S., and M. Barbaro. (2007). "Costco Bias Suit Is Given Class-Action Status." *New York Times,* January 12.

Griffin, S. (1979). *Rape, the Power of Consciousness.* New York: Harper and Row.

Griswold, A. (2014). "The American Concept of 'Prestige' Has Barely Changed in 37 Years." *Slate,* Moneybox, September 10. Retrieved 12/14, from http://www.slate.com/blogs/moneybox/2014/09/10/most_prestigious_jobs_in_america_the_short_list_has_barely_changed_in_37.html.

Griswold, W. (2013). *Cultures and Societies in a Changing World* (4th ed.). Thousand Oaks, CA: Pine Forge Press.

Grodsky, E., and D. Pager. (2001). "The Structure of Disadvantage: Individual and Occupational Determinants of the Black-White Wage Gap." *American Sociological Review* 66(4): 542–567. https://doi.org/10.2307/3088922.

Gross, J. (1992). "Suffering in Silence No More: Fighting Sexual Harassment." *New York Times,* July 13: A1.

Grosz, E. (1994). *Volatile Bodies: Toward a Corporeal Feminism.* Bloomington: Indiana University Press.

Guardian. (2002). "Top 1% Earn as Much as the Poorest 57%." Retrieved 1/10/05, from www.guardian.co.uk/business/story/0,,635292,00.html.

Guardian. (2019). "The Nigerian Film Industry." Nov. 26. Retrieved from https://guardian.ng/life/the-nigerian-film-industry/.

Gubernskaya, Z., and J. Treas. (2020). "Pathways to linguistic isolation among older US immigrants: Assessing the role of living arrangements and English proficiency." *The Journals of Gerontology: Series B* 75(2): 351–56.

Guilford, G. (2014). "Why the Girl-Power Blockbuster 'Frozen' Is the Most Popular Movie to Hit Japan in a Decade," *Quartz,* June 28, Retrieved from https://qz.com/226971/why-the-girl-power-blockbuster-frozen-is-the-most-popular-movie-to-hit-japan-in-a-decade/.

Guibernau, M. (1999). *Nations without States: Political Communities in a Global Age.* Cambridge, MA: Blackwell.

Gunderson, E. A., G. Ramirez, S. C. Levine, and S. L. Beilock. (2011). "The Role of Parents and Teachers in the Development of Gender-Related Math Attitudes." *Sex Roles* 66: 153–66.

Gupta, A. H. (2020). "Does Covid-19 Hit Women and Men Differently? U.S. Isn't Keeping Track." *New York Times,* April 3. Retrieved from https://www.nytimes.com/2020/04/03/us/coronavirus-male-female-data-bias.html.

Gurrentz, B. (2018). "For Young Adults, Cohabitation is Up, Marriage is Down: Living with an Unmarried Partner Now Common for Young Adults." U.S. Bureau of the Census, November 15. Retrieved from https://www.census.gov/library/stories/2018/11/cohabitaiton-is-up-marriage-is-down-for-young-adults.html.

Guzman, G. (2019). "U.S. Median Household Income Up in 2018 from 2017: New Data Show Income Increased in 14 States and 10 of the Largest Metros." U.S. Bureau of the Census, Sept. 26. Retrieved from https://www.census.gov/library/stories/2019/09/us-median-household-income-up-in-2018-from-2017.html.

Guzzo, K. B. (2009). "Marital intentions and the stability of first cohabitations." *Journal of Family Issues* 30(2): 179–205.

Ha, J.-H. (2008). "Changes in Support from Confidantes, Children, and Friends Following Widowhood." *Journal of Marriage and Family* 70: 306–18.

Habermas, J. (1975). *Legitimation Crisis* (T. McCarthy, trans.). Boston: Beacon Press.

Haberstick, B. C., J. M. Lessem, M. McQueen, J. D. Boardman, C. J. Hopfer, A. Smolen, and J. K. Hewitt. (2010). "Stable Genes and Changing Environments: Body Mass Index Across Adolescence and Young Adulthood." *Behavior Genetics* 40: 495–504.

Hadden, J. (1997a). "The Concepts 'Cult' and 'Sect' in Scholarly Research and Public Discourse." New Religious Movements. Retrieved 1/10/05, from http://religiousmovements.lib.virginia.edu/cultsect/concult.htm (site discontinued).

Hadden, J. (1997b). "New Religious Movements Mission Statement." New Religious Movements. Retrieved 1/10/05,

from http://religiousmovements.lib.
virginia.edu/welcome/mission.htm
(site discontinued).

Hadden, J. (2004). "Televangelism." Religious Broadcasting Website. Retrieved
1/3/05, from http://religious
broadcasting.lib.virginia.edu/
televangelism.html (site
discontinued).

Hagey, K. (2015). "Rupert Murdoch
Positions Sons to Lead 21st Century
Fox," The Wall Street Journal, June
11, Retrieved from https://www.wsj.
com/articles/rupert-murdoch-to-
step-down-as-ceo-of-21st-century-
fox-1434034508.

Haggerty, R. (2012). "To Cut Homelessness,
Cut the Red Tape." New York Times,
May 24. Retrieved 3/01/13, from www.
nytimes.com/roomfordebate/2012/
05/24/how-should-the-us-support-
returning-veterans/to-cut-veteran-
homelessness-cut-the-red-tape.

Hajnal, Z., N. Lajevardi, and L. Nielson.
(2017). "Voter Identification Laws and
the Suppression of Minority Votes,"
The Journal of Politics, 79, no. 2 (April
2017): 363–379.

Hales C. M., M. D. Carroll, C. D. Fryar,
and C. L. Ogden. (2017). "Prevalence
of obesity among adults and youth:
United States, 2015–2016." NCHS
data brief, no. 288. Hyattsville, MD:
National Center for Health Statistics.
Retrieved from https://www.cdc.gov/
nchs/data/databriefs/db288.pdf.

Hales, C. M., M. D. Carroll, C. D. Fryar,
and C. L. Ogden. (2020). "Prevalence
of obesity and severe obesity among
adults: United States, 2017–2018."
NCHS data brief, no. 360. Hyattsville,
MD: National Center for Health Statistics. Retrieved from https://www.
cdc.gov/nchs/products/databriefs/
db360.htm.

Hall, E. T. (1969). The Hidden Dimension.
New York: Doubleday.

Hall, S. (1992). "The Question of Cultural
Identity." In S. Hall, D. Held, and T.
McGrew, eds., Modernity and its Fu-
tures. Cambridge, UK: Polity Press.

Hall, S., D. Held, and T. McGrew. (1988).
"New Times." Marxism Today, October.

Hamel, G. (1991). "Competition for Competence and Inter-Partner Learning
within International Strategic Alliances." Strategic Management Journal
12 (Summer Special Issue): 83–103.

Hamer, D. H., S. Hu, V. L. Magnuson, N. Hu,
and A. M. Pattatucci. (1993). "A linkage between DNA markers on the X
chromosome and male sexual orientation." Science 261(5119): 321–27.

Hamilton, J. (2017). "Politics Aside, Counting Crowds Is Tricky," NPR, Jan. 23,
Retrieved from http://www.npr.org/

sections/thetwo-way/2017/01/23/
511267138/politics-aside-counting-
crowds-is-tricky.

Hamilton, L., and E. A. Armstrong. (2009).
"Double Binds and Flawed Options:
Gendered Sexuality in Early Adult-
hood," Gender & Sexuality 23: 589–616.

Hammond, P. E. (1992). Religion and
Personal Autonomy: The Third Dis-
establishment in America. Columbia:
University of South Carolina Press.

Hampton, K., L. Sessions Goulet, L. Rainie,
and K. Purcell. (2011). "Social networking sites and our lives." Washington, DC: Pew Internet and American
Life Project.

Hanks, A., D. Solomon, and C. E. Weller.
(2018), "Systematic inequality: How
America's structural racism helped
create the black-white wealth gap."
Center for American Progress. Retrieved from https://www.american-
progress.org/issues/race/reports/
2018/02/21/447051/systematic-
inequality/.

Harding, R. (2018). "Fukushima nuclear
disaster: did the evacuation raise the
death toll?" Financial Times, March
10. Retrieved from https://www.
ft.com/content/000f864e-22ba-11e8-
add1-0e8958b189ea.

Harknett, K., and S. McLanahan. (2004).
"Racial and Ethnic Differences in
Marriage after the Birth of a Child."
American Sociological Review 69:
790–811.

Harrington Meyer, M., and P. Herd. 2007.
Market Friendly or Family Friendly?
The State and Gender Inequality in Old
Age. New York: Russell Sage.

Harris. (2014). "Doctors, Military Officers,
Firefighters, and Scientists Seen as
America's Most Prestigious Occupations." September 10. Retrieved 12/14,
from http://www.harrisinteractive.
com/NewsRoom/HarrisPolls/tabid/
447/mid/1508/articleId/1490/ctl/
ReadCustom%20Default/Default.
aspx.

Harris, J. R. (1998). The Nurture Assumption: Why Children Turn Out the Way
They Do. New York: Free Press.

Harris, M. (1975). Cows, Pigs, Wars, and
Riches: The Riddles of Culture. New
York: Random House.

Harris, M. (1978). Cannibals and Kings:
The Origins of Cultures. New York:
Random House.

Harris, M. (1980). Cultural Materialism:
The Struggle for a Science of Culture.
New York: Vintage Books.

Hartig, T., G. Johansson, and C. Kylin
(2003). "Residence in the Social
Ecology of Stress and Restoration."
Journal of Social Issues 59 (3): 611–36.

Hartman, M., and H. Hartman. (1996).
Gender Equality and American Jews.
Albany, NY: State University of New
York Press.

Harvard Kennedy School Institute of
Politics. (2017). "Survey of Young
Americans' Attitudes Toward Politics
and Public Service 33rd Edition,"
Retrieved from http://iop.harvard.
edu/sites/default/files/content/
docs/170424_Harvard%20IOP%20
Poll_Spring%20_Exec%20Summary.
pdf.

Harvey, D. (1973). Social Justice and the
City. Oxford, UK: Blackwell.

Harvey, D. (1982). The Limits to Capital.
Oxford, UK: Blackwell.

Harvey, D. (1985). Consciousness and the
Urban Experience: Studies in the History and Theory of Capitalist Urbanization. Oxford, UK: Blackwell.

Harvey, D. (1990). The Condition of Postmodernity. Cambridge, MA: Blackwell.

Harvey, D. (2009). Social Justice and
the City: Volume 1 of Geographies of
Justice and Social Transformation.
Athens, GA: University of Georgia
Press.

Haskins, R. (2009). "Education and Economic Mobility," in J. B. Isaacs, I. V.
Sawhill, and R. Haskins, eds. Getting
Ahead or Losing Ground: Economic
Mobility in America (pp. 91–104).
Washington: Brookings and the Pew
Charitable Trusts. Retrieved 12/14,
from http://www.brookings.
edu/~/media/research/files/reports/
2008/2/economic%20mobility%20
sawhill/02_economic_mobility_
sawhill_ch8.pdf.

Haslam, D. W., and W. P. James. (2005).
"Obesity." Lancet 366 (9492):
1197–1209.

Haslett, B., F. L. Geis, and M. R. Carter.
(1992). The Organizational Woman:
Power and Paradox. Norwood, NJ:
Ablex.

Hatch, A. (2015). "Saying 'I Don't' to
Matrimony An Investigation of Why
Long-Term Heterosexual Cohabitors
Choose Not to Marry." Journal of Fam-
ily Issues, 0192513X15576200.

Hatch, J. (2017). "Hidden Figures' Is
Already Inspiring More Girls To
Go Into STEM." Huffington Post
(February 2, 2017). Retrieved from
http://www.huffingtonpost.com/
entry/hidden-figures-is-already-
inspiring-more-girls-to-go-into-stem_
us_588f4d4be4b0176377956501.

Hatch, N. O. (1989). The Democratization
of American Christianity. New Haven,
CT: Yale University Press.

Hathaway, A. D. (1997). "Marijuana
and Tolerance: Revisiting Becker's
Sources of Control." Deviant Behavior
18(2): 103–24.

Hawkes, T. (1977). *Structuralism and Semiotics*. Berkeley, CA: University of California Press.

Hawley, A. H. (1950). *Human Ecology: A Theory of Community Structure*. New York: Ronald Press Company.

Hawley, A. H. (1968). "Human Ecology." *International Encyclopedia of Social Science* (Vol. 4). New York: Free Press.

Hayden, R. M. (2000). "Rape and Rape Avoidance in Ethno-National Conflicts: Sexual Violence in Liminalized States." *American Anthropologist* 102(1): 27–41.

Hayflick, L. (1994). *How and Why We Age*. New York: Ballantine Books.

Hays, S. (2000). "Constructing the Centrality of Culture—and Deconstructing Sociology?" *Contemporary Sociology* 29(4): 594–602.

He, W, D. Goodkind, and P. Kowal. (2016). "An Aging World: 2015." U.S. Census Bureau. https://www.census.gov/content/dam/Census/library/publications/2016/demo/p95-16-1.pdf.

Healy, M. (2001). "Pieces of the Puzzle." *Los Angeles Times*, May 21. Retrieved 1/10/05, from http://articles.latimes.com/2001/may/21/health/he-533.

Hedegaard, H., S. C. Curtin, and C. Warner. (2018). "Suicide Mortality in the United States, 1999–2017." NCHS data brief, no. 330. Hyattsville, MD: National Center for Health Statistics.

Hegewisch, A. (2018). "The Gender Wage Gap: 2017; Earnings Differences by Gender, Race, and Ethnicity." Institute for Women's Policy Research, Sept. 13. Retrieved from https://iwpr.org/publications/gender-wage-gap-2017/.

Hegewisch, A., and A. Tesfaselassie. (2019). "The Gender Wage Gap by Occupation 2018, and by Race and Ethnicity." Institute for Women's Policy Research. Retrieved from https://iwpr.org/wp-content/uploads/2019/04/C480_The-Gender-Wage-Gap-by-Occupation-2018-1.pdf.

Hegewisch, A., and H. Hartmann. (2014). *Occupational Segregation and the Gender Wage Gap: A Job Half Done*. Washington, DC: Institute for Women's Policy Research

Hegewisch, A., and H. Hartmann. (2019). "The Gender Wage Gap: 2018 Earnings Differences by Race and Ethnicity." Institute for Women's Policy Research. Retrieved from https://iwpr.org/wp-content/uploads/2019/03/C478_Gender-Wage-Gap-in-2018.pdf.

Heidensohn, F. (1985). *Women and Crime*. London: Macmillan.

Heine, F. (2013). "M, F or Blank: 'Third Gender' Official in Germany from November." *Der Spiegel*, August 13. Retrieved from http://www.spiegel.de/international/germany/third-genderoption-to-become-available-on-german-birthcertificates-a-916940.html.

Held, D. (2006). *Models of Democracy*, 3rd ed. Stanford, CA: Stanford University Press.

Hendricks, J. (1992). "Generation and the Generation of Theory in Social Gerontology." *Aging and Human Development* 35: 31–47.

Hendricks, J., and C. D. Hendricks. (1986). *Aging in Mass Society: Myths and Realities*. Boston: Little, Brown.

Henig, R. M. (2010). "What is it about 20-Somethings?" *New York Times* (August 18, 2010). Retrieved from http://www.nytimes.com/2010/08/22/magazine/22Adulthood-t.html?pagewanted=all&_r=0.

Henry, W. E. (1965). *Growing Older: The Process of Disengagement*. New York: Basic Books.

Henry, M., A. Mahathey, T. Morrill, A. Robinson, A. Shivji, and R. Watt. (2018). "The 2018 Annual Homeless Assessment Report (AHAR) to Congress." U.S. Department of Housing and Urban Development. Retrieved from https://files.hudexchange.info/resources/documents/2018-AHAR-Part-1.pdf.

Henslin, J. M., and M. A. Biggs. (1971). "Dramaturgical Desexualization: The Sociology of the Vaginal Examination." In J. M. Henslin, ed., *Studies in the Sociology of Sex*. New York: Appleton-Century-Crofts.

Henslin, J. M., and M. A. Biggs. (1997). "Behavior in Public Places: The Sociology of the Vaginal Examination." In J. M. Henslin, ed., *Down to Earth Sociology: Introductory Readings*, 9th ed. New York: Free Press.

Hentges, B., and Case, K. (2013). "Gender Representations on Disney Channel, Cartoon Network, and Nickelodeon Broadcasts in the United States." *Journal of Children and Media*, 7(3), 319–333.

Herdt, G. (1981). *Guardians of the Flutes: Idioms of Masculinity*. New York: McGraw-Hill.

Herdt, G. (1984). *Ritualized Homosexuality in Melanesia*. Berkeley, CA: University of California Press.

Herdt, G. (1986). *The Sambia: Ritual and Gender in New Guinea*. New York: Holt, Rinehart and Winston.

Herdt, G., and J. Davidson. (1988). "The Sambia 'Urnim-Man': Sociocultural and Clinical Aspects of Gender Formation in Papua, New Guinea." *Archives of Sexual Behavior* 17.

Heritage, J. (1985). *Garfinkel and Ethnomethodology*. New York: Basil Blackwell.

Herrnstein, R. J., and C. Murray. (1994). *The Bell Curve: Intelligence and Class Structure in American Life*. New York: Free Press.

Hertz, T. (2006). "Understanding Mobility in America." Center for American Progress, April 26. Retrieved 12/14, from http://cdn.americanprogress.org/wp-content/uploads/issues/2006/04/Hertz_MobilityAnalysis.pdf.

Hesse-Biber, S. (1997). *Am I Thin Enough Yet? The Cult of Thinness and the Commercialization of Identity*. New York: Oxford University Press.

Hexham, I., and K. Poewe. (1997). *New Religions as Global Cultures*. Boulder, CO: Westview Press.

Hicks, M. J., and S. Devaraj. (2015). "The Myth and the Reality of Manufacturing in America," Retrieved from http://projects.cberdata.org/reports/MfgReality.pdf.

Highton, B. (2017). "Voter Identification Laws and Turnout in the United States," Annual Review of Political Science, Retrieved from http://www.annualreviews.org/doi/abs/10.1146/annurev-polisci-051215-022822.

Hill, K., and D. M. Upchurch. (1995). "Gender Differences in Child Health: Evidence from the Demographic and Health Surveys." *Population and Development Review* 21: 127–51.

Himes, C. L. (1999). "Racial Differences in Education, Obesity, and Health in Later Life." In N. E. Adler, M. Marmot, B. S. McEwen, and J. Stewart, eds., *Socioeconomic Status and Health in Industrial Nations: Social, Psychological, and Biological Pathways. Annals of the New York Academy of Sciences* 896: 370–72.

Hindman, M. (2008). *The Myth of Digital Democracy*, Princeton, NJ: Princeton University Press.

Hinn, S. (2014). "When Women Stopped Coding." National Public Radio, October 21. Retrieved 10/14, from http://www.npr.org/blogs/money/2014/10/21/357629765/when-women-stopped-coding.

Hirschi, T. (1969). *Causes of Delinquency*. Berkeley, CA: University of California Press.

Hirst, P. (1997). "The Global Economy: Myths and Realities." *International Affairs* 73: 409–25.

Hirst, P., and G. Thompson. (1992). "The Problem of 'Globalization': International Economic Relations, National Economic Management, and the Formation of Trading Blocs." *Economy and Society* 24: 357–96.

Hirst, P., and G. Thompson. (1999). *Globalization in Question: The International Economy and the Possibilities of Governance*, rev. ed. Cambridge, UK: Polity Press.

Hitchcock, R. K., ad Beisele, M. (2000). "Introduction." In P. P. Schweitzer, M. Biesele and R. K. Hitchcock, eds., *Hunters and gatherers in the modern world: Conflict, resistance, and self-determinations* (pp. 1–27), New York: Berghahn Books.

Hochschild, A. R. (1975). "Disengagement Theory: A Critique and Proposal." *American Sociological Review* 40: 553–69.

Hochschild, A. R. (1983). *The Managed Heart: Commercialization of Human Feeling*. Berkeley, CA: University of California Press..

Hofstede, G. (1997). *Cultures and Organizations: Software of the Mind*. New York: McGraw-Hill.

Holmes, L. D. (1983). *Other Cultures, Elder Years: An Introduction to Cultural Gerontology*. Minneapolis, MN: Burgess.

Holmes, S. A. (1997). "New Reports Say Minorities Benefit in Fiscal Recovery." *New York Times*, September 30: A1.

Holmstrom, N., ed. (2002) *The Socialist Feminist Project: A Contemporary Reader in Theory and Politics*. New York: New York University Press.

Holton, R. J. (1978). "The Crowd in History: Some Problems of Theory and Method." *Social History* 3: 219–33.

Homans, G. (1950). *The Human Group* New York: Harcourt, Brace.

Hopkins, T. K., and I. Wallerstein. (1996). *The Age of Transition: Trajectory of the World-System, 1945–2025*. London: Zed.

Horowitz, J. M., R. Igielnik, and R. Kochhar. (2020a). "Trends in income and wealth inequality." Pew Research Center, Jan. 9. Retrieved from https://www.pewsocialtrends.org/2020/01/09/trends-in-income-and-wealth-inequality/.

Horowitz, J. M., R. Igielnik, and R. Kochhar. (2020b). "What Americans see as contributors to economic inequality." Pew Research Center, Jan. 9. Retrieved from https://www.pewsocialtrends.org/2020/01/09/what-americans-see-as-contributors-to-economic-inequality/.

Horwitz, A. V. (2013). *Anxiety: A Short History* (Johns Hopkins Biographies of Disease). Baltimore: Johns Hopkins University Press.

Horwitz, A., and J. Wakefield. (2007). *The Loss of Sadness: How Psychiatry has Transformed Normal Sadness into Depressive Disorder*. New York: Oxford University Press.

House Committee on Education and the Workforce. (2014). "The Just in Time Professor: A Staff Report Summarizing eForum Responses on the Working Conditions of Contingent Faculty in Higher Education," Retrieved from http://democrats-edworkforce.house.gov/imo/media/doc/1.24.14-AdjunctEforumReport.pdf.

Huang, J., and A. Damico. (2015). "The Rising Cost of Living Longer: Analysis of Medicare Spending by Age for Beneficiaries in Traditional Medicare." Kaiser Family Foundation, Jan. 14. Retrieved from https://www.kff.org/medicare/report/the-rising-cost-of-living-longer-analysis-of-medicare-spending-by-age-for-beneficiaries-in-traditional-medicare/.

Huang, P. M., P. J. Smock, W. D. Manning, and C. A. Bergstrom-Lynch. (2011.) "He says, she says: Gender and cohabitation." *Journal of Family Issues* 32(7): 876–905.

Huesmann, L. R. (2007). "The Impact of Electronic Media Violence: Scientific Theory and Research." *Journal of Adolescent Health* 41(6): S6–S13.

Huggler, J. (2019). "Germany faces growing calls to delay phase-out of nuclear energy." *The Telegraph*, June 6. Retrieved from https://www.telegraph.co.uk/news/2019/06/06/germany-faces-growing-calls-delay-phase-out-nuclear-energy/.

Human Rights Campaign. (2017). "Marriage Equality Around the World." Retrieved from http://assets.hrc.org//files/assets/resources/WorldMarriageMap.pdf?_ga=2.123142070.07801559.1498332260-746855304.1498332260.

Hume, T. (2016). "Hundreds of Migrants Feared Dead in Latest Sinkings on Mediterranean," CNN, November 18, Retrieved from http://www.cnn.com/2016/11/18/world/mediterranean-refugees-migrant-deaths/index.html.

Humphreys, K. L., M. T. Myint, and C. H. Zeanah. (2020). "Increased risk for family violence during the COVID-19 pandemic." *Pediatrics* 145(4): e20200982.

Hunter, J. D. (1987). *Evangelism: The Coming Generation*. Chicago: University of Chicago Press.

Huntington, S. P. (1993). "The Clash of Civilizations?" *Foreign Affairs* 72(3): 22–49.

Huntington, S. P. (1998). *The Clash of Civilizations and the Remaking of World Order*. New York: Simon and Schuster.

Hursh, D. (2007). "Assessing No Child Left Behind and the Rise of Neoliberal Education Policies." *American Educational Research Journal* 44: 493–518.

Hurtado, A. (1995). "Variation, Combinations, and Evolutions: Latino Families in the United States." In R. Zambrana, ed., *Understanding Latino Families*. Thousand Oaks, CA: Sage.

Hviid, A., J. V. Hansen, M. Frisch, and M. Melbye. (2019). "Measles, Mumps, Rubella Vaccination and Autism: A Nationwide Cohort Study." *Annals of Internal Medicine* 170(8): 513–20.

Hyman, H. H., and E. Singer. (1968). *Readings in Reference Group Theory and Research*. New York: Free Press.

Ianni, F. A. J. (1974). *Black Mafia: Ethnic Succession in Organized Crime*. New York: Simon and Schuster.

Idler, E. L. (1993). "Age Differences in Self-Assessments of Health: Age Changes, Cohort Differences, or Survivorship?" *Journals of Gerontology: Series B: Psychological Sciences and Social Sciences* 48: P289–P300.

Iftikhar, U. (2018). "Nike's 3D Printed Elite Shoe Preparing for a Wider Release." 3D Printing Industry, Nov. 1. Retrieved from https://3dprintingindustry.com/news/nikes-3d-printed-elite-shoe-preparing-for-a-wider-release-142527/.

Illich, I. D. (1983), *Deschooling Society*. New York: Harper and Row.

Illinois State Board of Education. (2010). "Illinois Report Card." Retrieved from https://www.illinoisreportcard.com/Default.aspx.

Imbert, F. (2020). "Here's what happened to the stock market on Monday." CNBC, March 16. Retrieved from https://www.cnbc.com/2020/03/16/what-happened-to-the-stock-market-monday-stocks-plunge-despite-fed-stimulus.html.

Independent Sector. (2016). "Independent Sector's Value of Volunteer Time." Washington, DC: Independent Sector. http://www.independentsector.org/resource/the-value-of-volunteer-time/.

Independent Sector. (2019). "Independent Sector Releases New Value of Volunteer Time of $25.43 Per Hour." Retrieved from https://independentsector.org/news-post/new-value-volunteer-time-2019/.

Inequality.org, (2018). "Income Inequality in the United States." Retrieved from https://inequality.org/facts/income-inequality/#income-inequality.

Inglehart, R. (1997). *Modernization and Postmodernization: Cultural, Economic and Political Change in 43 Societies*. Princeton, NJ: Princeton University Press.

Inglis, D. (2005). *Culture and Everyday Life*. New York: Routledge.

Inman, P. (2020). "Will the coronavirus outbreak derail the global economy?" *Guardian*, Feb. 9. Retrieved from https://www.theguardian.com/news/2020/feb/10/will-the-coronavirus-outbreak-derail-the-global-economy.

Institute for College Access & Success. (2020). "Student Debt and the Class of 2018: 14th Annual Report, September 2019." Retrieved from https://ticas.org/wp-content/uploads/2019/09/classof2018.pdf.

Institute of International Education (IIE). (2016). "Open Doors Report on International Educational Exchange." Retrieved from http://www.iie.org/opendoors.

Institute of International Education (IIE). (2019a). "Fields of Study." Retrieved from https://www.iie.org/Research-and-Insights/Open-Doors/Data/International-Students/Fields-of-Study.

Institute of International Education (IIE). (2019b). "Places of Origin." Retrieved from https://www.iie.org/Research-and-Insights/Open-Doors/Data/International-Students/Places-of-Origin.

Intel. (2019). Annual Report. Retrieved from https://www.sec.gov/Archives/edgar/data/50863/000005086319000007/a12292018q4-10kdocument.htm.

Intergovernmental Panel on Climate Change (IPCC). (2015). "Climate Change 2014: Synthesis Report." Retrieved from http://www.ipcc.ch/pdf/assessment-report/ar5/syr/SYR_AR5_FINAL_full_wcover.pdf.

Intergovernmental Panel on Climate Change (IPCC). (2018). "Impacts of 1.5°C Global Warming on Natural and Human Systems." *IPCC Special Report on Global Warming of 1.5C*, Ch. 3. Retrieved from https://www.ipcc.ch/site/assets/uploads/sites/2/2019/06/SR15.

Intergovernmental Panel on Climate Change (IPCC). (2019a). "Food Security." *Special Report on Climate Change and Land*, Ch. 5. Retrieved from https://www.ipcc.ch/site/assets/uploads/2019/08/2f.-Chapter-5_FINAL.pdf.

Intergovernmental Panel on Climate Change (IPCC). (2019b). "The Ocean and Cryosphere in a Changing Climate: Summary for Policymakers." Retrieved from https://report.ipcc.ch/srocc/pdf/SROCC_FinalDraft_FullReport.pdf.

Intergovernmental Science-Policy Platform on Biodiversity and Ecosystem Services (IPBES). (2019). "UN Report: Nature's Dangerous Decline 'Unprecedented'; Species Extinction Rates 'Accelerating'," Retrieved from https://www.un.org/sustainabledevelopment/blog/2019/05/nature-decline-unprecedented-report/.

International Energy Agency. (2016). "Decoupling of Global Emissions and Economic Growth Confirmed," March 16. Retrieved from https://www.iea.org/news/decoupling-of-global-emissions-and-economic-growth-confirmed.

International Energy Agency. (2019). "World Energy Investment 2019." Retrieved from https://www.iea.org/reports/world-energy-investment-2019.

International Institute for Democracy and Electoral Assistance (IIDEA). (2004). *Voter Turnout in Western Europe since 1945*. Stockholm: International Institute for Democracy and Electoral Assistance.

International Labour Organization (ILO). (2016a). "Decent work for domestic workers: Achievements since the adoption of C189." Retrieved from http://www.ilo.org/wcmsp5/groups/public/—-ed_protect/—-protrav/—-travail/documents/briefingnote/wcms_490778.pdf.

International Labour Organization (ILO). (2016b). "Women at Work: Trends 2016." Retrieved from http://www.ilo.org/wcmsp5/groups/public/—dgreports/—dcomm/—publ/documents/publication/wcms_457317.pdf.

International Labour Organization (ILO). (2018). "Women and Men in the Informal Economy: A Statistical Picture," 3rd ed. Retrieved from https://www.ilo.org/wcmsp5/groups/public/—-dgreports/—-dcomm/documents/publication/wcms_626831.pdf.

International Pollutants Elimination Network (IPEN). (2019). "Plastic Waste Poisons Indonesia's Food Chain: Indonesia Egg Report Infographic." Retrieved from https://ipen.org/sites/default/files/documents/report_infographic_final_r2-tw-5a-01-web.pdf.

International Service for the Acquisition of Agri-biotech Applications (ISAAA). (2016). "Global Status of Commercialized Biotech/GM Crops: 2016." Retrieved from http://www.isaaa.org/resources/publications/briefs/52/executivesummary/default.asp.

International Telecommunication Union (ITU). (2019). "Measuring digital development: Facts and figures 2019." Retrieved from https://www.itu.int/en/ITU-D/Statistics/Documents/facts/FactsFigures2019.pdf.

International Telework Association and Council (ITAC). (2004). "Telework Facts and Figures." Retrieved 1/20/05, from www.telecommute.org/resources/abouttelework.htm.

Internet World Stats. (2017). "Internet users in the world by regions: December 31, 2017." Retrieved from http://www.internetworldstats.com/stats.htm.

Islam, S., and I. Hossain. (2015)."The Global Treadmill of Production and the Environment." In S. Islam and I. Hossain, eds., *Social Justice in the Globalization of Production* (pp. 144–158). London: Palgrave Macmillan.

Ives, M. (2017). "China Limits Waste. 'Cardboard Grannies' and Texas Recyclers Scramble." *New York Times*, November 25. Retrieved from https://www.nytimes.com/2017/11/25/business/energy-environment/china-waste-recycling.html.

Ives, M. (2019). "Recyclers Cringe as Southeast Asia Says It's Sick of the West's Trash." *New York Times*. Retrieved from https://www.nytimes.com/2019/06/07/world/asia/asia-trash.html.

Jacobs, J. (1961). *The Death and Life of Great American Cities*. New York: Random House.

Jacobson, C. K., and T. B. Heaton (1991). "Voluntary childlessness among American men and women in the late 1980s." *Social Biology*, 38(1–2), 79–93.

Jacobson, R. (2014). "Medical Marijuana: How the Evidence Stacks Up." *Scientific American*, May 1. Retrieved 10/26/14, from http://www.scientificamerican.com/article/medical-marijuana-how-the-evidence-stacks-up/.

Jacoby, H. (1995). "The economics of polygyny in Sub-Saharan Africa: Female productivity and the demand for wives in Cote d'Ivoire." *Journal of Political Economy* 103(5): 938–971.

Jacoby, S. (1998). *Modern Manors: Welfare Capitalism since the New Deal*. Princeton, NJ: Princeton University Press.

James, L. (2014). "The Cost of Improper Procedures: Using Police Body Cameras to Reduce Economic and Social Ills." The Public Advocate for the City of New York. August 2014. Retrieved 1/13/15, from http://pubadvocate.nyc.gov/news/2014-08-11/pa-james-releases-report-nypd-body-cameras-proposal.

Jänicke, M. (1991). *The Political System's Capacity for Environmental Policy*. Berlin: Department of Environmental Politics, Free University Berlin.

Jänicke, M., and H. Weidner. (1995). "Successful Environmental Policy: An

Introduction." In M. Jänicke and H. Weidner, eds., *Successful Environmental Policy. A Critical Evaluation of 24 Cases* (pp. 10–26). Berlin: Sigma.

Jarvis, P. (2007). *Globalization, Lifelong Learning and the Learning Society: Sociological Perspectives.* New York: Routledge.

Jencks, C., M. Smith, H. Acland, M. J. Bane, D. Cohen, H. Gintis et al. (1972). *Inequality: A Reassessment of the Effects of Family and School in America.* New York: Basic Books.

Jensen, A. (1979). *Bias in Mental Testing.* New York: Free Press.

Jensen, A. R. (1969). How much can we boost I.Q. and scholastic achievement? *Harvard Educational Review* 33: 1–123.

Jewkes, R. (2002). "Intimate Partner Violence: Causes and Prevention." *The Lancet* 359(9315), 1423–1429.

Jobling, R. (1988). "The Experience of Psoriasis under Treatment." In M. Bury and R. Anderson, eds., *Living with Chronic Illness: The Experience of Patients and Their Families.* London: Unwin Hyman.

Johns Hopkins University & Medicine. (2020). "COVID-19 Dashboard by the Center for Systems Science and Engineering." Retrieved from https://coronavirus.jhu.edu/map.html.

Johnson, D. (2010). "Will Supreme Court Rule for One Dollar, One Vote?" *Campaign for America's Future,* January 9. Retrieved spring 2011, from www.ourfuture.org/blog-entry/2010010109/will-supreme-court-rule-one-dollar-one-vote.

Johnson, K. (2006). "Demographic Trends in Rural and Small Town America." *Institute Reports on Rural America* 1.

Johnson, M., and J. Morton. (1991). *Biology and Cognitive Development: The Case of Face Recognition.* Oxford, UK: Blackwell.

Johnson-Odim, C. (1991). "Common Themes, Different Contexts: Third World Women and Feminism." In C. Mohanty et al., eds., *Third World Women and the Politics of Feminism.* Bloomington, IN: Indiana University Press.

Joint Center for Housing Studies of Harvard University (JCHS). (2013). "America's Rental Housing 2013: Evolving Markets and Needs." Retrieved 12/14, from http://www.jchs.harvard.edu/sites/jchs.harvard.edu/files/jchs_americas_rental_housing_2013_1_0.pdf.

Joint Center for Housing Studies of Harvard University (JCHS). (2014). "State of the Nation's Housing 2014: Key Facts." June 26. Retrieved 12/14, from http://www.jchs.harvard.edu/sites/jchs.harvard.edu/files/son_2014_key_facts.pdf.

Joint Center for Housing Studies of Harvard University (JCHS). (2020). "America's Rental Housing 2020." Retrieved from https://www.jchs.harvard.edu/sites/default/files/Harvard_JCHS_Americas_Rental_Housing_2020.pdf.

Joint Center for Political and Economic Studies. (2011). National roster of black elected officials. Retrieved from http://www.jointcenter.org/research/national-roster-of-black-electedofficials.

Jones, J. (1986). *Labor of Love, Labor of Sorrow: Black Women, Work, and the Family from Slavery to the Present.* New York: Random House.

Jones, N. (2009). "'I Was Aggressive for the Streets, Pretty for the Pictures:' Gender, Difference, and the Inner-City Girl." *Gender and Society* (2009): 89–93.

Jones, S. G. (1995). "Understanding Community in the Information Age." In S. G. Jones, ed., *CyberSociety: Computer-Mediated Communication and Community.* Thousand Oaks, CA: Sage.

Jones, R. P., and D. Cox. (2017). "America's Changing Religious Identity: Findings from the 2016 American Values Atlas." Public Religion Research Institute. Retrieved from https://www.prri.org/wp-content/uploads/2017/09/PRRI-Religion-Report.pdf.

Jordan, M. (2019). "No More Family Separations, Except These 900." *New York Times,* June 30. Retrieved from https://www.nytimes.com/2019/07/30/us/migrant-family-separations.html.

Judge, K. (1995). "Income Distribution and Life Expectancy: A Critical Appraisal." *British Medical Journal* 311: 1282–87.

Juergensmeyer, M. (1993). *The New Cold War? Religious Nationalism Confronts the Secular State.* Berkeley, CA: University of California Press.

Juergensmeyer, M. (1995). "The New Religious State." *Comparative Politics* 27: 379–91.

Juergensmeyer, M. (2001). *Terror in the Mind of God: The Global Rise of Religious Violence.* Berkeley, CA: University of California Press.

Juergensmeyer, M. (2008). *Global Rebellion: Religious Challenges to the Secular State, from Christian Militias to al Qaeda.* Berkeley, CA: University of California Press.

Juergensmeyer, M. (2016) "How ISIS Will End," *The Cairo Review of Global Affairs,* Retrieved from https://www.thecairoreview.com/essays/how-isis-will-end/.

Juergensmeyer, M., D. Griego, and J. Soboslai. (2015). *God in the tumult of the global square: Religion in global civil society.* Berkeley, CA: University of California Press.

Kaeble, D. (2018). "Time Served in State Prison, 2016." U.S. Department of Justice, Bureau of Justice Statistics. Retrieved from https://www.bjs.gov/content/pub/pdf/tssp16.pdf.

Kaeble, D., and L. Glaze. (2016). "Correctional Populations in the United States, 2015." U.S. Department of Justice, Bureau of Justice Statistics. Retrieved from https://www.bjs.gov/content/pub/pdf/cpus15.pdf.

Kalleberg, A. (2003). 'Flexible Firms and Labor Market Segmentation." *Work and Occupations* 30 (2): 154–75.

Kamal, R. (2019). "How does U.S. life expectancy compare to other countries? Peterson-Kaiser Family Foundation Health System Tracker. Retrieved from https://www.healthsystemtracker.org/chart-collection/u-s-life-expectancy-compare-countries/.

Kamenetz, A., and C. Turner. (2020). "Tips for Homeschooling During Coronavirus." *NPR,* March 23. Retrieved from https://www.npr.org/2020/03/23/820228206/6-tips-for-homeschooling-during-coronavirus.

Kann, L., T. McManus, W. A. Harris, S. L. Shanklin, K. H. Flint, B. Queen, R. Lowry, D. Chyen, L. Whittle, J. Thornton, and C. Lim. (2018). "Youth risk behavior surveillance—United States, 2017." *Morbidity and Mortality Weekly Report Surveillance Summaries* 67(8): 1–114.

Kanter, R. M. (1991). "The Future of Bureaucracy and Hierarchy in Organizational Theory." In P. Bourdieu and J. Coleman, eds., *Social Theory for a Changing Society.* Boulder, CO: Westview Press.

Kao, G., K. Joyner, and K. S. Balistreri. (2019). *Interracial Friendships and Romantic Relationships from Adolescence to Adulthood.* New York: Russell Sage.

Kaplan, T., and J. Eligon. (2012). "In Albany, Lawmakers Vote to Limit Public Pensions." *New York Times,* March 14. Retrieved 6/18/12, from www.nytimes.com/2012/03/15/nyregion/plan-to-reduce-pensions-for-new-public-workers-takes-shape-in-albany.html?_r=1&pagewanted=all.

Karraker, A., J. DeLamater, and C. R. Schwartz. (2011). "Sexual Frequency Decline from Midlife to Later Life." *The Journals of Gerontology, Series*

B: Psychological Sciences and Social Sciences 66B(4): 502–12.

Karabel, J. (2005). *The Chosen: The Hidden History of Admission and Exclusion at Harvard, Yale, and Princeton.* Boston: Houghton Mifflin Company.

Karas-Montez, J., and A. Zajacova. (2013). "Explaining the widening education gap in mortality risk among U.S. white women." *Journal of Health and Social Behavior*, 54(2), 165–181.

Karney, B. R., and T. N. Bradbury. (1995). "The longitudinal course of marital quality and stability: A review of theory, methods, and research." *Psychological Bulletin* 118(3): 34.

Kasarda, J. (1993). "Urban Industrial Transition and the Underclass." In W. J. Wilson, ed., *The Ghetto Underclass.* Newbury Park, CA: Sage.

Kassie, E. (2015). "Male Victims of Campus Sexual Assault Speak Out 'We're Up Against a System That's Not Designed To Help Us'." *Huffington Post* (January 27, 2015). Retrieved from http://www.huffingtonpost.com/2015/01/27/male-victims-sexual-assault_n_6535730.html.

Katz, L. F., and A. B. Krueger. (2016). "The Rise and Nature of Alternative Work Arrangements in the United States, 1995-2015," Retrieved from https://krueger.princeton.edu/sites/default/files/akrueger/files/katz_krueger_cws_-_march_29_20165.pdf.

Katz, V. (2014). "Children as Brokers of Their Immigrant Families' Healthcare Connections." *Social Problems*, 61(2), 194–215.

Kaufman, A. (2017)."China Proposes Major Green Investment Amid U.S. Retreat from Climate Change," *Huffington Post*, May 5. Retrieved from http://www.huffingtonpost.com/entry/china-climate-change-xi-jinping_us_5919c109e4b0fe039b3646ca.

Kautsky, J. (1982). *The Politics of Aristocratic Empires.* Chapel Hill, NC: University of North Carolina Press.

Kawachi, I., and B. P. Kennedy. (1997). "Socioeconomic Determinants of Health: Health and Social Cohesion: Why Care about Income Inequality?" *British Medical Journal* 314: 1037.

Kedouri, E. (1992). *Politics in the Middle East.* New York: Oxford University Press.

Keeter, S. (2008). "Young Voters in the 2008 Election." November 12. Retrieved fall 2010, from http://pewresearch.org/pubs/1031/young-voters-in-the-2008-election.

Kelley, J., and M. D. R. Evans. (1995). "Class and Class Conflict in Six Western Nations." *American Review of Sociology* 60(2): 157–78.

Kelling, G. L., and C. M. Coles. (1997). *Fixing Broken Windows: Restoring Order and Reducing Crime in Our Communities.* New York: Free Press.

Kelly, M. P. (1992). *Colitis: The Experience of Illness.* London: Routledge.

Kenkel, D., D. Lillard, and A. Mathios. (2006). "The Roles of High School Completion and GED Receipt in Smoking and Obesity." *Journal of Labor Economics* 24(3): 635–60.

Kennedy, S., and C.A. Fitch. (2012). "Measuring cohabitation and family structure in the United States: Assessing the impact of new data from the Current Population Survey." *Demography* 49(4): 1479–98.

Kennedy, S., and F. F. Furstenberg Jr. (2013). "The Changing Transition to Adulthood in the U.S.: Trends in Demographic Role Transitions and Age Norms Since 2000." Population Association of America 2013 Annual Meeting. Retrieved from http://paa2013.princeton.edu/papers/132789.

Kenworthy, L., and M. Malami. (1999). "Gender Inequality in Political Representation: A Worldwide Comparative Analysis." *Social Forces* 78(1): 235–69.

Kessler, G. (2014). "Does the NRA really have more than 4.5 million members?" *The Washington Post,* February 8. Retrieved 12/14, from http://www.washingtonpost.com/blogs/fact-checker/post/does-the-nra-really-have-more-than-45-million-members/2013/02/07/06047c10-7164-11e2-ac36-3d8d9dcaa2e2_blog.html.

Kharas, H., K. Hamel, and M. Hofer. (2018). "Rethinking Global Poverty Reduction in 2019." Brookings Institution, December 13. Retrieved from https://www.brookings.edu/blog/future-development/2018/12/13/rethinking-global-poverty-reduction-in-2019/.

Kibbey, J. (2016). "The Sustainable Apparel Coalition and the Higg Index: A New Approach for the Apparel and Footwear Industries." In R. P. Appelbaum and N. Lichtenstein (eds.), *Achieving Workers' Rights in the Global Economy* (pp. 229–38). Ithaca, NY: Cornell University Press.

Kiecolt, K. J., and N. M. Nelson. (1991). "Evangelicals and Party Realignment, 1976–1988." *Social Science Quarterly* 72: 552–69.

Kiger, P. (2012). "Boomers' 'Anxiety Index' High, Voter Survey Reveal Retirement Prospects Top Economic Issues, Concerns." American Association of Retired Persons (August 8, 2012). Retrieved 8/09/12, from www.aarp.org/politics-society/government-elections/info-08-2012/aarp-2012-voter-survey.html?cmp=RDRCT-VTR50PL_JUL30_012.

Kilachand, S. (2012). "Forbes History: The Original 1987 List of International Billionaires." *Forbes*, March 21. Retrieved from https://www.forbes.com/sites/seankilachand/2012/03/21/forbes-history-the-original-1987-list-of-international-billionaires/#3f38c6e1447e.

Kilbourne, J. (2010). *Killing Us Softly 4: Advertising's Image of Women.* Media Education Foundation.

King, G., R. O. Keohane, and S. Verba. (1994). *Designing Social Inquiry: Scientific Inference in Qualitative Research.* Princeton, NJ: Princeton University Press.

King, N. R. (1984). "Exploitation and Abuse of Older Family Members: An Overview of the Problem." In J. J. Cosa, ed., *Abuse of the Elderly.* Lexington, MA: Lexington Books.

Kinsey, A. C. (1953). *Sexual Behavior in the Human Female.* Philadelphia: Saunders.

Kinsey, A. C., W. R. Pomeroy, and C. E. Martin. (1948). *Sexual Behavior in the Human Male.* Philadelphia: Saunders.

Kinsley, D. (1982). *Hinduism: A Cultural Perspective.* Englewood Cliffs, NJ: Prentice Hall.

Kirk, C. (2014). "Publicly Funded Schools That Are Allowed to Teach Creationism," *Slate*, January 26. Retrieved 6/4/15, from http://www.slate.com/articles/health_and_science/science/2014/01/creationism_in_public_schools_mapped_where_tax_money_supports_alternatives.html.

Kjekshus, H. (1977). *Ecology, Control, and Economic Development in East African History.* Berkeley, CA: University of California Press.

Klinenberg, E. (2012a). *Going Solo: The Extraordinary Rise and Surprising Appeal of Living Alone.* New York: Penguin.

Klinenberg, E. (2012b). "One's a Crowd." *New York Times,* February 4. Retrieved 9/21/12, from www.nytimes.com/2012/02/05/opinion/sunday/living-alone-means-being-social.html?pagewanted=print.

Kling, R. (1996). "Computerization at Work." In R. Kling, ed., *Computers and Controversy,* 2nd ed. New York: Academic Press.

Kluckhohn, C. (1949). *Mirror for Man.* Tucson, AZ: University of Arizona Press.

Knodel, J. (2006). "Parents of Persons with AIDS: Unrecognized Contributions and Unmet Needs." *Journal of Global Ageing* 4: 46–55.

Knoke, D. (1990). *Political Networks: The Structural Perspective.* New York: Cambridge University Press.

Knop, K., R. Michaels, and A. Riles. (2012). "From Multiculturalism to Technique: Feminism, Culture, and the Conflict of Laws Style." *Stanford Law Review* 64: 589–656.

Kobrin, S. J. (1997). "Electronic Cash and the End of National Markets." *Foreign Policy* 107: 65–77.

Kochanek, K.D., R. N. Anderson, and E. Arias. (2020). "Changes in life expectancy at birth, 2010–2018." NCHS Health E-Stat. Retrieved from https://www.cdc.gov/nchs/data/hestat/life-expectancy/life-expectancy-2018.htm#Table1.

Kochhar, R. (2018). "The American middle class is stable in size, but losing ground financially to upper-income families." Pew Research Center, Sept. 6. Retrieved from https://www.pewresearch.org/fact-tank/2018/09/06/the-american-middle-class-is-stable-in-size-but-losing-ground-financially-to-upper-income-families/.

Kohut, A. (2008). "Post-Election Perspectives." November 13. Pew Research Center for the People and the Press. Retrieved fall 2010, from http://pewresearch.org/pubs/1039/post-election-perspectives.

Kollock, P., and M. A. Smith. (1996). "Managing the Virtual Commons: Cooperation and Conflict in Computer Communities." In S. Herring, ed., *Computer-Mediated Communication.* Amsterdam: John Benjamins.

Korzeniewicz, R. P., and T. P. Moran. (2012). *Unveiling Inequality: A World Historical Perspective.* New York: Russell Sage Foundation.

Kosciw, J. G., E. A. Greytak, N. M. Giga, C. Villenas, and D. J. Danischewski. (2016). *The 2015 National School Climate Survey: The Experiences of Lesbian, Gay, Bisexual, Transgender, and Queer Youth in Our Nation's Schools.* New York: GLSEN.

Kosmin, B. A., E. Mayer, and A. Keysar. (2001). "American Religious Identification Survey (ARIS)." December 19. New York: CUNY Graduate Center. Retrieved 1/3/05, from www.gc.cuny.edu/studies/aris.pdf (site discontinued).

Kotlikoff, L. J., and S. Burns. (2012). *The Clash of Generations: Saving Ourselves, Our Kids, and Our Economy.* Cambridge, MA: MIT Press.

Kotnik, P., M. E. Sakinç, and D. Guduraš. (2018). "Executive compensation in Europe: Realized gains from stock-based pay." Institute for New Economic Thinking, July 13. Retrieved from https://www.ineteconomics.org/uploads/papers/WP_78-KotnikSakincGudurasFinal.pdf.

Kozol, J. (1991). *Savage Inequalities: Children in America's Schools.* New York: Crown.

Kozol, J. (1995). *Amazing Grace: The Lives of Children and the Conscience of a Nation.* New York: Crown.

Kreager, D. A., S. E. Cavanagh, J. Yen, and M. Yu. (2014). "Where Have All the Good Men Gone? Gendered Interactions in Online Dating," *Journal of Marriage and Family* 76(April): 387–410. Retrieved from http://onlinelibrary.wiley.com/store/10.1111/jomf.12072/asset/jomf12072.pdf?v=1&t=i2yxzy00&s=963a085cd904a925749258368c160e356e827768.

Krebs, C. P. et al. (2007). "The Campus Sexual Assault Study." Bureau of Justice Statistics, National Institute of Justice, RTI Project Number 0209487. Retrieved 12/14, from https://www.ncjrs.gov/pdffiles1/nij/grants/221153.pdf.

Kristof, N. D. (2010). "The World Capital of Killing." *New York Times,* February 6.

Kristof, N. D., and S. WuDunn. (2009). *Half the Sky: Turning Oppression into Opportunity for Women Worldwide.* New York: Knopf.

Kristof, N. (2020). "America's True Covid Toll Already Exceeds 100,000." *New York Times,* May 13. Retrieved from https://www.nytimes.com/2020/05/13/opinion/coronavirus-us-deaths.html.

Krogstad, J. M. (2014). "Hispanics only group to see its poverty rate decline and incomes rise," Pew Research Center, Fact Tank, September 19. Retrieved 12/14, from http://www.pewresearch.org/fact-tank/2014/09/19/hispanics-only-group-to-see-its-poverty-rate-decline-and-incomes-rise/.

Krogstad, J. M. (2016). "Key facts about how the U.S. Hispanic population is changing," Pew Research Center, Sept. 8. Retrieved from http://www.pewresearch.org/fact-tank/2016/09/08/key-facts-about-how-the-u-s-hispanic-population-is-changing/.

Krogstad, J. M., J. S. Passel, and D. Cohn. (2017). "5 facts about illegal immigration to the U.S.," Pew Research Center, April 27. Retrieved from http://www.pewresearch.org/fact-tank/2017/04/27/5-facts-about-illegal-immigration-in-the-u-s

Krogstad, J. M., K. J. Starr, and A. Sandstrom. (2017). "Key findings about Puerto Rico," Pew Research Center, March 29. Retrieved from http://www.pewresearch.org/fact-tank/2017/03/29/key-findings-about-puerto-rico/.

Kroll, L. and K. A. Dolan, eds. (2019a). "Billionaires: The Richest People in the World. *Forbes.* Retrieved from https://www.forbes.com/billionaires/#Cornell767ff73d251c.

Kroll, L., and K. A. Dolan, eds. (2019b). "The Forbes 400: The Definitive Ranking of the Wealthiest Americans." *Forbes,* Oct. 2. Retrieved from https://www.forbes.com/forbes-400/#42d02e737e2f.

Kross, E., P. Verduyn, E. Demiralp, J. Park, D. S. Lee, N. Lin, H. Shablack, J. Jonides, and O. Ybarra. (2013). "Facebook Use Predicts Declines in Subjective Well-being in Young Adults." *PLOS One.* Retrieved from http://www.plosone.org/article/info%3Adoi%2F10.1371%2Fjournal.pone.0069841.

Kulish, N. (2011). "As Scorn for Vote Grows, Protests Surge Around the Globe." *New York Times,* September 27. Retrieved from http://www.nytimes.com/2011/09/28/world/as-scorn-for-vote-grows-protests-surge-around-globe.html?pagewanted=all.

Kumagai, F. (2010). "Forty Years of Family Change in Japan: A Society Experiencing Population Aging and Declining Fertility." *Journal of Comparative Family Studies* 41(4): 581–610.

Kuperberg, A., and A. M. Walker. (2018). "Heterosexual college students who hookup with same-sex partners." *Archives of Sexual Behavior* 47(5). 1387–1403.

Kwong, R. (2012). "Terry Gou: Managing "1m animals," Jan. 20, *Financial Times.* Retrieved from http://blogs.ft.com/beyond-brics/2012/01/20/terry-gou-managing-1-million-animals/.

Kyckelhahn, T. (2015). "Justice Expenditure And Employment Extracts, 2012," Bureau of Justice Statistics, Retrieved from https://www.bjs.gov/index.cfm?ty=pbdetail&iid=5239.

Lacy, K. R. (2007). *Blue-Chip Black: Race, Class, and Status in the New Black Middle Class.* Berkeley, CA: University of California Press.

Laing, R. D. (1971). *Self and Others.* London: Tavistock.

Lachs, M., and K. Pillemer. (2015). "Elder Abuse." *New England Journal of Medicine,* 373, 1947–56.

Lalich, J. (2004). *Bounded Choice: True Believers and Charismatic Cults.* Berkeley, CA: University of California Press.

LaMagna, M. (2018). "Who is really middle class in America? This chart shows just how much family size matters." MarketWatch. Retrieved from https://www.marketwatch.com/story/who-is-really-middle-class-in-america-this-chart-shows-just-how-much-family-size-matters-2018-12-28.

Lamb, M. E. (2012.) "Mothers, fathers, families, and circumstances: Factors affecting children's adjustment." *Applied Developmental Science* 16(2): 98–111.

Lamb, M. E. and C. Lewis. (2013). *Father-Child Relationships. Handbook of Father Involvement: Multidisciplinary Perspectives*, 2, pp.119–135.

Lam, B. (2017). "The Department of Labor Accuses Google of Gender Pay Discrimination." *The Atlantic* (April 7, 2017), Retrieved from https://www.theatlantic.com/business/archive/2017/04/dol-google-pay-discrimination/522411/.

Lamidi, E. and W. D. Manning. (2016). "Mariage and Cohabitation Experiences among Young Adults." Family Profiles, Bowling Green, OH: National Center for Family & Marriage Research. Retrieved from https://magic.piktochart.com/output/15665834-lamidi-marriage-cohabitation-young-adults-fp-16-17

Land, K. C., G. Deane, and J. R. Blau. (1991). "Religious Pluralism and Church Membership." *American Sociological Review* 56: 237–49.

Landale, N., and K. Fennelly. (1992). "Informal Unions among Mainland Puerto Ricans: Cohabitation or an Alternative to Legal Marriage?" *Journal of Marriage and Family* 54: 269–80.

Landry, B., and K. Marsh. (2011). "The Evolution of the New Black Middle Class." *Annual Review of Sociology* 37: 373–94.

Lane, J. (2018). *The Digital Street*. New York: Oxford University Press.

Lareau, A. (2011). *Unequal Childhoods: Class, Race and Family Life*, 2nd ed. Berkeley, CA: University of California Press.

LaRossa, R., and D. C. Reitzes. (1993). "Symbolic interactionism and family studies." In P. G. Boss, W. J. Doherty, R. LaRossa, W. R. Schumm, and S. K. Steinmetz (Eds.), *Sourcebook of family theories and methods: A contextual approach* (pp. 135-163). New York: Plenum Press.

Latner, J. D., and A. J. Stunkard. (2003). "Getting Worse: The Stigmatization of Obese Children." *Obesity Research* 11: 452–56.

Lattman, P. (2010). "3 Women Claim Bias at Goldman." *New York Times*, September 15. Retrieved spring 2011, from www.nytimes.com/2010/09/16/business/16bias.html.

Laumann, E. O., J. H. Gagnon, R. T. Michael, and S. Michaels. (1994). *The Social Organization of Sexuality: Sexual Practices in the United States.* Chicago: University of Chicago Press.

Laumann, E. O., S. A. Leitsch, and L. J. Waite. (2008). "Elder Mistreatment in the United States: Prevalence Estimates from a Nationally Representative Study." *Journal of Gerontology: Social Sciences* 63: 248–54.

Lawrence, B. B. (1989). *Defenders of God: The Fundamentalist Revolt Against the Modern Age.* San Francisco: Harper and Row.

Layte, R. (2011). "The association between income inequality and mental health: Testing status anxiety, social capital, and neo-materialist explanations." *European Sociological Review.* doi:10.1093/esr/jcr012.

Leach, E. (1976). *Culture and Communication: The Logic By Which Symbols Are Connected.* New York: Cambridge University Press.

Leaper, C., and R. S. Bigler. (2018). "Societal causes and consequences of gender typing of children's toys." In E. S. Weisgram and L. M. Dinella, eds., *Gender Typing of Children's Toys: How Early Play Experiences Impact Development* (pp. 287–308). Washington, DC: American Psychological Association.

Leckart, S. (2015). "The Hackathon Fast Track, from Campus to Silicon Valley." *New York Times* (April 6, 2015), Retrieved from https://www.nytimes.com/2015/04/12/education/edlife/the-hackathon-fast-track-from-campus-to-silicon-valley.html.

Ledford, H. (2016). "UK bioethicists eye designer babies and CRISPR cows." *Nature,* September 30, 2016. Retrieved from http://www.nature.com/news/uk-bioethicists-eye-designer-babies-and-crispr-cows-1.20713.

Lee, C., V. Tsenkova, and D. Carr. (2014). "Childhood trauma and metabolic syndrome in men and women." *Social Science & Medicine* 105: 122–30.

Lee, G. (1982). *Family Structure and Interaction: A Comparative Analysis,* 2nd ed. Minneapolis: University of Minnesota Press.

Lee, J. and M. Zhou. (2014). "From Unassimilable to Exceptional: The Rise of Asian Americans and 'Stereotype Promise'." *New Diversities* 16(1): 7–22. Retrieved 3/01/15, from http://newdiversities.mmg.mpg.de/wp-content/uploads/2014/11/2014_16-01_02_Lee.pdf.

Lee, W. (2019). "People Spend More Time on Mobile Devices than TV, Firm Says." *Los Angeles Times,* June 5. Retrieved from https://www.latimes.com/business/la-fi-ct-people-spend-more-time-on-mobile-than-tv-20190605-story.html.

Leif, D., I. Barbopuolos, I. Nilsson, L. Holmber, M. Thulin, M. Wendeblsad, L. Anden, and E. Davidsson. (2012). "Sweden's Largest Facebook Study," Gothenburg Research Institute. Retrieved from https://gupea.ub.gu.se/bitstream/2077/28893/1/gupea_2077_28893_1.pdf.

Leiss, W. (1994). *The Domination of Nature.* New York: Braziller.

Lemert, E. (1972). *Human Deviance, Social Problems, and Social Control.* Englewood Cliffs, NJ: Prentice-Hall.

Lemoyne, T., and T. Buchanan. (2011). "Does 'Hovering' Matter? Helicopter Parenting and Its Effect on Well-Being." *Sociological Spectrum* 31(4): 399–418.

Lenhart, A. (2015). "Teens, Social Media, and Technology Overview 2015," Retrieved from http://www.pewinternet.org/2015/04/09/teens-social-media-technology-2015/.

Lenhart, A. et al. (2015). "Teens, Technology, and Friendships." Retrieved from http://www.pewinternet.org/files/2015/08/Teens-and-Friendships-FINAL2.pdf.

Lenzer, R. (2011). "The Top 0.1% of the Nation Earn Half of All Capital Gains." *Forbes,* November 20. Retrieved 12/14, from http://www.forbes.com/sites/robertlenzner/2011/11/20/the-top-0-1-of-the-nation-earn-half-of-all-capital-gains/.

Leonhardt, D. (2014). "Is College Worth It? Clearly, New Data Say," *New York Times,* May 27. Retrieved 12/14, from http://mobile.nytimes.com/2014/05/27/upshot/is-college-worth-it-clearly-new-data-say.html?_r=1.

Lesane-Brown, C. (2006). "A Review of Race Socialization within Black Families." *Developmental Review* 26: 400–426.

Lesane-Brown, C. L., T. N. Brown, C. H. Caldwell, and R. M. Sellers. (2005). "The Comprehensive Race Socialization Inventory." *Journal of Black Studies* 36(2): 163–190

Lessig, L. (2011). *Republic, Lost: How Money Corrupts Congress—and a Plan to Stop It.* Mission Viejo, CA: Twelve.

Lcupp, G. P. (1995). *Male Colors: The Construction of Homosexuality in Tokugawa Japan.* Berkeley, CA: University of California Press.

LeVay, S. (1996). *Queer Science: The Uses and Abuses of Research into Homosexuality.* Cambridge, MA: MIT Press.

LeVay, S. (2011). *Gay, straight, and the reason why: The science of sexual orientation.* New York, NY: Oxford.

LeVine, R., and D. T. Campbell. (1972). *Ethnocentrism: Theories of Conflict,*

Attitudes and Group Behavior. New York: Wiley.

Levy, B., M.D. Slade, S. R. Kunkel, and S. V. Kasl. (2002). "Longevity Increased by Positive Self-Perceptions of Aging." *Journal of Personality and Social Psychology* 83(2): 261–70.

Levy, K. E. C. (2014). The Automation of Compliance: Techno-Legal Regulation in the United States Trucking Industry. Dissertation, Princeton University Department of Sociology.

Lewin, T. (2012). College of Future Could Be Come One, Come All. *New York Times*, November 19. Retrieved 8/26/13, from http://www.nytimes.com/2012/11/20/education/colleges-turn-to-crowd-sourcing-courses.html?pagewanted=all.

Lewis, J. (2018). "Economic Impact of Cybercrime—No Slowing Down." McAfee: Santa Clara, CA. Retrieved from https://www.mcafee.com/enterprise/en-us/assets/reports/restricted/rp-economic-impact-cybercrime.pdf.

Lewis, K. (2013). "The Limits of Racial Prejudice." *Proceedings of the National Academy of Sciences,* 110(47), 18814–18819.

Lewis, O. (1968). "The Culture of Poverty." In D. P. Moynihan, ed., *On Understanding Poverty: Perspectives from the Social Sciences*. New York: Basic Books.

Li, Z., and J. Dalaker. (2019). "Poverty Among Americans Aged 65 and Older." Congressional Research Service, July 1. Retrieved from https://fas.org/sgp/crs/misc/R45791.pdf.

Lichtenstein, N. (2006). "Wal-Mart: A Template for Twenty-First-Century Capitalism." In N. Lichtenstein, ed., *Wal-Mart: The Face of Twenty-First-Century Capitalism*. New York: New Press.

Lichtenstein, N. (2010). *The Retail Revolution: How Wal-Mart Created a Brave New World of Business*. New York: Metropolitan Books.

Lichtenstein, N. (2012a). "A New Era for Walmart Workers?" *Dissent* October 11. Retrieved 10/1/15, from http://www.dissentmagazine.org/blog/a-new-era-for-wal-mart-workers.

Lichtenstein, N. (2012b). "Wal-Mart, John Tate, and Their Anti-Union America." In N. Lichtenstein, ed., *The Right and Labor in America*. Philadelphia: University of Pennsylvania Press

Lightfoot-Klein, H. (1989). *Prisoners of Ritual: An Odyssey into Female Genital Circumcision in Africa*. New York: Haworth.

Lin, A. C., and D. R. Harris, eds. (2010). *The Colors of Poverty: Why Racial and Ethnic Disparities Persist*. New York: Russell Sage Foundation.

Lindau, S. T., P. Schumm, E. O. Laumann, W. Levinson, C. A. O'Muircheartaigh, and L. J. Waite. (2007). "A Study of Sexuality and Health among Older Adults in the United States." *New England Journal of Medicine* 357: 762–74.

Linden, E. (2019). "How Scientists Got Climate Change So Wrong." *New York Times*, Nov. 8. Retrieved from https://www.nytimes.com/2019/11/08/opinion/sunday/science-climate-change.html?smid=nytcore-ios-share.

Link, T. (2017). "The Total Cost of the 2016 Election Was Nearly $6.5 Billion: Report," *Salon*, April 15, Retrieved from http://www.salon.com/2017/04/15/the-total-cost-of-the-2016-election-was-nearly-6-5-billion-report/.

Lipka, M. (2017). "Muslims and Islam: Key findings in the U.S. and around the World," Pew Research Center, Feb. 27, Retrieved from http://www.pewresearch.org/fact-tank/2017/02/27/muslims-and-islam-key-findings-in-the-u-s-and-around-the-world/.

Lipka, M. (2019). "5 facts about religion in Canada." Pew Research Center, July 1. Retrieved from https://www.pewresearch.org/fact-tank/2019/07/01/5-facts-about-religion-in-canada/.

Lipsitz, G. (1997). *Dangerous Crossroads: Popular Music, Postmodernism and the Poetics of Place*. London: Verso.

Lipsky, D. (2003). *Absolutely American: Four Years at West Point*. Boston: Houghton Mifflin.

Liptak, A. (2010). "Justices, 5–4, Reject Corporate Spending Limit." *New York Times*, January 21. Retrieved spring 2011, from www.nytimes.com/2010/01/22/us/politics/22scotus.html.

Lister, T. (2017). "Islamic State 2.0: As the Caliphate Crumbles, ISIS Evolves," *CNN*, March 27, Retrieved from http://www.cnn.com/2017/03/22/europe/isis-2-0/

Livingston, G. (2015). "Childlessness Falls, Family Size Grows Among Highly Educated Women." Washington, D.C.: Pew Research Center. Retrieved from http://www.pewsocialtrends.org/files/2015/05/2015-05-07_children-ever-born_FINAL.pdf.

Livingston, G. (2016). "Among 41 nations, U.S. is the Outlier When it Comes to Paid Parental Leave." Pew Research Group (September 26, 2016), Retrieved from http://www.pewresearch.org/fact-tank/2016/09/26/u-s-lacks-mandated-paid-parental-leave/.

Livingston, G. (2018). "Stay-at-home moms and dads account for about one-in-five U.S. parents." Pew Research Center, Sept. 24. Retrieved from https://www.pewresearch.org/fact-tank/2018/09/24/stay-at-home-moms-and-dads-account-for-about-one-in-five-u-s-parents/.

Livingston, G., and A. Brown. (2017). "Intermarriage in the U.S. 50 Years After Loving v. Virginia." (Pew Research Center, May 18. Retrieved from https://www.pewsocialtrends.org/2017/05/18/intermarriage-in-the-u-s-50-years-after-loving-v-virginia/.

Locke, J., and E. Pascoe. (2000). "Can a Sense of Community Flourish in Cyberspace?" *Guardian*, March 11.

Loe, M. (2004). *The Rise of Viagra: How the Little Blue Pill Changed Sex in America*. New York: New York University Press.

Lofquist, D. (2011). "Same-Sex Couple Households." *American Community Survey Briefs*. Washington, DC: U.S. Department of the Census. Retrieved 9/20/12, from www.census.gov/prod/2011pubs/acsbr10-03.pdf.

Logan, J. R., and H. L. Molotch. (1987). *Urban Fortunes: The Political Economy of Place*. Berkeley, CA: University of California Press.

Long, C. (2020). "Parents-Turned-Homeschoolers Agree: Teachers Are Amazing!" neaToday, March 19. Retrieved from http://neatoday.org/2020/03/19/homeschooling-during-coronavirus-outbreak/.

Lopez, G. and K. Bialik. (2017). "Key findings About U.S. Immigrants," Pew Research Center, May 3, Retrieved from http://www.pewresearch.org/fact-tank/2017/05/03/key-findings-about-u-s-immigrants/.

Loprest, P. (1999). "Families Who Left Welfare: Who Are They and How Are They Doing?" Washington, DC: Urban Institute. Retrieved 1/03/05, from www.urban.org/Template.cfm?NavMenuID=24&template=/TaggedContent/iewPublication.cfm&PublicationID=7297.

Lorber, J. (1994). *Paradoxes of Gender*. New Haven, CT: Yale University Press.

Lorber, J. (1996). "Beyond the Binaries: Depolarizing the Categories of Sex, Sexuality, and Gender." *Sociological Inquiry*, 66(2), 143–160.

Lowe, G. S. (1987). *Women in the Administrative Revolution: The Feminization of Clerical Work*. Toronto: University of Toronto Press.

Luckerson, V. (2015). "Target Will Stop Separating "Girls" Toys From "Boys" Toys in Stores." *Time*, January 29. Retrieved from http://time.com/3989850/target-gender-signs/.

Lucy, F. (1997). "Linguistic Relativity." *Annual Review of Anthropology* 26: 291–312.

Lunney, J.R., J. Lynn, D. J. Foley, S. Lipson, and J. M. Guralnik. (2003). "Patterns of functional decline at the end of life." *Journal of the American Medical Association* 289(18): 2387–92

Luo, Y., J. Xu, E. Granberg, and W. M. Wentworth. (2011). "A Longitudinal Study of Social Status, Perceived Discrimination, and Physical and Emotional Health among Older Adults." *Research on Aging.* Advance online publication doi: 10.1177/0164027511426151.

Lyons, R. (2011). "The Spread of Evidence-Poor Medicine via Flawed Social-Network Analysis." *Statistics, Politics, and Policy* 2(1), Article 2.

Lyotard, J. (1985). *The Post-Modern Condition: A Report on Knowledge.* Minneapolis: University of Minnesota Press.

Lynd, R. S. and H. M. Lynd. (1929). *Middletown: A Study in Contemporary American Culture.* London: Constable.

Lytton, H., and Romney, D. M. (1991). "Parents' Differential Socialization of Boys and Girls: A Meta-analysis." *Psychological Bulletin,* 109(2), 267.

MacEnoin, D., and A. al-Shahi, eds. (1983). *Islam in the Modern World.* New York: St. Martin's Press.

Maddox, G. L. (1965). "Fact and Artifact: Evidence Bearing on Disengagement from the Duke Geriatrics Project." *Human Development* 8: 117–30.

Maddox, G. L. (1970). "Themes and Issues in Sociological Theories of Human Aging." *Human Development* 13: 17–27.

Madigan, F. C. (1957). "Are Sex Mortality Differentials Biologically Caused?" *Millbank Memorial Fund Quarterly* 25: 202–23.

Mahalik, J. R., S. M. Burns, and M. Syzdek. (2007). "Masculinity and Perceived Normative Health Behaviors as Predictors of Men's Health Behaviors." *Social Science and Medicine* 64(11): 2201–209.

Mahler, D. G., C. Lakner, R. A. C. Aguilar, and H. Wu. (2020). "The impact of COVID-19 (Coronavirus) on global poverty: Why Sub-Saharan Africa might be the region hardest hit." World Bank, April 20. Retrieved from https://blogs.worldbank.org/opendata/impact-covid-19-coronavirus-global-poverty-why-sub-saharan-africa-might-be-region-hardest.

Malone, C. (2106). "Clinton Couldn't Win Over White Women," *FiveThirtyEight,* Nov. 9, Retrieved from https://fivethirtyeight.com/features/clinton-couldnt-win-over-white-women/.

Malthus, T. (2003; orig. 1798). *Essay on the Principle of Population: A Norton Critical Edition,* rev. ed. (P. Appleman, ed.). New York: W. W. Norton.

Manchin, R. (2004). "Religion in Europe: Trust Not Filling the Pews." Gallup Poll, September 21. Retrieved fall 2010, from www.gallup.com/poll/13117/religion-europe-trust-filling-pews.aspx.

Mandavilli, A. (2019). "H.I.V. Is Reported Cured in a Second Patient, a Milestone in the Global AIDS Epidemic." *New York Times,* March 4. Retrieved from https://www.nytimes.com/2019/03/04/health/aids-cure-london-patient.html.

Manjoo, F. (2008). *True Enough: Learning to Live in a Post-Fact Society.* New York: Wiley.

Manning, W. D. (2015). "Cohabitation and Child Wellbeing." *The Future of Children* 25(2): 51–66.

Manning, J., and I. A. Brudnick. (2020). "Women in Congress: Statistics and Brief Overview." Congressional Research Service, January 15. Retrieved from https://fas.org/sgp/crs/misc/R43244.pdf.

Manning, J. T., K. Koukourakis, and D. A. Brodie. (1997). "Fluctuating Asymmetry, Metabolic Rate and Sexual Selection in Human Males." *Evolution and Human Behavior* 18(1): 15–21.

Manning, W. D., and S. L. Brown. (2011). "The Demography of Unions among Older Americans, 1980–Present: A Family Change Approach." In R. A. Settersten Jr., and J. L. Angel, eds. *Handbook of Sociology of Aging* (pp. 193–212). New York: Springer.

Manpower Inc. (2014). "About ManPower Group." Retrieved from www.manpowergroup.com/about/about.cfm.

Manton K. G., X. Gu, and G. R. Lowrimore. (2008). "Cohort Changes in Active Life Expectancy in the U.S. Elderly Population: Experience from the 1982–2004 National Long-Term Care Survey." *Journals of Gerontology: Series B: Psychological Sciences and Social Sciences* 63: P269–81.

Mare, R. (1991). "Five Decades of Educational Assortative Mating." *American Sociological Review,* 56(1).

Marsden, P. (1987). "Core Discussion Networks of Americans." *American Sociological Review* 52: 122–31.

Marsden, P., and N. Lin. (1982). *Social Structure and Network Analysis.* Beverly Hills, CA: Sage.

Marsh, K., W. A. Darity Jr., P. N. Cohen, L. M. Casper, and D. Salters. (2007). "The Emerging Black Middle Class: Single and Living Alone." *Social Forces* 86: 735–62.

Marshall, T. H. (1973). *Class, Citizenship, and Social Development: Essays by T. H. Marshall.* Westport, CT: Greenwood Press.

Martel, J. (2017). "What members of the Mega-Rich Trump Administration Are Worth," *Bankrate,* April, Retrieved from http://www.bankrate.com/lifestyle/celebrity-money/trumps-cabinet-is-rich-in-millionaires-and-billionaires-see-their-net-worth/#slide=1.

Martin, G. (1986). *Socialist Feminism: The First Decade, 1966–76.* Seattle: Red Letter Press.

Martin, J. A., B. E. Hamilton, S. J. Ventura, M. J. K. Osterman, E. C. Wilson, T. J. Mathews, and Division of Vital Statistics. (2013). "Births: Final data for 2011." *National Vital Statistics Reports* 62(1). Hyattsville, MD: National Center for Health Statistics. Retrieved 10/14, from http://www.cdc.gov/nchs/data/nvsr/nvsr62/nvsr62_01.pdf.

Martin J. A., B. E. Hamilton, M. J. K. Osterman, A. K. Driscoll, and T. J. Mathews. (2017). "Births: Final data for 2015." *National Vital Statistics Reports* 66(1). Hyattsville, MD: National Center for Health Statistics. Retrieved from https://www.cdc.gov/nchs/data/nvsr/nvsr66/nvsr66_01.pdf.

Martin, J.A., B. E. Hamilton, M. J. K. Osterman, A. K. Driscoll. (2019). "Births: Final Data for 2018." *National Vital Statistics Reports* 68(13). Retrieved from https://www.cdc.gov/nchs/data/nvsr/nvsr68/nvsr68_13-tables-508.pdf#I07.

Martin, J. A., and M. J. Osterman. (2019). "Is Twin Childbearing on the Decline? Twin Births in the United States, 2014–2018." NCHS data brief, no. 351. Hyattsville, MD: National Center for Health Statistics Retrieved from https://www.cdc.gov/nchs/products/databriefs/db351.htm#section_1.

Martin, R. C. (1982). *Islam: A Cultural Perspective.* Englewood Cliffs, NJ: Prentice Hall.

Martin, M. (2008). "The Intergenerational Correlation in Weight: How Genetic Resemblance Reveals the Social Role of Families." *American Journal of Sociology,* 114 (S1): S67–S105.

Martinovich, M.. (2017). "Stanford sociologist attempts to explain puzzling lack of grassroots climate change activism in U.S." *Stanford News,* June 15. Retrieved from https://news.stanford.edu/2017/06/15/sociologist-probes-lack-grassroots-climate-change-activism/.

Marvell, T. B. (1989). Divorce rates and the fault requirement. *Law and Society Review*: 543–67.

Marx, K. (1977; orig. 1867). *Capital: A Critique of Political Economy* (Vol. 1). New York: Random House.

Marx, K. (1983). *The Portable Karl Marx*. New York: Penguin.

Marx, K. (1994; orig. 1843–1844). "A Contribution to the Critique of Hegel's *Philosophy of Right*: Introduction." In J. J. O'Malley, ed., *Marx: Early Writings*. New York: Cambridge University Press.

Marx, K. (2000; orig. 1844). "The Economic and Philosophical Manuscripts." In D. McLellan, ed., *Karl Marx: Selected Writings*. New York: Oxford University Press.

Marx, K. (2008; orig. 1867). *Capital: A New Abridgement* (D. McClellan, ed.). New York: Oxford University Press.

Marx, K., and F. Engels. (2008; orig. 1848). *The Communist Manifesto*. New York: Oxford University Press.

Mascia, J. (2009). "A Landlord's Foreclosure Puts a Tenant in Trouble." *New York Times*, November 26. Retrieved 8/01/10, from ww.nytimes.com/2009/11/26/nyregion/26neediest2.html.

Massey, D. S. (1996). "The Age of Extremes: Concentrated Affluence and Poverty in the Twenty-First Century." *Demography* 33 (4): 395–412.

Massey, D. S., and N. A. Denton. (1993). *American Apartheid: Segregation and the Making of the Underclass*. Cambridge, MA: Harvard University Press.

Mather, M., and L. Kilduff. (2020). "The U.S. Population Is Growing Older, and the Gender Gap in Life Expectancy Is Narrowing." Population Reference Bureau, February 19. Retrieved from https://www.prb.org/the-u-s-population-is-growing-older-and-the-gender-gap-in-life-expectancy-is-narrowing/.

Mather, M., P. Scommegna, and L. Kilduff. (2019). "Fact Sheet: Aging in the United States." Population Reference Bureau, July 15. Retrieved from https://www.prb.org/aging-unitedstates-fact-sheet/.

Mathews, T. J., and B. E. Hamilton. (2014). "First births to older women continue to rise." NCHS data brief, no 152. Hyattsville, MD: National Center for Health Statistics.

Matisons, M. (2015). "3D Printing Shoes from Home "Not That Far Away," Nike COO Predicts," 3DPrint.com, Oct. 12, Retrieved from https://3dprint.com/99927/nike-coo-3d-printing-not-far/.

Matsueda, R. L. (1992). "Reflected Appraisals, Parental Labeling, and Delinquency: Specifying a Symbolic Interaction Theory." *American Journal of Sociology* 97: 1577–611.

Maugh, T. H., II. (1991). "Survey of Identical Twins Links Biological Factors with Being Gay." *Los Angeles Times*, December 15.

Maugh, T. H., II. (1993). "Genetic Compound Found in Lesbianism, Study Says." *Los Angeles Times*, March 12.

Maugh, T. H., II, and N. Zamichow. (1991). "Medicine: San Diego's Researcher's Findings Offer First Evidence of a Biological Cause for Homosexuality." *Los Angeles Times*, August 30.

Maxwell, A., and P. Riley. (2016). "Emotional Demands, Emotional Labour and Occupational Outcomes in School Principals." *Educational Management Administration & Leadership* 45(3): 484–502.

Maxwell, C. (2012). "Target launches gay wedding-registry advertisement" (August 1). Retrieved 3/27/15, from http://www.windycitymediagroup.com/lgbt/Target-launches-gay-wedding-registry-advertisement/38862.html.

May, E. T. (1997). *Barren in the promised land: Childless Americans and the pursuit of happiness*. Harvard University Press.

Mbaye, A. A., and N. Benjamin. (2014). "Informality, Growth and Development in Africa." In J. Lin and C. Monga eds., *The Oxford Handbook of Africa and Economics*. New York: Oxford University Press.

McAdam, D. (2017). "Social Movement Theory and the Prospects for Climate Change Activism in the United States." *Annual Review of Political Science* 20: 189–206.

McCabe, J., E. Fairchild, L. Grauerholz, and B. A. Pescosolido. (2011). "Gender in Twentieth-Century Children's Books: Patterns of Disparity in Titles and Central Characters." *Gender & Society* 25(2), 197.

McCall, L. (2005). "The complexity of intersectionality." *Signs* 30: 1771–1800.

McCarthy, M. M. (2015). "Sex Differences in the Brain: How Male and Female Brains Diverge is a Hotly Debated Topic, But the Study of Model Organisms Points to Differences that Cannot Be Ignored." *The Scientist* (October 2015), Retrieved from http://www.the-scientist.com/?articles.view/articleNo/44096/title/Sex-Differences-in-the-Brain/.

McDonough, S. (2005). "U.S. Prison Population Soars in 2003, 2004." ABC News, April 25. Retrieved spring 2006, from http://abcnews.go.com/US/LegalCenter/wireStory?id=699808&CMP=OTC-RSSFeeds0312 (site discontinued).

McFadden, D., and C. A. Champlin. (2000). "Comparison of Auditory Evoked Po-

tentials in Heterosexual, Homosexual, and Bisexual Males and Females." *Journal of the Association for Research in Otolaryngology* 1: 89–99.

McFadden, J. (2016). "Genetic Editing Is Like Playing God—and What's Wrong with That?" *Guardian*, February 2, Retrieved from https://www.theguardian.com/commentisfree/2016/feb/02/genetic-editing-playing-god-children-british-scientists-embryos-dna-diseases.

McGranahan, D. A., and C. L. Beale. (2002). "Understanding Rural Population Loss." *Rural America* 17.

McIntosh, P. (1988). "White Privilege and Male Privilege: A Personal Account of Coming to See Correspondences through Work in Women's Studies," Working Paper, Wellesley College Center for Research on Women.

McKibben, B. (2019). "The climate science is clear: it's now or never to avert catastrophe." *Guardian*, Nov. 20. Retrieved from https://www.theguardian.com/commentisfree/2019/nov/20/climate-crisis-its-now-or-never-to-avert-catastrophe.

McLanahan, S., and G. Sandefur. (1994). *Growing Up with a Single Parent: What Hurts, What Helps*. Cambridge, MA: Harvard University Press.

McLaren, P. (1985). "The Ritual Dimensions of Resistance: Clowning and Symbolic Inversion." *Journal of Education* 167(2): 84–97.

McLeod, J. (1995). *Ain't No Makin' It*. Boulder, CO: Westview Press.

McManus, P. A and T. A. DiPrete. (2001). "Losers and Winners: The Financial Consequences of Separation and Divorce for Men." *American Sociological Review* 66: 246–268.

McMichael, P. (1996). *Development and Social Change: A Global Perspective*. Thousand Oaks, CA: Pine Forge.

McMurrer, J. (2007). *Choices, Changes, and Challenges: Curriculum and Instruction in the NCLB Era*. Washington, DC: Center on Education Policy). Retrieved spring 2008, from http://www.cep-dc.org/displayDocument.cfm?DocumentID=312.

McNeil, Donald G. (2014). "Early Treatment is Found to Clear HIV in a 2nd Baby." *New York Times*, March 5. Retrieved from http://www.nytimes.com/2014/03/06/health/second-success-raises-hope-for-a-way-to-rid-babies-of-hiv.html?_r=0.

McPherson, M., L. Smith-Lovin, and M. E. Brashears. (2006). "Social Isolation in America: Changes in Core Discussion Networks over Two Decades." *American Sociological Review* 71(3): 185–203.

Mead, M. (1963; orig. 1935). *Sex and Temperament in Three Primitive Societies*. New York: William Morrow & Company.

Mead, M. (1972). *Blackberry Winter: My Earlier Years*. New York: William Morrow & Company.

Meadows, D. H., D. L. Meadows, J. Randers, and W. W. Behrens III. (1972). *The Limits to Growth*. New York: Universe Books.

Media Education Foundation. (1997). Study Guide: Gerbner Series. Retrieved from http://www.mediaed.org/assets/products/111/studyguide_111.pdf.

Medical Education Cooperation with Cuba (MEDICC). (2016). "About MEDICC." Retrieved from http://medicc.org/ns/.

Mehta, S. (2013). Treatment of HIV-AIDS still poses sociopsychological issues: Study. *Times of India* (November 30, 2013). Retrieved from http://articles.timesofindia.indiatimes.com/2013-11-30/visakhapatnam/44595899_1_hiv-aidspatients-treatment-study.

Melton, J. G. (1996). *The Encyclopedia of American Religions*, 5th ed. Detroit, MI: Gale Research Co.

Meyer, R. (2018). "The World Spends $400 Billion Propping Up Oil Companies. Is That Bad?" *The Atlantic*, Feb. 8. Retrieved from https://www.theatlantic.com/science/archive/2018/02/maybe-cutting-fossil-fuel-subsidies-wouldnt-do-much-good/552668/.

Minasians, C. (2016). "Where are the iPhone, iPad and Mac designed, made and assembled? A comprehensive breakdown of Apple's product supply chain," *Macworld*, April 18. Retrieved from http://www.macworld.co.uk/feature/apple/are-apple-products-truly-designed-in-california-made-in-china-iphonese-3633832/.

Merkyl, P. H., and N. Smart, eds. (1983). *Religion and Politics in the Modern World*. New York: New York University Press.

Merton, R. K. (1957). *Social Theory and Social Structure*, rev. ed. New York: Free Press.

Merton, R. K. (1968; orig. 1938). "Social Structure and Anomie." *American Sociological Review* 3.

Meyer, J. W., and B. Rowan. (1977). "Institutionalized Organizations: Formal Structure as Myth and Ceremony." *American Journal of Sociology* 83: 340–63.

Michalopoulos, S., and E. Papaioannou. (2012). "Pre-Colonial Ethnic Institutions and Contemporary African Development," July 2012, NBER Working Paper No. w18224. Retrieved from https://ssrn.com/abstract=2105969.

Michels, R. (1967; orig. 1911). *Political Parties*. New York: Free Press.

Michigan Department of Community Health. (2010). "Watch Out for Date Rape Drugs." Retrieved 9/20/10, from www.michigan.gov/documents/publications_date_rape_drugs_8886_7.pdf (site discontinued).

Mickelson, R. A. (1990). "The Attitude-Achievement Paradox among Black Adolescents." *Sociology of Education* 63: 44–61.

Migration Policy Institute. (2017). "Frequently Requested Statistics on Immigrants and Immigration in the United States." Retrieved from http://www.migrationpolicy.org/article/frequently-requested-statistics-immigrants-and-immigration-united-states#CurrentHistoricalNumbers.

Miles, R. (1993). *Racism after 'Race Relations'* London: Routledge.

Milgram, S. (1963). "Behavioral Study of Obedience." *Journal of Abnormal and Social Psychology* 67: 371–78.

Miller, M. (2017). "Protesters Outside White House Demand 'Pizzagate' Investigation," *Washington Post*, March 25, Retrieved from https://www.washingtonpost.com/news/local/wp/2017/03/25/protesters-outside-white-house-demand-pizzagate-investigation/?utm_term=.f3e27bc46861.

Mills, C. W. (1956). *The Power Elite*. New York: Oxford University Press.

Mills, T. J. (1967). *The Sociology of Small Groups*. Englewood, NJ: Prentice-Hall.

Minchin, T. J. (2016). "A Pivotal Role? The AFL-CIO and the 2008 Presidential Election," *Labor History*, Vol. 57, 3, 299-322.

Minkov, M., and G. Hofstede. (2012). "Is National Culture a Meaningful Concept? Cultural Values Delineate Homogeneous National Clusters of In-Country Regions." *Cross-Cultural Research* 46(2): 133–59.

Mirowsky, J., and C. E. Ross. (2005). "Education, Cumulative Advantage, and Health." *Ageing International* 30(1): 27–62.

Mishel, L., and J. Wolfe. (2019). "CEO Compensation has grown 940% since 1978." Economic Policy Institute, August 14. Retrieved from https://www.epi.org/publication/ceo-compensation-2018/.

Mitchell, A., J. Gottfried, M. Barthel, and E. Shearer. (2016). "The Modern News Consumer," Pew Research Center, July 7, Retrieved from http://www.journalism.org/2016/07/07/the-modern-news-consumer/pj_2016-07-07_modern-news-consumer_1-01/.

Mitchell, J. (1975). *Psychoanalysis and Feminism*. New York: Random House.

Mitnick, K., and W. L. Simon. (2011). *Ghost in the Wires: My Adventures as the World's Most Wanted Hacker*. New York: Little, Brown.

Miyazaki, I. (1981). *China's Examination Hell: The Civil Service Examinations of Imperial China*. (Conrad Schirokauer, trans). New Haven, CT: Yale University Press.

Mizoguchi, N., L. Walker, E. Trevelyan, and B. Ahmed. (2019). "The Older Foreign-Born Population in the United States: 2012–2016." U.S. Bureau of the Census. Retrieved from https://www.census.gov/content/dam/Census/library/publications/2019/acs/acs-42.pdf.

Moen, P. (1995). "A Life Course Approach to Postretirement Roles and Well-Being." In L. A. Bond, S. J. Cutler, and A. Grams, eds., *Promoting Successful and Productive Aging*. Newbury Park, CA: Sage.

Mohamed, B. (2016). "A New Estimate of the U.S. Muslim Population," Pew Research Center, Jan. 6, Retrieved from http://www.pewresearch.org/fact-tank/2016/01/06/a-new-estimate-of-the-u-s-muslim-population/.

Mohanty, C. T. (2003). *Feminism without Borders*. Durham, NC: Duke University Press.

Mohanty, C. T. (2013). "Transnational Feminist Crossings: On Neoliberalism and Radical Critique." *Signs*, 38(4), 967–991.

Mol, A. P. J., and D. A. Sonnenfeld. (2000). "Ecological Modernization Around the World: An Introduction." *Environmental Politics* 9(1): 3–16.

Molotch, H. (2012). *Against Security: How We Go Wrong at Airports, Subways, and Other Sites of Ambiguous Danger*. Princeton, NJ: Princeton University Press.

Monk Jr., Ellis P. (2016). "The Consequences of 'Race and Color' in Brazil." *Social Problems* 63(3): 413–430.

Monnat, S. M. (2019). "The Contributions of Socioeconomic and Opioid Supply Factors to Geographic Variation in U.S. Drug Mortality Rates." INET Working Paper no. 87. Retrieved from https://www.ineteconomics.org/uploads/papers/Monnat-WP-87.pdf.

Monnat, S. M., and C. B. Pickett. (2011). "Rural/Urban Differences in Self-Rated Health: Examining the Roles of County Size and Metropolitan Adjacency." *Health & Place* 17(1): 311–19.

Monticciolo, D. L., M. S. Newell, L. Moy, B. Niell, B. Monsees, and E. A. Sickles. (2018). "Breast Cancer Screening in Women at Higher-Than-Average Risk: Recommendations From the ACR." *Journal of the American College of Radiology* 15(3): 408–14.

Moore, G. (1990). "Structural Determinants of Men's and Women's Personal Networks." *American Sociological Review* 55: 726–35.

Moore, K. J. (2004). "Coding for Depression Without Getting Depressed." *Family Practice Management* 11: 23–25.

Moore, L. R. (1994). *Selling God: American Religion in the Marketplace of Culture.* New York: Oxford University Press.

Morgan, S. L., D. Gelbgiser, and K. A. Weeden. (2013). "Feeding the Pipeline: Gender, Occupational Plans, and College Major Selection." *Social Science Research* 42: 989–1005

Morin, R. and S. Motel. (2012). "A Third of Americans Now Say they are in the Lower Classes," Pew Research Social & Demographic Trends, September 10. Retrieved 12/14, from http://www.pewsocialtrends.org/2012/09/10/a-third-of-americans-now-say-they-are-in-the-lower-classes/.

Morland, K., S. Wing, A. Diez-Roux, and C. Poole. (2002). "Neighborhood Characteristics Associated with the Location of Food Stores and Food Service Places." *American Journal of Preventive Medicine* 22(1): 23–29.

Morris, E. W. (2007)."'Ladies' or 'Loudies'? Perceptions and Experiences of Black Girls in Classrooms." *Youth Society* 38: 490–515.

Morrow-Howell, N., N. Galucia, and E. Swinford. (2020). "Recovering from the COVID-19 Pandemic: A Focus on Older Adults." *Journal of Aging & Social Policy* 32(4–5): 526–35.

Moynihan, D. P. (1965). *The Negro Family: A Case for National Action.* Washington, DC: U.S. Government Printing Office.

Mukherjee, W. (2014). "iPhone 6 stock flows out of India to meet China demand and Black Friday sales in US." *Economic Times*, October 31. Retrieved from http://articles.economictimes.indiatimes.com/2014-10-31/news/55631596_1_apple-india-iphone-5s.

Mulligan, C. (2010). "In a First, Women Surpass Men on U.S. Payrolls." *New York Times*, February 5. Retrieved 12/14.

Mumford, L. (1973). *Interpretations and Forecasts.* New York: Harcourt Brace Jovanovich.

Murdock, G. P. (1949). *Social Structure.* New York: Macmillan.

Murdock, G. P. (1967). *Ethnographic Atlas.* Pittsburgh, PA. Pittsburgh University Press.

Murdock, G. P. (1981). *Atlas of World Cultures.* Pittsburgh, PA: University of Pittsburgh Press.

Murphy, J. (2012). *Homeschooling in America: Capturing and Assessing the Movement.* Thousand Oaks, CA: Sage.

Murray, C. A. (1984). *Losing Ground: American Social Policy, 1950–1980.* New York: Basic Books.

Murray, L. (2010). *Breaking Night: A Memoir of Forgiveness, Survival, and My Journey from Homeless to Harvard.* New York: Hyperion.

Murray, T. H. (2014). "Stirring the Simmering 'Designer Baby' Pot," *Science* (March 14) 343: 6176.

NAFSA. (2019a). "Communities will suffer economic loss if enrollment declines continue." Retrieved from https://www.nafsa.org/about/about-nafsa/new-nafsa-data-despite-stagnant-enrollment.

NAFSA. (2019b). "Trends in U.S. Study Abroad." Retrieved from https://www.nafsa.org/policy-and-advocacy/policy-resources/trends-us-study-abroad.

Najman, J. M. (1993). "Health and Poverty: Past, Present, and Prospects for the Future." *Social Science and Medicine* 36(2): 157–66.

National Academy of Sciences. (2015). "Report in Brief: Climate Intervention—Carbon Dioxide Removal and Reliable Sequestration Reflecting Sunlight to Cool Earth." Retrieved from https://www.nap.edu/resource/18988/climate-intervention-brief-final.pdf.

National Association for the Advancement of Colored People (NAACP). (2014). "Criminal Justice Fact Sheet." Retrieved from https://www.naacp.org/criminal-justice-fact-sheet/.

National Association of Anorexia Nervosa and Associated Disorders. (2020). "Eating Disorder Statistics." Retrieved from https://anad.org/education-and-awareness/about-eating-disorders/eating-disorders-statistics/.

National Center for Education Statistics (NCES). (2009). "NAEP 2009 High School Transcript Study, 2009." Retrieved 10/19/12, from http://nationsreportcard.gov/hsts_2009/.

National Center for Education Statistics (NCES). (2011). "Condition of Education 2011." Retrieved 10/19/12, from http://nces.ed.gov/programs/coe/analysis/2010-section3b.asp (site discontinued).

National Center for Education Statistics (NCES). (2016a). "Digest of Education Statistics: Table 219.75: Percentage of High School Dropouts among persons 16 to 24 years old by income level: 1970-2015." Retrieved from https://nces.ed.gov/programs/digest/d16/tables/d16_219.75.asp.

National Center for Education Statistics. (NCES). (2016b). "Digest of Education Statistics: 2015." Retrieved from https://nces.ed.gov/programs/digest/d15/.

National Center for Education Statistics. (NCES). (2016c). "Public High School Graduation Rates." Retrieved from https://nces.ed.gov/programs/coe/indicator_coi.asp.

National Center for Education Statistics. (NCES). (2017a). "The Condition of Education." Retrieved from https://nces.ed.gov/programs/coe/.

National Center for Education Statistics (NCES). (2017b). "Digest of Education Statistics 2018: Fast Facts, SAT Scores." Retrieved from https://nces.ed.gov/fastfacts/display.asp?id=80.

National Center for Education Statistics (NCES). (2018a). "Digest of Education Statistics: Table 206.10: Number and percentage of homeschooled students ages 5 through 17 with a grade equivalent of kindergarten through 12th grade, by selected child, parent, and household characteristics: Selected years, 1999 through 2016." Retrieved from https://nces.ed.gov/programs/digest/d18/tables/dt18_206.10.asp.

National Center for Education Statistics (NCES). (2018b). "Digest of Education Statistics: Table 219.70: Percentage of high school dropouts among persons 16 to 24 years old (status dropout rate), by sex and race/ethnicity: Selected years, 1960 through 2017." Retrieved from https://nces.ed.gov/programs/digest/d18/tables/dt18_219.70.asp.

National Center for Education Statistics (NCES). (2018c). "Digest of Education Statistics: Table 302.10: Recent high school completers and their enrollment in college, by sex and level of institution: 1960 through 2017." Retrieved from https://nces.ed.gov/programs/digest/d18/tables/dt18_302.10.asp.

National Center for Education Statistics (NCES). (2018d). "Digest of Education Statistics: Table 502.30: Median annual earnings of full-time year-round workers 25 to 34 years old and full-time year-round workers as a percentage of the labor force, by sex, race/ethnicity, and educational attainment: Selected years, 1995 through 2017." Retrieved from https://nces.ed.gov/programs/digest/d18/tables/dt18_502.30.asp?current=yes.

National Center for Education Statistics (NCES). (2018e). "Fast Facts, SAT Scores." Retrieved from https://nces.ed.gov/fastfacts/display.asp?id=171.

National Center for Education Statistics (NCES). (2018f). "Graduate Degree

Fields." Retrieved from https://nces. ed.gov/programs/coe/indicator_ctb. asp.

National Center for Education Statistics (NCES). (2019a). "Indicator 26: STEM Degrees." February. Retrieved from https://nces.ed.gov/programs/ raceindicators/indicator_reg.asp.

National Center for Education Statistics (NCES). (2019b). "Public High School Graduation Rates." The Condition of Education. Retrieved from https:// nces.ed.gov/programs/coe/ indicator_coi.asp.

National Center for Education Statistics (NCES). (2019c). "Table 1. Public high school 4-year adjusted cohort graduation rate (ACGR), by race/ ethnicity and selected demographic characteristics for the United States, the 50 states, and the District of Columbia: School year 2016–17." Common Core of Data. Retrieved from https://nces.ed.gov/ccd/tables/ACGR_ RE_and_characteristics_2016-17.asp.

National Center for Education Statistics (NCES). (2019d). "The Condition of Education 2019." U.S. Department of Education, May 29. Retrieved from https://nces.ed.gov/pubsearch/ pubsinfo.asp?pubid=2019144.

National Center for Education Statistics. (2020). "Annual Earnings." Retrieved from https://nces.ed.gov/programs/ coe/indicator_cba.asp.

National Center for Health Statistics. (2008a). "National Marriage and Divorce Rate Trends." Retrieved from www.cdc.gov/nchs/nvss/mardiv_ tables.htm.

National Center for Health Statistics. (2008b). "Women's Health." Retrieved 5/15/10, from www.cdc.gov/nchs/ fastats/womens_health.htm.

National Center on Elder Abuse (NCEA). (2012). Statistics Data. Retrieved 3/3/15, from http://www.ncea. aoa.gov/Library/Data/index.aspx. 12/14, from http://www.cdc.gov/ healthyyouth.

National Conference of State Legislatures. (2019). "State Minimum Wages, 2019 Minimum Wage by State." January 7. Retrieved from http://www.ncsl.org/ research/labor-and-employment/ state-minimum-wage-chart.aspx.

National Conference of State Legislatures. (2020a). "State Medical Marijuana Laws." Retrieved from https://www. ncsl.org/research/health/state-medical-marijuana-laws.aspx.

National Conference of State Legislatures. (2020b). "Voter Identification Requirements, Voter ID Laws." Retrieved from https://www.ncsl.org/research/ elections-and-campaigns/voter-id. aspx.

National Heart, Lung, and Blood Institute. (2015). "Aim for a Healthy Weight: Information for Patients and the Public." Retrieved from www.nhlbi.nih.gov/ health/public/heart/obesity/lose_wt/ risk.htm.

National Institutes of Health. (2019). "Decline in measles vaccination is causing a preventable global resurgence of the disease." U.S. Department of Health and Human Services, April 18. Retrieved from https://www.nih.gov/ news-events/news-releases/decline-measles-vaccination-causing-preventable-global-resurgence-disease.

National Law Center on Homelessness and Poverty (NLCHP). (2004). "Key Data Concerning Homeless Persons in America," July. Retrieved spring 2006, from www.nlchp.org/FA_HAPIA/ HomelessPersonsinAmerica.pdf (site discontinued).

National Law Center on Homelessness and Poverty (NLCHP). (2014). "Racial Discrimination in Housing and Home-lessness in the United States." July 3. Retrieved 12/14, from http://www. nlchp.org/CERD_Housing_Report_ 2014.pdf.

National Law Center on Homelessness and Poverty (NLCHP). (2015). "Homeless-ness in America: Overview of Data and Causes." Retrieved from https://nlchp. org/wp-content/uploads/2018/10/ Homeless_Stats_Fact_Sheet.pdf.

National Low Income Housing Coalition (NLIHC). (2000). "Out of Reach: The Growing Gap between Housing Costs and Income of Poor People in the United States." Washington, DC: The National Low Income Housing Coalition/Low Income Housing In-formation Service. Retrieved 1/03/05, from www.nlihc.org/oor2000/index. htm.

National Low Income Housing Coalition (NLIHC). (2015). "Child Poverty Rises in Rural America," Retrieved from http://nlihc.org/article/child-poverty-rises-rural-america.

National Oceanic and Atmospheric Ad-ministration (NOAA). (2019). "What is an Invasive Species?" Retrieved from https://oceanservice.noaa.gov/facts/ invasive.html.

National Public Radio (NPR). (2014). "Why do Ebola Mortality Rates Vary So Widely?" October 24. Retrieved 12/2014, from http://www.npr. org/2014/10/23/358363535/why-do-ebola-mortality-rates-vary-so-widely.

National Science Foundation (NSF). (2018). "Science & Engineering Indi-cators 2018." Retrieved from https:// nsf.gov/statistics/2018/nsb20181/.

National Snow and Ice Data Center (NSIDC). (2019). "Greenland Ice Sheet Today." Retrieved from http://nsidc. org/greenland-today/.

Neale, A. (1997). "Organising Environ-mental Self-Regulation: Liberal Governmentality and the Pursuit of Ecological Modernisation in Europe." *Environmental Politics* 6(4): 1–24.

Nederveen Pieterse, J. (2001). Develop-ment Theory: *Deconstructions/ Reconstructions*. London; Thousand Oaks, CA: SAGE Publications.

Nederveen Pieterse, J. (2011). "Global Re-balancing and the East-South Turn." *Development and Change* 42(1): 22–48.

Ness, R. B., and L. H. Kuller. (1999). *Health and Disease among Women: Biological and Environmental Influences.* New York: Oxford University Press.

New York Daily News. (2020). "Corona-virus Updates in NYC and the World: The News on April 24–27." April 28. Retrieved from https://www. nydailynews.com/coronavirus/ ny-coronavirus-nyc-us-world-updates-latest-20200424-kmaib3vuevhodfrm6cc4ljyaie-story. html.

New York Times. (2012). "How Obama Won Re-election: Romney's Shift Wasn't Enough." *New York Times*, November 7. Retrieved 3/03/13, from www. nytimes.com/interactive/2012/11/07/ us/politics/obamas-diverse-base-of-support.html?_r=0.

New York Times. (2014). "Ebola Facts: How many Ebola patients have been treated outside of West Africa?" *New York Times,* November 21 2014. Retrieved November 2014, from http://www. nytimes.com/interactive/2014/07/31/ world/africa/ebola-virus-outbreak-qa. html?_r=0#outside-africa.

New York Times. (2020). "U.S. Jobless Claims Pass 40 Million: Live Business Updates." Retrieved from https:// www.nytimes.com/2020/05/28/ business/unemployment-stock-market-coronavirus.html.

Newman, A. (2019). "On the Job, 24 Hours a Day, 27 Days a Month." *New York Times,* Sept. 2. Retrieved from https:// www.nytimes.com/2019/09/02/ nyregion/home-health-aide.html.

Newman. K. S. (1999). *Falling from Grace: Downward Mobility in the Age of Affluence.* Berkeley, CA: University of California Press.

Newman, K. S. (2000). *No Shame in My Game: The Working Poor in the Inner City.* New York: Vintage.

Newman, K. S., and D. Pedulla. (2010). "An Unequal Opportunity Recession." *The Nation,* July 19. Retrieved 3/01/13, from www.thenation.com/article/36883/unequal-opportunity-recession.

Newport, F. (2011). "For First Time, Majority of Americans Favor Legal Gay Marriage." Gallup Poll, May 20. Retrieved summer2013, from www.gallup.com/poll/147662/First-Time-Majority-Americans-Favor-Legal-Gay-Marriage.aspx.

Newport, F. (2015). "Many Americans Doubt they will get Social Security Benefits." Retrieved from http://www.gallup.com/poll/184580/americans-doubt-social-security-benefits.aspx.

Newport, F. (2016). "Five Key Findings on Religion in the U.S." Gallup, Dec. 23. Retrieved from https://news.gallup.com/poll/200186/five-key-findings-religion.aspx.

Newport, F. (2018). "Americans Big on Idea of Living in the Country." Gallup, Dec. 7. Retrieved from https://news.gallup.com/poll/245249/americans-big-idea-living-country.aspx.

Ng, Joyce. (2016). "The changing face of the Asian family." *Channel News Asia* (August 3, 2016). Retrieved from http://www.channelnewsasia.com/news/singapore/the-changing-face-of-the-asian-family-7848690.

Ngai, P., J. Chan, and M. Selden. (2014). "Dying for an iPhone: Apple, Foxconn, and a New Generation of Chinese Workers." Lanham, MD: Rowman & Littlefield.

Niahh, S. S. (2010). *Dancehall: From Slave Ship to Ghetto.* Ottawa: University of Ottawa Press.

Nibley, L. (2011). "Two Spirits." Retrieved 8/25/11, from www.pbs.org/independentlens/two-spirits/resources/two-spirits-discussion.pdf.

Niebuhr, H. R. (1929). *The Social Sources of Denominationalism.* New York: Holt.

Nielsen, F. (1994). "Income Inequality and Industrial Development: Dualism Revisited." *American Sociological Review* 59: 654–77.

Nien Hsing. (2012). "Our Customers." Retrieved 3/18/13, from www.nhjeans.com/en/client.php.

Noe-Bustamante, L., A. Flores, and S. Shah. (2019a). "Facts on Hispanics of Cuban origin in the United States, 2017." Pew Research Center, Sept. 16. https://www.pewresearch.org/hispanic/fact-sheet/u-s-hispanics-facts-on-cuban-origin-latinos/.

Noe-Bustamante, L., A. Flores, and S. Shah. (2019b). "Facts on Hispanics of Mexican origin in the United States, 2017." Pew Research Center, Sept. 16. Retrieved from https://www.pewresearch.org/hispanic/fact-sheet/u-s-hispanics-facts-on-mexican-origin-latinos/.

Noe-Bustamante, L., A. Flores, and S. Shah. (2019c). "Facts on Hispanics of Puerto Rican origin in the United States, 2017." Pew Research Center, Sept. 16. Retrieved from https://www.pewresearch.org/hispanic/fact-sheet/u-s-hispanics-facts-on-puerto-rican-origin-latinos/.

Nolan, K., and J. Anyon. (2004). "Learning to Do Time: Willis' Cultural Reproduction Model in an Era of Deindustrialization, Globalization, and the Mass Incarceration of People of Color." In N. Dolby, G. Dimitriadis, and P. Willis, eds., *Learning to Labor in New Times.* New York: Routledge.

Nolen-Hoeksema, S. (1993). *Sex Differences in Depression.* Palo Alto, CA: Stanford University Press.

Nordberg, J. (2010). "Afghan Boys Are Prized, So Girls Live the Part." *New York Times*, September 21. Retrieved 9/22/10, from www.nytimes.com/2010/09/21/world/asia/21gender.html.

Norman, J. (2015). "In U.S., Support for Tea Party Drops to New Low," Gallup, Oct. 26, Retrieved from http://www.gallup.com/poll/186338/support-tea-party-drops-new-low.aspx.

Norris, P., and R. Inglehart. (2004). *Sacred and Secular: Religion and Politics Worldwide.* New York: Cambridge University Press.

Norris, P. and R. Inglehart. (2018). *Cultural Backlash: The Rise of Populist Authoritarianism,* Retrieved from https://www.electoralintegrityproject.com/populistauthoritarianism/.

NPR Staff. (2014). "'Anything That Connects': A Conversation With Taylor Swift." Retrieved 10/31/2014, from http://www.npr.org/2014/10/31/359827368/anything-that-connects-a-conversation-with-taylor-swift.

Nugent, C. (2012). "Parents' Preferences for Mixed-Sex Children: Motivations, Fertility Behavior, and Psychological Well-Being." Unpublished doctoral dissertation. New Brunswick, NJ: Rutgers University.

Oakes, J. (1990). *Multiplying Inequalities: The Effects of Race, Social Class, and Tracking on Opportunities to Learn Mathematics and Science.* Santa Monica, CA: Rand.

Oakes, J., and G. Guiton. (1995). "Matchmaking: The Dynamics of High School Tracking Decisions." *American Educational Research Journal, 32*(1), 3–33.

Oakford, S. (2014). "Muslim Scholars Make the Theological Case Against the Islamic State," *Vice,* Sept. 24, Retrieved from https://news.vice.com/article/muslim-scholars-make-the-theological-case-against-the-islamic-state.

Oates, G., and J. Goode. (2012). "Racial Differences in Effects of Religiosity and Mastery on Psychological Distress: Evidence from National Longitudinal Data," *Society & Mental Health* 3: 40–58.

O'Connor, J. (1973). *The Fiscal Crisis of the State,* New York: St. Martin's Press.

O'Connor, M. (2012). "Boy or Girl? Only the Cake Knows." *Omaha World-Herald,* January 17. Retrieved 3/05/13, from www.omaha.com/article/20120117/LIVING/701179974.

Offe, C. (1984). *Contradictions of the Welfare State.* Cambridge, MA: MIT Press.

Offe, C. (1985). *Disorganized Capitalism.* Cambridge, MA: MIT Press.

Office of the U.S. Trade Representative. (2020). "United States-Mexico-Canada Agreement." Retrieved from https://ustr.gov/trade-agreements/free-trade-agreements/united-states-mexico-canada-agreement.

Ogbu, J. U., and S. Fordham. (1986). "Black Students' School Success: Coping with the 'Burden of Acting White.'" *Urban Review* 18: 176–206.

Ogburn, W. F. (1964). *Ogburn on Culture and Social Change, Selected Papers.* Chicago: University of Chicago Press Phoenix Books.

Ogrodnik, C., and S. Staggenborg. (2016). "The Ebb and Flow of Environmentalism." *Sociology Compass* 10(3): 218–20.

O'Hare, W., and M. Mather. (2008). "Child Poverty Is Highest in Rural Counties in U.S." Population Reference Bureau. Retrieved spring 2011, from www.prb.org/Articles/2008/childpoverty.aspx.

Ohmae, K. (1995). *The End of the Nation-State: How Regional Economies Will Soon Reshape the World.* New York: Simon and Schuster.

Ojanperä, S., M. Graham, and M. Zook. (2019). "The Digital Knowledge Economy Index: Mapping Content Production." *The Journal of Development Studies* 55(12): 2626–43.

Okahana, H., and E. Zhou. (2018). "Graduate Enrollment and Degrees: 2007–2017." Council of Graduate Schools. Retrieved from https://cgsnet.org/first-time-enrollment-holds-steady-application-counts-slightly-decline-us-graduate-schools.

Okoshi, Y. (2019). "China's research papers lead the world in cutting-edge tech." *Nikkei Asian Review,* Jan. 6. Retrieved from https://asia.nikkei.com/Business/China-tech/China-s-research-papers-lead-the-world-in-cutting-edge-tech.

Oldfield, F. et al. (2018X). *"The Anthropocene Review*: Its Significance, Implications, and the Rationale for a New Interdisciplinary Journal." *The Anthropocene Review* 1(1): 3–7.

Oliphant, J. B. (2018). "Public support for the death penalty ticks up." Pew Research Center, June 11. Retrieved from https://www.pewresearch.org/fact-tank/2018/06/11/us-support-for-death-penalty-ticks-up-2018/.

Oliver, J. G. J., and J. A. H. W. Peters. (2018). "Trends in Global CO2 and Greenhouse Gas Emissions," PBL Netherlands Environmental Assessment Agency. Retrieved from https://www.pbl.nl/sites/default/files/downloads/pbl-2018-trends-in-global-co2-and-total-greenhouse-gas-emissons-2018-report_3125_0.pdf.

Oliver, M. L., and T. M. Shapiro. (2006). *Black Wealth/White Wealth*, 2nd ed. New York: Routledge.

Olshansky, S. J., B. A. Carnes, and D. Grahn. (2003). "Biological Evidence for Limits to the Duration of Life." *Biogerontology* 4(1): 31–45.

Olshansky, S. J., T. Antonucci, L. Berkman et al. (2012). "Differences in Life Expectancy Due to Race and Educational Differences Are Widening, and Many May Not Catch Up." *Health Affairs* 31(8): 1803–13.

Olson, M. H., and S. B. Primps. (1984). "Working at Home with Computers." *Journal of Social Issues* 40(3): 97–112.

O'Neill, G. (2009). "The Baby Boom Age Wave: Population Success or Tsunami?" In R. B. Hudson, ed., *Boomer Bust? Economic and Political Issues of the Graying Society* (pp. 3–22). Westport, CT: Praeger Press.

Ongweso Jr., E. (2019). "The Walmart Subreddit Has Been Flooded with Pro-Union Memes." *Vice*, July 11. Retrieved from https://www.vice.com/en_us/article/mb8y9a/the-walmart-subreddit-has-been-flooded-with-pro-union-memes.

Oplinger, D., and D. J. Willard. (2004). "Claims of Academic Success Rely on Anecdote, Flawed Data Analysis." *Akron Beacon Journal*, November 15.

Oppel, R. (2011). "Steady Decline in Major Crime Baffles Experts." *New York Times*, May 23. Retrieved 1/13/15, from http://www.nytimes.com/2011/05/24/us/24crime.html?_r=0

Oppenheimer, M et al. (2019). *Discerning Experts: The Practices of Scientific Assessment for Environmental Policy.* Chicago: University of Chicago Press.

Oppenheimer, V. K. (1970). *The Female Labor Force in the United States.* Westport, CT: Greenwood Press.

Oreskes, N., M. Oppenheimer, and D. Jamieson. (2019). "Scientists Have Been Underestimating the Pace of Climate Change." *Scientific American*, Aug. 19. Retrieved from https://blogs.scientificamerican.com/observations/scientists-have-been-underestimating-the-pace-of-climate-change/.

Orfield, G., and E. Frankenberg. (2014). "Increasingly Segregated and Unequal Schools as Courts Reverse Policy," *Educational Administration Quarterly*, 50:5, 718–734.

Organisation for Economic Co-operation and Development (OECD). (2012). "Closing the Gender Gap: Act Now." December 17. Retrieved 12/14, from http://www.oecd.org/gender/closingthegap.htm.

Organisation for Economic Co-operation and Development (OECD). (2014a). "Income Inequality." *OECD Factbook 2014: Economic, Environmental and Social Statistics.* Paris: OECD Publishing. Retrieved 12/14, from http://www.oecd-ilibrary.org/economics/oecd-factbook-2014/income-inequality_factbook-2014-24-en.

Organisation for Economic Co-operation and Development (OECD). (2014b). *PISA 2012 Results in Focus: What 15-year-olds know and what they can do with what they know.* Retrieved from http://www.oecd.org/pisa/keyfindings/pisa-2012-results-overview.pdf.

Organisation for Economic Co-operation and Development (OECD). (2019). "OECD Family Database: SF3.1: Marriage and divorce rates." Retrieved from https://www.oecd.org/els/family/SF_3_1_Marriage_and_divorce_rates.pdf.

Organisation for Economic Co-operation and Development (OECD). (2020). "Life expectancy at birth." Retrieved from https://data.oecd.org/healthstat/life-expectancy-at-birth.htm.

Orloff, A. S. (1993). *The Politics of Pensions: A Comparative Analysis of Britain, Canada, and the United States, 1880–1940.* Madison: University of Wisconsin Press.

Ostroff, J. (2016). "Baby Storm Now: Dad David Stocker on the Uproar and Storm's Gender Identity." *Huffington Post* (June 30, 2016), Retrieved from http://www.huffingtonpost.ca/2016/06/30/baby-storm-gender_n_10756806.html.

Ott, B. L. (2017). "The Age of Twitter: Donald J. Trump and the Politics of Debasement," *Critical Studies in Media Communication* 34: 1 (59-68).

Oxfam International. (2019). "Billionaire fortunes grew by $2.5 billion a day last year as poorest saw their wealth fall." Jan. 21. Retrieved from https://www.oxfam.org/en/press-releases/billionaire-fortunes-grew-25-billion-day-last-year-poorest-saw-their-wealth-fall.

Oxford Geoengineering Programme. (2019). "What Is Geoengineering?" Retrieved from http://www.geoengineering.ox.ac.uk/www.geoengineering.ox.ac.uk/what-is-geoengineering/what-is-geoengineering/.

Ozimek, A. (2019). "Report: Overboard on Offshore Fears." *Upwork*. Retrieved from https://www.upwork.com/press/economics/report-overboard-on-offshore-fears/.

Padavic, I., and B. Reskin. (2002). *Women and Men at Work*, 2nd ed. Thousand Oaks, CA: Pine Forge Press.

Padawer, R. (2014). "Men of Wellesley: Can Women's Colleges Survive the Transgender Movement." *New York Times*, October 19.

Paddock, R. C. (2019). "To Make This Tofu, Start by Burning Toxic Plastic." *New York Times*, November 14. Retrieved from https://www.nytimes.com/2019/11/14/world/asia/indonesia-tofu-dioxin-plastic.html.

Pager, D. (2007). *Marked: Race, Crime, and Finding Work in an Era of Mass Incarceration.* Chicago: University of Chicago Press.

Pager, D., and H. Shepard. (2008). "The Sociology of Discrimination: Racial Discrimination in Employment, Housing, Credit, and Consumer Markets." *Annual Review of Sociology* 34: 181–209.

Palmore, E. (2015). "Ageism Comes of Age" *The Journals of Gerontology Series B: Psychological Sciences and Social Sciences,* 70(6), 873-875.

Paludi, M. A., and R. B. Barickman. (1991). *Academic and Workplace Sexual Harassment: A Resource Manual.* Albany, NY: State University of New York Press.

Paluck, E. L., H. Shepherd, and P. M. Aronow. (2016). "Changing Climates of Conflict: A Social Network Experiment in 56 Schools." *Proceedings of the National Academy of Sciences.*

Pande, R. (2015). "'I arranged my own marriage': Arranged marriages and postcolonial feminism." *Gender, Place & Culture* 22(2): 172–187.

Pandey, E. (2018). "How Barnes & Noble, the last big bookstore, fell to Amazon." AXIOS, Oct. 7. Retrieved from https://www.axios.com/barnes-and-noble-book-stores-sale-amazon-effect-4f2753d2-818c-49d1-878a-60f0c3a5b3f7.html.

Panico, R., and B. Duhart. (2020). "We can't go online, parents say. How will our kids learn if coronavirus closes schools?" NJ.com, March 12. Retrieved from https://www.nj.com/coronavirus/2020/03/we-cant-go-online-parents-say-how-will-our-kids-learn-if-coronavirus-closes-school.html.

Paoletti, J. B. (2012). *Pink and Blue: Telling the Boys from the Girls in America*. Bloomington, IN: Indiana University Press.

Parekh, B. (2010). "What Is Multiculturalism?" In Montserrat Guibernau and John Rex, eds., *The Ethnicity Reader: Nationalism, Multiculturalism, and Migration*, 2nd ed. (pp. 238–41). Malden, MA: Polity Press.

Parietti, M. (2019). "The World's Top 10 Telecommunications Companies." Investopedia, May 16. Retrieved from https://www.investopedia.com/articles/markets/030216/worlds-top-10-telecommunications-companies.asp.

Park, R. E. (1952). *Human Communities: The City and Human Ecology*. New York: Free Press.

Parker, K. (2012). *The Boomerang Generation Feeling OK about Living with Mom and Dad*. Washington, DC: Pew Social and Demographic Trends. Retrieved 8/07/12, from www.pewsocialtrends.org/2012/03/15/the-boomerang-generation/.

Parker, K. (2014). "Families may differ, but they share common values on parenting." Pew Research Organization, September 18. Retrieved 11/05/2014, from http://www.pewresearch.org/fact-tank/2014/09/18/families-may-differ-but-they-share-common-values-on-parenting/.

Parker, K., and R. Stepler. (2017). "Americans See Men as the Financial Providers, Even As Women's Contributions Grow." Pew Research Center, Sept. 20. Retrieved from https://www.pewresearch.org/fact-tank/2017/09/20/americans-see-men-as-the-financial-providers-even-as-womens-contributions-grow/.

Parker, K., and W. Wang. (2013). "Modern Parenthood." Pew Research Center. Retrieved 6/10/15, from http://www.pewsocialtrends.org/files/2013/03/FINAL_modern_parenthood_03_2013.pdf.

Parsons, T. (1960). "Towards a Healthy Maturity." *Journal of Health and Social Behavior* 1: 163–73.

Parsons, T. (1964; orig. 1951). *The Social System*. Glencoe, IL: Free Press.

Parsons, T., and R. F. Bales. (1955). *Family, Socialization, and Interaction Process*. Glencoe, IL: Free Press.

Parveen, S. (2014). "Rana Plaza factory collapse survivors struggle one year on," BBC News, April 23. Retrieved 4/8/15, from http://www.bbc.com/news/world-asia-27107860.

Pascoe, C. J. (2011). *Dude, You're a Fag: Masculinity and Sexuality in High School*, 2nd ed. Berkeley, CA: University of California Press.

Patten, E. (2016). "Racial, gender wage gaps persist in U.S. despite some progress." Pew Research Center, July 1. Retrieved from https://www.pewresearch.org/fact-tank/2016/07/01/racial-gender-wage-gaps-persist-in-u-s-despite-some-progress/.

Paul, D. Y. (1985). *Women in Buddhism: Images of the Feminine in the Mahayana Tradition*. Berkeley, CA: University of California Press.

Payscale. (2019). "Highest Paying Jobs With a Bachelor's Degree." College Salary Report. Retrieved from https://www.payscale.com/college-salary-report/majors-that-pay-you-back/bachelors?orderBy=midCareerMedianPay&ascending=true.

Pear, R. (2011). "Reshaping Medicare Brings Hard Choices." *New York Times*, April 12. Retrieved 8/10/12, from www.nytimes.com/2011/04/13/us/politics/13medicare.html.

Pearce, F. (1976). *Crimes of the Powerful: Marxism, Crime, and Deviance*. London: Pluto Press.

Peralta, E. (2013). "Court Overturns DOMA, Sidesteps Broad Gay Marriage Ruling." NPR. Retrieved 7/01/13, from www.npr.org/blogs/thetwo-way/2013/06/26/195857796/supreme-court-strikes-down-defense-of-marriage-act.

Pedulla, D. S., and S. Thébaud. (2015). "Can We Finish the Revolution? Gender, Work-Family Ideals, and Institutional Constraint." *American Sociological Review* 80(1): 116–139.

Pellow, D. N., and H. N. Brehm. (2013). "An Environmental Sociology for the 21st Century." *Annual Review of Sociology* 39: 229–50.

Pellow, D. N., and H. N. Brehm. (2015). "From the New Ecological Paradigm to Total Liberation: The Emergence of a Social Movement Frame." *The Sociological Quarterly* 56: 185–212.

Pellow, D. N. (2017). *What is Critical Environmental Justice?* Cambridge, UK: Polity Press.

Peluso, M., C. H. Baird, and L. Kesterson-Townes. (2019). "Women, Leadership, and the Priority Paradox." IBM Institute for Business Value. Retrieved from https://www.ibm.com/thought-leadership/institute-business-value/report/womeninleadership#

Penner, A. M. (2008). "Gender Differences in Extreme Mathematical Achievement: An International Perspective on Biological and Social Factors," *American Journal of Sociology*, 114(S1): S138–S170.

Perea, F. C. 2012. "Hispanic Health Paradox." In S. Loue and M. Sajatovic, eds., *Encyclopedia of Immigrant Health* (pp. 828–30). New York: Springer.

Perrin, A., and M. Anderson. (2019). "Share of U.S. adults using social media, including Facebook, is mostly unchanged since 2018." Pew Research Center, April 10. Retrieved from https://www.pewresearch.org/fact-tank/2019/04/10/share-of-u-s-adults-using-social-media-including-facebook-is-mostly-unchanged-since-2018/.

Perrin, A. J., P. N. Cohen, and N. Caren. (2013). "Are Children of Parents Who Had Same-Sex Relationships Disadvantaged? A Scientific Evaluation of the No-Differences Hypothesis." *Journal of Gay and Lesbian Mental Health*, 17(3), 327–336.

Persily, N. (2017). "The 2016 U.S. Election: Can Democracy Survive the Internet?" *Journal of Democracy*, 28, 2, 63–76.

Pescosolido, B. A., B. L. Perry, J. S. Long, J. K. Martin, J. I. Nurnberger, Jr., and V. Hesselbrock. (2008). "Under the Influence of Genetics: How Transdisciplinarity Leads Us to Rethink Social Pathways to Illness," *American Journal of Sociology*, 114(S1): S171–S201.

Pescosolido, B. A., T. R. Medina, J. K. Martin, and J. S. Long. (2013). "The 'backbone' of stigma: Identifying the global core of public prejudice associated with mental illness." *American Journal of Public Health*, 103, 853–860.

Peter G. Peterson Foundation (2019). "Budget Basics: Medicare." April 30. Retrieved from https://www.pgpf.org/budget-basics/medicare.

Peterson-Withorn, C. (2016). "Forbes 400: The Full List of the Richest People in America 2016." *Forbes*. Retrieved from https://www.forbes.com/sites/chasewithorn/2016/10/04/forbes-400-the-full-list-of-the-richest-people-in-america-2016/#3242e0ee22f4.

Petrovic, M., and G. G. Hamilton. (2006). "Making Global Markets: Wal-Mart and Its Suppliers." In N. Lichtenstein, ed., *Wal-Mart: The Face of Twenty-First-Century Capitalism*. New York: New Press.

Pew Research Center. (2003). Views of a Changing World 2003. Retrieved from https://www.pewresearch.org/global/2003/06/03/views-of-a-changing-world-2003/.

Pew Research Center. (2008). "U.S. Religious Landscape Survey." Pew Forum on Religion and Public Life, February. Retrieved spring 2011, frpm http://religions.pewforum.org/reports.

Pew Research Center. (2009). "Faith in Flux: Changes in Religious Affiliation in the U.S." Pew Forum on Religion and Public Life, April. Retrieved spring 2011, from http://pewforum.org/uploadedfiles/Topics/Religious_Affiliation/fullreport.pdf.

Pew Research Center. (2011a). "Common Concerns about Muslim Extremism: Muslim-Western Tensions Persist." Pew Global Attitudes Project, July 21. Retrieved spring 2013, from www.pewglobal.org/files/2011/07/Pew-Global-Attitudes-Muslim-Western-Relations-FINAL-FOR-PRINT-July-21-2011.pdf.

Pew Research Center. (2011b). "Global Survey of Evangelical Protestant Leaders." Pew Forum on Religion and Public Life, June 22. Retrieved spring 2013, from www.pewforum.org/uploadedFiles/Topics/Religious_Affiliation/Christian/Evangelical_Protestant_Churches/Global%20Survey%20of%20Evan.%20Prot.%20Leaders.pdf.

Pew Research Center. (2011c). "Social Networking Sites and Our Lives." Pew Research Internet Project. Retrieved from http://www.pewinternet.org/2011/06/16/social-networking-sites-and-our-lives/.

Pew Research Center. (2011d). "Cohabitation a Step Toward Marriage?" Pew (January 6, 2011). Retrieved from http://www.pewresearch.org/fact-tank/2011/01/06/cohabitation-a-step-toward-marriage/.

Pew Research Center. (2012a). "The Lost Decade of the Middle Class." Retrieved 3/5/15, from http://www.pewsocialtrends.org/2012/08/22/the-lost-decade-of-the-middle-class/.

Pew Research Center. (2012b). "The World's Muslims: Unity and Diversity." Pew Forum on Religion and Public Life, August 9. Retrieved summer 2012, from www.pewforum.org/Muslim/the-worlds-muslims-unity-and-diversity-executive-summary.aspx.

Pew Research Center. (2013a). "A Portrait of Jewish Americans." Retrieved 5/6/15, from http://www.pewforum.org/files/2013/10/jewish-american-full-report-for-web.pdf.

Pew Research Center. (2013b) "Online Dating and Relationships" October 21. Pew Research Center. Retrieved from http://www.pewinternet.org/files/old-media/Files/Reports/2013/PIP_Online%20Dating%202013.pdf.

Pew Research Center. (2013c). "The Rise of Asian Americans." Retrieved from http://www.pewsocialtrends.org/files/2013/04/Asian-Americans-new-full-report-04-2013.pdf.

Pew Research Center. (2014a). "2014 Political Polarization and Topline Survey." September 16. Retrieved 12/14, from http://www.people-press.org/files/2014/06/2014-Polarization-Topline-for-Release.pdf.

Pew Research Center. (2014b). "Most See Inequality Growing, but Partisans Differ Over Solutions." Pew Research Center for the People and the Press, January 23. Retrieved 12/14, from http://www.people-press.org/2014/01/23/most-see-inequality-growing-but-partisans-differ-over-solutions/.

Pew Research Center. (2014c). "The Rising Cost of Not Going to College." Pew Research Social Demographic Trends, February 11. Retrieved from http://www.pewsocialtrends.org/2014/02/11/the-rising-cost-of-not-going-to-college/.

Pew Research Center. (2014d). "Social Networking Fact Sheet." Pew Research Internet Project. Retrieved from http://www.pewinternet.org/fact-sheets/social-networking-fact-sheet/.

Pew Research Center (2014e). "How Americans Feel About Religious Groups." July 16. Retrieved summer 2014, from http://www.pewforum.org/2014/07/16/how-americans-feel-about-religious-groups/.

Pew Research Center. (2014f). "Faith and Skepticism about Trade, Foreign Investment." Retrieved from http://www.pewglobal.org/2014/09/16/faith-and-skepticism-about-trade-foreign-investment/.

Pew Research Center. (2015a). "The Future of World Religions: Population Growth Projections: 2010–2050." Retrieved 5/5/15, from http://www.pewforum.org/2015/04/02/religious-projections-2010-2050/.

Pew Research Center. (2015b). "Most Say Government Policies Since Recession Have Done Little to Help Middle Class, Poor." Retrieved 3/5/15, from http://www.people-press.org/2015/03/04/most-say-government-policies-since-recession-have-done-little-to-help-middle-class-poor.

Pew Research Center. (2015c). "America's Changing Religious Landscape." Retrieved from http://www.pewforum.org/2015/05/12/americas-changing-religious-landscape/.

Pew Research Center. (2015d). "U.S. Catholics Open to Non-Traditional Families." Retrieved from http://www.pewforum.org/2015/09/02/u-s-catholics-open-to-non-traditional-families/.

Pew Research Center. (2016a). "Behind Trump's victory: Divisions by race, gender, education," Nov. 9. Retrieved from http://www.pewresearch.org/fact-tank/2016/11/09/behind-trumps-victory-divisions-by-race-gender-education/.

Pew Research Center. (2016b). "Election 2016: Campaigns as a Direct Source of News," July 18. Retrieved from http://www.journalism.org/2016/07/18/candidates-differ-in-their-use-of-social-media-to-connect-with-the-public/.

Pew Research Center. (2016c). "Most Americans Say Government Doesn't Do Enough to Help Middle Class." Feb. 4. Retrieved from https://www.pewsocialtrends.org/2016/02/04/most-americans-say-government-doesnt-do-enough-to-help-middle-class/.

Pew Research Center (2016d). "On Views of Race and Inequality, Blacks and Whites Are Worlds Apart." Retrieved from http://www.pewsocialtrends.org/files/2016/06/ST_2016.06.27_Race-Inequality-Final.pdf.

Pew Research Center. (2016e). "Smartphone Ownership and Internet Usage Continues to Climb in Emerging Economies," p. 21. Pew Research Center (February). Retrieved from http://www.pewglobal.org/2016/02/22/social-networking-very-popular-among-adult-internet-users-in-emerging-and-developing-nations/.

Pew Research Center. (2016f). "State of the News Media 2015." Pew Research Center Journalism and Media. (April 29). Retrieved from http://www.journalism.org/files/2015/04/FINAL-STATE-OF-THE-NEWS-MEDIA1.pdf.

Pew Research Center. (2017a). "Internet and Broadband Fact Sheet. Retrieved from http://www.pewinternet.org/fact-sheet/internet-broadband/.

Pew Research Center. (2017b). "Social Media Factsheet," January 12. Retrieved from http://www.pewinternet.org/fact-sheet/social-media/.

Pew Research Center. (2017c). "The Changing Global Religious Landscape." Retrieved from http://www.pewforum.org/2017/04/05/the-changing-global-religious-landscape/.

Pew Research Center. (2018). "The Age Gap in Religion Around the World." Retrieved from https://www.pewforum.org/wp-content/uploads/sites/7/2018/06/ReligiousCommitment-FULL-WEB.pdf.

Pew Research Center. (2019a). "Attitudes on Same-Sex Marriage." May 14. Retrieved from https://www.pewforum.org/fact-sheet/changing-attitudes-on-gay-marriage/.

Pew Research Center. (2019b). "Internet/Broadband Fact Sheet." June 12. Retrieved from https://www.pewresearch.org/internet/fact-sheet/internet-broadband/.

Pew Research Center. (2019c). "In U.S., Decline of Christianity Continues at Rapid Pace." Oct. 17. Retrieved from https://www.pewforum.org/2019/10/17/in-u-s-decline-of-christianity-continues-at-rapid-pace/.

Pew Research Center. (2019d). "Little Public Support for Reductions in Federal Spending." April 11. Retrieved from https://www.people-press.org/2019/04/11/little-public-support-for-reductions-in-federal-spending/.

Pew Research Center. (2019e). "Mobile Fact Sheet." June 12. Retrieved from https://www.pewresearch.org/internet/fact-sheet/mobile/.

Pew Research Center. (2019f). "Public Trust in Government: 1958–2019." April 11. Retrieved from https://www.people-press.org/2019/04/11/public-trust-in-government-1958-2019/.

Pew Research Center. (2019g). "Same-Sex Marriage Around the World." Oct. 28. Retrieved from https://www.pewforum.org/fact-sheet/gay-marriage-around-the-world/.

Pew Research Center for the People and the Press. (2005). "GOP Makes Gains among the Working Class, While Democrats Hold On to the Union Vote," August 2. Retrieved spring 2011, from http://people-press.org/commentary/?analysisid=114 (site discontinued).

Pew Research Center for the People and the Press. (2011). "Public Wants Changes in Entitlements, Not Changes in Benefits: GOP Divided over Benefit Reductions." Retrieved 8/09/12, from http://pewresearch.org/pubs/2051/medicare-medicaid-social-security-republicans-entitlements-budget-deficit.

Pew Research Center for the People and the Press. (2012). "The Rise of Asian Americans." Pew Social and Demographic Trends. Retrieved from www.pewsocialtrends.org/files/2012/06/SDT-The-Rise-of-Asian-Americans-Full-Report.pdf.

Pew Research Hispanic Center. (2013). "Population Decline of Unauthorized Immigrants Stalls, May Have Reversed." September 23. Retrieved summer 2014, from http://www.pewhispanic.org/2013/09/23/population-decline-of-unauthorized-immigrants-stalls-may-have-reversed/.

Phelan, J. C. (2005). "Geneticization of deviant behavior and consequences for stigma. The case of mental illness." Journal of Health and Social Behavior 46, 307–22.

PHI National. (2019). "Direct Care Worker Projected Job Openings, 2018 to 2028." Workforce Data Center. Retrieved from https://phinational.org/policy-research/workforce-data-center/#tab=National+Data.

Picchi, A. (2019). "How much income you need to be in the 1%." CBS News, February 6. Retrieved from https://www.cbsnews.com/news/how-much-income-you-need-to-be-in-the-1/.

Pickett, K. and R. Wilkinson. (2011). The Spirit Level: Why Greater Equality Makes Societies Stronger. London: Bloomsbury.

Pierce, C., and J. Dimsdale (1986). "Suppressed anger and blood pressure: the effects of race, sex, social class, obesity, and age". Psychomatic Medicine. 48 (6): 430–36.

Pierce, F. (2013). "More Scientists Now Think Geoengineering May Be Essential." Wired, June 11. Retrieved from https://www.wired.com/story/more-scientists-now-think-geoengineering-may-be-essential/.

Piketty, T. and A. Goldhammer (translator). (2014). Capital in the 21st Century. Belknap Press.

Piketty, T. and Zucman, G. (2014). "Capital is back: Wealth-income ratios in rich countries, 1700–2010." Quarterly Journal of Economics, 129: 1255–1310. Retrieved 12/14, from http://piketty.pse.ens.fr/files/PikettyZucman2014QJE.pdf.

Pine, J. (1999). Mass Customization: The New Frontier in Business Competition. Cambridge, MA: Harvard Business School Press.

Pinquart, M., and S. Sorensen. (2006). "Gender Differences in Caregiver Stressors, Social Resources, and Health: An Updated Meta-Analysis." Journals of Gerontology, Series B (Psychological Sciences and Social Sciences) 61(1): 33–45.

Piore, M. J., and C. F. Sabel. (1984). The Second Industrial Divide: Possibilities for Prosperity. New York: Basic Books.

Pitts, S. (2011). "Research Brief: Black Workers and the Public Sector." Berkeley, CA: University of California–Berkeley Center for Labor Research and Education. Retrieved 6/18/12. http://laborcenter.berkeley.edu/blackworkers/blacks_public_sector11.pdf.

Poisson, J. (2013). "Remember Storm? We check in on the baby being raised gender-neutral." Star. November 15. Retrieved 10/14, from http://www.thestar.com/life/parent/2013/11/15/remember_storm_we_check_in_on_the_baby_being_raised_genderneutral.html.

Pollak, O. (1950). The Criminality of Women. Philadelphia: University of Pennsylvania Press.

Pollard, K. (2011). The Gender Gap in College Enrollment and Graduation. Washington, DC: Population Reference Bureau. Retrieved 10/19/12, from www.prb.org/Articles/2011/gender-gap-in-education.aspx.

Polletta, F., and J. M. Jasper. (2001). "Collective Identity and Social Movements." Annual Review of Sociology 27: 283–305.

Polonski, V. (2016). "Impact of Social Media on the Outcome of the EU Referendum," EU Referendum Analysis 2016, Retrieved from http://www.referendumanalysis.eu/eu-referendum-analysis-2016/section-7-social-media/impact-of-social-media-on-the-outcome-of-the-eu-referendum/.

Pomerleau, A., Bolduc, D., Malcuit, G., and Cossette, L. (1990). "Pink or Blue: Environmental Gender Stereotypes in the First Two Years of Life." Sex Roles, 22(5–6), 359–367.

Pomerleau, K. (2013). "Summary of Latest Federal Income Tax Data." Tax Foundation, December 28. Retrieved 12/14, from http://taxfoundation.org/article/summary-latest-federal-income-tax-data.

Ponciano, J., and S. Hansen. (2019). "World's Largest Public Companies 2019: Global 2020 by the Numbers." Forbes, May 15. Retrieved from https://www.forbes.com/sites/jonathanponciano/2019/05/15/worlds-largest-companies-2019-global-2000/#488727814ada.

Pope, H. G., K. A. Phillips, and R. Olivardia. (2002). The Adonis Complex: How to Identify, Treat and Prevent Body Obsession in Men and Boys. New York: Free Press.

Popenoe, D. (1993). "American Family Decline, 1960–1990: A Review and Appraisal." *Journal of Marriage and Family* 55: 527–55.

Popenoe, D. (1996). *Life without Father: Compelling New Evidence That Fatherhood and Marriage Are Indispensable for the Good of Children and Society.* New York: Martin Kessler Books.

Porter, S. R., and P. D. Umbach. (2006). "College major choice: An analysis of student-environment fit." *Research in Higher Education* 47(4): 429–49.

Posner, S. (2016). "How Donald Trump's New Campaign Chief Created an Online Ha-ven for White Nationalists," *Mother Jones,* Aug. 22, Retrieved from http://www.motherjones.com/politics/2016/08/stephen-bannon-donald-trump-alt-right-breitbart-news.

Pospisil, M., F. Foiadelli, P. Anton, and P. Dvorak. (2019). "Introducing the EBRD Knowledge Economy Index." European Bank for Reconstruction and Development. Retrieved from https://www.ebrd.com/documents/policy/download-the-ebrds-knowledge-economy-index.pdf.

Potter, K. H. (1992). "Hinduism." *The American Academic Encyclopedia* (online ed.). Danbury, CT: Grolier Electronic.

Poushter, J., and C. Huang. (2019). "Climate Change Still Seen as the Top Global Threat, but Cyberattacks a Rising Concern." Pew Research Center, Feb. 10. Retrieved from https://www.pewresearch.org/global/2019/02/10/climate-change-still-seen-as-the-top-global-threat-but-cyberattacks-a-rising-concern/.

Poushter, J., and D. Manevich. (2017). "Globally, People Point to ISIS and Climate Change as Leading Security Threats," Pew Research Center, Aug. 1, Retrieved from http://www.pewglobal.org/2017/08/01/globally-people-point-to-isis-and-climate-change-as-leading-security-threats/#in-middle-east-and-north-africa-overwhelming-concern-about-isis.

Powell, M. (2009). "Bank Accused of Pushing Mortgage Deals on Blacks." *New York Times,* June 6. Retrieved spring 2011, from www.nytimes.com/2009/06/07/us/07baltimore.html?pagewanted=1&_r=1.

Powell, W. W., and P. Brantley. (1992). "Competitive Cooperation in Biotechnology: Learning through Networks?" In N. Nohria and R. Eccles, eds., *Networks and Organizations: Structure, Form and Action.* Boston: Harvard Business School Press.

Powell, W. W., K. W. Koput, and L. Smith-Doerr. (1996). "Interorganizational Collaboration and the Locus of Innovation: Networks of Learning in Biotechnology." *Administration Science Quarterly* 41.

Prebisch, R. (1967). *Hacia Una Dinamica del Desarollo Latinoamericano.* Montevideo, Uruguay: Ediciones de la Banda Oriental.

Prebisch, R. (1971). "Change and Development—Latin America's Great Task." Report Submitted to the Inter-American Bank. New York: Praeger.

President's Commission on Organized Crime. (1986). "Records of Hearings, June 24–26, 1985." Washington, DC: U.S. Government Printing Office.

Presto, S., B. Gingras, and C. Welch. (2017). "Trump Voters to President: Stop Twitter Rants" *CNN,* March 29, Retrieved from http://www.cnn.com/2017/03/28/politics/trump-tweets-supporters-ccntv/.

Priest, N., J. Walton, F. White, E. Kowal, A. Baker, and Y. Paradies. (2014). "Understanding the Complexities of Ethnic-Racial Socialization Processes for Both Minority and Majority Groups: A 30-Year Review." *International Journal of Intercultural Relations,* 43, 139–155.

Proctor, B., J. Semega, and M. Kollar. (2016) "Income and Poverty in the United States: 2015." Retrieved from https://www.census.gov/content/dam/Census/library/publications/2016/demo/p60-256.pdf.

Prydz, E. B. and D. Wadhwa (2019). "Classifying countries by income." World Bank. Retrieved from https://datatopics.worldbank.org/world-development-indicators/stories/the-classification-of-countries-by-income.html.

Puglise, N. (2016). "Exit Polls and Election Results—What We Learned." *Guardian,* Nov. 12. Retrieved from https://www.theguardian.com/us-news/2016/nov/12/exit-polls-election-results-what-we-learned.

Puhl, R. M., and J. D. Latner. (2007). "Stigma, obesity, and the health of the nation's children." *Psychological Bulletin* 133: 557–80.

Qian, Z., and D. T. Lichter. (2017). "Racial Pairings and Fertility: Do Interracial Couples Have Fewer Children?" Population Association of America 2018 Annual Meeting. Retrieved from https://paa.confex.com/paa/2018/meetingapp.cgi/Paper/20332.

Quadagno, J. (1989). "Generational Equity and the Politics of the Welfare State." *Politics and Society* 17: 353–76.

Quadlin, N., and L. Doan. (2018). "Sex-Typed Chores and the City: Gender, Urbanicity, and Housework." *Gender and Society* 32(6): 789–813.

Quah, D. (1999). *The Weightless Economy in Economic Development.* London: Centre for Economic Performance.

Qureshi, S. (2016). "Annual determination of average cost of incarceration." Federal Bureau of Prisons. Retrieved from https://www.federalregister.gov/documents/2016/07/19/2016-17040/annual-determination-of-average-cost-of-incarceration.

Rabkin, A. (2011). "The Facebooks of China." *Fast Company.* Retrieved from http://www.fastcompany.com/1715041/facebookschina.

Radford, J. (2019). "Key findings about U.S. immigrants." Pew Research Center, June 17. Retrieved from https://www.pewresearch.org/fact-tank/2019/06/17/key-findings-about-u-s-immigrants/.

Raley, R. K., M. M. Sweeney, and D. Wondra. (2015). "The growing racial and ethnic divide in US marriage patterns." *The Future of Children* 25(2): 89.

Ramirez, F. O., and J. Boli. (1987). "The Political Construction of Mass Schooling: European Origins and Worldwide Institutionalism." *Sociology of Education* 60.

Ranis, G. (1996). *Will Latin America Now Put a Stop to "Stop-and-Go"?* New Haven, CT: Yale University, Economic Growth Center.

Ranis, G., and S. A. Mahmood. (1992). *The Political Economy of Development Policy Change.* Cambridge, MA: Blackwell.

Rank, M. R., H. Yoon, and T. A. Hirschl. (2003). "American Poverty as Structural Failing: Evidence and Arguments." *Journal of Sociology and Social Welfare* 30(4): 3–29.

Rao, A. (2019). "Uber was Designed to Exploit Drivers." *Vice,* May 8. Retrieved from https://www.vice.com/en_us/article/3k3kdn/uber-was-designed-to-exploit-drivers.

Ratcliffe, M., C. Burd, K. Holder, and A. Fields. (2016). "Defining Rural at the U.S. Census Bureau: American Community Survey and Geography Brief." U.S. Bureau of the Census. Retrieved from https://www.census.gov/content/dam/Census/library/publications/2016/acs/acsgeo-1.pdf.

Reardon, S. (2011). "The widening academic achievement gap between the rich and the poor: New evidence and possible explanations." In R. Murnane and G. Duncan, eds., *Whither Opportunity? Rising Inequality and the Uncertain Life Chances of Low-Income Children,* New York: Russell Sage Foundation Press.

Reardon, S. (2012). "The widening academic achievement gap between the rich and the poor." *Community Investments: Summer 2012,* 24(2): 19–39.

Reardon, S. (2015). "US science academies take on human-genome editing." *Nature,* May 18. Retrieved from http://www.nature.com/news/us-science-academies-take-on-human-genome-editing-1.17581.

Redford, J., D. Battle, and S. Bielick. (2017). "Homeschooling in the United States: 2012 (NCES 2016-096.REV)." National Center for Education Statistics, Institute of Education Sciences, U.S. Department of Education. Washington, DC.

Regnerus, M. (2012). "How different are the adult children of parents who have same-sex relationships? Findings from the New Family Structures Study." *Social Science Research* 41(4): 752–70.

Reich, R. (1991). *The Work of Nations: Preparing Ourselves for 21st Century Capitalism.* New York: Knopf.

Reinhart, R. J. (2018). "Global Warming Age Gap: Younger Americans Most Worried," Gallup, May 11. Retrieved from https://news.gallup.com/poll/234314/global-warming-age-gap-younger-americans-worried.aspx.

Renzetti, C., and D. Curran. (1995). *Women, Men, and Society,* 3rd ed. Needham, MA: Allyn and Bacon.

Reuter, P., and V. Greenfield. (2001). "Measuring Global Drug Markets: How Good Are the Numbers and Why Should We Care about Them?" *World Economics* 2(4).

Rhoades, G. K., S. M. Stanley, and H. J. Markman. (2009). "Couples' Reasons for Cohabitation. Associations with Individual Well-Being and Relationship Quality." *Journal of Family Issues* 30: 233–58.

Richardson, D., and H. May. (1999). "Deserving Victims? Sexual Status and the Social Construction of Violence." *Sociological Review* 47: 308–31.

Richardson, S. A., N. Goodman, A. H. Hastorf, and S. M. Dornbusch. (1961). "Cultural Uniformity in Reaction to Physical Disabilities." *American Sociological Review* 26: 241–47.

Riley, M. W., A. Foner, and J. Waring. (1988). "Sociology of Age." In N. J. Smelser, ed., *Handbook of Sociology.* Newbury Park, CA: Sage.

Rios, V. (2011). *Punished: Policing the Lives of Black and Latino Boys.* New York: New York University Press.

Ritzer, G. (1993). *The McDonaldization of Society.* Newbury Park, CA: Pine Forge Press.

Robinson, W. I. (2004). *A Theory of Global Capitalism: Production, Class and State in a Transnational World.* Baltimore, MD: Johns Hopkins University Press.

Robinson, W. I. (2014). *Global Capitalism and the Crisis of Humanity.* Cambridge, UK: Cambridge University Press.

Robinson, W. I. (2017). "Global Capitalism: Reflections on a Brave New World." Great Transition Initiative. Retrieved from http://www.greattransition.org/publication/global-capitalism.

Robinson, W. I. (2019). *Into the Tempest: Essays on the New Global Capitalism.* Chicago: Haymarket Books.

Robles, F. (2017). "23% of Puerto Ricans Vote in Referendum, 97% of Them for Statehood," *New York Times,* June 11. Retrieved from https://www.nytimes.com/2017/06/11/us/puerto-ricans-vote-on-the-question-of-statehood.html.

Roof, W. C. (1993). *A Generation of Seekers: The Spiritual Journeys of the Baby Boom Generation.* San Francisco: Harper San Francisco.

Roof, W. C., J. W. Carroll, and D. A. Roozen, eds. (1995). *The Post-War Generation and Establishment Religion: Cross-Cultural Perspectives.* Boulder, CO: Westview Press.

Roof, W. C., and W. McKinney. (1990). *American Mainline Religion: Its Changing Shape and Future Prospects.* New Brunswick, NJ: Rutgers University Press.

Rook, E. (2017). "Google Home Ad Reminds Us That Gay Parents Start Their Day Like Any Others." *LGBTQ Nation* (April 23, 2017). Retrieved from https://www.lgbtqnation.com/2017/04/google-home-ad-reminds-us-gay-parents-start-day-like-others/.

Roos, P., and B. Reskin. (1992). "Occupational Desegregation in the 1970s—Integration and Economic Equity." *Sociological Perspectives* 35: 69–91.

Rose, S. J., and H. I. Hartmann. "Still a Man's Labor Market." (2018). Institute for Women's Policy Research. Retrieved from https://iwpr.org/wp-content/uploads/2018/11/C474_IWPR-Still-a-Mans-Labor-Market-update-2018-1.pdf.

Rosen, D. (2008). "Rape as an Instrument of Total War." *Counterpunch.* Retrieved spring 2013, from www.counterpunch.org/2008/04/04/rape-as-an-instrument-of-total-war/.

Rosenau, J. N. (1997). *Along the Domestic-Foreign Frontier: Exploring Governance in a Turbulent World.* Cambridge, UK: Cambridge University Press.

Rosenfeld, J. (2014). *What Unions No Longer Do.* Cambridge, MA: Harvard University Press.

Rosenfeld, M. (2018). "Are Tinder and Dating Apps Changing Dating and Mating in the USA?" In J. Van Hook, S. M. McHale, and V. King, eds., *Families and Technology* (pp. 103–117). Cham: Springer.

Rosenfeld, M. J. (2010). "Nontraditional Families and Childhood Progress through School." *Demography* 47: 755–75.

Rosenstock, I. (1974). "Historical Origins of the Health Belief Model." *Health Education Monographs* 2(4).

Roser, M., and E. Ortiz-Espina. (2017). "Income Inequality," Our World in Data, Retrieved from https://ourworldindata.org/income-inequality/.

Ross, N., and A. Mohammadpur. (2016). "Imagined or Real: the Intersection of Tribalism and Nationalism in the Kurdish Regional Government (KRG)," *British Journal of Middle Eastern Studies.*

Rostow, W. W. (1961). *The Stages of Economic Growth.* Cambridge, UK. Cambridge University Press.

Rothenberg, P. (2007). *Race, Class and Gender in the United States,* 7th ed. New York: Worth.

Rothstein, R. (2017). *The Color of Law.* New York, NY: W. W. Norton & Company.

Rousselle, R. (1999). "Defining Ancient Greek Sexuality. *Digital Archives of Psychohistory* 26 (4). Retrieved 1/11/05, from www.geocities.com/kidhistory/ja/defining.htm (site discontinued).

Rowe, R. H., and R. L. Kahn. (1987). "Human Aging: Usual and Successful." *Science* 237: 10143–49.

Rubin, J., F. Provenzano, and Z. Luria. (1974). "The Eye of the Beholder: Parents' Views on Sex of Newborns." *American Journal of Orthopsychiatry,* 44, 512–519.

Rubin, K. H., W. Bukowski, and J. Parker. (2006). "Peer Interactions, Relationships, and Groups." In N. Eisenberg (Ed.), *Handbook of Child Psychology: Social, Emotional, and Personality Development* (6th ed., pp. 571–645). New York: Wiley.

Rubin, L. B. (1990). *Erotic Wars: What Happened to the Sexual Revolution?* New York: Farrar, Straus and Giroux.

Rubinstein, S., and B. Caballero. (2000). Is Miss America an undernourished role model? *Journal of the American Medical Association* 283: 12. Retrieved 10/23/14, from http://jama.jamanetwork.com/article.aspx?articleid=1731376.

Rudé, G. (1964). *The Crowd in History: A Study of Popular Disturbances in France and England, 1730–1848*. New York: Wiley.

Rudner, L. (1999). "Scholastic Achievement and Demographic Characteristics of Home Schooled Students in 1998." *Educational Policy Analysis Archive* 7(8).

Rummel, K. (2020). "Teacher's Note: How to homeschool during coronavirus." *Al Jazeera*, March 25. Retrieved from https://www.aljazeera.com/indepth/features/teacher-note-homeschool-coronavirus-200324172503525.html.

Russell Sage. (2014). "Future of Work: A History of the Program," Retrieved from http://www.russellsage.org/research/future-work-detailed.

Russell, S. T., and K. Joyner. (2001). "Adolescent sexual orientation and suicide risk: Evidence from a national study." *American Journal of Public Health* 91: 1276–81.

Rutgers. (2020). "Facts on Women of Color in Office." Center for American Women and Politics. Retrieved from https://cawp.rutgers.edu/fact-sheets-women-color.

Rutten, T. (2018). "Breaking the binary: exploring gender self-presentation and passing on #TransIsBeautiful on Instagram." Master's Thesis, Uppsala University. Retrieved from http://uu.diva-portal.org/smash/record.jsf?pid=diva2%3A1186144&dswid=9318.

Ryan C., D. Huebner, R. M. Diaz, and J. Sanchez. (2009). "Family rejection as a predictor of negative health outcomes in white and Latino lesbian, gay, and bisexual young adults." *Pediatrics* 123: 346–52.

Saad, L. (2018). "Catholics' Church Attendance Resumes Downward Slide." Gallup, April 9. Retrieved from https://news.gallup.com/poll/232226/church-attendance-among-catholics-resumes-downward-slide.aspx.

Sackmann, R., and M. Wingens. (2003). "From Transitions to Trajectories: Sequence Types." In W. R. Heinz, ed., *Social Dynamics of the Life Course: Transitions, Institutions, and Interrelations*. New York: Aldine de Gruyter.

Sadker, M., and D. Sadker. (1994). *Failing at Fairness*. New York: Scribner.

Saez, E. (2016). "Striking it Richer: The Evolution of Top Incomes in the United States," Retrieved from https://eml.berkeley.edu/,saez/saez-UStopincomes-2015.pdf.

Saez, E. (2018). "Striking it Richer: The Evolution of Top Incomes in the United States (updated with 2018 estimates)." Retrieved from https://eml.berkeley.edu/,saez/saez-UStopincomes-2018.pdf.

Saez, E., and G. Zucman. (2016). "Wealth Inequality in the United States since 1913: Evidence from Capitalized Income Tax Data." The *Quarterly Journal of Economics* 131 (2): 519-578.

Saguy, A. (2012). *What's Wrong with Fat?* New York: Oxford University Press.

Saguy, A. C. (2020). *Come Out, Come Out, Whoever You Are*. New York: Oxford University Press.

Sahliyeh, E., ed. (1990). *Religious Resurgence and Politics in the Contemporary World*. Albany, NY: State University of New York Press.

Saks, M., ed. (1992). *Alternative Medicine in Britain*. Oxford, UK: Clarendon.

Salganik, M. J., P. S. Dodds, and D. J. Watts. (2006). "Experimental Study of Inequality and Unpredictability in an Artificial Cultural Market." *Science* 311(5762): 854–56.

Saliu, O., and G. Jun. (2019). "Africa." *Xinhua News*, April 30. Retrieved from http://www.xinhuanet.com/english/africa/2019-04/30/c_138025503.htm.

SAMHSA. (2010). "Violent Behaviors among Adolescent Females." Retrieved from http://oas.samhsa.gov/2k9/171/171FemaleViolence.cfm.

Sampson, R. J., and J. Cohen. (1988). "Deterrent Effects of the Police on Crime: A Replication and Theoretical Extension." *Law and Society Review* 22(1).

Sandefur, G., and C. Liebler. (1997). "The Demography of American Indian Families." *Population Research and Policy Review* 16: 95–114.

Sandler, L. (2013). "The Childfree Life: When Having It All Means Not Having Children." *TIME Magazine* (August 12, 2013): 38-45.

Sarkisian, N., and N. Gerstel. (2004). "Kin Support among Blacks and Whites: Race and Family Organization." *American Sociological Review* 69: 812–37.

Sartre, J. (1965; orig. 1948). *Anti-Semite and Jew*. New York: Schocken Books.

Sassen, S. (1991). *The Global City: New York, London, Tokyo*. Princeton, NJ: Princeton University Press.

Sassen, S. (1996). *Losing Control. Sovereignty in the Age of Globalization*. New York: Columbia University Press.

Sassen, S. (1998). *Globalization and Its Discontents*. New York: New Press.

Sassler, S., K. Michelmore, and Z. Qian. (2018). "Transitions from Sexual Relationships into Cohabitation and Beyond." *Demography* 55(2): 511–534.

Sasson, I., and M. D. Hayward. (2019). "Association Between Educational Attainment and Causes of Death Among White and Black US Adults, 2010-2017." *Journal of the American Medical Association* 322(8): 756–763.

Savage, D. G. (1998). "Same-Sex Harassment Illegal, Says High Court." *Los Angeles Times*, March 5.

Sayers, J. (1986). *Sexual Contradiction: Psychology, Psychoanalysis, and Feminism*. New York: Methuen.

Schafer, M. H., and K. F. Ferraro. (2011). "Childhood misfortune as a threat to successful aging: avoiding disease." *Gerontologist* 52(1): 111–20

Schaie, K. W. (1983). *Longitudinal Studies of Adult Psychological Development*. New York: Guilford Press.

Schaie, K. W., and S. L. Willis. (2010). *Handbook of the Psychology of Aging*, 7th ed. New York: Academic Press.

Scheff, T. (1966). *Being Mentally Ill*. Chicago: Aldine.

Schiller, J. S., J. W. Lucas, B. W. Ward, and J. A. Peregoy. (2012). "Summary Health Statistics for U.S. Adults: National Health Interview Survey, 2010." *Vital Health Statistics* 10(252):1–207.

Schmidt, R. (1980). *Exploring Religion*. Belmont, CA: Wadsworth.

Schmitt, J. (2012). "Low-Wage Lessons," Center for Economic and Policy Research, January. Retrieved from http://www.cepr.net/documents/publications/low-wage-2012-01.pdf.

Schnaiberg, A. (1980). *The Environment: From Surplus to Scarcity*. New York: Oxford University Press.

Schneider, F., and D. Enste. (2002). "Hiding in the Shadows: The Growth of the Underground Economy." *International Monetary Fund*, March. Retrieved spring 2013, from www.imf.org/external/pubs/ft/issues/issues30/index.htm#3.

Schneider, S. K., L. O'Donnell, A. Stueve, and R. W. Coulter. (2012). "Cyberbullying, School Bullying, and Psychological Distress: A Regional Census of High School Students." *American Journal of Public Health*, 102(1), 171–177.

Schulman, M. (2013). "Generation LGBTQIA." *New York Times*, January 9. Retrieved 10/22/14, from http://www.nytimes.com/2013/01/10/fashion/generation-lgbtqia.html?pagewanted=all.

Schumpeter, J. (1983; orig. 1942). *Capitalism, Socialism, and Democracy*. Magnolia, MA: Peter Smith.

Schwartz, G. (1970). *Sect Ideologies and Social Status*. Chicago: University of Chicago Press.

Scott, R. E. (2015). "The Manufacturing Footprint and the Importance of U.S. Manufacturing Jobs." Economic Policy Institute. Retrieved from http://www.epi.org/publication/the-manufacturing-footprint-and-the-importance-of-u-s-manufacturing-jobs/.

Scott, S., and D. Morgan. (1993). "Bodies in a Social Landscape." In S. Scott and D. Morgan, eds., *Body Matters: Essays on the Sociology of the Body*. Washington, DC: Falmer Press.

Scully, D. (1990). *Understanding Sexual Violence: A Study of Convicted Rapists*. Boston: Unwin Hyman.

Sedlak, A., and D. Broadhurst. (1996). *Third National Incidence Study of Child Abuse and Neglect*. Washington, DC: U.S. Department of Health and Human Services.

Seeman, T. E., S. S. Merkin, E. M. Crimmins, and A. S. Karlamangla. (2009). "Disability Trends among Older Americans: National Health and Nutrition Examination Surveys, 1988–1994 and 1999–2004." *American Journal of Public Health* 100: 100–107.

Segura, D. A., and J. L. Pierce. (1993). "Chicana/o Family Structure and Gender Personality: Chodorow, Familism, and Psychoanalytic Sociology Revisited." *Signs* 19: 62–91.

Seidman, S. (1997). "Relativizing Sociology: The Challenge of Cultural Studies." In E. Long, ed., *From Sociology to Cultural Studies: New Perspectives*. Malden, MA: Blackwell.

Seidman, S., C. Meeks, and F. Traschen. (1999). "Beyond the Closet? The Changing Social Meaning of Homosexuality in the United States." *Sexualities* 2(1): 9–34.

Semega, J., M. Kollar, J. Creamer, and A. Mohanty. (2019a). "Income and Poverty in the United States: 2018." U.S. Bureau of the Census. Retrieved from https://www.census.gov/content/dam/Census/library/publications/2019/demo/p60-266.pdf

Semega, J., M. Kollar, J. Creamer, and A. Mohanty. (2019b). "Income and Poverty in the United States: 2018." Table A-1. U.S. Bureau of the Census. Retrieved from https://www.census.gov/data/tables/2019/demo/income-poverty/p60-266.html.

Semega, J., M. Kollar, J. Creamer, and A. Mohanty. (2019c). "Income and Poverty in the United States: 2018." Table B-1. U.S. Bureau of the Census. Retrieved from https://www.census.gov/data/tables/2019/demo/income-poverty/p60-266.html.

Semega, J., M. Kollar, J. Creamer, and A. Mohanty. (2019d). "Income and Poverty in the United States: 2018." Table B-2. U.S. Bureau of the Census. Retrieved from https://www.census.gov/data/tables/2019/demo/income-poverty/p60-266.html.

Semuels, A. (2015). "'Good' Jobs Aren't Coming Back." *The Atlantic*, October 26. Retrieved from http://www.theatlantic.com/business/archive/2015/10/onshoring-jobs/412201/.

Semmes, C. E. (2001). "E. Franklin Frazier's theory of the Black family: Vindication and sociological insight." *Journal of Sociology and Social Welfare* 28(2): 3–21.

Sen, A. (2010). "Equality of what?" In S. M. MacMurrin, ed., The Tanner Lectures on Human Values (pp. 195–220). Cambridge, UK: Cambridge University Press.

Senchuk, D. M. (1990). "Listening to a Different Voice: A Feminist Critique of Gilligan." *Studies in Philosophy and Education* 10(3): 233–49.

Sengupta, S. (2019). "Protesting Climate Change, Young People Take to Streets in a Global Strike." *New York Times*, Sept. 20. Retrieved from https://www.nytimes.com/2019/09/20/climate/global-climate-strike.html.

Sepúlveda, A. R., and M. Calado. (2012). "Westernization: The Role of Mass Media on Body Image and Eating Disorders." In I. J. Lobera, ed., Relevant Topics in Eating Disorders. InTech. Retrieved from http://cdn.intechopen.com/pdfs/29049/InTechWesternization_the_role_of_mass_media_on_body_image_and_eating_disorders.pdf.

Seville Statement on Violence. (1990). *American Psychologist* 45 (10): 1167–68. Retrieved 1/03/05, from www.lraino.com/swtaboo/taboos/seville1.html (site discontinued).

Sewell, W. H., Jr. (1992). "A Theory of Structure: Duality, Agency, and Transformation." *American Journal of Sociology* 98:1–29.

Sewell, W. H., Jr. (1999). "The Concept of Culture." In V. E. Bonnell and L. Hunt, eds., *Beyond the Cultural Turn*. Berkeley, CA: University of California Press.

Sewell, W. H., and R. M. Hauser. (1980). "The Wisconsin Longitudinal Study of Social and Psychological Factors in Aspirations and Achievements." In A. C. Kerckhoff, ed., *Research in Sociology of Education and Socialization*, vol. 1. Greenwich, CT: JAI Press.

Sezgin. (2012). "Assimilation versus Absorption." In Patrick Hayes (ed.), *The Making of Modern Immigration* (pp. 29–61). Santa Barbara, CA: ABC-CLIO.

Shah, A. (2011). "World Military Spending." *Global Issues*. Retrieved spring 2011, from www.globalissues.org/article/75/world-military-spending.

Shakya, H. B., and N. A. Christakis. (2017). "Association of Facebook Use with Compromised Well-Being: A Longitudinal Study." *American Journal of Epidemiology*, 185(3): 203–211.

Shariati, A. (1971). *Fatima Is Fatima*. Tehran, Iran: The Shariati Foundation. Retrieved spring 2011, from www.al-islam.org/fatimaisfatima/.

Shaw, M. (2000). *Theory of the Global State: Globality as an Unfinished Revolution*. Cambridge, UK: Cambridge University Press.

Shea, S., A. D. Stein, C. E. Basch, R. Lantigua, C. Maylahn, D. Strogatz et al. (1991). "Independent Associations of Educational Attainment and Ethnicity with Behavioral Risk Factors for Cardiovascular Disease." *American Journal of Epidemiology* 134(6): 567–82.

Shelbourne, M. (2017). "Infowars' Alex Jones Apologizes for Pushing 'Pizzagate' Conspiracy Theory," *The Hill*, March 25, Retrieved from http://thehill.com/homenews/325761-infowars-alex-jones-apologizes-for-pushing-pizzagate-conspiracy-theory.

Sheldon, A. (1990). "'Kings are Royaler than Queens': Language and Socialization." *Young Children*, 45, 4–9.

Shelton, B. A. (1992). *Women, Men, and Time: Gender Differences in Paid Work, Housework, and Leisure*. Westport, CT: Greenwood.

Shepard, W. (2016). "China Hits Record High M&A Investments in Western Firms." *Forbes*, October 9. Retrieved from https://www.forbes.com/sites/wadeshepard/2016/09/10/from-made-in-china-to-owned-by-china-chinese-enterprises-buying-up-western-companies-at-record-pace/#67b3a9285d87.

Sherman, R. (2017). *Uneasy Street: The Anxieties of Affluence*. Princeton: Princeton University Press.

Shils, E. (1972). *The Intellectuals and the Powers and Other Essays*. Chicago: University of Chicago Press.

Shin, H. B., and R. A. Kominski. (2010). *Language Use in the United States: 2007. American Community Survey Reports*, ACS-12. Washington, DC: U.S. Bureau of the Census. Retrieved 5/19/10, from www.census.gov/prod/2010pubs/acs-12.pdf.

Shkolnikov, V. D. (2010). *Nations in Transit 2009: Democracy's Dark Year*. Washington, DC: Freedom House.

Shollenberger, T. L. (2014). "Racial Disparities in School Suspension and Subsequent Outcomes. Closing the School Discipline Gap: Equitable Remedies for Excessive Exclusion," 31.

Shorrocks, A., J. Davies, and R. Lluberas. (2019a). "Global Wealth Databook 2019." Credit Suisse. Retrieved from https://www.credit-suisse.com/media/assets/corporate/docs/about-us/research/publications/global-wealth-databook-2019.pdf.

Shorrocks, A., J. Davies, and R. Lluberas. (2019b). "Global Wealth Report 2019." Credit Suisse. Retrieved from https://www.credit-suisse.com/about-us/en/reports-research/global-wealth-report.html.

Sigmund, P. E. (1990). *Liberation Theology at the Crossroads: Democracy or Revolution?* New York: Oxford University Press.

Silver, L., A. Smith, C. Johnson, K. Taylor, J. Jiang, M. Anderson, and L. Rainie. (2019). "Mobile connectivity in emerging economies." Pew Research Center, March 7. Retrieved from https://www.pewresearch.org/internet/2019/03/07/mobile-connectivity-in-emerging-economies/.

Simmel, G. (1955). *Conflict and the Web of Group Affiliations* (K. Wolff, trans.). Glencoe, IL: Free Press.

Simon, J. (1981). *The Ultimate Resource.* Princeton, NJ: Princeton University Press.

Simon, J. (1989). *The Economic Consequences of Immigration.* Cambridge, MA: Basil Blackwell.

Simpson, G. E., and J. M. Yinger. (1986). *Racial and Cultural Minorities: An Analysis of Prejudice and Discrimination.* New York: Plenum Press.

Simpson, J. H. (1985). "Socio-Moral Issues and Recent Presidential Elections." *Review of Religious Research* 27: 115–23.

Singh, G. K., and M. Siahpush. (2014). "Widening Rural-Urban Disparities in Life Expectancy, U.S., 1969-2009." *American Journal of Preventative Medicine* 46(2): e19–29.

SIPRI. (2017). "Trends in World Military Expenditure, 2016," Retrieved from https://www.sipri.org/sites/default/files/Trends-world-military-expenditure-2016.pdf.

Sjoberg, G. (1960). *The Pre-Industrial City: Past and Present.* New York: Free Press.

Sjoberg, G. (1963). "The Rise and Fall of Cities: A Theoretical Perspective." *International Journal of Comparative Sociology* 4: 107–20.

Sklair, L. (2000). *The Transnational Capitalist Class.* New York: Wiley-Blackwell.

Sklair, L. (2002a). Democracy and the Transnational Capitalist Class. *Annals of the American Academy of Political and Social Science* 581: 144–57.

Sklair, L. (2002b). *Globalization: Capitalism and Its Alternatives,* 3rd ed. New York: Oxford University Press.

Sklair, L. (2003). "Transnational Practices and the Analysis of the Global System." In A. Hulsemeyer, *Globalization in the Twenty-First Century.* New York: Palgrave Macmillan.

Skocpol, T. (1979). *States and Social Revolutions: A Comparative Analysis of France, Russia, and China.* New York: Cambridge University Press.

Skocpol, T. (1992). *Protecting Soldiers and Mothers: The Political Origins of Social Policy in the United States.* Cambridge, MA: Harvard University Press.

Slapper, G., and S. Tombs. (1999). *Corporate Crime.* Essex, UK: Longman.

Slater, M., and J. Bendel. (2019). "Why Deep Adaptation needs re-localisation." November 2. Retrieved from https://jembendell.com/2019/11/02/deep-adaptation-relocalisation/.

Slavich, G. M., S. M. Monroe, and I. H. Gotlib. (2011). "Early Parental Loss and Depression History: Associations with Recent Life Stress in Major Depressive Disorder." *Journal of Psychiatric Research,* 45(9): 1146–52.

Slevin, P. (2005). "Prison Experts See Opportunity for Improvement." *Washington Post,* July 26. Retrieved spring 2006, from www.washingtonpost.com/wpdyn/content/article/2005/07/25/AR2005072501484.html (site discontinued).

Slopen, N., T. T. Lewis, T. L. Gruenewald, M. S. Mujahid, C. D. Ryff, M. A. Albert, and D. R. Williams. (2010). "Early Life Adversity and Inflammation in African Americans and Whites in the Midlife in the United States Survey." *Psychosomatic Medicine* 72: 694–701.

Smart, N. (1989). *The World Religions.* Englewood Cliffs, NJ: Prentice Hall.

Smelser, N. J. (1963). *Theory of Collective Behavior.* New York: Free Press.

Smith, A. (1776). *An Inquiry into the Nature and Causes of the Wealth of Nations.* London: Methuen and Co., Ltd.

Smith, T. W., P. Marsden, M. Hout, and J. Kim. General Social Surveys, 1972-2016 [machine-readable data file] / Principal Investigator, Tom W. Smith; Co-Principal Investigator, Peter V. Marsden; Co-Principal Investigator, Michael Hout; Sponsored by National Science Foundation. -NORC ed.- Chicago: NORC at the University of Chicago [producer and distributor]. Data accessed from the GSS Data Explorer website at gssdataexplorer.norc.org.

Smith, A. (1988). *The Ethnic Origins of Nations.* Boston: Blackwell.

Smith, A. (2016). "15% of American Adults Have Used Online Dating Sites or Mobile Dating Apps." Pew Research Center: Internet & Technology. Retrieved from http://www.pewinternet.org/2016/02/11/15-percent-of-american-adults-have-used-online-dating-sites-or-mobile-dating-apps/.

Smith, N. (2019). "Japan's labor market is still rigged against women." *The Japan Times,* Oct. 1. Retrieved from https://www.japantimes.co.jp/opinion/2019/10/01/commentary/japan-commentary/japans-labor-market-still-rigged-women/#.Xli5i5NKgWo.

Smith, E. L., and A. Cooper. (2013). "Homicide in the U.S. Known to Law Enforcement, 2011," U.S. Department of Justice, Bureau of Justice Statistics, Retrieved from https://www.bjs.gov/content/pub/pdf/hus11.pdf.

Smith, P., and B. West. (2000). "Cultural Studies." In *Encyclopedia of Naturalism,* vol. 1. San Diego, CA: Academic Press.

Smith, T., and J. Son. (2014). Measuring Occupational Prestige on the 2012 General Social Survey. National Opinion Research Center GSS Methodological Report no. 122. http://gss.norc.org/Documents/reports/methodological-reports/MR122%20Occupational%20Prestige.pdf.

Smith-Bindman, R., et al. (2006). "Does Utilization of Screening Mammography Explain Racial and Ethnic Differences in Breast Cancer?" *Annals of Internal Medicine* 144(8): 541–53.

Smokowski, P. R., and M. Bacallao. (2011). *Becoming bicultural: Risk, resilience, and Latino youth.* New York: University Press.

Smolowe, J. (1994). " . . . and Throw Away the Key." *Time,* February 7.

Snider, S. (2019). "Where Do I Fall in the American Economic Class System?" *U.S. News and World Report,* Oct. 29. Retrieved from https://money.usnews.com/money/personal-finance/family-finance/articles/where-do-i-fall-in-the-american-economic-class-system.

Snow, Jon. (2020). "'There's no sign for us of a slowdown' - UCL's Prof Hugh Montgomery on coronavirus cases." Channel 4 News Dispatches. Retrieved from https://www.channel4.com/news/theres-no-sign-for-us-of-a-slowdown-ucls-prof-hugh-montgomery-on-coronavirus-cases.

Social Security Administration. (SSA). (2016a). "Fact Sheet: Social Security." Retrieved from https://www.ssa.gov/news/press/factsheets/basicfact-alt.pdf.

Social Security Administration. (SSA). (2016b). "Fast Facts and Figures 2016." Retrieved from https://www.ssa.gov/policy/docs/chartbooks/fast_facts/2016/fast_facts16.pdf.

Social Security Administration. (SSA). (2016c). "Income of the Aged Chartbook, 2014." Retrieved from https://www.ssa.gov/policy/docs/chartbooks/income_aged/2014/iac14.pdf.

Social Security Administration (SSA). (2019). "Annual Statistical Supplement to the Social Security Bulletin, 2019." Retrieved from https://www.ssa.gov/policy/docs/statcomps/supplement/2019/supplement19.pdf.

Social Security Administration. (2020). "Fact Sheet." Retrieved from https://www.ssa.gov/news/press/factsheets/basicfact-alt.pdf.

Solomon, R. P. (1992). *Black Resistance in High School: Forging a Separatist Culture.* Albany, NY: State University of New York Press.

Soros, G. (2000). *Open Society: Reforming Global Capitalism.* Jackson, TN: Public Affairs Books.

Soros, G. (2005). *George Soros on Globalization.* Jackson, TN: Public Affairs Books.

Soros, G. (2009). *The Crash of 2008 and What It Means: The New Paradigm for Financial Markets.* Jackson, TN: Public Affairs Books.

Sorvino, C. (2017). "The World's 56 Self-Made Women Billionaires: The Definitive Ranking." *Forbes.* Retrieved from https://www.forbes.com/sites/chloesorvino/2017/03/08/the-worlds-56-self-made-women-billionaires-the-definitive-ranking/#67e40f5a68a2.

Southwick, S. (1996). "Liszt: Searchable Directory of E-Mail Discussion Groups." Retrieved 1/03/05, from www.liszt.com (site discontinued).

Spaargaren, G., and A. P. J. Mol. (1992). "Sociology, Environment and Modernity. Ecological Modernisation as a Theory of Social Change." *Society and Natural Resources* 5(4): 323–44.

Specter, M. (2017). "Rewriting the Code of Life," *New Yorker,* January 2. Retrieved from http://www.newyorker.com/magazine/2017/01/02/rewriting-the-code-of-life.

Spencer, S. (2014). *Race and Ethnicity.* Abington: Routledge.

Speth, L. E. (2011). The Married Women's Property Acts, 1839–1865: Reform, Reaction, or Revolution? In J. R. Lindgren, et al, eds., *The Law of Sex Discrimination,* 4th ed. New York: Wadsworth. 12–15.

Springer, K. W. (2010). "Economic Dependence in Marriage and Husbands' Midlife Health: Testing Three Possible Mechanisms." *Gender & Society,* 24(3), 378–401.

Springer, K. W., and D. Mouzon. (2011). "'Macho Men' and Preventive Healthcare: Implications for Older Men in Different Social Classes." *Journal of Health and Social Behavior* 50(2): 212–27.

Stacey, J. (1998). *Brave New Families: Stories of Domestic Upheaval in Late Twentieth-Century America,* 2nd ed. Berkeley: University of California Press.

Stacey, J. (2011). *Unhitched: Love, Marriage and Family Values from West Hollywood to Western China.* New York: New York University Press.

Stacey, J., and T. Biblarz. (2001). "(How) Does the Sexual Orientation of Parents Matter?" *American Sociological Review* 66(2): 159–83.

Stack, C. B. (1997). *All Our Kin: Strategies for Survival in a Black Community.* New York: Harper Colophon.

Stampp, K. (1956). *The Peculiar Institution.* New York: Knopf.

Stark, R., and W. S. Bainbridge. (1980). "Towards a Theory of Religious Commitment." *Journal for the Scientific Study of Religion* 19: 114–28.

Stark, R., and W. S. Bainbridge. (1987). *A Theory of Religion.* New Brunswick, NJ: Rutgers University Press.

Statham, J. (1986). *Daughters and Sons: Experiences of Non-Sexist Childraising.* New York: Basil Blackwell.

Statista. (2019). "Number of apps available in leading app stores as of 2nd quarter 2019." Retrieved from https://www.statista.com/statistics/276623/number-of-apps-available-in-leading-app-stores/.

Statistics Bureau Japan. (2015). "Japan Statistical Yearbook 2015." Chapter 2: Population and Households, Table 2-8: Population by Age Group and Indicies of Age Structure. Retrieved 1/15, from http://www.stat.go.jp/english/data/nenkan/1431-02.htm.

Stebbins, S. (2018a). "Biggest Mergers of the Year." 24/7 Wall St., December 3. Retrieved from https://247wallst.com/special-report/2018/12/03/biggest-mergers-of-the-year-3/4/.

Stebbins, S. (2018b). "Biggest Mergers of the Year." 24/7 Wall St., December 3. Retrieved from https://247wallst.com/special-report/2018/12/03/biggest-mergers-of-the-year-3/.

Steel, E. and N. Chokshi. (2017). "Fox News Besieged by New Bias Lawsuit and Federal Inquiry," *New York Times,* May 4, Retrieved from https://www.nytimes.com/2017/05/04/business/media/fox-news-lawsuit-gender-discrimination-sky-takeover.html.

Steele, C. M., and J. Aronson. (1995). "Stereotype Threat and the Intellectual Test Performance of African-Americans." *Journal of Personality and Social Psychology* 69: 797–811.

Steele, C. M., and J. A. Aronson. (2004). "Stereotype Threat Does Not Live by Steele and Aronson (1995) Alone." *American Psychologist* 59: 47–48.

Stein, J. (2018). "The UN says 18.5 million Americans are in 'extreme poverty.' Trump's team says just 250,000 are." *Washington Post,* June 25. Retrieved from https://www.washingtonpost.com/news/wonk/wp/2018/06/25/trump-team-rebukes-u-n-saying-it-overestimates-extreme-poverty-in-america-by-18-million-people/.

Stein, P., S. Hendrix, and A. Hauslohner. (2017). "Women's Marches: More Than One Million Protesters Vow to Resist President Trump," *Washington Post,* Jan. 22, Retrieved from https://www.washingtonpost.com/local/womens-march-on-washington-a-sea-of-pink-hatted-protesters-vow-to-resist-donald-trump/2017/01/21/ae4def62-dfdf-11e6-acdf-14da832ae861_story.html?hpid=hp_hp-bignews2_banner-hed%3Ahomepage%2Fstory&utm_term=.b37f1a4425b0.

Steinberg, L., and Monahan, K. C. (2007). "Age Differences in Resistance to Peer Influence." *Developmental Psychology,* 43, 1531–1543.

Steinmetz, S. K. (1983). "Family Violence toward Elders." In S. Saunders, A. Anderson, and C. Hart, eds., *Violent Individuals and Families: A Practitioner's Handbook.* Springfield, IL: Charles C. Thomas.

Steklis, H. D., G. L. Brammer, M. J. Raleigh, and M. T. McGuire. (1985). "Serum testosterone, male dominance, and aggression in captive groups of vervet monkeys (Cercopithecus aethiops sabaeus)." *Hormones and Behavior* 19: 154–63.

Stepler, R., and A. Brown. (2016). "Statistical portrait of Hispanics in the United States." Retrieved from http://www.pewhispanic.org/2016/04/19/.

Stepler, R., and Lopez, M. H. (2016). "U.S. Latino Population Growth and Dispersion Has Slowed Since Onset of the Great Recession," Pew Research Center, Sept. 8, Retrieved from http://www.pewhispanic.org/2016/09/08/latino-population-growth-and-dispersion-has-slowed-since-the-onset-of-the-great-recession/statistical-portrait-of-hispanics-in-the-unitedstates/.

Stetz, M., and B. Oh, eds. (2001). *Legacies of the Comfort Women of World War II.* Armonk, NY: M.E. Sharpe.

Stevens, M. L. (2009). *Creating a Class: College Admissions and the Education of Elites.* Cambridge, MA: Harvard University Press.

Stiglitz, J. (2003). *Globalization and Its Discontents.* New York: W. W. Norton.

Stiglitz, J. (2007). *Making Globalization Work.* New York: W. W. Norton.

Stiglitz, J. (2010). *Freefall: America, Free Markets, and the Sinking of the World Economy.* New York: W. W. Norton.

Stiles, J. (2011). "Brain Development and the Nature versus Nurture Debate." *Progress in Brain Research* 189: 3–22.

Stockholm Environment Institute (SEI) et al. (2019). "2019 Report: The Production Gap: The Discrepancy between Countries' Planned Fossil Fuel Production and Global Production Levels Consistent with Limiting Warming to 1.5°C or 2°C. "Retrieved from http://productiongap.org/wp-content/uploads/2019/11/Production-Gap-Report-2019.pdf.

Stommel, M., B. A. Given, C. W. Given, H. A. Kalaian, R. Schulz, and R. McCorkle. (1993)."Gender bias in the measurement properties of the Center for Epidemiologic Studies Depression Scale (CES-D)." *Psychiatry Research* 49(3): 239.

Stone, L. (1980). *The Family, Sex, and Marriage in England, 1500–1800.* New York: Harper and Row.

Stonecash, J. M. (2000). *Class and Party in American Politics.* Boulder, CO: Westview Press.

Stow, K. (2000). *Theater of Acculturation: The Roman Ghetto in the Sixteenth Century.* Seattle, WA: University of Washington Press.

Stratton, L. S. (2012). "The role of preferences and opportunity costs in determining the time allocated to housework." *American Economic Review* 102(3): 606–11.

Street, D., and J. S. Cossman. (2006). "Greatest Generation or Greedy Geezers? A Life Course Approach to Social Spending Preferences." *Social Problems* 53(1): 75–96.

Stromberg, J. (2013). "What is the Anthropocene and Are We in It?" *Smithsonian.* Retrieved from http://www.smithsonianmag.com/sciencenature/what-is-the-anthropocene-and-are-wein-it-164801414/?no-ist.

Stryker, S., and Serpe, R. T. (1994). "Identity Salience and Psychological Centrality: Equivalent, Overlapping, or Complementary Concepts?" *Social Psychology Quarterly,* 16–35.

Sudworth, J. (2012). "China's Students Take on Tough Gaokao University Entrance Exam." BBC World News Website (June 8). Retrieved 7/08/12, from www.bbc.co.uk/news/world-asia-china-18349873.

Sue, D. W. (2010). *Microaggressions in Everyday Life: Race, Gender, and Sexual Orientation.* New York: Wiley.

Suitor, J. J., J. Sechrist, M. Gilligan, and K. Pillemer. (2011). "Intergenerational Relations in Later Life Families." In R. A. Settersten Jr. and J. L. Angel, eds., *Handbook of Sociology of Aging* (pp. 161–78). New York: Springer.

Sullivan, P. (2012). "The Tightwire Act of Living Only on Social Security." *New York Times,* September 11. Retrieved spring 2013, from www.nytimes.com/2012/09/12/business/retirementspecial/living-only-on-social-security-is-a-tightwire-act.html?pagewanted=all.

Sultan, N. (2017). "Election 2016: Trump's Free Media Helped Keep Cost Down, but Fewer Donors Provided More of the Cash," Center for Responsive Politics, April 13, Retrieved from https://www.opensecrets.org/news/2017/04/election-2016-trump-fewer-donors-provided-more-of-the-cash/.

Sung, K. (2000). "Respect for Elders: Myths and Realities in East Asia." *Journal of Aging and Identity* 5: 197–205.

Sunstein, C. (2012). *Republic.com 2.0.* Princeton, NJ: Princeton University Press.

Surowiecki, J. (2014). "The Mobility Myth." *New Yorker,* March 3. Retrieved 12/14, from http://www.newyorker.com/magazine/2014/03/03/the-mobility-myth.

Sustainable Apparel Coalition. (2019). "The Sustainable Apparel Coalition." Retrieved from https://apparelcoalition.org/the-sac/.

Sutherland, E. H. (1949). *Principles of Criminology.* Chicago: Lippincott.

Swidler, A. (1986). "Culture in Action: Symbols and Strategies." *American Sociological Review* 51: 273–86.

Swidler, A. (2001). *Talk of Love: How Culture Matters.* Chicago: University of Chicago Press.

Tabor, J. D., and E. V. Gallagher. (1995). *Why Waco? Cults and the Battle for Religious Freedom in America.* Berkeley, CA: University of California Press.

Tang, S., and J. Zuo. (2000). Dating Attitudes and Behaviors of American and Chinese College Students. *Social Science Journal* 37(1): 67–78.

Tarmann, A. (2003). "Fifty Years of Demographic Change in Rural America." Population Reference Bureau. Retrieved from https://www.prb.org/fiftyyearsofdemographicchangeinruralamerica/.

Tavernise, S. (2012). "Life Spans Shrink for Least-Educated Whites in the U.S." *New York Times,* September 20. Retrieved 9/22/12, from www.nytimes.com/2012/09/21/us/life-expectancy-for-less-educated-whites-in-us-is-shrinking.html?pagewanted=all&_moc.semityn.www&pagewanted=print.

Tharps, Lori L. (2014). "The Case for Black With a Capital B." *The New York Times.* Retrieved from https://www.nytimes.com/2014/11/19/opinion/the-case-for-black-with-a-capital-b.html.

The Institute for College Access and Success (TICAS). (2016). "Student Debt and the Class of 2015," Retrieved from http://ticas.org/sites/default/files/pub_files/classof2015.pdf.

Thayer, M. (2010). *Making Transnational Feminism: Rural Women, NGO Activists, and Northern Donors in Brazil.* New York, NY: Routledge.

Thompson, E. P. (1971). "The Moral Economy of the English Crowd in the Eighteenth Century." *Past and Present* 50: 76–136.

Thompson, W. S. (1929). "Population." *American Journal of Sociology* 34: 959–75.

Thorne, B. (1993). *Gender Play: Girls and Boys in School.* New Brunswick, NJ: Rutgers University Press.

Thoumi, F. (2003). "The Numbers Game: Let's All Guess the Size of the Illegal Drugs Industry!" Paper prepared for TNI seminar on the Economic Impact of the Illicit Drug Industry, December. Retrieved spring 2013, from http://jod.sagepub.com/content/35/1/185.abstract.

Thunberg, G. (2019). "Transcript: Greta Thunberg's Speech at the U.N. Climate Action Summit," National Public Radio, Sept. 23. Retrieved from https://www.npr.org/2019/09/23/763452863/transcript-greta-thunbergs-speech-at-the-u-n-climate-action-summit.

Tilly, C. (1978). *From Mobilization to Revolution.* Reading, MA: Addison-Wesley.

Tilly, C. (1992). "How to Detect, Describe, and Explain Repertoires of Contention." Working Paper No. 150. Center for the Study of Social Change. New York: New School for Social Research.

Time. (2014). "The 25 Most Influential Teens of 2014." *Time,* October 13. Retrieved from http://time.com/3486048/most influential teens-2014/.

Tjaden, P., and N. Thoennes. (2010). "Full Report of the Prevalence, Incidence, and Consequences of Violence Against Women," November. Washington, DC: U.S. Department of Justice. Retrieved spring 2011, from www.ncjrs.gov/pdffiles1/nij/183781.pdf.

Toedtman, J. (2016). "Americans Increasingly Frustrated With Government, Survey Finds," Pew Research Center, May 11, Retrieved from http://

magazine.pewtrusts.org/en/archive/spring-2016/americans-increasingly-frustrated-with-government-survey-finds.

Tolliver, S. O., J. L. Hefner, S. D. Tolliver, and L. McDougle. (2019). "Primary Care Provider Understanding of Hair Care Maintenance as a Barrier to Physical Activity in African American Women." *Journal of the American Board of Family Medicine* 32(6): 944–947.

Tong, R. (2009). *Feminist Thought: A More Comprehensive Introduction*. Philadelphia: Westview Press.

Toobin, J. (2011). "Betty Dukes v. Walmart." *New Yorker*, June 20. Retrieved spring 2013, from www.newyorker.com/online/blogs/newsdesk/2011/06/betty-dukes-v-walmart.html.

Torpey, E. (2018). "Measuring the value of education." U.S. Bureau of Labor Statistics (BLS). Retrieved from https://www.bls.gov/careeroutlook/2018/data-on-display/education-pays.htm.

Toufexis, A. (1993). "Sex Has Many Accents." *Time*, May 24.

Touraine, A. (1974). *The Post-Industrial Society*. London: Wildwood.

Touraine, A. (1977). *The Self-Production of Society*. Chicago: University of Chicago Press.

Touraine, A. (1981). *The Voice and the Eye: An Analysis of Social Movements*. New York: Cambridge University Press.

Townsend, P., and N. Davidson, eds. (1982). *Inequalities in Health: The Black Report*. Harmondsworth, UK: Penguin.

Tran, A. (2014). "Pre-Med Stress Hits New Heights As MCAT Exam Changes Loom." *WBUR's Common Health* (October 24). Retrieved 10/25/14, from http://commonhealth.wbur.org/2014/10/pre-med stress-hits-new-heights-as-mcat-exam-changes loom?utm_source=facebook.com&utm_medium=social&utm_campaign=npr&utm_term=nprnws&utm_content=2049.

Treas, J., J. Lui, and Z. Gubernskaya. "Attitudes on marriage and new relationships: Cross-national evidence on the deinstitutionalization of marriage." *Demographic Research* 30 (2014): 1495.

Trevelyan, E., C. Gambino, T. Gryn, L. Larsen, Y. Acosta, E. Grieco, D. Harris, and N. Walters. (2016). U.S. Bureau of the Census. "Characteristics of the U.S. Population by Generational Status: 2013." Retrieved from https://www.census.gov/content/dam/Census/library/publications/2016/demo/P23-214.pdf.

Troeltsch, E. (1931). *The Social Teaching of the Christian Churches* (2 vols.). New York: Macmillan.

Truman, D. B. (1981). *The Governmental Process*. Westport, CT: Greenwood Press.

Truman, J., and R. Morgan. (2016). "Criminal Victimization, 2015," Bureau of Justice Statistics. Retrieved from https://www.bjs.gov/content/pub/pdf/cv15.pdf.

Tu, W. (1989). "The Rise of Industrial East Asia: The Role of Confucian Values." *Copenhagen Journal of Asian Studies* 4: 81–97. Retrieved spring 2011. http://rauli.cbs.dk/index.php/cjas/article/view/1767/1787.

Tuller, D. (2009). "My Mother, the Octogenarian Activist." *New York Times*, December 11. Retrieved 8/01/10, from http://well.blogs.nytimes.com/2009/12/11/my-mother-the-octogenarian-activist/.

Tumin, M. M. (1953). "Some Principles of Stratification: A Critical Analysis." *American Sociological Review* 18: 387–94.

Turnbull, C. (1983). *The Human Cycle*. New York: Simon and Schuster.

Tutton, M. (2019). "Greenland's ice sheet just lost 11 billion tons of ice—in one day." CNN, August 15. Retrieved from https://www.cnn.com/2019/08/02/world/greenland-ice-sheet-11-billion-intl/index.html.

Twine, F. W. (1999). "Bearing blackness in Britain: The meaning of racial difference for white birth mothers of African-descent children." *Social Identities* 5(2). 185–210.

24/7 Wall St. (2016). "America's Most Segregated Cities," *Huffington Post*, Sept. 12, Retrieved from http://www.huffingtonpost.com/entry/americas most segregated cities_us_57d2c19ae4b0f831f7071b3d.

Uggen, C., and Blackstone, A. (2004). "Sexual harassment as a gendered expression of power." *American Sociological Review* 69: 64–92.

Uh, M. (2016). "Priced Out: Big Cities Are Becoming Too Costly for Lower-Income Residents," Retrieved from https://www.trulia.com/blog/trends/priced-out-migration/.

Umberson, D., K. Williams, D. P. Powers and M. D. Chen. (2005). "As Good As It Gets? A Life Course Perspective on Marital Quality." *Social Forces* 84:493–511.

Umberson, D., C. B. Wortman, and R. C. Kessler. (1992). "Widowhood and Depression: Explaining Long-Term Gender Differences in Vulnerability." *Journal of Health and Social Behavior* 33: 10–24.

UNAIDS. (2003). "AIDS Epidemic Update." December 2003. Retrieved 1/10/05, from http://data.unaids.org/Publications/IRC-pub06/JC943-EpiUpdate2003_en.pdf.

UNAIDS. (2019a). "Fact Sheet–Global HIV Statistics." Retrieved from http://www.unaids.org/sites/default/files/media_asset/UNAIDS_FactSheet_en.pdf.

UNAIDS. (2019b). "Global HIV & AIDS statistics—2019 fact sheet." Retrieved from https://www.unaids.org/en/resources/fact-sheet.

UN Conference on Trade and Development (UNCTAD). (2019). "UN Handbook of Statistics, 2019." Retrieved from https://stats.unctad.org/handbook/index.html.

UN Department of Economic and Social Affairs (DESA). (2016). "The World's Cities in 2016." Retrieved from http://www.un.org/en/development/desa/population/publications/pdf/urbanization/the_worlds_cities_in_2016_data_booklet.pdf.

UN Department of Economic and Social Affairs (DESA). (2017). "World Population Prospects, the 2017 Revision." Retrieved from https://esa.un.org/unpd/wpp/Publications.

UN Department of Economic and Social Affairs (DESA). (2018a). "2018 Revision of World Urbanization Prospects." Retrieved from https://www.un.org/development/desa/publications/2018-revision-of-world-urbanization-prospects.html.

UN Department of Economic and Social Affairs (DESA). (2018b). "Annual Percentage of Population at Mid-Year Residing in Urban Areas by Region, Subregion, Country, and Area, 1950-2050." Retrieved from https://population.un.org/wup/Download/Files/WUP2018-F21-Proportion_Urban_Annual.xls.

UN Department of Economic and Social Affairs (DESA). (2018c). "Annual Urban Population at Mid-Year by Region, Subregion, Country, and Area, 1950-2050 (thousands)." Retrieved from https://population.un.org/wup/Download/Files/WUP2018-F19-Urban_Population_Annual.xls.

UN Department of Economic and Social Affairs (DESA). (2018d). "Population of Urban and Rural Areas at Mid-Year (thousands) and Percentage Urban, 2018." Retrieved from https://population.un.org/wup/Download/Files/WUP2018-F01-Total_Urban_Rural.xls.

UN Department of Economic and Social Affairs (DESA). (2019). "World Population Prospects 2019: Highlights." Retrieved from https://population.un.org/wpp/Publications/Files/WPP2019_Highlights.pdf.

UN Development Programme (UNDP). (2019a). "The 2019 Global Multidimensional Poverty Index (MPI)." Retrieved from http://hdr.undp.org/en/2018-MPI.

UN Development Programme (UNDP). (2019b). "Human Development Report 2019: Beyond income, beyond averages, beyond today: Inequalities in human development in the 21st century." Retrieved from http://hdr.undp.org/sites/default/files/hdr2019.pdf.

UN Development Report. (2011). "The Real Wealth of Nations: Pathways to Human Development." Retrieved summer 2012, from http://hdr.undp.org/en/reports/global/hdr2010/chapters/.

UN Economic Commission for Africa. (2015). "Harnessing the Potential of the Informal Sector for Inclusive Growth in Africa." Retrieved from http://www.un.org/en/ecosoc/integration/2015/pdf/eca.pdf.

UN Economic and Social Commission for Asia and the Pacific (UNESCAP). (2010). "Global Financial Crisis Derails MDG Progress in Asia-Pacific Region." Press Release. Retrieved spring 2011, from http://mediaglobal.org/article/2010-02-23/global-financial-crisis-derails-mdg-progress-in-asia-pacific-region (site discontinued).

UN Environment Programme. (2019). "Emissions Gap Report 2019" Retrieved from https://wedocs.unep.org/bitstream/handle/20.500.11822/30797/EGR2019.pdf?sequence=1&isAllowed=y.

UNESCO. (2017a). "Cinema Data Release." Retrieved from http://uis.unesco.org/en/news/cinema-data-release.

UNESCO. (2017b). "Education: Literacy Rate," UNESCO Institute for Statistics, Retrieved from http://data.uis.unesco.org/index.aspx?queryid=166.

UNESCO. (2017c). "The United Nations World Water Development Report: 2017: Wastewater: The Untapped Resource." Retrieved from http://unesdoc.unesco.org/images/0024/002471/247153e.pdf.

UN Food and Agriculture Organization (UN FAO). (2010). "The State of Food Insecurity in the World 2010." Retrieved summer 2012, from www.fao.org/docrep/013/i1683e/i1683e.pdf.

UN Food and Agriculture Organization (UN FAO). (2011). "How to Feed the World in 2050." UN Issue Brief, October 12–13. Retrieved spring 2013, from www.fao.org/fileadmin/templates/wsfs/docs/expert_paper/How_to_Feed_the_World_in_2050.pdf.

UN Food and Agriculture Organization (UN FAO). (2015). "The State of Food Insecurity, 2015," Retrieved from http://www.fao.org/3/a-i4646e/index.html.

UN Food and Agriculture Organization (UN FAO). (2016). "The State of Food and Agriculture," Retrieved from http://www.fao.org/3/a-i6030e.pdf.

UN Food and Agriculture Organization (UN FAO). (2019a). "FAO framework on rural extreme poverty: Towards reaching Target 1.1 of the Sustainable Development Goals." Retrieved from https://reliefweb.int/report/world/fao-framework-rural-extreme-poverty-towards-reaching-target-11-sustainable-development.

UN Food and Agriculture Organization (UN FAO). (2019b). "The State of Food Security and Nutrition in the World 2020." Retrieved from http://www.fao.org/state-of-food-security-nutrition/en/.

UN Framework Convention on Climate Change. (2015). "Historic Paris Agreement on Climate Change: 195 Nations Set Path to Keep Temperature Rise Well Below 2 Degrees Celsius." Retrieved from http://newsroom.unfccc.int/unfccc-newsroom/finale-cop21/.

UNICEF. (2012). "Measuring Child Poverty: New League Tables of Child Poverty in the World's Rich Countries." May 2012. Retrieved 6/19/12, from www.unicef-irc.org/publications/pdf/rc10_eng.pdf.

UNICEF. (2019a). "Literacy among youth is rising, but young women lag behind." Retrieved from https://data.unicef.org/topic/education/literacy/.

UNICEF. (2019b). "Sanitation." Retrieved from https://data.unicef.org/topic/water-and-sanitation/sanitation/.

Union of International Associations (UIA). (2005). "Statistics on International Organizations and NGOs." Retrieved spring 2008, from www.uia.org/statistics/organizations/types-2004.pdf

United Auto Workers (UAW). (2014). "UAW: Uniting Academic Workers," Retrieved from http://www.uaw.org/page/uaw-uniting-academic-workers.

United States Institute of Peace. (2013). "Guide for participants in peace, stability, and relief operations." Retrieved from http://www.usip.org/node/5599.

University of Michigan Institute for Social Research. (2008a). "Chore Wars: Men, Women, and Housework." National Science Foundation. Retrieved 8/16/11, from www.nsf.gov/discoveries/disc_summ.jsp?cntn_id=111458.

University of Michigan Institute for Social Research. (2008b). "Exactly how much housework does a husband create?" http://ns.umich.edu/new/releases/6452.

University of Warwick. (2014). "Girls Feel They Must 'Play Dumb' to Please Boys, Study Shows." ScienceDaily (August 5, 2014), Retrieved from www.sciencedaily.com/releases/2014/08/140805090947.htm.

UN Office on Drugs and Crime (UNODC). (2016). "World Drug Report: 2016," Retrieved from https://www.unodc.org/documents/scientific/WORLD_DRUG_REPORT_2016_web.pdf.

UN Office on Drugs and Crime. (2019). "Afghanistan opium survey 2018: Challenges to sustainable development, peace and security." Retrieved from http://www.unodc.org/documents/crop-monitoring/Afghanistan/Afghanistan_opium_survey_2018_socioeconomic_report.pdf.

UN Population Division. (2015). "Trends in International Migrant Stock: the 2015 Revision." Retrieved from http://www.un.org/en/development/desa/population/migration/data/estimates2/estimates15.shtml.

UN Women. (2019). "Women in Politics: 2019." Retrieved from https://www.unwomen.org/-/media/headquarters/attachments/sections/library/publications/2019/women-in-politics-2019-map-en.pdf?la=en&vs=3303.

Urahn, S. K., E. Currier, D. Elliott, L. Wechsler, D. Wilson, D. Colbert, and Pew Charitable Trusts. (2012). "Pursuing the American Dream: Economic Mobility across Generations. Project Report." Retrieved 9/21/12, from www.pewstates.org/uploadedFiles/PCS_Assets/2012/Pursuing_American_Dream.pdf.

Urban Institute. (2010). "The Future of Social Security: Solvency, Work, Adequacy, and Equity." Washington, DC: Program on Retirement Policy. Retrieved 8/09/12, from www.urban.org/uploadedpdf/412253-Social-Security-Solvency.pdf.

U.S. Administration on Aging (AOA). (2016). "A Profile of Older Americans: 2015." Retrieved from https://aoa.acl.gov/Aging_Statistics/Profile/2015/4.aspx.

USAFacts. (2019). "Wealth in America: Inequality Persists in Household Wealth." U.S. News and World Report, Nov. 14. Retrieved from https://www.usnews.com/news/elections/articles/2019-11-14/wealth-in-america-inequality-persists-in-household-wealth.

U.S. Bureau of Justice Statistics (BJS). (2011). "Justice Expenditures and Employment, FY1982-2007—Statistical Tables." Retrieved 1/13/2015, from http://www.bjs.gov/content/pub/pdf/jee8207st.pdf.

U.S. Bureau of Justice Statistics (BJS). (2014a). "Criminal Victimization, 2013." Retrieved 1/13/15, from http://www.bjs.gov/content/pub/pdf/cv13.pdf.

U.S. Bureau of Justice Statistics (BJS). (2014b). "Justice Expenditures and Employment Extracts, 2011 — Preliminary." Retrieved 1/13/15, from http://www.bjs.gov/index.cfm?ty=pbdetail&iid=5050.

U.S. Bureau of Justice Statistics (BJS). (2017). "National Crime Victimization Survey, 2010–2016." Retrieved from https://www.bjs.gov/index.cfm?ty=dcdetail&iid=245.

U.S. Bureau of Labor Statistics (BLS). (2010). "Labor Force Statistics from the Current Population Survey." Feb. 5. Retrieved from https://www.bls.gov/cps/cpsatabs.htm.

U.S. Bureau of Labor Statistics (BLS). (2012). "National Census of Fatal Occupational Injuries in 2011." Retrieved 10/01/12, from www.bls.gov/news.release/pdf/cfoi.pdf.

U.S. Bureau of Labor Statistics (BLS). (2013). "Industry employment and output projections to 2022." Retrieved 3/19/15, from http://www.bls.gov/opub/mlr/2013/article/industry-employment-and-output-projections-to-2022.htm.

U.S. Bureau of Labor Statistics (BLS). (2014). Census of Fatal Occupational Injuries Summary (September 11, 2014). Retrieved 10/25/14, http://www.bls.gov/news.release/cfoi.nr0.htm. from

U.S. Bureau of Labor Statistics (BLS). (2016a). "American Time Use Survey: 2015." Retrieved from http://www.bls.gov/news.release/archives/atus_06242016.pdf.

U.S. Bureau of Labor Statistics (BLS). (2016b). "Labor force characteristics by race and ethnicity, 2015." Retrieved from https://www.bls.gov/opub/reports/race-and-ethnicity/2015/home.htm.

U.S. Bureau of Labor Statistics (BLS). (2016c). "The Economics Daily: Unemployment rate 3.2 percent for those 55 years of age and older." Retrieved from http://www.bls.gov/opub/ted/2016/unemployment-rate-3-point-2-percent-for-those-55-years-of-age-and-older.htm.

U.S. Bureau of Labor Statistics (BLS). (2016d). "24 percent of employed people did some or all of their work at home in 2015." Retrieved from https://www.bls.gov/opub/ted/2016/24-percent-of-employed-people-did-some-or-all-of-their-work-at-home-in-2015.htm.

U.S. Bureau of Labor Statistics (BLS). (2017a). "American Time Use Survey—2016 Results." Retrieved from https://www.bls.gov/news.release/pdf/atus.pdf.

U.S. Bureau of Labor Statistics (BLS). (2017b). "A profile of the working poor: 2015," Retrieved from https://www.bls.gov/opub/reports/working-poor/2015/home.htm.

U.S. Bureau of Labor Statistics (BLS). (2017c). "Highlights of Women's Earnings in 2016." Retrieved from https://www.bls.gov/opub/reports/womens-earnings/2016/home.htm.

U.S. Bureau of Labor Statistics (BLS). (2017d). "Labor Force Statistics from the Current Population Survey: Employment status of the civilian noninstitutional population by age, sex, and race." Retrieved from https://www.bls.gov/cps/cpsaat03.htm.

U.S. Bureau of Labor Statistics (BLS). (2017e). "Table 1. Work Stoppages Involving 1,000 or More Workers, 1947–2016." Retrieved from https://www.bls.gov/news.release/wkstp.t01.htm.

U.S. Bureau of Labor Statistics (BLS). (2017f). "Unemployment and earnings by educational attainment, 2016," Retrieved from https://www.bls.gov/emp/ep_chart_001.htm.

U.S. Bureau of Labor Statistics (BLS). (2017g). "Union Members Summary: 2016." Retrieved from https://www.bls.gov/news.release/union2.nr0.htm.

U.S. Bureau of Labor Statistics (BLS). (2017h). "Women in the Labor Force: a databook." Retrieved from https://www.bls.gov/opub/reports/womens-databook/2016/pdf/home.pdf.

U.S. Bureau of Labor Statistics (BLS). (2018a). "Labor Force Statistics from the Current Population Survey: Household Data, Annual Averages. Table 39. Median weekly earnings of full-time wage and salary workers by detailed occupation and sex." Retrieved from http://www.bls.gov/cps/cpsaat39.htm.

U.S. Bureau of Labor Statistics (BLS). (2018b). "Women in the Labor Force: A Databook." Retrieved from https://www.bls.gov/opub/reports/womens-databook/2018/home.htm#table-2.

U.S. Bureau of Labor Statistics (BLS). (2019a). "A profile of the working poor, 2017." Retrieved from https://www.bls.gov/opub/reports/working-poor/2017/home.htm.

U.S. Bureau of Labor Statistics (BLS). (2019b). "American Time Use Survey." Retrieved from https://www.bls.gov/news.release/atus.nr0.htm.

U.S. Bureau of Labor Statistics (BLS). (2019c). "American Time Use Survey—2018 Results." Retrieved from https://www.bls.gov/new.release/pdf/atus.pdf.

U.S. Bureau of Labor Statistics (BLS). (2019d). "Average hours per day spent in selected by sex and day." Retrieved from https://www.bls.gov/charts/american-time-use/activity-by-sex.htm.

U.S. Bureau of Labor Statistics (BLS). (2019e). "Civilian labor force participation rate by age, sex, race, and ethnicity." Retrieved from https://www.bls.gov/emp/tables/civilian-labor-force-participation-rate.htm.

U.S. Bureau of Labor Statistics (BLS). (2019f). "Employment by Major Industry Sector." Retrieved from https://www.bls.gov/emp/tables/employment-by-major-industry-sector.htm.

U.S. Bureau of Labor Statistics (BLS). (2019g). "Employment Characteristics of Families—2018." Retrieved from https://www.bls.gov/news.release/pdf/famee.pdf.

U.S. Bureau of Labor Statistics (BLS). (2019h). "Employment Situation Summary." Oct. 4. Retrieved from https://www.bls.gov/news.release/empsit.nr0.htm.

U.S. Bureau of Labor Statistics (BLS). (2019i). "Labor force characteristics by race and ethnicity, 2018." Retrieved from https://www.bls.gov/opub/reports/race-and-ethnicity/2018/pdf/home.pdf.

U.S. Bureau of Labor Statistics. (2019j). "Labor Force Statistics from the Current Population Survey: Household Data, Annual Averages. Table 11. Employed persons by detailed occupation, sex, race, and Hispanic or Latino ethnicity." Retrieved from https://www.bls.gov/cps/cpsaat11.htm.

U.S. Bureau of Labor Statistics (BLS). (2019k). "Labor Force Statistics from the Current Population Survey: Household Data, Annual Averages. Table 39. Median weekly earnings of full-time wage and salary workers by detailed occupation and sex." Retrieved from http://www.bls.gov/cps/cpsaat39.htm.

U.S. Bureau of Labor Statistics (BLS). (2019l). "Major Work Stoppages in 2019." Retrieved from https://www.bls.gov/news.release/wkstp.nr0.htm.

U.S. Bureau of Labor Statistics (BLS). (2019m). "National Census of Fatal Occupational Injuries in 2018." Retrieved from https://www.bls.gov/news.release/pdf/cfoi.pdf.

U.S. Bureau of Labor Statistics (BLS). (2019n). "The Employment Situation — February 2019." Retrieved from https://www.bls.gov/news.release/pdf/empsit.pdf.

U.S. Bureau of Labor Statistics (BLS). (2019o). "Union affiliation of employed wage and salary workers by occupation and industry." Jan. 18. Retrieved from https://www.bls.gov/news.release/union2.t03.htm.

U.S. Bureau of Labor Statistics (BLS). (2019p). "Union Members Summary." Jan. 18. Retrieved from https://www.bls.gov/news.release/union2.nr0.htm.

U.S. Bureau of Labor Statistics (BLS). (2019q). "Usual Weekly Earnings of Wage and Salary Workers Third Quarter 2019." Retrieved from https://www.bls.gov/news.release/pdf/wkyeng.pdf.

U.S. Bureau of Labor Statistics (BLS). (2019r). "Women's Earnings in 2018." Retrieved from https://www.bls.gov/opub/reports/womens-earnings/2018/pdf/home.pdf.

U.S. Bureau of Labor Statistics (BLS). (2019s). "Work Stoppages Involving 1,000 or More Workers, 1947–2019." https://www.bls.gov/web/wkstp/annual-listing.htm.

U.S. Bureau of Labor Statistics. (2019t). "29 Percent of Wage and Salary Workers Could Work at Home in Their Primary job in 2017–2018." Retrieved from https://www.bls.gov/opub/ted/2019/29-percent-of-wage-and-salary-workers-could-work-at-home-in-their-primary-job-in-2017-18.htm.

U.S. Bureau of Labor Statistics (BLS). (2020a). "Civilian Labor Force Participation Rate." Sept. 4. Retrieved from https://www.bls.gov/charts/employment-situation/civilian-labor-force-participation-rate.htm.

U.S. Bureau of Labor Statistics (BLS). (2020b). "Labor Force Statistics from the Current Population Survey: Household Data, Annual Averages. Table 13. Employed Hispanic or Latino workers by sex, occupation, class of worker, full- or part-time status, and detailed ethnic group." Retrieved from https://www.bls.gov/cps/cpsaat13.htm.

U.S. Bureau of Labor Statistics (BLS). (2020c). "The Employment Situation—June 2020." Retrieved from https://www.bls.gov/news.release/pdf/empsit.pdf.

U.S. Bureau of Labor Statistics (BLS). (2020d). "Unemployment Rate - Hispanic or Latino." Retrieved from FRED, Federal Reserve Bank of St. Louis, https://fred.stlouisfed.org/series/LNS14000009.

U.S. Bureau of the Census. (2003). *Statistical abstract of the United States 2000*. Washington, DC: U.S. Government Printing Office.

U.S. Bureau of the Census. (2010). "Selected Social Characteristics in the United States." *American Community Survey: 2010*. Retrieved spring 2011, from http://www.culvercity.org/./media/Files/Planning/Census2010/US%20Census%20DP-02%20Selected%20Social%20Char.%202010.ashx

U.S. Bureau of the Census. (2011). Census Bureau Releases Estimates of Same-Sex Married Couples. Retrieved 3/29/15, from http://www.census.gov/newsroom/releases/archives/2010_census/cb11-cn181.html.

U.S. Bureau of the Census. (2012a). "Mean Household Income Received by Each Fifth and Top 5 Percent, All Races: 1967 to 2010." Historical Income Tables: Households, Table H-3. Retrieved 8/27/12, from www.census.gov/hhes/www/income/data/historical/household/index.html.

U.S. Bureau of the Census. (2012b). "Self-Described Religious Affiliation of Adult Population: 1990, 2001, and 2008." *Statistical Abstract of the United States: 2012*, Table 75. Washington, DC: U.S. Bureau of the Census. Retrieved spring 2013, from www.census.gov/compendia/statab/2012/tables/12s0075.pdf.

U.S. Bureau of the Census. (2012c). "Unemployed and Unemployment Rates by Educational Attainment, Sex, Race, and Hispanic Origin: 2000 to 2010." *Statistical Abstract of the United States: 2012*, Table 627. Retrieved spring 2013, from www.census.gov/compendia/statab/2012/tables/12s0627.pdf.

U.S. Bureau of the Census. (2014a). "2014 National Population Projections Tables: Table 3. Projections of the Population by Sex and Selected Age Groups for the United States: 2015 to 2060," Retrieved from https://www.census.gov/data/tables/2014/demo/popproj/2014-summary-tables.html.

U.S. Bureau of the Census. (2014b). "Income Limits for Each Fifth and Top 5 Percent of All Households (All Races)." Historical Income Tables: Income Inequality, Table H-1 All Races. Retrieved 12/14, from https://www.census.gov/hhes/www/income/data/historical/inequality/.

U.S. Bureau of the Census. (2016a). "Current Population Survey Detailed Tables for Poverty, POV-01. Age and Sex of All People, Family Members and Unrelated Individuals Iterated by Income-to-Poverty Ratio and Race," Retrieved from https://www.census.gov/data/tables/time-series/demo/income-poverty/cps-pov/pov-01.html.

U.S. Bureau of the Census. (2016b). "Historical Families Tables: Table SHP-1. Parents and Children in Stay-At-Home Parent Family Groups: 1994 to Present." Retrieved from https://www.census.gov/data/tables/time-series/demo/families/families.html.

U.S. Bureau of the Census. (2016c). "Measuring America: 30-year-olds: Then and Now." Retrieved from http://www.census.gov/library/visualizations/2016/comm/30-year-olds.html.

U.S. Bureau of the Census. (2016d). "POV-02. People in Families by Family Structure, Age, and Sex, Iterated by Income-to-Poverty Ratio and Race." Retrieved from https://www.census.gov/data/tables/time-series/demo/income-poverty/cps-pov/pov-02.html.

U.S. Bureau of the Census. (2016e). "2016 Census Occupation Index." Retrieved from https://www.census.gov/people/io/methodology/indexes.html

U.S. Bureau of the Census. (2017a). "2017 National Population Projections Tables: Main Series." Table 10. Retrieved from https://www.census.gov/data/tables/2017/demo/popproj/2017-summary-tables.html.

U.S. Bureau of the Census. (2017b). "America's Families and Living Arrangements: 2016, Table A1. Marital Status Of People 15 Years And Over, By Age, Sex, and Personal Earnings: 2016." Retrieved from https://www.census.gov/data/tables/2016/demo/families/cps-2016.html.

U.S. Bureau of the Census. (2017c). "America's Families and Living Arrangements: 2016, Table AVG1. Average Number of People Per Household, by Race And Hispanic Origin, Marital Status, Age, and Education of Householder: 2016." Retrieved from https://www.census.gov/data/tables/2016/demo/families/cps-2016.html.

U.S. Bureau of the Census. (2017d). "America's Families and Living Arrangements: 2016, Table C3. Living Arrangements Of Children Under 18 Years and Marital Status of Parents, by Age, Sex, Race, and Hispanic Origin and Selected Characteristics of the Child for All Children: 2016." Retrieved from https://www.census.gov/data/tables/2016/demo/families/cps-2016.html.

U.S. Bureau of the Census. (2017e). "America's Families and Living Arrangements: 2016, Table H1. Households by Type and Tenure of Householder for Selected Characteristics: 2016," Retrieved from https://www.census.gov/data/tables/2016/demo/families/cps-2016.html.

U.S. Bureau of the Census. (2017f). "Educational Attainment in the United States: 2016, Table A-1. Years of School Completed by People 25 Years and Over, by Age and Sex: Selected Years 1940 to 2016." Retrieved from https://www.census.gov/data/tables/2016/demo/education-attainment/cps-detailed-tables.html.

U.S. Bureau of the Census. (2017g). "Historical Families Tables: Table FM-2. All Parent/Child Situations, by Type, Race, and Hispanic Origin of Householder or Reference Person: 1970 to Present." Retrieved from https://www.census.gov/data/tables/time-series/demo/families/families.html.

U.S. Bureau of the Census. (2017h). "Historical Living Arrangements of Adults, Table UC-1. Unmarried Couples of the Opposite Sex, by Presence of Children: 1960 to present." Retrieved from https://www.census.gov/data/tables/time-series/demo/families/adults.html.

U.S. Bureau of the Census. (2017i). "Historical Marital Status Tables: Table MS-2. Estimated Median Age at First Marriage, by Sex: 1890 to the Present." Retrieved from https://www.census.gov/data/tables/time-series/demo/families/marital.html.

U.S. Bureau of the Census. (2017j). "National Population by Characteristics Tables: 2010-2016: Annual Estimates of the Resident Population by Sex, Age, Race, and Hispanic Origin: April 1, 2010 to July 1, 2016," Retreived from https://www.census.gov/data/tables/2016/demo/popest/nation-detail.html.

U.S. Bureau of the Census. (2017k). "Older Americans Month: May 2017." Retrieved from https://www.census.gov/content/dam/Census/newsroom/facts-for-features/2017/cb17-ff08.pdf.

U.S. Bureau of the Census. (2017l). "Real Median Household Income by Race and Hispanic Origin: 1967 to 2017." Retrieved from https://www.census.gov/content/dam/Census/library/visualizations/2018/demo/p60-263/figure1.pdf.

U.S. Bureau of the Census. (2017m). "The Nation's Older Population Is Still Growing, Census Bureau Reports," June 22, Retrieved from https://www.census.gov/newsroom/press-releases/2017/cb17-100.html.

U.S. Bureau of the Census. (2017n). "Voting and Registration in the Election of November 2016." Retrieved from https://www.census.gov/data/tables/time-series/demo/voting-and-registration/p20-580.html.

U.S. Bureau of the Census. (2017o). "Wealth, Asset Ownership, and Debt of Households Detailed Tables: 2013," Table 1, Retrieved from https://www.census.gov/data/tables/2013/demo/wealth/wealth-asset-ownership.html.

U.S. Bureau of the Census. (2018a). "Fertility of Women in the United States: 2018." Tables 3A and 3B. Retrieved from https://www.census.gov/data/tables/2018/demo/fertility/women-fertility.html.

U.S. Bureau of the Census. (2018b). "Historical Estimates of World Population." Retrieved from https://www.census.gov/data/tables/time-series/demo/international-programs/historical-est-worldpop.html.

U.S. Bureau of the Census. (2018c). "Income and Poverty in the United States: 2017." Retrieved from https://census.gov/library/publications/2018/demo/p60-263.html.

U.S. Bureau of the Census. (2018d). National Marriage and Divorce Rate Trends: Fact Sheet. Retrieved from https://www.cdc.gov/nchs/fastats/marriage-divorce.htm#:~:text=Divorce%20rate%3A%202.9%20per%201%2C000,45%20reporting%20States%20and%20D.C.

U.S. Bureau of the Census. (2018e). "U.S. World and Population Clock." Retrieved from https://www.census.gov/popclock/data_tables.php?component=growth.

U.S. Bureau of the Census. (2019a). "Historical Families Tables." Table FM-2. Retrieved from https://www.census.gov/data/tables/time-series/demo/families/families.html.

U.S. Bureau of the Census. (2019b). "Historical Income Tables: Families." Table F-22. Retrieved from https://www.census.gov/data/tables/time-series/demo/income-poverty/historical-income-families.html/.

U.S. Bureau of the Census. (2019c). "Historical Income Tables: Households." Table H-2. Retrieved from https://www.census.gov/data/tables/time-series/demo/income-poverty/historical-income-households.html.

U.S. Bureau of the Census. (2019d). "Historical Marital Status Tables." Retrieved from https://www.census.gov/data/tables/time-series/demo/families/marital.html.

U.S. Bureau of the Census. (2019e). "Income and Poverty in the United States: 2018." Retrieved from https://www.census.gov/library/publications/2019/demo/p60-266.html

U.S. Bureau of the Census. (2019f). "New Census Bureau Estimates Show Counties in South and West Lead Nation in Population Growth." April 18. Retrieved from https://www.census.gov/newsroom/press-releases/2019/estimates-county-metro.html.

U.S. Bureau of the Census. (2019g). "Population Estimates Show Aging Across Race Groups Differs." June 20. Retrieved from https://www.census.gov/newsroom/press-releases/2019/estimates-characteristics.html.

U.S. Bureau of the Census. (2019h). "QuickFacts." Retrieved from https://www.census.gov/quickfacts/fact/table/US/RHI725218#RHI725218.

U.S. Bureau of the Census. (2019i). "U.S. and World Population Clock." Retrieved from https://www.census.gov/popclock/data_tables.php?component=growth.

U.S. Bureau of the Census. (2019j). "U.S. Families and Living Arrangements: 2019." Table C-3. Retrieved from https://www.census.gov/data/tables/2019/demo/families/cps-2019.html

U.S. Bureau of the Census. (2020). Educational Attainment in the United States: 2019. Retrieved from https://www.census.gov/data/tables/2019/demo/educational-attainment/cps-detailed-tables.html.

U.S. Department of Agriculture. (2018). "Rural America at a Glance: 2018 Edition." Retrieved from https://www.ers.usda.gov/webdocs/publications/90556/eib-200.pdf?v=5899.2.

U.S. Department of Commerce. (2010). "Middle Class in America." Washington, DC: U.S. Department of Commerce Economics and Statistics Administration for the Office of the Vice President of the United States Middle Class Task Force.

U.S. Department of Education. (2016). "Digest of Education Statistics: Fall enrollment in degree-granting historically Black colleges and universities, by sex of student and level and control of institution: Selected years, 1976 through 2014." Retrieved from https://nces.ed.gov/programs/digest/d15/tables/dt15_313.20.asp?current=yes.

U.S. Department of Education Office for Civil Rights. (2018). "2015–16 Civil Rights Data Collection: School Climate and Safety." Retrieved from https://www2.ed.gov/about/offices/list/ocr/docs/school-climate-and-safety.pdf.

U.S. Department of Health and Human Services (DHHS). (2016). "Child Maltreatment 2014." Retrieved from http://www.acf.hhs.gov/programs/cb/research-data-technology/statistics-research/child-maltreatment.

U.S. Department of Health and Human Services (DHHS). (2018). "Welfare Indicators and Risk Factors, Seventeenth Report to Congress." "https://aspe.hhs.gov/pdf-report/welfare-indicators-and-risk-factors-seventeenth-report-congress

U.S. Department of Health and Human Services. (2020). "HHS Poverty Guidelines For 2020." Retrieved from https://aspe.hhs.gov/2020-poverty-guidelines.

U.S. Department of Housing and Urban Development. (2016). "The 2016 Homeless Assessment Report (AHAR) to Congress." Retrieved from https://www.hudexchange.info/resources/documents/2016-AHAR-Part-1.pdf.

U.S. Department of Justice. (2014). "Rape and Sexual Assault Among College-Age Females, 1995–2013." Retrieved 12/14, from http://www.bjs.gov/content/pub/pdf/rsavcaf9513.pdf.

U.S. Department of Labor. (2018). "2018 Findings on the Worst Forms of Child Labor." Retrieved from https://www.dol.gov/agencies/ilab/resources/reports/child-labor/findings.

U.S. Director of National Intelligence (DNI) (2017). "'Background to "Assessing Russian Activities and Intentions in Recent US Elections:' The Analytic Process and Cyber Incident Attribution." Retrieved from https://www.dni.gov/files/documents/ICA_2017_01.pdf.

U.S. Elections Project. (2017). "Voter Turnout." Retrieved from http://www.electproject.org/home/voter-turnout/voter-turnout-data.

U.S. Energy Information Administration. (2017). "Independent Statistics and Analysis." Retrieved from http://www.eia.gov/beta/international/.

U.S. Energy Information Administration. (2019a). International Energy Outlook 2019, with Projections to 2050. September 24. Retrieved from https://www.eia.gov/outlooks/ieo/pdf/ieo2019.pdf.

U.S. Energy Information Administration. (2019b). "International Energy Statistics." Retrieved from https://www.eia.gov/beta/international/data/browser/#/?pa=000000001&c=41000000020 0006000000000000g00020000000 0000000001&vs=INTL.44-2-AFRC-QBTU.A&vo=0&v=H&start=1980& end=2016.

U.S. Energy Information Administration. (2019c). "Frequently Asked Questions: What Countries are the Top Producers and Consumers of Oil?" Retrieved from https://www.eia.gov/tools/faqs/faq.php?id=709&t=6.

U.S. Equal Employment Opportunity Commission (EEOC). (2012). "Sexual Harassment Charges, FY 2010–FY 2012." Retrieved spring 2013, from http://www.eeoc.gov/eeoc/statistics/enforcement/sexual_harassment_new.cfm.

U.S. Government Accountability Office (GAO). (2011). "Income Security: Older Adults and the 2007–2009 Recession." Retrieved spring 2013, from www.gao.gov/products/GAO-12-76.

U.S. International Trade Commission. (2016). "Nigeria's Film Industry: Nollywood Looks to Expand Globally." Retrieved from https://www.usitc.gov/publications/332/erick_oh_nigerias_film_industry.pdf.

U.S. Supreme Court. (2011). Wal-Mart Stores, Inc. v. Dukes et al. No. 10–277. Retrieved spring 2013, from www.supremecourt.gov/opinions/10pdf/10-277.pdf.

Valdes, J. G. (2008). Pinochet's Economists: The Chicago School of Economics in Chile. Cambridge, UK: Cambridge University Press.

Valenti, J. (2014). "Tinder's sexual harassment scandal is not a surprise. It's another wake-up call." Guardian, July 2. Retrieved 10/14, from http://www.theguardian.com/commentisfree/2014/jul/02/tinder-sexual-harassment-silicon-valley-sexism.

Valenzuela, A. (1999). Subtractively Schooling: U.S. Mexican Youth and the Politics of Caring. Albany, NY: State University of New York Press.

Vanacore, A. (2012). "Recovery School District Will Lay off Almost 200 Teachers." Times-Picayune, June 18. Retrieved 6/18/12, from www.nola.com/education/index.ssf/2012/06/recovery_school_district_will_2.html.

van de Kaa, D. J. (2003). "Second Demographic Transition." In P. Demeny and G. McNicoll, eds., Encyclopedia of Population, vol. 2 (pp. 872–75). New York: Macmillan.

Van de Velde, S., P. Bracke, and K. Levecque. (2010). Gender differences in depression in 23 European countries. Cross-national variation in the gender gap in depression. Social Science and Medicine, 71(2), 305–313.

van den Hoonard, D. K. (2002). "Attitudes of Older Widows and Widowers in New Brunswick, Canada toward New Partnerships." Ageing International 27: 79–92.

van der Veer, P. (1994). Religious Nationalism: Hindus and Muslims in India. Berkeley, CA: University of California Press.

van Gennep, A. (1977; orig. 1908). The Rites of Passage. London: Routledge and Kegan Paul.

Van Horn, C., C. Zukin, M. Szeltner, and C. Stone. (2012). Left Out, Forgotten? Recent High School Graduates and the Great Recession (June 2012). New Brunswick, NJ: John J. Heldrich Center for Workforce Development. Retrieved 6/18/12, from www.heldrich.rutgers.edu/sites/default/files/content/Left_Out_Forgotten_Work_Trends_June_2012.pdf.

Van Overtveldt, J. (2007). The Chicago School: How the University of Chicago Assembled the Thinkers who Revolutionized Economics and Business. Evanston, IL: Agate Publishing.

Vartanian, T. P., and L. Houser. (2010). "The Effects of Childhood Neighborhood Conditions on Self-Reports of Adult Health." Journal of Health and Social Behavior 51: 291–306.

Vaughan, D. (1986). Uncoupling: Turning Points in Intimate Relationships. New York: Oxford University Press.

Vaughan, A. (2019). "Could geoengineering really help us solve the climate crisis?" New Scientist, May 16. Retrieved from https://www.newscientist.com/article/2203085-could-geoengineering-really-help-us-solve-the-climate-crisis/#ixzz67L8IXyhM.

Vaupel, J. W., et al. (1998). "Biodemographic Trajectories of Longevity." Science 280 (5365): 855–60.

Veracini, L. (2010). Settler Colonialism: A Theoretical Overview. New York: Palgrave Macmillan.

Verizon (2018). "2018 Data Breach Investigations Report," 11th ed. Retrieved from https://enterprise.verizon.com/resources/reports/DBIR_2018_Report.pdf.

Verlie, B. (2019). "Bearing worlds: learning to live-with climate change." Environmental Education Journal 25(5): 751–766.

Versey, S. (2014). "Centering Perspectives on Black Women, Hair Politics, and Physical Activity." American Journal of Public Health 104: 810–15.

Veselinovic, M. (2015). "More than Feuds and Dramas, Nollywood Is a Mighty Economic Machine," CNN, Aug. 27, Retrieved from http://www.cnn.com/2015/07/10/africa/nollywood-mighty-economic-machine/index.html.

Vidal, J. (2018). "What Are Coastal Nuclear Power Plants Doing to Address Climate Threats?" Ensia, August 18. Retrieved from https://ensia.com/features/coastal-nuclear/.

Vinopal, C. (2020). "Coronavirus has changed online dating. Here's why some say that's a good thing." PBS News Hour, May 15. Retrieved from https://www.pbs.org/newshour/nation/coronavirus-has-changed-online-dating-heres-why-some-say-thats-a-good-thing.

Vitali, S., J. Glattfelder, and S. Battiston. (2011). "The Network of Global Corporate Control." Retrieved summer 2013, from http://arxiv.org/pdf/1107.5728v2.pdf.

Wacquant, L. J. D. (2010). *Deadly Symbiosis*. Cambridge: Polity.

Wade, L. (2011). "Separating the Heat from the Light: Lessons from 30 Years of Academic Discourse about Female Genital Cutting" *Ethnicities* 12(1): 26–49.

Wade, L. (2017). *American Hookup: The New Culture of Sex on Campus*. New York: W. W. Norton & Company.

Wadhera, R. K., P. Wadhera, P. Gaba, J. F. Figueroa, K. E. Joynt Maddox, R. W. Yeh, and C. Shen. (2020). "Variation in COVID-19 Hospitalizations and Deaths Across New York City Boroughs." *Journal of the American Medical Association* 323(21): 2192–95.

Wadud, A. (1999). *Qur'an and Women: Rereading the Sacred Text from a Woman's Perspective*. New York: Oxford University Press.

Wadwha, V. (2014). "We're heading into a jobless future, no matter what the government does." *Washington Post*. July 21. Retrieved from http://www. washingtonpost.com/blogs/ innovations/wp/2014/07/21/were-heading-into-a-jobless-future-no-matter-what-the-government-does/.

Wagner, L. A. (2015). "When Your Smartphone Is Too Smart for Your Own Good: How Social Media Alters Human Relationships." *The Journal of Individual Psychology* 71(2): 114–21.

Wagner, P., and B. Rabuy. (2017). "Following the Money of Mass Incarceration." Prison Policy Initiative. Retrieved from https://www.prisonpolicy.org/ reports/money.html.

Wakefield, J. (2016). "Foxconn replaces '60,000 factory workers with robots,'" May 25, *BBC*, Retrieved from http:// www.bbc.com/news/technology-36376966.

Waldron, I. (1986). "Why Do Women Live Longer Than Men?" In P. Conrad and R. Kern, eds., *The Sociology of Health and Illness*. New York: St. Martin's.

Walker, R. E., C. R. Keane, and J. G. Burke. (2010). "Disparities and access to healthy food in the United States: A review of food deserts literature". *Health & Place* 16: 876–84.

Waller, W. (1938). *The Family: A Dynamic Interpretation*. New York: Gordon.

Wallerstein, I. (1974a). *Capitalist Agriculture and the Origins of the European World-Economy in the Sixteenth Century*. New York: Academic Press.

Wallerstein, I. (1974b). *The Modern World-System*. New York: Academic Press.

Wallerstein, I. (1979). *The Capitalist World Economy*. Cambridge, UK: Cambridge University Press.

Wallerstein, I. (1990). *The Modern World-System II*. New York: Academic Press.

Wallerstein, I. (1996). *Historical Capitalism with Capitalist Civilization*. New York: W. W. Norton.

Wallerstein, I. (2004). *World-System Analysis: An Introduction*. Durham, NC: Duke University Press.

Wallis, L. (2019). "Private Households: Employing the Nation's Invisible Workforce." State of Oregon Employment Department, March 12. https:// www.qualityinfo.org/-/private-households-employing-the-nation-s-invisible-workforce.

Wallis, R. (1984). *The Elementary Forms of New Religious Life*. London: Routledge and Kegan Paul.

Walmart. (2019). "Walmart on Track to Reduce 1 Billion Metric Tons of Emissions from Global Supply Chains by 2030." Retrieved from https:// corporate.walmart.com/newsroom/ 2019/05/08/walmart-on-track-to-reduce-1-billion-metric-tons-of-emissions-from-global-supply-chains-by-2030.

Walmart. (2020). "Location Facts." Retrieved from https://corporate. walmart.com/our-story/locations/ united-states.

Walmsley, R. (2016). "World Prison Population List," Institute for Criminal Policy Research, Retrieved from http://prisonstudies.org/sites/ default/files/resources/downloads/ world_prison_population_list_11th_ edition_0.pdf.

Walmsley, R. (2018). "World Prison Population List," 12th ed. World Prison Brief and Institute for Criminal Policy Research. Retrieved from https:// www.prisonstudies.org/sites/default/ files/resources/downloads/wppl_12. pdf.

Walum, L. R. (1977). *The Dynamics of Sex and Gender: A Sociological Perspective*. Chicago: Rand McNally.

Wang, J-L., L. A. Jackson, D.-J. Zhang, and Z.-Q. Su. (2012). "Relationships and the Big Five personality factors. Self-esteem, narcissism, and sensation-seeking to Chinese University students' use of social networking sites." *Computers in Human Behavior* 28(2): 370–76.

Wang, W., and K. Parker. (2014). "Record Share of Americans Have Never Married: As Values, Economics and Gender Patterns Change." Washington, D.C.: Pew Research Center's Social & Demographic Trends project. Retrieved 12/26/14, from http://www.pewsocialtrends.org/ files/2014/09/2014-09-24_Never-Married-Americans.pdf.

Warner, J. (2010). "What the Great Recession Has Done to Family Life." *New York Times*, August 6. Retrieved 6/18/12, from www.nytimes.com/ 2010/08/08/magazine/08FOB-wwln-t.html.

Warner, S. (1993). "Work in Progress toward a New Paradigm for the Sociological Study of Religion in the United States." *American Journal of Sociology* 98: 1044–93.

Warren, B. (1980). *Imperialism: Pioneer of Capitalism*. London: Verso.

Washington Post. (2012). "Exit Polls 2012: How the Vote Has Shifted." Campaign 2012. Retrieved spring 2013, from www.washingtonpost.com/wp-srv/ special/politics/2012-exit-polls/ table.html.

Watts, D. J. (2007). "Is Justin Timberlake a Product of Cumulative Advantage?" *New York Times*, April 15. Retrieved 3/14/13, from www.nytimes.com/ 2007/04/15/magazine/ 15wwlnidealab.t.html.

Watts, J. (2018). "We have 12 years to limit climate change catastrophe, warns UN." *Guardian*, Oct. 8. Retrieved from https://www.theguardian.com/ environment/2018/oct/08/global-warming-must-not-exceed-15c-warns-landmark-un-report.

Watts, N. et al. (2019). "The 2019 report of The *Lancet* Countdown on health and climate change: ensuring that the health of a child born today is not defined by a changing climate." *The Lancet*, November 13. Retrieved from https://www. thelancet.com/action/showPdf?pii =S0140-6736%2819%2932596-6.

Weber, M. (1963; orig. 1922). *The Sociology of Religion*. Boston: Beacon Press.

Weber, M. (1978, orig. 1921). *Economy and Society: An Outline of Interpretive Sociology* (2 vols.). Berkeley, CA: University of California Press.

Weeks, J. (1977). *Coming Out: Homosexual Politics in Britain, from the Nineteenth Century to the Present*. New York: Quartet.

Weigel, M. (2017). *Labor of Love: The Invention of Dating*. New York: Farrar, Straus and Giroux.

Weise, E. (2019). "Climate change the new Vietnam War? Generation Z poised to change US politics with activism." *USA Today*, May 6. Retrieved from https://www.usatoday.com/story/ news/2019/05/06/generation-z-poised-change-us-politics-climate-change-activism/1090104001/.

Weitzman, L., et al. (1972). "Sex-Role Socialization in Picture Books for Preschool Children." *American Journal of Sociology* 77: 1125–50.

Wellman, B. (1994). "I Was a Teenage Network Analyst: The Route from the Bronx to the Information Highway." *Connections* 17(2): 28–45.

Wellman, B. (2008). "What is the Internet doing to community—and vice-versa?" In T. Haas, ed., *New Urbanism and Beyond* (pp. 239–42). Milan: Rizzoli.

Wellman, B., P. J. Carrington, and A. Hall. (1988). "Networks as Personal Communities." In B. Wellman and S. D. Berkowitz, eds., *Social Structures: A Network Approach.* New York: Cambridge University Press.

Wellman, B., J. Salaff, D. Dimitrova, L. Garton, M. Gulia, and C. Haythornthwaite. (1996). "Computer Networks as Social Networks: Collaborative Work, Telework, and Virtual Community." *Annual Review of Sociology* 22: 213–38.

Wessler, S. F. (2014). "Poll: Fewer Americans Blame Poverty on the Poor." ABC News, June 20. Retrieved 12/14, from. http://www.nbcnews.com/feature/in-plain-sight/poll-fewer-americans-blame-poverty-poor-n136051.

West, C., and D. H. Zimmerman. (1987). "Doing Gender." *Gender and Society* 1(2): 125–51.

Western, B. (1997). *Between Class and Market: Postwar Unionization in the Capitalist Democracies.* Princeton, NJ: Princeton University Press.

Westheimer, J. (Ed.). (2007). *Pledging Allegiance: The Politics of Patriotism in American's Schools.* New York: Teachers College Press.

Wezerek, G., and K. R. Ghodsee. (2020). "Women's Unpaid Labor is Worth $10,900,000,000,000." *New York Times,* March 5. Retrieved from https://www.nytimes.com/interactive/2020/03/04/opinion/women-unpaid-labor.html.

Whalen, J. (2016). "The Children of the Opioid Crisis." *The Wall Street Journal* (December 15, 2016). Retrieved from https://www.wsj.com/articles/the-children-of-the-opioid-crisis-1481816178.

Wheatley, P. (1971). *The Pivot of the Four Quarters.* Edinburgh: Edinburgh University Press.

White House. (2014). Let's Move: America's Move to Raise a Healthier Generation of Kids. Retrieved 10/24/14, from http://www.letsmove.gov/learn-facts/epidemic-childhood-obesity.

Widom, C. S., S. J. Czaja, and K. A. DuMont. (2015). "Intergenerational transmission of child abuse and neglect: Real or detection bias?" *Science,* 2015; 347 (6229): 1480 DOI: 10.1126/science.1259917.

Widra, E. (2019). "Stark racial disparities in murder victimization persist,

even as overall murder rate declines." Prison Policy Initiative. Retrieved from https://www.prisonpolicy.org/blog/2018/05/03/homicide_overtime/.

Wike, R., J. Poushter, J. Fetterolf, and S. Schumacher. "U.S. image generally favorable around the world, but mixed in some countries." Retrieved from https://www.pewresearch.org/global/2020/01/08/u-s-image-generally-favorable-around-the-world-but-mixed-in-some-countries/.

Wilcox, W. B., and L. DeRose. (2017). "In Europe, cohabitation is stable... right?" Brookings Institution, March 27. Retrieved from https://www.brookings.edu/blog/social-mobility-memos/2017/03/27/in-europe-cohabitation-is-stable-right/.

Wildsmith, E., J. Manlove, and E. Cook. (2018). "Dramatic increase in the proportion of births outside of marriage in the United States from 1990 to 2016." Child Trends, Aug. 8. Retrieved from https://www.childtrends.org/publications/dramatic-increase-in-percentage-of-births-outside-marriage-among-whites-hispanics-and-women-with-higher-education-levels.

Wilken, C. S. (2008). *Myths and Realities of Aging.* Gainesville, FL: University of Florida IFAS Extension. Retrieved 8/09/12, from http://edis.ifas.ufl.edu/pdffiles/FY/FY52400.pdf.

Wilkinson, L., and J. Pearson. (2009). "School culture and the well-being of same-sex-attracted youth." *Gender & Society* 23(4): 542–568.

Wilkinson, R. (1996). *Unhealthy Societies: The Afflictions of Inequality.* New York: Routledge.

Will, J., P. Self, and N. Datan. (1976). "Maternal Behavior and Perceived Sex of Infant." *American Journal of Orthopsychiatry* 46: 135–39.

Willen, L. (2020). "Ready or not, a new era of homeschooling has begun." The Hechinger Report, March 16. Retrieved from https://hechingerreport.org/ready-or-not-a-new-era-of-homeschooling-has-begun/.

Williams, C. L. (1992). "The Glass Escalator: Hidden Advantages for Men in the 'Female' Professions." *Social Problems* 39: 253–67.

Williams, C. L. (2013). "The Glass Escalator, Revisited: Gender Inequality in Neoliberal Times." *Gender & Society* 27: 609–29.

Williams County. (2019). "About Us." Retrieved from https://www.williamsnd.com/.

Williams, S. J. (1993). *Chronic Respiratory Illness.* London: Routledge.

Williams, T. (2012). "For Native American Women, Scourge of Rape, Rare Justice." *New York Times,* May 22. Retrieved 9/10/12, from www.nytimes.com/2012/05/23/us/native-americans-struggle-with-high-rate-of-rape.html.

Williams, D., N. Martins, M. Consalvo, and J. D. Ivory. (2009). "The virtual census: Representations of gender, race, and age in video games." *New Media and Society* 11: 815–83

Willis, P. (1977). *Learning to Labor.* Lexington, MA: Lexington Books.

Wilsdon, J., and J. Keeley. (2007). *China: The Next Science Superpower?* London: Demos. Retrieved summer 2013, from www.google.com/url?sa=t&rct=j&q=&esrc=s&source=web&cd=2&ved=0CGQQFjAB&url=http%3A%2F%2Fwww.naider.com%2Fupload%2F82_china_final.pdf&ei=dz8cUM-vG-n_igKi04D4Dg&usg=AFQjCNG_GZ6E6_9NIWk0ftR-ifla276GCA&sig2=8_7eKS0i7OaZvHOC6KDM0A.

Wilson, B. (1982). *Religion in Sociological Perspective.* New York: Oxford University Press.

Wilson, J. Q., and G. Kelling. (1982). "Broken Windows." *Atlantic Monthly,* March.

Wilson, W. J. (1987). *The Truly Disadvantaged: The Inner City, the Underclass, and Public Policy.* Chicago: University of Chicago Press.

Wilson, W. J. (1991). "Studying Inner-City Social Dislocations: The Challenge of Public Agenda Research." *American Sociological Review* 56: 1–14.

Wilson, W. J. (1996). *When Work Disappears: The World of the New Urban Poor.* New York: Knopf.

Wilson, W. J. (2011). "Being Poor, Black, and American: The Impact of Political, Economic, and Cultural Forces." *American Educator* (Spring): 10–23, 46.

Wimmer, A. (2012). *Waves of War: Nationalism, State Formation, and Ethnic Exclusion in the Modern World.* New York: Cambridge University Press.

Winkleby, M. A., D. E. Jatulis, E. Frank, and S. P. Fortmann. (1992). "Socioeconomic Status and Health: How Education, Income, and Occupation Contribute to Risk Factors for Cardiovascular Disease." *American Journal of Public Health* 82: 816–20.

Wirth, L. (1938). "Urbanism as a Way of Life." *American Sociological Review* 44: 1–24.

Witterick, K. (2013). "Dancing in the Eye of the Storm: The Gift of Gender Diversity to Our Family." In F. J. Green and M. Friedman, eds., *Chasing Rainbows: Exploring Gender Fluid Parenting Practices.* Ontario, CA: Demeter Press.

Wolff, P. M., and K. J. Holmes. (2011). "Linguistic Relativity." *Wiley Interdisciplinary Reviews: Cognitive Science* 2(May/June).

Wong, M. (2016). "Today's children face tough prospects of being better off than their parents, Stanford researchers find." Retrieved from: http://news.stanford.edu/2016/12/08/todays-children-face-tough-prospects-better-off-parents.

Wong, V. (2014). "Top CEOs Make 331 Times the Average Worker. Does Anyone Care?" *Bloomberg Businessweek*, April 18. Retrieved 12/14, from http://www.businessweek.com/articles/2014-04-18/top-ceos-make-331-times-the-average-worker-dot-does-anyone-care.

Wood, T. (2017). "Racism Motivated Trump Voters More Than Authoritarianism," *Washington Post*, April 17, Retrieved from https://www.washingtonpost.com/news/monkey-cage/wp/2017/04/17/racism-motivated-trump-voters-more-than-authoritarianism-or-income-inequality/?utm_term=.ec2fec462bc0.

Woodrum, E. (1988). "Moral Conservatism and the 1984 Presidential Election." *Journal for the Scientific Study of Religion* 27: 192–210.

Woodward, A. (2020). "Australia's fires are 46% bigger than last year's Brazilian Amazon blazes. There are at least 2 months of fire season to go." INSIDER, Jan. 8. Retrieved from https://www.insider.com/australia-fires-burned-twice-land-area-as-2019-amazon-fires-2020-1.

World Bank. (1997). *World Development Report: 1997: The State in a Changing World*. New York: Oxford University Press.

World Bank. (2000). *World Development Report: 2000*. New York: Oxford University Press.

World Bank. (2009). "World Development Indicators, GNI per capita, all countries, 1960-2018 (constant 2010 US$)." Calculated from http://api.worldbank.org/v2/en/indicator/NY.GNP.PCAP.KD?downloadformat=excel.

World Bank. (2012). "Knowledge Economy Index." Retrieved from http://info.worldbank.org/etools/kam2/KAM_page5.asp.

World Bank. (2016a). "Poverty and Shared Prosperity 2016: Taking on Inequality." Retrieved from https://openknowledge.worldbank.org/bitstream/handle/10986/25078/9781464809583.pdf.

World Bank. (2016b). "World Development Indicators: Poverty rates at international poverty lines Part 2."

Retrieved from http://wdi.worldbank.org/table/2.8.2.

World Bank. (2017a). "Life expectancy at birth, total (years) - United States." Retrieved from https://data.worldbank.org/indicator/SP.DYN.LE00.IN?locations=US&most_recent_year_desc=false.

World Bank. (2017b). "Urban Development: Overview." March 29, Retrieved from http://www.worldbank.org/en/topic/urbandevelopment/overview.

World Bank. (2017c). "World Development Indicators: Economy," July 1, Retrieved from http://data.worldbank.org/data-catalog/world-development-indicators.

World Bank. (2018a). "Decline of Global Extreme Poverty Continues but Has Slowed: World Bank." September 19. Retrieved from https://www.worldbank.org/en/news/press-release/2018/09/19/decline-of-global-extreme-poverty-continues-but-has-slowed-world-bank.

World Bank. (2018b). "GDP (Current US$)." Retrieved from https://data.worldbank.org/indicator/ny.gdp.mktp.cd.

World Bank. (2018c). "Literacy rate, adult total (% of people ages 15 and above)." Retrieved from https://data.worldbank.org/indicator/se.adt.litr.zs?end=2018&start=1970&view=chart.

World Bank. (2018d). "Poverty and Shared Prosperity 2018: Piecing Together the Poverty Puzzle." Retrieved from https://doi.org/10.1596/978-1-4648-1330-6.

World Bank. (2019a). "Birth rate, crude (per 1,000 people)." Retrieved from https://data.worldbank.org/indicator/SP.DYN.CDRT.IN.

World Bank. (2019b). "Death rate, crude (per 1,000 people)." Retrieved from https://data.worldbank.org/indicator/sp.dyn.cdrt.in?most_recent_value_desc=false.

World Bank. (2019c). "High income." Retrieved from https://data.worldbank.org/income-level/high-income.

World Bank. (2019d). "Indicators." Retrieved from https://data.worldbank.org/indicator/.

World Bank. (2019e). "Low income." Retrieved from https://data.worldbank.org/income-level/low-income/.

World Bank. (2019f). "Mortality rate, infant (per 1,000 live births)." Retrieved from https://data.worldbank.org/indicator/sp.dyn.imrt.in?end=2018&most_recent_value_desc=false&start=1960&view=chart.

World Bank. (2019g). "New country classifications by income level: 2019–2020." Retrieved from https://

blogs.worldbank.org/opendata/new-country-classifications-income-level-2019-2020.

World Bank. (2019h). "Population Ages 0-14 (% of total population)." Retrieved from https://data.worldbank.org/indicator/SP.POP.0014.TO.ZS?most_recent_value_desc=false.

World Bank. (2019i). "Population Ages 65 and Above (% of Total Population)." Retrieved from https://data.worldbank.org/indicator/SP.POP.65UP.TO.ZS?most_recent_value_desc=false.

World Bank. (2019j). "Population Growth (annual %)." Retrieved from https://data.worldbank.org/indicator/SP.POP.GROW?most_recent_value_desc=false.

World Bank. (2019k). "The World Bank in China." Retrieved from https://www.worldbank.org/en/country/china/overview#1.

World Bank. (2019l). "United States life expectancy at birth." Retrieved from https://data.worldbank.org/indicator/SP.DYN.LE00.IN?locations=US&most_recent_year_desc=false.

World Bank. (2019m). "Urban Population (% of Total Population)." Retrieved from https://data.worldbank.org/indicator/sp.urb.totl.in.zs?most_recent_value_desc=false.

World Bank. (2020a). "Pandemic, Recession: The Global Economy in Crisis." Retrieved from https://www.worldbank.org/en/publication/global-economic-prospects.

World Bank. (2020b). "The World by Income and Region." Retrieved from https://datatopics.worldbank.org/world-development-indicators/the-world-by-income-and-region.html.

World Bank. (2020c). "U.S. GDP (Current US$)." https://data.worldbank.org/indicator/NY.GDP.MKTP.CD

World Bank Institute. (2012). "Knowledge Economy Index." Retrieved summer 2012, from http://info.worldbank.org/etools/kam2/KAM_page5.asp.

World Commission on Environment and Development. (1987). *Our Common Future: The World Commission on Environment and Development*. New York: Oxford University Press.

World Food Programme. (2018). "Nearly two-thirds of the population in South Sudan at risk of rising hunger." Retrieved from https://www.wfp.org/news/nearly-two-thirds-population-south-sudan-risk-rising-hunger.

World Food Program U.S.A. (2019). "10 Facts about Conflict & Hunger in Burundi." Retrieved from https://www.wfpusa.org/stories/10-facts-about-conflict-hunger-in-burundi/.

World Health Organization (WHO). (1948). "Preamble to the Constitution of the World Health Organization as Adopted by the International Health Conference, New York, 19–22." June, 1946; signed on 22 July 1946 by the representatives of 61 States (Official Records of the World Health Organization, no. 2, p. 100) and entered into force on 7 April 1948. Retrieved spring 2013, from www.who.int/about/definition/en/print.html.

World Health Organization (WHO). (2016a). "Global Health Observatory (GHO) Data." Retrieved from https://www.who.int/gho/mortality_burden_disease/life_tables/situation_trends/en/.

World Health Organization (WHO). (2016b). "Life expectancy and Healthy life expectancy by WHO region." Retrieved from http://apps.who.int/gho/data/view.main.SDG2016LEXv?lang=en.

World Health Organization (WHO). (2017). "Female genital mutilation: Factsheet," Retrieved from http://www.who.int/mediacentre/factsheets/fs241/en/.

World Health Organization (WHO). (2018). "Elder Abuse." Retrieved from https://www.who.int/news-room/fact-sheets/detail/elder-abuse.

World Health Organization (WHO). (2019a). "Drinking Water." Retrieved from https://www.who.int/news-room/fact-sheets/detail/drinking-water.

World Health Organization (WHO). (2019b). "Measles—European Region." May 6. Retrieved from https://www.who.int/csr/don/06-may-2019-measles-euro/en/.

World Health Organization (WHO). (2020a). "Female Life Expectancy." Retrieved from https://www.who.int/gho/women_and_health/mortality/situation_trends_life_expectancy/en/.

World Health Organization (WHO). (2020b). "Malaria." Retrieved from https://www.who.int/news-room/fact-sheets/detail/malaria.

World Health Organization (WHO). (2020c). "Novel Coronavirus (2019-nCoV): Situation Report – 20." Retrieved from https://www.who.int/docs/default-source/coronaviruse/situation-reports/20200209-sitrep-20-ncov.pdf?sfvrsn=6f80d1b9_4.

World Health Organization. (2020d). "Novel Coronavirus Disease (COVID-19) Situation Report – 175 ." Retrieved from https://www.who.int/docs/default-source/coronaviruse/situation-reports/20200713-covid-19-sitrep-175.pdf?sfvrsn=d6acef25_2.

World Health Organization. (2020e). "WHO Coronavirus Disease (COVID-19) Online Dashboard." Retrieved from https://covid19.who.int.

World Intellectual Property Organization. (2018). "World Intellectual Property Indicators, 2018." Retrieved from https://www.wipo.int/edocs/pubdocs/en/wipo_pub_941_2018-chapter2.pdf.

World Meteorological Organization. (2019). "The Global Climate in 2015–2019." Retrieved from https://library.wmo.int/doc_num.php?explnum_id=9936.

World Nuclear Association. (2018). "Nuclear Power Plants and Earthquakes." Retrieved from https://www.world-nuclear.org/information-library/safety-and-security/safety-of-plants/nuclear-power-plants-and-earthquakes.aspx.

World Population Review. (2019a). "Birth Rate by Country 2019." Retrieved from http://worldpopulationreview.com/countries/birth-rate-by-country/.

World Population Review. (2019b). "Life Expectancy by Country 2019." Retrieved from http://worldpopulationreview.com/countries/life-expectancy-by-country/.

World Population Review. (2019c). "Most Polluted Countries 2019." Retrieved from http://worldpopulationreview.com/countries/most-polluted-countries/.

World Population Review. (2020). "United States by Density 2020." Retrieved from https://worldpopulationreview.com/states/state-densities/.

World Steel Association. (2013). Steel Statistical Yearbook 2013. Retrieved 11/25/2014, from https://www.worldsteel.org/dms/internetDocumentList/statistics-archive/yearbook-archive/Steel-Statistical-Yearbook-2013/document/Steel-Statistical-Yearbook-2012.pdf.

Worrall, A. (1990). *Offending Women: Female Lawbreakers and the Criminal Justice System.* London: Routledge.

Wortham, J. (2014). "Tinder is target of sexual harassment lawsuit." *New York Times,* July 1. Retrieved 10/14, from http://www.nytimes.com/2014/07/02/business/media/tinder-is-target-of-sexual-harassment-lawsuit.html?_r=0.

Wray, L. A., A. R. Herzog, R. J. Willis, and R. B. Wallace. (1998). "The Impact of Education and Heart Attack on Smoking Cessation among Middle-Aged Adults." *Journal of Health and Social Behavior* 39(4): 271–94.

Wright, E. O. (1997). *Class Counts: Comparative Studies in Class Analysis.* New York: Cambridge University Press.

Wright, E. O. (2010). *Envisioning Real Utopias.* New York: Verso. Retrieved spring 2013, from www.scribd.com/doc/55940923/Erik-Olin-Wright-Envisioning-Real-Utopias-Verso.

Wrigley, J. (1989). "Do Young Children Need Intellectual Stimulation? Experts' Advice to Parents, 1900–1985." *History of Education Quarterly* 29(1): 41–75.

Wu, C. (2019). "The Queen of the World's Largest Contract Footwear Manufacturer." Commonwealth, June 20. Retrieved from https://english.cw.com.tw/article/article.action?id=2446.

Wuthnow, R. (1976). *The Consciousness Reformation.* Berkeley, CA: University of California Press.

Wuthnow, R. (1978). *Experimentation in American Religion.* Berkeley, CA: University of California Press.

Wuthnow, R. (1988). "Sociology of Religion." In N. J. Smelser, ed., *Handbook of Sociology.* Newbury Park, CA: Sage.

Wuthnow, R. (1990). *The Restructuring of American Religion.* Princeton, NJ: Princeton University Press.

Wuthnow, R. (1998). *After Heaven: Spirituality in America since the 1950s.* Berkeley, CA: University of California Press.

Wuthnow, R. (2007). *America and the Challenges of Religious Diversity.* Princeton, NJ: Princeton University Press.

Wuthnow, R. (2010). *Boundless Faith: The Global Outreach of American Churches.* Berkeley: University of California Press.

Xin, L. (2019). "China and Coca-Cola: A Common Development Trajectory." *China Today,* March 4. Retrieved from http://www.chinatoday.com.cn/ctenglish/2018/et/201903/t20190304_800158961.html.

Xu, J., S. L. Murphy, K. D. Kochanek, and E. Arias. (2020). "Mortality in the United States, 2018." NCHS data brief, no. 355. Hyattsville, MD: National Center for Health Statistics. Retrieved from https://www.cdc.gov/nchs/products/databriefs/db355.htm.

Yale, A. J. (2018). "Black Home Buyers Denied Mortgages More Than Twice As Often As Whites, Report Finds." *Forbes,* May 7. Retrieved from https://www.forbes.com/sites/alyyale/2018/05/07/mortgage-loan-denials-more-common-with-minorities-new-report-shows/#676dbf4e509a.

Yang, D., S. Wegner, and A. Cowsky. (2019). "Apple iPhone 11 Pro Max Teardown." Tech Insights, October 1. Retrieved from https://www.techinsights.com/blog/apple-iphone-11-pro-max-teardown.

Yankelovich, C. S. (1991). "What's OK on a Date: Survey for Time and CNN," May 8.

Yeung, K.-T., and J. L. Martin. (2003). "The Looking Glass Self: An Empirical Test and Elaboration," *Social Forces*, 81(3): 843–879.

Yon, Y., C. R. Mikton, Z. D. Gassoumis, and K. H. Wilber. (2017). "Elder Abuse Prevalence in Community Settings: A Systematic Review and Meta-Analysis." *The Lancet Global Health* 5(2): e147–56.

Young, M., and P. Willmott. (1973). *The Symmetrical Family: A Study of Work and Leisure in the London Region.* London: Routledge and Kegan Paul.

Yourish, K., K. K. R Lai, D. Ivory, D., and M. Smith. (2020). "One-Third of All U.S. Coronavirus Deaths Are Nursing Home Residents or Workers." *New York Times*, May 11. Retrieved from https://www.nytimes.com/interactive/2020/05/09/us/coronavirus-cases-nursing-homes-us.html.

Yue Yuen (2007). "Yue Yuen Industrial (Holdings) Ltd: About Us: Corporate Profile." Retrieved 12/07, from www.yueyuen.com/about_corporateProfile.htm.

Zakaria, F. (2009). *The Post-American World and the Rise of the Rest.* New York: Penguin.

Zammuner, V. (1986). "Children's Sex-Role Stereotypes: A Cross-Cultural Analysis." In P. Shaver and C. Hendrick, eds., *Sex and Gender.* Beverly Hills, CA: Sage.

Zarcadoolas, C., A. Pleasant, and D. Greer. (2006). *Advancing Health Literacy: A Framework for Understanding and Action.* San Francisco: Jossey-Bass.

Zaveri, M., and E. Rueb. (2020). "How Many Animals Have Died in Australia's Wildfires?" *New York Times*, Jan. 11. Retrieved from https://www.nytimes.com/2020/01/11/world/australia/fires-animals.html.

Zerubavel, E. (1979). *Patterns of Time in Hospital Life.* Chicago: University of Chicago Press.

Zerubavel, E. (1982). "The Standardization of Time: A Sociohistorical Perspective." *American Journal of Sociology* 88: 1–23.

Zheng, H. (2009). "Rising U.S. Income Inequality, Gender, and Individual Self-Rated Health, 1972–2004." *Social Science and Medicine* 69: 1333–42.

Zheng, H. (2012). "Do People Die from Income Inequality of a Decade Ago?" *Social Science and Medicine* 75: 36–45.

Zillman, C. (2019). "The Fortune 500 Has More Female CEOs Than Ever Before." *Fortune*, May 26. Retrieved from https://fortune.com/2019/05/16/fortune-500-female-ceos/.

Zimbardo, P. G. (1969). "The Human Choice: Individuation, Reason, and Order Versus Deindividuation, Impulse, and Chaos." In W. J. Arnold and D. Levine, eds., *Nebraska Symposium on Motivation* 17. Lincoln, NE: University of Nebraska Press.

Zimbardo, P. G. (1992). *Quiet Rage: The Stanford Prison Experiment* (documentary). Available from www.prisonexp.org/.

Zimbardo, P. G., E. B. Ebbesen, and C. Maslach. (1977). *Influencing Attitudes and Changing Behavior.* Reading, MA: Addison-Wesley.

Zimmerman, J. (2010). "College Admissions: What Matters Most—SAT Scores, Grades, or Just Luck?" *Christian Science Monitor*, April 13. Retrieved spring 2011, from www.csmonitor.com/Commentary/Opinion/2010/0413/College-admissions-What-matters-most-SAT-scores-grades-or-just-luck.

Zoepf, S., S. Chen, P. Adu, and G. Pozo. (2018). "The Economics of Ride Hailing: Driver Revenue, Expenses and Taxes." MIT Center for Energy and Environmental Policy Research. Retrieved from https://orfe.princeton.edu/~alaink/SmartDrivingCars/PDFs/Zoepf_The%20Economics%20of%20RideHialing_OriginalPdfFeb2018.pdf.

Zosuls, K. M., D. N. Ruble, C. S. Tamis-LeMonda, P. E. Shrout, M. H. Bornstein, and F. K. Greulich. (2009). "The Acquisition of Gender Labels in Infancy: Implications for Gender-typed Play." *Developmental Psychology* 45, 688–701.

Zuboff, S. (1988). *In the Age of the Smart Machine. The Future of Work and Power.* New York: Basic Books.

Credits

Stock Photo; **p. 267:** Q. Sakamaki/ Redux; **p. 271:** Josh Edelson/AFP via Getty Images; **p. 275:** Xinhua/eyevine/ Redux; **p. 277:** Hulton Archive/Getty Images; **p. 282:** Erik Pendzich/Alamy Stock Photo.

Chapter 9: p. 284: © Miguel Caibarién/Novarc Images/age foto-stock; **p. 298:** Popperfoto/Getty Images; **p. 303:** Michael Kemp/Alamy Stock Photo; **p. 308:** Victor J. Blue/The New York Times/Redux; **p. 315:** Andy Ng Photography/Getty Images; **p. 318:** AP Photo/Matt Dunham; **p. 320:** © Miguel Caibarién/Novarc Images/age footstock.

Chapter 10: p. 322: AP Photo/Paul Sancya; **p. 327:** AP Photo/Noah Berger; **p. 328:** Chris Ratcliffe/Bloomberg via Getty Images; **p. 333:** Jennie Hart/ Alamy Stock Photo; **p. 336:** © Adam Ferguson; **p. 339:** Keystone Features/ Stringer/Getty Images; **p. 342:** John MacDougal/AFP via Getty Images; **p. 343:** Librado Romero/The New York Times/Redux; **p. 347:** Mary F. Calvert/ MCT via Getty Images; **p. 359:** Qilai Shen/Panos Pictures; **p. 361:** Aaron P. Bernstein/Stringer/Getty Images; **p. 363:** Gabe Souza/Portland Press Herald via Getty Images; **p. 365:** Jonathan Nackstrand/AFP via Getty Images; **p. 366:** Andrew Kelly/Reuters/ Newscom; **p. 369:** Andrew Burton/ Getty Images; **p. 372:** AP Photo/Paul Sancya.

Chapter 11: p. 374: John Moore/ Getty Images; **p. 377 (left):** U.S. Census Bureau; **p. 377 (right):** Jay Paul/ Bloomberg via Getty Images; **p. 378:** Alain Nogues/Sygma/Sygma via Getty Images; **p. 380 (left):** Albin Lohr-Jones/Pacific Press/Newscom; **p. 380 (right):** David Grossman/Alamy Stock Photo; **p. 384:** Spencer Platt/Getty Images; **p. 387:** Joshua Roberts/Reuters/ Newscom; **p. 391:** Mark Peterson/ Corbis via Getty Images; **p. 393:** © Hulton-Deutsch Collection/CORBIS/ Corbis via Getty Images; **p. 397:** National Archives; **p. 402:** David McNew/ Getty Images; **p. 403:** Spencer Platt/ Getty Images; **p. 410:** Jewel Amad/AFP via Getty Images; **p. 414:** John Moore/ Getty Images.

Chapter 12: p. 416: © 2020 Scott JonesPhotography; **p. 424:** Arterra Picture Library/Alamy Stock Photo; **p. 427:** Ed Kashi/VII/Redux; **p. 429:** Monty Rakusen/Cultura/Getty Images;

p. 436: Erin Moroney LaBelle/The Image Works/TopFoto; **p. 440:** Todd Heisler/The New York Times/Redux; **p. 445:** AP Photo/Louie Balukoff; **p. 448:** AFP/AFP via Getty Images; **p. 450:** Ed Kashi/VII/Redux.

Chapter 13: p. 452: Mark Peterson/Redux; **p. 456:** AP Photo/John Minchillo; **p. 459:** AP Photo/Harold Valentine; **p. 463:** Stephen Crowley/ The New York Times/Redux; **p. 469 (top):** Jim Watson/AFP via Getty Images; **p. 469 (bottom):** AP Photo/ John Locher; **p. 473:** Daniel Acker/ Bloomberg via Getty Images; **p. 476:** AP Photo/Alex Brandon; **p. 480:** © RMN-Grand Palais/Art Resource, NY, **p. 483:** Bryan Woolston/Reuters/Newscom; **p. 485:** Polaris Images; **p. 487:** Patrick Baz/AFP via Getty Images; **p. 489:** Craig Ruttle/Redux; **p. 496:** Suzanne Kreiter/The Boston Globe via Getty Images; **p. 502:** Mark Peterson/Redux.

Chapter 14: p. 506: Image China/ Newscom; **p. 510:** STR/AFP via Getty Images; **p. 513:** Scott Houston/Alamy Stock Photo; **p. 515:** From the Collections of Henry Ford; **p. 518:** Bettmann/ Corbis via Getty Images; **p. 524:** Qilai Shen/Bloomberg via Getty Images; **p. 526:** Blickwinkel/Alamy Stock Photo; **p. 532:** Stringer/EPA-EFE/ Shutterstock; **p. 533:** Null Marvel/ Disney/Kobal/Shutterstock; **p. 536:** Scott Olsen/Getty Images; **p. 545:** Andrew Link/The Rochester Post-Bulletin via AP; **p. 553:** Gideon Mendel/ Corbis via Getty Images; **p. 556:** Michael Gould-Wartofsky; **p. 558:** Image China/Newscom.

Chapter 15: p. 560: Linda Davidson/ The Washington Post via Getty Images; **p. 564:** NBC/Photofest; **p. 566 (left):** Reinhard Krause/Reuters/Newscom; **p. 566 (right):** VCG/VCG via Getty Images; **p. 568:** Elizabethsalleebauer/ Getty Images; **p. 572:** Christopher Gregory/Getty Images; **p. 576:** Jeremy Sutton-Hibbert/Alamy Stock Photo; **p. 577:** B. Christopher/Alamy Stock Photo; **p. 584:** Alvin Jornada/The Press Democrat; **p. 593:** Siri Stafford/Getty Images; **p. 598:** Ilana Panich-Linsman for The Washington Post via Getty Images; **p. 601 (left):** Hadas Parush/ Flash90/Redux; **p. 601 (right):** Allison Joyce/Redux; **p. 606:** Hero Images/ Getty Images; **p. 607:** Gordon Welters/ Laif/Redux; **p. 610:** Linda Davidson/ The Washington Post via Getty Images.

Chapter 16: p. 612: © Joseph Sohm/Visions of America LBRF/ age fotostock; **p. 616:** Michael Kirby Smith/The New York Times/Redux; **p. 619:** Image Source/Alamy Stock Photo; **p. 620:** Myung J. Chun/Los Angeles Times via Getty Images; **p. 621:** © Douglas R. Clifford/Tampa Bay Times/ZUMA Press; **p. 626:** AP Photo/Kamil Krzaczynski; **p. 628:** AP Photo/Michael Conroy; **p. 632:** © Ted Streshinsky/CORBIS/Corbis via Getty Images; **p. 633:** Marilynn K. Yee/The New York Times/Redux; **p. 635:** Keith Beaty/Toronto Star via Getty Images; **p. 640:** Christophe Archambault/AFP via Getty Images; **p. 645:** Michael F. McElroy/The New York Times/Redux; **p. 646:** Mark Leong/Redux; **p. 648:** © Joseph Sohm/Visions of America LBRF/age footstock.

Chapter 17: p. 650: Lorenzo Moscia/ Archivolatino/Redux; **p. 654:** Mark Peterson/Redux; **p. 660:** Kim Jae-Hwan/AFP via Getty Images; **p. 662:** DB Pictures/Alamy Stock Photo; **p. 665:** AP Photo/Elizabeth Dalziel; **p. 667:** Marka/UIG via Getty Images; **p. 670:** © World Religions Photo Library/ Bridgeman Images; **p. 671:** Robertus Pudyanto/Getty Images; **p. 675:** Chris Williams/Icon Sportswire/Corbis via Getty Images; **p. 679:** AP Photo/Nick Ut; **p. 681:** Frederic J. Brown/AFP via GettyImages; **p. 685:** James Estrin/ The New York Times/Redux; **p. 690:** Bettmann/Getty Images; **p. 692:** Veli Gurgah/Anadolu Agency/Getty Images; **p. 695:** James Estrin/The New York Times/Redux, **p. 700:** Lorenzo Moscia/ Archivolatino/Redux.

Chapter 18: p. 704: AP Photo/Mark Humphrey; **p. 707:** AP Photo/Richard Drew; **p. 709:** Mark Peterson/Corbis via Getty Images; **p. 712:** BSIP/UIG Via Getty Images; **p. 713:** Manny Crisostomo/Sacramento Bee/Tribune News Service via Getty Images; **p. 719:** Oxford Science Archive/Heritage-Images/TopFoto; **p. 723:** Amelie-Benoist/ BSIP/age fotostock; **p. 725:** Sarin Images/GRANGER; **p. 726:** Bettmann/Getty Images; **p. 729:** Vincent Laforet/The New York Times/ Redux; **p. 736:** Rick Gershon/Getty Images; **p. 737:** Jack Sullivan/Alamy Stock Photo; **p. 743:** Callista Images Cultura/Newscom; **p. 745:** Photo by NY Daily News Archive via Getty Images; **p. 746:** Michael Kappeler/dpa via AP; **p. 751:** Adam Gault/Science Photo Library/Getty Images; **p. 752:** Frederic

FIGURES

Index

education and literacy, 247–48
  academic achievement and differential outcomes
    gender and, 630–31
    intelligence, 616–17, 641–43
    race and, 121–22, 629–30
    school discipline, 628–29
    stereotype threat, 631
  China and, 92
  functional literacy, 632–33
  gender inequality in, 102, 346–49
  global inequality and, 312
  global rates of, 637
  in global south, 636–37
  health and, 731
  homeschooling, 644–45
  inequality in U.S. schools, 102, 262–63, 623–29
    between-school effects and, 623–24
    Kozol on, 624–26
    tracking and within-school effects, 627–28
  international, 645–47
  Internet use and, 169
  media, technology, and, 637–39
  No Child Left Behind Act and, 634
  as poverty-related indicator, 294
  race and, 248, 347–48, 404–6, 616, 623–29, 631
  reform in the United States, 632–33
  social mobility and, 260–64, 280
  theories of, 618–22
  unemployment and, 546
  voting behavior and, 495–96
egocentrism, 117
Egypt, 49, 487–88, 655
Ehrlich, Paul, 809
Eibl-Eibesfeldt, Irenäus, 140
Eisenhower, Dwight D., 465–66, 784
Ekman, Paul, 139–40
elder abuse, 439
Elder Mistreatment (NRC), 439
elections, U.S.
  in 2000, 468
  in 2008, 472, 476
  in 2012, 470, 472, 476
  in 2016, 376, 386, 468, 469, 472, 474, 476, 478, 483, 497–98, 500
  democracy and, 468–69
  voter turnout for, 495–96
electoral college, 468
electronic communications; see also information technology; Internet; telecommunications technologies
  emotional expression in, 141–42
  face-to-face communications replaced by, 160–61
  impression management and, 157–58
electronic data interchange (EDI) software, 522, 523
electronic economy, 835

Elementary and Secondary Education Act, 634
Elementary Forms of the Religious Life, The (Durkheim), 14, 662
el-Sisi, Abdel Fattah, 655
e-mail
  emotional expression in, 141–42
  face-to-face contact replaced by, 160–61
emerging economies, 76, 301–2, 315
emigration, 399
Eminem, 81
emotion, facial expressions of, 139–42
emotional intelligence, 617
emotional loneliness, 435
emotions, workplace and, 107
empirical investigation, 50
Employee Free Choice Act, 547
employment, see occupations; unemployment; work and the workplace
encounters, 143
energy consumption and environmental issues, 794, 795, 803–4
England, see Great Britain
England, Paula, 741
"English-only" movement, 65
entrepreneurs, 354, 514, 527
environment
  corporate crime and, 224–25
  manufactured risk, 840
  new ecological paradigm (NEP), 791
  population growth, urbanization, and, 767, 770, 821
  social change and, 821
  technological waste and, 306
  urbanization and, 778
Environment, The (Schnaiberg), 792
environmental ecology, 793, 798
environmental injustice, 800–801, 805
Environmental Kuznets Curve, 792
environmental social movements, 804, 806–8
environmental sociology, 792
Envisioning Real Utopias (Wright), 852
epidemiology, social, 728
Episcopal Church, 685
Equal Pay Act, 340
Esper, Mark, 465
Essay on the Principle of Population (Malthus), 808
Eternal Word Broadcasting Network, 697
ethical dilemmas and exploitation, 50
ethnic cleansing, 411, 654
ethnic conflicts, 411–12
ethnicity, 379–81
  census classifications of, 376–77
  colonization and, 389–90
  dating and, 579
  definition of, 379
  educational attainment and, 404–6
  environmental injustice and, 800
  family and, 582–88

health and, 408–9
income inequality and, 406–8
inequality and, 404–11
political power and, 410–11
poverty and, 268–69
race vs., 378–81
research on, see ethnic relations
residential segregation and, 392–93, 409–10
U.S. racial and ethnic composition, charts of, 395
wages and, 540–41
ethnic relations
  global migration and, 398–401
  historical perspective on ethnic antagonism, 389–91
  models of ethnic integration, 397–98
  rise of racism, 391–94
  in the United States, 389–401
    African Americans, 393–94
    Asian Americans, 397
    early colonization and, 389–91
    immigrants and the economy, 402–4
    Latinos, 394–96
ethnocentrism, 83–84
ethnography, 38–39
ethnomethodology, 148–50
European Union, 317–18, 357, 461, 827, 832, 833, 847
evangelicalism, 670, 695–97
Evangelical Lutheran Church in America, 685
everyday work, 722
Evicted (Desmond), 787
exchange mobility, 261
experimental group, 43, 45
experiments, 39, 43–46
exploitation, 50
exponential population growth, 766
Express Scripts, 529
extended family, 566, 574
external risk, 840
extreme poverty, 75, 313–14
eye contact, 143

F

Facebook, 58, 88, 92, 138, 157, 169, 257, 285, 471, 533, 838
  in China, 59
  data collection by, 231
  elections and, 478, 483
  ISIS and, 693
  online adults on, 160
  protests and, 487
  study on romantic relationships and, 32–33
  unfocused interaction on, 144
FaceTime, 141
Facial Action Coding System (FACS), 139–40, 140
facial expressions of emotion, 139–42
Fadiman, Anne, 713
failed states, 458

National Crime Victimization Survey, 218–19
National Health and Nutrition Examination Survey, 441
National Health and Social Life Survey (NHSLS), 742
National Health Service (NHS), 729
National Immigration Forum, 404
National Institute of Campus Sexual Assault, 368
National Intimate Partner and Sexual Violence Survey (NISVS), 603
nationalism, 89, 89–90, 458
  definition of, 89
  in global south, 492–93
  Islamic, 689–91
  modern society and, 490–91
  nations without states, 491–92
  religious, 658, 669–70, 687–94, 697–99
  in schools, 618
  social movements, 490–91
  states without nations, 492–94
National Labor Relations Board (NLRB), 546
National Longitudinal Study of Youth (NLSY), 579, 642
National Night Out, 233
National Organization for Women (NOW), 473, 477
National Research Council (NRC), 439
National Rifle Association, 473
National Security Agency, 231
National Social Life, Health and Aging Project (NSHAP), 741
National System of Interstate and Defense Highways, 784
nation-states, 72, 457, 494–95
Native Americans, 394
  families, 582–85, 602
  gender roles and, 336
  Hopi tribe, 20–21
  poverty among, 272
NATO (North Atlantic Treaty Organization), 411, 693
nature/nurture debate, 84–87, 330–31
Nazi Germany, 172, 381, 411, 673
NCES (National Center for Education Statistics), 629, 633
NCHS (National Center for Health Statistics), 599, 747, 750–51
NCLB (No Child Left Behind) Act, 634
Negro Family, The (Frazier), 586
Neng, Liu, 59
neoliberalism, 296
neoliberal theories of global inequality, 296–97, 303–4, 305
NEP (new ecological paradigm), 791–92, 799, 805
Nepal, 337
Netflix, 818, 838
Netherlandish Proverbs (Brueghel), 35
Netherlands, 666, 745
networks, 168–70
  Internet as, 160, 169–70

obesity and, 187–88
organizations as, 192
personal taste and, 186
and spread of COVID-19, 166
net worth, 244–45
New Age movements, 659, 681
New Deal, 244, 276
new ecological paradigm (NEP), 791–92, 799, 805
new economy, 553
New Guinea, 69
  gender roles among tribes in, 335
  same-sex norms in, 717
  study of facial expressions in, 140
New Jim Crow, The (Alexander), 213
newly industrializing economies (NIEs), see emerging economies
new religious movements, 678–83, 688
  world-accommodating, 682–83
  world-affirming, 680–82
  world-rejecting, 682
new social movements, 489–90
New York City, 513, 639, 776–78
New York City
  stop-and-frisk policy of, 228
  surveillance technologies and, 229–30
New York Police Department, 744
New York Times, 246
New York University, 556
New Zealand, 337, 601, 643, 745
NHS (National Health Service), 729
NHSLS (National Health and Social Life Survey), 742
Nicaragua, 299
Niebuhr, Richard, 658
Nien Hsing, 509
NIEs (newly industrializing economies), see emerging economies
Nietzsche, Friedrich, 653
Nigeria, 75, 84, 492–93, 691, 789, 818–19, 839
Nike, 523
"90 Day Fiance," 577
NISVS (National Intimate Partner and Sexual Violence Survey), 603
Nixon, Richard, 791
Nkrumah, Kwame, 17
NLRB (National Labor Relations Board), 546
NLSY (National Longitudinal Study of Youth), 642
"no bullshit Marxists," 253
No Child Left Behind (NCLB) Act, 634
Nolan, Kathleen, 628
Nollywood films, 819, 839
nonmarital childbearing, 591–93
nonmaterial culture, 62, 62–66
nonverbal communication, 139–42, 144, 148
norms
  conformity to, 63, 77–78
  definition of, 63, 199

deviance and, 201–2
social order and, 8–9
variation over time, 62–64
Norris, Pippa, 666–67
North Atlantic Treaty Organization (NATO), 411, 693
North Korea, 823
Norway, 577, 601, 745
Nostradamus, 659
NOW (National Organization for Women), 473, 477
NRC (National Research Council), 439
NSHAP (National Social Life, Health and Aging Project), 741
nuclear energy, 804
nuclear family, 565, 569, 574, 576
Nuer, 493
nursing homes, 440–41
N.W.A., 81

O

Oakes, Jeannie, 627
Oakland, California, 229
Obama, Barack, 371, 394, 410
  in 2008 election, 472, 476
  in 2012 election, 470, 472, 476
  education and, 634
  minimum wage and, 268
  as multiracial, 588
Obama, Michelle, 709
obedience to authority, 172–74
Obergefell v. Hodges, 744
obesity, 86, 109, 187–88, 706–9, 710
Ocasio-Cortez, Alexandria (AOC), 210
occupations
  definition of, 510–11
  gender typing or sex segregation, 351–52
  status and, 249
Occupy Wall Street, 208, 257, 275, 488
O'Connor, James, 500
Odle, Stephanie, 327
OECD (Organisation for Economic Co-operation and Development), 496, 547
offshoring, 550–51
Of Human Life (Humane Vitae), 677
Ogburn, John, 629
Ogburn, William, 37–38
Ohlin, Lloyd E., 204
Ohmae, Kenichi, 494
oil spill, 791
Oklahoma City bombing, 698
older adults, see aging and older adults
oldest old, 431
old old, 431
oligarchy, 189
oligopolies, 529
Oliver, Melvin, 245
online dating, 158–60, 578
On the Run (Goffman), 40
open-ended questionnaires, 40–41
opioid addiction, 783
Oracle, 324
O'Reilly, Bill, 355